ADVANCES
IN
SPORT
PSYCHOLOGY

THIRD EDITION

Thelma S. Horn

Miami University
Oxford, Ohio

Editor

Human Kinetics

Library of Congress Cataloging-in-Publication Data

Advances in sport psychology / Thelma S. Horn, editor. -- 3rd ed.
   p. ; cm.
 Includes bibliographical references and index.
 ISBN-13: 978-0-7360-5735-6 (hard cover)
 ISBN-10: 0-7360-5735-8 (hard cover)
 1. Sports--Psychological aspects. I. Horn, Thelma S., 1949-
 [DNLM: 1. Sports--psychology. 2. Achievement. 3. Exercise--psychology. 4. Goals. 5. Physical Fitness--psychology. 6. Sports Medicine--methods. QT 260 A2445 2008]

 GV706.4.A38 2008
 796.01--dc22

          2007045899

ISBN-10: 0-7360-5735-8
ISBN-13: 978-0-7360-5735-6

Copyright © 2008, 2002, 1992 by Human Kinetics, Inc.

The Web addresses cited in this text were current as of October 5, 2007, unless otherwise noted.

Acquisitions Editor: Myles Schrag; **Developmental Editor:** Judy Park; **Assistant Editors:** Lee Alexander and Jillian Evans; **Copyeditor:** Bob Replinger; **Proofreader:** Sarah Wiseman; **Indexer:** Bobbi Swanson; **Permission Manager:** Dalene Reeder; **Graphic Designer:** Bob Reuther; **Graphic Artist:** Denise Lowry; **Cover Designer:** Keith Blomberg; **Photographer (cover):** Mark Dadswell/Getty Images; **Photo Asset Manager:** Laura Fitch; **Photo Office Assistant:** Jason Allen; **Art Manager:** Kelly Hendren; **Associate Art Manager:** Alan L. Wilborn; **Illustrator:** Alan L. Wilborn; **Printer:** Edwards Brothers

Printed in the United States of America   10 9 8 7 6 5 4 3 2

Human Kinetics
Web site: www.HumanKinetics.com

United States: Human Kinetics, P.O. Box 5076, Champaign, IL 61825-5076
800-747-4457
e-mail: humank@hkusa.com

Canada: Human Kinetics, 475 Devonshire Road Unit 100, Windsor, ON N8Y 2L5
800-465-7301 (in Canada only)
e-mail: info@hkcanada.com

Europe: Human Kinetics, 107 Bradford Road, Stanningley, Leeds LS28 6AT, United Kingdom
+44 (0) 113 255 5665
e-mail: hk@hkeurope.com

Australia: Human Kinetics, 57A Price Avenue, Lower Mitcham, South Australia 5062
08 8372 0999
e-mail: info@hkaustralia.com

New Zealand: Human Kinetics, Division of Sports Distributors NZ Ltd., P.O. Box 300 226 Albany, North Shore City, Auckland
0064 9 448 1207
e-mail: info@humankinetics.co.nz

Contents

Chapter 6   Attributions and Perceived Control 99

Stephanie J. Hanrahan, PhD, and Stuart J.H. Biddle, PhD

Chapter 7   Motivational Orientations and Sport Behavior. 115

Maureen R. Weiss, PhD, and Anthony J. Amorose, PhD

Chapter 8   Achievement Goal Theories in Sport 157

Chris Harwood, PhD; Christopher M. Spray, PhD; and Richard Keegan, MSc

Chapter 9   Moral Development in Sport and Physical Activity. 187

Maureen R. Weiss, PhD; Alan L. Smith, PhD; and Cheryl P. Stuntz, PhD

PART III   SOCIOENVIRONMENTAL FACTORS AND SPORT BEHAVIOR   211

Chapter 10   Group Dynamics in Sport and Physical Activity 213

Albert V. Carron, EdD, and Lawrence R. Brawley, PhD

Chapter 11 Coaching Effectiveness in the Sport Domain. 239

Thelma S. Horn, PhD

Chapter 12 Social Influence in Sport 269

Julie A. Partridge, PhD; Robert J. Brustad, PhD; and Megan Babkes Stellino, EdD

PART IV PSYCHOLOGICAL SKILLS, INTERVENTION TECHNIQUES, AND SPORT BEHAVIOR   293

Chapter 13 Imagery in Sport, Exercise, and Dance 297

Shane Murphy, PhD; Sanna Nordin, PhD; and Jennifer Cumming, PhD

Chapter 14 Attentional Processes and Sport Performance 325

Stephen H. Boutcher, PhD

In its most generic sense, sport psychology can be defined as the psychological study of human behavior in sport settings. A close examination of the available literature in the field suggests that sport psychologists are particularly interested in the variation that occurs in the behavior of people in such contexts. This topic includes the variation between individuals in the same situation as well as the variation that occurs in the behavior of the same individual across situations. To illustrate variation between individuals, consider the case of two athletes from the same team who are both performing in a crucial athletic contest (e.g., league, state, or regional championship). Despite the fact that both athletes are performing in the same or similar context, their behavior in this situation may differ. That is, they may vary considerably in anxiety, confidence, motivation, and actual performance. Equally as interesting to sport psychologists is the variation in behavior that occurs when an individual athlete moves from one situation to another. For example, sport psychologists have consistently noted that the amount of anxiety that an individual athlete experiences depends largely on the situation (e.g., practice versus game, home versus away contest). Similarly, an athlete may exhibit a high level of motivation in a soccer practice but be considerably less motivated to achieve in a softball practice. Or a person who coaches both cross-country and track and field teams at the same high school may exhibit significantly different leadership styles and behaviors across the two sporting contexts.

To explain such behavioral variation, sport psychologists have identified and examined a number of factors that can be categorized as either individual difference factors or socioenvironmental factors. Individual difference factors can refer to either

- relatively stable traits, dispositions, or characteristics of the individual such as age, trait

anxiety, motivational orientation, self-esteem, or other personality characteristics; or

- differences that exist between people in their subjective appraisals of the world around them and the events that occur in that world.

Sport psychologists have used these individual difference variables in an effort to explain and predict the behavior of individual participants in sport contexts. From a related perspective, sport psychologists have also found that factors within the sport or broader social environment can affect the participants' behavior. Specifically, characteristics of the sport group (e.g., size, cohesion, composition) and the behaviors of group leaders (e.g., coach or peer leaders) have been found to affect the behavior of the group members. Similarly, significant others in the athletes' social environment (e.g., parents, siblings, teammates, and peers) can exert a strong influence. In addition, the sociocultural or sociopolitical context within which sport occurs can also determine or strongly affect not only the behaviors exhibited by individual athletes, coaches, and others in the sport environment but also their attitudes, beliefs, cognitions, and orientations.

Although much of the research in sport psychology has examined the influence of individual difference and socioenvironmental factors separately, recent consensus in the field suggests that these two entities exert an interactional effect. That is, the characteristics of the individual participant interact with factors in the social environment to determine the individual's behavior in specific sport or physical activity contexts.

The first edition of this text, *Advances in Sport Psychology*, was published in 1992 with the express purpose of summarizing the state of knowledge with regard to research in sport psychology. The second edition was published in 2002 under the same global purpose. Like its predecessors, this third edition of the text was also written to provide a comprehensive and up-to-date review of the major issues that are of current research interest in sport psychology. Thus, this third edition emphasizes a discussion and critical analysis of the current state of knowledge in each topical area combined with recommendations concerning future research directions. The text is primarily directed toward graduate students enrolled in research-oriented sport psychology courses and toward those currently conducting research in some area of sport psychology. Although the book is not intended to serve as a how-to text for practicing sport psychologists or to provide information oriented only toward the enhancement of sport performance, the individual chapters should be useful to current or future practitioners who need to understand the factors that affect the behavior of sport performers before they can hope to effect behavioral change.

Note that this text, as well as its predecessors, primarily focuses on research advances concerning the sport context. Although individual chapters in this third edition may include some discussion of the research conducted in such other physical activity contexts as exercise, dance, physical education, and recreation, the primary focus is on the competitive sport context. This decision was made because of the wealth of information that has been accumulated on psychological issues in each of the previously identified physical activity contexts. Trying to include research from all these disparate physical activity areas would be difficult. Furthermore, context appears to be important. Therefore, the results of research conducted to examine the psychological aspects of exercise participants do not necessarily apply in the same way to sport participants or to the performance and behavior of students in physical education classes. Thus, the overall focus of this book is on psychological research and theory in relation to the sport setting. Certainly, applications can be made to other contexts.

The first edition of this text contained 13 chapters. The second edition, published a decade later, was expanded to 17 chapters to reflect the proliferation of topics in the field. The current third edition also contains 17 chapters, but the specific chapter topics as well as their content have changed significantly, again in response to changes that have occurred in the field. The 17 chapters in this edition are organized into four parts. The three chapters in part I provide a comprehensive introduction to the field of sport psychology (e.g., definitions, history, research paradigms, research methodologies). The six chapters in part II examine the characteristics of individuals (i.e., individual difference factors) that

affect their behavior in sport and physical activity contexts. These characteristics include self-perceptions (self-concept, self-esteem, perceived ability or competence, self-confidence, self-efficacy), attributional patterns and perceptions of control, motivational orientations, achievement goal perspectives, and moral reasoning levels. The three chapters presented in part III provide a discussion concerning various agents in the social environment—members of the sport group, the coach, and the family and peers—who impinge on sport participants' behavior. Finally, the five chapters in part IV examine the research and theory concerning selected intervention techniques that can be and have been used to enhance the performance or modify the behavior of athletes. Individual chapters in this section discuss the research and theory pertaining to imagery and mental rehearsal, attentional processes, goal setting, flow and peak performance, and athletic injuries.

All chapters returning to this third edition have been either substantially revised or, in some cases, totally rewritten. Some of the chapters from the previous edition have been subdivided or reconceptualized to provide a more concise overview of the individual topics. This extensive revision of the previous edition of this text clearly and appropriately reflects the theoretical and empirical advances that have occurred within the last several years in the sport psychology field. Thus, returning readers will certainly see significant changes from the second edition to the third in the content of the individual chapters as well as in the book as a whole.

Despite the fact that different authors wrote the chapters in this edited text, an attempt was made to use a consistent format. Specifically, each chapter begins with a brief introduction to the topic area. This introduction includes definitions of terms, an explanation of the scope of the chapter, and a clear outline of the sections composing the chapter. In the main body of each chapter, the author or authors provide a review of the available research and theory on the chapter topic. This review goes beyond just summarizing the research to date by providing an analysis and, in most cases, a synthesis of the state of knowledge in the area. Finally, a section of each chapter is devoted to a discussion of future research directions.

The production of a textbook of this depth and breadth requires the coordinated efforts of a number of people. I wish at this time to recognize the major contributors. First, I want to acknowledge the contributions of the people at Human Kinetics Publishers. Myles Schrag was the acquisitions editor for this text. In this role, he provided the technical, administrative, and organizational support needed to get the third edition of the text from conceptualization to the publication stage. His technical assistance as well as his social support were greatly appreciated.

Of course, I also want to acknowledge the contributions of the authors who wrote the individual chapters for this text. Several authors (Deborah Feltz, Robin Vealey, Maureen Weiss, Albert Carron, Larry Brawley, Shane Murphy, Stephen Boutcher, and Damon Burton) have been with me since the first edition of this text. I appreciate their continuing loyalty to the field and their continuing contributions to this text. Several other authors (Anthony Kontos, Robert Brustad, Kenneth Fox, Alan Smith, Sue Jackson, Jay Kimiecik, Eileen Udry, and Mark Andersen) joined us for the second edition and are returning. As editor of this third edition, I truly appreciate the willingness of all these returning authors to rewrite and revise what were already high-quality summaries of the research in their respective topic areas. Finally, I want to welcome to this third edition a new cadre of authors. These include David Conroy, Stephanie Hanrahan, Chris Harwood, and Julie Partridge, each of whom agreed to take on the task of being the primary author for a chapter new to this edition of the text. In addition, several new coauthors were recruited. These include Stuart Biddle, Philip Wilson, Melissa Chase, Anthony Amorose, Cheryl Stuntz, Megan Babkes Stellino, Miranda Kaye, Lindsey Schantz, Christopher Spray, Richard Keegan, Sanna Nordin, Jennifer Cumming, and Cheryl Weiss.

From my perspective as the book's editor, the 33 authors or coauthors represented in this text have been, still are, or will soon be some of the most prolific researchers and scholars in the field. Despite their extremely busy schedules, these 33 individuals invested considerable time and effort in writing and rewriting their chapters. As several of them noted, condensing the research and theory that has been accumulated in each particular topic area into a reasonable manuscript length was not an easy task. In addition, each author was specifically requested to go beyond writing a summary of the available research and theory by providing a critical review of what we currently know and an outline of where we need to go in the future. In summary, the overall idea in writing the individual chapters for this book was to push at the boundaries that have defined and, in many cases, limited our field since its inception. This task was certainly formidable but one that each author accomplished with distinction.

In soliciting authors for the individual chapters in all three editions of this book, I found that of the many arguments that I had marshaled to encourage their participation, the one that was consistently the most successful was the one that appealed to their commitment to the field of sport psychology. I am convinced that each author's primary motivation in writing her or his chapter was to advance the field and, perhaps more important, to stimulate the interest and enthusiasm of current and future researchers. Our combined hope, then, is that this text will be of value to our readers not only in furthering their understanding of the field but also in motivating all of us toward continued and qualitatively better research work. May our passion for sport psychology continue to burn brightly!

Part I

INTRODUCTION TO SPORT PSYCHOLOGY

Despite the early and relatively isolated work of such individuals as Coleman Griffith and Norman Triplett, sport psychology as an area of academic research within the sport sciences did not really begin in earnest until the mid-1960s. As will become evident throughout this book, much has been accomplished over the last several decades. But as with any area of academic study, many changes have also occurred with respect to the field of study itself. Thus, it seems appropriate for this text to begin with three chapters that provide an introduction to, or an overview of, the area of study known as sport psychology.

In chapter 1 Anthony Kontos and Deborah Feltz describe the nature of sport psychology. They begin this overview by comparing and contrasting the various perspectives of sport psychology and linking these perspectives to divergent research objectives and methodologies. This section of the chapter includes a discussion concerning the differing views of sport psychology held by researchers both within and outside North America as well as a comparative analysis of the multiple roles that sport psychologists can choose or be expected to fulfill. Kontos and Feltz then offer a historical account of the last 60 years

of research in sport psychology and conclude by identifying and discussing current issues and future challenges in the field. The authors underscore the importance of these issues and challenges by noting at the end of their chapter that "those fields that work to resolve these issues and embrace its challenges will show continued growth and popularity."

In chapter 2 David Conroy, Miranda Kaye, and Lindsey Schantz provide an overview of some fundamental epistemological and research design concepts that are central to researchers who use quantitatively based approaches. Conroy and his colleagues begin by identifying the common goals of scientists and practitioners. They then provide an overview of the positivist research perspective and use this framework to discuss selected methodological and statistical issues that are important to researchers as they design, conduct, and evaluate quantitatively based research investigations. To examine current trends in sport psychology research, Conroy et al. report the results of a content analysis of all quantitatively based research studies published in the *Journal of Sport and Exercise Psychology* during the first 26 years of its existence (1979–2004). The authors use the results of this analysis to make recommendations for future researchers, scholars, and practitioners in sport psychology. Similar to the Kontos and Feltz chapter, this chapter provides a much-needed perspective about how future quantitatively based researchers might "think of ways that research methods can be used creatively to enhance understanding of psychological phenomena in sport and exercise settings."

In chapter 3 Robert Brustad examines the emergence and status of qualitative research approaches to knowledge generation in sport psychology. His chapter begins with an overview of the epistemological differences between quantitative and qualitative research approaches. This section includes a discussion of the assumptions and beliefs that underlie the positivist view of science. Brustad then presents the critiques that have been written concerning these dominant ways of knowing and uses this perspective to identify current limitations in our understanding of individuals' behavior in sport contexts. In discussing these varying perspectives on the pursuit of knowledge in sport psychology, Brustad clearly shows how our field's alliances with our parent discipline of psychology and with the other subdisciplinary areas within the sport sciences have influenced the content of our knowledge base and the means with which we pursue this knowledge. Brustad continues his chapter by providing an overview of five general types of qualitative research in sport psychology. Within each of these sections, Brustad describes research studies to illustrate each approach. His chapter concludes with a discussion regarding future directions for qualitative research in our field.

Although the chapters by Conroy and his colleagues and by Brustad focus on different methodological approaches to research in sport psychology, the authors of both chapters emphasize the importance and value that each approach has to the generation of knowledge in sport psychology. Furthermore, these authors are clear in specifying the need for researchers and scholars in sport psychology to understand the epistemological foundation on which their research methodologies are based. That is, all of us must reflect on our beliefs about what it means "to know" in our field of inquiry. Research in our field cannot advance quickly if we are unwilling to examine the assumptions, beliefs, values, and perspectives with which we approach our research studies.

In combination, then, the three chapters that make up this part of the book provide an introduction to, and overview of, sport psychology as an area of academic study. As such, they establish a foundation on which the following more topically oriented chapters will rest.

CHAPTER 1

The Nature of Sport Psychology

■ Anthony P. Kontos, PhD ■ Deborah L. Feltz, PhD ■

Describing the nature of sport psychology is difficult because many different perspectives on the field exist. Differences are present not only in the definition of the term itself but also in the roles that psychologists are presumed to play. A content review of the definitions of sport psychology provided in a number of recent books and articles shows that some writers view sport psychology as a subdiscipline of psychology whereas others view it as a subdiscipline of sport and exercise science. A brief survey of these definitions is provided in the following sidebar. In addition, sport psychology writers have differentiated between psychology focusing on athletics and psychology of physical activity (i.e., exercise psychology) encompassing all movement-related contexts (e.g., Cratty, 1989; Martens, 1974). Finally, some writers have created even more specialized terms, such as developmental sport psychology (Duda, 1987; Weiss & Bredemeier, 1983; Weiss, 2004), psychophysiological sport psychology (Hatfield & Landers, 1983), and cognitive sport psychology (Straub & Williams, 1983). Given such diversity of opinion, it is no wonder that almost 25 years ago Dishman (1983) suggested that the field of sport psychology was suffering from an identity crisis.

In this chapter we will describe the nature of sport psychology. The chapter begins with an overview of different perspectives on the field of study. Next comes a discussion of the various roles of sport psychologists. Then we present a historical overview of the research from 1950 to the present. Our chapter concludes with a discussion regarding current issues in the field and a presentation of future challenges.

Perspectives on Sport Psychology

Sport psychology, when viewed as a subdiscipline within the larger field of psychology, is defined as an applied psychology, or as a field of study in which the principles of psychology are applied to sport. Although sport psychology has not been recognized traditionally as a subdisciplinary area of study within the field of academic psychology, Smith suggested back in 1989 (Smith, 1989) that sport psychology was ready to be embraced by mainstream psychology. As evidence of this, sport psychology was approved as Division 47 within the American Psychological Association in 1986 and has long been recognized as a specialization

DEFINITIONS OF SPORT PSYCHOLOGY

Sport psychology has been defined in the following ways:

"The effect of sport itself on human behavior" (Alderman, 1980, p. 4)

"A field of study in which the principles of psychology are applied in a sports setting" (Cox, 1985, p. xiii)

"A subcategory of psychology focusing on athletes and athletics" (Cratty, 1989, p. 1)

"The branch of sport and exercise science that seeks to provide answers to questions about human behavior in sport" (Gill, 1986, p. 3)

"The educational, scientific, and professional contributions of psychology to the promotion, maintenance, and enhancement of sport-related behavior" (Rejeski & Brawley, 1983, p. 239)

"An applied psychology; the science of psychology applied to athletics and athletic situations" (Singer, 1978, p. 4)

"The scientific study of people and their behavior in sport and exercise activities" (Weinberg & Gould, 1995, p. 8)

within psychology throughout Europe. Some sport psychology specializations are present within graduate programs in clinical psychology (e.g., University of Washington) and educational or school psychology (e.g., Florida State University). Sachs and colleagues (2007) published a directory of these "clinically oriented" sport psychology graduate programs. Still, sport psychology has only recently begun to gain acceptance within the broader field of psychology.

The view of sport psychology as a subdiscipline within the field of sport and exercise science comes mostly from researchers in physical education (or kinesiology). Henry (1981), for example, argued that the academic discipline of physical education consists of the study of certain aspects of fields such as psychology, physiology, anatomy, and sociology rather than the application of those disciplines to physical activity settings. Dishman (1983) and others (e.g., Gill, 1986; Morgan, 1989; Roberts, 1989) support this view of sport psychology as a part of the broad area of sport science. Gill noted that although sport and exercise science is a multidisciplinary field that draws on knowledge from the broader parent disciplines, the subareas that make up sport and exercise science also draw on theories, constructs, and measures from each other. In fact, some sport psychology researchers (e.g., Brawley & Martin, 1995; Dishman, 1983; Feltz, 1989; Morgan, 1989) have suggested that sport psychology should include knowledge from other subdisciplines within sport and exercise science to gain a better understanding of phenomena specific to sport. McCullagh and Noble (1996) suggested that the emphasis placed on psychology or sport science will vary as a function of one's intended career goals (i.e., academic or research versus practitioner or applied). They did contend, however, that knowledge in both sport psychology and sport science will be necessary to address the issues facing academic and applied sport psychologists.

Whether one views sport psychology as a subdiscipline of psychology or as a subdiscipline of sport and exercise science is an important issue because the perspective chosen determines one's focus of study. For instance, if sport psychology is viewed as a subdiscipline of psychology, the focus of study would generally involve using activity as a setting to understand psychological theory and to apply psychological principles (see Goldstein, 1979; Martin & Hrycaiko, 1983). If, however, sport psychology is viewed as a subdiscipline of sport and exercise science, the focus of study would more likely involve trying to describe, explain, predict, and enhance behavior in sport contexts.

A third perspective is to view the relationship between sport psychology and psychology as an interface in which an interchange of concepts and methodology occurs (Brawley & Martin, 1995). Brawley and Martin viewed sport psychology as an extension of social psychology (the most influential force in sport psychology) into the sport context and as a window into the nature of human society. Many of the current research themes in sport psychology (e.g., self-efficacy, anxiety, attitudes, and goal orientations) were adapted from or based on social psychology research and theory. Sport psychology has, in turn, influenced social psychology by contributing to its theoretical knowledge base and contributing measurement and testing principles.

The perspective of this chapter is that Martens' (1974) concept of psychological kinesiology offers the most comprehensive view from which to study behavior in sport. Martens defined kinesiology as "the study of human movement, especially physical activity, in all forms and in all contexts" (1989, p. 101). Many departments of physical education and sport and exercise science have changed their names to kinesiology. Using this term to define the overall field, psychological kinesiology (sport psychology and motor learning and control) becomes the study of the psychological aspects of human movement. The other areas of kinesiology might then be labeled physiological kinesiology (exercise physiology), biomechanical kinesiology (sport biomechanics), social-cultural kinesiology (sport sociology), and developmental kinesiology (motor development).

Currently, scholars typically specialize in one of these subdisciplines and may engage in research within their own specialty, in multidisciplinary research, or in crossdisciplinary research. In multidisciplinary research, various subdisciplinary specialists investigate a common problem from their own subdisciplinary perspective, whereas in crossdisciplinary research, specialists integrate their views and theories with those of others from different backgrounds into a consolidated viewpoint to try to understand a human movement problem (Abernathy, Kippers, Mackinnon, Neal, & Hanrahan, 1997). A crossdisciplinary approach to the study of kinesiology has the potential to create greater understanding of phenomena in human movement than does a multidisciplinary or subdisciplinary perspective. Crossdisciplinary approaches also increase the potential for external (i.e., grant) funding and knowledge sharing beyond the sport psychology subdiscipline. As some sport psychologists (or psychological kinesiologists) have noted (e.g., Dishman, 1983; Feltz, 1989; Gill, 1986; Morgan, 1989), a thorough understanding of behavior in human movement settings requires the integration of knowledge from all subdisciplines of kinesiology and from psychology. A schematic representation of kinesiology and some research problems with a psychological focus that can be studied from this crossdisciplinary perspective are shown in figure 1.1.

Figure 1.1 indicates the nature of potential interrelationships between sport psychology and other disciplines within kinesiology. Developmental, biomechanical, psychological, social-cultural, and physiological subdisciplines represent the major perspectives in understanding human movement. The lines connecting these perspectives show where they might converge on a specific research problem. Note that the location of "psychological" in the center of this figure is not meant to imply that sport psychology is the focal point of kinesiology.

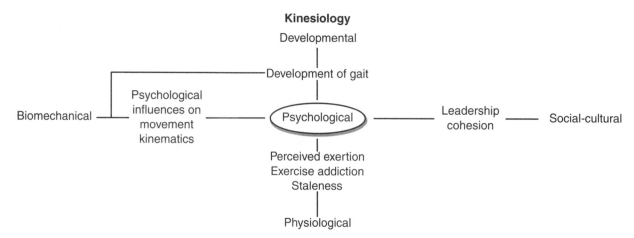

Figure 1.1 A schematic representation of the interdisciplinary nature of kinesiology with a focus on the psychological aspects, including examples of research problems.

On the contrary, sport psychology is one of several equally important dimensions of kinesiology. Several examples are provided to illustrate this crossdisciplinary view.

For instance, in the first example, the study of the development of gait patterns could include biomechanical, developmental, and psychological factors. In the second example, a study of the areas of leadership and cohesion necessitate knowledge of social, cultural, and psychological variables. In the third example, perceived exertion, exercise addiction, and staleness are research topics that involve physiological and psychological factors. In the last example, Beuter and Duda (1985) studied the psychological influences on movement kinematics using a biomechanical approach (movement kinematics) to examine the effect of arousal on stepping movements of children.

As has been the case for psychology in general, sport psychology has been examined primarily from a North American perspective. The North American perspective continues to be dominated by an applied (i.e., consulting) versus academic (i.e., research, teaching) dichotomy. This dualistic approach is in contrast to other international approaches to sport psychology. Therefore, a brief examination of the perspectives of sport psychology that emanate from outside North America, particularly those from Europe, will be useful.

The perspective of sport psychology in Europe, particularly Western Europe, is relatively similar to that in North America and, as Biddle (1995) has suggested, "there are undoubtedly more similarities than there are differences (between European and North American sport psychology)" (p. xii). There are, however, different emphases in the

research, theory, and application of sport psychology in Europe. In Germany, for instance, a holistic orientation to sport psychology has developed that includes both basic and applied research (Hackfort, 1993). Much of the basic research centers on action control theory (Kuhl, 1985) and includes work on the attentional demands of sport (e.g., Maxeiner, 1989) and motor memory (Janssen, Stoll, & Volkens, 1987). Most applied research in Germany has been designed specifically for integration into the training of elite-level athletes. In Eastern Europe and Russia, the traditional perspective of sport psychology has focused primarily on elite-level athletics. Recently, this research has begun to examine the development of psychological skills in youth sport participants as well (Kantor & Ryzonkin, 1993).

Another difference in sport psychology in Europe involves the emphasis placed on applied work with athletes. Evidence of this appears in the Directory of European Sport Psychologists (FEPSAC, 1993), in which counseling was cited as a special skill more frequently than either teaching or research. In addition, many of the more common research themes in European sport psychology, including anxiety and stress reduction, mental training, and motivation, are applied in nature. In affirmation of this, Great Britain has seen a marked increase in applied research and work with athletes in the last decade (Biddle, 1995).

European perspectives in sport psychology, although not entirely different from those in mainstream North American sport psychology, are valuable in providing a culturally different perspective of the field. Perspectives from non-Western countries are also important in the development of sport psychology. In China, for instance, sport psychology researchers (which include coaches, psychologists, and kinesiologists) have examined the psychological selection of athletes into sport (Qiu & Qiu, 1993). In Japan the focus has been primarily on achievement motivation, perceptual motor behaviors, and developmental aspects of sport psychology (Fujita & Ichimura, 1993). Unfortunately, much of this work has not been translated into English, which discourages many Western researchers from examining it. As we move toward a more global community within sport psychology, this barrier will likely become easier to cross.

Australia and New Zealand, while following similar research paradigms as North America and Europe, have been at the forefront in integrating sport psychology into mainstream psychology and university education. Examples include the creation of the Board of Sport Psychologists within the Australian Psychological Society in 1991 and a twofold increase in academic sport psychology positions within universities during 1993 (Morris, 1995; Morris & Summers, 1995). Future sport psychology researchers and practitioners alike will need to incorporate the body of applied and basic knowledge from European, Asian, and other countries to meet the current and future challenges facing sport psychology.

Roles of Sport Psychologists

The discussion in the previous section noted the increase of applied research and consulting with athletes outside North America (e.g., Eastern Europe, Russia). Although integration of applied and research roles appears to exist outside North America, a schism between the two roles has developed, particularly in the United States. This schism is reflected in the decades-old debates regarding the location, coursework, and accreditation of sport psychology graduate programs and applied certifications in sport psychology in the United States. The dichotomy (applied versus academic) in sport psychology mentioned earlier is reflected in the roles that sport psychologists assume.

Sport psychologists traditionally have worked from two perspectives: (a) academic oriented and (b) practitioner oriented. The academic sport psychologist focuses primarily on theoretical research and educational pursuits, whereas the practitioner emphasizes applied work and research. Although these two roles appear to differ considerably, some sport psychologists play both roles. Roberts (1989) expressed concern that a gulf was rapidly emerging between the academic- and practitioner-oriented

sport psychologists. Recently, in parallel with debates in psychology in general, sport psychology has struggled with the adoption of either a practitioner-academic- or an academic-practitioner-oriented model of training and practice. Moreover, sport psychology, which straddles the fields of psychology and kinesiology and is usually located within kinesiology departments, has struggled to find its place in academe. The Association for Applied Sport Psychology (AASP) has adopted a set of broad guidelines for applied sport psychology coursework. But a true model of training and its implementation across the discipline has not yet taken root in the field of sport psychology. This circumstance is a result of the expanding view that psychologists should have responsibility for both research and applied work, instead of working or learning in delineated academic or applied roles only. Furthermore, the research versus practice distinction is oversimplistic and unproductive. Applied work can provide questions, problems, observations, and issues that can guide research, which, in turn, should guide future practice.

Some sport psychologists have argued that professional services should not be sanctioned until we possess an applied body of knowledge and a reliable technology (Dishman, 1983; Morgan, 1989). Others have contended that the need for professional services in sport psychology is now present and that those providing such service should not "sit idle until scientific evidence has validated their particular application or technique" (Landers, 1989, p. 477).

Throughout this debate, there has been a problem regarding who should be certified to "practice" sport psychology and what titles and roles a sport psychologist should fulfill. As a result of this quandary, AASP developed a certification process for sport psychology practitioners in 1989. This action resulted in creation of the title "Certified Consultant, AASP" rather than "certified sport psychologist," which is legally regulated by individual state psychology licensing boards. In 1995 AASP, in conjunction with the United States Olympic Committee (USOC), formed a joint certification program for sport psychology professionals who were both APA members and AASP certified (McCann & Scanlan, 1995). Similar certification processes recently have been instituted in Canada (Canadian Mental Training Registry) and Great Britain (British Association of Sport and Exercise Sciences–psychology section). In spite of these apparent advances in certification, some researchers believe that the certification process excludes those from an academic or kinesiology-based sport psychology background (Anshel,

1992, 1993). The members of the AASP certification committee acknowledged this issue and reexamined the certification process to revise the requirements to be more inclusive of people from kinesiology backgrounds and those with master's degrees in sport psychology or related disciplines (Burton, 2000). The result of this process was a more inclusive certification process that reflects understanding of psychology and kinesiology topics, and offers both master's-level and doctoral-level certifications (see www.aaasponline.org for more information). The certification committee is also considering a certifying examination similar to those currently used in psychology and counseling certifications. Unfortunately for the field of sport psychology, some groups of sport psychology professionals have taken it upon themselves to create their own licensing boards and pseudo-certifications. These actions only confuse consumers of sport psychology and discredit the field to other professionals. Moreover, many psychologists and other mental health professionals practice sport psychology without any background in sport or kinesiology, and many professionals in kinesiology provide services to athletes that go beyond performance enhancement without the necessary background in psychology.

Further widening the gulf between academic and practitioner-oriented sport psychologists are the growing number of professional journals and organizations that have developed along either scientific research (e.g., *Journal of Sport and Exercise Psychology*) or applied sport psychology lines (e.g., *The Sport Psychologist*). Refer to the following sidebar for a list of prominent sport psychology journals and organizations. A recent addition to the journal field is *Psychology of Sport and Exercise*, which includes academically rigorous articles that reflect both academic and applied research.

Controversy continues in the field today regarding the basic nature of sport psychology and the roles that sport psychologists can or should play. Roberts (1989) has contended that the controversy in sport psychology is due primarily to the lack of a generally accepted conceptual paradigm to drive the research and applied efforts of sport psychologists. To appreciate the controversial issues in this field and understand why sport psychology lacks a generally accepted paradigm, we need to examine where sport psychology has been in the past. Because several individuals have already written excellent historical overviews (e.g., Cox, 1985; Landers, 1983; Ryan, 1981; Wiggins, 1984), we shall present only a brief overview of how the current paradigms in sport psychology evolved.

PROMINENT SPORT PSYCHOLOGY JOURNALS AND ORGANIZATIONS

Journals

International Journal of Sport and Exercise Psychology (IJSEP)

Journal of Applied Sport Psychology (JASP)

Journal of Sport Behavior

Journal of Sport and Exercise Psychology (JSEP)

Perceptual and Motor Skills

Research Quarterly for Exercise and Sport

The Sport Psychologist

Professional Organizations

Association for Applied Sport Psychology (AASP)

British Association for Sports and Exercise Science (BASES)

Board of Sport Psychology, Australian Society of Psychology

Canadian Society of Psychomotor Learning and Sport Psychology (SCAPPS)

Division 47 of the American Psychology Association (Div. 47 APA)

European Congress for Sport Psychology

International Society for Sport Psychology (ISSP)

North American Society for the Psychology of Sport and Physical Activity (NASPSPA)

Historical Evolution of Sport Psychology

Perspectives in sport psychology have tended to parallel those in general psychology (Morgan, 1980). As Landers (1983) noted, the research conducted in sport psychology during the 1950–1965 period was characterized by empiricism, and most of the studies investigated personality. In contrast the period 1966–1976 was characterized by a social analysis approach involving the selection of one theory at a time from mainstream psychology and testing that theory in the area of sport and motor performance

(Landers, 1983). Topics such as social facilitation, achievement motivation, social reinforcement, and arousal and motor performance were investigated. Research conducted from the late 1970s to the mid-1980s was influenced by sociological forces in psychology and sport psychology. These forces included causal attributions, intrinsic motivation, and self-efficacy or self-confidence. During the late 1980s and into the 1990s, research in sport psychology became more sport specific and measurement driven. Atheoretical and clinical research, as well as sport-specific theoretical research, became more prominent, suggesting that sport psychology matured considerably from the 1980s through the 2000s. We shall examine the research perspectives that characterized each of the four periods in detail in an effort to describe the evolution of sport psychology. Specifically, we describe a research topic from within each period to illustrate the primary focus from that period.

Personality Research

The relationship of personality to participation in sport and physical activity has been one of the most popular research areas in sport psychology. Much of the early research took a trait approach to studying personality profiles in athletes or athletic groups. This approach has been described as being of the "shotgun" variety (Ryan, 1968). Researchers would gain access to a sample of athletes (from high school to Olympic caliber) and test them on the most convenient personality test. Leaders in sport psychology (e.g., Kroll, 1970; Martens, 1975) criticized this research approach for its theoretical and methodological shortcomings. The applicability of general personality assessment techniques for sport and physical activity that may not have a logical link to participation or performance has been questioned (Kroll).

Martens (1970, 1975), one of the most vocal critics of this research approach, began advocating the use of a social analysis approach that combined empirical methods with theory, which represents the second major stage in the history of sport psychology research.

Social Facilitation and the Arousal– Performance Relationship

The typical research paradigm during this period involved taking a social-psychological theory and testing its applicability to motor skill performance. The most popular topics of research were social facilitation and the arousal–performance relationship. Much of the research in social facilitation and arousal in sport psychology was based on Zajonc's (1965) theory of social facilitation. Reviewers of this research have generally concluded that the evidence for a drive theory explanation of social facilitation effects in motor performance has been mixed (Carron, 1980; Landers, 1980; Wankel, 1984). In addition, the size of social facilitation effects has been shown to be very small (Bond & Titus, 1983). The most frequently cited alternative to drive theory for social facilitation and arousal–performance research was the inverted-U hypothesis (Carron). This hypothesis predicted that performance improved progressively as a subject's arousal level increased up to some optimal point, beyond which further increases in arousal progressively decreased performance efficiency. Much of the arousal–motor performance literature of the 1970s also tested the inverted-U hypothesis (e.g., Klavora, 1978; Martens & Landers, 1970). Researchers of this period became dissatisfied with the laboratory-oriented social psychological paradigm and started looking to cognitive approaches and field methods to answer their research questions.

Cognitive Approaches and Field Methods

In the late 1970s and early 1980s a variety of cognitive models in the sport personality, social facilitation, arousal–performance, and other motivation areas were proposed as a response to the general dissatisfaction with the simplistic and mechanistic drive theory perspective for explaining complex human behavior (Landers, 1980; Wankel, 1975, 1984). For example, Landers (1980) advocated a cognitive arousal-attention model based on Easterbrook's (1959) cue utilization theory. This model suggests that increased arousal leads to a narrowing of attentional focus and cue utilization, thus limiting performance. Rejeski and Brawley (1983) called for innovative approaches and broader conceptual views to help us understand motivation in sport. The cognitive concepts of perceived ability, self-efficacy, and achievement orientation (Bandura, 1977; Harter, 1978; Maehr & Nicholls, 1980) were proposed to play a key role in mediating motivation. These concepts were subsequently incorporated into the sport psychology research in this area (Feltz, 1982, 1988; Roberts, Kleiber, & Duda, 1981; Weiss, Bredemeier, & Shewchuk, 1986). At the same time, Martens (1980) pointed out the limitations of laboratory studies and suggested switching from laboratory settings to field settings to observe behavior more accurately and to understand the real world of sport. But as Landers (1983) noted, some investigators misinterpreted Martens' position and abandoned both theory and laboratory when they became field researchers, thus slowing the development of sport psychology. Landers (1983) suggested that sport psychology must develop its own logically formulated alternative explanations and test them against the predictions of broader psychological theory. Dishman (1983) argued that sport psychology had been applying general psychology theories and trying to validate general psychology models in sport, rather than developing "applied theories" to answer sport-specific questions. As more researchers began to view sport psychology as a subdiscipline within sport science rather than as a field of study in which psychological principles were tested and applied, they began to advocate the development of theories or conceptual frameworks and measures within sport psychology to understand sport behavior (Alderman, 1980; Dishman; Martens, 1980; Morgan, 1989).

Extension to Sport-Specific Theory and Advances in Measurement and Acceptance

Since the late 1980s progress has been made in the development and extension of the conceptual frameworks or models within sport, including movement confidence (Griffin, Keogh, & Maybee, 1984), sport confidence (Vealey, 1986), sport enjoyment (Scanlan & Lewthwaite, 1986), sport motivation orientations (Duda & Nicholls, 1992; Gill & Deeter, 1988; Treasure & Roberts, 1994; Vealey), and sport leadership (Chelladurai, Haggerty, & Baxter, 1989; Smoll & Smith, 1989). Accompanying the development of conceptual frameworks specific to sport has been the development of sport-specific measures that are construct valid. The TEOSQ (Duda & Nicholls, 1992), State-Trait Sport Confidence Inventory (Vealey, 1986), and the Group Environment Questionnaire (Carron, Widmeyer, & Brawley, 1985) are three examples of sport-specific measures that have used a construct validation approach and have strong links from concept to operational definition. Although sport-specific measures are being developed using a construct validation approach, some are concerned about the possible mislabeling of these constructs (Marsh, 1994). Some researchers in sport psychology (e.g., Brawley, Martin, & Gyurcsik, 1998; Duda, 1998; Gauvin & Spence, 1998) have acknowledged the existence of this "jingle-jangle fallacy" (Marsh). The jingle fallacy refers to scales that have the same label but may not measure the same constructs. The jangle fallacy, on the other hand, pertains to scales with different labels that may not represent different constructs.

During the past few years, applied sport psychology has gained broader acceptance from both psychology and the public. Many athletes, coaches, and sport organizations now openly acknowledge the contribution of their sport psychologists to their successes in sport. For example, the dramatic turnaround and subsequent College World Series Championship for the California State University at Fullerton men's baseball team was attributed in large part by their coach to their work with sport psychologist Kenneth Ravizza. The recent acceptance and successes of applied sport psychology have increased the visibility of the field and provided more opportunities for researchers to assess the practical application of theoretical research.

In each of the first three periods discussed (i.e., 1950–1965; 1966–1976; 1977–mid-1980s), researchers started with theories (e.g., personality traits, social facilitation, attribution) that were borrowed from psychology and applied to sport settings. They often obtained mixed results because of theoretical or methodological shortcomings. Their discouragement and dissatisfaction led them to abandon either the research area or the methodology and search for a new approach. Until the mid-1980s, this historical pattern resulted in, or contributed to, the development of three problems: (a) few programs of sustained research, (b) a lack of a generally accepted conceptual paradigm, and (c) slow growth in advancing knowledge in sport psychology. In the last period discussed, researchers began to expand the realm of sport-specific theoretical research. This activity has helped sport psychology begin to distinguish itself as a more theoretically driven science as opposed to a place where theories from other disciplines are tested. In addition, the increased and better use of statistics in validating and developing sport-specific measures has done much to further the legitimacy of the field. The increased acceptance and use of sport psychology services across sport has provided the field with access to a wider audience and more opportunities for applied research. Still, many aspects of sport psychology are in their infancy (e.g., sustained research lines, accepted conceptual paradigms, systematic construct validation studies) or more appropriately stated, just entering into childhood, and need to be continually advanced. We will discuss the current issues and challenges facing sport psychology in the remainder of this chapter.

Current Issues

The following examples show how sport psychology has expanded beyond its own context. Theoretically driven research, crossdisciplinary approaches, and a broader conceptual framework will continue to be relevant issues in research and applied work in sport psychology. The ever-changing demographics of sport participants will continue to influence the research, applied work, and perspectives of sport psychologists. As these changes evolve and continue to shape the field, sport psychology practitioners and researchers will face a variety of new challenges.

Integration of Applied and Theoretical Work

One of the immediate issues facing sport psychology continues to be the need for integrating applied and theoretical work. Currently, research studies and the journals that publish them, as well as professional organizations, are divided between applied (e.g., *Journal of Applied Sport Psychology*, AASP) and theoretical (e.g., *Journal of Sport and Exercise Psychology*, NASPSPA) camps. Theoretical concepts often are not tested in applied settings, and applied concepts often do not serve as the basis for theory development. This lack of integration between applied work and theoretical research has slowed the growth of sport psychology and created a disconnect between practice and research in sport psychology.

Several researchers have begun to address the issue of theory versus application. Hardy (1996) reexamined the cusp catastrophe model of anxiety (Fazey & Hardy, 1988) for its practical value to sport psychology. Williams and Andersen (1998)

reviewed and critiqued their original model of stress and injury (Andersen & Williams, 1988) in relation to its use in applied and research settings. Gilbourne and Taylor (1998) made an initial foray into integrating goal perspective theory and injury rehabilitation. Their research suggested that this area holds potential, but it too needs further empirical validation.

The bidirectional flow of information between theory and practice is important to the growth of the field. A model adapted from Rivenes (1978) (see figure 1.2) illustrates how a working relationship between researchers and practitioners in sport psychology can be mutually beneficial. This model can be a useful tool when trying to gain a new perspective on a research or professional problem. For instance, direct observation and clinical case studies may help create new constructs or explain conflicting findings in existing studies. Such was the case with the concept of relaxation-induced anxiety, which was first noted in anecdotal reports in clinical psychology (Heide & Borkovec, 1983). After documenting the occurrence of relaxation-induced anxiety (the display of increases in anxiety as a consequence of engaging in relaxation training), Heide and Borkovec (1984) hypothesized several mechanisms to explain the phenomenon. They also proposed a theoretical model wherein relaxation-induced anxiety was viewed within a broader framework designed to explain the development and maintenance of the more generalized anxiety disorders.

Sport Psychology Theory

A second issue pertains to whether we need a singular conceptual paradigm to drive our research and applied efforts. Roberts (1989) maintained

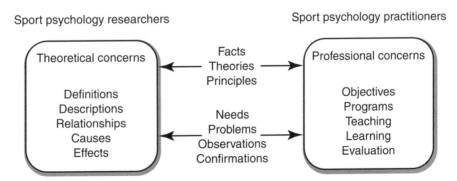

Figure 1.2 A bidirectional relationship between theoretical research and practice in sport psychology.

R.S. Rivenes, *Foundations of physical education,* copyright © 1978 Houghton Mifflin Company. Adapted with permission.

that the slow growth is due to a lack of a generally accepted conceptual paradigm to drive our work. He advocated that we use cognitive models to understand behavior in sport and exercise and become better acquainted with the epistemological concerns of mainstream psychology, in which the cognitive paradigm has dominated research since the late 1970s. But Roberts also conceded that sport psychology researchers should be open to the work of those using other paradigms (e.g., psychobiological, social psychological). Other writers (Landers, 1989; Morgan, 1989) have suggested that shifting to one conceptual paradigm would be a mistake. They advocate broadening the prevailing zeitgeist to provide a better understanding of problems in sport behavior.

We believe that the development of theoretical formulations within the context of sport and exercise should draw from multiple sources. As Landers (1989) suggested, theory cannot be developed in a vacuum. He contended that sport psychology researchers need to continue to borrow theories, methods, and approaches from academic psychology as a starting point from which to examine their applicability and modify them accordingly. But as we stated in the beginning of this chapter, these models may also be inadequate to understand some of the psychological phenomena specific to sport unless researchers begin to integrate knowledge from other subdisciplines within sport and exercise science. Dishman (1983) advocated that researchers within kinesiology combine their talents across subdisciplines to answer questions of practical effect. Dishman termed this a recycled suggestion, one that has more frequently been ignored than followed. For instance, in trying to explain why children drop out of youth sports, sport psychology researchers have previously considered only psychological reasons (Feltz & Petlichkoff, 1983; Gould, Feltz, Horn, & Weiss, 1982; Klint & Weiss, 1986). As a result of this narrow focus, training and conditioning or maturational explanations for dropping out have often been overlooked.

An example, previously illustrated in figure 1.1, of a crossdisciplinary approach to examining a sport-specific question is Beuter and Duda's (1985) analysis of the arousal–motor performance relationship. These researchers used movement kinematics (an assessment of the quality of performance) to examine the effect of arousal on motor performance. This approach allowed them to focus on the process by which arousal influences performance rather than simply on the outcome of performance.

Crossdisciplinary studies may uncover explanations that a study based solely on psychological models cannot provide.

A third issue has been the lack of response to the call for innovative approaches and broader conceptual views to understanding psychological phenomena in sport (Landers, 1983; Rejeski & Brawley, 1983). Broadening our conceptual views is not an easy task, given the human tendency to think recurring thoughts that constrain our research efforts (Wicker, 1985). Wicker offered some strategies to help researchers get out of their conceptual ruts and gain new perspectives on familiar problems. One category of strategies was playing with ideas, and another was considering contexts. Researchers and practitioners can play with ideas by working with metaphors, drawing graphic representations of ideas, and rethinking concepts in terms of process. For example, Selye's (1946) concept of stress in the human body was taken from the domain of physics.

Consideration of contexts includes placing specific research problems in a larger domain, such as within the larger domain of kinesiology, as mentioned earlier, and making comparisons to other domains. McCormack and Challip (1988) advocated making comparisons to social contexts outside the sport domain to help define the unique attributes of sport, but these comparisons may also generate new ideas. For instance, by examining the moral reasoning of athletes within and outside a sport context, Bredemeier and Shields (1986) postulated that sport involves a "bracketed morality," a legitimated, temporary suspension of the usual moral obligations to consider the needs and desires of all persons equally.

Changing Populations

A final issue is the changing demographics of sport participants and the realization of the need for new research and applied perspectives to match the population shift. Traditionally, sport psychology research and applied work has focused on elite, collegiate, and, more recently, youth sport participants. Older adult, recreational, and other sport participants were largely ignored. As North American and international population demographics continue to change (with expansions at both the older adult and youth levels), researchers and practitioners have begun to examine sport psychology from a developmental perspective. Weiss (2004) edited a new textbook that uses a lifespan perspective to examine sport and exercise psychology. This trend, although recent, is likely to expand in the coming years.

North America and the United States, in particular, have experienced a shift to a more multicultural and global sport environment. Recent articles in sport psychology have attested to the need for sport psychologists to adopt a multicultural perspective in their work with athletes (Kontos & Arguello, 2005; Kontos & Breland-Noble, 2002). Martens, Mobley, and Zizzi (2000) presented a multicultural model for training in applied sport psychology. But sport psychology graduate programs and practitioners have yet to embrace these suggestions. Although 30 to 40% of the U.S. population is made up of ethnic minorities and an even greater percentage of many sports' participants are ethnic minorities, multicultural issues and training are still scarce in sport psychology. Moreover, much as the larger field of psychology is characterized by low representation (less than 5%, as reported in a 1997 *APA Monitor* report [Martin, 1999]) of culturally diverse professionals, so too is sport psychology. To understand and meet the needs of the increasingly multicultural world of sport, sport psychology will need to embrace a multicultural approach and more closely reflect the population that it serves.

Future Research Directions

The field of sport psychology and the discipline of kinesiology are in exciting stages of development. Journals, professional societies, graduate programs, and professional avenues in sport psychology have proliferated around the globe. This growth poses challenges for the next generation of researchers and practitioners. We see four major challenges in sport psychology as researchers move forward—balancing specialization and integrative knowledge, keeping abreast of the knowledge expansion, using new statistical methods, and obtaining funding for research.

Balancing Specialization and Integrative Knowledge Researchers and graduate programs will need to balance specialization and integrative knowledge to develop the theoretical models that will ultimately answer questions of sport and human movement (Alderman, 1980; Dishman, 1983; Martens, 1980). To achieve this integrated body of knowledge in kinesiology, departments may have to change their reward structure so that researchers receive greater rewards for publishing within kinesiology than for publishing in their parent

disciplines (Hoffman, 1985). Researchers should not be subject to penalties for doing collaborative research (Mahoney, 1985). In addition, graduate curricular programs may need to be modified to prepare students better for interdisciplinary research (Hoffman). An integrated knowledge of sport and exercise science, however, does not eliminate the need for intensive study in psychology. Both will be necessary if students are to be successful in conducting state-of-the-art research.

Knowledge Expansion A second challenge will be to keep abreast of the knowledge being generated in sport psychology and the broader fields of psychology and kinesiology. The incredible expansion of information in sport psychology and its easy access on the internet has allowed for rapid exchange of ideas and progression of research in our field. However, the lack of refereed editing and secondary sourcing of information that is prevalent on the internet (e.g., Google, Wikipedia), and the tendency for the public, students, and professionals alike to rely on this information without critically examining it presents concerns regarding the quality of such information. In spite of the recent growth in online and hard copy outlets for publication in sport psychology, the turnaround times and immediacy of published empirical information for many journals has become slower (up to 2-3 years lag time in some journals). This slowing of information flow can be attributed to the increased need for editors and reviewers for the growing number of publication outlets in our field. The costs of access to some journals have been reduced through online databases; however, the increase in publication outlets means there are more journals now to buy. Unfortunately, in this era of higher education budget reductions, library funding and recurrent costs for journals are among the first budget casualties. To keep up with the constantly evolving literature in sport psychology researchers will need to adapt to new information technologies (e.g., online journals, search engines, Pod casts), be more involved in the reviewing process, become better critical consumers of online information, and advocate for increased institutional library funding. There will also be an increased need for meta-analytical reviews of the growing numbers of empirical studies to synthesize the large amount of research being generated.

Keeping Up With Statistics and Research Methodologies A third challenge will be the need to keep current regarding the statistical and research methods available to investigate the complex questions at the cutting edge of research in sport psychology and kinesiology. Many more tools are available now than there were 20 years ago, such as hierarchical linear modeling, structural equation modeling, confirmatory factor analysis, simultaneous factor analysis, log-linear analysis of categorical data, and computer simulations of social interactions, to name just a few. Schutz and Gessaroli (1993) observed a gradual shift away from experimental analysis toward complex statistical applications in the areas of inventory development, comprehensive model building, reliability and validity studies, survey analyses, and longitudinal intervention studies. They suggested that researchers will need to change continually and use the best tools available as our knowledge about a phenomenon grows. They also warn, however, against becoming method (or instrument) bound and ritualizing statistics instead of remembering that they are tools to help researchers answer well-formulated, theoretically based questions. Helping researchers keep abreast of statistical advances in the field may require leaders in the field to devote more journal space and conference time to covering new methods and statistical techniques as they are developed. Moreover, a renewed emphasis on understanding the assumptions and application of the appropriate statistical procedures for the various research questions and designs is warranted.

External Funding   A final challenge is the increased pressure to obtain external funding. All researchers at institutions of higher education, including sport psychology professors, face this challenge as the relative proportion of support from public sources continues to decline and competition for other funds increases. Departments and individual faculty who want to succeed must demonstrate solid extramurally funded research programs (Moore, 1998; Wilmore, 1998). Graduate students will need to demonstrate their grant activity if they want faculty positions at research-intensive universities. If sport psychology as a field cannot demonstrate that its research can attract funding, fewer sport psychology positions may be available at research universities in the future. One way to increase fundability within the field is to adopt a more crossdisciplinary approach involving multi-

dimensional perspectives from within and outside kinesiology and psychology. One example of this involves the current push for more physical activity among youth. The acknowledgment of obesity and physical inactivity as major health problems in the United States (Hedley et al., 2004) has refocused interest in sport and physical activity programs. This renewed focus provides an opportunity for researchers and practitioners from sport psychology, exercise physiology, health psychology, and pedagogy to obtain funding to study the effects of sport on participants.

Garnering outside funding for research in sport psychology can have a positive influence on the field, as Moore (1998) indicated, by enhancing a researcher's ability to answer important scientific questions and make significant scholarly contributions to the field. The availability of external grant money will also strongly influence the direction of research in sport psychology toward those areas that funding sources deem worthwhile. For instance, governmental funding for research on exercise behavior exceeds funding for research on sport behavior. Sport psychology has already witnessed the results of this influence through the increasing number of textbooks devoted to exercise psychology, the large number of research articles on issues of health and exercise, and the change in the name of the *Journal of Sport Psychology* to the *Journal of Sport and Exercise Psychology*. The challenge will be not only to obtain funding for research but also to resist changing research orientations to chase money.

The issues surrounding the nature of sport psychology (e.g., its definition, roles, specialization, academic preparation, ecological validity, theoretical versus applied emphasis) are not unique to the field, nor are the future challenges. The fields that work to resolve these issues and embrace their challenges will show continued growth and popularity. The fields whose members are more concerned with self-serving pursuits than with working together to advance the field will eventually dwindle and die. Sport psychology, within the broader fields of kinesiology and psychology, has experienced increased growth, exposure, and popularity. This growth and popularity brings with it challenges and opportunities for sport psychology researchers and practitioners alike.

CHAPTER 2

Quantitative Research Methodology

David E. Conroy, PhD ▪ **Miranda P. Kaye** ▪ **Lindsey H. Schantz, MS** ▪

There are many ways of learning about psychological phenomena in movement settings. Quantitative research has been the dominant approach in the sport and exercise psychology literature. The aim of this chapter is to unpack some of the mystery surrounding quantitative research methods for students who are learning how to read, evaluate, and conduct research using this approach. In doing so, we hope to highlight the boundaries of how quantitative research methods have been employed so that readers might think of ways that research methods can be used creatively to enhance understanding of psychological phenomena in sport and exercise settings.

We begin the chapter by reviewing some fundamental epistemological and research design concepts that are relevant when conducting and evaluating quantitatively based investigations. We also report an original content analysis of empirical articles with quantitative data in a leading sport and exercise psychology journal to highlight some research design patterns and trends in this literature. These patterns and trends provide the basis for a series of recommendations that we offer for consideration by current and future researchers whose work will fill these journals in the years ahead.

We recognize that epistemology and research design are not topics that tend to inspire excitement among most readers, perhaps especially so among readers whose interests focus on the practice of sport and exercise psychology. Science and practice have been uneasy partners in the modern history of psychology. Scientists sometimes view practitioners as unsystematic and insufficiently rigorous in their efforts to change human behavior. Practitioners sometimes view scientists as being disconnected from practically significant problems and simplistic in their worldview. In reality, scientists and practitioners share common goals and simply pursue them through different paths.

Common Goals of Scientists and Practitioners

For a given phenomenon, the goals of both scientists and practitioners involve observation, description, explanation, prediction, and control. These five goals provide one context for understanding the methods used to conduct sport and exercise psychology research. To illustrate how scientists pursue these goals, we will periodically refer to an example involving the effects of fear of failure on motor performance in a high-stakes situation. This phenomenon may appeal to readers' scientific or practical interests but, given the focus of the chapter, we will focus primarily on how it illustrates research-related concepts.

Goal 1: Observation Observation is a primary goal of scientists and practitioners. Empirical work refers to scholarship based on observations and data. Careful observation can even lead to unintended discoveries, an occurrence known as serendipity. Many important discoveries have been serendipitous (e.g., anesthetic qualities of nitrous oxide and ether, antidepressant effects of monoamine oxidase inhibitors, hallucinogenic effects of LSD; see Roberts, 1989; Valenstein, 1998).

Scientists strive to witness relations that exist in the natural world as well as responses to their manipulations of the natural environment. Similarly, practitioners observe their clients during assessments using a variety of tools (e.g., interviews, paper-and-pencil tests, behavior observations). Observation may be the single most important task of scientists and practitioners because the accuracy of their observations will largely determine the success of their efforts toward all other goals.

Goal 2: Description Having observed a phenomenon of interest, scientists seek to describe that phenomenon in detail so that others can understand what the phenomenon involves and identify it in their own observations. In psychological work, description is a critical task because many of the phenomena of interest are not directly observable (e.g., fear of failure, anxiety, self-efficacy, perceived competence). That is, these elements are latent and must be inferred based on other observations. We often refer to such unobserved variables as constructs because the investigator forms or synthesizes them based on other observations.

In a classic paper MacCorquodale and Meehl (1948) formalized the distinction between intervening variables and hypothetical constructs. From their perspective, intervening variables can be reduced to strictly empirical formulations (e.g., scores on a psychometric instrument, checklists of diagnostic criteria), whereas hypothetical constructs cannot be reduced to strict empirical laws. In other words, hypothetical constructs contain surplus meaning beyond what is contained in an empirical law; thus, the validity of the law is insufficient for determining the truth of the hypothetical construct. In some ways, this distinction parallels the difference between constitutive and operational definitions of a construct. Constitutive definitions are general and abstract; they focus on the conceptual nature of the construct (thus incorporating surplus meaning). On the other hand, operational definitions specify how a construct will be defined for a particular purpose.

To illustrate this difference, let's consider our example involving an achievement motive construct (e.g., fear of failure). A constitutive definition of achievement motives refers to socialized associations between anticipated achievement outcomes and pleasant or unpleasant self-conscious affects that energize achievement behavior toward competence (approach) or away from incompetence (avoidance). This definition helps us understand what achievement motives are and the role they play in motivation, but it does not indicate how we would measure such motives. An operational definition would distinguish whether we were focusing on implicit or self-attributed motives, approach- or avoidance-valenced motives, and the specific techniques being used to quantify the motive (e.g., responses to pictorial content or to standardized statements).

In the scientific literature, descriptions of relations between hypothetical constructs can be referred to as models. Returning to the example mentioned previously, we can construct a model indicating that people who fear failure perform poorly in high-stakes situations because their attention is biased toward failure-related cues that they find threatening. Models can often be depicted graphically by path diagrams such as figure 2.1. These path diagrams represent relations between constructs (typically focusing on the direction but not magnitude of relations) but provide little in the way of explanation for why specific relations exist. Much like scientists, practitioners seek to describe their observations of a client's affect, behavior, and cognition to build rapport with the client, develop their understanding of the client's situation, and define the nature of their focus with the client.

Goal 3: Explanation After observing and describing a phenomenon, scientists and practitioners seek to synthesize their observations into the simplest explanation that most completely accounts for the observations made for a particular phenomenon. Scientists refer to these explanations (for a set of observations) as theories. Theories must (a) provide a viable explanation for a phenomenon including relations between hypothetical constructs associated with that phenomenon, (b) be stated in testable terms (a requirement that led Sigmund Freud to draw the ire of the scientific community of his day), and (c) be refutable or falsifiable (i.e., they can be demonstrated to be wrong if they are in fact incorrect explanations of the phenomena of interest). The best theories also offer the simplest explanation for the widest range of phenomena with the fewest assumptions possible, a characteristic referred to as parsimony. Scientists are encouraged to use what is known as Occam's razor to trim away the nonessential assumptions and select the most parsimonious explanation in their theory-building or theory-revising enterprises.

Practitioners develop their explanations of a specific client's affect, behavior, and cognition in their case formulations. Similar to theories, case formulations attempt to connect all the information known about a particular phenomenon in the simplest explanation possible. They provide the basis for the development of interventions that address the core issue behind the symptoms that led the client to seek consultation. Whether the phenomenon of interest is occurring in a controlled laboratory setting or in a high-pressure situation such as a playoff, both scientists and practitioners are intimately (if not always explicitly) involved in theory development.

Goal 4: Prediction The explanations (theories) that scientists and practitioners develop provide the basis for their predictions about the phenomenon in question. Scientists call these predictions

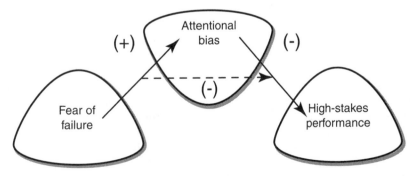

Figure 2.1 Model of relations between fear of failure, attentional bias, and performance in a high-stakes test. This model describes relations between the constructs, but it does not explain why specific relations are proposed.

hypotheses. The hypothesis testing process (i.e., the scientific method) is likely to be familiar to many readers, and we will review some of its key logical tenets later in this chapter in discussing the process of establishing causal relations between variables. Practitioners may be less formal in developing and testing their predictions, but this goal is just as important in their work. For example, every intervention should be based on a prediction that the intervention will alter a person's thoughts, feelings, or behaviors in an adaptive fashion. This prediction should be followed by an ongoing process of monitoring and evaluating the person's thoughts, feelings, and behaviors.

Goal 5: Control Of course, the ultimate goal of both scientists and practitioners is to control a particular phenomenon. Scientists seek to identify causal relations that exist in the natural world as well as manipulations that can induce desired causal effects. Practitioners seek to modify the thoughts, feelings, and behaviors of athletes and exercisers to optimize some aspect of their experience (e.g., performance, well-being).

The five goals just outlined illustrate many of the parallels between the work of scientists and practitioners in sport and exercise psychology. Ultimately, both scientists and practitioners confront the challenge of uncovering causal relations responsible for creating specific phenomena.

The Scientific Method for Inferring Causality

The epistemological movements of logical positivism and postpositivism have had a tremendous influence on how social and behavioral scientists test and evaluate causal relations. Logical positivists are rational empiricists who believe that truth can be found through the verification and replication of observable findings involving directly perceivable entities or processes. They logically deduce hypotheses to test their theories. From this perspective, theory must be verifiable and falsifiable through observation. Postpositivists reject a central tenet of positivism by asserting that observations are fallible and potentially inaccurate. From this perspective, scientific discoveries are influenced by human motives, biases, and institutions, not just by the cold, logical progression of empiricism. Postpositivists emphasize the importance of multiple measures of constructs for managing sources of error and approaching an understanding of objective reality.

This section of the chapter summarizes some of the key requirements for inferring causality from a generally postpositivist perspective. It is heavily influenced by Cook and Campbell's (1979) analysis of different theories of causation.

David Hume (1739/2000), a Scottish philosopher of science, proposed that three necessary and sufficient conditions exist for demonstrating causal relations between two variables: (a) association between the putative cause and effect variables, (b) temporal precedence of the putative causal variable, and (c) constant conjunction of the two variables. In other words, the putative cause and effect variables must covary, changes in the cause variable must precede changes in the effect variable, and the effect variable must not change without prior changes in the cause variable. This perspective has some limitations, most of which concern the interpretation of the constant conjunction requirement. For example, a strong association between temporally sequenced cause-and-effect variables may have been observed in the past, but that historical association provides no guarantee that this functional relation will be observed in the future (i.e., such empirically derived conclusions are matters of belief rather than reason).

John Stuart Mill (1846) offered an alternative perspective to Hume's notion of constant conjunction. Instead of requiring constant conjunction between the putative cause-and-effect variables, Mill indicated that researchers instead bear the burden of eliminating other plausible explanations for associations between those variables. Thus, reason plays a more prominent role, and the researcher must be creative in seeking plausible rival explanations for observed relations. Popper (1959) extended this notion in his writing on the importance of falsification. Given that we can never know a theory to be correct, we must rule out competing theories (i.e., falsify them).

This emphasis on falsification gave rise to what is often referred to as the hypothetico-deductive method, in which researchers use a process of elimination to increase their confidence that a given explanation is true. By treating hypotheses as assumptions about the nature of reality, successful predictions produce conclusions that the theory leading to the hypothesis was not incorrect. Likewise, unsuccessful predictions produce conclusions that either the theory or method used to test the theory was flawed. At that point, scientists return to the drawing board to review and refine their methods while considering plausible alternative explanations for the new empirical observations (i.e., the unsuccessful predictions). Although proving that one explanation is correct is impossible because testing *all* possible competing theories in all possible situations is not practical, it is possible to rule out plausible alternative explanations for results by demonstrating that their predictions are consistently incorrect. As such, scientists strive to enhance their confidence in the conclusions that they draw about a given theory by ruling out plausible alternative explanations. Obviously, a single study cannot eliminate all plausible rival hypotheses, so science must be a cumulative process.

To illustrate how this epistemology influences scientists' approaches to solving a research problem, consider how one might investigate the effects of fear of failure on a golfer's performance in a high-stakes situation, such as a playoff to determine a tournament champion. We can come up with several plausible explanations for why fear of failure might influence a golfer's accuracy. For instance, fear of failure may bias the golfer's attention in that situation toward failure-related cues in the environment. Because information-processing capacity is limited, this attentional bias will reduce the amount of task-relevant information that the golfer is processing and thereby lead to performance decrements (an information-processing-based explanation). Alternatively, fear of failure may lead people to experience higher levels of state anxiety, which might increase their activation beyond an optimal level for the task (an affective explanation). These are just two of several possible explanations. Both explanations involve mediation. That is, both explanations specify a mechanism responsible for the relation between fear of failure and performance in the playoff. Mediation hypotheses are central to psychological theorizing because they speak directly to why causal variables have the effects that they do. Another important type of relation that is commonly hypothesized involves moderation. Moderation hypotheses test specific conditions under which relations between variables may vary or subgroups within a sample for which relations may vary. For example, one could suggest that fear of failure will be a much stronger predictor of performance (a) following failure feedback than it would following success feedback or (b) for people with low perceived competence compared with people with high perceived competence. In this case, the prior feedback and individual differences in perceived competence would be framed as moderators of the effects of fear of failure on performance. With a set of plausible explanations in hand (whether they involve mediation or moderation), the researcher

is positioned to design an experiment to test competing models.

Readers interested in learning more about the concepts of mediation and moderation should refer to the classic article by Baron and Kenny (1986) or more recent presentations by MacKinnon and colleagues (e.g., MacKinnon, Lockwood, Hoffman, West, & Sheets, 2002).

Basic Research Designs

The investigator interested in testing competing explanations for the effect of fear of failure on high-stakes task performance may choose from three broad classes of research designs. Passive observation designs involve data collected without any experimental manipulation. Data are typically collected on a single occasion in this design, but it is possible to collect data on multiple occasions in a passive observation research design. Passive observation designs are sometimes referred to as correlational designs. Given that correlations are statistics that can be employed in any research design, we use the term *passive observation* to describe these designs. At the opposite end of the spectrum from passive observation designs and their relative lack of experimental manipulations and control are experimental designs.

Experimental designs involve random assignment of participants to conditions, implementation of one or more manipulations that vary across conditions, and assessment of participants before and after the manipulation. Random assignment is critical in experimental designs because it permits assumptions that all factors beyond experimental assignment are equivalent, thus limiting the number of possible explanations of any observed differences between experimental groups (i.e., such differences cannot be attributed to preexisting differences between groups). Randomization, and the assumption of equivalence that it permits, afford the experimenter a tremendous advantage when the time comes to draw conclusions about relations between variables.

A third category, quasi-experimental designs, was proposed in the middle of the last century (Campbell, 1957; Stouffer, 1950). These designs are identical to experimental designs in every way except for a lack of random assignment to experimental conditions (Cook & Campbell, 1979). The quasi-experimenter may assign participants to different treatment groups nonrandomly, and data may be collected longitudinally to assess treatment-related differences in change. These designs are common in field research settings where random assignment is often not possible. For example, an investigator may not be able to assign individuals to teams or exercise classes randomly. Even if multiple teams or classes are sampled, the investigator is left with the possibility that differences observed between the experimental groups may have been because of systematic differences in the groups that existed before the manipulation. We will revisit this issue later in the chapter in the section about contemporary issues in research design.

Experimental designs are the sine qua non for investigating causal relations. They provide the strongest possible approach to testing hypotheses and falsifying theories because they afford investigators the greatest control and limit the number of possible explanations for results. In reality, employing an experimental design is not always feasible because of practical limitations in the potential for randomly assigning participants to conditions. In such situations, the quasi-experiment is the next best option for investigators. Use of such designs requires that investigators temper their conclusions somewhat relative to what might be drawn from a truly experimental design. Nevertheless, a quasi-experimental design is superior to a passive observation design for questions concerning causal relations between independent and dependent variables. Passive observations are the weakest design for studying causal relations because they rely solely on uncontrolled variation between the variables. They serve a useful role in the early stages of inquiry that emphasize observation, description, and preliminary explanation but are insufficient for drawing conclusions about causal relations.

The main difference between the three major research designs described above involves the level of control afforded to the investigators. As a literature matures, one would expect to see evidence of increasing experimental control. To our knowledge, the relative frequency of these designs in the sport and exercise psychology literature has not been documented to date.

A related issue of interest is the temporal structure of data collected in sport and exercise psychology. Some studies involve data collection at a single time point for all measures (referred to as concomitant data collection), whereas others collect data at multiple time points. The former strategy allows for the possibility that observed relations between variables result from situational parameters or participants' states at the time of data collection. Thus, concomitant data collection limits investigators' ability to draw conclusions about change. Collecting data at multiple time points, either prospectively or in a repeated measures design, affords researchers greater confidence in ruling out state effects and may enable them to study how dependent variables change over time (typically in response to some manipulation or covariate).

The use of repeated measures is standard in quasi-experimental and experimental designs, but the time interval between the first and last measurement may vary tremendously between studies. Some studies collect all their repeated measurements during a single experimental session that may last less than an hour, whereas others collect their repeated measures over extended intervals (e.g., days, weeks, years). Although human development occurs in brief as well as extended time frames, longer intervals for repeated measures can strengthen conclusions about the long-term consequences of manipulations (as well as the permanence of change in some cases). Clearly, substantive considerations should guide decision making about research design. Nevertheless, the frequency with which investigators employ concomitant versus repeated measures data collection designs (as well as the interval for the repeated measures) will reveal some of the priorities in the literature. Frequent use of concomitant data collection would suggest an emphasis on describing relations between variables, whereas frequent use of repeated measures would suggest an emphasis on testing explanations of why variables change.

The final research design issue of interest for our purposes involves the multilevel structure of samples that are collected. As noted previously, sport and exercise participants are often organized into groups, such as teams or classes, before the investigator becomes involved. Unfortunately, these preexisting groupings can be a threat to the randomization scheme used by investigators because team or class assignments may be determined (intentionally or not) by some characteristic of the participants. For example, parents may register their children for teams based on proximity to their homes. If characteristics of neighborhoods or parts of town vary systematically (e.g., by race, ethnicity, or socioeconomic status), these community characteristics may be responsible for differences between participants on different teams (instead of differences in experimental group assignments). Thus, such groupings represent an additional level of analysis that requires attention. To illustrate how data can exist at multiple levels, consider that an outcome (e.g., performance in high-stakes competitions) may be assessed repeatedly within an individual (level 1), who is on a team (level 2), in a particular league (level 3). Scholars have begun to urge the sport and exercise psychology research community to attend to these nested effects (e.g., Papaiouannou, Marsh, & Theodorakis, 2004).

Sampling

Sample Size and Statistical Power A major issue with regard to sample characteristics is the size of a sample. Sample size has a direct effect on statistical power—the probability that an analysis will detect significant effects in the population. The probability that a study will fail to detect an effect that exists in the population is referred to as the Type II error rate (β); thus, power is $(1 - \beta)$. (Effect refers simply to an association or relation between two variables.) Power is a function of three factors: (a) the size of an effect in the population, (b) the a priori Type I error level (i.e., the probability of incorrectly rejecting a null hypothesis), and (c) the sample size (Cohen, 1988). Power is a critical consideration in quantitative research because it influences how much confidence investigators can place in their conclusions.

Most investigators place great importance on avoiding Type I errors (i.e., false positives) and pay less attention to the cost of Type II errors (i.e., false negatives). For this reason, readers who have taken an introductory statistics course are probably familiar with the meaning of p values (e.g., $p < .05$; $p < .01$) reported after every inferential statistical test but may be less familiar with the concept of statistical power. A brief explanation of p values may be useful for readers who have not taken an introductory statistics course recently (or those who do not remember much from the one they took). In traditional null-hypothesis significance testing, investigators assume that no relations actually exist between the variables they are studying; this assumption forms the null hypothesis that is tested. Of course, when data are collected from a sample of participants, rarely are the observed effects perfectly zero (even when no effect exists in the population). Thus, the investigator must determine the likelihood of the observed effects (in the sample) if the null hypothesis is true at the level of the population. The p value refers to the probability of obtaining the observed result if the relation is truly nonexistent in the population. By arbitrary convention, scientists typically require less than a 5% probability ($p < .05$) of obtaining the observed difference by chance before they will reject the hypothesis that no relation exists in the population (i.e., the null hypothesis). Type I errors refer to situ-

ations in which the investigator mistakenly rejects the null hypothesis (i.e., claims to have observed a nonzero association between two variables that are, in fact, unrelated). There is a tradeoff between Type I and Type II error rates. As an investigator's risk of Type I errors decreases (i.e., fewer false positives), his or her risk of Type II errors increases (i.e., more false negatives). Cohen (1988) suggested somewhat arbitrarily that Type I errors may be four times as undesirable as Type II errors. Thus, for studies with an a priori alpha level (i.e., Type I error rate) of .05, the optimal statistical power for the analysis is .80 $(= 1 - [4 \times .05])$.

Statistical power is a practical concern for investigators. Consider the case of two investigators who are studying whether fear of failure is associated with golfers' performance in a high-stakes task. Investigator A collects data from a sample of 96 athletes, whereas investigator B collects data from a sample of 25 athletes. Both find that the correlation between dispositional fear of failure and performance in the high-stakes task is .20 and not statistically significant ($p > .05$, meaning that the effect does not appear to be significantly different from zero). The power of these two investigators' analyses (given the observed effect size, the stated sample sizes, and a two-tailed alpha level of .05) is estimated to be .50 (investigator A) and .16 (investigator B). (Readers can consult Cohen (1988) to learn more about conducting power analyses.) Although neither investigator can entirely rule out low statistical power as an explanation for his or her results, investigator A is in a much better position than investigator B. If a small association ($r = .20$) truly existed between these variables in the population, investigator A would have had a greater likelihood of detecting it than would investigator B. In contrast investigator B is left to wonder whether he or she should conclude (a) that no association exists in the population or (b) that the association in the population is too small for the analysis to detect. Both investigators will likely struggle to publish their null results, but investigator B is going to have a more difficult time than investigator A because of the relatively inferior statistical power of her or his study.

In a review of the statistical power of research in the 1960 volume of the *Journal of Abnormal Psychology*, Cohen (1962) found that the average level of power for detecting medium-sized effects was .48. A quarter of a century later, the mean power for detecting medium effects in the same journal had dropped to .25 (Sedlmeier & Gigerenzer, 1989; Cohen, 1992). Clearly, this trend is heading in the wrong direction in the abnormal psychology literature. Little is known about the level of statistical power in sport and exercise psychology research or longitudinal trends in the power of research in this literature.

Qualitative Characteristics of Samples Beyond sample size and its effect on power, qualitative differences in samples are worth considering. Gender, age, and race or ethnicity are the most common qualities of human research participants used to describe the members of a sample. This information helps readers appreciate to whom the findings may be generalized. When appropriate, the American Psychological Association (2001) encourages investigators to report socioeconomic status, disability status, and sexual orientation. Depending on the focus of the study, descriptions of other characteristics also may be useful (e.g., education, health status; APA, 2001).

Gender is perhaps the characteristic most commonly used to describe participants in a sample. Concerns have emerged that the sport and exercise psychology literature has neither focused sufficiently on gender as a variable of interest nor sampled the genders equally (e.g., Krane, 1994). Claims have been made that males have been sampled disproportionately more than females (Gill, 1992; Landers, Boutcher, & Wang, 1986).

The age of research participants has become increasingly important in recent years as interest in developmental sport psychology has increased (Weiss & Bredemeier, 1983; Weiss, 2004). The number of sport psychology studies focused on children and youth has increased recently (Weiss & Raedeke, 2004), and a lifespan developmental perspective is gaining popularity in the literature (Weiss). Age is commonly used as a proxy measure of the cognitive-developmental level of people. Emerging research clearly indicates that the antecedents and consequences of physical activity vary as a function of age (Weiss). Additionally, the meaning of scores from a particular measure may not be the same for younger and older people (Brustad, 1998). Accordingly, generalizing findings from one population to another without considering the potential role of age differences is inappropriate. Age is becoming a more central theoretical variable and appears to be a common descriptor of samples. Yet little is known about how frequently participants' ages have been reported by sport and exercise psychology researchers, what the range of ages studied has been, or whether the mean age of research participants has changed over the past quarter century. Even if the mean age of research participants is roughly stable

over time, greater interest in developmental issues suggests that one might expect to see a wider range of ages being studied over time.

Race and ethnicity are other characteristics commonly used to describe samples. Investigators have tended to generalize research results to individuals of all races and ethnicities although these populations have not always been included in the research (Duda & Hayashi, 1998; Duda & Allison, 1990; Ram, Starek, & Johnson, 2004). Indeed, recent investigations have revealed widespread neglect of race and ethnicity in the sport and exercise psychology literature. From 1979 to 1987, fewer than 4% (7 out of 186) of the empirical papers published in the *Journal of Sport & Exercise Psychology* investigated the influences of race and ethnicity on physical activity (Duda & Allison). A more recent content analysis revealed that from 1987 to 2000 approximately 19% of empirical papers published in the *Journal of Applied Sport Psychology*, the *Journal of Sport & Exercise Psychology*, and *The Sport Psychologist* included a reference to race or ethnicity; however, fewer than 2% of the papers published in that period dealt with race or ethnicity as a substantive construct (Ram et al.). Although the fivefold increase in attention to race and ethnicity as qualitative descriptors of research samples is laudable, it may be inadequate for a society as diverse as ours. The apparent neglect of race and ethnicity in the sport and exercise psychology literature may be confounded by investigators' decisions to publish work substantively focused on race and ethnicity in sociological journals. Several calls have been issued in the sport and exercise psychology literature for investigators to identify and recruit samples from more diverse populations (Duda & Allison; Gill, 1992; Ram et al., 2004). At a minimum, we support this recommendation for future research because research bias occurs when one group's experience and behavior is considered normative and serves as the basis for interpreting the experiences and behaviors of other groups (Herek, Kimmel, Amaro, & Melton, 1991; Iijima-Hall, 1997; Sue, 1999).

Instrumentation

A variety of methods are available to investigators when collecting data to test their hypotheses. These methods include self-reports, informant reports (e.g., coach, peer, or parent ratings), behavior observations, and psychophysiological indices. Each of these assessment approaches is valuable but limited in its own way. Self-reports are perhaps the easiest to obtain but are associated with many potential biases (e.g., social desirability, recall accuracy). Informant reports provide information from a unique perspective but are accompanied by questions about accuracy and bias as well. Behavior observations provide invaluable insight into what is objectively taking place but are expensive, time consuming, and dependent on the assumption that the coding scheme is sensitive to the most relevant behaviors. Psychophysiological measures offer unique and objective insight into mind–body processes but may be invasive and require expensive and specialized equipment or training to use.

Ideally, investigators can vary the assessment method and arrive at the same findings about a phenomenon. From a postpositivist perspective, that hope may be viewed as naïve, so researchers should prepare themselves for variability in their results depending on their assessment method. This variability can be highly informative in the process of theory building because it can provide investigators with closer access to the hypothetical constructs of interest. From another perspective, overreliance on any single approach can create a methodological monism that threatens theory development. The breadth of assessment methods used in the sport and exercise psychology literature has not been documented previously and will be examined in our content analysis.

Data Analysis

When data have a multilevel structure, statistically teasing apart the effects of the different levels of analysis is important. Recent advances in multilevel modeling analyses provide a means for decomposing outcome variance and linking it to the different levels of analysis (e.g., individual characteristics, team characteristics, league characteristics; Raudenbush & Bryk, 2002). Although such analyses are not a substitute for random assignment, they provide a compromise solution given our inability to assign every unit of analysis randomly in real-world studies. Although multilevel modeling techniques have been available since the early 1980s, they have only recently begun to appear in the sport and exercise psychology literature.

The majority of data analyses are conducted using statistics based on the general linear model (GLM). This model is the basis for a variety of analyses including t-tests, ANOVAs, correlations, multiple regressions, factor analysis, discriminant function analyses, and (in its most general expression) structural equation modeling. The GLM is an amazingly flexible model for data analysis because it can test linear as well as curvilinear (e.g., quadratic, cubic) patterns of relations between independent and dependent variables. Linear effects are likely to account for most of the variance in outcomes, but the addition of curvilinear effects may provide a more complete and accurate accounting of the variability in an outcome. As a literature matures and understanding of phenomena increases, we expect to see more sophisticated hypotheses about the specific shape of effects that are being modeled.

The final issue that we considered in our content analysis was the extent to which investigators report effect sizes in their research. Over the years, investigators have often misinterpreted the meaning of p values and mistakenly implied that smaller Type I error rates equated to larger effects. The American Psychological Association (2001) requires that investigators report effect sizes when possible, but it is not clear to what extent investigators have followed this dictum.

Reporting Scientific Research

Regardless of the specific research design employed, scientists rely on the research report to communicate results from their investigations. Research reports have a clear and well-defined structure consisting of separate sections for the introduction, methods, results, and discussion. The major tasks of the introduction are (a) to identify the research problem, (b) to convince readers of the significance of this problem, (c) to develop a theoretical framework that will guide the present investigation, and (d) to state a purpose and hypotheses based on the theoretical framework developed previously.

The methods section focuses on describing the sample, materials, and procedures employed in the investigation. The materials used may include equipment as well as specific instrumentation used to collect data. Methods sections also may include an overview of the methods used to analyze data from the sample. This section must provide detail sufficient to allow a reader to replicate the study if desired.

The results section reviews the findings of the study and may include tables and figures to provide details on specific results or illustrate key findings. The *Publication Manual of the American Psychological Association* (2001) requires investigators to report effect sizes for their analyses, especially for key analyses; these effect sizes indicate the direction and magnitude of relations between variables and should be reported in addition to probability (e.g., p, α) levels.

The discussion section interprets the findings in the context of the theoretical framework that guided hypothesis development and previous findings in the literature. Alternative explanations for the findings should be identified. Authors should also note the limitations and implications of the findings from both theoretical and practical perspectives. Ultimately, the discussion section provides a forum for convincing readers that an investigation advances understanding of a phenomenon and thus contributes positively to the literature.

Given that this chapter focuses on research methods, the four components of the methods section provide the structure for the rest of this chapter. Specifically, these issues (i.e., research design, sampling, instrumentation, data analysis) will be revisited in the context of describing patterns and trends observed in the existing sport and exercise psychology literature, and our recommendations for the next generation of research in sport and exercise psychology.

Research Trends

Given our emphasis on quantitative methods in this chapter, we thought it fitting to analyze the quantitative research literature in sport and exercise psychology to document patterns and trends. To increase the efficiency of this content analysis, we limited our review to a single journal. Several journals are dedicated to publishing empirical research in sport and exercise psychology. These outlets include (in order of longevity) the *International Journal of Sport and Exercise Psychology* (*IJSEP*; first published in 1970 as the *International Journal of Sport Psychology*), the *Journal of Sport & Exercise Psychology* (*JSEP*; first published in 1979 as the *Journal of Sport Psychology*), *The Sport Psychologist* (*TSP*; first published in 1987), the *Journal of Applied Sport Psychology* (*JASP*; first published in 1989), and *Psychology of Sport & Exercise* (*PSE*; first published in 2000). These journals differ in focus, and each makes a valuable contribution to the field. Nevertheless, we limited our analysis to a single journal that has had considerable influence on the sport and exercise psychology literature.

Several quantitative indices of journal influence are available from *Journal Citation Reports (JCR)*. These indicators include impact factors ("average number of times recent articles in a specific journal were cited in the *JCR* cover year"), immediacy indices ("average number of times current articles in a specific journal were cited during the year they were published"), total citations ("number of cita-

tions published in the current *JCR* year to all years of the journal"), and cited half-life of publications ("number of journal publication years going back from the current year which account for 50% of the total citations given by the citing journal in the current year") (*Journal Citation Reports*, 2004, pp. 10–11). To select a journal to examine, we used the admittedly imperfect impact factor index because it is among the most commonly used indicators of the scientific quality of a journal.

To provide some context for interpreting these impact factors, table 2.1 provides the 2006 impact factors for some other journals likely to be familiar to readers. Figure 2.2 presents the available impact factors for the four major sport and exercise psychology research journals since 1977—the *JSEP*, *JASP*, *IJSEP*, and *TSP*. Clearly, the influence of research in the specialized sport and exercise psychology journals is limited in comparison with the influence of research in journals from other kinesiology subdisciplines or the parent discipline of psychology. Figure 2.2 also indicates that articles published in

Table 2.1 Impact Factors for Selected Journals Outside Sport and Exercise Psychology

Journal name	2006 impact factor
Kinesiology journals	
Journal of Applied Physiology	3.178
Journal of Biomechanics	2.542
Journal of Motor Behavior	1.450
Medicine and Science in Sports and Exercise	2.909
Research Quarterly for Exercise and Sport	0.982
Psychology journals	
Developmental Psychology	3.556
Journal of Experimental Psychology: Human	2.261
Journal of Personality and Social Psychology	4.223
Major scientific journals	
Nature	26.681
Science	30.028

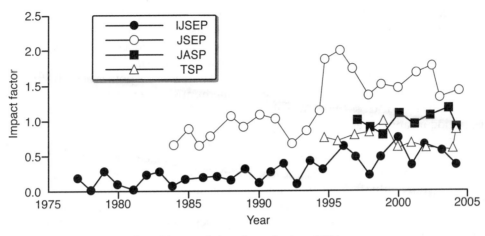

Figure 2.2   Impact factors for sport and exercise psychology journals since 1977.

the *JSEP* are more likely to be cited in future research than are articles published in the other specialized outlets. We infer that the *JSEP* articles are among the most influential in shaping the sport and exercise psychology literature. Accordingly, our content analysis focused on original, quantitatively based, empirical articles published in the *JSEP*.

Given that our content analysis is not the sole focus of this chapter, we will provide only a brief description of the methods that we used to conduct the study. Five coders were trained to code

characteristics of study sampling, instrumentation, design, and analysis (each coder coded part or all of one of those four aspects). Approximately 84% of the articles published in the first 26 volumes of the *JSEP* were original empirical reports (annual estimates ranged from 67% to 97% across the 26 years). Of those empirical reports, approximately 93% were based on quantitative data.

The lead author coded 15% of these articles to estimate agreement and reliability with the coders (agreement and reliability estimates are noted

AGREEMENT BETWEEN CODERS

A number of empirical articles (15% of the total) were coded by the coding team and the first author to estimate agreement. Given the variability in what was reported, we first calculated agreement with respect to identifying whether or not a particular type of information was reported. Following is a summary of those agreement statistics: number of studies or articles ($\kappa = .96$), age ($\kappa = .78$), gender ($\kappa = 1.00$), SES ($\kappa = .91$), whether any effect sizes were reported ($\kappa = .85$), type of measures used ($\kappa = .70$), data structure (single occasion, repeated measures in a single day, repeated measures over multiple days; $\kappa = .72$); whether the data had a multilevel structure ($\kappa = .86$), whether multilevel modeling was used for multilevel data ($\kappa = 1.00$), and the nature of effects that were tested (i.e., linear, curvilinear, nonlinear; $\kappa = .91$). Because details on race or ethnicity and SES were rarely provided, we did not include them in further analyses.

A more stringent test of agreement involved calculating agreement (or reliability) of the specific type of information reported. Following is a summary of the agreement (or reliability) statistics for relevant variables: age ($r = 1.00$), gender ($\kappa = .92$), type of measures used ($\kappa = .70$), design ($\kappa = .65$), data structure (single occasion, repeated measures in a single day, repeated measures over multiple days; $\kappa = .98$); whether the data had a multilevel structure ($\kappa = .86$), whether multilevel modeling was used for multilevel data ($\kappa = 1.00$), and the nature of effects that were tested (i.e., linear, curvilinear, nonlinear; $\kappa = .91$).

Although the level of agreement varied somewhat depending on the characteristic being coded, the level of agreement for each characteristic exceeded conventional minimum values (e.g., Fleiss, 1981; Landis & Koch, 1977). This level of agreement is generally viewed as being acceptable.

below). As indicated in the highlight box, agreement levels were generally sufficient to provide a basis for interpreting trends in the data. For maximum clarity, we focus here on averages for the following three periods: 1979–1989, 1990–1999, and 2000–2004. Annual averages for each coding category were estimated and then averaged across the years in the period. Thus, period means represent the average article in the average year within that period.

Besides calculating means, we estimated linear trend lines to describe longitudinal trends in each category of interest. The R^2 value for each trend line indicated how well the linear trend fit the observed trend across the three periods. Values close to .00 indicated that the linear trend did not describe the observed trend well, and values close to 1.00 indicated that the linear trend did an excellent job of describing the observed trend. When the linear trend line fit well (i.e., large R^2 value), the slope (b) of the line was examined. This slope indicated the average rate of change in a category between each of the three periods. (The three periods are not of equal size, so these slope estimates should be interpreted with caution.) Patterns and trends in sampling, instrumentation, research design, and data analysis are described here along with our recommendations for designing future research in sport and exercise psychology.

Research Design

As seen in the top panel of figure 2.3, passive observation designs accounted for approximately 63% of the studies from 1979 through 2004. This proportion did not vary predictably over the three periods examined ($R^2 = .12$). Experimental and quasi-experimental designs, the next most common design ($M = 34\%$), also did not vary predictably across time ($R^2 = .00$). Single-case research designs were extremely rare ($M < 1\%$). A reliance on passive observation research designs is appropriate in the early stages of inquiry because these designs are well suited to describing phenomena of interest. This descriptive emphasis can also be a limiting factor for theory development in sport and exercise psychology.

Sample Size

The average sample size each year increased dramatically through the three periods that we examined ($b = 62.2$, $R^2 = .96$). From 1979 through 1989, the average sample size each year was approximately 143 participants. From 2000 through 2004, the aver-

age sample size each year was 267 participants. This increase in sample sizes is encouraging because it has a direct and positive effect on the statistical power of data analyses.

The statistical power of each study for detecting medium-sized effects was estimated using essentially the same procedure used by Cohen (1962). Across the three periods the average level of statistical power for analyses was .80, and mean annual estimates ranged from .70 to .90 (means for the three periods ranged from .79 to .82). A linear trend did not fit the data extremely well ($R^2 = .17$), but it is reasonable to conclude that the level of statistical power has not changed appreciably across the three periods examined.

We caution readers that these findings were based on some extremely liberal assumptions in our power calculations. For example, we assumed that only one significance test was conducted with each dataset. Multiple tests will inflate the experiment-wise Type I error rate (Bland & Altman, 1995), and corrections to that error rate typically involve lowering the alpha level, a change that reduces power substantially. We also assumed that the relation being tested was a main effect, not an interaction effect. Interaction effects involving variables with measurement error are considerably underpowered relative to main effects of the same variables (Aiken & West, 1991). With those caveats in mind, the actual power of the analyses that we examined is likely to be substantially less than the .80 level that we documented. Improving the statistical power of analyses should continue to be a goal in sport and exercise psychology research.

Sample Composition

Samples can be described in many ways. Some common descriptors include the gender, age, race or ethnicity, and socioeconomic status (SES) of participants. To our surprise, approximately 20% of the studies did not describe the gender breakdown of participants. Overall, males (N = 52,478, or 55% of total gender-identified participants) have been sampled more frequently than females (N = 42,189, or 45% of total gender-identified participants). As seen in the middle panel of figure 2.3, an interesting longitudinal trend emerged to indicate that males are being sampled less frequently ($b = -0.05$, $R^2 = .90$), whereas females are being sampled more frequently ($b = 0.03$, $R^2 = .99$) over the three periods examined. In the 2000–2004 period, males and females appeared to be sampled equally for the first time (at least in studies that reported gender breakdowns).

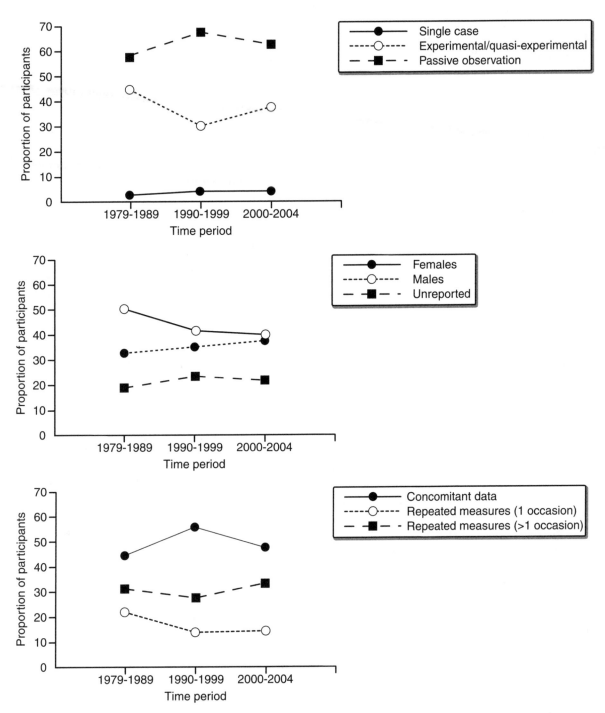

Figure 2.3 Longitudinal trends in experimental designs (top panel), gender sampling (middle panel), and temporal structures of data (bottom panel).

The average sample comprised participants with a mean age of 23.2 years (the mean age of the average participant across all studies was 22.5 years). The mean age of participants was relatively stable over time, and only a slight negative trend was observed ($b = -0.45$, $R^2 = .43$). Participants ranged in age from 4 to 96 years, but 95% of the mean ages

for samples each year ranged between 20.3 and 24.7 years. Clearly, the most research in sport and exercise psychology has focused on college-aged and young adult populations.

Given the recent review of race and ethnicity in sport and exercise psychology research (Ram et al., 2004), we did not include this variable in our content analysis. Socioeconomic status (SES) was rarely reported in the *JSEP* articles that we reviewed. In fact, fewer than 5% of all studies reviewed included any information about the SES of participants.

Instrumentation

Five types of assessment methods were coded: self-report, informant report, interview, behavior observation, and psychophysiological measures. Approximately 80% of the studies from 1979 through 2004 employed self-report measures, and this proportion increased by about 5% across each time period examined ($R^2 = .99$). Behavior observation was the next most common method of assessment ($M = 29\%$). Although the frequency of behavior observations dropped dramatically in the 1990s, no clear linear longitudinal trend was present ($R^2 = .19$). Psychophysiological measures became slightly more common over the three periods ($b = 0.01$; $R^2 = .99$) and were employed in approximately 15% of the studies from 2000 through 2004. Both interviews ($M = 7\%$) and informant reports ($M = 3\%$) were relatively uncommon in the studies analyzed. No longitudinal trend was evident for interviews ($R^2 = .19$), but the use of informant reports appeared to be on the decline ($b = -0.02$, $R^2 = .97$).

These results are disconcerting because they suggest a methodological monism in the sport and exercise psychology literature. That is, self-report methods may be having undue influence on theory development. The selection of measurement tools should be driven by substantive considerations. Although self-report methods are entirely appropriate for many studies on theoretical grounds, some research studies could certainly benefit from diversifying their sources of data.

Data Analysis

There are several interesting data analysis trends, particularly in the nature of effects examined, the temporal structure of data collection, multilevel modeling, and increased reporting of effect sizes.

Nature of Effects The vast majority of studies (95 to 99% across the three periods) examined linear effects. Far fewer studies have attempted to model curvilinear (e.g., quadratic or cubic, 2–5% across the three periods) or nonlinear (e.g., discontinuous, 0–1% across the three periods) relations between variables. Curvilinear effects have been examined since the early 1980s, but nonlinear relations have only recently been examined. Linear trend lines adequately captured longitudinal trends for linear

($R^2 = .93$, $b = -0.02$), curvilinear ($R^2 = .73$, $b = 0.02$), and nonlinear ($R^2 = .99$, $b = 0.00$) effects. These slope estimates suggested that curvilinear trends were becoming slightly more popular, but linear effects are clearly still the dominant focus of data analyses.

Temporal Data Structure As seen in the bottom panel of figure 2.3, concomitant data collection on a single occasion was the most common temporal structure for data across the three periods (M = 49%, annual range = 17–70%). Repeated measures on multiple occasions were second most common (*M* = 31%, range = 11–58%), and repeated measures on a single occasion were the least common temporal structure (*M* = 18%, range = 0–35%). Linear trend lines captured changes in the repeated measures across occasions ($R^2 = .40$, $b = 0.02$) and repeated measures within occasion ($R^2 = .65$, $b = -0.02$) data structures but did not fit the trends for concomitant data collection structures ($R^2 = .07$). None of the slope terms was especially large, so these temporal data structure patterns appear to be fairly stable.

Hierarchical Data Structure Approximately 64% of the studies reviewed combined data from multiple existing groups into a single sample (annual range = 41–90%). The first appearance of multilevel modeling in the *JSEP* was in 1999. Although still vastly underutilized, this statistical technique is gaining in popularity and was employed for approximately 17% of the studies published in 2004 that clearly combined data from multiple identifiable groups.

Effect Sizes Investigators have steadily increased the rate at which they report effect sizes for their analyses across the three periods that we examined ($R^2 = .84$, $b = 0.15$). For the period from 1979 through 1989, effect sizes were reported in approximately half of the studies, whereas in the period from 2000 through 2004, they were reported in approximately 80% of the published studies. These values may be liberal estimates because most of the effect sizes found were correlation statistics that also yielded inferential significance tests that were more likely the focus of investigators' interests. Also, we coded only whether studies reported at least one effect size estimate. Most studies do not report effect sizes for all (or even most) of their analyses. Despite these cautions, this trend toward reporting effect sizes more frequently is encouraging.

Having reviewed the research design, sampling, instrumentation, and data analysis trends in a leading sport and exercise psychology journal that presumably publishes some of the best research in our field, we can step back and evaluate the state of this literature. We observed several encouraging trends. Some other trends suggested opportunities for researchers to extend their use of quantitative methods to study sport and exercise psychology phenomena. The following recommendations reflect our assessment of the current state of the literature and are offered as one blueprint for increasing the rigor and theory-developing potential of our best research.

■ Recommendation 1: Investigators should include statistical power considerations (e.g., anticipated effect sizes, Type I error rate, number of analyses planned, types of effects being examined) in their sample size planning.

■ Recommendation 2: Efforts should be made to include younger and older participants in research samples. Diversifying the ages of participants will shed light on developmental differences and the boundaries for generalizing some conclusions.

■ Recommendation 3: Researchers should collect and report the race and ethnicity of research participants, as well as their socioeconomic status if that is relevant. This information identifies the population to which findings may be generalized.

■ Recommendation 4: When possible, investigators should incorporate multiple assessment methods into their research designs. Doing so will limit the threat to theory development posed by exclusive or excessive reliance on a single method.

■ Recommendation 5: Future research should strive to employ quasi-experimental or experimental research designs more frequently to enhance understanding of causal relations that exist for psychological phenomena in sport and exercise settings.

■ Recommendation 6: As understanding of sport and exercise phenomena becomes more refined, investigators should increasingly explore the potential of curvilinear functions for adding predictive power to their statistical models. The desire to maximize explained variance should also be balanced by the principle of parsimony in theory development.

■ Recommendation 7: Unless investigations are preliminary, investigators should seek ways to integrate temporal delays or repeated assessments into their research designs to reduce the threats presented by concomitant data collection.

■ Recommendation 8: Investigators should be more attentive to the hierarchical (multilevel) structures that exist in their data because neglecting nested effects from multilevel data structures can bias results and distort conclusions from a study.

■ Recommendation 9: Effect sizes should be reported for all inferential statistical tests that lead to nonnull results. Investigators should also focus on the magnitude of effect sizes when interpreting results instead of relying solely on binary reject-or-fail-to-reject hypothesis tests. As the literature becomes better developed, investigators should be able to specify point estimates of effect sizes that can be tested in lieu of the null hypothesis of no effect.

Conclusion

This chapter presented some fundamental concepts that are relevant when conducting or evaluating quantitative research from a logical positivist or postpositivist tradition. Establishing causal relations is both a central objective and a major challenge for scientists and practitioners alike. The process of explaining why changes in one variable lead to changes in another is an integral component of theory development. Although the term *theory* and its derivatives can have pejorative undertones that suggest a disconnect from reality (e.g., "that's just theoretical"), theory is intimately intertwined with reality. Theories must account for existing observations of a phenomenon while simultaneously casting an explanation for why those observations exist as they do. Thus, theory development can be viewed as a highly practical endeavor. As such, the methods used to generate observations will greatly influence the rate at which theory develops.

Several methodological issues related to research design, sampling, instrumentation, and data analysis were reviewed because of their salience when conducting and evaluating quantitative research. A content analysis of original research published in the *Journal of Sport & Exercise Psychology* revealed a number of patterns and trends that have shaped the state of theory development in this literature. Based on the current status of the literature and trends that we documented, several recommendations were offered for consideration by current and future researchers. Not all these recommendations are appropriate for every research study, but we hope that considering them might stimulate researchers to stretch the methodological boundaries of their work and consequently enhance theory development in sport and exercise psychology.

Acknowledgments

The authors wish to thank Mollie Dunn, Lynn Gregorwicz, and Darbee Nelson for their assistance in coding journal articles for the content analysis. Thanks also go to Danielle Symons Downs for her comments on a draft of this chapter.

CHAPTER 3

Qualitative Research Approaches

Robert J. Brustad, PhD

Knowing how research is conducted in sport psychology allows us to understand a great deal about the history, traditions, and philosophies that have shaped who we are as a scientific discipline. The role and status of qualitative research within our field reflects the various forces that have affected our scholarly growth and evolution. The purpose of this chapter is to discuss the emergence and status of qualitative research approaches to knowledge generation in sport psychology. Doing so will require a close and critical look at both our past and our present.

As both an academic and applied discipline, sport psychology has a unique lineage. Our heritage includes close links to our parent discipline of psychology as well as a strong grounding in the sport sciences. Our link to psychology means that we have been strongly influenced by many of the research traditions that have shaped scholarship in psychology. Academic programs in sport psychology, however, are usually housed in departments of sport science, which means that we have been greatly influenced by developments within the sport sciences and the natural science traditions (Harris, 1981, 1983; Sparkes, 1998). Researchers in sport psychology, a relatively young area of investigation, have had to be aware of concerns for scientific acceptance and legitimacy, which have shaped our approach to scholarship in both subtle and overt ways (Sparkes, 1998).

Qualitative forms of research have been present in sport psychology scholarship for roughly 15 years. The relative recency of their arrival reflects on the legitimacy issue and trends in the preparation of our young researchers. But qualitative forms of research have a strong current presence in our field. In their review of publication trends in sport psychology, Culver, Gilbert, and Trudel (2003) found that roughly 17.3% of data-based articles published in the major North American sport psychology research journals during the 1990s relied primarily on qualitative research methods. This proportion of research is likely to grow in the coming years. The focus of this chapter will be on identifying the current and potential contributions of qualitative research approaches to our knowledge base. The chapter will not discuss how to do qualitative research. Instead, it will concentrate on identifying the underlying philosophical principles of qualitative research because they generally differ from the fundamental principles of the quantitative research tradition. In addition, exemplars of qualitative research will be provided to describe the various expressions of qualitative research within our field of study.

Defining Qualitative Research

No simple explanation can describe the differences between qualitative and quantitative forms of research. At a superficial level, qualitative research can be regarded as the form of research that relies primarily on qualitative forms of data as opposed to quantitative forms of data. Qualitative forms of data could thus include interview data or narrative data, observational or ethnographic data, or written texts and accounts. Conversely, quantitative research could be characterized simply as research that relies on numbers for data. But focusing only on the form of our data obscures important philosophical orientations about knowledge development that typically differentiate the two traditions.

Characteristics other than the nature of the data distinguish the qualitative and quantitative research traditions. This distinction rests not in methodological differences but in epistemological differences. Epistemology refers to the branch of philosophy concerned with knowledge generation and the knowledge that we value and trust. Epistemology refers to how we know what we know or, in essence, the nature, sources, and validity of knowledge.

From an epistemological standpoint, qualitative research comes out of a constructivist, interpretivist, or naturalistic tradition of inquiry, whereas quantitative research comes from the positivist, experimentalist tradition (Guba & Lincoln, 1994; Schwandt, 1994). We are much more familiar with the positivist, experimentalist tradition because this tradition is most frequently associated with "good science" or the "hard sciences," such as physics and chemistry (Martens, 1987). The positivist, experimentalist tradition focuses on theory or hypothesis testing through the process of deduction. In general, this tradition seeks to provide understanding of general laws of nature. The classic laboratory, experimental design is considered the apotheosis of knowledge generation. The constructivist, interpretivist, or naturalistic research traditions that underlie the qualitative paradigm to knowledge development reflect a greater interest in understanding than in explanation. Theory testing through deductive processes does not occur in this tradition, but theory may emerge from the data by processes of induction. Furthermore, qualitative researchers have relatively little interest in trying to discover universal laws of nature because they generally conduct research that focuses on knowledge that is situated and constructed by people in interaction with others, in relation to the meaning and purpose that this interaction has for them in a given context. Greater focus rests as well in understanding the particular, whether that might be a particular culture or group of people, or even a particular individual. In line with these fundamental underlying differences between the two traditions, Schwandt (1997, p. 39) commented, "Rather than conceiving of the differences between so-called qualitative and quantitative inquiry in terms of tools and methods, students of qualitative inquiry might be better served by examining the differences between epistemologies." This chapter will focus on the epistemological differences that exist between the two research traditions. I will argue not that one tradition is better than the other but only that researchers need to be aware of the underlying philosophical differences between the traditions because these differences influence our research goals, research methods, and eventually the development of new knowledge in sport psychology.

Qualitative research first began to demonstrate a presence in sport psychology in the early 1990s. Why were qualitative approaches to knowledge development so late in arriving in sport psychology, and why do they not have a greater role in current efforts to generate knowledge? By nature, knowledge development in any field rests on particular sets of philosophical assumptions that have been developed in relation to prevailing belief systems, historical traditions, and social conventions of science (Guba & Lincoln, 1994; Kuhn, 1970). Knowledge generation is inherently a social process that reflects the beliefs of a scientific community about the best ways to understand a phenomenon at any given time (Dewar & Horn, 1992; Kuhn, 1970). As a rapidly emerging field of study, sport psychology has been influenced by these same beliefs, traditions, and social conventions as have more mature disciplines (Dzewaltowski, 1997; Martens, 1987). An explanation of some of the traditions that have shaped knowledge generation in sport psychology in the past will help us understand our present status and future trends.

Research Traditions in Sport Psychology

Although the knowledge base in sport psychology has been generated relatively recently, the empirical foundation of our knowledge rests largely on research carried out using traditional scientific approaches. Like other emerging scientific disciplines in search of acceptance, sport psychology has relied on established scientific conventions to guide its approach to research (Sparkes, 1998). The

positivist philosophy of knowledge generation has had the greatest singular influence on the course of science in general, as well as on the scientific legacy in psychology, the social sciences, and the sport sciences.

The Positivist Scientific Legacy

The predominant influence on the Western scientific tradition has been the theory of knowledge known as positivism, or logical positivism. Positivism emerged out of the modernist era, which experienced its fullest expression during the Enlightenment of 18th century Europe, which had been stimulated through the earlier writings of philosophers such as Auguste Comte, John Stuart Mill, and David Hume. A defining feature of modernism was the belief that the natural world follows systematic, orderly, and predictable laws. The belief in the lawful nature of the physical world inspired efforts to identify underlying causative mechanisms. A modernist conviction of importance for the growth of modern science was the belief that humans possess the requisite mental capacities to comprehend the laws that regulate the natural and social worlds. From a modernist perspective, the world was understandable by employing reason. Modernist thought thus differed substantially from all preceding worldviews, such as that of the romantic era, because for the first time humans were considered capable of understanding and thus shaping the world for their own benefit (Gergen, 1991). The tremendous optimism of the modernist era was accompanied by an unrelenting faith in both the epistemology and methodology of positivism.

The epistemological foundation of positivism was grounded in a mechanistic worldview predicated on the assumption of predictable cause-and-effect patterns of relationships. Positivist philosophy strongly adhered to the "machinelike" explanations characteristic of Newtonian physics (Capra, 1982; Gergen, 1991). Furthermore, positivism was grounded in the belief that there exist immutable laws in the natural and social worlds that are unaffected by one's perspective and that can best be understood through reliance on objective scientific processes. In other words, this tradition adhered to the notion that there exists a singular, concrete reality that reasonable people using logical means can understand. The methodology of positivism relied heavily on the principles of reductionism and quantification for acquiring new knowledge and employed the hypothetico-deductive method of theory testing, which is best epitomized by controlled laboratory experimentation. Finally, positivists considered reliance on subjective or unobservable processes, including emotional experiences, to be outside the realm of good science. Thus, only that which was measurable, quantifiable, and objectifiable was appropriate for study from a positivist perspective. Although the scientific method that we are familiar with emerged gradually over a period of many years, the core beliefs that drive orthodox science are directly attributable to positivist philosophy. To this day, social science researchers occasionally have to face the contention that their approach is somehow less scientific or "softer" than natural science research because of the powerful hold that the positivist tradition has had over the way that we judge the quality of research.

The assumption that there exist invariant, general laws of nature is an important dimension of positivist philosophy and has had a powerful influence on social science research. This viewpoint recognizes the existence of concrete, universal laws that are unaffected by perspective or context. This perspective results in the pursuit of nomothetic explanations of human behavior, or attempts to provide general laws across all individuals, rather than the search for idiographic forms of explanation that direct attention toward particular groups of people or individuals in specific situations.

Belief in the possibility of objectivity is a core component of positivist philosophy and of the Western scientific tradition. Objectivity is the assumption that the researcher can engage in the scientific process without interjecting his or her views, beliefs, or biases in a way that might influence scientific conclusions or affect the object of study through his or her presence. The concept of objectivity is also based on the premise that reasonable people who follow systematic procedures can agree on a singular absolute truth.

Reliance on reductionist practices is also an important component of positivist methodology. Reductionism is the belief that the best means of understanding reality is through analysis of the functioning of individual entities in isolation from other influences. Through the reductionist approach, the scientist attempts to understand the unique functioning of constituent parts but is less concerned with interactive relational patterns. Thus, reductionist practices are in direct contrast with dynamic systems and systems theory perspectives on the functioning of the physical and social worlds (Capra, 1996).

Dependence on quantifiable forms of knowledge is an additional characteristic of positivism. The reliance on quantifiable information was the result of an inherent distrust in the subjective and intuitive forms of knowledge that was characteristic of the premodernist era. From the positivist perspective on quantification, that which is not measurable is not understandable and thus not appropriate for study.

Inherent trust in the logic of the experimental method is another cornerstone of positivism. The experimental method is based on a hypothetico-deductive model of science in which testable hypotheses are derived from prevailing theories. Through the process of deduction, a determination is made as to whether specific observations conform to hypothetical expectations that have been proposed a priori. The experimental method is based on implicit belief in cause-and-effect patterns of relationships in the world that can be accurately assessed only through controlled experimental procedures, typically in a laboratory setting.

Positivist philosophy has profoundly affected the course of Western science. Given the widespread belief that this philosophy of knowledge is the most trustworthy form of inquiry, philosophers of science have labeled this form of knowledge development as "orthodox science" (Martens, 1987) and "normal science" (Kuhn, 1970). Other approaches to knowledge development are much less familiar to students because they have not been exposed to alternative philosophies or because practitioners of orthodox science denigrate such approaches. In Martens' (1987) words, the influence of the positivist paradigm cannot be underestimated because "orthodox science exerts a comprehensive power over most of us today, not unlike religion once did" (p. 36).

Critiques of Positivism

Until the 20th century, positivism was rarely challenged as the singular route to knowledge development in the sciences. But limitations of the positivist worldview in the natural sciences became apparent early in the 20th century, particularly in theoretical physics, and these shortcomings sparked closer examination of positivist doctrine. Philosophers of science (e.g., Capra, 1982; Feyerabend, 1975; Hesse, 1980) have strongly contested many of the fundamental beliefs about the world upon which positivist epistemology is grounded. Within the social sciences, some argue that the positivist paradigm of knowledge development is much less useful for understanding the complexities of human cognition and social behavior than it is in our explanations of natural phenomena (Guba & Lincoln, 1994). These perspectives on the limitations of positivist inquiry resulted in the call for alternate paradigms for knowledge development, or at least the recognition that multiple approaches to knowledge development exist (e.g., Dewar & Horn, 1992; Harris, 1983; Martens, 1987; Sparkes, 1992).

The epistemological foundations of positivism are also grounded in the belief that there exist systematic, orderly, and immutable laws of nature. Within the social sciences, we might question how well a guiding belief in absolute, unchangeable laws serves our research interests. Specifically, do we really believe that universal laws of human behavior extend across all cultures and contexts?

The complexities inherent in studying human behavior might further argue against a strict positivist perspective. Current cognitive psychology is based on the premise that people act with intention and in relation to situational interpretation and personal reflection, which highlights the intricacy and dynamic nature of human behavior in relation to meanings that are both personal and socially constructed. The recognition that humans are conscious of their behavior and thus capable of altering their behavior under observation contributes a complexity that is not present in the natural sciences and argues against a narrow deterministic model of social science. Human behavior cannot be readily understood without reference to context. Social context provides the frame of reference from which any singular behavior takes on meaning. Context can be considered to include not only the objective characteristics of any situation but also individuals' experiences, their subjective interpretation of those experiences, and their expectancies for current encounters. Such recognition suggests that viewing behavior from a dynamic systems perspective rather than the simpler mechanistic paradigm may be more appropriate within the social sciences.

The principle of objectivity in research, which is a core foundation of positivist epistemology, represents an additional area of contention. Trust in objectivity rests on the belief that the investigator can detach himself or herself from the subject matter of interest and thereby avoid influencing the interpretation of research outcomes. To illustrate the difficulty associated with maintaining objective detachment in social science research, Pagels (1982) provided the example of an anthropologist who visits a remote culture for study and, in so doing, cannot help but affect the course of village life and thus his interpretation of what is characteristic of that life. The objectivity assumption is further grounded in the belief that there exists a singular material reality unaffected by perspective. But Einstein's relativity principle asserts that our understanding of time and motion is itself related to perspective. This conceptualization contributed to a relativist, rather than an absolutist, view of the physical world that conflicts with the positivist notion of a singular, absolute reality.

Reductionism as a means of knowledge development in social science research is compromised because the interaction of personal and social influences cannot be fully understood by focusing on singular entities in isolation. Within sport psychology, many of the primary issues of interest inherently call for a systems perspective (Brustad & Ritter-Taylor, 1997; Foon, 1987). In particular, research in the social psychology of sport requires an interactionist perspective. For example, to study leadership effectiveness, group processes, or self-presentational influences in sport and exercise, we must direct our attention to the interactions that occur among individuals and the reciprocal forms of influence that take place over time. In our quest to understand the whole in social science research, we must identify and understand the functioning of constituent parts. But the functioning of those parts in isolation is meaningless without reference to the other parts that make up the whole (Hesse, 1980). A systems view rather than a mechanistic view may be more appropriate in many situations in sport psychology research.

The emphasis on quantification in orthodox science reflects both epistemological and methodological assumptions that constrain knowledge development. Because positivist philosophy only supported science that studied observable and measurable phenomena, subjective processes inherently fell outside the realm of "good science." For psychologists, however, the domain of study consists of subjective cognitive processes that pertain to thought and emotion. Furthermore, the emphasis on quantification implies a false dichotomy between quantitative and qualitative approaches in psychological research. In reality, each form of data analysis relies heavily on human interpretive processes in assessing the dimensions of interest. For example, self-confidence levels may be quantified through use of a research questionnaire because a number may be applied to any response. But the questions and response options that make up the questionnaire require considerable interpretation on behalf of the respondent, so language and subjective interpretation mediate the responses. When interview techniques are used as a form of qualitative methodology, the same issues of interpretation are present. Thus, the idea that quantitative and qualitative methodologies are fundamentally different is inaccurate.

Postpositivism

In response to 20th century research developments and internally and externally generated forms of criticism, a scientific philosophy known as postpositivism has emerged. Overall, postpositivism is closely aligned with the worldview of its predecessor and thus will not be considered a distinct philosophical tradition in its own right. In general, postpositivists have a more restrained view of our capacity to ever "know" reality than do positivists. Postpositivists recognize limitations in the ability of humans to cognize and understand the world fully (Guba & Lincoln, 1994). In addition, postpositivists are more open to a variety of methodologies than their predecessors are. The methodology of postpositivism relies more heavily on critical multiplism, which is similar to triangulation, in that the researcher employs a variety of methodological approaches to assess whether the phenomenon under study adheres to expectations. Thus, the postpositivist might employ various methodologies. Although postpositivism represents an important departure from some of the traditions of positivism, the fundamental worldview of this approach does not differ substantially from that of its predecessor. Thus, postpositivist work will be considered to fall within the framework of positivist epistemology for the remainder of this chapter.

The purpose of this chapter is to highlight the epistemological assumptions that guide our research. Given that all forms of knowledge development have unique limitations, few critics of positivism would argue that "orthodox science" should be discarded. In this chapter I do not seek to minimize the contributions of the positivist tradition to knowledge generation. I wish only to highlight the assumptions of the tradition that have profoundly shaped how we typically conduct research. The dominance of orthodox science in the training of young researchers ignores current developments in the philosophy of science and provides the false impression that there exists only one route to knowledge (Brustad, 1997, 2002; Dewar & Horn, 1992; Sparkes, 1992; Strean & Roberts, 1992).

Influences of the Psychological Tradition

Although the positivist philosophy of science has had the greatest influence on our approach to knowledge development in sport psychology, research traditions within our parent discipline of psychology have also had a profound effect on the content and form of our inquiry. In fact, a common critique of sport psychology research has been that sport psychologists have been excessively reliant on the research conventions of psychology proper in generating questions for study and in devising methodological approaches to studying these issues (Foon, 1987; Martens, 1979, 1987). An appreciation of the sociohistorical context within which North American psychology emerged is useful in understanding the influences that have shaped this tradition.

In comparison with the natural sciences, psychology and the other social sciences are relatively young fields of study. A critical issue in the emergence of psychology as a social science was whether, as a new scientific discipline with human behavior as its subject matter, psychology would adhere to the strict positivist traditions of the natural sciences or generate unique approaches to the study of human behavior. In contrast with other social sciences such as anthropology and sociology, psychological research has adhered closely to the orthodox science traditions of positivism. Thus, issues of "legitimization" have been a constant concern that have affected these research traditions (Sparkes, 1998).

Psychological researchers in North America clung to the positivist scientific tradition of the natural sciences. Before the late 1800s, the perception that psychology was unsystematic and unscientific hindered its recognition a unique discipline of study. This perception held back the emergence of each of the social sciences (Collins, 1985). Use of the methodology of the natural sciences was an important step in gaining credibility as a science. Second, the successes of the positivist model in the natural sciences led to the unwarranted expectation that the use of this methodology would be similarly effective in explaining human behavior. Little concern was expressed at the time about the unique problems inherent in attempting to explain human behavior through a scientific model developed for use in the natural sciences.

In the United States, psychological researchers exhibited strong trust in the experimental method as the means for producing the purest forms of knowledge about the mechanisms underlying human behavior. The rise of behaviorism and its affiliation with the experimental methodology of positivism was directly attributable to a common mistrust of subjective and unobservable features of being human (Collins, 1985). During the decades when behaviorism ruled American psychology, the behavior of rats, pigeons, and other laboratory animals became the focus of study. As Gergen (1991) noted, "In retrospect, we find it disturbing that the scholarly world could believe that the fundamentals of human nature could be laid bare by the antics of a small number of laboratory animals" (p. 40). This outcome was directly attributable to the conviction that truth could be known through the methodology of positivism.

The legacies of experimentalism and behaviorism within American psychology have had a lasting effect on the content and breadth of the knowledge base in psychology. Because our parent discipline has strongly influenced knowledge traditions in sport psychology, these concerns extend to our field of study as well. As Sparkes (1998) commented, "Given that psychology has been historically linked with the positivist stance of the natural sciences in an attempt to establish itself within a scientific framework that emphasizes quantitative methods, it is not surprising that many members of the sport psychology community hold a positivistic or postpositivistic perspective" (p. 365). In this light, Martens (1987, pp. 30-31) described the operative mind-set when he began to pursue sport psychology research:

> I recall how we were enraptured with the American social psychological experimental paradigm, devoured the theories of the day, and charged into the laboratories to lift the field of sport psychology to a true science. . . . We created unique, controlled, and artificial environments to observe people compete, imitate, be reinforced, cheat, and cope with stress. (We never once thought that these studies might in turn produce artificial, contrived behavior unique to the environment we created.) With strong convictions based on our ability to use the scientific method, we saw ourselves as the new generation of sport psychologists who were going to build a solid foundation of scientific facts for the field of sport psychology. Thus began the modern era of the academic discipline of sport psychology.

The cognitive revolution (Gardner, 1985) that has gained increasing prominence within North American psychology over the past several decades continues to have an important effect on the nature of knowledge development within psychology, and by implication, within sport psychology. Cognitive psychology focuses on individual differences in subjective appraisal processes, so the reductionist, experimentalist research tradition does not serve the field effectively. From the cognitive theoretical worldview, the focus of knowledge development is on the world as cognized and the variability among individuals' subjective appraisals of the world. Such

a perspective takes a relativist rather than an absolutist approach to understanding because the research focuses on understanding the nature of individual differences rather than identifying universal psychological laws. To the extent that cognitive theorists also examine context-specific cognitions, psychological research will use dynamic, relativistic, and context-bound approaches to knowledge development that are inconsistent with the determinism of orthodox science (Gergen, 1985). Thus, cognitive theoretical perspectives in psychology have paved the way for greater utilization of constructivist and interpretivist approaches to knowledge development characteristic of the qualitative tradition.

Sport Science Influence

A third influential research tradition in sport psychology is the consequence of the traditionally close association between sport psychology and the other sport sciences. Although the theoretical foundations of most of our research were generated within psychology, most academic programs in sport psychology have been housed in departments of exercise and sport science, kinesiology, or physical education. The influence of our allegiance with the other sport sciences has been experienced in various ways.

Sport psychologists have been strongly inclined to use the research methods of their sport science counterparts. Although the sport and exercise sciences represent an interesting mix of subdisciplines grounded in the natural (exercise physiology, biomechanics) and social sciences (sport psychology, sport sociology), these subdisciplinary areas are not necessarily of similar size or status within most academic programs. In terms of status, number of academic positions, and program size, sport psychology has historically been relegated to a relatively minor role within sport science departments. Given the visibility and status accorded to exercise physiology within sport science departments, it is not surprising that sport psychology research has been prone to rely on the positivist scientific tradition characteristic of the physical sciences.

Qualitative Research in Sport Psychology

Qualitative research has had an increasing presence in the sport psychology knowledge base since the early 1990s. Two papers written by Rainer Martens (1979, 1987) were instrumental in helping researchers reconsider the traditional approach to knowledge generation in sport psychology. As early as 1979, Martens expressed displeasure with the prevailing laboratory-based, experimental research that characterized inquiry in sport psychology at that time. Because of his displeasure with this extreme positivist model, Martens called for sport psychologists to shed their lab coats and study psychological dimensions of sport in their natural context. But it was not until the appearance of Martens' 1987 paper, in which he encouraged "greater diversification" of knowledge approaches in sport psychology, that qualitative research began to appear regularly in our journals.

Qualitative research began to appear more frequently in sport psychology journals in the early 1990s, so we currently have roughly 15 years of history with this form of research. In this chapter I will discuss five general types of qualitative research in sport psychology and try to describe some of the ways that each method has been used to address research questions. Just as the categorization of quantitative and qualitative research is not straightforward, the categorization of types of qualitative research is complicated by the fact that individuals using similar methodologies (e.g., interview techniques) can approach their research from distinct epistemological standpoints (Schwandt, 1994). Thus I will try to consider research from the standpoint of epistemological, rather than methodological, similarities to be consistent with previous arguments. The five general categories of qualitative research approaches to be discussed include individual interviews; phenomenological, narrative, and life history approaches; grounded theory methodology; case studies; and ethnographic and participant observation approaches.

Interviews

The contemporary emergence of qualitative research in sport psychology was sparked by the publication of a series of studies by Scanlan and colleagues (Scanlan, Ravizza, & Stein, 1989a, 1989b; Scanlan, Stein, & Ravizza, 1991) that investigated the psychological and emotional experiences of elite figure skaters. Shortly thereafter, Gould and colleagues (Gould, Eklund, & Jackson, 1992a, 1992b; Gould, Jackson, & Finch, 1993) examined the cognitive and emotional experiences of wrestlers during their preparation for, and participation in, the Olympic Games. These investigations were seminal in the growth of qualitative research in sport psychology because they clearly illustrated the utility of

qualitative research as a form of knowledge development and helped solve the credibility issue that surrounded qualitative research in our field at that phase of our maturation (Sparkes, 1998).

The primary purpose of the research as conducted by both sets of investigators was to increase understanding of the psychological and emotional characteristics of elite-level athletic participation. These investigations were excellent examples of how interview methods can generate greater depth of explanation of particular psychological and emotional phenomena than can be attained through questionnaire or survey methods. More important, individual interviews enable the interviewee to express novel concepts, thoughts, and feelings that the researcher may not have considered. Interviews can thus be instrumental in generating new knowledge and even new theoretical perspectives. This inductive use of interview data constitutes an important potential benefit.

The work of Scanlan, Gould, and colleagues has contributed greatly to the knowledge base in sport psychology. Their methodological approach has come to serve as the most common template for qualitative research in sport psychology (Biddle, Markland, Gilbourne, Chatzisarantis, and Sparkes, 2001; Cote, Salmela, Baria, & Russell, 1993; Culver et al., 2003). In both lines of research, the investigators relied on a standardized set of interview questions that was consistent across all participants. The researchers also carried out a generalized, nomothetic type of explanation of the experience of the elite athlete in that they were looking for general similarities across individuals rather than seeking to identify and address individual difference characteristics. In each line of research, the authors commented that they used inductive procedures with the purpose of using data to generate new theoretical or conceptual perspectives on the issues of interest.

Since the publication of this work, this methodological approach has been exceptionally common in sport psychology. In their review of trends and tendencies in qualitative research in sport psychology, Culver et al. (2003) examined all data-based publications in the three primary North American sport psychology journals, the *Journal of Sport & Exercise Psychology*, *The Sport Psychologist*, and *Journal of Applied Sport Psychology*, over the 10-year period from 1990 through 1999. Culver and colleagues found that 84 (or 17.3%) of the 485 full-length, data-based research studies relied primarily on qualitative methods. Of the 84 published qualitative studies, a full 67 relied on interview techniques such as those employed by Scanlan, Gould, and colleagues. In other words, 80% of the published qualitative research in sport psychology for the decade followed this template. Only 17 qualitative studies published in the three journals over the decade used other qualitative methods.

The knowledge that qualitative research within sport psychology is heavily associated with interview techniques is important in understanding how qualitative research has evolved in sport psychology. Clearly, we have a dominant methodological paradigm for conducting research in sport psychology. A particular concern expressed in the review by Culver et al. (2003) was that most interview approaches have used a one-shot interview method to data collection. If the purpose of interviewing is to gain greater depth of understanding of a particular phenomenon, a one-shot method is not likely to provide great insight nor does it necessarily establish sufficient rapport with the respondent to ensure appropriate openness and depth of responses.

In their review of issues relevant to quantitative and qualitative research in sport psychology, Biddle et al. (2001) voiced an additional concern about this template of qualitative research. These authors argued that the highly structured interview protocol, in which the same questions are posed to the respondents in the same order, might restrict the range of possible responses and result in a grouping of response data into anticipated or previously established categories. In this way, the highly structured interview can run contrary to a true inductive approach (Biddle et al., 2001). This concern echoed the commentary of Krane, Andersen, and Strean (1997), who argued that a true inductive approach is unlikely to be taken with a highly structured interview protocol because the researcher probably already has specialized knowledge in the content area of interest and has structured the interview format in line with that knowledge. Krane et al. (1997) considered this type of methodology to be a "compromise between qualitative and quantitative procedures" (p. 215), and Culver et al. (2003) similarly labeled this a quasi-qualitative approach. Culver et al. further commented:

> Like the wolf in sheep's clothing, much of the qualitative research in sport psychology has been conducted from a descriptive/quantitative approach under the guise of qualitative research. We are not challenging the credibility or significance of this body of work; instead, we are challenging qualitative researchers in sport psychology to critically examine the epistemological beliefs that guide their methodological decisions. (pp. 7-8)

In sum, the one-shot, semistructured interview method is the most visible expression of qualitative research in sport psychology. Critics have questioned whether this approach conforms closely enough to the general constructivist–interpretivist–naturalistic paradigm that it is intended to represent. A second form of qualitative research that is relatively similar methodologically, but considerable different epistemologically, is represented by phenomenological, life history, and narrative practices.

Phenomenology, Life History, and Narrative Practice

Dale (1996) called attention to alternative uses of interview methodology in sport psychology, most notably the use of the existential phenomenology tradition. Although this approach also relies heavily on interviewing methodology, the purpose differs from the more common and traditional forms of interviews that have been relied on to date. The phenomenological interview approach is unstandardized and focuses on the subjective experiences of the individual in relation to his or her social environment. From this perspective, the athlete is considered to be situated within a given social context or framework in which personal attributes and social or environmental factors combine to influence thought, behavior, and emotion (Dale, 1996). Language is considered the best medium through which to understand personal meaning for an individual (Holstein & Gubrium, 1995). The phenomenological interview process is regarded as a discourse or conversation (Mishler, 1986, as cited by Dale, 1996), which provides considerable flexibility for both interviewee and interviewer. The method also differs from other descriptive and qualitative approaches because it focuses on the participant's experienced meaning rather than a description of his or her overt actions or behaviors. Dale contrasted the phenomenological method with the more typical interview methodology in sport psychology:

> It seems that by asking all of the participants the same question from a preconceived guide, we are assuming all participants will find each topic figural in their experience. Rather, what might be relevant for one person in his or her experience might not be at all relevant for another. Therefore, if we are interested in the experience of the athlete, we should identify the topic of interest for the study and then allow the participant to describe that experience as he or she lived it. (pp. 310–311)

A life history approach to data collection originates from a perspective similar to that of the phenomenological approach. The life history approach is well represented in the work of Rees, Smith, and Sparkes (2003). These researchers examined the role of social support in the lives of six men who had experienced spinal cord injuries in sport that had left them disabled. The primary data collection technique was the interview process. Through the interviews, the respondents provided considerable discussion of their life histories, in relation to both their injuries and their lives apart from their injuries. The life history account entailed at least two interviews with each participant, with each interview lasting from two to six hours. The interviews were structured around some general common questions, but for the most part the interviews were informal. Because this approach represented a new line of research in sport psychology, most of the data was used in an inductive manner to build knowledge about the nature of the social support experiences of male athletes who were responding to spinal cord injury. Deductive elements were also present because the researchers were interested in determining whether the same types of social support (emotional support, esteem support, informational support, and tangible support) were present for athletes in this situation as had been previously identified in the social support knowledge base. An implicit purpose of the research was to use these narrative accounts as a means of empowering people with this type of injury to tell their stories and better understand how the experience has shaped their lives. Furthermore, the specific quotes from the interviews were considered potentially salient to others who have incurred a similar injury or to those who assume a supportive role with an athlete who has had a spinal cord injury.

Narrative practice is a related form of qualitative methodology that relies extensively on the linguistic technique of telling one's personal story. This research method comes from the perspective that humans are inherently "story-telling animals" (Sparkes & Partington, 2003, p. 293) and that to provide people with voice is the best means of understanding them and their thoughts and behaviors in relation to social circumstances and relationships. As such, the focus is on how people construct or structure their life experiences and the meaning and purpose that those experiences have for the individual. Sparkes and Partington provided an example of narrative practice methodology in relation to the topic of flow or peak performance. Their focus was not strongly directed toward adding to the knowledge base regarding the flow experience but rather toward understanding the social forms of

influence that affect who gets to provide an account of a personal flow experience within a given social context such as a sport club.

The category of qualitative research methods that includes phenomenological, life history, and narrative accounts uses a methodology similar to that used in the individual interview approach, but clear differences exist between the two forms. These differences revolve primarily around issues of depth and generalizability. The phenomenological, life history, and narrative accounts are intended to provide greater depth of discussion and understanding, but the generalizability of these methods is clearly limited by considerations relative to the number of participants who can take part in this type of research. Thus, researchers should weigh issues of depth and generalizability before choosing their approach.

Case Study

A third general category of qualitative research in sport psychology is the case study approach, or instrumental case study approach, as it is sometimes known (Faulkner & Biddle, 2004). Stake (1994) explained that the case study seeks to provide great depth of explanation about the particular. In this regard, a specific phenomenon or individual constitutes the case, and the goal of the researcher is to gain as much knowledge as possible about that individual case. Stake provided the examples of a doctor who studies a child because the child is ill and a social worker who studies a child because the child is neglected. In each circumstance, the case is the child, with special consideration for his or her particular set of circumstances. The manner in which the researcher studies the child varies according to his or her purposes, and the researcher is likely to rely on both qualitative and quantitative forms of data.

Case studies have been used infrequently in sport psychology. An example of case study research done in the domain of exercise psychology is Faulkner and Biddle's (2004) study of the influence of exercise on depression. The researchers' purpose was to examine the role of exercise on depression with specific consideration for the role of contextual and individual differences in this relationship. The researchers approached this topic with the idea that the nature of the relationship between exercise and depression is likely to be both complex and individualistic. A further stimulus for this line of research was the recognition that medically based research tends to adhere strongly to the positivist tradition but that, in accordance with the views of Mutrie (1997), qualitative methods may provide unique insights into understanding the effects of exercise on quality of life. Furthermore, "qualitative studies with a focus on change at the individual level might permit greater insight and understanding of personal level changes than are possible through a randomized controlled trial" (Faulkner & Biddle, 2004, p. 4).

Six individuals were included in the study, each of whom experienced chronic depression. Each participant took part in five semistructured interviews. These interviews took place before the exercise program began and then periodically throughout the duration of the yearlong exercise program. The advantage of these multiple interview opportunities was that they enabled the researchers to get a sense for the nature of change over time in the exercise–depression relationship, an outcome that would not have been possible with the one-shot interview method. Furthermore, repeated interviews allowed the researchers to establish strong rapport with the participants, which likely resulted in greater openness and depth of understanding of the exercise–depression relationship. The repeated interviews also allowed more accurate identification of the specific factors that may have moderated the effects of exercise on depression. The findings from this study indicated that the relationship between exercise and depressive symptomology is highly idiosyncratic for this population and needs to be understood not in terms of a standard dose–response relationship but rather in relation to the broader context of participants' lives.

Grounded Theory

Grounded theory is a general methodology used to develop new concepts or theories through data that have been obtained and analyzed in an ongoing, systematic manner (Strauss & Corbin, 1994). In this sense, a system of data analysis known as the constant comparative method (Strauss & Corbin, 1994) is utilized. This method has a strongly inductive orientation but also contains deductive elements (Strauss & Corbin, 1998). In this regard, data that are initially obtained are analyzed. Certain responses trigger new questions, but some response categories may become saturated. Data collection is an ongoing process. Data are collected as needed, and new categories of knowledge may be necessary to address particular questions.

Holt and Dunn (2004) used grounded theory methodology to attempt to understand the psychosocial competencies and environmental conditions associated with success in soccer for young professional players. In their study, Holt and Dunn relied primarily on data obtained from repeated interviews with the players. In addition, the authors used field notes taken during three trips to a youth soccer academy in England and to two national training camps in Canada. The researchers also relied on data gained through interviews with coaches of these elite young soccer players. Findings from this study built on the existing knowledge base on developing talent in young athletes. Specifically, the authors identified competencies related to success that were linked with discipline, resilience, social support, and commitment. These findings will be instrumental in conceptualizing the social and intrapersonal factors associated with high levels of sport success for athletes at relatively young ages.

Cote (1999) examined the role of the family in shaping talent development in sport through the constant comparative method. The primary purpose of the study was to understand patterns of familial influence on talented athletes during the developmental phases of their sport involvement. In grounded theory, as with virtually all forms of qualitative inquiry, the selection of the sample is crucial because the sample size is likely to be quite small. Consequently, individuals need to be included who can best represent the phenomena of interest. Cote used four families who were identified as likely to be able to provide the requisite depth of interest. The four families were studied simultaneously so that similarities, dissimilarities, and redundancies among the families would be more salient. The data collection involved in-depth open-ended interviews with each family member. Each family member was interviewed individually. By interviewing the parents, the athletes, and the siblings, greater opportunity was available to triangulate data sources and examine perceptions of family members for consistency and differences. Findings from this study revealed three distinct phases of participation—the sampling, specializing, and investment years—each of which involved different patterns of family influence.

Ethnographic Research

A final type of qualitative research is ethnographic research, sometimes called field research. As with other forms of qualitative research, providing a simple definition of this approach is difficult because many variations can fit under the umbrella of ethnographic research (Sands, 2002). However, Atkinson and Hammersley (1995) described the most important considerations related to this line of work. These core characteristics include the view that the purpose of ethnographic research is to understand particular social phenomena, commonly a group or culture. Ethnographic researchers have no implicit interest in testing hypotheses or theories. Instead, they seek to explain or illuminate a unique group, culture, or social environment. Analysis of data from ethnographic studies revolves around the interpretation of the meanings and functions of human actions, which typically requires verbal description and explanation on behalf of the participants as well as considerable observation by the researcher. In addition, researchers typically adopt an "emic" perspective in which they attempt to understand the world from the viewpoint of the group or culture, as opposed to an "etic" perspective that reflects the researcher's a priori perspective.

Holt and Sparkes (2001) conducted an ethnographic study of group cohesiveness of a university soccer team over an eight-month competitive season. A primary reason that they chose an ethnographic approach rather than the quantitative approach typical of previous research on group cohesion is that they wished to understand how cohesion varied over time because of social and personal influences. Although group cohesion is conceptualized as a dynamic process that fluctuates according to interpersonal relationships, leadership practices, task and social expectancies, and performance outcomes, cohesion has commonly been measured using quantitative assessments that reflect a one-shot view of cohesion. In their study, Holt and Sparkes used a variety of data collection approaches including participant observation, formal and informal interviews, documentary sources, a field diary, and a reflexive journal. This multifaceted approach to data collection is typical of ethnographic research, particularly as practiced by anthropologists and sociologists. The authors identified four key factors that appeared to influence cohesion. These underlying themes were athletes' beliefs about the importance of clear and meaningful roles within the group, the balance between self-concern and sacrifice for the group, communication within the group, and team goals.

Faulkner and Sparkes (1999) examined the role of exercise as an adjunct therapy for the treatment of schizophrenia. They used an ethnographic approach to study this phenomenon. The importance of the research question is underscored by the knowledge that people with schizophrenia tend to have levels of physical fitness appreciably below population norms. An ethnographic approach was considered appropriate for use in this study because of the researchers' strong interest in a specific group of individuals that has been highly underrepresented in the literature dealing with exercise and mental health. In addition, the researchers were curious about the social interaction patterns of people with schizophrenia; thus, studying the nature of their social interaction within a naturally occurring context made sense. These purposes align with general ethnographic goals of understanding a phenomenon in relation to contextual characteristics and individual uniqueness, as opposed to the goal of generalizability across a particular population.

A particularly intriguing aspect of Faulkner and Sparkes' research involved the participant observation role of the lead author. To gain an appropriate understanding of the exercise experience of the individuals within their daily context, Faulkner obtained employment at the housing site as a substitute caseworker, which allowed him to serve as a participant observer on a regular basis for 17 weeks. Because the primary purpose of ethnographic research is to understand a group or culture in depth, having regular extensive access to that group or culture within a naturally occurring context is essential. The findings from this study shed new light on the role of exercise in contributing to positive mental health outcomes for people with schizophrenia. In this case, positive outcomes included a reduction in participants' perceptions of auditory hallucinations, increased self-esteem, improved sleep patterns, and better overall behavior in general. The authors concluded that these positive outcomes were not the direct consequence of the exercise per se, but the result of the distraction and possibilities for social interaction afforded by the exercise opportunities.

In a sport context, Adler and Adler (1987) conducted a four-year study of a major college basketball program using a combination of methods that they referred to as field research strategies and participant observation methods. The primary purpose of this research was to examine how three dimensions of identity salience changed over time in college basketball players during their experience in a high-powered Division I program. The researchers had extensive first-hand experience with the team because one of the researchers worked regularly with the players on team-related issues and group processes. Thus, the research was fully contextualized in the day-to-day experiences of these athletes. The results of the study (Adler & Adler, 1987, 1991) provided a fascinating account of the influence of social factors on various psychosocial outcomes for the athletes. In particular, the manner in which the athletic identity took precedence over the academic and social dimensions of identity provided great insight into understanding how social forces affect individual psychological characteristics in big-time sport programs.

Future Research Directions

Qualitative research has an increasing presence and role in sport psychology, and the "legitimization issue" regarding this form of research is much less of an issue than it was in the past. As has been argued throughout the chapter, traditions have restricted knowledge generation practices in sport psychology. Although the positivist tradition has been the primary influence, we currently witness relatively rigid traditions with regard to qualitative research methods in our field. In line with the arguments advanced by Cote et al. (1993), Biddle et al. (2001), and Culver et al. (2003), a current influential tradition in sport psychology research is the strong reliance on a single type of qualitative research—the individual interview. Although this form of knowledge generation offers many benefits, other forms of knowledge generation using different qualitative methods continue to be overlooked.

Researchers must recognize the epistemological foundations that underlie their choice of methodology. The primary purpose of this chapter was to highlight the philosophical assumptions that generally differentiate the quantitative and qualitative traditions. These distinctions are somewhat murky in that much of the qualitative research in sport psychology has been carried out in a way that reflects confidence in the safety of a positivistic approach rather than a true understanding of what qualitative research has to offer. As has been argued, the researcher's epistemological viewpoint should determine his or her methodological approach. Therefore, further attention needs to be devoted to the fundamental philosophical assumptions that differentiate the two traditions.

Part II

INDIVIDUAL DIFFERENCE AND SPORT BEHAVIOR

A major focus in the sport psychology research literature over the past several decades has been the identification of particular characteristics of individuals that can be used to explain and predict their behavior in sport and physical activity contexts. As noted in the preface to this book, such individual difference factors were first defined in our field to consist of relatively stable traits, dispositions, or characteristics of individuals that can be measured with varying degrees of ease and accuracy. More recently, however, researchers have also begun to investigate differences between people in their subjective appraisals of the world around them. These cognitive appraisal processes may be somewhat less stable in nature than the earlier mentioned traits and dispositions, but the research reveals significant variability between individuals in the way in which they process, analyze, interpret, and evaluate events that occur in the sport environment. Furthermore, such interindividual variability in subjective appraisal processes has been linked to subsequent

differences in sport participants' performance and behavior.

The six chapters contained in part II of this text examine the theoretical frameworks and the research studies that have been conducted to test the hypothesized relationship between selected individual difference factors and subsequent sport behavior. This section begins with a chapter by Kenneth Fox and Philip Wilson that focuses on individuals' perceptions of themselves and their competencies, abilities, and worth in sport and physical activity contexts. Fox and Wilson begin by detailing why research on self-esteem and its related self-perception constructs has attracted so much attention in both the academic literature and the popular press. They then review the theoretical and empirical research that has focused on the self-system, with consideration of how the self is structured and how it develops and changes both over the lifespan and as a consequence of environmental factors. Fox and Wilson also discuss the bidirectional and, probably, reciprocal link between aspects of the self-system and individuals' participation in sport and physical activity. The authors offer recommendations and guidelines regarding the measurement of physical self-perceptions and conclude their chapter by identifying avenues for future research that ultimately should enhance our understanding of the role played by sport, exercise, and health in the self-system.

In chapter 5 Robin Vealey and Melissa Chase contribute a chapter new to this text that focuses on self-confidence as a crucial, but also fragile, psychological characteristic. Their chapter begins with an overview of the various definitions and conceptual approaches to the study of self-confidence in sport. These conceptual approaches cover research and theory from several areas, including self-efficacy, self-confidence, movement confidence, and performance expectancy. Vealey and Chase then provide a critical review of the multiple ways in which the construct of self-confidence has been measured in sport contexts. This section is followed by a comprehensive overview of the empirical research on sport self-confidence. The chapter concludes with an identification of several key issues on self-confidence in sport that remain to be examined. As Vealey and Chase point out in their concluding section, "Many personal, social, and cultural forces influence the development and manifestation of feelings of personal agency in the intensely public and comparative subculture of competitive sport. Considering those many possibilities is the challenge for sport psychology researchers who seek to understand self-confidence in sport."

In chapter 6 Stephanie Hanrahan and Stuart Biddle examine the attributions that people make for their sport performance and behavior and the consequences or effects that such attributions have on subsequent performance and behavior. In reviewing and critiquing the research and theory in this area, Hanrahan and Biddle argue that the notion of perceived control is central to understanding attributions. Thus, they also present a perspective on control as an important construct to consider in analyzing and interpreting the relationship between attributions, behavior, and performance. As part of their review of this body of work, Hanrahan and Biddle examine a variety of theoretical and measurement approaches to the study of attributions and perceived control. They also provide a summary of the research pertaining to the factors that may serve as antecedents of individuals' attributional and control beliefs and the consequences that attributions and perceptions of control may have on individuals'

performance and behavior. These authors conclude their chapter by identifying critical issues and future research directions for investigators interested in conducting research on these topics.

In chapter 7 Maureen Weiss and Anthony Amorose provide a comprehensive review of the research and theory related to motivational orientations in the sport domain. These authors begin by summarizing the early descriptively based research on participation motivation and attrition in the sport context. They use this early research as the basis for their discussion regarding four theoretical approaches to motivation in the sport domain. These theories include competence motivation theory, self-determination theory, the expectancy-value model, and the sport commitment model. Within each of these areas, Weiss and Amorose provide an overview of the theory with a particular focus on motivational aspects. They then summarize the research and conclude the section with a critical perspective on the current state of knowledge, along with clear directions for future research work. In their concluding section, the authors summarize the main tenets of each of the four theories and identify several commonalities across the theories. As Weiss and Amorose note, sport researchers as well as sport and physical activity practitioners would do well to study and understand the processes that underlie motivation in physical activity settings. Such an understanding will inspire interventions that can help people adopt a physically active lifestyle or remain involved in the sport context.

In chapter 8 Chris Harwood, Christopher Spray, and Richard Keegan provide an inclusive and contemporary review of the theoretical and empirical literature on achievement goal approaches in sport contexts. In particular, these authors review the theoretical work of Nicholls, Dweck, Elliot, and Ames, comparing and contrasting the perspectives of each scholar and summarizing the empirical research using each approach. This review is not only complete in its coverage of the research to date but also keenly critical of the limitations of this body of research. Harwood et al. conclude their chapter by identifying a number of sport-specific, conceptual, and methodological issues that should be central to future research on this topic. As Harwood and his colleagues point out, although a significant amount of research on goal orientation theories has been conducted over the past couple of decades, new and innovative approaches are now needed to guard against intellectual complacency that can result in plateaus in the process of knowledge development.

As Maureen Weiss, Alan Smith, and Cheryl Stuntz note at the beginning of chapter 9, "Character development and sport participation is one of the hottest topics in contemporary society." Perhaps because of this real-world interest in morality, research on moral reasoning and moral development in relation to participation in competitive sport has burgeoned over the last two decades. Weiss and her colleagues begin this chapter by providing a historical perspective on the role of sport in contributing to moral development in young athletes. They then review the theoretical and empirical research that has been conducted to examine moral reasoning levels in athletes and others who participate in physical activity. Much of this research is developmentally based and reflects a continuing interest among researchers and practitioners in identifying how sport participation can and does affect children's and adolescents' moral growth and development. This review of the theoretical and empirical literature ends with a section that examines the rather limited research conducted to examine the effectiveness of moral development interventions in sport contexts and to spotlight the growing field of positive youth development. Weiss et al. conclude their chapter by identifying obstacles that currently limit the pursuit of knowledge concerning moral development, but they also offer a number of suggestions for future research in this area.

Although all six chapters in part II are written from the perspective that individual difference factors can serve as predictors of sport behavior, all the authors clearly recognize that these individual difference factors must be used in combination with situational or contextual factors if an adequate understanding of sport behavior is to be obtained. Thus, although the six chapters in part II focus on individual difference characteristics whereas the three chapters in part III focus on socioenvironmental factors, the overriding theme of all nine chapters has to do with the interactional approach to the study of behavior in sport.

CHAPTER 4

Self-Perceptual Systems and Physical Activity

Kenneth R. Fox, PhD ▪ **Philip M. Wilson, PhD**

It is hard to imagine a topic that has generated more interest than the self. Perhaps even more surprising is the infancy of sustained academic study of the self. Its rise to prominence did not take place until about 1950, following the fall of behaviorism as the dominant mode of thinking in psychological sciences (Leary & Tangney, 2003). Not unlike other areas of scientific inquiry, the self as a topic of study blossomed after scholars from diverse fields converged on a unifying topic. The latter half of the 20th century saw anthropologists, theologians, sociologists, and psychologists sharing a goal of seeking greater understanding about the development, structure, importance, and function of the self across life domains. Currently, the self as a topic remains at the forefront of psychological research.

Few would currently argue with the importance of the self, and it is impressive that a psychological entity has attracted so much empirical attention. Researchers focus on the self and related self-perceptions for several good reasons:

■ Self-esteem is an index of emotional stability and adjustment to life demands. High self-esteem, for example, is positively associated with a number of desirable qualities including life satisfaction, vitality, psychological adjustment, functionality, integration, leadership, and resilience to stress (Wylie, 1989). Conversely, low self-esteem has been linked with suicidal ideation, clinical depression, high trait anxiety, and feelings of inadequacy or helplessness (Leary & Tangney, 2003). Considering this pattern of relationships with health indices, it is hardly surprising that self-esteem is considered a critical indicator of psychological well-being.

■ Self-esteem and domain-specific self-perceptions influence engagement and persistence decisions in various life pursuits (Harter, 1996), including physical activities such as sport and exercise, work, relationships, and health behaviors such as smoking, substance use, alcohol consumption, and dietary practices (Martin Ginis & Leary, 2004).

Self-esteem is one of the few psychological constructs to acquire meaning outside the ivory tower of academia, and it emerges frequently in media accounts and everyday conversations. For example, the promotion of self-esteem shapes curriculum design (including physical education) in many countries, serves as a barometer for staff welfare in occupational settings, acts as a target for the evaluation of health-care initiatives in various populations, and provides a vehicle for explaining a broad array of human functioning (Baumeister, 1987; Fox, 2000). Campbell (1984) described self-

esteem seeking as the first law of human nature given that people continually invest energy into validating who they are, who they want to be, and what they do. Empirical support corroborates this claim, indicating that self-esteem is the most important self-perception experienced during satisfying events in collectivistic and individualistic cultures (Sheldon, Elliot, Kim, & Kasser, 2001). Attention to self-perceptions is required for understanding the function, actions, and psychological well-being of participants engaged within the sporting arena. Moreover, increased participation in physical activity will undoubtedly shape the self-perceptions contributing to identity development and self-worth (Fox, 2002). These contributions will likely be most evident during transitional periods such as moving from adolescence to adulthood or retiring from professional sport when the sense of self is challenged to grow, adjust, and realign with other pursuits and demands of life.

This chapter examines relevant theory and research pertaining to the self in the context of physical activity and sport. Attention will be given to how the self is structured, how it develops and changes, how it influences physical activity participation, and conversely how the self is influenced by involvement in physical activities. Guidelines on the measurement of physical self-perceptions are offered and suggestions for further research are provided.

The Self-System

Any meaningful overview of the self requires consideration of the constructs underpinning this aspect of the human psyche. Harter (1996) provided an excellent account of early self-concept research that has remained an influential contributor to contemporary thinking and research on the self. Central to most approaches is the idea that the self is a complex arrangement of constructs that make up the self-system. This idea is clearly reflected in Epstein's (1991) work, self-schemata theory (Markus & Wurf, 1987), and self-determination theory (Deci & Ryan, 2002). Theorists generally agree that the self has an organized structure that is managed by a self-director whose role is to assimilate information pertinent to the self during interfaces with the social world. The idea of a self-director is not novel and emerged in the seminal work of William James (1898), who distinguished between the "I" and the "Me" as the subjective and objective facets of the self. The "I" represents the aspect of the self that is capable of knowing and making judgments about the objective self (i.e., "Me"). A useful analogy is the function of a large professional organization such as a sports franchise, commercial bank, or industry headquarters. The "I" is analogous to the chief executive officer who oversees the managerial system, directs the production strategy, and keeps account of performance. The "Me" in this analogy would be the structure of the company, including its various subdivisions, departments, and activities that support the organization's global structure and goals.

The self-as-organization analogy clarifies several terms and concepts that permeate the self-system literature and tend to foster confusion when used interchangeably. The terms most often confounded are *self-concept* and *self-esteem*. Self-concept is a description of "the individual as known by the individual" (Murphy, 1947, p. 996) and includes all relevant abilities, activities, qualities, morals, values, roles, and responsibilities. In essence, the notion of self-concept is the "Me" as known by the "I." Sociologists have used the term *identity* in a similar vein, although this term seems to encompass a greater entity that integrates values with the various roles that the self performs.

Self-esteem represents the main outcome of the self and is equivalent to the annual financial report that details how well the company is achieving its mission. Self-esteem is evaluative in nature and is defined by Campbell (1984) as "an awareness of good possessed by self" (p. 9). The criteria on which self-esteem is based are idiosyncratic. For the company director, certain factors such as profit margins and public relations cannot be ignored. Similarly, the dominant culture in which an individual exists will be influential to the formation of self. In Western society, areas such as sporting prowess, educational attainment, job performance, physical appearance (slenderness and muscularity), and financial success are particularly valued, and self-ratings in these areas usually contribute to an individual's self-esteem. People also invest in subcultures and adopt their values. Athletic groups will likely emphasize physical prowess and competitive status along with other characteristics considered integral to athletic performance such as assertiveness and self-belief. Some people may be unbound by cultural constraints and express individualism or even quirkiness, whereas others may be primarily conformist and perhaps be seen as victims of fashion, toeing the line, or susceptible to peer pressure. In this sense, Cooley (1902) argued that we adopt a looking-glass self that simply reflects how others see us. Symbolic interactionists (Hall, 1992) have

followed Cooley's arguments and feel that the self can largely be explained in terms of the fragmented set of social roles that it has to play and that any central core epitomizing the self is nonexistent, weak, or transient.

The foregoing suggests that the criterion on which self-esteem is determined reflects the value and priority systems adopted by the person. Self-esteem is therefore based on being an OK person, depending on what the person considers as OK within his or her culture. This underpinned James's (1892) argument that self-esteem is a function of the degree to which an individual perceives that he or she has achieved personal aspirations. These points suggest that self-esteem can only be fully understood with an accompanying analysis of (a) the cultures to which the individual ascribes, (b) the value systems operating within those cultures, and (c) the degree to which a person infuses his or her own sense of self with these cultural demands. These matters have been considered too infrequently in self-esteem research.

The self has become more complex as the shackles of social class, familial roles, and religious dictums have waned and the scope for individuality has increased (Baumeister, 1987). The self now commonly has multiple roles and contrasting identities (e.g., a CEO who is also a father, friend, partner, and golfer) that make the organizational role of the self-director more demanding. Integrating the relevant elements of the self into a coherent and congruent system has traditionally been seen as the major task of adolescence. But because patterns of fragmentation transcend areas such as marriage, education, employment, and income, the organizational role of the self-director will likely become increasingly complex and multifaceted, and be a lifelong undertaking.

Strategies That the Self Uses for Enhancement

The self-director determines where to invest time and energy in serving the mission of the company. This responsibility involves directing choices, commitment, and persistence to relevant tasks, and deploying public relations strategies to present the company in a successful light. The self-director may use several strategies internally to convince the self that it is doing well or externally to convince others that it is successful:

▪ One strategy is to minimize the amount of negative information that influences self-esteem by attaching less value to arenas of life where inadequacies prevail. This process has been termed the *discounting principle* (Harter, 1996). Some areas that carry a high cultural currency, however, may be too overpowering for a person to discount. Attractiveness is one such area that is troublesome to discount for girls (Harter, 1996), young women, and increasingly for males (Fox, 1990).

▪ Another approach is to use self-presentation strategies to convince others that the self is doing well (Leary, 1995). Such external relations strategies could include emphasizing the positive dimensions of the self while concealing the troublesome aspects that leave the self vulnerable to negative evaluation (Martin Ginis & Leary, 2004).

▪ Employing a self-serving bias when deciphering incoming information is a third common strategy. The self ignores or forgets negative information while embellishing and claiming successes. The self is more likely to ascribe failure to external sources such as luck or lack of control while attributing success to personal ability and effort.

▪ Some of this processing may operate at the conscious level, although much will remain inaccessible (Guidano, 1986). Self-serving strategies are beneficial in building confidence and buffering adversity, and their absence is linked with low self-esteem (Blaine & Crocker, 1993). The potential exists, however, for the self to become overdependent on these strategies and thus defensive or conservative to the point where the self excludes stimuli for development, promotes delusions of grandeur, and ultimately fails to connect successfully with the social world. These types of excesses usually result in impaired social functioning and curtailed development. Moreover, discounting behaviors such as physical activity that are integrally linked with health promotion could be detrimental.

Establishing and maintaining self-esteem is a complex process. The self is nurtured by an innate drive to explore and develop while concomitantly establishing a coherent base from which to operate. Thus, stability across time and consistency across situations in patterns of behaviors and emotional reactions provide the sense of identity and predictability that ties the self together. This base, in turn, nurtures the necessary roots for individuals to seek challenges that facilitate personal learning and growth. The self is left with a delicate balancing act of establishing a solid and recognizable core while retaining sufficient flexibility to accept the challenges of individual development and not stifle opportunities for change and growth. A strong, stable self provides the wings for exploration and positive change. These processes become transparent during major transitional periods across the lifespan such as adolescence and retirement.

The Construct of the Self-System

The self's ascendance to the forefront of psychological research during the 1950s and 1960s was accompanied by a naively simplistic view of the construct. During this initial phase of self-esteem research, the self was viewed as a unidimensional entity. This perspective was reflected in instrument design and selection. Items that tapped personal characteristics ranging from facial features to social skills were combined to form an omnibus measure of self-esteem. The central focus of this early work was concerned with comparing self-esteem scores across known groups classified by demographic variables such as age, gender, and educational status. This unsophisticated view of the self placed little emphasis on domain-specific perceptions that contribute to the self's overall evaluation but served as a useful platform for more advanced work that examined the structure, function, and malleability of the self (Wylie, 1979, 1989).

A number of crucial developments spearheaded what has been labeled the second phase of self-esteem research (Fox, 1997). The first development involved recognition that the self is multidimensional in nature and is composed of subdomains that contribute to overall self-worth. Early work indicated that competence, power, moral self-approval, love worthiness, virtue, and significance were key elements operating within the self-system to promote overall self-esteem (Coopersmith, 1967; Epstein, 1973). Building on this idea, Fitts (1965) developed the Tennessee Self-Concept Scale (TSCS), considered one of the first multidimensional self-perception instruments. The TSCS has been featured prominently in research related to physical activity during the past 40 years, in part because it includes a subscale that measures the physical self. The original version of the TSCS has since been revised to include the assessment of physical, social, family, personal, and moral components of the self-system (Roid & Fitts, 1994).

Subsequent instrument development research concerning the self-system has focused on establishing perceived competence profiles within domains. The advent of self-perception profiles solidified the importance of weighting life domains according to their differential contribution to global self-esteem and prompted the development of instruments designed to capture relevant content domains. Harter and her colleagues developed a series of multidimensional self-perception profiles for children (Harter, 1985), adolescents (Harter, 1988), college students (Neemann & Harter, 1986), and adults (Messer & Harter, 1986) that included cohort-specific measures incorporating progressively more differentiated profiles to reflect age-related changes in the self (Fox, 1998). Along similar lines, Marsh and colleagues developed the Self-Description Questionnaire (SDQ) for use in preadolescent children (SDQ–I, Marsh; 1992a), adolescent high school students (SDQ–II; Marsh, 1992b), and young adults (SDQ-III; Marsh, 1992c).

Central to these instrument development efforts was the theoretical argument that self-esteem or global self-worth is a function of an array of self-ratings made by a person across multiple domains. In other words, self-esteem resides at the apex of a self-system composed of perceived competencies in specific life domains. Self-esteem is thereby considered a generic appraisal of pride in oneself. Rosenberg's (1965) Global Self-Esteem Scale was designed as a domain-free measure of overall self-regard, and test developers have included similar measures of self-esteem in their instruments. The major advantage of the profile approach to self-perception measurement exemplified by Harter and Marsh's work has been clarifying the relationship of perceived competencies across life domains with global self-esteem.

Self-System Structure

Following the acceptance of multidimensional approaches to measuring self-perceptions, subsequent research investigated how subcomponents of the self-system were organized in relation to each other. Marsh discussed the notion of self-concept structure in depth and presented various models that correspond to research detailing the structure of intelligence (Marsh, 1997; Marsh & Hattie, 1996). One influential model depicting the structure of the self-system was proposed by Shavelson, Hubner, and Stanton (1976) with specific reference to educational contexts. This model posits that the self is multidimensional and hierarchical in nature with self-esteem sitting at the apex of a dendritic self-system. Within this configuration, self-perceptions ranging from highly specific to more general abstractions within life domains formulate beneath the apex. According to Shavelson et al., four life domains—the physical, social, emotional, and academic selves—form the cornerstone of this rootlike system that has the capacity to nurture (or forestall) the development of self-esteem (see figure 4.1). The model contends that daily experiences with specific tasks provide immediate confirmation of perceived competencies that generalize over time into more global feelings of worth. The notion of different levels of abstraction within the model is consistent with the trait–state debate in areas of psychological research and implied varying degrees

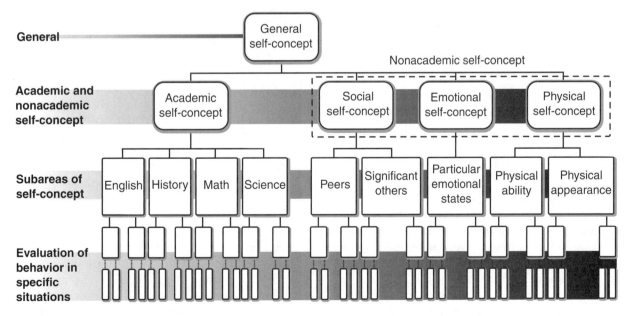

Figure 4.1 A hierarchical structure of self-concept.

From G.R. Shavelson, J.J. Hubner, and G.C. Stanton, 1976. "Self-concept: Validation of construct interpretations." *Review of Educational Research* 46: p. 413. Copyright by the American Educational Research Association; reproduced with permission from the publisher.

of stability ascribed to self-perceptions at different levels (Fox, 2002). Marsh and colleagues developed the SDQ instruments based on the model proposed by Shavelson et al. and have pursued a vigorous approach to construct validation using advanced statistical procedures that has generally supported the configuration of the model.

Considerable advances in understanding the nature and function of the self have been made in the past 50 years (Leary & Tangney, 2003). Self-esteem is now considered an integral component of psychological health and a useful index of adjustment to the demands of life. Complementing the importance of self-esteem as a marker of well-being, the foregoing review illustrates the advances made in understanding how the self operates and identifies the components that unite to form the self-system. The following section examines the role afforded the physical self in the process of constructing and maintaining self-esteem with particular emphasis placed on the nature and measurement of physical self-perceptions.

The Physical Self and Self-System Instrument Development

Given that sport and exercise activate the physical system of the body, it comes as no surprise that the physical self has been prominent in recent developments of self-concept theory and measurement in sport psychology. Physical self-perceptions have consistently emerged as salient components of self-concept, and they account for the contributions made by a variety of health and achievement behaviors to one's self-esteem. Early attempts to capture the physical dimensions of the self-system did not benefit from the clarity provided by Shavelson and colleagues' (1976) conceptual model. For example, the Body Cathexis Scale (Secord & Jourard, 1953) and the Physical Estimation Scale (Sonstroem, 1978) were created as unidimensional self-perception instruments. Construct validation studies using early physical self-perception measures indicated little association between the physical self and other domain-level components of the self-system, but the studies supported a strong relationship between the physical self and global self-esteem. Consistent observations of strong links between physical self-perceptions (particularly aspects of physical appearance) and global self-esteem have led some theorists to argue that the physical self is a manifestation of the public self that is lucidly tied to self-presentational processes (Leary, 2004). Its importance lies in its salience as a vehicle for expression and social interaction.

Following early work on the physical self, greater attention to the content, structure, and function of physical self-perceptions emerged in the 1980s. The Physical Self-Efficacy Scale (Ryckman, Robbins, Thornton, & Cantrell, 1982) was created to assess people's confidence in displaying physical skills in the presence of others. Lintunen (1987) developed the Perceived Physical Competence Scale for Children, which incorporated assessments of physical performance capacity and physical appearance. Although these instruments provided a useful starting point for physical self-perception research, the nature of their development was based largely on statistical analyses of existing item pools as opposed to careful consideration of substantive content. This approach was later criticized for not systematically representing the content of the physical self-system (Wylie, 1989).

Considering these shortcomings, two instruments emerged that blended theoretical considerations with careful attention to measurement principles. These were the development of the Physical Self-Perception Profile (PSPP; Fox & Corbin, 1989) and the Physical Self-Description Questionnaire (PSDQ; Marsh, Richards, Johnson, Roche, & Tremayne, 1994). The PSPP includes 30 structured alternative response items that capture four salient subdomains of the physical self-system (perceived sport competence, physical conditioning, physical strength, and body attractiveness) and an index of overall physical self-worth. The original version of the PSPP was developed through content analysis of interviews and open-ended responses from college students to inform item development using normative perceptions of the physical self. Subsequent modifications stemming from the original PSPP have been made to produce the Children and Youth Physical Self-Perception Profile (CY–PSPP; Whitehead, 1995) as well as a version for older adults that included health and physical functioning items along with other PSPP subscales (Chase & Corbin, 1995).

The PSDQ (Marsh et al., 1994) comprises 70 items that assess nine subdomains relevant to the physical self (strength, body fat, activity, endurance, sport competence, coordination, appearance, flexibility, and health), one domain (labeled physical self-concept), and a global index of overall self-esteem using Likert response scales. Marsh and colleagues developed these instruments using the format of the SDQ as a frame of reference and created subsequent instruments for specific populations such as the Elite Athlete Self-Description Questionnaire (EASDQ; Marsh & Perry, 2005). Corroborating the importance of physical self-perceptions has been a proliferation of instruments designed to measure specific elements of the physical self-system including sport ability, body image, and self-presentational processes, or self-efficacy for surmounting physical challenges (Duda, 1998).

Despite minor differences between the content and structure of the PSDQ and PSPP and their population-specific variants, the development and ongoing validation of these instruments generally supports the multidimensional and hierarchical nature of the self-system. Self-referenced evaluations of personal ability are made at the foundational level of the hierarchy. Combined with mastery experiences, these evaluations generalize to increasingly abstract perceptions of adequacy within a particular domain of the self-system over time. Thus, self-perceptions can be organized and assessed at multiple levels ranging from microlevel evaluations of personal ability to macrolevel evaluations of self-worth. Figure 4.2 provides an illustration of self-relevant constructs at various levels of the self-perception hierarchy along with relevant examples from sport and health domains.

Additional work on the self-system connected with the physical self has emerged in the area of identity development. The notion of an athletic identity, or the degree to which a person describes himself or herself as athletic, has been of interest to sport psychologists because of the connection between identity formation and the physical self (Brewer, Van Raalte, & Linder, 1993; Grove, Fish, & Eklund, 2004). Moreover, exercise psychologists have examined self-schema theory (Markus, 1977)

to investigate the influence of different exercise identities. Self-schemata develop from beliefs, behaviors, or personal descriptions and formulate into semidiscrete identities that have logical relationships with physical activity behavior and cognitive and affective concomitants (Boyd & Yin, 1999; Estabrooks & Courneya, 1997). Despite the challenges inherent in classifying identities based on self-schema (Estabrooks & Courneya), the integration of psychological processes with the emotional attachment that people afford certain behavioral roles is logically linked with physical self-perceptions and development of what some theorists have labeled the true self (Deci & Ryan, 2002). On a more practical level, the study of self-schema and identity may be useful in unraveling the mysteries involved in exercise participation and termination decisions (Anderson, 2004). Conversely, an identity restricted solely to physical prowess seems counterproductive to positive attitudes toward aging and opportunities for identity expansion across the lifespan (Pheonix, Faulkner, & Sparkes, 2005). This kind of restricted identity is particularly salient in illnesses that challenge physical performance such as arthritis (MacSween, Brydson, & Fox, 2004) and congenital or acquired physical disability (Sherrill, 1997).

The development of theory in conjunction with instrumentation to assess relevant self-perceptions has clarified previous work and motivated interest in the study of the self within physical activity domains. Given the focus on physical activity that permeates this chapter, a number of important

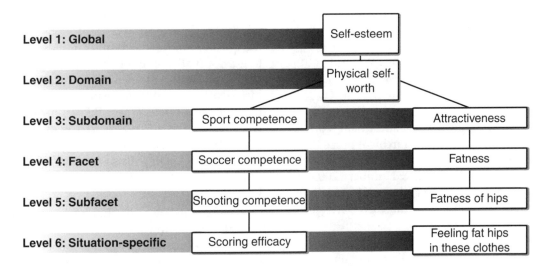

Figure 4.2 Levels of specificity of self-perceptions within the physical domain.

Reprinted, by permission, from K.R. Fox, 1998, "Advances in the measurement of the physical self." In *Advances in sport and exercise psychology measurement*, edited by J. Duda (Morgantown, WV: Fitness Information Technology), 297.

observations can be offered to guide future research in this area:

■ The physical self is multidimensional in nature. The sustained focus on the structural validity of physical self-perception scores has established the multidimensional nature of instruments designed to capture such processes in adults (Fox, 1990; Marsh, 1997) and children and youth (Eklund, Whitehead, & Welk, 1997; Welk & Eklund, 2005). More recent evidence supports the cross-national and cross-cultural generalizability of PSDQ and PSPP scores (Asçi, Asçi, & Zorba, 1999; Atenzia, Balaguer, Moreno, & Fox, 2004; Fonseca & Fox, 2002; Guérin, Marsh, & Famose, 2004; Marsh, Asçi, & Marco, 2002; Van de Vliet, Knapen, Onghena, Fox, Van Coppenolle, et al., 2002b), and to a lesser extent CY–PSPP scores (Asçi, Eklund, Whitehead, Kiraszci, & Koca, 2005; Hagger, Biddle, Chow, Stambulova, & Kavussanu, 2003). Collectively, these studies highlight potential measurement issues worthy of additional research such as the presence of methods effects for particular item response formats and content validity issues when considering self-perception profiles across cultural groups. Perceptions of sport or athletic competence remain integral components of self-esteem throughout the lifespan although evidence of invariance across age cohorts would enhance the credibility of cross-sectional data on this issue.

■ The physical self-system is, at least in part, hierarchically organized. Consistent with the conceptual model proposed by Shavelson et al. (1976), the wealth of available evidence suggests that perceptions of physical self-worth mediate the relationship between global perceptions of self-esteem and more situation- or task-specific perceptions of competence or adequacy at lower levels of abstraction (Fox & Corbin, 1989; Eklund et al., 1997; Sonstroem, Harlow, & Josephs, 1994; Van de Vliet, Knapen, Onghena, Fox, David, et al., 2002a). Despite this assertion, one study of Canadian adolescent girls suggested that additional work is needed to corroborate the hierarchical processing of self-perception development over time (Kowalski, Crocker, Kowalski, Chad, & Humbert, 2003) in which shifts in physical and global self-perceptions can inform theoretical links within self-perception models.

■ The development of the physical self is likely accompanied by individuals' embracing of particular identities such as weightlifter, football player, dancer, gymnast, or physically fit person. The degree to which people incorporate (or repel) these identities into the formation of the physical self has motivational currency (Ryan & Deci, 2003) and offers insight into the processes influencing physical activity participation decisions.

Measuring Physical Self-Perceptions

Although attention to instrument development and construct validation has improved the knowledge base tied to physical self-perceptions, the proliferation of instruments designed to capture salient self-perceptions (especially as they relate to the physique) has become daunting. Several useful monographs have been prepared to guide researchers interested in selecting the most suitable physical self-perception instrument. These include Byrne's (1996) *Measuring Self-Concept Across the Lifespan*, Duda's (1998) *Advances in Sport and Exercise Psychology Measurement*, Ostrow's (1996) *Directory of Psychological Tests in Sport and Exercise Sciences, 2nd Edition*, and Fox's (1997) *The Physical Self: From Motivation to Well-Being*. Given the evidence available from the past three decades of physical self-perception research, we can offer some guidance for instrument selection in the physical domain:

■ **Determine the focus of the research question and target population in relation to self-relevant content.** The physical domain is composed of numerous self-perceptions including body image, sports competence, athletic identity, social physique anxiety, perceived fitness, and efficacy beliefs. Being mindful of this diversity is required to select the most appropriate instrument to capture the dimensionality and specificity of relevant self-perception content. Consideration of the question under study in conjunction with the target population of interest should aid instrument selection. Self-perception theorists have given careful attention to these issues and created scales for general use (PSPP and PSDQ) in conjunction with scales that address a narrower segment of the population such as the CY–PSPP (Whitehead, 1995) or the EASDQ (Marsh & Perry, 2005) in which salient content within the physical self-system may warrant more scrutiny.

■ **Select instruments that have a strong theoretical foundation.** Measurement experts have extolled the virtues of linking theory with measurement during the process of instrument development and theoretical refinement (Cronbach & Meehl, 1955; Messick, 1995). Atheoretical research can be useful in the early stages of scientific inquiry.

But the field of physical self-perception research has moved past description to a focus on explanation. We need a theoretical basis to improve our understanding of the interplay between physical activity participation and self-perception development or degradation.

■ **Choose instruments with established psychometric properties.** The process of construct validation is ongoing and requires the constellation of evidence from multiple sources to inform the user of test score utility (Messick, 1995). To enhance our understanding of self-perceptions, we must use instruments that have demonstrated evidence of reliability and validity for the target population. Fortunately, we have two self-perception profiles germane to physical activity (PSPP and PSDQ) that were created with self-concept theory as a foundational guide and appear to demonstrate characteristics indicative of sound measurement across divergent samples.

■ **Consider assessing domains of interest and relevance other than physical self-perceptions.** Research questions focusing on abstract concepts such as subjective well-being may include assessment of physical self-perceptions as an integral component of the research question. Self-referent perceptions outside the physical domain have been developed with careful attention to construct validation issues. Given the abstract nature of psychological and social health, careful consideration of relevant constructs would be wise because good mental health and subjective well-being are unlikely to result solely from the contributions of the physical self. Where well-being is the issue, the inclusion of indices such as life satisfaction (Diener, 2000) and vitality (Ryan & Frederick, 1997) might be informative alongside measures of social self-concept if this domain is seen as a potential mechanism for global self-perception development and change.

The choice of instrumentation is never easy, yet it remains fundamental to scientific development in any field, including physical self-perception research. Kerlinger (1979) noted that measurement can be "the Achilles heel of behavioral research" (p. 141), and in this vein we echo his sentiments with reference to the measurement of self-perceptions in general and physical self-perceptions in particular. Studies frequently fail to produce relevant findings because the instrumentation used to capture self-perceptions was insufficiently sensitive or psychometrically troubled, irrespective of the design or execution of the study.

The Self in Physical Activity

The ubiquitous nature of the self predisposes this system to a continual series of interactions with different life domains. The physical self assists the development of individualized personas, contributes to self-worth, and motivates physical activity engagement and commitment. The role of the physical self in these processes can be viewed from two contrasting perspectives that illuminate the causal processes operating in the self's nomological network (Cronbach & Meehl, 1955). The first perspective, termed the self-enhancement hypothesis (Fox, 1997), suggests that people constantly strive for situations in which they can demonstrate laudable qualities. By contrast, the skill-enhancement hypothesis (Fox, 1997) contends that physical activity interventions improve physical abilities, fitness, and health, which in turn serve to fortify self-perceptions. Complementing these approaches, Marsh (1990) has forwarded the reciprocal effects hypothesis, whereby a bidirectional flow of causative energy is transmitted between behaviors and self-perceptions. Although this hypothesis is not unique to psychological theory (Bandura, 1986), it probably reflects the iterative nature of the self's interaction with the social world. Data support reciprocal effects with respect to physical self-perceptions (Kowalski et al., 2003; Marsh & Perry, 2005), and this hypothesis will likely stimulate useful avenues of research about the synergies between the self and health behaviors.

In the following sections of this chapter, we review the available evidence pertaining to the self-enhancement and skill-enhancement hypotheses. Our initial focus in this section concerns the role played by perceived adequacies or competencies, self-presentational processes, and "importance" profiles with reference to the self-enhancement hypothesis. Next, we examine the narrative (Fox, 2000) and hypothesis-testing (Heian, Hagen, Abbott & Nordheim, 2005; Spence, McGannon, & Poon, 2005) approaches taken to evaluate the role of physical activity behavior in self-perception formation advocated by the skill-enhancement hypothesis. Considerations for future research on the interface between self-perceptions and physical activity behaviors are offered throughout this section in an attempt to encourage further theoretical development in physical self-perception research.

Self-Enhancement Hypothesis

The self-enhancement hypothesis posits the self-system as a primary determinant of activity choice and behavior. This hypothesis contends that humans seek to maximize positive feelings or effectively master challenging tasks (Campbell, 1984; Deci & Ryan, 2002; Harter, 1978; Nicholls, 1989; White, 1959). This drive manifests itself through activity choice, intensity of engagement, and persistence over time in the face of obstacles. The central tenet of this approach is that a flow of motivational energy stems from the self to regulate investment in behaviors that offer positive benefits while simultaneously avoiding negative outcomes such as shame or embarrassment.

Role of Perceived Competence and Perceived Ability Perceptions of competence and ability are no strangers to the self-perceptual web that influences physical activity. Research consistently reveals that physically active people report higher levels of perceived competence and greater expectations for success (Biddle, 1997), suggesting that the self seeks domains where ability can be demonstrated and avoids situations where incompetence is prominently displayed to others. Whether such actions are intrinsically motivated by the activity itself or regulated by extrinsic forces such as social recognition that are separable from the activity remains unclear. Moreover, the extent to which developmental epochs influence these processes represents a fruitful area for further investigation given that previous research indicates that the self becomes increasingly differentiated with age (Harter, 1996; Raudsepp, Kais, & Hannus, 2004). Deci and Ryan's (2002) self-determination theory presents an interesting framework from which to address these and related questions pertaining to the interplay between motivational processes and self-development. Preliminary findings indicate that self-determined motives, regardless of their intrinsic or extrinsic nature, correlate with elevated physical and global self-worth (Georgiadis, Biddle, & Chatzisarantis, 2001; Wilson & Rodgers, 2002) that is consistent with theoretical arguments concerning the source of "true" self-esteem (Deci & Ryan, 1995).

Research with both the PSDQ and the PSPP, along with microlevel assessments of self-efficacy, supports a robust relationship between elevated levels of perceived competence and physical activity involvement. The strength of the perceived competence–activity relationship appears consistent across children and youth (Crocker, Eklund, & Kowalski, 2000; Crocker et al., 2003; Raudsepp, Liblick, & Hannus, 2002), university students (Fox & Corbin, 1989; Hayes, Crocker, & Kowalski, 1999), middle-aged adults (Sonstroem, Speliotis, & Fava, 1992),

older adults (Chase & Corbin, 1995), and older old adults (Fox, Stathi, McKenna, & Davis, 2007). Most of the evidence supports the prominent role of sports competence and conditioning perceptions with respect to physical activity behavior. These effects appear to be unaffected by self-presentational concerns pertaining to physique in North American women (Kowalski, Crocker, & Kowalski, 2001). Interestingly, perceptions of body attractiveness have not been strong predictors of physical activity in Canadian youth or adults when other self-perceptions are considered (Crocker et al., 2003). Recent data from Estonian youth, however, indicate that body-related perceptions of competence were the dominant predictor of activity in young females (Raudsepp et al., 2004). The extent to which this can be attributed to the ambient differences between Eastern and Western cultures remains a topic for further investigation.

The predictive influence of physical self-perceptions on physical activity involvement has been explored to a greater extent than the effect attributable to global self-esteem. In one longitudinal study, Sonstroem and colleagues noted that self-esteem was predictive of performance in male varsity high school swimmers (Sonstroem, Harlow, & Salisbury, 1993). Marsh and Perry (2005) augmented earlier work by demonstrating that an athletic self-concept accounts for an additional 10% of the variability in championship performance in elite swimmers after controlling for objective performance indices. Contrary to these findings, Crocker et al. (2003) reported weak ($r = .19$) relationships between global self-esteem and physical activity changes over one year in adolescent females that were expunged by the contributions of physical self-perceptions. The role of global self-esteem in sport and exercise participation warrants further investigation to determine the underlying direction of causal flow between the self and behavior. High self-esteem may conceivably provide a solid foundation from which people can be more adventurous, engaged, and willing to endure the inherent risks associated with trying new activities. On the contrary, people with low self-esteem may be conservative, recalcitrant, and unwilling to try new activities, thereby stifling opportunities for self-development. These questions along with their concomitant effects on persistence behavior and identity formation in various spheres of physical activity have yet to be fully explored.

Although sound theoretical and intuitive reasons appear to support the perceived competence–physical activity relationship, most of the evidence provides marginal support for the causal role played by the self as a determinant of physical activity behavior. Although the notion of causality has a long and turbulent history in scientific inquiry (Okasha, 2002), many scholars agree that the mere presence of a relationship is insufficient for a causative argument without evidence of temporal precedence and refutation of plausible alternative hypotheses (Trochim, 2001). Although evidence supports the relationship between physical self-perceptions and activity levels, few studies in comparison have employed longitudinal approaches or controlled experimental designs that permit greater confidence in causal inference. Early work by Sonstroem and Kampper (1980) demonstrated that physical self-concept was predictive of subsequent decisions to enroll in sports programs in junior high school boys. More recently, Crocker et al. (2003) demonstrated a similar pattern of relationships in Canadian adolescent females. In that study, changes in physical self-perceptions (especially perceived conditioning) accounted for changes in physical activity participation across a one-year period.

A comprehensive understanding of causal ordering between self-perceptions and physical activities will require more than longitudinal modeling of self-report data. Fox (1997) noted that the relationship between activity involvement and self-perceptions is dynamic and reciprocal, thereby requiring more advanced design and analytical procedures to elucidate these processes. In-depth studies using intrasubject designs may elucidate the role of self-perceptions in decision making at crucial transitional periods. Additional work clarifying the role afforded social agents in self-perception formation irrespective of participant ability would be insightful. Studies examining the role of friendship or peer networks (McDonough & Crocker, 2005), coaches (Gagné, Ryan, & Bargmann, 2003), and physical educators (Standage, Duda, & Ntoumanis, 2006) have emerged and will verify the importance of social agents in self-perception development.

Self-Presentational Processes Given that we are "physical" entities, our bodies form a medium between the public and private personas that shape our physical activity endeavors. The desire to look fit and attractive according to societal ideals represents a strong motivational force geared toward compliance rather than integration of the behavior into a coherent self. In the context of sport, this might be true of events and activities in which the physique is overtly displayed such as in aesthetically evaluated sports (Crocker, Snyder, Kowalski, & Hoar, 2000). The salience of such image-laden motives may be safeguarded in team sports in which

hiding from the coach's evaluative gaze is possible. Alternatively, these processes are implicated in an attraction to exercise contexts where the physique can be displayed and publicly admired.

Much of the literature examining image-based motives has been explored using self-presentational frameworks (Leary, 1992). Although self-presentational processes may play a role in motivating physical activity behavior, an emerging body of evidence implies that these processes can curtail physical activity involvement directly or indirectly (Martin Ginis & Leary, 2004). For example, athletes who report self-presentational concerns such as appearing fatigued, unfit, unathletic, or incapable of performance experience elevated trait anxiety (Wilson & Eklund, 1998). Moreover, self-presentational concerns inspire smoking and drug use because of impression management ties with the self-system (Martin Ginis, & Leary). The comparative nature of impression management is evident in the big-fish-little-pond-effect model as a frame of reference for self-concept development, which seems worthy of additional investigation (Chanal, Marsh, Sarrazin, & Bois, 2005).

The major focus of self-presentational research in physical activity domains has been on the construct of social physique anxiety (SPA; Hart, Leary, & Rejeski, 1989). This emphasis is hardly surprising given the relationship between the physical self and activity involvement coupled with the challenge of motivating at-risk groups to incorporate activity into their daily lifestyle. According to Hart et al., SPA is "a subtype of social anxiety that occurs as a result of the prospect or presence of interpersonal evaluation of one's physique" (p. 96) and has been measured with the Social Physique Anxiety Scale (SPAS; Hart et al.). Conroy and colleagues extended this line of research by developing the Self-Presentation in Exercise Questionnaire (SPEQ; Conroy, Motl, & Hall, 2000; Conroy & Motl, 2002) as a measure of impression motivation and construction based on the self-presentational nature of exercise motives such as the desire to lose weight or increase muscularity. Although self-presentational frameworks have intuitive appeal in relation to physical self-perceptions, the measurement of constructs pertinent to Leary's (1992) approach remains controversial. Neither the SPAS nor the SPEQ has received overwhelming psychometric support. Scale dimensionality and item content relevance issues are evident in the literature. Considering the importance of measurement to progress in self-perception research, future research may wish to embrace a rigorous construct validation approach advocated by Messick (1995) to improve the measurement of self-presentational constructs.

Self-Deficiency Motives Although perceived competencies and self-presentational processes clearly influence physical activity, the self-enhancement hypothesis may not apply in some situations. People may have good reasons to engage in activities without having an overall sense of competence or despite having heightened self-presentational concerns. Such situations are likely to occur when outcomes stemming from the behavior are central to the person's identity or desires such that any perceived competence inadequacies are overridden. This circumstance could occur in sport when an athlete plays through pain given the importance ascribed to winning at all costs, or in a rehabilitative context when a morbidly obese person has a desire for health improvement or weight loss that overrides feelings of ineptness. Such activities could be linked to self-worth improvement by overcoming trepidations or could be driven by a focus on the benefits derived from the activity itself even though the behavior is unrewarding (Deci & Ryan, 2002).

Other motives such as a desire to belong to a group or feel accepted by one's peers may affect physical activity choices and persistence behaviors. The extent to which social motives operate based on perceived deficiencies within the self-system or from an innate need to feel meaningfully connected within one's environment (known as relatedness in self-determination theory parlance; Deci & Ryan, 2002) remains unclear and is an area worthy of further inquiry. Despite this caveat, preliminary support exists for the relatedness–motivation link in sport and physical education settings (Kowal & Fortier, 2000; Ntoumanis, 2001; Sarrazin, Vallerand, Guillet, Pelletier, & Guay, 2002). Moreover, relatedness is associated with positive changes in self-esteem across training sessions in female gymnasts (Gagné, Ryan, & Bargman, 2003) and with increased physical self-worth and global self-esteem in female exercise participants (Wilson, Rodgers, Fraser, Murray, & McIntyre, 2004). Such findings call for greater research attention to the role of the deficiency-based motives in physical activity decision making and their long-term behavioral consequences.

Role of Perceived Importance in Self-Enhancement Given our understanding of the self's structure, there is logic to the idea that aspects of the self deemed unimportant to the person will not influence overall self-worth. One extension of this view is that people will strategically reduce the importance affixed to life domains where they feel inadequate. The centrality of importance has attracted considerable attention from self-theorists ranging from James (1892) to Rosenberg (1965) and is encapsulated in contemporary reviews of the self (Leary & Tanguay, 2003). Harter (1996) advocated the use of discrepancy scores that weighted self-perceptions by their importance to people across life's domains. Fox (1990) and Whitehead (1995) both developed perceived importance profiles for use alongside self-perception measures.

The use of perceived importance profiles with self-perception instruments has yielded mixed findings. Fox (1990) reported a graded pattern of relationships between subdomain self-perceptions and higher-order constructs when stratified by perceived importance discrepancies. Subsequent research (Chase & Corbin, 1995; Whitehead, 1995) corroborated Fox's work by showing comparable trends in other populations, suggesting some support for Harter's (1996) discounting principle. Moreover, discounting appears to be greatest in the most culturally permissible areas, reaffirming the important link between cultural ideals and self-development. In contrast, Marsh and Sonstroem (1995) failed to provide convincing support for the use of importance–competence discrepancy scores in the prediction of self-esteem. These anomalies may reflect deviation from the discounting principle during applications of sophisticated regression modeling, or alternatively, to limitations associated with the measurement of perceived importance pertaining to item content representation. Current instrumentation assessing perceived importance has demonstrated psychometric concerns (Fox, 1998). Nevertheless, measurement development efforts to assess perceived importance seem worthwhile in light of the theoretical and practical merit that this approach offers future physical self-perception research.

Skill-Enhancement Hypothesis

The corollary to self-enhancement is skill enhancement, which is concerned with improving the global sense of self through developing physical abilities, fitness, appearance, or health attributes. The central premise here is that participation in certain activities or behaviors will (perhaps through actual or perceived physical changes) exert a positive effect on elements of the self-system. Given the current ethos concerning health promotion and disease prevention through lifestyle physical activity, a better label for this approach is the *intervention hypothesis* given that the goal here is to improve aspects of the self through behavioral change (Fox, 1997, 2002). This hypothesis has underpinned the rationale for a broad array of programmatic decisions and policy arguments. Consider the maxim "Sport builds character" that is often the basis for delivering youth sport programs and physical education curricula. The intervention hypothesis also frames many of the approaches to mental health promotion and disease prevention that have established links with physical activity involvement and have permeated the field of behavioral medicine (Sallis & Owen, 1999). Early work in this area focused on the effect of increased physical ability, because of participation, to influence global aspects of the self-system such as self-esteem. More recent work has examined changes in microlevel aspects of the self-system and physical self-system, including body image, perceived sports competence, and self-efficacy for physical activity. Irrespective of the criterion variable studied, improvement may be driven by perceptual changes as much as by objective changes in physical or performance parameters, although recent meta-analytic work suggests that fitness gains and program type moderate the exercise–self-esteem relationship (Spence et al., 2005).

Following the advent of the positive psychology movement (Seligman & Czikszentmihalyi, 2000), outcomes such as high self-esteem have gained greater acceptance as viable end products of multifaceted programs. Even so, research linking physical activity with self-esteem has been slow to evolve compared with comparable research examining depression, anxiety, and personality dysfunctions. Cross-sectional research has dominated the landscape and can serve as a useful starting point when examining the relationship between physical activity participation and changes within the self-system. Many of these studies, however, have been one-shot comparisons of known groups on relevant self-perceptions or have correlated physical activity involvement with a plethora of self-system constructs that give little attention to models of self-esteem function or change. Such designs constrain our ability to draw causal inferences and offer limited insight into the merit of the intervention hypothesis. Selection bias, for example, is likely a major cause of the inconsistent findings. Participants involved in physical activity already exhibit greater confidence, better achievement motivation, and higher self-worth compared with those who have elected to avoid physical activity engagement. Cross-sectional research also fails to account for plausible alternative influences affect-

ing self-perception change and does little to omit temporal precedence concerns that plague these designs (Trochim, 2001).

Several recent reviews of studies that address the intervention hypothesis through pre- and posttest assessment attest to the merit of physical activity participation as a vehicle for promoting self-esteem. Fox (2000) summarized the outcomes of randomized controlled (n = 36) and nonrandomized (n = 44) studies conducted between 1970 and 1999. Randomized controlled studies provide a strong approach to evaluating the intervention hypothesis given that they counteract many of the threats to internal validity that are a feature of cross-sectional and nonequivalent group designs (Trochim, 2001). Fox reported that 50% of the studies showed an improvement in global self-esteem. He attributed this inconsistency to problems with instrumentation but also suggested that short (usually less than 12 weeks) engagement in physical activity may not be sufficiently powerful to change a fundamentally important construct, especially when it is susceptible to other events occurring simultaneously in many life domains.

The narrative review conducted by Fox (2000) is complemented by the results of two recent quantitative reviews that support the tenability of the intervention hypothesis. Spence and colleagues' (2005) meta-analysis reported an overall weak to moderate effect (d = +0.23) of exercise participation on changes in global self-esteem in adults. Corroborating this study was a separate meta-analysis that supported the influence of physical exercise on global self-esteem in children and youth (standardized mean difference values ranged from 0.21 to 1.33 [all 95% CIs > 0]; Heian et al., 2005), although the studies included in this review varied in quality. Both meta-analyses suggested that the intervention hypothesis is supported as far as global self-esteem is concerned, although the effect may be modified by factors within individuals, specific groups of people, and exercise settings. Moreover, small effects may still provide important contributions to positive changes in self-esteem (Prentice & Miller, 1992), a benefit that seems as important as reducing psychological maladies such as depression and anxiety.

A consistent finding from experimental studies is that physical activity interventions positively influence physical self-perception change (Asçi, 2003; Li, Harmer, Chaumeton, Duncan, & Duncan, 2002; Taylor & Fox, 2005). Fox (2000) reported that 78% of the randomized controlled studies indicated that positive changes in the physical aspects of the self-system occurred after intervention. Furthermore, evidence is emerging that the physical self is associated with emotional well-being and mental health in its own right, independent of global self-esteem or social desirability. Sonstroem and Potts (1996) were among the first to report this evidence. Similar findings have been seen with patients undergoing treatment for depression and anxiety (Van de Vliet, Knapen et al., 2003a; Van de Vliet, Onghena et al., 2003b) and in administrative staff in a large organization (Thogersen-Ntoumani & Fox, 2005). This work suggests that global aspects of the physical self are worthy outcome indicators of mental well-being in themselves as well as a potential mediating route by which self-esteem might change.

Given the paucity of research employing controlled experimental designs and psychometrically sound measures of self-perceptions, considerable scope remains for research examining the influence of physical activity participation in psychological health promotion. Theoretical arguments warrant careful consideration during the planning and implementation of future intervention-based studies of self-perception change. Sonstroem and Morgan (1989) advocated use of the exercise and self-esteem model (EXSEM; see figure 4.3), which articulates the processes of change in self-esteem attributable to physical activity. Spence et al. (2005) used this model in their meta-analytic study. According to the EXSEM, changes in physical competence underpin more global perceptions of self-esteem, and micro-level perceptions of efficacy for the activity trigger changes in perceived physical competence. Physical acceptance, or the degree to which people have

self-regard irrespective of their physical abilities and attributes, works in tandem with competency to bolster self-esteem changes following intervention. The model depicted in figure 4.3 has also been adapted to incorporate the subdomains featured in the PSPP (Sonstroem, Harlow, & Josephs, 1994). Research has confirmed the structure of the model in both its original and adapted forms and has supported the importance of physical acceptance to the study of perceived self-esteem (Baldwin & Courneya, 1997; Levy & Ebbeck, 2005; Sonstroem, Harlow, Gemma, & Osbourne, 1991). A complete test of the utility of the model in the documentation of change in various self-perception levels awaits future research.

Conclusion and Future Research Directions

This chapter has delineated progress on the study of the self with a particular emphasis on the role played by physical-self perceptions within the self-system. Self-esteem provides the core component of the self-system as an index of overall psychological well-being. Instruments have been designed with a specific focus on the physical self (for example, the PSDQ and PSPP) that adopt a profile approach to the measurement of self-perceptions in the physical domain. Both instruments have contributed to our understanding of the structure and function of the physical self-system, and more important, have articulated the contributions of the physical self to the promotion and maintenance of self-esteem. The

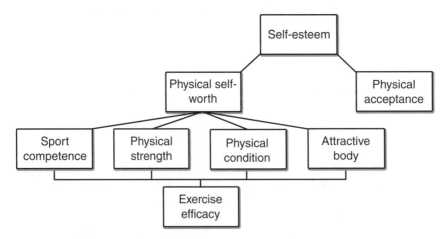

Figure 4.3 Adaptation of the exercise and self-esteem model (EXSEM) to include the Physical Self-Perception Profile (after Sonstroem, Harlow, and Josephs, 1994).

differentiated approach taken by both instruments has facilitated preliminary groundwork on the role of micro- and macrolevel self-perceptions in physical activity promotion, and conversely, identified potential mechanisms of change through which sport, exercise, and lifestyle physical activities can contribute to bolstering the self. Identification and support for mechanisms of change await the next phase of physical self-perception research (Fox, 1997).

Given the burgeoning literature on the self and the associated interest in physical self-perceptions, we will offer several general recommendations for future research to improve understanding of the self. Based on the level of integration represented in self-perception research in recent years, issues pertaining to cultural sensitivity, methodological diversity, developmental trajectories, and agents of change warrant attention to move the field of self-perception research in new directions.

The intimate link between self and culture is hardly novel and has represented an important caveat in the study of the self and self-perceptions for some time. Because the self embodies values, norms, ideals, and aspirations within a fabric of intertwined systems, researchers need to be mindful of the important role played by culture when studying self-perceptions and processes associated with the development and maintenance of healthy self-regard. Research has solidified the importance of self-esteem across cultures irrespective of their independent or interdependent orientation (Sheldon et al., 2001) and has suggested that the drive for positive self-worth transcends ambient cultural differences. Recognizing that the empirical study of the self is dominated by Western samples, research is beginning to explore the role of culture more carefully in relation to context-specific and global self-perceptions (Sheldon et al.), as well as physical self-perceptions (Asçi et al., 2005; Hagger et al., 2003). Cross-cultural research examining the source of self-perception development would be fruitful along with continued examination of the contributions made by different elements of self-perceptions to self-esteem promotion and physical activity participation.

A major challenge to advancing our understanding of the influence afforded the pervading cultural ethos in self-perception formation will be the utility of instruments designed to measure self-perceptions. The majority of physical self-perception instruments were originally developed on samples drawn from Western cultures (i.e., Australia and the United States) with little consideration of cross-cultural idio-syncrasies in terms of either item content or salient self-perceptions during instrument development. Recent research that has focused on the cross-cultural generalizability of scores derived from physical self-perception instruments has yielded interesting results (Asçi et al., 1999; Atienza et al., 2004; Fonseca & Fox, 2002; Hagger et al., 2003; Marsh et al., 2002; Van de Vliet, Knapen, Onghena, Fox, Van Coppenolle, et al., 2002b). Although most of the evidence supports a multidimensional conceptualization of physical self-perception systems, questions have arisen pertaining to the hierarchical structure of self-perception models, especially when examined over time (Kowalski et al., 2003). Future research would do well to attend to the issue of how physical self-perceptions are organized both within and between levels of the self-concept hierarchy across different cultures. Furthermore, the integrity and meaning of constructs such as sport competence and physical fitness vary across cultures. In Spain, Portugal, and Belgium, for example, athleticism, "sportiness," and fitness are more closely aligned than they are in the United States or United Kingdom.

Given the utility and widespread use of the PSDQ and PSPP instruments, it is not surprising that alternative methodological approaches for understanding the self have been slow to emerge. The interaction between cultural dynamics and self-perceptual changes is vibrant. Therefore, detailed qualitative work or innovative methods such as daily diary studies may complement traditional nomothetic approaches by illuminating mechanisms of self-perceptual change (Gagné et al., 2003; McGannon & Mauws, 2000). One example of innovative methodological work emerging in this area is provided by Ninot and colleagues (Fortes, Delignières, & Ninot, 2004; Fortes, Ninot, & Delignières, 2004, 2005) from the University of Montpellier, France. They have begun to address the dynamics of change in self-esteem and the physical self-system using single-item markers drawn from the PSPP (Fox & Corbin, 1989) measured several times daily and have documented diurnal and weekly change in individuals. Through the application of time trend analysis (borrowed from the field of economics), they are pioneering an approach that allows the documentation of change stimulated by an event such as a single exercise session, a program, or an injury at the individual level. Although the method remains in development, it could offer tremendous advantages over the traditional randomized controlled studies, which rely on mean group change in the outcome variables of interest that often mask important idiosyncratic effects (Bouffard, 1993).

Considerations of development trajectories have been prominent in Harter's (1996) contributions to our understanding of the self-system and represent two important considerations for future research into the study of the physical self. First, do developmental changes occur in the composition of the physical self-system that correspond with biological markers of growth and maturation? If so, critical landmarks for healthy physical and psychological development may be identifiable. Harter's work has supported a differentiated approach to studying the self, and she has already documented the changes in composition within the self-system across stages of human development. One application of Harter's work to the physical domain concerns extending Marsh's research (Marsh & Perry, 2005) to examine how the self-concept of elite athletes evolves over time and what effects those developmental changes have on the self-esteem of the athletically gifted. Second, what effect do developmental changes in self-perceptions have on behavioral indices such as physical activity participation and psychological well-being? The study of self-perception development across the lifespan presents formidable challenges to researchers in terms of measurement, design, and analyses of longitudinal data (Rogasa, 1995).

We are moving toward an era when greater emphasis will be placed on agents of change that have evidence-based links with outcomes such as mental health and physical activity. Toward this end, further examination of reciprocal effects models as suggested by Marsh and Perry (2005) will undoubtedly contribute to our understanding of the flow of causative energy to and from the self-system. The identification of intermediary variables relevant to self-perception change remains a major challenge. Concomitant changes in physical fitness measures have been a focus in current self-perception models and research. But note that current self-perception profiles and related instruments rely heavily on perceptions of competence as the cornerstone of a functional self-system (Fox, 1990; Marsh, 1997). Arguments from the perspective of self-determination theory contend that satisfaction of the psychological needs for autonomy and relatedness are also crucial to a healthy self-system.

Initial research supports these arguments in the physical domain (Georgiadis et al., 2000; Wilson & Rodgers 2002; Wilson et al., 2004).

Finally, given the emerging interest within the field of sport and exercise psychology on the health benefits of physical activity, researchers have been slow to embrace the demands and realities of the health services domain. If we are to see changes in policy involving the promotion of physical activity for mental and physical health, then we must develop the right kinds and amounts of evidence. Researchers must apply theory to practice by probing solutions to questions such as these: Does it work? Why does it work? Does it work better than the extant treatments or interventions? Ironically, theory and the mechanisms of change become secondary in importance. More carefully monitored trials need to be launched in ecologically meaningful settings. Intention-to-treat analyses with more sophisticated methods to deal with dropout and missing data need to become standard practice. Shorter instruments that have shown evidence of validity alongside clinical symptomology are required. These steps away from the parent discipline require effort and courage but are necessary if the field is to extend itself beyond academic inquiry.

Clearly, these avenues for future research represent difficult challenges that will fuel the next generation of self-perception research in the physical domain. Such challenges are likely to present obstacles and rewards in terms of theoretical development, methodological approaches, and population accessibility issues. Given the centrality of self-esteem and self-perceptions to human functioning, these challenges are worthy of our attention. We must confront them if we are to understand the role played by sport and exercise in the promotion and maintenance of psychological health and welfare.

Acknowledgments

The authors gratefully acknowledge the research assistance provided by Ms. Virginia Lightheart (Brock University) during the preparation of the literature review for this chapter.

CHAPTER 5

Self-Confidence in Sport

■ Robin S. Vealey, PhD ■ Melissa A. Chase, PhD ■

Most athletes, coaches, and sport psychology consultants strongly believe that confidence is a crucial psychological requisite for success in sport. International-level elite athletes identified self-confidence as the most critical mental skill defining mental toughness (Bull, Shambrook, James, & Brooks, 2005; Jones, Hanton, & Connaughton, 2002), and self-confidence consistently appears as a key skill possessed by successful, elite athletes (Gould, Dieffenbach, & Moffett, 2002; Gould, Greenleaf, Chung, & Guinan, 2002; Kitsantas & Zimmerman, 2002). Elite field hockey players identified the development and maintenance of self-confidence as one of their biggest needs in terms of mental training (Grove & Hanrahan, 1988). Acclaimed sport psychology consultant Terry Orlick (2000) puts confidence at the core of his mental skills model for athletes, and the ability to build confidence in athletes has been identified in the sport psychology literature as one of the "secrets" of successful coaches (Janssen & Dale, 2002).

Although it is a mental skill critical to sport performance, self-confidence is fragile. Mia Hamm, all-time leading goal scorer in elite women's soccer, stated, "The thing about confidence I don't think people understand, is it's a day-to-day issue. It takes constant nurturing. It's not something you go in and turn on the light switch and say, 'I'm confident,' and it stays on until the light bulb burns out." Former professional football quarterback and NFL Hall of Fame member Joe Montana admitted, "Confidence is a fragile thing." Indeed, fluctuations in confidence have been identified as accounting for differences in best and worst performances in sport competition (Eklund, 1994, 1996; Greenleaf, Gould, & Dieffenbach, 2001). Elite athletes state that the key to mental toughness is an unshakable self-confidence that is robust and resilient (Bull et al., 2005).

The fact that self-confidence in sport is crucial yet fragile makes it an intriguing and fruitful area for scholarly inquiry in sport psychology. Thus, the purpose of this chapter is to review the conceptual and research literature on self-confidence in sport. The intent is to provide an overview and synthesis of the state of knowledge in this area. The chapter is divided into four sections. First, we review various definitions of and conceptual approaches to the study of self-confidence in sport. Second, the multiple methods that have been used to measure the construct of self-confidence in sport are explained. Third, a broad overview of research examining self-confidence in sport is presented. Finally, in the fourth section, we provide suggestions for future research.

Definitions and Conceptual Approaches

Self-confidence is the belief that one has the internal resources, particularly abilities, to achieve success. This definition underscores the fact that self-confidence is rooted in beliefs and expectations. Although there are multiple definitions of self-confidence, they all refer to individuals' beliefs about their abilities or their expectations about achieving success based on those abilities. The five conceptual approaches that have been used to study self-confidence in sport are presented in this section, including self-efficacy theory, two sport-confidence conceptualizations, movement confidence, and performance expectancy.

Self-Efficacy Theory

Much of the research on self-confidence in sport has used Bandura's (1977, 1986, 1997) self-efficacy theory as an explanatory theoretical framework. Self-efficacy refers to "beliefs in one's capabilities to organize and execute the courses of action required to produce given attainments" (Bandura, 1997, p. 3). These capabilities include regulating not only physical performance execution (e.g., ability to execute a jump shot in basketball) but also thought processes, emotional states, and actions needed in relation to changing environmental conditions. An athlete might believe that she has the ability to shoot a jump shot successfully in practice, but her self-efficacy about shooting might differ in competitive conditions if she has missed her last few shots, is feeling anxious, or is being guarded by a skilled defender. Self-efficacy is a dynamic, fluctuating property, not a static trait, and it involves the control of physical performance execution, disruptive thinking, and affective states. Thus, self-efficacy takes different forms, such as behavioral self-efficacy (belief in one's ability to perform the specific actions needed to gain mastery over a problem situation), cognitive self-efficacy (belief in the ability to exercise control over one's thoughts), and emotional self-efficacy (belief in the ability to perform actions that influence one's moods or emotional states) (Maddux & Lewis, 1995).

Self-Efficacy Versus Outcome (Consequence) Expectancies   A definitional point of confusion in sport psychology is Bandura's (1997) differentiation between self-efficacy and outcome expectancies. According to Bandura, self-efficacy is a judgment of one's ability to organize and execute given types

of performances, whereas an outcome expectation is a judgment of the likely consequences such performances will produce. Thus, performance is an accomplishment, and an outcome is something that follows from it and is the consequence of the performance. The confusion persists in the sport psychology literature because Bandura uses the term *outcome expectancies* to describe the physical, social, material, and self-evaluative consequences that people expect as a result of their performance. However, the term *outcome* in sport psychology is widely used to refer to the outcomes of competitive events, such as winning or losing or beating a particular opponent. For example, in the sport psychology literature, outcome goals are standards based on results such as winning (Gould, 2006), and outcome

orientation is a personality disposition in which people tend to define success and failure based on winning and losing (Vealey, 1986). Yet in self-efficacy theory, winning is not an outcome expectancy, but rather a performance marker, and the outcome expectancies are the perceived consequences (e.g., social status, pride) that follow the achievement of the performance marker of winning.

To avoid the definitional confusion based on the popular use of the term *outcome* in sport psychology, a modified illustration of Bandura's (1997) distinction between self-efficacy and outcome expectancies is shown in figure 5.1. Bandura's terms *person, behavior,* and *outcomes* have been replaced with the sport-specific terms *athlete, performance,* and *consequences.* The term *consequence* replaces the term *outcome* in

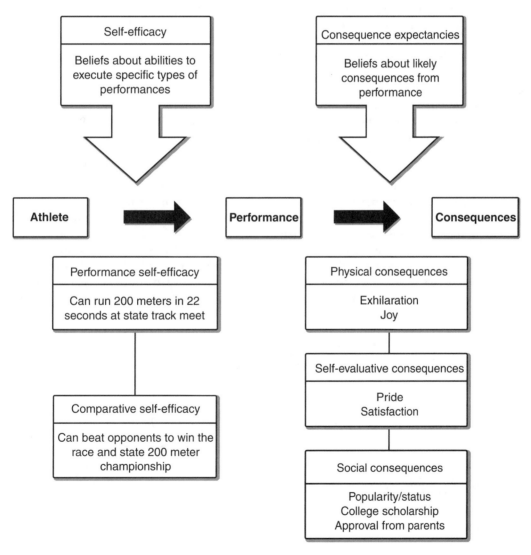

Figure 5.1 Modified version of Bandura's (1997) distinction between self-efficacy and outcome expectancies.

Adapted from A. Bandura, 1997, Self-efficacy: The exercise of control (New York: Freeman). Reprinted, by permission, from D.L. Feltz and M.A. Chase, 1998, The measurement of self-efficacy and confidence in sport. In *Advances in sport and exercise psychology measurement,* edited by J.L. Duda (Morgantown, WV: Fitness Information Technology).

the model. A sprinter's belief that he can run 200 meters in 22 seconds is a self-efficacy judgment, and because it is based on personal performance standards, it may be referred to as performance self-efficacy. The sprinter's belief that he can beat the other runners and win the race and state title is also a self-efficacy judgment, and because it is based on normative comparisons with others, it may be referred to as comparative self-efficacy (Feltz & Chase, 1998). The sprinter's beliefs about the likely consequences of performing well and winning include physical sensations of joy and exhilaration, self-evaluative reactions of pride and satisfaction, and social consequences of popularity, status, a college scholarship, and approval from his parents.

The important point about this distinction is that consequence expectancies, along with self-efficacy, influence performance (Bandura, 1997). People take action when they possess self-efficacy and consequence expectancies that make the effort worthwhile. In the 1960s and 1970s, many people in a society that viewed sport as a male bastion of physical superiority ridiculed female athletes and derogated their performance. A female college athlete during that time may have had strong efficacy beliefs about her sport abilities but may also have perceived negative social, and even negative self-evaluative, consequences from performing well in sport. Such consequence expectancies could influence the athlete to depress her performance subconsciously or even consciously, particularly in comparison with male athletes, even though her self-efficacy about that performance was strong. Even today, what may often be viewed as a lack of confidence in females may really be negative consequence expectancies, particularly in sports traditionally dominated by males. Research is

needed to examine more fully the interactive influence of self-efficacy and consequence expectancies on behavior and performance in sport.

Exercising Human Agency Through Self-Efficacy

The key point of self-efficacy theory is that people's engagement and persistence in behavioral actions are determined primarily by their beliefs in their capabilities and their perceived likelihood of successfully mastering or coping with environmental demands and challenges. Bandura (1997) stated, "Beliefs of personal efficacy constitute the key factor of human agency. If people believe they have no power to produce results, they will not attempt to make things happen" (p. 3). Self-efficacy theory is based on a social cognitive approach that assumes that people engage in self-reflection and self-regulation to shape their environment rather than react to it. This social cognitive perspective for understanding personality and behavior is distinct from the three alternative approaches: psychodynamic theories, trait theories, and radical behaviorism. Thus, the study of self-confidence in sport from a self-efficacy perspective views confidence not as a static internal trait or a simple response to environmental events, but as the key personal cognitive factor in the triadic reciprocal causation model of social cognitive theory (Bandura, 1997).

This principle of triadic reciprocal causation posits that inner personal factors, environmental events, and behavior are mutually interacting influences and that a complete understanding of human behavior in any situation requires understanding the interactive effects of person, environment, and behavior (see figure 5.2). The social cognitive approach to the study of human behavior attempts to avoid dualism between individuals or personal

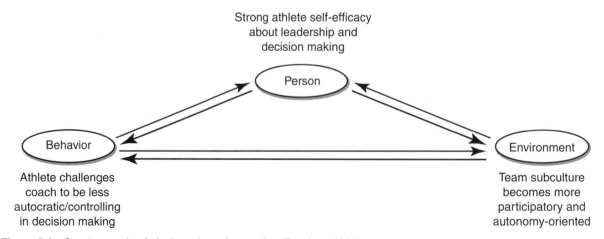

Figure 5.2   Sport example of triadic reciprocal causation (Bandura, 1997).

Adapted from A. Bandura, 1997, Self-efficacy: The exercise of control (New York: Freeman).

agency and society or social structure. This aspect is critical for the future study of confidence in sport to account for the interaction of social structural influences and athlete self-confidence in the unique subculture of competitive sport. The example shown in figure 5.2 illustrates the role of self-efficacy in the exercise of human agency, in which people are producers as well as products of social environments (Bandura, 1997). A strong sense of self-efficacy about leadership and decision making in an athlete leads her to challenge her coach to be less autocratic and controlling in her decision making and leadership style. The coach engages in self-reflection and attempts to change her behavior, which alters the team subculture, which becomes more participatory and autonomy-supportive. The increase in autonomy support within the team reciprocally enhances the self-efficacy and intrinsic motivation of the athletes and influences them to behave in more personally responsible and assertive ways. The autonomous environment reciprocally influences the coach and enhances her personal efficacy about communication. Her leadership and communication behaviors thus become more effective.

Processes Through Which Self-Efficacy Produces Effects Self-efficacy, or efficacy beliefs, influences the way that people behave, think, and feel. As shown on the right side of figure 5.3, efficacy beliefs influence individuals' behavioral choices or their selection of specific situations and activities in which to participate as well as the type of environments that they choose to produce. People avoid activities and environments that they believe exceed their capabilities, yet they choose to engage in situations in which they judge themselves capable of succeeding. The higher their perceived self-efficacy, the more challenging the activities they select (Bandura, 1997). Besides influencing behavioral choices and selections, self-efficacy influences the effort and persistence applied to mastering challenges when they arise.

Efficacy beliefs also influence various cognitions, or thought patterns, that can be either productive or dysfunctional. This point is important because thought shapes most courses of action. Self-efficacy influences how people cognitively construe, or make sense of, things that happen to them. A strong sense of self-efficacy fosters cognitive constructions of optimism, opportunities for self-growth, and effective courses of action. People with stronger self-efficacy set higher goals, commit to goals more strongly (Bandura & Wood, 1989; Locke & Latham, 1990), and engage in more productive attributions to explain their successes and failures (e.g., Courneya & McAuley, 1993) than do people with weaker beliefs about their abilities. Also, people who believe strongly in their problem-solving abilities remain efficient and effective problem solvers and decision makers, whereas those who doubt their abilities are cognitively inefficient and ineffective in solving

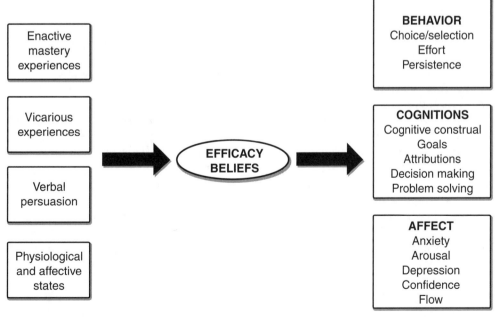

Figure 5.3 Theoretical model of self-efficacy.

Adapted, by permission, from D. Feltz.

problems and making decisions (e.g., Bandura & Jourden, 1991).

The final process through which efficacy beliefs influence human functioning involves the self-regulation of affective or emotional responses to life events. According to Bandura (1997), efficacy beliefs create attentional biases and influence whether life events are construed in ways that are positive, innocuous, or emotionally upsetting. Thus, self-efficacy influences the type and intensity of affect, so that low self-efficacy for attaining highly desired goals leads to anxiety or depression, whereas strong self-efficacy leads to feelings of confidence (Hanin, 2000) or the ultimate enjoyment state of flow (Jackson, 1995). The term *confidence* is used in this context to describe an affective feeling. Although self-confidence is typically defined as a belief system, research with athletes shows that *confident* is a positive emotion described as facilitative to performance, whereas *uncertain* is a negative emotional feeling described by athletes as dysfunctional for their performance (Hanin, 2000). Also, efficacy beliefs about one's ability to control the cognitions related to aversive emotions influence subsequent emotional responses. Low self-efficacy for managing one's thoughts related to anxiety, depression, or anger, called affective control efficacy (Bandura, 1997), can become self-perpetuating because these expectations for poor control produce the very emotions that one wishes to prevent (Hanton, Mellalieu, & Hall, 2004; Hardy, Woodman, & Carrington, 2004; Maddux, 1995).

Sources of Self-Efficacy   Self-efficacy is constructed through a complex process of self-persuasion. Bandura (1997) identifies four sources of self-efficacy, as shown on the left side of figure 5.3. Enactive mastery experiences are the most influential source of efficacy information because they provide direct evidence that one can succeed at a specific task (Bandura, 1997). Vicarious experiences (observational learning, modeling, imitation) influence self-efficacy when people observe the behavior of others to form expectancies about their own behavior and its consequences. Verbal, or social, persuasion occurs when significant others express faith in or support for one's capabilities. This source of self-efficacy is theorized to be weaker and less enduring than self-efficacy built through performance or vicarious experiences. Physiological and affective states influence self-efficacy when people associate unpleasant physiological arousal or specific emotions with poor performance or when they experience comfortable physiological sensations or pleasant emotions that lead them to feel confident in their abilities in a particular situation.

But it is not the sheer intensity of physiological and affective reactions that is important in influencing self-efficacy, but rather how they are perceived and interpreted (Bandura, 1997). The development and maintenance of self-efficacy involves a complex weighting and integration of these diverse efficacy sources, and the importance of efficacy sources to people varies across situations and life domains. That is, athletes may use different sources to enhance their self-efficacy in different ways in different situations.

Collective Efficacy   Although most of the discussion within self-efficacy theory focuses on personal efficacy in individual pursuits, the theory also defines a collective efficacy, which is a group's shared belief in its combined abilities to execute the actions needed to produce given levels of attainment (Bandura, 1997). This addition to the theory is particularly relevant for the study of self-confidence in sport, in which the complex psychology of team dynamics strongly influences the success of sport teams (Carron, Colman, Wheeler, & Stevens, 2002). Although personal efficacy and collective efficacy differ in the unit of agency, they share similar sources and influence performance through the same processes (see figure 5.3). Because the focus of this chapter is on individual self-perceptions of confidence, the research area of collective efficacy is not extensively reviewed (see chapter 11 for a review of the research on collective efficacy in sport). Measurement approaches to the assessment of collective efficacy are included in this chapter, however, because they are related to and often include the measurement of personal efficacy.

In summary, self-efficacy theory serves as an elegant and complex conceptual framework within which to study the manifestation of self-confidence in sport. Using this perspective, self-confidence in athletes is a multifaceted belief system, not a single personality trait or disposition. Bandura (1997) stated that self-efficacy is different from the more popular term *confidence* because confidence refers to strength of belief but does not specify what the certainty is about. In this view, a person can be extremely confident that she or he will fail at a task. Self-efficacy is the preferred term for Bandura because it includes both an affirmation of ability as well as the strength of that belief. But because the term *self-confidence* is widely understood and accepted in sport, it is used in this chapter as the main descriptor for constructs like self-efficacy that focus on the beliefs of people about their ability to achieve success.

Sport-Confidence

Building on self-efficacy theory, Vealey (1986) developed a conceptual model of self-confidence in sport and companion inventories to measure the key constructs in the model.

The sport-specific term *sport-confidence* was used to represent an athlete's belief or degree of certainty that she or he has the abilities to perform successfully in sport. Although sport-confidence is similar to self-efficacy, the conceptual model and measurement instruments were developed to create a sport-specific conceptual framework and inventories to operationalize self-confidence in relation to the unique context of competitive sport (Vealey, 2001). The original model of sport-confidence was based on a dispositional-state approach in which dispositional confidence (SC–trait) was predicted to interact with situational factors to elicit state sport-confidence (SC–state). The model was revised, however, to move beyond the dichotomy of dispositions ("how you *usually* feel") and states ("how you feel *right now*") to think about sport-confidence being on a continuum from more generalized to more specific, depending on the frame of reference used in the research question (confidence about today's competition versus confidence about the upcoming season versus typical level of confidence over the past year).

The revised model, shown in figure 5.4, suggests that the organizational culture of sport and society, along with various individual difference characteristics, influences the manifestation of sport-confidence in athletes, including the types of confidence they possess as well as the sources or antecedents on which their confidence is based. Nine sources of sport-confidence (defined in table 5.1) were identified to be specifically salient to athletes within the unique sport context (Vealey, Hayashi, Garner-Holman, & Giacobbi, 1998). These sources of sport-confidence clearly overlap with the sources

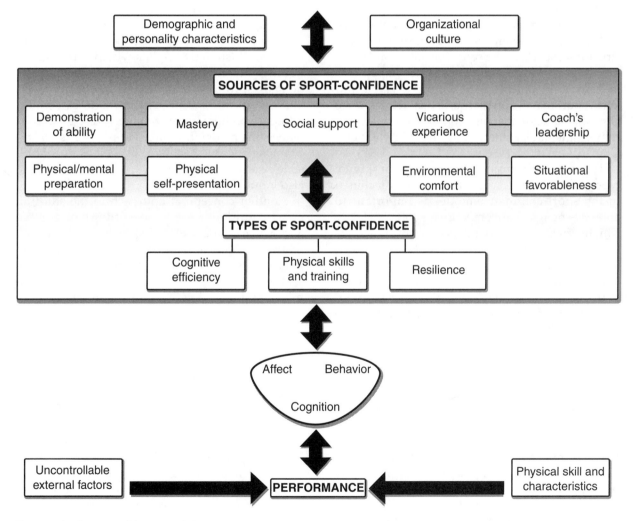

Figure 5.4 Sport-confidence model.

Table 5.1   Sources of Sport-Confidence

Source	Confidence derived from . . .
Mastery	Mastering or improving personal skills
Demonstration of ability	Showing off skills to others or demonstrating more ability than one's opponent
Physical and mental preparation	Feeling physically and mentally prepared with an optimal focus for performance
Physical self-presentation	Perceptions of one's physical self (how one perceives that he or she looks to others)
Social support	Perceiving support and encouragement from significant others in sport, such as coaches, family, and teammates
Vicarious experience	Watching others, such as teammates or friends, perform successfully
Coach's leadership	Believing coach is skilled in decision-making and leadership
Environmental comfort	Feeling comfortable in a competitive environment
Situational favorableness	Feeling that the breaks of the situation are in one's favor

of efficacy beliefs identified in self-efficacy theory, yet they focus more specifically on the competitive and training environments of sport. Certainly, the structural aspects of the sport subculture influence the ways in which confidence is developed and manifested in athletes. For example, Olympic athletes report that the pressure and distractions at the Olympic Games render their confidence levels atypically fragile and vulnerable to instability (Gould, Guinan, Greenleaf, Medbery, & Peterson, 1999).

Three multidimensional components, or specific types, of confidence were identified and included in the sport-confidence model as important to athletes engaging in competitive sport (Vealey & Knight, 2002). Sport-confidence in physical skills and training (termed *SC-physical skills and training*) is an athlete's belief or degree of certainty about her or his ability to execute the physical skills necessary to perform successfully. *SC-cognitive efficiency* is an athlete's belief or degree of certainty that she or he can mentally focus, maintain concentration, and make effective decisions to perform successfully. *SC-resilience* is an athlete's belief or degree of certainty that she or he can regain focus after performance efforts, bounce back from performing poorly, and overcome doubts, problems, and setbacks to perform successfully. The three dimensions of sport-confidence have been shown to be differentially predictive of competitive anxiety, coping skills, and sport performance, supporting the multidimensionality of sport-confidence (Vealey & Knight).

Beliefs about one's sport-confidence influence performance through the mediating effects of the athlete's affect, behavior, and cognition, or the ABCs of human functioning (see figure 5.4). Because the ABCs are interactive, or reciprocally determined, they are illustrated together within a triangle in figure 5.4 to emphasize their continuous interactional reciprocity. And although sport-confidence, like self-efficacy, is viewed in the model as a critical influence on human functioning and sport performance, the model indicates that physical skill and characteristics of the athlete as well as uncontrollable external factors (e.g., luck, weather, opponents) also influence performance.

Another conceptual approach to the study of sport-confidence, developed by Manzo, Silva and Mink (2001), defined sport-confidence as a relatively enduring belief system that results from the interaction between processing an expectation that good things will happen (dispositional optimism) and believing that one's skills and abilities can successfully fulfill the demands of a sport task (sport competence). Dispositional optimism was included in the model because Manzo and colleagues believed that it provided insight about how individuals' perceptions of external events influenced their thoughts, feelings, and behaviors, and because this disposition has been shown to result in greater effort, more persistence, and more successful outcomes as compared with that seen in pessimistic individuals (Scheier & Carver, 1993). As conceptualized in this approach, the relatively enduring nature of the disposition of sport-confidence is predicted to predispose situation-specific responses.

Movement Confidence

Whereas the sport-confidence conceptual approach focuses on confidence as manifested in competitive sport, the movement confidence conceptual approach was developed to examine confidence in basic movement, or physical activity, situations (Griffin & Crawford, 1989; Griffin & Keogh, 1982; Griffin, Keogh, & Maybee, 1984). Specifically, movement confidence is "an individual feeling of adequacy in a movement situation" (Griffin & Keogh, 1982, p. 213). Like self-efficacy and sport-confidence, movement confidence involves a cognitive evaluation of one's abilities in relation to the perceived demands of a task. But the movement confidence model differs from self-efficacy and sport-confidence because it includes a sensory component along with a perceived competence component. Movement confidence is the consequence of a cognitive evaluation of perceived movement competence (evaluation of personal skills and situational demands) and movement sensation (evaluation of expected and preferred movement sensation). Movement sensation has two subcomponents: the perceived potential for enjoying moving (E) and the perceived potential for physical harm (H). The model is represented by this formula: movement confidence (MC) = perceived movement competence (C) + movement sensation (E − H).

Research has supported the importance of the three model factors of competence, enjoyment, and harm in influencing movement decisions (Crawford & Griffin, 1986; Crocker & Leclerc, 1992; Griffin & Crawford, 1989; Griffin et al., 1984). The relative importance of the model factors has differed depending on the type and nature of movement experience. For example, perceived potential for physical harm was the most important predictor of overall movement confidence in the high-risk movement activity of performing a back dive from a one-meter diving board (Crocker & Leclerc). In contrast, in lower-risk scenarios, perceived movement competence was found to be the most important factor in the model (Griffin & Crawford; Griffin et al.). The significance of this research is that it shows that confidence is more than perceived competence or an evaluation of one's ability and that the determinants of confidence vary in different movement situations.

Performance Expectancy

Performance expectancy is a term used in some sport psychology research as a way to define and operationalize self-confidence in sport by asking participants how well they expect to perform (Corbin, Landers, Feltz, & Senior, 1983; Cox & Whaley, 2004; Passer, 1983; Scanlan & Passer, 1979, 1981) or whether they expect to beat their opponents (Corbin, 1981; Corbin & Nix, 1979; Nelson & Furst, 1972; Scanlan & Lewthwaite, 1984). This operational definition is useful because self-confidence as a judgment about personal capabilities is closely tied to expectancies about the outcomes in various situations. Many motivational theories over the years have emphasized the role of expectancies in the regulation of behavior (Atkinson, 1964; Carver & Scheier, 1981; Eccles & Wigfield, 2002; Feather, 1982). For example, expectancy-value theory predicts that the higher the expectancy that certain behavior will lead to specific outcomes, and the more that these outcomes are valued, the greater is the motivation to perform the activity (Eccles & Wigfield, 2002; Feather, 1982). Self-confidence, or one's belief in personal capabilities, partly governs the motivating potential of performance and outcome expectancies.

Most research on self-confidence in sport has used self-efficacy theory as a conceptual basis, because of its theoretical sophistication, multitude of theoretical predictions that have spawned empirical research in the sport domain, and precise guidelines about how to operationalize or assess self-efficacy (Bandura, 1997). Vealey's sport-confidence model has generated a fair amount of research, because of its specification of antecedents and consequences of confidence, as well as the validation of multiple measurement instruments to assess constructs within the conceptual model. The performance expectancy approach was adopted in earlier research on self-confidence in sport in the 1970s and 1980s, or is used today within expectancy-value theoretical approaches. Manzo and colleagues' (2001) sport-confidence model and the movement confidence model have yet to be tested extensively.

These multiple conceptual approaches provide a broad understanding and theoretical diversity to the study of self-confidence in sport. Debating which approach is right or representative of the true nature of self-confidence is fruitless. Maddux (1999) reminds us that psychological concepts are called constructs because they are socially constructed by theorists, as opposed to being discovered in the way that we discover archeological treasures or biological viruses. Thus, there is no true nature of self-confidence. Rather, researchers attempt to conceptualize and study self-confidence in useful ways. We should continue to examine how the different conceptual approaches to the study of self-confidence inform our attempts to understand and enhance human behavior in sport, and we should be open to reconstructing our psychological constructs of self-confidence as our knowledge about them evolves in more sophisticated ways.

Measuring Self-Confidence in Sport

Emanating from the conceptual approaches to the study of self-confidence in sport are the specific ways that the various approaches operationalize self-confidence. Self-confidence, like other psychological characteristics studied in sport psychology, is not directly observable or overtly measurable because it is an abstraction of a theoretical construct. This circumstance creates particular concerns regarding the validity and reliability of the methods used to assess self-confidence in sport. Thus, it is important to understand the various types of measurement strategies available for the study of self-confidence. This section is an overview of the ways that self-confidence has been operationalized for study in sport contexts (as related to the conceptual approaches discussed in the previous section). Detailed psychometric analyses of the measures are not presented here, so researchers are urged to consult the primary references that explain the development of the measures when deciding

how to operationalize self-confidence for specific research questions.

Self-Efficacy Measurement Approaches

The measurement of self-efficacy involves assessing people's beliefs in their ability to produce specific levels of attainment (Bandura, 1997). The self-efficacy measurement approaches reviewed in this section include task-specific self-efficacy measures, task-specific collective efficacy measurement approaches, the collective efficacy questionnaire for sports (Short, Sullivan, & Feltz, 2005), task-specific role efficacy measures, and the coaching efficacy scale (Feltz, Chase, Moritz, & Sullivan, 1999).

Task-Specific Self-Efficacy Measures Bandura (1997) advocates measuring task-specific self-efficacy on the two dimensions of level and strength. *Level* refers to levels of task demands that represent varying degrees of challenge. As shown in the left-hand column of figure 5.5, athletes assess their efficacy on varying levels of basketball free-throw shooting performance. Performance levels should be developed from conceptual analysis and knowledge of appropriate levels of challenge and impediments to successful performance. For example, a hierarchy of performance levels against which to judge self-efficacy in pitching a curveball in softball is shown in the following sidebar. The

How certain are you that you can successfully shoot a basketball from the free throw line?

	0%	10%	20%	30%	40%	50%	60%	70%	80%	90%	100%
10 out of 100											
20 out of 100											
30 out of 100											
40 out of 100											
50 out of 100											
60 out of 100											
70 out of 100											
80 out of 100											
90 out of 100											
100 out of 100											

Figure 5.5 Hierarchical measure of level and strength of free-throw shooting self-efficacy.

range of perceived capability for softball pitchers is measured against task demands that represent varying degrees of challenge in relation to successfully pitching a curveball. If performance levels lack appropriate challenge, the results will likely yield ceiling effects in which all respondents have uniformly high self-efficacy to succeed at the task.

PERFORMANCE LEVELS TO JUDGE SELF-EFFICACY IN SOFTBALL PITCHING

How certain are you that you can throw a curveball for a strike in these situations?

1. In practice?
2. When warming up before a game?
3. In early innings with no score and no runners on base?
4. In early innings with runners on base?
5. In middle innings with the scored tied and runners on base?
6. In late innings with the score tied?
7. In late innings with the score tied and runners on base?
8. In the final inning with a one-run lead and runners on base?
9. In the final inning with a one-run lead, two outs, full count, and bases loaded?

Strength refers to an athlete's degree of certainty that she or he can successfully perform at each level. As shown in the top row of figure 5.5, athletes rate the strength of their belief ranging in 10-unit intervals from 0% to 100%. The stem questions shown in the sidebar and figure 5.5 use the verb *can* rather than *will* to emphasize a judgment of capability as opposed to a statement of intention (Bandura, 1997). Two self-efficacy scores may be computed in this task-specific self-efficacy measurement approach. The efficacy strength scores are summed and divided by the total number of items to provide a measure of self-efficacy strength for that activity. A measure of efficacy level can also be obtained by identifying the last item before respondents judged themselves incapable of successfully performing the task (0% as shown in figure 5.5).

The levels of task demands shown in figure 5.5 and the sidebar constitute hierarchical self-efficacy measures, because the items vary in difficulty, complexity, or stressfulness. Task-specific self-efficacy may also be assessed using nonhierarchical measures that use a list of items representing subskills of specific sports. A nonhierarchical measure of self-efficacy in wrestling included 10 items representing various wrestling moves, such as escape, get reversal, get takedown by throw, ride opponent, and so forth (Treasure, Monson, & Lox, 1996).

Task-Specific Collective Efficacy Measures   Collective, or team, efficacy refers to "a group's shared belief in its conjoint capabilities to organize and execute the courses of action required to produce given levels of attainments" (Bandura, 1997, p. 477). Early research on team efficacy in sport psychology used one-item questions that assessed comparative efficacy at the team level by asking, "What do you think your team's chances are of winning?" and "How confident are you of your prediction?" (Hodges & Carron, 1992) or "What placing do you expect your team to attain?" and "How confident are you that your team will attain this placing?" (Spink, 1990). But the measurement of team efficacy has evolved in complexity, and this methodology is important because collective perceptions of efficacy and confidence are rooted in individual perceptions of task self-efficacy (Bandura, 1997).

Contemporary research has used two methods for measuring team efficacy, as advocated by Bandura (1997). The first method involves aggregating team members' appraisals of *their own* abilities for the functions that they perform on the team by summing all team members' responses to various items using the stem question "How confident are you that you can . . . ?" The second method involves aggregating team members' appraisals of *their team's* capability as a whole using items that assess competitive task components as well as coordination, communication, and coordination within the team. This second method has been operationalized using two different stem questions. The stem question "How confident are you in your team's ability to . . . ?" has been used to assess individuals' perceptions of the collective efficacy of the team (Feltz & Lirgg, 1998; Magyar, Feltz, & Simpson, 2004; Myers, Feltz, & Short, 2004; Myers, Payment, & Feltz, 2004; Stanimirovic & Hanrahan, 2004). The stem question "What is your team's confidence that they can . . . ?" has been used to assess individuals' estimates of the team's collective efficacy (Bray, Brawley, & Carron,

2002; Heuzé, Raimbault, & Fontayne, 2006; Heuzé, Sarrazin, Masiero, Raimbault, & Thomas, 2006; Paskevich, Brawley, Dorsch, & Widmeyer, 1999; Short et al., 2005).

The relative merits of the competing stem question approaches to assessing collective efficacy have been debated (Short et al., 2005; Moritz & Watson, 1998). The issue is whether the stem question should direct a respondent to focus on his or her individual belief in the team or his or her perception of the team's belief. Although no differences were found between the two stem questions on team efficacy ratings (Short, Apostal, et al., 2002), Feltz and colleagues (Feltz, Short, & Sullivan, 2008; Myers & Feltz, 2007) prefer the "How confident are you in your team's abilities?" question stem. Their argument in favor of this question stem is that individuals are more able to access their own beliefs about their team's capabilities than they are to estimate what the team believes. Additional research is needed about how each type of stem question influences the measurement of and advances our understanding of team efficacy.

Bandura (1997) indicates that the appropriateness and predictability of using either the aggregate measure of personal ability appraisals or the aggregate measure of team ability appraisals (using either stem question) depends on the degree of interdependence needed among team members to achieve success. The first method may be an appropriate measure of team efficacy in sports with low interdependence, such as golf or wrestling, whereas the second method is warranted in teams where interdependence is critical for performance success (e.g., volleyball, basketball, hockey). Measuring both types of team efficacy is advantageous in examining their relative influence in different types of sports (Feltz & Chase, 1998) as well as in avoiding overgeneralization or misrepresentation of the data (Moritz & Watson, 1998). Researchers are urged to assess both self-efficacy and team efficacy within a multilevel conception of efficacy because individuals, groups, and organizations are not separate entities but are parts of a whole that influence and are influenced by each other. A multilevel model of efficacy, or confidence, may enable researchers to examine how sociocultural contexts influence self-efficacy and team efficacy as well as to examine parallels and divergence in efficacy across athletes, subgroups within teams, and intact teams (Moritz & Watson, 1998; Rousseau & House, 1994). The statistical technique of hierarchical linear modeling (HLM) is recommended for simultaneously examining individual and team-level predictors of collective efficacy because of the hierarchical nesting of athletes within teams (Bryk & Raudenbush, 1992). HLM used with sport teams has shown different predictors of team efficacy at the individual and group levels (Magyar et al., 2004) as well as different predictors across levels at different times during the competitive season (Watson, Chemers, & Preiser, 2001).

In addition, because collective efficacy is defined as a group's shared belief, researchers have examined whether team members' judgments of their team's capabilities are similar within the group (Moritz & Watson, 1998). Consensus analyses have typically used an index of within-group interrater reliability (James, Demaree, & Wolf, 1984) or a consistency analysis using intraclass correlations (Kenny & La Voie, 1985; Kozlowski & Hattrup, 1992) for each team on each measure of collective efficacy. Research examining interrater reliability on team efficacy in sport has shown a high degree of consensus within groups (Feltz & Lirgg, 1998; Myers, Feltz, & Short, 2004; Myers, Payment, & Feltz, 2004), and research examining intraclass correlations has shown that responses within teams are more homogeneous than would occur by chance (Paskevich et al., 1999). That is, both methods have been successful in statistically demonstrating the sharing of beliefs about a team's capabilities. But Feltz et al. (2008) stated that the aggregation of efficacy data should not, as previously thought, require high levels of consensual validation (e.g., > .70), and that consensual estimates should be used as a variable to help researchers understand issues related to team efficacy and team performance.

Collective Efficacy Questionnaire for Sports   The Collective Efficacy Questionnaire for Sports (CEQS), developed by Short et al. (2005), was developed as a multidimensional measure of collective or team efficacy to be used in sport research. Unlike the task-specific collective or team efficacy measures just discussed, the CEQS was developed to assess team sport functioning in general, which allows researchers to examine team efficacy across different types of sports. The CEQS was developed as a state measure, with specific instructions to respondents to base their perceptions on the upcoming competition. The CEQS measures five interrelated team efficacy factors: ability, effort, preparation, persistence, and unity. The overall team efficacy score can be computed as the average of these subscales.

Task-Specific Role Efficacy Measures   Role efficacy has been conceptualized as athletes' perceived capabilities to execute the primary interdependent functions within their formal roles within the team (Bray et al., 2002). Role efficacy differs from self-efficacy in that self-efficacy is based on perceived capabilities to perform skills independent of other athletes. Role efficacy differs from collective efficacy in that collective efficacy is a team-level perception about the group's shared beliefs in its collective capabilities. Role efficacy may be assessed by asking athletes to list their primary interdependent role functions within their teams and then having them rate their confidence in their ability to perform each role function successfully. Research has shown that role efficacy and self-efficacy were positively, but only moderately, correlated, indicating that these constructs are distinct, yet related (Bray et al., 2002; Bray, Balaguer, & Duda, 2004). The examination of role efficacy as another layer in the multilevel analysis of confidence of athletes within teams seems to be an important research consideration.

Coaching Efficacy Scale The Coaching Efficacy Scale (CES) was developed by Feltz et al. (1999) to measure the extent to which coaches believe they have the capacity to affect the learning and performance of their athletes. The CES consists of 24 items with four subscales: motivation (coaches' beliefs in their abilities to affect the psychological skills and mood of their athletes), character building (coaches' beliefs in their abilities to affect the personal development of their athletes), game strategy (coaches' beliefs in their abilities to lead during competition), and technique (coaches' beliefs in their instructional and diagnostic skills). The four subscales represent four specific types of efficacy in a multidimensional model of coaching efficacy. In addition, a total score of coaching efficacy is computed as an average of all subscale scores.

Sport-Confidence Measurement Approaches

Several inventories have been developed to measure sport-specific self-confidence, termed *sport-confidence*. Vealey (1986) developed a dispositional and a state measure of sport-confidence named the Trait Sport-Confidence Inventory (TSCI) and the State Sport-Confidence Inventory (SSCI), respectively. Both the TSCI and SSCI are 13-item inventories that assess sport-confidence as a unidimensional construct based on an amalgamation of athletes' perceived abilities to execute skills successfully, perform under pressure, make critical decisions, and so on. The TSCI and SSCI have been successfully translated and validity supported for various international samples (e.g., Balaguer, Castillo, Tomás, & Vealey, 2004; Fung, Ng, & Cheung, 2001).

The Sport-Confidence Inventory, or SCI, was developed as a 14-item multidimensional measure of sport-confidence, with three subscales representing athletes' confidence in physical skills and training, cognitive efficiency, and resilience (Vealey & Knight, 2002). The three subscales can be summed to form an overall sport-confidence score. The SCI was designed so that the instructions can be modified to provide athletes with specific temporal frames of reference on which to base their responses (e.g., confidence about tomorrow's competition or the upcoming season). In addition, the Sources of Sport-Confidence Questionnaire, or SSCQ, was developed to measure nine sources of self-confidence (41 total items divided into nine subscales) particularly salient to athletes in competitive sport (Vealey et al., 1998). These sources were previously defined in table 5.1 and illustrated within the sport-confidence model in figure 5.4. Finally, the 13-item Carolina Sport Confidence Inventory was developed as a dispositional sport-confidence inventory that measures dispositional optimism and perceived sport competence (Manzo et al., 2001). The two subscales can be summed to form an overall sport-confidence score, which in this case is the combined effect of dispositional optimism and perceived sport competence.

Movement Confidence Measurement Approaches

Three inventories have been developed within the movement confidence conceptual approach. The Movement Confidence Inventory, or MCI, assesses a person's feeling of adequacy in a movement situation. It asks respondents to rate their experience and confidence in 12 movement tasks (e.g., shooting basketball free throws, roller skating, swimming under water) (Griffin et al., 1984). Besides assessing confidence levels, the MCI assesses how feelings of competence, enjoyment, and possible harm contribute to a person's confidence in doing each task. The MCI can easily be modified to assess movement confidence in specific tasks, as with the investigation of movement confidence in the high-risk sport of diving (Crocker & Leclerc, 1992). Two additional modifications of the original MCI have been published. The Playground Movement Confidence Inventory was developed to measure children's confidence in movement situations in relation to six playground activities (Crawford & Griffin, 1986), and the Stunt Movement Confidence Inventory was developed to measure children's confidence in the six movement skills of "jumping" a bicycle, performing a stunt on a skateboard, walking on stilts, jumping on a Pogo stick, jumping while on roller skates, and climbing a rope (Griffin & Crawford, 1989).

Self-Confidence Subscales Within Multidimensional Sport Psychological Inventories

Several multidimensional inventories used in sport psychology research include a self-confidence subscale. The Ottawa Mental Skills Assessment Tool (OMSAT–3) includes a four-item self-confidence subscale as one of 12 mental skills viewed as "important for performing consistently at a high level" (Durand-Bush, Salmela, & Green-Demers, 2001, p. 2). The Athletic Coping Skills Inventory–28 (ACSI–28) includes a four-item subscale that is a combination of self-confidence and achievement motivation (Smith, Schutz, Smoll, & Ptacek, 1995). The Psychological Skills Inventory for Sport (PSIS) includes self-confidence as one of six subscales that represent mental skills relevant to exceptional athletic performance (Mahoney, Gabriel, & Perkins, 1987). But the PSIS failed to meet adequate psychometric standards after its initial publication, so it is not recommended for use (Murphy & Tammen, 1998). A personality state measure ("how you feel right now—at this moment") of self-confidence in sport is included as one of three subscales of the Competitive State Anxiety Inventory–2, or CSAI–2 (Martens, Burton, Vealey, Bump, & Smith, 1990). A revision of this inventory (called the CSAI–2R) produced a better fit of the data to the multivariate model and yielded a revised self-confidence subscale of five items (Cox, Martens, & Russell, 2003).

Assessing Performance Expectancies

Assessing athletes' performance expectancies as a measure of self-confidence typically involves a single question about personal performance expectancies such as "How well do you think you will play in the game today?" or "How well do you expect to do in basketball?" (Cox & Whaley, 2004; Scanlan & Passer, 1978, 1979, 1981). A variation on this approach is the use of a single question to assess outcome expectancies in terms of comparison with others or winning and losing, such as "Do you think you will win or lose?" or "How many times out of 10 do you think you can beat this opponent at this game?" (Corbin & Nix, 1979) or "How sure are you that you will win this match?" (Scanlan & Lewthwaite, 1984). Although one-item measures of self-confidence have been criticized because they

cannot demonstrate reliability (Feltz & Chase, 1998), recent psychometric analyses indicated that one-item measures are useful because of their practical relevance, high face validity, and high predictive validity (Tenenbaum, Kamata, & Hayashi, 2007).

Qualitative and Idiographic Measurement of Self-Confidence in Sport

Most research on self-confidence in sport has used quantitative, nomothetic approaches. Quantitative measurement means that numbers are used to represent athletes' self-evaluation of their confidence (typically in Likert scale formats). The nomothetic approach (Allport, 1937) assumes that a common set of descriptors or dimensions can characterize all persons and that groups' results represent general tendencies about self-confidence that apply to all people (e.g., labeling an individual athlete as high or low confident based on his or her score on the SCI compared with the scores of all other individuals).

Deductive interviews (based on existing conceptual frameworks) with athletes have yielded qualitative results (verbal descriptions as opposed to numbers) that describe manifestations of self-confidence in athletes and how these manifestations of confidence influenced perceptions of anxiety and performance (Hanton & Connaughton, 2002; Hanton et al., 2004). Also, inductive interviews to derive information about each athlete's personal constructs and experiences related to self-confidence in sport have yielded qualitative data about the sources and types of self-confidence identified by world-class athletes (Hays, Maynard, Thomas, & Bawden, 2007). The inductive approach, which allows important patterns or findings about self-confidence to emerge from the data without presupposing what the important dimensions will be (Patton, 2002), seems to be a fruitful area for inquiry because of the preponderance of deductive-based research in this area as well as the need to conduct more holistic studies about how the unique subculture of competitive sport influences self-confidence in athletes. Finally, performance profiling (Hays, Thomas, Maynard, & Butt, 2006), single-subject designs (Barker & Jones, 2006), and case study methods (Mamassis & Doganis, 2004; Pensgaard, & Duda, 2002; Savoy, 1993) have been used as idiographic measurement approaches to assess athletes' self-confidence in sport. More idiographic research on self-confidence in sport is needed because it better meets the applied needs of athletes and coaches by illuminating the nature of self-confidence within people. Such research may suggest specific interventions that can be adopted to enhance athletes' self-confidence in sport.

Summary of Approaches to the Measurement of Self-Confidence in Sport

Four inventories have been developed that measure sport-specific self-confidence in athletes, along with a questionnaire assessing sources of sport-confidence in athletes. Inventories that assess the confidence of coaches and teams have also been developed. Three movement confidence measurement inventories have been developed, and five multidimensional sport-specific inventories contain self-confidence subscales that were developed for athletes. Along with psychometrically developed inventories, other approaches to measuring self-confidence in sport include task-specific self, team, and role efficacy measures, performance expectancy measures, qualitative interview techniques, idiographic profiling, and case studies.

The various measurement approaches to the study of self-confidence in sport represent a smorgasbord from which researchers should carefully select in relation to their specific research purposes. Obviously, task-specific measures of self-efficacy enhance the prediction of a particular performance under a specific set of conditions (as shown in figure 5.5 and table 5.2). But it is often useful to assess self-confidence at a more global level, as when examining more general patterns of behavior (e.g., using the Sport-Confidence Inventory to assess changes in confidence as the result of interventions or to assess confidence as one of a group of mental skills important to athletes at various levels of competition). Also, inventories such as the Sport-Confidence Inventory, the Collective Efficacy Questionnaire for Sports, and the Coaching Efficacy Scale allow researchers to compare results from different sports without having to apply artificial standards to different measures used in different sports. Finally, researchers are encouraged to adopt inductive and idiographic research designs to enhance conceptual advances in self-confidence in sport as well as to incorporate the study of how confidence is developed, experienced, and affected by the sociocultural context within which athletes, coaches, and teams perform.

Research Advances

Thus far, the chapter has focused on the conceptual frameworks and measurement approaches used in the study of confidence in sport. This section reviews the research findings about self-confidence in sport. These findings are grouped in subsections based on the focus of the research (e.g., influence of self-confidence on performance), and the various conceptual and measurement approaches previously discussed separately in the chapter are now integrated within each research focus area. Basic proposition statements are provided throughout the research review to emphasize key findings in each area.

Types of Self-Confidence Salient to Athletes in Sport

Most research on self-confidence in sport has assessed confidence as a unidimensional construct. For example, items on the TSCI and SSCI (Vealey, 1986) assessed athletes' confidence about various areas (e.g., skill execution, focusing, refocusing after errors), but the inventories provided a single confidence score, which integrated all types of confidence into a unitary sport-confidence construct. But self-efficacy theory indicates that self-efficacy, and thus sport-confidence, are indeed multidimensional constructs based on the idea that athletes judge their abilities to respond successfully in relation to many task demands in competitive sport. Thus, research has begun to examine what types of self-confidence are viewed as important for athletes in competitive sport.

In a multiphase study, Vealey and Knight (2002) found support for three types of sport-confidence particularly salient to athletes. These types of sport-confidence, defined previously as part of the sport-confidence model (see figure 5.4), were SC–physical skills and training, SC–cognitive efficiency, and SC–resilience. Their relative independence was supported by their differential relationships to competitive anxiety, coping skills, and performance.

An inductive qualitative analysis of confidence in 14 world-class athletes identified six types of confidence viewed as important for athletes in sport, including confidence in skill execution, achievement, physical factors, psychological factors, superiority to opposition, and tactical awareness (Hays et al., 2007). Confidence in skill execution and physical factors (Hays et al., in press) are similar to SC–physical skills and training (Vealey & Knight, 2002), and confidence in psychological factors and tactical awareness (Hays et al., 2007) are similar to Vealey and Knight's SC–cognitive efficiency. Interestingly, the data themes in Hays and colleagues' research indicated that athletes believed it was important to be confident about attaining personal mastery (e.g., swimming a certain time, meeting own expectations) as well as attaining normative performance outcomes (e.g., winning, beating opponents, being superior to opponents).

Martin (2002) has distinguished between performance confidence, self-regulatory confidence, and outcome confidence. Self-regulatory confidence is athletes' confidence that they can successfully perform in the face of obstacles or setbacks (Bandura, 1997), whereas performance confidence is athletes' confidence that they can achieve a certain level of performance (e.g., race times). Martin's self-regulatory confidence incorporates Vealey and Knight's (2002) SC–cognitive efficiency and Hays et al.'s (2007) psychological factors and tactical awareness. Martin's performance confidence is similar to Hays et al.'s achievement confidence. Martin's outcome confidence is athletes' confidence that they can achieve performance outcomes, such as winning or placing high in a race compared with competitors. Outcome confidence has been also defined as comparative efficacy (Feltz & Chase, 1998), and is similar to Hays et al.'s superiority to opposition confidence.

Overall, this research indicates that self-confidence in sport is uniquely multidimensional based on the competitive demands on athletes. Athletes need to believe in their abilities to execute physical skills, attain high levels of physical fitness, make correct decisions, execute mental skills such as focusing attention and managing nervousness, bounce back from mistakes and overcome obstacles and setbacks, achieve mastery and personal performance standards, and win and demonstrate superiority over opponents. Figure 5.6 offers a categorization of these various types of confidence indicated by research as important for athletes in sport. Athletes develop and maintain beliefs about their abilities to (a) win (outcome self-confidence), (b) perform successfully in relation to certain standards (performance self-confidence), (c) self-regulate to manage their thoughts and emotions as well as bounce back in demonstrating resilience (self-regulatory self-confidence), and (d) execute physical skills, achieve fitness or training levels, and learn new skills needed to be successful in their sports (physical self-confidence). Future research may illuminate other types of confidence and different conceptualizations of confidence unique to the sport milieu.

Research is needed to examine how various types of self-confidence may differentially influence performance and competition-related thoughts, emotions, and behavior in athletes. For example, are some types of confidence more important or facilitative for athletes at certain times? And, like the matching hypothesis used to link intervention strategies to specific types of anxiety (Martens et al., 1990), intervention research should examine the effectiveness of matching specific confidence-enhancing strategies to the specific confidence needs of athletes. In summary, the study of unidimensional confidence in sport should continue to evolve to a multidimensional perspective with a focus on specific types of confidence essential for

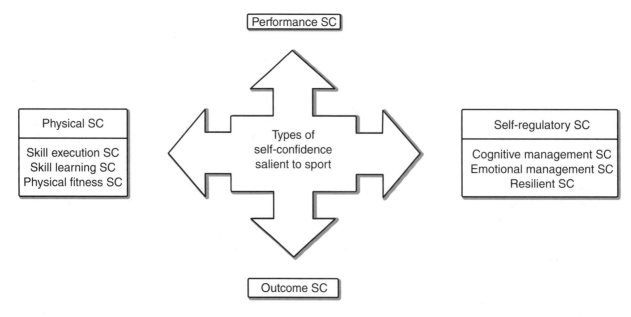

Figure 5.6 Types of self-confidence salient to athletes in sport.

particular athletes based on particular demands in particular sport situations.

Influence of Self-Confidence on Athletes' Performance

A great deal of research in sport psychology has examined the influence of self-confidence on athletes' performance. This section reviews this research, including (a) studies in which athletes and coaches identify self-confidence as critical to performance, (b) studies that examine the relationships between confidence and athlete performance in natural competitive sport settings, and (c) studies that examine the effects of self-confidence on physical performance in controlled experimental settings.

Athletes and coaches have generally identified self-confidence as important for success in sport. Overall, research supports the view that athletes and coaches perceive self-confidence to be a crucial psychological requisite for success in sport. International-level elite athletes identified self-confidence as the most critical mental skill in defining mental toughness (Bull et al., 2005; Jones et al., 2002). Over half of a sample of elite, university, and club athletes ranked self-confidence as the most important mental skill related to their performance (Durand-Bush et al., 2001). In interviews, U.S. Olympic champions, their coaches, and parents or significant others identified self-confidence as a key mental skill in successful performance at the elite level (Gould, Dieffenbach, & Moffet, 2002). U.S. Olympic coaches identified self-confidence as an important influence on their athletes' performance at the 1996 and 1998 Olympic Games (Gould, Guinan, Greenleaf, & Chung, 2002), and junior tennis coaches rated self-confidence as an important mental skill for young tennis players (Gould, Medbery, Damarjian, & Lauer, 1999).

Self-confidence is a key factor in discriminating between successful and less successful athletes. Self-confidence has differentiated successful and less successful athletes at the elite level (the term *unsuccessful* is relative in these studies). Mahoney and Avener (1977) demonstrated that Olympic gymnastics qualifiers were higher in self-confidence than nonqualifiers. This result was replicated with college wrestlers at a championship meet (Gould, Weiss, & Weinberg, 1981). Highlen and Bennett (1979) found self-confidence to be the factor that most effectively discriminated qualifiers from nonqualifiers in international competition; the qualifiers, of course, possessed greater confidence and less self-doubt.

Relationships between self-confidence and performance in natural competitive sport settings As described in the previous sections, athletes and coaches believe that self-confidence is significantly related to performance, and self-confidence is a key discriminator between successful and less successful athletes. Moving beyond these descriptive studies, much research has statistically examined the relationship between self-confidence and performance. These studies typically employ correlational designs, with the relationship explained by Pearson correlations, regression analyses, and path analyses. Most of the research since the mid-1980s has examined the relationship between self-confidence and performance with athletes in natural competitive settings.

Self-confidence and performance are positively, yet moderately, related when assessed in natural competitive sport settings. Three meta-analyses have examined the relationship between self-confidence and sport performance (Craft, Magyar, Becker, & Feltz, 2003; Moritz, Feltz, Fahrbach, & Mack, 2000; Woodman & Hardy, 2003). By statistically analyzing the findings of many individual analyses, meta-analyses yield statistical values that represent the combined or integrated findings of previous research and thus allow us to make broad conclusions about a specific research area. In these meta-analyses, self-confidence was shown to have a positive, yet moderate, relationship with performance (.38, .25, and .24).

The relationships between self-confidence and performance are influenced by many factors, such as the types of measures used in research and the time of assessment of confidence. Several factors were found to moderate the relationship between self-confidence and performance in the meta-analyses (Craft et al., 2003; Moritz et al., 2000; Woodman & Hardy, 2003). Readers should consult the original meta-analysis articles for a complete list of all moderator variables examined, because only two are discussed here based on their conceptual and methodological significance.

Higher correlations (.43) were found in those studies in which self-confidence and performance measures were concordant as compared with nonconcordant (.26). Concordance means that the confidence and performance measures match, or tap similar capabilities. A concordant study would assess confidence in various golf skills (putting, driving, iron play, course management) and then assess performance on those characteristics. A nonconcordant study would assess confidence in those golf skills and then relate them to whether or not the golfer won the match. Moritz and colleagues (2000) indicated that concordance is not necessarily good and nonconcordance bad. In the case of performance prediction, concordance certainly should enhance the ability of the confidence measure to predict performance more accurately. But if a researcher was interested in how the mental skill of confidence would predict longevity in a professional sports career (e.g., Smith & Christensen, 2005), nonconcordance in measures may be warranted to test the predictive validity of specific psychological inventories that profile important mental skills such as confidence (e.g., ACSI–28).

In addition, self-confidence assessed after performance was more strongly related to performance than confidence assessed before performance, suggesting that prior performance influences confidence more strongly than confidence influences performance. This finding is supported by causal studies of the self-confidence–performance relationship (Feltz, 1982, 1988; Feltz & Mugno, 1983; Fitzsimmons, Landers, Thomas, & van der Mars, 1991; George, 1994; Theodorakis, 1995).

Different types of self-confidence relate differently to athletes' performance. Vealey and Knight (2002) found that SC–physical skills and training was the strongest predictor of college swimming performance for the first two meets after a winter training program. However, SC–resilience and SC–cognitive efficiency were the strongest predictors of performance for a late-season, highly competitive meet against a main rival. Thus, confidence in one's physical abilities was predictive of performance immediately following an intense training period, whereas confidence in one's ability to focus, manage emotions, and cope with obstacles and distractions was more predictive of confidence later in the season in a pressurized competitive meet. Martin (2002) found that outcome confidence was the only significant predictor of final place in a road race, although self-regulatory confidence and confidence in one's training showed moderate yet insignificant correlations with performance. Additional research is needed to investigate how various types of confidence influence performance in different ways and perhaps at different times of the season based on varying competitive demands and athletes' changing socioenvironmental contexts.

The relationship between self-confidence and performance in sport has been tested within numerous conceptual frameworks. The meta-analyses provided useful summary information that integrates a plethora of studies examining the

relationship between self-confidence and sport performance. This relationship has been tested within numerous sports and using various conceptual frameworks, including self-efficacy theory (Beauchamp & Whinton, 2005; George, 1994; Kane, Marks, Zaccaro, & Blair, 1996; Treasure, Monson, & Lox, 1996; Weiss, Wiese, & Klint, 1989), expectancy-value theory (Martin & Gill, 1995), achievement goal theory (Kane, Marks, Zaccaro, & Blair, 1996), stress and coping theory (Haney & Long, 1995), multidimensional anxiety theory (Butt, Weinberg, & Horn, 2003; Edwards & Hardy, 1996; Martens et al., 1990), self-discrepancy theory (Beattie, Hardy, & Woodman, 2004), expectancy theory (Solomon, 2001), the sport-confidence model (Gayton & Nickless, 1987; Martin & Gill, 1991; Vealey, 1986; Vealey & Campbell, 1988), the mental skills model (Smith & Christensen, 1995), the cusp catastrophe model (Hardy, 1996; Hardy et al., 2004), processing efficiency theory (Edwards, Kingston, Hardy, & Gould, 2002; Hanton et al., 2004), the control process model (Hanton & Connaughton, 2002; Hanton et al., 2004; Jones & Hanton, 1996), and the individualized zones of optimal functioning (IZOF) model (Annesi, 1998).

Several notable findings can be identified from these conceptual approaches. First, in examining athletes' actual versus ideal (what you would like to have) confidence, the closer athletes' actual confidence was to their ideal confidence, the better they performed (Beattie et al., 2004). Self-discrepancies in self-confidence predicted athletes' performance better than self-confidence alone did. Future research should consider key aspects of the self, especially the effects of competition on ego threat or threat to the self, when attempting to understand the influence of confidence on performance. Second, a test of confidence within expectancy theory found that coaches' evaluations of athletes' confidence significantly predicted athletes' performance, whereas coaches' predictions of athletes' abilities and athletes' own levels of self-confidence did not predict performance (Solomon, 2001). This finding extends coaching expectancy theory to emphasize that the study of coaches' expectations of athletes should include coaches' perceptions of athletes' confidence as well as their assessment of athletes' physical abilities. Third, a study of equestrian performance found that riders' self-confidence and riders' self-confidence in their horses were both significant predictors of dressage performance (Beauchamp & Whinton, 2005). (And no, they didn't measure the horses' confidence!) Lent and Lopez (2002) refer to this as other-efficacy, which is defined as "an individual's beliefs about his or her significant others' ability to perform particular behaviors" (p. 264). They theorize that confidence in the abilities of one's partner can influence a person's level of commitment, effort, and various behaviors and cognitions crucial to joint performance with a partner. This idea indicates that an important future research direction is the study of one's confidence in key performance partners in sport, such as tennis doubles partners, figure skating pairs, or pitchers' confidence in their catchers.

Self-confidence serves as an important cognitive mediator of the effects of anxiety on athletes' performance. Research within multiple conceptual frameworks has demonstrated that self-confidence is critical in buffering the negative effects of anxiety on athletes' performance. Within the cusp catastrophe model, self-confidence mediates the effects of cognitive anxiety and physiological arousal on performance by increasing the probability that cognitively anxious athletes will be able to tolerate higher levels of arousal before experiencing decrements in performance (Hardy, 1996; Hardy et al., 2004). Within the control process model (Carver & Scheier, 1988), the key factor in whether anxiety facilitates or debilitates performance is perception of control. If athletes feel in control, they maintain positive expectancies of goal attainment and coping abilities (self-confidence), and respond in pressurized situations with increased effort, persistence, and performance. But for athletes who doubt their ability to cope and succeed, anxiety is debilitating because they withdraw effort based on their belief that they cannot control themselves or their environments. These predictions have been demonstrated with athletes in sport situations (Edwards et al., 2002; Hanton & Connaughton, 2002; Hanton et al., 2004; Jones & Hanton, 1996). Finally, processing efficiency theory (Eysenck & Calvo, 1992) posits that if cognitively anxious performers believe that the probability of success is at least moderate (confidence), they will exert additional effort, which acts as a compensatory mechanism to enable performance despite the reduction of cognitive resources that results from worry. Researchers have demonstrated the predictions from this theory with athletes (Edwards et al.; Hanton & Connaughton, 2002).

These findings emphasize the point that self-confidence is not the absence of anxiety but rather a facilitative quality that enables athletes to engage in self-regulatory responses (e.g., reframing, effort, coping) to manage their anxiety in productive ways and perform effectively. An elite gymnast explains this perfectly: "I had doubts, that everyone has, like what happens if I fall off again . . . but I mean that's only momentarily and then you start telling yourself just to calm down and get back on and do it cleanly . . . I knew I could do it easily . . . But . . . I was confident that . . . I could do it—and, it's just [that] your heart rate goes up and you feel your chest pounding" (Edwards et al., 2002, p. 8).

Influence of self-confidence on performance in controlled experimental settings Beginning in the 1970s, a line of experimental research studies using nonathletes as research participants investigated the influence of self-confidence on motor performance. Although this research was not directly generalizable to competitive sport contexts, it established a causal link between self-confidence and performance and provided a foundation of theory testing for subsequent naturalistic field research on self-confidence. Several of these studies used anxiety-inducing tasks to examine avoidance behavior. The results showed that confidence in the form of self-efficacy predicted performance (Feltz, 1982, 1988; Feltz & Mugno, 1983; McAuley, 1985). As discussed previously, these studies also found that confidence more strongly predicted performance than vice versa.

People who were experimentally manipulated to have higher confidence outperformed those who were experimentally manipulated to have lower confidence. From the classic Nelson and Furst (1972) study on arm wrestling, several studies followed that experimentally induced high and low levels of confidence in research participants using deception (Weinberg, Gould, & Jackson, 1979; Weinberg, Gould, Yukelson, & Jackson, 1981; Weinberg, Yukelson, & Jackson, 1980). In all instances, participants manipulated to have high self-confidence outperformed participants who were manipulated to have low self-confidence. Other experimental research showed that "cognitive psyching" by using self-confidence exhortations to oneself increased strength performance as compared with a control group who did not psych themselves up (Wilkes & Summers, 1984), and the use of false feedback (Escartí & Guzmán, 1999; Fitzsimmons et al., 1991) and goals (Miller, 1993) to induce high self-confidence significantly improved performance.

Summary of research on self-confidence–performance relationship Experimental, correlational, and descriptive research has established the positive influence of self-confidence on athlete performance, as well as the stronger influence of performance on self-confidence. Many conceptual frameworks have been adopted to study the self-confidence–performance relationship, increasing the complexity of this research area by examining the role of self-confidence as a key cognitive mediator between anxiety, perceptions of control, attention, achievement goals, and sport performance. Research has begun to examine the relationship between different types of self-confidence and performance as well as the ways in which self-discrepancies, other-efficacy, and coaches' perceptions of athlete confidence influence athlete performance. Undoubtedly, research examining the influence of self-confidence on sport performance will continue to evolve in complexity and sophistication as we attempt to understand the ways in which athletes' beliefs affect how they perform.

Influence of Self-Confidence on Athletes' Behavior, Cognitions, and Affect

As discussed previously in the chapter and shown in figure 5.3, self-confidence influences performance by affecting athletes' behavior, cognitions, and affect. Vealey (2001) called self-confidence the mental modifier because confidence seems to modify how athletes feel about, respond to, and think about everything that happens to them in sport. This section reviews the research that has examined these relationships.

Self-confidence in athletes significantly influences their achievement choices, effort, and persistence. Athletes' self-confidence has been shown to predict effort and persistence in sport (Cox & Whaley, 2004; George, 1994). Effort and persistence has also been inferred because of heightened self-confidence in experimental studies in which participants in high-confidence conditions persisted longer on muscular endurance tasks as compared with those in low-confidence conditions (Weinberg et al., 1979, 1980, 1981). An elite athlete explained how confidence increases effort: "When I feel confident, it just drives me on more and makes me try harder, raises my game and the intensity of my effort and preparation" (Hanton et al., 2004, p. 487).

Besides predicting effort and persistence, self-confidence has predicted achievement choices. Youth wrestlers who remained in the sport had higher self-confidence than did wrestlers who dropped out (Burton & Martens, 1986), children with higher confidence chose to participate more in the future than did children with lower confidence (Chase, 2001), and runners with higher self-confidence chose more difficult tasks than did those with less self-confidence (Escartí & Guzmán, 1999). These findings support self-efficacy theory (Bandura, 1997), expectancy-value theory (Eccles

& Wigfield, 2002), and the sport-confidence model (Vealey, 2001) predictions that confidence influences individuals' behavioral choices, the amount of effort produced, and the persistence applied in overcoming challenges.

Self-confidence is positively related to productive self-perceptions and achievement-related cognitions. As the mental modifier, self-confidence is related to a host of other self-perceptions and cognitions. Obvious positive relationships between self-confidence and perceived ability (Hall & Kerr, 1997; Rudisill, 1989; Scanlan & Lewthwaite, 1985; Sheldon & Eccles, 2005), self-esteem (Scanlan & Passer, 1979, 1981; Scanlan & Lewthwaite, 1985; Vealey, 1986), perceived success (Vealey, 1986), internal locus of control (Fallby, Hassmen, Kentta, & Durand-Bush, 2006), and sport identity (Cox & Whaley, 2004) have been shown. In addition, self-confidence has been positively correlated with the use of problem-focused coping strategies and negatively correlated with the use of emotion-focused coping strategies for dealing with performance slumps (Grove & Heard, 1997). With regard to motivational constructs, self-confidence has been positively correlated with competitiveness (Martin & Gill, 1991; Swain & Jones, 1992), productive causal attributions (Bond, Biddle, & Ntoumanis, 2001; Chase, 2001; Gernigon & Delloye, 2003; Vealey, 1986), setting challenging goals (Kane et al., 1996; Lerner & Locke, 1995; Theodorakis, 1995, 1996), importance of and thoughts about goals (Martin & Gill, 1995), goal commitment (Lerner & Locke, 1995), and task or mastery achievement goal orientations (Hall & Kerr, 1997; Mills, 1996; Vealey, 1986).

Self-confidence is positively related to decision making and concentration, and the relationship between self-confidence and imagery is equivocal. With regard to cognitive processing, self-confidence is a strong predictor of decision-making processes and response executions (Tenenbaum, Levi-Kolker, Sage, Lieberman, & Lidor, 1996) and is related to effective concentration (Smith et al., 1995; Vealey & Knight, 2002). Because imagery is a popular cognitive performance enhancement technique, it has been studied in relation to athlete self-confidence. Although Bandura (1997) stated that people's self-efficacy influences the types of anticipated scenarios and visualized futures that they construct, no clear pattern between self-confidence and imagery use has emerged from research in this area (Abma, Fry, Li, & Relyea, 2002; Callow & Hardy, 2001; Mills, Munroe, & Hall, 2000; Moritz, Martin, Hall, & Vadocz, 1997; Vadocz, Hall, &

Moritz, 1997). The research on the relationship between self-confidence and imagery ability is also equivocal. High self-confident athletes have been shown to possess better kinesthetic and visual imagery ability than low self-confident athletes (Moritz et al., 1996), yet in another study no differences were found in imagery ability based on confidence levels (Abma et al., 2002). Future research is needed to gain better understanding of the relationships between self-confidence and imagery use and ability.

Self-confidence is positively related to positive affective feelings and negatively related to negative affective feelings that athletes experience in sport. Research supports the idea that self-confidence in athletes is positively related to positive affective feelings (e.g., satisfied, excited, proud) and negatively related to negative affective feelings (e.g., distressed, nervous, ashamed) (Kane et al., 1996; Martin, 2002; Theodorakis, 1996; Treasure et al., 1996). Interestingly, Martin (2002) found that positive affect was related more strongly to self-regulatory confidence than it was to performance or outcome self-confidence. Self-confidence has also been predictive of athletes' mood states (Prapavessis & Grove, 1994a, 1994b), and happy moods have been linked to higher self-confidence (Kavanagh & Hausfeld, 1986). Athletes identify self-confidence as an important facilitator of flow, or optimal experiences, in sport (Jackson, 2000). And although self-confidence is typically defined as a belief system, research indicates that athletes view feeling confident as a positive emotion that is facilitative to performance (Hanin, 2000).

Without question, the affective feeling most often studied in relation to self-confidence is anxiety. This interest is due to the contrasting nature of anxiety and confidence as precompetitive achievement states, multiple conceptual models that include both constructs (catastrophe model, multidimensional anxiety theory, control process model, processing efficiency theory), and the wide use of the CSAI–2, which assesses both state anxiety and self-confidence. Early research in this area demonstrated that lower levels of self-confidence predicted precompetitive anxiety (Scanlan & Lewthwaite, 1984; Scanlan & Passer, 1978; Yan Lan & Gill, 1984) and that high competitive trait anxiety predicted lower levels of self-confidence (Passer, 1983). The negative relationship between self-confidence and anxiety in sport has been widely supported through the years (Beattie et al., 2004; George, 1994; Man, Stuchlíková, & Kindlmann, 1995; Martens et al., 1990; Smith et al., 1995). An important research finding is that different types of confidence were differentially related to

anxiety (Vealey & Knight, 2002). SC–resilience was negatively related to worry and managing pressure, whereas SC–cognitive efficiency was negatively related to concentration disruption. Additional research is needed to understand more fully how specific types of confidence are related to various affective states.

Another important development in the study of the self-confidence–anxiety relationship is the finding that self-confidence enables athletes to perceive their anxiety as more facilitative and controllable (Chartrand, Jowdy, & Danish, 1992; Edwards & Hardy, 1996), or conversely that athletes who perceive their anxiety as facilitative for their performance exhibit higher self-confidence (Jones & Hanton, 2001; Mellalieu, Hanton, & Jones, 2003; Perry & Williams, 1998; Thomas, Maynard, & Hanton, 2004). Bandura (1997) used the term *affective control efficacy* to describe this process.

Research has clearly supported the basic tenets of self-efficacy theory that self-confidence influences the way that athletes behave, think, and feel. This area of research is critical to our understanding of the processes through which self-confidence influences athletes' performance. The literature has evolved from early research that established the link between confidence and performance to more complex multivariate analyses of the mechanisms underlying the self-confidence–performance relationship.

Temporal Stability of Self-Confidence in Sport

Because sport competition is an ongoing process involving athletes' progression of precompetitive, competitive, and postcompetitive thoughts and feelings (Martens, 1975), research has examined how self-confidence fluctuates across time in relation to competitive events.

Self-confidence has shown stability as well as fluctuation as time to compete nears. Some research has supported the multidimensional anxiety theory prediction that self-confidence should remain fairly stable in the days and hours preceding competition because performance expectancy remains unchanged until actual competition begins (Gould, Petlichkoff, & Weinberg, 1984; Martens et al., 1990; Wiggins, 1998). Other research, however, has shown fluctuations in confidence, indicating that individual difference and environmental factors influence confidence as time to compete nears (Butt et al., 2003; Hall & Kerr, 1997; Jones & Cale, 1989; Jones, Swain, & Cale, 1991; Swain and Jones, 1992; Thomas et al., 2004).

Future research grounded within guiding theoretical frameworks (e.g., Hall & Kerr, 1997) is needed to understand how personality characteristics interact with salient social factors to influence athletes' self-confidence as time to compete nears.

The resilience of athletes' confidence has been superficially examined, and future research is needed in this area. Although Bandura (1997) emphasized the importance of a resilient sense of confidence, the stability or resilience of confidence across training and competitive events as well as through obstacles and setbacks has not been systematically studied in sport. An interesting study predicted that injured athletes would have a drop in confidence immediately after their injuries, after which confidence would increase as they recovered, only to find the opposite (Quinn & Fallon, 1999). Athletes showed the highest levels of confidence immediately after their injuries. Confidence then dropped during rehabilitation before rebounding at full recovery. This finding was attributed to the long and grueling nature of the rehabilitation process, which athletes did not fully understand at the time of their injuries. Vealey and Sinclair (1987) found that performance or mastery orientation, previous practice performance, and dispositional confidence predicted the stability of athletes' precompetitive self-confidence over the course of a season. Because self-confidence is fleeting and fragile, research that assesses the patterning of self-confidence over time seems important to investigate how and why confidence remains resilient for some and unstable for others.

Sources of Self-Confidence in Sport

As shown in the previous sections, a growing body of research supports the idea that self-confidence is a key influence on athletes' behavior and performance in sport. In addition, researchers are beginning to conduct systematic studies of the effects of the competitive environment in influencing changes in self-confidence across time. In this section, the focus turns to research that has examined the antecedents, or sources, of self-confidence for athletes in sport. As Bandura (1997) stated, self-confidence is constructed through a complex process of self-persuasion, because athletes choose and interpret internal and environmental sources of information that affect their beliefs about their abilities to succeed.

Sources of self-confidence have been identified that are uniquely salient to athletes in competitive sport contexts. The sources of self-confidence described in self-efficacy theory were presented

previously in this chapter (see figure 5.3). Research in sport psychology has expanded upon the four sources of self-confidence theorized within self-efficacy theory (Bandura, 1997) to identify sources that are specifically salient to athletes within the unique subculture of competitive sport. The nine sources of self-confidence identified by Vealey et al. (1998) were presented previously in the chapter within the sport-confidence model (see figure 5.4 and table 5.1). Recent research inductively analyzed interview data from 14 world-class athletes to identify the sources of self-confidence that they used (Hays et al., 2007). The sources of self-confidence identified in the two sport-specific studies are shown in figure 5.7, along with Bandura's (1997) theorized four sources of self-efficacy.

The point of figure 5.7 is that the sport-specific sources represent contextually relevant descriptors of the broader categories of sources conceptualized by Bandura. Enactive mastery experiences perceived by athletes as important sources of confidence include mastery, demonstration of ability, performance accomplishments in training and competition, experience, and physical and mental preparation. Social support and coaches' leadership relate to verbal persuasion, and trust in team seems related to vicarious experience. Feelings about one's physical self-presentation, feeling comfortable in the competitive environment, perceptions of a favorable situation or competitive advantage, and self-awareness seem related to physiological and affective states. The intent is not to force sources into categories but rather to indicate overlap and congruency between the overarching theory of self-efficacy and the identification of specific sources of self-confidence in competitive sport. Clearly, some sport-specific sources relate to more than one self-efficacy source category (e.g., physical and mental preparation is relevant to all four self-efficacy source categories).

Enactive mastery experiences are the most important source of self-confidence in sport. Research has strongly supported the notion that the most important source of self-confidence for athletes in sport is enactive experience. First, several descriptive studies have indicated that athletes and coaches identify these sources as extremely important. Vealey et al. (1998) found that mastery, physical and mental preparation, and demonstration of ability were rated as important sources of confidence for high school and college athletes. All the world-class athletes in Hays et al.'s (2007) study identified preparation and competition accomplishments as important sources of self-confidence. In a study of

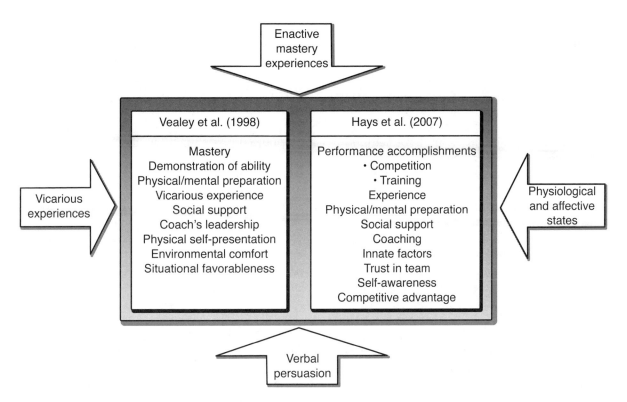

Figure 5.7 Sources of self-confidence in sport.

female collegiate basketball players, the frequency of reasons that they cited as to why they were confident were past performance (48%), physiological or affective states (35%), outside sources (9%), vicarious experience (4%), and verbal persuasion (3%) (Chase, Feltz, & Lirgg, 2003). Four descriptive studies have examined coaches' use and perceived effectiveness of confidence-enhancing techniques (Gould, Hodge, Peterson, & Giannini, 1989; Vargas-Tonsing, Myers, & Feltz, 2004; Weinberg, Grove, & Jackson, 1992; Weinberg & Jackson, 1990). Three studies found that coaches ranked "enhancing performance through instruction and drilling" as the confidence-enhancing technique that they used most frequently and thought was most effective. The other study ranked that technique second.

Enactive mastery experiences are shown to be important at all developmental levels. The highest frequency of responses for sources of self-confidence for 8- to 9-year-old children was successful performance, and successful performance was in the top three most frequent sources of confidence for 10- to 12-year-olds and 13- to 14-year-olds (Chase, 1998). Wilson, Sullivan, Myers, and Feltz (2004) found that mastery and physical and mental preparation were the highest ranked sources of confidence for masters athletes over age 50. An interesting study found that movement confidence (or feelings of

competence in one's physical skills) in childhood was an important predictor of later-life self-confidence in fitness activities for women aged 70 to 98 years (Cousins, 1997). Even when controlling for age, educational level, and perceived well-being, the movement confidence that these women experienced as young girls predicted 22% of the variance in their confidence as older adults (a great plug for motor skill development in young girls!).

Enactive mastery experiences have been shown to be the strongest predictor of self-confidence in both experimental field studies (Brody, Hatfield, & Spalding, 1988; Feltz, 1982, 1988; Feltz & Mugno, 1983, Fitzsimmons et al., 1991; Gernigon & Delloye, 2003; Wise & Trunnel, 2001) and naturalistic field studies (George, 1994; Haberl & Zaichkowsky, 1999; Pensgaard & Duda, 2002; Scanlan & Lewthwaite, 1985). Participant modeling, in which people first watch a model and then are guided through successful performance of the task (Bandura, 1977), has enhanced confidence (and performance) more so than unguided participant modeling, watching another person model the task, or watching a videotaped model perform the task (Feltz, Landers, & Raeder, 1979; McAuley, 1985).

Wise and Trunnel (2001) found that performance accomplishments increased self-confidence in weightlifting more than observing a model did, and that observing a model enhanced self-confidence more than verbal persuasion did. An interesting finding was that verbal persuasion was more effective in increasing self-confidence when it followed a performance accomplishment. This study indicated that knowing how to combine and sequence different sources can produce a greater effect on athletes' self-confidence. A similar example of combining sources is Escarti and Guzman's (1999) use of bogus feedback to manipulate participants' perception of past performance, which may be thought of as combining performance experience, social support, and verbal persuasion. Those who received positive feedback increased their self-confidence more than those who received negative feedback. Physical and mental preparation and mastery emerged as the strongest positive predictor of self-confidence for high school, college, and master athletes (Vealey et al., 1998; Wilson et al., 2004), and mastery and demonstration of ability were the confidence sources significantly related to self-confidence restoration in injured athletes (Magyar & Duda, 2000).

The research reviewed in this section demonstrates the powerful influence of successful performance in sport on self-confidence. A member of the U.S. women's ice-hockey team, which won the gold medal in the 1998 Olympic Games, described the effect this way:

> Having played Canada 15 times was a huge factor, because they went from having this kind of aura about them, of being . . . the best team, and after you play them several times, you're, "Hey, they are just another team, and we're [just] as good." With each win that we had against Canada, and even each loss, because it was a one-goal loss . . . or it was a really close game . . . so each victory or each close loss kind of built that confidence up. (Haberl & Zaichkowsky, 1999, p. 224)

This quotation emphasizes that even a loss can serve as a successful performance experience for the enhancement of confidence if athletes perceive that they performed well and gained insights from the experience. Bandura (1997) emphasized that past performance alone does not automatically enhance self-confidence but that athletes interpret and appraise performance successes and failures in a complex inferential process to weigh the relative contributions of personal abilities as well as other factors to arrive at some sense of mastery that then enhances self-confidence.

Research supports other sources of self-confidence besides enactive mastery experiences. Although enactive mastery experiences in sport, such as performance success and hard training, are the most influential sources of confidence, research has indicated that several of the other sources shown in figure 5.7 are important sources as well. A major source of confidence in sport is modeling, which involves the vicarious experience of watching another person perform. Experimental studies have supported modeling as an effective source of self-confidence, especially when people observe a model similar to themselves (George, Feltz, & Chase, 1992; Gould & Weiss, 1981) or a highly skilled model (Lirgg & Feltz, 1991). High school and college athletes viewed vicarious experience as an important source of self-confidence. The coach who served as a confident model and effective leader was identified by both coaches and athletes as an important source of confidence (Gould et al., 1989; Hays et al., 2007; Vargas-Tonsing et al., 2004; Vealey et al., 1998; Weinberg et al., 1992; Weinberg & Jackson, 1990). Imagery, a common performance-enhancement technique, has been shown to enhance self-confidence (Feltz & Riessinger, 1990). Athletes described imagery as a useful way to review their previous good performances in what may be thought of as vicarious mastery experiences (Hanton et al., 2004).

Social support and verbal persuasion have also been identified as sources of confidence for athletes in sport (Chase, 1998; Haberl & Zaichoksky, 1999; Hanton et al., 2004; Scanlan & Lewthwaite, 1985; Wise & Trunnel, 2001). Coaches have identified encouraging self-talk, verbal persuasion, and use of reward statements as effective confidence-enhancing techniques that they use (Gould et al., 1989; Vargas-Tonsing et al., 2004; Weinberg et al., 1992; Weinberg & Jackson, 1990). An elite athlete explained,

> Being verbally persuaded by your coach is the best protection against any worries or concerns. It's linked to your confidence. . . . You don't think negative when you've got positive thoughts in your mind and your coach is saying to you that you are going to do it. You know it's going to be a . . . good performance. (Hanton et al., 2004, p. 489)

Athletes also use self-talk as a personalized verbal persuasive technique to enhance their self-confidence (Hardy, Gammage, & Hall, 2001). Physiological and affective states have been shown to influence individuals' perceptions of their confidence in sport and physical activity (Chase et al., 2003; Feltz & Mugno, 1983), and the previous discussion on the complex relationship between anxiety and self-confidence supports this as well.

Research with injured athletes found that they selected environmental sources (social support, athletic trainers' leadership, environmental comfort) as particularly salient in their recovery (Magyar & Duda, 2000). Similarly, elite distance runners identified the suitability of the external environment as an important source of their confidence. Athletes identified trust (in coach and teammates) as an important source of confidence (Hays et al., 2007). Future research should examine this source based on the finding that trust in one's coach has been shown to be significantly predictive of winning percentages in men's college basketball (Dirks, 2000). Feelings of confidence and control have been linked to the phenomenon of psychological momentum (Shaw, Dzewaltowski, & McElroy, 1992; Vallerand, Colavecchio, & Pelletier, 1988), which as a form of situational favorableness (Vealey et al., 1998) may be a fruitful area to study as a source (or result) of self-confidence. Finally, affective feelings about one's sense of physical self-presentation offers an interesting area to study in relation to confidence. Research indicates that certain types of clothing and body language influence how people are perceived by others (Greenlees, Buscombe, Thelwell, Holder, & Rimmer, 2005). Thus, athletes' perceptions of their physical selves should be investigated more fully as a source of confidence.

The research on sources of self-confidence in sport is rapidly expanding and has begun to examine sources in relation to unique sport contexts. Various forms of enactive mastery experiences in sport have demonstrated their primary importance as a source of self-confidence in sport, although many other sources have been identified as useful to athletes as well. Future research should heed Bandura's (1997) suggestion to examine more fully how athletes select, weigh, and integrate sources of confidence, and how they use different sources to enhance their confidence in different ways in different situations.

Individual Differences in Self-Confidence

Research has examined individual differences in self-confidence within the context of sport. Most of the studies examined differences based on gender and skill level of athletes.

Research examining gender differences in self-confidence in sport is equivocal and is influenced by the sex typing of activities, performance feedback, and conception of ability. Some studies have shown that male athletes have more self-confidence than female athletes do (Crocker, 1989; Jones et al., 1991; Krane & Williams, 1994;

Martens et al., 1990; Petruzello & Corbin, 1988), but other studies have found no gender differences in self-confidence (Cox & Whaley, 2004; Perry & Williams, 1998). A meta-analysis of gender differences in self-confidence generated a .40 effect size that favored males, but the effect size was not homogenous (meaning that the effect sizes in the analysis varied a great deal).

To gain a better understanding of the equivocal findings, researchers began to test Lenney's (1977) suggestion that females are not dispositionally different from males but rather lack self-confidence in achievement situations that are (a) perceived as inappropriate for their gender, (b) extremely socially comparative, and (c) lacking in performance feedback. Females showed lower self-confidence on "gender-inappropriate" activities (Corbin & Nix, 1979; Corbin, Stewart, & Blair, 1981; Corbin, Landers, Feltz, & Senior, 1983), but no gender differences in confidence emerged for performance on gender-neutral activities (Corbin et al., 1981). Meta-analytic results demonstrated that the more "masculine" an activity was considered, the greater was the differences in self-confidence between males and females (Lirgg, 1991). Sex typing worked both ways. Males showed higher confidence on "male" tasks, whereas females showed higher confidence on "female" tasks (Clifton & Gill, 1994; Lirgg, George, Chase, & Ferguson, 1996; Sanguinetti, Lee, & Nelson, 1985). Males who possessed a more "masculine" sex role had higher self-confidence than the other male and female sex role groups did during the week preceding competition (Swain & Jones, 1991).

Performance feedback increased the confidence of low-confident females so that it was no different from males' levels of confidence (Petruzello & Corbin, 1988; Stewart & Corbin, 1988). Conception of ability also influenced the relationship between gender and self-confidence because females who believed ability to be an acquired attribute were more confident in a "masculine" activity than were females who believed ability to be an innate condition (Lirgg et al., 1996). Vealey (1988) found gender differences in self-confidence in high school and college athletes (males higher), but also found that gender differences in self-confidence were not apparent for elite athletes.

Males and females identify different sources for their confidence. Gender differences have also been found among athletes in the sources of confidence that they identify. Vealey and colleagues (1998) found that college female athletes in individual sports rated social support and physical self-presentation as more important sources for their confidence as compared with college male athletes in individual sports. This study also found that high school female team-sport athletes rated social support as a more important source than male athletes did, and conversely that male athletes rated demonstration of ability as a more important source of confidence than female athletes did. This finding was supported by Jones et al. (1991), who found comparison and winning as significant antecedents of male athletes' confidence, and personal goals and standards as significant antecedents of female athletes' confidence.

Elite and expert athletes have higher self-confidence than nonelite and nonexpert athletes. A robust finding in the literature is that advanced, elite, expert athletes have higher levels of self-confidence than beginner, nonelite, nonexpert athletes (Cleary & Zimmerman, 2001; George, 1994; Kitsantas & Zimmerman, 2002; McPherson, 2000; Perry & Williams, 1998; Tenenbaum et al., 1996).

In summary, perceptions of the gender appropriateness of activities and the availability of performance feedback influence gender differences in self-confidence. Future research is needed to examine research participants' perceptions of sex typing or perceived gender appropriateness. Such studies would be in contrast to designs in which the investigators defined activities as either gender appropriate or nongender appropriate. Gender differences also have appeared with regard to sources of self-confidence. Finally, elite and expert athletes have been repeatedly shown to have higher self-confidence than nonelite and nonexpert athletes do.

Regarding race, Cox and Whaley (2004) found that African American male and female high school basketball players had higher self-confidence than white players did. Coaches, however, rated African American players lower on effort and persistence, attributed by the investigators to stereotypical beliefs about race, which raises the possibility of negative expectancy effects on African American athletes. Additional research is needed to examine subcultural influences on confidence and sources of confidence used with regard to race and gender. Self-confidence as a mediating factor within the phenomenon of stereotype threat (Beilock & McConnell, 2004) is an example of a conceptual approach that could be useful.

Self-Confidence in Coaches

The study of self-confidence in sport has progressed to focus on confidence in coaches as well as athletes.

The importance of self-confidence for coaches is apparent in the following remarks of inexperienced coaches: "I wasn't as confident as I wished I had been from the start . . . and I think that weakened the power of my coaching." "I should have started out just being more confident in myself. If I had been a little stronger, I would have been more effective throughout the season" (Weiss, Barber, Sisley, & Ebbeck, 1991, p. 348). Feltz and colleagues developed and tested a conceptual model of coaching efficacy (confidence) that included four dimensions, or important types, of coaching confidence (Chase, Feltz, Hayashi, & Hepler, 2005; Feltz, Chase, Moritz, & Sullivan, 1999). These dimensions, defined previously in the chapter as subscales within the Coaching Efficacy Scale (CES), are game strategy, motivation, technique, and character building. Research has supported the conceptual relationships shown in the model of coaching efficacy illustrated in figure 5.8.

Coaches' confidence is derived from prior success, playing experience, coaching experience, perceived athlete talent, social support, player improvement, and education. Research using the CES indicated that coaches' efficacy was predicted by prior success, coaching experience, perceived athlete talent, and social support (Feltz et al., 1999; Tsorbatzoudis, Daroglou, Zahariadis, & Grouios, 2003). Social support was a stronger source of confidence for female coaches as compared with male coaches (Myers, Vargas-Tonsing, & Feltz, 2005). In structured interviews, coaches identified the development of their athletes, their own coaching education and development, knowledge and preparation, leadership skills, athlete support, and experience as sources for their coaching confidence (Chase, Feltz, Hayashi, & Hepler, 2005). Coaches' confidence before competitive events was predicted by the coaches' perceived ability of their opponents for that event (Chase, Lirgg, & Feltz, 1997). Coaches who were highly confident that their teams would perform well attributed that confidence to good competitive and practice performance, preparation, favorable social comparison with the opponent, and a belief in their team's resilience (Chase et al., 1997). Coaches who were less confident that their teams would perform well attributed that lack of confidence to unfavorable social comparison with the opponent, poor competitive and practice performance, inconsistency in the team's performance, physical problems, and low athlete self-confidence.

In examining sources for specific types of coaching efficacy, previous performance predicted coaches'

Sources of coaching efficacy information

Extent of coaching experience/preparation
Playing experience
Prior success (win-loss record)
Perceived skill of athletes/player improvement
School/community
Parents/player support

Coaching efficacy dimensions

Game strategy
Motivation
Technique
Character building

Outcomes

Coaching behavior
Commitment
Player/team satisfaction
Player/team performance
Player/team efficacy

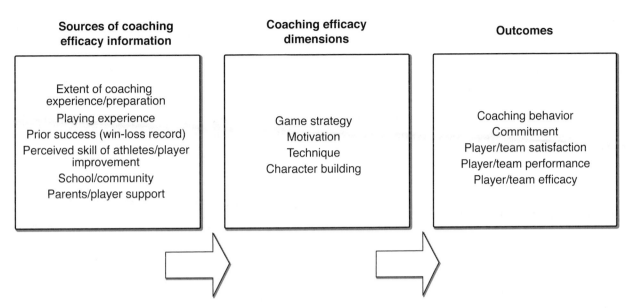

Figure 5.8 Model of coaching efficacy.
Adapted, by permission, from D. Feltz.

confidence in using game strategy, previous performance and athlete affect predicted coaches' confidence in motivating their athletes, and athlete feedback, athlete affect, and social comparison predicted coaches' confidence in character building (Marback, Short, Short, & Sullivan, 2005). Overall, the sources of coach confidence are similar to the sources of athlete confidence, in that both coaches and athletes viewed enactive mastery experiences, preparation, and social support as important sources of confidence. The difference is that coaching confidence is based on the perception of having had a positive effect on others, so that coaches gain confidence when they see their athletes improve their skills and experience satisfaction in their sport experiences.

Coaches' confidence influences coaching behavior, commitment, athlete satisfaction, team performance, and team confidence. As shown in figure 5.8, coaching efficacy affects coaches' own behaviors and self-perceptions, as well as the behaviors, self-perceptions, and affective responses of athletes on the team. High-efficacy coaches provided more praise and encouragement to athletes and had higher winning percentages than did low-efficacy coaches, whereas low-efficacy coaches provided more instructional and organizational behaviors than did high-efficacy coaches (Feltz et al., 1999). These findings are similar to research that has shown that more confident and effective teachers demonstrate more effective interaction skills and spend more time with their students on active learning as opposed to instruction and management (Behets, 1997; Woolfolk, Rossoff, & Hoy, 1990).

Coaching efficacy also was related to coaches' perceived use of confidence-enhancing behaviors with their athletes (Myers et al., 2005), coaches' perceived control over an upcoming competitive event (Chase et al., 1997), and assistant coaches' desire to become head coaches (Cunningham, Sagas, & Ashley, 2003; Everhart & Chelladurai, 1998).

With regard to performance, high-efficacy coaches had higher winning percentages than did low-efficacy coaches (Feltz et al., 1999), and coaching efficacy was predictive of team basketball performance in terms of successful free-throw shooting and fewer turnovers (Chase et al., 1997). Myers et al. (2005) found that coaching efficacy predicted winning percentages for men's teams but not for women's teams. Because both studies have linked coaches' confidence to winning only with male coaches, future research should examine the influence of gender on this relationship. Coaching efficacy has also been positively associated with team confidence, yet in the same study no relationship was found between coaching efficacy and athlete self-confidence (Vargas-Tonsing, Warners, & Feltz, 2003).

Coaching efficacy has been positively related to athlete satisfaction in male teams (Feltz et al., 1999; Myers et al., 2005), but the gender of the coach moderated the relationships between coach confidence and athlete satisfaction in female teams. Motivation coaching efficacy was positively related to athlete satisfaction in female teams with female coaches, but character-building coaching efficacy was negatively related to athlete satisfaction in female teams with male coaches. These findings are difficult to interpret, but they suggest that some sort of gender bias is operating that moderates the complex relationships between coach confidence, coach behavior, and athlete satisfaction. With regard to gender differences, coaching efficacy has been found to be no different between male and female head coaches (Everhart & Chelladurai, 1998; Myers et al., 2005). Male assistant coaches, however, were found to have higher coaching confidence than female assistant coaches (Cunningham et al., 2003), and head female college coaches were less confident than male coaches in game strategy efficacy, coaching during competition, knowledge of strategies and tactics, and ability to motivate their athletes (Marback et al., 2005).

The conceptualization of a model for coaching efficacy (see figure 5.8) and development of the multidimensional Coaching Efficacy Scale (CES) has established an important line of research on coaching confidence. Research has identified sources of coaches' confidence and has linked coaches' confidence to important outcomes like team success, team confidence, and athlete satisfaction. Future research is needed to increase our understanding of the role of gender in the complex relationship between coaching confidence, coaching behavior, and athletes' perceptions and performance. Additional research is also needed to untangle the relative relationships of the different types of coach confidence with various sources and outcomes. None of the sources in the coaching efficacy model predicted coaches' confidence in character building (Feltz et al., 1999); thus, research should more fully investigate the relevance and antecedents of this dimension of coaching confidence. Research on coaches' confidence provides a strong conceptual foundation for coaching education programs, and intervention research is warranted to examine the effectiveness of interventions to enhance coaches' confidence (e.g., Malete & Feltz, 2001).

Role and Team Confidence

As discussed previously in the theoretical and measurement sections of the chapter, the study of self-confidence has evolved to focus on confidence beyond the self. Role efficacy, or confidence, has been conceptualized as athletes' perceived capability to perform successfully in interdependent ways within their roles on teams (Bray et al., 2002).

Athletes' confidence in their roles within teams influences their performance beyond their self-confidence to execute specific skills. Research has shown that role efficacy and self-efficacy were

positively correlated but only to a moderate extent, providing support that these constructs are distinct, yet related (Bray et al., 2002; Bray et al., 2004). Starting basketball players reported greater role efficacy than nonstarters, although no differences were found in self-efficacy between groups. After controlling for self-efficacy, role efficacy was significantly related to athletes' performance as assessed by teammates and coaches (Beauchamp, Bray, Eys, & Carron, 2002; Bray, Brawley, & Carron, 2002; Bray et al., 2004).

Team confidence is more predictive of team performance than is an aggregated measure of team members' self-confidence. Team confidence, or collective efficacy, was defined previously in the chapter as the team's belief in their collective ability to perform successfully (Bandura, 1997), and the research on collective efficacy in sport is reviewed in chapter 11. But it seems important to mention here that team confidence is much more than a simple aggregation of the individual confidence levels of team members. Because of required task interdependence and close interpersonal relations within sport teams, team confidence is a better predictor of team performance than is the aggregate of team members' confidence (e.g., Feltz & Lirgg, 1998). Although research in this area has focused on the relationship of team confidence to team outcomes (performance, cohesion), research should also consider relationships between self and team confidence, focused particularly on differential interpersonal requirements within teams. For example, individual self-confidence was the strongest predictor of personal perceptions of team confidence in the sport of rowing, which requires almost perfect synchronicity among teammates (Magyar et al., 2004). That is, rowers who were more confident in their own ability to row were more likely to feel confident about their crew's ability to row. Research could also examine the relative influence of team confidence on positions in sport in which confidence in team members is critical, such as softball and baseball pitchers, football quarterbacks, and soccer goalkeepers. Such research could be part of a multilayer analysis of confidence within teams, discussed later in the chapter as a future research direction.

Interventions to Enhance Self-Confidence

Because self-confidence is viewed as an important mental skill for athletes, intervention research using different types of mental training strategies and techniques has focused on the enhancement of athletes' self-confidence. Vealey (2007) identified self-confidence as one of four foundation skills in a comprehensive mental skills conceptual model.

Various mental training interventions have been successful in enhancing the self-confidence of athletes in sport. Athletes who extensively used the mental training techniques of relaxation, self-talk, and goal setting had higher levels of self-confidence before competition than athletes who reported a lower frequency of using these techniques (Fletcher & Hanton, 2001). Self-confidence has been significantly increased through mental training interventions using imagery (Callow, Hardy, & Hall, 2001; Evans, Jones, & Mullen, 2004; Feltz & Riessinger, 1990; Garza & Feltz, 1998; Hale & Whitehouse, 1998; McKenzie & Howe, 1997; Short, Bruggerman, et al., 2002), self-talk (Landin & Hebert, 1999; Maynard, Smith, & Warwick-Evans, 1995), goal setting (Burton, 1989; Kingston & Hardy, 1997; Zimmerman & Kitsantas, 1996), and relaxation training (Maynard, Hemmings, & Warwick-Evans, 1995).

Self-confidence has also been facilitated by numerous multimodal interventions, which use a combination of mental training strategies and techniques to enhance self-confidence (e.g., Mamassis & Doganis, 2004). A few of these are highlighted based on notable features. An effective strategy for intervention programs has been to preselect athletes who score high in debilitative anxiety interpretation and then investigate the effects of mental training on their interpretations of anxiety and self-confidence. Hanton and Jones (1999) used a combination of goal setting, imagery, and self-talk with anxiety-debilitated swimmers and found that the intervention resulted in significant improvements in self-confidence. Future research should consider identifying athletes with low confidence for specific interventions and even attempt to intervene with programs to facilitate athlete confidence based on sources of confidence important to individual athletes.

Harwood and Swain (2002) implemented a season-long player, parent, and coach intervention program with elite youth tennis players that resulted in enhanced self-confidence for three program participants and no increases in confidence for the control participant. The intervention focused on goal enhancement to achieve a competitive performance mentality that emphasized self-challenge and game challenge. The program also worked to enhance the motivation of parents and coaches, a particularly effective approach to attempting to facilitate the sociocultural context within which athletes perform. This social-psychological approach to mental training interventions is sorely needed in sport psychology.

Barker and Jones (2006) used a combination of hypnosis, technique refinement, and self-modeling to enhance the self-confidence of a cricket leg-spin bowler. The single-subject design showed a significant increase in self-confidence as the result of the intervention. This intervention was noteworthy because it combined mental and physical training. Hypnosis and self-modeling through video were augmented by coaching sessions dedicated to technique refinement. This integration of mental and physical training is a powerful enactive mastery approach to enhancing confidence in athletes. Future research should also examine the effects of mental training interventions on coach, role, and team confidence.

Conclusion and Future Research Directions

Research examining self-confidence in sport has evolved from laboratory-based experimental verification of key tenets of self-efficacy theory to naturalistic field studies of how self-confidence is developed and the ways in which it influences the behavior, thoughts, feelings, and performance of athletes and coaches in sport. The list of conceptual frameworks within which confidence has been studied in sport is extensive, because self-confidence seems to be a metacognition, or mental modifier, that influences many other relationships between psychological constructs and human behavior (e.g., self-efficacy theory, expectancy-value theory, processing efficiency theory, cusp catastrophe model, control process model). The study of confidence in athletes has expanded from the study of self-confidence to the study of coach, partner, role, and team confidence. The assessment of self-confidence has evolved from one-item questions to multidimensional questionnaires tapping sport-specific constructions of various types of confidence, complex methodological and statistical procedures, and idiographic and qualitative approaches to gain a more context-rich view of how athletes and coaches experience confidence in sport. The first 30 years of research have provided a solid foundation from which research may evolve in greater complexity, theoretical importance, and practical usefulness in the next 30 years.

Research begets research. A comprehensive review of any research area should illuminate shadowy areas where our understanding is unclear, areas without light that have gone uninvestigated, and epiphanies for new ways of knowing that have not been considered. This section suggests some directions for investigating self-confidence in sport. These are broad suggestions. Specific research ideas have been sprinkled throughout the preceding research review.

Multilevel Investigations of Confidence

Most theory and research on confidence has focused on the individual level—hence the term *self-confidence*. As previously discussed (and discussed in chapter 11), collective efficacy within sport teams has received increasing attention. Also as noted in this chapter, new conceptualizations of role confidence (Bray et al., 2002, 2004) and partner confidence (Beauchamp & Whinton, 2005; Lent & Lopez, 2002) have been developed. Research is needed to investigate athletes' confidence in successfully fulfilling an interdependent performance requirement as well as their confidence in key performance partners. The self-confidence of athletes is embedded within various layers that represent increasingly broader aspects of confidence. As shown in figure 5.9, a multilevel model of confidence in sport begins at the self level and then extends to role, partner, cohort, team, and organizational confidence. Cohort confidence refers to the confidence of an interdependent subset within a team, such as defensive backs in football or lines in ice hockey. Organizational confidence could be represented by the confidence of a collegiate athletic department or a professional sports franchise.

Research has begun to examine confidence using the multilevel perspective (Chen et al., 2002; Lindsley, Brass, & Thomas, 1995; Magyar et al., 2004; Moritz & Watson, 1998). As discussed in the measurement section of the chapter, multilevel analyses through hierarchical linear modeling (HLM) have been used to test for similarities and dissimilarities in multilevel confidence models at different levels of analysis. For example, in a study of community league basketball teams, experience and achievement motivation significantly predicted self-efficacy (Chen et al., 2002). Team-level results found that team motivation predicted team efficacy but that team expertise did not. Thus, achievement motivation predicted confidence at multiple levels of analysis, but other variables did not. Similar research designs could examine various multilevel models of confidence moving from individual self-confidence to the broad notion of organizational confidence.

Resilient Self-Confidence

Bandura (1997) talked about the importance of developing a resilient self-confidence that can withstand the constant obstacles and setbacks inherent in life. Athletes in sport constantly face obstacles such as losing, making mistakes, receiving critical feedback from coaches, and returning from injuries. A belief in their abilities to weather these setbacks and succeed is critical. Elite athletes identified not just confidence but rather a *resilient* confidence in the form of "unshakable self-belief" as the key to mental toughness and success in sport (Bull et al., 2005; Jones et al., 2002). But research has not extensively examined the resiliency, or stability of, self-confidence across time and throughout experiences. An interesting study showed that gymnasts at the 2000 Olympic Games did not allow a major equipment malfunction (vault set five centimeters too low during competition) to affect their subsequent performance after the error was corrected (Grandjean,

Figure 5.9 Multilevel model of confidence in sport.

Taylor, & Weiner, 2002). The investigators attributed this result to the gymnasts' extensive mental and physical training, which allowed them to remain confident and focused despite the distraction. This mental resilience was not directly tested but rather inferred from the gymnasts' performance.

Future research is needed to examine the resiliency of athletes' self-confidence across time and in response to various obstacles. Stability of confidence could be studied across a competitive season or a span of competitions within a tournament. Research could assess factors that influence confidence stability or examine differences in athletes with stable confidence versus athletes with unstable confidence. This problem could be studied quantitatively or with qualitative methods such as interviews and ethnography. Research is equivocal in assessing changes in confidence as time to compete nears, so future studies should move beyond the mere description of how confidence changes to try to understand why it changes in relation to upcoming competition. Research examining the stability of coach confidence and team confidence is also warranted. In fact, adopting the multilevel analysis model could provide insights about how changes in confidence over time at one level affect the patterning of confidence at other levels within the model (self, coach, and team confidence across a series of practices and competitions).

Confidence–Performance Spirals

Another important area for future research is the examination of confidence–performance relationships over time, termed *confidence-performance spirals* (Lindsley et al., 1995). When performance affects self-confidence, which in turn affects performance and so on, these iterative loops often become deviation amplifying. In this process, a deviation in one variable (decrease in confidence) leads to a similar deviation in another variable (lower performance), which in turn continues to amplify. Thus, the cyclic nature of the self-confidence–performance relationship can result in a downward (decreasing confidence and performance) or upward (increasing confidence and performance) spiral. Terms such as "progressive deterioration" (Bandura & Jourden, 1991), "downward spirals," (Hambrick & D'Aveni, 1988), and "self-fueling spirals" (Hackman, 1990) are used to describe this process. Sport phenomena that may be related to confidence–performance spirals include momentum, slumps, and hot streaks.

Interestingly, upward spirals are not always viewed as beneficial, because mastery learning and outstanding achievements typically occur when athletes encounter failures and then learn from their mistakes (Lindsley et al., 1995). Consistent success has been linked to complacency and overconfidence (Bandura & Jourden, 1991); successful people often reduce their attention because they have no reason to change strategies or standards. Thus, self-correcting spirals are more beneficial than upward spirals because a person who analyzes performance can make adjustments in future efforts and reverse the previous decrease (or increase) in performance and self-confidence. Athletes commonly do this in sport. When teams are successful and gain confidence, coaches often set higher goals and standards to push athletes to remain focused and effortful. This approach results in self-correction by thwarting overconfidence and depressing performance, at least momentarily, based on the new, more difficult goals. Athletes then self-correct again by gaining confidence and performance success as they adapt to the new challenges set for them. This redefining of success by applying information gained from task attempts is called intelligent failure by Sitkin (1992) and informative failure by Lindsley et al. (1995). Continued success occurs only when athletes focus on what went wrong, thus obtaining information that leads to improvement. Focusing on the mistakes of a success prevents athletes' self-confidence from leaping to overconfidence within an upward spiral. Because overconfidence in sport is a common attribution for poor performance in a situation in which success is expected, research should examine these ideas about confidence–performance spirals and the importance of intelligent or informative failure in building and reestablishing confidence.

These ideas about confidence–performance spirals seem to question whether we want confidence to be stable, as discussed in the previous section. Perhaps resilient confidence means that confidence is optimal at the time of performance but should decrease between competitive events to gain the full benefits of increased effort and attention and to avoid complacency. Bandura (1997) has suggested this idea by differentiating between preparatory efficacy and performance efficacy. The optimal level of self-confidence during the development of skills is theorized to be lower than the optimal level of self-confidence for performing. Thus, the confidence–performance relationship seems to change depending on whether athletes are in training or in competition. At the point of competition, actual feelings of efficacy might never be too high, yet in training, extremely high levels of efficacy might interfere with the preparatory effort needed to gain the most from the training session. Some self-doubt is useful in preparatory situations because it provides the incentive to focus attention and expend effort to acquire knowledge and skills (Bandura, 1997). Bandura and Locke (2003) recommended that coaches reduce their athletes' self-confidence during training periods between competitions. Optimal zones of self-confidence may exist for different situations, similar to the individual zones of optimal functioning for cognitive and somatic anxiety (Hanin, 1997).

In summary, the idea that extremely high levels of confidence are desired because they will enhance performance in all situations is simplistic and appears to be unfounded. Research at the within-person level of analysis has supported the idea that self-confidence was negatively related to motivation and performance in a learning context (Vancouver & Kendall, 2006). All these ideas regarding confidence–performance spirals and the differences in optimal preparatory and performance confidence provide interesting research questions for researchers in sport psychology. In the spirit of multilevel analysis discussed in the previous section, research on the confidence–performance relationship should be conducted at both the individual level and the collective level.

Extending Various Conceptual Predictions About Self-Confidence in Sport

Research questions abound in relation to the many predictions emanating from conceptual models that include the construct of self-confidence. The interactive effects of self-confidence and consequence expectancies, called outcome expectancies by Bandura (1997), on athletes' behavior should be examined. The increasing specialization practices and award inducements in sport serve as a rationale for the field to consider how consequence expectancies (e.g., approval from parents, gaining a college scholarship) may influence self-confidence or interact with self-confidence in different ways to influence behavior. This kind of research may help explain how high expectations viewed in a positive way ("I'm prepared and have a great chance to win based on my abilities") differ from or change to high expectations that create pressure for athletes ("I'm supposed to win, so I hope I don't screw up"). Negative consequence expectancies may debilitate athletes' self-confidence, and this result has occurred with champion athletes who feel pressure after they reach the top (Gould, Jackson, & Finch, 1993a, 1993b; Jackson, Dover, & Mayocchi, 1998). Consequence

expectancies also seem to interfere with athletes' ability to engage in automatic processing without conscious attention—an ability required for high-level performance (Schneider, Dumais, & Shiffrin, 1984). The paradox is that self-confidence is a positive expectancy for performance, whereas trust to engage in automatic processing is the absence of expectancy (Moore & Stevenson, 1991). Research is needed to understand how self-confidence, anxiety, and consequence expectancies interact to affect athletes' ability to relinquish conscious control and to trust in their performance.

Research is needed to examine how various sources and combinations of sources of self-confidence influence different types of confidence and, as suggested by Bandura (1997), to investigate the ways in which athletes choose, weigh, and combine sources of confidence. The ways in which athletes' sources of confidence change over time, based on competitive demands as well as their own skill development, is another area that has not been examined. The multidimensionality of self-confidence, coach confidence, and team confidence should continue to be explored, particularly the ways in which different types of confidence influence important outcomes. The area of coaching efficacy is relatively unexplored, and many conceptual predictions from the various self-confidence models could be tested with coaches. Although coaches' leadership has been identified as an important source of self-confidence for athletes, athletes' confidence in their coaches (confidence in leadership) is another layer in the multilevel model of confidence in sport that could be examined. The movement confidence model is largely untested, and the movement sensation scale (evaluation of expected and preferred movement sensation related to enjoyment and potential for harm), coupled with perceived movement competence, might be useful in helping to understand sedentary individuals' motivation and persistence in physical activity. Research could use expectancy theory or stereotype threat as conceptual frameworks to examine the influence of gender and race on self-confidence.

Social Structure and Personal Agency

Brustad & Ritter-Taylor (1997) stated that the social-cultural context serves as the backdrop against which all thoughts, feelings, and behaviors by athletes and coaches take on meaning. Self-confidence, as a belief in one's personal agency, may only be understood by understanding how people are influenced by their social-cultural surroundings.

Multilevel analyses of confidence may shed light on the social-structural influences on self-confidence of athletes within partner, cohort, team, organization, and cultural systems (see figure 5.9). Adopting idiographic case study approaches and qualitative techniques such as participant observation, ethnography, and interviewing may provide rich insights that complement quantitative research examining confidence in sport.

Many personal, social, and cultural forces influence the development and manifestation of feelings of personal agency in the intensely public and comparative subculture of competitive sport. Considering those many possibilities is the challenge for sport psychology researchers who seek to understand self-confidence in sport, with the intent to infuse all sport participants with the belief that "they can."

CHAPTER 6

Attributions and Perceived Control

Stephanie J. Hanrahan, PhD ■ Stuart J.H. Biddle, PhD

In sport and exercise settings we constantly seek explanations for our own behavior and that of others. Attributions, the explanations that we give for events, can influence our future expectancies, emotions, performance, and persistence. A number of attributional theories have been developed, and these theories have had a significant influence on the study of attributions in sport contexts. Using various methods of measuring attributions, researchers have investigated predictors of attributions, consequences of attributions, and the trainability of attributions. Although attributions identify the perceived causes of outcomes, they also involve beliefs about control over the causes.

The purpose of this chapter is to review the research and theory on attributions, attributional style, and control beliefs. This chapter begins with definitions of relevant terms and a review of the theoretical approaches. The second section presents measurement issues, and the third section reviews the research pertaining to antecedents, consequences, and retraining of attributions. The fourth section contains a discussion of other perspectives on control. The chapter ends with consideration of future areas of research in the field.

Definitions and Conceptual Approaches

In this section we start by describing what attributions are, and we outline the concepts of attributional style and attributional dimensions. Attributions are the reasons that people give to explain events related to themselves or others. Attributions may not be the actual causes of events, but they are the perceived causes of events. For example, a basketball player may attribute limited success with shooting layups to being short, when in fact the player's technique is poor and height has nothing to do with it. We tend to make attributions because we want to explain, understand, and predict the behaviors of ourselves and others.

Attributional style can be defined as the generally consistent way in which people tend to account for outcomes. Relatively stable, individual differences in the types of attributions that people make have been related to loneliness, depression, and achievement behavior.

Early attribution research in achievement behavior focused on the four attributions of ability, effort, task difficulty, and luck. Research in sport, however, found that these four attributions account for much less than half of the attributions made by athletes

(e.g., Roberts & Pascuzzi, 1979; Yamamoto, 1983). Because interactive competitive sporting situations are likely to elicit more diverse attributions than academic situations (the focus of much of the early attribution research in achievement behavior), researchers generally should focus on attributional dimensions instead of actual attributions.

Attributions can be placed along attributional dimensions. For example, the four attributions of ability, effort, task difficulty, and luck were placed within the attributional dimensions of internality (originally called locus of control) and stability (Weiner, 1972). Internality refers to whether the perceived cause was due to something inside the person (internal) or to something outside the person (external). Stability refers to whether the perceived cause will always be present in the future (stable) or will rarely if ever be present again (unstable). Table 6.1 shows how the four attributions are placed within these two dimensions.

Table 6.1 Two-Dimensional Model of Attributions (Weiner, 1972)

	Stable	Unstable
Internal	Ability	Effort
External	Task difficulty	Luck

As will be discussed later in this chapter, the attributional dimensions are related to expectancies for future success and emotions. For example, if someone attributes failure to a stable cause, the expectancy for future success will be limited. On the other hand, if the person attributes failure to an unstable cause, future success is possible. Problems can arise, however, when it is the researchers who determine how a particular attribution falls along attributional dimensions. Although originally it was believed that the attribution of ability is stable, some people may perceive it to be unstable. For example, the ability to run 10K depends on fitness, which can change over time. Similarly, some athletes may perceive effort to be a stable characteristic, because they always try no matter what. Additionally, task difficulty may be relatively stable in sports such as diving or gymnastics but highly variable in interactive sports in which the skill level of the opposition determines the level of challenge. Given this variability in the way that particular attributions may be perceived to fall along the attributional dimensions, researchers should allow participants to place their attributions within the dimensions (Russell, 1982), thus avoiding interpretation problems.

Internality and stability are not the only attributional dimensions that have been proposed. Controllability is a self-explanatory dimension that ranges from controllable to uncontrollable. For example, the basketball player mentioned earlier cannot control her or his height but could conceivably control technique. In the early 1990s researchers suggested that there are two types of controllability—personal control and external control (McAuley, Duncan, & Russell, 1992). Although an athlete might not be able to control the perceived cause of performance, someone else could. For example, an athlete may attribute a loss to poor officiating. This attribution would probably be rated low in terms of personal control but high in terms of external control (or control by others).

Research initiated in the area of depression considered the dimensions of internality, stability, and globality (Seligman, Abramson, Semmel, & vonBaeyer, 1979). The globality dimension measures the breadth of the effect of the perceived cause. The cause may be specific and influence only one situation, or it may be global and affect a variety of situations. Attributing negative events to global factors may lead to feelings of depression and helplessness (Abramson & Martin, 1981). For example, if athletes attribute poor officiating to the poor training of officials and a general lack of concern about the quality of officiating by the league (a global attribution), they are likely to perceive that the quality of officiating will not change for other games or other venues even when different officials are present. However, if the poor officiating is attributed to a specific cause, say the illness of a particular official in that game, then the athletes may have more positive expectations for the quality of officiating in future games. From a performance perspective, Prapavessis and Carron (1988) found that tennis players who exhibited symptoms of learned helplessness attributed losses to global factors to a greater extent than did players who did not exhibit those symptoms.

The attributional dimension of intentionality was originally introduced by Heider in 1958 but was integrated with controllability by Russell in 1982. Hanrahan, Grove, and Hattie (1989) provided support for distinguishing between intentionality and controllability, particularly for attributions for negative events. Although the correlation between the two dimensions for attributions made for positive events was relatively strong ($r = .67$), this correlation was notably weaker for attributions made for negative events ($r = .38$). The distinction between the two dimensions is logical when thinking of some attributions for failure or poor performances. For example, I may attribute my poor tennis performance to being distracted by the crowd. With practice I can learn to control my attention and not be distracted by the crowd, so this attribution is personally controllable. I did not, however, enter the tennis court intending to be distracted, so the attribution was unintentional.

This section has defined attributions, attributional style, and attributional dimensions, and has explained the dimensions of internality, stability, controllability, globality, and intentionality. The following text will describe the perspectives of the major theorists relevant to sport-related attribution research.

Despite the current interest in cognitive and social cognitive paradigms in psychology, attribution theory can be traced back to the work of Heider (1944, 1958). Later theories that have had a considerable influence on the field are also based on Heider's original work. The perspectives put forward by Jones and Davis (1965), Kelley (1967), and Weiner (Weiner, 1986; Weiner et al., 1972) have been dominant, although the works of Bem (1972), Kruglanski (1975), Schacter and Singer (1962), Seligman and coworkers (Abramson, Seligman, & Teasdale, 1978), and Peterson et al. (Peterson, 1990; Peterson, Maier, & Seligman, 1993) have all had a significant influence on the theory and application of attributions. Although some of these theoretical perspectives have not been used much in the sport and exercise psychology literature, a brief historical sketch of all these theories will increase the understanding of the attribution processes that have been studied in sport contexts.

Heider Heider is considered the founding father of attribution theory. Although his seminal book, *The Psychology of Interpersonal Relations* (Heider, 1958), is often used as the benchmark against which other attribution perspectives are compared, his 1944 article in *Psychological Review* should be cited as the beginning of the contemporary literature on attributions. In this paper, Heider suggested that the determination of the locality ("locus") of an attribution was related to the concept of "unit formation." By this he meant that both causes (origins) and effects constituted causal units and that by studying the similarity between origins and effects, inferences or attributions about the event could be made. Similarly, Heider suggested that "person" attributions were more common than situational attributions because he believed that people were the "prototype of origins." Such suggestions have fuelled a great deal of research into attribution errors and biases, as well as the attribution of responsibility. Developing these ideas in his book, Heider (1958) began formulating his "naive psychology," or what became known as the phenomenology of the layperson. Three fundamental propositions stem from this approach. First, to understand the behavior of individuals, one must understand how they perceive and describe their social environment. Second, Heider assumed that people seek a stable and predictable environment in their effort to control their surroundings and anticipate the behavior of others. Finally, Heider suggested that the processes of perceiving objects and people were similar and that to understand behavior, people will look toward the dispositional qualities of the individual.

Jones and Davis In 1979 Edward Jones (Jones, 1979) commented that "getting from acts to dispositions, or more generally, making inferences from behavior about personality, is a ubiquitous activity of paramount significance for all of us" (p. 107). Some 14 years earlier, Jones and Davis had formulated their theory of correspondent inferences, in which they attempted to explain how people infer dispositions, or personality characteristics, of individuals from their behavior (Jones & Davis, 1965).

This approach, therefore, is one of social ("other person") attribution rather than the self-perception more commonly found in the sport psychology literature. For example, one might gain more information about athletes' commitment by observing their enthusiasm for training in adverse conditions than one would get from observing athletes in conditions that are comfortable and positive.

Kelley Kelley's perspective (Kelley, 1967, 1972) is similar to that of Jones and Davis (1965). Using his "principle of co-variation," Kelley suggested that people arrive at a cause for an event by processing information about whether accompanying conditions and circumstances vary or not as the event varies. This process was considered analogous to experimental methods in which the event or outcome (dependent variable) is studied in relation to associated conditions (independent variables). Hence, Kelley and Michela (1980) said, "The effect is attributed to the factor with which it covaries" (p. 462).

Weiner Bernard Weiner's contribution to the field of attribution theory has been highly significant, nowhere more so than in the area of attribution

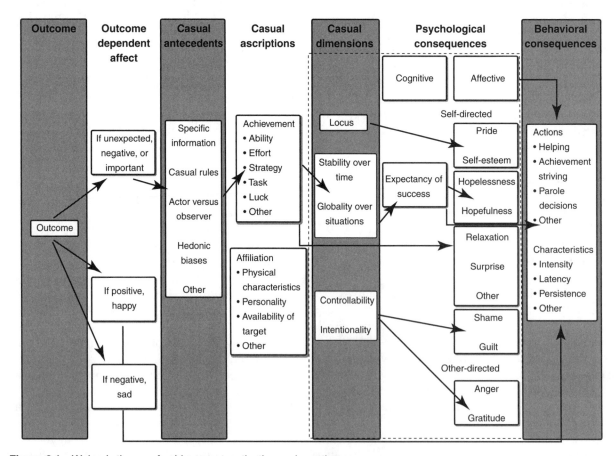

Figure 6.1 Weiner's theory of achievement motivation and emotion.

Reprinted, by permission, from B. Weiner, 1972, *Theories of motivation: From mechanism to cognition* (United Kingdom: Markham Publishing). By permission of B. Weiner.

processes associated with achievement contexts (Weiner, 1979, 1980, 1985a, 1986, 1992, 1995; Weiner et al., 1972). Weiner's research originated with investigations into the attributional responses to academic success and failure in the classroom. This work was extended into research on links between attributions and emotions, behavioral correlates of the attribution–emotion relationship, whether people make spontaneous attributions in everyday life, and the consequences of attributional thinking associated with social conduct. For a summary of Weiner's attributional theory of achievement motivation and emotion, see figure 6.1. The theory is organized around the simple notions of certain outcomes generating attributional thinking, which, in turn, are organized into dimensions. These have particular psychological and behavioral consequences (Weiner, 1986, 1992, 1995).

This theory shows that an outcome may generate positive or negative emotion (attribution-independent affect) and, especially in the case of negative, unexpected, or important outcomes, a search for the reasons for the outcome. Various antecedent factors will affect the nature of these attributions. The attributions themselves are thought to be organized into key dimensions that, in turn, influence the psychological consequences of the attributions, such as expectancy change or emotional feeling (attribution-dependent affect), such as, for example, pride. Finally, these consequences may affect behaviors such as offering help or achievement motivation.

Aspects of Weiner's model have been tested in many contexts, including achievement and affiliation settings. Central to the model is the belief that people organize their attributional thinking around dimensions of locus of causality, stability, and controllability.

Because of its focus on achievement contexts, Weiner's theory has had more recent and more direct application to sport and physical activity than have the theories of Heider, Jones and Davis, or Kelley. On whichever theory they base their investigations, researchers need tools to measure attributions or attributional style. The next section presents a discussion of measurement issues and instruments.

Measuring Attributions and Attributional Style

Self-report questionnaires are the most commonly used method of assessing attributions or attributional style within sport and exercise. Assessing attributions about a specific situation at a specific time is known as measuring states. Trait measures are those that assess attributional style, the generally consistent manner in which people account for outcomes across time and situations. Whether measuring states or traits, investigators must think carefully about the focus of the attributions.

Performance Versus Outcome

Many studies have investigated the different attributions of winners and losers. Winners are often found to make more internal and stable attributions than losers do (e.g., Aiken, McClure & Siegert, 1998). Other studies have compared attributions of individuals' best and worse performances. These studies also found that attributions for best performances tend to be more internal, stable, and controllable than attributions for worst performances (Hamilton & Jordan, 2000). Unfortunately, sometimes people equate winning with success and losing with failure. Although many winners feel successful, some athletes who win do not feel successful (e.g., win the gold medal in swimming but fail to achieve a personal best time). Similarly, many athletes do not win yet feel successful. In major marathons, for example, technically only one runner wins and thousands lose, yet many nonwinners may feel successful because they completed their first marathon or achieved a personal time goal.

Athletes may make different attributions depending on whether they are asked to make attributions for their performance or for the outcome. Biddle and Hill (1992) found that competitive squash players made attributions of personality, motivation, and effort for outcome, but not performance. Similarly, Hanrahan and Gross (2005) asked masters athletes competing in swimming and track to make attributions for their performances before they knew the outcomes and then later to make attributions for the outcomes when they were announced at the end of the day. The attributions were for the same swims or runs, but the responses were in terms of performance first and outcome later. Participants rated their performances as more successful than their outcomes. In addition, performances were perceived to result more from internal and intentional causes than were outcomes (Hanrahan & Gross). The point here is that researchers may get one result if they ask athletes to make attributions for the outcome and a different result if they ask for attributions for their performances.

Before the development of psychometrically sound questionnaires, researchers simply asked participants for their attributions or used a checklist approach (e.g., Vallerand, 1987). The attributions were then analyzed as individual attributions (e.g., winners made more attributions to ability than did losers), or the researchers coded the attributions along dimensions, possibly assuming dimensional properties that were not perceived or intended by the participants.

Causal Dimension Scale

Using Weiner's (1979) three dimensions of internality, stability, and controllability, Russell (1982) developed the Causal Dimension Scale (CDS). Russell designed this scale specifically to eliminate possible errors caused by researchers' assumptions. In the CDS the participants decide on the dimensional properties of their attributions. The CDS was developed using eight hypothetical achievement scenarios. Respondents were supplied with attributions that they rated on the three dimensions. In the final version of the CDS, three subscales were used to measure each dimension. For example, the stability dimension was measured by rating the attribution on nine-point Likert scales anchored by permanent–temporary, variable over time–stable over time, and changeable–unchanging (Russell).

Although the CDS was later used with actual situations that allowed participants to create their own attributions (e.g., Grove, Hanrahan, & McInman, 1991; McAuley & Gross, 1983; Van Raalte, 1994), a number of potential problems existed. First, the assumption that the measure developed using hypothetical events could be used in real situations was not tested. Second, the assumption that the psychometric properties of the CDS remain the same when free-response attributions are used in place of supplied attributions was not tested. Third, the wording of the CDS allows respondents to make more than one attribution for a particular situation but allows them only one opportunity to rate the attributions on the dimensions. If more than one attribution is made, are the respondents averaging across their responses for the dimensional ratings or just rating the attribution that is most salient to them? Fourth, controllability and intentionality are confounded in the same subscale. As mentioned earlier, intentionality and controllability are separate dimensions, particularly when rating attributions for negative events. Finally, a number of studies questioned the reliability and validity of the controllability subscale (e.g., McAuley & Gross; Russell, McAuley, & Tarico, 1987; Vallerand & Richer, 1988).

Causal Dimension Scale II

Overall, the CDS was a good first step in allowing respondents to rate their own attributions along dimensions. The methodological concerns, however, prompted the development of the CDSII (McAuley, et al., 1992). In this second version of the instrument, the internality and stability subscales remained unchanged. New items were added to the controllability subscale to represent both personal control and external control. Psychometric analysis resulted in the deletion of all the original controllability items, and the creation of two new subscales (personal and external control) with three items each. In the development of the CDSII only actual achievement events were used, and respondents made their own attributions. Intentionality items were deleted, so controllability and intentionality were no longer confounded. The CDSII still has the potential problem that individuals rate multiple attributions for the single situation.

In a study of the psychometric properties of the CDSII with adolescent athletes, Crocker, Eklund, and Graham (2002) suggested the need for further instrument development. Although designed to measure the stability dimension, the item changeable–unchangeable was also related to internality and personal control. In addition, a high correlation (> .8) was present between the internality and personal control subscales, suggesting that at least for adolescents, they are not distinct constructs.

Sport Attributional Style Scale

Hanrahan et al. (1989) developed the Sport Attributional Style Scale (SASS) as a sport-specific measure of attributional style. Similar to the CDS and the CDSII, the SASS allows a variety of attributions and requires the respondents to classify their attributions along dimensions. Unlike the CDS measures, the SASS asks respondents to provide the single most likely cause of each event, avoiding the problem of making dimensional ratings across multiple attributions. Two other main differences between the CDS measures and the SASS are that the SASS measures attributional style (i.e., a trait measure) and considers five attributional dimensions. The dimensions included are internality, stability, globality, controllability, and intentionality.

To measure attributional style, researchers need respondents to make attributions about a number of events. The SASS initially involved 12 positive and 12 negative situations that were matched for content. Almost 300 undergraduate physical education students completed this initial version of the SASS (Hanrahan, et al., 1989). Confirmatory factor analysis provided reasonable support for the five dimensions for both positive and negative events. After further psychometric analyses, four pairs of items were deleted, resulting in a 16-item measure.

To determine whether the use of hypothetical situations is a valid method of measuring sport-related attributional style, Hanrahan and Grove (1990a) examined the consistency between responses to the hypothetical events of the SASS and responses to actual sporting situations. Athletes rated their attributions about real-life sporting situations along the same dimensions as those used in the SASS and then completed the SASS. Correlations between actual sporting situations and hypothetical situations were significant for 9 of the 10 subscales.

To check that the SASS is appropriate for use with nonuniversity samples, an additional study tested the factor structure and internal consistency of the SASS with athletes outside the university environment (Hanrahan & Grove, 1990a). Confirmatory factor analysis again supported the factor structure, and the internal consistency was stronger for the nonuniversity sample than it was for the original student sample. Because the 16-item version of the SASS is somewhat lengthy, taking 20 to 30 minutes to complete, the feasibility of using a shortened 10-item version was investigated (Hanrahan & Grove, 1990b). Using three different versions of the 10-item form and four samples, correlations between the 16-item and 10-item forms were found to be consistently high (mean = .94). Using the longer version does not appear to offer any advantage.

Revised SASS Recently the SASS was revised to reflect the split of the controllability dimension into personal and external control, as noted in the CDSII. This revised version (SASS–R) has not been psychometrically tested, but it has revealed results in expected directions, particularly for personal control (Hanrahan & Seefeld, 2005). The SASS–R (as well as the original SASS) also has been modified and used to measure state attributions rather than attributional style. Respondents are simply asked to make attributions about specific outcomes or performances and then rate the attribution along the same dimensions used in the trait version. See figure 6.2 for the state version of SASS–R worded to measure performance attributions. As mentioned earlier, correlations between the state (real-life) and trait (hypothetical) versions were found to be significant on 9 of the 10 subscales (Hanrahan & Grove, 1990a). Future

work is needed to establish the psychometrics of the SASS–R in both its trait and its state forms, particularly because the state version has only one response per dimension.

Exercise Version of SASS Recently work has been done to create a version of the SASS to measure attributional style in exercise (Muller, 2005). Significant differences in attributional style were found between exercisers and nonexercisers on the internality, stability, and globality dimensions but not on the controllability or intentionality dimensions. Muller confirmed these results using other measures.

Qualitative Analysis of Spontaneous Attributions

The question has arisen whether people spontaneously make attributions or whether they make them only when prompted by questionnaires. In a review of 17 studies Weiner (1985b) found clear support for the proposition that attributions do occur as part of everyday life. Spontaneous attributions are most likely to be made when unexpected outcomes occur or when goals are not achieved, suggesting that naturally occurring attributions for success may be less frequent than those for failure (Weiner, 1985b). Interviews with elite triathletes, however, found that these athletes provided more explanations for success than for failure (Minniti & Hanrahan, 2005).

Researchers need to consider how to measure naturally occurring attributions, regardless of their frequency. Stratton, Munton, Hanks, Hard, and Davidson (1988) developed the Leeds Attributional Coding System (LACS) to explore attributions in qualitative material with quantitative analysis. Although the LACS was initially devised to be used in family therapy settings, it can be used with any qualitative material including naturally occurring dialogue, interviews, focus group discussions, and speech material. Specific attributions or any answers to the question "Why?" are then identified and extracted from the text. Causes and outcomes are then separated. For example, in the statement "I fell off the beam because I got distracted," falling off the beam is the outcome and being distracted is the cause. The next step in the LACS is to identify the speaker (the person making the attribution), the agent (the person or circumstance that is bringing about the outcome), and the target (the person or circumstance affected by the cause and located in the outcome). The attributions are then coded along the dimensions of internality, stability, controllability,

Please rate how well you think you performed in your main event. (Circle one number.)

1	2	3	4	5	6	7
Very poor performance			Average			Very good performance

Please write down what you believe was the single most likely cause of your level of performance (e.g., why you performed well or poorly today):

Is this cause something about you or something about other people or circumstances? (Circle one number.)

1	2	3	4	5	6	7
Totally due to other people or circumstances						Totally due to me

In the future when performing in a competition, will this cause be present again? (Circle one number.)

1	2	3	4	5	6	7
Will never again be present						Will always be present

Is the cause something that influences just your performance in competitions, or does it also influence other areas of your life? (Circle one number.)

1	2	3	4	5	6	7
Influences just this particular event						Influences all my life events

Is the cause something that is controllable by you? (Circle one number.)

1	2	3	4	5	6	7
Controllable						Uncontrollable

Is the cause something that is controllable by others? (Circle one number.)

1	2	3	4	5	6	7
Controllable						Uncontrollable

Is the cause something that is intentional or unintentional? (Circle one number.)

1	2	3	4	5	6	7
Intentional						Unintentional

Figure 6.2 The state version of the SASS–R worded to measure performance attributions.

universality, and globality. The coded and quantified data can then be put in a data file for use with statistical packages. See Munton, Silvester, Stratton, and Hanks (1999) for a detailed description of the process or Biddle, Hanrahan, and Sellars (2001) for a simplified example. Others have suggested that discourse analysis, a thriving field in social psychology, should be used more for the analysis of attributions in sport (Faulkner & Finlay, 2002; Finlay & Faulkner, 2003).

The bulk of research related to sport has used versions of either the CDS or the SASS to measure attributions or attributional style. Qualitative research in the area remains relatively sparse. The following section considers the major topics of sport-related attribution research.

Research on Attributions in Sport Contexts

Most research on sport-related attributions has focused on one of four main areas: attributional bias, predictors of attributions, consequences of attributions, or attribution retraining. This section reviews research in each of these areas.

Attributional Bias

People tend to attribute success to their own efforts, abilities, or dispositions while attributing failure to luck, task difficulty, or other external factors (Heider, 1958; Kelley, 1971). Two explanations may account for this bias. The ego-defensive explanation states that the attributional bias allows people to maintain or enhance their self-esteem (Miller & Ross, 1975). Researchers who adhere to this explanation often refer to the attributional bias as the self-serving bias. By taking credit for success and blaming external factors for failure, people can feel good about themselves. For example, De Michele, Gansneder, and Solomon (1998) found that winning collegiate wrestlers made attributions that were significantly more internal, stable, and personally controllable than did losers.

An alternative explanation of the attributional bias is based on the assumption that successful outcomes are intended and failures are unintended. Therefore, people logically attribute success to their own efforts or abilities because things went as planned. If things did not go as planned, some outside, interfering factor must have been the cause (Miller & Ross, 1975). People do not intend to fail, so if failure occurs they attribute it to external factors. Individuals are not trying to protect their egos; they are just being logical. This is the cognitive explanation for the bias that appears to exist.

Whether the attributional bias is due to cognitive or self-serving reasons, it has been repeatedly demonstrated in multiple sports including table tennis (McAuley & Gross, 1983), volleyball (Gill, Ruder, & Gross, 1982), squash and racquetball (Mark, Mutrie, Brooks, & Harris, 1984), and Australian rules football and soccer (Patchell, 2004). Interestingly, the attributional bias has been found to exist even when participants were unaware of how successful they had been in the task (Zientek & Breakwell, 1988). In the sporting environment, attributional bias has been found to exist not only in athletes but also in coaches and spectators (Grove et al., 1991). This bias in spectators increases in strength as the degree to which fan identification with their teams increases (Wann & Wilson, 2001). Wann and Wilson also found that the more fans identified with their team, the more attributions they made for their team's performance. This increase in attributions could be because they found the situations to be more personally relevant than did those who had weaker team identification.

Predictors of Attributions

A number of recent studies have been conducted to identify possible predictors of the attributions that people make in sport contexts or the attributional styles that they exhibit. The presence of mental retardation, year in school, age, gender, and type of sport have not been found to influence attributions. Kozub (2002) found no differences in the attributions made between children with and without mental retardation. Similarly, no significant differences have been found in the attributions made by high school freshmen and senior track athletes (Hamilton & Jordan, 2000). No significant differences due to age were found in the attributions made by children aged 8 to 14 years (Chase, 2001). In a study of masters athletes no significant gender differences in attributions were identified (Hanrahan & Gross, 2005). Athletes from objectively and subjectively evaluated sports made similar attributions, so the type of sport also appears to have no influence on attributions (Leith & Prapavessis, 1989).

Some variables, however, have been found to be related to differences in attributions. Attributions have been found to differ depending on levels of expertise, self-efficacy, self-esteem, task orientation, and team cohesion. In basketball, experts make more strategy attributions than do either nonexperts or novices (Cleary & Zimmerman, 2001). Children higher in self-efficacy showed a tendency to attribute failure to lack of effort, whereas those with lower self-efficacy made attributions of failure to lack of ability. Similarly, children high in self-esteem made attributions that were more internal, stable, and personally controllable for physical and social competence than did children low in self-esteem (Weiss, Ebbeck, McAuley, & Wiese, 1990). Although ego orientation was not found to predict attributions, task orientation did (Hanrahan & Gross, 2005). Specifically, task orientation significantly predicted globality ratings for performance and both globality and stability ratings for outcome. A higher task orientation predicted more global and more stable attributions (Hanrahan & Gross). In terms of cohesion, athletes who perceived high task and social cohesion attributed significantly more personal control for a poor performance than athletes who perceived lower levels of cohesion (Patchell, 2004). In addition, athletes who perceived high social cohesion were more apt to attribute poor performance to unstable and specific causes, and good performance to global causes, than were athletes who perceived lower levels of team cohesion (Patchell).

Consequences of Attributions

Recent research studies have been conducted to identify possible consequences of different types of attributions or attributional styles. Outcome variables that have been identified to date include expectancies, emotions, performance, and persistence. As mentioned earlier in this chapter, Weiner (1986) argued that the stability of attributions determines changes in expectancies for future success. Attributions of success to stable factors lead to expectancies of future success, and attributions of failure to stable factors lead to expectancies of future failure. Attributions of success or failure to unstable causes can lead to expectancies of either success or failure. A study by Singer and McCaughan (1978) supported this theory by finding that attributions of success to stable factors enhanced positive expectations. Rudisill (1989) noted that attributions for failure to internal, unstable, and controllable causes were related to positive expectations for future success. Attributions of failure to effort rather than ability have been found to relate to future expectancies of success (Grove & Pargman, 1986). Effort can be considered as both more unstable and more controllable than ability. The controllability dimension may be as related to future expectations as is the stability dimension of attributions. Not all research, however, supports the relationship between the stability dimension and expectancy of success. In a study of 98 athletes, Belciug (1991) found no significant correlation between stability scores and future expectancy of success, although when prior expectancy was high, confirmation of that expectancy was related to stable factors.

Weiner's (1986) theory also indicates that the attributional dimensions relate to emotions in different ways. We already know that the stability dimension relates to expectancies. Logic tells us that emotions related to expectancy, such as hope, also are related to the stability dimension. The internality dimension is associated with self-esteem emotions such as pride, and the controllability dimension is related to social emotions such as pity and guilt. Social emotions such as shame and guilt are self-directed, and social emotions of anger and pity are other-directed (Weiner, 1995). Most research on attributions and emotions in physical activity only partially supports Weiner's theory. The attributions that middle-aged adults gave for dropping out of an exercise program were only moderately associated with emotional reactions (McAuley, Poag, Gleason, & Wraith, 1990). Vlachopoulos, Biddle, and Fox (1997) found that attributions added a small amount of additional variance to positive affective reactions but much less than that of perceptions of success and task involvement. Attributions did not contribute at all to the prediction of negative affect. More recently, Graham, Kowalski, and Crocker (2002) found that attributional dimensions predicted emotion but did not support the theoretical links between dimensions and specific emotions. Overall, perceptions of success and performance satisfaction predict emotion in physical activity, and attributions account for some additional variance (Biddle et al., 2001).

In the previous section we stated that self-efficacy predicted attributions. Attributions, however, have also been found to predict self-efficacy. In a study of competitive sprinters, success feedback increased self-efficacy and failure feedback decreased self-efficacy (Gernigon & Delloye, 2003). For males, however, the stability of attributions mediated the relationship between feedback and self-efficacy, and for females the personal controllability dimension predicted self-efficacy. In a study of golfers, the stability dimension predicted postcompetition self-efficacy but only under conditions of perceived success (Bond, Biddle, & Ntoumanis, 2001). Under conditions of perceived failure, there were no attributional predictors of postcompetition self-efficacy.

Attributions for positive events also appear to be more relevant than attributions for negative events to predictions of performance and persistence. Competitive athletes with a more desirable attributional style for positive events (i.e., internal, stable, personally controllable, externally uncontrollable, and intentional) exhibited a higher level of both self-rated and coach-rated performance than did athletes with a less desirable attributional style for positive events, particularly for those with an ego orientation above the sample mean (Hanrahan, Cerin, & Hartel, 2003). Figures 6.3 and 6.4 graphically demonstrate the interaction between attributional style for positive events and ego orientation. Besides predicting performance, attributional style for positive events also significantly predicted athletes' persistence as rated by coaches (Hanrahan, et al., 2003).

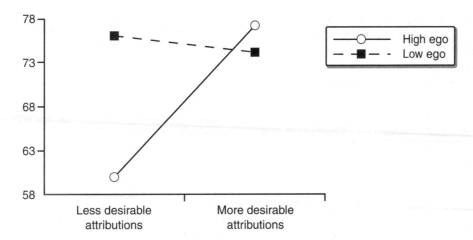

Figure 6.3   The interaction effect of desirable attributions for positive events and ego orientation on athletes' self-ratings of performance (Hanrahan et al., 2003).

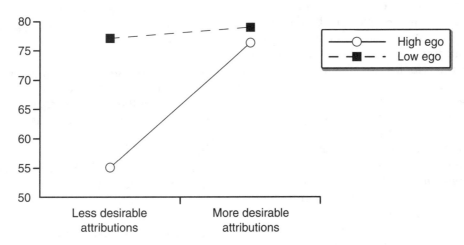

Figure 6.4   The interaction effect of desirable attributions for positive events and ego orientation on coaches' ratings of athletes' performances (Hanrahan et al., 2003).

Attribution Retraining

Interventions have been designed to change attributions based on the premise that people can revise their attributional styles. The objective is to alter attributions that are unsuitable and may lead to cognitive, emotional, or behavioral deficits by replacing them with more appropriate attributions that lead to positive and future-oriented thoughts. Forsterling (1985, 1988, 2001) identified three theoretical approaches that can be used in attribution retraining: Weiner's (1986) attributional model, Bandura's (1986) self-efficacy model, and Abramson et al.'s (1978) learned helplessness model. Weiner (1986) stated that people need to create positive emotional states and expectations. Therefore, favorable attribu-

tions for success include ability, and desirable attributions for failure include poor strategy. Bandura's self-efficacy model indicates that the attributions that people make create positive or negative perceptions of their ability to perform specific behaviors. As with the attributional model, desirable attributions for success include ability, and favorable attributions for failure include poor strategy as well as low effort. The learned helplessness model focuses on avoiding a perceived lack of control as well as changing attributions for failure that are associated with depression. Numerous researchers have tested the effectiveness of attribution retraining in a variety of areas including education (e.g., Dodds, 1994; Miranda, Villaescusa, & Vidal-Abarca; 1997), social skills (e.g., Carlyon, 1997), forgiveness (e.g.,

Al-Mabuk, Dedrick, & Vanderah, 1998; Fincham, Paleari, & Regalia, 2002), and therapeutic recreation (Dieser & Ruddell, 2002).

In sport settings, most attribution-retraining research has emphasized altering attributions for failure among recreational, novice, or youth athletes. In a study with collegiate recreational basketball players, retraining attributions for failure to controllable and unstable causes resulted in an increase in functional attributions as well as improvement in performance (Orbach, Singer, & Murphey, 1997). Replicating this study with tennis players, Orbach, Singer, and Price (1999) found that those who learned to make controllable and unstable attributions for failure had greater expectations for future success and more positive emotions than those who were trained to make uncontrollable and stable attributions or were in a nonattributional control group. Also demonstrating the effectiveness of attribution retraining in a sport setting, Sinnott and Biddle (1998) used modeling and information techniques to retrain maladaptive attributional profiles by focusing on strategy attributions for failure. After training, these 11- and 12-year-old children made more internal and controllable attributions for success. Furthermore, they showed corresponding increases in perceived success and had higher intrinsic motivation scores. Miserandino (1998) found that feedback with attribution retraining was more effective than feedback alone in improving the shooting performance of high school basketball players. The attribution training focused on attributing failure to lack of effort rather than lack of ability. After the four-week intervention, the attribution training group not only significantly improved their shooting performance but also had stronger mastery orientation.

In summary, attribution-retraining research has demonstrated that attributions can be changed and that these changes in attributions appear to result in alterations in other variables related to performance and motivation. Many of these attribution-retraining studies have focused on increasing perceptions of control.

Additional Perspectives on Control

Central to attributional and other social-cognitive perspectives in recent years has been the notion of perceived control. Most of this research has centered on the old construct of locus of control (i.e., the internality dimension), but more recently Skinner (1995, 1996) has reconceptualized control with an interesting and important model.

Agent–Means–Ends and Different Belief Systems

Skinner (1995, 1996) made the point that one way to conceptualize the vast array of control constructs is to analyze them in relation to their place within the tripartite model of agent (person), means (behaviors), and ends (outcomes), as illustrated in figure 6.5.

Agent–Means and Capacity Beliefs Agent–means connections involve expectations that the agent (self) has the means to produce a response (but not necessarily an outcome). This concept involves capacity beliefs—beliefs concerning whether the agent has the ability to produce the appropriate cause. For example, if effort is deemed important to produce success in sport, then positive capacity beliefs must involve the belief that "I can try hard in sport." Self-efficacy research has adopted this approach and has become a major force in motivational research in exercise and sport psychology (Bandura, 1997). Similarly, perceived competence approaches adopt the agent–means approach (Harter, 1978).

Means–Ends and Strategy Beliefs Means–ends connections involve beliefs about the link between potential causes and outcomes. This concept involves strategy beliefs—beliefs concerning the necessary availability of means to produce the

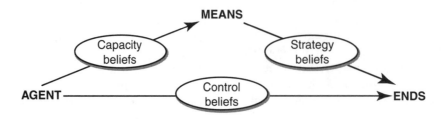

Figure 6.5 Agent–means–ends model of Skinner.

desired outcomes. For example, if trying hard is necessary in sport, a strategy belief is "I need to try hard to be successful at sport," a belief that contrasts with the capacity belief "I can try hard in sport." Typically, means–ends relations involve attributional approaches, outcome expectancies, and locus of control (Rotter, 1966, 1975), constructs familiar in sport and exercise psychology.

Agent–Ends and Control Beliefs As Skinner (1995) put it, "Connections between people and outcomes prescribe the prototypical definitions of control" (p. 554). Hence this connection involves control beliefs. This idea involves the belief by the agent that a desirable outcome is within his or her capability: "I can be successful at sport if I want to." This viewpoint must involve both capacity and strategy beliefs.

Agent–ends connections are less easy to recognize in sport and exercise psychology. Some of Bandura's writings (e.g., Bandura, 1989, 1997) suggest that self-efficacy can have an agent–ends connection as well as the more traditional agent–means connection. For example, Bandura (1989) said, "Self-beliefs of efficacy influence how people feel, think, *and act*" (p. 3; emphasis added). Similarly, outcome expectancies can involve agent–ends as well as means–ends. Behavioral regulations, as depicted in self-determination theory (Deci & Ryan, 1985) and now popular in physical activity (Chatzisarantis, Hagger, Biddle, Smith, & Wang, 2003; Markland, 1999), may suit an agent–ends analysis.

Plotting Beliefs on a Competence System

Skinner (1995) proposed that humans have a need to seek competence. If this is the case, we can analyze control-related beliefs within a system of competence seeking, or what Skinner (1995) referred to as the competence system (figure 6.6). This model shows that action is regulated by initial control beliefs. Action, in turn, produces some form of outcome that is evaluated and interpreted in respect of other beliefs (self, causes); these can lead to further control beliefs. The place of beliefs within this system may be important in analyzing the contributions of control-related constructs in exercise and sport. For example, locus of control beliefs precede performance and are proximal to behavior, whereas attributions are beliefs that interpret past behavior and are likely to be less proximal or even quite distal to future actions.

Locus of Control

Locus of control of reinforcements refers to the extent to which people perceive that reinforcements are within their own control, are controlled by others, or are due to chance. The construct is a means–ends (contingency) approach according to Skinner's (1995, 1996) model. The locus of control (LOC) construct stems from a social learning theory approach to personality (Rotter, 1954) in which general beliefs are thought to develop from expectations based on prior reinforcements. When the value attached to such reinforcements is added, it becomes an expectancy-value approach to motivation. Rotter (1966), in his seminal monograph, formalized the construct of LOC and suggested that a generalized belief existed for internal versus external control of reinforcement.

Note, however, that Rotter (1966) stated that his psychometric measure of LOC (the internal–external scale, or I–E scale) was a measure of generalized

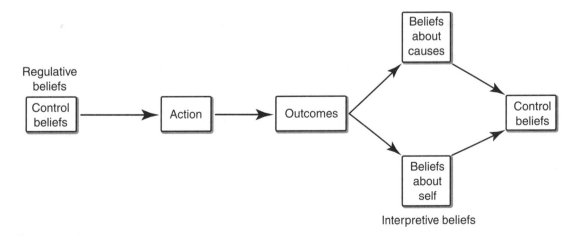

Figure 6.6 Skinner's competence system model.

Reprinted, by permission, from E. Skinner, 1995, *Perceived control, motivation, and coping* (Thousand Oaks, CA: Sage Publishing).

expectancy and therefore was likely to have a relatively low behavioral prediction, although across a wide variety of situations. The measure was also likely to have greater predictive powers in novel or ambiguous situations because in specific well-known contexts more situation-specific expectancies will be used. These might be outcome expectancies in a means–ends analysis or efficacy expectations in an agent–means analysis. This point raises the issue of measurement specificity.

A well-known typology in our field is to categorize constructs within a hierarchy ranging from global levels of measurement (e.g., global self-esteem) through contextual, or domain-related, perceptions (e.g., in sport), to situation-specific perceptions (e.g., "right now"). Such typologies have been used to good effect in physical self-perception measurement (Fox, 1997) and intrinsic motivation (Vallerand, 1997). Research investigating the link between perceived control (LOC) scales and physical activity has mainly been in the area of participation in exercise and has taken three routes. First, some researchers have tried to identify links between generalized LOC and exercise, some have used domain-related (health) LOC, and others have used exercise- and fitness-specific measures.

Collectively, the literature provides weak support for LOC in predicting fitness and exercise behaviors. The extent to which this could be a reflection of the inadequacies of the activity or LOC measures remains to be seen. At best these studies suggest that some group differences may exist between exercisers and nonexercisers at a cross-sectional level on LOC. One cannot ascertain, however, whether such differences developed because of involvement or whether they were influential in individuals' initial decisions to become active.

Analysis of Control-Related Properties

The conclusion from these studies appears to be that LOC or health LOC does not strongly relate to exercise behavior. Such a conclusion has prompted researchers to ask why this is the case. Four main possibilities exist. First, the theory could be wrong or not applicable to exercise. Second, the measuring tools may not be sensitive enough or appropriate enough to assess the relationship between LOC and exercise participation. Third, fitness or exercise "externals" are rare people, thus making it difficult from a research perspective to find relationships between exercise participants' LOC or to discriminate between groups.

The final possible reason requires us to return to Skinner's model and her notion of the competence system. By plotting LOC onto the competence system in figure 6.6, we can conceptualize LOC as a set of regulative beliefs that precedes action and outcome. Thus, we would expect LOC to have a strong influence on behavior. So why are the data weak or inconsistent? Given the potential for regulative beliefs to influence behavior, it may be that LOC has been inadequately assessed or poorly operationalized. Rotter (1966) said that generalized LOC beliefs should have a wide range of application but lack predictive strength. Given the weak research designs in much of the LOC literature in sport and exercise psychology, the weakness of relations between LOC and behavior should perhaps not be surprising.

Given that we seem to allocate greater importance to studies that demonstrate strength of relationships rather than stability and width of application, we may be applying LOC in a suboptimal way. In addition, if LOC is primarily involving means–ends relations, and hence strategy beliefs, it is concerned with thoughts about what is required for success (contingency) rather than beliefs about whether one actually possesses such requirements (competence). The predictive power of LOC on behavior may thus be limited. By using Skinner's (1995) competence system and tripartite models, we may have some explanations for why LOC has not been particularly successful in predicting motivated behavior in sport or exercise.

Analyzing Attributions Using the Skinner Framework

Attributional thinking, placed within the competence system shown in figure 6.6 is, as we know, primarily about interpretation of outcomes, the consequences of which may affect future regulative beliefs and actions (Weiner, 1986). Outcomes are, therefore, more distant from (future) actions and outcomes than most regulative beliefs, such as LOC. This explanation may account for the difficulty that researchers have had in demonstrating strong relationships between attributions and behavior in sport. Only prospective studies can test this notion, and these types of studies are rare. We must also assume that little will change between making the attributions and subsequent behavior, yet we have not tested the longevity or consistency of attributions over time. To make matters worse, we have nearly always assessed attributions immediately after performance. At the anecdotal level, however, coaches, athletes, and sport psychologists tell us that attributions are an important part of the sport experience, are reflected in subsequent thoughts, feelings, and actions, and change with time.

If attributional processing reflects means–ends connections, the same criticism leveled at LOC can be made of attributions. Means–ends connections involve strategy, not capacity, beliefs. Accordingly, attributional thinking looks to identify causes of outcomes (e.g., ability, effort, and luck) rather than to appraise whether the agent has access to these causes (e.g., effort). In reality, one could argue that true attributional thinking, while primarily being about identification of causes, is also a response to questions such as "Why did I fail at this task?" thus necessitating control beliefs (i.e., strategy and capacity beliefs). For example, athletes are unlikely to be interested in whether a particular game strategy caused success unless they think that they can produce that strategy. If so, attributions are more central to control beliefs and will involve agent–ends connections. True perceptions of control, through control beliefs, require a combination of competence and contingency. Attributions, but not LOC, include both. Attributional processing involves, as just argued, both means–ends (contingency) and agent–ends (competence). LOC, however, is primarily concerned with means–ends (contingency).

Although attributions traditionally are seen as means–ends connections, further support for attributions involving agent–ends processes comes from matching attributions against other agent–ends constructs. For example, outcome expectancies involve agent–ends connections, and attributions have been linked, mainly by the stability dimension, to beliefs concerning outcome expectancies.

Future Research Directions

The need for prospective studies to investigate the link between attributions and behavior in sport was mentioned earlier. Additional research is also needed on attribution retraining, attributions in team situations, and coach attributions.

As noted in the section on attribution retraining, physical activity studies in this area have focused on retraining attributions for failure. The potential importance of the role of attributions for success or positive events has been virtually ignored. Attributions for positive events have been found to play a bigger role than attributions for negative events in predicting postcompetition efficacy, performance, and persistence. Yet intervention studies focused on retraining attributions for positive events have only recently been considered. Hanrahan and Seefeld (2005) designed an intervention to have participants understand the interaction of thoughts, feelings, and behaviors; to focus on process rather than outcome; to attribute positive events to stable, global, and controllable factors; and to attribute negative events to specific, unstable, and controllable causes. The intervention group significantly increased the internality of their attributions for positive events from pretest to posttest and maintained an elevated score at follow-up. Internality and personal controllability of their attributions for negative events significantly increased from pretest to posttest but returned to original levels at follow-up. Attributions of positive events remained relatively stable in terms of perceived personal control for the intervention group but became significantly less personally controllable for the control group (Hanrahan & Seefeld). This study represents only initial research examining the effectiveness of retraining attributions for both positive and negative events. The results do suggest that training can influence at least some dimensions of attributions for positive events. Randomized control trials that include pretests, posttests, and follow-ups and that measure changes in attributions as well as variables affected by attributions such as efficacy, persistence, and performance need to be conducted.

Although research has suggested that people spontaneously make attributions (e.g., Weiner, 1985b), little research has investigated whether athletes are aware of the effect of attributions on their future thoughts, feelings, or behaviors. In interviews, elite triathletes said that they had considered definitions of success and attributions for success and failure before the interviews but were relatively unclear about the possible role of attributions in performance, and few had given any thought to maintaining or modifying attributions (Minniti & Hanrahan, 2005). The perceived effects of attributions for positive events related to an improved race or confident and positive feelings. Attributions for failure sometimes resulted in negative emotions, but some triathletes felt that these attributions could have positive effects (Minniti & Hanrahan). Athletes apparently may have varying levels of awareness related to the attributional process. What is not known is whether this awareness will influence the attribution-retraining process or increase the chances that athletes will experience positive effects following attributions for negative events.

A relatively unexplored area in attribution research is the investigation of attributions for individual versus team performance. Although both individual and team-sport athletes have participated in attribution research, we were unable to find research that has compared the attributions that athletes make for their own performance versus the attributions that they make for the performance of the team as a whole. Perceived team cohesion can influence individual performance attributions (Patchell, 2004), so it would be logical to hypothesize that cohesion would also influence attributions for team performance. Additional variables such as communication could potentially influence these attributions as well as moderate or mediate the effect of attributions on other variables.

Another underinvestigated area is the attributions of coaches. Do the attributions that coaches make about their own performance influence their emotions, performance, persistence, and expectancies? In addition, it could be useful to know whether the attributions that coaches make about the performance of their athletes influence self-fulfilling prophesies, coaches' decisions about selection, or starting lineups.

Conclusion

In this chapter we have defined key terms associated with the study of attributions, including the placement of attributions along dimensions of internality, stability, globality, intentionality, personal control, and external control. Work on attributions began more than 60 years ago when Heider investigated how people explain the behavior of others. Other theorists expanded this initial work to include how individuals explain events that happen to them, not just others. Most attribution research in the area of sport has been based on the work of Weiner, which considers how attributions can influence emotions and expectancies for future success.

The majority of attribution research both in and out of sport has relied on self-report questionnaires. Versions of the Causal Dimension Scale and the Sport Attributional Style Scale have dominated the physical activity attribution research. Regardless of the questionnaire or qualitative format used, researchers must make it clear to athletes whether they are to make attributions for performance or outcome.

Attributions have been found to differ depending on levels of expertise, self-efficacy, self-esteem, task orientation, and team cohesion, but they do not appear to be influenced by age, gender, or type of sport. Research has determined that attributions affect expectancies for future success, emotions, performance, and persistence. Because some attributions or attributional styles have been found to be more beneficial than others, attribution-retraining interventions have been developed to help people make more effective attributions. Traditionally, retraining has focused on attributions for failure, but current research suggests that attributions for success are equally if not more important. In the future, research may be extended to consider attributions for individual versus team performance as well as the attributions of coaches.

CHAPTER 7

Motivational Orientations and Sport Behavior

Maureen R. Weiss, PhD ▪ **Anthony J. Amorose, PhD**

The term *motivation* can perhaps be conceived best as *because* answers to a number of *why* questions (Weiss & Williams, 2004). Why do people start participating in physical activity or sport? Why do some participate primarily for the inherent pleasure of the activity, whereas others participate more because of social or external rewards? Why do some people try hard and persist in skill learning and competitive situations, whereas others give up easily? Ultimately, why do people discontinue a particular sport or activity? Implicit within these *why* questions and *because* answers is an understanding of the antecedents (i.e., what or who influences these variations in behavior) and anticipated consequences of motivation (i.e., physical, psychological, and social benefits or costs). This perspective helps us understand why motivation is one of the most important topics in sport psychology as we strive to maximize participation levels and the positive benefits of an active lifestyle.

Contemporary theory and research on motivation in sport and physical activity embrace an interactionist approach, or one that considers a combination of social-environmental and individual difference factors to explain motivated behavior (Weiss & Ferrer-Caja, 2002). Such approaches recognize that neither social nor personal factors alone are adequate for understanding variations in motivational orientations and behaviors in physical activity contexts. Both are instrumental for understanding motivational orientations and participation behaviors. As such, the theories and related research that we review in this chapter share common features in the social-contextual factors (e.g., parent feedback, coaching style, learning climate) and individual differences (e.g., perceived competence, perceived autonomy, subjective task values) that are highlighted in their respective models for understanding motivation.

In this chapter we review theories or conceptual models that have been supported in physical achievement contexts in terms of understanding participation motivation and behavior. These theories include competence motivation theory, self-determination theory, expectancy-value model, and sport commitment model. Second, we synthesize and consolidate relevant sport-related research for each conceptual framework. Finally, we present some ideas for future research that may help explain motivational orientations and behavior from each conceptual perspective. We begin the chapter, however, with a review of the early descriptive research on participation motivation and attrition, because these studies were crucial in shaping the way that we conceptualize motivational orientations and sport behavior today.

From Description to Theory Development in Participation Motivation and Attrition Research

Participation motivation and attrition entail the reasons why people continue and discontinue participation in sport or physical activity. In this section we trace the evolution of participation motivation and attrition research from descriptive to theory-based studies.

Early Research on Participation Motivation in Sport

Interest in participation motivation emerged in the 1970s with a study conducted by Alderman and Wood (1976) with Canadian young athletes. These authors found that incentives for participation such as affiliation (making friends), excellence (doing something well), arousal (seeking excitement), and esteem (recognition of one's achievements) were valued most strongly. Similar motives for participation were reported by sport type, gender, and age. Sapp and Haubenstricker (1978) conducted a large-scale study of participation motivation that was completed by more than 1,000 boys and girls 11 to 18 years of age. Major reasons cited for sport participation included having fun, learning and improving skills, becoming physically fit, and being with friends.

Many descriptive studies on participation motivation followed in the 1980s to build the knowledge base and glean findings that might be used to develop theory (see Gould & Petlichkoff, 1988; Weiss, 1993; Weiss & Petlichkoff, 1989). Some studies targeted participation motives across several sports (e.g., Gill, Gross, & Huddleston, 1983; Longhurst & Spink, 1987), and others focused on specific sports such as gymnastics (Klint & Weiss, 1986), swimming (Gould, Feltz, & Weiss, 1985), and ice hockey (Ewing, Feltz, Schultz, & Albrecht, 1988). Several common themes emerged for why young people participate in sport (see Weiss & Williams, 2004), including (a) to develop or demonstrate physical competence (i.e., learn and improve skills, become physically fit), (b) to gain social acceptance or approval (i.e., be with and make friends, receive approval from parents and coaches), and (c) to enjoy one's experiences (i.e., have fun, be challenged). These three common themes—physical competence, social acceptance, and enjoyment—are essential components of the theories that have been productive for understanding motivation in physical activity settings.

Concurrent with the research on reasons for participating in sport was the troubling finding that a large percentage (at least 35%) of participants drop out from a program each year (Gould, 1987). The topic of retention remains important for researchers and practitioners alike. Research on attrition from sport gained momentum in the 1980s to understand factors leading to discontinued involvement that might be helpful in reducing dropout rates.

Early Research on Attrition from Sport

An early study by Orlick (1974) inspired interest in why individuals drop out of sport. Orlick interviewed 60 former participants (ages 7 to 19 years) who cited negative reasons for discontinued involvement. Children under 10 years old cited lack of success and lack of playing time as their exclusive reasons, whereas older youth gave reasons such as pursuing other interests and school conflicts. A study of age-group swimmers conducted by McPherson, Marteniuk, Tihanyi, and Clark (1980) supported Orlick's finding that negative reasons were the cause of youth sport attrition. A majority identified at least one friend who had quit swimming the previous year, citing reasons such as too much pressure, lack of fun, too time consuming, and conflict with the coach. Moreover, 48% said that they wanted to quit at some time because of boredom, dislike for the coach, time demands, and interest in other activities.

These discouraging findings were not replicated in a large-scale study conducted by the Institute for the Study of Youth Sports at Michigan State University (Sapp & Haubenstricker, 1978; State of Michigan, 1978). Although 24% of 6- to 10-year-olds and 37% of 11- to 18-year-olds indicated a desire to discontinue their sport the following year, negative experiences identified in Orlick's study accounted for less than 15% of the reasons for sport withdrawal. Instead, primary reasons for discontinuing sport were interests in other activities and work responsibilities.

Several studies suggested that withdrawing from a program may be temporary or sport specific for most participants. Klint and Weiss (1986) reported that 95% of former club gymnasts were participating in another sport or gymnastics at a lower level of intensity; similarly, Johns, Lindner, and Wolko (1990) reported that 78% of former gymnasts had entered another sport. Gould, Feltz, Horn, and Weiss (1982) found that 68% of former youth swimmers were active in other sports and 80% planned to reenter swimming. Perhaps athletes found that alternative programs were better able to meet their needs for physical competence, social acceptance, and enjoyment motives. To determine if this was the case, Klint and Weiss (1986) and McClements, Fry, and Sefton (1982) assessed current *and* former participants about participation reasons. Klint and Weiss found that current gymnasts rated skill development, physical fitness, and competition as important, whereas former gymnasts rated fun and skill development as important reasons. McClements et al. found that boys who continued in ice hockey reported higher achievement reasons and fewer social and fun reasons than did boys who were no longer involved. These studies suggest that youth who discontinue sport may do so because their motives for initially joining were not satisfied.

In a review of research on participation motivation and attrition, Weiss and Petlichkoff (1989) stated that *dropout* is an inappropriate term because many youth transfer to other sports or activities, continue in the same sport at a different level, or make decisions based on developmental needs. That many youth drop in and drop out of sport suggests a developmental phenomenon of sampling activities and choosing those that allow for interests, competencies, and goals (i.e., do what friends are doing, demonstrate ability in a valued achievement area, pursue a career-related activity).

The 1990s and Beyond

Weiss and Petlichkoff (1989) suggested a number of important research directions in participation motivation and attrition. First, individuals should be assessed at multiple time periods during participation rather than at a single point in time (e.g., preseason, midseason, end of season) to determine whether motives change as a function of success, coaching style, and playing time, among other reasons. Second, people could be monitored through participation phases such as initiation, continuation, cessation, and reentry to get a better idea of factors related to dropping in and dropping out. Third, developmental differences in participation and attrition motives are important to consider, because transitions (e.g., elementary to middle school, middle to high school) may be crucial to participation decisions. Finally, social-contextual variables such as gender, program type, ethnicity, culture, and playing status were identified as a missing link in the majority of studies.

Researchers in the 1990s responded to several of these recommendations. Studies considered social-contextual factors such as gender (e.g., Ebbeck,

Gibbons, & Loken-Dahle, 1995; Ryckman & Hamel, 1995), culture (e.g., Hayashi & Weiss, 1994; Kolt et al., 1999; Wang & Wiese-Bjornstal, 1996), sport type (e.g., Ebbeck et al., 1995; Hellandsig, 1998), and time of season and player status (Petlichkoff, 1993a, 1993b; Weiss & Frazer, 1995). Early research primarily examined participation motives in Western societies (United States, Canada, Australia, Great Britain). Studies of participants from Eastern societies (Hayashi & Weiss, 1994; Wang & Wiese-Bjornstal, 1996) show that sociocultural factors influence reasons for participating in sport. For example, Hayashi and Weiss found that Anglo-American and Japanese marathoners were similar in participating for health and fitness, enjoyment, and personal challenge reasons. Anglo-American runners, however, cited competition and social recognition reasons, whereas Japanese runners cited having a good experience and being part of a running group.

The biggest change in participation motivation research over the past 16 years has been adoption of theoretical approaches to study continued and discontinued involvement in sport. Given consistent findings that people participate to demonstrate physical competence, obtain social acceptance and approval, and experience fun and enjoyment, several theories from educational and developmental psychology were natural candidates for research in this area. Theories that highlight perceptions of competence, social influence, and positive affect account for variations in motivated behavior based on reasons of physical competence, social acceptance, and enjoyment. We review three of these theories and related research in the physical domain: Harter's (1978) competence motivation theory, Deci and Ryan's (1985a) self-determination theory, and Eccles et al.'s (1983) expectancy-value model. We also review the sport commitment model (Scanlan, Carpenter, Schmidt, Simons, & Keeler, 1993) that was developed based on the literature in enjoyment and commitment to relationships. This model has been productive for understanding the desire to continue sport involvement.

Competence Motivation Theory

People primarily participate in physical activities for intrinsic reasons such as enjoyment and sense of mastery that come from learning and improving skills. Social reasons are also important, such as support from and positive interactions with significant adults (parents, coaches) and peers (teammates, friends). Harter's (1978, 1981a) competence motiva-

tion theory, an educationally relevant approach to understanding motivation in achievement domains such as sport, addresses these concepts. Moreover, model constructs and relationships are sensitive to developmental change and individual differences. Since her classic article was published in 1978, Harter's model has been a productive theory for applications to the physical domain. The following sections review theoretical underpinnings, empirical research in the physical domain, and directions for future research.

Theoretical Underpinnings

Imagine a young girl playfully turning cartwheels in the grass. What about a young boy mustering the courage to try a new swimming skill? Can you identify with the curiosity and sense of mastery that they experienced from their efforts? Researchers would describe these types of behaviors as intrinsic in nature—behaviors motivated by curiosity, challenge seeking, self-reward, and the need to have an effect on one's environment. R.W. White (1959) originated the concept of effectance, or competence motivation, which describes the antecedents and consequences of intrinsic or self-rewarding motivation. His concept of effectance was later operationally defined, revised, and extended by Harter (1978, 1981a, 1981b).

White's (1959) thesis was that individuals are intrinsically motivated to interact with their social and physical environment and do so by engaging in mastery attempts. If people are successful in these attempts (i.e., they demonstrate competence), they experience feelings of efficacy and pleasure, which maintain or enhance effectance motivation, or the desire to have an effect on their environment. White viewed motivation to develop mastery, satisfy curiosity, and enjoy challenge as examples of an effectance motive. White's article was embraced as an appealing approach to understanding motivated behavior. Nevertheless, empirical testing of his theory lay dormant for nearly 20 years because constructs such as effectance motivation, feelings of efficacy, and intrinsic pleasure were not operationally defined and could not be measured.

Susan Harter refined White's original ideas and developed valid measures of constructs that allowed empirical testing of predictions stemming from competence motivation theory. Her articles on competence motivation cast the theory within a developmental perspective (Harter, 1978, 1981a, 1981b) and had considerable influence in a variety of achievement domains including sport. Harter viewed competence motivation as a multidimensional construct that influences domain-specific mastery attempts and subsequent cognitions, emotions, and behaviors such as perceived competence, joy, and effort.

Extensions to the Original Effectance Model

Harter (1978, 1981a, 1981b) revised White's (1959) original model in several ways (see figure 7.1). First, she specified that competence motivation varies depending on the achievement domain in which mastery attempts occur (i.e., cognitive, physical, social). Children will differ in level of desire, curiosity, interest, and challenge seeking (i.e., motivational orientation) to master skills in sports, mathematics, and computers. Perceived competence, perceived control, and reinforcement by significant others also will vary with achievement domain. Therefore, Harter refined White's global construct of effectance motivation to a multidimensional one that considers variations in different achievement domains.

A second refinement related to performance outcomes. Whereas White addressed only the consequences of successful mastery attempts, Harter also considered the consequences of unsuccessful experiences and the relative balance or interaction between success and failure experiences on self-perceptions, affective responses, and motivated behavior. Moreover, Harter contended that success at any task or activity is insufficient to alter competence motivation; rather, success at optimal challenges, or difficult but realistic goals, provides the greatest feelings of positive affect and intrinsic motivation.

Third, Harter added the role of socializing agents such as important adults and peers in developing children's self-perceptions, affective responses, and motivational orientations. Harter contended that adult caregivers, especially parents, should approve and reinforce independent mastery attempts and not reserve such responses for successful outcomes. Positive and contingent feedback given for effort and improvement nurtures children's perceptions of competence and control, positive affect, and intrinsic motivation.

Fourth, Harter added perceptions of competence and control as crucial outcomes as well as mediators of affective responses and competence motivation. Perceived competence, the most frequently studied construct within this theory, is a strong predictor of cognitive (i.e., self-esteem), affective (i.e., enjoyment, anxiety), and behavioral (i.e., achievement) outcomes. Because perceived competence is a predictor of achievement outcomes, significant research has focused on understanding the processes by which children and adolescents form judgments about how competent they are in sport (see Horn, 2004; Horn & Amorose, 1998).

Fifth, Harter positioned inherent pleasure in response to successful mastery within the larger concept of positive affect, which she considered a central variable driving intrinsic motivation. Harter's call to "restore affect and emotion to its rightful

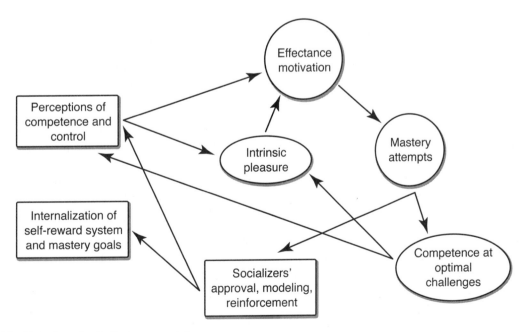

Figure 7.1 Harter's revised effectance model.

place, as central to an understanding of behavior" (Harter, 1981b, p. 4) is consistent with enjoyment as a primary participation motive and lack of enjoyment as a reason for attrition from sport.

Relationships Among Model Constructs

Putting together antecedents, mediators, and consequences of competence motivation (see figure 7.1), the theory posits that intrinsically oriented people (those with high competence motivation) are motivated to develop or demonstrate competence in a particular achievement domain (e.g., academic, physical, social). This urge to be effective leads them to try to master a task or activity (mastery attempts). They prefer challenging rather than easy tasks and ones that will satisfy their curiosity and interest. If mastery attempts are successful (success at optimal challenges) and significant adults and peers respond with approval and reinforcement, the child will experience increased perceptions of competence and control, positive affect, and motivation to continue demonstrating competence.

From a developmental perspective, children's positive socialization and cognitive maturation will pull them away from depending on social reinforcement and externally defined goals and push them toward relying on internal criteria (i.e., improvement, effort) and mastery goals to judge competence. This process should occur throughout the childhood years so that by early adolescence individuals are capable of using self-rewarding behavior, internal criteria, and independent judgments to define success. If this does not occur, the opposite scenario unfolds—one in which unsuccessful mastery attempts and inappropriate reinforcement from significant others lowers self-perceptions, increases anxiety, and shapes an extrinsic motivational orientation. Harter (1978) acknowledged that the balance between successful and unsuccessful mastery attempts and the pattern of reinforcement over time determines motivational orientation, self-perceptions, affect, and participation behavior.

Competence motivation theory specifies mastery attempts and performance outcomes in specific achievement domains and includes constructs that are salient to the physical domain (e.g., significant others, perceived competence, affective responses). Moreover, Harter and colleagues operationally defined competence motivation, thus allowing for tests of theoretical relationships. Because of its educational appeal, support of Harter's theory in the physical domain has flourished in the last 20 years. This research is presented in the following

sections along with specific model relationships: (a) perceived competence, participation motives, and attrition from sport; (b) developmental trends in perceived competence; (c) influence by significant others; and (d) perceived competence and achievement-related cognitions, affect, and behavior.

Perceived Competence, Participation Motives, and Attrition From Sport

The theory posits that people strive to demonstrate mastery and continue in achievement domains in which they feel competent. Thus, one might hypothesize that continuing sport participants should be higher in perceived physical competence than nonparticipants or former participants. Roberts, Kleiber, and Duda (1981) found that youth sport participants reported higher perceived physical competence than nonparticipants did. Feltz and Petlichkoff (1983) reported similar findings for interscholastic participants versus dropouts, as did Burton and Martens (1986) for current versus former youth wrestlers. Gibbons and Bushakra (1989) found that Special Olympics participants were higher on perceived physical competence than were nonparticipants. But Klint (1985) did not find differences in perceived physical competence between continuing and former youth and adolescent gymnasts, nor did Ulrich (1987) with 5- to 10-year-old participants and nonparticipants.

These discrepant findings prompted Klint and Weiss (1987) to examine the relationship between perceptions of competence and particular motives for participation. It may have been erroneous to assume that people who are no longer involved in sport were initially motivated to demonstrate physical competence but then dropped out when they perceived lower physical competence. Youth participate for many reasons including skill development, enjoyment, and social acceptance. Klint and Weiss hypothesized, based on competence motivation theory, that participants higher in perceived physical competence would cite skill development reasons as more important, whereas those higher in perceived social acceptance would rate friendship and team affiliation as more important, compared with participants with lower perceived competence. Results supported these contentions. Ryckman and Hamel (1993) also found that 14-year-old sport participants who were higher in perceived physical ability cited skill motives as more important than did those lower in perceived ability. These findings may explain the discrepant results relevant to perceived competence and participant status.

An alternative approach was to investigate the relationship between player status and perceived competence. Players vary in amount of playing time or, stated in competence motivation terms, opportunities to develop and demonstrate mastery. Petlichkoff (1993a, 1993b) found that starters on high school teams were higher in perceived physical competence than primary substitutes (first players into the game) or secondary substitutes (bench-warmers) were. Weiss and Frazer (1995) assessed high school basketball players on perceived success, perceived basketball competence, and enjoyment at preseason, midseason, and end of season. No differences existed at preseason, but by midseason and at postseason starters and primary substitutes were higher on all variables than secondary substitutes were. Results from these studies offer support that perceptions of competence are stronger in participants who receive more opportunities to demonstrate competence in an achievement domain.

Developmental Trends in Perceived Competence

Harter's empirical efforts (1981a, 1981c, 1982, 1990) clearly delineated developmental trends in dimensions of competence motivation such as perceived competence and motivational orientation. Understanding children's conceptions of these motivational components is important to explaining variations in achievement behavior and to devising strategies for enhancing competence perceptions, affect, and intrinsic motivation. But a developmental focus does not preclude examining individual variations within developmental level. That is, most but not all young children depend primarily on parental feedback to determine whether they are physically competent. A developmental approach allows for understanding between and within age-group differences on key motivational constructs. This section summarizes developmental trends in (a) differentiation of competence dimensions, (b) level and accuracy of perceived competence, and (c) sources of information used to assess physical competence.

Differentiation of Competence Dimensions
According to Harter (1990, 1998), the number and content of competence areas increases from early childhood through adolescence because of cognitive maturation and social experiences. Young children (ages 4 to 7 years) conceive of competence along general competence and social acceptance dimensions (Harter & Pike, 1984). General competence combines school subjects and sport skills; in other words, being good at something. Social acceptance combines acceptance by peers and mothers.

In middle and late childhood (ages 8 to 13 years), children are able to differentiate among several specific competence domains such as academic, athletic, social acceptance, physical appearance, and behavioral conduct (Harter, 1982, 1985). By adolescence (ages 14 to 18 years), the number and content of competence dimensions changes yet again (Harter, 1988). Beyond the five specific dimensions for middle to late childhood, three additional areas emerge as salient for teenagers—close friendship, romantic relationships, and job competence. Collectively these findings indicate that children and youth at varying levels of cognitive and social maturity conceive of competence in different ways.

Level and Accuracy of Perceived Competence
Because level of perceived competence (i.e., how high or low one's beliefs are) is a strong predictor of achievement-related cognitions, affect, and behavior, several developmentally oriented questions remain. Does level of perceived competence change with age (i.e., increase or decrease)? Does the relationship between perceived and actual competence become stronger with age (i.e., do people become more accurate in assessing their competence)? With age do people use different information sources to judge physical competence, and could this be a reason for observed variations in level and accuracy of perceived competence?

Research on children's evaluations of academic competence indicates that levels decline across early and middle childhood (Fredricks & Eccles, 2002; Harter, 1992; Stipek & Mac Iver, 1989). Along with this decline is a concomitant increase in accuracy of perceived competence (i.e., higher correlations between actual and perceived competence). Age trends in perceived physical competence, however, have been mixed. Harter (1982) and Feltz and Brown (1984) found relatively stable perceived competence levels across ages 8 to 13 years, but Ulrich (1987) found an age-related decrease in competence perceptions among 5- to 10-year-olds. Harter (1988) reported a progressive decline in perceived physical competence for girls in grades 8 to 10 but no change for boys. Duncan and Duncan (1991) showed an increase in boys' perceived physical competence across the adolescent years, as did Wigfield, Eccles, Mac Iver, Reuman, and Midgley (1991) in the transition from elementary to junior high school.

Trends for perceived physical competence are not as consistent as for academic competence. This may be due to sport being a voluntary activity while school is compulsory. Stable trends or even increases may occur because some youth discontinue sport if they do not believe they are good enough or are cut by the coach. Alternatively, those who advance to higher competition levels may see this as a positive source of competence information. By contrast, observed decreases in perceived competence could be due to a big fish-little pond effect whereby moving up in competitive level provides opportunities to compare oneself to others of similar or better ability. Further research is needed to tease out the underlying reasons explaining varying trends in perceived physical competence over the childhood and adolescent years.

Research on accuracy of competence judgments in the academic domain suggests that young children possess unrealistically high perceptions of competence (i.e., perceived competence is much higher than objective assessments). Gradually, perceptions become more accurate during middle and late childhood (see Harter, 1998). Explanations given for increase in accuracy of perceived competence include children's cognitive maturity to differentiate ability and effort as causes of success, change in information sources used to judge competence, and change in social environmental factors encountered in achievement domains (see Eccles, Wigfield, & Schiefele, 1998; Harter, 1999).

Horn and Weiss (1991) assessed accuracy of perceived competence in the physical domain. Children ages 8 to 13 years completed measures of level and sources of perceived competence, and teachers rated each child's actual sport competence. Correlations between perceived and actual competence revealed a progressive increase with age, indicating that children's self-judgments about ability become more accurate over the childhood years. Second, 8- to 9-year-old participants cited parent feedback as a more important source than did 10- to 13-year-olds, who rated peer comparison and evaluation as more important. This finding implies that accuracy and sources of perceived competence are related. Finally, children varying in accuracy (underestimating, accurate, overestimating) differed in the importance that they placed on social and self-comparison sources. McKiddie and Maynard (1997) replicated Horn and Weiss' age-related differences in accuracy and sources of perceived competence in 11- to 12-year-old students and 14- to 15-year-old students. Together, findings support age-related improvements in accuracy of competence judgments that are linked to information sources used by younger versus older children.

More recently, Weiss and Amorose (2005) uncovered profiles of youth who differed in age, actual competence, and level and accuracy of perceived competence. Comparison of these groups on sources of information for judging physical ability revealed that they placed different emphasis on norm- and self-referenced sources. Youth with similar levels of perceived competence who differed in accuracy of perceived competence rated peer comparison, skill improvement, and parent/coach feedback as more or less important for determining how physically capable they were. Findings revealed between- and within-age variability in level and accuracy of perceived competence, and these variations were linked to sources of information used to judge physical ability. According to competence motivation theory, youth varying in level and/or accuracy of perceived competence should also exhibit differences in cognitive and affective responses and motivational orientations. This study provides a nice segue to developmental trends in sources of competence information.

Sources of Information Used to Assess Physical Competence Knowing the types of information that children use to determine how good they are in sport and physical activities improves understanding of why they are low or high, or accurate or inaccurate, in their assessments of competence. Research has evaluated variations in use of information sources based on age, gender, skill, and psychological characteristics (e.g., self-esteem, anxiety, goal orientation). We summarize findings from these studies in the following paragraphs.

Several studies investigated which sources are used during middle childhood and early adolescence (ages 8 to 14 years). Horn and Hasbrook (1986) assessed girls and boys in a soccer league and divided them into three age groups: 8 to 9 years old, 10 to 11 years old, and 12 to 14 years old. The two younger groups rated evaluative feedback by parents and spectators, as well as winning and losing, as more important sources than did 12- to 14-year-olds, who scored higher on peer comparison. Results showed that reliance on parent feedback declines with age and use of peer comparison increases. Horn and Weiss (1991) extended these findings with 8- to 13-year-old youth participating in a variety of sports. Weiss, Bredemeier, and Shewchuk (1985) found a decline in preference for external criteria (e.g., coach feedback) and an increase in internal criteria (e.g., effort) to judge performance among 8- to 13-year-old sport participants.

Other studies focused on sources of competence information among adolescents. Horn, Glenn, and

Wentzell (1993) assessed adolescent athletes on sources of competence information; 14- to 15-year-olds played at the freshman or junior varsity level and 16- to 18-year-olds played at the varsity level. The younger/lower competitive level group rated peer evaluation more important, whereas the older/higher competitive level athletes scored higher on self-comparison and internal information (i.e., skill improvement, effort), goal achievement, and attraction to sport. To separate age from competitive level, Halliburton and Weiss (2002) assessed 12- to 14-year-old gymnasts who varied in competitive level. Gymnasts who competed at lower levels used effort and enjoyment (self-referenced sources) more than did gymnasts who competed at higher levels, who used feelings of nervousness and spectator feedback (norm-referenced sources) more frequently. Similar to the conclusions of Weiss and Amorose (2005), these findings suggest that, beyond typical findings of between-age differences, within-age variability is important for understanding preferences for information sources to judge physical ability.

Gender differences emerge in sources of competence information starting in adolescence. In Horn et al. (1993), male athletes indicated competitive outcomes and speed of learning skills as more important than female athletes did, who cited self-comparison, internal information, and evaluation by peers, coaches, and spectators. McKiddie and Maynard (1997) also found that 14- to 15-year-old girls rated adult feedback as more important than boys did, but no gender differences were found between 11- to 12-year-old boys and girls. Ebbeck (1990) uncovered gender differences in sources of performance information among college-age men and women who participated in weight-training classes. Women reported using goal setting, learning, effort, improvement, and outside-gym changes more frequently than men did, who relied more heavily on student feedback.

Sources of information for judging competence have also been linked to individual differences in psychological characteristics (Horn & Hasbrook, 1987; Weiss, Ebbeck, & Horn, 1997; Williams, 1994). For example, Horn and Hasbrook (1987) found that youth with higher perceived competence placed greater importance on peer comparison, effort, improvement, and positive affect, and those higher in perceived external control assigned higher ratings to game outcome. Weiss et al. uncovered a positive profile of children—higher in perceived competence and self-esteem and lower in trait anxiety—who used self-referenced criteria and parent evaluation to assess ability (i.e., multiple sources). They found

a negative profile of younger children—lower in perceived competence and higher in trait anxiety—who used pregame anxiety information. Older youth with a similar negative profile used social comparison and evaluation.

In all these studies, significant adults (parents, coaches) and peers (comparison to and evaluation by) emerge as important sources whereby youth derive information about their ability. The important role of socializers on competence motivation variables is reviewed next.

Influence by Significant Others

Competence motivation theory highlights the role of significant others in shaping children's self-perceptions, affect, and motivational orientation. Moreover, Harter has shown that beliefs and behaviors communicated about mastery attempts, rather than performance outcomes, are essential to children's adoption of internal standards and a self-reward system. Harter (1990) showed that social regard or support is a powerful predictor of self-conceptions in children through middle-age adults but that the most important source of support varies developmentally. Parents are salient for children and adolescents, whereas acceptance and support by general peers (i.e., classmates) and close friends are important throughout the life span.

Parents Studies illustrate a strong link between parent beliefs, expectancies, and behaviors with children's self-perceptions, affective responses, motivation, and participation. According to Harter (1978, 1981a, 1990), parents are especially important as transmitters of information about the child's competence through mechanisms of modeling, feedback, and reinforcement of mastery attempts and performance. In youth sport, these behaviors are readily observed in both positive (e.g., support, encouragement) and negative ways (e.g., pressure to perform, criticism for errors). In the following paragraphs, we summarize findings on the relation between parent beliefs and behaviors and children's competence motivation variables.

Brustad (1988; Brustad & Weiss, 1987) was interested in children's perceptions of parental pressure and evaluation-related worries as correlates of positive (enjoyment) and negative (anxiety) affective outcomes in youth sport. Although Brustad and Weiss did not find a link between social evaluation worries and competitive anxiety, Brustad found that children who perceived less pressure from parents to perform well reported higher levels of sport enjoyment. He also found that children higher in competitive anxiety reported more frequent worries about negative evaluation from parents than those lower in anxiety did. Weiss, Wiese, and Klint (1989) found that youth gymnasts stated "what my parents will say" and "letting my parents down" as the two most frequent worries before competitive events.

Perceptions of parent support are related to competence perceptions, motivational orientations, and behaviors. For example, Rose, Larkin, and Berger (1994) assessed perceptions of parent support among children in physical education classes who were divided into low, moderate, and high motor coordination (e.g., actual competence). Highly coordinated boys and girls perceived greater support from parents than did low or moderately coordinated children. Thus, children who would benefit most from supportive parents reported the least positive responses to their involvement. Other studies have also shown moderate or strong relationships between parent support (i.e., encouraging, being involved, attending competitions) and youths' psychosocial and behavioral outcomes (e.g., Babkes & Weiss, 1999; Brown, Frankel, & Fennell, 1989; Brustad, 1993, 1996; Leff & Hoyle, 1995; Weiss & Hayashi, 1995).

McCullagh, Matzkanin, Shaw, and Maldonado (1993) examined relationships between child and parent motives for participation and between child and parent perceptions of child's competencies. According to competence motivation theory, parent modeling, approval, and reinforcement should result in children internalizing parent-held motives and beliefs. Parents and children cited intrinsic motives (e.g., skill development, fun) as most important for involvement and extrinsic motives (e.g., competition, recognition) as least important. A moderate relationship was found for parents' and children's perceived social acceptance and athletic competence. Thus some support was found for compatibility between parent-held and children's participation motives and perceptions of competence.

An important aspect of parent influence within competence motivation theory is children's perceptions of parents' beliefs about their competence. *Reflected appraisals* refer to the child's interpretation of what others think about their abilities, which in turn influences self-appraisals such as perceived competence. Babkes and Weiss (1999) examined parents' actual appraisals (parent-reported beliefs about child's competence), reflected appraisals (child's perceptions of parents' beliefs), and self-appraisals (child's perceived competence) among 9- to 12-year-old soccer players. Boys and girls who reported more positive perceptions of parents' competence beliefs reported greater soccer competence themselves. Parents' actual appraisals, however, were not related to self-appraisals of ability, demonstrating the importance of children's interpretations of parents' beliefs. The mediating role of reflected appraisals in the relation between parents' actual appraisals and child's self-appraisals of sport ability was also shown in a longitudinal study (Bois, Sarrazin, Brustad, Chanal, & Trouilloud, 2005).

Modeling is another important mechanism by which parents influence children's competence beliefs, enjoyment, motivational orientations, and participation. When parents are active in sports and exercise, or express positive affect about their involvement, the child's observational learning translates to change in attitudes, emotions, and behaviors (Babkes & Weiss, 1999; Bois, Sarrazin, Brustad, Trouilloud, & Cury, 2005; Brustad, 1993, 1996; Weiss & Fretwell, 2005). For example, Babkes and Weiss found that youth who perceived their mothers and fathers as positive exercise role models reported greater perceived competence, enjoyment, and intrinsic motivation about soccer participation. Others found a direct relationship between parent and child levels of physical activity (Freedson & Evenson, 1991; Moore et al., 1991).

In youth sport programs in the United States, parents often coach their own children. Despite the prevalence of parent-coaches, little research has explored psychosocial and behavioral outcomes among child-athletes. Weiss and Fretwell (2005) interviewed father-coaches, son-athletes, and teammates about benefits and costs of being coached by one's parent. Consistent with competence motivation theory (and others), positive behaviors (e.g., praise, modeling, instruction) and negative behaviors (e.g., pressure, criticism for mistakes) by father-coaches were related to son-athletes' beliefs about competence, emotional responses, and motivational orientations. McCann (2006) reported similar findings with father–daughter, father–son, and mother–daughter dyads. These studies lend a nice segue from parent to coach influence within competence motivation theory.

Coaches Along with parents, coaches are powerful socializing agents in the physical domain (Horn, 2002). Coaches significantly affect children's and adolescents' competence perceptions, affect, and motivation in the way that they structure practice or respond to participants' performance. Coaches' feedback and reinforcement comprise informational (i.e., instruction) or evaluative (i.e., praise, criticism) responses to performance. For example, Smoll and Smith (2002) have demonstrated that quantity and quality of coaches' feedback resulted in higher perceived competence, self-esteem, enjoyment, and intention to continue playing and lower anxiety and attrition rates in male youth baseball players.

Several studies have examined coaches' influence on youths' psychosocial responses based on competence motivation theory. Horn (1985) studied whether coaches' reinforcement contributed beyond season-long skill improvement to self-perceptions in adolescent female softball players. Results indicated that players who received more frequent praise after successful performances scored lower in perceived physical competence, whereas players who received greater frequency of criticism following errors reported higher perceptions. Horn explained these paradoxical results in terms of contingent and appropriate feedback. Coaches did not give praise for specific and challenging skill accomplishments but instead for mastering easy skills or exhibiting mediocre performance. In contrast, coaches gave criticism based on specific performance levels combined with information about how to improve on subsequent mastery attempts. To support this inference further, Horn (1984) reported that lower-skilled players received more praise whereas the more talented athletes received more criticism for their efforts.

Black and Weiss (1992) extended Horn (1985) by assessing swimmers' perceptions of coaches' praise, information, encouragement, and criticism after successful and unsuccessful performance (i.e., contingent reinforcement). For 12- to 18-year-old swimmers, greater perceived praise combined with information after successful swims and greater encouragement combined with information after poor swims were associated with higher perceived competence, enjoyment, and intrinsic motivation. For 15- to 18-year-olds, more frequent criticism after poor performances was also associated with lower values on these variables. These results support competence motivation predictions and help to explain the contradictory findings by Horn (1985). Allen and Howe (1998) assessed the relationship between coaching behaviors and self-perceptions in adolescent female field hockey players. Consistent with Horn and Black and Weiss, more frequent praise was positively associated with perceived competence; however, counter to previous findings, more frequent encouragement plus instruction after skill errors was negatively related to perceived competence. To help explain this finding, Wilko (2004) extended Allen and Howe by examining the influence of coaching behaviors and motivational climate on female athletes' competence motivation. Greater praise plus instruction, encouragement plus instruction, mastery climate, and lower-performance climate were related to higher perceived competence, enjoyment, and intrinsic motivation. Thus, it is conceivable that players in Allen and Howe's study perceived an emphasis on a performance-oriented climate and that coaches' encouragement plus instruction after errors was interpreted within that social context.

Amorose and Weiss (1998) used an experimental protocol to determine age differences in use of coaches' feedback as a source of competence information. Children 6 to 8 and 12 to 14 years of age watched videotapes of athletes of similar age and gender and rated the athletes' ability after they received evaluative, informational, or neutral feedback following performance (hitting a baseball or softball). For both age groups, athletes who received praise after success were rated as higher in ability than athletes who received neutral or informational feedback. For unsuccessful performances, both age groups rated athletes as higher in ability if they received informational feedback and lower in ability if they received criticism. Amorose and Smith (2003) found similar results with informational feedback divided into descriptive and prescriptive conditions. Collectively, findings suggest that quality and type of feedback are important influences on youths' perceptions of ability. Contingent praise following success and informational feedback following skill errors are related to higher ability perceptions in young athletes.

Amorose (2002, 2003) also conducted studies to examine the relationship between reflected appraisals of parents, coaches, and teammates with self-appraisals of sport competence among middle school, high school, and college athletes. Reflected appraisals by coaches were significantly related to perceived competence for all three age groups, offering support for the importance of the coach's beliefs and behaviors in shaping perceptions of sport competence. Besides identifying the influence of coaches' reflected appraisals, Amorose found that perceptions of teammates' beliefs about one's sport ability were strongly related to athletes' self-reported competence. This conclusion leads us to an examination of the role of significant peers such as teammates, classmates, and friends within competence motivation theory.

Peers   One's peers, such as teammates, classmates, and close friends, are powerful socializing agents who contribute beyond the influence of adults to children's cognitions, emotions, and behaviors in the physical domain (see Smith, 2003; Weiss & Stuntz, 2004). Within Harter's (1978, 1981a) theory, social comparison to and evaluation by peers are important sources of information by which children and adolescents judge how competent they are. In addition, peers influence each other's general self-beliefs (i.e., self-worth), emotional experiences, motivational orientations, and participation behaviors. Peer acceptance and close friendship are two types of relationships that investigators have studied in relation to youths' psychosocial and behavioral outcomes in the physical domain.

Peer acceptance is the degree to which a person is liked or accepted by members of his or her peer group and can range from popular to rejected. In contrast, friendship refers to a close, dyadic relationship, such as mutual liking, similarity, and social support (companionship, esteem, loyalty, intimacy). Finally, social competence refers to the skills necessary for having successful peer interactions and relationships, such as social perspective taking, cooperative problem solving, and communication skills (Rubin, Bukowski, & Parker, 1998). Several studies support Harter's (1978, 1981a, 1987) theorizing of relationships among peer variables and cognitive, emotional, and motivational consequences in the physical domain.

Studies consistently show that peer acceptance and perceived physical competence are strongly related. For example, children and teenagers identify being good at sports as an important quality for being popular with one's peers (e.g., Adler, Kless, & Adler, 1992), and those who are more skilled in sports are afforded greater peer status within their group (Evans & Roberts, 1987; Glenn & Horn, 1993). Weiss and Duncan (1992) tested the direct link between physical competence and peer acceptance among 8- to 13-year-old participants. A strong relationship emerged between competence and acceptance variables. Children who believed that they were skilled and were rated by instructors as such also rated themselves as liked by their peer group and were rated by instructors as such.

Other studies have shown strong relationships between peer acceptance and competence motivation variables (perceived competence, affect, motivation, participation behavior). Kunesh, Hasbrook, and Lewthwaite (1992) used interviews, observations, and peer nominations to demonstrate that peer acceptance was strongly related to girls' emotional responses and motivation to participate

in physical activities. Those who were rejected by peers reported anxiety, embarrassment, and lack of desire to participate in sports, especially in contexts in which peer behaviors were particularly negative (i.e., school physical education). Smith (1999) found that adolescents who reported greater peer acceptance also rated higher in physical self-worth, positive affect, intrinsic motivation, and physical activity levels. Ullrich-French and Smith (2006) found that higher peer acceptance was related to greater perceived competence, enjoyment, and intrinsic motivation among youth soccer players. In sum, several studies have demonstrated an intimate linkage between peer acceptance and competence motivation variables, notably perceived competence, affect, motivational orientation, and participation behavior.

Close friendship is also strongly related to perceptions of competence, affect, and motivational orientation and behavior. For example, Duncan (1993) found that adolescents' perceptions of companionship and esteem support from classmates were related to greater enjoyment and motivation to participate in physical activity. Weiss and colleagues (Weiss & Smith, 1999, 2002; Weiss, Smith, & Theeboom, 1996) conducted a series of studies on youths' perceptions of friendships in the physical domain. Emergent themes from interview data included several competence and affect-related dimensions such as esteem enhancement, help and guidance, companionship, emotional support, and intimacy. In turn, certain friendship qualities were related to enjoyment of and commitment to tennis participation. Similarly, Patrick et al. (1999) found that friendships were important contributors to adolescents' enjoyment of a talent activity (music, sports, art) and their decisions to continue or discontinue involvement.

Some researchers examined the combined influence of friendship and peer acceptance on competence motivation variables (Smith, 1999; Ullrich-French & Smith, 2006). In addition to the earlier reported findings of peer acceptance, Smith found that perceptions of having a close friend in sport and physical activity were associated with greater positive affect, intrinsic motivation, and physical activity levels. Ullrich-French and Smith found that positive friendship quality predicted perceived competence and enjoyment when coupled with higher peer acceptance among youth soccer players. Collectively, studies indicate that peer group acceptance, close friendship, and friendship quality are contributors to self-perceptions, affective responses, and motivation.

Perceived Competence and Achievement-Related Cognitions, Affect, and Behavior

Pathways in Harter's (1978, 1981a) model suggest relationships between perceptions of competence and achievement-related cognitions (e.g., perceived control, self-esteem, motivational orientation), positive and negative affect, and behavior (e.g., effort, physical activity level). To date, studies designed to test these relationships have gleaned strong support for competence motivation theory. In the following paragraphs, we review empirical research of relationships between perceived competence and cognitions, affect, and behaviors.

Perceived physical competence consistently emerges as a strong correlate of perceptions of control. In Harter's (1978, 1981a) model, perceived control refers to the degree to which the child understands who or what is responsible for success and failure in an achievement domain. Perceptions of control are strongly related to perceived competence, motivational orientation, and behavioral consequences (Weigand & Broadhurst, 1998; Weiss, Bredemeier, & Shewchuk, 1986; Weiss & Horn, 1990; Weiss, McAuley, Ebbeck, & Wiese, 1990). For example, Weiss et al. (1990) found that children higher in perceived competence made internal, stable, and personally controllable attributions for performance compared with peers lower in perceived competence. Weiss et al. (1986) reported that participants higher in perceived physical competence and lower in perceived unknown control scored higher in intrinsic motivational orientation.

Several studies show that perceptions of physical competence are related to positive and negative affective experiences and motivational orientations (e.g., Scanlan & Lewthwaite, 1986; Scanlan, Stein, & Ravizza, 1989, 1991). For example, Ebbeck and Weiss (1998) assessed multiple positive (i.e., proud, satisfied, happy) and negative affects (i.e., unhappy, guilty, angry) and found that perceived competence was strongly related to positive affect and, to a lesser degree, negative affect. Smith (1999) uncovered a strong relationship between physical self-worth (consisting of sport competence, physical appearance, strength, and conditioning) and attraction to physical activity among female and male middle school youth. Amorose (2001) found that both level and intraindividual variability of perceived physical competence predicted affect toward physical activity and intrinsic motivation among middle school students.

A handful of studies demonstrated relationships between perceived sport competence and behav-

ioral outcomes. As part of the study by Weiss et al. (1986), perceptions of competence and control and motivational orientation were examined in relation to actual competence in three sports (baseball, swimming, gymnastics). Perceived competence was strongly related to its corresponding sport performance (perceived swimming competence with swimming ability) or generally related (perceived athletic competence with baseball ability). Ulrich (1987) found that children higher in perceived physical competence demonstrated superior motor performance in playground and sport skills (e.g., ball dribble, softball throw, broad jump) compared to those lower in competence perceptions. Ebbeck (1994) found a strong relationship of perceptions of tennis competence and preference for optimally challenging activities with tennis skill rating.

Smith (1999) focused on physical activity levels among 12- to 15-year-old adolescents, a developmental period marked by declines in participation. A model that included several competence motivation variables was analyzed in relation to frequency and intensity of physical activity. Results indicated that peer influence (acceptance and close friendship), physical self-worth, positive affect, and challenge motivation directly or indirectly (through mediating variables) predicted physical activity levels in both girls and boys. This study was important in that it included social, cognitive, affective, and behavioral variables as specified by Harter's (1978, 1981a) competence motivation theory (and her model of global self-worth).

Results suggest that children with higher levels of perceived competence are more likely to adopt a functional pattern of cognitions and affect, reflected by perceptions of personal control, higher global self-esteem, intrinsic motivational orientation, and higher positive affect and lower negative affect. Such cognitions and affect translate to achievement behaviors such as effort; persistence; continued involvement; and level, frequency, and duration of physical activity.

Conclusion and Future Research Directions

As shown by this review, Harter's (1978) competence motivation theory is strongly supported in the physical domain. Robust findings exist for links between perceived competence and cognitions, affect, and behavior; developmental trends in perceived competence; and influence by significant adults and peers on competence motivation. These theoretical links translate to applications for teaching and coaching youth, most notably strategies for enhancing perceived competence, enjoyment, and social support to enhance physical activity and psychosocial outcomes (see Weiss, 2004; Weiss & Ebbeck, 1996). Despite the strong existing knowledge base, several directions for future research are offered.

First, we need better understanding of the factors that influence perceived competence and participation behaviors over time. For example, Petlichkoff (1993a, 1993b) and Weiss and Frazer (1995) studied athletes who were categorized as cuttees, those dropped from their teams during tryouts. Little is known about those who continue to participate in sport up until adolescence but then fail to "make the cut" because of lack of skill, experience, and physical characteristics. What are the motivational implications for the cuttee, whether eliminated by a coach or self-selected? Is perceived competence lowered and, consequently, is motivation for physical activity lowered? If so, are the effects temporary or enduring? What alternative programs exist for teenagers who are not skilled enough to make a school team but value the importance of physical activity for social, fitness, or enjoyment reasons? Participation rates decline dramatically during the adolescent years for both females and males. This developmental period reflects a prime window of time for researchers to assess activity levels, participation motives, and self-perceptions to understand factors that will retain greater numbers in sport and physical activity.

A second direction is considering youths' entire social network to understand competence beliefs, enjoyment, and motivation in physical activity. Most studies have looked at parents, coaches, or peers, but we know that significant adults and peers all contribute, in varying ways, to youths' activity outcomes. Some researchers have considered children's perceptions of multiple socializers (e.g., Amorose, 2002, 2003; Ullrich-French & Smith, 2006), and findings show that a combination of sources explain more of the variance in self-perceptions, affect, and motivation than one source alone. Besides knowing about sources of influence, understanding the processes by which people might effect change in youths' motivation is critical both to extending theoretical knowledge and to applying strategies to improve psychosocial and behavioral outcomes. Garcia Bengoechea and Strean (in press) recently investigated sources, dimensions, and processes of social influence on adolescents' sport motivation. Their model of adolescents' interpersonal context on motivation offers promising directions for future research.

Finally, given consistent findings that perceived competence, enjoyment, and positive social interactions strongly predict intrinsic motivation and motivated behaviors, more intervention studies are needed to evaluate effectiveness of strategies designed to enhance psychosocial and behavioral outcomes. Some researchers have shown that perceived ability, enjoyment, and motivation increase as a result of training teachers and coaches (e.g., Ebbeck & Gibbons, 1998; Marsh & Peart, 1988; Smoll, Smith, Barnett, & Everett, 1993). Others delineated guidelines for promoting physical activity among youth (Centers for Disease Control and Prevention, 1997), which include psychological (confidence), emotional (enjoyment), and social-contextual (positive environment, parent support) factors compatible with competence motivation theory (and other theories in this chapter). Integrating theories and research in developmental, sport and health psychology, and pediatric exercise science should optimize our knowledge of enhancing positive experiences in sport and physical activity.

Self-Determination Theory

A theory increasingly used as a framework for understanding motivation in sport and physical activity is self-determination theory (SDT) (see Hagger & Chatzisarantis, 2007). This theory, developed and refined by Deci and Ryan (1985a; Ryan & Deci, 2000, 2002) over the past three decades, is more than a theory of motivation. The underlying principles and processes explicated in the theory have implications for understanding not only motivation but also personality, social development, and overall psychological functioning. SDT is really a metatheory composed of four related minitheories, including cognitive evaluation theory, organismic integration theory, causality orientation theory, and basic needs theory.

Although each minitheory provides a unique contribution to the overall SDT framework, all four share some fundamental assumptions. First, Deci and Ryan (1985a; Ryan & Deci, 2000, 2002) have argued that all people have an innate tendency toward psychological growth, integration of the self, and behavioral self-regulation. This organismic view considers people as active and growth oriented, with the natural inclination to seek optimal challenges, extend themselves, and strive to learn and master new skills by freely applying their talents and abilities. SDT also specifies that social-contextual factors can either support or hinder these processes. In other words, the social environment can either nurture or impede one's active, integrating human nature. Thus, SDT is also considered a dialectical framework insomuch as the theory specifies that development, psychological functioning, and motivation will result from ongoing interaction between human nature and the social context.

The minitheories that represent the SDT framework also share the concept of fundamental psychological needs. Specifically, the theory posits that three universal needs—for competence, autonomy, and relatedness—are essential for optimal functioning and development. The need for competence reflects the need to perceive our behavior and interaction with the social environment as effective (Deci, 1975; Harter, 1978, White, 1959). The need for autonomy represents the need to perceive our behaviors and thoughts as freely chosen and that we are the origins of our own actions (deCharms, 1968; Deci & Ryan, 1987; Ryan & Connell, 1989). In other words, a person needs to experience a sense of self-determination. The need for relatedness represents the need to perceive that we are connected to those around us and that we experience a sense of belongingness (Baumeister & Leary, 1995; Ryan, 1995). The extent to which these needs are fulfilled or thwarted provides a mechanism by which the social context affects individual outcomes such as personal and social development, motivation, and well-being. Situations that satisfy these needs will promote optimal functioning, whereas situations that inhibit satisfaction of these needs will lead to nonoptimal outcomes.

These basic assumptions provide the foundation of SDT and are detailed either implicitly or explicitly in each of the four minitheories. Ryan and Deci (2002) indicated that their approach to building SDT has been to research specific phenomena and construct minitheories to explain the findings and make predictions about the underlying processes at work. The following sections review the basic elements of each of the four minitheories comprising SDT and present some examples of research studies specific to sport and physical activity that support the theories.

Cognitive Evaluation Theory

First formulated by Deci (1975) and subsequently extended by Deci and Ryan (1985a), cognitive evaluation theory (CET) was developed to explain the effects of the social context on people's intrinsic motivation. Deci and Ryan (1985a) defined intrinsic motivation as behavior based on the inherent satisfaction or pleasure associated with an activity itself. When intrinsically motivated, people will freely engage in an activity and experience a sense of enjoyment while doing so as opposed to performing to obtain some separable outcome, as is the case with extrinsic motivation. CET specifies that any event that facilitates or undermines the needs for competence or autonomy will ultimately affect intrinsic motivation. Ryan and Deci (2000, 2002) acknowledge the potential influence of people's need for relatedness as a determinant of intrinsic motivation, particularly when the activity is social in nature. Nevertheless, they argue that feelings of relatedness will play a more distal role and that intrinsic motivation for an activity is primarily affected by the extent to which people feel competent and autonomous.

Events capable of influencing intrinsic motivation are assumed to possess both controlling and informational aspects (Deci & Ryan, 1985a). The controlling aspect of an event relates to the need for autonomy and perceived locus of causality. Events that promote an external locus of causality (i.e., behavior is perceived to be initiated and controlled by factors outside oneself) will lessen feelings of autonomy and undermine intrinsic motivation, whereas events that promote an internal locus of causality (i.e., behavior is seen as determined by one's freedom of choice) will facilitate autonomy and ultimately intrinsic motivation. The informational aspect of an event, on the other hand, relates to the need for competence. An event that provides positive information about one's ability will support or enhance intrinsic motivation. Conversely, experiencing negative competence information will reduce the degree to which behavior is intrinsically motivated by lowering perceived competence.

The initial development of CET focused on understanding social-contextual factors such as the distribution of rewards or feedback. However, Deci and Ryan (1985a, Ryan & Deci, 2000, 2002) contend that intrapersonal events, like external events, can also influence perceived competence, autonomy, and intrinsic motivation. Based on Ryan's (1982) work, they use the terms *internally controlling* and *internally informational* to refer to events that occur within the person. Internally informational events (e.g., self-reward) enhance perceived competence and, as a result, maintain or increase intrinsic motivation. In contrast, internally controlling events (e.g., self-imposed pressure, guilt, ego involvement) may decrease autonomy and intrinsic motivation.

A critical component of CET is that the influence of intrapersonal or social-contextual events on intrinsic motivation will be a function of the meaning attached to the event by the individual (Deci & Ryan, 1985a). To use CET terminology, the *functional significance*, or salience, of the event dictates whether intrinsic motivation is facilitated or diminished. For example, an athlete may perceive receiving an external reward (e.g., money, trophy) as a positive indicator of her sport competence (informational), whereas another athlete may perceive the same reward as coercion to keep her involved in the activity (controlling). Thus, the aspect of the event that is perceived as salient will determine level of autonomy and perceived competence experienced, and ultimately affect intrinsic motivation for that activity.

CET has generated a considerable amount of research within and outside the physical domain (see Deci & Ryan, 1985a; Ferrer-Caja & Weiss, 2000, 2002; Frederick & Ryan, 1995; Ryan & Deci, 2002; Vallerand, Deci, & Ryan, 1987). Results show that the extent and diversity of events that can act on one's need satisfaction and intrinsic motivation are manifold. For instance, the extent to which people become ego involved versus task involved in an activity is an intrapersonal factor shown to affect perceptions of competence, autonomy, and intrinsic motivation (see Harwood, Spray, & Keegan, this volume; Rawsthrone & Elliot, 1999; Ryan, Koestner, & Deci, 1991). Achievement goal theory has elaborated the distinction between task-involved and ego-involved goals. This theory suggests that the goals people adopt, or how they personally define success and failure, will influence various motivational outcomes. For instance, those who are more ego involved, who define success as performing better than others or winning competitions, should theoretically have lower intrinsic motivation because they are participating as a means to an end (i.e., for more extrinsic reasons) and are more likely to experience pressure to perform well to ensure that they demonstrate competence relative to others. Thus, they are likely to perceive participation in sport as internally controlling, leading to lower feelings of autonomy and intrinsic motivation. On the other hand, those who adopt more task-involved goals, who define success as learning a new task, improving, or trying their best, should generally report higher levels of intrinsic motivation because they are more likely to experience situations as providing positive information about their ability (i.e., informational).

Relationships consistent with these predictions have consistently emerged in the literature (see Harwood, Spray, & Keegan, this volume). Studies that explore achievement goal orientations, which reflect the dispositional tendency to define success and failure using self-referenced or norm-referenced criteria, show that task-involved goals positively relate to intrinsic motivation, whereas ego-involved goals negatively relate to intrinsic motivation (e.g., Brunel, 1999; Duda, Chi, Newton, Walling, & Catley, 1995; Ferrer-Caja & Weiss, 2000, 2002; Goudas, Biddle, & Fox, 1994; Standage, Duda, & Ntoumanis, 2003b; Standage & Treasure, 2002).

Intrinsic motivation is also associated with achievement goals emphasized in the environment, otherwise referred to as motivational climate (see Ames, 1992; Harwood, Spray, & Keegan, this volume). Intrinsic motivation is supported in a mastery (also called task-involving) motivational climate that emphasizes learning, improvement, and effort as keys to success (e.g., Newton, Duda, Yin, 2000; Seifriz, Duda, & Chi, 1992; Standage et al., 2003b; Theeboom, De Knop, & Weiss, 1995). In contrast, intrinsic motivation is undermined when people participate in a performance (also called ego-involving) motivational climate that emphasizes competition, winning, and outperforming others (e.g., Newton et al., 2000; Seifriz et al., 1992). Studies exploring motivational climate in physical education classes support the prediction that need satisfaction mediates the relationship between the social context and intrinsic motivation (e.g., Ferrer-Caja & Weiss, 2000, 2002; Ntoumanis, 2001; Standage, Duda, & Ntoumanis, 2003a). For example, Ferrer-Caja and Weiss (2000) assessed high school physical education students' perceptions of motivational climate and teaching style, as well as perceived competence, autonomy, intrinsic motivation, achievement goals, and motivated behavior (e.g., effort and persistence). Students who perceived a task-involving class (mastery climate) displayed task-involving goals, reported a positive sense of competence and autonomy, indicated that they participated for intrinsic reasons, and demonstrated greater motivated behavior. In contrast, students who perceived an ego-involving class (performance climate) displayed ego-involving goals and reported that they were less likely to participate for intrinsic reasons such as fun and enjoyment.

Numerous other social-contextual events have been associated with intrinsic motivation, such as rewards, feedback, imposed deadlines, competition, surveillance, and interpersonal styles (see Deci, Koestner, & Ryan, 2001; Henderlong & Lepper, 2002; Mageau & Vallerand, 2003; Ryan & Deci, 2002). For instance, much of the early research testing CET focused on the motivational implication of rewards (e.g., Orlick & Mosher, 1978, Thomas & Tennant,

1978). Typically, these early experimental studies showed that rewards, especially when distributed in a controlling manner, tend to undermine intrinsic motivation (see Deci, Koestner, & Ryan, 2001). Field-based studies in sport have also shown a relationship between rewards in the form of scholarships and athletes' intrinsic motivation (e.g., Amorose & Horn, 2000; Ryan, 1977, 1980). For example, in two studies Ryan found that football players on scholarship reported lower intrinsic motivation than their nonscholarship teammates did. In contrast, Ryan found that scholarship wrestlers and female athletes had higher levels of intrinsic motivation than their nonscholarship teammates did. Using CET, Ryan explained the results by suggesting that football players might have perceived the scholarship as controlling, thus lowering intrinsic motivation. On the other hand, wrestlers and female athletes might have found scholarships to be a sign of their sport competence given the relatively few scholarships available, thus raising intrinsic motivation by making the informational aspect of the reward salient. These results highlight the processes of CET, which indicate that the motivational implication of events such as distribution of rewards will depend on the meaning attached to the event, that is, whether it is perceived as informational or controlling (Deci & Ryan, 1985a).

Another social contextual event relevant in sport and physical activity is the feedback provided by significant others such as coaches and teachers (see Amorose, 2007; Horn, 2002). Early studies focused on the basic content of the feedback provided (e.g., Vallerand, 1983; Vallerand & Reid, 1984; Whitehead & Corbin, 1991). For example, Vallerand and Reid assessed intrinsic motivation and perceived competence on a stabilometer task among undergraduate males. Students who initially reported moderate levels of intrinsic motivation for the task were tested a second time in conditions in which positive, negative, or no feedback was provided after performing. Results indicated that positive feedback increased intrinsic motivation and perceived competence and negative feedback had the opposite effect. Consistent with CET, perceived competence mediated the relationship between feedback and intrinsic motivation. Although other studies have found that providing praise inappropriately and noncontingently leads to lower perceived competence in athletes (Horn, 1985), in general research shows that positive feedback from others is associated with higher levels of perceived competence and intrinsic motivation, whereas negative feedback has the opposite effect (see Henderlong & Lepper, 2002).

Studies in the physical domain that explored a wider range of feedback behaviors have also shown a link with intrinsic motivation consistent with CET predictions (e.g., Amorose & Horn, 2000; Black & Weiss, 1992). For instance, Amorose and Horn examined the relationship between a host of coaching behaviors and indices of intrinsic motivation in collegiate athletes. Athletes were asked about the frequency of feedback that they perceived their coaches provided using a questionnaire version of the Coaching Behavior Assessment System (see Smoll & Smith, 2002). Despite some subtle gender differences in the pattern of relationships, results showed that the feedback dimensions related to greater intrinsic motivation included higher frequencies of positive and information-based feedback and lower frequencies of punishment-oriented feedback and ignoring players' performances. Amorose and Horn explained the results using CET, suggesting that these patterns of coaching behavior should lead to more positive perceptions of competence and higher intrinsic motivation.

Research has shown that not only will type, frequency, and quality of feedback have motivational implications, so too will the general interpersonal style that significant others demonstrate (see Amorose, 2007). For example, a series of studies by Amorose and colleagues (Amorose & Horn, 2000, 2001; Hollembeak & Amorose, 2005) have explored the links between athletes' intrinsic motivation and perceptions of coaches' leadership styles. Although some unique relationships emerge in each study, overall the results highlight coaches' decision-making styles as key predictors of intrinsic motivation. Hollembeak and Amorose, as an example, had athletes from a variety of university sports complete measures that assessed their coaches' leadership style as well as their perceptions of competence, autonomy, relatedness, and intrinsic motivation. Similar to those studied by Amorose and Horn (2000, 2001), athletes who reported lower intrinsic motivation perceived that their coaches engaged in higher frequencies of autocratic behavior, in which they stressed their personal authority and made decisions independent of the athletes, and lower frequencies of democratic behavior, in which they involved the athletes in the decision-making process. Furthermore, consistent with CET, analyses showed that the effect of coaches' decision-making style was mediated primarily by the athletes' perceptions of autonomy.

Although many dimensions of coaching and teaching behavior may affect intrinsic motivation, one that is particularly relevant within the SDT framework is the extent to which participants perceive their coach or teacher to be autonomy supportive versus controlling in their interactions (see Mageau & Vallerand, 2003). An authority figure, like a coach, who is autonomy supportive engages in behaviors that acknowledge the thoughts and feelings of others; encourages choice, self-initiation, and self-regulation of behavior; and minimizes use of pressure and demands to control others. Conversely, an authority figure who pressures others to think, feel, and act in a way consistent with his or her needs and wants characterizes a controlling interpersonal style. Basically, then, authority figures who are autonomy supportive satisfy the needs of those with whom they work, whereas controlling behaviors diminish need satisfaction and intrinsic motivation (Deci & Ryan, 1985a, 1987).

Considerable research outside the physical domain has shown that an autonomy-supportive interpersonal style is an effective motivational technique, such that a higher level of intrinsic motivation is associated with an autonomy-supportive interpersonal style (see Baard, 2002; Reeve, 2002; Williams, 2002). Comparable results are reported in sport settings (see Mageau & Vallerand, 2003). For example, Pelletier, Fortier, Vallerand, Tuson, et al. (1995) and Pelletier, Fortier, Vallerand, and Briére (2001) reported positive relationships between athletes' intrinsic motivation and perceived autonomy support from their coaches. Similarly, studies in physical education classes have shown that students who perceive that their teachers exhibit a more autonomy-supportive style report greater need satisfaction and intrinsic motivation (e.g., Hagger, Chatzisarantis, Culverhouse, & Biddle, 2003; Standage, Duda, & Ntoumanis, 2005).

CET has been a common framework for studying motivation in sport and physical activity settings. This popularity is due, at least in part, to the fact that people often engage in sport and physical activity for fun, therefore making intrinsic motivation a critical motivational concept. Nevertheless, extrinsic factors can also lead to motivated behavior in sport and physical activity. As such, exploring the nature of extrinsic motivation is critical and is the primary focus of the next minitheory in the SDT framework—organismic integration theory.

Organismic Integration Theory

Having fun is typically one of the most important reasons cited for sport participation. Nevertheless, not all sport and physical activity behavior will be intrinsically motivating. When activities are not inherently interesting, optimally challenging, or enjoyable, participation will require extrinsic motivation (Ryan & Deci, 2002). Extrinsic motivation is defined as engaging in an activity for instrumental reasons (Vallerand, 1997). Extrinsic motivation is viewed as antithetical to intrinsic motivation and is believed to represent a controlled, nonautonomous form of behavior (e.g., deCharms, 1968). But SDT, and specifically organismic integration theory (OIT), indicates that people can participate in an activity to attain some separable outcome yet do so more or less autonomously. Thus, one of the main contributions of OIT to the SDT framework is the distinction and elaboration of types of extrinsic motivation and other forms of motivated behavior.

According to Deci and Ryan (1985a; Ryan & Deci, 2000, 2002) all motivated behavior, whether intrinsic or extrinsic, varies in terms of locus of causality (i.e., whether behavior is initiated and controlled by internal versus external sources) and the degree to which the behavior is regulated autonomously (i.e., the extent to which action emanates from the self). Table 7.1 presents the self-determination continuum of motivation, which illustrates the basic categories of motives underlying behavior according to OIT. To the far left is amotivation, which represents nonmotivated behavior. Amotivation involves lack of intention to act and is characterized by relative absence of motivated behavior resulting from not valuing the activity, feelings of incompetence, or lack of perceived contingency between the action and desired outcomes (see Ntoumanis, Pensgaard, Martin, & Pipe, 2004; Ryan & Deci, 2000).

The remaining five classifications reflect specific forms of motivated behavior. Shown on the far right is the most autonomous form, namely intrinsic motivation. Intrinsically motivated behavior emanates entirely from within the individual (i.e., has an internal locus of causality) and involves doing an activity for the sense of pleasure and satisfaction derived from the behavior itself. Situated between amotivation and intrinsic motivation on the self-determination continuum is extrinsic motivation. Ryan and colleagues (Ryan & Connell, 1989; Ryan & Deci, 2000, 2002) identified four specific forms of extrinsic motivation based on underlying regulatory processes driving behavior. External regulation involves behavior controlled by external means such as rewards or punishments. This form of motivated behavior is the least self-determined and represents the classic form of extrinsic motivation discussed in the literature. Introjected regulation is also considered a non-self-determined form of motivation despite the fact that with this type of motivation

Table 7.1 Self-Determination Continuum

Type of motivation	Amotivation	Extrinsic motivation				Intrinsic motivation
Type of regulation	Nonregulation	External	Introjected	Identified	Integrated	Intrinsic
Example motive	*"I participate in sport because . . .*					
	I have nothing better to do with myself."	*my parents are making me."*	*I don't want to let others down by quitting."*	*it will help me open doors for my future career as a coach."*	*it helps to confirm my identity as an athlete."*	*I love the rush I feel when running down the field."*
Locus of causality	Impersonal	External	Somewhat external	Somewhat internal	Internal	Internal
Degree of autonomy	Non-self-determined					Self-determined

a person has internalized an external regulation. Nevertheless, this form of regulation still represents an external locus of causality in the sense that the person does not experience the behaviors, although internal, as part of the true self. With introjected regulation, internal pressures such as worry, shame, or a desire to enhance the ego will be the driving force behind these actions.

The next two forms of extrinsic motivation—identified regulation and integrated regulation—represent behaviors that have been internalized and thus reflect an internal locus of causality (Ryan & Connell, 1989; Ryan & Deci, 2000, 2002). Identified regulation represents behavior performed out of choice because a person values or finds benefits in the activity. The most autonomous form of extrinsic motivation is integrated regulation. In this type of motivation, the person brings regulations into the self and assimilates them with his or her other values, goals, and needs. These behaviors are similar in nature to intrinsic motivation, but they are still extrinsic in nature because the person expects to obtain some separable outcome from the behavior.

Researchers have developed measures designed to assess the various motives identified by OIT in the context of sport (e.g., Pelletier et al., 1995), physical education (e.g., Goudas et al., 1994), and exercise (e.g., Li, 1999; Markland & Tobin, 2004; Mullan, Markland, & Ingledew, 1997). Although identified regulation is typically omitted from these measures, evidence of the distinction between the various forms of behavioral regulation is clear (see Vallerand

& Fortier, 1998). Furthermore, studies have shown support for the validity of the self-determination continuum in that a simplex pattern of relationships among the various forms of motivation consistently emerges (e.g., Chatzisarantis, Hagger, Biddle, Smith, & Wang, 2003; Li & Harmer, 1996). These measurement tools have enabled researchers to study various forms of behavioral regulation as separate constructs, as well as combine them in a weighted relative autonomy index used to reflect people's overall motivational orientation (see Vallerand & Fortier, 1998).

The importance of understanding what regulates people's behavior is clear when considering the consequences associated with engaging in an activity for more or less self-determined reasons (see Ryan & Deci, 2000, 2002; Vallerand, 1997; Vallerand & Ratelle, 2002). Studies in the physical domain have shown a host of positive behavioral, cognitive, and affective outcomes associated with more self-determined motivation. For instance, self-determined forms of motivation are positively associated with attendance and participation in sports and physical activities (e.g., Chatzisarantis & Biddle, 1998; Chatzisarantis, Biddle, & Meek, 1997; Gagné, Ryan, & Bargmann, 2003; Hagger et al., 2003; Hagger, Chatzisarantis, & Harris, 2006; Vansteenkiste, Simons, Soenens, & Lens, 2004; Williams, Grow, Freedman, Ryan, & Deci, 1996), exerted effort in physical education (e.g., Ferrer-Caja & Weiss, 2000, 2002; Ntoumanis, 2001; Standage, Duda, & Ntoumanis, 2006; Vansteenkiste, Simons, Soenens, & Lens, 2004), and lower intention to discontinue and actually drop out in sport (e.g.,

Pelletier et al., 2001; Sarrazin, Vallerand, Guillet, Pelletier, & Cury, 2002). More self-determined forms of motivation are also associated with greater positive affect (e.g., Amiot, Gaudreau, & Bachard, 2004; Standage et al., 2005), lower levels of burnout (e.g., Cresswell & Eklund, 2005a, 2005b; Lemyre, Treasure, & Roberts, 2006; Raedeke & Smith, 2001), and higher incidences of flow experiences (e.g., Kowal & Fortier, 1999). Studies have also shown links with greater concentration (e.g., Standage et al., 2005) and more effective coping strategies and goal attainment (e.g., Amiot et al., 2004).

Given these benefits, understanding the processes by which people develop more self-determined motivation, particularly when the initial motive for the activity is not inherently enjoyable but rather instrumental in nature, has been a critical goal of the SDT framework (Ryan & Deci, 2002). To this end, OIT has focused on understanding the processes by which people internalize and integrate their experiences. As noted, a basic assumption of SDT is that people by nature are prone to assimilate their ongoing experiences into a unified and integrated sense of self (Deci & Ryan, 1991; Ryan & Deci, 2002). Thus, as people confront external regulations they will attempt to take in the regulation and integrate it with their sense of self, especially when supports for their needs are in place (Deci & Ryan, 1991). For instance, an athlete whose coach tells her that she has to show up to lift weights in the morning before school will attempt to find meaning and connection with herself in the request. Consequently, she might decide to comply with the request and engage in the behavior, not just because she was told to (external regulation) but also because she would not want to let her coach down (introjected regulation). Alternatively, she may decide to participate in practices after concluding that weight training will help her achieve her goal of being a successful athlete (identified regulation), or she may even comply because she views extra practice and training as consistent with her self-view as a motivated, hard-working athlete (integrated regulation). Thus, although the athlete may never come to view early morning practice as inherently enjoyable, she can develop a more self-determined form of motivation for the activity.

Ryan and Deci (2002) argue that the self-determination continuum of motivation specified in OIT is heuristic rather than a strict developmental continuum. People will be able to internalize a new behavior at any point on the continuum, and on occasion these processes will be incomplete insomuch as behaviors may never be fully internalized and integrated. According to OIT, the extent to which these processes function depends on the social context. For example, studies have found that the way in which instructions are provided for engaging in a nonintrinsically motivated activity has important implications (e.g., Reeve, Jang, Hardre, & Omura, 2002; Vansteenkiste, Simons, Sheldon, Lens, & Deci, 2004; Vansteenkiste, Simons, Soenens, & Lens, 2004). Specifically, framing an activity to emphasize the intrinsic goals of the activity (e.g., emphasizing personal value and relevance, presenting a clear and meaningful rationale for engagement), especially when presented in an autonomy-supportive context, leads people to engage in the activity for more self-determined reasons as well as to perform with greater effort, persistence, and achievement.

Ultimately, OIT posits that the degree to which people's needs for competence, autonomy, and relatedness are supported in the social environment will facilitate or obstruct their natural tendencies toward integration, a unified sense of self, and autonomous regulation of behavior (Ryan & Deci, 2002). A number of studies in the physical domain provide support for the link between need satisfaction and various forms of behavioral regulation identified by OIT. For instance, studies show that the extent to which physical education students perceive higher levels of competence, autonomy, and relatedness predicts intrinsic, extrinsic, and amotivation (e.g., Ntoumanis, 2001; Standage et al., 2003a, 2003b, 2005). Greater need satisfaction positively relates to more self-determined forms of motivation and negatively relates to less self-determined forms, although introjected regulation, which is considered a controlled form of motivation, positively relates to need satisfaction in these studies. The strongest relationships between the needs and motives occur at the two ends of the self-determination continuum; positive relationships emerge with intrinsic motivation and negative relationships with amotivation. Consistent with OIT, these studies have shown that various elements of the class environment (e.g., motivational climate, autonomy-supportive teaching behavior) predict students' motivation through their effect on students' needs for competence, autonomy, and relatedness.

Support also exists for the relationship between the psychological needs and motivational orientation using a relative autonomy index (e.g., Amorose & Anderson-Butcher, 2007; Hagger et al., 2006; Sarrazin et al., 2002; Standage et al., 2006). For example, Standage et al. (2006) reported that adolescent physical education students' perceptions of their teacher's autonomy support were positively related to their perceptions of competence, autonomy, and relatedness. Each of the three needs, in turn, positively predicted students' motivational orientation for physical education. Sarrazin et al. reported similar results with adolescent female handball players. In this case, athletes' perception of the motivational climate was the key social contextual factor. A mastery climate was a positive predictor of athletes' perceived competence, autonomy, and relatedness, which in turn were positively associated with athletes' levels of self-determined motivation. A performance motivational climate, on the other hand, negatively related to athletes' motivation through effects on perceived autonomy. Interestingly, athletes who reported higher levels of self-determined motivation had lower intentions to discontinue participation and were less likely to drop out the following season.

In summary, the distinction between various forms of behavioral regulation made in OIT have allowed for a more comprehensive examination of motivation in sport. Research on OIT that explores the social-contextual factors affecting processes of internalization and integration should ultimately help practitioners develop strategies for promoting more self-determined motivation in sport and physical activity participants. People's motivation, however, will not necessarily be a function of only what happens to them in the environment. Rather, behavior will also result from enduring personal characteristics. Deci and Ryan (1985a; Ryan & Deci, 2002) have elaborated on one salient intrapersonal characteristic in the next minitheory—causality orientation theory.

Causality Orientation Theory

In the SDT framework, Deci and Ryan (1985a; Ryan & Deci, 2000, 2002) argue that development, motivated behavior, and psychological functioning are the result of both social-contextual and intrapersonal factors. Whereas CET focuses primarily on the motivational effect of the social context, causality orientation theory (COT) details enduring personal characteristics. In particular, COT focuses on the relatively stable individual differences in people's motivational orientation, which Deci and Ryan (1985b) refer to as causality orientations.

COT specifies three main causality orientations—autonomous, controlled, and impersonal (Deci & Ryan, 1985b). These orientations are motivational in nature and reflect the general organizing processes that affect people's ongoing experience (e.g., interpretation of situations), particularly the regulation of their behavior (Ryan & Deci, 2002).

All three orientations, which develop over time as a result of people's ongoing interaction with the world in which they live, are believed to exist to a certain extent in everyone. An autonomous orientation describes regulation of behavior guided by self-selected goals and interests. People who endorse this orientation display high levels of self-initiation, seek activities that are interesting and challenging, and take responsibility for their own behavior. In this case, people tend to engage in actions for intrinsic or self-determined forms of extrinsic motivation. A controlled orientation, on the other hand, involves the tendency for other-directed or self-directed pressures to regulate behavior. People with a high controlled orientation depend on rewards, deadlines, or ego involvement, and focus more on what others demand rather than what they want personally. Thus, the driving motivation of this general tendency is external or introjected regulation. Finally, an impersonal orientation is consistent with amotivation. People with this orientation tend to lack intention to act and find themselves with feelings of incompetence and helplessness.

Much of the research examining elements of COT has used the General Causality Orientation Scale (Deci & Ryan, 1985b), which assesses the likelihood that people will respond in an autonomous, controlled, and impersonal manner to various hypothetical life situations (e.g., interpersonal relationships, the work environment, socializing). Thus, typical assessment of one's causality orientation is considered a general personality dimension, not unlike Vallerand's global level of motivation (Vallerand, 1997). Studies using this global indicator of causality orientation have shown that a high autonomy orientation is associated with higher levels of self-esteem, ego development, and self-actualization (Deci & Ryan 1985b) and greater integration in personality (Koestner, Bernieri, & Zuckerman, 1992). Williams and colleagues (1996) found that severely obese patients who endorsed a more autonomous causality orientation and perceived an autonomy-supportive climate reported participating in a clinical weight reduction program for more autonomous reasons, had better attendance at the program, and ultimately lost and kept off more weight. Considerably less positive outcomes have been associated with endorsement of the other two orientations. For instance, a controlled orientation has been related to a type A personality pattern and to high levels of public self-consciousness, whereas an impersonal orientation has been found to predict higher levels of social anxiety, depression, and self-derogation (Deci & Ryan, 1985b).

Although research supports the prediction that one's global causality orientation has important implications, Deci and Ryan (1985b) acknowledge that the strength of one's causality orientation may vary across contexts. In other words, despite being a relatively enduring characteristic, causality orientations can be domain specific. In one of the few attempts to explore causality orientations at the contextual level, Rose, Markland, and Parfitt (2001) developed the Exercise Causality Orientation Scale (ECOS). The scale measures the degree to which people approach and interpret information in an autonomous, controlled, and impersonal nature. But unlike the GCOS, which references multiple and diverse life situations, this scale asks about situations relevant to the exercise setting. As an example, when a respondent is presented with a hypothetical scenario in which he or she is just beginning a exercise program, the scale assesses the likelihood that the person would (a) attend a gym where they decide which exercises to complete (autonomous), (b) attend a structured exercise class where an exercise leader tells them what to do (controlled), and (c) tag along with friends and do what they do (impersonal).

Results from initial validation testing of the ECOS were generally consistent with expectations (Rose et al., 2001). The three exercise causality orientations each positively related to their global orientation counterpart. Further, the orientations related to the expected form of exercise motivation. For instance, an autonomy orientation related to more self-determined reasons for participating in exercise (intrinsic motivation, identified regulation), whereas positive associations between the controlled and impersonal orientations and non-self-determined motivation (external regulation) emerged. Rose, Parfitt, and Williams (2005) reported a similar pattern of relationships between exercise causality orientations and behavioral regulation.

COT represents one of the least studied portions of the SDT framework in the context of sport and physical activity. The lack of attention is likely due to the relatively global nature of the causality orientation construct. Nevertheless, recent research suggests that these orientations may have implications for understanding motivated behavior at a more contextual level. Another area within the SDT framework only recently generating research attention comes from the final minitheory—basic needs theory.

Basic Needs Theory

One of the basic assumptions underlying all elements of the SDT framework is the concept of basic needs. Deci and Ryan (1985a, 1991; Ryan & Deci, 2000, 2002) have argued from the initial development of SDT that there are a set of universal needs and that the degree to which these needs are satisfied will have important implications. Basic needs theory (BNT) was recently added to the SDT framework to clarify the role of these needs, particularly as they relate to psychological functioning and well-being (Ryan & Deci, 2002).

Central to BNT is the notion that needs for competence, autonomy, and relatedness are universal. This idea does not mean that the mechanism by which the needs are satisfied or thwarted will be identical across all people, places, and times. In fact, Ryan and Deci (2002) acknowledge that a particular social context may support the needs for one group of people but undermine them for another. Instead, the concept of universality reflects the belief that everyone, regardless of age, gender, race, or ethnicity, requires a sense of competence, autonomy, and relatedness for optimal functioning. In other words, the extent to which these needs are satisfied will result in positive well-being for all people.

Research on BNT has taken a few approaches. For instance, supporting research has looked at the link between the content of life goals and well-being (Kasser & Ryan, 1996, 2001). These studies have shown that people with more intrinsic aspirations (e.g., personal growth, affiliation, community contribution), which provide relatively direct support for a person's basic needs, achieve higher levels of well-being. Those with extrinsic aspirations (e.g., wealth, fame, image), on the other hand, typically attain lower levels of well-being. An important point here is that this pattern of relationships is independent of actual goal attainment (e.g., Kasser & Ryan, 2001).

Other studies that tested BNT have looked at the direct relationship between need satisfaction and indicators of physical and psychological well-being. For example, Kasser and Ryan (1999) linked perceived autonomy and relatedness to well-being and perceived health in nursing home residents, and Deci, Ryan, Gagné, et al. (2001) found positive relationships between basic need satisfaction and indices of well-being with a workforce sample. A few recent studies within the physical domain have also tested these relationships (e.g., Reinboth & Duda, 2006; Reinboth, Duda, & Ntoumanis, 2004). For example, Reinboth, Duda, and Ntoumanis examined the relationship between dimensions of coaching behavior and adolescent players' need satisfaction and psychological and physical well-being. Specifically, these researchers tested a model in which the extent to which athletes perceived their coaches to be autonomy supportive (i.e., provided athletes with choices and options), to promote a mastery motivational climate, and to provide social support influenced athletes' perceptions of competence, autonomy, and relatedness. The three needs, in turn, were predicted to influence various dimensions of well-being such as subjective vitality, intrinsic interest in sport, and physical well-being. Results showed that autonomy support, motivational climate, and social support were positive predictors of athletes' needs for autonomy, competence, and relatedness, respectively. In turn, perceived competence and autonomy, but not relatedness, positively related to athletes' psychological and physical well-being.

Another approach to testing BNT predictions comes from research examining relationships between indices of well-being and daily fluctuations that people experience in their need satisfaction (e.g., Reis, Sheldon, Gable, Roscoe, & Ryan, 2000; Sheldon, Ryan, & Reis, 1996). Gagné and colleagues (2003) recently took this approach in a diary study with young female gymnasts. Gymnasts were asked before each practice to offer their reason for attending that day and to report their current well-being. Immediately after each practice, they were asked to indicate how their needs had been satisfied during practice and again to report on their level of well-being, including positive and negative affect, subjective vitality, and self-esteem. Data collection occurred before and after 15 practices spanning a total of four weeks. Analyses revealed that athletes experienced increases in well-being when they perceived that their needs were satisfied during practices.

In sum, research supports the importance of need satisfaction on well-being as outlined in BNT. Although the minitheory does not specifically relate to understanding motivated behavior, the basic propositions have important implications for the overall experiences of participants in sport and physical activity. Clearly, promotion of optimal psychological function and positive well-being through satisfying needs for competence, autonomy, and relatedness will have affective, cognitive, and behavioral implications for those involved in all forms of physical activity. Thus, the theory makes an important contribution to the literature.

Conclusion and Future Research Directions

Each of the four minitheories contributes to the SDT framework, and together they provide a comprehensive explanation of human behavior and functioning. The theory makes important distinctions between motives that underlie people's actions, suggesting that regulation of behavior varies along a continuum of self-determination. The framework also describes how social-contextual and intrapersonal events facilitate or thwart people's tendency toward psychological growth, integration of the self, and self-regulation of behavior. Specifically, the theory specifies that the extent to which events affect the basic human needs for competence, autonomy, and relatedness will influence motivation and psychological functioning.

A model summarizing some of the key relationships outlined in SDT is presented in figure 7.2. Clearly, this model is an oversimplification of

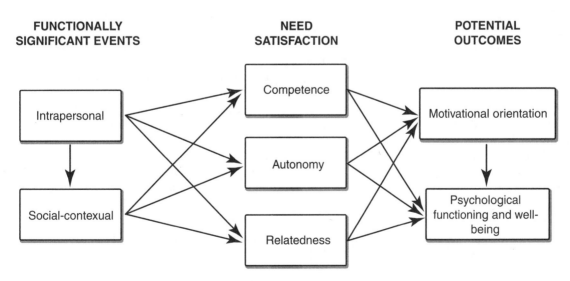

Figure 7.2 A model of the key relationships outlined in SDT.

motivational processes, but it illustrates how the minitheories work in concert to form the SDT framework. The model is similar to the basic motivational sequence identified in the hierarchical model of intrinsic and extrinsic motivation (see Vallerand & Ratelle, 2002), which proposes that social-contextual factors affect satisfaction of people's needs for competence, autonomy, and relatedness, which in turn influence motivation and a host of behavioral, cognitive, and affective outcomes. But the model has a few subtle differences. For instance, consistent with CET, not only do social factors influence satisfaction of needs, but so too will intrapersonal characteristics such as achievement goals or beliefs about the nature of ability. Behavioral, cognitive, and affective outcomes will be directly influenced by motivational orientation and indirectly influenced by perceptions of competence, autonomy, and relatedness as specified by BNT.

Despite the explosion of research in the physical domain testing SDT (see Hagger & Chatzisarantis, 2007), many important questions remain. First, much of the early research testing elements of SDT in sport and physical activity omitted relatedness. Recent research has incorporated satisfaction of relatedness along with competence and autonomy as a key predictor of motivation and psychological functioning (e.g., Hagger et al., 2006; Pelletier et al., 2001; Reinboth & Duda, 2006; Sarrazin et al., 2002; Standage et al., 2003a). Relatedness should continue to be included with perceived competence and autonomy in future tests of SDT.

Second, the amount of variance explained in motivational outcomes has often been small. For instance, Reinboth and colleagues (2004) found that various coaching behaviors and athletes' need satisfaction accounted for 25% of the variance in subjective vitality and intrinsic interest and only 4% of the variance in physical symptoms. Consistent with SDT, perceptions of competence, autonomy, and relatedness relate to participants' motivation and well-being. Nevertheless, the magnitude of variance explained suggests that other factors may contribute to an understanding of outcomes. Thus, a second area of future research could involve expanding the scope of the need constructs. For example, most studies have assessed perceived autonomy using items referencing perceived choice (e.g., Hollembeak & Amorose, 2005; Ntoumanis, 2001). Reeve (2002) argued, however, that perceived autonomy is a multifaceted construct composed of perceptions of choice, perceived locus of causality, and volition (i.e., feeling free versus feeling pressured in one's behavior). Adopting a more comprehensive autonomy construct may help

enhance prediction of motivation and psychological functioning. In support of this, Reinboth and Duda (2006) found that change in athletes' perceived locus of causality across a season predicted change in athletes' subjective vitality, whereas changes in perceived choice were not significant.

A third research direction that may be fruitful would be an exploration of the interactive effects of the three basic needs on outcomes. In the original formulation of CET, Deci and Ryan (1985a) argued that increased perceptions of competence should facilitate intrinsic motivation only when people feel a sense of autonomy. Markland (1999), however, found that variations in perceived competence positively influenced intrinsic motivation for exercise only under conditions of low perceived autonomy. These findings demonstrate that the needs interact to predict motivational outcomes. Increased attention should be directed to interaction effects of not only the three needs but also the intrapersonal and social-contextual determinants of need satisfaction and motivation (see Amorose, 2007; Pintrich, 2003). For instance, in their motivational model of the coach–athlete relationship Mageau and Vallerand (2003) suggested that autonomy-supportive behaviors should have positive effects on athletes' self-determined motivation only when accompanied by adequate structure and social support by the coach. Other determinants are likely to work together to influence motivation. For example, Standage and colleagues (2003b) found that the interaction of dispositional and situational achievement goals predicted intrinsic motivation above and beyond independent effects of these determinants.

Fourth, researchers should consider how the processes outlined in SDT function over time. Motivational processes are not static but rather are constantly changing as a function of intrapersonal and social-contextual variations (Weiss & Ferrer-Caja, 2002). Most SDT research in sport and physical activity, however, has employed cross-sectional designs. Consequently, information is limited to inferences about relationships among the variables at a particular time, rather than patterns of change in antecedents, motivational orientations, and cognitive, affective, and behavioral consequences. A few notable exceptions highlight the value of adopting a longitudinal approach (e.g., Gagné et al., 2003; Pelletier et al., 2001; Reinboth & Duda, 2006). For instance, Pelletier et al. followed a group of swimmers over two competitive seasons and found that forms of motivation functioned differently as predictors of persistence over time.

Finally, support for relationships described in SDT signals a readiness to develop and test interventions designed to satisfy the needs of physical activity participants and thus promote self-determined motivation, actual participation, and optimal psychological functioning. There are good examples of interventions in sport and physical activity that have manipulated elements of the social context, such as feedback patterns (Smoll & Smith, 2002), motivational climate (Harwood, Spray, & Keegan, this volume), and autonomy-supportive behaviors (Mageau & Vallerand, 2003). Scholars should expand these programs and attempt to (a) explore which aspects of interventions are more or less effective for promoting self-determined forms of motivation, (b) identify the optimal length of time required to effect meaningful changes in motivational processes, and (c) examine ways to train coaches, teachers, and other practitioners involved in sport and physical activity to adopt promotive behaviors.

Expectancy-Value Theory

Eccles and her colleagues formulated a model that embraces a multidimensional view of achievement choices and behaviors (Eccles et al., 1983, Eccles, Adler, & Kaczala, 1982; Eccles, Wigfield, & Schiefele, 1998; Wigfield & Eccles, 1992, 2000). Eccles's worldview expresses the relationship between self-beliefs and task beliefs with activity choices and participation behaviors, and specifies the social and psychological determinants of ability perceptions and task

value. Several motivational questions stem from this framework. For example, given similar competence levels, why do some children believe that they can succeed at just about any skill or activity, whereas others linger in self-doubt? Why do some children want to succeed in a particular achievement area, whereas others discount the importance of doing well in the same domain?

Consistent gender differences in educational and career decisions, especially in mathematics, sparked Eccles's initial interest in understanding achievement motivation (e.g., Eccles, Adler, & Meece, 1984). Despite having similar ability and test scores in elementary school, girls were less likely than boys were to choose advanced math courses that would prepare them for high-status professions and careers. Eccles contended that girls' lower self-concept of ability in math and their assigning less importance to being good in math were primary predictors of lack of motivation to take math courses. What are the sources of such beliefs? Will an understanding of determinants help in planning interventions to abate self-fulfilling tendencies?

Eccles et al.'s (1983) comprehensive model describes and explains behavioral variations in choice, persistence, and performance in children and adolescents across achievement domains. This model is depicted in figure 7.3. Achievement behavior is directly influenced by expectancies of success and subjective task value, and indirectly influenced by psychological factors such as

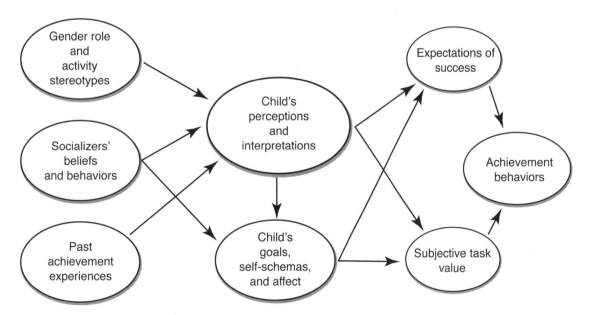

Figure 7.3 Eccles' expectancy-value model of activity behaviors.

self-schema, goals, perceived task difficulty, and affect as well as social-contextual factors such as parents' beliefs and behaviors, cultural norms, and the structure or climate of achievement situations. It is important to note that youths' interpretations or perceptions of socializers' beliefs and behaviors, previous achievement experiences, and situational factors shape their competence beliefs, values, and achievement behaviors, rather than actual ability or past successes and failures. The following sections overview theoretical underpinnings, research applying the model to the physical domain, and future research directions.

Theoretical Underpinnings

The expectancy-value model (Eccles et al., 1983, 1998) attempts to explain variations in youths' achievement choices and behaviors despite similar talent, opportunities to achieve, and history of successes in a particular domain. Achievement choices and behaviors refer to decisions about whether to participate in an activity, whether to select an easy or challenging task, how much effort to expend, and how much persistence to apply to a difficult skill. Two primary determinants of achievement choices and behaviors are (a) the person's expectancies of success or competence beliefs in a particular domain and (b) the subjective task value or importance that the person places on being successful in a domain. These model components and relationships will be discussed in turn, with supporting research provided by Eccles and her colleagues across achievement domains.

Expectancies of Success According to Eccles et al. (1998), expectancies of success reflect the question "Can I do this task?" Thus, success expectancies are akin to efficacy expectations or confidence in being successful at an achievement activity. Domain-specific ability beliefs (i.e., perceived competence) are determinants of activity-specific confidence ratings. Eccles and her colleagues have consistently found expectancies or perceived ability to be strong predictors of achievement behaviors (Eccles et al., 1983; Eccles & Harold, 1991; Wigfield et al., 1997). For example, Eccles and Harold found that by the first grade, girls reported lower ability perceptions than boys did in math and sport, and that among sixth graders ability beliefs in sport explained gender differences in physical activity levels.

Given the crucial role that success expectancies or perceived competence plays in achievement choices, understanding the factors that influence such self-beliefs is essential. The main determinants

of success expectancies are self-schema, perceived task difficulty, perceptions of socializers' beliefs and behaviors, causes of past successes and failures, and gender and activity stereotypes. Eccles and Harold (1991), for example, reported that children's perceptions of their parents' beliefs about participating and performing well in sport, and their parents' importance ratings for boys and girls being good in sports (i.e., gender-role stereotype), were significantly related to children's self-ability ratings in the athletic domain. Perceptions of parents' beliefs were a stronger source of gender differences in children's self-ability ratings than were objective measures of sport ability.

Subjective Task Value Subjective task value is the second major determinant of achievement choices and behaviors in the expectancy-value model. This construct addresses the question "Do I want to do this task and why?" (Eccles et al., 1998; Wigfield & Eccles, 1992). Task value alludes to the importance that a person attaches to being successful in a particular achievement area. The extent to which an individual perceives that a task meets personal needs or goals determines the value attached to participating in that activity. Eccles and colleagues identified four components of subjective task value: attainment value, interest value, utility value, and cost.

Attainment value refers to the importance of doing well in a particular achievement domain that confirms self-identity (e.g., athletic, intelligent). Interest value refers to the enjoyment experienced from participating in the activity (i.e., intrinsic rewards of the activity). Utility value describes perceived usefulness of the activity in relation to short- or long-term goals such as investment in a career (i.e., extrinsic value of the activity). Finally, perceived cost refers to time, energy, and opportunities that may be lost by engaging in a particular achievement activity or engaging in one activity over another. Ultimately, people weigh the positives (values) and negatives (costs) of engaging in an activity and make choices accordingly.

As with expectancies, the model identifies several antecedents of task value. Directly influencing value are the affective memories associated with achievement experiences. Experiences associated with feelings such as pride, joy, and happiness will positively affect task value, whereas negative memories will relate to devaluing the activity. In addition to affective experiences, individuals' goals and self-schemas, perceptions of socializers' beliefs and behaviors, and perceptions of gender and activity stereotypes will affect subjective task value.

Relationships Among Success Expectancies, Task Values, and Achievement Behaviors

To demonstrate relationships among expectancies, task values, and achievement choices, Eccles and her colleagues engaged in several studies that cut across achievement domains such as math, reading, English, music, and sports (e.g., Eccles et al., 1983; Eccles & Harold, 1991; Fredricks & Eccles, 2002; Jacobs, Lanza, Osgood, Eccles, & Wigfield, 2002; Wigfield et al., 1997). Strong support emerged for relationships among these variables, especially as they relate to gender. For example, Eccles et al. found that among 5th- to 12th-grade students, boys reported higher success expectancies, lower task difficulty, and greater utility value for mathematics. The researchers also found that perceived math ability was positively related to task value, expectancies of success, and plans to continue taking math courses. Children's perceptions of parents' expectancy beliefs and value toward math mediated the effect of gender and history of success on achievement beliefs and behaviors. Parents were seen as having higher competency beliefs and greater attainment value for their sons than for their daughters in math.

Eccles and Harold (1991) tested the expectancy-value model with elementary and middle school students in English, reading, math, and sport. Boys rated themselves as more competent than girls in sport. They rated sports as more important, useful, and enjoyable; and they reported greater participation rates. Girls reported higher expectancies, value, and participation in reading and English than boys. Gender effects on participation rates were not significant when self-concept of ability and task value were included as mediating variables. These studies demonstrate that children's perceptions of ability and task values drive achievement behavior in domains that vary in gender stereotyping. These early studies stimulated others who examined relationships among expectancy-value constructs in the physical domain and connections to gender and socializers' influence (e.g., Cox & Whaley, 2004; Fredricks & Eccles, 2005; Stuart, 2003). Before delving into these results, we first highlight the developmental component of Eccles' model.

Developmental Component Eccles and colleagues couch the expectancy-value model within a developmental perspective (e.g., Eccles & Wigfield, 1995; Wigfield, 1994). Conceptualization of success expectancies and subjective task value varies with age, as do relationships with model constructs (e.g., socializers' beliefs, achievement behaviors).

As seen in figure 7.4, levels of and relationships among model constructs change over time, and such change will produce variations in subsequent relationships. For example, success expectancies and task values decline across the childhood and adolescent years (e.g., Eccles & Wigfield, 1995; Fredricks & Eccles, 2002; Wigfield, et al., 1991, 1997). Rodriguez, Wigfield, and Eccles (2003) found that sport competence beliefs and value toward sport decreased over a three-year period among elementary-age children. Jacobs et al. (2002) found varying rates of decline in levels of girls' and boys' competence beliefs and task values for math, language arts, and sport from grades 1 to 12, and they found that competence beliefs contributed to gender differences and trajectories of change in task values. Age-related changes in self-beliefs and task beliefs have implications for subsequent motivation and achievement behaviors.

Wigfield et al. (1997), in a three-year study of achievement beliefs in math, reading, music, and sport, found that young children were very optimistic about their abilities, but self-beliefs, attainment and utility values declined in each domain over the elementary years. Interest value, however, depended on domain: Interest in music and reading decreased, whereas interest in math and sport did not. A positive relationship between success expectancies and attainment value increased over time (i.e., children came to value those domains at which they succeeded), and relationships of children's competence and value beliefs with parents' beliefs about child's competence became increasingly stronger over the elementary years. Fredricks and Eccles (2002) followed boys and girls from grade 1 to grade 12 on competence beliefs and task values in math and sport. Competence beliefs in both domains progressively decreased but were more pronounced for sport. Attainment value for math increased, but interest value decreased over the middle and high school years; by contrast, interest value remained high for sport over this same period while attainment value decreased. Parents' beliefs about children's competence in math and sport strongly related to youths' own ability beliefs and task values.

Collectively, these studies demonstrate that developmental issues are important for understanding variations in level of and relationships among competence beliefs, task values, parents' influence, and achievement behaviors. Eccles and colleagues (Eccles et al., 1998; Fredricks & Eccles, 2004) have devoted particular attention to mechanisms of parental socialization that contribute to developmental trends in children's achievement beliefs and behaviors. We review this literature next.

Socializers' Influence on Expectancy-Value Constructs Considerable research exists on parents' beliefs and behaviors conveyed to children concerning their capability for performing a task and the importance of being successful in a domain (see Eccles et al., 1983, 1998; Fredricks & Eccles, 2004). According to Eccles and colleagues, parents can shape children's perceived competence, task values, and achievement behaviors in three ways: (a) as providers of experience, (b) as interpreters of experience, and (c) as role models. Parents provide experiences when they sign their children up for sports and provide transportation to and from practices and games. Parents interpret experiences by conveying some degree of confidence about their child's probability of success, communicating evaluative feedback, or expressing beliefs about the importance of being successful in a domain. Finally, through observation of their parents' behavior, children derive a sense of their competence and learn which achievement domains are important, interesting, and useful. As such, parents model, provide, and interpret salient information and experiences for children that influence their ability beliefs, task values, and achievement behaviors.

Several studies have shown support for these mechanisms of parent influence and children's expectancies and values (see Fredricks & Eccles, 2004). For example, Jacobs and Eccles (1992) explored the influence of mothers' gender-role stereotypes and competence beliefs for their children in math, sport, and social domains. Consistent with expectancy-value predictions, mothers who held stronger gender-stereotyped beliefs were more likely to possess ability estimates that favored boys for math and sport and girls for social activities. Mothers' perceptions of their children's abilities in these domains, in turn, predicted children's self-perceptions of ability. Moreover, mothers' perceptions of their children's abilities were stronger determinants of children's self-ratings than were children's actual abilities based on teachers' ratings. Several other studies have shown that parents' beliefs about their children's competence are strongly related to children's own ability beliefs and the value that they place on being successful (e.g., Babkes & Weiss, 1999; Fredricks & Eccles, 2002, 2005; Wigfield et al., 1991).

Eccles' model emphasizes cognitive (competence beliefs, task values), affective (memories of achievement experiences), and social (adults' and peers' beliefs and behaviors) influences on achievement choices and behaviors. Moreover, tests of model hypotheses have held up across a variety of achievement domains. Since the previous version of our chapter appeared, several studies were conducted to extend the knowledge base of expectancy-value theory to the physical domain. In the following sections we review research conducted in physical activity contexts along the following topics: (a) correlates of success expectancies and task values; (b) relationships among expectancies, task values, and achievement behaviors; (c) gender differences in expectancy-value constructs and relationships; (d) parent influence on expectancies, task values, and physical activity behaviors; and (e) contextual influences on expectancies, task values, and physical activity behaviors.

Correlates of Success Expectancies and Task Values in the Physical Domain

Some researchers have been interested in correlates of expectancies and task values. Stephens (1998) integrated constructs within expectancy-value and achievement goal theories to examine goal orientations, perceived ability, enjoyment (interest value), and importance, or utility value, among youth soccer players. Those higher in task orientation and lower in ego orientation reported higher enjoyment and value than those lower in task orientation (regardless of ego). For players with lower perceived ability, those of higher task and lower ego orientation reported greater value toward soccer than all other groups. Players with higher perceived ability who were higher in task orientation (regardless of ego) reported greater enjoyment than those higher in ego orientation and lower in task orientation. Thus, those who primarily used self-referenced means to define success (effort, improvement) viewed sport as an enjoyable, important, and useful domain in which to succeed. Variations depended on beliefs about soccer competence.

Stuart (2003) was interested in identifying sources of attainment, utility, and interest value toward sport. Boys and girls (ages 12 to 14) completed items pertaining to each component of task value, and then 10 youth who scored low, medium, and high in these dimensions were interviewed about why they thought sport was interesting, important, and useful (or not). Findings confirmed Eccles et al.'s (1983) origins of subjective task value—affective memories (positive movement sensations, performance concerns) and significant adult (coach, parent) beliefs about the importance of sport. Stuart's findings also extended Eccles' sources in that peers (teammates, friends) were frequently named as sources of task value (e.g., lack of friendship led to low interest value). Study participants named attractive alternative activities as contributors to low task value, such as opportunities to make money, engage in noncompetitive activities, and hang out with friends. Both common and unique sources of value components were identified among low, medium, and high value groups.

Relationships Among Expectancies, Task Values, and Physical Activity Behaviors

Several researchers have explored relationships of success expectancies and task values with achievement behaviors. Deeter (1989, 1990) assessed these relationships among university students in physical activity classes. Trait sport confidence and self-efficacy were used to assess expectancy of success, whereas sport orientations (competitiveness, win, goal) represented attainment and utility values. Achievement behavior was represented by instructors' evaluations of students' performance and objective measures (win percentage, number of laps run). Results revealed that success expectancy variables were stronger predictors of achievement behavior than task values. Paxton, Estabrooks, and Dzewaltowski (2004) took an alternative approach. They found that perceived physical competence significantly predicted attraction to physical activity (i.e., subjective task value) among 9- to 14-year-old youth, which in turn predicted physical activity behavior (i.e., attraction mediated the relationship between perceived competence and physical activity).

Papaioannou and Theodorakis (1996) integrated constructs from three theories (expectancy-value, planned behavior, achievement goal) to predict intention to participate among high school physical education students. Their study supported Eccles' model in that perceived competence and interest and utility values were significant predictors of intention. They also found perceived behavioral control and attitude toward physical activity to be important predictors, indicating that additional variables may contribute beyond expectancies and value to explain achievement intentions. Similarly, Xiang, McBride, Guan, and Solmon (2003) found that beliefs about physical ability and task value among fourth graders predicted intention to participate in future physical education classes. An important follow-up to these studies would be to assess whether intentions, in turn, are predictive of actual behaviors such as choosing to participate, effort, and persistence.

Cox and Whaley (2004) extended previous research by assessing relationships among expectancies, value, and achievement behaviors in high school basketball players and determining whether relationships differ by race. In addition, they investigated whether athletic identity (self-schema) contributes to variations in expectancies, value, and achievement behavior, as suggested by Eccles' model. For players of both races, success expectancies and task values significantly predicted effort and persistence shown on the court, with expectancies contributing more strongly. Athletic identity was strongly related to expectancies and attainment, interest, and utility values but was not significantly related to effort and persistence through the mediation of expectancies and values.

Application of the expectancy-value model has also been supported in unstructured physical activity settings such as school recess and at home (e.g., Shapiro & Ulrich, 2002; Watkinson, Dwyer, & Nielsen, 2005). For example, Watkinson et al. interviewed children about decisions to participate in school recess activities. Reasons reflected success expectancies (being good at the activity), positive task values (e.g., it's interesting, it's cool), and cost of participating in activities (e.g., get tired, made fun of). Shapiro and Ulrich assessed expectancy-value constructs among children with and without learning disabilities in three physical activity contexts (physical education class, school recess, and at home), and found moderate to strong relationships between perceived competence and subjective task values.

Gender Differences in Expectancy-Value Constructs in the Physical Domain

Given that Eccles' conceptualizing about determinants of achievement choices and behaviors stemmed from gender variations in self-concept of ability and subjective task values, a number of studies have investigated gender differences in expectancy-value constructs in physical activity contexts. Others have included gender as a moderator variable in relationships among expectancy-value constructs. In the following paragraphs, we review relevant studies with an eye toward gender-specific findings.

Because females report lower success expectancies or ability beliefs about sport than do males, Lirgg (1991) conducted a meta-analysis to determine the magnitude of such differences and possible moderators of these effects. She reported an overall effect size of 0.40 favoring males but also considerable variability in magnitude of differences. Using gender stereotyping of task as a moderator, Lirgg produced an effect size of 0.65 favoring males for masculine-typed tasks and –1.02 favoring females for the only study that examinined a feminine-typed task (ballet). Clifton and Gill (1994) examined self-confidence among female and male cheerleaders, because cheerleading subtasks vary in perceived gender appropriateness (e.g., dance, partner stunts, cheers and motions, jumps). Males rated overall athletic ability higher than females did, whereas females were more confident in overall cheerleading ability, cheers and motions, jumps, and dance. Findings lend support for Eccles' model in that individuals' perceptions of activity stereotypes influenced ability beliefs, which should influence activity choice and behavior.

As part of larger studies examining relationships among expectancy-value constructs, researchers reported male–female differences in expectancies of success, subjective task values, and achievement behaviors (Bois et al., 2002; Bois, Sarrazin, Brustad, Trouilloud, et al. 2005; Brustad, 1993, 1996; Eccles & Harold, 1991; Fredricks & Eccles, 2002, 2005; Jacobs & Eccles, 1992; Lirgg, 1993). Boys report higher levels of physical ability and value toward sport, and are more physically active than girls. Gender differences in expectancies, values, and achievement behaviors, however, do not exist within a social vacuum. Social and contextual factors, which are explicitly embedded within Eccles' model, serve as important sources whereby girls and boys derive a sense of how capable they are and what domains they value, which together drive their achievement choices and behaviors. The next two sections review these social-contextual factors.

Parents' Influence on Children's Expectancies, Task Values, and Physical Activity Behaviors

Eccles' model highlights parents as important socializers of children's achievement beliefs and behaviors. In fact, Eccles et al. (1998) expanded the expectancy-value model into a comprehensive model of parental influence (see figure 7.4) that specifies sources of parents' beliefs and behaviors (family, characteristics, child characteristics, parents' general beliefs) that affect child outcomes (beliefs, values, behaviors). According to Eccles and colleagues (1983, 1998; Fredricks & Eccles, 2004), parents influence their children through mechanisms as providers, interpreters, and role models of beliefs and behaviors. Strong support exists for these types of parental influence in the physical domain. This body of knowledge has been informed by programmatic research studies.

Brustad (1993, 1996) studied parents' beliefs and behaviors in relation to children's perceived competence and value toward physical activity. In the first study, fourth-grade boys and girls completed measures of perceived competence and attraction toward physical activity, which included interest value (e.g., liking of vigorous exercise) and utility value (i.e., importance of activity to good health). Parents rated their enjoyment of physical activity (interest value), fitness level (modeling), and importance of physical activity (utility value). They also indicated how frequently they encouraged their children to be active and how often they participated with their children. Parents who reported greater enjoyment of activity, but not importance or fitness, gave more encouragement to their chil-

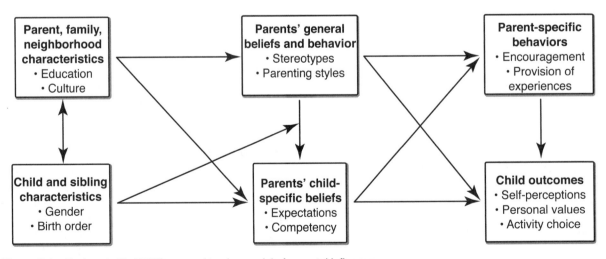

Figure 7.4 Eccles et al.'s (1998) comprehensive model of parental influence.

dren to be active. Greater parent enjoyment and encouragement were associated with higher levels of children's perceived competence and attraction to physical activity. Brustad (1996) replicated these results with a more diverse ethnic and socioeconomic group of children.

Kimiecik and colleagues conducted three studies of parent influence on children's physical activity beliefs and behaviors (Dempsey, Kimiecik, & Horn, 1993; Kimiecik & Horn, 1998; Kimiecik, Horn, & Shurin, 1996). Dempsey et al. found that parents' perceptions of their child's competence, but not role modeling, contributed beyond gender to explain moderate to vigorous physical activity (MVPA). Kimiecik et al. examined the relationship between children's fitness beliefs, children's perceptions of parent beliefs, and MVPA. The association between children's ability beliefs and MVPA was moderately strong, and children who perceived that their parents held high competency beliefs reported higher competence. Kimiecik and Horn examined mothers' and fathers' beliefs about their child's MVPA, the link between parents' and child's MVPA, and the relationship between parent beliefs and child's MVPA. Mothers and fathers did not differ in perceived competence or value for daughters or sons. This finding contrasts gender differences reported by others (e.g., Eccles & Harold, 1991; Jacobs & Eccles, 1992). Parent-reported MVPA was not related to children's MVPA (i.e., no support for role modeling), but parents' competence beliefs for their child were significantly related to their child's MVPA.

Bois and his colleagues (Bois et al., 2002; Bois, Sarrazin, Brustad, Chanal, et al., 2005; Bois, Sarrazin, Brustad, Trouilloud, et al. 2005) conducted longitudinal studies that tested relationships between parent beliefs and behaviors with those of their children in the physical domain. Bois et al. (2002) assessed mothers' perceptions of the child's competence in relation to the child's own perceived physical competence over the course of a year. Mothers' beliefs contributed beyond the child's perceived competence and physical performance at time 1 to explain perceived competence at time 2. These results were stronger for daughters than for sons. Bois, Sarrazin, Brustad, Chanal, et al. (2005) assessed mothers' and fathers' competence beliefs and physical activity behavior in relation to those of their child. Mothers' beliefs predicted the child's perceived competence that, in turn, predicted activity level, and mothers' physical activity directly predicted the child's physical activity. For fathers, competence beliefs for the child directly predicted the child's physical activity. These results support

both parent role modeling and interpretation effects, and suggest that processes of child influence may be different for mothers and fathers. Finally, Bois, Sarrazin, Brustad, Trouilloud, et al. (2005) assessed relationships among parent appraisals of children's physical competence, children's reflected appraisals of parents, and children's self-appraisals of physical ability. Strong support emerged for children's reflected appraisals as mediators of parents' actual appraisals on children's self-appraisals of physical competence. Collectively, these studies demonstrate support for the parent–child linkages in Eccles et al.'s (1983, 1998) models.

Fredricks and Eccles (2005) extended previous studies in several ways. They examined parent–child relationships in physical activity beliefs and behaviors in three cohorts of children concurrently and over the course of a year. They used regression and pattern-centered analyses to assess the nature and strength of parents' provisions, beliefs, and modeling on children's perceptions of competence, task value, and sport participation. Regression analyses (both cross-sectional and longitudinal) revealed that parents' beliefs about their child's sport ability were strongly related to the child's achievement beliefs and sport involvement. For pattern-centered analyses, a total support score was created based on parents' beliefs (e.g., child's sport ability, value of sport) and behaviors (e.g., encouragement, time involvement in sports). A variable was considered a "promotive" socialization factor if the score was in the top 25% of the distribution. Assessment of children's outcomes as a function of promotive factors revealed an additive effect for parent socialization and children's self-beliefs, value, and sport participation. Greater number of promotive factors (parent beliefs, value, behaviors) was associated with children's higher perceived competence, value toward sport, and time spent in sport.

Collectively these studies strongly support Eccles's model in the physical domain. First, children's perceptions of parent beliefs and behaviors strongly relate to children's competence beliefs, attraction toward activity, and activity behavior. Second, children's reflected appraisals mediate the relationship between parents' appraisals and children's self-appraisals of ability. Similarly, children's beliefs about ability mediate the relationship between perceptions of parents' beliefs and activity behavior. Finally, all three socialization mechanisms—parents as providers, interpreters, and role models—contribute to children's achievement beliefs and behaviors. Besides parents, the social context of sport including climate, norms, and structure contributes to feelings of competence, value of doing well, and motivation to achieve. Studies that addressed contextual factors within Eccles et al.'s (1983) model are reviewed next.

Contextual Influences on Expectancies, Task Values, and Physical Activity Behaviors

Following research by Eccles and Blumenfeld (1985) that implicated classroom context as a predictor of achievement behavior, Lirgg (1993, 1994) examined the influence of same-sex and coed physical education classes on students' self-perceptions, task values, and perceptions of the classroom environment. In the first study, Lirgg examined self-confidence, utility value, and perceived gender appropriateness of basketball as a function of class context. Middle and high school boys exhibited greater confidence in coed versus same-sex classes, whereas girls showed a trend toward higher confidence in same-sex classes than did those in coed classes. Regardless of class context, boys rated basketball as a more masculine activity and as more useful for future leisure time than did girls. These results partially support class context as an important contributor to self-perceptions, value, and gender typing of activities.

In the second study (Lirgg, 1994) examined environmental perceptions of same-sex versus coed classes by focusing on participants' evaluations of student behavior, involvement, and social interaction tendencies, as well as teacher behavior. Girls in same-sex classes rated their classes as better behaved and more cooperative than did all other groups. Boys in same-sex classes recorded the highest ratings for competitiveness. Lirgg found more student involvement for same-sex versus coed classes. These results highlight that classroom climate in the form of same-sex versus coeducational classes is perceived quite differently by gender. These perceptions, according to Eccles, are likely to affect the quantity and quality of opportunities afforded for developing competence beliefs and task values and influencing activity choices and behaviors.

Besides Lirgg's studies (1993, 1994), we did not locate any others in the physical domain that looked at connections between social context and expectancy-value constructs. This dearth of research is surprising given that Eccles' model identifies contextual factors such as classroom climate, evaluation practices, and quality of teacher–student relationships as contributors to variations in success expectancies, task values, and achievement behav-

iors, especially during developmental transitions such as elementary to middle school (e.g., Eccles & Midgley, 1990; Roeser & Eccles, 1998). A similar argument could be made for sport transitions, such as when youth move from a lower-skilled league (i.e., recreational) to a higher level (i.e., select or travel league). Weiss and Williams (2004) suggested that ability beliefs and task values change as a function of the motivational climate, coaching philosophy, and extent of social support that exists in varying competitive contexts. Change in perceptions of competence and value toward sport as a function of shift in contextual influence is likely to influence motivated behaviors such as continued participation, level of effort expended, and intensity of involvement. Thus the linkage among contextual factors, expectancies, values, and behaviors is an important direction to pursue.

Conclusion and Future Research Directions

Considerable research by Eccles and colleagues and researchers in sport psychology shows that the expectancy-value model is conceptually sound and practical for understanding relations among expectancies, values, and achievement behaviors in sport and physical activity. Notable is the quantity and quality of findings relative to parent beliefs and behaviors on youths' psychosocial and behavioral outcomes. One direction for future research is to consider linkages in Eccles et al.'s (1998) comprehensive model of parent influence on children's motivation and achievement. In this model (see figure 7.5), antecedents of parents' beliefs and behaviors include parents' general beliefs and behaviors (e.g., stereotypes, parenting styles), child and sibling characteristics (e.g., birth order, gender), and parent and family characteristics (e.g., culture, education). Sources of parents' child-specific influences have been given scant attention, and findings would inform educators about why parents believe and act the way they do. For example, sport exists with a multicultural context but little is known about how parents of differing background value sport as an achievement domain and consequently convey certain expectancies to their children.

Similarly, social-contextual variables represent an important antecedent in Eccles et al.'s (1983) expectancy-value model. Achievement behaviors occur within social contexts that vary in cultural norms, gender and activity stereotypes, psychological climate, and significant adults' and peers' behaviors. Thus, a second important research direction is to consider the social context in which children's success expectations, attraction toward activity, and participatory behaviors occur. For example, physical activity contexts differ in the degree to which certain practices and values are endorsed. Is the emphasis on learning or performance? Does the coach allow autonomy or exert significant control? Is the process or product of performance reinforced? Is ability grouping practiced? The preceding are only some of the contextual influences that bear directly on self-judgments of ability, perceptions of what is valued, and desire to continue participation. Eccles' model posits that the organization, structure, and teaching practices within particular social contexts affect achievement beliefs and behaviors. Future research might examine perceptions of the motivational climate, teachers' management and decision-making styles, and gender and activity stereotypes as they influence self-beliefs, task beliefs, and achievement behaviors.

A third promising area for future research in the physical domain is developmental transitions. A focus of Eccles and colleagues' empirical work has been on transitions from one school context to another (i.e., elementary to middle school, middle school to high school). Eccles and Midgley (1990), for example, documented social contextual changes in the transition from elementary to junior high school that included class size, organizational structure for instruction, grading practices, and motivational goals. These changes were deemed negative motivational effects because fewer opportunities for autonomy and greater emphasis on social comparison, normative grading, and public evaluation practices equated to a poor fit between the needs of early adolescents and their classroom environment. Changes in the social context were implicated as a source of decreased competence perceptions and interest value in many school subjects across older childhood and early adolescence.

Transitioning across social contexts is particularly relevant to the physical domain. Children often begin their sport careers in programs in which skill development and fun are the primary goals. Evaluation and recognition are based on effort and improvement, activities are interesting and varied, and coaches provide ample playing and practice time. As children climb the athletic skill ladder (e.g., move up to a select team), coaches are stricter with rules, criteria differ for defining successful performance, and drills become less varied and interesting. Fewer youth are talented enough to make select or travel squads, resulting in a narrower comparison group by which to judge athletic competence. Thus, competence ratings likely decline, and interest

in the activity, as well as importance and utility values, may wane. The pyramid of athletic success is complete when only the fittest survive eventual cuts at the higher levels of sport (e.g., all-star and state team selections). Eccles' model suggests that differences in program philosophy, importance of winning, and coaching behaviors have important effects on participants' expectancies, value, and participation. Research supports such hypotheses in the academic domain, but testing needs to be done in sport. Studies on sport transitions may help tease out whether variations in competence beliefs and task values reflect age-related changes in cognitive abilities (e.g., differentiating effort and ability), sources of information for judging competence, structure of sport (task or ego involving), or an interaction of these factors.

Sport Commitment Model

The robust finding that enjoyment or fun is a dominant motive for participating in sport led Scanlan and her colleagues to conduct a series of studies on sources of enjoyment in diverse athletic samples varying in age, gender, ethnicity, and sport type (Scanlan, Carpenter, Lobel, & Simons, 1993; Scanlan & Lewthwaite, 1986; Scanlan, Stein, & Ravizza, 1989; Stein & Scanlan, 1992). Findings across samples revealed that positive social interactions (parents, coach, teammates), perceptions of competence, social recognition of competence, effort, mastery, and movement sensations were primary determinants of sport enjoyment. Despite these consistent findings of sources of enjoyment, the construct remained largely atheoretical in nature.

In a synthesis of their own and others' empirical work on enjoyment sources, Scanlan and Simons (1992) introduced sport enjoyment as a central construct within a larger conceptual model of motivation that they called the sport commitment model. Sport commitment is defined as the desire and resolve to continue sport participation and is thus viewed as a psychological rather than behavioral construct (Scanlan, Carpenter, Schmidt, et al., 1993). The model was adapted from social exchange theory (Kelley & Thibaut, 1978; Thibaut & Kelley, 1959) and Rusbult's (1980a, 1980b, 1983) investment model of personal relationships. These models identify three major antecedents of commitment: (a) attraction toward the relationship or activity (e.g., benefits minus costs; level of satisfaction), (b) attractiveness of available alternatives, and (c) constraints or barriers to ceasing involvement (e.g., investment of time, energy, and money; social pressures or feelings of obligations to others to continue). Attraction and constraints maximize commitment, whereas attractive alternatives minimize commitment to the current activity. Scanlan and her colleagues customized these determinants of commitment as well as the commitment construct to the specific social context of sport and physical activity.

The sport commitment model originally proposed by Scanlan and colleagues (Scanlan, Carpenter, Schmidt, et al., 1993; Scanlan, Simons, Carpenter, Schmidt, & Keeler, 1993) consists of five determinants (see figure 7.5). Enjoyment is defined as a positive affective response that reflects feelings of pleasure, liking, and fun. Involvement opportunities are anticipated or expected benefits afforded from continued participation such as friendships, positive interactions with adults, skill mastery, travel, and physical conditioning. Involvement alternatives reflect attractiveness of other activities that could compete with continued participation in the current activity. Personal investments pertain to time, effort, financial, and other resources put into the activity that would be lost if participation was discontinued. Social constraints refer to expectations from significant others that instill a sense of obligation to continue involvement. Perceptions of higher enjoyment, investments, involvement opportunities, and social constraints should increase commitment, whereas perception that other activities are more attractive lowers commitment. Determinants and level of sport commitment can be investigated at different levels of analysis such as sport in general, a specific sport program, or a specific sport or physical activity (e.g., swimming, baseball).

Measurement Development and Model Testing

Initial validation of the sport commitment model involved developing theoretically consistent items for key constructs and investigating the magnitude of relationships between determinants and level of sport commitment (Carpenter, Scanlan, Simons, & Lobel, 1993; Scanlan, Carpenter, Schmidt, et al., 1993; Scanlan, Simons, et al., 1993). Multiple items were developed and modified for original model constructs based on the commitment and youth sport literatures, feedback from experts, and evaluation by teachers to ensure comprehension and readability in children of varying backgrounds. Validity testing was conducted with several diverse samples varying in gender, ethnicity, and age, including youth in a variety of team and individual sports in community and school contexts (Scanlan, Carpenter, Schmidt, et al., 1993).

In the first test of relationships within the sport commitment model, only enjoyment and personal investments significantly predicted level of commitment in youth baseball and softball players (Scanlan, Carpenter, Schmidt, et al., 1993). Although nonsignificant, involvement opportunities were moderately correlated with sport commitment and sport enjoyment. A subsequent study with athletes (ages 10 to 19) in three sports revealed that enjoyment, investments, and involvement opportunities were significant predictors of sport commitment, with social constraints also emerging as a significant but weak contributor (Carpenter et al., 1993). Contrary to model hypotheses, social constraints were negatively related to commitment.

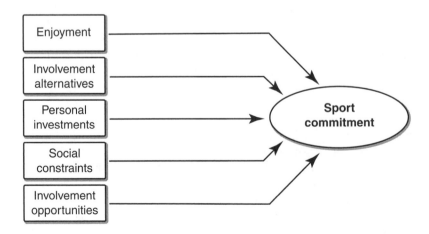

Figure 7.5 The sport commitment model.

Carpenter (1992) studied commitment among adolescent sport participants and added several determinants in an effort to increase predictability, including negative affect, satisfaction, rewards, costs, available alternative activities, social support, and perceived ability. Six variables emerged as significant determinants of sport commitment: enjoyment, personal investments, recognition opportunities, attractive alternatives, parent support, and coach obligation. Several findings were noteworthy. One was the positive relationship between perceived social constraints (by the coach) and sport commitment. Second was the link between social (parent) support and commitment, suggesting that the positive side of social influence is important to consider along with the negative side (i.e., social constraints). Third, consistent with previous studies, enjoyment, investment, and involvement opportunities were strong predictors of commitment. Finally, moderate correlations among several determinants (e.g., enjoyment and social support from friends; enjoyment and perceived ability) suggested that additional variables should be considered in further tests of the sport commitment model.

Subsequent studies by Carpenter (Carpenter & Coleman, 1998; Carpenter & Scanlan, 1998) tested relationships among commitment constructs assessed at several points during the season. Model predictions suggest that variation over time in determinants should correspond with change in commitment. Carpenter and Scanlan had soccer players complete measures of commitment constructs at midseason and near the end of the season (five- to seven-week span). Players were categorized as increasing, decreasing, or showing no change in constructs from time 1 to time 2. Athletes whose enjoyment decreased and whose involvement opportunities lessened showed a significant decrease in sport commitment over the season. Carpenter and Coleman assessed elite (ages 9 to 17) cricket players at the beginning and end of a season (about eight weeks) on original determinants and ones added by Carpenter (1992). Fluctuations in sport enjoyment and involvement opportunities were associated with similar changes in commitment. Increases in social support and negative affect also were associated with an increase and decrease, respectively, in commitment. Findings from these studies offer partial support for the sport commitment model in that change over time in some determinants was associated with concomitant change in commitment.

Collectively, early studies of the sport commitment model showed general support for relationships specified between determinants and level of commitment. In addition, social support emerged as an important determinant in two studies (Carpenter, 1992; Carpenter & Coleman, 1998). More research was needed to test hypothesized relationships at various levels of analysis (sport in general, specific program, specific sport) and with diverse participants who vary in talent, age, sport type, and competitive level. Since the appearance of our previous version of this chapter, several studies have been conducted to extend the knowledge base in sport commitment. One direction was expansions to the model (i.e., additional determinants, inclusion of consequences) and testing of alternative models that specify relationships among commitment variables.

Expansions to the Sport Commitment Model and Testing of Alternative Models

Initial testing of the sport commitment model included children and adolescents involved in recreational and competitive sports. Scanlan and colleagues (Scanlan, Russell, Beals, & Scanlan, 2003; Scanlan, Russell, Wilson, & Scanlan, 2003) extended their early work by testing the sport commitment model using mixed methods with elite male rugby players (New Zealand's All Blacks). Besides providing further support for the role of enjoyment, personal investments, and involvement opportunities to explaining players' commitment to the All Blacks, results revealed two important considerations for modifying the model. First, the researchers relabeled involvement alternatives as *other priorities* to capture activities or responsibilities in a participant's life that would make continued involvement difficult (family, job, education). Second, they found that feeling encouraged and supported by family, the rugby community, the public, and friends was an important contributor to team commitment. This finding supports studies with youth athletes (Carpenter 1992; Carpenter & Coleman, 1998; Weiss, Kimmel, & Smith, 2001) that suggest including social support as a determinant of sport commitment.

Weiss et al. (2001) tested an alternative sport commitment model—one in which enjoyment mediated the relationship between other determinants (investments, involvement alternatives, social constraints, social support) and level of commitment. Including enjoyment as a mediator made sense in light of high correlations between enjoyment and sport commitment ($r \geq .70$) found in previous studies. Thus, it is possible that other constructs are suppressed as contributors to commitment. In addition, enjoyment has been moderately correlated with involvement opportunities (e.g., make friends, improve skills) and personal investments. Finally, sources of enjoyment include social support from adults and teammates; low perceived pressure from parents and coaches; perceived competence; and social and life opportunities (Scanlan & Simons, 1992). These constructs are all contained within the sport commitment model. Thus, Weiss et al. tested a mediational model using junior tennis players. The model showed a good fit and supported enjoyment as a filter through which other determinants influence commitment. Enjoyment was the strongest predictor of commitment and mediated the influence of attractive alternatives and personal investments on the desire and resolve to continue participation. A mediational model is theoretically appealing because it accounts for sources and consequences of enjoyment.

Recently, Weiss and Weiss (2006a) also found that a mediational model best explained relationships among commitment variables in female gymnasts. Along with original determinants, several other variables based on the youth motivation literature were included: perceived costs, perceived competence, and motivational climate. Behavioral commitment in the form of effort and persistence in the gym was included as a consequence of sport (psychological) commitment, because ultimately we are interested in actual participation behaviors. With a correlation of .80 between enjoyment and sport commitment, multicollinearity resulted in misfit of the model and suppression of variables that contribute to sport commitment. Thus, enjoyment was specified as a mediator; this model resulted in a good fit and revealed that involvement opportunities, perceived costs, and attractive alternatives predicted enjoyment that, in turn, directly predicted psychological commitment and indirectly predicted participation behavior. Gymnasts who perceived greater benefits and lower costs of participating and fewer attractive alternative activities scored higher in enjoyment, psychological commitment, and effort and persistence in the gym. Other researchers have also found that enjoyment and perceived benefits predicted participation behavior (i.e., continued involvement) through effects on psychological commitment (Guillet, Sarrazin, Carpenter, Trouilloud, & Cury, 2002; VanYperen, 1998).

Based on the developmental sport psychology literature, Martin (2006) chose specific social and psychological constructs as determinants of commitment among participants in youth disability sport. Specific constructs included sport enjoyment, perceived physical competence, parent encouragement, and friendship quality. Given the high correlation between enjoyment and commitment (r = .66), it is not surprising that enjoyment emerged as the sole predictor of sport commitment, even though perceived competence was moderately correlated with both enjoyment and commitment, and parent encouragement and positive friendship quality were significantly related to both. Given previous comments, it would be interesting to test a mediational model with perceived competence, parent encouragement, and friendship quality as antecedents of enjoyment, which in turn is specified to predict commitment.

In summary, a mediational model is appealing on both theoretical and practical grounds. This model suggests that strategies should be designed to enhance athletes' enjoyment of participating, which in turn increases motivation and continued involvement. Strategies include enhancing sources of enjoyment such as social support by parents, coaches, and peers; perceived competence; benefits of participating (skill improvement, positive interactions, achieving goals); and a mastery motivational climate; and reducing sources of lack of enjoyment such as social constraints by adults and teammates and a performance climate. Figure 7.6 presents a schematic in which constructs of sport commitment and sport enjoyment are intertwined. Antecedents of commitment include enjoyment and its sources, and consequences include behavioral indicators of the desire and resolve to maintain involvement, such as continued participation; effort and persistence; and frequency, intensity, and duration of involvement.

Developmental Considerations in Sport Commitment

Most studies that have investigated sport commitment combined female and male samples ranging in age from 9 to 19 years. This approach allowed for measurement development and model testing that generalized across diverse youth populations. Now that measures have been validated and the nature of relationships is better understood, an important direction is to determine whether relationships between determinants and sport commitment vary by age, competitive level, and gender. A strong rationale exists for exploring developmental differences in the relationship between determinants and level of commitment, given variations in self-perceptions, emotions, social relationships, and motivational ori-

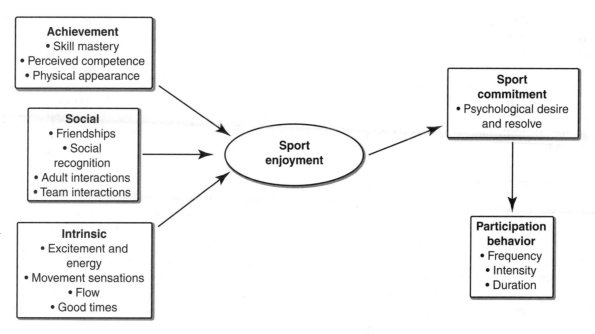

Figure 7.6 Schematic of the sources and consequences of sport enjoyment.

entations across childhood and adolescence (Harter, 1999; Horn, 2004; Weiss & Stuntz, 2004; Weiss & Williams, 2004).

Weiss and Weiss (2007) examined age and competitive level differences in commitment among female gymnasts. Gymnasts were classified into three age groups: 8 to 11 years (middle to late childhood), 11 to 14.5 years (early to middle adolescence), and 14.5 to 18 years (middle to late adolescence). Because of high correlations between enjoyment, involvement opportunities, and attractive alternatives, the latter two variables were removed from analysis. Enjoyment emerged as the strongest predictor of commitment for all age groups, explaining nearly all the variance. Based on this finding and the high correlation between enjoyment and sport commitment ($r = .80$), enjoyment was removed from the equation to see whether other variables emerged as predictors of commitment. Regression analyses revealed significant relationships for all age groups. For 8- to 11-year-olds, parent and best friend social constraints and perceived costs were negatively related to commitment. Perceived costs and parent social constraints were also significant for 11- to 14.5-year-olds, but so was personal investment: Greater investment translated to higher commitment. For the oldest gymnasts (14.5- to 18-year-olds), lower perceived costs and higher perceived gymnastics competence were associated with greater commitment.

Gymnasts were also grouped into two competitive levels—levels 5 and 6 (introductory, compulsory levels) and levels 8 to 10 (highly competitive,

optional levels). Again, relationships between determinants and level of commitment were significant. For lower-level gymnasts, personal investments, best friend and teammate social constraints, and coach social support were positively related to commitment. Greater perceived costs and coach social constraints were associated with lower commitment. For higher-level gymnasts, greater personal investments and teammate social constraints were associated with greater commitment, and greater perceived costs were related to lower commitment. Collectively, results show that developmental factors such as age and competitive level are important in exploring relationships within the sport commitment model. Age and variations in competitive level provide insight into motivational strategies that should positively influence psychological and behavioral commitment.

The importance of considering developmental needs, goals, and interests in relation to sport commitment was demonstrated in a study of adolescents' continued motivation in sports, music, and performing arts (Fredricks et al., 2002; Patrick et al., 1999). The researchers chose to study adolescents because peer relationships are especially salient and play a significant role in influencing activity choices and degree of involvement. Although the study was not couched within the sport commitment model, adolescents were interviewed about factors that influenced their enjoyment of and commitment to their talent activity. Prevalent sources included perceived competence, supportive peer relationships, perceived challenge, benefits and costs of involvement, and self-definition or identity (i.e., athlete, musician, actor). These factors are all reminiscent of sources of sport enjoyment and commitment discussed earlier (i.e., involvement opportunities, personal investments, social support, social constraints, perceived competence).

Although both female and male adolescents identified social benefits of involvement, females were more likely to highlight the influence of peers in contributing positively or negatively to their decisions to continue or quit, and this was especially true of nonschool activities rather than school-based activities. The emergence of identity, gender differences, and contextual influences contributes to understanding variations in commitment to sport and physical activity. Gender differences reinforce findings by Coakley and White (1992) that adolescent girls report greater social constraints from opposite-sex friends and greater social support from same-sex friends to participate than do boys. Moreover, adolescent girls made decisions to participate based on concerns about competence, their perceptions of whether physical activity was compatible with becoming an adult, and past negative affective experiences in sport. Again, social constraints, social support, and affect are prime determinants of sport commitment, so we might expect differences between male and female adolescents on relative influence of determinants on psychological and behavioral commitment.

Attraction Commitment Versus Entrapment Commitment

Rusbult (1980a, 1980b, 1983), in her investment model, not only identified the conditions necessary for commitment to a relationship (high satisfaction, low attractive alternatives, high investments) but also differentiated between those who stayed in a relationship for positive reasons (i.e., out of attraction) and those who stayed for negative reasons (i.e., felt entrapped). Those who were committed for attraction reasons reported high benefits, satisfaction, and investments and low costs and attractive alternatives. People who were committed to a relationship for entrapment reasons reported decreasing benefits and satisfaction and increasing costs associated with the relationship. Despite this negative profile, individuals remained in the relationship because they had already invested so much and did not perceive available or appealing options.

Schmidt and Stein (1991) translated this notion of types of commitment to competitive sport. They contended that as long as people perceive high benefits, enjoyment, and investments and low costs and attractive alternatives, they will be committed to their sport for attraction reasons. Alternatively, individuals may be committed because they think that they have to stay involved. That is, even though enjoyment and perceived benefits of the activity are decreasing and perceived costs are increasing, alternative activities may not be available or attractive and individuals have invested so much of their time, energy, and money. This type of commitment has been labeled *entrapment*. Schmidt and Stein proposed that, similar to athletes who stay for attraction-based reasons, people committed out of entrapment perceive low alternatives and high investments but also perceive low rewards, high costs, and low enjoyment. Both types of commitment result in similar behavior, however, in that people remain in the sport but do so for highly different reasons.

Raedeke (1997) tested Schmidt and Stein's (1991) predictions of attracted and entrapped committed athletes. He assessed adolescent swimmers on benefits, costs, enjoyment, investments, and attractive alternatives. Attraction and entrapment profiles emerged. The entrapment profile (called malcontented swimmers) reported lower enjoyment and benefits and higher costs relative to the sample mean. Contrary to predictions, however, these swimmers reported lower investments and higher attractive alternatives. An attraction commitment profile emerged that supported predictions. The malcontented swimmers were significantly higher on burnout and lower in level of commitment than attraction-committed swimmers. Thus, Raedeke suggested that athletes comprising the entrapped profile were experiencing burnout and thinking of leaving the sport, thereby decreasing their investments and viewing other activities or options as highly appealing. Raedeke's study was the first empirical test of attraction and entrapment commitment in sport and showed that people who reflected these profiles could be distinguished on level of commitment (desire and resolve to continue) and burnout.

Weiss and Weiss (2003, 2006b) replicated and extended Raedeke (1997) using high-level competitive female gymnasts. The researchers used cluster analysis to determine profiles and compared emergent groups on social support, social constraints, motivational orientation, and training behaviors. A profile of attracted gymnasts was consistent with Schmidt and Stein's (1991) predictions and Raedeke's findings, characterized by higher enjoyment, benefits, and investments, and lower costs and attractive alternatives. An entrapped profile also emerged that was characterized by lower enjoyment and benefits and higher costs, investments, and attractive alternatives. This profile supported predictions by Schmidt and Stein except for attractive alternatives, which was consistent with Raedeke's findings. Attracted athletes were higher than entrapped athletes were on level of commitment, parent and coach support, intrinsic motivation, and effort and persistence, and lower on parent social constraints and amotivation.

Weiss and Weiss (2006b) followed up a subsample of these gymnasts one year later to determine whether they were still participating, whether commitment type stayed the same or changed, and whether levels of social influence and commitment could still differentiate commitment types. Findings revealed that a higher percentage of entrapped gymnasts had discontinued gymnastics at year 2, that the same cluster types and patterns of variables emerged one year later, that 63.5% of gymnasts stayed in the same group while the remaining 36.5% "cluster-hopped," and that attraction-committed gymnasts reported greater parent and coach support and level of commitment, and lower teammate and parent constraints, than entrapped gymnasts did. Collectively, these studies lend further support to the notion that athletes vary in type of commitment and that these groups differ in theoretically consistent ways on social, motivational, and behavioral variables. Such findings carry implications for coaches and parents who strive to provide athletes with positive sport experiences and maximize their continued involvement.

Coaching Commitment

The sport commitment model has also been applied to understanding coaches' dedication to the profession (Raedeke, 2004; Raedeke, Granzyk, & Warren, 2000; Raedeke, Warren, & Granzyk, 2002). Raedeke et al. (2000) assessed current age-group swim coaches on perceived benefits, costs, satisfaction, investments, social constraints, and attractive alternatives. A cluster analysis revealed three commitment profiles: attracted, entrapped, and less interested. Coaches committed out of attraction reported higher benefits and satisfaction and lower costs and attractive alternatives. Entrapped coaches scored higher on costs, investments, and social constraints, and moderately lower on benefits and satisfaction. Less interested coaches were lower on benefits, satisfaction, and investments and higher on attractive alternatives. In support of hypotheses,

entrapped coaches scored higher on burnout than other groups did and were similar in level of commitment to attracted coaches. These same coaches were compared with former coaches (Raedeke et al., 2002) on commitment constructs. Current coaches reported higher investments and social constraints than did former coaches, who scored higher on attractiveness of alternative options. Finally, Raedeke followed a subsample of current coaches one year later and similar commitment profiles emerged. Entrapped coaches reported higher burnout and lower commitment than attracted coaches but higher commitment than less interested coaches. Collectively, these studies demonstrate that commitment for entrapment reasons is linked to burnout in coaches and supplement Raedeke's (1997) similar findings with athletes.

Conclusion and Future Research Directions

The sport commitment model did not emanate from the achievement motivation literature but rather from social exchange and investment models that emphasize benefits, costs, and satisfaction within relationship contexts. Scanlan and colleagues integrated these ideas with those from youth sport motivation to customize a model that specifies conditions in which people express desire to continue their involvement in a program or activity. Since our previous chapter, research has provided further validity for the sport commitment model. In addition, researchers tested variations of the model including additional determinants, enjoyment as a mediator, developmental differences, and attracted and entrapped forms of commitment. Considering these studies, we offer several directions for future research.

An important direction in future research is to improve measurement of commitment constructs. One example is the high correlation ($r > .70$) between enjoyment and sport (psychological) commitment found in most studies (e.g., Raedeke, 1997; Weiss et al., 2001; Weiss & Weiss, 2006a, in press). These constructs are conceptually distinct but nonetheless overlap empirically. This issue may explain why enjoyment has been the overriding predictor of sport commitment in studies conducted to date and why other theoretical determinants of commitment (involvement opportunities, investments, social constraints, attractive alternatives) are weak or nonsignificant predictors. In addition, enjoyment is often strongly correlated with attractive alternatives. Again, these concepts are distinct but overlap, perhaps because high enjoyment in one activity is likely to correspond with low attractiveness toward other activities.

Enjoyment has also been moderately related to involvement opportunities. This empirical overlap also makes sense because involvement opportunities are assessed with questions such as "Would you miss the good times you have had?" and "Would you miss your friends [your coach]?" These items represent perceived benefits or sources of enjoyment. In addition, Scanlan, Russell, Beals, and Scanlan (2003) found that enjoyment and its sources (e.g., friendships, travel) were mentioned as valuable (involvement) opportunities among elite athletes. This overlap may have resulted in the suppression of involvement opportunities and other determinants as predictors of commitment. In some studies, theoretical determinants were eliminated to avoid multicollinearity, whereas in others enjoyment was specified as a mediator to test other constructs' contribution to commitment through their linkage with enjoyment. The sport commitment model is conceptually sound, but empirical testing of relationships is sometimes limited by measurement of certain constructs. Thus future research might devote attention to improving measures or adopting alternative models (i.e., mediational model) to address these issues.

Another potentially useful research direction is inclusion of participation behaviors as a consequence of sport commitment. Sport commitment is defined as the psychological desire and resolve to continue participation in sport. Therefore, a test of the sport commitment model would be incomplete without investigating behavioral consequences of commitment. Are highly determined people more likely to maintain participation over time, sustain involvement under challenging times, and exhibit greater effort and persistence compared with less determined peers? By including behavioral outcomes, the commitment framework allows a comprehensive look at participation motivation: Do individuals stay in or leave a program as a function of determinants and level of sport commitment? What factors most strongly affect decisions to continue or discontinue involvement? Figure 7.6 includes sources and consequences of psychological commitment, and provides a roadmap for investigating these questions. Some researchers have included measures of behavior (Raedeke, 2004; VanYperen, 1998; Weiss & Weiss, 2003, 2006a), and others chose highly committed athletes as study participants because of their sustained time and training in their sport (Scanlan, Russell, Beals, & Scanlan, 2003). We encourage researchers to include

behavioral assessments in tests of the sport commitment model.

Because sport commitment is defined as "the desire and resolve to continue sport participation over time" (Scanlan, Carpenter, Schmidt, et al., 1993, p. 7), another important research direction would be to conduct intervention studies with a longitudinal component. The integration of enjoyment and commitment within a broader framework provides a heuristic model (figure 7.6) that identifies antecedents and consequences of both constructs. As such, several possibilities exist for testing the validity of the sport commitment model through intervention research. For example, findings to date and figure 7.6 suggest that structuring the situation to realize involvement opportunities (e.g., affirm friendships, skill mastery), emphasize social support (e.g., coaches' encouragement and positive behaviors), and minimize social constraints (e.g., pressure to perform, controlling behaviors) will result in higher enjoyment and psychological commitment. Higher desire and resolve should result in greater effort, persistence, and continued involvement in the activity. These conditions set the stage for intervention in which one group is exposed to conditions that maximize enjoyment and commitment while a control group is taught in the standard way. Change over the course of the program in determinants and consequences of enjoyment and commitment could be assessed along with behavioral measures at appropriate times. The sport commitment model would be validated if corresponding change in theoretical determinants, psychological commitment, and behavior occurred at multiple times during the intervention. Moreover, a retention test months later would determine whether change as a result of intervention was enduring or temporary.

Conclusion

Researchers can use a variety of theoretical approaches to investigate motivational orientation and sport behavior. Our intent was to provide an overview of several conceptual models, associated empirical research, and directions for future research. We chose four theoretical approaches that are suitable and effective when applied to sport and physical activity contexts. These included competence motivation theory, self-determination theory, expectancy-value model, and sport commitment model.

Certain nuances characterize each perspective. Competence motivation theory views positive affect or enjoyment as central to motivational processes.

Perceptions of competence and influence by significant adults and peers are important determinants of affect, desire for optimally challenging activities, and intrinsic interest in mastering challenges. Self-determination theory considers individuals' interpretations of experiences as controlling or informational; needs for competence, autonomy, and relatedness; and a variety of intrinsic and extrinsic motivational orientations and their consequences. The expectancy-value model highlights individuals' success expectations and subjective value toward activities as predictors of achievement behaviors, as well as the developmental sources of competence beliefs and values. The sport commitment model accounts for enjoyment within a broader motivational framework. Sources and consequences of sport enjoyment and commitment are considered, which provides opportunities to locate which variables best explain the desire and resolve to continue participation.

Along with their unique twists to understanding motivated behavior, these approaches possess several commonalities. Each theory implicates the importance of the social context, including social support and constraints by significant adults and peers, and situational factors such as culture, gender, and the climate in which learning and performance take place. A number of individual differences make up a common denominator: self-perceptions (perceived competence, success expectancies), perceived choice or autonomy, and subjective task value or the importance of doing well in a domain. Affect is key to all theories, whether it is positive (enjoyment, pride, satisfaction) or negative (anxiety, boredom). Intrinsic motivation, or doing an activity for its own sake, is central to each theory, along with behavioral consequences such as activity choice, intensity of effort, persistence, and continued involvement. Finally, most theories contain a developmental component in terms of differentiating competence beliefs and task values; showing preference for socializing agents; and using sources of competence information.

One of the major goals of sport psychology is to determine what factors maximize participation in physical activity. Research should focus on identifying factors that promote continued activity from youth through older adulthood. This kind of sustained activity will allow people to achieve physical, psychological, and social benefits available from a physically active lifestyle. A critical element that affects whether people sustain their involvement and attain these benefits is their motivational orientation. An intrinsically motivated or mastery-oriented person embraces optimal challenges, those that enhance perceptions of competence and value toward physical activity. Enhanced self-perceptions and value (importance, enjoyment, usefulness) will maintain or enhance intrinsic motivation and activity choices, effort, persistence, and involvement. The extrinsically motivated or performance-oriented person who doubts his or her ability, in contrast, will likely select easy activities, exert minimal effort, and give up when the going gets tough. Perceptions of competence, affect, and motivational consequences are compromised in this case. Thus, focusing efforts on determinants of an intrinsic motivational orientation will help promote positive outcomes.

Practitioners who face challenges related to youth and adult program enrollment or persistence must understand the underlying processes that explain motivation in physical activity settings. Similarly, sport psychology scholars need an accurate conceptualization of these processes to conduct research that contributes to theory development and asks questions of practical significance. Such an understanding will also inspire interventions that make a difference when it comes to helping people adopt a physically active lifestyle or choose to remain involved in sport. We hope that the theoretical and empirical issues presented in this chapter will stimulate researchers and educators to pursue these objectives with a desire for mastery and feelings of competence, positive affect, and intrinsic interest.

CHAPTER 8

Achievement Goal Theories in Sport

Chris Harwood, PhD ▪ Christopher M. Spray, PhD ▪ Richard Keegan, MSc

It is perhaps a fortunate coincidence that modern-day society's ever-increasing emphasis on competition and achievement is matched by the staggering endeavor of researchers focused on understanding achievement motivation in sport. The past 20 years have been a watershed for our understanding of sport achievement behavior—our ability to appreciate why some people eagerly approach difficult challenges, exert consistent effort, and persist in adversity, whereas others avoid certain competitive encounters, restrain effort, and give up at the first sign of things going wrong. Such understanding is needed if national governing bodies, coaches, parents, and athletes themselves are keen to sustain growth, mastery, and long-term participation in sport at all levels. Since the mid-1980s sport psychologists have been blessed with a cluster of achievement goal theories, largely from the educational domain (Dweck, 1986; 1999; Nicholls, 1984, 1989), that triggered a penetrating wave of research into the intrapersonal and environmental influences on athlete behavior in achievement settings.

Achievement goals represent the meaning that individuals assign to achievement situations. These goals provide a cognitive structure that organizes a person's definitions of success and failure, motivational processes (e.g., attributions), affective reactions, and subsequent motivated behaviors (e.g., task choice, effort, persistence). The central objectives for researchers interested in achievement goal approaches have been to understand more precisely what achievement goals exist, the mechanisms by which they are developed or adopted, and the subsequent influence that they have on psychological parameters associated with participation, performance, and overall psychological well-being.

In the late 1970s and early 1980s the work in classroom settings of John Nicholls, Carol Dweck, Martin Maehr, and Carole Ames provided the early foundation for our understanding of achievement goals in sport, and readers are encouraged to access these original papers (Ames, 1984a; Dweck, 1986; Maehr & Nicholls, 1980; Nicholls, 1984, 1989). Alongside more contemporary theorists (Elliot, 1999; Elliot & Church, 1997), each scholar formulated his or her own viewpoint of how achievement goals determine motivated behavior. Theoretical differences exist in the antecedents of particular achievement goals and the number of achievement goals in operation. Their common thread lies in their explanation of not only the primary reason why people engage in achievement contexts (e.g., to demonstrate or develop competence) but also the criteria that they employ for judging successful or unsuccessful competence outcomes.

The original works of Glyn Roberts (1984, 1992) and Joan Duda (1987, 1992) launched achievement goal research in sport, and it has largely been Nicholls' theoretical approach to achievement goals that researchers have mapped onto the sporting landscape. Since then a number of major review papers and books have emerged (Duda, 1993, 2001; Duda & Hall, 2001; Duda & Whitehead, 1998; Weiss & Ferrer-Caja, 2002), and this chapter does not seek to replicate this work. Rather, its purpose is to review the key theoretical principles of the varying approaches and directions that research has taken in recent years and then to challenge researchers to consider a number of sport-specific, conceptual, and methodological avenues that we believe are salient to the continued popularity and progress of achievement goal approaches in sport.

The chapter is divided into five main sections. First, we present John Nicholls' conceptualization of achievement goals and follow up by looking at the central themes of literature in sport and some critical future directions. Second, Carol Dweck's approach, often given lesser attention within sport, will be outlined comprehensively here together with examples of past, present, and future research endeavors. Third, we explain Andrew Elliot's integrated theory of approach-avoidance motivation alongside specific ideas to advance the validity of his two-by-two framework. Penultimately, we appraise the current state of research into motivational climate (Ames, 1992b), a key situational factor of significance to all the approaches mentioned earlier. Finally, with each of these complementary approaches in mind, we offer a number of future research recommendations to guide researchers over the next decade and drive them to adopt more challenging and sophisticated questions in this area.

Nicholls' Approach to Achievement Goals

To Nicholls (1984, 1989) the concept of ability (often used interchangeably with the term *competence*) was fundamental to understanding achievement motivation in educational settings. He maintained that a person's internal sense of ability was a central achievement motive but proposed that ability could be construed in two different manners. Drawing from one of his key publications, Nicholls states

> Achievement behavior is defined as behavior directed at developing or demonstrating high rather than low ability. It is shown that ability can be conceived in two ways. First, ability can be judged

high or low with reference to the individual's own past performance or knowledge. In this context, gains in mastery indicate competence. Second, ability can be judged as capacity relative to that of others. In this context, a gain in mastery alone does not indicate high ability. To demonstrate high capacity, one must achieve more with equal effort or use less effort than do others for an equal performance. (Nicholls, 1984, p. 328)

These two conceptions of ability identified by Nicholls underpin two contrasting achievement goals that represent how people define success in an achievement task. People are task involved when gains in personal mastery of a skill or task enrich them with a sense of competence. In this respect, self-referent improvement or learning on a task is sufficient to generate feelings of personal achievement. In contrast, people are ego involved when their sense of competence depends on demonstrating superior performance to others or an equal performance to others but with less effort exhibited. These two achievement goals, therefore, focus on different aspects of the self. An individual in a state of task involvement (i.e., a task-involved goal is most salient), focuses mainly on the development of the self irrespective of others. A person in a state of ego involvement (i.e., an ego-involved goal is most prevalent) is primarily concerned with the perceived ability of the self compared with others and the external demonstration of this ability.

Developmental Processes

Nicholls' theory emerged from developmental ideas about how young children move through a temporal process whereby they gradually differentiate the concept of ability from effort, task difficulty, and luck (Nicholls & Miller, 1984). In the early stages, from 5 to 7 years of age, children do not differentiate between the concepts of ability and effort, and ability and task difficulty. Tasks that children are uncertain of completing are viewed as difficult. They see these tasks as requiring more effort, which when mastered through effort, provide them with a sense of ability. Effort is positively correlated with ability, reflecting what is known as an undifferentiated conception of ability. In this state, an internal sense of ability is simply equated with (and guaranteed by) trying hard, learning, and understanding something more fully (Nicholls, 1989). This undifferentiated state, at least on cognitive grounds, might be viewed as the earliest or indeed purest form of task involvement. It represents a mind-set that perhaps Nicholls and all achievement goal researchers are eager to hold constant. But maturity ensures that children move

through a series of cognitive-developmental stages whereby at 11 or 12 years, they are able to conceptualize ability as a capacity (see Fry, 2001, for a detailed discussion of this process in the sport domain). Children at this stage understand that difficult tasks are those that only few can perform and that normative ability as opposed to effort determines whether they can complete such tasks. Effort and ability become inversely related; ability sets the limit on what effort alone can accomplish, and exerting high effort is simply not enough for a person to feel successful or competent. When children achieve this mature understanding and differentiated conception of ability, they are capable for the first time of being ego involved. Nicholls' body of work is powerful in its keen emphasis on how maintaining optimal motivation in youth revolves around fostering task involvement even after children become capable of being ego involved.

Achievement Goal Orientations

One of the critical features of Nicholls' approach with respect to subsequent research in sport is that he promoted the existence of two dispositional goal orientations that reflected "individual differences in proneness to different types of involvement" (1989, p. 95). Because of socialization experiences in childhood and adolescence, individuals develop a tendency to adopt task- or ego-involved goals in achievement situations. Nicholls viewed these dispositional goals as representative of a worldview or theory about success in a given achievement domain (i.e., education). Subsequent research in education and sport (Duda, 1989; Duda & Nicholls, 1992) has found that a task goal orientation is associated with the belief that sport and education provide opportunities for personal growth and mastery and that success stems from working hard, learning, and collaborating with others. Conversely, an ego goal orientation has been consistently associated with the belief that sport and education provide opportunities for social status, superiority, and wealth and that success stems from outperforming others and even using deceptive or illegal tactics.

This line of research into the more global beliefs associated with the two dispositional achievement goals is noteworthy. Further, an understanding of the correlates of these dispositional goal orientations became the focus of early research in sport. The fact that goal orientations are orthogonal (i.e., largely independent; uncorrelated), however, means that people can vary in their levels of each goal orientation. For example, a person could possess a high level of task orientation and a high level of ego orientation, or any of the other three basic combinations (i.e., high task and low ego, low task and high ego, low task and low ego). Nicholls never studied these combinations in his own research, but as noted later in this chapter, these dispositional goal profiles (Fox, Goudas, Biddle, Duda & Armstrong, 1994; Hodge & Petlichkoff, 2000) have provided a better understanding of the person as a two-part whole as opposed to the more limited predictions gleaned from being labeled as task oriented or ego oriented.

Situational Factors and Goal Involvement

Nicholls' theory was interactionist in nature in that he proposed that the adoption of task-and ego-involved goals for a specific activity would rest on the interaction between an individual's dispositional goal orientations and situational cues specific to that achievement environment. For example, a person may tend to be more ego involved than task involved (i.e., a higher ego orientation and lower task orientation profile) in his or her approach to achievement situations. But if the person is placed in a noncompetitive environment where working on improving skills is valued and social recognition is given purely for personal improvement and effort exerted, his or her conception of achievement for that particular situation may be different. With an activity devoid of ego-involving situational cues, a state of task involvement may be induced, depending on the strength of the person's ego orientation.

Nicholls did not specifically test these propositions, and research in sport has not fully examined the interaction of disposition by situation on goal involvement (i.e., at the situational, or state, level). An overview of the key issues will be reported later, but for in-depth coverage of this topic, see Duda (2001), Harwood and Swain (1998), Swain and Harwood (1996), and Williams (1998).

Core Theoretical Predictions

Nicholls proposed that when an individual experiences a state of task involvement, a positive and adaptive pattern of cognitive, affective, and behavioral responses is likely to emerge. The person will engage in positive achievement striving through effort, persistence, challenging task choices, and intrinsic motivation (Nicholls, 1984). At a dispositional level, people high in task orientation will have a positive belief and value structure about sport as a whole, including the causes of success in sport, its role and purpose in society, and the moral behaviors

associated with such pursuits (Duda, 1992; 2001; Roberts, 2001).

Nicholls suggested that although a task-involved athlete and a person in a state of ego involvement would have divergent belief and value systems, a similar pattern of motivational responses could be expected. But this proposal was strictly on the proviso that the person maintained a high perception of ability. In sport terms, an athlete whose perception of adequacy depends on winning but who is confident of doing so is likely to approach the task with at least enough effort to win. The sense of self in achievement terms is under less normative threat. But because of the external source of control implicit in ego involvement, perceptions of ability are much more fragile. Thus when perceived ability is low or when ego-involved athletes are uncertain of normative success, Nicholls suggested that a negative and maladaptive pattern of psychological responses would result. These responses include dysfunctional behaviors (i.e., effort withdrawal, low persistence, avoidance of moderately challenging tasks), unhealthy or self-serving attributions for outcomes, greater stress and anxiety, and a tendency toward morally unacceptable behaviors within such a domain (e.g., cheating, intention to injure).

Over the past 15 years, many of Nicholls' predictions have been addressed vigorously in the sport domain, whereas others remain to be tested conclusively. In the next section we will address the scope of this literature and offer a critical appraisal of areas in need of greater scrutiny.

Application of Nicholls' Theory in Sport

Of the immense amount of research conducted on Nicholls' achievement goal theory, the majority has focused on understanding the psychosocial correlates and potential implications of task and ego orientations. A recent systematic review of these correlates of achievement goal orientations in sport and physical activity contexts uncovered 98 published studies of an accumulated 21,076 participants (see Biddle, Wang, Kavussanu, & Spray, 2003b). Studies of the antecedents and implications of task- or ego-involved goals (i.e., where state measures of task and ego involvement are taken in situ) are limited in sport (see Gernigon, D'Arripe Longueville, Delignieres, & Ninot, 2004; Harwood & Swain, 1998). The scarcity of this research is an issue not only of accessibility and timing of completion but also of the need for a valid and reliable measurement technology for the situational context (see Harwood, 2002). The assessment of dispositional goal orientations (i.e., in sport in general) is ostensibly less constrained by time and place.

Task and ego orientations in sport have been assessed using one of two principal scales: the Task and Ego Orientation in Sport Questionnaire (TEOSQ; Duda & Nicholls, 1992) and the Perceptions of Success Questionnaire (POSQ; Roberts, Treasure, & Balague, 1998). Both scales have demonstrated a reliable internal structure over a large number of studies investigating the correlates of goal orientations (see Duda, 2001; Duda & Whitehead, 1998; Roberts, 2001).

Participation and performance-related factors in sport such as effort exerted, achievement beliefs, attributions, learning and achievement strategies, enjoyment and intrinsic interest, anxiety and coping, perfectionism, moral behaviors, and psychological skills have all been significantly associated with task and ego orientations. This body of literature forms the attempt by researchers to explain both positive and negative roles that certain achievement goals may play in human functioning in the context of sport. The following section draws on some of the most interesting and popular topics from this menu of research.

Goals, Beliefs, and Cognitive-Affective Responses
Considerable research endeavor has been plowed into understanding relationships between goal orientations and belief systems, cognitive content, enjoyment, interest, and emotional responses in athletes. Task orientation is consistently linked to the belief that hard work is a cause for success in sport (Duda & Nicholls, 1992; Duda & White, 1992; Lochbaum & Roberts, 1993; Roberts & Ommundsen, 1996) and that the purposes of sport are to foster mastery, cooperation, and social responsibility. Further, high task orientation has been associated with greater enjoyment, reported satisfaction, and intrinsic interest in sport (Duda, Chi, Newton, Walling, & Catley, 1995; Ntoumanis & Biddle, 1999), as well as the experience of entering a flow state in sport (Jackson & Roberts, 1992). As alluded to earlier, ego orientation has been associated with the belief that high ability and deceptive strategies (e.g., cheating) lead to success (Duda & Nicholls, 1992; Roberts, Treasure, & Kavussanu, 1996) and that the purposes of sport revolve around enhancing popularity, wealth, and social status (Duda, 1989; Roberts & Ommundsen, 1996). When ego orientation was combined with high task orientation, a positive relationship was found between ego orientation and levels of enjoyment (Biddle, Akande, Vlachopoulos, & Fox, 1996), but much of the remaining research has found either negative

relationships or no relationships between an ego orientation and enjoyment, intrinsic interest, and satisfaction (see Biddle et al., 2003b).

Of interest to coaches and practitioners in competitive settings is awareness of the links between achievement goals and the stress process (see Hall & Kerr, 1997; Newton & Duda, 1995; Ntoumanis & Biddle, 1998). Hall and Kerr found ego orientation to be a significant predictor of precompetitive cognitive anxiety in young fencers. Correlations between ego orientation and cognitive anxiety for fencers with low perceived ability were positive and very high 2 days, 1 day, and 30 minutes before competition. Task orientation scores were negatively associated, indicating that increasing levels of task orientation were associated with lower cognitive anxiety. Similar findings for ego orientation have emerged for concentration disruption (White & Zellner, 1996) and cognitive interference (Hatzigeorgiardis & Biddle, 1999), in which thoughts of escape during competition were less likely to be reported by snooker and tennis players high in task orientation but more likely for players high in ego orientation with low perceived competence.

A further research strand has explored how athletes cope with stress and anxiety. Ntoumanis, Biddle, and Haddock (1999) found that task orientation was associated with the use of problem-solving coping strategies, such as trying hard, seeking social support, and curtailing competing activities. Athletes with high ego orientation were more likely to use the emotion-focused strategy of venting emotions, including becoming upset, losing their cool, and letting out negative feelings. Initial research on the interplay between perfectionism and achievement goals has revealed that athletes with strong ego orientation, in spite of a moderate level of task orientation, tend to report greater neurotic/maladaptive perfectionism (i.e., concern over personal mistakes and perceived parental criticism) than do athletes with high task and low ego orientation (Hall, Kerr & Matthews, 1998). Interest in the construct of perfectionism in sport has grown recently and further research exploring the working relationship between achievement goals and perfectionism is merited.

Goals, Information Processing, and Strategy Use
An innovative avenue of research has targeted how goal perspectives may affect skill development and performance by examining how practice strategies and use of feedback and information processing differ according to levels of task and ego orientation. High levels of task orientation have been associated with valuing practice and

committing to it for skill development reasons, whereas high levels of ego orientation have been linked to avoiding practice and preferring simply to compete (Lochbaum & Roberts, 1993; Roberts & Ommundsen, 1996). In addition, Cury, Famose, and Sarrazin (1997) investigated how athletes high in task and ego orientation used the opportunities for feedback in different manners on a basketball dribbling task. When offered the opportunity to receive personal feedback to aid their skill development and performance, athletes high in ego orientation who doubted their ability refused to take advantage of the opportunity. Those high in ego orientation who were confident of their ability preferred only normative information (i.e., did I win?) and refused the opportunity of receiving self-referenced feedback and information on strategies to help them improve. Athletes high in task orientation sought out both self-referent feedback on levels of personal progress as well as tips on how to improve their dribbling score. This finding prompted Cury and his colleagues (1997) to speculate that

> an (highly) ego-involved participant is not interested in learning, even if he/she has tools on hand allowing him/her to progress and perform better; he/she tried primarily to situate him/herself in relation to others. Moreover, if he/she meets difficulties in this situation, he/she rejects all information, and notably task information which will be important to him/her . . . exhibiting a "learned helpless psychological state." (p. 220)

In a similar vein, Thill and Brunel (1995) reported that highly task-involved soccer players engaged in more spontaneous and deeper processing of information when they received either positive or negative feedback on their performance in a shooting task compared with highly ego-involved players. They concluded that highly ego-involved athletes allocate mental resources to how they compare and what the consequences are, leaving little capacity to allocate to how to improve on the task and learn. This latter approach is precisely how task-involved players used the information.

Finally, recent studies by Berlant and Weiss (1997); Cumming, Hall, Harwood, and Gammage (2002); Harwood, Cumming, and Fletcher (2004); and Harwood, Cumming, and Hall (2003) have offered an initial understanding of how goal orientations relate to the experience or use of psychological strategies in sport. Cumming and colleagues showed that young athletes who ranged from moderate to high in both task and ego orientation reported using more imagery and mental rehearsal than did athletes with lower levels of both goal orientations.

Athletes reported engaging in imagery associated with both skill mastery and winning in preparation for competition; these imagery functions are closely associated with the natural features of task and ego goal orientations. Harwood et al.'s (2004) study revealed that elite young athletes high in both goal orientations reported using goal setting, imagery, and self-talk strategies in practice and competition significantly more than did athletes with other goal orientation profiles. Although our understanding of the exact cognitive-behavioral functioning of athletes with both high task and high ego orientation remains limited, these studies make an interesting case for the functionality of an ego orientation if it is counterbalanced by a high task orientation.

Goals, Moral Functioning, and Fair Play An area of research that has received consistent, albeit cross-sectional, attention over the past decade has been the link between achievement goals and moral functioning. A number of studies have examined whether goal orientations relate to indices of fair play, including intentions to take illegal advantage, break the rules, promote aggression, endorse intentionally injurious acts, and cheat per se (Carpenter & Yates, 1997; Duda, Olson, & Templin, 1991; Dunn & Dunn, 1999; Kavussanu & Roberts, 2001; Lemyre, Roberts, & Ommundsen, 2002). Most studies in this area support Nicholls' (1989) predictions that athletes with high ego orientation, low task orientation, and low perceived ability are more likely to engage in unsporting behaviors and take any advantage to ensure that they achieve their normative goal. More prosocial patterns of behavior are reported for athletes high in task orientation and low in ego orientation, regardless of their perceived ability (Kavussanu, 2006; Sage, Kavussanu & Duda, 2006).

Methodological Challenges

Research applying Nicholls' approach in sport has progressed on both methodological and data analytical grounds whenever the research question has challenged investigators to find a more sophisticated approach. But many of these advancements need to be further consolidated and refined. The following section discusses some of the main progressions and issues.

Goal Profiling A limitation of initial research throughout the 1990s was a tendency for studies to investigate the correlates of each goal orientation separately as opposed to examining the athlete as an individual who possessed certain levels of each goal orientation (i.e., the principle of orthogonality). For example, to say that task orientation is positively correlated with good behavior and that ego orientation is positively correlated with bad behavior greatly oversimplifies the reality of human behavior. Because task and ego goal orientations are theoretically independent of each other (most research in sport reports either no significant correlation between task and ego orientations or occasionally small positive or negative correlations), we would not be any closer to understanding the behavioral pattern of an athlete who was high or low in both goal orientations.

Although early correlational research failed to examine the interaction between task and ego orientations, recent studies have considered both goal orientations in combination. This trend or method in data analysis, commonly referred to as goal profiling, has emerged as a popular feature of the research process in the last decade (see Cumming et al., 2002; Fox et al., 1994; Harwood et al., 2003, 2004; Hodge & Petlichkoff, 2000; Roberts et al., 1996; White, 1998). Researchers have used either a mean or median split technique that effectively forces the sample into the four basic high–low combinations or cluster analysis (Aldenderfer & Blashfield, 1984), which allows distinct clusters of participants with similar goal orientation profiles to emerge from the data. Both methods have advantages and disadvantages, but cluster analysis has recently become the preferred method, perhaps because of the realness of the profiles that emerge and the large sample sizes required in the four-combination approach to locate enough participants for each quadrant (see Hodge & Petlichkoff, 2000). As a collective body of evidence, the findings from these studies attest to the potential benefits of a moderate to high task orientation combined with corresponding levels of ego orientation. For example, Hodge and Petlichkoff found that athletes who report the desire both to demonstrate superior abilities over others and to develop through personal mastery appeared to have the edge in terms of reported self-concept and perceived ability compared with other profiles.

Ultimately, the studies that have investigated athlete goal profiles tend to show that a high ego orientation is not necessarily detrimental (rather the opposite in fact) provided that it is tempered by high task orientation. This body of evidence should not be ignored, particularly in the context of high-level sport, which clearly emphasizes gaining the normative edge. Nonetheless, as a cautionary note, more research is needed to understand more explicitly the mechanisms by which high task and high ego orientations tend to function productively together. We must also study the behavioral pattern of athletes who might be characterized by a high–high profile but who possess differential perceptions of ability. Research examining the moderating role of perceived ability on the relationship between goal profiles and psychosocial patterns is nonexistent. Most studies of this nature have failed to measure perceived ability, and the findings have largely stemmed from relatively high-level samples of those whose perceived ability is likely to have been higher than average.

Situational Level Measurement Most studies that use Nicholls' approach have measured achievement goals at a dispositional level (i.e., goal orientations). Nicholls' theory, however, talks to situational level goals (i.e., states of task and ego involvement) far more than it does to goal orientations. Today, like almost 20 years ago, the most challenging research remains with the antecedents and assessment of achievement goals at the situational level (i.e., the personal theories of achievement operating right now, within a given achievement situation). Our understanding of task and ego goal involvement states, their specific antecedents, and how these states potentially interact throughout an athletic contest remains relatively shallow.

One research method has been to provide task- or ego-involving feedback or information about a particular task to a participant in order to induce an actual state of task or ego involvement experimentally (e.g., Hall, 1990; see also later section on motivational climate). This technique does not account for the strength of the participant's goal orientations and, in terms of verifying the treatment effect, actual states of task and ego involvement were not assessed. Nevertheless, by carefully controlling for extraneous variables, sophisticated experimental studies can be exceptionally useful in enhancing our understanding of goal involvement. Further, we may need to gain a deeper understanding of goal involvement in laboratory-controlled tasks before testing in the field what we subsequently learn from these experiments.

With this latter point in mind, field attempts to measure achievement goal states and their antecedents have been conducted in precompetition circumstances by altering the stem of the TEOSQ to read with relevance to that context (see Harwood, 2002; Williams, 1998) or by using more crude but practical single-item assessments of achievement goals just before performance (see Harwood & Swain, 1998; Swain & Harwood, 1996). These latter pieces of research with elite tennis players and swimmers illustrated how reported precompetition levels of task and ego involvement were predicted not only by dispositional goal orientation but also by situational factors. In tennis, these factors included expectancy of winning the match, the perceived importance and value of the match, and players' perceptions of the achievement goal most preferred and recognized by parents, coaches, and the national governing body in the context of that match. These findings from assessments just before competition do complement dispositional research in which athletes' perceptions of significant others' goal orientations (i.e., parents, coach) have been associated with their own levels of task and ego orientation (see Duda & Hom, 1993; Ebbeck & Becker, 1994; Escarti, Roberts, Cervello, & Guzman, 1999).

Finally, recent research has attempted to access states of task and ego involvement in performance by employing a retrospective performance recall protocol. Smith and Harwood (2001) tracked a professional tennis player over four tournament matches. One hour after the match, the player was taken through his videotaped performance point by point, responding to single-item questions that assessed his achievement goals, cognitions, and levels of performance satisfaction. Self-reported levels of task and ego involvement were subject to dynamic fluctuations according to set score, game score, and whether serving or receiving. Specifically, the player reported higher levels of ego involvement and lower task involvement on game and break points, when serving compared with receiving, and at later stages in the set. This in-depth analysis provided a detailed insight into the interactive dynamics of a player's goal states in specific match situations compared with the information gathered from merely dispositional or prematch assessments of achievement goals. Continuing this theme, Gernignon et al. (2004) have recently investigated the dynamic fluctuations of goal involvement states across a judo contest using Elliot's (1999) approach-avoidance framework (see later section). In this study, using a technologically advanced video recall method and follow-up interview, they showed how performance-approach, performance-avoidance, and mastery-approach goals interacted in multifaceted ways during a five-minute combat.

Intervention Methods Researchers have been consistently encouraged toward intervention projects that essentially put achievement goal theory into practice (Duda, 1993). But besides a few notable exceptions, the amount of research embracing longitudinal and field-based intervention methodologies

is disappointing given the applied nature of the theory. Early studies by Goudas, Biddle, Fox, and Underwood (1995), Lloyd and Fox (1992), and Theeboom, DeKnop, and Weiss (1995) investigated the motivational responses of sport participants exposed to task- or ego-involving teaching styles or learning conditions. In each case, the task involving style or learning condition was found to be most adaptive.

Most recently, using features of a single-case design methodology, Harwood and Swain (2002) conducted three one-to-one interventions with junior national tennis players targeted not only at enhancing their task involvement for competitive matches but also at encouraging a complementary balance between their task and ego goals. Resourced by qualitative insights from the elite tennis context (Harwood & Swain, 2001), their multimodal intervention program actively involved coaches and parents in educational and behavior change activities, alongside individual education and tasks for players. Following the three-month intervention, results showed increases in precompetition task involvement, higher indices of self-regulation, and more positive cognitive appraisals in response to a series of matches with highly ego-involving stimuli. Furthermore, although players reported moderate to high levels of ego involvement, the social approval element of their ego-involved goal measured in the study fell considerably postintervention.

We could not locate any subsequent intervention research that adopted a longitudinal methodology targeted at influencing achievement goals in athletes. Despite the time-consuming nature of multimodal and socially driven interventions, this area is certainly worthy of much greater toil.

Recent Debates in the Literature

The sheer density of published research using Nicholls' approach inevitably causes academics to reflect on the state of the literature and the effectiveness of theory testing in sport settings. Active researchers in the field have interpreted this body of literature through their personal lenses and have provided stimulating insights and recommendations for the new intake of achievement goal enthusiasts (see Duda, 2001; Duda & Hall 2001; Roberts 2001). A number of recent research papers have also tackled various issues in detail. Harwood (2002) presented important caveats for both researchers and practitioners when employing the TEOSQ and POSQ to assess the achievement goals of athletes in competitive sport. The paper illustrated how elevations and decreases in reported dispositional goal orientations occur merely as a function of the context when altering the stem of the questionnaire (e.g., in sport, in competition, in practice settings). This finding reinforces the importance of tackling contextual-level research questions (e.g., the influence of achievement goals on prematch cognitive-affective processes) with contextual-level assessments (i.e., prematch) to increase the validity of the investigation. The development of sensitive, contextual measurement technologies is a key recommendation from this research.

In addition, the application of Nicholls' approach to sport has not progressed without critique. Harwood, Hardy, and Swain (2000) and Harwood and Hardy (2001) raised a number of conceptual and measurement issues associated with the continued progress of the theory within competitive sports. Their issues focused on clearer definitions and corrections in terminology, and questioned how the concept of task involvement might be more accurately represented and measured in sport terms. Specifically, they proposed that task involvement could comprise two distinctly different achieve-

ment states (see figure 8.1). They offered the term *task involvement-product* to reflect a state in which a subjective sense of achievement rests on adequate mastery, improvement, and favorable perceptions of intraindividual performance as an end product. In contrast, they forwarded the term *task involvement–process* to represent the more traditional notion of a task goal in which a sense of achievement is derived merely from positive perceptions of effort exerted, task understanding, and learning without necessarily any objective improvement in task execution or performance. Harwood and Hardy proposed that failing to experience a sense of definite intraindividual improvement or mastery (i.e., task product), particularly at higher levels of sport, can be as motivationally crippling over the long haul as failing to outperform others (i.e., a state of ego involvement). Only with a high level of task involvement–process in which the source of achievement stems purely from self-referent task investment (e.g., consistent effort) and perceived learning (e.g., better read of the opponent) would an individual athlete be able to motivationally reconcile the nonachievement

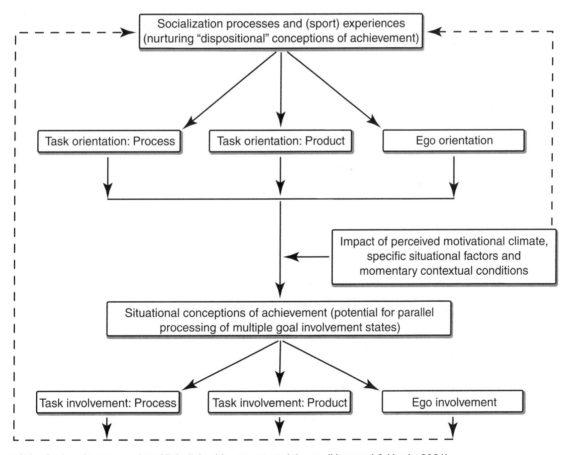

Figure 8.1 A tripartite approach to Nicholls' achievement goal theory (Harwood & Hardy, 2001).

Reprinted, by permission, from C.G. Harwood and L. Hardy, 2001, "Persistence and effort in moving achievement goal research forward: A response to Treasure and colleagues," *Journal of Sport and Exercise Psychology* 23: 330-345.

of task-involved product or ego-involved goals. A key point to Harwood's argument was that traditional measures of achievement goals tend to mix processes and products within a single task subscale, thereby limiting understanding of the competitive athlete that might be gained from two separate subscales.

Treasure and colleagues (Treasure et al., 2001) responded to these issues by arguing for misinterpretations of the theory and reinforcing the traditional principles on which the theory was founded. In both countering and integrating Treasure et al.'s points, Harwood and Hardy (2001) closed the debate by offering a number of avenues for future research, including the importance of tighter terminology, continued testing in the field, and greater attention to the study of achievement goal states. These three commentaries in the *Journal of Sport and Exercise Psychology* are worthy of close reading for those who wish to form their own opinions on the points and counterpoints made.

Future Research Directions

As this section conveys, researchers have applied Nicholls' approach in a diverse manner and at a furious pace. Much of this research has involved cross-sectional assessments of goal orientation that have led to a sound foundation of understanding about task and ego orientation. Although original, applied, and scholarly research questions supported this body of literature, a trend is nevertheless developing toward repetitious or basic cross-sectional studies that attempt to hunt down further correlational links with task and ego orientation, however tenuous the link may be theoretically. The level of research that was conceptually and methodologically satisfactory in the 1990s is not satisfactory in 2007 if we are to advance our understanding of achievement goals. Researchers are encouraged to pursue more conceptual or finely grained population- and context-specific questions (see Harwood & Hardy, 2001). The following areas represent some of the more sophisticated, important, and topical avenues open to the next decade of research.

Contextual Levels of Measurement and Understanding
Developments in our measurement technology for specific contexts would furnish researchers with a closer understanding of athletes from different sports in their different settings. The TEOSQ and the POSQ target general tendencies in sport, and as Duda (2001) rightly argues, simply altering the stem and instruction set of a questionnaire for a sample, context, or question that fails to fit the questionnaire is inappropriate. A valid instrument that sensitively assesses whether tendencies to be task or ego involved in competition differ from tendencies in unsupervised practice and supervised training would be one example of obtaining this closer, contextual understanding of an athlete. Tracking age-related changes in these contextual goal orientations would also give researchers and practitioners a clearer appreciation of how goal orientations may be subject to domain-specific changes over time. This avenue of study could be supplemented by a finer-grained investigation of context-specific antecedents and consequences, which may give practitioners clearer guidance about when certain goal orientations are most susceptible to shaping.

Auditing the High–High Profile
Researchers are becoming clear on the benefits of task orientation and the potential downside of ego orientation. But the positive results emerging for a high task–high ego orientation profile continue to ruffle a few feathers in the achievement goal fraternity. We need to be careful of construct discrimination and be aware that a bias toward the niceties of task orientation may cloud our empirical objectivity as academics. Researchers have not fully audited the high–high profile and have not investigated the moderating influence of perceived ability on psychosocial outcomes. The mechanics of the (working) relationship between the two goals needs to be scrutinized, and the profile needs to be subjected to a more thorough test. The message here is to embrace the challenge of understanding this profile, target high–high athletes, and conduct research that helps us appreciate the why, when, and how of this profile and its role at different levels of sport.

Role of Social Approval
Within the academic context, Maehr and Nicholls (1980) supported the relevance of social approval goals in their original theory of achievement motivation. Subsequent research by Ewing (1981), Vealey and Campbell (1988), and Whitehead (1995) have all attempted to measure social approval orientation in sport using the Achievement Orientation Questionnaire (Ewing). Nicholls (1984) omitted social approval goals from his conceptualization, later noting that the study of social goals was a motivational topic in its own right and that blending them with task or ego goals could confound our understanding of motivation (Nicholls, Cheung, Lauer, & Patashnick, 1989).

Unlike the classroom, however, competitive sport is typically highly public. Significant others and social evaluation processes associated with sport competition may be so salient to athletes that their perceptions of physical competence may be intertwined with certain socially oriented motives.

Interest in, and recognition of, the need to study the social aspects of achievement goals have increased in recent years (Allen, 2003; Stuntz & Weiss, 2003). Allen proposed a separate theory of social motivation in sport that focuses on athletes' desire for social competence in achievement settings, their definition of social competence, and the role of perceived belonging. Further, Harwood and Swain (2001, 2002) documented how either intrapersonal or socially controlled antecedents could underpin the achievement goals of young tennis players. Players reported that their perceptions of competence indeed depended on whether they had improved or mastered a stroke (task) or demonstrated superior ability to another player (ego). For some players, however, these goals represented purely internal motives initiated by themselves for themselves to achieve (self-directed, intrapersonal), whereas for others the goals represented external motives shaped by a more controlling need to prove themselves to significant others (social approval).

Work on developing an alternative four-factor model (self-directed task, self-directed ego, social approval task, social approval ego) of achievement goal orientations in competitive sport has been conducted (Harwood, Wilson, & Hardy, 2002). Wilson, Hardy, and Harwood (2006) have recently shown how either a self-directed task orientation or a self-directed ego orientation positively predicts the use of process goals in competition, whereas a social approval ego orientation served as a negative predictor of employing process-oriented activities. A much greater understanding of the role of social approval in the constitution of personal theories of achievement is needed. Because competitive sport is a highly social achievement context, the composition of achievement goals reflected within athletes in this context represents a worthy area of investigation.

Sport-Specific Considerations: Teams and Partnerships The study of achievement goals in team sports has essentially reflected attempts to associate goal orientations with indices of group cohesion and leadership (e.g., Duda & Balaguer, 1999). But when assessing achievement goals in a team setting, researchers must direct careful attention to context or the culture under study. At an individual level, a team member, like any other athlete, will possess a certain level of task and ego orientation as measured by the TEOSQ or POSQ. Placed in a team setting with competition for places, however, a major difference emerges between being highly ego oriented with respect to the opposition and

being highly ego oriented with respect to teammates and peers. The TEOSQ would not be able to offer the researcher or practitioner this specific information on intrateam ego orientation and the motivational composition of the team as a whole as opposed to the individuals who compose it. A subcultural approach to measurement, in this case an assessment of inter- and intrateam achievement goals, may open up a more dedicated vein of research into the interplay between Nicholls' theory and important group-dynamic processes. A similar line of thinking applies to partnership or pair sports, notably the effect of achievement goal compatibility on short-term performance and long-term partnership stability (Harwood & Lacey, 2001; see final section).

Conclusion

Some academics would argue that the body of literature applying Nicholls' approach in sport continues to build, whereas others might argue that it has reached a plateau and is being overtaken by more fashionable approaches. Time will perhaps tell, but to the current authors at least, lack of fashion will not cause Nicholls' approach to fall out of favor. Rather, the failure of researchers to integrate Nicholls' core concepts into research themes and measurement tools that strike at the heart of sport subcultures and specific contexts is what will bring to a halt this line of inquiry. Research that peddles Nicholls' concepts through mundane cross-sectional research runs the risk of creating stagnancy in the literature and boredom in its readership. In addition, measures that fail to capture the "language" and properties of the sport situation under study will cause researchers to risk offering applied implications that may be inappropriate, inaccurate and of limited use to the practitioner. Researchers can choose among several routes to avoid this plateau and approach the required methodological advancements while keeping Nicholls' core concepts intact. That said, other theories complementary in nature to Nicholls' are receiving further attention, and we now turn our own attention to these approaches.

Dweck's Model of Achievement Motivation

Like Nicholls (1984, 1989), Carol Dweck formulated a framework based on the theme of goals to explain achievement-relevant phenomena (Dweck, 1986, 1999; Dweck & Bempechat, 1983; Dweck & Elliott,

1983; Dweck & Leggett, 1988). Dweck's work sought to provide an explanation of the underlying psychological processes that account for individuals' mastery and helpless responses to failure on competence-based tasks. The mastery response is associated with adaptive cognitions, affect, and behavior in the face of adversity, such as enhanced concentration, determination, and effort. Conversely, the helpless response is characterized by a belief that high effort signifies low ability, heightened experience of anxiety, a concomitant threat to self-esteem, and reduced effort. Dweck argued that performance (ego) goals are linked to the helpless response when perceptions of competence are low, whereas learning (task) goals are associated with the mastery response irrespective of perceived competence (see table 8.1).

Comparing Nicholls' and Dweck's Theoretical Perspectives

The inherent aims of performance (ego) goals and learning (task) goals, along with the predicted consequences of pursuing these two types of goals, are essentially similar in Dweck's and Nicholls' theoretical perspectives. Both proffer a performance- or ego-based goal that refers to normative perceptions of ability, and both argue that the motivational ramifications of pursuing such a goal depend on perceived competence. If competence perceptions are high, adaptive or mastery responses are predicted; if doubts about competence exist, maladaptive or helpless patterns result. In both perspectives, therefore, perceived competence is proposed to moderate the influence of normatively based competence goals. In addition, both Nicholls and Dweck postulate a self-referenced task or learning goal that leads to adaptive competence-based processes and outcomes even if perceived competence is low.

In contrast to Nicholls, however, Dweck has proposed specific individual differences variables that lead to the pursuit of different goals. These individual differences variables have become known as implicit theories. Initially, the links between implicit theories and achievement goals were articulated within an achievement motivation model in the educational domain. More recently, the study of implicit theories and goals has broadened to encompass social judgments, stereotyping, romantic relationships, and conceptions of morality (see, for example, Chiu, Dweck, Tong, & Fu, 1997; Franiuk, Cohen, & Pomerantz, 2002; Gervey, Chiu, Hong, & Dweck, 1999).

According to Dweck (Dweck, 1999; Dweck, Chiu, & Hong, 1995a), attributes of the self, other people, places, and the world in general can be conceived as fixed, uncontrollable factors or, alternatively, as malleable and controllable factors open to development. The first approach has been termed an *entity theory*, the second is called an *incremental theory*, and people can be described as entity theorists or incremental theorists depending on their views of human attributes. Dweck proposed that entity theorists are more likely to endorse performance (ego) goals, whereas incremental theorists are more likely to pursue learning (task) goals (see table 8.1). In achievement settings such as education, sport, or PE, performance goals serve to demonstrate or prove the adequacy of a person's stable ability (or to avoid displaying the inadequacy of the person's stable ability). Learning goals, on the other hand, serve to develop a person's unstable, malleable ability. Goals and implicit theories combine to determine achievement-related cognitions, affect, and behavior. Therefore, individuals can interpret the achievement setting quite differently depending on underlying personality variables (implicit theories) and their concern with proving, relative to improving, competence in that setting.

Table 8.1 Implicit Theories, Goals, and Achievement Behavior

Implicit theory	Goal orientation	Perceived competence	Behavior pattern
Entity (ability is fixed)	Performance (seek positive judgments and avoid negative judgments of competence)	High	Mastery (seek challenge to prove competence, high persistence)
		Low	Helpless (avoid challenge, low persistence)
Incremental (ability is malleable)	Learning (increase competence)	High or low	Mastery (seek challenge that fosters learning)

Adapted, by permission, from C.S. Dweck and E.L. Leggett, 1988, "A social-cognitive approach to motivation and personality," *Psychological Review* 95: 256-273.

Application of Dweck's Theory in Sport

Investigators have begun to examine implicit theories in the physical domain, as well as their relationships with achievement goals and motivation. Because students have typically formed the participant base in these investigations, implicit theories and goals have been assessed with reference to sport and physical education. This line of inquiry has differed from that of Dweck and her colleagues in two ways. First, whereas Dweck's experimental approach has in the main sought to manipulate entity or incremental views temporarily to examine the effect on goal choice and motivational outcomes, physical activity researchers have been more concerned with assessing naturally occurring incremental and entity beliefs. Second, investigations in the physical domain have focused at a general level (i.e., sport or PE) and have primarily targeted links between naturally occurring implicit theories and goal orientations (assessed using either the TEOSQ or POSQ), rather than state or situational goals. The purpose has been to determine whether beliefs about the stability and controllability of a person's ability are related to that person's (independent) dispositional tendencies for judging competence and defining success as conceptualized within Nicholls' theory.

Although nascent, investigations into goals and implicit theories in sport and PE have provided initial support for Dweck's theoretical propositions. Incremental beliefs about sport ability have been linked with task goal orientation, whereas entity beliefs have been linked with ego goal orientation (e.g., Biddle, Soos, & Chatzisarantis, 1999; Biddle, Wang, Chatzisarantis, & Spray, 2003a; Cury, Da Fonseca, Rufo, & Sarrazin, 2002; Lintunen, Valkonen, Leskinen, & Biddle, 1999; Ommundsen, 2001a, b; Sarrazin et al., 1996).

In line with Dweck's acknowledgment that individuals can hold blends of incremental and entity theories but to differing degrees (Dweck, Chiu, & Hong, 1995b; Dweck & Leggett, 1988), work by Sarrazin et al. (1996), Biddle et al. (2003a), and Wang, Liu, Biddle, and Spray (2005) has culminated in the development of the Conceptions of the Nature of Athletic Ability Questionnaire–Version 2 (CNAAQ–2). This instrument permits the independent assessment of implicit ability beliefs in sport and PE and consists of two second-order dimensions (entity and incremental), underpinned by first-order stable and gift beliefs (entity) and learning and improvement beliefs (incremental). The factor structure of the CNAAQ–2 has been found invariant across age and gender among English youth and across samples of secondary school students from the United Kingdom and Singapore. Moreover, convergent and discriminant validity have been supported (Biddle et al., 2003a; Wang et al., 2005). Correlations between higher-order incremental and entity dimensions are typically negative in direction but weak, lending weight to the suggestion that people can hold blends of the two theories (Dweck & Leggett).

Biddle et al. (2003a) revealed links between entity and incremental views of ability, goal orientations, and amotivation and enjoyment in sport and PE. Specifically, entity beliefs directly predicted self-reported amotivation, whereas task orientation and incremental beliefs directly predicted enjoyment. Researchers have also investigated implicit theories of ability, goals, and their links with self-handicapping in PE (Ommundsen, 2001a), anxiety and satisfaction in PE (Ommundsen, 2001b), physical activity intentions among youth (Biddle et al., 1999; Lintunen et al., 1999), and physical activity levels in youth (Biddle & Wang, 2003). These investigations have furthered our understanding of the wider meaning of physical settings for school students and the determinants of physical activity in young people. The extant research has, to date, highlighted the adaptive consequences of holding incremental views of athletic ability and pursuing task (learning) goals, relative to holding entity views and pursuing ego (performance) goals.

Although most investigations in physical settings have been correlational in nature, recent work has started to examine implicit theories using arguably stronger research designs. Spray, Wang, Biddle, Chatzisarantis, & Warburton (2006) manipulated secondary school students' incremental and entity beliefs with respect to a golf task to determine their influence on goal choice, attributions, affect, and intentions for future participation in golf. Although support was not found for all theoretically driven hypotheses, students in the entity condition were more likely to endorse normatively referenced goals and to attribute failure at the task to ability rather than effort. Moreover, individuals in the incremental condition were more likely to endorse self-referenced goals in relation to the golf task.

Future Research Directions

A number of lines of inquiry emanate from the preceding discussion of Dweck's contribution to achievement goal theories in sport. These research directions are outlined in the following section.

A Hierarchy of Implicit Theories One line of inquiry concerns the extent to which implicit theories are domain specific. Can a person be described as an entity theorist in one domain, such as sport ability, but as an incremental theorist in another domain, such as conceptions of morality or social judgments regarding stereotypes? Moreover, do self-theories of ability in sport apply at lower levels, that is, at specific subcomponents and skills (e.g., kicking versus heading skills in soccer; throwing-in skills for the rugby hooker versus scrummaging, rucking, and mauling skills)? A related question is whether self-theories operate at the situational level in naturally occurring sport or PE contexts. Within Dweck's model, implicit theories are conceived as individual differences variables, yet her experimental work has suggested that such theories can be temporarily manipulated. How do self-theories regulate motivation and achievement in these field settings, and how do incremental and entity beliefs relate to situational perceived competence or self-efficacy?

Developmental Issues A second area for investigation relates to the development of theories of athletic ability. Longitudinal investigations tracing the development of implicit theories in children and adolescents as they proceed through youth sport are required. How are such theories socialized in ongoing interactions with parents, peers, teachers, and coaches? For example, how might different types of praise, or criticism and punishment in reaction to failure and mistakes, cultivate an entity theory in young people (see, for example, Mueller & Dweck, 1998)? Further, how do young people perceive competition in sport in terms of developing an entity theory versus an incremental theory? In short, research is required into the circumstances that elicit the different beliefs. The applied ramifications of such research are potentially profound. For example, if an entity theorist previously successful in sport fails to make a successful transition to a higher level, thus eroding perceptions of ability, can the person develop an incremental belief structure that serves to maintain motivation, optimism, and ultimately participation?

Research into individuals' implicit theories of athletic ability has focused entirely on youth. There is a pressing need to examine differences in implicit theories, achievement goal pursuit, and motivational outcomes among adults involved in team and individual sports.

Methodological Issues A third area of consideration concerns research designs. Experimental studies are necessary to examine the efficacy of temporarily inducing entity and incremental beliefs and determining their motivational ramifications.

Such work is not without challenges to researchers (see Spray et al., 2006, for a discussion). For example, in line with the finding that, at least among youth, incremental beliefs about athletic ability are high relative to entity beliefs, researchers will need to control for these existing differences in such designs. Moreover, if goals are manipulated, what is the effect on beliefs and motivation? In other words, are beliefs causal antecedents of goals or vice versa (see Dweck et al., 1995b)?

Conclusion

Implicit theories of ability offer researchers the opportunity to advance understanding of athletes' motivation in sport. The extant research is limited in scope and design, however, and Dweck's overall contribution to achievement goal theory has received less attention than that of Nicholls in the realm of sport. This situation may change with the incorporation of implicit theories of ability into a more contemporary theory of achievement goals, one that (re)introduces the concept of avoidance motivation into the goal perspectives framework. We now turn to this theory of approach-avoidance achievement goals.

Elliot's Model of Approach-Avoidance Achievement Goals

In his seminal paper on conceptions of ability, subjective experience, task choice, and performance in the achievement domain, Nicholls (1984) examined the notion that people, under certain circumstances, are concerned with how to avoid demonstrating incompetence (avoidance achievement motivation). He suggested that people with low perceived competence can belong to one of three mutually exclusive groups in achievement situations: those committed to demonstrating competence despite perceptions of inadequacy, those committed to avoiding demonstrating incompetence, and those who are not concerned with how to avoid demonstrating low ability. Differential predictions were formulated for these types of individuals in terms of, for example, task choice and subjective experiences. Nicholls (1984, p. 332) argued that the goal of not demonstrating low ability is the next most attractive alternative to demonstrating competence and that people adopt this less attractive goal when they are certain that they cannot achieve the goal of showing high normative ability.

The contributions to achievement goal theory by Dweck and colleagues (Dweck & Bempechat, 1983; Dweck & Elliott, 1983; Dweck & Leggett, 1988) also highlighted that concern with showing incompetence can be a focal point of attention for people in achievement contexts. Her framework seems to imply that concerns with competence and incompetence coexist for those who adopt performance goals. In her achievement motivation model in the intellectual domain, Dweck proposed that individuals who possess low perceived ability and tend to view human attributes such as intelligence as fixed are more likely to want to avoid negative judgments of competence and seek to gain positive judgments of that (stable) attribute. Early work showed that children with entity theories of intelligence were most likely to choose a challenge-avoidance performance goal in which the concern was to want to do well on easy tasks and avoid making mistakes (cited in Dweck & Leggett).

Despite these early contributions to the development of achievement goal theory, the army of researchers in sport that followed ignored the concept of seeking to avoid demonstrating incompetence in achievement settings. As evidenced in the current chapter and in recent reviews of the application of achievement goal theory to sport (see, for example, Duda, 2001; Duda & Hall, 2001), empirical investigations have focused overwhelmingly on approach motivation, specifically the motivational ramifications of wanting to demonstrate competence in self-referenced and normatively referenced terms, and the related criteria employed to judge feelings of success. More recently, however, led by the theoretical and empirical work of Elliot (1997, 1999, 2005; Elliot & Church, 1997), researchers in the educational achievement domain have (re)introduced the concept of avoidance goals (i.e., striving to avoid displaying inadequacy). Before examining the major theoretical tenets and empirical research concerned with the approach-avoidance framework, however, we offer a comparison of the conceptualization of the achievement goal construct in this more recent formulation with the traditional approaches of Dweck and Nicholls.

Alternative Conceptualizations of Achievement Goals: Nicholls, Dweck, and Elliot

Nicholls (1984, 1989) emphasized that achievement goals emanate from conceptions of ability and effort. In this regard, his theorizing centered on the precursors of goal involvement. For example, if a person believes that effort is clearly distinct from ability and that ability limits the influence of effort on performance, then that person may become ego involved while engaged in a competence-relevant task, particularly if situational influences such as competition are salient. But the vast majority of research, especially in the sport domain, has not addressed the motivational antecedents and consequences of ego and task involvement. Rather, the focus has been on goal orientations that are conceptualized as relatively stable tendencies to be task or ego involved. As noted earlier, these tendencies have been shown to be independent such that a person can be high in both ego and task orientation, low in both, or possess a dominant orientation. When measuring goal orientations, participants in sport are asked to indicate the criteria (task- and ego-related) that make them feel successful. Items therefore tap an individual's personal definition of success in sport.

In contrast to the correlational research that has stemmed from Nicholls' approach, educationally based work employing Dweck's framework has typically used experimental designs to induce state performance (ego) and learning (task) goals, along with low or high perceptions of competence. Here, performance and learning goals are viewed as bipolar at the state level, and participants must choose a task that embodies either goal (following manipulation of goals and perceived ability). This type of investigation has been far less prevalent in sport-based work. In this line of inquiry, however, learning goals are viewed as seeking to increase competence, whereas performance goals are viewed as seeking to gain favorable judgments of ability and avoiding negative judgments of competence.

Elliot and colleagues argued that the achievement goal construct should focus solely on whether the aim is to demonstrate competence (approach-valenced goal) or to avoid demonstrating incompetence (avoidance-valenced goal), defined in either self-referenced or normatively referenced terms (see, for example, Elliot & Thrash, 2001). Thus, valence and definition are the central components of an achievement goal. Some argue that measures of goals using Nicholls' and Dweck's approaches go beyond the definition and valence of competence per se (accepting that avoidance-valenced motivation is omitted in contemporary measures of goal orientations in sport such as the TEOSQ and POSQ). People are asked to indicate what makes them feel successful, or they are oriented to a focus on how others judge their (in)competence. Such self-worth and self-presentational concerns should not be bound up in the conceptualization and measurement of a goal, according to Elliot, because it becomes unclear whether it is these concerns or the definition and valence of competence that influence motivational processes and outcomes. Empirically, researchers should strip self-presentational aspects from the assessment of achievement goals.

Elliot (1997, 1999) asserted that equivocal findings in the achievement goal literature concerning the motivational influence of performance goals result partly from the failure to distinguish both approach and avoidance forms of this normatively referenced goal. Moreover, he argued persuasively for the relevance of the mastery-avoidance goal whereby the individual is concerned with (and strives to avoid) demonstrating incompetence from a self-referenced perspective (see Elliot, 1999). He also illustrated the fundamental importance of the approach-avoidance distinction in the history of psychological inquiry generally, and achievement motivation approaches specifically (e.g., need achievement theory; Atkinson, 1957) (see Elliot, 1999; Elliot & Covington, 2001). Consequently, failure to account for the approach-avoidance distinction within both self- and normatively defined goals will lead to incomplete understanding of achievement motivation phenomena.

Trichotomous and Two-by-Two Frameworks

The approach-avoidance goal framework was initially incorporated into a hierarchical model that specified three types of goals: mastery (approach) goals, in which the concern is to demonstrate self-referenced competence; performance-approach goals, in which the concern is to demonstrate normatively referenced competence; and performance-avoidance goals, in which the concern is to avoid demonstrating normatively referenced incompetence (trichotomous model—Elliot, 1997; Elliot & Church, 1997). Although both definition and valence were incorporated into the performance goal at this stage, it was not until a few years later that the mastery goal was also bifurcated into approach and avoidance forms, providing a full two-by-two crossing of approach and avoidance forms of performance and mastery goals (see Elliot, 1999; Elliot & McGregor, 2001). Therefore, in contrast to Nicholls' and Dweck's early writings that alluded to avoidance goals from the point of view of individuals pursuing ego (performance) goals, it is now argued that people can also be preoccupied with inadequacy from a self-referenced perspective. These four goals are construed as "concrete cognitive representations that serve a directional function in motivation by guiding the individual toward or away from specific possible outcomes" (Elliot & Thrash, 2001, p. 143). In achievement settings such as sport, the cognitive representation refers to a competence-based possibility (i.e., demonstrating competence in sport or avoiding demonstrating incompetence in sport). To illustrate these four goals with reference to swimming, an elite performer may enter an important gala concerned that she will do poorly in relation to other swimmers in each event (performance-avoidance goal) or poorly in relation to her own previous times for each event (mastery-avoidance goal). She may well be concerned with wanting to win all her races (performance-approach goal) or simply to swim well from a technical perspective and improve on her own previous times (mastery-approach goal). Each of the four types of concern (i.e., goals) may be salient to differing degrees. Consequently, in Elliot's approach, achievement goals are considered neither orthogonal (cf. Nicholls' goal orientations) nor bipolar (cf. Dweck's state goals). People can pursue different goals simultaneously. Empirically, positive associations have been found among all four goals (see Conroy, Elliot, & Hofer, 2003; Guan, Xiang, McBride, & Bruene, 2006; and Wang, Biddle, & Elliot, 2007 for sport- and PE-based examples).

In Elliot and coworkers' two-by-two framework, a goal serves as the aim (direction) of behavior, and individuals can pursue each of the four goals for a host of reasons (antecedents). These antecedents of achievement goals provide the energizing force to act (e.g., need for achievement, fear of failure), whereas the goals themselves channel this energy toward or away from specific desirable and aversive possibilities. The reasons for pursuing a goal and the goal itself combine (forming goal complexes) to determine motivational outcomes and processes. Key antecedents, besides fear of failure and need for achievement, include implicit theories of ability, competence expectancies, self-esteem, need for approval, fear of rejection, as well as situational factors such as perceived motivational climate (see figure 8.2). Therefore, people may experience sport settings very differently depending on the goals adopted and the reasons for their adoption (see Elliot, 1999).

The framework allows for the testing of predictions in terms of both antecedents of the four goals and their achievement-related consequences, despite the fact that the variety of individual and environmental factors potentially underpinning achievement goal pursuit will affect processes and

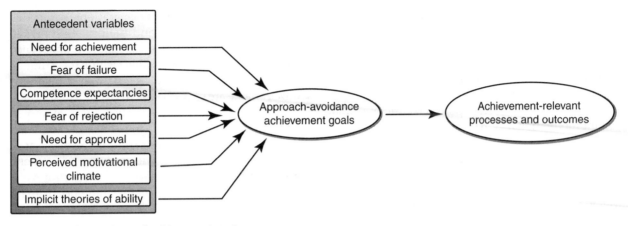

Figure 8.2 Antecedents of achievement goals.

Reprinted, by permission, from A.J. Elliot, 1999, "Approach and avoidance motivation and achievement goals," *Educational Psychologist* 34(3): 469-489.

outcomes in diverse ways. Mastery-approach goals are predicted to bring about positive outcomes, particularly in terms of positive affect and self-determination experienced in sport. Success-oriented factors such as need for achievement and incremental beliefs underpin these goals. Performance-avoidance goals, rooted in failure-oriented antecedents such as fear of failure, are thought to lead to a host of negative processes and outcomes, such as high state anxiety, lower self-determination, and impaired performance. Predicting the consequences of pursuing performance-approach goals is complex given that they can be underpinned by factors that orient an athlete to success or failure. For example, a sport participant pursuing performance-approach goals underpinned by a strong fear of failure may work hard and persist in the short term but is likely to experience greater anxiety and lower self-determination than is a participant pursuing performance-approach goals underpinned by a strong need for achievement and high competence expectancy. In a similar vein, the adoption of performance-approach goals for reasons of gaining social approval is likely to lead to yet more differences in the phenomenological experience of sport. Finally, mastery-avoidance goals are likely to be rooted in fear of failure, incremental beliefs, low perceptions of competence, and situational cues that highlight not only self and task improvement but also the possibility of failure rather than success (Elliot, 1999). The consequences of pursuing such goals, as with the other three types of goals, will depend on their antecedent profile. Mastery-avoidance goals underpinned by fear of failure may lead to more negative consequences than mastery-avoidance goals underpinned by incremental beliefs. In general, it is postulated that the motivational effect of adopting mastery-avoidance

goals will be less positive than the effect of adopting mastery-approach goals but more positive than the effect of adopting performance-avoidance goals (Elliot, 1999; Elliot & McGregor, 2001).

Application of Elliot's Theory in Sport and PE

The trichotomous and two-by-two achievement goal frameworks have been examined extensively within educational and personality–social psychology domains yet have been underutilized within the sport psychology domain (Elliot & Conroy, 2005). In PE, Cury, Da Fonseca, et al. (2002) found entity beliefs to be positively associated with performance-approach and performance-avoidance goals. On the other hand, incremental beliefs were negatively linked with both forms of performance goals. Perceived competence showed a positive relationship with performance-approach goals but a negative association with performance-avoidance goals. Both types of performance goal were positively correlated with perceived performance climate in PE. Mastery-approach goals were linked with incremental beliefs, competence perceptions, and perceived mastery climate. Experimental work by Cury, Elliot, Sarrazin, Da Fonseca, and Rufo (2002) using a basketball dribbling task identified competence valuation, task absorption, and state anxiety as mediators of the relationship between goals and intrinsic motivation. The performance-avoidance condition reduced competence valuation and task absorption but heightened state anxiety relative to the performance-approach and mastery-approach conditions. Carr (2006) demonstrated that goal profiles (e.g., high mastery/high performance-approach/low performance-avoidance or high mastery/low performance-approach/low performance-avoidance) were differentially associated with motivational outcomes in PE. Adaptive outcomes such as self-determined motivation, positive affect, and sporting activity in school were positively associated with profiles that included high mastery goals. Moreover, some students' goal profiles evidenced change over a school year dependent upon perceptions of the extant motivational climate in PE classes.

Two studies have examined the two-by-two framework in the context of school PE. Guan et al. (2006) showed that mastery-approach, mastery-avoidance, and performance-approach goals positively predicted students' self-reported persistence in classes. Using cluster analysis, Wang et al. (2007) examined the intraindividual goal profiles among Singaporean students and established that these profiles were related to motivational regulation and important affective and behavioral outcomes. Specifically, the "high achievement goals" group, along with the "mastery achievement goals" group evidenced the most adaptive pattern of responses in terms of autonomy, enjoyment, effort, and boredom, compared to the "moderate achievement goals" and "low achievement goals" groups.

Future Research Directions

With research into the two-by-two framework in its infancy in sport and PE, abundant questions and areas await future study.

Measurement of Approach-Avoidance Goals
In terms of the measurement of the four goals, Conroy et al. (2003) recently introduced the AGQ–S. These authors report promising psychometric properties in terms of factorial and temporal stability, along with external validity. But from a conceptual standpoint, some of the items could be misinterpreted. For example, the item "I just want to avoid doing poorly in this class" is purported to assess a performance-avoidance goal but arguably is vague with respect to whether the focus of doing poorly is self- or normatively referenced. In addition, the mastery-avoidance items should focus more clearly on goals rather than merely reflect concerns and worries. Future research efforts in this area may therefore result in modification to the AGQ–S items.

Temporal and Situational Stability
Studies that have measured the four goals in sport and PE have revealed positive intercorrelations. Does this mean that people can and do pursue these goals simultaneously to differential degrees? Does goal adoption fluctuate moment to moment (cf. goal involvement in Nicholls' perspective), or does it

represent less variable preoccupations with how competence is valenced and defined in sport? If approach-avoidance goals are adopted for specific sport activities in a more stable fashion (cf. a unit of work in PE that typically lasts six to eight weeks), how variable are such goals across different sporting activities and environments? The issue of temporal and situational stability of approach and avoidance goals in sport and PE offers exciting research possibilities. As with the dichotomous achievement goal approach reviewed earlier, greater efforts are required to examine the dynamic influence of goals at the situational rather than contextual level (cf. Gernigon et al., 2004).

Mastery-Avoidance Goals
The bifurcation of the mastery goal into approach and avoidance forms has been a relatively recent advance in achievement goal theory. More research is needed into the unique antecedents and consequences associated with these goals, in order to provide support for the utility of the approach-avoidance distinction. The salience and influence of mastery-avoidance goals in sport across different populations also await examination. Initial research endeavors point to the negative effect of mastery-avoidance goals on young participants' sense of autonomy (Conroy, Kaye, & Coatsworth, 2006). Elliot's argument that for many athletes longitudinal decreases in self-referenced competence become a focus of attention as they age appears credible, particularly to the current authors! (see Elliot, 1999, 2005; Elliot & Conroy, 2005). Striving to avoid the demonstration of one's declining physical capacities may be a powerful yet ultimately unrewarding experience.

Goal Complexes
Given the major tenet of the approach-avoidance framework that goals intertwine with their antecedents, future work should examine how goal complexes affect achievement behavior in sport. Possibilities here are numerous and will likely involve a range of qualitative and quantitative approaches that will aid understanding of the meaning of sport to athletes. For example, how do concerns with social approval, fear of rejection by peers, quality of friendships, or perceptions of motivational climate combine with approach and avoidance goals to determine competence-based behavior, cognition, and affect in sport?

Conclusion

The approach-avoidance distinction offers researchers in sport the new opportunity to test a host of questions relating to avoidance goals. It may be tempting to revisit the correlates described in the section on Nicholls' theory to examine relationships with mastery-avoidance and performance-avoidance goals using cross-sectional designs. No doubt such studies would yield useful information regarding the influence of avoidance goals. But we also urge academics to use the approach-avoidance distinction in addressing the future research directions outlined in the section devoted to Nicholls' work, thereby rising to the challenge of designing more innovative and more significant studies. In pursuing these lines of inquiry, studies that employ the TEOSQ or POSQ as the sole measure of goals may be viewed as old hat or flawed because these measures do not address the concept of avoidance motivation. We suggest that this view is shortsighted. As described earlier, many important motivation questions in sport remain to be answered using Nicholls' (and Dweck's) core concepts.

Situational Factors in Achievement Goal Research

So far in this chapter we have presented three theoretical approaches from the achievement goal domain that represent individual differences in the goals that are most salient to athletes at dispositional or situational levels. A central feature of the three approaches is that they recognize the role played by the situation or environment in manipulating a person's achievement goals for a specific task or activity. As Dweck and Leggett (1988) noted, "Dispositions are seen as individual difference variables that determine the a priori probability of adopting a particular goal and displaying a particular behavioral pattern, and situational factors are seen as potentially altering these probabilities" (p. 269).

The study of these situational factors has been a popular area of research in achievement goal theory. Much of our knowledge is drawn from the initial work of Carole Ames. This section will begin with an overview of Ames' research before moving on to a broad discussion of the literature on motivational climate—the construct attributed to Ames' work. Subsequently, a number of future directions for motivational climate research are proposed.

Ames' Approach

Although the initial work on motivational climate is credited to Ames and her colleagues (Ames, Ames, & Felker, 1977; Ames, 1984a), her early work did not draw on achievement goal theory per se but instead examined the influences of the environment (reward structures, incentives) on motivational processes (e.g., attributions following success and failure). Ames et al. (1977) examined the behaviors of 40 sixth-grade boys following success and failure in competitive and noncompetitive situations. Boys were placed in matched-ability pairs and assigned either to fail or to succeed. Under competitive conditions only the winner received a reward, but under noncompetitive conditions both could choose a prize for participating. Competitive conditions led to significant increases in self-punitive behaviors following failure (rating self as lower ability and undeserving of reward), but ego-enhancing behaviors increased following success (rating self as higher ability and deserving of rewards). No differences in attribution were found in the noncompetitive condition. In a later study Ames (1984a) created a competitive goal structure by testing children in pairs against each other and an individualistic goal structure by testing children on their own and encouraging them to improve their scores. The outcome (high versus low success) was manipulated by changing the number of solvable puzzles given to a child. Following testing, children were asked questions about what they were thinking during the tasks. In the competitive condition, children tended to link their ability to the outcomes, whereas in the individualistic condition, children attributed outcomes (success or failure) to effort. Further, the individualistic condition led children to self-instruct (e.g., "I need to take my time with this," "I'm going to think carefully about this") more than they did in the competitive condition. In Ames' words, these children "behaved much like Diener and Dweck's (1980) mastery-oriented children and reflected what Nicholls has called task involvement" (p. 485). These differences in behavior as a function of situational conditions (cf. goal or reward structures) suggested that differing reward structures influence the salience of various informational sources in self-evaluations of ability, the affective influence of success and failure, and subsequent perceptions of ability. From there, Ames (1984b) defined qualitatively different motivational systems in children, which bore more than passing resemblance to the conceptualizations of task and ego involvement. Although not directly grounded in achievement goal theory, the competitive and individualistic conditions (as well as cooperative goal structures that formed her work) are closely analogized to what were later termed *ego-involving* and *task-involving* climates, respectively.

Ames and Archer (1988) and Ames (1992a) continued investigating these ego-involving versus task-involving classroom environments, proposing that situational cues, chiefly controlled by the teacher, will influence the salience of different achievement goals. In nonclassroom settings, significant others and important social agents were proposed to determine goal salience by the nature of their instructional demands (Ames, 1992a, p. 262). Further, Ames (1992b) asserted that the subjective meaning, or the individual's perception of the motivational environment, was the critical factor in predicting subsequent achievement goals and patterns of behavior. This body of literature helped researchers define two types of motivational climate: a mastery climate in which the criteria for evaluation are self-referenced and people are viewed as competent when they have made progress, accomplished a task, or learned something new; and a performance climate in which the criteria for evaluation are heavily other-referenced and the emphasis is on outperforming others and making as few mistakes as possible (Blumenfeld, 1992). Based on Epstein (1989), Ames (1992a) then described specific classroom structures that were likely to invoke mastery or performance climates; these six achievement structures were task (design of tasks), authority (location of decision making), recognition (distribution of rewards), grouping (manner and frequency of grouping), evaluation (standards for performance), and time (pace of learning). The initial letters of the six structures create the acronym TARGET. Using each structure, a performance or mastery climate could be emphasized by the teacher or other salient social agents (see table 8.2).

Manipulations of Situational Goal Structures in Sport

By manipulating these climatic structures in the TARGET framework, early research attempted to create environmental conditions that would foster task (mastery) or ego (performance) involvement in participants. Examples of these studies include Duda and Chi (1989, basketball), Lloyd and Fox (1992, fitness classes), Marsh and Peart (1988, aerobics classes), and Theeboom, De Knop, and Weiss (1995, children's martial arts classes). All four of these studies supported theoretically specified links between climate or involvement and participants' behaviors or cognitions. In Lloyd and Fox's six-week study, low ego-oriented participants in the ego-involving climate became more ego oriented over the course of the study, and high ego-oriented participants in the task climate became less ego oriented. This study is one of the few that demonstrate an influence of climate on goal orientation. Such a theoretical link between climate and orientation has been suggested on a number of occasions (Duda, 1992; 1993; Nicholls, 1989; Treasure & Roberts, 1995), but experimental, relatively well-controlled investigations of sufficient length have been scarce.

Although noteworthy for their field-based experimental designs, the preceding studies contained several gaps given that they each adopted Nicholls' tenets. First, in some cases no account was taken of the independent effect of goal orientations on motivational outcomes. Therefore, limited

Table 8.2 Descriptions of Mastery and Performance Climates Within the TARGET Framework

	Mastery	Performance
Tasks	Challenging and diverse, offering chance for all to find involvement	Absence of variety and challenge, favoring participants who excel in these few tasks
Authority	Choices and leadership roles available to students	Students not involved in decision-making processes
Recognition	Private and based on individual progress	Public and based on social comparison
Grouping	Mixed-ability groups that promote cooperative learning and peer interaction	Groups formed based on ability (best to worst)
Evaluation	Based on mastery of tasks and individual improvement	Based on winning or outperforming others
Time	Time requirements adjusted to personal capabilities	Uniform time allocated for learning to all students, favoring those who are already adept

Adapted, by permission, from N. Ntoumanis and S. Biddle, 1999, "A review of motivational climate in physical activity," *Journal of Sports Sciences* 17: 643-665.

For TARGET framework, see Ames, 1992b and Epstein, 1989.

insight can be gained about the relative influence of dispositional and situational characteristics on task and ego involvement. Second, no measure was taken of participants' perceptions of the climate. Researchers perhaps misguidedly assumed that participants uniformly interpreted and applied the climate manipulation within each condition. Further, no measures of task and ego involvement were taken to determine degrees of situational change in achievement goals.

Nevertheless, such studies laid down a marker for testing achievement goal theory in true-to-life settings, and it is disappointing that such research waned in the following years. Perhaps in part, this design gave way to what has since become the dominant means of assessing situational factors in achievement goal theory—the measurement of *perceived* motivational climate.

Perceived Motivational Climate in Sport and Physical Education

Following Ames' (1992b) assertion that the perception of the motivational environment was critical, a number of questionnaires emerged to assess the perceived situational and contextual goal emphases in sport and physical education settings. The main scales are presented in table 8.3 alongside a

Table 8.3 Measures of Perceived Motivational Climate in Sport and Physical Education

	Questionnaire	Researchers	Primary factors	Subscales and supporting factors
Physical education climate scales	Learning and Performance Orientations in Physical Education Classes Questionnaire (LAPOPECQ)	Papaioannou (1994, 1998)	Performance climate	Students define success as outperforming others. Students worry about mistakes. Outcome-without-effort-orientation.
			Mastery climate	Teacher-initiated learning orientation. Students define success as learning. Teacher-initiated competitive orientation.
	Physical Education Class Climate Scale (PECCS)	Goudas and Biddle (1994)	Performance climate	Students define success as outperforming others. Students worry about mistakes.
			Mastery climate	Teacher-initiated learning orientation. Students define success as learning. Students' perceptions of choice. Students' perceptions of teacher support.
	L'Echelle de Perception du Climat Motivational (EPCM)	Biddle, Cury, Goudas, Sarrazin, Famose, & Durand (1995)	Performance climate	Pupils pursue comparisons. Pupils worry about mistakes. Teacher promotes comparison.
			Mastery climate	Pupils pursue progress. Teacher promotes learning.
Sport climate scales	Perceived Motivational Climate in Sport Questionnaire (PMCSQ)	Seifriz, Duda, and Chi (1992)	Performance climate	Items emphasizing outplaying teammates and punishment for mistakes.
			Mastery climate	Items emphasizing hard work, skill improvement, and seeing mistakes as part of learning.
	Perceived Motivational Climate in Sport Questionnaire–2 (PMCSQ–2)	Newton, Duda, and Yin (2000)	Performance climate	Unequal recognition. Punishment for mistakes. Intrateam rivalry and competition.
			Mastery climate	Emphasis on effort and improvement. Perceived important role. Cooperative learning.
	Parent Initiated Motivational Climate Questionnaire (PIMCQ–1 and PIMCQ–2)	White, Duda, and Hart (1992) and White (1996)	Performance climate	Worry-conducive climate. Success-without-effort climate.
			Mastery climate	Learning- and enjoyment-oriented climate.

description of the subscale composites that support the overall perceptions of mastery or performance climate. To summarize these subfactors, (a) effort, (b) learning or skill improvement, (c) perceived important role, (d) cooperative learning, and (e) "mistakes are part of learning" are all key themes of mastery climates; whereas (a) interpersonal comparison (and rivalry), (b) punishment and fear of mistakes, (c) unequal treatment of players, and (d) achieving without effort are consistent themes of performance climates. Notionally, any individual leading or participating in sporting activities can influence the motivational climate by differentially emphasizing those themes, and it is immediately clear that coaches or teachers, parents, and peers are important social protagonists of such climates. Although the development of these questionnaires has contributed significantly to our understanding of the role played by situational perceptions, the measurement of climate continues to court a great deal of deserved scrutiny. Duda and Whitehead (1998) provided some excellent critical insights into the different measures of perceived climate, the origins and properties of each instrument, and the conceptual appropriateness of certain scales. Ideas for advancements in measurement and other methodological directions will follow shortly. First, however, we will summarize what has been learned from the research that has employed these scales (see Ntoumanis and Biddle, 1999, for a further review).

Correlates of Motivational Climate

In a similar vein to research investigating dispositional goal orientations (Duda & Nicholls, 1992), interest has been high in the motivational, affective, and behavioral correlates of perceived mastery or performance climates in sport and PE. To date, the motivational variables linked to motivational climate include (a) beliefs about causes of sporting success; (b) beliefs about the purpose of sport; (c) positive affect—enjoyment, intrinsic interest, and satisfaction; (d) negative affect—pressure, tension, anxiety, distress, and worry; (e) perceived competence; (f) adoption of learning versus competitive strategies; (g) goal orientations; (h) moral development; (i) motor learning and development; and (j) the experience of flow (optimal involvement and distorted experience of the passage of time with an absence of effortful or cognitive thought; Csikszentmihalyi, 1990). For a comprehensive overview of this evidence see table 8.4. In summarizing these findings, a strong case can be made that the creation of an environment high in mastery cues is likely to produce numerous adaptive and desirable consequences for the participation and development of sport performers. In contrast, when participants perceive performance climates, positive or adaptive motivational patterns are rarely displayed. In fact, perceived performance climates are often associated with undesirable beliefs and patterns of behavior.

Table 8.4 A Summary of Research Investigating Correlates of Perceived Motivational Climate

Correlate of motivational climate	Theoretical associations	Studies examining the link	Associations supported
Beliefs about causes of sporting success	According to theory, (1) a perceived mastery climate will be linked to belief that *effort* is necessary for success while (2) a perceived performance climate will link to beliefs that success stems from greater (a) *ability* (finite and unchangeable), and possibly (b) deception or gamesmanship.	Seifriz, Duda, & Chi (1992)	1, 2a, and 2b
		Treasure & Roberts (1998)	1, 2a, and 2b
		Treasure & Roberts (2001)	1, 2a, and 2b
		Newton & Duda (1999)	1, 2a, and 2b
		Carpenter & Morgan (1999)	1 and 2b; 2a not tested
Beliefs about the purpose of sport	According to theory, (3) only perceived mastery climates link to the belief that sport serves the purpose of improving and challenging ourselves. Perceived performance climates (4), on the other hand, appear to link to the belief that sport is for the enhancement of social status.	Ommundsen & Roberts (1999)	3 and 4
		Ommundsen, Roberts, & Kavussanu (1998)	

Correlate of motivational climate	Theoretical associations	Studies examining the link	Associations supported
Positive affect—enjoyment, intrinsic interest and satisfaction (Representative sample only)	Theoretically, (5) a perceived mastery climate should promote challenge and autonomy, and cause sport participation to be seen as the end in itself (intrinsic motivation and enjoyment), whilst (6) a perceived performance climate should promote the idea that the activity is a means-to-an-end: the demonstration of superior ability. This should create pressure and tension and reduce positive affect.	Balaguer, Duda, & Crespo (1999)	5 and 6
		Digelidis, Papaioannou, Laparidis, & Christodoulidis (2003)	5
		Kavussanu & Roberts (1996)	5 and 6
		Whitehead, Andrée, & Lee (2004)	5 and 6
		Newton, Duda, & Yin (2000)	5
		Newton & Duda (1999)	5
		Parish & Treasure (2003)	5 and 6
		Seifriz, Duda, & Chi (1992)	5
		Treasure & Roberts (2001)	5 and 6
		Liukkonen, Telama, & Biddle (1998)	5 and 6
		Dorabantu & Biddle (1997)	5
		Boixadós, Cruz, Torregrosa, & Valiente (2004)	5 and 6
		Treasure & Roberts (2001)	5 and 6
Negative affect—anxiety, tension and boredom	According to theory, (7) a perceived mastery climate will either a) reduce negative affective experiences, or b) show no relationship. Whereas there should be (8) a positive association between perceptions of a performance climate and anxiety, worry, distress, and dissatisfaction with the team.	Newton, Duda, & Yin (2000)	7a and 8
		Newton & Duda (1999)	7b and 8
		Ntoumanis & Biddle (1998)	7b and 8
		Escarti & Gutierrez (2001)	7b and 8
		Papaioannou & Kouli (1999)	7a and 8
		Pensgaard & Roberts (2000)	7a and 8
		Walling, Duda, & Chi (1993)	7a and 8
Perceived competence	According to theory, (9) a perceived mastery climate is likely to promote perceived competence due to focus on personal improvement and effort. Whereas (10) a perceived performance climate implies ability is the main determinant of success so any failures reduce perceived competence, meaning an (a) negative relationship or (b) no relationship.	Escarti & Gutierrez (2001)	9 and 10b
		Goudas & Biddle (1994)	9 and 10b
		Cury, Da Fonseco, Rufo, & Sarrazin (2002)	10a
		Cury, Biddle, Famose, Goudas, Sarrazin, & Durand (1996)	9 and 10b
		Balaguer, Duda, & Crespo (1999)	9 and 10b
		Dunn (2000)	9 and 10b
		Balaguer, Duda, Atienza, & Mayo (2002)	9 and 10b
		Standage, Duda, & Ntoumanis (2003a; b)	9 and 10b
		Kavussanu & Roberts (1996)	9 and 10b
		Digelidis, Papaioannou, Laparidis, & Christodoulidis (2003)	9 and 10b
		Liukkonen, Telama, & Biddle (1998)	9 and 10b
		Ommundsen & Roberts (1999)	9
		Ferrer-Caja & Weiss (2000)	9 and 10a
		Sarrazin, Vallerand, Guillet, Pelletier, & Cury, (2002)	9 and 10b

(continued)

Table 8.4 *(continued)*

Correlate of motivational climate	Theoretical associations	Studies examining the link	Associations supported
Adoption of learning versus competitive strategies	Roberts & Treasure (1992; 1995) suggest that (11) a perceived mastery climate leads to internal standards of comparison and striving for improvement—leading to seeking challenging tasks, persistence and participation in training, while (12) a perceived performance climate promotes interpersonal comparisons, which are relatively unstable outcomes and therefore result in the use of varied strategies (e.g., no association).	Gano-Overway & Ewing (2004)	11 and 12
		Yoo (1999)	11 and 12
		Xiang & Lee (2002)	11 and 12 (+ older groups more prone to performance)
		Magyar & Feltz (2003)	11 and 12
		Ntoumanis, Biddle, & Haddock (1999)	11 and 12
		Ommundsen & Roberts (2001)	11 and 12
		Ommundsen, Roberts, & Kavussanu (1998)	11 and 12
		Ryska, Yin, & Boyd (1999)	12
		Treasure & Roberts (2001)	11 and 12
Goal orientations (Representative sample only)	Either task-orientation biases towards perceiving a mastery climate or perceptions of a mastery climate promote task orientation (13). Either ego-orientation biases towards perceiving a performance climate or a perceived performance climate promotes ego orientation (14).	Standage, Duda, & Ntoumanis (2003)	13 and 14
		Digelidis, Papaioannou, Lapraridis, & Christodoulidis (1993)	13 and 14
		Xiang & Lee (2002)	13 and 14
		Williams (1998)	13, no link for 14
		Todorovich & Curtner-Smith (2002)	13 and 14
Moral development	According to theory, (15) a perceived mastery climate links to concern over effort and improvement so opponents are seen as allies in testing and improving skill; hence foul play and cheating are considered amoral and unsportsmanlike, meaning a negative relationship with rough/foul play. Whereas (16) a perceived performance climate emphasizes winning at all costs and so foul-play and cheating are considered acceptable means to this end, meaning a positive relationship with rough/foul play.	Kavussanu, Roberts, & Ntoumanis (2002)	15 not tested 16 supported link at *team level*
		Ommundsen, Roberts, Lemyre, & Treasure (2003)	15 and 16
		Fry & Newton (2003)	15 and 16
		Gano-Overway, Guivernau, Magyar, Waldron, & Ewing (2005)	15 (Mastery climate promotes "respect for the game") and 16 (No effect for performance climate)
		Boixadós, Cruz, Torregrosa, & Valiente (2004)	15 and 16
		Miller, Roberts, & Ommundsen (2004)	15 and 16
Motor learning or development	No theoretically specified links between motivational climate and motor development or skill learning.	Valentini & Rudisill (2004a)	Creation of a mastery climate led to improved motor learning versus control groups for both disabled and non-disabled
		Valentini & Rudisill (2004b)	Creation of a mastery climate led to improved motor learning versus control groups—including retention effects
		Theeboom, De Knop, & Weiss (1995)	Improved karate kick learning in mastery climate as opposed to traditional climate

Correlate of motivational climate	Theoretical associations	Studies examining the link	Associations supported
Flow	No theoretically specified links between motivational climate and flow.	Kowal & Fortier (2000)	Perceived mastery climate positively correlated with reported flow experiences; perceived performance climate showed no relationship.

Future Research Directions

Investigations over the past two decades have reinforced the key role played by motivational climate within the interactionist principles of (largely) Nicholls' achievement goal theory. Nevertheless, before moving into our final section, we will mention a number of methodological, contextual, and conceptual challenges that researchers should address over the next two decades.

Experimental Designs Besides conducting cross-sectional examinations of perceived motivational climate, researchers need to manipulate a motivational climate over a period of time and track those manipulations while examining behavioral and affective consequences in participants. This experimental or intervention-type research will require some sophisticated thinking about methods of assessment specific to the context, a sound intervention process, an appropriate length of time, and perhaps a matched control group (see Harwood & Swain, 2002). Correlational investigations have given us a basic map, but only by testing these hypotheses in a more experimental manner will we be able to infer causality with greater confidence. Further to this, a more advanced research question would be to determine the degree to which the manipulation of climates in one setting (e.g., organized sport, soccer) will not only influence motivational patterns in this situation (e.g., Lloyd & Fox, 1992) but also transfer between domains to other sports (e.g., tennis) or settings (e.g., school, music). A further possibility may be to examine what facilitates such a transfer (e.g., a perceived change in parental orientations, beliefs, and behavior through parent education with parental interaction being common to all these settings).

Orthogonal Versus Bipolar When employing the Physical Education Class Climate Scale (PECCS), Goudas and Biddle (1994) reported that a class environment high in both mastery and performance cues led to more enjoyment than did any other combination (low and high, high and low, low and low). This finding suggests that the different goal emphases do not cancel out or cause confusion but rather complement each other (cf. Hodge & Petlichkoff, 2001; goal profiling). At first glance, it may appear difficult to see how, for example, a climate on a sport team can be both task and ego involving. But the general climate of a sport team includes perceptions of the values, attitudes, and behaviors of a variety of social agents (e.g., coach, teammates), and effort, improvement, and social comparison might be equally emphasized. Existing questionnaires (e.g., PMCSQ–2) assess perceptions of a general climate as opposed to perceptions of a climate in a specific situation or moment in time (e.g., prematch before important games, in training, at halftime). Therefore, it may not be surprising that the constructs of mastery and performance climate behave independently when assessments are made about what happens generally "on this team" or "in this class."

Little research has specifically examined the orthogonality (conceptual independence) or bipolarity of performance and mastery climates (Goudas & Biddle, 1994; Ntoumanis & Biddle, 1999). A more situational-level measurement technology would be required to do this research question justice. Such research may also help us understand whether motivational climate (in a particular situation) is more influential than goal orientation in predicting situational task and ego involvement (Papaioannou & Kouli, 1999) and in influencing other immediate motivational variables (e.g., in vivo moral behavior, precompetition anxiety). Our knowledge of the interaction of motivational climate and goal orientation on goal involvement and motivational outcomes is constrained by studies that have not measured climate at a situational level.

Levels of Measurement and Intrateam Variability The interest of researchers in establishing relationships between perceived motivational climate and motivation-related outcomes in sport has demanded relatively large sample sizes. This requirement has effectively led to cross-sectional assessments of groups of participants in a variety of teams, without considering the effect of each separate team on the data and the degree of variability of participant responses from the same intact team.

Researchers have recently proffered that the motivational climate construct is inherently group-like in nature (see Papaioannou, Marsh, & Theodorakis, 2004) and that investigations should consider group-level as well as individual-level variability in members' climate perceptions. The key concern here is that the term *climate* suggests that all members of intact teams are exposed to similar environmental influences, which may have a homogenizing effect on player motivation (i.e., they are influenced in a similar way by similar factors). Therefore, multilevel modeling statistical procedures to examine these group-level effects have been introduced into recent work.

The counterpoint to this proposal is that individual team members will carry perceptions of their direct relationship with the coach and the highly personal motivational climate that surrounds that relationship, as well as their perceptions of the climate existing within the team as a whole. Therefore, although the athlete's personal climate may be embedded within the team climate, the unique relationship that each athlete has with the coach (and others) may mean that personal climates differ amongst members of each team. A recent study by Cumming, Smoll, Smith & Grossbard (2007) found very small intra-class correlations for task and ego climates in a sample of basketball teams, suggesting that individual team members had very different perceptions of the team's motivational climate. This high intra-team variability led Cumming and colleagues to conclude that athlete-perceived motivational climate is better regarded as an individual-level as opposed to group-level variable (see Harwood & Beauchamp, in press).

Essentially, intra-team variability represents the level of consensus of climate perceptions between individuals in the same team (Chan, 1998; Schneider, Salvaggio, & Subirats, 2002). For example, as alluded to earlier, members of a team may report different levels of mastery and performance climate. Why and how would this occur, and what are the implications of such differences to the functioning of the team? These represent important practical questions that are worth addressing. Certainly, at an applied level, the congruence of team members' perceptions may offer greater understanding of the quality of group dynamics, the appropriateness of the coach's and teammates' behavior, and subsequent team outcomes (e.g., productivity, stability).

Researchers are encouraged to conduct more intimate intra-team research not only to explore levels of variability but also to consider interventions that may yield strong, positive congruence of team members' perceptions (e.g., congruent high-mastery, lower-performance climates).

As a summary point, whilst these multilevel issues should make for an interesting phase of future research, consideration might be given to the current stems of existing questionnaires. At present, the PMCSQ-2 and most climate scales use the team as the point of reference for the respondent (e.g., on this team, the coach favors some players more than others). The athlete is perceiving what he or she feels goes on in the team as a whole. However, if climate is to be measured as an individual-level variable, then it makes most sense to have an individual-level reference point (e.g., on this team, I am rewarded for high levels of effort; on this team, I am punished for my mistakes by the coach). If these perceptions are what the researcher is really trying to capture, then using a group-reference point may not be appropriate. This point also applies to any practitioner who considers employing such questionnaires to understand the athlete in his or her environment or team from a motivational perspective.

Giving Practitioners the Real Picture   As noted earlier, a number of climate measures such as the PMCSQ–2 comprise separate lower-order subscales that combine to provide the total score for perceived mastery and performance climate (e.g., on this team). Unfortunately, the habit is developing whereby researchers rarely report or analyze these subscale scores, although the ostensible purpose for their development was to enhance our understanding of the specific elements behind such climates. At a theoretical and applied level, researchers need to examine how these climate subscales (e.g., learning and skill improvement, punishment for mistakes) independently relate to psychosocial or motivational outcomes. Further, if researchers do investigate the perceived motivational climate (of a team) within the different situations that a team comes together (e.g., practice, competition), does the climate change, and, if so, what specific elements change? For example, we could hypothesize a lower skill-improvement climate and a higher punishment-for-mistakes climate in competition compared with practice situations. This kind of research is important for applied practitioners and certainly questions the utility of using a general scale to predict situation-specific cognitive, affective, and behavioral responses. Finally, such an investigation may shed light on the orthogonal versus bipolar debate by presenting the degree to which such elements are correlated when participants respond to a situation as opposed to circumstances in general. In sum, from the point of view of conducting good research and promoting more informed applied practice, researchers must develop measures that differentiate these two levels of analysis (Duda & Whitehead, 1998).

Integrative Measures of Specific Sport Environments A look at the measurement of climate in sport reveals two issues. First, separate questionnaires cover various social dimensions of climate in a general manner. Second, no measure targets the motivational climate of a sport performer in an individual sport context. Certainly, it is a concern that studies assessing motivational climate with measures strictly designed for team sports (i.e., PMCSQ; PMCSQ–2) have included data from individual sport participants. The use of the PMCSQ–2 within individual sports (even with severe item editing and removal) is inappropriate, not only psychometrically but also because the composition of influences and nature of the two contexts are qualitatively different. A key step forward for research, in our opinion, is to consider both the person or persons and the social context when developing measures that seek to assess the climate influencing the athlete. For example, Harwood, Smith, and Treasure (2005) have conducted initial work on the Individual Sport Motivational Climate Scales (ISMC scales), a holistic measure of motivational climate for individual sport performers. The overall measure consists of five separate scales targeted at the perceived climate from the athlete's perspective created by coach, father, mother, peers, and the sport reward structure. The intention here is to understand the influence of different social agents on the individual athlete and to assess social agents' perceived behaviors and conveyed beliefs. This approach will allow researchers and practitioners to target their interventions more specifically. A similar idea would follow for team-sport performers, again reinforcing the need to specify the context under study (i.e., practice versus competition environments).

Other Social Agents Current studies of climate are essentially limited to our appreciation of the behavioral roles played by coach or teacher, parents, and teammates. Some research, however, has made the case for examining the motivational influence of sporting heroes and role models (Carr & Weigand,

2001), and recent studies have conceptualized the role played by peers (Vazou, Ntoumanis, & Duda, 2005), leading to a new measure of peer motivational climate (in broadly team sport contexts; see Ntoumanis & Vazou, 2005). The media is a further social agent of relevance to higher-level and professional athletes. All these avenues are worthy of greater investigation.

Level Versus Strength of Influence An increasing body of evidence suggests that the quality of relationships in a sporting context has a significant influence on the motivation of sport participants. Vazou, Ntoumanis, and Duda (2005) and Smith (1999, 2003) presented strong arguments for the consideration of peer relationships and the influence of their quality on motivation. Olympiou, Jowett, and Duda (under review) have examined the influence of the quality and nature of the coach–athlete relationship on motivational variables. They found that the quality of this relationship correlates positively with perceived mastery climate and negatively with perceived performance climate. These studies offer an insight into how relationships exert a direct influence on motivation and may serve to illustrate the salience of certain social agents (e.g., how likely are athletes to be influenced by the behavior or values of coaches, parents, or peers whom they do or do not respect, value, or like?). Most significantly in previous research, we have assumed that individual responses to a questionnaire accurately reflect the intensity or level of perceived mastery and performance climates that influence achievement goals and motivational processes. Although an athlete may report the task- or ego-involving behavior of a certain social agent, he or she may not internalize or be affected by the behavior that is promoted by that agent. In simple terms, the level of task- or ego-involving behaviors or values reported on a 5-point Likert scale may not necessarily have a salient psychological influence on the individual. This issue of level versus strength of influence is an important measurement issue for researchers in determining whether the climate being reported is indeed a *motivational* climate or simply the reported actions of a non-salient significant other.

Approach Versus Avoidance Climates We reiterate that motivational climate research to date has been based on Ames', Dweck's, and Nicholls' two-goal conceptualizations. The propensity of a mastery and performance climate to invoke approach or avoidance goals has not been studied. Nevertheless, although certain items on existing scales may correspond to some of Elliot's dimensions (e.g., mastery approach, performance approach, performance avoidance), there is perhaps a need to conceptualize climate in a manner that explicitly corresponds with the two-by-two approach-avoidance framework (see Papaioannou, Tsigilis, Kosmidou and Milosi, 2007). Investigating the precise constituents of two-by-two (mastery or performance by approach or avoidance) climates may help further our understanding of human motivation, particularly the construct of avoidance motivation that remains understudied within achievement goal theory.

Future Research Directions

This chapter has focused on the principles and related research of four major theoretical approaches to achievement goals in sport and physical activity settings. Each section has also addressed a number of unanswered or underexplored research questions that seek to maintain the impetus of that particular approach in a sport context. Some common challenges, however, apply to all these approaches if they are to advance our understanding of motivated behavior in sport. The final section of this chapter proposes three broad areas of study that we feel should occupy the interests and time of researchers over the next decade. These areas focus on enhancing our understanding of the individual athlete, the team dynamic, and the performance situation.

The Individual: Developmental Transitions in Young Athletes

When it comes to understanding the young athlete and achievement goals, we need to refocus our picture of the developmental process on a number of levels. According to Nicholls (1989), children are incapable of being ego involved before age 11, yet we witness behaviors and comments of children on and off the sports field symptomatic of ego involvement at far younger ages (see Fry, 2001; Fry & Duda, 1997). What exactly is happening here? Indeed, if true ego involvement can only be experienced at 11 years of age, then does an ego orientation only come into play at that point as well, and is it safe to assume that covert socialization of task and ego orientations has been occurring up until 11 years of age? Similarly, do approach and avoidance goals become socialized and form orientations? If so, what situational behaviors promoted by adults lead to the development of such goals? At what age does that occur? As noted earlier, what is the outcome of the interplay between Dweck's theory of entity and incremental beliefs

and Nicholls' differentiation process with respect to young athletes in search of competence?

As researchers we probably hypothesize about the actual mechanics of these early organized youth sport processes more than we actually study them. Observant coaches in workshops (of the first author) have asked keen questions about what is happening during these early transitions. As researchers we have a responsibility to answer these questions.

Continuing this theme of individual transitions, are certain achievement goal profiles, implicit belief profiles, and motivational climates more optimal than others in facilitating the athlete's transition to a higher level (see Wylleman & Lavallee, 2003)? On what grounds is a high task, high ego orientation profile optimal, and does Elliot's two-by-two model of approach-avoidance goals offer more insight into an adaptive motivational profile? Further, if the motive for social approval is high during adolescence, what are the potential advantages and disadvantages of this social orientation in terms of achievement goals from Nicholls' and Elliot's perspectives?

All these questions charge researchers to take a closer look at the individual athlete in real life and to investigate the positive (and negative) role of these motivational constructs in the context of changes that take place as an athlete makes the journey toward fulfilling his or her potential in sport.

The Team: Maximizing Compatibility and Team Functioning

Beyond a few cross-cultural studies (e.g., Hayashi, 1996), achievement goal researchers tend to have isolated their investigations to exploring outcomes and correlates of achievement goals as opposed to individuals and groups per se. The lack of individually targeted intervention research is noteworthy, but perhaps not as noteworthy as the absence of research into team functioning. Even with a measure of perceived motivational climate geared toward sport teams, we could not locate an intervention or intrateam-based case study that tackled issues of incompatible achievement goal orientations, role or position-specific variations in achievement goals, or variability versus congruence of team members' perceptions of motivational climate. Research has also yet to consider the role that the approach-avoidance framework may play or whether other types of competence-based goals exist in team settings (e.g., intrateam ego involvement).

The relevance of studying team functioning from an achievement goals perspective can be seen in a discrete study of 36 sport acrobat pairs by Harwood and Lacey (2001). Using adapted versions of the POSQ (Roberts et al., 1998), this study examined the levels of compatibility and perceptual agreement between each individual's reported goal orientations and his or her partner's perception of that individual's goal orientations. The POSQ was adapted to contain a directional subscale that asked acrobats to rate on a scale of +3, or very positive, to –3, or very negative, the degree to which they felt that their response to each POSQ item had a positive or negative effect on their performance as a pair. Bases (older athletes who form the base of the pair) reported lower levels of ego orientation and higher levels of task orientation than did their respective tops (younger athletes who form the top of the pair). Bases also perceived their level of task orientation to be more positive to the performance as a pair than did their respective tops. When analyzing their perceptions of each other's goal orientations, bases perceived their tops to be lower in task orientation than the tops' self-reported responses, and bases appraised this level of task orientation to be less positive to performance than did tops. In addition, although predictions made by bases about the level of ego orientation of their tops were accurate, they perceived their tops' ego orientation to be less positive to performance than the tops' self-reported perceptions of their ego orientation. These findings illustrated the importance of perception (and misperception) in team or pair sport settings, as well as the issue of compatible versus incompatible individual motivational differences in terms of team functioning. Group outcome variables such as cohesion, collective efficacy, enjoyment, satisfaction, role acceptance, stability, and ultimately performance may rest on the development of climates that facilitate compatible (or position-specific) motivational orientations and states in team members. A beneficial climate may also help team members understand their individual motivational differences when working together as a team. Researchers should consider the role that achievement goal theory plays in team settings and direct some effort toward intra- and interteam designs that will help further this understanding.

The Performance Situation: Goal Involvement and Dynamic Fluctuations

Nicholls, Dweck, and Elliot offer differing perspectives on both the number and activation of achievement goals at the state or situational level (i.e., goal involvement; achievement goal states).

Within Nicholls' approach, the constructs of task and ego involvement in sport are badly in need of some sophisticated research attention. The same is true for Elliot's theory. The transience or dynamic properties of achievement goal states, including their potential orthogonality and momentary flipping mechanisms, represent a rich, applied, and experimental field of study. How do states of task and ego involvement or approach and avoidance goals interact during performance? What should the relative intensities of each goal perspective be before and during performance for optimal skill execution? Does this optimal profile differ in competition versus practice settings? What effect do sport type, duration, and positional demands have on these predictions? What are the biopsychosocial antecedents and consequences of these momentary shifts? Readers are guided to Gernigon et al. (2004) and the *Journal of Sport & Exercise Psychology* debates for further insights into a research area that probably represents the most salient advances that we can make as academics. Nicholls' theory is built on notions about goal involvement, yet in sport settings we have only stretched ourselves to the ease of measuring dispositions and scratched the surface at a situational level. Dweck's and Elliot's constructs require similar academic scrutiny over the duration and heat of in vivo sport competition.

Conclusion

The endeavor of researchers in achievement goal theory over the past 20 years has immeasurably aided the field of sport psychology. These findings have been gradually translated to the practice of sport psychology, and it is certainly in the field of applied practice that achievement goal theories have the most gravitas.

This chapter has addressed both traditional and contemporary approaches to achievement goals, and has suggested areas in need of attention that are specific to each. To the reader, we hope that we have furnished you with the same sound understanding of sport motivation that the past 20 years of literature has offered us. Nevertheless, we affirm the need to approach the next 20 years with investigations that are more context specific to individual athletes, teams, and performance or activity situations. Such research will continue to challenge researchers conceptually and guard against any complacency that might cause analytical efforts to reach a plateau in this field.

CHAPTER 9

Moral Development in Sport and Physical Activity

Maureen R. Weiss, PhD ▪ Alan L. Smith, PhD ▪ Cheryl P. Stuntz, PhD

© SportsChrome

Character development and sport participation is one of the hottest topics in contemporary society. ESPN's *SportsCenter* and *Outside the Lines* highlight controversial moral issues in sport every evening. Numerous media outlets offer the latest news about such topics as steroids in major league baseball, violence in professional ice hockey, bribery in international soccer, and incidences of sexism, racism, and homophobia. Less often do consumers learn about actions that reflect "doing the right thing" in sports. Although critics are quick to draw the public's attention to athletes' behaviors that fall below ethical standards expected of everyday citizens, proponents convincingly argue that sport is an appropriate and powerful developmental context for teaching fair play and sportsmanship. To this end, advocates claim that sport builds character (honesty, respect, responsibility), while opponents implore that, instead, sport develops *characters* by endorsing cheating and aggressive play as a means of attaining the goal of winning. Ultimately, sport is like a double-edged sword—it has the potential to build character *or* characters.

The question of whether sport builds character or characters depends on the quality of adult leadership and the types of experiences afforded participants in skill-learning and competitive environments. As such, most educators agree that sport participation by itself is not associated with developing character or other developmental outcomes such as interpersonal, emotion management, and self-regulation skills. These outcomes do not occur automatically because of mere participation in sport or physical activity, or for that matter because of participation in any meaningful context for children and adolescents. Instead, positive developmental outcomes are likely to occur when competent and caring adults teach for character by designing appropriate activities, identifying appropriate role models, reinforcing prosocial behaviors, discussing varying perspectives, and taking advantage of teachable moments. If developing character through sport participation requires deliberate activities and curricula combined with trained teachers and coaches who are sensitive, motivated, and committed to instilling character in their participants, what activities and teaching strategies should they employ? What does the body of knowledge on character development through sport say about the factors that are most likely to influence moral development in sport?

In this chapter we provide a comprehensive and inclusive review of theory, research, and application pertaining to moral development in sport and physical activity contexts. First, we trace the history of the role of sport in contributing to moral values among youth. Second, we distinguish among character-related terms and definitions, and summarize theoretical perspectives of moral development. Third, we synthesize and consolidate the body of knowledge on moral development and sport, including research focusing on social-contextual factors followed by research examining individual difference factors that influence moral thoughts and behaviors. Fourth, we describe studies that were explicitly designed to investigate the effects of interventions on moral reasoning and prosocial behaviors. Finally, we offer suggestions for further research to enhance the knowledge base on moral development in sport and physical activity contexts.

Historical Perspectives

The belief that sport participation promotes development of character can be traced to the ancient belief that being of sound body is to be of sound spirit and mind. Modern conceptions of this relationship can be linked to mid-19th century Britain, where elite schools promoted sport participation as a means to developing leadership, self-control, honesty, and other virtues (see Shields & Bredemeier, 1995). In promoting these virtues, school leaders believed that sport was a vehicle for boys (of the upper class) to develop into military, industry, and political leaders of the highest caliber. Underlying this conception of sport were assumptions that sport held to an amateur model and that sport was youth governed. Linking sport with professionalism was believed to corrupt the character-building process because material gain would supplant spiritual gain (Shields & Bredemeier). Self-governance was believed critical for the development of leadership, conflict resolution, and other skills associated with organizing and negotiating.

As the United States was rapidly industrializing in the mid- to late-19th century, attitudes about the character-building qualities of sport became consonant with those in British society. This development was largely the result of the Muscular Christianity movement, in which American Protestants promoted sport as a means to develop the spirit (see Wiggins, 1996). The YMCA began to develop competitive sport programs in the late 19th century and was at the forefront of the Muscular Christianity movement. Further perpetuating belief in the character-building capacity of sport, the playground movement took hold in the early 20th century. This movement fostered the creation of play and sport opportunities for youth of a variety of backgrounds, with particular attention to the waves of immigrant youths entering the country. With inclusion of sport activities in the schools, access to sport was widespread and believed to be critical to the socialization of the country's youth.

In the 1920s and 1930s youth sport began to emulate highly competitive sport, with emphasis on winning and elite-level competition. Physical educators and medical professionals distanced themselves from organized sport (see Berryman, 1996), believing that this new emphasis placed undue physical and psychological stress on youth and was contrary to the inclusive, character-building emphasis of the playground movement. Agencies outside the school system filled the void left by the decrease in school-related opportunities for children, resulting in the development and later success of sport organizations such as Little League Baseball. Indeed, youth sport programs proliferated to the degree that today organized sport participation is a ubiquitous feature of childhood in the United States.

Resolutions and policy statements on youth competitive sport were vigorously developed from the 1930s to 1960s, yet little empirical research was conducted to explore the character-building or character-endangering nature of sport. In a historically significant article published in *Research Quarterly*, C.H. McCloy (1930) noted the importance of deliberately teaching character within physical education and presented challenges associated with measuring character, issues that continue to be discussed by contemporary sport philosophers (e.g., Gough, 1995; Stoll, 1999) and sport psychology researchers (Weiss & Gill, 2005). Nonetheless, research on the topic was sporadic until the 1980s. The intensified interest may be attributed in part to increased media attention on negative acts in sport, increasing numbers of boys *and* girls involved in organized sport, concerns about the diminished role of the sandlot in the youth sport experience (see Coakley, 1998, and Martens, 1978, for discussions of this issue), and perceptions that society has become morally bankrupt, making social institutions such as sport more critical to the socialization of youth.

Also contributing to the increase in scientific investigations of sport and character development were the production and advancement of theoretical perspectives on moral development. Early research on the topic not only was sporadic but also relatively atheoretical. With the advancement of moral development theory and social psychological training

within the sport sciences, researchers in the past two and a half decades have vigorously tackled this research topic. The following section will address the dominant theoretical perspectives that have allowed sport psychologists to both advance the knowledge base and design physical education and sport-based intervention strategies for developing character.

Theoretical Perspectives

The academic term *moral development* is rarely used in everyday language or in stories of role models or transgressors at any level of sport. Instead we tend to use the more common terms *sportsmanship* (or sportspersonship), *character*, or *fair play*, among others. But what exactly do these terms mean? *Sportsmanship* and *character* are often considered cliché and, as such, everybody knows or thinks they know what the terms mean. But depending on individuals' perceptions or worldviews, these words can reflect a number of meanings.

Consider the child's perspective. Bovyer (1963) asked children in fourth through sixth grades to write down what the term *sportsmanship* meant to them. Children's responses were content-analyzed, and the most frequent categories were (a) plays by the rules and exhibits fair play; (b) respects the decisions, requests, opinions, and ideas of other people; (c) is a good loser; (d) is even-tempered; (e) respects the feelings of other people; and (f) takes turns and lets others play.

Forty years later, Stuart (2003) found similar results to those of Bovyer, albeit from a problem-focused view. She interviewed 15 youth sport participants, ages 10 to 12 years, about perceptions of right and wrong actions in sport. She asked them to describe events from their sport experience that they thought were a problem, defined as a situation in which some people are negatively affected by what another person does. Responses included disrespecting opponents, physical and verbal intimidation, teammates' selfishness, losing self-control, and dishonesty. Children also mentioned inappropriate adult behaviors: favoritism by officials and coaches, unfair treatment by coaches, and parental pressure.

Similarly, Entzion (1991), in a practitioner-oriented article, summarized his sixth-grade students' top 10 descriptors of fair play:

▪ Don't hurt anybody.

▪ Take turns.

▪ Don't yell at teammates when they make mistakes.

- Don't cheat.
- Don't cry every time you don't win.
- Don't make excuses when you lose.
- *Try* for first place.
- Don't tell people they're no good.
- Don't brag.
- Don't kick anyone in the stomach.

Collectively, children in these three studies were consistent with how they defined sportsmanship. Their responses depict behavioral norms and conventions that are expected within society (e.g., follow the rules, take turns, be honest) as well as concerns about the physical and psychological well-being of others (e.g., don't make fun of others, don't hurt others physically, show respect for others). Children seem to understand the golden rule (i.e., treat others the way you would want to be treated) and "doing the right thing" when it comes to defining sportsmanship and fair play.

Children's definitions are in line with the two most prevalent theoretical frameworks of moral development—social learning theory and structural developmental approaches—that have guided inquiry into sport and character development. This congruence is not surprising given Kohlberg's (cited in Turiel, 1998) observation of "the child as a moral philosopher," referring to children's use of their social experiences to form judgments about what is just, fair, and right. Detailed descriptions of these theories are found in the mainstream psychology (e.g., Eisenberg & Fabes, 1998; Kurtines & Gewirtz, 1995) and sport psychology literature (e.g., Shields & Bredemeier, 1995; Solomon, 2004; Weiss & Bredemeier, 1986, 1990; Weiss & Smith, 2002). In the following section, we describe social learning and structural developmental approaches to help set up the subsequent section on moral development research in physical activity settings.

Social Learning Theory

According to social learning theory (Bandura, 1986), morality is defined as prosocial behaviors that are consistent with societal norms and conventions, such as honesty, respect, and helping. Children internalize these behaviors through observational learning of and reinforcement by significant adults and peers within the larger socialization process. They may learn antisocial behaviors, of course, through the same mechanisms. Modeling of high-status models (e.g., professional athletes), perceiving approval by significant adults (e.g., believing that parents and

coaches would approve of retaliating after a foul), and experiencing vicarious reinforcement (e.g., seeing another player being congratulated for an aggressive action) are powerful means of learning sportsmanlike or unsportsmanlike behaviors from the perspective of social learning theory.

Bandura's (1991) social-cognitive theory of moral thought and action emphasizes the integration of individual differences and social factors as they govern moral behavior. Bandura contended that personal factors (e.g., moral reasoning, affective reactions), environmental influences (e.g., parental socialization), and moral behavior operate interactively in a reciprocal way. According to Bandura, "The self is not disembodied from social reality" (p. 69). Because Bandura believes that moral conduct is influenced strongly by affective self-reactions aside from the environment, self-regulation skills are paramount to instigating change and mobilizing efforts in behaving morally. Self-regulation includes self-monitoring of one's actions, self-judgment of behavior in relation to personal standards and environmental circumstances, and affective self-reaction. Effective self-regulation of moral behavior requires not only monitoring, judgment, and evaluation but also strong belief in one's capabilities to achieve personal control, referred to as self-regulatory efficacy. The stronger one's perceived self-regulatory efficacy, the more the person will adhere to his or her own moral standards and resist social pressures to transgress.

Eisenberg (1995; Eisenberg & Fabes, 1998) also takes an integrated approach to moral development while primarily working within a social-cognitive model. Her focus is on the factors that influence development of prosocial behavior in children. She developed a heuristic model that proposes a variety of developmental and social-psychological factors that influence prosocial behavior: (a) moral reasoning and social perspective-taking ability; (b) influence by parents, teachers, and peers; (c) personality qualities (e.g., self-esteem and personal values); (d) affective factors such as empathy, sympathy, and personal distress; and (e) situational factors that play a role in decision making. Eisenberg claims that all types of personal competencies and environmental influences interact to profoundly affect the development and expression of prosocial behavior.

Structural Developmental Approaches

Structural developmental theories focus on individuals' reasoning that underlies behavior, or why individuals act the way that they do. As such, children actively construct meaning about moral issues by interacting with adults and peers in a variety of social contexts. The two components of the term *structural developmental* vividly portray this perspective. A moral reasoning *structure* underlies judgments about what is right and wrong; this structure undergoes *developmental* change because of cognitive maturation and social interactions. Change generally proceeds from a focus on self-interest to an other-orientation and eventually to a principled reasoning level of mutual interest and welfare. A number of key theorists have made substantive contributions to the structural developmental way of thinking about morality, including Piaget, Kohlberg, Gilligan, and Haan (see Weiss & Smith, 2002, for an in-depth discussion of these theorists).

According to structural developmental approaches, morality is defined as concern for the physical and psychological welfare of self and others and is shaped through social interactions in response to moral *dilemmas*. Haan's (1977) emphasis on *dialogue and balance* reflects the processes of conflict and conflict resolution that are necessary to achieve moral balance among people facing situational dilemmas. She labeled her three phases of morality as assimilation, accommodation, and equilibration. The assimilation phase is characterized by seeking moral balance that gives preference to one's own needs and concerns. In the accommodation phase, people seek to resolve moral conflict by giving more to the moral exchange than they receive. Finally, the equilibration phase is characterized by recognizing all individuals' interests, rights, and needs.

Table 9.1 summarizes the social-learning and structural developmental approaches to moral development. The theories are distinguished based on their definition, sources, and basis of intervention of moral development.

Rest's Model of Moral Action

Rest (1984, 1986; Narváez & Rest, 1995) argued morality is more than development of moral reasoning or judgment. He derived a four-component model of morality that describes the factors that affect the relationship between moral thoughts and actions. Rather than merely divide these factors into cognitions, affect, and behavior, Rest (1984) asked, "What must we suppose happens psychologically in order for moral behavior to take place?" And so emerged his four components or processes that influence moral behavior.

The first component, *interpreting the situation*, involves an awareness of how actions affect other people. It involves imagining a range of possible courses of action and the effect that each may have on individuals. Rest alternatively labeled this component as *moral sensitivity* and noted that empathy and role-taking skills are essential for interpreting the situation as a moral one. The second component is *moral judgment*, or deciding which action is morally right or wrong. This component is reflected by one's *moral reasoning*, or the reasons why a person decides which course of action is more justifiable. The third component, *deciding what one intends to do*, or *moral motivation*, concerns weighing the importance of choosing among various competing values. The fourth component, *implementing a moral plan of action*, or *moral character*, refers to how the person actually behaves and may be influenced by ego strength, courage, and strength of conviction. Although the four components are presented in a logical sequence, they are thought to interact with and reciprocally influence one another. Narváez and Rest (1995) indicated that the model depicts an "ensemble of processes" and that failure to act morally could represent a problem with any of the four components. All components need to work in

Table 9.1 Theoretical Approaches to Moral Development

Approach	Definition of morality	Sources of moral development	Basis for intervention
Social learning	Prosocial behaviors in accordance with societal norms	Observational learning, reinforcement, approval by significant others	Role models, moral mentors, tangible and social rewards
Structural developmental	Concern for physical and emotional welfare of self and others	Cognitive or social disequilibrium when confronted with a moral dilemma; dialogue and balance with involved persons	Activities prompting discussion and resolution of moral dilemmas; role-playing, cooperative problem solving; empowering students to make decisions

concert for people to act morally. The model ultimately was developed as a framework for conducting research and moral education programs.

As discussed in later sections, researchers have embraced Rest's four-component model as a viable means of addressing research questions related to moral thoughts and behaviors in sport. For example, the components served as dependent variables before and after a moral education program (Gibbons, Ebbeck, & Weiss, 1995) and as correlates of variables such as perceived social approval of antisocial behaviors (Stuart & Ebbeck, 1995). Because Rest's model was so thorough in considering the range of thoughts, feelings, and behaviors that influence morality, Shields and Bredemeier (1995) adapted his model to one of moral action in sport.

Shields and Bredemeier's (1995) Model of Moral Action in Sport

Shields and Bredemeier embedded three sources of influence (personal competencies, social contextual factors, and ego processes) within their model for each of the four components of morality within Rest's model: interpretation, judgment, intention, and behavior. Shields and Bredemeier expanded Rest's model from 4 to 12 components to account for factors that may explain variations in moral behavior in sport. Rest actually delineated the factors that were likely to affect each of the four components but did not explicitly include them in the model itself.

As shown in table 9.2, a number of individual difference and social-contextual factors may influence moral processes. To date, moral reasoning, goal orientations, and legitimacy beliefs reflect the dominant personal competencies studied in relation to prosocial and antisocial behaviors in sport. Social-contextual factors thought to affect the relationship between moral thought and moral behavior include situational ambiguity, motivational climate, team norms (e.g., teammates' and coach's beliefs), and leadership style.

Shields and Bredemeier's (1995) 12-component model offers a useful way of organizing research on the relationship between moral thoughts and actions in physical activity contexts. The model describes possibilities for examining personal and social factors as correlates of moral processes. Since the publication of the previous version of this chapter, several studies have extended the knowledge base on personal and social-contextual factors as they relate to understanding moral development in sport. We turn to this body of knowledge next.

Moral Development Research in Physical Activity Settings

One of the many benefits of theory is that its principles can be tested through empirical research in specific social contexts and ultimately applied to practical teaching and coaching situations. In expanding Rest's (1984, 1986) four-component model of moral action, Shields and Bredemeier (1995) focused on two major sources of influence—social-contextual and individual difference factors—on moral interpretation, judgment, intention, and behavior. Several studies have explored ways in which our social settings influence personal beliefs and behaviors about what is right and wrong.

Table 9.2 Twelve-Component Model of Moral Action

	Moral interpretation	Moral judgment	Moral intention	Moral behavior
Personal competency influences	Role taking, social perspective taking	Moral reasoning, moral beliefs and values, legitimacy beliefs	Responsibility judgments, goal orientation, self-concept	Self-regulation skills, problem-solving skills
Social-contextual influences	Situational ambiguity, goal-reward structure	Moral atmosphere or collective norms	Domain cues, mastery versus performance climate	Power structures, leadership style
Ego-processing influences	Empathy, tolerance of ambiguity	Objectivity, intellectuality, logical analysis as coping; isolation, intellectualizing, rationalization as defending	Sublimation, substitution, suppression as coping; displacement, repression, reaction formation as defending	Concentration as coping; denial as defending

Adapted, by permission, from D.L.L. Shields and B.J.L. Bredemeier, 1995, *Character development and physical activity* (Champaign, IL: Human Kinetics), 92.

Other work has closely examined how individual differences or cognitive factors influence our moral beliefs and actions. Taken together, this body of knowledge shows that both social-contextual and individual difference factors are important contributors to moral development in physical activity settings. In the following sections, we systematically review the empirical research on social-contextual and individual difference factors, respectively, in relation to moral functioning in sport and physical activity.

Social-Contextual Factors

The social context in which we live is a strong contributor to our moral development. Relationships with teammates, coaches, officials, and parents, as well as influence from the media, mold our views of which behaviors are acceptable and which are unacceptable in sport. Socialization of normative moral beliefs and behaviors occurs through many pathways. The social-contextual pathways to moral development in sport have been studied within topics such as (a) socialization of prosocial behaviors, (b) observational learning of sportsmanlike and unsportsmanlike behaviors, (c) social approval of aggressive and unfair play, (d) moral atmosphere, and (e) motivational climate.

Socialization of Prosocial Behaviors
Prosocial behaviors include altruism, honesty, cooperation, and peer encouragement, as well as the demonstration of respect, empathy, responsibility, and equity. From a social learning perspective, morality is defined in terms of promoting prosocial behaviors that voluntarily benefit another (Eisenberg & Fabes, 1998). Reducing antisocial behaviors such as physical and verbal aggression, selfishness, and lack of responsibility is also a focus of the social learning perspective. Studies indicate that sport experiences contribute to promoting prosocial and reducing antisocial behaviors.

Early work on moral development in sport contexts examined the learning of character and prosocial behaviors. For example, Orlick (1981) showed that young children (5 years of age) exhibit more sharing behaviors after experiencing an 18-week *cooperative* games intervention. This games program had children work together, potentially fostering empathy, interdependence, and cooperative learning. Although participation in cooperative games may be related to increases in prosocial behavior, Kleiber and Roberts (1981) investigated the effect of participating in *competitive* games on altruistic behavior of 10- and 11-year-old boys and girls.

Children either competed in an eight-day kickball tournament or were assigned to a control group. Results provided little evidence that competition results in negative or positive effects on prosocial behavior.

In a series of studies, Sharpe, Brown, and Crider (1995; Sharpe, Crider, Vyhlidal, & Brown, 1996) taught respect for peers, helping behaviors, and conflict resolution skills to elementary school physical education students using a behaviorally based curriculum. Using a multiple baseline design, children exhibited better leadership and conflict resolution skills and less off-task behavior; children in the control group showed no change in behavior. Moreover, prosocial behaviors that improved in the gymnasium generalized to regular classroom settings. Giebink and McKenzie (1985) also employed a behaviorally based intervention during physical education to enhance social interaction skills in four at-risk boys characterized as unsportsmanlike. Intervention strategies included direct instruction, teacher modeling, praise for sportsmanlike behavior, and a contingent reward system (i.e., points for good behavior that counted toward a lottery for gaining tangible rewards). Although the intervention was successful at enhancing sportsmanlike behaviors (e.g., complimenting, supporting, and encouraging others) and reducing unsportsmanlike ones (e.g., intimidating, provoking, and disapproving of others) in all four boys, generalization from the physical education to recreational setting was unsuccessful.

Clearly, sport and physical activity represent socializing situations that offer the possibility to develop prosocial and reduce antisocial behaviors, especially with youth in physical education and recreational settings. However, it is unclear how successful organized sport is at developing and promoting prosocial behaviors, especially as competitive level and accompanying win orientation increases. We will revisit this theme later.

Observational Learning of Sportsmanlike and Unsportsmanlike Behaviors
The belief that role models exert considerable influence on children's learning of right and wrong behaviors in sport has historically been popular (Smith, 1988; Wiggins, 1996). Role models include significant adults such as parents, teachers, coaches, community leaders, and professional athletes as well as peer models such as teammates, classmates, and siblings. In recent years, professional hockey, baseball, basketball, and football instituted codes of ethics in an effort to curtail aggressive and other inappropriate behaviors (e.g., touchdown celebrations, drug use). Developing a

code of ethics is, in part, a means of acknowledging the influential role that professional athletes play in youths' development of moral and social norms in sport. Aside from anecdotal accounts of role-modeling effects, what does the empirical research say about such influence?

Studies show that observing an aggressive model leads people to engage in more physically and verbally aggressive behaviors. Bandura, Ross, and Ross' (1961) classic Bobo doll experiment strongly demonstrated the observational learning of aggressive behaviors. Children ages three to six years were exposed to aggressive or nonaggressive models. Children in the aggressive model condition watched an adult engage in physical and verbal aggression toward a 5-foot-tall (150-centimeter-tall) inflated Bobo doll. The behaviors were ones unlikely to be naturally produced by children (e.g., saying "Sock him in the face," striking a toy mallet on the doll's head). Children in the nonaggressive model condition observed the adult quietly assemble tinker toys while totally ignoring the Bobo doll. Observers in the aggressive model condition used more physical and verbal aggressive behaviors than did children in the nonaggressive group in a subsequent free-play period.

Social learning of aggression has also been demonstrated in sport settings. An early line of research by Michael D. Smith (1974, 1975, 1978, 1979) showed that aggressive behaviors in amateur ice hockey can be learned through and influenced by significant others. Smith (1974) asked male adolescent ice hockey players to name their favorite professional player and most-admired teammate. Players who selected role models that were more violent received more assaultive penalties (fighting, slashing, high-sticking) than did players who chose less aggressive players.

Smith (1978) surveyed a large number of 12- to 21-year-old hockey players on their consumption of the sport through the mass media. He contended that observers' perceived similarity to professional models and expectations of rewards for expressing similar behaviors should result in modeling of such behaviors. Smith found that 70% of players watched hockey on television at least once a week and 60% said they learned from watching professional hockey how to hit another player illegally, including spearing, elbowing, tripping, slashing, and high-sticking. Among players who learned illegal tactics, 64% stated that they performed these actions at least once or twice during the season. This study showed that media portrayals of violence in ice hockey contribute to attitudes and behaviors of youth and amateur hockey players.

Mugno and Feltz (1985) replicated Smith (1978) by investigating the social learning of aggression among youth football players. They assessed middle school (ages 12 through 14) and high school (ages 15 through 18) boys on mass media consumption of football and extent of learning and performing aggressive actions through watching football. Players watched (94%) and read (83%) about football and reported learning about 10 illegal aggressive actions (e.g., spearing, face-masking, late hits, clipping). Some 82% of players reported using at least one aggressive behavior that they learned through watching high-level football. Moderately strong correlations emerged between number of aggressive acts learned and number of behaviors players reported using in their games ($r = .50$ for middle school and $.62$ for high school). Collectively, these studies reinforce the importance of observational learning in youths' adoption of aggressive attitudes and playing behaviors.

Children can also learn sportsmanlike qualities through other forms of social influence. White and O'Brien (1999) examined children's conceptions of heroes as a source of values beliefs and moral development. Youth ages 5 to 16 years were asked to define, name, and identify characteristics of a hero. Parents were the most frequent response across all age levels. The 5- to 9-year-olds named cartoon characters and then family members and friends next, whereas 11- to 16-year-olds cited sports figures second after parents. When asked why a person was their hero, youth cited helping behaviors, caring traits, and unique qualities (e.g., courage, athletic ability). A characteristic beyond talent was essential to being named a hero (e.g., Penny Hardaway was named because he helps the homeless). Across age levels, characteristics essential to defining a hero included being good, courageous, nice, and trustworthy. The authors concluded that youth identify with their heroes because they demonstrate moral excellence.

In light of the powerful influence of role models in moral development, Damon (1990) proposed that children be exposed to "moral mentors"—people in their communities who have distinguished themselves through exemplary moral behavior (e.g., speaking out against discrimination, helping the needy). Interactive workshops and discussions among moral mentors and children, Damon contended, could inspire children to develop moral awareness and adopt moral responsibility to engage in socially relevant actions.

Social Approval of Aggressive and Unfair Play

Perceiving that significant adults and peers approve or disapprove of aggressive behaviors strongly influences participants' beliefs about and engagement in such actions. Smith (1975) interviewed male adolescent ice hockey players about perceptions of their reference groups' views toward violence during game play. Players responded to questions concerning fathers', mothers', teammates', nonplaying peers', and coaches' approval of body-checking, fighting, boarding, and cross-checking. Players reported that most groups approved or strongly approved of body-checking and that mothers were most likely to disapprove. They also said that fathers, peers, and teammates were favorable toward fighting back if someone else started a fight. In particular, players viewed teammates and nonplaying peers as supporting fighting and cross-checking. In another study, Smith (1979) surveyed select and house league hockey players, ages 12 through 21, about their own and reference groups' approval of fighting during game play. Greater disapproval of fighting was reported by 12- to 15-year-olds and house league players, but approval percentages dramatically increased for 16- to 21-year-olds and select league players. For all age groups and competitive levels, rankings were consistent for approval of violence: teammates, spectators, self, coach, father, and mother.

Mugno and Feltz (1985) extended Smith's (1975) work to young football players' perceptions of significant others' attitudes toward aggressive behaviors. Youth (ages 12 through 14) and high school (ages 15 through 18) players rated whether father, mother, teammates, nonplaying friends, and spectators viewed aggressive actions as acceptable if officials do not call them and if they help the team win. Frequency percentages revealed that players rated teammates, friends, and spectators as most approving of such actions. Over 40% of youth players stated that teammates, coach, and father exerted a great deal of influence (highest rating possible) on their own use of illegal hits, and over 30% of high school players cited teammates and coach as encouraging of such actions.

Stuart and Ebbeck (1995) bridged social learning and structural-developmental theories by considering the association of significant adults' and peers' approval of unsportsmanlike play with youths' moral thoughts and actions. Players in grades 4 through 5 and 7 through 8 rated the degree to which their father, mother, coach, and teammates approved of actions in five situations (e.g., injure a player to prevent a basket, push an opponent when the referee is not looking). For both age groups, teammates were rated as more favorable toward engaging in antisocial behaviors than were coaches and parents. A strong relationship emerged between significant others' approval and moral variables. For younger players, perception of greater disapproval of antisocial behaviors by parents, coach, and teammates was associated with players judging such behaviors as inappropriate and intending not to engage in them. For older players, perception of greater disapproval by teammates, coach, and parents was associated with higher moral judgment and intention as well as more mature moral reasoning and more frequent prosocial behaviors. Although approval from all socializers was significantly associated with moral variables, mothers for younger players and teammates for older players recorded the strongest relationship.

Recently, Stuntz (2005) also showed that when adolescents perceive that their coaches, teammates, and sport friends were more approving of unsportsmanlike play, they were more likely to view such play as legitimate and to intend to use those actions. Although the primary purpose of Stuntz's study was to examine how achievement goal orientations and perceived approval from significant others regarding unsportsmanlike play *interact* to predict individuals' beliefs about unsportsmanlike play, results highlighted the strong influence of the social context on moral beliefs and the relatively minimal influence of goal orientations on such beliefs. Perceived approval from significant others was by far the strongest predictor of self-beliefs about aggression.

Moral Atmosphere According to Shields and Bredemeier (1995), central components of the moral atmosphere are the collective norms and conventions guiding appropriate behavior that team members adopt, develop, and condone over time and that are consonant with the image of a particular sport. This notion is reminiscent of Smith's (1974, 1975, 1978, 1979) work on young ice hockey players' sources of beliefs and behaviors toward violence. Teammates' and coaches' beliefs about what denotes appropriate and inappropriate behavior are a salient part of the moral atmosphere.

Stephens (2000, 2001; Stephens & Bredemeier, 1996; Stephens, Bredemeier, & Shields, 1997) conducted a series of studies on the influence of moral atmosphere on youth participants' beliefs about aggression and unsportsmanlike play. Perceptions of pro-aggressive team norms were assessed by having players indicate how many of their teammates would be likely to lie to an official, hurt an opponent, and violate a game rule. Respondents were asked to imagine themselves in the protagonist's position and think about how the protagonist might decide what she or he should and would do by considering desire for winning, what coach and teammates would want, and what would be fair. Team norms condoning aggressive behavior were the strongest predictor of players' self-reported aggressive tendencies followed by a smaller contribution of coach's ego goal orientation (Stephens, 2000; Stephens & Bredemeier, 1996). When players believed that most of their teammates would use aggressive actions, they were more likely to use such actions in their own play.

Stephens (2001) found that team norms for aggressive behavior and willingness to injure an opponent if requested by the coach predicted self-described likelihood to aggress equally well among 11- to 14-year-old beginning players. For 15- to 17-year-old advanced players, however, willingness to injure an opponent if requested by the coach was more predictive of self-described likelihood to aggress than team norms regarding aggression. Guivernau and Duda (2002) also found that perception of pro-aggressive team norms predicted self-reported aggression among male and female soccer players (ages 13 through 19). In another study, elite adolescent male athletes attributed their respect for rules compliance or transgression in competitive settings to the moral atmosphere. Specifically, their decisions related to the coach's pressure to play fairly or cheat in order to win and to team norms pertaining to sportsmanship or lack thereof (Long, Pantaléon, Bruant, & d'Arripe-Longueville, 2006).

Duquin and Schroeder-Braun (1996) adopted an alternative approach to study moral atmosphere in sport by examining coach–athlete conflicts. Adolescent and college students (93% athletes) read scenarios depicting types of coach–athlete conflicts and then rated the degree to which the coach behaved immorally. Physical abuse of athletes (pushing or shoving to make a point, forcing an athlete to play with an injury) was rated as most serious, followed by emotional abuse (being made to feel like a loser, being humiliated in front of others). Athletes were also asked to recall a time when their coach did something that they felt was immoral; responses included physical abuse (e.g., forced to diet), emotional abuse (e.g., name calling), punishment for errors (e.g., run laps), and favoritism. About half of the participants indicated that they did not act on the perceived injustice because of the coach's power. The authors concluded that sources of coach power create a sport environment that may inhibit athletes from learning and developing empathy, prosocial behavior, and conflict resolution.

Collectively, these studies show that team norms for aggression, perception of the coach's goal orientation, coach–athlete conflict, and players' willingness to comply with the coach's expectations are salient contributors to attitudes toward what is considered appropriate behavior in sport as well as associated moral behaviors. Closely aligned with moral atmosphere are perceptions of the motivational climate in sport, which we turn to next.

Motivational Climate The motivational climate represents the goal-reward structure typically implemented by the coach, and characterizes what is recognized, rewarded, and emphasized within the social context of the team environment (Ames, 1992). Mastery or task-involving climates emphasize improvement and effort in pursuit of personal mastery, whereas performance or ego-involving climates emphasize norm-referenced achievement and favorable comparisons to others. It is important to note that sport environments contain varying degrees of both mastery and performance climates, and this mixture is assessed through athletes' perceptions of the emphasis placed on self-referenced and norm-referenced ability. Several studies have examined links between athletes' perceptions of the motivational climate created by their coaches and their own moral beliefs and behaviors.

Kavussanu, Roberts, and Ntoumanis (2002) examined the relationship of perceived performance climate and moral atmosphere with moral functioning (self-reported beliefs and behaviors) of college basketball players. Moral atmosphere was significantly related to moral functioning, but performance climate was not. When athletes perceived that their teammates and coach were approving of improper actions, athletes judged these actions as more legitimate, intended to engage in them, and did engage in similar actions more frequently. Although performance climate did not *directly* relate to moral functioning, performance climate was significantly related to moral atmosphere and thus may be *indirectly* related to moral functioning. In general, perceiving that coaches emphasized winning or being the best was related to believing that coaches and teammates approved of unsportsmanlike play.

Other studies have shown that motivational climate and moral beliefs are directly related. In a study of male youth soccer players, Ommundsen, Roberts, Lemyre, and Treasure (2003) found that perceptions of a mastery climate were related to team norms with greater disapproval of aggression, use of higher-level moral reasoning, and greater respect for rules, officials, and conventions. Perceptions of a performance climate were related to greater pro-aggressive team norms and amoral behavior, and less respect for rules, officials, and conventions. Miller, Roberts, and Ommundsen (2004) found that youth soccer players who perceived a stronger mastery climate endorsed sportsmanship more than players with lower perceptions did; similarly, athletes who perceived a stronger performance climate endorsed sportsmanship less than athletes with lower perceptions did. In a follow-up study, Miller, Roberts, and Ommundsen (2005) found relationships between performance climate and moral variables. Greater perceptions of a performance climate were related to lower levels of moral judgment, reasoning, and intention; greater perceived legitimacy of injurious actions and self-reported unsportsmanlike behavior; and team norms that condoned aggression. Other studies report similar findings for motivational climate and moral beliefs and behaviors (Boixados, Cruz, Torregroa, & Valiente, 2004; Laparidis, Papaioannou, Vretakou, & Morou, 2003). Thus, the coach-created motivational climate is related to moral atmosphere of the team, beliefs about aggression, and unsportsmanlike play.

Some studies have examined motivational climate and goal orientation simultaneously as predictors of moral beliefs. Fry and Newton (2003) examined the relationship among motivational climate, goal orientations, and a variety of variables, including sportspersonship, among youth tennis players. Higher task orientation was related to greater sportspersonship, but perceived motivational climate was more influential than task and ego goal orientations as a predictor of sportspersonship. Stronger perceptions of a mastery climate and weaker perceptions of a performance climate were related to greater endorsement of good sport behavior. Similarly, Kavussanu (2006) found that perceived mastery climate was a stronger predictor of prosocial behaviors than task and ego orientations among 12- to 17-year-old male football players and that ego orientation and perceived performance climate were comparable predictors of antisocial behaviors.

Gano-Overway, Guivernau, Magyar, Waldron, and Ewing (2005) examined the interaction of motivational climate and goal orientation on sportspersonship among 12- to 18-year-old female volleyball players. In contrast to Fry and Newton (2003), task orientation and a three-way interaction between task orientation, ego orientation, and mastery climate were significant predictors of respect

for the game. When ego orientation was high and perceptions of a mastery climate were low, increases in task orientation did not relate to changes in sportspersonship. However, when perception of mastery climate was high and ego orientation was high or low, increasing from low to high task orientation was related to increased respect for the game.

In contrast to the coach-created climate, d'Arripe-Longueville, Pantaléon, and Smith (2006) assessed the relationship of parent- and peer-created motivational climates as well as task and ego orientations with sportspersonship attitudes in young judo competitors. For both 8- to 10-year-olds and 13- to 15-year-olds, those higher in task orientation and perceptions of a learning climate promoted by parents and peers reported greater respect for opponents, rules and officials, and social conventions of the sport. Thus motivational climate not only pertains to the values and goals endorsed by coaches but also can extend to other social agents.

This section highlighted research examining social-contextual influences on moral beliefs and actions. Studies show that youth learn aggressive actions by watching elite athletes and then put those actions into play. In addition, believing that significant others approve of unsportsmanlike play is related to athletes' own approval of similar behaviors. The moral atmosphere, or collective group norms about legitimacy of behaviors, and perceptions of the motivational climate also influence moral attitudes and behavioral tendencies in sport. The social context clearly plays a significant role in shaping moral beliefs and behaviors. The next section examines predictors of moral beliefs and actions from an individual differences perspective.

Individual Difference Factors

According to Shields and Bredemeier (1995), many individual difference factors will influence moral functioning. Social perspective-taking ability, moral reasoning level, values, moral motives, self-conceptions, self-regulation skills, and problem-solving skills compose some of the individual differences specified by Shields and Bredemeier as essential for understanding moral development in sport. In the following sections, we review empirical research on the relation between moral functioning and several individual difference factors: (a) moral reasoning, (b) goal orientations, (c) moral identity, and (d) self-regulatory efficacy.

Moral Reasoning Moral reasoning reflects the reasons why people intend to act in certain ways.

Moral reasoning has typically been characterized as either self-interested, other-oriented, or principled. Some of the earliest work to assess levels of moral reasoning was conducted over 50 years ago (Haskins, 1960; McAfee, 1955). In perhaps the first theory-driven moral development study in sport, Jantz (1975) extended Piaget's ideas of children's moral thinking to youth basketball by asking participants a series of questions about the rules of the game. He found that younger boys (ages 7 to 8) were more likely to think about rules using a morality of constraint and that older boys (ages 9 to 12) were more likely to use a morality of cooperation, supporting Piaget's moral development stages in a physical activity context. In the last two and a half decades, empirical work on moral reasoning, attitudes, and behaviors has increased considerably.

Moral reasoning in sport and daily life contexts. Bredemeier and her colleagues pioneered efforts to obtain a scientific understanding of moral reasoning in sport and relationships with moral attitudes and behaviors (see Shields & Bredemeier, 1995). Their early work compared athletes' and nonathletes' moral reasoning in sport and nonsport domains. Bredemeier and Shields (1984a, 1986a, 1986b) interviewed high school and college basketball players, swimmers, and nonathletes about moral issues in daily life and sport contexts. Moral reasoning for sport was significantly lower than daily life dilemmas for all subgroups (female, male; high school, college; athlete, nonathlete). Athletes and nonathletes at the high school level did not differ on life or sport moral reasoning; college athletes, by contrast, scored lower on life and sport reasoning than nonathletes did. Females scored higher than males did on sport moral reasoning at all levels. Finally, basketball players scored lower in sport moral reasoning than swimmers and nonathletes did.

Beller and Stoll (1995) extended the study of moral reasoning in athletes and nonathletes by asking high school students to judge legitimacy of sport issues such as retaliation, drug use, fairness, heckling the visiting team, and rule violations. Team-sport athletes exhibited lower moral reasoning for sport dilemmas than nonathletes did but not compared with individual-sport athletes. Moreover, female athletes and nonathletes reasoned at a higher level than males did. Priest, Krause, and Beach (1999), by contrast, found that both male and female team-sport athletes scored lower in moral reasoning than individual-sport athletes did at the beginning and end of their college careers.

Bredemeier (1995) further examined the life–sport moral reasoning divergence among 9- to 13-year-old youth participating in a summer sport program. Participants were presented with life and sport dilemmas about whether to act honestly and whether to injure another child who had acted unfairly. Only the sixth and seventh graders diverged in their moral reasoning level about daily life and sport contexts. Bredemeier graphed sport and daily life reasoning scores in this study relative to scores in her earlier studies with high school and college athletes (Bredemeier & Shields, 1984a, 1986b). She concluded that divergence in moral reasoning regarding life and sport appears at about age 12 or 13 and continues to broaden as age and sport experience increase.

Game reasoning. To explain differences in levels of moral reasoning in life and sport contexts, Bredemeier and Shields (1985, 1986a, 1986b; Shields & Bredemeier, 1995) coined the term *game reasoning*. Game reasoning reflects one's viewpoint of sport as a form of *bracketed morality*—one that is set apart from the broader morality of everyday life. Game reasoning involves a moral transformation during athletic contests in which a self-interest perspective is considered a legitimate means of pursuing the goal of winning. Features of the sport context help form the "brackets" of sport morality that are embedded within daily life reasoning, such as rules of the game, officials' deciding on rule infractions, and spatial and temporal separation of sport and everyday life experiences. Loland (2006) recently argued, "The 'bracketed morality' of sport in which conduct is allowed that is otherwise banned, is expanding. In fact, the brackets seem to fall off. Aggression is internalized and constitutes a disposition for action in all spheres of life" (pp. 62–63). A vivid example of game reasoning was offered by NFL player Bryan Cox: "When I'm on the field, I think about causing as much pain to the person lined up across from me as possible. During the three hours of the game on Sunday evening, I figure I can commit as many crimes as I want to without going to jail."

Game reasoning as a legitimate worldview within sport suggests that athletes who reason at an egocentric level of moral reasoning are likely to express their thoughts and emotions differently than people who hold higher moral reasoning levels. The "game reasoner" should be more likely to endorse aggressive actions and unfair play as an accepted means of maximizing winning as well as engage more frequently in behavior that may physically or psychologically injure others. What does the empirical research reveal about relationships among moral reasoning, legitimacy of aggression and unfair play, and sport behavior?

Moral reasoning, perceived legitimacy of aggression, and sport behavior. The studies reported in this section explore relationships between (a) moral reasoning and sport behavior (prosocial, aggressive), (b) moral reasoning and legitimacy of aggressive actions, and (c) legitimacy of and engagement in aggressive behavior. In so doing, the literature on moral reasoning differences in life and sport is extended to the linkage among moral reasoning, endorsement of fair and unfair play, and behavioral consequences in sport.

Horrocks (1979) conducted one of the first studies to link moral reasoning and prosocial behaviors. Children in fifth and sixth grades were presented with life and sport dilemmas, and teachers rated children on sharing, taking turns, consoling a teammate after a mistake, and abiding by the rules of the game. Relationships between moral reasoning and prosocial behavior were moderately strong ($r = .55$ for life, .63 for sport). Children moderate or high in life moral reasoning were higher in prosocial play behavior than were children with low moral reasoning. For sport moral reasoning, children in the high, moderate, and low groups all differed on prosocial behaviors. This study established a strong linkage between children's moral reasoning and behaviors considered reflective of good sportsmanship.

Romance (1984; Romance, Weiss, & Bockoven, 1986) implemented a moral intervention with fifth-grade children in physical education (the intervention itself is described more fully in the interventions section). Teachers reported behavioral changes in the experimental group (higher moral reasoning) compared with the control group over the course of the program. Children became more active in discussions that led to more effective conflict resolutions, were cited for fewer misconduct and disciplinary problems, showed cooperation and sensitivity to less-skilled peers, and showed reduced verbal aggression.

Bredemeier and colleagues have consistently linked level of moral reasoning with beliefs about and expression of aggressive and unfair play. Several studies (Bredemeier, 1985, 1994; Bredemeier & Shields, 1984b; Bredemeier, Weiss, Shields, & Cooper, 1986, 1987) uncovered associations between levels of moral reasoning and perceived legitimacy for injurious and aggressive actions in sport among youth through college sport participants. Bredemeier and Shields found that moral reasoning at preconventional levels was positively related to aggression, whereas reasoning at postconventional levels was negatively related to aggression.

In companion studies examining moral reasoning, legitimacy judgments, and self-reported sport behavior in 9- to 13-year-old youth, Bredemeier (1994; Bredemeier, Weiss, Shields, & Cooper, 1986, 1987) found moral reasoning to be moderately related to legitimacy judgments of injurious actions. Children with lower moral reasoning levels viewed aggressive play as more justified within the context of sport. Sport moral reasoning scores were moderately related to self-reported assertive and aggressive actions. Boys' legitimacy judgments, but not girls', were moderately related to self-reported sport aggression; those who saw physically aggressive actions as justified were more likely to report that they too engaged in such behaviors. Similarly, Ryan, Williams, and Wimer (1990) found that preseason legitimacy judgments of aggression in college basketball positively predicted season-long self-reported aggressive behaviors.

Sport type, age, competitive level, and gender: Associations with moral variables. Beliefs about what behaviors are acceptable in sport vary with sport type, age, competitive level, and gender. With regard to sport type, boys' participation in high-contact and collision sports, and girls' participation in medium-contact sports, is related to less mature moral reasoning, greater legitimacy of aggressive behavior, and more frequent aggressive tendencies (Bredemeier, Weiss, Shields, & Cooper, 1986; Levin, Smith, Caldwell, & Kimbrough, 1995; Silva, 1983; Tucker & Parks, 2001). Bredemeier and colleagues (1987) found moderately strong relationships among boys' legitimacy judgments, moral reasoning, aggression tendencies, and interest and participation in high-contact sports. Gardner and Janelle (2002), however, found that athletes in high-contact (football, basketball, soccer) and low-contact sports (baseball, softball, volleyball) did not differ in perceived legitimacy of assertive and aggressive actions.

Other studies demonstrate how age and competitive level are related to moral beliefs and value orientations in sport. As competitive level and age increase, participants rate aggressive actions as more legitimate (Bredemeier, 1985, 1995; Bredemeier et al., 1987; Silva, 1983; Visek & Watson, 2005). In addition, athletes place greater emphasis on a win orientation or playing to beat others, in comparison to a skill or fairness orientation, with increasing age and competitive level (Dubois, 1986; Knoppers, Zuidema, & Meyer, 1989; Visek & Watson, 2005; Webb, 1969). Along the same lines, Conroy, Silva, Newcomer, Walker, and Johnson (2001) showed that greater perceived legitimacy of aggressive behavior was linked to being older, being male, and participating longer in contact sports. Loughead and Leith (2001) found that older ice hockey players (ages 12 to 15) approved of hostile aggression more than younger players (ages 10 to 11) did, but younger players were more approving of instrumental aggression, perhaps to compensate for lower technical abilities.

Gender has also been linked to moral reasoning, beliefs about legitimacy of actions, and sport behavior. As reported earlier, male youth and adults generally score lower in sport moral reasoning than females do. Males also report sport aggression to be more legitimate behavior than females do (Beller & Stoll, 1995; Bredemeier, Weiss, Shields, & Cooper, 1986, 1987; Gardner & Janelle, 2002; Silva, 1983). Weinstein, Smith, and Wiesenthal (1995) found that males who embraced traditional ideas of masculinity engaged in more hockey violence than did males who held less traditional beliefs.

Crown and Heatherington (1989) tested Gilligan's (1982) notions of gender variations in justice and care reasoning within sport contexts. Female and male undergraduate students read scenarios about competitive athletic encounters between friends and were interviewed about what they thought the protagonist should do. Women and men were equally likely to use justice and care reasoning, but women were more likely than men were to consider the situation and consequences as moral ones. Fisher and Bredemeier (2000) criticized Crown and Heatherington on several grounds: (a) participants were not athletes but college students in introductory courses, (b) hypothetical dilemmas may elicit different responses than personal experiences do, and (c) the authors were not trained in Gilligan's methodology. Fisher and Bredemeier designed a study to examine moral reasoning orientations in female athletes who face real-life dilemmas in their sport—competitive bodybuilding. Findings indicated that female athletes use care *and* justice orientations when reasoning about personally meaningful dilemmas.

Summary. Collectively, studies suggest that continued participation in sport, especially high-contact sports, is linked to lower moral reasoning and greater acceptance of aggression. Male athletes use lower levels of moral reasoning and are more approving of unsportsmanlike play than female athletes, and older youth tend to be more approving of aggressive acts than younger participants are. The ability of sport to build character may decrease as the focus shifts to winning and outperforming others with increasing competitive level. In addi-

tion, significant others become more approving of aggression at higher levels, suggesting that socialization plays a role in influencing moral beliefs and behaviors in sport.

Goal Orientations Achievement goal orientations denote worldviews or theories about success in a particular domain. Nicholls (1989) suggested that the way in which people define success (i.e., goal orientation) is related to attitudes towards sportsmanship and aggression. Specifically, Nicholls suggested that those who conceptualize success predominantly in terms of outperforming others should be more likely to approve of or intend to engage in unsportsmanlike behavior. Highly ego-oriented individuals, because they are concerned more with demonstrating superior ability than with mastering the task itself, are more likely to adopt dishonest means to reach their goals. People higher in task orientation, however, focus on the process itself and are less likely to adopt dishonest means to reach their goal. Several studies have empirically examined the relationship between goal orientations and moral beliefs and behaviors.

Task and ego orientations. Duda, Olson, and Templin (1991) examined the linkage between goal orientations and sportsmanlike attitudes among high school basketball players. Athletes higher on ego orientation reported greater approval of unsportsmanlike play and verbal or physical aggression. Similarly, Kavussanu and Roberts (2001) found that college basketball players who were higher in ego (but not task) orientation believed that intimidating opponents, risking injury to an opponent, and faking injury were appropriate behaviors and intended to engage in such actions. Dunn and Causgrove Dunn (1999) studied 11- to 14-year-old ice hockey players; those players higher in ego orientation were more likely to approve of intentionally injurious acts and less likely to show respect for rules and officials. A nonsignificant relationship emerged between task orientation and legitimacy of injurious acts, but those higher on task orientation showed greater respect for social conventions, rules, and officials.

Among youth soccer players, Lemyre, Roberts, and Ommundsen (2002) showed that higher task orientation was related to greater sportsperson-ship and that ego orientation was related to lower sportspersonship, including respect for social conventions, rules, officials, and opponents. However, higher task orientation combined with higher ego orientation was related to lower respect for rules, officials, and opponents, suggesting that ego orientation may have a stronger influence on antisocial beliefs. Sage, Kavussanu, and Duda (2006) found that task orientation predicted prosocial judgments, but not behaviors, under conditions of low ego orientation among adult soccer players, whereas ego orientation was positively related to antisocial judgments and behaviors.

Tod and Hodge (2001) interviewed rugby players about goal orientations and moral dilemmas. Support emerged for a link between goal orientations and beliefs about unsportsmanlike play. Players with a dominant ego orientation tended to use less mature levels of moral reasoning, be more self-centered, and believe that winning at all costs was important. In contrast, players with a more balanced endorsement of task and ego orientations used more mature levels of moral reasoning. Similarly, Boixados et al. (2004) found that male youth soccer players who were low on task orientation and high on ego orientation expressed the highest level of acceptance of rough play, whereas the lowest level of acceptance occurred among the high task and low ego subgroup.

Kavussanu and Ntoumanis (2003) examined whether ego orientation mediates the relationship between sport participation and moral functioning among college athletes. A direct path between sport participation and moral functioning became nonsignificant when ego orientation was included as a mediator variable. Athletes who participated in sport longer were more highly ego oriented, which in turn predicted lower moral judgment, intention, and behavior.

Interestingly, when both social-contextual and goal orientation variables are included in analyses, the influence of goal orientations on moral beliefs is often nonsignificant. For example, Stephens (2000; Stephens & Bredemeier, 1996) found that, in addition to team norms, perception of the coach's ego orientation was a significant predictor of likelihood to aggress in youth soccer. Girls who perceived their coaches to focus on winning and outperforming others were more likely to say that they intended to use aggression. Athletes' own task or ego orientation did not significantly predict likelihood of aggression. Similarly, Stephens (2001) did not find an individual's own task or ego orientation to predict likelihood of aggression in the presence of team norms as a predictor variable. Stuntz (2005) also demonstrated that, in the presence of perceived approval from middle school students' teammates, friends, and coaches regarding unsportsmanlike play, task and ego orientations were not significant predictors of beliefs about unsportsmanlike play.

Social orientations. Although most work using achievement goal theory has focused on task and ego orientations, other types of goal orientations exist including social orientations (ways of viewing the world and defining success in terms of social relationships). Recently, researchers have examined links between social orientations and moral beliefs. Stuntz and Weiss (2003a) sought to understand the combined influence of social orientations and social contextual information on beliefs about unsportsmanlike play. Besides task and ego orientations, three types of social goal orientations were assessed: friendship orientation, group acceptance orientation, and coach praise orientation. Stuntz and Weiss hypothesized that individuals who valued social goal orientations would think and behave differently depending on the beliefs of significant peers. Results confirmed that social goal orientations influenced beliefs about unsportsmanlike play above and beyond influence by task and ego orientations. For boys, but not girls, defining success in terms of having strong friendships and being accepted by teammates was related to greater intention to use unsportsmanlike play than those with lower friendship and group acceptance orientations.

Stuntz (2005) further explored the simultaneous relationship of social goal orientations and the social context with beliefs about unsportsmanlike play. Contrary to findings of Stuntz and Weiss (2003a), social orientations did not significantly predict beliefs about unsportsmanlike play. Instead, believing that significant others (teammates, best friend, coach) approved of unsportsmanlike actions was strongly related to beliefs about unsportsmanlike play. A cluster analysis that considered combinations of goal orientations showed that the relationship between social orientations and beliefs about unsportsmanlike play varied depending on the perceived level of approval by significant others. This finding suggests that social orientations may influence moral beliefs but that this relationship may be best uncovered by considering individual profiling approaches.

Summary. Despite a few inconsistencies, higher levels of ego orientation tend to relate to lower levels of moral reasoning and greater endorsement of aggression, cheating, and unsportsmanlike behavior. In contrast, higher task orientation is related to good sportsmanship and less tolerance for aggression and cheating. Social orientations should also be considered because recent research demonstrates the efficacy of considering a wider array of goal orientations. However, situational influences such as motivational climate, social approval of actions, and perceived goal orientation of the coach may be more influential than an individual's own goal orientation in predicting moral beliefs.

Moral Identity and Self-Regulatory Efficacy

Aside from moral reasoning level and goal orientations, several other individual difference factors may influence moral thoughts and actions, including moral identity and self-regulatory efficacy. Damon (2004) defined moral identity as a person's use of moral beliefs to define the self (i.e., "the kind of person I am or want to be"). He (Damon, 1984, 2004) suggested that effective translation of moral reasoning into moral behavior depends on how essential the individual considers morality to his or her personal conceptualization of the self. Damon (1984) stated, "...persons with the same moral beliefs may differ in their view on how important it is for them to be moral in a personal sense. Some may consider their morality to be central to their self-identities, whereas others may consider it to be peripheral" (p. 110). Bergman (2002) also argued that people feel compelled to maintain consistency between a strong moral identity and their behavior. Thus, strong moral identity should be a predictor of moral beliefs and behaviors.

Empirical work by Aquino and Reed (2002; Reed & Aquino, 2003) demonstrated a positive relationship between moral identity and level of moral reasoning as well as between moral identity and a perceived obligation to show concern for the welfare and interests of others. Considering moral beliefs to be centrally related to one's self concept is related to less egocentric thinking and more concern and positive involvement with others. However, the concept of moral identity has yet to be fully explored in the physical domain. One exception is a study by Ebbeck and Gibbons (2003), who examined the relationship of moral reasoning, intention, and behavior with moral self-concept. Perceived behavioral conduct (a moral self-concept variable) showed a moderately strong association with moral reasoning, moral intention, and prosocial behavior among 9- to 12-year-old physical education students, offering support for the linkage between moral identity and moral functioning. In addition, Sage et al. (2006) found that adult male soccer players who rated moral traits (e.g., kind, compassionate, helpful, caring) as more central to their self-concept were less likely to judge antisocial behaviors as appropriate and less likely to report that they had engaged in such behaviors (e.g., retaliating to a bad tackle, body-checking an opponent).

Bandura and colleagues have emphasized the importance of self-regulatory mechanisms in influencing moral attitudes and behaviors in work conducted outside the sport domain. Bandura (1991) suggested that the link between moral reasoning and moral behavior occurs through self-regulatory efficacy. That is, people who have lower efficacy to resist peer pressure are more vulnerable to negative social pressures even if they can rationalize their behaviors. Bandura, Caprara, Barbaranelli, Gerbino, and Pastorelli (2003) showed that self-regulatory efficacy was negatively related to delinquency, whereas empathic efficacy (perceived capability to sense another's feelings and needs) was positively related to prosocial behavior.

Similarly, Bandura, Caprara, Barbaranelli, Pastorelli, and Regalia (2001), using structural equation modeling, demonstrated that greater self-regulatory efficacy to resist peer pressure was related to lower incidence of transgressive behavior, both directly and indirectly through lower levels of moral disengagement. Moral disengagement allows individuals to pursue amoral behaviors but still maintain higher moral standards (e.g., Bandura, 1999, 2002; Bandura, Barbaranelli, Caprara, & Pastorelli, 1996). Mechanisms of moral disengagement include moral justification (portray negative action as a valuable service), euphemistic labeling (use sanitized language), advantageous comparison (compare to worse actions), displacement of responsibility (attribute actions to social pressure from others), diffusion of responsibility (share or subdivide decisions or actions), distortion of the consequences (minimize the harm caused), dehumanization (dissociate from human qualities), and attribution of blame onto others.

Recently, d'Arripe-Longueville, Weiss, Pantaléon, and Raimbault (2005) tested a model of self-regulatory mechanisms governing beliefs about unsportsmanlike play among adolescent athletes. Results showed that self-regulatory efficacy to resist peer pressure to engage in moral transgressions was negatively related to legitimacy judgments of and intentions to engage in unsportsmanlike play, primarily through the mediating role of moral disengagement. The constructs of self-regulatory efficacy to resist peer pressure and moral disengagement are relevant ones to explore in the sport domain and represent a salient future research direction.

In summary, research suggests that a number of individual differences influence moral beliefs. Individuals who use higher levels of moral reasoning, embrace higher task and social orientations and lower ego orientation, have a central moral identity, and possess higher levels of self-regulatory efficacy to resist peer pressure tend both to disapprove of aggressive and unsportsmanlike actions and not to engage in such actions themselves. Considering previously discussed research on social-contextual factors, it is clear that both personal and contextual factors influence moral beliefs and behaviors. Only by considering both sets of constructs can we comprehensively understand the nature of moral development in sport and physical activity.

Moral Development Interventions in Physical Activity Contexts

The research covered in the previous section represents a dramatic increase in activity since the publication of this chapter in 2002. Many of these studies employ group difference or correlational designs, which assess associations of social-contextual factors (e.g., motivational climate) or individual differences (e.g., moral reasoning) with moral attitudes and behaviors. The significant growth in number of these studies has not been matched by a similar increase in intervention studies of moral development in sport. This discrepancy is surprising given the optimistic results shown by early research of theory-based interventions designed to enhance moral reasoning and prosocial behaviors. In this section, we synthesize the knowledge about moral development interventions in sport contexts and review literature in the growing field of positive youth development, offering this framework as an appealing way to design intervention programs and conduct evaluation research.

General Theory-Based Intervention Studies

A handful of studies employed social learning or structural developmental principles in designing field-based interventions targeted toward improving moral reasoning and prosocial behaviors among youth in physical education or sport settings. Collectively, these studies demonstrated promise for the efficacy of physical activity contexts in enhancing moral beliefs and behaviors. Moreover, these studies laid the groundwork for subsequent interventions by identifying program components that made an impact on moral functioning among participants.

Bredemeier, Weiss, Shields, and Shewchuk (1986) designed a program to enhance moral reasoning within a children's summer sports camp. Partici-

pants (ages 5 to 7) were assigned to social learning, structural developmental, or control groups for six weeks. Activities highlighted fairness, sharing, verbal aggression, physical aggression, distributive justice, and retributive justice. Teacher and peer modeling and verbal and tangible reinforcement were the social learning strategies, and participants in the structural development group were prompted to discuss and resolve conflicts following activity dilemmas. Children in the control group were encouraged to follow game rules and teacher guidelines. Both experimental groups increased in moral reasoning from pre- to postintervention, but the control group did not. Group differences at postintervention approached significance. This study showed that a moral intervention could be implemented successfully with children as young as 5 years old.

Romance (1984; Romance et al., 1986) theorized that more meaningful effects on moral reasoning and behavior should occur with youth older than the 5-year-olds in Bredemeier, Weiss, Shields, & Shewchuk's (1986) study, given older youths' cognitive, social, and emotional maturity to engage in discussion and resolution of moral dilemmas. An eight-week structural developmental intervention was employed with fifth-grade children (ages 10 to 11) in a school physical education setting. Pre- and postassessments of moral reasoning in life and sport contexts were compared to a control group. Students in the experimental group were involved in moral dilemmas, discussed dilemmas in a group setting, and created moral balances that considered the rights and responsibilities of all students. The experimental group showed significant pre- to postintervention improvement in life and sport moral reasoning, whereas the control group showed no change. The structural developmental group was significantly higher in moral reasoning and exhibited more prosocial and less antisocial behaviors than the control group at posttest.

Wandzilak, Carroll, and Ansorge (1988) implemented a nine-week moral development program with male adolescent basketball players. A mix of social learning and structural developmental strategies was used, such as having players offer examples of good and bad sportsmanship and discuss basketball-specific moral dilemmas daily. The researchers assessed moral reasoning, perceptions of sportsmanship, and prosocial behaviors. Although significant between-group differences did not emerge, pre- to postintervention improvement occurred in the experimental group but not in the control group. DeBusk and Hellison (1989) also used social learning and structural developmental teaching strategies with 10 delinquency-prone fourth-grade boys in a physical education program for six weeks. Interventions included daily teacher talk, student sharing, reflection time, modeling, teacher praise, and dialogue and balance activities. Case study results indicated that the boys' affect, behavior, and knowledge improved during the program.

Solomon (1997) implemented a moral intervention program through physical education with second-grade students identified as at-risk for dysfunctional behavior. The goals of the program were to improve personal and social responsibility by targeting communication skills, cooperation, and sharing among classmates. During the 13-week intervention, four moral themes guided the activities during class: trust, helping, problem solving, and body awareness. Lesson plans were structured to ensure teaching of social values and skills. Children participating in the intervention significantly improved on moral reasoning scores, whereas students in a second-grade class who were not exposed to the themes and activities did not show change. Moreover, the classroom teacher of the experimental group reported positive behavior change in her students compared to the start of the program.

These five studies demonstrate the value of field experiments in gauging effectiveness of theory-driven moral intervention programs. Unfortunately, these studies did not include follow-up investigations to determine retention of growth in moral variables. The first four studies were instrumental in the development of a curriculum implemented within Canadian elementary school systems called *Fair Play for Kids*. This nationally based program, and others like it, has better sustaining value than one-shot field experiments. These programs are described next.

Fair Play for Kids

In 1990 the Commission for Fair Play joined with Sport Canada to develop a teacher's resource manual for grades 4 through 6 with the goal of bringing fair play activities into the classroom—in language arts, health, art, social studies, science, drama, and physical education. Activities focused on developing attitudes and behaviors that exemplify the ideals of fair play identified as (a) respect the rules, (b) respect the officials and accept their decisions, (c) respect opponents, (d) give everybody an equal chance to participate, and (e) maintain self-control

at all times. Learning processes are specified in the manual as (a) identifying and resolving moral conflicts through discussion and conflict resolution and (b) changing roles and perspectives (e.g., simulation games, social perspective–taking). Although these processes emanate from a structural developmental view, social learning strategies are emphasized in the form of modeling by Canadian Olympians, role playing, and rewarding of "fair players." *Fair Play for Kids* was developed from moral development theory and research, and created activities emphasizing social perspective–taking, dialogue and balance, and modeling and reinforcement of prosocial behaviors.

In the first evaluation of *Fair Play for Kids*, Gibbons et al. (1995) sampled 452 students in 18 fourth-, fifth-, and sixth-grade classrooms. Six classrooms at each grade level were randomly assigned to three groups: (a) control (no fair play curriculum), (b) physical education only (fair play curriculum conducted by physical education teachers only), and (c) all classes (fair play curriculum conducted in physical education and other subjects including health, language arts, social studies, and fine arts). The experimental protocol lasted seven months, with at least one fair play activity implemented weekly. Students completed self-reports of moral judgment, reasoning, and intention, and teachers rated each student on frequency of prosocial behaviors before and after the intervention. Strong support emerged for the effectiveness of *Fair Play for Kids*. Children in both experimental groups recorded significantly higher posttest scores on all moral variables compared with those in the control group. Moreover, effect sizes were moderate to large in magnitude, suggesting that strength of group differences was meaningful. The two experimental groups did not differ from one another, meaning that moral development can be effectively addressed in the physical education classroom only or in a combination of classes.

Gibbons and Ebbeck (1997) extended the first study in two ways. First, given the strong pre- to postintervention changes in moral variables during the seven-month program, they determined whether changes occurred more quickly by assessing moral variables at pre-, mid-, and postintervention. Second, they compared whether strategies unique to social learning (modeling, reinforcement) and structural developmental (dialogue and problem solving) approaches are equally effective for influencing moral growth. Students from fourth- to sixth-grade classes participated in a control group or one of two experimental groups (social learning, structural development) during physical education for seven months. Fair play activities were implemented at least once weekly. At mid- and postintervention, structural development and social-learning participants scored significantly higher than controls did on moral judgment, intention, and prosocial behavior. The structural development group scored higher on moral reasoning than the social learning and control groups at both time periods. These differences were again meaningful (i.e., large effect sizes). Moral growth occurred within four months into the intervention and in theoretically consistent ways (experimental groups were higher than controls on moral judgment, intention, and behavior; the structural developmental group was higher than social-learning and control groups on moral reasoning).

In sum, the two studies that evaluated the efficacy of *Fair Play for Kids* strongly support the strategies and activities promoted by the program. Perhaps the most important aspect of the studies is that the teachers embraced the program and enthusiastically participated in and implemented the program. In the end, if an intervention is to have an impact on participants' moral and social development, commitment by the social change agents themselves is crucial.

Personal-Social Responsibility Model

Hellison (1985, 1995) developed a physical activity–based responsibility model, designed to balance empowering students with teaching explicit values to develop personal and social skills among underserved youth. A particularly far-reaching goal of the responsibility model is promoting resiliency in youth vulnerable to risks of poverty and crime (Martinek & Hellison, 1997). The responsibility model has been applied in a broad variety of settings with children and adolescents from diverse backgrounds.

Five levels of responsibility are specified in the model (Hellison & Walsh, 2002): (a) respect for the rights and feelings of others (i.e., self-control, inclusion, resolve conflicts), (b) effort and teamwork (i.e., self-motivation, cooperation, and coachability), (c) self-direction (i.e., independent work, goal-setting progression with courage to resist peer pressure), (d) helping and leadership (i.e., sensitivity to others' needs, contributing to the well-being of individuals and the group), and (e) application outside the gym (i.e., trying these ideas outside the physical activity program, being a role model). Each of the responsibilities is designed to build on one another. Respecting others lays the foundation for developing social

responsibility, because refraining from verbal and physical aggression, resolving conflicts, and including everyone in activities are minimal requirements for protecting the rights of all participants (Hellison, Martinek, & Cutforth, 1996). Self-motivation and self-direction challenge youth to take responsibility for their effort and goals, which in turn stimulate social responsibility in the form of caring about and helping others.

The responsibility levels describe what needs to be learned, but implementation strategies that distribute power between teacher and students describe how students attain personal and social responsibility toward others. These strategies include awareness talks, direct instruction, individual decision-making, group evaluation meetings, and reflection time to enable self-evaluation of goal attainment. Awareness talks and direct instruction are designed to teach students the levels of responsibility and integrate them into physical activity lessons. Individual decision making, group meetings, and reflection time shift the onus of responsibility onto the participants themselves. Reflection time allows students the opportunity to monitor, evaluate, and reinforce themselves for being responsible during the lesson (i.e., respecting others' feelings, helping others). Detailed accounts of specific responsibility-based physical activity programs are found in the literature (Cutforth, 1997; Georgiadis, 1990; Hellison et al., 1996).

A prototype program exemplifying the responsibility model was one designed to teach values through basketball to at-risk African American boys (Hellison & Georgiadis, 1992). Basketball was chosen as the vehicle by which to promote personal and social responsibility because it is valued within the subculture of African American teenage boys. Empowerment was accomplished by challenging students to control their behavior when interacting with others, develop appropriate rules for themselves in class, and evaluate their own behavior in class. Success in attaining responsibility goals was assessed through evaluation in the form of attendance, students' journal entries, and number of youth achieving higher levels. This evaluation revealed that students accepted program goals and worked to improve themselves within the basketball context. Researchers' field notes and school staff evaluations provided evidence that the program was successful with this vulnerable group of teenage youth.

Overall evaluation of the responsibility model across various projects has been conducted primarily with case study or ethnographic methods. Hellison and Walsh (2002) examined the influence of the responsibility model on participants' improvement of in-program goals and transfer outside the gym by synthesizing outcomes and processes of 26 empirical studies. They concluded that strong evidence exists for improvement in self-control, effort, helping others, and self-direction for in-program goals, and improvement in self-control, effort, self-esteem, and making better choices in the classroom (transfer from physical activity context). Hellison and Wright (2003) also provided evidence of positive youth development (technical skills, attitude/responsibility, transfer outside the program) because of participation in urban extended day programs based on the *Personal-Social Responsibility Model.*

The *Personal-Social Responsibility Model* is based on sound youth development principles and processes that should maximize positive outcomes. Such processes include relationships with caring adult leaders and opportunities to learn important life skills. Mostly qualitative data substantiate attainment of model goals among a broad spectrum of youth demographics. Future evaluation studies may benefit from a mixed-method design using qualitative and quantitative data to evaluate the responsibility model's effect on achievement (graduation rate, test scores), social (cooperation, respect), and psychological (empathy, perspective-taking) outcomes.

Sport for Peace

The *Sport for Peace* curriculum is an intervention devised by Ennis (1999; Ennis et al., 1999) to address problems of disruptive and disengaged students in urban high schools. The program was customized to meet the specific needs of urban students, who are often challenged by poverty, living in single-parent households, and limited educational opportunities for peer affiliation. The *Sport for Peace* initiative included personal and social responsibility, conflict negotiation skills, nonviolent verbal and physical behavior, and a sense of community. Ennis et al. implemented the *Sport for Peace* curriculum in six urban schools. A three-phase research design included (a) a baseline period; (b) training, staff development, and experimentation with the curriculum for eight weeks; and (c) application of the *Sport for Peace* curriculum in a nine-week basketball unit. All teachers and students were interviewed after this phase of the study. The investigators collected field notes and observational data during all three phases of the research design.

Results revealed that during phase 1 (baseline), teachers taught skills briefly and allowed students to organize games for the remainder of the period. Skilled boys had the advantage in this scenario, and few girls participated in the activities. During phase 2 (training), teachers experimented with modifications to curricular and teaching strategies consistent with the *Sport for Peace* program. During this phase, students assumed responsibility to discuss problems, express their feelings, and negotiate solutions with class members. In phase 3 (implementation), students expressed responsibility toward teammates, showed them respect, and developed a sense of trust. The authors concluded, "The *Sport for Peace* curriculum appeared to be instrumental in building the care and concern for others essential to creating mutually trusting and respectful relationships that these students said felt like family" (Ennis et al., 1999, p. 284).

Recently, Ennis and McCauley (2002) addressed the essential curricula and teaching strategies that maximize trusting relationships and student engagement among at-risk students. They conducted interviews with teachers and students to discern strategies that both groups indicated were effective in engaging difficult students. A consistent emergent theme was the need for teachers to create a curriculum and learning climate that invited opportunities for student engagement, nurtured positive social interactions, and promoted feelings of autonomy. These qualities, Ennis and McCauley argued, lay the foundation for trusting teacher–student relationships based on shared expectations, persistence, commitment, and voice.

Ennis and Hellison are teacher–educators who conceived *Sport for Peace* and the *Personal-Social Responsibility Model* by developing curricula and instructional strategies that address the developmental needs of youth. *Fair Play for Kids* also embraces curricular content and teaching strategies that target children's social and moral development. All three programs are grounded in theory and empirical literature specifying the conditions under which character development and other positive qualities are likely to occur. Collectively, these programs demonstrate that to modify moral and social attitudes and behaviors, a curriculum must target personal skill development that students can transfer beyond the playing field (e.g., self-control, interpersonal skills) and implement strategies that endorse caring teacher–student relationships. These qualities—teaching of life skills and ensuring positive social relationships within a youth-friendly environment—are central to an approach known as positive youth development.

Positive Youth Development Perspective

In recent years, child development scholars have identified structured, community-based activities, including sport, as important contexts in which youth may learn life skills and positive qualities such as moral, social, emotional, and behavioral competencies (Damon, 2004; Larson, 2000; Lerner, Almerigi, Theokas, & Lerner, 2005). The positive youth development approach emphasizes promotion of desired outcomes, not only prevention of undesirable behaviors. The five Cs—character, caring, competence, confidence, and connection—is one way of conceptualizing positive youth development (Lerner, Lerner, et al., 2005) and offers an appealing framework for understanding moral development in sport.

A comprehensive analysis of effective youth development programs identified those that foster personal skill development through carefully designed curricula and emphasize positive interactions and relationships with adults and peers (Catalano, Berglund, Ryan, Lonczak, & Hawkins, 2002). These features are often referred to as developmental assets; caring and competent adults and mentors connote the external assets, and moral (and other psychosocial) dimensions, such as responsibility, integrity, social justice, and compassion, reflect the internal assets (Catalano et al.; Damon, 2004). Although none of the 25 "effective" positive youth development programs identified by Catalano et al. were sport related, the sport context is clearly amenable to constructs and processes promoted by the positive youth development perspective.

Petitpas, Cornelius, Van Raalte, and Jones (2005) synthesized the youth development literature and identified the conditions for maximizing positive social and psychological outcomes through sport. These conditions are (a) a *context* in which activities are optimally challenging and intrinsically interesting, participants feel accepted by their peers, and personal mastery and group cooperation are emphasized; (b) *external resources* characterized by close relationships with caring adult mentors, parental monitoring, positive peer relationships, and community involvement; and (c) *internal assets* consisting of skills that youth can learn and transfer to domains outside sport (e.g., interpersonal, self-management, resistance skills). Petitpas et al. suggested that implementing and evaluating youth development through sport programs are essential to documenting the efficacy of sport to contribute to positive psychosocial outcomes.

To our knowledge, two sport-based youth development programs have the components of context, external resources, and internal assets in place. These are the *Play It Smart* and *The First Tee* programs; the former uses football and the latter golf as the platform by which to teach developmental assets and promote psychosocial growth. Both programs use coaches, parents, and community members as external resources and provide structured training to educate coaches on how to maximize positive development and embrace a youth-centered philosophy. Both programs also employ curricula based on the youth development literature that are designed to teach interpersonal, self-management, goal-setting, and resistance skills. Together, the context, external resources, and internal assets combine to maximize positive developmental outcomes in youth participants.

Preliminary evidence for the effectiveness of *Play It Smart* exists for academic outcomes (Petitpas, Van Raalte, Cornelius, & Presbrey, 2004). Grade point average, SAT scores, and graduation percentage for program participants compared favorably to those of the general population. Efficacy of *The First Tee* in achieving its goals of positive youth development also exists (Weiss, Bhalla, Price, Bolter, & Stuntz, 2006). Data from the first year of a longitudinal investigation indicated that over 90% of the 11- to 17-year-old youth interviewed showed transfer of skills learned through the context of golf to other salient domains (e.g., school, home, peer contexts), such as showing respect, managing negative emotions, engaging in healthy behaviors, and helping others. This evidence was corroborated through interviews with parents and coaches. Synergy among the climate, curriculum, and program delivery in *The First Tee* was implicated as a key process in realizing positive youth development.

In the second year of the study, the main purpose was to assess retention of life skills knowledge and transfer through interviews with 20 returning participants who provided in-depth responses the previous year. Qualitative analysis revealed that 90% of the interviewees provided compelling evidence of retaining knowledge and transfer of life skills learned in *The First Tee* (see Weiss, 2007). Domains in which life skills were used (e.g., school, family, friends, sports teams) and themes for using life skills (e.g., *Goal Ladder*) were consistent over time, with some differences (e.g., more emphasis on using life skills for job and college preparation). Other data collected in year 2 showed that participants in *The First Tee* compared favorably to youth involved in other activities (e.g., sports, band, youth organizations) on life skills transfer, general life skills usage, and developmental outcomes. Collectively, findings indicate that *The First Tee* is an effective youth development program in attaining its goals of teaching life skills and promoting positive developmental outcomes.

In summary, the positive youth development perspective offers a viable means for planning and evaluating character development programs through sport. The framework, components, and assessment tools are in place for designing curricula to assist programs in targeting youth development. Relevant studies in youth sport psychology go back 25 years, so it is ironic that, up until recently, child development researchers showed little interest in sport and physical activities as contexts for developing character and other psychosocial outcomes. We encourage youth sport researchers to seize the opportunity to help practitioners develop coach training and curricula and then evaluate the potential of these components to influence the lives of young people through sport.

Future Research Directions

Although considerable enhancement of the knowledge base has occurred over the past 25 years, many avenues for future research on moral development in sport are available. There is room to improve assessment of moral development constructs as well as our understanding of key predictors of such constructs, moral development trajectories, and the elements that make intervention programs effective. Indeed, several interesting and challenging research questions require answers. For example, how do we best assess group norms regarding moral behavior? Do differing motivational climates foster different moral development trajectories over the course of a season? What does and does not enable sport-related intervention effects to transfer to other contexts?

One of the key challenges to the pursuit of sport (and general) moral development research is the measurement of moral constructs. Measures that are conceptually and psychometrically sound, carefully constructed, and convenient to use are in short supply (Bredemeier & Shields, 1998). Therefore, efforts to evaluate existing measurement tools and develop new instruments would meaningfully contribute to the sport moral development research literature. Particularly valuable would be the development of tools or strategies for assessing group-level constructs such as team moral norms. Interest in situational predictors of sport moral constructs has intensified in recent years, and such pursuits will be essential to realizing significant knowledge gains from this work.

Social relationships clearly link with moral development outcomes in sport, and we believe that focused attention on relationships with significant others such as coaches, parents, teammates, and nonsport peers will improve the knowledge base. Existing work has focused predominantly on sport participants' perceptions of what significant others would or would not condone. However, rarely has such assessment been conducted along with an evaluation of the degree to which participants value these relationships or perceive them to be of high or low quality. These factors are likely to dictate the degree to which perceptions of others' beliefs link with one's own moral beliefs. Our work on youth sport friendships (see Weiss & Stuntz, 2004) highlights the relevance of prosocial behavior, conflict, and conflict resolution to youth sport participants, suggesting that close friendships can provide a context for moral development. To provide deeper understanding of this connection, comparative examination of relationships (e.g., friends versus acquaintances), assessment of how people negotiate impartiality (e.g., conflicts between friends and nonfriends), and attention to affective aspects of friendship would be valuable (see Bukowski and Sippola, 1996). Comparative examinations would be particularly interesting because most sport moral development work incorporating multiple significant-other variables has examined their predictive value in parallel. How does a young athlete reason or behave, for example, when teammates hold expectations for moral behavior that differ from the coach's expectations, parents' expectations, or a particular friend's expectations?

Social relationships also figure into alternative types of aggression that may occur in sport. Although most of the research examining aggression in sport has focused on overt, physical forms of aggression, other types of aggression exist, such as social or relational aggression. In the general psychology literature, relational aggression is a hot topic and refers to manipulating and damaging social relationships as a mechanism for harming others. Several books (e.g., Simmons, 2002; Underwood, 2003) and numerous research articles (e.g., Crick, 1995, 1996, 1997) have examined relational aggression in general contexts. To our knowledge, few studies have examined relational aggression in sport settings. One qualitative study by Stuntz and Weiss (2003b) examined athletes' responses when asked about what they do when they are angry with others in sport (and school) settings. Besides direct physical and verbal aggression, several relational behaviors emerged including spreading rumors, involving authority figures (e.g., coaches, team captains), and forming alliances against others. Still, relational aggression use was higher in school situations than it was in sport situations. In addition, a study by Storch, Werner, and Storch (2003) reported a positive link between peer nominations for relational aggression and peer rejection in a sample of college athletes. Given the importance of positive team dynamics, strong interpersonal relationships (friendship, group acceptance, coach–athlete), and group cohesion in sports, further examination of relational aggression in sport is warranted.

Beyond more in-depth study of the role of social relationships in moral development, the adoption of an interactionist approach that examines individual and contextual variables simultaneously is sorely needed. Rest's (1984, 1986) and Shields and Bredemeier's (1995) models of moral action are interactionist and therefore cannot be fully tested without such a research strategy. The simultaneous examination of individual and social-contextual variables to understand their respective and combined contributions to moral development in sport is rare. We believe that such efforts have the greatest potential to advance the boundaries of knowledge on moral development in sport and are particularly essential to the development of more parsimonious and effective intervention protocols.

As is the case in many areas of sport psychology research, use of longitudinal research designs will significantly enhance the knowledge base on moral development in sport. Indeed, an understanding of development necessitates such work, and it is surprising that more longitudinal studies on theoretical questions of interest have not been conducted. Instead, the few longitudinal studies have been directed toward the evaluation of intervention programs. Longitudinal investigations could help us understand how moral intentions are translated into actions, the degree to which significant others' beliefs and behaviors cause moral developmental change, degree of stability and change in relationship and aggression variables, and how group norms form over time. Debate continues about whether the decline in moral reasoning across increasingly competitive levels of sport involve-

ment stems from bona fide change or merely reflects selection and attrition processes. Carefully designed longitudinal research is labor intensive and involves a multitude of challenges (e.g., retaining subjects), but the payoff in conceptual understanding of moral development processes in sport would be well worth the effort.

The intervention literature identifies a number of efficacious sport-based character-building programs. Better understanding of the strengths and shortcomings of these programs would be useful. Intervention programs that have been evaluated are characterized by holistic, multimodal strategies drawn from multiple theoretical frameworks. Therefore, it has been difficult to acquire understanding of the specific program components that drive change in participants. We encourage finer-grained assessment of intervention programs, with careful attention to capturing potential *mechanisms* of change as well as outcomes. We also encourage careful examination of potential moderators of intervention effects, such as gender, age, and developmental level (e.g., cognitive age, social perspective-taking level). Furthermore, longer-term retention assessments than those that have been employed in the intervention literature are necessary to determine if character has been *developed* or if effects are only temporary.

Finally, an important research challenge is to determine whether intervention programs yield effects that generalize to other contexts. If we argue that sport represents a "bracketed" context in which typical moral functioning may be suspended, then we must be cautious about making arguments that sport-based moral development interventions will have wide-reaching effects. The intervention effects may be bracketed as well. Careful assessment of what elements of an intervention program enable its effects to be realized in other contexts would be valuable, allowing the development of wide-reaching intervention protocols that would be attractive to both sport and nonsport administrators and policy makers.

In summary, we believe that deliberate attention to measurement issues, the predictive value of social relationships, interactionist and longitudinal research designs, and fine-grained assessment of intervention approaches will significantly enhance the moral development literature. Each of these items has potential to enhance not only the conceptual knowledge base on moral development in sport but also the efficiency and effectiveness of sport-based character development interventions.

Conclusion

Does sport develop character or characters? We comprehensively reviewed the body of knowledge on moral development theory, research, and interventions, which suggests that either is possible through sport. Whether positive or negative outcomes occur depends on the quality of adult leadership as well as the mission, goals, and activities of specific programs. Several questions remain regarding personal and social factors that may affect moral interpretation, judgment, intention, and behavior (i.e., character). Work that addresses such issues would provide important information to guide practitioners in developing new interventions and refining existing ones to enhance character. There is a dire need to conduct evaluation studies that test the efficacy of sport programs in modifying moral beliefs and behaviors in the larger context of positive youth development, and to examine whether moral reasoning and behavioral changes that occur in sport contexts generalize to other life domains. Only through further theory-based studies and intervention programs can we be confident in saying that sport *can* build character in youth participants.

Part III

SOCIO-ENVIRONMENTAL FACTORS AND SPORT BEHAVIOR

The six chapters presented in part II of this text identified and discussed the relationship between selected individual difference factors and sport behavior. The collective research and theory reviewed there have clearly shown that psychological characteristics of individual participants can be used to explain and predict how they will behave in sport and physical activity settings. But it has also become apparent that individual difference factors cannot be completely understood without an accompanying analysis of the context within which the person lives and within which the sport behavior occurs. Thus, taking into account socio-environmental and sociocultural influences will allow more accurate and complete interpretation of sport behavior.

As Julie Partridge and her coauthors note at the beginning of chapter 12, the sport involvement of children, youth, adolescents, and young adults takes place within a social context. Thus, the psychological outcomes of athletes are strongly affected by individuals within that context. These influential individuals include teammates, coaches, peers, siblings, and parents. The chapters in this section of the text highlight the roles that these significant others play. Collectively, then, the three chapters in part III present a socioenvironmental perspective on the behavior of people in sport contexts.

Part III begins with chapter 10, written by Albert Carron and Lawrence Brawley to review current research and theory on group dynamics and to identify directions for future research. As these authors note, the primary rationale for studying group dynamics in the sport and exercise setting stems primarily from the importance of groups. Furthermore, because groups can be perceived as microcosms of larger societies, they represent a good context for the study of social relations and social interactions. Carron and Brawley begin their chapter with an overview of the major theoretical approaches to the study of groups in general as well as in sport contexts. They then review the empirical research on three of the more extensively researched or potentially important aspects of group dynamics: group size, collective efficacy, and group cohesion. Finally, they identify and examine recent advances in sport and exercise research, with specific reference to remedying previously identified pitfalls to research, and conclude by offering new directions for research in group dynamics.

I wrote chapter 11 to focus on a more specific aspect of the sport group environment—the behavior of the coach. This chapter begins with a discussion of the various conceptual approaches that have been used to design and conduct research oriented toward the identification of particular coaching characteristics, leadership styles, and behavioral patterns that will be most effective (or ineffective) in facilitating the performance and psychosocial growth of athletes. These multiple conceptual approaches are used to specify a composite working model of coaching effectiveness. This working model is then used as a framework to review the current state of knowledge about coaching effectiveness as well as to identify gaps in our knowledge base and to provide recommendations for future researchers interested in identifying how and why coaches behave as they do in practice and competitive situations and how such leader behavior can affect athletes' performance and psychosocial growth.

In a chapter that is new to the third edition of this text, Julie Partridge, Robert Brustad, and Megan Babkes Stellino explore the role that parents, peers, and siblings may play in affecting the behavior, attitudes, perceptions, and beliefs of children and youth in sport contexts. This chapter begins with a discussion regarding the notion of social influence as a general concept and then outlines the way in which social influence must be conceived within a developmental framework. Following this introductory section, Partridge and her colleagues provide a review of the research on the effects of parents, peers, and siblings on the sport participation of children and adolescents. Although most of the research conducted to date has focused on each of the three social influences separately, the authors conclude their chapter with a call for research that examines the effects of these three groups in an interactional manner.

As Kontos and Feltz noted in chapter 1 of this text, the research focus in the early years of the field of sport psychology was primarily on the relationship between individual difference variables (e.g., traits and dispositions) and sport performance and behavior. Relatively quickly, however, sport psychology researchers recognized the value of incorporating socioenvironmental factors into their work. As the research cited in this part of the book shows, this more inclusive focus has provided valuable information to the understanding of individuals' behavior and psychosocial responses in sport, particularly when such social factors are examined in combination with individual difference variables.

CHAPTER 10

Group Dynamics in Sport and Physical Activity

Albert V. Carron, EdD   Lawrence R. Brawley, PhD

Since the beginning of social psychology, group dynamics has been recognized as a major branch of the discipline. The term *group dynamics* has been used in two major ways. First, it has been used to depict the vitality and changing nature of groups. Second, it has been seen as the field of study that focuses on the behavior of groups. Although Kurt Lewin (1943) is credited with coining and popularizing the term, Dorwin Cartwright and Alvin Zander (1968) are recognized as two of the most prolific early researchers in this area (see Forsyth, 1983). In their classic text *Group Dynamics*, they stated that this field of inquiry is "dedicated to advancing knowledge about the nature of groups, the laws of their development, and their interrelationships with individuals, other groups, and larger institutions" (1968, p. 7). Group dynamics is not normally recognized as a discipline unto itself but instead as an area of study within social psychology and sociology. In this chapter, we recognize that groups are not static and use the term *group dynamics* to refer to the scientific study of these changing entities.

The importance of group dynamics stems primarily from the importance of groups. Groups are important because of the large number that each person encounters or has membership in and because of the effect that such groups can have on a person's life. Besides being part of a family, most people simultaneously belong to a variety of recreational, social, and work groups, all of which can influence and be influenced by the person's thoughts, feelings, and actions. Thus, it is not surprising that group dynamics has been a major interest area for social psychologists. Also, because groups can be seen as microcosms of larger societies, they represent a convenient place for sociologists to study broader social systems. In addition, Forsyth (1983) identified anthropology, political science, education, business, speech and communication, social work, criminal justice, and sports and recreation as other fields that recognize the importance of understanding group dynamics. One consequence of the broad interest in groups (as well as their inherent complexity) has been that theoreticians in the various disciplines have advanced a wide variety of definitions.

A Group Defined

In their recent book *Group Dynamics in Sport*, Carron, Hausenblas, and Eys (2005) classified the various approaches that have been taken in defining a group into four broad categories. One general category, which is illustrated by a definition advanced by Fiedler (1967), emphasizes the common fate of members. Thus, Fiedler defined a group as "a set of individuals who share a common fate, that is, who are interdependent in the sense that an event which affects one member is likely to affect all" (p. 6).

In a second general category of definitions, the group is perceived as an avenue through which group members experience mutual benefit. The definition forwarded by Bass (1960) provides a good example. Specifically, Bass defined a group as a "collection of individuals whose existence as a collection is rewarding to the individuals" (p. 39).

Third, groups can be differentiated from happenstance collections of individuals in terms of the social structure that they develop. As a consequence, some theoreticians have capitalized on this characteristic to define a group. The definition advanced by the Sherifs (Sherif & Sherif, 1956) is typical: "(A) group is a social unit which consists of a number of individuals who stand in (more or less) definite status and role relationships to one another and which possess a set of values or norms of its own regulating the behavior of individual members, at least in matters of consequence to the group" (p. 144).

A fourth approach emphasizes important group processes that distinguish a group from a collection of individuals. The definition proposed by Shaw (1981) is typical of this category. He proposed that a group is "two or more persons who are interacting with one another in such a manner that each person influences and is influenced by each other person" (p. 8).

Although each of the general categories of definition is useful, group dynamics theoreticians realized that the presence of a common fate, mutual benefits, a social structure, and group processes in some instances could characterize a happenstance collection of individuals. For example, the relationship between two strangers shooting baskets in a gym could be characterized by a common fate (e.g., eviction if they are caught by the custodians), mutual benefit (e.g., retrieving the other person's basketball), social structure (e.g., establishing a teacher–learner relationship), and group processes (e.g., interacting and communicating with one another). Thus, theoreticians have suggested that a fifth component or characteristic, self-categorization, should be added to the definition of a group. A good example of this fifth component is evident in Brown's (1988) definition: "A group exists when two or more people define themselves as members of it and when its existence is recognized by at least one other" (pp. 2–3).

The sport team as a group obviously possesses all five characteristics. Therefore, drawing on the five general categories of definitions, Carron, Hausenblas, and Eys (2005) defined a sport team as "a collective of two or more individuals who possess a common identity, have consensus on a shared purpose, share a common fate, exhibit structured patterns of interaction and communication, hold common perceptions about group structure, are personally and instrumentally interdependent, reciprocate interpersonal attraction, and consider themselves to be a group." Given their pervasiveness and their prevalence in society, sport teams offer a particularly important and interesting environment for the study of group dynamics.

Group Dynamics in Sport Teams

In North America today, the team sports of baseball, basketball, football, and, more recently, hockey, soccer, and volleyball attract millions of competitors and countless spectators. Next to the family, the sport team may be the most influential group to which an individual belongs. Teams are organized for children of both sexes as young as age 7 and for adults as old as 90. "Old-timers" leagues in sports such as hockey and softball typically begin at age 30, and people often participate into their 60s and 70s.

Team sports are especially prevalent in high school, where students participate in interscholastic, intramural, and recreational groups. Many businesses not only adopt a team approach for work but also encourage participation on company-endorsed teams. Because the team can be a major social group for an individual for 10 to 30 years, it has the potential to have a socializing influence of similar magnitude to that of a church or school. In spite of the prevalence of sport teams and the potential effect that such groups may have on people, most research conducted within sport has focused on individual participants (i.e., their performance, enjoyment, adherence, and so on). The team has been studied much less frequently, both as an entity unto itself and as a factor that influences individuals, other teams, or larger organizations.

From an academic perspective, because the sport team is a small group, the sociological and social psychological reasons for studying any group apply. As Loy, McPherson, and Kenyon (1978) pointed out, "Sport groups possess unique structural features that offer special advantages with respect to small group research" (p. 68). Schafer (1966) identified four such advantages. First, because the sport team is a naturally occurring group rather than an experimenter-created laboratory entity, it can provide information about group development and group relationships with other groups and the broader social environment. Second, sport research can control a number of confounding variables such as group size and rules of conduct by automatically holding them constant. Third, because sport groups typically pursue zero-sum goals (i.e., in most sports teams either win or lose), they provide an ideal context for the study of cooperation, competition, and conflict. Finally, sport offers objective measures of group effectiveness (e.g., number of errors made, points scored, and percentage of games won). Thus, the sport team offers an excellent setting for research on group dynamics.

An examination of group dynamics texts in social psychology, organizational psychology, and sociology shows that outside the realm of sport the topics most frequently covered include

- group formation,
- group tasks,
- group development,
- group composition,
- group size,
- group structure,
- group cohesion,
- group motivation,
- group leadership,
- group conformity,
- intergroup relations,
- group decision making, and
- collective efficacy.

For the most part, the same topics that have been studied in nonsport settings have also been investigated in sport. But the emphasis on specific topics is not the same. In sport, the topics of cohesion and leadership and to a lesser extent collective efficacy are overrepresented, whereas size, for example, one of the most extensively examined small-group variables, has had minimal attention in sport. Note that the paucity of research into certain small-group topics in sport does not necessarily mean that these topics are not important or not of interest to sport practitioners or researchers. These topics may simply be difficult to examine in sport, and other topics may have been seen as more central to the functioning of athletic teams.

In summary, group dynamics, the scientific study of groups, is a worthwhile endeavor because of the prevalence of groups and the effect that they have on individuals. Likewise, the study of the dynamics of sport groups is equally significant, given the important role that athletic teams play in the lives of many humans. Although numerous relationships between groups, between groups and individuals, and between groups and larger institutions could be examined, group dynamics research to date has primarily focused on interrelationships within groups.

The primary purpose of this chapter is to review current research and theory on group dynamics and identify directions for future research. The chapter is organized into eight major sections. In the first section, we outline theoretical approaches to the study of groups. In the second and third sections, findings from two representative areas within the group dynamics of sport and exercise—group size and collective efficacy—are presented. In the fourth section, we provide our perspective on the nature of group cohesion in sport teams. Cohesion, the group construct that we consider the most important for group effectiveness, is the one that we have spent the most time studying. In the fifth section, we provide a relatively comprehensive overview of research examining the correlates of cohesiveness in sport and exercise groups. In the sixth section, recent advances in sport and exercise with specific reference to remedying pitfalls to research are presented. Finally, in the last section, we propose new directions for research in group dynamics in sport.

Theoretical Approaches in Group Dynamics

Scholars in a variety of disciplines have espoused the importance of theoretical perspectives. In discussing group dynamics, McGrath (1984) emphasized that theory is as important as data. Specifically, he stated

> Theory strengthens a data-based science in several ways: (a) as a means for identifying problems worthy of study; (b) as a means for connecting one problem or one piece of evidence with another, even when they have been given different labels; (c) as a means for estimating (hypothesizing/predicting) the pattern of data likely to be found in a yet-unstudied area; (d) as a means for anticipating what aspects of a problem are most likely to be important. (p. 27)

Thus, theory helps people understand previous research findings and serves as a guide for future research.

In categorizing theoretical approaches to the study of group dynamics, Shaw (1981) distinguished between theoretical orientations (e.g., field theory), which apply to a broad range of social contexts, not just groups, and limited theories (e.g., leadership theory), which apply to specific phenomena within groups. Between these two extremes lie middle-range theories (e.g., exchange theory), which explain more than one, but not all, aspects of group life (see Shaw & Costanzo, 1982).

After considering a number of theoretical approaches, most authors conclude that no one theory can explain all group behavior but that each adds something to the understanding of groups. In contrast to such optimistic statements, Zander (1979) proposed,

> There are few well-developed theories about behavior in groups. The theories that do exist, moreover, seldom aid in understanding groups as such, or even the behavior of members on behalf of their groups, because the theories often are based on ideas taken from individual psychology, and these are primarily concerned with the actions of individuals for the good of those individuals. (p. 423)

Extensive review of the research on group dynamics in sport indicates that none of the general theoretical orientations identified by Shaw have been tested or used as a guide in the study of athletic teams. Likewise, rarely have any middle-range theories been employed in sport. Thus, when theoretical approaches have been used to study athletic teams, they have been what Shaw referred to as limited theories. They are limited in the sense that they focus on single specific group-related phenomena such as leadership (e.g., Chelladurai, 1978), group structure (Grusky, 1963), cohesion (e.g., Carron, Widmeyer, & Brawley, 1985), effectiveness (Steiner, 1972), home territorial advantage (Carron, Loughead, & Bray, 2005), and role ambiguity (e.g., Beauchamp, Bray, Eys, & Carron, 2002).

Theory and research pertaining to the home advantage and cohesion are presented later in this chapter, and another chapter in this text deals with the theory of leadership in sport. We do not discuss here Grusky's theory of formal structure, which has been used primarily by sport sociologists to explain both racial discrimination and ascendancy to leadership positions in sport organizations. The theory is described in detail by Loy, McPherson, and Kenyon (1978). Three limited theories—Steiner's (1972) theory of group productivity, the Beauchamp et al.

(2002) theory of role ambiguity in sport, and the Carron et al. conceptual model for home territorial advantage—are discussed briefly below.

Group Productivity

According to Steiner (1972), a group's actual productivity is equal to its potential productivity minus process losses, which result from either faulty coordination of member resources or less-than-optimal motivation by members. Thus, a group of physical education students might not have moved a wrestling mat as effectively as they could have because they did not all lift and move simultaneously or because some of them did not give maximum effort. The amount of relevant resources determines potential productivity (e.g., sewing ability is not a relevant resource for moving a wrestling mat). Similarly, communication is more relevant for a football team than it is for a bowling team because coordination of effort is more crucial in the former.

Using Steiner's theory, one can predict that team A will perform better than team B if any of the following scenarios is present:

- Team A possesses greater relevant resources than team B does and experiences equal process losses, or

- Team A possesses equal relevant resources but experiences fewer process losses than team B does, or

- Team A possesses greater relevant resources and experiences fewer process losses than team B does.

These predictions suggest that the primary role of a coach is to increase relevant resources (through instruction, training, and recruiting) and reduce process losses (through strategies for motivating players and combining their contributions). Because sport is performance oriented, Steiner's theory has innumerable applications. For example, it has been used to determine the relative contributions of ability and cohesion to performance outcome (Gossett & Widmeyer, 1978) and to look at social loafing in rowing performance (Ingham, Levinger, Graves, & Peckham, 1974).

Role Ambiguity

A role is the pattern of behavior expected of an individual in a social situation. For a team to be successful, each athlete must clearly understand the responsibilities associated with his or her role; this circumstance represents role clarity. The opposite cognitive state—a group member's lack of understanding—represents role ambiguity. In 1964 Kahn and his colleagues developed a conceptual framework to explain role ambiguity in industrial settings. Recently, Beauchamp, Bray, Eys, and Carron (2002) modified Kahn and colleagues' conceptual model so that it was more applicable to sport teams (see figure 10.1). In interdependent sports such as hockey and basketball, athletes must understand four aspects associated with their role responsibilities on both offense and defense. One aspect pertains to the individual's degree of understanding about the scope of his or her responsibilities. For example, a point guard in basketball might have multiple offensive responsibilities and be fully aware of only a fraction of them. A second pertains to the degree of understanding of the behaviors necessary to carry out role responsibilities. A young, inexperienced athlete just elected captain might be unsure about the degree to which he or she should be vocal, critical, or supportive with teammates. A third relates to uncertainty regarding how role performance will be evaluated. An athlete playing a point guard role

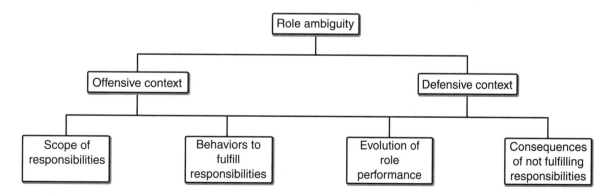

Figure 10.1 A conceptual model for role ambiguity in sport.

Adapted, by permission, from M.A. Eys, 2005, *Development of a measure of role ambiguity in sport*, Thesis, University of Western Ontario (London, Ontario).

may not know whether the evaluation criteria for the position is based on statistics (e.g., points scored and assists made) or by more subjective criteria such as leadership displayed on the court. Finally, a fourth type of ambiguity arises from uncertainty about the consequences of failing to fulfill role responsibilities. Will poor role performance from a point guard lead to benching, public criticism, apathy, extra repetitions in practice, or all of these?

In a series of studies, Beauchamp and his colleagues found that role ambiguity in sport teams is associated with several important group constructs. For one, the greater the athlete's understanding of his or her role, the more likely it is that he or she will perform the role successfully (Beauchamp et al., 2002). Also, greater role clarity is related to decreased competitive state anxiety (Beauchamp, Bray, Eys, & Carron, 2003) and increased athlete satisfaction (Eys, Carron, Bray, & Beauchamp, 2003a).

Home Advantage

In 1992 Courneya and Carron defined the home advantage as "the term used to describe the consistent finding that home teams in sport competitions win over 50% of the games played under a balanced home and away schedule" (p. 13). They also advanced a conceptual model to both explain and facilitate research on the phenomenon. Recently, Carron, Loughead, and Bray (2005) modified that model slightly. The conceptual framework proposed by Carron et al. includes three categories of factors thought to affect the home advantage (or performance outcomes): game location, game location factors, and critical psychological states (see figure 10.2).

The first, game location, represents simply the site—home versus away—for the competition. The game location factors include four major elements that are different for teams competing at home versus away: (a) crowd factors (e.g., crowd size, crowd density, crowd support); (b) learning and familiarity factors (e.g., idiosyncrasies in the facility with which the home team would be familiar); (c) travel factors (e.g., distance that the visiting team must travel, time zones that they must cross, and so forth); and (d) rule factors (e.g., last line change in ice hockey). As figure 10.2 shows, the four game location factors, in turn, are thought to influence first the critical psychological states (e.g., confidence, anxiety, and so on) and then the critical behavioral states (e.g., assertiveness, strategic decisions, and so on) of two groups of principals involved in the outcome—coaches and competitors. Finally, all the preceding are considered to influence three levels of performance outcomes (i.e., the home advantage): primary outcomes (e.g., free-throw percentage in basketball), secondary outcomes (e.g., points scored in basketball), and tertiary outcomes (e.g., win–loss ratio).

A considerable amount of research has been carried out to examine various aspects of the home advantage. A brief overview of the results of that research follows (see Carron, Hausenblas, and Eys, 2005, for a more comprehensive summary).

- A home advantage is present in both professional and amateur team sports.
- A home advantage is present in individual sports.
- Competing in a home territory positively benefits countries in international competitions.

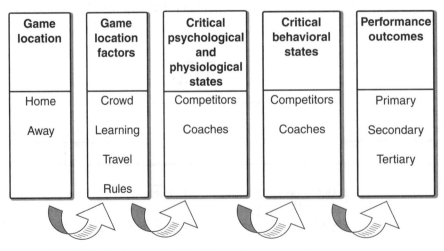

Figure 10.2 A conceptual model for the home advantage in sport.

Adapted, by permission, from A.V. Carron, T.M. Loughead, and S.R. Bray, 2005, "The home advantage in sports competitions: Courneya and Carron's (1992) conceptual model a decade later," *Journal of Sport Science* 23(4): 395-407.

- The home advantage is generalizable across gender.

- The home advantage is generalizable across the age spectrum.

- The home advantage is not a recent phenomenon; for example, the extent of the home advantage in English soccer has remained relatively unchanged since 1888 (Pollard, 1986)

- Research (see Carron, Hausenblas, & Eys, 2005) has shown that the rules category does not seem to contribute to the home advantage. Visitor team travel and lack of familiarity with the other team's venue make a small contribution. The home crowd is the factor that seems most influential both directly (i.e., crowd support) and indirectly (i.e., influence on officiating).

Beginnings to an Overall Theory

We have already noted that no overall theory explains the dynamics of sport teams or even groups in general. But certain models, or conceptual frameworks, identify and organize the categories of variables that operate within groups. In a framework advanced by McGrath (1984), member interaction is hypothesized to be the central factor in group life. McGrath then identified a number of factors that influence, and are influenced by, interaction processes. Specifically, he proposed that interaction is influenced by member characteristics, group structure, environmental properties, and processes internal to interaction itself. In turn, interactions can influence group members, the environment, and group relationships.

Although Carron, Hausenblas, and Eys (2005) reiterated the advantages of conceptual models identified by Shaw (and discussed earlier), they also pointed out that models have some disadvantages. One is that any conceptualization, because it is a simplified representation of reality, can never

adequately portray the total phenomena. Another is that conceptual frameworks tend to present a static picture, whereas groups (and their members) are dynamic and evolving entities. A third, somewhat related point is that conceptual frameworks generally represent interrelationships within dynamic constructs in a linear causal fashion. Life does not unfold in a similar linear fashion. For example, group-related variables such as communication (or role acceptance, conformity, collective efficacy, or other facets) contribute to improvements in a group variable such as cohesion, but cohesion, in turn, contributes to improvements in communication (and role acceptance, conformity, collective efficacy, and so on). In short, relationships among most group variables are dynamic and circular in nature, not linear.

After emphasizing these qualifiers, Carron, Hausenblas, and Eys (2005) presented a linear model (see figure 10.3) that they believed helps depict most inputs (also called antecedents), throughputs, and outputs (also called consequences) operating within athletic groups. The inputs (antecedents) identified are member attributes (e.g., social, psychological, and physical characteristics of team members) and the group's environment (e.g., the location and task of the group). According to Carron et al. these inputs contribute to the development of throughputs, which include group structure (e.g., positions, roles, and status of members), group cohesion (i.e., task and social unity), and group processes (e.g., motivation, communication, and decision making). Finally, two general categories of outputs from these inputs and throughputs were proposed: individual member consequences (e.g., their satisfaction, adherence, performance, and so on) and group-level consequences (e.g., group performance, stability).

The limited use of theory in group dynamics across all disciplines has undoubtedly restricted the advancement of knowledge in this area. Nevertheless, a considerable amount of research has been conducted. This research from other disciplines

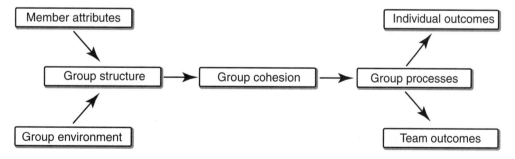

Figure 10.3 A conceptual model for group dynamics in sport teams.

Adapted, by permission, from A.V. Carron and H.A. Hausenblas, 1998, *Group dynamics in sport*, 2nd ed. (Morgantown, WV: Fitness Information Technologies).

has been discussed in a number of excellent books such as *Individual and Group Decision Making: Current Issues* by John Castellan (1993), *Group Communication in Context: Studies of Natural Groups* by Lawrence Frey (1994), *Groups, Teams, and Social Interaction: Theories and Applications* by Paul Hare (1992), *Perspectives on Socially Shared Cognition* by Lauren Resnick, John Levine, and Stephanie Teasley (1991), *Teamwork and the Bottom Line: Groups Make a Difference* by Ned Rosen (1989), *Groups at Work: Theory and Research* by Marlene Turner (2001), and *Understanding Group Behavior* by Erich Witte and James Davis (1996).

Because the field of group dynamics encompasses many areas of research, we will restrict ourselves to the examination of three major topics: group size, collective efficacy, and group cohesion. We selected these topics because of the amount of research conducted in each area or the importance of the topic for sport practitioners. Although we recognize that investigations have been conducted within sport dealing with such topics as group structure and selected group processes (e.g., motivation and attribution), space limitations prevent discussion of such topics here. In addition, researchers have examined other important aspects of groups, but not in conjunction with sport teams. For now, information on such group topics as development, communication, and decision making must be gleaned from nonsport research.

Group Size

Historically, one of the most frequently examined variables in nonsport research on group dynamics has been size. Research on this topic has been stimulated by interest among researchers and practitioners in determining how many individuals constitute the ideal for group productivity, morale, cohesion, satisfaction, and other outcomes. Specific examples of this research include determining the optimal unit size for a work group carrying out a manual labor project, an army platoon entering combat, a group of friends going on a social outing, or a secretarial pool within a large corporation.

Popular wisdom says, "The more the merrier," "Two heads are better than one," and "Many hands make the work lighter." But as Ivan Steiner (1972) pointed out, popular wisdom also says, "Three is a crowd," "Too many cooks spoil the broth," and "A chain is as strong as the weakest link." Scientists, of course, attempt to resolve these conflicting notions.

Steiner's theory of group productivity has guided much of the research on group size. This conceptual framework can be used to explain the effect of group size on a variety of factors related to group effectiveness. The graph presented in figure 10.4 illustrates how Steiner's framework explains effects of group size on group productivity. Examination of this graph shows that as the number of members in a group increases, the potential for the group to be more productive also increases. The reason for this is simple—more resources are available. Note, however, that the curve for potential productivity eventually reaches a plateau. This occurrence reflects the fact that at some point, all the expertise necessary for a group to complete its mission is available. Adding new members beyond this point does not increase productivity.

When group size increases beyond the optimal point, members have more difficulty interacting and communicating about both task and social concerns.

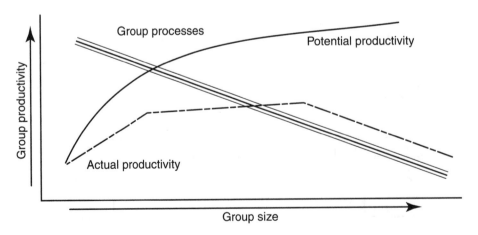

Figure 10.4 The relationship between group size and group productivity.

Based on A.V. Carron and H.A. Hausenblas, 1998, *Group dynamics in sport*, 2nd ed. (Morgantown, WV: Fitness Information Technologies).

Planning and coordinating each group member's activities to ensure minimal duplication and maximal individual involvement also becomes more difficult. These are examples of group processes. As figure 10.4 illustrates, when group size increases, group processes decrease.

The final relationship depicted in figure 10.4 is between group size and the relative productivity of each member. Relative individual productivity declines with increasing group size. This result occurs because of two factors. First, because of the coordination problems already discussed, the efficiency of the group suffers. Second, in larger groups, individual members do not give maximum effort. This motivation loss, known as social loafing, is discussed later.

Steiner's predictions regarding group size effects are based primarily on research with nonsport groups. Recently, however, several sets of researchers have examined the effects of group size in both sport and exercise contexts.

Sport Teams

In 1990 Widmeyer, Brawley, & Carron (1990) reported two studies on the effect of group size in sport teams. The first study primarily concerned effects of size on cohesion and is discussed later in this chapter. In designing these studies, researchers considered using different functional definitions of group size, including the number of players carried on the overall roster of the team and the number on the field of action at one time.

In the second study, the number of athletes on the field of action was varied in recreational volleyball teams to produce 3-on-3, 6-on-6, and 12-on-12 competitions. When the participants evaluated these three situations, they indicated that their sense of enjoyment, their perceptions of cohesiveness, their feelings of having obtained exercise and being fatigued, of having had influence and responsibility on the team, and of being organized and using strategies were greatest in the 3-on-3 teams and least in the 12-on-12 teams. At the same time, feelings of being crowded increased with increasing team size. The smallest teams were associated with the most positive experiences for the participants. The results from this study on sport teams showed that group size has an effect on productivity, perceptions about contributing to the group, individual perceptions about the attractiveness of the group, and the nature and amount of cohesiveness that develops. More about the effect on cohesion from these studies is presented later.

Social Loafing

Research on the productivity of groups has identified a phenomenon referred to as social loafing. Social loafing represents a reduction in individual effort that occurs when people work collectively on a problem (Latané, Williams, & Harkins, 1979). A considerable amount of research has subsequently verified the presence of social loafing in laboratory and nonlaboratory situations (see Hardy, 1989). In 1993 Karau and Williams undertook a meta-analysis to summarize the results from over 80 studies. Karau and Williams found that social loafing reliably occurs across a wide cross-section of situations including activities involving physical effort or skill (e.g., swimming), cognitive skills (e.g., generating ideas), evaluation (e.g., rating the quality of poems), and perceptual skills (e.g., vigilance on the computer), and is not a characteristic of one population (i.e., North Americans) or either gender. Karau and Williams noted that a number of conditions in the situation increase the probability that social loafing will occur. These include those instances in which

■ the individual's output cannot be evaluated independently,

■ the task is low in meaningfulness,

■ the individual's personal involvement is low,

■ a comparison of the individual's effort against group standards is not possible,

■ other individuals contributing to the collective effort are strangers,

■ the individual's coworkers are expected to do well, and

■ the individual believes that his or her efforts to the outcome are redundant.

Numerous explanations have been proposed to account for the social-loafing phenomenon (Harkins, Latané, & Williams, 1980). The allocation strategy proposal is based on the assumption that people are motivated to work hard in groups but save their best efforts for solitary work because it is personally most beneficial. The minimizing strategy proposal suggests that people are motivated to get by with as little effort as possible. Because individuals have minimal personal accountability, groups provide an optimal environment in which to loaf. In the free rider proposal, the assumption is that people in groups reduce their personal efforts and go for a free ride because they feel that their efforts are not essential to the outcome. Finally, the basis for the sucker effect proposal is the assumption that individuals in groups reduce their personal efforts because they do not want to provide a free ride to less productive individuals.

Collective Efficacy

In its broadest sense, efficacy is the strength of the belief that an objective can be achieved or that the responsibilities necessary to produce a desired outcome can be carried out successfully. Although his original theory and earliest research focused principally on individuals, Albert Bandura (1982) pointed out that "people do not live their lives as social isolates. Many of the challenges and difficulties they face reflect group problems requiring sustained collective effort to produce any significant change" (Bandura, 1982, p. 143). So, as with individuals, groups vary in the strength of their belief that the group can achieve an objective or carry out the responsibilities necessary to produce a desired outcome.

In 1995 Steven Zaccaro and his colleagues (Zaccaro, Blair, Peterson, & Zazanis, 1995) advanced a definition that captures the comprehensive, complex nature of collective efficacy. They suggested it is "a sense of collective competence shared among individuals when allocating, coordinating, and integrating their resources in a successful concerted response to specific situational demands" (p. 309). Research on collective efficacy has provided empirical confirmation that collective efficacy does exist—that group members do come to share common perceptions about their group's capabilities (Bandura, 1997; Feltz & Lirgg, 1998; Paskevich, 1995; Paskevich, Brawley, Dorsch, & Widmeyer, 1996; Prussia & Kinicki, 1996).

As figure 10.5 shows, collective efficacy can develop from a number of sources including prior performance, vicarious experiences, verbal persuasion, leadership behaviors, group size, and group cohesion (Bandura, 1977, 1982, 1986; Zaccaro et al., 1995). Gully, Incalcaterra, Joshi, and Beaubien (2002) undertook a meta-analysis to summarize the relationship between collective efficacy and performance among teams from a variety of situations, including business, industry, management, and social psychology (only one sport-related study was included). The result was a collection of 67 studies and 114 effect sizes (i.e., comparisons). Based on the statistical analysis of these studies, Gully and colleagues concluded that collective efficacy is positively related to performance. They also reported that the degree of group interdependence serves as a moderator in the collective efficacy–performance relationship. That is, for tasks that require considerable interaction and coordination, and have goals shared among group members (in contrast to group tasks carried out relatively independently), the collective efficacy–performance relationship is stronger.

Research in sport situations with ice hockey teams (Feltz, Bandura, Albrecht, & Corcoran, 1988; Feltz, Corcoran, & Lirgg, 1989) and with volleyball teams (Paskevich, 1995; Spink, 1990) supports the conclusion that prior performance has a major influence on collective efficacy. Success breeds confidence.

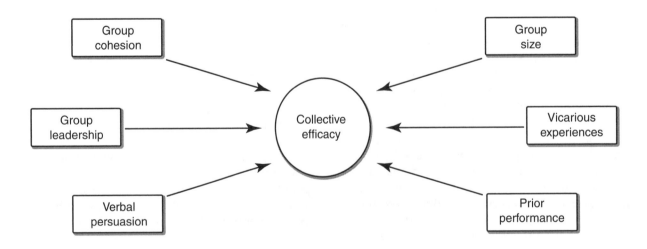

Figure 10.5 Sources of collective efficacy.

Adapted from A.V. Carron and H.A. Hausenblas, 1998, *Group dynamics in sport*, 2nd ed. (Morgantown, WV: Fitness Information Technologies).

A considerable body of research examining the nature and consequences of observational learning provides support for the supposition that vicarious experiences (see figure 10.5 again)—seeing other groups have success—has an influence on collective efficacy (e.g., McCullagh, 1987). A model (i.e., the other who is being observed) who is highly similar to the observer in important characteristics (e.g., competence, ability) has more influence on collective efficacy.

Zaccaro and his colleagues (1995) argued that verbal persuasion in the form of "leadership actions that persuade and develop subordinate competency beliefs may be as critical a determinant . . . as the group's prior performance experiences, if not more so" (p. 317). To date, however, no evidence supports this suggestion.

The relationship of group size, the final variable presented in figure 10.5, to collective efficacy is unclear. Zaccaro et al. (1995) proposed two possible scenarios. One is that increasing the size of the group will lead to an increase in members' belief that the group has sufficient skills, knowledge, and abilities within its membership for task success; thus, collective efficacy will increase. A second is that increasing the size of the group will lead members to believe that coordinating group actions will be more difficult and that social loafing will increase; thus, collective efficacy will diminish.

Recent research has been equivocal regarding the influence of group size. Watson, Chemers, and Preiser (2001) found that increasing group size in basketball teams was predictive of lower collective efficacy, whereas Magyar, Feltz, and Simpson (2004) found no relationship between these two variables in rowing crews.

Nature of Group Cohesion

Group cohesion is one of the most frequently examined group concepts in sport science. A number of reviews and book chapters provide extensive reports on the current state of knowledge concerning group cohesion in sport and exercise (e.g., Carron & Brawley, 2000; Carron, Brawley, & Widmeyer, 1998; Carron & Hausenblas, 1998; Carron, Hausenblas, & Eys, 2005; Gill, 1979; Paskevich, Estabrooks, Brawley, & Carron, 2000; Widmeyer, Brawley, & Carron, 1985). In this section of the chapter, we provide a contemporary definition of sport group cohesion and summarize the research captured by these sources to give a brief glimpse of the state of knowledge.

Problems With Pre-1985 Research on Sport Cohesion

A major problem with the early sport cohesion research was the failure to define and measure sport cohesion in more than a unidimensional manner. This problem affected both sport research and social science in general. Mudrack (1989) noted that researchers not only defined cohesion poorly but also failed to link measures to the various definitions of cohesion. Another problem in the early research was the arbitrary borrowing of measures of cohesion from other fields of study. In the sport sciences before the early 1980s, little thought was given to the limitations of borrowing definitions or measures from other fields of study. Borrowed operational definitions of cohesion do not have universal application to other settings.

At the root of the definition problem was the global problem that no conceptual or theoretical model could be used as the basis for the definition of cohesion and its measurement. Without some common foundation to guide research efforts, the variety of cohesion definitions and measures made subsequent comparisons between studies (e.g., comparing cohesion–performance relationships) difficult, if not impossible.

The problems of lack of a conceptual foundation, a poor definition of cohesion, and a poor operational definition to measurement link created a kind of domino effect in research error. Research problems of measurement cannot be solved without correcting the more basic problem of lack of a theory or model. We (Carron et al., 1985) addressed the related problems of cohesion theory, definition, and measurement by developing a conceptual model and measurement instrument that would enable comparisons between studies and permit subsequent meta-analyses. The next section describes these developments in response to the problems in sport cohesion research.

Developing a Conceptual Model and Definition of Cohesion

Several research groups developed new cohesion ideas and measures in the early 1980s (e.g., Gruber & Gray, 1981, 1982; Yukelson, Weinberg, & Jackson. 1984). Our research team was one of those groups. We (Carron et al., 1985) employed a theory-driven approach to develop the Group Environment Questionnaire (GEQ). Carron's (1982) definition of cohesion—"a dynamic process that is reflected in the tendency for a group to stick together and remain united in pursuit of its goals and objectives" (p. 124)—was used to assist the development of the conceptual model of sport group cohesion. The model then served as the basis for instrument development and validation.

The report of the entire validation process can be found elsewhere (see the recent GEQ, *Group Environment Questionnaire Test Manual*; Carron, Brawley, & Widmeyer, 2002), but key points appear here. To develop the model and the GEQ, we extensively reviewed the group dynamics literature. Two major themes consistently emerged. These themes centered on the distinction between individual and group aspects of group involvement and the distinction between the task and social functions of groups (e.g., Mikalachki, 1969; Van Bergen & Koekebakker, 1959). An example of the individual distinction is that group involvement has been examined with respect to the motives that individual members have for belonging to their group. In other words, what does the individual team member get out of being on the team? By contrast, for the group distinction, group involvement has been considered relative to decisions or perceptions that the entire group has about the group's behavior. For example, the group as a whole may set goals for performance or goals for a season, or the group as a whole may decide why it should continue postseason training.

A distinction between task and social reasons arises in examining why groups stay together. Work groups, competitive sport groups, and other physical activity and exercise groups form and pursue task-related activities relative to their goals and objectives, and stay together primarily for task reasons. By contrast, some leisure and recreational sport groups may form for social reasons, set social goals and objectives, and stay together primarily to socialize regularly.

A Conceptual Model of Group Cohesion for Sport

Using the themes and distinctions drawn from the literature, we proposed a conceptual model of cohesion that includes the distinctions between groups and individuals and between task reasons and social reasons (Carron et al., 1985; see figure 10.6). Our conceptual model and thus our measure derive from three fundamental assumptions: (a) Cohesion is a group property that can be assessed through the perceptions of individual members, (b) the nature of the social cognitions (beliefs) that members obtain through group experience reflect shared beliefs about the group, and (c) the primary orientation of these group perceptions is multidimensional. In the following section we discuss the evidence that supports the validity of these assumptions.

Assumption 1: Measuring Cohesion Through Perceptions of Group Members
Our belief that cohesion can be assessed through the perceptions of individual group members is founded on five principles: (a) A group has observable properties to define its stability, (b) members are socialized into their groups and thus develop a set of beliefs about the group and its properties, (c) these beliefs are a product of the selective processing and integration of group-relevant information, (d) the strength of the perceptions that individual group members hold about their group is an estimate of the strength of characteristic aspects of group unity, and (e) these perceptions can be measured quantitatively.

Assumption 2: The Group and the Individual
Our second assumption arose from the general distinctions apparent from reviewing group dynamics research. Social cognitions that a group member holds about cohesion concern the group and the

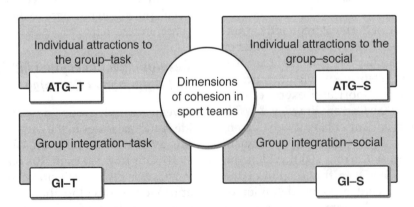

Figure 10.6 A conceptual model of group cohesion.

Adapted from A.V. Carron, W.N. Widmeyer, and L.R. Brawley, 1985, "The development of an instrument to assess cohesion in sport teams: The Group Environment Questionnaire," *Journal of Sport Psychology* 7: 244-266.

individual—those about the group as a totality and those about the manner in which the group satisfies an individual member's personal needs and objectives. These social cognitions are labeled in this way: (a) group integration—individual members' perceptions about the way that their group unites, is close, and is similar as a whole, and (b) individual attraction to the group—individual members' perceptions about (i) their personal motives brought to the group that function to retain and maintain them in that group and (ii) their perceptions or feelings about what the group provides or gives back to them. Group members learn these social cognitions by being in the group over time. Inasmuch as all members of the group are exposed to this learning through group processes, it follows that the social cognitions that members obtain through this group experience are shared beliefs about the group.

Assumption 3: Cohesion Beliefs Are Both Task and Social Our third assumption also stems from the general distinctions observed in the group literature—the distinction between task and social orientations. We assume that individual members' social cognitions about their group as a unit and about their attractions to the group have two fundamental orientations: (a) a task orientation that relates to the group's various task objectives for itself and its members and (b) a social orientation that relates to the development and maintenance of various social relationships and activities within the group.

To summarize, our multidimensional conceptual model of cohesion comprises four related dimensions. These are group integration–task (GI–T), group integration–social (GI–S), individual attractions to the group–task (ATG–T), and individual attractions to the group–social (ATG–S). The group integration dimensions are reflected in "us, our, or we" beliefs, whereas the individual attractions dimensions are reflected in "I, my, or me" beliefs. Each is potentially sufficient to bind people to their group, but depending on the developmental level of the group (i.e., reflected by the stability of various group properties such as organizational structure and role and status relationships), several dimensions could be relatively more reflective of a group's cohesiveness. The strength of the perceptions that define each dimension is assumed to indicate the strength of characteristic aspects of group cohesion at a given time in the group's life. Note, however, that other forces not explicitly identified by us may contribute to a group's cohesiveness. Thus, we do not assume that our conceptual model is all encompassing. Like all models or theories, research evidence accumulated over time should dictate how these dimensions might need to be modified.

A Developmental Perspective on Cohesion

Following the reasoning behind the conceptual model, it is expected that groups at different developmental stages in their group life may exhibit different profiles or pictures of cohesiveness. For example, early in a group's development or early in a team's season, the task-related aspects of cohesiveness (i.e., ATG–T and GI–T) are more likely to characterize a team's cohesiveness than are social aspects of cohesiveness (i.e., ATG–S and GI–S). The rationale for such a hypothesis comes from group research that has considered the way that groups develop (e.g., Moreland & Levine, 1988; Sherif & Sherif, 1969). For example, task-oriented groups like sport teams focus on the motivational basis for their existence—performance and competition. For task-oriented groups that are early in their development, a focus on social relationships and social cohesiveness is of less importance than is a focus on the group's task. Consequently, social cohesion likely develops gradually over time as a function of the interactions that occur as a part of group life. Why might researchers observe slow developmental growth in social cohesion? An understanding of group structure and process provides a hypothesis.

Team social cohesion may develop more slowly because socially oriented interactions occur less frequently and are less systematically imposed by coaches and players than are task-oriented interactions. Observations of increased social cohesiveness may be more likely later in a team's development or season after key aspects of the interactions necessary for group task performance become stable. Social cohesiveness may conceivably always be weaker than task cohesiveness in groups that struggle for effective task performance. Furthermore, many sport and physical activity groups inherently possess structural properties (e.g., size, leadership, rules, individual member responsibilities) that facilitate member task interaction and rapidly order a group's function around its tasks, thus encouraging task cohesion. By contrast, the same groups may not have formalized norms or structural properties that encourage a similar level and consistency of social interaction, thereby limiting development of strong social cohesion. To the extent that formalized norms relating to social interactions make this type of group member-to-member contact more systematic or frequent, observation of earlier emergence of social cohesion might be possible.

Because the profile of a group's cohesiveness may vary with changes in membership, tenure of group members, and over the group's life, a measure that examines the multiple dimensions of the construct and allows for change is necessary. Multiple indicators are required to detect the various aspects of the construct salient to members at the time of assessment. What this means, of course, is that each dimension of cohesiveness is not a trait property of a group but is more statelike. That is, change is a characteristic of the various dimensions—a reflection of changes occurring within the group. Accordingly, some aspects of cohesiveness may be more stable than others depending on the group's history, its current state of development, and its motivational base.

Group Environment Questionnaire

Based on the conceptual model just described and on the assumption that group members perceived cohesiveness in several ways, we developed the Group Environment Questionnaire (GEQ). The GEQ is an 18-item, four-scale instrument that has been shown to be reliable and valid in numerous ways. The validation process for the GEQ has evolved over the 20 years since the instrument was published. The studies that contribute to validation are described in detail elsewhere (e.g., Brawley, Carron, & Widemeyer, 1987, 1988; Carron, Brawley, & Widmeyer, 1998; Carron et al., 2005; Carron, Widmeyer, & Brawley, 1988; Carron et al., 1985, 1988; Widmeyer et al., 1985, 1990).

Correlates of Cohesiveness

A summary of the cohesion research in sport that followed the development of the GEQ is best discussed within the framework presented by Carron et al. (2005). This framework, which is illustrated in figure 10.7, is a modification of a framework originally proposed by Carron (1982) to help investigators systematically organize the research pertaining to cohesion.

As figure 10.7 shows, the correlates of cohesion can be considered within four categories: situational, personal, leadership, and team. In each category, we present a few illustrative examples. For a more complete overview of social and contextual variables related to cohesion (i.e., as assessed by the GEQ and other measures), consult Carron et al. (2005).

Situational Correlates

A number of situational constraints have an influence on the level of cohesiveness present in a team. For example, athletes may cohere in a team because of a variety of contractual considerations—eligibility rules, geographical restrictions, legal contracts, and so on. Also, normative pressures discourage quitting in our society. As a further example, the orientation of the organization can influence the nature and amount of the cohesiveness that is present. In this regard, Spink and Carron (1994) reported that task cohesion was associated with adherence in exercise programs in a university setting, whereas in private fitness clubs it was social cohesion. Also, Granito and Rainey (1988) found that social cohesion was greater in elementary and junior high school basketball teams than it was in senior high school teams.

Group size is another situational variable that differentially impinges on different aspects of cohesion. In 1990 we (Widmeyer, Brawley, & Carron, 1990) reported on two studies on the effect of group size on cohesion in sport teams. In designing these studies, different functional definitions of group

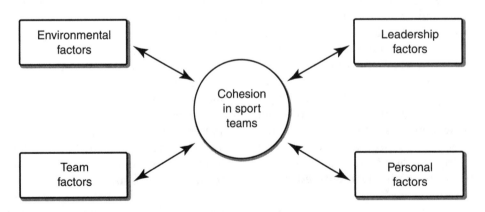

Figure 10.7 A schematic representation of the correlates of cohesiveness.

Adapted, by permission, from A.V. Carron and H.A. Hausenblas, 1998, *Group dynamics in sport*, 2nd ed. (Morgantown, WV: Fitness Information Technologies).

size, including the number of players carried on the overall roster of the team and the number on the field of action at one time, were considered and used. In study 1, the rosters of three-on-three recreational basketball teams were manipulated to produce teams that carried three, six, and nine members. Each team played two games per week for a 10-week period.

The results revealed that in the smallest teams, task cohesiveness was highest although win–loss success was not greatest. That is, unity, consensus, and commitment to the group's goals and objectives (i.e., reflected as perceptions of task cohesion) was greatest in the three-person groups. But because of the relatively limited number of resources available, the three-person teams were less successful than larger teams. Also, social cohesion (i.e., closeness among players) was lowest in these smallest teams, either because athletes were constantly competing or because of the relatively limited number of attractive others with whom to interact. In the largest teams (nine-person teams) task and social cohesion were lowest. Among that many players, obtaining consensus and commitment to the group's goals and objectives and developing a strong sense of social cohesion were more difficult. The intermediate-size groups—the six-person teams—were highest in social cohesion and the most successful in terms of win–loss outcomes.

In study 2, the number of athletes on the field of action was varied in recreational volleyball teams to produce 3-on-3, 6-on-6, and 12-on-12 competitions. When the participants evaluated these three different situations, they indicated that their perceptions of cohesiveness and their feelings of contributing to the team were greatest in the 3-on-3 teams and least in the 12-on-12 teams. At the same time, feelings of being crowded increased with increasing team size. In summary, we (Widmeyer et al., 1990) found that recreational volleyball players assigned to teams of varying size playing in a 10-week season expressed greatest task cohesion in small teams and least cohesion in large teams.

Personal Correlates

A wide cross-section of personal factors also are associated with the cohesion present in sport teams. Carron et al. (2005) found it convenient to organize these personal factors within three categories: cognitions (social cognitions), motivations (affective reactions), and behaviors.

Relationships With Social Cognitions Social cognitions refer to multiple psychological variables that characterize our daily reflections about ourselves and our circumstances and often represent the forethought that we have about future actions (cf. Bandura, 1997). Examples are attributions for causality, efficacy beliefs, attitudes, and goals including behavioral intentions. The relationship between group-member social cognitions and cohesion is likely reciprocal in nature—member similarity in social cognitions contributes to cohesion and, in turn, cohesion contributes to member similarity in various social cognitions. In cohesive groups, members may share social cognitions about the group (Carron et al., 2003). Some examples of findings concerning the relationship between social cognitions and cohesion serve to illustrate the point. One important cognition that is influenced by cohesion is attributions for responsibility (Bird, Foster, & Maruyama, 1980; Brawley, Carron, & Widmeyer, 1987; Schlenker & Miller, 1977). On cohesive teams, team-enhancing attributional strategies are used. That is, the members of highly cohesive teams distribute the credit for success and share the responsibility for failure. On the other hand, if the team is low in cohesion, the individual members use self-enhancing strategies—they take inordinate credit for success and deny responsibility after failure. Consistent with attribution theory (Weiner, 1986), members of highly cohesive teams find their self-esteem maintained by the division of responsibility for both success and failure, whereas members of teams low in cohesion use a strategy to enhance their individual self-esteem when the team is successful but deny responsibility to protect their individual self-esteem when the team is unsuccessful.

In most theoretical conceptualizations of social cognitions (e.g., social-cognitive theory; Bandura, 1986), behavioral intentions are considered a form of goal (i.e., a specific action plan for future behavior). Relative to their team, individuals have intentions for their future involvement, and their expressed intent is positively related to group cohesion. Specifically, in a series of studies, Spink and colleagues (Spink, 1995, 1998; Spink & Odnokon, 2001) found that regardless of the performance outcome of the season, elite and recreational female ringette players and elite male ice-hockey players on teams high in social cohesiveness (as assessed by the GEQ) indicated that they would return to play with their team the following season.

Affective Relationships Members also experience less anxiety in group situations than when they are alone. Also, members of a cohesive group have less anxiety than do members of a noncohesive group. For example, Martens and his colleagues (1990) noted that individual-sport athletes experience greater cognitive and somatic anxiety and lower state self-confidence than team-sport athletes do. Also, in a study examining the social anxiety that emanates from self-presentation concerns, Carron and Prapavessis (1997) found that individuals were less anxious in a group or with a best friend than they were when alone. Prapavessis and Carron (1996) found that athletes in a variety of sports who possessed higher perceptions of task cohesion reported less cognitive state anxiety.

Mark Eys and his colleagues (Eys, Hardy, Carron, & Beauchamp, 2003) took a slightly different approach. Athletes from a variety of sports rated both their state anxiety before competition and the degree to which that anxiety was either facilitative or debilitative. An athlete may, for example, be quite nervous before competition but consider that state as either positive (i.e., facilitative: "I'm ready") or negative (debilitative: "I'm too nervous to play well"). Eys and his colleagues found that athletes higher in task cohesion perceived their cognitive and somatic state anxiety symptoms as more facilitative.

Satisfaction is another affective measure related to cohesion. Jean Williams and Colleen Hacker (1982) tested the cause–effect relationships among performance, cohesion, and satisfaction in women's intercollegiate field hockey teams. They reported that the presence of cohesiveness contributes to team performance and, ultimately, to team success. In turn, success produces higher satisfaction in the individual athlete, which leads to the development of a greater sense of cohesiveness.

In co-acting sports such as golf, satisfaction may be one of the most important positive correlates of team cohesion. The relative importance to cohesion of team size, athlete satisfaction from team membership, athlete similarity, the coach's efforts to foster cohesion, prior team success, the presence and importance of team goals, participation in team goal setting, communication, and prior liking were assessed by Widmeyer & Williams (1991). They found that the best single predictor of both task and social cohesion in female golfers from Division I intercollegiate teams was satisfaction.

Behavior in Groups Cohesion has been found to be associated with a wide variety of individual behaviors. For example, adherence in exercise classes is positively associated with greater cohesion—whether adherence is operationalized as dropout behavior (Carron, Widmeyer, & Brawley, 1988; Spink & Carron, 1994), absenteeism and lateness (Spink & Carron, 1992), or resistance to disruptive events (Brawley, Carron, & Widmeyer, 1988, study 2).

Another operational measure of adherence used in business and industry is effort expended. When Prapavessis and Carron (1997) tested athletes from a variety of sports, they found that athletes holding higher perceptions of their team's task cohesiveness worked in practice at a level significantly closer to their maximum.

Social loafing is yet another behavior (and cognition) that is influenced by the team's cohesiveness. Research has shown that athletes on teams higher in cohesion are not only less likely to think that their teammates will socially loaf (Naylor & Brawley, 1992) but also less likely to loaf socially themselves (McKnight, Williams, & Widmeyer, 1991).

Leadership Correlates

The complex interaction between coach and players also appears to influence the development of cohesion. For example, a considerable body of research has examined the association between leader decision style and cohesion (Carron & Chelladurai, 1981; Kozub, 1993; Lee, Kim, & Lim, 1993; Westre & Weiss, 1991). The results from that research have been unequivocal. That is, a participative style of decision making is related to greater perceptions of cohesiveness.

The type of leadership behavior exhibited by the coach also has been found to be associated with the development of cohesiveness. But the specific type of leader behavior that is optimal is not clear. For example, Westre and Weiss (1991) found that higher levels of training and instruction behavior, social support behavior, and positive feedback with high school football players were associated with higher levels of task cohesion in athletes. In a study conducted with high school basketball teams, however, Kozub (1993) found that only higher levels of training and instruction behavior and social support behavior were related to greater task cohesion.

In a recent study, Sophia Jowett and Victoria Chaundy (2004) showed that it may not be leader behaviors alone that are important for team cohesion. They found that athletes' perceptions of the coach–athlete relationship (commitment, closeness, complementarity) explained more variance in task and social cohesion than did leader behaviors by themselves.

Team Correlates

Cohesion is both associated with (i.e., correlated with) and a causal agent in the development of collective efficacy in the group. Collective efficacy is the sense of shared competence held by team members that they can successfully respond to the demands of the situation (Zaccaro et al., 1995). In a study of volleyball teams, Spink (1990) found a correlation between cohesion and collective efficacy. Individual volleyball players who perceived their team to be more task cohesive also perceived their team to be more collectively efficacious. Paskevich (1995, study 3) inferred causation because teams higher in task cohesion early in the season had greater collective efficacy later in the season. Similarly, the teams that were higher in collective efficacy early in the season had greater task cohesion later in the season. Kozub and McDonnell (2000) found similar results with rugby teams.

A second important group (team) variable that has been extensively examined for its relationship to cohesion is performance. In 2002 Carron, Colman, Wheeler, and Stevens undertook a meta-analysis of 46 studies that had examined the association between team cohesiveness and team success. An overall moderate to large relationship was found. They also found that the type of cohesiveness present—task versus social—is irrelevant insofar as team success is concerned. That is, when the cohesion measures were subdivided according to whether they represented task or social cohesiveness, moderate to large relationships between both types of cohesion and performance were noted.

Carron and his colleagues also examined whether gender, level of competition, or type of sport served as moderator variables in the cohesion–performance relationship. As the term suggests, a moderator is a factor that modifies (changes) the relationship between an independent variable (e.g., cohesion) and a dependent variable (e.g., team success).

Females and Males   The group dynamics literature is replete with instances in which gender has been found to be a moderator of fundamental relationships (see Carron et al. 2005, for a review). Carron et al. found that the cohesion–performance relationship is no exception; the association between cohesion and performance is substantial for female and male teams but the relationship is significantly greater in female teams.

Type of Sport   In some of the earliest research on cohesion and performance, negative relationships were found for sports such as bowling (e.g., Landers & Lüschen, 1974). This led some authors (e.g., Carron & Chelladurai, 1981) to propose that cohesion may be important for team success in interactive sports such as volleyball, basketball,

and hockey but detrimental to team success in independent sports such as wrestling, tennis, and badminton. This proposal has now been shown to be unwarranted. Carron and his colleagues found that cohesion is equally important for both coactive and interactive teams.

Level of Competition   Carron and his colleagues also found that the magnitude of the cohesion–performance relationship varied according to level of competition (i.e., with the highest relationship present in high school sport and the lowest in professional sport). But possibly because of the large variability of results in each of those levels or because of the small number of studies at some levels (e.g., professional, high school), these substantial differences were not statistically significant. Thus, the question of whether cohesion is equally important for teams at every level of competition requires further research.

Conclusion

In summarizing the results of the sport-related research concerning recent developments in the study of cohesion, five points are notable:

- The Group Environment Questionnaire (GEQ) has been the sport-related multidimensional measure of cohesion that has been the most extensively validated.
- The GEQ instrument is based on a four-dimensional conceptual model and has been validated in numerous studies.
- The development of a conceptual model of cohesion and the GEQ instrument filled the pre-1985 void in the otherwise atheoretical study of cohesion in sport, and the GEQ became the dominant measure used to study sport cohesion.
- Use of the four-dimensional model and the related GEQ instrument avoids the common research error of not linking conceptual operational definitions of cohesion to their measurement.
- The four aspects of group cohesion specified by the conceptual model are related to both the antecedents (e.g., situational: size effects; personal: gender or social background; leader style; team: shared success and failure) and the consequences (e.g., individual outcomes: attribution of outcome responsibility, satisfaction with season's performance; group outcomes: collective efficacy; greater effort toward group goals) of cohesiveness in sport.

Remedying Research Pitfalls

Carron et al. (1998) and Carron, Hausenblas, and Eys (2005) have noted that although sport groups represent a major social structure across cultures and provide the context within which much of participation and competition occurs, the amount of sport and exercise group research is surprisingly limited compared with the amount of research focused on the individual. Carron et al's (2005) recent book on group dynamics in sport offers evidence of a number of new directions that suggest this trend is slowly changing.

What sport and exercise psychologists often fail to recognize is that the group has a major influence on individual behavior and performance (e.g., motivation, goal setting, performance attributions; Carron et al., 2005). Ignoring this influence of the group on individual behavior may be a major conceptual and methodological error. The failure to examine group influence on individual member actions excludes a major source of variance in the sport behavior prediction equation. This exclusion has implications for the accuracy of many of the interpretations in research studies about what influenced behavior. Was it an individual trait (i.e., unique individual variability), or was it the group (i.e., patterned group variability)? Was group cohesion or collective efficacy a mediator of individual reactions toward success or failure? If progress is to occur in understanding individual sport behavior, we cannot continue to examine individuals as if they exist in a social vacuum.

In the previous editions of this book (e.g., Widmeyer, Brawley, & Carron, 1992; Carron, Brawley, & Widmeyer, 2002), we argued that it was important to alert those who aspire to investigate sport groups to the problems characteristic of the research in this area. We suggested that if problems are identified and then remedied, the quality and quantity of research in sport group dynamics would improve. A reasonable question to ask here is whether we have developed any remedies for problems and made any advances during the last 15 years (i.e., since the first edition of this book).

In sport group research, the scientist can function as an architect or as a laborer. The architect establishes a plan and works toward it, whereas the laborer makes single bricks not necessarily destined for a particular building. Using a blueprint for research such as a conceptual or theoretical model avoids the work of simply collecting unrelated bricks of fact about the dynamics of sport groups. Also, developing or using remedies for research problems avoids the perpetuation of incorrect research. Have we made progress toward these two ends? Some examples illustrate that we have.

Remedy 1

The greatest general pitfall in the study of group dynamics in sport before 1990 was the failure to develop and use theory in a systematic way. Much earlier, both McGrath (1984) and Zander (1979) noted that group research had been highly fragmented, involving the collection of many bricks or data sets but using no theory to guide the collection, ordering, and interpretation of the results. From 1990 to the present, sport scientists have made advances by using theoretical frameworks advanced by authors such as Bandura (1997), Carron (1988), Carron and Hausenblas (1998), Carron, Hausenblas, and Eys (2005), and McGrath (1984).

For example, Bray, Brawley, and Carron (2002) used Bandura's self-efficacy theory to examine the interdependent roles of members of teams. The investigators argued that group members could have efficacy beliefs about the integration of specific interdependent skills and abilities unique to their particular role on a team. For example, a center on a basketball team could have efficacy beliefs about the way that the center's role interdependently functions with a power forward and guard on the strong side of the team's offensive plays. Role efficacy was shown to be distinct from both collective efficacy and players' efficacy beliefs about their individual basketball skills, and role efficacy was higher for the most competent interdependent players (i.e., starters versus nonstarters). No differences were found between starters and nonstarters for collective efficacy and individual self-efficacy.

Using Bandura's (1997) theorizing, Bray and Brawley (2002) also examined the clarity of players' roles with the expectation that role clarity would moderate the relationship between role efficacy and role performance. They argued that role efficacy should be a good predictor of role performance effectiveness but only under conditions of high role clarity. The result for role clarity expressed by elite basketball players was that it moderated the prospective relationship between role efficacy and role performance effectiveness in the predicted direction for offensive role functions. It was also hypothesized that athletes reporting higher role clarity would be more efficacious and would be rated by coaches as performing better than those with lower role clarity. The results generally supported the hypotheses. Other research by Beauchamp and Bray also supports the relationship between role efficacy and role performance (Beauchamp, Bray, Eys, & Carron, 2002), which is affected by role clarity (Beauchamp & Bray, 2001) among different sports and teams.

Remedy 2

A second general pitfall for sport scientists is conducting snapshot research about groups. This form of investigation, although offering a concise picture of a specific aspect of group life, fails to capture the dynamic nature of groups as they change over time. Most group studies conducted in the sport context (including a number of our own) are of the snapshot variety, with specific games or seasonal time points as their focus. But to understand the changing and reciprocal relationships among input and output variables, prospective, longitudinal studies are needed. A few such attempts have been made in examining the changing relationships among group dynamics variables over the course of a competitive season. These attempts include studies of the group cohesion–performance relationship (see Carron et al., 2002, for an overview), the role ambiguity–satisfaction relationship (Eys, Carron, Beauchamp, & Bray, 2003b), the cohesion–collective efficacy relationship (Paskevich, 1995), and the role of cohesion in the leader behavior–satisfaction relationships (Loughead & Carron, 2004). Research of a longitudinal nature also has been conducted in the exercise domain; the exercise-related studies are considered in later comments in the "Advances" section.

Remedy 3

The third pitfall to avoid is reliance on a univariate approach in examining groups. The univariate approach is often characterized by simple, bivariate correlations between one independent and one dependent variable. What is required is a multivariate approach. Multivariate research involves several independent predictors of one dependent variable or multiple dependent variables (e.g., multiple or multivariate multiple regression). This approach takes into account the complexity of group phenomena and acknowledges interrelationships among group variables that occur simultaneously. For example, Zaccaro et al. (1995) discuss the various interactive processes that occur concurrently within a group whose task demands require member interdependence. Numerous team functions such as offense, defense, coordination, communication, and motivation are hypothesized as contributing factors to the multivariable concept of collective efficacy. Paskevich (1995; Paskevich et al., 1999)

examined Zaccaro et al.'s contentions and found that a multifaceted collective efficacy predicted task-related aspects of team cohesion as well as team performance outcome.

As yet another example, in research that was discussed earlier, Beauchamp and his colleagues (e.g., Beauchamp et al., 2002; Eys et al., 2003) advanced a multidimensional concept of role ambiguity in interdependent sport teams. In their research, they found that different dimensions of role ambiguity for offense and defense differentially predicted group-related variables such as intention to return to the team, satisfaction, anxiety, and personal performance (see Carron, Hausenblas & Eys, 2005, for a comprehensive overview).

Remedy 4

The fourth major pitfall has been that group physical activity research has focused only on sport teams. Previously, we argued that the influence of the unique characteristics of teams (i.e., unique rules, properties, and physical structure) were not necessarily generalizable to other types of physical activity groups. We thus encouraged research that concerned the variety of other groups in physical activity (Widmeyer, Brawley, & Carron, 2002). These groups may strongly influence how people exercise (e.g., fitness classes), rehabilitate (cardiac and athlete rehabilitation groups), and learn motor activities (physical skill classes, music classes). In addition, we suggested that researchers explore group influences in groups that focus on physical activity during different parts of the life span, from groups for the very young (play groups) to groups for retired and older adults (masters' clubs, fitness for seniors). We also argued that the types of groups that influence an individual's physical activity are numerous, complex, and unique. Extending research to include these groups would lead to a broader view of group dynamics in physical activity. Today, we see many signs that group research in physical activity has diversified. One of the better examples of this trend is in the literature about group interventions to promote exercise adherence.

Team Building as a Way to Foster Adherence For example, Carron, Spink and Prapavessis (1997) reviewed several examples of the use of their indirect team-building (TB) strategies to develop cohesion and promote adherence to structured exercise classes for young adults. This approach was labeled indirect because the group leaders rather than the investigators directed the interventions and because the TB interventions were applied to intact groups of fitness classes. In an early study, Spink and Carron (1993) first taught the instructors in the TB condition how to use group-building strategies and then had the leaders employ the strategies when working with their participants over the course of 13 weeks. By contrast, instructors in the control condition taught their classes in their normal fashion without systematically attempting to build cohesive groups. Spink and Carron found that fitness classes randomly assigned to the TB intervention had better exercise adherence and greater perceptions of group cohesion than did classes assigned to the control condition. In subsequent investigations using the same intervention approach, Carron and Spink (1995) found reliable effects in producing greater perceptions of cohesion and satisfaction among members of young adult fitness classes (see Carron, Spink, & Prapavessis, 1997).

Among older adults, Estabrooks and Carron (1999, 2000) also used the indirect approach to conduct a TB intervention among intact seniors' exercise groups. They found promising results for increasing adherence and cohesion that were similar to the effects observed for young adults. More recently, Spink and his colleagues conducted team building among very old individuals (80 years of age and older) engaged in a structured exercise class for seniors and found that strengthening various components of group distinctiveness, structure, and process encouraged class adherence and modestly increased group cohesion (Watson, Martin Ginis, & Spink, 2004).

Groups as Agents of Individual Behavior Change Whereas Carron and Spink and colleagues used TB strategies to promote cohesion and adherence outcomes in ongoing, intact exercise groups, Brawley, Rejeski, and Lutes (2000) used a different approach to group intervention. Brawley and collaborators employed a group-mediated intervention in which they developed a group to facilitate the learning of skills that would assist home-based exercise adherence of the elderly. They compared this treatment to a wait-list control condition and to a condition in which participants received only age-appropriate exercise training in structured, instructor-led classes. The Brawley et al. intervention was based on principles of social-cognitive theory (Bandura, 1986) and group dynamics (Cartwright, 1972). The group was used as a motivational agent of change in which asymptomatic but sedentary participants learned exercise self-management skills. After practicing these skills within the group, seniors followed a schedule of increasing independent exercise at home (i.e., they practiced

being independent and then discussed successes and failures within the safe environment of their group). Participants were gradually weaned away from reliance on their group. After three months of this center-based instruction in both physical activity and self-management, the older adults then pursued their independent, self-managed exercise program for *another* three months. Compared with the control group, the group-mediated treatment participants steadily increased their volume of exercise during a following three-month, home-based period (six months). Finally, these same older adults persisted and increased their exercise frequency in comparison with both a group of older adults who had received standard exercise instruction and lifestyle counseling and a control group of apparently healthy but sedentary older adults. The older adults who received the group-mediated instruction had a much higher rate of exercise adherence than the other two groups did, particularly during the months (i.e., months six through nine) when they were completely independent of support or instruction (i.e., during a no-contact follow-up period). The results have implications for the strength of group-mediated procedures in encouraging more enduring behavior change than that produced by other individually oriented approaches.

This type of group-mediated intervention has also been used successfully in the context of cardiac rehabilitation (CRP) with older adults (Rejeski, Brawley, Ambrosius, Brubaker, Focht, Foy, et al., 2003) as well as in the context of exercise adoption among postnatal mothers (Gardner & Brawley, 2004). In the former investigation (12 months' duration), the group-mediated intervention was compared with a standard CRP exercise and lifestyle counseling intervention. Exercise adherence for older adults (age 65 and older) during the CRP (i.e., class attendance plus home-based activity during the first 3 months) was best for the group-mediated intervention that received CRP exercise therapy plus cognitive-behavioral counseling. In addition, at 12 months, after 6 months of home-based exercise and 3 months of no contact, the group-mediated intervention demonstrated superior fitness, greater frequency of independent exercise, and higher self-regulatory efficacy than the standard CRP did. Note that although the standard CRP was successful in improving initial fitness and physical function, the group-mediated intervention encouraged superior effects overall.

In the postnatal intervention context involving two months of exercise adoption (Gardner & Brawley, 2004), the group-mediated intervention was superior to a standard exercise intervention in encouraging postnatal mothers (20 to 46 years old) to (a) initiate and participate in self-managed exercise (exercise frequency) during the postnatal period (nine months postdelivery), (b) perceive achievement of immediate outcomes relevant to mothers, and (c) increase efficacy for self-managing their exercise. In this short intervention of eight weeks (four weeks of structured classes followed by four weeks of self-managed home-based exercise), the postnatal mothers in the group-mediated intervention sustained effects during the second month when they exercised on their own, whereas the mothers who completed standard exercise classes began to lose the improvements observed during the first four weeks.

What can we learn from the collective results of these team-building and group-mediated interventions? The findings tell us that groups promote interactions among their members that have powerful influences on individual exercise adherence. Furthermore, these studies illustrate that groups can encourage the kind of exercise persistence recommended to promote health and prevent disease in two different social contexts—the continuing group and individual management of exercise after a group disbands.

Carron and Spink and colleagues' work with intact and continuing groups indicates that simply being in an exercise group to participate, while convenient, does not guarantee adherence. By contrast, being in a group in which the group property of cohesion is systematically promoted around the motivational objectives of the group increases both exercise adherence and participant satisfaction. If structured group participation is the means by which people gain their exercise, a prevalent social phenomenon, then the power of the group must be developed to create conditions that maximize participant adherence.

Many groups have a defined life, such as rehabilitation groups using exercise therapy or groups led by unpaid volunteers. In addition, some individuals do not have access to groups or cannot afford long-term group membership. In these circumstances, the group must be used differently to encourage change and adherence. Brawley and Rejeski and colleagues' work uses the development of a group and group cohesion as a powerful social environment in which people learn how to exercise independently and self-manage so that they can fit regular, independent exercise into their lives. The use of the group as a social agent for learning change that leads to individual exercise adherence has a clear advantage over standard training and education programs. The use of the group simply to train and educate people without providing opportunity to practice what they will encounter after they leave the group fails to use the group as a social agent in which group members collaborate and learn from one another. Group leaders who disband training groups under the assumption that instructor-provided training and education will carry over to individual exercise adherence need only consider the 50% attrition rate in the six months that follow to know that the assumption is wrong (cf. Dishman, 1994; Meichenbaum & Turk, 1987). By contrast, when the group serves as the means of learning how to change in addition to being the venue for training, the adherence observed in the group training environment continues to occur after the group disbands and individuals must manage on their own.

Research Advances

Two issues that have received attention recently in group dynamics in sport and physical activity pertain to assessment. One of these involves testing the degree to which individual group members possess common beliefs about a group construct such as collective efficacy or group cohesion. The second is associated with the appropriate statistical analysis of data obtained from members of intact groups.

Shared Beliefs

The notion that group members share beliefs about things that matter to the group has been associated with group dynamics generally, and with cohesion specifically, for some time (Hinsz, Tindale, & Vollrath, 1997). For two of the concepts that we have discussed in this chapter, collective efficacy and cohesion, the assumption that group members share perceptions about their group's skills and abilities (i.e., collective efficacy) or about the group's unity (i.e., cohesion) is central to the concepts and their measurement. As noted earlier, a fundamental assumption of the predominant approach to thinking about and measuring cohesion is that "perceptions about the group held by a group member are a reasonable estimate of various aspects of unity characteristic of the group" (Carron et al., 1998, p. 217). Another basic assumption is that these beliefs are shared. The idea that individuals share cognition or beliefs may refer to both divisions of knowledge shared by members of a group (e.g., what other members of the offense on a football team are doing besides me) and ideas held in common (e.g., if we work hard as a team in every practice, we will achieve our team goals). In the former case, group members might have a common goal but divide the cognitive work into different areas of responsibility so that they share the workload in the group's striving toward its common goal. In the latter case, there is a commonsense notion that members of the group will share thoughts and beliefs because of common knowledge and experience. But as Cole (1991) noted, no one knows everything about his or her group or culture.

How much sharing of thoughts and beliefs occurs within groups and how much is necessary before we can say that we are studying a group-level perception versus an individual one? Some answer to this question seems necessary to validate the sharing assumption that is central to predicting how groups will respond to questions about their actions and behaviors. Obviously, we have to measure to be able to use concepts like cohesion to predict. When we measure, the normal protocol is to ask individual group members about their perceptions of cohesion. In the past, researchers have simply averaged group-member responses and defined that average as the group level of cohesion. But if individual group members do not perceive cohesion to the same extent, is it appropriate to consider an average score of all group-member responses as representative of the level of cohesion for the group? The answer to this question becomes critical to the way in which we analyze and eventually draw conclusions about the relation between the cohesion expressed by groups and group-level behavior (e.g., team performance). Thus, we must be able to demonstrate that these individual perceptions of group members represent shared beliefs about cohesion before we aggregate individual member responses to the group level.

Moritz and Watson (1998) suggested the need for strong evidence to demonstrate sharing lest we violate first principles associated with measurement of concepts like collective efficacy and cohesion. In discussing collective efficacy, they note that we need evidence that group members share judgments about their group's capabilities, and they stress that such evidence is required to aggregate individual responses to represent a group-level attribute. If this sharing index value was not reached, then the assumption was that no collective attribute for a particular group was present. They suggested that not meeting this standard would eliminate a group from the group level of analysis. Their comments were in reference to collective efficacy but would also hold for a concept like group cohesion.

These researchers were attempting to advance group dynamics research by providing a strong rule about the necessary degree of sharing in order to improve analysis at the group level. Part of their intent was to provide clarity for quantitative purposes. On their own, their suggestions seem logical and have merit. Questions arise, however, when their suggestions are considered in the light of what we know about groups and how they influence group members. If cohesion includes multiple aspects (e.g., the four aspects assessed by the GEQ) and multiple factors that can influence any of them, then Moritz and Watson's criterion of a high degree of shared beliefs as being necessary for a concept to exist would seem to be conceptually improbable and not quantitatively measurable. This important idea about extent of sharing required answers because it challenged the existence of collective group concepts and the way that we analyze in order to answer research questions.

Carron, Brawley, Eys, and colleagues (2003) attempted to provide some initial insight about extent of shared beliefs about group cohesion. They used GEQ-assessed cohesion responses from a heterogeneous sample of 192 intact teams and 2,107 athletes from different sports to describe extent of sharing in four cohesion beliefs. They used Moritz and Watson's suggestion that calculating an index of agreement would provide a quantitative indication of the degree to which members of a team shared beliefs (in this case, about cohesion). A more complete explanation about this index can be found elsewhere and is beyond the intended scope of this chapter (James, Demaree, & Wolf, 1984; Kozlowski & Hattrup, 1992). Briefly, however, the index of agreement provides a statistical measure of the degree to which a set of individuals (e.g., a team) is in consensus about a target stimulus (e.g., an item about the team's level of cohesiveness). Carron et al. (2003) examined the range and absolute magnitude of shared beliefs—the index of agreement—that was present for group cohesion in their large sample of sport teams. They also examined how the type of cohesion, the task interactive nature of the group, and the absolute level of cohesion present were related to the index of agreement exhibited for team cohesiveness.

The results showed that the absolute level of cohesion present on a team is strongly related to the average amount of consensus present. Team members are more likely to show higher consensus about their team's cohesiveness when that cohesiveness is greater. The researchers also concluded that the amount of agreement that would reflect "groupness" on a sport team might vary according to the dimension of cohesion examined. Specifically, some aspects of cohesion concern the group (i.e., GEQ measures of group integration–task and group integration–social), and others concern the individual needs that the group meets for the individual member (i.e., GEQ measures of individual attractions to the group–task and individual attractions to the group–social). Thus, what researchers might suggest as a probable degree of expected sharing of these beliefs might differ according to the type of belief. For example, greater agreement might be expected before researchers suggest that sufficient sharing on group task perceptions had occurred, whereas lesser sharing might be expected among members relative to the group's meeting individual social needs. Obviously, this issue has implications for whether the analysis of results should be at the group level or the individual level. Finally, the researchers noted that the amount of interaction demanded by a team's task appeared to be unrelated to the extent of agreement on various aspects of cohesion assessed.

Recently, Burke, Carron et al. (2005) examined the notion of shared beliefs among members of exercise classes to investigate the question of whether members of these classes shared views of their cohesiveness in a manner characteristic of true groups (i.e., versus ad hoc collections of individuals). They obtained responses from 1,700 participants in 130 classes. The average class size was 12 participants, and the age range of the participants was from 19 to 84 years. With the exception of one of four dimensions of cohesion on the GEQ, all index of agreement values were moderate to high, regardless of the type of cohesion measure used. In addition, the investigators found sufficient between-group variability differences to support the conclusion that members of exercise classes perceive their group's cohesiveness in a manner unique from other groups. When the investigators considered both the extent of shared beliefs (i.e., index of agreement values) and unique group variability, they concluded that exercise classes are true groups.

The importance of the descriptive research in both large-sample studies lies in the implications that they have for examining shared beliefs. A gold standard criterion value for the index of agreement may not be necessary. Understanding degree of agreement as another means of interpreting group data is more important than using it to eliminate teams or other physical activity groups from an analysis. The latter action could produce selective samples and eliminate intact groups that share less but stick together nevertheless. The implication is that we would not understand processes in these

eliminated groups that prevent them from being on the same page but at the same time allow them to stick together in cohesive fashion. Dion (2000) has noted that cohesiveness means different things for different groups with different goals and tasks. Thus, we still have much to learn about shared beliefs in physical activity groups and sport teams.

The Group and the Individual as the Unit of Analysis

For years, an important question in the study of group dynamics has concerned the use of the appropriate unit of analysis. Should it be the individual or the group? Group investigators are still wrestling with this question. Elsewhere, we (Carron, Brawley, & Widmeyer, 1998) suggested three criteria, both conceptual and empirical, to help investigators choose the appropriate level of analysis. The first criterion concerned the question being asked. For example, the individual can be used as the unit of analysis if the question involves the relationship between individual group-member satisfaction and individual need for affiliation. The second criterion involved the type of theory being tested. If the theory concerns social influence within groups, the group could be used as the unit of analysis. The third criterion concerned the statistical nature of the data. In this case, perhaps both group and individual levels might provide information of interest. Consider the following point.

A statistical consideration that cannot be ignored is that individual team-member responses are nested within their groups. That is, in real groups, individual responses are interdependent and reflect group influences. This circumstance presents a case of statistical nonindependence. A statistical dilemma in group research is that traditionally used analysis procedures such as ANOVA proceed from the assumption that observations are independent; thus, individual effects are analyzed and group effects are ignored. The consequence of violating this assumption is that estimates of error are biased because group effects make the scores of members more similar than different if a true group effect (i.e., cohesion) is present.

In past group dynamics research in sport, few studies have acknowledged the multilevel nature of the data in which team members are nested within teams. Data have been typically analyzed at the individual level. To avoid overlooking either individual or group effects when examining groups, investigators should consider alternative approaches to the analysis of group data.

Kenny and LaVoie (1985) have suggested methods allowing investigators the strategy of simultaneously studying the group and the individual. Moritz and Watson (1998) have discussed multiple ways of performing this analysis. One of their suggestions is to use a technique called multilevel modeling (MLM). This technique allows the examination of hierarchically structured data, in which a hierarchy consists of lower-level observations (i.e., individual players) nested within higher-level units such as teams (Kreft & de Leeuw, 2002). Advocates of MLM (Raudenbush & Bryk, 2002) suggest this type of modeling of data because it accounts for the dependence among responses within teams when examining relationships that involve some type of nesting. MLM can also provide information on both individual-level and group-level influence if both types of information are useful in answering research questions pertaining to groups. In this case, a choice between units of analysis is not necessary if both types can help answer the research question of interest.

As an example, consider a recent study by Spink, Nickel, Wilson, and Odnokon, (in press). Using multilevel modeling, they chose to examine the relationship between team cohesion and team task satisfaction in 10 ice-hockey teams (194 players). They argued that these measures might well be related at two different levels and both types of variation might account for the relationship. Their results revealed that team task cohesion predicted variance in team task satisfaction at both the individual (33%) and team (55%) levels. Thus, athletes on a team who have similar, shared cohesion beliefs (i.e., group integration–task) reflect a high degree of groupness, which predicted the group variance in perceptions of team satisfaction. But individuals on teams provide a certain amount of unique variability in their responses to each set of questions about their group. The fact that both concepts were also related at the individual level argues that some individual variability in both measures is correlated. If the research question is to account for as much variance as possible through a predictive model and to identify the sources of that variation by taking into account both the interdependency of players and the uniqueness in their individual responses, then the researcher can do this using MLM procedures. The finding that cohesion variables predicted team task satisfaction at both the individual and group level suggests that decisions about whether to analyze at the individual versus group level may not be a simple either–or decision, as it often has been in the past (cf. Florin, Giamartino, Kenny, & Wandersman, 1990, for a discussion of this issue).

Future Research Directions

The future research opportunities that can be found in the dynamics of physical activity groups are challenging. In the previous edition of this book, we asked whether future investigators would attempt to meet the challenge. We suggested that their first approach might be to move our research beyond description by attempting to answer related research questions of increasingly greater complexity. The second approach that we suggested was to conduct systematic and theoretically driven research that addressed the functions of sport groups and thus would further our understanding of function-driven group behavior. Have these suggestions received research attention?

Moving Beyond Description

Although description is an important aspect of science, it is still the major source of evidence about sport group dynamics. But we have begun to move toward answering a three-generation hierarchy of research questions (see Carron, 1988; Zanna & Fazio, 1982). The first and simplest generation of research question is whether a relationship exists between two variables. For example, does a relationship exist between cohesion and team performance? What are its strength, direction, and reliability? As outlined earlier, we have many answers to this first-generation question. But whether this relationship occurs for all types of teams, for both genders, and for all types of conditions that might influence the variables studied is not always known. Seeking this information leads us to the second generation of research question.

Accordingly, the second-generation question is one that encourages an examination of conditions moderating a relationship. For example, task cohesion might relate to performance in team sports but not in coactive sports. When the answers to these two generations of questions are provided, the boundaries of the phenomenon are better known and may be placed within some potential theoretical framework (see Carron, 1988). It is gratifying to see that research of this nature is now regularly taking place in sport and exercise, as reflected in a number of the examples outlined earlier in this chapter.

Explanations for why these boundaries occur are still tentative, however, unless we ask and answer the third-generation question: What are the causes of the relationships observed in the first- and second-generation evidence? For example, task cohesion may influence team performance because team members perceive coordination interdependence as a requirement for success and demanded by their task (e.g., basketball). Conversely, no great influence of cohesion on performance is observed for coactive teams. These athletes do not perceive its necessity, and task completion does not require team member interaction (e.g., bowling). Fortunately, studies that attempt to detect mediators of a relationship have been conducted (e.g., Beauchamp et al., 2002; Loughead & Carron, 2004). Only by considering answers to the three generations of research questions can we gain understanding of the cohesion–performance relationship and make progress toward a theory.

Expanding Existing Research

Although numerous issues require attention, we do not wish to encourage an asystematic approach to their study. Instead we suggest systematic and theoretically driven initiatives that investigate the different functions of physical activity groups. As one example, McGrath (1984) identified three broad categories of group functions. These functions concern groups as systems that perform tasks, structures that organize social interaction, and mechanisms that deliver social influence. Thus, hypotheses and interpretations about a future research issue would be stated relative to the group function. The following example illustrates how this approach can be productive.

If a group functions as a means of organizing social influence interactions that promote training or rehabilitation, how are member roles and communication organized, or how are they used for intervention? The previously reported studies of team building and use of the group as an agent of behavior change offer examples about how steps can be applied to make the social influence function of groups systematically effective in promoting exercise adherence. Also, the degree and type of social influence (e.g., through a collaborative or prescriptive group leader or interventionist) that is promoted or inhibited could provide clues about the member beliefs that are developed, whether or not these beliefs are shared. Social satisfaction and type of member motivation (i.e., collective or self-efficacy) may be issues related to this function.

Continuing with this example, if the team functions as a powerful social influence over, for example, the efforts of members, do its normative rules bias their thinking (a possible negative effect)? The research of James Hardy and his colleagues is illustrative here (Hardy, Eys, & Carron, 2005). They had athletes advance possible disadvantages of high task cohesion on a team. Some athletes "expressed concern that high task cohesion could lead to a general team atmosphere that was incompatible with their interests" (Hardy et al., 2005, p. 181). The issues of conformity and group attributions are obviously related to this function. Does the degree of team unity exert a normative influence on members in the direction of either a realistic or a false sense of team confidence? The notion of group efficacy would be studied as part of this function.

In summary, the present chapter has attempted to provide an overview of some of the constructs and theoretical propositions that form the basis for group dynamics in sport. We were certainly able to discuss considerably more in this third edition than we could in the previous two. More important, perhaps, we were able to present some conceptual (theoretical) models advanced to account for various aspects of the dynamics of sport teams. This should not be surprising. As Sir Arthur Conan Doyle (1989) had his main character, Sherlock Holmes, point out, "[When you don't have data] it is a capital mistake to theorise . . . insensibly one begins to twist facts to suit theories, instead of theories to suit facts" (p. 119). Data on group dynamics in sport are accumulating at an impressive rate. Thus, we should expect scholars in the field to advance theories to account for the patterns in those data. We hope that in a fourth edition of *Advances in Sport Psychology*, we will be able to report on even more theorizing.

CHAPTER 11

Coaching Effectiveness in the Sport Domain

Thelma S. Horn, PhD

Research in the coaching effectiveness area has been conducted under the general assumption that coaches exert a large influence not only on the performance and behavior of their athletes but also on the athletes' psychological and emotional well-being. In this research context, leadership has been rather generally conceived of as "the behavioral process of influencing individuals and groups toward set goals" (Barrow, 1977, p. 232). Obviously, this broad definition encompasses many dimensions of coaches' leadership behavior, including the goals and objectives that they set for themselves and their athletes, the processes that they use to make decisions, the types of learning activities that they employ in practice situations, the type and frequency of feedback that they give in response to athletes' performances, the techniques that they use to motivate or discipline individual athletes, and the type of relationship that they establish with athletes.

Most of the research that has been conducted in the coaching effectiveness area within the last three decades has been motivated by a desire to identify the particular coaching characteristics, competencies, cognitions, practice strategies and techniques, leadership styles, or behavioral patterns that are most effective. Under this research approach, coaching effectiveness is typically operationalized in terms of outcome scores or measures. That is, effective coaching is defined as that which results in either successful performance outcomes (measured either in terms of win–loss percentages, individual player development, or success at the national or international level) or positive psychological responses on the part of the athletes (e.g., high perceived ability, high self-esteem, intrinsic motivational orientation, or high levels of sport enjoyment and satisfaction). Because the text as a whole focuses on psychological issues as they relate to sport, the review and analysis of the literature in this chapter is primarily limited to those studies that have examined the effect of coaches' behavior on the psychosocial growth and development of athletes. Thus, the chapter does not include a review of the research that has examined the relationship between coaches' behavior and athletes' sport performance and skill learning. Interested readers should consult the literature in sport pedagogy and motor learning.

Despite the number of studies that have been conducted over the last three decades to examine the effects of coaches' behavior on athletes' psychosocial responses, much remains to be done. Therefore, the dual purpose of this chapter is (a) to review the available research and theory pertaining to coaching effectiveness in sport settings and (b) to provide specific directions for future research in this area. This chapter begins with a discussion of the various conceptual approaches that researchers have used in their quest to identify the correlates of coaching effectiveness. The second section of the chapter consists of a review of the current research on coaching effectiveness. The third, and final, section contains a discussion of the current gaps in our knowledge base combined with recommendations for future research in the coaching effectiveness area.

Conceptual Approaches

Although the research studies conducted in the coaching effectiveness area over the past several decades have shared a common purpose or goal (i.e., the identification of effective coaching characteristics, competencies, cognitions, behaviors or leadership styles), the studies themselves have varied considerably in the methodologies used to measure coaching behavior and in the conceptual basis underlying the study of coaching effectiveness. This section offers a brief review of the different conceptual approaches to coaching or leadership effectiveness. These approaches are categorized into two groups: those based on theoretical models and those that use a more grounded theory approach to the study of coaching effectiveness.

Theoretically Based Research

Much of the coaching effectiveness research conducted over the past couple of decades has been guided by one of several theoretical models that have been proffered in the literature. These models include those proposed by Chelladurai (1978, 1990, 2007), Smoll and Smith (1989), and, more recently, by Mageau and Vallerand (2003). These theoretically based models are briefly reviewed in the following paragraphs.

Chelladurai (1978, 1990, 2007) constructed his multidimensional model of leadership to provide a framework for the specification and identification of effective leadership behavior in specific sport situations. Specifically, Chelladurai proposed that leadership effectiveness could be multidimensionally measured in terms of performance outcomes and member satisfaction. The particular leadership behaviors that will produce such desired outcomes are a function of three interacting aspects of leader behavior. These include the actual behavior exhibited by the coach or leader, the type of leader behavior preferred by the athletes, and the type of leader behavior appropriate to or required in that situational context. Each of these constructs is, in turn, driven by corresponding antecedent factors or conditions. Specifically, characteristics of the athletes themselves (e.g., age, gender, skill level, psychological characteristics) and factors within the situation (e.g., organizational expectations, social norms, cultural values) will primarily determine the type of leader behaviors that the athletes prefer their coaches to exhibit. In addition, the actual behavior exhibited by a coach or leader will be a direct function of her or his personal characteristics (e.g., gender, age, years of experience, psychological characteristics), situationally shaped requirements for coaches' behavior (e.g., sport competitive level), and the preferences of the individual athletes. Finally, certain aspects of the particular sport situation (e.g., type of sport, program structure, organizational goals, sociocultural environment) and the characteristics of the team members will determine the behaviors required by the situation.

To put the model as a whole into perspective, Chelladurai (1978, 1990, 2007) hypothesized that the positive outcomes of group performance and member satisfaction on the part of the athletes can be obtained if congruence between the three aspects of leader behavior is present. That is, if the coach exhibits the leadership behaviors that are dictated for the particular situation and that are consistent with the preferences or desires of the members, then optimal performance and member satisfaction will be achieved. In more recent writings, Chelladurai has added feedback loops that suggest that a coach's actual behavior may be influenced by his or her athletes' level of satisfaction as well as their performance. Thus, a reciprocal relationship exists between the consequences of the coaches' behavior and the type of behaviors that they will actually exhibit in practice and game contexts.

Smoll and Smith (1989) proposed the mediational model of leadership, which emphasizes relationships among situational, cognitive, behavioral, and individual difference variables. Similar to Chelladurai (1978, 1990, 2007), Smoll and Smith incorporated a situational approach to leadership behavior in their argument that the coaching behaviors that are most effective will vary as a function of situational factors within the athletic context (e.g., nature of the sport, level of competition). Smoll and Smith also argued, however, that "a truly comprehensive model of leadership requires that consideration be given not only to situational factors and overt behaviors, but

also the cognitive processes and individual difference variables which mediate relationships between antecedents, leader behaviors, and outcomes" (p. 1532). Thus, Smoll and Smith's cognitive-mediational model proposes that the effects of coaches' behaviors on their athletes are mediated not only by situational factors but also by the meaning that the athletes attribute to those coaching behaviors.

As indicated in Smoll and Smith's (1989) cognitive-mediational model, coaches' behavior is influenced by, or is a function of, both their own personal characteristics (e.g., coaching goals and motives, behavioral intentions) as well as by situational factors (nature of the sport, level of competition). Additionally, the behaviors that the coach exhibits in practices and games are interpreted by players in individualized ways. That is, players' interpretations and evaluation of the coaches' behaviors are influenced by, or are a function of, their personal characteristics (e.g., age, sex, competitive trait anxiety), and, again, situational factors (e.g., nature of the sport, level of competition).

Recently, Mageau and Vallerand (2003) presented the motivational model of the coach–athlete relationship. This model incorporates Vallerand's (2001) hierarchical perspective on intrinsic and extrinsic motivation as well as Deci and Ryan's (1985) cognitive-evaluation theory. As the Mageau and Vallerand model illustrates, three factors (coach's personal orientation, the coaching context, and the coach's perceptions of the athletes' behavior and motivation) affect or determine the degree to which the coach employs or exhibits autonomy-supportive behaviors toward and with her or his athletes. The coach's autonomy-supportive behaviors, in combination with the structure instilled by the coach and the coach's level of involvement with her or his athletes, affects or determines the athletes' perceptions of competence, autonomy, and relatedness. These three athlete perceptions, in turn, affect or determine athletes' level of intrinsic and self-determined extrinsic motivation. According to this model, then, the critical elements of effective coaching behavior are those that support athletes' perceptions of autonomy (autonomy-supportive behaviors) but also provide structure for athletes in the sport setting (e.g., setting of guidelines, limits, standards) and show involvement in athletes' welfare (e.g., encouragement, emotional support).

In their presentation and discussion of this motivational model, Mageau and Vallerand (2003) identified personal, social, and contextual variables that may affect both the coach's behavior and the coach–athlete relationship. These variables include the three antecedents of the coach's behavior: the coach's personal orientation (controlling versus autonomy-supportive interpersonal style), the coaching context (e.g., level of competition, external pressure on the coach to win or perform well), and the athletes' behavior and motivation (i.e., coach's perception of individual athletes' temperament, talent, level of motivation).

Besides the three models described in the previous paragraphs, a few other theoretically based perspectives on coaching effectiveness have also been offered. These include Duda's (2001) model that incorporates elements from both the mediational model of leadership (Smoll & Smith, 1989) and the multidimensional model of leadership (Chelladurai, 1978, 1990, 2007) and also include constructs from achievement goal theory (Ames, 1992a; Dweck, 1999; Nicholls, 1984, 1989) to provide a more mechanistic perspective as to how and why coaching behaviors affect athletes' psychosocial growth and development. In addition, Sophia Jowett and her colleagues (Jowett, 2005; Jowett & Cockerill, 2002; Jowett & Meek, 2000) have offered the "3Cs" (closeness, commitment, and complementarity) model, and, more recently, the 3+1Cs (coorientation) model to describe and investigate the quality of the coach–athlete interpersonal relationship. The importance and relevance of examining interpersonal relationships in sport (e.g., coach–athlete, parent–athlete, coach–parent) has also been demonstrated or advocated by other writers and researchers (e.g., Gould, Guinan, Greenleaf, & Chung, 2002; LaVoi, 2005; Poczwardowski, Barott, & Jowett, 2006). In particular, LaVoi (2005) has argued for the use of relational cultural theory in examining the coach–athlete relationship. Finally, the transformational leadership model (Bass, 1999), which was developed and tested in nonsport settings (e.g., industry, military, education), has also been used by a few writers (e.g., Vealey, 2005) to address effective leadership in sport contexts. Moreover, Chelladurai (2007) has recently discussed the inclusion of elements of the transformational leadership perspective into his multidimensional model. Although the transformational leadership model has yet to be extensively tested in its applicability to the study of coaching effectiveness, it appears to have promise (see, for example, recent studies by Charbonneau, Barling, & Kelloway, 2001; Rowold, 2006; and Vallee & Bloom, 2005).

Grounded Theory Research

A number of studies have been conducted over the last decade using a qualitative or heuristic approach to explore a variety of dimensions of effective coaching. These studies have not only used different methodological procedures (e.g., in-depth interviews, field observation, videotaping, document analysis, and other ethnographic techniques) than those used in the previously reported theoretically derived and primarily quantitative studies but also have focused on different aspects of the coaching experience. Some researchers in this area have, for example, conducted in-depth interviews or collected observational data with expert or successful coaches to identify the characteristics, behaviors, cognitions, or actions that they exhibit or use in practice and competitive contexts (e.g., Bloom, Durand-Bush, & Salmela, 1997; Gould, Collins, Lauer, & Chung, 2007; Hardin & Bennett, 2002; Vallee & Bloom, 2005). Other researchers have begun focusing on the processes by which expert or talented coaches have acquired their expertise or developed their coaching behaviors, styles, and decision-making skills (e.g., Bloom, Durand-Bush, Schinke, & Salmela, 1998; Gilbert, Cote, & Mallett, in press; Werthner & Trudel, 2006). The results of such research studies are particularly useful in providing information about how coaching education programs can or should be structured to develop expertise and competence in novice coaches.

From a somewhat more cognitive perspective, some researchers have used qualitative procedures to identify the cognitions, thoughts, beliefs, or perceptions that coaches have before or during practice or competitive events and how they use such cognitions or thoughts to guide their actions or behaviors in actual field situations (e.g., Gilbert & Trudel, 2004a; Gilbert, Trudel, & Haughian, 1999). Along the same lines, Jean Cote and his colleagues (e.g., Cote & Salmela, 1996; Cote, Salmela, & Russell, 1995; Cote, Salmela, Trudel, Baria, & Russell, 1995) have conducted several qualitative studies designed to obtain information about how expert coaches think and act as they prepare for their seasons and then design and conduct their practice and competitive events so as to develop successful and competent athletes. As part of this line of research, Cote, Salmela, Trudel, et al. (1995) have proposed a coaching model that provides a framework for identifying and understanding how coaches approach their work and how and why they make the training and competitive decisions that they do. Saury and his colleagues (e.g., d'Arripe-Longueville, Saury, Fournier, & Durand, 2001; Saury & Durand, 1998) have used an ergonomic approach to the study of coaching effectiveness. In particular, d'Arripe-Longueville et al. used a course of action perspective to examine the collective actions exhibited by both coaches and athletes as they worked together in the sport setting. These ergonomic research approaches are characterized by the point of view that "cognition (or action) must be studied in situ and that the points of view of actors have to be considered" (p. 277).

Obviously, the research studies conducted to examine the correlates of coaching effectiveness have used a variety of conceptual and methodological approaches. This variety certainly can and should contribute to the richness of the information now available. The results of this wide array of research studies are reviewed in the following section of this chapter.

Working Model of Coaching Effectiveness

Given the variability in the conceptual and methodological approaches to coaching effectiveness described in the previous section, a review of this disparate literature would be difficult without use of an organizing framework. The framework that will

be used in this chapter is diagrammed in figure 11.1. This framework provides a comprehensive working model that specifies an outline of the antecedent factors that affect or determine the coach's behavior as well as the way in which the coach's behavior can affect the performance and psychosocial growth and development of the athletes. This working model incorporates elements of the theoretical models described in the previous section as well as elements from several other theoretical models from the developmental and social-cognitive literatures (see list in table 11.1) that describe the processes by which children, adolescents, and young adults form self-perceptions, social perceptions, and motivational orientations.

Although the working model depicted in figure 11.1 may initially appear complex, three major points can summarize it. First, consistent with both Chelladurai's (1978, 1990, 2007) and Smoll & Smith's (1989) models of leadership effectiveness, the current working model emphasizes that coaches' behavior in athletic contexts (e.g., games, practices) does not occur in a vacuum. Rather, identifiable antecedent

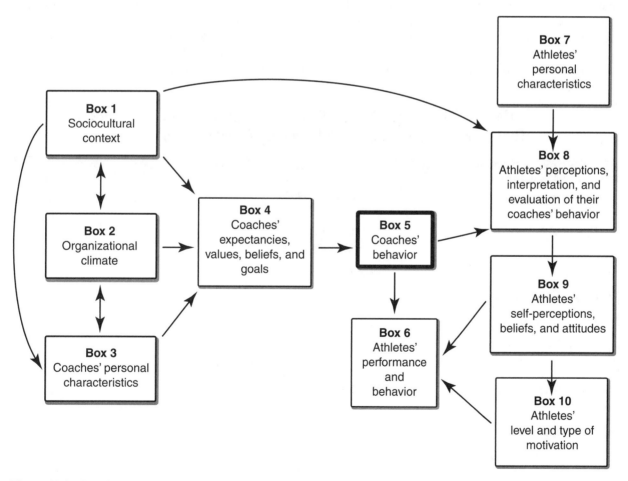

Figure 11.1 A working model of coaching effectiveness.

factors lead up to, or explain, the types of behaviors that coaches will exhibit in sport settings. These antecedent factors are illustrated in the left side of the model (boxes 1 through 5). Similar to Chelladurai's and Smoll and Smith's models, such factors as the sociocultural context (box 1), the organizational climate (box 2), and the coaches' own personal characteristics (box 3) can combine to determine the behaviors that the coach will exhibit (box 5). But based on research and theory in the social-cognitive literature (see table 11.1), this working model also proposes that the effects of these three factors (boxes 1 through 3) on the coaches' behavior (box 5) may be, at least in part, mediated through the coaches' expectancies, values, beliefs, and goals (box 4).

The second major point about the working model is that the coaches' behavior in practices and games exerts not only a direct effect on the athletes' performance and behavior (i.e., the hypothesized link between boxes 5 and 6) but also an indirect effect. This indirect effect is illustrated in the right side of the model (boxes 5 and 7 through 10). Specifically, consistent with Smoll and Smith's (1989) theoretical model, the current working model also specifies that the meaning that the athletes attach to the coaches' behavior mediates the indirect effects of the coaches' behavior on athletes' performance and behavior. That is, this model proposes that athletes may perceive or interpret the coaches' behavior in individualized ways. These individualized perceptions of the coaches' behavior are what actually affect the athletes' self-perceptions, beliefs, and attitudes (e.g., their self-confidence, perceptions of competence, self-esteem, attributional beliefs). In turn, such self-perceptions, beliefs, and attitudes affect the athletes' motivation (box 10) as well as their performance and behavior (box 6).

The third point regarding this working model is that it clearly specifies, similar to the models of Chelladurai (1978, 1990, 2007) and Smoll and Smith (1989), that the effectiveness of different types of coaching behaviors will be mediated by both situational and individual difference variables. Specifically, a variety of sport contextual variables (e.g., competitive level, type of sport) and athlete variables (e.g., age, skill level) mediate the direct link between the coaches' behavior and the athletes' performance and behavior. Similarly, athletes' personal characteristics (e.g., age, gender, psychological traits and dispositions) and the sociocultural context mediate, or influence, athletes' perceptions and interpretations of their coaches' behavior. Thus, as these aspects of the working model indicate, we can no longer assume that one set of coaching behaviors will be effective for all athletes and in all sport situations. Rather, we should recognize that effective coaching behaviors will vary as a function of the athlete and the sport context.

Table 11.1 Relevant Theoretical Perspectives From the Nonsport Literature That May Inform Research on Coaching Effectiveness

Theory or model	References
Achievement goal theories	Ames (1992a, 1992b)
	Dweck (1986, 1999)
	Elliot (1999)
	Nicholls (1984, 1989)
Attribution theory	Weiner (1986, 1992)
Perceived control theories	Skinner (1995, 1996)
Competence motivation theory	Harter (1981, 1999)
Expectancy-value model	Eccles (2005)
	Eccles, Wigfield, & Schiefele (1998)
Self-determination theory	Deci & Ryan (1985)
	Ryan & Deci (2000)
Self-efficacy theory	Bandura (1986, 1997)
Relational cultural theory	Jordan, Kaplan, Miller, Stiver, & Surrey (1991)
	Miller & Stiver (1997)

As illustrated in figure 11.1, the cornerstone of the working model on coaching effectiveness is the box labeled coaches' behavior (box 5). The primary assumption underlying the research on coaching effectiveness is that the coaches' behavior can have a significant effect on athletes' performance as well as their psychological or emotional well-being. This influence can, of course, be either positive or negative. Thus, the review of the research on coaching effectiveness begins with a discussion concerning the construct of coaches' behavior.

Coaches' Behavior

A review of the literature on coaching effectiveness reveals that a number of different methodologies and instruments are used to assess coaching behavior. These instruments or methodologies can be divided into three categories: questionnaires, observational measures, and interviews. In the following sections, examples of instruments within each of these categories are identified and briefly discussed.

Coaching Behavior Questionnaires

Researchers have developed a variety of questionnaire or survey instruments to assess aspects or dimensions of coaches' leadership styles or behaviors (see table 11.2). Many of these instruments were developed based on theoretical approaches to coaching effectiveness. For example, Chelladurai and Saleh (1978, 1980) developed the Leadership Scale for Sports (LSS) to measure a broad spectrum of leadership behaviors. The LSS consists of five subscales, two of which measure the coach's decision-making style (democratic and autocratic), two of which measure the coach's motivational tendencies (social support and positive feedback), and one that measures the coach's instructional behavior (training and instruction). Since its inception, the LSS has been subjected to a number of statistical and methodological procedures to assess its psychometric properties (see summary of this work in Chelladurai, 2007; Chelladurai & Riemer, 1998). Although these procedures have generally provided support for the reliability and validity of the LSS, Chelladurai (2007) and Chelladurai and Riemer (1998) do note some concerns that remain with regard to some of the subscales and identify suggestions for future psychometric testing and instrument revision (e.g., the autocratic subscale may need to be divided into two or more separate subscales). In addition, some researchers (e.g., Price

& Weiss, 2000; Zhang, Jensen & Mann, 1997) have modified the LSS in an effort to increase the reliability and validity of the instrument.

Another instrument that has been used to a great extent in the coaching effectiveness literature is the Perceived Motivational Climate in Sport Questionnaire–2 (PMCSQ–2) (Newton, Duda, & Yin, 2000). This instrument was developed to measure the type of motivational climate coaches create in practices and competitive events. The PMCSQ–2 consists of a set of items that ask individual respondents to indicate the degree to which their team climate is characterized by a task-involving (mastery-oriented) or an ego-involving (performance-oriented) goal perspective. The items in the scale have been found to be hierarchically ordered into two first-order factors (a task-involving, or mastery-oriented, team climate and an ego-involving, or performance-oriented, team climate) and six subscales (three subsumed under each of the two first-order factors) (Newton et al., 2000). A task-involving (mastery-oriented) team climate is characterized by perceptions among athletes that trying hard will be rewarded and that all players have an important role to fill and thus will be encouraged by the coach. In contrast, in an ego-involving (performance-oriented) climate, athletes perceive that teammates try to outdo each other, players are punished for their mistakes, and individual recognition is limited to a few stars. The PMCSQ–2, as well as its earlier versions, was developed based on a strong theoretical and empirical research base, and has been subjected to numerous procedures to test its reliability and validity (see summary and analyses of these procedures provided by Duda, 2001; Duda and Whitehead, 1998; Newton et al., 2000; Ntoumanis & Biddle, 1999).

Pelletier and his colleagues (Pelletier, Fortier, Vallerand, & Briere, 2002) have developed and used a questionnaire that measures athletes' perceptions of their coaches' interpersonal behaviors. This scale (adapted from one used by Pelletier, Tuson, & Haddad, 1997, and Pelletier & Vallerand, 1996) asks athletes to rate their coaches' behavior toward them using eight items designed to assess coaches' autonomy-supportive behaviors (i.e., coaches' tendencies to exhibit respect for athletes' desire and choice) and coaches' controlling behaviors (i.e., coaches' tendencies to exhibit coercive behaviors). Pelletier et al. (2002) reported acceptable estimates of the internal consistency of the two subscales. In addition, they found both subscales to be significantly predictive of athletes' level and type of motivation. Thus, this scale appears to provide a good measure of two of the components or dimensions of effective coaching

Table 11.2   Instruments to Measure Coaching Behavior: Questionnaires

Instrument	What it measures	Subscales or scale components	Relevant references
Leadership Scale for Sports (LSS)	Dimensions of leader behavior Note: Three versions have been developed to measure (a) athletes' preferences for different types of coaching behavior, (b) athletes' perceptions of their coaches' behavior, and (c) coaches' self-evaluation of their own behavior.	1. Autocratic behavior 2. Democratic behavior 3. Training and instruction behavior 4. Positive feedback behavior 5. Social support behavior	Chelladurai & Saleh (1978, 1980) Chelladurai & Riemer (1998) Zhang, Jensen, & Mann (1997)
Decision-style questionnaires	How coaches make decisions in sport contexts Note: Different versions have been developed to assess athletes' perceptions of their coaches' style and coaches' perceptions of their own style.	Range of decision-making styles (e.g., autocratic, consultative, participative, delegative) that reflect degree to which the coach allows athletes to participate in the decision-making process.	Chelladurai & Arnott (1985) Chelladurai & Quek (1991)
Perceived Motivational Climate in Sport Questionnaire–2 (PMCSQ–2)	Athletes' perceptions of the motivational climate that their coaches initiate or create in practice and game contexts Note: See Harwood et al. (2005) for motivational climate scale more applicable to individual sports.	Each of two higher-order factors—task-involving climate and ego-involving climate—has three subscales.	Newton, Duda, & Yin (2000) Duda & Whitehead (1998) Harwood, Smith, & Treasure (2005)
Coaches' interpersonal behavioral style	Athletes' perceptions of their coaches' interpersonal behaviors toward and with them	1. Autonomy-supportive interpersonal style 2. Controlling interpersonal style	Pelletier, Tuson, & Haddad (1997) Pelletier & Vallerand (1996) Pelletier, Fortier, Vallerand, & Briere (2002)
Coaching Behavior Questionnaire (CBQ)	Athletes' perceptions and evaluative reactions to both positive and negative coaching behaviors	1. Negative activation 2. Supportiveness and emotional composure	Kenow & Williams (1992, 1999) Williams et al. (2003)
Greek Coach–Athlete Relationship Questionnaire (GrCART–Q)	Coaches' and athletes' direct perspective of their interpersonal relationship Note: A modified GrCART–Q2 has also been developed to assess athletes' and coaches' metaperspective of the coach–athlete relationship.	1. Closeness 2. Commitment 3. Complementarity	Jowett & Ntoumanis (2003) Jowett (2006)
Coaching Behaviour Scale for Sport (CBS–S)	Coaching behaviors exhibited in training, competitive, and organizational settings	Seven dimensions of coaching behavior (e.g., physical training and planning, goal setting, personal rapport)	Cote, Yardley, Hay, Sedgwick, & Baker (1999) Mallett & Cote (2006)
Multifactor Leadership Questionnaire (MLQ–5X)	Individuals' perceptions of their leaders' attributes, behaviors, and leadership styles	Nine leadership factors composed of five transformational factors, three transactional factors, and one non-leadership or laissez-faire factor	Avolio & Bass (2004) Rowold (2006)
Questionnaires based on the CBAS (e.g., CFQ, CBAS–PBS)	Athletes' perceptions of their coaches' behavior Note: A modified version can be used to assess coaches' perceptions of their own behavior.	Twelve or 13 CBAS categories that can be reduced to a smaller number of factor scores	Smith, Smoll, & Curtis (1978) Cumming, Smith, & Smoll (2006) Amorose & Horn (2000) Smith, Fry, Ethington, & Li (2005)

behavior as specified in the Mageau and Vallerand (2003) motivational model.

A more limited number of research studies have used the remaining questionnaires identified in table 11.2. But these scales may be valuable to future researchers who are interested in examining aspects or dimensions of coaching behavior different from those found in the commonly used instruments.

Coaching Behavior Observation Systems

A second major approach to the measurement of coaching behavior involves the assessment of such behavior in actual practice and game contexts either directly or by using videotaped sequences of the coach's behavior. Trained observers conduct this assessment using a systematic observation and recording device (see list provided in table 11.3). The most commonly used instrument in this category is the Coaching Behavior Assessment System (CBAS) (Smith, Smoll, & Hunt, 1977), which was developed and validated over a period of several years. The CBAS provides a direct, observationally based assessment of 12 categories of coaching behavior. The 12 empirically derived categories can be broadly classified into reactive and spontaneous coaching behaviors. Reactive behaviors are those that a coach exhibits in response to a variety of player behaviors. Specifically, the CBAS allows for two coaching responses to a player's desirable or successful performances (reinforcement and non-reinforcement) and five coaching responses to a player's performance errors or mistakes (mistake-contingent encouragement, mistake-contingent technical instruction, punishment, punitive technical instruction, and ignoring mistakes). In addition, the CBAS specifies one coaching response (keeping control behaviors) to player misbehaviors. In the spontaneous coaching behavior category, the CBAS provides for four types of coaching behaviors: spontaneous general technical instruction (not given in response to a particular player performance attempt), spontaneous general encouragement, team organizational

Table 11.3 Instruments to Measure Coaching Behavior: Observational Systems

Instrument	What it measures	Coding categories	Relevant references
Coaching Behavior Assessment System (CBAS)	Coaches' overt leadership behaviors during both practices and competitive events Note: CBAS can be used to assess coaches' behaviors in general or coaches' behaviors toward individual athletes.	Twelve or 13 coding categories divided into reactive and spontaneous coaching behaviors	Smith, Smoll, & Hunt (1977) Smith & Smoll (1990) Smith, Smoll, & Christensen (1996) Horn (1984, 1985) Coatsworth & Conroy (2006)
Arizona State University Observation Instrument (ASUOI)	Coaches' instructional and other behaviors in practice settings	Fourteen categories of coaching behavior, seven of which are directly related to instruction	Lacy & Darst (1984) Cushion & Jones (2001) Darst, Zakrajsek, & Mancini (1989) Brewer & Jones (2002)
Coaching Behavior Recording Form	Coaches' behavior in practices and competitive events	Ten to 12 categories of coaching behavior including performance feedback, instruction, encouragement, and modeling	Tharp & Gallimore (1976) Darst et al. (1989) Bloom, Crumpton, & Anderson (1999) Gallimore & Tharp (2004)
Coach Analysis Instrument (CAI)	Coaches' verbal behavior	Computer-based system that uses hierarchical form of event recording so that coaches' comments can be analyzed at up to five levels: direction, focus, timing, delivery, and emphasis. Note: An appropriateness level can be added.	Franks, Johnson, & Sinclair (1988) More & Franks (1996)

behaviors, and game-irrelevant general communication. Smith and his colleagues (Smith et al., 1977) conducted extensive procedures to document the reliability and validity of the CBAS. Furthermore, the recommended training procedures for data collection are extensive and rigorous. An analysis of the psychometric properties of the CBAS can be found in recent chapters by Chelladurai (2007) and Chelladurai and Riemer (1998).

Although the CBAS was originally developed as an observationally based instrument, it has been adapted into questionnaire form (see last entry in table 11.2). These adapted questionnaires are based on either all 12 (or 13) of the CBAS behavioral categories (e.g., Cumming, Smith, & Smoll, 2006; Smith, Smoll, & Curtis, 1978) or only the reactive feedback behavioral categories (e.g., Allen & Howe, 1998; Amorose & Horn, 2000; Black & Weiss, 1992; Smith, Fry, Ethington, & Li, 2005). These questionnaires appear useful for the assessment of coaching behaviors in studies using large samples of athletes. However, only initial estimates of the reliability and validity of these questionnaire versions of the CBAS have so far been provided.

Although the CBAS is one of the most frequently used systematic observation instruments for the assessment of coaching behavior, others have been developed and used (see table 11.3). In 1976, for example, Tharp and Gallimore conducted one of the earliest systematic observation studies using an early version of the Coaching Behavior Recording Form to analyze the practice behaviors of a single coach—John Wooden, men's intercollegiate basketball coach at UCLA. This instrument (and its revisions) contains 10 to 12 categories that provide an assessment of the frequency of different types of coaches' instructional behaviors (e.g., praise, hustle, modeling). Subsequent research studies with adapted versions of this instrument have been conducted (e.g., Bloom, Crumpton, & Anderson, 1999; Seagrave & Ciancio, 1990). In addition, Gallimore and Tharp (2004) have recently provided a more qualitatively based reanalysis of the data that they collected in 1976 with John Wooden.

One of the main issues involved in using these observational systems is that each has often been developed within a particular sport context (e.g., the CBAS was developed with male Little League baseball players). When other researchers attempt to use the systems in other contexts (different ages, different sports, different culture), reliability and validity can be lower. Recently, Brewer and Jones (2002) proposed a five-stage process for establishing both reliability and validity in systematic observa-

tion instruments. Their article provided a much-needed perspective for the field on the processes that researchers should follow when attempting to obtain a psychometrically sound assessment of coaching behavior within a particular context.

Other Coaching Behavior Assessment Procedures

As noted in the previous section on conceptual approaches to coaching effectiveness research, an increasing number of researchers are using grounded theory to identify and define the coaching experience. Some of these researchers (e.g., Bloom et al., 1997; Cote & Salmela, 1996; Cote, Salmela, & Russell, 1995; Cote, Salmela, Trudel, et al.1995; Gould et al., 2007) have used in-depth interviews with coaches (typically expert or successful coaches), whereas other researchers have interviewed both coaches and athletes (e.g., d'Arripe-Longueville, Fournier, & Dubois, 1998) or have used interviews in combination with other techniques (e.g., videotaping, audiotaping, document analysis, field observation) (e.g., d'Arripe-Longueville et al., 2001; Gilbert et al., 1999; Gilbert & Trudel, 2001; Hardin & Bennett, 2002). Potrac and his colleagues (Potrac, Brewer, Jones, Armour, & Hoff, 2000) advocated using a combination of systematic observation of coaches' behavior and interpretive interviews with both coaches and athletes to identify not only the behaviors that coaches exhibit in practice and competitive situations but also their cognitions regarding such behaviors, their rationale for employing them, and their athletes' perceptions of such coaching behaviors. Potrac et al. suggested that such a multimethod approach may be necessary to obtain a fuller understanding of the correlates of effective coaching within particular sport contexts.

Summary: Instrumentation to Assess Coaches' Behavior

Although the information presented in the previous section and in tables 11.2 and 11.3 indicates that researchers may choose from among a number of instruments or methodologies to measure coaches' behavior, the choices are still somewhat limited (especially for researchers who choose to use a quantitative approach) to only a few aspects of coaches' behavior. Thus, many other dimensions of coaches' behavior remain untapped and equally relevant to explore. Discussion regarding these potential other dimensions of coaching behavior is presented in the last section of this chapter.

As indicated in the working model of coaching effectiveness (see figure 11.1), coaches' behavior does not occur in a vacuum. Rather, there are identifiable antecedents of such behavior. In particular, the working model indicates that coaches' behavior is directly influenced by their expectancies, values, beliefs, and goals. This link between boxes 4 and 5 is explored in the next section.

Direct Antecedents of Coaches' Behavior

The research that can be used to provide support for the hypothesized link between coaches' expectancies, values, beliefs, and goals (box 4) and their subsequent behavior (box 5) comes from a diverse set of research literatures, including the research on expectancy (self-fulfilling prophecy) theory; the research on individuals' stereotyped beliefs about gender, race and ethnicity, and sexuality; and the research on goal orientation theory. These issues are discussed in the following paragraphs.

Coaches' Expectations

In all likelihood, the best available empirical evidence for the hypothesized link between coaches' expectancies, values, beliefs, and goals and their subsequent behavior in sport contexts comes from the research that has investigated the self-fulfilling prophecy theory as it may occur in sport contexts. Most of these research studies (see recent review by Horn, Lox, & Labrador, 2006) were based on a four-step self-fulfilling prophecy model proposed by researchers in educational contexts (e.g., Brophy, 1983; Harris & Rosenthal, 1985) to explain how teachers' expectations can affect the performance of their students. Adapting this four-step process to the athletic setting, it has been hypothesized that (a) coaches develop, at the beginning of the season, an expectation for each athlete that predicts the level of performance and type of behavior that the athlete will exhibit over the season; (b) the coaches' expectations affect their behavior toward individual athletes on their teams; (c) the differential ways in which coaches treat individual athletes affect each athlete's performance and self-perceptions; and (d) the athletes' performance and behavior conforms to the coaches' original expectations.

Most of the research studies conducted to examine the self-fulfilling prophecy theory in the sport setting have focused on the second step in the model. Early studies conducted by Rejeski, Dar-

racott, and Hutslar (1979) and by Horn (1984) used the CBAS in the youth sport setting to compare coaching behaviors directed toward high-expectancy athletes (those identified by the coaches as the higher-ability athletes on the team) with behaviors directed toward their lower-expectancy teammates. Subsequent expectancy-biased observation studies focused on older athletes were conducted by Sinclair and Vealey (1989) and Solomon and colleagues (e.g., Solomon, Golden, Ciapponi, & Martin, 1998; Solomon et al., 1996). In general, the results of these disparate studies provided support for the self-fulfilling prophecy theory in that high-expectancy and low-expectancy athletes were found to receive different frequencies and different types of feedback from their coaches.

More recently, Solomon and her colleagues (e.g., Solomon, 2001, 2002; Becker & Solomon, 2005) focused on the first step in the self-fulfilling prophecy phenomenon (the formation of coaches' expectations) by conducting studies designed to identify the sources of information that collegiate coaches use to form their judgments, evaluations, or expectations of individual athletes. This research has rather consistently indicated that coaches predominantly use their perceptions of players' psychological characteristics (e.g., confidence, receptivity to coaching, willingness to learn) to form their expectations about an individual athlete's athletic ability.

From a somewhat different perspective, Papaioannou (1995) used goal perspective theory (Ames, 1992a, 1992b; Dweck, 1986; Nicholls, 1989) to investigate differential teacher behavior in junior high and high school physical education contexts. The results of this study clearly showed a connection between the type of achievement climate in individual classrooms and students' perceptions of their teachers' expectancy-biased behavior. Specifically, students who perceived that their teachers created a performance-oriented climate also believed that their teachers favored high achievers in their classes. In contrast, students who believed that their teachers created a learning-oriented climate perceived that their teachers did not exhibit differential behavior toward the high and low achievers in the class. This study was unique in that it linked expectancy-biased behaviors on the part of the teachers to the overall climate that they create in the classroom. Thus, this study provides additional information regarding the ways in which teachers allow their expectations to affect their behavior. Additional research is needed to determine if such a link occurs in the athletic setting.

Coaches' Stereotyped Beliefs

Besides coaches' expectancies, coaches' beliefs (especially their stereotype-based beliefs) are likely to affect their behavior. Specifically, coaches who hold strong gender-stereotypical beliefs might well behave differently toward their male and female athletes. That is, coaches who believe that girls are less physically or psychologically capable than boys in sport contexts might treat their female players as low-expectancy athletes. On coeducational teams, for example, female athletes may be given less time, attention, and instruction by their coaches in practices and less playing time in games. When they do get playing time, they may be put in positions where they will be less active (e.g., right field in baseball) or less likely to touch the ball. Coaches of all-girls teams who subscribe to such gender-stereotypical beliefs may hold lower standards of performance for all their athletes (based on the belief that girls cannot reach a high standard of performance or proficiency) and thus reduce the amount and quality of the instruction and feedback that they provide their athletes.

The gender-stereotypical beliefs that some coaches hold may interact or intersect with athletes' age or with their maturational status. Horn et al. (2006) make this argument in their recent chapter on the self-fulfilling prophecy theory in sport contexts. Furthermore, their arguments regarding the differential expectations that coaches may hold for early, average, and late-maturing girls (and boys) are also consistent with Malina's (1994, 2002) biosocial hypothesis, which suggests that proportionately more late-maturing girls and women participate in competitive sport after age 12 because coaches, parents, and sport administrators perceive the linear body build of the late maturer (narrow hips, flat chest, relatively low body fat) to be more conducive to sport proficiency and performance. Thus, early maturing girls may be cut from sport teams or may be socialized out of sport at a relatively early age (i.e., by age 12) because coaches and sport administrators no longer perceive them as athletic.

A few recent research studies provide some perspective on the way in which gender of athletes may affect some coaches' attitudes, expectancies, beliefs, and behaviors. In a small but interesting field study with kindergarten children participating in a coeducational tee ball league, Landers and Fine (1996) used participant observation procedures to document how individual coaches reinforced traditional gender-role stereotypes through their behavior, modeling, instructional comments, and disciplinary techniques. Messner (2000) used similar field-based participant observation procedures in his study of early youth sport participants. As the authors of these studies correctly point out, such gender-differential treatment at the earliest ages of youth sport participation may certainly affect the athletic and psychosocial progress of both boys and girls.

Gilbert and Trudel (2004a) completed a qualitative study with six model youth sport coaches (of athletes ranging in age from 10 to 14) to determine how such coaches framed their roles. As part of their results, Gilbert and Trudel found that two of the six coaches (the only ones in the sample who had experience working with both boys and girls) identified gender of the athlete as an important influence on how they planned and conducted their practice activities. Thus, these coaches indicated that they adjusted their role frame depending on whether they were coaching boys or girls. The results of this study suggest that at least some youth sport coaches go into their seasons with expectations about how boys and girls will differ in their performance and behavior in practice and field contexts. Such gender-differential expectations may affect their coaching decisions and coaching behavior.

Coaches who endorse or hold gender-stereotypical beliefs may also hold homophobic views regarding both male and female athletes. Such coaches of male athletes might, for example, act positively toward the players on their team who fit the masculine stereotype (e.g., have broad shoulders, possess a muscular body shape, and act in aggressive ways) but act negatively toward the male athletes on their team who do not fit this masculine stereotype (e.g., are more slender and do not consistently act in what the coach believes to be gender-appropriate ways). Similarly, gender-biased and homophobic (i.e., personal attitude or belief characterized by dislike for, or fear of, homosexually identified individuals) coaches of female athletes may act more positively toward female athletes on their team who fit the feminine stereotype (i.e., athletes who have boyfriends, wear their hair long, and dress off the court or field in more feminine-typed clothing) than they would toward the athletes on their team who do not conform to this feminine stereotype. For further discussion on this topic, see Griffin (1998), Harry (1995), Krane (1996), and Messner and Sabo (1990).

Another aspect of coaches' stereotyped beliefs that has attracted the attention of researchers is race and ethnicity. A number of race-related stereotypes exist in sport contexts (see chapters in the text edited by Brooks and Althouse, 2000) including notions that African American people are naturally gifted in particular sports or sporting activities (e.g., basketball, sprinting events) and that European American athletes are more competent in mental capabilities (e.g., decision making) whereas African American athletes are more competent in physical capabilities (e.g., speed, reaction time). Coaches who hold such race-related stereotypes might show greater differences in their behavior toward African American and European American athletes on their teams than would coaches who do not hold such stereotypes (see in-depth discussion on this issue in Horn et al., 2006). The likelihood of such race-related expectancy effects occurring in the sport context is suggested by research in educational contexts (e.g., Jussim, Eccles, & Madon, 1996; McCormick & Noriega, 1986; Steele, 1997; Steele & Aronson, 1995) that has demonstrated the effects of negative racial and gender stereotypes on children's, adolescents', and young adults' academic performance.

Solomon and her colleagues (Solomon et al., 1996) conducted initial attempts to examine racial biases in coaches' behavior by recording the frequency and type of feedback given to athletes from two college basketball teams. Although examination of mean scores indicated that African American athletes received more instruction and European American athletes received more praise, the statistical analysis revealed no significant differences. Solomon et al. cited the small sample size as a possible explanation for the nonsignificant findings. Obviously, more research on this topic is needed. One suggestion for future researchers would be to assess coaches' attitudes and beliefs with regard to race and ethnicity. Assuming that variability in endorsement of race-related stereotypes would occur within a sample of coaches, observational data of coaches' behavior toward athletes on their teams could be examined to determine whether the degree to which coaches endorsed stereotypes would be reflected in differential behavioral patterns toward athletes on their teams (i.e., would coaches who exhibited the strongest race-related stereotyped beliefs also show the greatest differential treatment of their African American and European American athletes?). Such research would provide a strong test of the hypothesized link between coaches' attitudes, values, and beliefs and their subsequent behavior in practice and game context.

Note that the examination of race and ethnicity in regard to coaching behavior should not be limited to comparisons of African American and European American athletes. As Coakley (1994) notes, little research has been conducted to examine the experi-ences of other racial and ethnic groups (e.g., Asian Americans, Hispanic Americans) in sport contexts. Furthermore, race and ethnicity likely interact with gender, social class, and other diversity characteristics to affect individual athletes' experiences in sport contexts. Thus, for researchers in sport psychology, the examination of the coach–athlete relationship, especially as it concerns ethnicity, race, gender, sexual orientation, or social class, should probably be conducted in more complex ways.

Coaches' Achievement Goal Perspectives

As another example of the hypothesized link between boxes 4 and 5 in the working model of coaching effectiveness (figure 11.1), we can use the tenets of achievement goal orientation theory (Ames, 1992a, 1992b; Nicholls, 1984, 1989) to suggest that coaches who hold a predominantly task-oriented perspective regarding their sport programs would exhibit behaviors in practices and games consistent with such a goal perspective. That is, task-oriented coaches should provide feedback that emphasizes task mastery and individual skill improvement. They should also show persistence in working with all athletes and continually emphasize the important contributions that all athletes make to the team. In contrast, coaches who are predominantly ego-oriented should be observed to exhibit behaviors in practices and games that focus attention on the peer comparison process. That is, they should be expected to give feedback to individual athletes contingent on whether they performed better than teammates rather than on whether they demonstrate skill improvement or task mastery.

Another interesting perspective to use in identifying antecedents of coaches' behavior would be the implicit theories notion forwarded by Dweck and her colleagues (e.g., Dweck, Chiu, & Hong, 1995; Levy, Stroessner, & Dweck, 1998). Specifically, Dweck and her colleagues distinguish between people who believe that such individual difference factors as intelligence, ability in achievement contexts, and personality traits or characteristics are fixed (entity theorists) and those who believe that such individual difference factors are malleable and that they can and do change over time (incremental theorists). Horn and her colleagues (Horn et al., 2006) have argued that coaches who hold or adhere to an entity perspective (i.e., strongly believe that their athletes' traits and abilities are fixed) would be more likely to exhibit expectancy-biased or stereotyped behaviors toward and with individual athletes. In contrast, coaches who subscribe to a more incremental perspective (i.e., believe that athletes' traits and abilities are malleable) might keep an open mind with regard to their initial observations of individual athletes and continue to believe that athletes can improve their ability with instruction and practice. Recently, Butler (2000) has presented evidence suggesting that such a relationship between teachers' theories about the nature of students' mathematical ability (entity versus incremental theorists) and the teachers' subsequent judgments about the students' performance in a laboratory task does exist. Thus, research comparing the behaviors of coaches identified as entity theorists with those who are incremental theorists might provide an interesting perspective on why coaches behave as they do in sport contexts.

Antecedents of Coaches' Expectancies, Values, Beliefs, and Goals

As the research and theory cited in the previous section suggest, we have reason to believe that the behavior exhibited by coaches in practices and games can be linked to, or predicted by, their expectancies, values, beliefs, and goals. Furthermore, as illustrated in the working model of coaching effectiveness (figure 11.1), coaches' expectancies, values, beliefs, and goals may actually be determined by three sets of interrelating factors: the sociocultural context (box 1), the organizational climate (box 2), and the coaches' personal characteristics (box 3). The supporting research and theory for these hypothesized links are discussed in the following sections.

Sociocultural Context

Although the link between the sociocultural context (box 1) and coaches' expectancies, values, beliefs, and goals (box 4) specified in the working model (figure 11.1) has not been well researched in the sport psychology literature, relevant research has been conducted on the sociocultural context in regard to athletes' perceptions and goals. Specifically, several researchers (see Li and Lee, 2004, for a review of this research) who have investigated cross-cultural variation in athletes' perceptions or interpretations of selected achievement goals have found that athletes' achievement goal perspectives do vary, at least to a certain extent, as a function of their sociocultural background. Thus, we might expect similar links between coaches' sociocultural

background and their expectancies, beliefs, and goals. In general, as Ram, Starek, and Johnson (2004) noted in a recent content analysis of the sport and exercise psychology journals, our field still lacks sufficient understanding of the degree to which race, ethnicity, and sexual orientation affects the experiences and behaviors of individuals who participate in sport and physical activity. Thus, the link between the sociocultural context and other aspects of the coach–athlete relationship require further examination.

Organizational Climate

The second factor identified in the working model (figure 11.1) as an antecedent of coaches' expectancies, values, beliefs, and goals is organizational climate (see the hypothesized link between boxes 2 and 4). This link refers to the effect that the particular sport program structure might have on the coach. Perhaps the most important or relevant example of this hypothesized link comes from the research that has looked at differences in coaches' behavior as a function of sport level.

A few studies (e.g., Chaumeton & Duda, 1988; Haliburton & Weiss, 2002; Jambor & Zhang, 1997) have been conducted to examine how coaches' behavior (as measured either through athletes' perceptions of such behavior or through coaches' self-perceptions) may differ as a function of the age level of the teams that they coach. The results of these studies have indicated that coaches' behavior at the older age levels may be less democratic and more ego involving (reinforcement and punishment based on performance outcome rather than on performance process) than it is at the younger age levels. But note that in most of these studies, athletes' age was confounded with level of competition. Thus, future researchers might seek to separate these two factors by comparing coaches' expectations, values, and beliefs as well as their behavior *within* specific age levels but across levels of competition.

Further support for the notion that coaches' beliefs, values, expectancies, and goals are affected by the age or competitive level at which they coach comes from the qualitative data obtained by Gilbert and Trudel (2004a) in their work with six model youth sport coaches. All six coaches in the sample identified athletes' age group as well as the competitive level at which the teams played as boundary components that framed their role as coaches and were the important factors in determining their approach to practice and game situations over the season.

At the collegiate level as well, organizational structure may be a factor affecting coaches' behavior. Amorose and Horn (1999), for example, collected data that showed significant differences in the perceptions of Division I and Division III collegiate male and female athletes regarding their coaches' behavior. Specifically, Division I athletes (as compared with Division III athletes) perceived that their coaches exhibited a leadership style that was more autocratic, offered less social support, and provided lower frequencies of positive and informationally based feedback. These researchers also found significant differences in perceived coaching behavior as a function of the number of athletes on each Division I team who were on scholarship. In particular, coaches of teams in which more than 75% of the athletes were on scholarship were perceived by their athletes to be more autocratic, less socially supportive, and more likely to give punishment-oriented feedback than were coaches of teams who had fewer athletes on scholarship. Based on Mageau and Vallerand's (2003) motivational model of the coach–athlete relationship, a reasonable hypothesis is that college coaches who are given relatively more scholarships than are other coaches may perceive greater pressure to win. In turn, such a win-oriented goal perspective may cause them to be more autocratic or controlling in their interactions with individual athletes. This interpretation of the data is consistent with the results of a recent study conducted by Pelletier and his colleagues (Pelletier, Sequin-Levesque, & Legault, 2002). These researchers found that teachers (of grades 1 through 12) who perceived higher levels of constraints in their workplace (i.e., perceptions that they had to comply with a curriculum, with colleagues' teaching methods, and with administration-determined performance standards) demonstrated lower self-determined motivation toward their teaching, which, in turn, was associated with lower levels of autonomy-supportive behavior and higher levels of controlling behavior toward and with their students. Similar relationships may be evident in the competitive sport setting, especially given external pressure exerted on coaches by administrators, parents, media, and fans to produce successful (i.e., winning) teams.

Coaches' Personal Characteristics

The third antecedent factor hypothesized in the working model of coaching effectiveness (figure 11.1) to affect coaches' expectancies, values, beliefs, and goals, and ultimately their behavior, is the coaches' personal characteristics (i.e., the hypothesized link between boxes 3 and 4). A few researchers in the sport psychology field have examined this link. Feltz and her colleagues (e.g., Feltz, Chase, Moritz, & Sullivan, 1999; Myers, Vargas-Tonsing & Feltz, 2005), along with Sullivan and Kent (2003) investigated relationships between coaches' level of self-efficacy for coaching (using the Coaching Efficacy Scale developed by Feltz et al., 1999) and their behavior toward and with their athletes.

Other researchers have used the motivational literature to examine links between coaches' personal characteristics and their behavior. Fredrick and Morrison (1999) measured motivational style (intrinsic versus extrinsic motivational orientation) in coaches and related this interpersonal characteristic to coaches' decision-making style in sport contexts. Similarly, Losier, Gaudette, and Vallerand (1997) developed a scale to measure coaches' motivational orientation toward coaching. This scale, based on self-determination theory (Vallerand, 2001), provides a mechanism to assess the possibility that coaches' personal orientation can affect the behaviors that they exhibit in practice and competitive contexts. From a somewhat different perspective, Price and Weiss (2000) and Vealey and her colleagues (Vealey, Armstrong, Comar, & Greenleaf, 1998) found a link between coaches' level of burnout and their behaviors in practice and game contexts.

Factors other than level of self-efficacy, motivational orientation or style, and level of burnout may also be predictors of coaches' expectancies, values, beliefs, goals, and behaviors. Abraham and Collins (1998) and Strean and colleagues (Strean, Senecal, Howlett, & Burgess, 1997) published articles in which they argued that such individual difference variables as self-reflectiveness, critical-thinking aptitude, decision-making ability, knowledge bases or structures, and sport or coaching experience may serve as predictors of coaching behavior or coaching effectiveness. Support for this idea is evident in a recent study conducted by Gilbert and Trudel (2001) using a season-long multiple case study approach with six model youth sport coaches to examine how they learned to coach through experience. The results of this study indicated that the process of reflection was critical to the learning experience. Given that these six coaches were specifically selected for participation because they were identified as model coaches, it is certainly possible that not all coaches engage in self-reflection and that this ability (or desire) to engage in self-reflection may be a critical correlate of coaching effectiveness.

As indicated in the last several paragraphs, evidence suggests that coaches' personal characteristics serve as predictors or determinants not only of their expectancies, values, beliefs, and goals but also of their behavior in practice and game contexts. Of course, as the model in figure 11.1 clearly illustrates, coaches' personal characteristics probably work in combination with, and actually interact with, the sociocultural context and the organizational climate to influence coaches' behavior.

As noted earlier in this chapter, the left side of the working model provides a framework to investigate how or why coaches exhibit the types of behaviors that they do in practice and game situations. As is evident, relatively little research in sport psychology has been conducted on this side of the model, but the initial studies in this area have provided some support for the linkages specified. The right side of the working model focuses on the effects of coaches' behavior on athletes' performance, behavior, and psychosocial responses. These linkages and the supporting research are discussed in the following sections.

Direct Effects of Coaches' Behavior on Athletes' Performance and Behavior

As the model (see figure 11.1) illustrates, a direct link is present between coaches' behavior (box 5) and athletes' performance and behavior (box 6). This arrow specifies that certain behaviors that a coach exhibits in practices and games will directly affect her or his athletes' performance and their ability to master the skills. Because the focus of this chapter is on the effect that coaches' behavior exerts on the psychosocial growth and development of athletes, the research on the direct link between coaches' behavior and their athletes' performance and behavior is not reviewed further here. Readers interested in this direct link should consult the motor learning and sport pedagogy literatures (e.g., see the recent book edited by Starkes and Ericsson, 2003, on factors related to the development of sport expertise) as well as some of the grounded theory research studies cited earlier in this chapter (e.g., Bloom et al., 1997; Cote & Salmela, 1996; Cote, Salmela, & Russell, 1995; Cushion & Jones, 2001; Gilbert et al., 1999).

The effects of coaches' behavior on athletes' psychosocial growth and development, and ultimately (or indirectly) on the athletes' motor skill learning and performance, is illustrated on the right side of the model (figure 11.1). In particular, the right side of the current working model hypothesizes that the coach's behavior in practice and game situations (box 5) is interpreted or perceived by the athletes (box 8) in ways that affect the athletes' self-perceptions, beliefs, and attitudes (box 9). Such self-perceptions, beliefs, and attitudes, in turn, affect the athletes' level or type of motivation (box 10) that then affects their performance and behavior in the sport context (box 6). An important point in this process is the athletes' perception or interpretation of their coaches' behavior. This model incorporates the notion that the coach's actual or observable behavior may not be as important as the way in which the athletes perceive or interpret that behavior. Therefore, the review of the research concerning the right side of the working model (the effects of coaches' behavior on athletes' psychosocial responses) begins with a discussion of box 8.

Athletes' Perceptions or Interpretations of Their Coaches' Behavior

As indicated in the working model, the actual behaviors exhibited by coaches in practice and game contexts (box 5) will have an effect on athletes' self-perceptions (box 9) and level of motivation (box 10) only as such coaching behaviors are mediated by athletes' perceptions and interpretations of the coaches' actual behavior (box 8). This notion is also embedded in Smoll and Smith's (1989) cognitive-mediational model. As these authors clearly note, "The ultimate effects of coaching behaviors are mediated by the meaning that players attribute to them" (p. 1527). In addition, however, individual athletes' perceptions of their coaches' behavior are affected or determined by the athletes' personal characteristics (i.e., as illustrated in the model in figure 11.1 by the arrow that links boxes 7 and 8). The research to date clearly supports this idea in that individual athletes have been found to differ significantly in their perception, interpretation, and evaluation of their coaches' behavior. This research is discussed in the following paragraphs.

Interindividual Variability in Athletes' Perceptions of Their Coaches' Behavior

One of the characteristics of athletes that may affect their perceptions of their coaches' behavior is age or developmental level. A few researchers in the developmental and educational literatures (see reviews by Deci, Koestner, & Ryan, 1999, and Henderlong & Lepper, 2002) have found differences between children and adolescents of varying ages in regard to how they interpret the feedback provided by adults in response to their (children's or adolescents') performance attempts. Furthermore, such age or developmental differences in interpretation or perception of adults' feedback appear to be consistent with developmental theory from the goal orientation theoretical literature (see, for example, Fry & Duda, 1997, and Xiang & Lee, 1998). Note, however, that two recent laboratory-based studies conducted by Amorose and his colleagues (Amorose & Weiss, 1998; Amorose & Smith, 2003) have not found age or developmental differences concerning children's interpretation of coaches' feedback. As these authors point out, the developmental differences found in the academic setting may not transfer to the sport setting. Conversely, the lack of developmental effects found by Amorose and his colleagues in laboratory-based studies may not necessarily represent what occurs in field contexts. Thus, further research on this topic is necessary.

In addition to age or developmental level, gender may be another factor that affects athletes' interpretation or perception of their coaches' behavior. Some researchers have found, for example, that the type of perceived coaching behaviors that are most effective in facilitating athletes' self-perceptions and level of intrinsic motivation varies with the athletes' gender (Amorose & Horn, 2001; Black & Weiss, 1992). Furthermore, Vargas-Tonsing and her associates (Vargas-Tonsing, Myers, & Feltz, 2004) recently found that male and female college athletes differed somewhat in their perceptions or evaluations regarding the effectiveness of different types of efficacy-enhancing behaviors used by their coaches. Two large research reviews published in the general psychology literature (Deci et al., 1999; Henderlong & Lepper, 2002) have also found differences between male and female participants in their perceptions or interpretation of the performance feedback given to them. The results of this research, then, support the notion that the effects of coaches' behavior on male and female athletes may differ because they perceive or interpret their coaches' behavior in different ways.

From a different but certainly related perspective, an interesting study would be to examine whether the actual behaviors exhibited by coaches in practice and game contexts (box 5) are perceived differently by athletes as a function of the coaches' gender. Given pervasive gender-stereotypical beliefs in

regard to sport behaviors, a reasonable hypothesis is that a male coach and a female coach who exhibited the same actual behavioral style might be perceived or evaluated by the athletes, as well as others in the sport environment (e.g., administrators, spectators, parents), in different ways. In support of this idea, Vargas-Tonsing et al. (2004) found that female college athletes' perceptions of the effectiveness of different efficacy-enhancing techniques that their coaches used varied as a function of their coach's gender. In addition, Riemer and Toon (2001) in their discussion regarding the preferences of male and female athletes for different types of coaching behavior noted that the gender of the coach may be a confounding factor. In particular, Riemer and Toon point out the possibility that homophobia among female athletes may affect how such athletes perceive their coaches' behaviors. Specifically, Riemer and Toon speculate that homophobic perceptions may affect or determine athletes' preferences for different types of coaching behaviors from their male versus their female coaches (i.e., female athletes who are homophobic may prefer social support behaviors from male coaches but not from female coaches). These studies, then, provide support for the idea that athletes may perceive the same coaching behaviors differently depending on whether the coach is a male or female. Obviously, additional research on this topic is needed (see also Kilty, 2006, for related discussion).

At least initial evidence is also available to show that athletes' perceptions or evaluations of their coaches' behavior may vary as a function of the athletes' psychological characteristics. In three studies, Williams and her colleagues (Kenow & Williams, 1992, 1999; Williams et al., 2003) have found that high school and college athletes' level of trait and state anxiety and state self-confidence affected their perception and evaluation of their coaches' behavior. Furthermore, several sets of researchers (e.g., Coatsworth & Conroy, 2006; Smoll, Smith, Barnett, & Everett, 1993) have found that athletes who began the season with lower self-esteem were more susceptible to their coaches' behavior than were their teammates who began the season with higher self-esteem. Cury, Famose, and Sarrazin (1997) discovered that boys' goal orientation combined with their perceptions of their ability affected the type of feedback that they sought in a performance situation. Finally, Briere and colleagues (Briere, Vallerand, Blais, & Pelletier, 1995) found that athletes' motivational reactions to autonomy-supportive and controlling coaches varied as a function of the athletes' motivational profile at the beginning of the season. Thus, athletes' psychological characteristics may affect their perceptions of, or their reactions to, their coaches' behavior.

Interindividual Variability in Athletes' Preferences for Different Types of Coaching Behavior

As further support for the notion that athletes differ in their perceptions or interpretation of their coaches' behavior, we can look at the extensive research base on athletes' preferences for different types of coaching behavior. This research, based predominantly on Chelladurai's (1978, 1990, 2007) multidimensional model of leadership effectiveness, has examined the extent to which selected characteristics of athletes may affect the type of leadership styles they would prefer their coaches to exhibit. Chelladurai (1990, 2007) reviewed the results of this research in considerable detail and clarity in his chapters on leadership effectiveness in the sport domain. In general, these reviews have indicated that athletes do differ from each other in the type and frequency of the behaviors that they want their coaches to exhibit and in the type of leadership styles they prefer their coaches to use. In addition, such interindividual variability in athletes' preferences appears to be a function of their developmental age, sport level, gender, nationality, sport type (individual versus team, open versus closed, interdependent versus independent), playing position (offensive versus defensive), and possibly their psychological characteristics (e.g., trait anxiety, self-efficacy, locus of control). For recent studies on interindividual variability in athletes' preferred coaching behavior, see articles by Beam, Serwatka, and Wilson, 2004; Riemer and Toon, 2001; and Sherman, Fuller, and Speed, 2000.

In summary, the extensive research base on athletes' preferences for particular types of coaching behavior as well as the more limited research on interindividual variability in athletes' perceptions or interpretations of their coaches' behavior provides support for the hypothesized link between boxes 7 and 8 in the working model (figure 11.1). Such interindividual variability in athletes' perceptions, interpretations, and preferences for particular types of coaching behavior provides support for the need to include box 8 as the mediating factor between boxes 5 and 9. The next section of this chapter offers a review of the research that has been conducted to examine the effects of different types of actual and perceived coaching behaviors on athletes' self-perceptions.

Links Between Coaches' Behavior and Athletes' Self-Perceptions and Level of Motivation

Over the past 30 years, a number of research studies have been conducted to test the relationship between coaches' behavior (measured either through observational means or through athletes' perceptions of their coaches' behavior) (boxes 5 or 8) and selected dimensions of their athletes' psychosocial responses (e.g., perceived competence, self-esteem) (box 9), level of motivation (box 10), or behavior (e.g., sport discontinuation) (box 6). In the following sections of this chapter, these research studies are reviewed. This review is organized into three main sections corresponding to the way in which the coaches' behavior was measured. Specifically, the literature review begins with the research studies that have examined the effects of the coaches' leadership style on athletes' self-perceptions and level of motivation. The second section focuses on the research studies that have examined the effects of coaches' feedback patterns. The third section includes research articles that have used a variety of other instrumentation or other methodological approaches to examine coaching effectiveness.

Effects of Coaches' Leadership Style

As noted earlier, research about the effects of coaches' leadership style on their athletes' psychosocial growth and development has been conducted primarily using three types of instruments. Thus, the review of the research in this section is organized around this measurement component.

Studies Using the Leadership Scale for Sports A considerable amount of research about the effects of coaches' leadership style has been conducted using the Leadership Scale for Sports (LSS), which measures five different dimensions of leadership style (see table 11.2). In addition, these research studies have been based predominantly on Chelladurai's (1978, 1990, 2007) multidimensional model of leadership effectiveness. According to this model, athletes will perform optimally and have maximum satisfaction if the coach behaves in a way that is congruent with the leadership behaviors that the athletes prefer their coaches to exhibit and with the behaviors required by or appropriate to the particular sport situation. The results of the research conducted to test the relationship between satisfaction and performance and leader behavior provide general support for Chelladurai's model. This body of research has been summarized in some detail by Chelladurai and Riemer (Chelladurai, 2007; Chelladurai & Riemer, 1998). In general, these reviews have shown that the leadership dimensions that are most typically positively associated with, or predictive of, athletes' level of satisfaction are the subscales representing a democratic leadership style and high frequencies of social support, positive feedback, and training and instruction. In contrast, the subscale assessing an autocratic leadership style has been linked to low levels of satisfaction on the part of athletes.

In regard to the notion contained in Chelladurai's (1978, 1990, 2007) multidimensional model that optimal performance and satisfaction on the part of athletes will result if congruency is present between the behaviors that athletes perceive their coach to exhibit (or the behaviors that coaches perceive themselves to exhibit) and the behaviors that athletes prefer their coaches to exhibit, mixed results have been obtained (see summaries of this research by Chelladurai, 1990, 2007; Chelladurai & Riemer, 1998). That is, some studies have found support for the congruency hypothesis, whereas others have not. Some of the variability in these study results may be due to the measurement of the congruency hypothesis; some researchers used discrepancy scores (preferred minus perceived), and others used hierarchical regression statistical procedures. In addition, the degree to which the congruency hypothesis may hold true appears to vary across the particular leadership styles represented on the LSS (e.g., Riemer & Chelladurai, 1995), as a function of the athletes' personal characteristics (e.g., Chelladurai, Imamura, Yamaguchi, Oinuma, & Miyauchi, 1988), and which of the three sets of scores (athlete preferred, athlete perceived, coach perceived) are used in the calculation of the discrepancy (see, for example, study by Shields, Gardner, Bredemeier, & Bastro, 1997). Obviously, further research on the relative contributions of the three measures of coaching behavior to athletes' positive outcomes is needed.

The few studies that have been conducted to examine the relationship between athletes' perceptions of their coaches' behavior (using the LSS) and their subsequent level of performance have supported these hypothesized links (see reviews by Chelladurai, 1990, 2007). A study conducted by Trail (2004) provides evidence for an indirect link between the LSS subscales and athletes' level of performance (i.e., coaches' behavior did not affect athletes' performance and satisfaction directly but rather indirectly as mediated through athletes' perceptions of their team's cohesion). In discussing this study, Chelladurai (2007) pointed out that other factors may also serve a mediating role in the link between the LSS subscales and athletes' performance and behavior in the sport setting.

Because most research studies that have used the LSS as the primary measure of coaches' leadership style have been based on Chelladurai's (1978, 1990, 2007) multidimensional model, the dependent variables in these studies have tended to center on the construct of satisfaction on the part of the athletes or on the athletes' level of performance. A subset of studies, however, has used the LSS to examine the effect of particular coaching leadership styles on such other outcome variables as athletes' perceptions of their team's cohesion (e.g., Pease & Kozub, 1994; Shields et al., 1997) and athletes' level of burnout, anxiety (e.g., Price & Weiss, 2000), and intrinsic motivation (Amorose & Horn, 2000, 2001). In the second of the two Amorose and Horn studies, a longitudinal research design was used with a sample of first-year Division I athletes from a variety of sports. The results of this study indicated that first-year athletes whose level of intrinsic motivation increased over the season perceived that their coaches provided high frequencies of training and instructional behaviors, low frequencies of social support, and low levels of autocratic behavioral style. These results, then, linked changes in first-year collegiate athletes' level of intrinsic motivation over a season to their perceptions of their coaches' behavior.

More recently, Hollembeak and Amorose (2005) examined components of the self-determination theory (Deci & Ryan, 1985; Ryan & Deci, 2000) using the LSS scales. Specifically, these researchers used structural equation modeling to test the possibility that collegiate athletes' perceptions of their coaches' behavior would directly affect their perceptions of competence, autonomy, and relatedness, which would, in turn, affect their level of intrinsic motivation. Results supported this model. In particular, perceived democratic behavior on the part of the coach was positively linked to athletes' perceptions of autonomy, and coaches' positive feedback behavior was positively linked to athletes' perceptions of relatedness but negatively linked to their perceptions of sport competence. An autocratic coaching style was negatively linked to athletes' perceptions of autonomy and relatedness, and training and instructional coaching behavior was negatively linked to athletes' perceptions of autonomy. In turn, athletes' perceptions of autonomy, competence, and relatedness directly predicted athletes' level of intrinsic motivation. These results provide support for SDT but also indicate the relevance of the LSS dimensions of coaching behavior to the prediction of athletes' level of intrinsic motivation.

In general, then, the results of the research conducted to examine the relationship between coaches' leadership style (as assessed using the LSS) and various dimensions of athletes' psychosocial responses have shown that the LSS subscales of democratic behavior, training and instruction, positive feedback, and social support may be the most effective leadership styles or behaviors in facilitating athletes' performance and psychosocial well-being. In contrast, an autocratic leadership style appears to be more negative in regard to athletes' psychosocial outcomes. But there is a possibility that such a behavioral style (or something similar, such as an authoritarian style) may be effective in certain sport contexts, with selected types of athletes, or in certain situations within a particular sport context (i.e., at different points in a competitive season or in relation to particular rules, behaviors, and so forth). d'Arripe-Longueville and colleagues (d'Arripe-Longueville et al., 1998) made this point, and Chelladurai (2007) recently alluded to the same idea in his argument that different types of coaching behaviors may be necessary or effective at different levels of competition and skill.

Studies Using the Autonomy-Supportive and Controlling Leadership Scales

As noted earlier in this chapter, Mageau and Vallerand (2003) forwarded a motivational model of the coach–athlete relationship that describes how different types of coaching behavior may influence athletes' motivation. This model proposes that three dimensions of coaches' behavior (autonomy supportive, provision of structure, and involvement) will affect athletes' perceptions of competence, autonomy, and relatedness. In turn, these constructs will affect or determine athletes' intrinsic and self-determined extrinsic motivation. In support of this model, Mageau and Vallerand reviewed a number of studies from the education, leisure, exercise, and sport literatures that provide evidence for the value of the three dimensions of coaching behavior. In particular, an autonomy-supportive coaching style has been identified as having positive effects on athletes, whereas a controlling style appears to have a negative effect on athletes' self-perceptions and their intrinsic and self-determined extrinsic motivation. In their review

of this research, Mageau and Vallerand provided a comprehensive list of coaching behaviors that characterize an autonomy-supportive approach to coaching.

Recently, Pelletier and his colleagues (Pelletier, Fortier et al., 2002) presented the results of a two-year, three-wave, longitudinal research project with 369 competitive swimmers, ranging in age from 13 to 22. At the beginning of the study (wave 1), swimmers completed self-report questionnaires assessing their perceptions of their coaches' interpersonal style (autonomy supportive versus controlling) and their motivational orientation toward their sport (Sport Motivation Scale). At waves 2 and 3 (10 months and 22 months later), an assessment of swimmers' sport persistence (sport continuation or sport discontinuation) was obtained. Structural equation modeling procedures indicated that the two measures of coaching behavior (autonomy supportive and controlling) directly predicted athletes' motivation, with autonomy-supportive behaviors positively associated with self-determined motivation and controlling behaviors positively associated with non-self-determined forms of regulation. Moreover, self-determined types of regulation (as assessed at wave 1) were significant predictors of persistence at both wave 1 and wave 2 time points.

Additional support for the positive effects of coaches' autonomy-supportive behaviors was provided in a case study conducted by Mallett (2005) with two men's Olympic-level relay teams and by Gagne, Ryan, & Bargman (2003) in a four-week diary study conducted with female gymnasts. Because these studies used somewhat different methodological approaches, they produced richer detail regarding the day-to-day implementation of autonomy-supportive coaching behaviors.

In general, then, the studies conducted to examine the effectiveness of the coaching behaviors identified by Vallerand and his colleagues (Vallerand, 2001; Mageau & Vallerand, 2003) have provided support for the autonomy-supportive coaching approach. Keep in mind, however, that Mageau and Vallerand also specified the value of coaching behaviors that provide structure and show involvement in, and concern for, athletes' welfare. Thus, Mageau and Vallerand stated, "It becomes apparent that autonomy-supportive behaviours can only be beneficial for people's motivation when they accompany structure and support." (p. 893). Although Mageau and Vallerand provide some evidence (mainly from nonsport domains) in support of the value of structure and involvement as dimensions of coaching effectiveness, further research is certainly needed on the interrelationships of these three coaching behavior dimensions as they affect athletes' performance and psychosocial well-being.

Studies Using the PMCSQ and Related Instrumentation The relatively strong relationship between coaches' leadership style and their athletes' level of motivation and self-perceptions has also been demonstrated by researchers who have followed the tenets of Nicholls' (1984, 1989), Dweck's (1986, 1999), and Ames' (1992a, 1992b) achievement goal orientation theories. Much of this work has been conducted using the Perceived Motivational Climate in Sport Questionnaire–2 (PMCSQ–2) (Newton et al., 2000) or one of its earlier versions (see Duda & Whitehead, 1998, for description of scale development). The PMCSQ–2 measures the type of motivational climate that coaches and others create in practice and game contexts. This body of research has provided consistent support for the value of a more task-involving (mastery-oriented) team climate (see comprehensive reviews of this research by Duda, 2001; Duda & Whitehead, 1998; Ntoumanis & Biddle, 1999). Specifically, a task-involving climate has been linked to a variety of positive outcome variables, such as athletes' level of self-determined motivation, sport enjoyment, satisfaction, personal effort, persistence, a more task-oriented goal perspective, and perceptions of sport competence. Furthermore, some studies have found evidence of the negative effects of an ego-involving (performance-oriented) motivational climate. That is, this type of climate has been linked to higher levels of athletes' anxiety, worry, tension, perceived performance pressure, maladaptive coping strategies, and a more ego-involved goal orientation perspective.

More recently, researchers have expanded the research base on motivational climate to examine other outcome variables. A few researchers, for example, have found that athletes' perceptions of their team's motivational climate are linked to the sources that they use to evaluate their sport competence (Halliburton & Weiss, 2002) and determine their level of self-confidence in regard to their sport (Magyar & Feltz, 2003). Additional research has indicated that a coach-initiated task-involving motivational climate is positively related to several team variables, including team cohesion (e.g., Heuze, Sarrazin, Masiero, Raimbault, & Thomas, 2006), perceptions of team improvement in regard to the technical, tactical, physical, and psychological aspects of the sport (Balaguer, Duda, Atienza, & Mayo, 2002), and collective efficacy (Heuze et al.,

2006; Magyar, Feltz, & Simpson, 2004). Sarrazin and his colleagues (Sarrazin, Vallerand, Guillet, Pelletier, & Cury, 2002) used a more longitudinal approach with a large sample (N = 335) of female handball athletes to show a predictive and causal relationship between athletes' perceptions of a task-involving motivational climate; their perceptions of competence, autonomy, and relatedness; and their level of self-determined motivation. Furthermore, over time, athletes' self-determined motivation predicted their intention to drop out as well as their actual dropout behavior.

Other researchers have examined team motivational climate as a potential factor affecting athletes' moral judgments, sportspersonship values and beliefs, and fair-play attitudes (e.g., Boixados, Cruz, Torregrosa, & Valiente, 2004; Fry & Newton, 2003; Kavussanu & Spray, 2006; Ommundsen, Roberts, Lemyre, & Treasure, 2003; see also an in-depth review of this body of research by Weiss and her colleagues in their chapter in this text). In general, these studies have found a positive relationship between a coach-initiated task-involving motivational climate and athletes' sportspersonship orientations, and a positive relationship between a coach-initiated ego-involving motivational climate and players' tendencies to engage in amoral sport behaviors (e.g., cheating, aggression).

In her chapter on achievement goal research in sport, Duda (2001) also recommended further research on the relationship between motivational climate and measures of athletes' physical and mental health. The few initial studies that have been conducted in this area (Duda, Balaguer, Moreno, & Crespo, 2001; Reinboth & Duda, 2004) have found a link between a highly ego-involving team climate and athletes' scores on emotional and physical exhaustion scales as well as on their self-report of physical ailments that they had experienced in the previous two weeks. In a recent, more longitudinally based study, Reinboth and Duda (2006) found that the degree to which collegiate athletes perceived an increase over the competitive season in a coach-initiated task-involving motivational climate was associated with a corresponding increase in athletes' satisfaction of the needs for autonomy, competence, and relatedness. In turn, increased perceptions of satisfaction for autonomy and relatedness were predictive of increases in athletes' perceptions of their vitality (perceived physical and mental vigor and alertness).

Using a somewhat different approach, Conroy, Kaye, and Coatsworth (2006) recently extended the motivational climate construct to include Elliot's

(1999) notions about approach and avoidance goals. Specifically, Conroy et al. assessed young swimmers' perceptions of the goals that their coaches used to evaluate their competence. Their analysis of the data indicated that swimmers' perceptions of the degree to which their coaches created an avoidance-oriented climate predicted corresponding changes in the athletes' own achievement goals over the season. In turn, changes in athletes' mastery-avoidance goals were linked to changes in athletes' external regulation and amotivation scores.

Within the past few years, a few sets of researchers (e.g., Cervello et al., 2007; Gernigon, d'Arripe-Longueville, Delignieres, & Ninot, 2004) have argued for the need to examine athletes' goal orientations at a more statelike level. Specifically, these researchers suggest that athletes' own goal involvement, as well as other aspects of their performance, behavior, beliefs, cognitions, and affective states, can perhaps best be studied within a particular performance context (e.g., within a single practice session, match, meet, or game). Initial attempts to use this more situationally based approach (e.g., Cervello et al., 2007; Gernigon et al., 2004; Kowall & Fortier, 2000; Simons, DeWitte, & Lens, 2003) have demonstrated the value of such an approach in understanding individuals' cognitions, beliefs, and affective reactions during a performance but have also documented the role that the coach's (or teacher's) comments can play in affecting the athlete's (or student's) goal involvement relative to a specific performance event. That is, the coach's instructions or comments just before the athlete's performance are one of the factors that affect the athlete's goal involvement as well as her or his performance and behavior within that situational context. Furthermore, Cervello et al. found that athletes' perceptions of the motivational climate that their coach initiated in relation to a specific competition was a better predictor of athletes' task involvement (concentration, autotelic experience) within that competition than was the athletes' perception of the general motivational climate that the coach created. The results of this research provide support for the value of considering motivational climate from both a more stable (general or contextual type of climate created by the coach over a season) and a more situational (climate created within particular situations) perspective.

Despite the considerable amount of research conducted on the effects of the motivational climate on athletes' cognitions, beliefs, affective responses, performance, and behavior, a number of important methodological and conceptual issues or questions have recently been raised. Some of these issues or questions are identified here (see the chapter in this text by Harwood et al. for an in-depth discussion on these topics).

■ Do athletes' dispositional goal orientations interact with their perceptions of the motivational climate to affect their performance, behavior, and psychosocial responses? In reviewing the research on this issue, Duda (2001) suggested that how significant the interaction effect will be and whether dispositional or climate measures will be better predictors may be a function of a number of contextual factors (e.g., age of the athlete, outcome variable assessed, type of sport setting).

■ Are the two types of climates (task involving and ego involving) related to each other, or are they orthogonal in nature? In general, most of the research on motivational climate has operated from the assumption that team motivational climates are predominantly either task involving or ego involving. But certainly both types of climates may be promoted, created, or initiated within a team (see recent research by Boixados et al., 2004, on this issue).

■ Is interindividual variability present within teams in athletes' perceptions of their team's motivational climate (see studies by Cumming, Smoll, Smith, & Grossbard, 2007; Gano-Overway, Guivernau, Magyar, Waldron, & Ewing, 2005; Magyar et al., 2004)? If so, what are the contextual or individual difference factors that explain such variability (see the discussion by Duda, 2001)? Should multilevel research designs and analytical procedures be used to incorporate both individual and group effects in the examination of the effect of motivational climate on athletes' performance, behavior, and psychosocial responses (e.g., Cumming et al., 2007; Gano-Overway et al., 2005; Magyar et al., 2004)?

■ Is the coach-initiated team climate generally stable across a competitive season, or does it change over time during the season or as a function of the competitive schedule (i.e., is it more ego involving in days leading up to important competitive events or during end-of-the-season playoffs)?

■ Although a task-involving motivational climate generally appears to be more facilitative of athletes' psychosocial growth, can an ego-involving climate also exert positive or facilitative effects, especially on athletes' and the team's performance but also on their psychosocial responses (see, for example, Balaguer et al., 2002; Cervello et al., 2007; Chelladurai, 2007; Steinberg, Singer, & Murphy, 2000; Treasure, 2001)? If so, what are the contextual factors (e.g., age of athlete, level of play, dispositional goal orientation, time in season) that determine the facilitative or debilitative effects of an ego-involving climate?

▪ Does the coach-initiated motivational climate interact with (or add to or subtract from) the peer-initiated motivational climate (see Ntoumanis & Vazou, 2005; Vazou, Ntoumanis, & Duda, 2006)?

▪ What specific game and practice behaviors and techniques characterize a coach-initiated task-involving climate versus a coach-initiated ego-involving climate (see Duda, 2001, and Smith et al., 2005, for recent research on this issue)?

As the research cited in this section has indicated, strong and consistent empirical evidence shows that the type of leadership style that coaches exhibit in practice and game contexts has a significant effect on the self-perceptions, level of motivation, and emotional well-being of their athletes. In the next section of this chapter, the research that has been conducted to examine the effects of coaches' feedback patterns on athletes' psychosocial development is reviewed.

Effects of Coaches' Feedback Patterns

Much of the research work in this area was stimulated by the series of studies conducted by Smith and Smoll and their colleagues at the University of Washington. They began their work by developing the Coaching Behavior Assessment System (CBAS), an observational instrument designed to assess the frequency with which individual coaches exhibit 12 behavioral dimensions (see table 11.3) (Smith et al., 1977). Following the development and testing of the CBAS, Smith and Smoll and their colleagues conducted a series of research studies to examine the link between coaches' behaviors and young athletes' psychosocial development. Some of these studies (e.g., Smith et al., 1978; Smith, Zane, Smoll, & Coppel, 1983) were descriptive in research design and looked at the correlational relationship between observed coaching behaviors and athletes' self-esteem and postseason attitudes. Consistent support was found for the value of an encouraging, supportive, and instructionally based coaching feedback style. In contrast, high levels of punishment-oriented feedback were negatively related to players' attitudes.

Based on these early descriptive study results, Smith and Smoll and their colleagues (e.g., Barnett, Smoll, & Smith, 1992; Smith, Smoll, & Barnett, 1995; Smoll et al., 1993) conducted more experimentally

based research studies to test for causal links between coaches' behavior and young athletes' psychosocial growth. In these studies, Smith and Smoll and their associates developed a coaching effectiveness training program (CET) and then assigned youth sport coaches to either an experimental (training) group or to a control (no training) group. The experimental coaches participated in the preseason cognitive-behavioral training program (CET) designed to teach and encourage them to develop the coaching behaviors identified as effective in the earlier descriptive studies. The results of these experimental studies indicated that young athletes who played for the trained coaches exhibited more positive attitudes at postseason, increased levels of self-esteem, decreased trait anxiety, higher levels of enjoyment and fun, and lower levels of sport discontinuation.

Recently, Conroy and Coatsworth conducted studies designed to extend Smith and Smoll's research model. In a 2004 study Conroy and Coatsworth employed a coach training program that was largely based on the CET but that added elements from the mastery program. These researchers also used experimental procedures to determine whether coach training would have an effect on young swimmers' (ages 7 to 18 years) fear of failure in the sport competition setting. Latent growth curve analyses of the longitudinal (season-long) data indicated that the training that coaches received did not significantly predict the rate of change in the fear of failure observed in the swimmers over the course of their competitive season. In a later study, however, Coatsworth and Conroy (2006) found some evidence that the self-esteem of young swimmers was affected by whether they were coached by individuals who had received coach effectiveness training or by those who had not. The effect of such coach training was particularly evident for female swimmers who began the season with lower levels of self-esteem and for younger children (i.e., age 11 or younger).

Besides those who conducted observational studies using the CBAS, other researchers have examined the link between coaches' feedback patterns and athletes' psychosocial responses by using questionnaire versions of the CBAS, thus assessing athletes' perceptions of the feedback patterns that their coaches exhibit in practice and competitive settings (see table 11.2). Participants in these studies have included intercollegiate athletes (Amorose & Horn, 2000) as well as youth and adolescent athletes (Allen & Howe, 1998; Black & Weiss, 1992; Cumming et al., 2006). Study results have generally indicated that higher frequencies of encouraging, supportive, and information-based feedback in response to both player successes and performance errors are characteristic of an effective coaching feedback pattern. In contrast, high frequencies of punishment-oriented feedback or coaches' tendencies to ignore players' performance errors as well as their successes were found to be detrimental to athletes' psychosocial well-being.

In general, the research on the effects of coaches' feedback patterns (or verbal behaviors) has primarily been focused either on the frequency with which coaches provide particular types of feedback or on the total amount of particular types of feedback that coaches provide their athletes. But alternative and perhaps more critical aspects of coaches' feedback may be important to assess. Horn and her colleagues (1985, 1987; Horn & Harris, 2002; Horn et al., 2006) have argued that the appropriateness and contingency of coaches' feedback might be more critical than the frequency or amount. In a review and synthesis of the empirical and theoretical literature on the effects of praise on children's intrinsic motivation, Henderlong and Lepper (2002) concluded that praise (as given by adults to children in response to their performance attempts in an achievement context) can undermine, enhance, or have no effect on children's intrinsic motivation for the achievement task at hand. Furthermore, Henderlong and Lepper used the available research to suggest that the effects of praise will depend on five factors: the perceived sincerity of the praise, the performance attributions contained in the praise, the degree to which the praise contributes to the child's perception of autonomy, whether the praise conveys positive information about the child's competence without relying on social comparisons, and the level or standard of performance and future expectancies contained in the praise.

From a similar perspective, Deci and his colleagues (Deci, Koestner, & Ryan, 1999) as well as Mageau and Vallerand (2003) distinguished positive feedback (praise) administered in an informational format from positive feedback offered in a controlling format. Positive feedback delivered by adults (teachers, parents, coaches, laboratory experimenters) in a controlling way typically contains the word *should*. For example, an adult might say, "Excellent! You should keep up that level." Positive feedback may also carry the implication that the future performance of the learner or performer should conform to the wishes of the person giving the praise. For example, a coach might say, "Keep it up! I would like you to do even better in the next game." Although

such feedback is positive, the athlete may perceive it as a form of control. This perception of external control or external pressure may lower the athlete's perception of autonomy and do nothing to increase her or his perception of competence. The result may be a decrease in the athlete's level of intrinsic, or self-determined, motivation.

Another component of coaches' feedback that we have not yet consistently measured is its attributional content. Based on available research and theory in the attributional literature (Weiner, 1986, 1992), a reasonable hypothesis is that the type of attributions contained in a coach's feedback to her or his players would significantly affect the athlete's perception of competence, level of motivation, and affective reactions. For example, compare "That was a lucky catch you made, Joe" to "Great hustle to get to that ball, Joe." For further discussion on the possible effects of attributional feedback in the sport context, see the chapter by Hanrahan and Biddle in this volume, chapters by Horn and colleagues (1987; Horn & Harris, 2002; Horn et al., 2006), and work by other writers in the developmental and educational psychology literatures (e.g., Henderlong and Lepper, 2002; Mueller & Dweck, 1998; Schunk, 1995).

Another interesting perspective on the assessment of coaches' feedback patterns was recently provided by Smith (2006), who reanalyzed data collected with the CBAS in the earlier described series of studies (e.g., Smith et al., 1978; Smith & Smoll, 1990). In those earlier studies, the data obtained from individual coaches had been aggregated in each coding category and then expressed as percentages of total behaviors (i.e., 62% of coach A's emitted behaviors were praise). But because the observational data had been coded per half inning and the time and score had been noted at the beginning of each half inning, Smith (2006) could develop situationally based behavioral profiles for two coaches in the reanalysis of this data. The results of these behavioral profiles were collated to show the stability (or instability) of three forms of coaching behavior (supportive, instructional, and punitive) across three types of game situations (own team was winning, teams were tied, own team was losing). One coach showed a reasonable level of stability in the three forms of behavior across all three game outcome situations (relatively high levels of supportive and instructional behavior and relatively low punitive behaviors across all three game situations). The other coach's profile was much more unstable (e.g., instructional behavior was relatively high when the team was winning and much lower when the team was tied or losing). The interesting point is that the two coaches looked similar in overall percentages of the three behaviors summed across the three game-situation categories. As Smith noted in his discussion of this reanalyzed data, it would be informative to measure coaches' behavioral patterns using this more situationally based profile to determine whether and how such profiles relate to athletes' performance and psychosocial growth. Furthermore, the degree to which coaches are (or are not) stable in their behaviors across situations may be, as Smith pointed out, an individual difference factor linked to other coach characteristics or to athlete outcomes.

Effects of Other Dimensions of Coaches' Behavior

A few studies conducted over the past several years have examined different dimensions of coaches' behavior toward and with their athletes. Bloom, Stevens, and Wickwire (2003), for example, used focus group interviews with 29 intercollegiate coaches to identify team-building strategies. Analysis of this data resulted in the identification of six main themes. Key points highlighted the role of the coach in building a team atmosphere or environment through use of core peer leaders, the importance of preseason and seasonal planning and organization, and the value of finding and using relevant team-building activities. This paper provided rich detail regarding the strategies that these coaches found effective in building team cohesion and unity.

Turman (2003) conducted a study on team building to investigate the coach's role in facilitating team cohesion. He used a two-phase study to identify coaching techniques and behaviors that athletes perceive to be motivating and demotivating, and then to assess the effect of these coaching behaviors on team cohesion. The results of this study provided considerable description of athlete–coach interactions that appear to be related to athletes' level of motivation or to their perceptions of team unity.

Vargas-Tonsing and her colleagues (Vargas-Tonsing et al., 2004) used more quantitative procedures to identify and compare coaches' and athletes' perceptions of the strategies that coaches use to enhance efficacy in athletes as well as the perceived effectiveness of these strategies. Study participants were college athletes. The results of this study provided insight into what may be effective and ineffective efficacy-enhancing strategies and identified how coaches and athletes can differ in their perceptions of the coaches' behavior.

Finally, the research studies conducted by Sophia Jowett and her colleagues provided support for the notion that coach–athlete relationships characterized by high levels of closeness, commitment, and complementarity are linked to higher levels of team cohesion (Jowett & Chaundry, 2004) as well as higher levels of satisfaction and performance (e.g., Jowett & Cockerill, 2003). Studies such as these highlight the importance of relational issues in identifying the correlates of coaching effectiveness.

Summary: Linking Coaches' Behavior to Athletes' Psychosocial Growth and Development

In summary, the results of the research reviewed in the previous section provide considerable support for the hypothesized connections between coaches' behavior in practice and game situations (as measured either directly or indirectly through athletes' perceptions of their coaches' behavior) and athletes' psychosocial growth and development. The links have been demonstrated through both correlational and experimental research approaches. Furthermore, the leadership styles, behaviors, and feedback patterns listed in table 11.4 have been most consistently identified as positive or negative in relation to athletes' psychosocial growth and development.

The results of the coaching effectiveness research discussed in the previous sections of this chapter are consistent with the current theoretical literature in the general psychology and sport psychology fields (see table 11.1). For example, according to self-determination theory (Deci & Ryan, 1985; Ryan & Deci, 2000), social or situational factors within the achievement environment that promote feelings of autonomy (i.e., the perception that one is self-initiating in the regulation of one's own actions), competence (i.e., the perception that one can interact effectively with the environment), and relatedness (i.e., the perception that one is connected with significant others) within the individual should increase the person's level of intrinsic or self-determined motivation. In contrast, situational factors that rob a person of feelings of autonomy, competence, and relatedness will undermine his or her intrinsic or self-determined motivation. Based on these theoretical tenets, it is easy to see how an autocratic or controlling coaching style can undermine athletes' perceptions of autonomy and thus lead to lower intrinsic or self-determined motivation whereas an autonomy-supportive or democratic coaching style can facilitate athletes' perceptions of autonomy and thus enhance their intrinsic or

Table 11.4 **Summary Listing of Coaching Behaviors and Styles Consistently Found to be Facilitative or Detrimental to Athletes' Psychosocial Growth and Development**

Facilitative coaching styles or behaviors	Detrimental coaching styles or behaviors
High frequency of training and instructional behavior	Ignoring athletes' skill errors
High level of social support and positive feedback	High frequency of punishment-oriented feedback (especially feedback not accompanied by skill-relevant information)
Democratic or autonomy-supportive leadership style	Autocratic or controlling leadership style
Creation of a mastery-oriented (task-involving) motivational climate	Creation of a performance-oriented (ego-involving) motivational climate
Provision of positive, supportive, and informationally based feedback in response to athletes' performance successes and failures	Failure to recognize or respond to athletes' performance successes

self-determined motivation. Furthermore, coaches who provide athletes with significant social support should promote athletes' perceptions of relatedness and thus facilitate athletes' level of intrinsic or self-determined motivation.

In regard to feedback patterns, self-determination theory (Deci & Ryan, 1985; Ryan & Deci, 2000) also postulates that events or situational factors that provide the individual with information about her or his competence should facilitate the development of the person's intrinsic or self-determined motivation. Conversely, events or situational factors that convey negative information about personal competence should undermine individuals' intrinsic or self-determined motivation. Extending these notions, Ryan and his colleagues (Ryan, Connell, & Deci, 1985) and Horn and colleagues (1987; Amorose & Horn, 2001; Horn & Harris, 2002) have argued that coaches' frequent provision of positive *and* informationally based feedback in response to athletes' performance successes and particularly their performance errors should constitute strong situational sources of information that confirm athletes' perceptions of competence, which should, in turn, increase their levels of intrinsic, or self-determined, motivation. In contrast, punishment-oriented feedback can undermine athletes' perceptions of competence, and no feedback (nonreinforcement and ignoring mistakes) from coaches can be a neutral or even negative source of competence information. Again, then, based on self-determination theory, these low perceptions of competence can lead to low levels of intrinsic or self-determined motivation (see also discussion by Mageau and Vallerand, 2003, and Vallerand and Losier, 1999, on the further use of

self-determination theory in the study of coaching effectiveness).

Harter's competence motivation theory (1981, 1999) also provides a strong theoretical framework for the interpretation of the coaching behaviors that appear to be most effective or ineffective. According to Harter, people need to receive positive and contingent feedback in response to their mastery attempts in any achievement domain. Receiving such positive and contingent feedback allows children to develop high perceptions of competence and an internal perception of control. Furthermore, receipt of this type of feedback during the childhood years is especially important because it assists children in internalizing achievement goal standards and thus developing independence from others. Therefore, the research on coaches' feedback patterns that has rather consistently demonstrated the effectiveness of providing athletes with high frequencies of positive and informationally based feedback and the corresponding ineffectiveness of responding to athletes' successful and unsuccessful performance attempts with nonreinforcement or ignoring of mistakes is consistent with Harter's competence motivation model.

Obviously, the theoretical models espoused by Nicholls (1984, 1989), Dweck (1986, 1999), and Ames (1992a, 1992b) can also be used to interpret and support the leadership styles and behaviors found to be most effective or ineffective. Specifically, the creation and maintenance of a mastery-oriented motivational climate, with its emphasis on individual task mastery, self-referenced evaluation, individualized goal structures, and group cooperation rather than competition would be expected to facilitate a task goal orientation on the part of athletes. A task goal orientation (in contrast to an ego goal orientation) has been linked to positive affect, high levels of perceived competence and intrinsic motivation, and adaptive achievement beliefs.

Although the other theoretical models listed in table 11.1 have not been used with any consistency in the investigation of the correlates of coaching effectiveness, they certainly have the potential to do so. That is, although these theories may not specifically address the role of the coach, each of them recognizes the contributions that significant others play in the facilitation of individuals' psychosocial growth and development. Thus, these theories may be useful in identifying effective coaching behaviors.

In general, then, both empirical research and the theoretical literature in the field support the notions regarding the coaching styles, behaviors, and feedback patterns identified earlier as the most effective or ineffective with regard to athletes' psychosocial growth and development. Despite the rather significant advances that have occurred over the last two decades in our knowledge base on coaching effectiveness, much remains to be learned. In the next (and last) section of this chapter, suggestions and directions for future researchers are presented.

Future Research Directions

The suggestions concerning future directions in leadership research discussed in this section are framed on the working model of coaching effectiveness (figure 11.1). The suggestions fall into three major areas: (a) the measurement of coaching behavior (box 5), (b) the examination of the consequences of coaching behavior (boxes 6 through 10), and (c) the examination of antecedents of coaches' behavior (boxes 1 through 4).

Measurement of Coaching Behavior

As noted earlier in this chapter, most quantitative research on coaching effectiveness in the psychosocial area has been conducted using only a few instruments that have been developed for the purpose of measuring coaches' behavior (e.g., the LSS, CBAS, and the PMCSQ–2). Although the use of these instruments has provided interesting and valuable information regarding effective coaching behaviors and leadership styles, the instruments do have limitations. Specifically, concerns remain about the reliability and validity of all or portions

of each instrument (see, for example, critical reviews by Chelladurai, 2007; Chelladurai & Riemer, 1998; Duda, 2001; Ntoumanis & Biddle, 1999). Thus, further work is needed to examine the content, format, and structure of these instruments and to incorporate revisions that will produce a more accurate and valid measure of coaches' behavior. In addition, continued work with the less often used instruments listed in tables 11.2 and 11.3 is needed to ascertain their psychometric properties and value for the field.

Future researchers should expand the research on coaching effectiveness by identifying and investigating other dimensions or aspects of coaches' behavior that may be relevant to athletes' performance and psychosocial well-being. Examples of such potential aspects or dimensions of coaching behavior include the following:

- Coaches' nonverbal behaviors (see, for example, Allen & Howe, 1998; Crocker, 1990; Kenow & Williams, 1992)
- Coaches' communication and coordination capabilities (see, for example, Cunningham, 2004; Eccles & Tenenbaum, 2004)
- Coach–athlete interactional patterns (see, for example, d'Arripe-Longueville et al., 1998; d'Arripe-Longueville et al., 2001)
- Coaches' cognitions, perceptions, and decision-making processes (see arguments made by Gilbert & Trudel, 2004b; Potrac et al., 2000; and Nash & Collins, 2006)
- Coaches' ability to clarify team members' roles (see, for example, recent research by Beauchamp, Bray, Eys, & Carron, 2003; Eys, Carron, Bray, & Beauchamp, 2005)

One final point pertaining to the measurement of coaching behavior concerns the relative value of assessing coaches' behavior directly (e.g., observationally based procedures) or indirectly (e.g., through the perceptions of athletes, coaches, or others in the sport environment). As the empirical research and theory reviewed in this chapter should indicate, both forms of assessment have provided valid and valuable information concerning the effective or ineffective forms of coaching behavior. Furthermore, as portrayed in the working model of coaching effectiveness (figure 11.1), both constitute important constructs or components in the coaching effectiveness process. Box 5 (in figure 11.1) represents the actual behavior exhibited by the coach, and box 8 represents the athletes' perceptions or interpretations of that behavior. Ultimately, both measures of coaching behavior (the direct measure and athletes' perceptions of that behavior) are linked to athletes' psychosocial growth and development as well as their performance and behavior. Thus, future researchers have a choice about which component they wish to assess. In reports of these studies, however, researchers need to be clear about which component (box) they are assessing, and they need to interpret the results of studies relative to that component. Of course, the field would probably benefit if both components (both boxes) could be measured in single studies. Such procedures would allow a direct comparison of their relative effects on athletes and allow researchers to test the model as a whole.

Consequences of Coaches' Behavior

The research regarding the consequences of coaches' behavior has typically been limited to examination of only selected aspects of athletes' psychosocial growth and, ultimately, their performance and behavior. Specifically, in regard to athletes' perceptions, beliefs, attitudes, and level of motivation (boxes 9 and 10), researchers have concentrated mostly on such constructs as athletes' (a) self-perceptions (e.g., perceived competence, self-esteem, success expectancies); (b) affective reactions (e.g., anxiety or stress, satisfaction, enjoyment, interest); and (c) level of motivation (intrinsic, or self-determined). Considerably less information is available concerning the coaching styles and behaviors that might affect athletes' level of self-efficacy, their attributional beliefs, their tendencies to experience feelings of learned helplessness, their perceptions of performance control (locus of control), or their commitment to the sport and the team. In regard to athletes' behaviors, we have only a little knowledge about the effects of different types or forms of coaching behaviors on athletes' work ethic, their willingness to persist in the face of failure, their tendencies to experience athletic burnout, or their decisions to discontinue (or continue) their sport participation (see discussion on this type of research by Vallerand and Losier, 1999). Furthermore, as pointed out by Duda (2001), relatively little information is available regarding the link between coaching behavior and athletes' physical and mental health. Exploration of this link could also focus on the possible effects of different types of coaching behaviors on athletes' body image or their tendencies to engage in disordered eating patterns (see, for example, Duda & Kim, 1997; Kerr, Berman, & DeSouza, 2006; Krane,

Greenleaf, & Snow, 1997). Thus, much research needs to be conducted to improve the knowledge base regarding the effects of coaches' behavior on multiple aspects of athletes' psychosocial growth, performance, and behavior.

As indicated in the working model (figure 11.1) and as pointed out numerous times in this chapter, we cannot forget that the particular coaching styles, behaviors, or feedback patterns identified as effective or ineffective will vary as a function of the sport context and as a function of the athletes themselves. We cannot generalize the results found in individual studies to all contexts or to all athletes. As Gilbert and Trudel (2004b) point out in their review of the coaching science literature, much of the research has focused on coaches of team-sport athletes or coaches of school-based sport teams. Less research has been conducted with coaches of adult teams, coaches of elementary or middle school teams, female coaches, assistant coaches, or coaches from individual-sport programs. Obviously, then, continued research is necessary to investigate and determine the correlates of coaching effectiveness in a variety of contexts and with a variety of athletes. Furthermore, research is also needed to compare the effects of coaching behaviors across different sport contexts or across different athletes or to compare the effects of different types of coaching behavior on athletes with varying psychological profiles. Finally, conducting research projects just to identify how athletes' personal characteristics affect their interpretation, evaluation, perception, or preference for different types of coaching behaviors (i.e., see link between boxes 7 and 8) would improve understanding of the potential effects of coaches' behavior on athletes' psychosocial growth and development.

Recently, Chelladurai (2007) made an interesting point regarding the role of context in determining or identifying the correlates of effective coaching. Specifically, Chelladurai distinguished between two different purposes of sport participation: sport as the pursuit of pleasure and sport as the pursuit of excellence. Because these two purposes entail different philosophies, goals, and processes, effective coaching behaviors will likely vary across these two sport contexts. In his chapter, Chelladurai identified a set of leader behaviors that may be essential to the development of sport excellence. As part of this section, Chelladurai recognized that the pursuit of excellence (as opposed to the pursuit of pleasure) may require coaching behaviors that are more demanding and directive, at least at certain points in the athlete's development, and that coaches may need to emphasize winning (along with skill development) and foster a sense of competitiveness in the athlete. Furthermore, athletes involved in sport for the pursuit of excellence may need to develop both a task goal orientation and an ego goal orientation. To accomplish this objective, the coach may need to foster a climate involving both task and ego, particularly concerning competition (see the previous discussion in this chapter regarding the possibility that a climate involving both task and ego may be facilitative in some contexts). Chelladurai concluded by noting that some of the leader behaviors identified as necessary for the pursuit of excellence would not be recommended in a sport context that emphasizes the pursuit of pleasure. Thus, Chelladurai suggested the "need for researchers and practitioners to be clear about the purposes of the two enterprises and resist from imposing a set of processes appropriate to one enterprise on the other."

Antecedents of Coaches' Behavior

As stated earlier in this chapter, the working model of coaching effectiveness (figure 11.1) illustrates the fact that coaches' behavior does not occur in a vacuum. Rather, identifiable reasons cause coaches to exhibit the leadership styles, behaviors, and feedback patterns that they do. The working model specifies or identifies some possible antecedents. But as the review of the literature on these antecedents showed, we have little research-based information regarding the hypothesized links between these constructs and coaches' behavior. Thus, this area of research is wide open. Specific suggestions and directions regarding the types of questions that could be addressed in this area were provided earlier in this chapter. Such research studies should not only provide theoretical and empirical information regarding the antecedents of coaches' behavior but also be useful in designing coaching education programs. After all, developing intervention programs designed to change individuals' behavior will be easier after we know *why* such individuals exhibit the behaviors that they do. Thus, the examination of the antecedents of coaches' behavior should be valuable for both theoretical and practical reasons.

Conclusion

The review of the research contained in this chapter clearly indicates that athletes' psychosocial growth and development as well as their performance and behavior within sport contexts are significantly influenced by the leadership styles, behaviors, and feedback patterns exhibited by their coaches in practice and game situations. The review also clearly shows that our current knowledge base on the correlates of coaching effectiveness has been limited to specific dimensions of coaching behavior and selected measures of the consequences of such behaviors on athletes' psychosocial growth and development. In addition, our current knowledge suggests that the particular correlates of effective coaching are context specific. Thus, the current knowledge base cannot be generalized to all athletes or all sport contexts. Contrary to the opinion of some, much remains to be learned in this area of study. Given what we already know about the influence that coaches can have on their athletes, further study to identify the effective and ineffective forms of coaching behavior across a wide range of athletic contexts is certainly warranted.

CHAPTER 12

Social Influence in Sport

■ Julie A. Partridge, PhD ■ Robert J. Brustad, PhD ■
■ Megan Babkes Stellino, EdD ■

The sport involvement of children and youth takes place within a social context, and parents, peers, and siblings can strongly influence the psychological outcomes of this involvement. The purpose of this chapter is to summarize essential knowledge about how each set of socialization agents can affect the psychological development of youngsters in sport. We will identify differences in how parents, peers, and siblings exert their own particular forms of influence. We will also address some of the developmental considerations that affect the salience and effect of each form of social influence at various points in time. We will review the most relevant contemporary research on parents, peers, and siblings, although we wish to mention at the outset that much more extensive research has been conducted on parents than on peers or siblings. Parent socialization research in sport dates back to the 1970s, whereas research on peer influence did not commence until the early 1990s and the examination of sibling influence in sport has been virtually nonexistent. Thus we will have to lean heavily on knowledge about siblings that has been gained from outside the sport context.

This chapter begins with a discussion concerning the conceptual and developmental nature of social influence. A detailed examination of parental influence on children's sport participation follows. Specifically, we will explore parental influence on children's motivational and emotional experiences in the sport domain. Next, we will examine the influence of various forms of peer relationships on children's psychosocial development, as well as the importance of peer leadership within sport. Lastly, we will focus on theoretical perspectives regarding the influence of siblings on developmental outcomes, as well as discuss sibling influences in the sport domain. Future research directions in each component of social influence will also be discussed.

Conceptualizing Social Influence

At the broadest and most general level, we will rely on Lewin's (1934) classic formulation in which he conceptualized behavior as being the consequence of the interaction between the personal characteristics of the individual and his or her environment. As humans, the significant others that are involved in our lives are the most important components of our social environment and clearly shape our attitudes, beliefs, and values. Bronfenbrenner (1979,

1993) later proposed, through ecological systems theory, a more developmentally sensitive extension of Lewin's conceptual framework, in which he recommended that we consider behavior to be a function of the developmental status of a particular individual in interaction with the environment. This extension of Lewin is even more appropriate for our purposes because it encourages us to recognize that the individual is not a stable entity but rather one who is engaged in a dynamic process of developmental change, and that the role of social influence needs to be considered in relation to developmental status. Furthermore, when studying youngsters in sport it is appropriate to recognize that the child or adolescent is part of a much larger network of influences that is dynamic in the sense that the system is constantly undergoing change. From this perspective, which is at the core of family systems theory (e.g., Carter & McGoldrick, 1989), any change in one member of the system will influence other members (e.g., family members, peers). This influence is clearly reciprocal, and although we normally focus on how parents influence children, we must remember that children influence their parents through their interests, experiences, and aptitudes (Cote, 1999; Weiss & Hayashi, 1995). In sum, we ask the reader to maintain the image of children's sport participation as just one part of a larger integrated system that is dynamic, reciprocal, and strongly affected by the young person's stage of development.

Developmental Considerations in Relation to Social Influence

Developmental considerations are not the focal point of this chapter, but social influence needs to be examined with consideration for the developmental characteristics of the individual to understand the influence of socialization agents (Csikszentmihalyi & Rathunde, 1998). The sport involvement of youngsters can extend from early or middle childhood to late adolescence or beyond, and sport involvement thus transcends many important developmental phases.

The most relevant developmental consideration is that the three most important socialization agents (parents, peers, and siblings) vary in the extent and nature of their influence according to the youngster's age and stage of development. At younger ages, children tend to spend the bulk of their time within the family unit and typically do not have sufficient cognitive and social developmental capacities necessary to sustain peer relationships. Parents also are the ones who introduce children to sport and enroll them in sport programs (Green & Chalip, 1998; Greendorfer, Lewko, & Rosengren, 1996). During the early sport years, parents are likely to be present at their children's games, and given the highly public nature of competitive sport, parents tend to have ample opportunities to communicate their values and beliefs about sport to their children (Scanlan, 1996). From a developmental standpoint it is important to note that children tend to base their estimates of personal competence or ability on adult feedback and behavior (Frieze & Bar-Tal, 1980; Horn & Weiss, 1991). Although children could use many different sources of information in forming judgments about their competence, the feedback provided by adults is particularly salient to youngsters before about 10 years of age (see Horn, 2004). Recent trends toward early sport specialization (Wiersma, 2000) also highlight the role of the family because the time, energy, and cost demands of specialized involvement can have a profound effect on the family as a whole.

By the time children have entered later childhood (10–12 years), they typically have the perspective-taking abilities that underlie reciprocity and social exchange, and which are essential to maintain mature social relationships (Laursen & Hartup, 2002). These developmental advancements stimulate youngsters to pursue relationships with friends and peers, and these nonfamily members become increasingly important to them. In addition, youngsters' increased cognitive development allows them to use and integrate multiple sources of information in assessing their competence (see Horn, 2004). Rather than rely heavily on adult feedback, they now use peer comparison processes in which they compare their skills in various achievement domains with their peers and consider how much effort and practice they require to succeed on tasks relative to their peers. In this regard, peers become highly salient sources of information for youngsters in making judgments about their competence. Although parents likely continue to be highly important socialization agents, their roles have probably changed. Parents are now likely to be primarily responsible for managing the time, transportation, and financial needs of participation (Cote, 1999). With regard to social development, the later childhood and adolescent years also constitute a developmental phase in which youngsters have both a strong need for social acceptance and a strong desire for personal uniqueness. The desire for uniqueness also reflects on the greater diversification that characterizes the self-concept of adolescents, in contrast with younger children (Csikszentmihalyi & Rathunde, 1998; Harter, 1999). The "more diverse self" or "more complex self" is reflected in adolescents' tendencies to see many more dimensions of their personality and character than they had at younger ages. The peer group serves an important function as a "mirror onto the self" that helps adolescents identify these various personal qualities and dimensions (Csikszentmihalyi & Rathunde, 1998). Although a simple formula cannot explain the relative influence of each set of significant others at any developmental stage, the nature and extent of social influence varies in accordance with developmental issues that characterize a person at any stage in the maturational process.

In this chapter, we will address the manner in which parents, peers, and siblings influence the nature of sport experiences for children and adolescents. This discussion will require continued attention to developmental forms of influence as such influence becomes manifest over the childhood and adolescent years. Our presentation will address current theoretical perspectives in each of the three areas of parental, peer, and sibling influence. Subsequent attention will be dedicated to the empirical knowledge base related to each form of social influence.

Parental Influences on Children's Sport Participation

Parents are extensively engaged in their children's sport experiences. Parents typically facilitate children's initial entree into sport (Green & Chalip, 1998; Greendorfer et al., 1996), and they play vital support roles by providing the transportation and financial support necessary for their child's ongoing participation. Apart from these practical considerations, however, the way in which parents influence the psychological and emotional dimensions of children's sport experience has the most important and enduring effect on the child's involvement. From a psychological perspective, it is essential to consider how parents influence children's motivational patterns, achievement characteristics, emotional experiences, and subsequent interest in maintaining or discontinuing their sport participation (Brustad, 1992). Parents have many essential roles in the youth sport context, but no role is more important than establishing the psychological climate in which the child's sport participation will take place. With regard to the psychological climate, we are referring to the parental values and beliefs that structure the meaning, interpretation, and evaluation of children's sport participation within the family. Although several motivational theories address parental influence on children's sport experiences, the expectancy-value theory (Eccles et al., 1983) is considered the most relevant and will be the focal point of our examination of parental influence in this chapter.

Theoretical Perspectives

Eccles' expectancy-value theory (Eccles, 1993; Eccles et al., 1983) is the primary contemporary theoretical perspective on parental socialization influence on children's motivation in achievement settings. Widely used in academic contexts, this theory has also served to guide research in the sport and physical activity domain (see Fredericks & Eccles, 2004). The theory can be used to explain how parents shape children's self-perceptions about their abilities in sport, parental beliefs about the relative value of various achievement domains, parental gender-related stereotypes about the adequacy and importance of various achievement domains for their sons and daughters, and children's subsequent levels of motivation to pursue achievement in various domains. Therefore, Eccles' theory links parental socialization practices with children's motivational characteristics.

At its core, Eccles' theory proposes that parents play a fundamental role in providing achievement experiences for their children as well as in interpreting for them the outcomes of those experiences. Parents perform these tasks in relation to their own belief systems, and these belief systems are reflected by their expectancies, values, and gender-related beliefs. In turn, children's belief systems are shaped through the combination of the experiences provided for them and through the feedback that they receive from their parents. A discussion of the three fundamental components of the model—expectancies, values, and gender stereotypes—will aid in developing a more complete understanding of the theory. The best way to begin the discussion is to focus on the value component.

Parental value refers to the perceived relative importance to parents of various achievement domains. Achievement domains can include academics, sport, music, and performing arts. The question is, What value does the parent place on sport as an achievement domain for his or her child? More specifically within a given domain, the question could be, How important for the parent is the child's

gymnastics participation relative to the child's participation in soccer? In Eccles' model, achievement domains are of unequal value to parents because of parents' personal experiences and beliefs. According to Eccles' (1993) theory, however, the greater the value that is ascribed to a particular achievement domain, the more frequent will be the opportunities provided by the parent to their children within that achievement domain. The concept of value includes different dimensions. Utility value refers to how well a task relates to the child's current or future goals, including career goals. Intrinsic value refers to the amount of enjoyment or satisfaction that the person receives from doing the activity and her or his intrinsic interest in the activity. Attainment value is the value associated with the activity because it is perceived to highlight salient aspects of the self. Finally, cost refers to the negative consequences associated with pursuing the task, including time and financial demands, missed opportunities to pursue other interests, and unfavorable psychological consequences such as anxiety and fear of failure that may occur as a consequence of participation.

Parental expectancies refer to parents' beliefs about the likelihood that a particular child will experience success in a given domain. A parent may expect that a child will have greater success in gymnastics than in basketball, for example. This expectation may be grounded in observations of the ease with which the child learns gymnastics skills, his or her intrinsic interest in gymnastics, the child's temperament, and perhaps the child's physical characteristics. Because children cannot have high levels of success in all achievement domains, parents interpret achievement-related information for them and offer more encouragement in those domains or activities in which they perceive that their children are likely to have the greatest success. Consequently, parents provide unequal levels of opportunity and encouragement across domains. Thus, the child in this example is much more likely to receive opportunities in gymnastics than in basketball, more encouragement and positive feedback about gymnastics progress, and more specialized camps and experiences. Note that although parents may highly value a given achievement area (e.g., basketball), not all children within a family will receive the same level of encouragement in this domain because parents will have different expectancies about their children's natural aptitudes and abilities. Thus, Eccles' theory helps to understand individual differences within the same family in the socialization process.

As a consequence of her or his parents' beliefs, specifically the parents' expectancies and values, a child will receive a differential pattern of encouragement and opportunity across varying achievement domains. Eccles (1993) argued that in accordance with this socialization history the child will typically adopt both parents' expectancies about his or her ability or competence, as well as the parents' values about the relative importance of differing achievement domains. The most important socialization component of the model is precisely that children are likely to adopt their parents' beliefs and thus that their motivation in various domains will reflect a belief system that originated with their parents. If children believe that they are highly competent in a given area, they are more likely to be motivated in that area of achievement. Eccles' theory is consistent with current motivational theories that emphasize self-efficacy (Bandura, 1977, 1986) and perceived competence (Harter, 1978, 1981) in that greater perceived ability is believed to predict greater motivation. But the value component of the model involves the question, Do I want to do this? Many other contemporary motivational theories do not address this question, but it seems fundamental in understanding the achievement motivation of children and adolescents.

Eccles' (1993) theory also contains a third related element that pertains to the influence of possible gender-related parental beliefs. The theory was initially used to help explain possible gender differences in academic achievement relative to stereotyping. In particular, this perspective was used to examine how gender-related stereotypes about math ability might differentially affect the motivation and achievement of boys and girls in math. A seminal early study (Parsons, Adler, & Kaczala, 1982) indicated that girls tend to adopt their parents' beliefs about their abilities in math even when more objective criteria of math ability (e.g., grades, achievement test scores) contradict those beliefs. This research indicated that children's beliefs about their abilities affect dimensions of motivation (self-perceptions) as well as subsequent interest and achievement levels.

Extensive research in both academic and sport and physical activity contexts provides good support for many of the major contentions of Eccles' theory. Probably the most well supported component of the model is the link between parents' expectancies, or perceptions of their child's competence, and the child's own success expectancies or perceptions of competence. In the academic realm, research indicates that parents' beliefs about their child's competence predict the child's own perceptions of academic competence, independent of the child's

previous academic performance (Frome & Eccles, 1998; Parsons et al., 1982; Phillips, 1984, 1987). In sport and physical activity contexts, researchers have also found significant relationships between parents' perceptions of their child's competence and the child's own perceived physical competence (Babkes & Weiss, 1999; Eccles, 1993; Fredricks & Eccles, 2002; McCullagh, Matzkanin, Shaw, & Maldonado, 1993), even in cases in which actual levels of physical ability have been statistically controlled (Bois, Sarrazin, Brustad, Trouilloud, & Cury, 2002; Felson & Reed, 1986; Jacobs & Eccles, 1992).

In their three-year longitudinal study, Eccles and Harold (1991) found that parents' perceptions of their child's sport competence contributed to explaining differences in children's own perceived sport competence and their subsequent motivation to participate in sport and physical activity contexts. Babkes and Weiss (1999) found that players who perceived that their parents had more positive beliefs about their competency and who received more frequent and positive contingent responses to their athletic performance had higher perceptions of soccer competence, as well as higher levels of intrinsic motivation to participate in soccer, than did their peers who reported less favorable perceptions of parental influence. In a longitudinal study conducted in France, Bois et al. (2002) found that mothers' perceptions of their child's physical competence predicted their child's own perceived physical competence one year later, independently of the child's initial level of perceived competence and actual competence (as assessed by physical skill tests).

Additional research supports the notion that parents who have favorable perceptions of their child's ability in physical activity and sport provide more opportunities and encouragement for their children in this domain than do parents with lower perceptions of their children's ability in sport and physical activity (Brustad, 1993). This study found that parental self-reported expectancies of their child's physical activity and sport competence explained the level of encouragement that the parent provided for the child's sport and physical activity involvement, which, in turn, explained the child's own self-reported perceived physical competence and level of attraction (value) to sport and physical activity. A subsequent study (Brustad, 1996) also found that children's attraction to sport and physical activity was predicted by children's perceptions of the level of encouragement that they received from their parents to participate in this domain.

Whereas the link between parent and child success expectancies seems well established, there is much less knowledge about the strength of the relationship between parental value and child value with regard to achievement domains. To date, the value component of the theory has only infrequently been included in research. In a recent study of second- to fifth-grade children and their parents, Fredricks and Eccles (2005) found significant but moderate relationships (r = .27 and .29) between parents' perceptions of the value of sport and their child's perception of sport value at two different time points. The researchers examined mothers' and fathers' value perceptions separately and found that mothers' level of value was significantly related to their perception of their child's ability. In addition, mothers' perceptions of the value of the sport domain were significantly and positively related to their sport equipment purchases and their level of encouragement of the child's sport involvement. Fathers' value was significantly related to the perception of the child's ability but not to other socialization variables.

Eccles and Harold (1991) found a link between children's perceptions of the value placed on sport by their parents and the child's perceived competence. The link between parental value and child value, however, was not supported. In a study addressing children's engagement in moderate to vigorous physical activity, Kimiecik and Horn (1998) did not find a significant association between parents' perception of the utility value and cost of moderate to vigorous physical activity involvement and children's own moderate to vigorous physical activity behavior.

Further research is highly encouraged because many parents in the United States place high value on sport. Because sport constitutes a free-choice activity in contrast to a required academic subject, both parental and child value should be relatively easy to assess. Academic research supports the notion that children distinguish competence from subjective task value as early as the elementary school years (Eccles et al., 1993; Eccles & Wigfield, 1995; Wigfield et al., 1998). In this regard, children of this age are able to make the distinction between what they perceive they are good at and what they value.

The third component of Eccles' (1993) theory involving the influence of parental gender stereotypes has recently received a fair amount of attention. Research conducted to date reveals that parental gender stereotypes remain in the sport and physical activity domain and that these stereotypes influence children's physical activity opportunities in relation to the child's gender. Research indicates that parents are more likely to engage in physical activity and sport with their sons than with their daughters and are more likely to take their sons to sporting events (Eccles, 1993). Parents are also more likely to report that their sons have high ability in sport and that sport involvement is of greater value to their sons than to their daughters (Eccles, 1993; Eccles, Jacobs, & Harold, 1990; Fredricks & Eccles, 2005; Jacobs & Eccles, 1992). In turn, boys generally rate themselves as more competent than girls on sport and physical activities (Eccles, Jacobs, & Harold, 1990; Fredricks & Eccles, 2005; Jacobs & Eccles, 1992). This line of research indicates that, in general, parents retain gender stereotypes that influence their interactions with their sons and daughters in the physical domain. But more individual difference research is needed to address how variations in the strength of parental stereotypes affect the socialization process. Clearly, not all parents hold stereotypes relative to gender in sport and physical activity. Individual difference research could shed light on the relationship between stereotypes and socialization patterns relative to the child's gender.

Overall, Eccles' (1993) model has proved to be highly useful for the examination of parental influence on children's sport and physical activity engagement. Research has provided strong support for the importance of parental expectancy beliefs, but the influence of parental value beliefs has not yet received sufficient consideration. Although gender stereotypes are an important contributor to physical activity outcomes for boys and girls, we need to know more at the level of the individual family how these stereotypic beliefs shape opportunities for children.

Parental Influence on Children's Emotional Experiences in Sport

In addition to the research that has increased our understanding of the role of parents in shaping the motivational characteristics of children's sport involvement, a body of knowledge has developed regarding the role of parents in shaping the emotional characteristics of children's involvement. Within this line of research, the most frequently investigated research questions have addressed parental influence on children's competitive state and trait anxiety, enjoyment, and burnout. Logically, these emotional experiences are also tied to youngsters' level of motivation to continue sport participation.

Competitive Anxiety Some of the initial research that directly addressed the nature of parental influence on children's emotional response to youth sport participation focused on state and trait anxiety related to sport. Competitive state anxiety constitutes a situation-specific form of anxiety in sport, whereas competitive trait anxiety represents a relatively enduring personal disposition to view sport competition as threatening and to respond customarily with elevated levels of state anxiety (Martens, 1977). Note that much of the sport anxiety research was conducted in the 1970s and 1980s because of concerns at that time that sport was too stressful for youngsters (e.g., Smilkstein, 1980). This concern seems to have been replaced by contemporary concerns about the excessive time demands of sport for youngsters and families and the increasing concern for the effects of early sport specialization on the psychological and physical development of young people (Wiersma, 2000).

Researchers have identified a relationship between parental behaviors and children's tendency to experience precompetition state anxiety. In their study of young competitive wrestlers, Scanlan and Lewthwaite (1984) found that youngsters who perceived greater parental pressure to wrestle also experienced higher levels of competitive state anxiety. Research on young male gymnasts by Weiss, Weise, and Klint (1989) revealed that the two principal sources of worry for these young athletes were about "what my parents will think" and "letting my parents down." An investigation by Gould, Eklund, Petlichkoff, Peterson, and Bump (1991) revealed that young wrestlers' prematch state anxiety was significantly related to the youngsters' feelings that their parents put pressure on them to wrestle. Parental beliefs and practices have also been linked to children's tendency to experience competitive trait anxiety. This line of investigation is important because competitive trait anxiety represents an enduring tendency to perceive sport competition as threatening, a predisposition that would logically be associated with ongoing distress and sport dropout. Passer (1983) found that children high in competitive trait anxiety tended to worry more frequently about incurring negative evaluations from significant others, including parents. Brustad (1988) found that young basketball players with high competitive trait anxiety were highly concerned about receiving negative evaluations from others. Parallel research in the academic realm revealed that youngsters with high test anxiety tended to have strong concerns for incurring negative evaluations from their parents (Wigfield & Eccles, 1990).

Burnout   The role of parents in affecting the likelihood that their children will experience burnout in sport is a topic that has also generated research

interest. This topic is an important issue because sport specialization in the United States has become increasingly common, as reflected both by sport involvement at progressively younger ages and by highly demanding practice and competitive schedules for youngsters in a single sport (Wiersma, 2000). Raedeke (1997) conceptualized sport burnout as a negative, long-term emotional state characterized by physical and emotional exhaustion and a reduced sense of personal accomplishment. The burnout experience would likely occur during adolescence, rather than childhood, through the accumulation of years of intensive involvement and in relation to normal developmental tendencies of adolescents to differentiate unique aspects of themselves that may not be reflected in their narrow sport involvement (Coakley, 1992). In his investigation of adolescent swimmers, Raedeke (1997) proposed that adolescents who experience burnout might do so because they feel trapped by social expectations to concentrate solely on the role of swimmer. His research indicated that, in general, swimmers who reported stronger feelings of entrapment in the swimmer role had higher burnout levels than did those who felt less trapped in this role.

Sport Enjoyment   Parental practices can also be associated with favorable emotional outcomes for youngsters in sport. Scanlan and Lewthwaite (1986) found that when young wrestlers perceived high parental satisfaction with performance, positive parental involvement and interactions related to wrestling, and low frequency of negative maternal interactions, they were likely to experience significantly greater enjoyment in the sport. In his study of young male and female basketball players, Brustad (1988) found that when youngsters perceived less parental pressure to participate, they were likely to experience higher levels of sport enjoyment. In an investigation involving young skiers, Hellstedt (1988) found that athletes who perceived their parents' involvement as positive and supportive reported more favorable emotional and motivational outcomes, such as enthusiasm, for their continued involvement. Similarly, Leff and Hoyle (1995) found that young male and female tennis players who perceived parental behaviors to be supportive of their continued involvement in tennis demonstrated higher levels of enjoyment in the sport. In their research with adolescent Norwegian soccer players, Ommundsen and Vaglum (1991) found that athlete enjoyment was favorably associated with the positive emotional involvement of parents (and coaches). In research conducted on high-ability youth soccer players, Babkes and Weiss (1999) found that players who perceived that their parental influence was positive and who reported that their fathers were regularly involved in their participation without exerting strong pressure to perform well experienced greater enjoyment.

The research conducted to date clearly indicates that parenting practices affect the favorability of children's emotional experiences in sport. This link is consistently evident across differing outcome variables for youngsters, including competitive state and trait anxiety, sport burnout, and sport enjoyment. Although research has clearly established a link between parental practices and affective outcomes for youth, much about this topic remains unknown. One of the most important areas to investigate in this line of research is which parental practices young athletes perceive as involving pressure. Sources of pressure, for example, could include unrealistic parental expectations and parental emotional responses that vary according to performance outcome. Second, longitudinal studies are needed to address how the emotional experiences of youngsters are related to persistence in sport or to discontinuance because of dropout or burnout.

Parental Influence Across Stages of Sport Involvement An important consideration in the understanding of parental influence involves the dynamics of family influence in sport over time, specifically the manner in which parental roles change in relation to the developmental characteristics of the young athlete and the increasing demands of sport involvement at higher levels of engagement. Bloom and colleagues (1985) initiated a line of research about the nature of family influence over time in relation to youngsters who were highly talented in achievement domains such as science, art, and athletics. These researchers concluded that predictable changes occur within the family. During the early years of their children's involvement, parents tended to provide a supportive role that allowed their children to make the decisions about whether to pursue the activity formally. When the child decided to pursue the activity at a high degree of commitment and dedication, parents typically provided the necessary support and encouragement to allow the child to focus her or his efforts on the activity. During the later stages of involvement, parents tended to provide more limited support that consisted primarily of financial support that enabled the teenager to continue participation at a high level of engagement.

Csikszentmihalyi, Rathunde, and Whalen (1993) presented the idea of complex families as the family structure most likely to result in highly accomplished teenagers. They characterized complex families as being both integrated and differentiated. Integration refers to the sense that children are securely integrated within the family in that they receive consistent support for achievement efforts within a secure and stable environment. Differentiation refers to the idea that individual members of the family are all encouraged to develop their individuality through the pursuit of personally relevant challenges and opportunities. The characterization of complex families in this way is consistent with Hellstedt's (1988) idea that a continuum of parental involvement patterns exists in which parents should be neither underinvolved nor overinvolved.

Cote (1999) examined the dynamics of families related to the development of highly talented young athletes. The participants in his study were elite rowers, tennis players, and their families. He used the framework provided by Ericsson, Krampe, and Tesch-Romer (1993), which explained family influence on expert performance in relation to three types of constraints: motivational, effort, and resource. The results indicated the presence of three phases of involvement consisting of the sampling years, the specializing years, and the investment years. The first stage of sport involvement, the sampling years, occurred between the ages of 6 and 13 years for all participants. During the sampling years, parental involvement primarily consisted of stimulating their child's interest in the sport but with the primary emphasis being on the play and enjoyment aspects of involvement. During the specializing years that typically occurred between the ages of 13 and 15 years, the young athlete tended to decrease involvement in additional talent activities and to commit to just one or two sports. During this phase, the parents reported that they typically developed a growing interest in the child's sport involvement and made financial and time commitments to facilitate the athlete's continued development. Finally, during the investment years both athletes and families demonstrated strong commitment to sporting excellence. During this phase, parents tended to demonstrate great interest in their child's sport involvement and to help their child fight through setbacks and difficulties. Cote's research also indicated that an imbalance in the distribution of family resources caused sibling jealousy and bitterness that influenced the family system as a whole. Overall, this research helps explain differential patterns of parent involvement over time.

Future Research Directions

A number of recommendations for future research flow out of this review of the current knowledge base. In accordance with the closing discussion of change in the nature of parental involvement over time because of the child's developmental status and level of sport engagement, conceptual perspectives on how and why parental behaviors change are warranted. Eccles et al. (1993) proposed that we need models of socialization influence that include a stage–environment fit to further our understanding of the interaction between social influence and developmental experiences for youngsters. This concept is in line with Bronfenbrenner's (1979, 1993) ecological systems theory and highlights the need to understand parental influence in relation to specific developmental periods of youngsters, as opposed to adhering to a global view on parenting practices. Clearly, longitudinal studies of parental influence are warranted.

Eccles' (1993) expectancy-value theory has demonstrated, for lack of a better term, great utility value with regard to understanding parental influence on motivational outcomes for youngsters in sport. As previously mentioned, we know a relatively great deal about the influence of parental expectations, a moderate amount about gender stereotypes, but relatively little about how the value characteristics of parents affect their children's value orientations with regard to sport. In addition, more research is needed on other parental motivational influences, such as parental achievement goal orientations and reinforcement patterns along intrinsic and extrinsic lines.

Peer Influence in Sport and Physical Activity

Although sport-specific research on peer influence has not traditionally been studied as extensively as parental and coaching influences, our understanding of the importance of peers on children's psychosocial development has grown considerably in recent years. Youth sport researchers have increasingly used theoretical approaches and findings from the existing knowledge base in educational and developmental psychological literature to address parallel issues in the sport domain. Peer influence in sport is a salient line of study for a variety of reasons. First, children and adolescents in our culture place high value on competence in sport (Adler, Kless, & Adler, 1992; Buchanan,

Blankenbaker, & Cotten, 1976; Chase & Dummer, 1992). Because participation in these activities has great potential to affect psychosocial development, peer influence is an important avenue of study for youth sport researchers. A second important consideration is that children have consistently reported that the desire for affiliation and social recognition are primary participatory motives for their initial involvement in sport programs (Weiss & Petlichkoff, 1989). Humans are a social species born with innate tendencies toward sociability, and social motivation has been suggested as an important determinant of social behaviors (Allen, 2003; Baumeister & Leary, 1995). These points underscore the importance of our reliance on these social motivators. Last, and perhaps most important, the peak years of youth sport involvement coincide with the developmental shift that occurs when children begin to use information from their peer group to judge their own level of competence (Horn & Hasbrook, 1986; Horn & Weiss, 1991). Given the importance of peers in shaping children's perceptions of competence, understanding the myriad ways in which these peer relationships may occur is imperative.

Peer relationships may take many forms. Peer acceptance, friendship development, friendship quality, and peer victimization all contribute to a person's unique peer relational pattern, and these relationships may influence several psychosocial outcomes in a variety of achievement domains. Although these relationships have been studied frequently in educational domains, they are also present in the physical domain. Therefore, understanding peer relationships as they affect youngsters in sport and physical activity contexts is important.

Acceptance

Peer acceptance is conceptualized as one's status or popularity within a peer group and the degree to which members of the group like and accept one another (Ladd, Kochenderfer, & Coleman, 1997). Conversely, a lack of status or popularity is categorized as peer rejection. A child's degree of acceptance or rejection among peers is a complex issue and may depend on any number of factors, many of which may be out of the child's control, such as physical appearance and perceived normalcy of a given name (Ladd et al., 1997). Understanding peer acceptance is an important developmental topic, given that experiencing acceptance or rejection by the peer group may have a profound effect on a child's psychosocial development. In the educational domain, self-esteem, liking and avoidance of school, dissatisfaction with school, and loneliness have all been linked to a child's individual pattern of peer acceptance or rejection (Bukowski & Hoza, 1989; Ladd et al., 1997; Parker & Asher, 1993).

Other less arbitrary factors may also influence peer acceptance and rejection levels. Physical ability is a fundamental contributor to acceptance or rejection within the peer group. Gender may be a mediating variable in this relationship, because boys have consistently indicated that being successful in physical endeavors is of the highest importance for peer acceptance, whereas among girls a weaker relationship exists between physical ability and peer acceptance (Adler et al., 1992; Buchanan et al., 1976; Chase & Dummer, 1992). When children fail to achieve acceptance from their peer group (i.e., they are rejected), feelings of social isolation may result (Parker & Asher, 1993).

Ability and Peer Acceptance in Sport Research has consistently supported the existence of a connection between physical competence and peer acceptance. Evans (cited in Evans & Roberts, 1987) conducted one of the early studies on this topic. This research examined the processes of team selection that third- through sixth-grade children used on school playgrounds. Children who were considered to have the highest athletic ability were selected to be team captains, and all other children were sorted into teams in a social hierarchy according to where each fit on the ability continuum. Children who were not as skilled typically had more trouble being accepted into games on the playground, highlighting the importance of physical ability for peer acceptance levels. Frequently, the children who were not accepted into the playground games also displayed lower social skills (i.e., they tried to force their way into games in which they were not wanted), indicating a need for possible social skill intervention to facilitate peer acceptance. These types of interventions have been virtually nonexistent in sport research to date.

Affiliation Reviews of youth sport motivation literature indicate that for both boys and girls, affiliative motives are at least as strong as achievement motives in influencing children's interest in becoming involved in sport, and children's levels of perceived physical competence influences perceptions of peer acceptance (Weiss & Chaumeton, 1992; Weiss & Duncan, 1992; Weiss & Petlichkoff, 1989). This interest in affiliation further reinforces the degree to which children view sport as a viable means through which to gain acceptance from peers.

The connection between perceived competence in an achievement domain and peer acceptance has also been established in an older adolescent population. Patrick et al. (1999) conducted a qualitatively based study that incorporated interview data from 41 adolescents in grades 9, 10, and 12, and their parents. Each of the adolescents had been identified as being talented in a variety of "nonacademic" domains (e.g., sport, drama, art, music). Themes that emerged from the data indicated that peers are salient sources of information for adolescents and that they can have an important influence on commitment to talent activities. The participants perceived that social relationships were integral to activity commitment. Over half of the participants mentioned that their activity provided them with an opportunity to make friends or continue friendships. Similar numbers of participants commented about the importance of their talent activity for developing more intense friendships based on similarities that they had with peers in their particular talent domain. This study indicated that peers provide several important benefits to adolescents outside the academic domain, such as enhancement of social skills and confidence in relating to peers. Both boys and girls made equal mention of the potential socially related benefits associated with participating in a talent domain.

Not all peer relationships described, however, facilitated commitment to an achievement domain. Some of the adolescents believed that their participation in a nonsport talent activity produced negative reactions from members of their peer group. For example, one girl who was a violinist mentioned that peers rejected her by labeling her an "orch dork" because of her participation in orchestra (Patrick et al., 1999). Note that only females reported negative comments received from peers. The authors commented that these types of negative comments could be potentially damaging for adolescents who engage in activities that are not highly valued by peers and could be detrimental to commitment to the domain. The likelihood that this result would occur in the sport and physical activity domain seems low, however, given the importance and prestige that most adolescents ascribe to sport.

Friendship

The second component of peer influence is friendship. Friendship consists of a mutual, affective bond that develops between two people (Bukowski & Hoza, 1989). Research on friendships in both educational and sport-specific domains has focused on friendship expectations, domain-specific friendship qualities, and influence on psychosocial outcomes. Although friendships and peer acceptance are both considered positive forms of peer influence and are frequently studied together, note the conceptual distinctions between the two. Friendship is considered critical in moving a young person from an egocentric perspective to a more other-oriented perspective by allowing him or her to take the role of another individual (i.e., the friend). This capacity is crucial to the individual's psychosocial adjustment (Sullivan, 1953). The importance of friendship in adolescence lies in its potential ability to provide validation of a person's worth in the face of feelings of rejection from a peer group. Consequently, children who do not have a strong friendship bond (even though they may be highly accepted in the peer group) are more likely to experience feelings of loneliness. A further distinction is that peer acceptance refers to levels of acceptance from generalized others, whereas friendships refer specifically to the approval and support provided by a specific other.

Two basic psychosocial goals for children and adolescents may be met through positive peer interactions such as those experienced with friendship—connectedness and individuation (Shantz & Hobart, 1989). Connectedness refers to activities that are noncompetitive, are primarily relationship focused, and facilitate the establishment of feelings of connectedness with peers (e.g., conversing on the telephone, watching TV, or listening to music). Individuation refers to activities that are competitive and promote development of children's individuality and uniqueness through opportunities to compare their skills and abilities with others (e.g., sports or games and academic activities).

Research from developmental literature supports the conceptualization of friendships as extremely important social relationships that can provide a number of psychosocial benefits to children and adolescents. A meta-analysis of 82 research studies that used friend versus nonfriend comparisons completed by Newcombe and Bagwell (1996) provided evidence that there are positive differences in psychosocial outcomes and properties associated with engaging in a friendship that are not present in relationships that do not include that mutual, dyadic bond. Four broadband categories were identified. Positive engagement, conflict management, task activity, and subjective properties of friendships (e.g., similarities, dominance, mutual liking, and closeness) were all found to differ significantly between friends and nonfriends, with friendships providing more intense social interactions, more frequent conflict resolution, and more effective task performance.

Given the importance of friendship in developmental outcomes, several specific issues related to friendships have been studied within both educational and sport domains. These include friendship quality, the relationship between friendships and peer acceptance in school settings, friendship expectations, and the influence of friendship expectations and quality in sport.

Friendship Quality Hartup (1995) proposed that all friendships are not alike and do not carry the same expectations or consequences for individuals; therefore, a distinction should be made between having friends, the identity of one's friends, and the quality of friends in children's and adolescents' lives. Bukowski and Hoza (1989) identified three aspects of friendship: whether a child is in a mutually reciprocated friendship, the number of friends that a child has, and the quality of the friendship. These friendship qualities include features such as support, companionship, and conflict resolution. Friendship quality provides important functions such as validation and helping behaviors that can facilitate greater levels of psychosocial development than would be experienced by children who have lower quality friendships.

Note that Parker and Asher (1993) found some gender differences in friendship quality. Girls reported that their friends provided them with higher levels of validation and support, help and guidance, conflict resolution, and intimate exchange than did boys. This finding suggests that gender differences in friendship qualities may be related to the tendency for boys and girls to play differently and, therefore, to adopt different group structures and dynamics that may facilitate the development of different patterns of interaction. For example, boys are more likely to play in larger groups, a setting that may encourage a more hierarchical structure. Girls, conversely, are more likely to participate in smaller groups, a setting that may encourage closer (and perhaps more equal) relationships. These findings are of particular interest in the sport and physical activity context, which contains both hierarchical and dyadic relationships.

Friendships and Peer Acceptance in the Educational Domain Connections between friendships and peer acceptance have been well established in educational and developmental literature. Parker and Asher (1993) conducted a study of third- through fifth-graders to determine the relationships among friendships, friendship quality, and peer acceptance. Results showed that experiencing high levels of peer acceptance provided no guarantee that a child would have close friendships. Feelings of loneliness were greater in children without best friends than among those children who had best friends. This relationship held true regardless of the acceptance level of the child, which indicated the importance of friendship in providing a positive psychosocial environment for a child. Children who do not have high-quality friendships are likely to be lacking a support system that can provide a buffer against feelings of loneliness, particularly if the child is already experiencing greater overall feelings of loneliness because of lack of peer acceptance.

Friendship Expectations People carry different expectations for friends based on the context of the relationship, and even young children are capable of distinguishing among different friendship processes (Ladd, Kochenderfer, & Coleman, 1996). Children report more satisfaction with friendships that provide higher levels of validation and exclusivity, and that include less conflict. Therefore, in the early stages of friendship formation, children show preference for relationships that provide positive features rather than ones with high levels of negative interactions. Moreover, children may try to maintain these types of relationships over time because they provide children with more positive outcomes than other types of friendships.

Conflict in friendships has been associated with difficulty adjusting to school, particularly among boys. First, this circumstance may reflect the fact that boys, who generally play in larger peer groups than girls do, tend to have fewer friendships and may therefore be more vulnerable to negative affect stemming from these relationships. Second, boys and girls tend to resolve their conflicts differently. Girls resolve disagreements more quickly and with greater satisfaction (Ladd et al., 1996; Parker & Asher, 1993).

Ladd et al. (1996) also found that positive friendship qualities were associated with more positive school adjustment. Specifically, children who believe that their friendships provide validation or aid tended to be happier in school, considered their classmates more supportive of them, and were more likely to develop positive school attitudes. But it is unclear whether positive outcomes of certain friendship processes are found in contexts other than school adjustment (e.g., sport and physical activity).

Friendship Expectations and Friendship Quality in Sport The existing knowledge of friendship and friendship quality in developmental psychol-

ogy literature has led the way for recent increases in popularity of research on sport friendships. In an early study, Bigelow, Lewko, and Salhani (1989) found that sport-involved boys and girls (ages 9 to 12 years) regarded team membership and team-sport involvement to be positive features affecting friendship expectations. Furthermore, children perceived to have less sport skill were regarded less favorably than were children who were considered better players, possibly because of the perception that lower-ability children were less likely to provide important sport friendship expectations, such as helping and sharing.

Zarbatany and colleagues (Zarbatany, Ghesquiere, & Mohr, 1992; Zarbatany, Hartmann, & Rankin, 1990) investigated children's (ages 10 to 12 years) perceptions of liked and disliked friendship behaviors when engaging in a variety of activities. The authors found that children hold different expectations for their friends in different activities; however, these expectations do not differ with respect to gender. For academic activities, friends were expected to provide helping behaviors, whereas noncompetitive activities were expected to elicit including and accepting behaviors. In activities such as sports and games, Zarbatany and colleagues (1992) found that friends were expected to demonstrate behaviors meant to enhance positive self-evaluations (e.g., ego reinforcement and preferential treatment). This expectation may be due to the competitive nature of these activities and the importance of maintaining a positive self-image among peers by being successful at these activities.

An important series of studies conducted by Weiss and colleagues (Weiss, Smith, & Theeboom, 1996; Weiss & Smith, 1999, 2002) sought to provide a better definition of the friendship expectations that children have within the sport domain. Weiss et al. (1996) first conducted in-depth interviews with 8- to 16-year-old sport program participants to discover what characteristics these children preferred their best sport friend to exhibit. The children varied considerably in their interpersonal relationship success (i.e., some participants were viewed as popular or had many friends, and others were considered less well liked and had fewer friends). The researchers identified 12 higher-order themes. These included the positive friendship dimensions of companionship, pleasant play or association, self-esteem enhancement, help and guidance, prosocial behavior, intimacy, loyalty, things in common, attractive personal qualities, emotional support, absence of conflicts, and conflict resolution. Moreover, four negative friendship dimensions emerged: conflict, unattractive personal qualities, betrayal, and inaccessibility.

The Weiss et al. study (1996) demonstrated that although the positive friendship dimensions found in the developmental literature were similar to those found in sport-specific situations, unique dimensions to sport friendships necessitate further exploration. For example, a positive dimension that emerged as being highly important to children in sport friendships was self-esteem enhancement. Children in the study expected their sport friends to provide them with reinforcement for favorable aspects of their sport abilities. Given the importance that children place on physical competence, it is not surprising that children expect their friends to try to facilitate self-esteem in sport activities. Failure to engage in this type of behavior could be potentially damaging to a friendship between children, particularly if a child perceives him- or herself to be less successful in sport.

The emergence of the four negative dimensions further indicated the complexity of friendships and the need for research that addresses all potential components of friendship for adolescents, particularly in the sport domain. Although most friendship research focuses on the positive aspects of friendships, negative dimensions are also present, and a better understanding of these negative aspects of friendship would yield greater insight into sport friendship.

As a follow-up to the findings of the Weiss et al. (1996) study, Weiss and Smith (1999, 2002) developed and validated a friendship quality scale based on the specific expectations that children have for their sport-related friendships. Their instrument, the Sport Friendship Quality Scale (SFQS) is a six factor, Likert-type scale. The six factors include self-esteem enhancement and supportiveness, loyalty and intimacy, things in common, companionship and pleasant play, conflict resolution, and conflict. Self-esteem enhancement and supportiveness is indicative of a friend's efforts to praise and encourage. Loyalty and intimacy refers to a friend's lending important support to another person (e.g., defending someone), as well as sharing interactions of a close nature. Things in common reflects similarities among friends on interests, values, and thinking. Companionship and pleasant play indicates the degree to which friends get along well and participate in fun activities together. Conflict refers to whether friends get mad and fight with one another. Last, conflict resolution consists of efforts made by friends to resolve disagreements. Examination of this measure has indicated a developmental preference for certain forms of friendship quality. Older adolescents (ages 14 to 18 years) rated loyalty and intimacy, things in common, and conflict

higher than did younger participants (ages 10 to 13 years), who rated companionship and pleasant play higher (Weiss & Smith, 2002).

Although the SFQS is still a relatively new instrument in the field of sport psychology, it represents an important step toward creation of valid, reliable, sport-specific tools for measuring such complex constructs as friendship quality in a sport context. By recognizing the physical domain as a distinct area within which unique contributions to psychosocial development are made, sport and exercise psychologists can begin to examine more closely the numerous facets that make it an important aspect of childhood and adolescent development.

Smith (1999) further extended the peer influence literature work within sport and exercise psychology. This study was grounded in Harter's (1978, 1981) competence motivation theory and used 12- to 15-year-old male and female participants to examine the relationships among peer relations, physical self-worth, affective responses toward physical activity, cognitive and behavioral physical activity motivation, and physical maturity. Smith's model posited that more positive perceptions of peer relationships (i.e., friendships and peer acceptance) would be predictive of motivation to participate in physical activity because of increased levels of self-worth and positive affect. The model was tested separately for boys and girls.

Perceptions of friendships and peer acceptance were found to influence children's affective responses to physical activity, as well as their physical self-worth. The results indicated that these two aspects of peer influence represent important components of children's youth sport and physical activity participation and, perhaps, discontinuation of their sport involvement.

Friendship is a positive form of peer relationship that is crucial to psychosocial development in both educational and sport domains. Friendships must be reciprocal between two people, and both members expect their friendship to provide specific qualities, such as support, validation, and helping, depending on the type of achievement domain in which the friendship exists. Although friendships and peer relationships are both positive forms of peer influence, they can be mutually exclusive, which necessitates further exploration to understand the unique contribution of each to developmental outcomes.

Victimization

Although the majority of peer relationship research in developmental sport and exercise psychology focuses on the positive constructs of peer acceptance and friendship, a third component of the peer influence puzzle, peer victimization, is also linked to children's psychological and social development. Note that peer victimization is not the same concept as peer rejection. Rejection describes a situation in which a child has achieved little or no liking or status within the peer group. Victimization refers to behaviors that can be considered physically or verbally threatening (Ladd, Kochenderfer, & Coleman, 1997). Victimization is a more active outcome of a peer relationship in which the recipient of the negative behaviors not only fails to gain acceptance (i.e., is rejected) but also may be subjected to a variety of negative behaviors including general outcomes (e.g., being picked on), physical outcomes (e.g., being pushed or hit), direct verbal victimization (e.g., having other kids say mean things to him or her), or indirect verbal victimization (e.g., being the target of gossip or rumors). This concept could be particularly important in sport.

In their body of childhood peer victimization research, Kochenderfer and Ladd (1996a, 1996b, 1997) have investigated such topics as negative psychosocial outcomes (e.g., school avoidance and maladjustment), effective strategies for coping with victimization, and the unique contributions of victimization to maladjustment. This line of research with victimized children suggests that the presence or absence of victimizing behaviors was the catalyst for future school maladjustment and avoidance behaviors.

We will now extend the discussion of existing research on peer victimization by exploring findings on psychosocial outcomes of victimization within educational contexts, the responses that children make to being victimized, and the limited research on victimization within sport.

Outcomes of Victimization in the Educational Domain

Kochenderfer and Ladd (1996a) identified victimized children by administering a self-report scale known as the Perceptions of Peer Support Scale (PPSS; Kochenderfer & Ladd, 1996a). The PPSS allows children to report whether they have been victimized and to identify what form the victimization has taken (general, direct physical, direct verbal, and indirect verbal). School liking or avoidance, loneliness, academic progress, and a variety of behavioral responses (e.g., anxiousness) were also assessed. More than 50% of the children reported being victimized in some form either "sometimes" or "a lot." The direct and indirect verbal victimization behaviors were the best predictors of school disliking, indicating that different forms of victimization behaviors may result in different behavioral or cognitive outcomes. Although no significant gender differences were found, the trend among highly victimized children was that boys were more likely to be targeted for direct forms of aggression and girls were more likely to experience indirect verbal aggression. Other lines of research into peer victimization behaviors have found the same trend. Several studies have indicated that girls may be more likely to engage in relational aggression than boys are and that these types of behaviors may have different psychosocial implications than do more direct forms of victimization (Crick, 1996; Crick & Gropeter, 1995). No clear evidence is currently available about whether these gender differences may be present in a physical setting such as sport and physical activity.

Children who experienced victimization behaviors at the hands of peers are also more likely to be lonely at school and to express a desire to avoid school altogether (Kochenderfer & Ladd, 1996b). Not surprisingly, the greater the amount of victimization, the greater the amount of maladjustment experienced by the victim. Children who experience relatively stable patterns of victimization experience school maladjustment at a greater level. These findings supported the idea that peer victimization is a cause of school maladjustment problems, such as the desire to avoid school.

Responses to Victimization

Because of the potentially negative outcomes associated with peer victimization, understanding what actions may be effective in responding to being victimized is crucial. Kochenderfer and Ladd (1997) found a gender difference among children who were recipients of any form of aggression. Boys were more likely to fight back, whereas girls were more inclined to walk away from the aggressor. Moreover, both boys and girls were more likely to be victimized by male children. For that reason, girls may be less likely to fight back if they perceive themselves to be at a physical disadvantage with a bully. When the effect of fighting back on subsequent victimization behaviors was assessed four to six months later, Kochenderfer and Ladd found that victims of aggressive behaviors who fought back were more likely to maintain a pattern of stable victimization throughout the school year. This result was attributed to the possibility that these children were ineffectual at fighting-back behaviors. Given the apparent ineffectiveness of fighting back for victimized children (particularly boys), other strategies may be necessary for reducing the levels of victimization behaviors in children.

Victimization behaviors typically involve abusive or exploitative experiences that can lead children to develop strong negative, affective associations with school. Similarly, these negative associations that may occur because of victimization can have an effect on school avoidance behaviors. This information could be of particular relevance for contexts other than school (e.g., sport and physical activity) in determining reasons for attrition or avoidance in achievement domains. Understanding the implications of all forms of peer influence on psychosocial outcomes is crucial for creating positive sport and physical activity experiences for children and adolescents.

Victimization in Sport Systematic study of negative peer relationships in sport has lagged well behind other areas of peer influence in the sport domain, although some studies do exist. Kunesh, Hasbrook, and Lewthwaite (1992) provided some insight into the potential pattern of victimizing behaviors surrounding peer group physical activity influence by conducting interviews, observations, and sociometric evaluations with eight 11- to 12-year-old girls about their peer interactions in, and affective responses to, three different physical activity settings. The settings used for the study were formal sport (physical education classes), informal activity (e.g., tetherball or four-square), and exercise contexts. Results showed that negative peer interactions occurred most consistently during evaluative activities. These negative peer interactions were characterized by repeated stable criticisms of girls' athletic abilities and by casting girls in a role subordinate to that of the boys in the class. Although the authors did not directly label these behaviors as peer victimization behaviors, this may be considered a starting point for studies in sport and physical activity that address those behaviors. Given the negative affect associated with peer victimization and the gender-specific nature of the behaviors, more knowledge is needed about how victimization behaviors can operate as a negative socialization mechanism that may discourage adolescents (particularly girls) from participation altogether.

In an effort to explore the unique pattern of positive and negative peer relationships, Partridge (2003) used a cluster analysis to describe 10- to 13-year-old athletes on peer acceptance, friendship, friendship quality, peer victimization, perceived social and physical competence, and affective responses to participation. Approximately 49% of the sport sample reported experiencing some form of victimization, which was consistent with previous educational samples (Kochenderfer & Ladd, 1996a), but only 5.8% of the sample indicated that the victimization occurred "a lot." This figure was below that found in previous studies of classroom incidence rates of victimization, which were between 10% (Perry, Kusel, & Perry, 1988) and 18% (Olweus, 1991). Moreover, physical victimization behaviors were almost nonexistent in the sport sample. Given the importance of peer victimization in affecting affective and behavioral outcomes in education, additional systematic study is needed to explore the incidence and nature of victimization behaviors in sport.

Much remains unknown about victimization in sport and physical activity contexts. Research is needed in this area of peer influence to increase knowledge about what effect victimization behaviors may have on youth sport athletes. Additionally, more research is necessary to delineate how different forms of peer relationships (i.e., peer acceptance or rejection, friendship, friendship quality) may or may not affect each other within the specific context of sport and physical activity.

Leadership

Coaching and leadership behaviors have been popular topics for many years in sport and exercise psychology (see chapter 11 of this volume). Studies of peer leadership behaviors, however, are scarce. The importance of this topic is underscored by the usefulness of having team members who can guide and motivate their peers on a team to achieve success and attain higher levels of motivation. The few empirical studies that have assessed peer leadership behaviors have done so primarily to identify specific personality traits that could be used to separate peer leaders from nonleaders on a team. In these early studies, such identifiers as high skill level, higher levels of internal locus of control (Yukelson, Weinberg, Richardson, & Jackson, 1981), player position (Lee, Coburn, & Partridge, 1981), and greater levels of masculinity sex-role orientation (Andersen & Williams, 1987; Wittig, Duncan, & Schurr, 1987) were found to be associated with perceptions of peer leadership. These findings have supported approaches to leadership that state that leadership effectiveness is context specific (Chelladurai, 1990). That is, the traits that may produce an effective peer leader on a volleyball team may not be in agreement with the traits that create effective leadership in student government.

Glenn and Horn (1993) found support for this approach in an important early study on this topic with female high school soccer athletes. These participants completed inventories on perceptions of competence, sex-role orientation, competitive trait anxiety, and global self-worth. Actual sport competence was measured through coach ratings. Leadership behavior was measured with coach, peer, and self-ratings on the Sport Leadership Behavior Inventory (SLBI). Results indicated that athletes who rated themselves higher in perceived competence, femininity, and masculinity also rated themselves higher on leadership ability. Peer ratings revealed that athletes who were rated high in leadership by their peers exhibited a profile of high levels of competitive trait anxiety, masculinity, skill, and perceived competence. Finally, the coach ratings of peer leadership were associated primarily with levels of skill. Moreover, consistent with previous work (Lee et al., 1981), athletes in central field positions were more likely to be rated high on leadership ability than were athletes in noncentral field positions.

Todd and Kent (2004) conducted a more recent and comprehensive look at perceptions of peer leadership behaviors. Using Bales' (1950) role differentiation theory, the authors asked a sample of interscholastic athletes to describe idealized peer leadership behaviors through ordinal ranking of leader characteristics. Bales' theory proposed the existence of two categories of leadership behaviors: instrumental behaviors, which are concerned with tasks, and expressive behaviors, which are concerned with morale and relationships among group members. Overall, the athletes identified "working hard in games and practice" as the most important leadership behavior. Interestingly, a gender difference was found in the sample. Male athletes reported that instrumental behaviors were significantly more important, whereas female athletes showed no preference for either form of leadership behavior. Therefore, the effectiveness of a peer leader seems to be guided by a series of psychological and personal characteristics and is influenced by the gender of the athletes involved. Clearly, more research is needed to provide a more robust understanding of how peer leadership is cultivated and expressed in sport and how peers may take advantage of leadership opportunities to facilitate success in sport.

Future Research Directions

The relative deficiency of peer influence as a research topic provides a number of areas for future research. Sport researchers should endeavor to assess parental,

sibling, coach, and peer influences concurrently to provide a more complete picture of the influence of social relationships on an individual's sport experience. By definition, social influence is a dynamic process, and the research process should reflect that concept. The existing literature has approached social influence as a series of parts. These studies have provided detailed information on each component, but our understanding of how these parts interact with each other is insufficient. This gap in our understanding needs to be addressed if we are to understand social influence in a multidirectional manner.

To gain a more complete understanding of the dynamic nature of children's peer relationships in sport and their effects on psychosocial outcomes, lines of longitudinal research should be initiated in youth sport. This type of research can provide valuable information pertaining to age-related changes in peer relationships, perceptions of competence, and affect. Age-related changes in preferred sources of competence information (Horn & Amorose, 1998; Horn & Hasbrook, 1986) and friendship qualities (Weiss & Smith, 1999) have been found in the sport domain, and these developmental shifts underscore the importance of using a longitudinal approach to understanding how peer influence may change over time.

Lastly, development of an intervention-based system for children and adolescents in sport should be the ultimate goal of this line of research. By gaining a better understanding of how youth sport participants affect each other through their peer relationships, sport researchers have a better chance of structuring sport experiences that can encourage both physical and social benefits in the physical activity domain.

Sibling Social Influence

The study of various forms of social influence is prolific in the sport psychology literature. One form of social influence that has virtually been neglected is the influence of siblings on individuals' sport and physical activity involvement and achievement. Nearly 85% of all American adults have at least one biological sibling, and almost 95% have a sibling of some relation (Crispell, 1996). The sibling relationship possesses a number of unique characteristics that provide merit for including this form of social influence in the study of children's socialization processes.

The sibling relationship is potentially the longest-lasting relationship that people will experience across their lifetime (Cicirelli, 1995). Given this longevity, the sibling relationship has considerable potential to serve as a significant and meaningful form of social influence throughout the lifespan. The time spent with one's siblings is estimated to be much longer than the time spent with one's parents because the typical child–parent relationship lasts approximately 30 to 50 years whereas the average sibling relationship lasts between 50 and 80 years (Bank, 1995; Waters, 1987). Sibling relationships during the developmental years are especially important because these relationships differ from most other relationships, including parent–child and child–peer. The sibling relationship has the potential to influence a wide range of processes throughout one's life (Dunn & Kendrick, 1981; Stoneman & Brody, 1982).

The acquisition of a sibling relationship is ascribed, rather than chosen (Cicirelli, 1995). People do not choose who their sibling or siblings will be; the brothers or sisters who ultimately exert some degree of influence in the socialization process result from choices made by parental figures or because of family expansion. The relationship, in other words, is the result of assigned social forms of influence or the assigned existence of the others with whom one will live. The ascribed aspect of sibling influence and relationships is powerful in terms of the type of influence that a brother or sister can or may exert (e.g., roles, expectations, and values) as well as in relation to a child's experiences within her or his particular family. Furthermore, brothers' and sisters' lives are often composed of a variety of shared experiences as well as separate experiences that collectively affect the socialization process of each sibling.

The sibling relationship is also unique because during childhood and adolescence, children may spend more time in the company of their brothers or sisters than their parents or peers. Research on early childhood social influence revealed that before children were school age they spent a significant portion of the day in intimate contact with their siblings (Lawson & Ingleby, 1974). Even after children enter school, researchers suggest that the majority of nonschool time is spent in close interaction with siblings (Bigner, 1974; Stoneman, Brody, & MacKinnon, 1984). According to Cicirelli (1995), the sibling relationship, in contrast to the parent–child or peer relationship, is relatively egalitarian because the power difference between the members of the dyad eventually becomes small.

Although social influences have constituted a large area of inquiry in sport, the focus has been on parents, peers, and coaches. Little information exists about how siblings, who during youth, may serve as a bridge between parents and peers and thus contribute to the socialization processes of sport. Fortunately, the empirically based efforts to understand this relationship and its effect on sport socialization and achievement have a solid basis in relevant theories, developmental psychological research on siblings, and the studies to date that have included brothers and sisters in the sport psychology literature.

Relevant Theoretical Perspectives

The study of social influence in youth sport and physical activity in recent years has often been grounded in socialization or developmentally based motivational theories (Brustad, Babkes & Smith, 2001). Many socialization and motivational theories contend that significant others play a critical role in the development of achievement beliefs and behaviors (Weiss & Ferrar-Caja, 2002). Therefore, brothers and sisters, like parents, have the capacity to influence whether a person chooses to play sport or not, as well as the nature of his or her athletic experiences. Harter's (1978, 1981) competence motivation theory and Eccles et al.'s (1983) expectancy-value theory in particular emphasize the critical role that significant others play as agents in shaping the patterns of beliefs and behaviors that contribute to children's activity choices and achievement outcomes. These theories further highlight the importance of the people whom children consider significant others and how children receive and perceive those influences. Most important, these theories provide a framework for investigations into the factors that may influence children's sport and physical activity socialization and psychosocial correlates.

Research conducted to date within Harter's (1978, 1981) competence motivation theory has targeted parents, peers, and coaches as forms of social influence that have the potential to contribute to children's sense of competence, control, affect, and motivation such that they engage in future mastery attempts within the athletic domain. According to theoretical contentions, sibling influence could contribute to a person's competence motivation. Theoretically based study of siblings becomes increasingly more relevant when the findings on developmental shifts in the sources of competence information are considered in combination with Stevenson's (1990) findings that siblings affect one another's sport socialization process somewhat later than parents do but not parallel to peers. Horn and colleagues' (Horn & Hasbrook, 1986, 1987; Horn & Weiss, 1991) line of research suggests that younger children tend to rely on adult feedback to determine their competence, whereas older children shift to using their peers and ultimately themselves as sources of information for evaluation of ability. Because siblings, during youth, may serve as an enduring source of competence information over a long span of years, examinations guided by Harter's model may further our understanding of the role of brothers and sisters.

Expectancy-value theory (Eccles et al., 1983) is also well suited for the study of social influence, such as siblings, on children's sport and physical activity choice behavior. Tenets of the theory maintain that significant others' expectancies for children's success in a particular domain as well as their value of success in that domain predict socialization practices that ultimately influence children's likelihood of participation and achievement in that specific domain. Although the research conducted within the expectancy-value framework has mainly focused on adults, particularly parents, as relevant significant others, Weiss and Ferrar-Caja (2002) poignantly noted that siblings are a form of social influence neglected in the research on activity choice behavior framed by Eccles and colleagues' model. Siblings, like parents, therefore theoretically have the potential to influence youth activity choices through their expectancy-related and value-related beliefs for particular achievement domains or activities.

Both of the aforementioned theories provide valid means of examining the influence of siblings as contributors to the experiences of youth in sport and physical activity. Note, however, that research has typically examined social influence entities, typically parents, in isolation rather than as components of a functioning system that has the potential to exert reciprocal and multidimensional effects. Studies have traditionally looked at the effect of parents on children and to a lesser extent the reverse influence of children on parents (e.g., Weiss & Hayashi, 1995), both at the exclusion of considering the effects of other significant individuals, such as siblings, who may exert an influence on both parents and other children, thus contributing to socialization and motivational outcomes.

A complete understanding of the influence that significant others, specifically family members, have on achievement and activity behaviors requires the inclusion of siblings in the examination of socialization processes (Stoneman & Brody, 1993). Based on

this contention, family systems theory should also be considered a suitable framework for examinations of brothers' and sisters' effect on one another. In the initial conception of family systems theory, Bowen (1960) conceptualized the family as a unit that functions because of a network of interlocking relationships. Accordingly, family systems theorists maintain that any change within the family can create change within the family system (Walsh & McGraw, 2002). In this process siblings can serve several functions. Families, like other systems, are composed of multiple components that interact with each other in a reciprocal manner. Cicirelli (1995) contended that systems consist of parts that have direct and reciprocal interactions that can ultimately cause indirect effects on various other components.

Family structures have changed drastically in recent years (Greendorfer, Lewko & Rosengren, 2002), necessitating research into how these changes have affected the processes of youth sport socialization. One result of these changes may be the increased salience of sibling influence in youth socialization processes because of higher rates of maternal employment and potentially more time for siblings to be exclusively with one another in the absence of adults. Given the nature of sport today, children's participation may affect the entire family. One child's participation in an activity can inadvertently influence the roles and expectations for other children in the family. Family systems theory, therefore, is a potentially ideal framework for understanding the sibling relationship and brothers and sisters' influence on one another in the sport and physical activity arena.

We now provide a brief review of the research on siblings from the developmental psychology literature. This overview is intended to illuminate the existing knowledge on brothers' and sisters' influence and sibling relationships outside the physical domain. We hope that the summary of research will inform the research conducted within the sport and physical activity realm.

Sibling Influence Research From Developmental Psychology

The extant research on siblings has focused primarily on three areas: constellation variables' effect on the sibling relationship, the effect of one sibling's unique circumstances on other siblings, and aspects of the quality of sibling relationships. The study of sibling constellation variables has historically been the focus in this area of sibling research. Cicirelli (1995) defines a sibling constellation as

> a hierarchical network of sibling positions within the family that identifies the status of each sibling relative to other siblings in the family. The positions in the network are defined or determined in terms of the number of siblings (or size of the network), the birth order associated with each position, gender, age and age spacing between siblings. (p. 18)

Most early research focused on the effect that birth ordinal position (i.e., when a child was born in relation to other siblings) had on outcomes such as educational attainment and other achievement outcomes (Bigner, 1974; Butcher & Case, 1994; Paulhus, Trapnell, & Chen, 1999). Much of the research on the effects of birth order among siblings was directed at the nature of power imbalances between siblings. These studies revealed that the roles adopted by siblings relative to one another often result in older children taking on more authority or management and younger siblings typically being compliant (Burhmester & Furman, 1990). Although evidence of power differentials among siblings does exist, most research on the effects of birth order is equivocal. Moreover, their meaningfulness has been questioned because the nature of sibling relationship appears to become more egalitarian with development (Bank & Kahn, 1982; Dunn, 1983; Schachter, 1963; Stoneman, Brody, & MacKinnon, 1984; Sutton-Smith & Rosenberg, 1968).

With regard to gender, research suggests that siblings generally prefer their same-sex sibling (Bowerman & Dobash, 1974). Same-sex sibling dyads tend to engage in more caretaking, to assist and support one another, and to experience more closeness than opposite-sex sibling dyads (Akiyama, Elliott, & Antonucci, 1996; Mendelson, DeVilla, Fitch, & Goodman, 1997). Same-sex siblings, however, tend to experience more conflict in young adulthood despite having provided one another with a strong influence on identity formation (Martin, 1990; Stocker, Furman, & Lanthier, 1997).

Findings related to how age spacing affects the sibling relationship suggest that the amount of age disparity is the discriminating factor. Generally, the greater the age disparity, the less likely siblings are to play with one another and the less positive and prosocial their behaviors are toward one another (Koch, 1960). Siblings with less age disparity tend to form coalitions and report strong psychological closeness to one another. The younger sibling tends to have stronger feelings toward an older sibling than the reverse (Bowerman & Dobash, 1974).

Despite these positive factors associated with close age proximity between siblings, researchers have also found that conflict and aggression are common among brothers and sisters close in age (Minnett, Vandell, & Santrock, 1983).

The effect of one sibling's uniqueness on another has been studied in relation to a variety of circumstances, notably when a sibling has a disability or illness (see Stoneman & Berman, 1993, for a comprehensive review) or when one sibling is gifted (Chamrad, Robinson, & Janos, 1995; Colangelo & Brower, 1987; Grenier, 1985; Tuttle & Cornell, 1993). For example, the presence of an academically gifted child in the family has consistently been found to have an influence on the sibling relationship. Researchers in this area contend that the special recognition given to a gifted child by parents has an effect on the sibling relationship. Outcomes such as more aggression by the nonacademically gifted sibling toward his or her gifted sibling have been observed among brothers and sisters (Tesser, 1980). These and other potential negative effects, however, were found to subside by late adolescence (Colangelo & Brower, 1987). Findings also indicate that in sibling dyads with one academically gifted child the siblings have different experiences with respect to one another. For example, gifted children reported enjoyment from engaging in competition with their nongifted sibling, whereas the nongifted child did not enjoy this competition (Grenier, 1985). Second borns labeled as gifted reported lower feelings of warmth and closeness with their siblings as compared with first borns' sentiments about their connection to younger siblings (Tuttle & Cornell, 1993). Overall, the presence of a gifted child in a family does not reveal prolonged detrimental effects on the sibling relationship. In some cases parents have viewed the presence of a gifted child as the catalyst for fewer problems between brothers and sisters (Chamrad et al., 1995).

Findings indicate that siblings relate to one another along a number of dimensions (Buhrmester & Furman, 1990; Furman & Buhrmester, 1985). The most salient qualities of the sibling relationship that appear across the lifespan are warmth, conflict, rivalry, and relative status or power (Furman & Buhrmester, 1985; Stocker et al., 1997). During childhood, adolescence, and adulthood, warmth consists of intimacy, prosocial behavior, companionship, admiration, and affection. Conflict has typically been composed of quarreling, antagonism, and competition, and rivalry has been linked to parental favoritism (Burhmester & Furman, 1990). Power, which reflects the relative nurturance or dominance of one sibling over another, tends to be more important when children are young and usually dissipates during adulthood. Extensive research has been conducted on how these qualities of sibling relationships vary depending on the composition of the dyad (e.g., age disparity, ordinal position, and gender) (see Dunn, 1983, 1992, for complete reviews). With this review of some of the research on siblings from developmental psychology in mind, we shift attention to the extant literature on siblings in the sport and physical activity domain.

Sibling Research in Sport and Physical Activity

Despite the logical arguments for investigating the contribution of brothers and sisters to sport participation and achievement, relatively few empirical findings exist about siblings in the sport and physical activity domain. Researchers consistently identify the family as an important influence in the youth sport and physical activity socialization process (Greendorfer, Lewko, & Rosengren, 1996). The nature or specific constitution of the family, however, is often not defined or delineated (Martin & Dodder, 1991). Therefore, when sibling influence has been examined in sport and physical activity, it has more often than not been under the umbrella of investigations that have focused on multiple family members or more general sources of social influence. The studies that have examined siblings in the context of sport and physical activity initially focused on the effect of family constellation variables, such as birth order and gender of siblings, on individual's activity choices and other psychosocial outcomes. Later research moved to explorations of siblings' effects on sport socialization and the forms of influence that facilitate this effect.

Findings from research focused on the relationship between sibling birth order and choice of activity consistently indicated that older siblings usually avoid sports considered dangerous, whereas younger siblings typically engage in sports that are considered more risky (Casher, 1977; Longstreath, 1970; Nisbett, 1968; Yiannakis, 1976). For example, Casher (1977) found that birth order among male Ivy League university individual-sport athletes was significantly related to participation in dangerous sports. First borns avoided dangerous or harm-inducing sports. Furthermore, the proportion of athletes in dangerous sports increased as birth order increased. More third- and fourth-born individuals participated in harm-inducing sports as compared with first and second borns. No differences were found in the proportion of first- and second-born individuals involved in dangerous sports.

Relative birth order among siblings has also been associated with anxiety in sport performance (Flowers & Brown, 2002). College-aged male and female track athletes who were first-born siblings reported greater cognitive and somatic anxiety than did their later-born siblings. Findings on birth order and attraction to more risky or dangerous sports and the anxiety experienced in athletics may be accounted for by variations in parental socialization factors or parent behaviors toward their first born as compared with their later-born children. For example, parents have been found to attend more closely to their older children, to be more overprotective and cautious, and to be more directive than they are with their younger children (Koch, 1960; Lasko, 1954). As a result older children seem to have a stronger sense of fear instilled in them as compared with their younger siblings. Despite the logic described, evidence of parents' differential behaviors toward their children born into various ordinal positions and the subsequent effect on attraction to various sports and physical activities has yet to be thoroughly explored.

The research focused on whether siblings have a meaningful influence on the sport and physical activity involvement of their brothers and sisters has been equivocal to date. Findings from early sport socialization research suggested that siblings play at most a minimal role in one another's sport socialization and that they are less significant than parents are in accounting for the variance in sport involvement in both male and female children (Greendorfer & Lewko, 1978). Subsequent examinations of the contribution of siblings to the sport socialization process differ. These later studies consistently indicated that brothers and sisters affect their siblings' sport participation in a variety of ways (Ebihara, Ikeda, & Mylashita, 1983; Lewko & Ewing, 1980; Raudsepp & Viira, 2000; Stevenson, 1990; Weiss & Barber, 1995; Wold & Anderssen, 1992).

Siblings have long been thought to influence the play, sport, and physical activities of one another (Sutton-Smith, Roberts, & Rosenberg, 1964). In particular, brothers were initially believed to have a meaningful influence on their sister's sport involvement (Portz, 1973, cited in Greendorfer & Lewko, 1978; Zoble, 1973, cited in Greendorfer & Lewko, 1978). Greendorfer and Lewko's (1978) research did not support this belief and, more important, provided indirect evidence to contradict this previously popular sibling-opposite hypothesis, which suggested that older brothers influenced female sport participation by exerting role-modeling effects that contributed to sport socialization.

Although little support exists for the sibling-opposite hypothesis in sport socialization, results from some studies indicate that a sibling-similarity hypothesis may have merit (Lewko & Ewing, 1980; Wold & Anderssen, 1992). For example, in addition to mothers, sisters contribute significantly to high levels of female sport involvement but do not appear to contribute to male sport participation (Lewko & Ewing, 1980). Wold and Anderssen found that sport participation of same-sex family members was more strongly associated with male and female youth sport participation than was the sport participation of opposite-sex family members. Ebihara and colleagues (1983) found that although the father was consistently identified as the primary sport-socializing agent, if he was dethroned as the most significant socializing role model his role was entrusted to older like-sex siblings.

The research also suggests that older siblings play a central role in their younger siblings' sport participation. Besides the influence of parents and peers, older siblings' physical activity levels and support for sport participation were found to influence the level of sport involvement among European adolescents (Wold & Anderssen, 1992). Results also revealed that males who did not have an older brother were more likely to be involved in sport than were males who had an older male sibling who was inactive. Given that a corresponding relationship was also found for females, having an inactive older sibling of the same sex seems to be more of a negative influence than having no older sibling at all.

Besides parents, older brothers and sisters were perceived as providing more influence to girls who were highly involved in sport as compared with those who were not (Lewko & Ewing, 1980). These socialization effects have consistently been more profound for females as exemplified by Weiss and Barber's (1995) findings that the effects of interest and encouragement by older siblings on younger siblings' sport participation significantly increased for females in terms of their athletic involvement between 1979 and 1989. They further found that female collegiate athletes reported stronger perceptions of older sibling support for their sport participation than did male and female nonathletes. The research clearly establishes the foundation for continued investigations into the meaningfulness of the influence of older siblings and those of the same sex on youth sport socialization processes.

Studies focused on the identification of specific forms of influence exerted by brothers and sisters have been rare. The limited empirical evidence suggests that siblings' role modeling and support are the primary mechanisms that influence one another's sport involvement (Ebihara et al., 1983; Stevenson, 1990). In a study conducted with Japanese youth, two prominent features of interaction patterns between siblings were apparent; younger borns had reinforcing functions for *sport* involvement of older borns, and older borns served as role models for later borns' *socialization* into *sport* within their family (Ebihara et al., 1983). Stevenson's (1990) interviews with Canadian national team members revealed that siblings played a role in the sponsored recruitment, or introductions, that the athletes had to sport and that the mechanism for sibling socialization into sport was mainly through role modeling. His data further indicated that siblings contribute to the entanglement that athletes encounter when they become involved in an activity because of personal relationships. Specifically, the support of a brother or sister for an individual's sport involvement or the older sibling's confirmation of the younger sibling's role identity as an athlete was evident (Stevenson, 1990).

Sibling influence on the amount of physical activity in which youth engage has recently received more substantial interest (Davison, 2004; Duncan, Duncan, Stryker, & Chaumeton, 2004; Raudsepp & Viira, 2000). Davison found that higher levels of physical activity among middle school aged males and females were associated with higher levels of activity support from their siblings. Activity-related support from family members besides parents appears to be a crucial mechanism for the promotion and maintenance of physical activity among adolescents. Findings from another study of sibling effects on physical activity levels among 930 siblings nested within 371 families indicated that siblings within the same family tend to have more similar physical activity habits to one another as compared with children in other families (Duncan et al., 2004). In terms of birth-order effects, results revealed that younger siblings participated in less physical activity than did older siblings. Furthermore, these researchers suggested that the correlation of physical activity levels among siblings may be higher than the correlation in physical activity levels between children and their parents. Raudsepp and Viira (2000) also studied the influence of parents and siblings on physical activity in Estonian adolescents who had both a brother and sister and who lived in a two-parent home. Results revealed that male adolescents' physical activity levels were significantly associated with moderate to very hard physical activity levels of the father and brother, whereas female adolescents' physical activity levels were related to both parents' moderate intensity and sister's physical activity. Based on the existing set of research, siblings clearly appear to be important agents of physical activity socialization. Mechanisms of influence were hypothesized to be instruction, advice, and support, but no evidence of the exact process of siblings' influence on one another's physical activity has been revealed.

Future Research Directions

Although sibling research clearly exists in the sport domain, the studies have been intermittent and lack the continuity of more popular social influence topics. The findings of previous research indicate the need for further theoretically based study of the influence of siblings on athletes and the subsequent effect of athletic participation on the entire family dynamic. Given the noted dearth in literature focused on siblings as a form of social influence in youth sport and physical activity, several directions for future research in this area are worthy of attention.

First, although existing research in developmental psychology has provided a solid foundation regarding the quality of sibling relationship dimensions (e.g., conflict, warmth, and rivalry), there is to date no knowledge of the dimensions relevant to the quality of sibling relationships in the physical domain. Second, extensive research in developmental psychology has revealed how the sibling relationship varies and is affected when one sibling is gifted or disabled. Corresponding research is needed to understand how the sibling relationship is affected when a brother or sister is a highly competitive athlete or extremely inactive.

An understanding of the specific dimensions of influence that siblings exert on one another's participation and achievement in the physical domain appears warranted as well. Considerable research has been devoted to understanding parents' influence on youth sport and physical activity participation and achievement, but no parallel work has been conducted to determine the specific ways in which children and adolescents perceive their siblings' influence on their athletic endeavors. This future research should furthermore seek to uncover whether there are distinct ways in which siblings contribute to the physical activity patterns of their brothers or sisters as compared with their competitive sport involvement. Building on the research in pediatric sport psychology that has examined

coach, parent, and peer influence on psychosocial predictors and outcomes associated with sport and physical activity involvement, investigators could expand the line of research on social influence by exploring the effect that siblings have on variables such as attraction to physical activity, perceived physical competence, sport enjoyment, stress, and motivation.

Conclusion

Parental influence has been the primary focus of social influence research in youth sport. Within this area of study, the most popular theoretical approach has been Eccles' expectancy-value theory (Eccles, 1993; Eccles et al., 1983), which has examined the influence of parental values and expectancies on youngsters' motivational and achievement outcomes in sport. Parents are also known to be extremely influential in shaping the emotional response that their children experience through their sport involvement. Such emotional responses include enjoyment, stress, and burnout. Although parents clearly influence their children's psychosocial experiences in sport, many avenues remain for continued investigation. A particularly important area of study involves the examination of the nature of parental influence throughout the child's development to understand the dynamic nature of parent influence over time.

The social influence of peers has been studied more recently as researchers began to understand the importance of peers on perceptions of competence. Acceptance, friendships, friendship quality, and victimization have all been studied within the sport domain, either in concert, or, more frequently, separately. These forms of peer influence have been found to influence psychosocial variables such as enjoyment, self-perceptions of competence, and feelings of self-worth. In addition to the importance of peer relationship variables, the importance of peers as leaders in the sport domain has also been explored and has been found to be influenced by various personal and psychological characteristics.

Sibling influence was the final form of social influence discussed in this chapter. Siblings serve as a type of bridge between parents and peers. Sibling studies have been conducted more frequently within developmental psychology and have documented the importance of such topics as birth order, presence of a gifted or exceptional child, and the existence of sibling rivalry. Within sport and exercise, the limited number of studies has suggested the importance of siblings' role modeling and support behaviors on participation and activity choice. Clearly, further study is warranted.

The future research directions identified in this chapter represent only a small portion of the exploration inspired by expanding our definition of potential social influence in sport and physical activity. We hope that these ideas will spur further research that examines the combined influences of parents, peers, siblings, coaches, and the many other significant others present in a person's life who may play a role in her or his sport and physical activity participation and achievement.

Part IV

PSYCHOLOGICAL SKILLS, INTERVENTION TECHNIQUES, AND SPORT BEHAVIOR

Interest in applying sport psychology knowledge to athletes and other physical activity participants has increased over the last couple of decades. Because of this burgeoning interest, a variety of intervention techniques have been developed and promoted as ways of helping athletes develop psychological skills and thus enhance their performance or modify their behavior in sport and physical activity contexts. In line with this more clinical perspective of sport psychology, the five chapters included in part IV of this text examine the extent to which selected psychological skills or intervention techniques can be linked to performance enhancement or behavioral change.

In their overview of the sport psychology field in chapter 1, Kontos and Feltz identify the integration of applied and theoretical work as one of the immediate challenges facing the field. Specifically, they suggest that the lack of integration between the applied and theoretical parts of the field have "slowed the growth of sport psychology and created a disconnect between practice and research in sport psychology." Given this perspective, the chapters in part IV of this text are presented with the assumption that researchers and practitioners can and must work together toward the common goal of understanding sport behavior. These chapters are therefore written from the perspective that (a) intervention techniques should be based as much as possible on research and theory and that (b) applied practices may provide valuable information that researchers can use to design research studies and develop theoretical models of sport behavior. Thus, the five chapters in part IV not only discuss the efficacy of selected intervention techniques but also examine potential mechanisms that may explain why and how these intervention strategies bring about performance or behavioral change.

In chapter 13 Shane Murphy, Sanna Nordin, and Jennifer Cumming present a comprehensive examination of imagery as it is, or can be, used in sport, exercise, and dance contexts. The authors begin with an overview of the neuroscience of imagery. In this section of the chapter, they describe three main and two applied imagery theories in light of functional equivalence theory. This perspective allows a more integrated perspective of the research to date. Murphy and his colleagues then propose a comprehensive neurocognitive information-processing model of applied imagery use in sports. This model is subsequently used as a framework for examining the current empirical and theoretical state of knowledge on imagery use in physical activity contexts and for identifying directions for future researchers. As Murphy and his coauthors note in their introductory section, this chapter represents the third version of their work, and as such incorporates an evolving view of imagery in sport. This approach provides the reader with an innovative perspective on the topic.

In chapter 14 Stephen Boutcher examines the complex relationship that exists between attention and sport performance. He begins his chapter by noting that attention is one of the core themes in psychology and has been explored in many areas of the psychological sciences. Boutcher then provides a review of the attention–performance link as it has been studied from three research perspectives—information processing, social psychology, and psychophysiology. Boutcher uses these disparate views of the attentional process to develop an integrated, multidimensional model of attention in sport. As Boutcher notes, "Viewing attention from a multidimensional perspective may generate more systematic research and provide a more reliable and valid research paradigm." Boutcher concludes his chapter with an examination of issues related to attentional training in athletes and other physical activity participants.

In chapter 15 Damon Burton and Cheryl Weiss begin by describing two real-life examples that illustrate the positive and negative effects that goal setting can have on individuals' performance and behavior. Continuing with their Jekyll and Hyde analogy, Burton and Weiss review the theoretical and empirical research on goal setting in sport with the specific intent of obtaining a better understanding of the goal-setting process and ways to maximize the effectiveness of goal setting in sport contexts. This review begins with an overview of goals and the goal-setting process. In the second section Burton and Weiss present an updated competitive goal-setting model and then summarize the research corresponding to this model. The third section includes a review and discussion of the types of goals that appear to be most effective, and the fourth section identifies some important measurement issues that may thwart research in goal setting. Burton and Weiss conclude their chapter with specific suggestions for future researchers.

In chapter 16 Susan Jackson and Jay Kimiecik suggest that optimal experiences in physical activity provide a rich and valuable source for understanding individuals' participation in such activities. Thus, these authors focus on the research that has been conducted on optimal experiences in sport and physical activity from a flow perspective. They begin by providing a brief history of the scholarly study of optimal experience in sport and other life contexts. This section includes a discussion of two constructs closely related to flow—peak performance and peak experience. Furthermore, Jackson and Kimiecik frame their discussion of these constructs in the context of positive psychology. In the main body of their chapter, these authors present a review and analysis of the research on flow not only in sport but also in exercise and recreation contexts. Along the way, Jackson and Kimiecik analyze current measurement issues and research paradigms. They conclude their chapter by identifying ideas for future (creative) researchers who wish to explore the role of flow in athletes' sport and physical activity experiences.

In chapter 17 Eileen Udry and Mark Andersen discuss the research and theory concerning the psychological correlates of athletic injury. In particular, they explore the dual possibilities that (a) psychological factors may serve as antecedents to athletic injuries and that (b) psychological techniques may be used to ameliorate the stress associated with an athletic injury and thus facilitate the recovery and rehabilitation process. Udry and Andersen begin their chapter with a discussion of operational definitions and measurement issues on the topic of sport injuries. They then review the empirical and theoretical literature pertaining to both the psychological antecedents of sport injury and athletes' psychological and behavioral responses to such injuries. These sections include a discussion of four theoretical approaches that researchers and practitioners can use to understand injury rehabilitation adherence in athletes and their behavioral responses to injury. Udry and Andersen conclude their chapter by identifying and discussing future directions for research on the psychological correlates of injury in sport contexts.

Collectively, the five chapters in this part of the text provide the reader with a comprehensive discussion of selected topics from the more applied literature in sport psychology. All of the chapter authors not only review the research linking these psychological skills and intervention techniques to participants' performance and behavior but also provide a mechanistic view about how and why sport psychological interventions may work. Therefore, these chapters may serve our field as an effective bridge between research and practice.

CHAPTER 13

Imagery in Sport, Exercise, and Dance

Shane Murphy, PhD ■ Sanna Nordin, PhD ■ Jennifer Cumming, PhD

As we move further into the 21st century, the field of sport psychology faces two key challenges with respect to understanding imagery in sport. First, researchers and theorists need to develop a comprehensive model that will guide imagery investigations. Second, development of guidelines for the applied use of imagery must continue, and knowledge about imagery effects must be widely disseminated. This chapter attempts to move the discussion forward in both areas and to suggest ways in which a comprehensive model of imagery in sport, exercise, and dance can inform both research and practice. We will propose a neurocognitive model of imagery and examine the implications of this model for the application of imagery in performance contexts.

This chapter is the third version of our work and represents an evolving view of imagery in sport. The first version of the chapter (Murphy & Jowdy, 1992) reviewed the experimental literature on imagery and mental practice in sport and discussed two explanations of imagery effects that had guided much of the mental practice research—psychoneuromuscular theory (Schmidt, 1987) and the symbolic learning hypothesis (Sackett, 1934). We argued that sport psychologists should examine two recently proposed theories of imagery as better potential models of imagery in sport—the bioinformational theory of Peter Lang (1977, 1979), which Hecker and Kaczor (1988) had applied to sports research, and the triple-code model of imagery (Ahsen, 1984), which was largely unknown to sport psychologists at the time. We concluded with the proposal that

> [a]n appropriate recommendation at the present time would be that researchers utilize some version of an information-processing model of imagery. . . . Information-processing models are sufficiently broad to incorporate the study of many related areas within the imagery field, such as the effect of imagery on performance, attention, emotional state, physiological arousal and self-efficacy. (Murphy & Jowdy, 1992, p. 240)

In the second version of this chapter (Murphy & Martin, 2002), we were more critical of the mental practice literature and, elaborating on previous critiques (Murphy, 1994), we discussed problems with the continuing study of mental practice. We proposed that a recently published applied model of imagery use in sport (Martin, Moritz, & Hall, 1999) provided a useful framework for integrating research and practice by sport psychologists in the imagery field. We also expressed the hope that further imagery theory development would occur:

> The use of rigorous imagery models in sport psychology will bring many benefits to researchers and practitioners. As theory development becomes a more integral part of the research process, the study of imagery in sport psychology will enter its most productive and exciting stage. (Murphy & Martin, 2002, p. 433)

For this third version of the chapter, we are in the fortunate position of being able to review a large amount of recent research that has greatly furthered our understanding of imagery in sport. A new applied model of imagery in sport has appeared (Holmes & Collins, 2001), and theory-based investigations of imagery in sport are now the rule rather than the exception. In this chapter we will not review the material that is readily available in the previous editions. Instead, we will focus on reviewing recent research, describing and analyzing recently published models of imagery use in sport, and proposing a neurocognitive model of imagery. The substantial quantity of new research about imagery in exercise and dance will be incorporated into our review. We will also examine how our model and others can guide the application of imagery by sport psychologists, athletes, performers, and coaches.

The Neuroscience of Imagery

In the ongoing search for an explanation of the workings of imagery, several key imagery theories have guided the sport psychology research base. A perusal of recently published book chapters reveals that authors still commonly refer to three main imagery theories (Hall, 2001; Lavallee, Kremer, Moran, & Williams, 2004; Moran, 2004; Morris, Spittle, & Perry 2004; Murphy & Martin, 2002; Vealey & Greenleaf, 2001)—the psychoneuromuscular theory (Jacobson, 1930; Richardson, 1967), the symbolic learning theory (Sackett, 1934), and the bioinformational theory of emotional imagery (Lang, 1977, 1979). Receiving lesser mention are the triple-code theory (Ahsen, 1984), dual coding theory (Paivio, 1986), the action-language-imagination (ALI) model (Annett, 1988), and the arousal or attentional set theory (Feltz & Landers, 1983; Suinn, 1993). Each theory has enhanced our understanding of the nature of imagery use in different ways. These approaches, however, clearly leave many questions unanswered, and few offer guidance about how performers may use imagery beyond simply rehearsing a skill (see Murphy & Martin, 2002, for a detailed review). To meet this need, several researchers have proposed applied theories of imagery that offer explicit guidelines for sport psychology practitioners who incorporate imagery techniques in their work with athletes (Holmes & Collins, 2001; Martin et al., 1999). We will examine the contributions of these applied theories in a subsequent chapter section.

Rather than repeat a review of older theories of imagery, we propose that a more sophisticated understanding of the imagery process will likely be achieved by taking an integrated approach that builds on previous research. One such approach has gained prominence in the sport psychology literature over the last few years, and we will now examine it in detail. Termed *functional equivalence*, this theory accounts for the strengths and limitations of the three most traditional imagery theories (i.e., psychoneuromuscular, symbolic learning, and bioinformational) and also incorporates recent cognitive neuroscience research (Lavallee et al., 2004; Moran, 2004).

Theory of Functional Equivalence

Imagery theories have generally been criticized for providing a vague or inadequate explanation for the underlying mechanism behind imagery's beneficial effects on performance. Moreover, with the exception of Lang's bioinformational theory, the majority of imagery theories have not been subjected to rigorous testing procedures (Holmes & Collins, 2001; Perry & Morris, 1995). By comparison, the mechanism proposed by functional equivalence theory has been more clearly articulated. With the developments of advanced neuroimaging techniques such as positron emission tomography (PET) and functional magnetic resonance imaging (fMRI), a growing body of evidence supports this explanation of imagery.

As we explained in our previous edition of the chapter,

> recent psychophysiological research into the neuronal processes underlying motor imagery suggests that motor images share the same neural mechanisms as those that are responsible for preparation and programming of actual movements (Decety, 1996a). This relationship has been called "functional equivalence" (Moran, 1996), and has also been suggested with respect to the relationship between visual imagery and the neural substrates for vision (Finke, 1980). (p. 416)

Functional equivalence theory proposes that imagery draws on the same neural network that is used in actual perception and motor control, and can also activate neural circuits used in memory

and emotion (Kosslyn, Ganis, & Thompson, 2001). As a result, a certain degree of overlap is found between these processes, which can be measured in terms of brain activity. If imagery is similar to perception, for example, then the same parts of the brain should engage when we imagine things as when we actually perceive them (Moran, 2004). Indeed, researchers have found a large degree of overlap between imagery and perception of the same sensory modality, including visual imagery (Kosslyn, Thompson, & Alpert, 1997), auditory imagery (Halpern & Zatorre, 1999), and olfactory imagery (Djordjevic, Zatorre, Petrides, Boyle, & Jones-Gotman, 2005). Data such as these have led Kosslyn et al. (2001) to conclude that "imagery, in many ways, can stand in for (re-present, if you will) a perceptual stimulus or situation" (p. 641). This assertion fits well with how performers actually use imagery. Within our field, imagery has long been acknowledged as a multisensory experience that occurs in the absence of actual perception. Indeed, imagery has been defined as "perception without sensation" (Moran, 2004, p. 133). White and Hardy (1998) also suggested that through imagery "we can be aware of 'seeing' an image, feeling movements as an image, or experiencing an image of smell, taste or sounds without experiencing the real thing" (p. 389). Imagery is thought to draw on the same neural processes involved in perception to create what is seen in the "mind's eye" or heard in the "mind's ear." Besides re-creating previous perceptual experiences, imagery creates new ones by combining or modifying stored perceptual information in different ways (Kosslyn et al., 2001). Research using advanced brain-imaging techniques supports this viewpoint and reinforces recommendations made by practitioners for performers to use all their senses to increase the vividness of their imagery (e.g., Holmes & Collins, 2001; Marks, 1999; Vealey & Greenleaf, 2001).

The belief that functional equivalence exists between imagery and physical practice is based on the assertion that the brain stores memories in the form of mental representations that can be similarly accessed through both actual and imagined behaviors (Holmes & Collins, 2001). In other words, imagery is related to the same central mental representation system that guides physical performance (e.g., Decety, 1996a, 1996b; Decety & Grèzes, 1999; Farah, 1988; Gabriele, Hall, & Lee, 1989; Hall, 2001; Holmes & Collins, 2001, 2002; Jeannerod, 1995; Jeannerod & Frak, 1999). If this is true, then similar levels of brain activation should be found whether a skill is imagined or performed. Seminal work by Ingvar and Philipson (1977) involved measuring regional cerebral blood flow (rCBF) when participants either imagined or actually carried out a clenching hand movement in a slow rhythm. During the imagery condition, a significant increase in rCBF was found in the premotor and frontal regions of the brain. Similar areas were activated when participants were physically engaged in the behavior. More recently, Lotze et al. (1999) compared brain activation during executed and imagined movements of the left and right hand using fMRI. They found that the supplementary motor area (SMA), the premotor cortex (PMC), and the primary motor area (M1) are equally activated during both actual and imagined movement. This finding is important because both the SMA and PMC have been found to play important roles in the planning, generation, and execution of complex motor tasks (Abbruzzese, Trompetto, & Schieppati, 1996).

In addition to brain-imaging techniques, interference paradigms provide evidence in support of the functional equivalence between imagery and physical practice (Boschker, Bakker, & Rietberg, 2000; Gabriele et al., 1989; Hall, Bernoties, & Schmidt, 1995; Johnson, 1982). Because, as noted by Jeannerod and Frak (1999), "if a motor image bears any relationship to the action it stimulates, then properties pertaining to the action should be expressed in the image" (p. 736). For example, Boschker et al. (2000) provided evidence for functional equivalence between imagery and physical practice of movement speed. In their study, participants were required to practice (physically or mentally) a sequential motor action (12 rhythmic steps) either two times faster or two times slower than their preferred speed. The speed of this practiced motor action, regardless of whether the practice was physical or imagery, subsequently affected performance in the retention test.

Together, these different lines of evidence support the notion that imagery engages the same processes involved with programming and preparing actual actions. Because these actions occur in the central nervous system, functional equivalence has also been referred to as the central control theory (Jeannerod, 1995) or central representation theory (Mulder, Zijlstra, Zijlstra, & Hochstenbach, 2004). Mental representations have been described as internal models of the intended action (Jeannerod, 1995), which are stored, modified, and retrieved through specific cognitive processing (Decety, 1996a, 1996b). As demonstrated earlier, images seem to share many of the properties of a mental representation of the skill to be performed (Jeannerod, 1995). Conse-

quently, imagery enables performers to prepare and plan for movement by accessing and strengthening these mental representations.

Functional Equivalence and Psychoneuromuscular Theory

Although imagery is involved with the planning and preparation of movements, actual execution is blocked at some level of the corticospinal flow (Decety, 1996a, 1996b). Thus, according to functional equivalence, imagery benefits are explained in terms of a top-down effect or central regulation (Mulder et al., 2004), and less attention is paid to what is happening at the peripheral musculature. This explanation is in stark contrast to claims of the psychoneuromuscular theory that imagery can be explained in terms of a bottom-up effect (Mulder et al., 2004). Taking a more peripheral approach, psychoneuromuscular theory proposes that imagery will cause small innervations to occur in muscles that are actually being used in the physical performance of the skill being imagined. The resulting muscular activity would be similar to, but of a smaller magnitude, than activity generated by actual physical performance. More specifically, the muscular activity produced during imagery would be sufficient to be detected by electromyographic (EMG) devices but would not produce any actual movement. Because nervous impulses sent to target muscles are thought to follow the same nervous pathways used in actual execution of the movement, the muscular activation experienced is thought to provide kinesthetic or proprioceptive feedback to the central nervous system. For this reason, psychoneuromuscular theory is also known as the inflow-processing explanation (Kohl & Roenker, 1983).

A number of studies have shown increased EMG activity in target muscles while imaging movement (e.g., Bakker, Boschker, & Chung, 1996; Bird, 1984; Hale, 1982; Harris & Robinson, 1986). For instance, Hale found that internal imagers demonstrated increased activity of the biceps muscle during an imagined dumbbell curl. This increased EMG activity has also been shown to increase proportionally to the amount of imagined effort. In their study, for example, Bakker and colleagues found a significant difference in EMG activity when participants were asked to imagine lifting 9-kilogram or 4.5-kilogram weights. Other studies, however, have not found EMG activity during imagery of movement execution (Mulder et al., 2004; Yue & Cole, 1992). Furthermore, a fundamental assumption made by the inflow explanation that the pattern of EMG activity should be similar during imagined and actual movements has not always been shown to exist (Hale; Slade, Landers, & Martin, 2002). If imagery did produce similar patterns of EMG activity, then a triphasic pattern should be shown, whereby an initial burst of EMG activity should occur in the agonist muscle, followed by a burst in the antagonist muscle, and finishing with a second burst of the agonist muscle (Slade et al.). In Hale's study of EMG activation during imagery of a dumbbell curl, a triphasic sequence would include activation of the biceps muscle (agonist) and triceps muscle (antagonist). Instead of finding this pattern, Hale reported that both muscles were activated at the same time during imagery, suggesting that the bicep and triceps activity represented a "bracing," or cocontraction, of the muscles. Using both dumbbell and manipulandrum curls, Slade et al. also found increased activity in both the biceps and triceps muscle during imagery. The pattern of activation again did not match the triphasic sequence generated when participants actually performed the curls, leading the authors to conclude that little support existed for an inflow explanation.

Alternatively, an outflow-processing explanation that is more consistent with functional equivalence maintains that imagery produces changes to the central motor program (Lutz, 2003). Jeannerod (1997) explained that minute muscular activity may result from an incomplete inhibition of motor output during imagery and can be interpreted as leakage from a centrally generated image. Thus, any EMG activity observed is a consequence of imagery rather than a cause of imagery effects (Decety & Ingvar, 1990). As we will see in a later section, this concept is also similar to Lang's notion that imagery is accompanied by efferent outflow or leakage (Lang, 1977, 1979). According to these explanations, any performance enhancement resulting from imagery practice is unrelated to the EMG activity occurring in peripheral muscles. Instead, adaptations are more likely occurring at higher levels of the motor system (i.e., planning and preparation), which in turn serve to strengthen the motor program and prime the system for the upcoming action (Mackay, 1981). Few studies, however, have attempted to link neural or muscular activity to the performance changes that occur following imagery.

An exception is the work done by Lutz (2003) to determine whether muscle activation experienced during imagery was related to subsequent improvements in dart-throwing performance. Although increased muscular activity was found in the biceps muscle during imagery, this excitation did not pre-

dict motor task acquisition or retention error. These findings led Lutz to conclude that EMG activity was mainly a by-product or outflow of a centrally generated image and did not relate to any meaningful changes in performance. Pascual-Leone et al. (1995), on the other hand, found that physical and mental practice led to similar changes in functional brain organization after participants either physically or mentally practiced a one-handed piano exercise for five days. Moreover, the level of performance for the mental practice group after five days of practice was comparable with the physical practice group's performance after three days. With an additional day of physical training, the mental practice group was able to perform at the level of the physical practice group, leading the authors to conclude that imagery had a preparatory effect on the task, which in turn increased the efficiency of subsequent physical practice.

Functional Equivalence and Symbolic Learning Theory

Although symbolic learning theory and functional equivalence are similar, they are not identical. Both theories suggest that imagery enhances skill learning by repeatedly activating mental representations of that action. But whereas functional equivalence accounts for beneficial effects across a variety of tasks, symbolic learning theory seems more limited to tasks that are cognitive or symbolic in nature. An early study by Sackett (1934) showed that performance on a finger-maze task improved following imagined rehearsal of the movement patterns involved. The explanation offered for these effects was that imagery may function as a coding system to help people understand and acquire movement patterns. In other words, imagery enables people to become more familiar with the symbolic or cognitive aspects of the skill to be performed. Not surprising, therefore, are the number of studies that have found imagery to be most beneficial for tasks with many cognitive or symbolic elements (see Murphy & Martin, 2002, for a more detailed review).

Symbolic learning theory has been criticized, however, for its inability to explain why imagery enhances strength and motor tasks. Take, for example, research that has found imagery to enhance muscular strength of little-used muscles (Ranganathan, Siemionow, Liu, Sahgal, & Yue, 2004; Smith, Collins, & Holmes, 2003; Yue & Cole, 1992). Yue and Cole found an increase in peak abduction force by 22% when participants were asked to image maximal isometric contractions of the abductor digit minimi muscle on the little finger. Imagery group participants in Smith et al.'s study reported a similar increase of 23.27% in peak force of the same muscle, and this was accompanied by increased EMG activity. By comparison, participants in the physical practice group showed a 53.36% increase from pre- to posttest, whereas the control group decreased their scores by 5.36%. The strength gains achieved through imagery could be attributed to training-induced changes to the central control system as predicted by functional equivalence theory. In support of this notion, Ranganathan et al. found that a 35% increase in abduction strength of the little finger was accompanied by increased brain activation following a 12-week imagery intervention. Using EEG signals as a measure of brain activity, the authors concluded that imagery trained the brain to produce a stronger signal output.

A functional equivalence perspective on imagery differs from the original concept of imagery in symbolic learning theory as a way to rehearse the elements of a motor task cognitively by improving performance through planning order effects, understanding spatial requirements of a task, and solving potential problems. Rather than just thinking about action, the functional equivalence approach suggests that imagery is much like action as far as the central nervous system is concerned. Thus imagery can benefit the performance of predominantly motor tasks, a result not possible in symbolic learning theory.

Functional Equivalence and the Bioinformational Theory of Emotional Imagery

Functional equivalence has also been closely associated with Lang's (1977, 1979) bioinformational theory. Borrowing heavily from Lang's work, proponents of functional equivalence have suggested that imagery can provoke an emotional response similar to what would be expected to occur during the real-life situation (Holmes & Collins, 2001, 2002; Kosslyn et al., 2001). As evidence, Holmes and Collins (2001, 2002) described work previously done by Harrigan and O'Connell (1996) to investigate facial gestures following imagery of previously experienced anxiety-producing events. In this study, reexperiencing anxiety-producing events through imagery led to facial movements involving fear expressions, more facial movement, and increased arousal. These responses are to be expected, according to Lang (1977, 1979), because an emotional image will tap into a powerful associative memory network resulting in efferent outflow (i.e., increased arousal) that is highly congruent with actual behavior.

Lang argued that all information, including imagery, is coded in the brain in a common abstract manner. Logical relationships between concepts are termed *propositions*. According to Lang, each emotional image comprises at least three types of propositions: stimulus propositions, response propositions, and meaning propositions. Stimulus propositions are information concerning external stimuli and the context in which they occur. Response propositions describe the cognitive, behavioral, and affective responses of a person to the stimuli in that scene and represent how a person would react in the real-life situation. Finally, meaning propositions elaborate on the relationships between the stimuli and response propositions and describe the perceived importance of the imagined scene to the person.

Functional equivalence theory and bioinformational theory thus share the view that people use some of the same cognitive concepts for perception, action, and imagination. According to Lang (1979),

> A more fundamental characteristic of the image is the fact that its information network includes propositions related not just to content but also to the modality specific operations of perceptual processing. That is to say, the image network includes information about perceptual responses, e.g., sense organ adjustments, body orientation to the stimulus, postural set, as well as psychological processing factors such as ease in resolving the image or picking it out from a background. (p. 500)

Hence, a physiological response is produced when response propositions are activated in imagery, and these responses are measurable through concurrent physiological recordings. Lang regarded these measurable motor patterns as a real-time index of the image processing going on in the brain. In support of Lang's theory, Hecker and Kaczor (1988) found that heart rates increased when softball players imaged a competitive anxiety scene that included response propositions such as "Your heart is pounding and your mouth is dry" (p. 368). More recently, Smith and Collins (2004) found that a combination of stimulus- and response-oriented imagery produced the expected EEG response for a finger strength task, but that stimulus-oriented imagery by itself did not. Their findings not only support bioinformational theory but also highlight the importance of activating response information during imagery. Performance benefits have also been found when imagery scripts include response propositions. Calmels, Holmes, Berthomieux, and Singer (2004) demonstrated that imagery vividness could be significantly improved for national-level softball players when imagery scripts were heavily laden with response propositions.

Physiological responses to imagery have also provided support for functional equivalence. Earlier in the chapter, we discussed the role of EMG activity. Here, we turn our attention to the other indices that suggest that emotional images can produce physiological and neural activation similar to what would be expected to occur in the corresponding real-life situation. For instance, Gallego, Denot-Ledunois, Vardon, and Perruchet (1996) found changes in breathing and cardiac frequency when 13 competitive swimmers and 16 judo athletes were asked to imagine a past sporting event. In comparison with responses during a no-imagery baseline, breathing and cardiac frequency increased when the athletes imaged the environment in which the competition took place. Further increases were found when the athletes began to imagine themselves performing. In another study, Pietrini, Gauzelli, Basso, Jaffe, and Grafman (2000) found that participants experienced greater anger, frustration, and anxiety along with significant increases in blood pressure when they imagined scenes that involved aggressive behavior compared with an emotionally neutral scene. Using PET scans, a significant decrease in rCBF was also noted in the areas of the brain responsible for inhibiting aggressive behavior.

Thus, many parallels can be drawn between the functional equivalence and bioinformational theories. One distinct difference worth mentioning concerns whether an image is considered to be a picture in the mind (picture theory; Kosslyn, 1994) or an abstract description of what the image is intended to represent (description theory; Pylyshyn, 1973). Adopting the latter view, Lang (1977, 1979) conceptualized an image as a cognitive schema made up of propositional information stored in long-term memory. Similar to language, these propositional representations are abstract codes that do not physically resemble the stimuli to which they refer (Moran, 2004). By comparison, some proponents of the functional equivalence theory would probably argue that imagery is more pictorially based. In their review of the literature, for example, Kosslyn et al. (2001) cited evidence that demonstrated that the early visual cortex (areas 17 and 18) is activated during imagery. They argue that activation of these areas substantiate the belief that images depict information, not describe it (proposi-

tional viewpoint). In other words, mental imagery depends on actual images.

Our proposed integrative model differs from Lang's theory in endorsing the distinct nature of imagery-based cognitive processing. We chose this approach in part because the research that we will discuss indicates that the neural mechanisms involved in imagery processing are distinctly different from those underlying verbal processing. In part, our approach simply reflects the fundamental wisdom of trying to understand what makes the conscious experience of imagery different from other types of thought experiences. If verbal and imagery cognitive processes were more alike than different, it would make little sense to have a chapter on imagery separate from a chapter on, say, self-talk. In any event, we hope that this debate will be settled over time as more research is done. We should point out that predictions based on both Lang's theory and our own neurocognitive model might be very similar whether imagery turns out to be perceptually based or propositionally based.

Conclusion

We have used the modern concept of functional equivalence here to illuminate the three main historically significant imagery theories used in sport psychology and the research that has been done using these approaches. This integrated theory suggests that imagery is probably best understood "as a centrally mediated cognitive activity that mimics perceptual, motor, and certain emotional experiences in the brain" (Moran, 2004, p. 149). From psychoneuromuscular theory, functional equivalence shares the idea that imagery involves activity of the central nervous system. Whereas psychoneuromuscular theory explains imagery in terms of a bottom-up effect, evidence favors the top-down effect advocated by functional equivalence theory. Symbolic learning theory and functional equivalence have in common the belief that a central representation system mediates imagery. But functional equivalence appears to provide a clearer explanation of the mechanism behind the beneficial effects of imagery for strength and motor-type tasks. Finally, and despite fundamental differences in how images are viewed, both bioinformational theory and functional equivalence suggest that imagery can elicit physiological and emotional responses.

Our review of functional equivalence research has enabled us to reexamine earlier models of imagery and mental practice in sport psychology and identify the important contributions they made to our understanding of imagery in sport. But functional equivalence theory has some limitations as a general theory of imagery in sport psychology. First, it focuses almost solely on explaining imagery when it occurs as part of motor preparation and execution. Although this aspect of imagery is important in sport psychology, imagery is also an important influence on many other processes, such as motivation, confidence, and arousal. Second, the functional equivalence approach does not address specific applied issues of concern to sport psychologists. We will therefore present a more comprehensive model of imagery in sport, dance, and exercise, but before we do so we will examine the contributions of two important applied models of imagery that have been proposed to help guide research and intervention in this area.

Applied Models of Imagery in Sport Psychology

The two models discussed next are strongly influenced by some of the theory and research that we discussed earlier. Each has made important contributions to our understanding of imagery use in sport.

The PETTLEP Model

A cognitive neuroscience approach to motor imagery in sport was presented by Holmes and Collins (2001). They examined current research efforts in neuroscience and applied the findings to developing a deeper understanding of motor imagery as athletes commonly use it. In particular, they highlighted the implications of the notion of the

functional equivalence of the motor imagery and motor execution systems for sport psychologists. Their PETTLEP model is strongly influenced by Jeannerod's (1997) motor preparation theory.

As mentioned earlier, a fundamental premise of functional equivalence is the idea that imagery operates by activating selected brain structures that would be used during physical practice (Lutz, 2003). Thus, the efficacy of an imagery intervention depends on how well the imagery activates these similar areas of the brain (Holmes & Collins, 2002). With this aim in mind, Holmes and Collins (2001, 2002) developed the PETTLEP model (illustrated in figure 13.1) as a guide for practitioners to use in creating functionally equivalent imagery. The model, essentially a seven-point checklist for practitioners to consider when writing an imagery script, includes the following elements: physical, environment, task, timing, learning, emotion, and perspective. The PETTLEP approach also draws on Lang's bioinformational theory by suggesting that each of the seven elements should contain important stimulus, response, and meaning propositions. Holmes and Collins (2002) likened these propositions to addresses used during the imagery process to find and locate the correct mental representation. For imagery to be effective in strengthening the memory trace for a particular behavior, therefore, imagery scripts would need to include information about the environment in which the behavior will take place (stimulus information), what is felt in response to that behavior (response information), and the perceived importance of the behavior to the individual (meaning information). When imagery scripts incorporate details from each of these classes of information that are relevant to the individual's experiences, the likelihood increases that the indi-

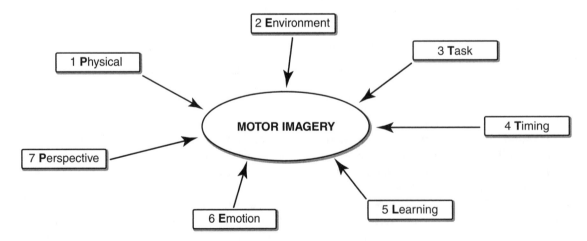

Figure 13.1 The PETTLEP model.
Adapted from Holmes and Collins, 2001, 2002.

vidual will access a functionally equivalent memory trace through imagery. As a result, imagery should be more effective.

The physical component of the PETTLEP model refers to individuals being actively involved in the imagery process by moving or by holding sport implements. A basketball player, for example, might imagine a man-to-man defensive strategy by adopting the appropriate stance and carrying out typical movements during imagery rehearsal. When the physical nature of the imagery process is manipulated in this way, resulting images are considered more likely to approximate the demands of the task (see, for example, Garza & Feltz, 1998). Consideration for the environment being imaged is the second component of the model. For response and meaning propositions to be relevant to the person, imagery should be personalized through full multisensory involvement. Imagery scripts should therefore include specific details about the environment in which the behavior will take place. Similarly, perceptual experiences (i.e., sights, sounds, smells, tastes) should replicate real life as closely as possible. Viewing videotapes of past performances may help performers access the correct mental representation.

The degree of task specificity is the third element to consider within the PETTLEP approach to imagery. Depending on task type and degree of task mastery, differences will occur in what individuals will attend to when performing a skill. The recommendation for imagery interventions is that the athlete should focus on the same thoughts, feelings, and actions as he or she does when physically performing the skill. Timing, the next component of the model, refers to the temporal characteristics of the skill being imagined. According to the PETTLEP approach, imagery would be most effective when it corresponds to actual movement time, particularly when timing is an important element of the task. Slow-motion imagery or imagery that is speeded up may not access the correct mental representation for a movement. The fifth element, learning, reflects the idea that memory representations will change over time as a function of learning and practice. Consequently, imagery content must evolve to accommodate learning that has taken place, and imagery scripts should be reviewed regularly to retain functional equivalence. As a guideline, the imagery scripts should describe characteristics about the task that most closely approximate the individual's current stage of learning. Emotion is another element through which imagery may access and strengthen memory representations. Lang (1985) has stated that efferent outflow or leakage will be more elaborate during emotional imagery. Imaging inappropriate emotions may have a debilitative effect on subsequent performance, and appropriate emotions should be included in imagery scripts to ensure that participants will experience them during the real-life situation.

The final element is the consideration of the visual imagery perspective of the performer. An internal perspective has traditionally been advocated as the best perspective for performers to use (e.g., Mahoney & Avener, 1977). From this viewpoint, performers are able to see the movement being performed as it would happen in the real-life situation. The external perspective, on the other hand, has been argued as being limited only to visual imagery and leaving the performer somewhat removed from the action of the skill (Decety, 1996a, 1996b; Epstein, 1980; Hinshaw, 1991). Empirical testing, however, has generally not supported the superiority of internal imagery for learning and performance (e.g., Glisky, Williams, & Kihlstrom, 1996; Gordon, Weinberg, & Jackson, 1994; Mumford & Hall, 1985). Researchers have also questioned the long-held assumption that kinesthetic imagery could be experienced only alongside an internal visual perspective. A number of studies have provided evidence that performers are capable of experiencing kinesthetic sensations from either an internal or an external perspective (Callow & Hardy, 2004; Cumming & Ste-Marie, 2001; Gates, DePalma, & Shelley, 2003; Glisky et al.; Gordon et al.; Hardy & Callow, 1999; Nordin & Cumming, 2005b; White & Hardy, 1995). Consequently, imagery perspective is now more appropriately conceived as the viewpoint that an individual takes during imagery (i.e., first vs. third person), and athletes are encouraged to use kinesthetic imagery regardless of their visual perspective (Glisky et al.; Hall, 1997; Hardy, 1997).

In sum, the PETTLEP model proposes how to maximize functional equivalence by considering seven elements of the imagery process either singularly or in interaction with each other. Given its theoretically based and evidence-based approach, this model will likely serve as a useful guide for designing imagery interventions and writing imagery scripts. Additional studies, however, are necessary for further testing of the different predictions made by the model.

The Applied Model of Imagery Use

A second approach to understanding imagery use in sport has strong applied implications and is based on sound theoretical concepts. The applied model of imagery use developed by Martin et al. (1999) draws on the ideas of Ahsen's (1984) triple-code model, Lang's (1977) bioinformational theory, and Paivio's (1985) influential framework describing imagery as having cognitive and motivational functions. Martin et al. constructed a model that emphasizes the central role of imagery content in determining imagery outcomes for athletes. Their model conceptualizes the sport situation, the type of imagery used, and imagery ability as the three main factors that affect how an athlete can use imagery to change performance, cognitions, and arousal. This model was a centerpiece of our second edition of this chapter (Murphy & Martin, 2002), and thus we will review it only briefly here.

The applied model proposes that different types of imagery will be used for different athletic goals and that athletes use imagery to achieve a variety of cognitive, behavioral, and affective changes. The model centers on imagery content (i.e., what the athlete images) as a key determinant of these changes. The imagery content includes the five types of imagery identified by Craig Hall and his colleagues (Hall, Mack, Paivio, & Hausenblas, 1998) through the development of the Sport Imagery Questionnaire (SIQ). Brief descriptions of the five types follow.

Motivational Specific (MS) Paivio (1985) suggested that a crucial function of mental practice for athletes is to serve in a motivational role when reinforcers are rare. Motivational specific imagery represents specific goals and goal-oriented behaviors such as imagining oneself winning an event, standing on a podium receiving a medal, and receiving congratulations from other athletes for a good performance.

Motivational General-Mastery (MG-M) General imagery that serves a motivational and mastery function is included in this category. The content of such imagery represents effective coping and mastery of challenging situations, such as imagining being mentally tough, confident, and focused during sport competition.

Motivational General-Arousal (MG-A) The content of athletic imagery in this category focuses on emotional and somatic experiences in sport. Imagery that represents feelings of relaxation, stress, arousal, and anxiety in conjunction with sport competition are classified in this category.

Cognitive Specific (CS) The content of cognitive specific imagery is based on imagery rehearsal of specific athletic skills. Imagery of specific sport skills such as penalty shots in soccer or balance beam dismounts in gymnastics are examples of this category. Most of the mental practice literature deals with imagery of this type.

Cognitive General (CG) Little research attention has been paid to the use of imagery to develop cognitive plans for athletic events. Cognitive general imagery refers to the strategies related to a competitive event, such as imaging using full-court pressure in basketball or a baseline game in tennis.

The applied model of imagery use predicts that athletes should employ the type of imagery that will be most useful in achieving their desired outcome, but the authors have acknowledged the need for testing the various predictions made by the model. The main prediction is best summed up as "What you see is what you get." Accordingly, skill-based imagery should be employed to enhance the execution of skills, and mastery-based imagery should be employed to enhance, for example, self-confidence (Martin et al., 1999).

Just over half a decade after the model was published, the amassing of a significant amount of research allows us to evaluate how well the predictions of the model have held up. The results obtained so far have varied in the extent to which they support the predictions made. On the supportive side, many studies have found CS imagery to be beneficial for skill learning, and MG–M imagery has been linked to increased state and trait self-confidence (for reviews, see Hall, 2001; Martin et al., 1999; Murphy & Martin, 2002). But several studies have found that more than one imagery type is in fact related to self-confidence (Abma, Fry, Li, & Relyea, 2002; Callow & Hardy, 2001; Mills, Munroe, & Hall, 2000; Moritz, Hall, Martin, & Vadocz, 1996). Moreover, a number of investigations have found that one imagery type can be related to several outcomes (Callow & Waters, 2005; Calmels, D'Arripe-Longueville, Fournier, & Soulard, 2003; Evans, Jones, & Mullen, 2004; Fish, Hall, & Cumming, 2004; Nordin & Cumming, 2005a; Short et al., 2002; Short, Monsma, & Short, 2004). For example, Calmels et al. (2003) found that elite gymnasts imaged their routines not only to enhance performance but also to forget feelings of pain and to increase engagement, to name but a few reasons.

The likely explanation for the somewhat inconsistent findings regarding imagery type, function, and outcome is that any given image can serve one or several functions, depending on the meaning that the image holds for a person. Short et al. (2002) highlighted this problem when trying to design imagery scripts to measure a certain function

(CS or MG–M) by asking, "Can we be absolutely certain that a participant in the CS + facilitative imagery group, for example, considered their imagery to be only cognitive? No, it is possible that the content was motivational to him/her, or even that the content served both functions" (p. 64). Several other researchers have raised the same point (e.g., Callow & Hardy, 2001; Hall et al., 1998; Short, Monsma, et al., 2004; Vadocz, Hall, & Moritz, 1997), but confusion still exists in the literature regarding imagery type and imagery function. In their paper describing the development of the applied model, for example, Martin et al. (1999) considered imagery type and function to be one and the same, and explain that "our model centers on the type of imagery used by the athlete (i.e., the function or purpose that imagery is serving)" (p. 249). Paradoxically, in this same paper, Martin et al. (1999) also alluded to the possibility that cognitive types of imagery could serve motivational functions by stating that CS and CG could facilitate focus in competitive settings. Similarly, the SIQ measures the frequency with which athletes use various images (*what*) based on the assumption that these images are reflective of certain functions (*why*). In their investigation of the perceptions that athletes have about imagery and its various functions, however, Short, Monsma, et al. found that all items of the SIQ were in fact perceived to serve more than one function.

In light of the evidence just reviewed, it has become imperative to clarify the constructs of imagery type, imagery function, and imagery outcome (the result of imagery). Rather than consider imagery type and imagery function as synonymous terms, we propose that the expression *imagery type* should be used to denote the actual content of an image (e.g., seeing oneself performing a dive, feeling oneself executing a penalty kick). By comparison, the term *imagery function* should refer to the purpose or reason why an athlete employs an image (e.g., to enhance motivation, to learn a skill). In other words, imagery function relates to the goals that an athlete is trying to achieve through imagery. Finally, the term *imagery outcome* should indicate the result of the imagery process (e.g., enhanced motivation, improved skill level). When defined in this manner, the subscales of the SIQ (i.e., CS, CG, MS, MG–M, and MG–A) would be considered imagery types, which may or may not be employed for particular functions. For instance, a basketball player might image a free-throw shot to improve his technique, increase his confidence, reduce his anxiety, and improve his focus (i.e., one type → several

functions). Likewise, he might combine images of skills, strategies, and mastery for the sole purpose of improving his confidence (i.e., several types → one function). A similar discussion can take place between imagery function and imagery outcome, and we will address and clarify this issue when we present our integrative model of imagery in a later section of the chapter.

Conclusion

The PETTLEP model and the applied model of imagery use in sport have generated substantial new research, but the models have some limitations. First, both models are descriptive and prescriptive, but not explanatory. That is, they do an excellent job of describing some of the most important factors to consider when using imagery with athletes, but they do not try to explain why imagery changes behavior. The authors themselves acknowledged this shortcoming. For example, Martin et al. (1999) were careful to point out that they were offering a model that represents the psychological aspects of imagery, not a theory that explains the phenomenon of imagery. Holmes and Collins (2001) described the PETTLEP model as an approach and a checklist rather than a theory.

Second, although the PETTLEP model clarifies the implications of adopting the functional equivalence viewpoint for applied sport psychology imagery interventions, the functional equivalence approach and the PETTLEP model focus on motor imagery and motor preparation. Many other kinds of imagery are important in sport psychology. For example, the applied model of imagery use in sport discusses the use of imagery for increasing motivation and lowering anxiety, which are functions of imagery that are outside the motor domain.

For those reasons we offer a theoretical framework to guide both research and practice in the area of imagery in sport. The theoretical framework that we now present draws on the research described earlier but considers the specific interactions between imagery and other cognitive processes to improve understanding of why imagery changes behavior. The framework also describes the imagery process itself with greater specificity than the original Martin et al. (1999) model, using evidence from a variety of recent studies to guide identification of key elements to be considered when using or studying imagery. Finally, the model also considers how imagery can be used in a variety of situations that extend beyond mental practice and preparation of motor skills.

A Neurocognitive Model of Imagery in Sport, Exercise, and Dance

The first author of this chapter proposed a comprehensive information-processing model of imagery use in sport in 1985. That model suggested the framework for studying a variety of cognitive processes that might both influence and be influenced by imagery use (Murphy, 1986). At the time, however, specific systems for explaining such cognitive processes were poorly understood. As reviewed earlier, the subsequent 20 years have seen an explosion of research in cognitive neuroscience and psychology, fueled by advances in brain-imaging techniques and in advanced technologies for studying brain processes. Current neuroscientific models of cognition incorporate both detailed explanations of the specific processes involved in cognition and an attempt to link such processes to specific brain areas, neural pathways, and even specific neurotransmitter systems (e.g., LeDoux, 1996). We feel that it is time for another look at cognitive and information-processing models of imagery in sport. The original model (Murphy, 1986) dealt with the cognitive processes of perception, memory, executive functions, and motor control, as well as emotions and physiological arousal. The model presented here describes the interaction between these same processes and the cognitive process of imagery using current models of brain processing whenever possible. Our proposed model borrows the computer-modeling language of cognitive psychologists to discuss how mental functions deal with sensory input and direct behavior (Johnson-Laird, 1981). The model is also guided by recent advances in neuroscience that suggest that neural relationships may underlie cognitive processes. Hence we propose that the model is a neurocognitive model of imagery for movement disciplines.

Our proposed model is shown in figure 13.2. The components of this model are based on current psychological theories that we hope give our model an explanatory power that is missing in other recent approaches to imagery in sport. Note that our model is organized around the functions that imagery serves in support of the attainment of a person's goals. This is the *why* of imagery in our preceding

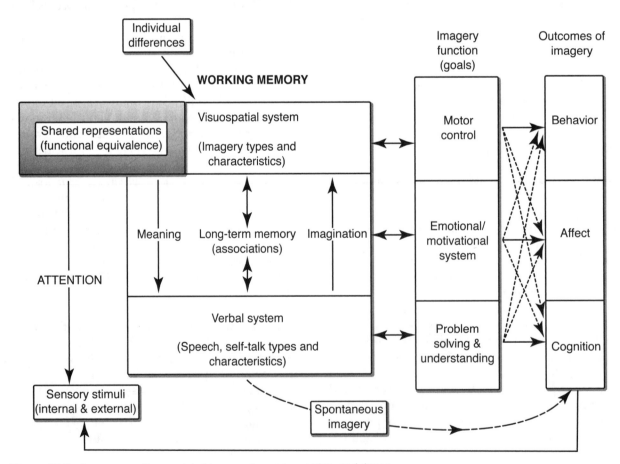

Figure 13.2 A neurocognitive model of imagery in sport, exercise, and dance.

analysis. Thus the column labeled *imagery function* is in some ways the most important part of the model, because the choice of goals will highly influence the nature and process of the ensuing cognitive activities. Our model is therefore a top-down model of imagery and action, congruent with evidence from the research of cognitive scientists such as Lutz (2003). Some goals will best be accomplished by the verbal system, whereas others will be better served by the visuospatial system. As Jeannerod (1997) explained,

> The mode of processing to which an object is submitted and the corresponding representation that is created for acting on that object, depend on the task in which the subject is involved. If the task refers to the semantic content of the object, in the context of an explicit operation like naming, describing, evaluating, etc., the processing mode will involve mechanisms for perceptual recognition, verbalization, semantic memory. If, on the other hand, the object is an element in an action as a tool or an instrument, the processing mode will involve mechanisms for visuomotor transformation, kinematics, procedural memory. (p. 9)

The central feature of our model of imagery is that it resides in conscious awareness, contained in the idea of working memory, a cognitive concept developed by psychologist Alan Baddeley (1986). He proposed that memory is not a single storage system but a system that processes multiple sources of information to solve problems and understand the environment. The visuospatial sketchpad is where visual and spatial information is stored during comprehension and problem solving, whereas verbal information is processed by the phonological rehearsal loop. In our model, imagery is the primary cognitive process of the visuospatial system and is an integral component of memory and consciousness.

In the next section we will describe the neurocognitive model in detail and evaluate empirical research on the influence of imagery on performance, using the model as a framework for organizing our review.

Research Advances

In this section we will deal with each component of our model in turn. We begin with the first step in the cognitive process of imagery, attention to stimuli, and then move through the model step by step, examining the research relevant to each stage of the model. We discuss the implications of our model for applied interventions and highlight potential new avenues of research. Note that although we describe our model from start to finish (left to right), the experience of imagery will usually be initiated when an athlete or performer selects a goal, thus triggering the chain of events described in our model.

Imagery, Perception, and Attention

The starting point for our study of imagery is sensory stimuli, both external (sights, sounds) and internal (feelings, motion), available to our awareness. People constantly process information from the world around them at the perceptual level, but the information that enters their consciousness is selected by their attention, as shown by the arrow from working memory in our model.

Functional equivalence theory states that similar representations in the cortex are activated during both visual imagery and perception. Thus imagery is closely tied to perception, and it is believed that the experience of imagery is largely constructed by brain mechanisms also involved in perceptual and memory processes (Kosslyn et al., 1997). Several experiments have demonstrated that asking subjects to use certain images can influence their perception of external stimuli (Farah, 1989; Podgorny & Shepard, 1978). In figure 13.2 we illustrate the set of neural processes shared between imagery and perception and between motor images and movement control mechanisms as a shaded area in working memory.

Neisser (1978) has described imagery as a readiness to perceive something, leading to the investigation of the role of imagery in anticipation. Attention, or concentration as it is usually described in sport, refers in part to the selection of certain perceived stimuli to be processed in working memory (Nougier, Stein, & Bonnel, 1991). The prefrontal cortex directs the visual processing brain areas to attend to and stay focused on those objects and spatial locations that are being processed in working memory (LeDoux, 2002). Think about a baseball batter waiting for a pitch. If he expects a fastball he may have an image of a fastball thrown by this pitcher in his awareness. When the pitch is delivered he "sees" a fastball and swings. Only as the umpire calls "strike" does the batter realize that in fact the pitch was a splitter, not a fastball at all. In this case the batter's imagery led to an incorrect perception and hindered his performance. This analysis suggests that imagery can cause people to be more or less accurate in attending to and perceiving external stimuli. If their imagery is congruent with their actual experience, their perceptions may be enhanced as demonstrated in the experiments by Farah (1989). If their images are incorrect anticipations of actual experience, then their reactions may be slower or lead to mistakes in performance. Imagery is thus an active process that prepares people to receive information, not a passive internal representation of stored information. The arrow labeled *Attention* indicates this relationship between imagery and the perception of selected stimuli.

Sport psychology researchers Deborah Feltz and Dan Landers first identified attention as a potential source of imagery effects on sport behavior. They proposed that mental practice of motor skills may facilitate the development of an attentional set for the athlete (Feltz & Landers, 1983). They argued that mental practice helps athletes focus on the relevant aspects of performance, thus reducing the risk that they will direct their attention toward irrelevant or distracting cues. The applied implication of this concept is that after the cognitive template that develops when athletic skills are well learned is in place, athletes with good imagery skills may be better able to access information critical to successful task execution of the template. A vivid image of a well-learned sport skill may enable an athlete to focus quickly and effectively on the elements needed for successful performance. Although most of the imagery research in cognitive psychology has focused on visual imagery, anecdotal reports from athletes suggest that kinesthetic imagery is more important in helping them focus for performance. In fact, the common saying among athletes warming up for competition is that they are trying to get the feel for the game. In an interview Tiger Woods reported that he has unreliable and largely uncontrolled visual imagery of his golf game and therefore relies almost exclusively on the feel of shots for his imagery rehearsal (Woods, 2005).

Unfortunately, evidence from applied research with athletes is insufficient to suggest concrete guidelines about how imagery can be best used to help focus attention. Indeed, in his review of the research, psychologist Aidan Moran concluded that evidence is insufficient to conclude that "visualization is a valid concentration strategy for athletes" (1996, p. 230). Recent research, however, is more encouraging. For instance, a study by Calmels, Berthomieux, and d'Arripe-Longueville (2004) found that the selective attention (i.e., concentration) of national-level softball players could be improved through structured imagery practice. Contrary to Moran (1996), therefore, Calmels et al. (2004) suggested that "the use of imagery as an additional technique to more popular concentration techniques . . . is strongly suggested" (p. 293).

One of the implications of this analysis of the interaction between imagery and perception and attention for sport performance is that in many situations athletes may want to prevent some types of images from entering their awareness immediately before performance. Otherwise, they may be prepared for an event that does not occur. Of course, the value of this suggestion based on our model awaits empirical testing, but the wisdom of this attitude towards preperformance imagery may be reflected in the common practice of clearing one's mind before performance. For example, when asked what he was thinking about in the batter's box after delivering the key hit in a stirring game-winning rally during the 1986 World Series, New York Mets player Ray Knight responded, "Nothing. I was trying to keep my mind absolutely empty and just think of nothing." This notion suggests some interesting avenues for research that explores differences in preperformance imagery for open skills such as hitting a baseball versus closed skills such as dart throwing or putting.

Imagery and Memory

In our model, as shown in figure 13.2, imagery is one aspect of working memory—the nonverbal system for processing information about the world that depends on the functioning of our sensory systems, such as vision, hearing, and movement awareness. Baddeley's influential concept of working memory (1986) posits that it consists of both a visuospatial sketchpad, where information is represented by mental images, and a phonological rehearsal loop, where speech is used to describe information. The central executive function coordinates the information in the two systems, which can be stored in the episodic buffer. Both processes, the verbal and the visuospatial, are shown in figure 13.2. The important differences between the ways that the central nervous system uses verbal information as compared with how it uses visual and spatial information have been recognized in other influential approaches to the study of imagery, such as Paivio's dual-coding theory (Paivio, 1971; 1986). Combining the approaches of Baddeley and Paivio allows us to recognize imagery as a key aspect of working memory. Paivio argued that this type of information is represented in the central nervous system in a distinct way; he called the units of information in the nonverbal system *imagens*. (For a critique of Paivio's theory and a review of other theories of imagery, see Pinker & Kosslyn, 1983. Although these experts consider Paivio's theory an oversimplification, the essential point remains that mental imagery involves a neural process different from that used in abstract thought.)

Our model also shows the relationship between working memory and long-term memory. Nonstructural theories of memory, such as Craik and Lockhart's levels of processing model (1972), help us understand why imagery is important for the creation of long-term memories. According to their model, cognitive brain processes have evolved to help people perceive and understand information about the external world. The more people cognitively analyze information, the more they comprehend it. Greater levels or degrees of cognitive analysis have been described as "depth of processing." Memory traces occur whenever people analyze perceptions, and the deeper the level of analysis, the more elaborate and long lasting are the memory traces. The construction of images represents a deep level of processing of information. For example, in the classic demonstration, subjects have much better recall of sentences they were asked to visualize than sentences they were told to rehearse verbally (Bugelski, Kidd, & Segmen, 1968).

We propose that the deep processing nature of imagery accounts for the many associations that images hold for individuals. Recalling a memory using imagery activates memory traces that are associated with many other memory traces. Indeed, the human hippocampus seems to associate multiple memories naturally and rapidly (Eichenbaum, 2000). Given the highly associative nature of the neural structure of the human brain (LeDoux, 2002), recalling single images without also recalling related images is difficult. (This analysis fits well with current parallel distributed processing (PDP) models of cognition, which posit that memory for visual images or motor skills can be explained as connectionist networks depending on patterns of activation of neural networks; see, for example, McClelland, 1992.) The associative nature of the neural structure of the brain may at least partly explain why imagery seems to have personal and unique meaning for every individual (Ahsen, 1984) because when asked to imagine (or "picture") the same scene according to a verbal description, each individual will use his or her unique experiences to construct the image, which will immediately have connections to other images. Thus, when used as a stimulus for rehearsal or preparation, a proposed image (e.g., "imagine hitting a good forehand with lots of topspin down the line") will produce a different outcome (both experientially and neurally) for each individual.

We illustrate the interconnection between long-term memory and the images in working memory with a two-way arrow to show that imagery can help store information in long-term memory, which in return is a plentiful source of imagery.

A complication for applied sport psychologists using imagery interventions is that neuroscience research has demonstrated that many memories occur outside conscious awareness. According to LeDoux (2002, p. 116), "[Many] aspects of our outward behavior and inner life are controlled by brain systems that store and use information implicitly, that is, without our awareness of their operation. Implicit memories are reflected more in the things we do, and the way we do them, than in the things we know." Because understanding the "doing" rather than the "knowing" is of paramount importance to sport psychologists, research and practice must attempt to account for the unconscious associations that imagery is likely to produce when used by athletes. The analysis of imagery with respect to memory suggests that imagery is likely to produce unanticipated outcomes of which the athlete is unaware, although research is yet to be done on this proposition.

Finally, although our model proposes that the verbal and imagery systems employ different neural structures and pathways to process information, we recognize links must be present between these systems. In Baddeley's (2001) memory model, integration of the two systems occurs in the executive workspace, which deploys and divides attention as needed, and in an episodic buffer, a limited capacity store allowing for integration of the various components of working memory and serving as an interface between working memory and long-term memory. We propose that when imagery material is explicitly translated by the verbal system, meaning occurs. The importance of understanding the meaning of an image to an individual has been emphasized by other theorists (e.g., Lang, 1977, 1979) but in particular by Akhter Ahsen (1984). Ahsen developed a triple-code model of imagery, suggesting that imagery experiences can be described in three ways: The image (I) is a cognitive template—a set of sensations arising in the brain; the somatic response (S) is the set of physiological reactions that occur in response to the image; and the meaning (M) is the unique significance of the imagery to the individual. Our neurocognitive model suggests that the I component of imagery is related to the links of imagery with perceptual and attentional processes; that the S response is due to the links between imagery and the somatic and autonomic nervous systems;

and that the M component of imagery reflects the highly associative nature of imagery and memory and the interpretation of images through executive functions. A number of research studies support the notion that a person's interpretation of imagery content will have a significant effect on imagery outcome (e.g., Abma et al., 2002; Callow & Hardy, 2001; Callow & Waters, 2005; Calmels et al., 2003; Evans et al., 2004; Fish et al., 2004; Nordin & Cumming, 2005b; Short et al., 2002; Short, Monsma, et al., 2004). As an example, Hale and Whitehouse (1998) showed that the perception of challenge versus pressure in a game-situation image was crucial in determining the effect of imagery on the person. All athletes engaged in the same imagery construction, but this imagery was found to cause less anxiety and greater confidence when perceived as a challenge and not as pressure.

Words and thoughts can also generate imagery in working memory, as when a baseball pitcher hears the name of an opposing player, bringing to mind a visual image of that opponent hitting a home run in their last confrontation, accompanied by a feeling of anxiety. In our model we call this relationship between the verbal and imagery systems *imagination*. Sport psychologists who teach or guide athlete clients in the use of specific imagery usually do so through verbal instructions about what to imagine, but our model suggests that the actual content of the athlete's *imagination* in response to such verbal stimuli may vary greatly depending on the athlete's experience and her or his imagery ability. Holmes and Collins (2001) also emphasized this point in their PETTLEP model, in which they suggested that one way to help guide imagination of sport situations might be through the use of video cues.

We now turn to a consideration within our model of two aspects of imagery that have been of great interest to sport psychology researchers in recent years. First, some researchers have suggested that people vary widely in their ability to use imagery (Isaac & Marks, 1994). Clearly, individual differences in imagery ability, experience, and even attitudes toward imagery use will have an effect on the outcome of imagery. Second, many researchers have tried to identify the dimensions of imagery that influence the effect of imagery on athletic behaviors. The type of imagery employed has been identified as an important dimension, as have a number of characteristics of imagery such as duration and modality. Most of the factors that researchers have studied have been based on the self-report of individuals concerning their imagery experience, but

some of these factors may eventually be tied to underlying neural processes that regulate imagery. We examine the research in these two areas next.

Individual Differences

Differences between individuals in their imagery and the effects of their imagery on their performance are important topics for both applied and theoretical reasons. Practitioners need to assess how well athletes can use imagery to manage performance, what types of imagery they prefer, how familiar they are with imagery techniques, and so on. Researchers who can demonstrate differences in outcome between individuals who vary on specific dimensions of imagery will uncover an important piece of evidence that imagery is a cognitive process separate from verbal thought. Researchers have studied a number of individual difference variables including imagery ability, age, gender, level of participation, and years of experience. Preliminary evidence indicates that additional individual difference variables should be considered in future research, namely the individual's knowledge about imagery as a psychological strategy, the individual's perceptions about the relevance and value of imagery, his or her motivational profile, and the amount of encouragement that the individual receives to use imagery. In figure 13.2, individual differences are shown as influencing the imagery system in working memory directly. For example, an athlete who is a good imager of her upcoming performance may perform better in competition than an athlete with poor imagery skills. Athletes may differ in their use of imagery because of underlying neurological differences in the brain structures and pathways that make up the imagery system in working memory. Alternatively, the differences may result from learning experiences such as differing reinforcement for imagery use or different exposure to systematic instruction in imagery skills.

Imagery Ability A person's ability to image is probably the most well-acknowledged individual difference variable in imagery studies. Indeed, Martin et al. (1999) predicted that imagery ability will moderate the effect that different functions of imagery will have on achieving a desired outcome. They made this prediction based on studies that have shown greater performance improvements following a CS imagery intervention for people with higher imagery ability (e.g., Goss, Hall, Buckolz, & Fishburne, 1986). Paivio (1986) explained that these individual differences in imagery ability are likely due to the combination of genetic variability and experience. That is, some variations in imagery ability are likely attributed to brain differences that give some athletes more ability than others to imagine visual, kinesthetic, auditory, or other aspects of imagery. But athletes can be taught to improve the quality of their imagery experience. For example, Rodgers, Hall, and Buckolz (1991) administered an imagery ability measure to figure skaters before and after a 16-week imagery training program. They reported significant improvements in the subjects' visual imagery ability scores compared with a control group that did not receive imagery training. This finding suggests that imagery, to some degree, can be considered a skill that is modifiable with training. Further, a cyclical relationship may exist between imagery use and ability. In other words, better imagers are more likely to engage in imagery, and greater imagery use will likely result in enhanced imagery ability (Vadocz et al., 1997). Hall (1985) has also suggested that imagery interventions will likely be more effective for performers with better imagery ability.

Gregg, Hall, and Nederhof (2005) examined whether imagery ability influenced the relationship between imagery use and track and field performance. Although the ability to image visually and kinesthetically predicted greater CS imagery use, the test for moderation was not successful. In other words, the interaction between CS imagery use and imagery ability failed to predict an athlete's best performance at a track and field meet held during the indoor season. The authors suggested that their measure of performance might not have been sensitive enough to show support for imagery ability as a moderating variable. A related issue concerns the instrument used to assess imagery ability. In their study, Gregg et al. employed the revised version of the Movement Imagery Questionnaire (MIQ–R; Hall & Martin, 1997; Hall & Pongrac, 1983), a popular and useful instrument for assessing ability to image simple movements (e.g., knee raise). Hall (2001) has cautioned, however, that the MIQ–R was not designed to assess the ability to image other aspects of sport performance such as arousal (MG–A) and affect (MG–M). Additional instruments will have to be created before researchers can properly test the moderating effects of imagery ability on types of imagery other than CS.

Age Research regarding differences in imagery use between athletes who differ in age is abundant. For instance, children and youth can and do use imagery in sport and dance settings (e.g.,

Afremow, Overby, & Vadocz, 1997; Li-Wei, Qi-Wei, Orlick, & Zitzelsberger, 1992). Although visual and kinesthetic imagery abilities have been shown to improve with age (Isaac & Marks, 1994), authors such as Campos, Pérez-Fabello, and Gómez-Juncal (2004) have found that the ability for mental rotation decreases throughout adulthood. From both research and applied standpoints, establishing more clearly how age differences affect imagery use would be useful. For example, we do not yet know whether age affects any imagery-related variables other than imagery ability.

Gender The effects of gender on imagery use are also unclear. Hall (2001) concluded in a review that gender probably does not greatly affect imagery use. But some researchers have found evidence to the contrary (e.g., Campos, Pérez-Fabello, & Gómez-Juncal, 2004; Gammage, Hall, & Rodgers, 2000; Weinberg, Butt, Knight, Burke, & Jackson, 2003). For instance, Weinberg et al. found that men used imagery more frequently than women did and found cognitive-specific images to be more effective. Investigating gender differences in imagery ability, Campos et al. (2004) found that men had higher scores than women did for visuospatial ability, but no differences existed concerning visual imagery control. It is tempting to speculate that the known differences in brain development between men and women underlie some of the gender differences observed in imagery research. Differences in lateralization of functions such as verbal and visuospatial processing have been a focus of cognitive research into gender differences (Ernest & Paivio, 1971). Drawing such conclusions would be premature, however, and much research remains to be done to specify possible gender differences in neural pathways underlying imagery.

Level of Participation and Years of Experience More consistent evidence has been obtained regarding level of participation. Athletes at higher competitive levels or with more experience in a sport use more imagery than those at lower levels or those with less experience (e.g., Barr & Hall, 1992; Calmels et al., 2003; Cumming & Hall, 2002a, 2002b; Gregg et al., 2005; Hall, Rodgers, & Barr, 1990; Hall et al., 1998; Salmon, Hall, & Haslam, 1994). Similarly, those who exercise more frequently use more imagery (Gammage et al., 2000; Hausenblas, Hall, Rodgers, & Munroe, 1999). The reason behind these differences, however, is not yet known. Hall (2001) has suggested that people who are more dedicated and spend more time in sport or exercise spend more time thinking about it. Further, Abbott and Collins (2004) proposed that imagery and other metacognitive strategies are in fact critical to moving people into higher developmental stages. Further research into this intriguing possibility is encouraged.

Additional Individual Difference Variables A number of other variables may explain differences in athletes' motivation and adherence to imagery training programs as well as outcomes achieved. The first to consider is the athlete's knowledge about imagery as an intervention strategy. It makes sense that athletes who know more about imagery will be able to use it more effectively. For instance, Calmels et al. (2003) found that national-level gymnasts who received a psychological skills training (PST) program were able to use psychological skills (including imagery) in a manner similar to that used by international-level gymnasts. Their imagery was also more advanced than the imagery used by national-level gymnasts who had not received a PST program and had learned their psychological skills through self-discovery. A related variable is athletes' perceptions about how beneficial and relevant imagery is to them and their performance improvement. Cumming and colleagues have found that athletes who view imagery as more relevant use it more frequently (Cumming & Hall, 2002a; Cumming et al., 2006). Moreover, athletes at higher competitive levels found imagery to be more relevant than did athletes at lower levels, leading these authors to suggest that lower-level athletes may not understand the benefits that imagery can bring them. Additional research is warranted, therefore, to investigate whether increasing one's knowledge about the potential benefits and relevance of imagery will lead to greater usage, particularly for lower-level athletes who may benefit most.

A direct link between motivation and use of imagery among athletes and exercisers has been made by investigating basic tenets of achievement goal (AGT) and self-determination (SDT) theories. These theories both describe the relationship between goal-directed behavior of individuals, the meaning behind such achievement striving, and how individuals interpret their social situations (for a review, see Duda, Cumming, & Balaguer, 2005). SDT refers more directly to the positive motivational outcomes associated with self-determination, whereas AGT explains the affective, behavioral, and cognitive consequences of being task and ego oriented in achievement settings. Based on the argument that different combinations of task and ego orientation will reflect varying levels of behavioral investment, studies have found that

combinations of moderate to higher levels of task and ego goal orientations are related to greater frequencies of imagery use (Cumming, Hall, Harwood, & Gammage, 2002; Harwood, Cumming, & Hall, 2003; Harwood, Cumming, & Fletcher, 2004). Similar results have been found in studies of the relationship between imagery use and self-determination. Bisig and Spray (2005) found that golfers with higher levels of self-determination reported using more imagery than did players with lower self-determination indexes. Thus, variations in personal motivation appear to influence imagery use. A useful research avenue would be to explore whether more task-oriented athletes engage in more effective imagery, such as deliberate practice imagery, whereas more ego-oriented athletes perhaps engage in more outcome-oriented, winning-focused imagery.

Finally, research also points to the benefit of being encouraged to image by one's teachers, coaches, or others. For instance, White and Hardy (1998) found that gymnasts' and canoe slalomists' use of imagery outside training was largely dependent on receiving encouragement from their coaches. Only 30% of participants in a study with rowers, however, reported that their coaches had encouraged them to use imagery (Barr & Hall, 1992). Further, it has been found that higher-level soccer players are more likely to receive encouragement from their coaches than are lower-level players (Salmon et al., 1994). A study comparing instructors from three different activities indicated that dance teachers and figure-skating coaches encouraged their performers to use imagery more than did the soccer coaches, although none of the instructors used imagery in an organized way (Overby, Hall, & Haslam, 1997). Moreover, figure skaters noticed an increase in the use of psychological skills in practices and evaluated their sessions as more effective after their coaches had attended a PST workshop (Hall & Rodgers, 1989). Thus, coaches and teachers will also likely benefit from receiving education about imagery use.

To conclude, a variety of individual difference variables may affect the imagery use of sport, exercise, and dance performers. Some of these variables reflect different learning and socialization processes that influence an athlete's subsequent attitude toward and frequency of use of imagery as a tool for behavior change. Other differences, for example, the differences between high imagers and low imagers, may turn out to result from differences in brain structure and organization in areas responsible for the nonverbal processing of information in working memory (Charlot, Tzourio, Zilbovicius, Mazoyer, & Denis, 1992).

Imagery Types and Characteristics

In our previous edition of this chapter we focused exclusively on imagery type as the defining aspect of imagery content. Martin et al. (1999) pointed out, however, that characteristics such as imagery duration, imagery modality, and imagery perspective may also find a place after more research has been conducted. After reviewing the imagery literature that has emerged over the past decade, we would like to suggest that these be considered as additional variables that influence the effectiveness of imagery use. Further, we would like to make the case for imagery amount, imagery speed, perceived direction, and degree of deliberation. We include these imagery types and characteristics in our model as a useful way of describing the nature of imagery. This area of research is continually evolving, and our focus here is to point the reader to relevant research rather than attempt to describe the many studies that have been recently published in this area.

Imagery Type Imagery type is concerned with the content of an image. The most common images in sport research have been CS, CG, MS, MG–A, and MG–M. In line with Martin et al.'s (1999) prediction, however, other types of imagery have been identified and integrated into the model. Our focus here is on newly identified imagery types that have emerged mainly from research conducted with exercisers and dancers but are arguably also applicable to athletes. Rather than associate an imagery type with a particular function for the reasons previously outlined, we also describe the more traditional imagery types using slightly different terms than those used by researchers employing the SIQ (Hall et al., 1998).

The imagery type most commonly referred to is that depicting various skills and technique, represented in the SIQ as CS imagery. When these skills are combined into a routine, such as those performed by gymnasts and figure skaters, the imagery is known as CG imagery. Exercisers and dancers have also been found to image their skills and routines (e.g., Gammage et al., 2000; Giacobbi, Hausenblas, Fallon, & Hall, 2003; Hanrahan & Vergeer, 2000; Nordin & Cumming, 2005b; Overby, 1990; Short, Hall, Engel, & Nigg, 2004). Second, images of plans and strategies are also captured by the CG subscale of the SIQ. Few studies have specifically focused on this imagery type. Recently, however, a single-case intervention study with elite footballers found that an imagery intervention consisting of skills and strategies improved exploratory visual activity for two out of the three players involved

(Jordet, 2005). Third, images depicting progress toward goals and goal achievement are captured by the MS subscale of the SIQ. Exercisers have similarly been found to image various health outcomes (e.g., Giacobbi et al., 2003). Fourth, images of cognitions such as mastery and control are captured by the MG–M subscale of the SIQ. Interestingly, MG–M is the imagery type most frequently used by athletes (e.g., Abma et al., 2002; Cumming & Hall, 2002a, 2002b; Gregg et al., 2005; Hall et al., 1998; Munroe, Hall, Simms, & Weinberg, 1998; Short, Monsma, et al., 2004; Vadocz et al., 1997; Weinberg et al., 2003). Similarly, exercisers have been found to image being confident and concentrated (e.g., Giacobbi et al., 2003).

Lastly, images of arousal and anxiety are captured by the MG–A subscale of the SIQ. Similar images are those depicting emotions, energy, effort, and other feelings associated with movement. One might argue that all these images are related to the body in some way. Other forms of body-related images also exist. For instance, dancers use anatomical images related to their posture and alignment (e.g., Hanrahan & Vergeer, 2000; Nordin & Cumming, 2005b). Images of appearance have been reported in both exercise (Gammage et al., 2000) and dance (Nordin & Cumming, 2005b). Finally, athletes, exercisers, and dancers have all been reported to engage in images of healing and injury (e.g., Hanrahan & Vergeer, 2000; Short, Hall, et al., 2004; Sordoni, Hall, & Forwell, 2000, 2002).

A prominent imagery type in dance settings is metaphorical imagery (e.g., Hanrahan & Vergeer, 2000; Nordin & Cumming, 2005b; Overby, 1990; Overby et al., 1997; Sawada, Mori, & Ishii, 2002). Athletes are thought to use this imagery type in various sporting contexts to aid communication, help identify and express thoughts and emotions, assist focus and concentration, maintain confidence, help relaxation, and enhance performance (Efran, Lesser, & Spiller, 1994; Hanin & Stambulova, 2002; Orlick & McCaffrey, 1991; Ruiz & Hanin, 2004). For instance, coaches may instruct runners to imagine running on eggs to help them understand that they need to be light on their feet. Using an approach similar to metaphorical imagery, dancers may use images of characters and roles to help them generate the performance that they seek (e.g., Hanrahan & Vergeer, 2000; Nordin & Cumming, 2005b). Finally, context images may depict content such as places and people. These images have been mentioned by athletes (Munroe, Giacobbi, Hall, & Weinberg, 2000), exercisers (Giacobbi et al., 2003; Short, Hall, et al., 2004), and dancers (Nordin & Cumming, 2005b).

Imagery Amount and Duration Few experimental studies have investigated the amount of imagery use necessary for bringing about desirable effects on performance. Contrary to expectations perhaps, Etnier and Landers (1996) found that a shorter bout of imagery (one to three minutes) was more beneficial for basketball performance than a slightly longer bout (five to seven minutes). Nevertheless, studies of a more applied nature have found that imagery interventions should be long to obtain meaningful outcomes. Thus far, intervention lengths have been as brief as a single workshop (Cumming, Hall, & Shambrook, 2004) or have ranged from a few weeks (e.g., Callow, Hardy, & Hall, 2001; Callow & Waters, 2005; Calmels, Berthomieux, & d'Arripe-Longueville, 2004; Cumming & Ste-Marie, 2001; Jones, Mace, Bray, MacRae, & Stockbridge, 2002) to a season-long program (e.g., Calmels et al., 2003; Evans et al., 2004; Fournier, Calmels, Durand-Bush, & Salmela, 2005; Jordet, 2005; Li-Wei et al., 1992; Munroe-Chandler & Hall, 2004; Munroe-Chandler, Hall, Fishburne & Shannon, 2004). Despite the abundance of these imagery intervention studies, they do not provide clear guidance for practitioners about the duration of imagery interventions. For now, the best recommendation that can be advanced is that more imagery is probably better (Hall, 2001). A worthwhile pursuit for researchers would be to establish the optimal length of imagery interventions.

Imagery Direction Traditionally, studies concerned with comparing imagery of successes and mistakes have termed the imagery as *positive* and *negative* respectively. These studies have often produced inconsistent findings. Some studies have found that positive and negative imagery had no effect on performance (Epstein, 1980; Meyers, Schleser, Cooke, & Cuvillier, 1979), whereas other investigations have found that performance was enhanced following positive imagery and impaired by negative imagery (e.g., Shaw & Goodfellow, 1997; Short et al., 2002; Woolfolk, Parrish, & Murphy, 1985). Further, others have found no effect for positive imagery and that negative imagery produced deleterious effects (e.g., Taylor & Shaw, 2002; Woolfolk, Murphy, Gottesfeld, & Aitken, 1985). Consequently, Short et al. (2002) introduced the term *imagery direction* to refer to the degree to which an image either assists performance (facilitative imagery) or hurts performance (debilitative imagery). Rather than assume that a negative image (e.g., poor golf putt) is synonymous with a negative outcome (e.g., narrowly missing the hole), this conceptualization of

imagery direction allows personal meaning to be applied to the image. That is, in certain situations, narrowly missing the hole may be seen as a successful outcome (e.g., for novice golfers). Thus, imagery that helped achieve this outcome, despite being negative in content, would be considered facilitative. Using this distinction, Nordin and Cumming (2005a) found that debilitative imagery has an apparently stronger effect on dart-throwing performance and self-efficacy than does facilitative imagery. With the help of manipulation checks, they were also able to establish that facilitative images were indeed perceived as facilitative and debilitative images were perceived as debilitative by the participants. Applied practitioners will also find it useful to establish whether an athlete perceives a particular image as being facilitative or debilitative to achieving their desired outcome (Short, Monsma, et al., 2004).

Imagery Deliberation Although some researchers involve the notion of volitional control in their definition of imagery (e.g., Perry & Morris, 1995), note that performers also experience images that they do not generate deliberately or consciously control. Thus, images can range on a continuum of deliberation from spontaneous to deliberate. In support of this notion, Nordin and Cumming (2005b) found that dancers not only experience spontaneous images of skills and different situations but also intrusive, debilitative images (e.g., being in pain, making a mistake). In a more direct investigation of this issue, Nordin, Cumming, Vincent, and McGrory (2006) found that athletes engaged in CS, CG, and MG–M imagery more deliberately than they did in MG–A and MS imagery. Moreover, higher-level (elite and intermediate) athletes could be distinguished from their lower-level counterparts by their more deliberate use of imagery. This finding is consistent with previous evidence that elite athletes have more structured and regular imagery sessions than do novices (Barr & Hall, 1992; Hall et al., 1990). Future research is necessary to improve understanding of how spontaneous images are triggered and how these images may affect desired outcomes. We will return to this issue shortly.

Imagery Modality The sensory modalities involved in imagery represent an imagery characteristic that has attracted a reasonable amount of research attention. Although visual imagery is most often considered, kinesthetic imagery has recently received increased recognition. To clarify what is meant by kinesthetic imagery, Callow and Waters (2005) recently offered the following definition: "Imagery involving the sensations of how it feels to perform an action, including the force and effort involved in movement and balance, and spatial location (either of a body part or piece of sports equipment)" (pp. 444-445). Moran and MacIntyre (1998) found that canoe slalomists differentiated between movement of limbs and force or effort. Similarly, Nordin and Cumming (2005b) found that when discussing "feel" with professional dancers, the responses included not only the traditional kinesthesia but also such things as rhythm, being in pain or being pain free, texture, touch, feeling someone's presence, and more. Clearly, kinesthetic imagery is multifaceted in nature.

Additional senses involved in imagery include the auditory, gustatory, and olfactory senses, although these are less prevalent in movement settings. Both athletes and exercisers have reported using some auditory imagery, but these images occurred less often than visual and kinesthetic ones (Calmels et al., 2003; Giacobbi et al., 2003; Moran & MacIntyre, 1998; Salmon et al., 1994; White & Hardy, 1998). By comparison, dancers describe images of music as well as their own voices, representing an overlap with self-talk (Hanrahan & Vergeer, 2000; Nordin & Cumming, 2005b).

The PETTLEP model suggests that using several senses will increase the vividness and effectiveness of one's image. But an intriguing possibility to consider would be whether the addition of certain senses can be distracting to the performer. For instance, a soccer player would probably not want to be directing her attention to the smell of grass when she is trying to focus on how to score a goal. Although this smell may help set the scene, it may be irrelevant to helping the performer achieve the desired outcome.

An impressive amount of research is being carried out on the characteristics of imagery that influence imagery outcomes. A variety of factors have been identified as being related to outcomes or have been suggested as possible factors that influence outcomes. We hope that over time this research will help identify the most crucial characteristics for athletes and practitioners to consider. In the next two sections we turn to the final components of our neurocognitive model—imagery function and imagery outcome.

Imagery Function

As outlined in the introduction to this section, the concept of imagery function refers to the reason that an image is employed, and includes motor control, emotional and motivational reasons, and cognitive reasons. We suggest that the goal of the individual will strongly influence the type of cognitive process that he or she employs to reach that goal, including the nature of the imagery process, although research on this hypothesis is yet to occur in the sport psychology literature. We describe research into some of the ways in which imagery has been used to attain specific tasks and goals under each of the three main functions of imagery—motor control, emotional and motivational management, and problem solving and understanding.

Motor Control The process of motor control has been the focus of sport psychology imagery research for the past 40 years, often to the exclusion of the study of the relationship of imagery with other processes being described in this model. Even recent applied models such as PETTLEP focus only on explaining motor imagery, which Holmes and Collins (2001) defined as "a force-generating representation of the self in action from a first person (internal) perspective" (p. 62). The research described earlier in the section on functional equivalence is directly relevant to understanding the role that imagery plays in the control of motor actions. Indeed, the functional equivalence approach suggests that "[t]he fundamental point for applied sport psychology is that . . . physical and mental practice are equivalent" (Holmes & Collins, 2001, p. 62). This notion in turn suggests that many of the principles used to make physical practice more effective can also be applied to imagery use.

Evidence from the expertise literature suggests that differences in the attained level of performance between elite and subelite athletes can be best explained by examining the person's engagement in demanding activities termed *deliberate practice* (Ericsson, 2003). In sport, this form of practice consists of activities that are extremely relevant to performance improvements, require physical effort or mental concentration, and may or may not be enjoyable (Helsen, Starkes, & Hodges, 1998; Hodges & Starkes, 1996). An assumption made is that the amount of time that a person is engaged in deliberate practice activities will be monotonically related to his or her acquired level of performance (Ericsson, Krampe, & Tesch-Römer, 1993). Consequently, performers should attempt to maximize the amount of time that they spend in deliberate practice activities.

After reviewing the evidence in favor of functional equivalence, Hall (2001) recommended that cognitive specific imagery (CS, imagery of skill rehearsal) should be treated similarly to physical practice. Further, this type of imagery should be considered a form of deliberate practice, and athletes and performers should be encouraged to use as much CS imagery as possible. Investigating this possibility, Cumming and Hall (2002b) found that athletes generally perceived imagery as being highly relevant for improving overall performance, requiring a great deal of mental effort, and being enjoyable in a similar fashion to physical practice. Differences were also found in the amount of imagery practice accumulated by national- and recreational-level athletes throughout their careers. In a second study, Cumming, Hall, & Starkes (2005) examined different types of sport-specific and sport-related images. They identified CS imagery (skill learning, skill execution) and, as a natural extension, cognitive general imagery (CG; strategy learning, strategy execution) as fulfilling the criteria for the sport-specific definition of deliberate practice. Thus, the recommendation for athletes to supplement their regular physical practice with imagery seems to make sense from a deliberate practice point of view. Moreover, imagery may be a potential avenue for accumulating deliberate practice amounts when athletes are injured or unable to train for some reason (Hall, 2001). Holmes and Collins (2002) further point out that through imagery, athletes will benefit from central reinforcement without the usual fatigue and possible injury risk associated with physical practice.

Throughout this chapter we have reflected on the implication that imagery used for motor behavior control might have different properties than imagery used for other functions. Marks (1999) has expressly made this argument:

> In this paper, it is argued, contra Jeannerod (1995), that conscious imagery provides one of the primary mechanisms for goal-directed action planning and that unconscious forms of representation are used only when action is part of an automatic, habitual routine (such as walking, typing) rather than planned, goal-directed actions adapted to novel circumstances. (p. 568)

Of course, athletes have as a primary goal making many of their actions as habitual and automatic as possible, so the study of imagery for this goal is important.

Enhancing Motivation How does our neurocognitive model explain the role that imagery plays in the life of a 13-year-old figure skater who wakes up at 4 a.m. every day and is on the ice practicing by 5 a.m., motivated by her images of one day representing her country in the Olympics? As Alan Paivio pointed out in 1985, imagery serves both a motivational role and a cognitive role in the brain. Imagery helps the athlete select goals and helps fuel the motivation to achieve them. Imagery may play a role in the selection of both direction and intensity of effort (Cumming et al., 2002). For example, ego-oriented athletes tend to want to defeat specific opponents and be seen as winners. They may focus on images of winning specific competitions and bask in the imagined glory of their success. These images have the potential to influence the direction of their goals—which competitions they enter, what results they want to achieve, and so on. Such imagery may also help fuel the intensity of effort that they expend in pursuit of their goals. Repeated imagery of a desired result helps bridge the gap between a far-off outcome and present-day reality, seeming to bring the desired goal closer and motivating the athlete to work hard to achieve it.

The process is probably similar for task-oriented athletes, although the goals are different. These athletes appear inclined to imagine themselves making constant progress, setting personal bests, and mastering difficult challenges. These images may influence their choice of training programs, type of coach, and competitions that will help them judge their progress. They want to see the image of a better, improved athlete become a reality, which serves as motivation to work hard, seek critical feedback, and make necessary adjustments. Exercise imagery studies have indeed found that exercisers use images of themselves looking and feeling fitter and healthier, which have also been found to serve motivational effects (Gammage et al., 2000; Giacobbi et al., 2003; Short, Hall, et al., 2004).

Changing Arousal and Affect Performers in sport, exercise, and dance can and do engage in many types of imagery to affect their arousal and affective states. Most of this research has been concerned with performance anxiety and has generally shown that imagery can help reduce anxiety symptoms or make the interpretation of such symptoms more facilitative (Fish et al., 2004; Fletcher & Hanton, 2001; Hanton & Jones, 1999; Hanton, Mellalieu, & Hall, 2004; Munroe et al., 2000; Page, Sime, & Nordell, 1999; Vadocz et al., 1997). Another arousal- and affect-related function that imagery may serve is to help a performer psych up or calm down. Again, research suggests that imagery is used for this reason by athletes (Munroe et al., 2000; White & Hardy, 1998), exercisers (Giacobbi et al., 2003; Short, Hall, et al. 2004), and dancers (Hanrahan & Vergeer, 2000; Nordin & Cumming, 2005b; Vergeer & Hanrahan, 1998). Imagery can further be used to change mood. Some findings have indicated that imagery may be used to experience fun and satisfaction, as well as to relieve boredom (e.g., Giacobbi et al., 2003; Nordin & Cumming, 2005b; Short, Hall, et al., 2004).

Problem Solving and Understanding People also use working memory to solve problems and better understand the challenges of sport, exercise, and dance. Although this task is perhaps best suited to the verbal system of working memory, several research studies have indicated that athletes also use imagery to change their thoughts and beliefs (Murphy, 1994; Rushall, 1988; Suinn, 1993).

Case study reports have documented the benefits of imagery for rehearsing football plays (Fenker & Lambiotte, 1987; Jordet, 2005), wrestling strategies (Rushall, 1988), and entire canoe slalom races (MacIntyre & Moran, 1996). A study by Rotella et al. (1980) indicated how athletes use imagery to plan for upcoming performances. In their study of competitive skiers, they found that in the time between inspecting the course and reaching the starting gate, successful skiers developed a visual image of the course and used it to plan an effective strategy for negotiating the course layout. This function of imagery is still probably the least studied by sport psychology researchers, although in nonsport settings a variety of studies have explored this function of imagery (see Taylor, Pham, Rivkin, & Armor, 1998, for a review of what they term *mental simulation*).

Another reason that performers may engage in imagery practice is to memorize or remember what they need to do. This function of imagery reflects the close relationship between imagery and the memory systems of the brain. Because this relationship was extensively outlined earlier, the information will not be repeated here. But note that although dancers report that memorizing is a key reason for imagery use (e.g. Nordin & Cumming, 2005b; Poon & Rodgers, 2000), this function is not as frequently alluded to in sport and exercise imagery research. Still, people may spontaneously image when trying to recall movements (Hall & Buckolz, 1982; Hall, Moore, Annett, & Rodgers, 1997; Kim, Singer, & Tennant, 1998).

Confidence and Self-Efficacy Cognitive-behavioral therapists, who have long recognized the positive effects of imagery on self-confidence, have developed imagery strategies that encourage behavior changes. These imagery strategies, which ask clients to imagine more successful behaviors than they presently exhibit, include systematic desensitization, flooding, coping imagery, and covert modeling. Indeed, in his comprehensive theory of behavior change, psychologist Albert Bandura (1977) stated that although successful performance is the greatest influence on confidence, vicarious experience—imagining success or watching someone else achieve success—is also a consistent source of confidence.

Many studies have found that using imagery is related to higher levels of self-confidence. But as noted earlier, the types of imagery associated with confidence have varied. The most consistent finding has been that images of mastery (e.g., MG–M) are related to confidence (e.g., Callow et al., 2001; Feltz & Riessinger, 1990; Fish et al., 2004; Monsma & Overby, 2004; Vadocz et al., 1997), but other studies have found that several other imagery types can also be employed for this function (Abma et al., 2002; Callow & Hardy, 2001; Jones et al., 2002; Mills et al., 2000; Moritz et al., 1996).

Artistic Functions of Imagery Another function of imagery that has been studied in the domain of the performing arts is its use to help lend artistic power and meaning to a performance. By their self-report, dancers use imagery for this reason, as do athletes in aesthetic sports such as gymnastics, figure skating, and synchronized swimming. Performance in these activities depends not only on the correct execution of motor skills but also on the artistic or aesthetic qualities of those movements. Thus, perhaps predictably, these performers use imagery to aid them in their striving to improve the artistic aspects of their performances. Examples of artistic functions include using imagery to communicate with one's audience, to add meaning, to enhance the quality of one's movements, and to choreograph a sequence or routine (e.g., Hanrahan, 1995; Nordin & Cumming, 2005b; Overby et al., 1997; Vergeer & Hanrahan, 1998).

Healing Functions of Imagery Researchers have recently realized that athletes, exercisers, and dancers all recognize that they can use imagery for healing purposes. For example, the exercisers in Short, Hall, et al.'s (2004) study claimed that imagery had the potential to prevent injury or aid in recovery from injury. The existing sport healing imagery research indicates that a multitude of positive benefits stand to be obtained from such imagery use, including preventing injuries in the first place, shortening recovery times, coping with pain, and enhancing self-efficacy (Ievleva & Orlick, 1991; Sordoni et al., 2000, 2002). Ievleva and Orlick

(1991) found that athletes recovered more quickly from injury if they did not engage in replay images depicting their injury. Thus, imagery appears capable of both speeding up and slowing down the process of healing from injury.

Spontaneous Imagery

Imagery can be experienced for no apparent reason (spontaneous imagery) at all, or it can be triggered. This circumstance would appear to be a problem for our model because it indicates that imagery may sometimes arise for no purpose and is thus not initiated as part of a goal or for completing a task. For example, Smith and Holmes (2004) found that imagery could be triggered in a golfer simply by his or her reading a book about golf. The background noise provided for the swimmers and judokas in Gallego et al.'s (1996) study could be considered triggers to image. Despite abundant mentions of triggered imagery in the literature (e.g., Franklin, 1996a, 1996b; Giacobbi et al., 2003; Hall & Buckolz, 1982; Hall et al., 1997; Hanrahan, 1995; Hanrahan & Salmela, 1990; Hanrahan, Tetréau, & Sarrazin, 1995; Hanrahan & Vergeer, 2000; Overby et al., 1997; Short, Hall, et al., 2004; Smith & Holmes, 2004; Vergeer, 2003), no research has directly investigated its prevalence or significance in sport, exercise, and dance settings. But studies with normal populations indicate that most imagery experienced on an everyday basis is in fact generated for no specific reason (Kosslyn, Seger, Pani, & Hillger, 1990; Vecchio & Bonifacio, 1997). Kosslyn and his colleagues (1990) also mentioned that "some of this type of 'day dreaming' or 'free association' imagery may have ended up being useful, but was not generated with the particular use in mind" (p. 138). Thus, triggered imagery is probably prevalent among performers. Therefore, this topic presents interesting avenues for future research. For instance, is the increase in imagery use in association with competition compared with training (Barr & Hall, 1992; Hall et al., 1990; Munroe et al., 1998; Weinberg et al., 2003) a result of increased dedication, or is it simply triggered by anxiety? Perhaps triggered imagery is one way that the central nervous system tries to manage certain situations when the person does not make a conscious choice to use imagery (see also Singer & Antrobus, 1972). We view this topic as an open area of research, and until the nature of spontaneous imagery is clarified we show it in our model as a separate imagery process, bypassing imagery function but perhaps having an (unintended) outcome for the person.

Imagery Outcome

The potential outcomes of the imagery process correspond closely to the functions of imagery. That is, change can occur for the individual in terms of his or her motor behavior (motor control function), emotions (emotional or motivational function), and cognitions and verbal behavior (problem solving and understanding function). More simply, imagery outcomes can be behavioral, affective, and cognitive. As we discussed earlier, the outcome is often congruent with the intention or purpose of imagery. Congruence between function and outcome would be the case if, for example, a karate athlete rehearses imaginally to learn a specific kata (function) and consequently improves her performance (outcome). But the outcome may be in an area that was not part of the athlete's goal. For example, a cyclist preparing for a race may decide that he will be more confident about the race if he imagines a strategy for staying close to his main rival (cognitive goal) but instead finds that his heart is racing and that he feels nauseous after the imagery (emotional outcome). (This scenario is an example of an unintended outcome from experiencing a debilitative image. Other examples of harmful consequences exist in the literature, and this notion will be further explored when we discuss future research directions.) In figure 13.2, we show that each of the three overall functions of imagery may affect the outcome of each of three primary outcomes of imagery.

By this analysis, outcomes may be beneficial or harmful, and intentional or unintentional. Presumably, the intended result for most athletes and sport psychology practitioners using imagery interventions is intentional and beneficial outcomes, such as skill learning, anxiety reduction, and motivation enhancement. Physiological responses such as increased temperature and heart rate can be unintended outcomes, or by-products, of imagery use. The elicitation of physiological responses through imagery plays a central role in Lang's (1977) explanation of how imagery works. Although presumably a relationship exists between imagined sensations and responses that are by-products of imagery use, distinguishing between the two is important. Experimental evidence suggests that both heart rate and total ventilation can increase proportionally with mental effort (Decety, Jeannerod, Germain, & Pastène, 1991), and Giacobbi et al. (2003) mentioned that one of their participants experienced increased heart rate when imaging exercising. Similarly, Gallego et al. (1996) found that competitive swimmers' breathing and heart rates increased when imaging competitive situations. The importance of such effects is unknown, although they may possibly contribute to increased functional equivalence and thereby enhanced effectiveness.

Another example of an outcome of imagery use is enjoyment, which can be described as an affective outcome. Performers probably engage in imagery for instrumental reasons (e.g., learning), and enjoyment is more likely a by-product. Nonetheless, research into the use of imagery as deliberate practice has revealed that athletes find imagery relatively enjoyable (Cumming & Hall, 2002a; Cumming et al., 2005; Nordin et al., in press). In addition, some evidence suggests that MS images are perceived to be the most enjoyable imagery type (Nordin et al., in press). Images over which athletes experience less control and perceive as debilitative are perhaps more likely to be experienced as unenjoyable.

Besides being unintentional or harmful, outcomes of imagery use can be subject to delays. Specifically, several studies have mentioned that a time lag can occur between using imagery and its effects on self-efficacy (Callow et al., 2001; Callow & Waters, 2005; Calmels et al., 2004; Feltz, 1984; Hall & Martin, 1997). Shambrook and Bull (1996) suggested that this delay occurs because psychological skills need to be learned before they reveal their effects. As with the research findings regarding intervention length, however, the expected duration of this time lag is unknown, and researchers might want to explore this variable to understand better how imagery can best enhance self-efficacy.

Finally, our model illustrates that a performer's actions generate feedback regarding outcomes that may alter the dynamic process. For example, an anxious athlete, worried by his fluttering heart and queasy stomach, uses calming imagery to relax and soon notices that his heart rate has slowed and that his stomach feels better. We show this feedback loop as an arrow linking the outcomes of imagery back to the stimuli that might be the subject of attention within an athlete's conscious awareness.

This concludes the presentation of our neurocognitive model and the accompanying analysis of the related research. We end our discussion on imagery in sport, exercise, and dance with suggestions for future research based on some of the knowledge gaps that we have identified in the research.

Future Research Directions

Throughout our review and synthesis of imagery research we have noted problem areas in the knowledge base. We will now highlight some of the major areas that we have identified and provide suggestions or ideas for future research directions in these areas.

Identification of Effective Imagery Prompts

Our analysis of the neural basis of motor imagery suggested that even expert performers may not be consciously aware of some of the important elements of imagery rehearsal of motor skills. This notion suggests that research is needed on how to guide motor rehearsal imagery that effectively accesses neural representations of action. Holmes and Collins (2001) suggested that one way to do this is to use imagery prompts, such as a self-model video of the skill to be rehearsed. Cognitive psychologists who have studied the problem of conscious identification of relevant factors in unconscious processing have suggested that people use a priori, implicit causal theories about the extent to which a particular stimulus is a plausible cause of a given response (Nisbett & Wilson, 1977). This research suggests that athletes may reasonably be expected to be accurate in identifying the important mental components of successful performance when the possibilities for causal agents (a) are few in number, (b) are salient to perception or memory, (c) are highly plausible causes of the given outcome, and (d) have been reliably associated with the outcome in the past. Under these specific conditions we should be reasonably confident in the athlete's assessment of cognitive processes leading to good outcomes. Under other conditions we should be suspicious of an athlete's ability to report his or her own cognitive experience accurately. We therefore share the concern of Holmes and Collins (2001) that sport psychologists should proceed cautiously in constructing verbal imagery scripts to aid in the rehearsal of sports skills, even with the input of athletes themselves. Collaborative research on this topic between sport psychologists and neuroscience researchers may yield knowledge gains that would be valuable to both fields.

Use of Imagery Immediately Before Performance

During our analysis of imagery and perception we suggested that athletes should treat imagery cautiously when using it immediately before performance. If the imagery involves mainly actions that the athlete has direct control over (e.g., a diver rehearsing her dive) or if the athlete has a high degree of certainty that the image will correctly anticipate the actions about to take place, then the imagery may benefit performance. But in most open, dynamic sports situations in which an athlete must be prepared to react quickly to a variety of situations, imagery may hinder performance if it leads to incorrect anticipation of events. Moreover, the paralysis by analysis phenomenon deserves mention here. This state occurs when cognitive analysis (e.g., through imagery) acts as a distractor, detracting from the automaticity of learned movements. This circumstance has been reported in both sport (Rushall & Lippman, 1998) and dance imagery research (Hanrahan & Vergeer, 2000; Nordin & Cumming, 2005b; Vergeer & Hanrahan, 1998). Still, the imagery itself may not be the problem. Just before competing, for example, athletes might want to focus on experiencing feelings of mastery as they image global aspects of performance (higher stage of learning) rather than on specific parts of the skill (lower stage of learning) that they normally perform without much thought. Metaphorical imagery may do this particularly well. For example, dance teachers have previously reported that preperformance imagery of skills can make a move too mechanical, whereas metaphorical imagery "takes them out of themselves; they let the particular movement happen" (Overby, 1990). Further research on this topic is warranted.

Lack of Assessment of Imagery Type, Function, and Outcome

No valid instrument is currently available to measure imagery abilities for motivational imagery, metaphorical imagery, or emotional imagery, to name but a few broad imagery types that athletes typically engage in. This issue was raised in the previous edition of this chapter (Murphy & Martin, 2002) as well as by Hall (1985). But as far as we are aware, little has been done to tackle the problem. The Movement Imagery Questionnaire–Revised (MIQ–R; Hall & Martin, 1997) has been the most widely used questionnaire to assess athletes' abilities to image movements both visually and kinaesthetically, but it focuses singularly on what the Sport Imagery Questionnaire (SIQ; Hall et al., 1998) would class as cognitive-specific imagery (i.e., images of skills). And despite the SIQ's measurement of imagery use, a wide variety of imagery-related variables are not accounted for in its questions. For example, we know that athletes (e.g., Gorecki, Vadocz, Mensch, & French, 2002; Hall, Buckolz, & Fishburne, 1992; Rodgers et al., 1991), exercisers (Short, Hall, et al.,

2004), and dancers (Nordin & Cumming, 2005b) all experience occasional debilitative images. But no measure currently exists to investigate the prevalence, antecedents, correlates, or consequences of such images. Given that debilitative images can decrease both self-efficacy and performance (e.g., Nordin & Cumming, 2005a; Short et al., 2002), better delineation of debilitative imagery would aid in the design and implementation of appropriate interventions.

Consistent with our descriptions of type, function, and outcome in our neurocognitive model, we emphasize that CS, CG, MS, MG–M, and MG–A are imagery types, not functions, as they are often called. This distinction highlights the fact that to date, no instrument allows us to examine *why* performers image. But Short, Monsma, et al. (2004) investigated the reasons why athletes engaged in the various images on the SIQ. They found that most (25 of 30) images were engaged in for the reasons predicted by the creators of the SIQ (Hall et al., 1998). For instance, CS images were employed to enhance skills, and MG–M images were used to enhance mastery-related cognitions. But the researchers also established that different athletes may use the same image for different functions and that a single image can serve multiple functions for a single athlete. We believe that researchers will benefit if further elaborations of imagery assessment instruments take into account the type, function, and outcome of imagery use.

Validity Issues in Current Imagery Assessment Instruments

The main focus when measuring imagery use has been to measure the relative frequency with which performers engage in various imagery types. This type of measurement is used because frequency is the response format for the SIQ (Hall et al., 1998), the Exercise Imagery Questionnaire (EIQ; Hausenblas et al. 1999), and the more recent Exercise Imagery Inventory (EII; Giacobbi, Hausenblas, & Penfield, in press). Similar to the MIQ–R, these questionnaires have been useful in producing informative research findings, but they also have shortcomings. One such limitation of the SIQ pertains to its motivational general–arousal (MG–A) subscale. Namely, some studies have found that this subscale correlates with anxiety (e.g., Monsma & Overby, 2004; Vadocz et al, 1997). Inspection of the items provides the reason for this finding. Specifically, the MG–A subscale includes items such as "I image the stress and anxiety associated with my sport" and "When I image myself participating in sport, I feel anxious." Findings such as these do not mean that the MG–A subscale is not valuable, but they probably mean that the suggestion that more imagery is better is not necessarily true for the items in the SIQ.

Note that the items on the SIQ should be taken only as some indicators of what an imagery type might entail, not the only ones. For example, the MG–A subscale focuses on arousal and anxiety but does not mention images of being calm. Nonetheless, when imagery scripts and interventions are created that do not employ the SIQ, images of calm clearly fall into the same category as those of psyching up, excitement, stress, and anxiety, because they are all related to arousal. For this reason, studies that use MG–A type images may not be comparable because the SIQ subscales are not all encompassing. In addition, although the literature consistently identifies CS as referring to images of skills, several items in the CS subscale appear to tap into imagery ability ("I can consistently control the image of a physical skill"; "I can easily change the image of a skill"; "I can mentally make corrections to physical skills"). Further assessment development is warranted.

The Problem of Spontaneous Imagery

Our review has highlighted a hitherto neglected aspect of imagery in sport, namely the occurrence of spontaneous images that the individual does not regard as serving any purpose. Indeed, these spontaneous images may sometimes interfere with ongoing imagery. For example, Vergeer (2003) reported that spontaneous images can interfere with deliberate imagery use. We encourage researchers to document and explore this interesting phenomenon in greater depth.

The Problem of Adverse Outcomes With Imagery Use in Sport

One troubling finding from decades of imagery research is that many research subjects experience performance degradation after mental practice. Budney and Woolfolk (1990) pointed out that a reexamination of the Feltz and Landers (1983) meta-analysis revealed that 33 of the 146 effect sizes analyzed were in the negative direction. All 33 of these tasks fell into the motor or strength categories. This finding suggests that many subjects experience performance deterioration with mental practice. In response to the question, "Describe any experience where imagery has inhibited performance," 35% of the athletes, 25% of the coaches, and 87% of the sport

psychologists surveyed by Jowdy, Murphy, and Durtschi (1989) gave examples of imagery use that inhibited performance. This survey clearly indicates that imagery can have negative as well as beneficial effects on performance.

Under what conditions might we expect imagery problems to occur? People with poor imagery ability may be especially likely to experience harmful outcomes from imagery use, especially if their problem is in controlling imagery. We do not know enough about the frequency and nature of debilitative images to have a full understanding of their effects. In addition, if athletes imagine incorrect actions in their imagery rehearsal, they may very well be programming mistakes into their action sequence. Novice or beginner athletes may need to be particularly cautious in their use of imagery for skill learning. Martin et al.'s (1999) model suggests that athletes might experience poor outcomes with imagery use if the type of imagery that they use is not suitable for the performance outcome desired. This proposal has received some research support, at least when imagery characteristics have been studied. For example, White and Hardy (1995) found that internal visual imagery was more effective for a simulated canoe slalom task, but that external visual imagery was more helpful for a simulated gymnastics task emphasizing technical execution. Finally, the individual's interpretation of and associations with the imagery used may have a major influence on the effect of the imagery. As we have suggested in previous editions of this chapter, both researchers and practitioners should be careful to assess the imagery experience and the meaning of the imagery for each individual because our neurocognitive model indicates that imagery prompts may lead to an imagery experience different from what was intended.

Conclusion

We have presented a neurocognitive model of imagery use in sport that builds on functional equivalence theory and several cognitive theories of working memory, such as Baddeley's (1986), to explain how imagery generates behavioral, cognitive, and affective changes in the areas of sport, exercise, and dance. We used this model to review a wide range of research, and we generated a number of testable assumptions based on the model. Although many specifics of the model await empirical study, we hope that by attempting to explain the imagery process rather than merely describing and cataloging imagery, we are moving the field forward, in conjunction with other recent theoretically based attempts to understand imagery, such as the PETTLEP model. We also expanded our review to include research from the closely related areas of exercise and dance to broaden the generality of our model and to utilize some of the novel research concepts generated in those areas. Our model aims to integrate the recent relevant imagery research in both neuroscience and applied sport psychology, and we hope that it will prove useful in guiding new imagery research in sport, exercise, and dance.

CHAPTER 14

Attentional Processes and Sport Performance

■ Stephen H. Boutcher, PhD ■

The study of attention has a rich and varied history. In the late 1800s and early 1900s, the laboratories of Wundt, Titchener, and Helmholtz carried out many experiments examining different aspects of attention. Surprisingly, however, interest in attention waned over the next 25 years and was not rekindled until the advent of World War II. The war challenged psychologists with many applied problems concerning attention (e.g., how long could a radar operator watch a screen without a decline in attention?). Attention, currently one of the core themes in psychology, is viewed as a complex multidisciplinary field of study. According to Parasuraman (1998), research in attention is being conducted in many areas of the psychological sciences including cognitive psychology, psychophysiology, neuropsychology, and developmental psychology.

In the sport context, several authors have suggested that attention is a vital aspect of athletic performance (Abernethy, 1993; Boutcher, 1990; Moran, 1996; Wulf, 2007). The research examining the role of attention in sport, however, is underdeveloped. Furthermore, few studies have examined the attentional mechanisms underpinning athletic performance. Thus, a suitable framework to study the influence of attention on sport skills has not been established.

In this chapter I review the research and theory pertaining to attention with a view toward synthesizing various perspectives to develop a better understanding of the relationship between attention and performance. The first part of this chapter focuses on a review of the attention–performance literature as it has been studied from three different perspectives: information processing, social psychology, and psychophysiology. At the conclusion of this section I present a synthesis of the three perspectives and an integrated model of attention in sport. The last part of this chapter focuses on a more applied perspective, discussing several issues related to attentional training in athletes.

Theoretical and Empirical Perspectives of Attention

Attention in sport has been studied from three perspectives: information processing, social psychology, and psychophysiology. Each of these research thrusts has emphasized a different but related perspective of the attentional process. Research in information processing has established the existence of two related forms of processing; control processing requires effort and is slow and cumbersome, whereas automatic processing is effortless, quick, and efficient. Social psychologists have focused on individual differences and environmental influences on attentional processes and have documented the ability of extraneous, inappropriate cues to disrupt performance. Sport psychophysiologists have attempted to examine the underlying mechanisms of attention by monitoring cortical and cardiac activity; both cortical and autonomic indicants of attention have been used successfully to assess attentional style in athletes during performance. The following three sections discuss the relevant aspects of these approaches necessary to develop an integrated model of attention and sport performance.

Information-Processing Perspective

Cognitive psychologists consider humans to be processors of information. The information-processing approach attempts to understand the stimulus–response relationship, stimulus being some kind of information entering the body through the sensory system and response being the resulting behavior. This approach assumes that a number of processing stages occur between the stimulus and response initiation. Although the names of the different stages vary, most information-processing models include perceptual, short-term memory, and long-term memory stages. For overviews of different information-processing models, see O'Donnel and Cohen (1993) and Schmidt (1999).

Information-processing models provide a framework for examining the characteristics of perception, memory, decision making, and attention. Attention is conceptualized as the ability to switch focus from one source of information to another and as the amount of information that can be attended to at any one time. Thus, attention is a central concept in the information-processing approach. Researchers working from this perspective have focused primarily on three aspects of attention—the three interacting processes of selective attention, capacity, and alertness (Posner & Bois, 1971). Because the literature examining these processes is extensive, only those aspects pertinent to the theme of this chapter are examined here (for more complete overviews, see Abernethy, 1993; Pashler, 1998; Schmidt, 1999; Styles, 1997).

Attentional Selectivity

Selective attention refers to the process by which certain information from the internal or external environment enters the information-processing system while other information is screened out or ignored. In any situation, the organism is constantly bombarded with a mass of information from both the internal and external environments, and it can assimilate only a certain amount at a particular moment. Therefore, selection is necessary so that only a few stimuli are processed. The organism focuses on certain aspects that directly affect behavior, whereas the remaining stimuli serve as background. Selection can be voluntary or involuntary depending on whether the selection is due to the organism or to the stimuli itself. Selection can take place in a large variety of behavioral situations. That is, an individual may choose to focus inwardly on certain strategies and experiences or outwardly on a wide range of environmental cues. Thus, selection is multifaceted and appears to be an essential condition for sport performance. William James (1890) expressed this succinctly in his classical statement that "without selective interest, experience is an utter chaos."

Selective attention is believed to play a central role in both the learning and performing of sport skills. But the stimuli that are essential for a particular performance change as a function of practice and skill improvement. For example, neophytes learning to dribble a basketball must devote much attention to watching the ball and are unable to lift their heads to focus on the players around them. With practice, however, players can dribble without watching the ball, and the skill becomes more synchronized and automatic. Eventually, after many years of practice, players can dribble with either hand while simultaneously defending the ball from an opposing player and monitoring the positions of fellow players. In this latter situation, most of the performer's attention is focused externally on surrounding players rather than on the process of dribbling. In contrast, the player sent to the foul line does not have to attend to much external information. But because the foul shot is typically well learned, attention that was previously available to focus on teammates and opponents now has the potential to focus on task-irrelevant cues and internal information such as worry about missing, spectators, and so forth.

This basketball example shows that with practice, attention can be changed from a cumbersome, conscious process to a smooth, unconscious process. These two aspects of attention have been called control and automatic processing (Badgaivan,

2000; Schneider, Dumais, & Shiffrin, 1984). Control processing is used to process novel or inconsistent information and is slow, effortful, capacity limited, and controlled by the individual. In sport, control processing is involved when decisions are required. For example, a golfer who is considering distance, wind conditions, and the position of hazards to determine club selection would use control processing. In contrast, automatic processing, which is responsible for the performance of well-learned skills, is fast, effortless, and not under direct conscious control. In sport, automatic processing occurs when athletes have developed skills through many years of practice. Thus, the professional golfer uses automatic processing when swinging the club. The major differences between automatic and control processing are that automatic processing requires little effort, attention, or awareness, whereas control processing requires high awareness, much attention, and intensive effort. All sports require a combination of automatic and control processing because athletes need to perform many skills in a reflexive, automatic manner yet also must make decisions and process inconsistent cues and new information. Closed-skill sports such as golf, archery, and shooting probably require more automatic processing, whereas open-skill sports involve a combination of the two. Thus, control processing (slow, effortful, capacity limited, and controlled by the individual) and automatic processing (fast, effortless, and not under direct conscious control) have the potential to play important roles in sport performance.

Attentional Capacity

A second aspect of attention that has been examined relative to performance is attentional capacity. This term refers to the fact that control processing is limited in the amount of information that can be processed at one time. Specifically, a person can perform only one complex task at a time and thus would have difficulty focusing attention on two sources of information simultaneously. Consequently, control processing can be viewed as having a limited capacity for processing information from either the internal or external environments. Thus, performing multiple tasks or attempting to focus on more than one source of information may impair performance. An example of control processing overload in the sport context would be two coaches simultaneously giving a basketball player a stream of instructions during a time-out.

The restrictions on attentional capacity are due to both structural and central capacity limitations.

Structural interference involves two tasks performed at the same time using the same receptor or effector systems. For example, listening for the sound of a starter's gun while at the same time listening to a voice in the crowd could provoke auditory structural interference. Capacity interference occurs when two tasks compete for limited central information-processing capacity simultaneously. Fixed-capacity and undifferentiated theories represent two different views for explaining how task performance will be affected if capacity for processing is exceeded. Fixed-capacity theories (e.g., Broadbent, 1958; Keele, 1973; Kerr, 1973; Norman, 1969) assume that capacity is fixed in size and remains the same for different tasks. In contrast, theories of undifferentiated capacity (e.g., Kahneman, 1973) view attention as a resource that can be channeled to various processing operations. This approach is a more flexible view of attention and suggests that capacity changes as task requirements change. Multiple resource theory (Navon & Gopher, 1979; Wickens, 1984) is an extension of flexible attentional capacity and suggests that attention may consist of a set of pools of resources, each with its own capacity to handle information processing. This view suggests that processes requiring attention may be able to handle more than one stimulus at any one time (parallel processing). The ability of the human information-processing system to process multiple sources of information simultaneously would depend on the importance of the tasks involved, task difficulty, and structural considerations. Resource theory generally is viewed as an attractive framework for understanding attention. Critics of the theory, however, have focused on issues regarding practice and divided attention and the number of resources necessary to cover all aspects of attention (see Hirst, 1986; Logan, 1988).

Whereas control processing is fragmentized; requires much attention, effort, and awareness; and can handle only relatively simple tasks, automatic processing is just the opposite. Automatic processing requires little attention, effort, or awareness; is not serial dependent; and is holistic rather than fragmentized in nature. The capacity limitations of automatic processing are less restrictive than are those of control processing. For instance, performing a golf swing involves a variety of muscles initiated by millions of efferent neural impulses. If a person had to monitor this process consciously, the task would be overwhelming. Thus, control processing, which may be dominant in the early stages of learning (Shiffrin, 1976), eventually will give way to automatic processing if the skill is to be performed in an effortless, efficient manner. For skill performance, then, the greater attentional capacity limitation of control processing compared with that of automatic processing is important.

Attentional Alertness

The third aspect of attention that has been examined in information-processing research concerns the effects of alertness and arousal on the breadth of the attentional field. Easterbrook (1959), in a comprehensive review of the available literature, cited numerous research studies supporting the hypothesis that increases in emotional arousal narrow the attentional field because of systematic reduction in the range of cue utilization. Landers (1980a, 1980b, 1981) used the work of Easterbrook (1959) to examine the effects of emotional arousal on athletes' visual field during performance. Numerous studies have indicated that in stressful situations, performance on a central visual task decreases the ability to respond to peripheral stimuli (Bacon, 1974; Hockey, 1970; Landers, Qi, & Courtet, 1985). Thus, it appears that arousal can bring about sensitivity loss to cues that are in the peripheral visual field. In sport, point guard play in basketball provides an example of how overarousal can affect the visual attentional field. If a point guard is looking for teammates outside the key (scanning the periphery of his or her attentional field), overarousal may bring about perceptual narrowing. This narrow focus may prevent the point guard from detecting open players in the periphery. Because many sport skills are performed in aroused states, the phenomenon of attentional field narrowing may be an important determinant of sport performance. Also the attentional narrowing phenomenon has been associated with sport injuries. For example, negative life event stress has been shown to induce peripheral narrowing that is associated with increased athletic injuries (Rogers, Alderman, & Landers, 2003; Rogers & Landers, 2005).

Conclusion

Researchers using the information perspective have focused primarily on selection, alertness, and capacity aspects of attention. Important aspects of selective attention are control and automatic processing. Control processing is slow, requires effort, and is controlled by the individual. In contrast, automatic processing is fast, effortless, and not under conscious individual control. Control processing is important in the early stages of learning and for dealing with novel and inconsistent information, whereas automatic processing is responsible for skills that are so well learned that they require little attention or effort. Regarding alertness, it has been demonstrated that increases in emotional arousal can narrow the attentional field because of systematic reduction in the range of cue utilization. Research has also shown that the capacity limitation of control processing is more restrictive than that of automatic processing.

Social Psychological Perspectives

Because sport typically requires performance of well-learned skills, automatic processing appears to be an important aspect of athletic performance. But successful sport performance also requires use of control processing. For instance, receivers and quarterbacks must constantly monitor the environment through control processing to attend to vital cues. In these performance situations, focusing attention on task-irrelevant information while attempting to perform well-learned skills may impair performance. Social psychologists have conducted most of the research about this aspect of control processing (i.e., the possibility that task-irrelevant rather than task-relevant stimuli may enter the information-processing system, thus disrupting performance). Most theories and explanations concerning this phenomenon have evolved from research in test anxiety, self-awareness, and pain. Three areas of this attentional research are pertinent to the role of attentional control and performance of well-learned skills: distraction theories, automatic functioning, and attentional style.

Distraction Theories

Distraction theories focus on the loss of attention caused by factors that attract attention to task-irrelevant cues. Thus, if task-irrelevant cues attract an athlete's attention, performance may suffer. If an archer focuses solely on thoughts of missing the target, attention might be disrupted and performance degraded. Similarly, if a baseball or softball batter does not focus visual attention on the pitcher, he or she probably will not make contact with the ball. Thus, even momentary loss of concentration during the initial flight of the ball may have devastating results.

One factor that may divert attention to irrelevant stimuli is worry. Sarason (1972) and Wine (1971)

suggested that worry as an emotional state distracts attention and thus can explain the negative effects of test anxiety on performance. According to Sarason and Wine, anxious people typically focus their attention on task-irrelevant thoughts and ignore critical task cues during testing. Thus, individuals who dwell on thoughts such as "I know I'll fail because I'm not as good as the others" are not focusing their attention on task-relevant cues and will not produce performance results that reflect their ability. Acute anxiety, in the form of self-debilitating thoughts, has been associated with competitive athletic situations (Gould, Greenleaf, & Krane, 2006). Thus, this research on distraction seems to be especially relevant to the study of sport. Processing task-irrelevant information can explain performance decrements in a wide range of athletic settings. In highly competitive situations, for example, performance could be hampered because the athlete focuses on self-defeating thoughts. In contrast, in nonstimulating, low-arousal environments (e.g., competitions that occur over hours or days), a lack of intensity in attention may cause the athlete to miss important task-relevant cues.

Another source of distraction information is self-awareness. Carver and Scheier (1981) suggested that attending to oneself while performing may take attention away from task cues, thus degrading performance. Other authors (Duval & Wicklund, 1972; Scheier, Fenigstein, & Buss, 1974) have suggested that attending to oneself and to the environment at the same time is impossible. Because social facilitation generally tends to increase self-awareness (Carver & Scheier, 1978), the presence of spectators and cameras at sporting events has the potential to increase focus on the self, thus distracting the athlete. Thus, distraction in the form of worry or self-awareness is another attentional factor that can affect skill performance.

Automatic Functioning

The second area of study in the social psychology research literature that is relevant to the disruptive effects of inappropriate attentional focus concerns the automatic execution of sport skills. This concept relates to the automatic-processing idea that was discussed in the section on information processing. Baumeister (1984) suggested that competitive pressure makes people want to do so well that they tend to focus on the process of performance. In competitive situations, when individuals realize the importance of correct skill execution, they attempt to ensure success by consciously monitoring the process of performance. That is, they attempt to put the execution of a skill, which is typically under automatic-processing control, under the control-processing mechanism. Unfortunately, consciousness (control processing) does not contain the necessary information regarding the muscle movement and coordination essential for effective performance. Thus, attempting to exert active or conscious control over the process involved in a skill can degrade performance (Kimble & Perlmuter, 1970). An example of the effect of consciously controlling well-learned skills was provided by Langer and Imber (1979), who demonstrated that attempting to ensure accuracy by consciously monitoring finger movements during typing was detrimental to performance. Keele (1973) found that focusing attention on hand movements during piano playing detracted from performance. Krings et al. (2000), using magnetic functional imaging, also found that professional compared to amateur piano players exhibited less cognitive effort during performance. Baumeister (1984) demonstrated this effect by using laboratory tasks when he found that increasing subjects' attention to the process of performing debilitated performance. Thus, attempting to ensure success by consciously monitoring performance during competition is another inefficient use of attention.

Attentional Style

Individual differences may exist regarding the distraction and automatic-processing concepts discussed in the previous sections. Thus, in competitive situations, certain athletes might use an attentional style that hinders performance. Variations in attentional style and their effect on sport performance have formed the focus of much of the attentional research in sport psychology. For instance, Nideffer (1976b), using concepts developed by Easterbrook (1959), Wachtel (1967), and Bacon (1974), suggested that the attentional demands of any sporting situation will vary along two dimensions: width (broad or narrow) and direction (internal or external). A broad external focus requires people to focus on a wide area of the external environment (e.g., a quarterback scanning the width of the field), whereas with a broad internal focus, people focus attention internally on a variety of strategies and past experience. A narrow external focus is appropriate for activities that require people to focus on a narrow aspect of the external environment, such as a golf ball or the ring in foul shooting. A narrow internal attentional focus is most suited to attending to specific images or cognitive cues.

The challenge for the athlete, according to Nideffer, is to match the attentional demands of the sporting environment with the appropriate attentional style. Therefore, an individual who uses an inappropriate style for a particular activity (e.g., a baseball batter who broadly focuses his attention on players and spectators rather than using a narrow focus on the pitcher) may experience impaired performance. Nideffer (1976b) also used Easterbrook's notion of attentional narrowing to explain the effects of anxiety and arousal on attentional processes. As discussed previously, the suggestion is that arousal produces an involuntary narrowing in attention and may interfere with the person's ability to shift attentional focus.

Nideffer (1976b) proposed that individuals may possess a particular attentional style. These styles, which are relatively stable across situations and over time, may affect performance in certain situations if the athlete's style is incompatible with the attentional requirements of that situation. For example, a basketball player may consistently focus on thoughts of missing when shooting foul shots. In contrast, the aspects of attention that are state dependent are situation specific and thus are amenable to change. Nideffer (1976b) developed the Test of Attentional and Interpersonal Style (TAIS) to assess the strengths and weaknesses of an individual's attentional style. The subscales of the TAIS are broad external, external overload, broad internal, internal overload, narrow effective focus, and errors of underinclusion. Although Nideffer provided preliminary support for the reliability and validity of the TAIS (Nideffer, 1976c), more recent research has suggested that the TAIS has limited validity and predictive properties for sport performance. Landers (1981, 1985a), who reviewed research examining the TAIS and sport performance, concluded that the scale seems to measure the narrow versus broad dimension but not the internal versus external dimension. Furthermore, he found no evidence that the TAIS is a good predictor of sport performance. Other researchers have developed sport-specific versions of the TAIS for tennis (Van Schoyck & Grasha, 1981) and baseball (Albrecht & Feltz, 1987) in an attempt to increase the reliability and validity of questionnaire assessment of attentional style. Although these versions of the TAIS increased internal consistency and were better predictors of performance, the prediction–performance relationship was still weak.

Any questionnaire assessment of attention is inherently limited in at least two ways. For instance, the assumption underlying questionnaire assessment is that athletes are able to make accurate assessments of their attentional focus across varying situations. The veracity of this assumption has not been established. Second, the assumption that self-analysis and language can accurately describe attention has problems. As discussed earlier, the automatic-processing aspect of attention appears to be free of conscious monitoring (Schneider et al., 1984). Thus, a paradox may exist when athletes are asked to assess nonconscious attentional states by way of conscious processing.

A related aspect of attentional style is the association–dissociation attentional strategies that elite and nonelite marathon runners use. Exploratory interviews with such athletes (Morgan & Pollack, 1977) have revealed that elite runners were less likely to use dissociative strategies when running (focusing on distractive thoughts to divert attention from physical discomfort) than were nonelite runners. Rather, elite marathoners reported that they used associative strategies (focusing on bodily sensations such as breathing and feelings in legs) more often than did nonelite runners.

Schomer (1986) suggested that postinterview data, postrace questionnaires, and anecdotal reports do not accurately assess the continuous thought flow of runners while running. To test this suggestion, Schomer (1986) used a tape recorder to record runners' thoughts while they ran on a treadmill. The tapes were then content analyzed by coding thoughts into mental strategies. From this analysis, 10 categories emerged as mental strategy subclassifications. Comparison of elite and nonelite runners' use of the 10 categories did not support the results of Morgan and Pollack (1977), who found that elite marathoners used associative mental strategies, whereas non-world-class runners preferred to dissociate. In contrast, the results of the Schomer study suggest that regardless of the marathon runners' status, increased running pace was accompanied by a predominately associative mental strategy.

In a second study, Schomer (1987) trained marathon runners to use associative thinking. A five-week mental strategy training program taught nonelite marathon runners to use associative thought processes similar to those of superior marathon runners. Eight of the 10 marathon runners undergoing the program exhibited increased associative thought processes and an increase in perceived training effort. Schomer concluded that using associative mental strategies during marathon running and training might enable athletes to achieve optimum running threshold. Overall, these results suggest that an associative attentional

focus may be most beneficial for long-distance sporting events such as marathon running. Acute (e.g., cycling on a stationary bike for 20 minutes) and chronic exercise (e.g., walking three times per week for 40 minutes) have also been found to influence certain aspects of attention. Overall, results indicate that moderately vigorous aerobic exercise lasting up to 60 minutes enhances cognitive function but that extended exercise reduces information-processing efficiency. Reviews in this area include the effect of acute exercise on cognitive ability of adults (Brisswalter, Collardeau, & Arcelin, 2002; Tomporowski, 2003) and the effect of chronic exercise on cognitive ability of older adults (Colcombe & Kramer, 2003).

Social psychologists' interest in attention has focused primarily on the disruptive influence of nonrelevant task stimuli such as worry and self-consciousness. In well-learned tasks, inappropriate use of control processing appears to have the potential to hamper the performance of well-learned skills that are typically under the control of automatic processing. In sport, in which many skills are well learned, athletes may interfere with automatic nonconscious performance by focusing on distracting information such as worry and fear of failure and by consciously attempting to control movement.

Social psychologists also have been interested in potential individual differences in attentional capabilities. These differences in attentional style of different athletic groups have been assessed through questionnaires. The rationale behind such questionnaires is that assessment of an athlete's attentional style can predict future performance. Unfortunately, no evidence exists that attentional questionnaires are good predictors of sport performance. Also, because of the nature of automatic processing, the validity of assessing attentional states by retrospective recall is uncertain. Other ways of assessing attentional style include interviews and thought-sampling techniques. The latter strategy may have greater potential for attentional assessment because it does not rely on retrospective recall.

Psychophysiological Perspectives

In contrast to cognitive psychologists who have attempted to understand attention by studying the whole process (receptor, information processing, and motor output), psychophysiologists have attempted to identify the mechanisms of attention by examining its component parts. In psychophysiological research, electroencephalogram (EEG), evoked response potentials (ERPs), heart rate, and gaze behavior primarily have been used to examine attention and its relationship to performance. For instance, EEG (obtained by monitoring general cortical activity through scalp electrodes) has been studied in relation to a variety of cognitive tasks including vigilance detection, perceptual structuring, and object recognition and discrimination. ERPs, which are averaged brain responses to a series of stimuli, also have been examined as indicants of attention and have been found to be sensitive to the level of concentration on a task.

Psychophysiological indicants of attention also have been used in sport research. Hatfield, Landers, and Ray (1984), for example, examined left and right brain alpha EEG activity of elite rifle shooters while subjects were shooting and while they performed a series of mental tasks. Results indicated that progressive electrocortical lateralization occurred toward right hemispheric dominance before the trigger pull. Thus, seconds before pulling the trigger, shooters exhibited more alpha activity in their left hemisphere compared with their right. The authors suggested that elite shooters may possess such a high degree of attentional focus that they can effectively reduce conscious mental activities of the left hemisphere, thus reducing cognitions unnecessary to performance of the task. This cognitive efficiency phenomenon found in shooting is a robust finding because a series of recent studies have replicated it (Deeny, Hillman, Janelle, & Hatfield, 2003; Haufler, Spalding, Santa Maria, & Hatfield, 2000; Janelle, Singer, & Williams 1999; Kerick, Douglass, & Hatfield, 2004; Kerick et al 2001).

Crews and Landers (1992) found similar decreases in left hemispheric alpha EEG activity immediately before golfers struck the ball when putting. Unlike shooters, however, golfers showed decreased right hemispheric alpha activity before putting. The authors suggested that the different EEG responses during putting may be caused by the need for both hands to be actively involved in putting.

Landers et al. (1994) showed that as novice archers improve performance, their EEG asymmetries change to resemble those of elite archers. These authors found that left hemisphere alpha activity of novice archers before releasing the arrow increased as archers improved performance. An extreme increase, however, was associated with poorer performance. Also, after the 15-week archery class, heart rates of the novice archers were observed to decelerate seconds before shooting. The authors concluded that EEG asymmetries and heart rate deceleration are markers of attention that change with learning.

Other sport scientists have examined ERPs before and during shooting. In this research, investigators record multiple ERPs and then separate them from other electrocortical noise by signal averaging techniques. For example, Konttinen and Lyytinen (1992) and Konttinen, Lyytinen, and Konttinen (1995) examined an ERP known as slow wave. They found that increases in frontal negative shifts were associated with successful performance if central-right slow waves were more positive than central-left slow waves. The authors suggested that the results reflected the ability of elite shooters to eradicate irrelevant motor activity while concentrating on visuospatial processing.

These data support the notion that there are general processing differences between the left and right cerebral hemispheres of the brain. For example, studies of split-brain patients' performance (LeDoux, Wilson, & Gazzaniga, 1977; Sperry, 1968) and EEG patterns (McKee, Humphrey, & McAdam, 1973) and lateral eye movements (Schwartz, Davidson, & Maer, 1975; Tucker, Shearer, & Murray, 1977) have demonstrated that for most people, verbal and linguistic processing occurs in the left cerebral hemisphere, whereas spatial cognitive processing occurs in the right hemisphere. Also, the left hemisphere appears to process information analytically, breaking down a concept into discrete parts, whereas the right hemisphere processes holistically in a gestaltic fashion (Springer & Deutsch, 1998; Tucker et al., 1977).

Another variable that has been used to explore attentional states in athletes is cardiac deceleration. For example, a number of studies have found heart rate deceleration with elite rifle shooters just before the trigger pull (Helin, Sihvonen, & Hanninen, 1987; Konttinen & Lyytinen, 1992; Landers, Christina, Hatfield, Doyle, & Daniels, 1980). Similar results have been found with archers, who exhibited a progressive deceleration in heart rate seconds before the release of the arrow (Landers et al., 1994). But another study of elite archers did not find heart rate deceleration before arrow release (Salazar et al., 1990). The authors explained the absence of heart rate deceleration in their elite archers because of the physiological strain imposed when drawing a 14- to 22-kilogram bow. They concluded that cardiac deceleration can be used as an attentional index only when the preparatory state is not physiologically demanding.

Boutcher and Zinsser (1990) also found similar deceleration effects with elite and beginning golfers on a putting task. Both groups displayed heart rate deceleration during performance of 4- and 12-foot (1.2- and 3.6-meter) putts, although the elite golfers showed significantly greater deceleration. The elite golfers also possessed significantly less variable preshot routines. The authors suggested that the different heart rate deceleration patterns may reflect the more efficient attentional control of the elite golfers. Other researchers who examined old and young golfers found similar results (Molander & Backman, 1989).

Gaze behavior is another measure used to examine attention and sport performance. Gaze behavior is believed to represent visual attention organization during closed-skilled performance (Vickers, 1996a) and has typically been measured by video-based eye movement systems (Janelle et al., 2000). Vickers (1996b) has shown that the quiet eye period, defined as the duration between the final fixation to a target and the initiation of the motor response, is a major performance determinant among expert and novice free-throw shooters. Highly skilled free-throw shooters recorded significantly longer quiet eye periods before performing a free throw compared with less skilled players. Vickers (1996b) suggested that the longer the gaze is fixated on the target (the quiet eye period), the more optimal is the preparatory period. The quiet eye phenomenon has also been shown to be characteristic of elite volleyball players (Vickers & Adolphe, 1997) and expert small-bore rifle shooters (Janelle et al., 2000).

Sport psychophysiologists have studied attention by monitoring cortical and autonomic responses during athletic performance. EEG studies have indicated that elite shooters display cortical lateral asymmetry during shooting performance. Cardiac deceleration has been associated with attentional states in archery, shooting, and putting. Eye gaze has been shown to influence the preparatory period in sports such as basketball, volleyball, and rifle shooting.

Synthesis of Theoretical Perspectives

The review of the research and theory presented in the first half of this chapter has revealed that the attention–performance relationship has been studied from three different viewpoints. Despite the relatively diverse nature of these three perspectives,

they actually represent complementary approaches and together provide a unique, integrated perspective on the relationship between attention and sport performance. Therefore, I recommend that future research into the attentional processes underlying athletic performance take into account the principles outlined in the previous sections on information processing, social psychology, and sport psychophysiological research. Thus, attention should be viewed as a multifaceted, multilevel phenomenon that can be assessed through questionnaires, thought sampling, observation analysis, performance, and psychophysiological measures. The appropriateness of the measure would depend on whether the performer carries out the skill in the control-processing mode or the automatic-processing mode. Other factors that need to be considered when investigating the attention–performance relationship include individual differences, environmental influences, and changes in the performer's level of arousal. A preliminary framework based on this multidimensional approach is illustrated in figure 14.1. This proposed model integrates relevant aspects of the research and theory on attention from all three perspectives. As shown in figure 14.1, enduring disposition (e.g., high trait anxiety), demands of the activity (e.g., putting versus sprinting), and environmental factors (e.g., spectators and television cameras) initially will determine the level of physiological arousal of the individual. During task performance, the individual could channel this arousal into control processing, automatic processing, or a combination of both. The nature of the task would determine the appropriateness of using either control or automatic processing. The individual would achieve an optimal attentional state, then, by reaching or attaining the exact balance of control and automatic processing essential for that particular task. Obviously, disruption in attentional processes would occur if internal or external factors caused the individual to reach a level of arousal that would cause an imbalance in control and automatic processing.

The arrows linking the ellipses and boxes in figure 14.1 indicate feedback mechanisms that would allow factors to interact and influence attention both during and after performance. An example of the interaction of these factors is a golfer attempting to hole an important putt. The perceived importance of the putt (e.g., a putt to win a tournament) could increase physiological arousal and anxiety, which, in turn, could reduce the golfer's attentional capacity. This anxiety could generate thoughts of missing the putt, which could direct attention away from

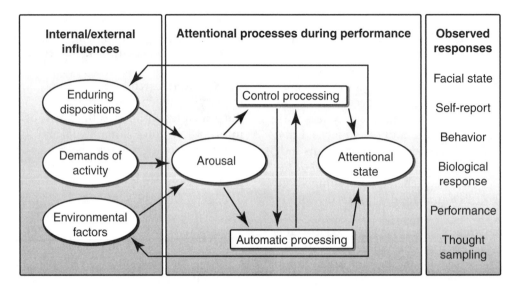

Figure 14.1 Interactions between internal and external factors and attentional processing.

task-relevant cues. Thus, the golfer may focus attention mostly on irrelevant information and be primarily in the control-processing mode. This state may be detrimental to putting performance, which the golfer should probably perform in the automatic-processing mode.

Possible ways to measure either control or automatic processing are illustrated in the end column. Self-report may be most useful for people engaging in control processing, although this notion does not preclude the use of retrospective recall to assess feelings and emotions associated with automatic processing. Variables such as facial state, eye gaze (discussed further in the next section), and psychophysiological variables also appear to have potential for measuring attention during athletic performance.

In summary, researchers who study the relationship between attention and performance need to consider integrated models of attention. Viewing attention from a multidimensional perspective may generate more systematic research and provide a more reliable and valid research paradigm.

Applied Perspectives on Attentional Control

As shown in this review, attentional theories of sport performance are not well developed. In addition, the empirical research that has been conducted on attention in sport has lacked a unifying model. Consequently, techniques to improve athletes' atten-

tional capabilities have not been developed within a theoretical framework and have proceeded largely by trial and error. Certainly, applied research needs to be conducted to advance understanding of how athletes' attentional capabilities can be improved. Specifically, qualitative strategies (e.g., single-subject research) should be wedded to the idiographic framework suggested earlier.

Given the lack of empirical research on attentional training, sport psychologists who want to provide attentional training for individual athletes will need to develop programs based on the research and theory discussed previously. The purpose of this last section is to outline a preliminary attentional training program. This proposed training program is based on the research and theory described in the previous sections. These recommendations are consistent with the principles outlined in the integrated model illustrated in figure 14.1. Considerably more field research, however, is needed to test the suitability and efficacy of these proposed techniques. This final section is divided into three parts: assessment of athletes' attentional strengths and weaknesses, basic attentional training, and advanced attentional training.

Assessment of Attentional Strengths and Weaknesses

Before an attentional training program can be designed and conducted for an individual athlete, an assessment of the athlete's attentional strengths and weaknesses will be necessary. Given the multifaceted nature of attention, it follows that assessment strategies will be most effective if they are also multifaceted. Some possible ways to assess an individual's attentional capabilities include questionnaires, interviews, thought-sampling techniques, observational analysis, performance tests, and psychophysiological measurement. These assessment strategies are examined further in the following paragraphs.

Sport-specific questionnaires seem to be more reliable and predict more variance associated with performance than do general measures of attention (Zaichkowsky, 1984). As discussed previously, sport-specific forms of the TAIS have been developed for tennis (Van Schoyck & Grasha, 1982) and baseball (Albrecht & Feltz, 1987). These questionnaires should be used with caution, however, and only as one part of a multidimensional assessment of attention because of their inherent limitations, which were discussed previously. The thought-sampling technique (Klinger, 1984; Schomer, 1986) appears to be a more valid way of assessing what athletes focus their thoughts on during performance. This technique involves recording individuals' thoughts during actual activity (usually by tape recorder); it seems especially appropriate for continuous activities such as running but could be adapted to other sports. For instance, golfers could record on a tape or write on a scorecard (see Boutcher & Rotella, 1987) their thoughts and feelings after shots. The researchers could then perform content analysis and estimate attentional foci during task performance.

Athletes' attentional strengths also could be measured through laboratory tasks such as choice reaction time tasks, the Stroop test, and the grid test. For instance, in research with elite and nonelite archers, Landers, Boutcher, and Wang (1986) found that the better archers recorded lower reaction times when performing a reaction–anticipation time task than did their lesser-skilled counterparts. Better archers' lower reaction times were due to greater consistency across performance trials, not because they were innately faster. Thus, these elite athletes' responses may have been more consistent because they could concentrate more effectively in this testing situation. Whether this difference in concentrational capabilities is linked to actual performance differences between elite and nonelite archers has not been established.

Another laboratory task that could be used to assess attentional capabilities is the Stroop test (Stroop, 1935). This test involves watching a series of slides flashed on a screen at the rate of one per second. On each slide is a word of a color in a contrasting color. For example, the word *red* may appear in green letters. Participants are required to report the color of the letters rather than the word. This task has been used extensively in a variety of research areas and usually produces heart rate increases of approximately 10 to 20 beats per minute. The task requires people to learn to focus attention on the color aspect of the slide while ignoring the letters. Stroop performance could be collected and used to assess both the efficacy of the Stroop as a training strategy and the efficacy of other attentional techniques. The grid test is another task that has been used with athletes (Schmidt & Peper, 2001). This test involves checking off random numbers on a sheet as quickly as possible in a one-minute period. This test is administered easily and requires little equipment. As discussed in the section on advanced attentional training, other more sport-specific attentional strategies involving computers and videos could be used after initial experience with these laboratory tasks.

Another form of attentional assessment involves the use of observational behavioral analysis. Crews and Boutcher (1987) developed an observational analysis technique that they have used to assess the consistency of professional golfers' preshot routines. In a series of studies, they found that elite golfers possessed more consistent preshot routines than collegiate or beginning golfers did (Boutcher & Crews, 1987; Crews & Boutcher, 1986). Thus, behavioral analysis through observation or videotaping appears to be an effective way of examining the behavioral concomitants of attention during actual performance.

Another potential indicant of attention is the assessment of facial or eye states. A well-developed body of literature has examined facial reactions as an indicant of affective states (Camras, Holland, & Patterson, 1993; Ekman & Friesan, 1975; Izard, 1977; Tomkins, 1983), although facial reactions associated with attentive states do not appear to have been examined. Similarly, the direction and characteristics of eye gaze have not been tested with regard to athletic performance. Facial responses and eye gaze, however, may reflect the general control and automatic-processing styles discussed earlier. For instance, Tucker et al. (1977) characterized an individual's hemispheric usage by observing lateral eye movements. As discussed previously, research has established that most people perform verbal and linguistic processing in the left hemisphere of the brain and perform spatial cognition and perception in the right hemisphere. Kocel, Galin, Ornstein, and Merrin (1972) suggested that people who are responding to a question will tend to look left if the response requires spatial thinking and right if the question requires verbal thought. Thus, lateral eye movement to different types of questions may indicate primary activation of the contralateral hemisphere. Although this lateral eye movement assessment has not been used in sport, research in cognitive behavioral therapy suggested that cognitive behavioral methods were most effective if they employed cognition of the participants' nonpreferred hemisphere (Tucker et al., 1977). Consequently, it may be possible to characterize athletes as to their primary patterns of hemispheric usage based on the frequency of leftward and rightward eye movement when responding to different types of sport-related questions.

Psychophysiological indicants of attention also could be used to assess attention. Equipment to collect indicants of attentional style is becoming cheaper, more portable, and easier to use. Several companies offer relatively inexpensive, user-friendly biofeedback systems that can collect a host of physiological variables. Thus, EEG, heart rate, pulse amplitude, respiration, EMG, skin temperature, and other physiological variables can be either used in a biofeedback setting or stored for research or applied purposes. Autonomic indicants of attention such as heart rate are less affected by movement and, therefore, lend themselves to collection during actual performance. For example, wrist telemetry monitors (Polar heart watches) can record up to 24 hours of heart rate during actual athletic performance. The data can then be downloaded to a computer and displayed graphically. Because cardiac patterns seem to be associated with attentional style (Boutcher & Zinsser, 1990; Crews & Landers, 1992), this variable seems to have potential for assessing cognitive activity during performance.

Finally, techniques to assess the attentional demands of sporting situations also need to be developed. As Nideffer (1976a) pointed out, athletes need to match the attentional demands of the sporting environment with the appropriate attentional style. Thus, the athlete's attentional strengths and weaknesses should be assessed and compared with the attentional demands of the particular sport. Table 14.1 illustrates some of the factors that need to be considered when analyzing the attentional demands of an individual position in a particular sport. Open-skill activities involve continuous and repetitive movement patterns (e.g., swimming or basketball), whereas closed-skill activities are of a stop-and-start nature (e.g., golf or archery). Fine skills require accuracy and generally involve more delicate movements (e.g., putting or dart throwing), whereas gross skills are more dynamic and involve larger muscle groups (e.g., sprinting). Generally, athletes performing fast, gross, open-skill sports are less prone to sources of distraction because attentional capacity is more limited during performance. In contrast, performers participating in closed-skill activities may be more susceptible to disruption of attention because of the extra time and capacity available.

This section has described possible ways to assess an individual's attentional capabilities. Techniques include questionnaires, interviews, thought-sampling techniques, observational analysis, performance tests, and psychophysiological measurement. A method to categorize the attentional demands of different sports was also described.

Basic Attentional Training

Based on the multidimensional profile that can be obtained from the assessment of an athlete's attentional capabilities, a training program could be designed around the athlete's attentional strengths and weaknesses. If basic attentional training is required, the program would start at a basic level and gradually progress to more complex, sophisticated attentional skills. But whether attentional training on laboratory or nonsport tasks will transfer to athletic performance is not clear. Considerably more research needs to be conducted to assess the generalizability of attentional training as well as other forms of training (e.g., relaxation and imagery). Nevertheless, there appears to be potential in viewing attentional skills in a similar fashion

Table 14.1 Nature of Sport Skills and External Demands

Nature of the task	External factors	Attentional processing
Slow–fast	Game demands	Control processing
Open–closed	Environmental demands	Automatic processing
Fine–gross	———	Combination of control and automatic processing

to motor skills in which the learning environment is most productive if structured in a graduated fashion (Cote, Baker, & Abernethy, 2003). Thus, attentional training on laboratory tasks such as the Stroop, reaction time, and grid tests could form the first phase of the attention-training program, with training on more sport-specific skills conducted in later phases.

Besides the laboratory training tasks already identified, biofeedback is another technique that can be used to develop basic attentional skills. Biofeedback requires people to be able to self-monitor and eventually control autonomic and somatic responses by interacting with some form of feedback loop (usually a computer). Thus, athletes can practice basic attentional control by learning to focus their attention on a variety of biofeedback cues. When athletes are directed to watch the screen or listen to an auditory cue, their attentional efficiency could be assessed by monitoring the resultant effects on the physiological variables being used. Because biofeedback reinforces the subject, this type of training task gives instant feedback to the person about his or her ability to focus and adjust to the appropriate cue.

Thus, basic attentional training programs could be structured around a variety of laboratory tasks and organized so that attentional tasks become progressively more difficult. Through these types of training activities, athletes could attempt to acquire basic control of variables such as heart rate, respiration, and attentional focus.

Advanced Attentional Training

An extension of basic attentional training may take the form of a sport-individualized program. At this advanced phase, the first step should be verification that the athlete has acquired basic attentional control and is ready to develop sport-specific attentional skills. For closed-skill athletes, much of the initial work at the advanced attentional training level needs to focus on the development of sound, effective preperformance routines (Boutcher, 1990; Moran, 1996). Thus, the precursor to successful attentional control during actual performance may be the establishment of a series of behavioral, physiological, and cognitive cues, which optimally prime both body and mind for the ensuing skill.

Although an increasing number of researchers are examining preperformance states, little research has explored attentional states during actual athletic performance. This lack of inquiry is probably due to the general reluctance of cognitive psychologists to examine processes that are not readily available to conscious processing. Consequently, unconscious or subconscious processing has been confined largely to psychodynamic theory and has remained relatively unexplored in cognitive psychology (Kissin, 1986). In sport, optimal attentional states have been labeled peak performance (Privette, 1982; 1983) or flow states (Csikszentmihalyi, 1975; Jackson, 1996). Unfortunately, these states have been mainly assessed through retrospective self-report of athletes. This approach views optimal attentional functioning as an outcome rather than a process and does not tell us much about the underlying process (Hatfield & Landers, 1983). Thus, an outcome approach may not be helpful in designing programs to improve attentional flow during performance.

A tentative hypothesis based on the concepts of control versus automatic processing and left versus right brain functioning, which were discussed earlier, may help stimulate research into the process of attentional flow. As noted earlier, previous research has demonstrated that elite shooters exhibit patterns of left and right brain cortical activity different from those of less elite shooters (Hatfield & Landers, 1983; Kerick et al., 2004). Specifically, the elite shooters showed suppressed left hemisphere activity and enhanced right brain activity. This particular pattern may represent the optimal attentional state during automatic skill execution. Furthermore, because performing in competitive environments is likely to generate physiological arousal (Moran, 1996), attentional flow may be achieved when physiological arousal is channeled into automatic processing rather than control processing. Thus, focusing attention on the task at hand when physiologically aroused may increase attentional flow. Because arousal tends to focus and narrow attention (Easterbrook, 1959), increased arousal and task-appropriate processing may generate the positive emotion, focused attention, and oneness with the task that are associated with attentional flow states (Jackson, 1996). Thus, the athlete who directs arousal away from task-irrelevant information and into the task itself may create optimal attentional flow. This relationship is diagrammed in figure 14.1. Consequently, the challenge for the athlete or any other performer may be to learn how to direct competition-generated arousal into automatic processing of the task at hand while suppressing analytical processing. Thus, athletes who are actively thinking of "nothing" while allowing themselves to perform skills reflexively and automatically may be using the most efficient attentional style for performing in competitive, challenging situations.

Because a large body of research indicates that brain-wave activity can be self-regulated, sport-specific EEG biofeedback seems to be of value in teaching athletes appropriate attentional focus during performance. For instance, research has established that people can learn to suppress cortical activity by learning to enhance alpha waves (Bauer, 1976; Elder et al., 1985; Jackson & Eberly, 1982). Other studies have demonstrated that participants can self-regulate EEG activity. For example, Schwartz, Davidson, and Pugwash (1976) trained participants to develop both symmetrical and asymmetrical EEG patterns. Suter, Griffin, Smallhouse, and Whitlach (1981) also found biofeedback control of EEG asymmetries.

In the sport context, one study has examined the effect of brain-wave biofeedback on archery performance. Landers et al. (1991) administered right hemispheric alpha feedback, left hemispheric alpha feedback, or no feedback to three groups of archers. The left hemisphere group improved performance, whereas the right hemisphere group exhibited significantly worse performance.

Although the efficacy of these EEG biofeedback techniques has yet to be established in sport, the increasing use of biofeedback in a variety of athletic situations (Landers, 1985b) suggests that this technique has potential. For example, biofeedback techniques could be combined with sport-specific videos. Thus, the athlete could be trained to produce the appropriate attentional focus while participating in a video experience of the sport. Progressing from the video to sporting situations on the practice ground and then eventually to the actual competitive setting appears to be logical. But research is clearly needed to establish the efficacy of these techniques in the sport domain.

Exploration of applied aspects of attentional control in sport is only beginning. Many of the ideas and suggestions expressed in this section are speculative and unsubstantiated by empirical research. My intent was not to provide the reader with untried techniques but rather to provide a broad review of potential strategies that need to be investigated. I hope that this attempt to synthesize related research in attention to applied interests in sport will generate both basic and applied investigations into the attention phenomenon.

Conclusion

In this chapter I have attempted to integrate research examining different aspects of attention from the areas of information processing, social psychology, and psychophysiology. Each of these research thrusts has emphasized a different but related perspective of the attentional process. Research in information processing has established the existence of two related forms of processing. Control processing requires effort and is slow and cumbersome, whereas automatic processing is effortless, quick, and efficient. Social psychologists have focused on individual differences and environmental influences on attentional processes. The ability of extraneous, inappropriate cues to disrupt performance has been established. Sport psychophysiologists have attempted to examine the underlying mechanisms of attention by monitoring cortical and cardiac activity. Both cortical and autonomic indicants of attention have been used successfully to assess attentional style in athletes during performance. I outlined a preliminary model encapsulating these principles. This multileveled, multifaceted nature of attention was developed further in the applied section, and I described a variety of assessment and training strategies. Assessment strategies included questionnaire, performance, thought-sampling techniques, behavioral analysis, and psychophysiological indicants. I outlined a preliminary model of attentional flow during peak performance and then described training strategies to enhance attentional abilities, including performance tests, computer and video tasks, and biofeedback strategies.

CHAPTER 15

The Fundamental Goal Concept: The Path to Process and Performance Success

Damon Burton, PhD ▪ Cheryl Weiss, MFA, EdM ▪

© Human Kinetics/Kelly J. Huff

Research on goal setting in sport has proliferated at an amazing rate in the 14 years since the first draft of this chapter was published, and two inescapable conclusions have emerged since the most recent version of this chapter came out four years ago: (a) goals work, although with varying degrees of success, and (b) the fundamental goal concept that emphasizes process and performance over outcome goals plays the biggest role in determining goal-setting effectiveness in sport.

Recent studies of the goal-setting patterns of adolescent, collegiate, and Olympic athletes (Burton, Weinberg, Yukelson, & Weigand, 1998, 2005; Weinberg, Burke, & Jackson, 1997; Weinberg, Burton, Yukelson, & Weigand, 1993, 2000) have confirmed that almost all athletes set goals, a process that they find moderately effective. Although athletes know that goals can be beneficial to their performance, too few understand that outcome goals can undermine confidence and motivation if not used effectively, and too many fail to recognize that goals can make a significant difference in their success.

Several years ago I worked with a perennial top 25 collegiate women's volleyball team. I had admired the coach for a number of years and jumped at the chance to work with a coaching staff who bought into mental training and seemingly did a great job developing the mental skills of their players. But their season took an abrupt right turn almost immediately, an event that taught me that any athlete or team, no matter how talented or well coached, can become failure oriented under the right set of circumstances.

The senior-dominated squad of the previous season had made the NCAA volleyball tournament Elite 8. Although extremely talented, the new team was inexperienced, returning only one starter. Moreover, it was young, starting four freshmen, a sophomore, and a senior. Although the coaching staff knew that the team was in a rebuilding year, they expected a successful season. Twenty wins was a realistic possibility. Unfortunately, the team experienced a disastrous run of injuries, putting in motion a series of events that prompted the team to become failure oriented. Four starters battled chronic injury problems the entire year, and several other players experienced minor injuries that required them to miss both practices and games. The worst injury was a chronic ankle sprain to the team's talented setter. The major effect of these injuries was to prevent this talented, well-coached team from making normal development technically and tactically because many key players were unavailable during practice. The result was a team

that became "learned helpless," or what we term *failure oriented*.

Learned helplessness is the belief that one lacks the ability to change the course of negative events. Failure-oriented athletes believe that failure is insurmountable. After failure accumulates, they eventually focus on not failing rather than striving for success. As long as the team was ahead or the score was close, they played well. But as soon as they fell behind by more than a few points, their performance deteriorated sharply. Confidence plunged, anxiety mounted, and players started blaming themselves and each other. The team's tempo of play sped up noticeably, support for teammates declined sharply, and players made numerous foolish mistakes. Most losses could be traced back to opponents' making many runs of 3 to 10 points. Seldom do elite collegiate teams allow negative runs of even 3 points, typically giving up less than 1 such run per game. This team gave up an average of 2.8 runs of 3 points or more per game while scoring only 1.2 runs per game. Opponents' runs also were normally longer and came at more crucial times. Thus, stretches of good play in which the team played as well or better than their opponent were punctuated with disastrous and ill-timed streaks of poor performance.

The pattern for most losing matches was alarmingly similar. The team would easily win the first two games and look unbeatable, only to lose a hard-fought game 3 because of several negative runs and many missed opportunities to put the match away. After they lost that first game, their mind-set changed. Their play would became tentative and self-destructive in game 4, which they usually lost by 8 to 12 points. They were seldom competitive in game 5 and usually lost by a large margin. Although I had observed for several decades the negative outcomes of athletes and teams who became failure oriented, I would not have believed that a talented and well-coached team like this one could have fallen into this mind-set had I not observed it so many times throughout the season. This experience convinced me that under the right circumstances, almost any athlete or team can fall victim to this failure mentality.

The fundamental goal concept does not suggest that outcome goals (i.e., winning) are unimportant in sport. Rather, it suggests that striving to win is essential, and that process and performance goals are the key stepping-stones to pursuing victory. Commitment has been shown to be a prerequisite to effective goal setting, and outcome goals are crucial to developing necessary goal commitment (Hardy, 1997). The following semester, one of my doctoral students, Bernie Holliday, conducted an intervention study for his dissertation with this failure-oriented volleyball team. One of the first mental training tools that Bernie introduced to the team was goal setting, because he could guarantee that athletes who set goals systematically could count on improving their performance at least 5%. Saying that the team was unimpressed was an understatement—as far as they were concerned, a 5% improvement was trivial. Recognizing that commitment was essential to making goals work, Bernie looked for a way to quantify how much difference 5% could make in volleyball. He decided to calculate what effect 5% more points would have made during the previous season in which this failure-oriented team finished with a record of 9-20. Interestingly, by scoring just 5% more points each match (i.e., 1.5 points per game) the team would have finished with a much more palatable 18-11 record. The team then recognized that 5% was a huge improvement and immediately bought into setting goals, helping make the mental skills training (MST) intervention a huge success. Most important, the team showed few signs of its previous failure orientation during spring tournaments. This example suggests that the most important role of outcome goals may be to promote commitment, even though the key steps to winning are established by setting process and performance goals that maximize players' opportunity to win.

These two stories demonstrate the complex nature of the fundamental goal concept. The two faces of goals can be as different as Dr. Jekyll and Mr. Hyde, and this Jekyll and Hyde nature of goals is an important reason why we must strive to understand the goal-setting process. The extensive research on goal setting, both within (Burton, 1992, 1993; Burton & Naylor, 2002; Burton, Naylor & Holliday, 2001; Kyllo & Landers, 1995; Weinberg, 1994) and outside sport (Locke & Latham, 1990), has confirmed that setting goals can be an effective performance enhancement strategy. The challenge to both researchers and practitioners is to understand the goal-setting process while maximizing the motivational and self-confidence benefits that goals can provide, thereby enhancing performance.

Therefore, the primary purpose of this chapter is to review existing theory and research on goal setting with the intent of better understanding the goal-setting process and ways of maximizing the effectiveness of setting goals in sport. In the first section, we define goal setting, clarify what goals are, examine their primary functions, describe how they work, illustrate the role of goals in such divergent constructs as motivation and stress, and review the

research that tests general goal-setting effectiveness. In the second section, we discuss the fundamental goal concept in sport, describe an updated competitive goal-setting model, briefly review model predictions, and summarize research that tests the model. The third section focuses on reviewing theory and research on the most effective types of goals, highlighting such goal attributes as specificity, difficulty, valence, proximity, and collectivity. The fourth section outlines several important measurement issues that currently limit our ability to test our updated competitive goal-setting (CGS–3) model and provide practical implementation of goal-setting programs. Finally, we address future directions in goal-setting research, highlighting three important issues that seemingly have an effect on goal effectiveness.

Defining Goals

Setting goals is not new to practitioners. Since the first contests of ancient times, athletes have set goals for themselves. Goal setting is one of the most commonly used performance enhancement strategies in sport, and both researchers and practitioners assume that goals have a straightforward meaning. Ed Locke, the world's most prolific goal-setting researcher, defined a goal simply as "what an individual is trying to accomplish; it is the object or aim of an action" (Locke, Shaw, Saari, & Latham, 1981, p. 126). In a more passionate description, Lessin suggested that "Goals are like magnets that attract us to higher ground and new horizons. They give our eyes a focus, our mind an aim, and our strength a purpose. Without their pull, we would remain forever stationary, incapable of moving forward. . . A goal is a possibility that fulfills a dream."

Locke (1968) took an objective approach to conceptualizing goal setting that emphasized behavior as purposeful and human beings as rational creatures who survive by using their intellect to govern their behavior. Although goal setting has gone by a number of terms over the years including "level of aspiration" in the 1930s and "management by objectives" in business contexts, the term *goal* is used today in an array of disciplines and contexts to refer to this type of cognitive regulator of behavior. As easy as it might be to accept goals as the tools used to pursue goal-directed behavior, they do not necessarily work at a conscious level all the time. Locke and Latham (1990) emphasized that goals go in and out of conscious awareness at different times. For example, focusing on winning a game may disrupt performance by interfering with actions needed to reach the goal, particularly habitual actions such as automated sport skills (e.g., jump shots in basketball or drop volleys in tennis). Goals help initiate action, but once initiated, little conscious control is needed to pursue goals effectively.

Three other important concepts must be examined as part of the process of defining goals, including (a) goal dimensions, (b) the benefits of goals, and (c) the importance of enjoying the process of setting goals and not just their results.

Goal Dimensions   Locke and Latham (1990) emphasized that every goal includes two basic components: direction and a comparison standard. Direction implies choice, specifically the choice about how to direct or focus one's behavior. For example, when a high school athlete sets a goal to make the varsity basketball team, he or she makes a choice to pursue basketball instead of competing in other winter sports, working, or participating in other extracurricular activities. The comparison standard suggests that a minimum quantity or quality of behavior or performance must be attained. The athlete's choice to play basketball constitutes a commitment to work on developing his or her skills to a level high enough to be selected for the high school varsity team, earn extensive playing time, or become a team leader.

Benefits of Setting Goals   Sport and exercise readily lends itself to setting goals, whether individual or collective in nature. Goal setting is a versatile mental training tool that can be used in a variety of ways to enhance enjoyment and performance. Goals are often thought of primarily as motivational tools, designed to help performers train or compete more successfully (Locke, 1996). But goals produce other benefits. Goals help enhance focus and concentration and boost self-confidence. Keeping goals realistic is an important strategy for preventing and managing stress, creating a positive mental attitude, and remaining optimistic in the face of failure and adversity. Goals also are instrumental in fostering a positive and cohesive team climate. Finally, goals can be an important tool in enhancing playing skills, techniques and strategies.

Enjoying the Journey   The most important lesson for goal setters to learn is that the process of striving to reach goals is ultimately more important than whether or not they are actually reached. Goals are the beacon, but the joy is in the journey. There are never any guarantees that we will reach our goals, but there is a promise that the journey will provide meaning to our lives and enrich us for the striving.

Bill Russell, the captain of the most successful dynasty in sport history, the Boston Celtics of the 1950 and 1960s, believes that success is a "journey not a destination." He reflected that he profited more from striving for excellence than from winning 11 NBA titles in 13 seasons (Russell & Branch, 1979). He emphasized that lofty goals prompt us to strive to perform our best and give our lives purpose whether we reach them or not. Russell characterized winning as determined by talent but success as the product of character. Goals allow us to take the risk to find out who we are and how good we can become. Even if we never reach our ultimate goals, the experience enhances our lives. Goal setting emphasizes savoring the quest to reach challenging standards and exalting when your efforts are rewarded.

How Goals Work

Goals are believed to work in two ways: (a) as a motivational strategy that takes advantage of four direct functions of goals and (b) as a self-confidence strategy that works long term over a number of goal-setting cycles that gradually lead to changes in performers' beliefs about themselves and their ability.

How Goals Enhance Motivation   Goals enhance performance primarily by increasing motivation. Goal theorists (e.g., Locke, 1996; Locke & Latham, 1990) have identified four direct ways that goals influence behavior motivationally:

- Focus attention on a specific task or tasks
- Increase effort and intensity
- Encourage persistence in the face of failure or adversity
- Promote the development of new task or problem-solving strategies

Goals enhance motivation most directly through the first three goal mechanisms (i.e., focusing attention, increasing effort, and enhancing persistence), whereas the development of new task strategies is often a more long-term process that may be necessary when tackling complex tasks or attempting to overcome failure or adversity. As long as the task is relatively simple and straightforward and athletes can perform it effectively, the motivational benefits of goals should prompt relatively rapid improvement in the quantity or quality of performance. But when performing highly complex tasks or confronting persistent problems, direct motivational mechanisms may not be enough to ensure that athletes reach their goals. Developing new task strategies involves working smarter as well as longer and harder. Goals typically take longer to achieve for complex tasks compared with simple tasks, because athletes must first execute the fundamentals correctly before the motivational benefits of goals can enhance skill execution. Thus, correcting flaws in form is a prerequisite before goal-inspired practice can pay dividends to automate skills.

For example, a basketball coach may set a team goal to increase free-throw percentage. He or she develops an action plan to have every player shoot a minimum of 50 free throws each practice. Unfortunately, the motivational benefits of this goal will be minimal if players have major flaws in their free-throw mechanics, do not use the same routine in shooting free throws in practice that they use in competition, or become distracted while shooting free throws in pressure-packed competitive situations. Thus, developing new task strategies is a two-stage process that focuses first on making desirable changes in shooting form, developing a consistent free-throw routine, and learning to remain focused during critical free-throw situations. In stage 2 the motivational benefits of goals can take over and automate the new shooting fundamentals.

How Goals Boost Self-Confidence The second way that goals work is more indirect. The process involves altering athletes' self-confidence over time through accumulating goal-setting successes or failures that prompt changes in performers' beliefs about their abilities. Each time performers set and attain their goals, their confidence receives a boost. As goal attainment accumulates, performers develop a strong and highly stable level of confidence. Conversely, extensive failure also develops stable underconfidence or diffidence patterns. Combinations of successes and failures in attaining goals should prompt confidence levels somewhere between those extremes. Thus, goal attainment history should have a significant effect on confidence levels. Moreover, although the motivational and self-confidence development functions of goals seem somewhat different, they are complementary, with the motivation function of goals serving as the stepping-stones for achieving long-term gains in self-confidence.

State and Trait Conceptions of Goals

Several subdisciplines within psychology use the term *goal* as a major component in both motivational and stress theories, prompting confusion about the exact meaning of the term in specific contexts.

The notion of goals is currently used in two major ways. First, business psychologists such as Edwin Locke and his colleagues (Locke, 1996; Locke & Latham, 1990; Locke et al., 1981) view goals as a direct motivational strategy. In this context, goals function primarily like a psychological state, providing a specific standard that motivates people to focus attention and improve efforts at attaining a particular quantity or quality of performance. Similarly, stress researchers such as Richard Lazarus (1991, 1999; Lazarus & Folkman, 1984) use goals as an important component of stress models, conceptualizing that stress will occur when people become challenged or threatened about their ability to attain important goals. In both cases, this state conception of goals focuses on attaining a goal in a particular situation for a specific purpose; in one case the prospect of success should engender personal motivation, whereas in the other, the threat of failure should elicit stress.

Several motivation theorists (Duda & Hall, 2001; Dweck, 1980, 1999; Elliott & Dweck, 1988; Maehr & Braskamp, 1986; Maehr & Nicholls, 1980; Nicholls, 1984a, 1984b) have used the notion of goals to suggest a more global purpose for involvement in particular activities. Goals in this context are more like personality traits, implying predispositions for participation based on underlying motives about how people view ability and what they want to attain or accomplish. Motivation theorists often use the term *goal orientation* to denote these more global goals (e.g., Duda & Hall, 2001; Dweck, 1999; Elliott & Dweck, 1988; Maehr & Braskamp, 1986; Maehr & Nicholls, 1980; Nicholls, 1984a, 1984b). Inherent in the idea of goal orientations is the premise that success and failure are subjective perceptions, not objective events. Thus, people can attain success in any situation in which they are able either to infer personally desirable characteristics, qualities, or attributes about themselves or to attain personally meaningful objectives (Maehr & Braskamp, 1986). Dweck (1999) emphasized that goal orientations reflect underlying theories of ability, both what it means and how it develops. In attempting to integrate these two notions of goals, we believe that the two conceptions are complementary. Discrete goals serve as the tools for achieving global goal orientations.

Goal Effectiveness

Effectiveness is the acid test of any intervention strategy. Goal setting has been a topic of great interest to researchers and practitioners, and research that tests the efficacy of goals for enhancing performance has been the primary focus of both the general (Locke & Latham, 1990) and sport goal-setting literatures (Burton, 1992, 1993; Burton & Naylor, 2002; Burton et al., 2001; Kyllo & Landers, 1995; Weinberg, 1994). Several specific questions have guided this research:

- How consistently do goals enhance performance?

- What is the magnitude of performance enhancement effects from setting goals?

- How well do goal-setting effects generalize across tasks, populations, and time spans?

The consensus of more than 500 goal-setting studies (e.g., Burton, 1992, 1993; Burton & Naylor, 2002; Burton et al., 2001; Chidester & Grigsby, 1984; Hunter & Schmidt, 1983; Kyllo & Landers, 1995; Locke & Latham, 1990; Locke et al., 1981; Mento, Steel, & Karren, 1987; Tubbs, 1986; Weinberg, 1994; Wood, Mento, & Locke, 1987) is that specific, difficult goals prompt higher levels of performance than vague do-your-best goals or no goals. Of the 201 studies reviewed by Locke and Latham (1990), goal-setting effects were demonstrated totally or contingently in 183 studies, a 91% success rate. Moreover, five meta-analyses of general goal-setting research (Chidester & Grigsby, 1984; Hunter & Schmidt, 1983; Mento et al., 1987; Tubbs, 1986; Wood et al., 1987), each containing between 17 and 53 goal-setting studies and including from 1,278 to 6,635 subjects, demonstrated mean effect sizes ranging from .42 to .80, representing performance increases of 8.4% to 16%.

A comprehensive review of the goal-setting literature convincingly demonstrates the generalizability of goal-setting findings (Burton, 1992, 1993; Burton & Naylor, 2002; Burton et al., 2001; Chidester & Grigsby, 1984; Hunter & Schmidt, 1983; Kyllo & Landers, 1995; Locke & Latham, 1990; Locke et al., 1981; Mento et al., 1987; Tubbs, 1986; Weinberg, 1994; Wood et al., 1987). Locke and Latham's (1990) review of nearly 500 goal-setting studies confirmed tremendous consistency in the frequency and magnitude of goal-setting effects across different tasks, settings, performance criteria, and types of participants. Locke and Latham documented goal-setting effects across 90 different tasks, ranging from simple laboratory experiments (e.g., listing nouns, computation) to complex tasks such as prose learning and management simulation, as well as across a great diversity of subject populations that varied

in gender, age, race, socioeconomic status, and type of employment (e.g., loggers, factory workers, engineers and scientists, and college professors). Finally, goal-setting effects have been demonstrated for time spans as short as 1 minute and as long as 36 months (Ivancevich, 1974). Clearly, these data confirm that goal setting is a highly consistent and robust performance enhancement strategy that works almost universally for participants across a variety of tasks and settings. Overall, these results confirm that goal setting is arguably the most effective performance enhancement technique in the behavioral sciences.

SPORT AND EXERCISE META-ANALYSES AND REVIEWS

Beggs (1990)

Burton (1992)

Burton (1993)

Burton & Naylor (2002)

Burton, Naylor, & Holliday (2001)

Kyllo & Landers (1995)

Rawsthorne & Elliot (1999)

Weinberg (1994)

A perusal of sport-specific goal research (Burton, 1992, 1993; Burton & Naylor, 2002; Burton et al., 2001; Kyllo & Landers, 1995; Weinberg, 1994) confirms that setting goals is also an effective performance enhancement technique in the physical activity domain. In the only meta-analysis of goal research in sport, Kyllo and Landers (1995) examined 49 goal-setting studies in sport and physical activity, using 36 of them in their analysis. When compared with no goals or do-your-best goals, goal setting yielded an effect size of .34, a slightly smaller value than the effect sizes of .42 to .80 found in the general goal literature. Our most recent review has summarized findings solely from published research, and we have identified 94 goal-setting manuscripts published with physical activity samples, 88 of which met our inclusion criteria. Of those 88 goal-setting studies in sport and physical activity, 70 demonstrated moderate to strong goal-setting effects, an 80% effectiveness rate (table 15.1).

Table 15.1 Summary of Goal Research in Sport and Physical Activity

Study	Subjects	Results	Level of support
General goal effectiveness (goal versus no-goal or control conditions: strong or partial support for general goal effectiveness in 21 out of 25 studies)			
Annesi (2002)	100 Italian adult male exercise participants	Goal-setting condition resulted in higher attendance and lower program dropout rates compared with non-goal-setting condition.	Strong
Anshel, Weinberg, & Jackson (1992)	54 undergraduate students	All goal conditions (easy, difficult, and self-set) resulted in better performance than a no-goal condition on a juggling task.	Strong
Bar-Eli, Levy-Kolker, Tenenbaum, & Weinberg (1993)	184 army trainees	No differences were found between five goal-setting conditions and a no-goal condition on physical fitness tasks.	Weak
Barnett (1977)	93 female high school students	No difference was found in juggling performance between two student-set goal conditions and three no-goal conditions.	Weak
Barnett & Stanicek (1979)	30 university archery students	Goal condition resulted in superior archery performance compared with a no-goal condition.	Strong
Boyce & Wayda (1994)	252 female university weight-training students	Self-set and assigned goal conditions resulted in better performance than did the no-goal condition.	Strong
Burton, Weinberg, Yukelson, & Weigand (1998)	321 male and 249 female college athletes	Most college athletes reported setting goals but found them to be only moderately effective.	Moderate
Croteau (2004)	8 male and 29 female adult college employees	Goal-setting conditions resulted in significantly greater gains than did the maintenance condition.	Strong
Evans & Hardy (2002a)	33 male and 6 female injured adult athletes	Goal condition resulted in significant gains over no-goal condition.	Strong
Goudas, Ardamerinos, Vasilliou, & Zanou (1999)	17 male and 23 female undergraduate physical education students	Significant difference was found between difficult goal condition and easy, personal, and no-goal conditions.	Moderate
Hollingsworth (1975)	90 junior high school students	No difference was found between performance goal condition, do-your-best condition, and no-goal condition on a juggling task.	Weak
Humphries, Thomas, & Nelson (1991)	60 college males	Goal conditions led to superior mirror-tracing performance compared with no-goal condition.	Strong
Lerner, Ostrow, Yura, & Etzel (1996)	12 female basketball players	Goal-setting condition resulted in superior free-throw shooting improvement compared with goal setting plus imagery condition and imagery condition.	Moderate
Nelson (1978)	100 college males	Assigned goal condition resulted in better performance on a muscular endurance task compared to a no-goal condition.	Strong
Shoenfelt (1996)	12 female collegiate basketball players	Goals and feedback condition increased free-throw accuracy more than did the control condition.	Strong

(continued)

Table 15.1 *(continued)*

Study	Subjects	Results	Level of support
General goal effectiveness (goal versus no-goal or control conditions: strong or partial support for general goal effectiveness in 21 out of 25 studies) *(continued)*			
Smith & Lee (1992)	51 university students	Public and private goals improved performance during a novel motor task compared with a no-goal condition.	Strong
Tenenbaum, Bar-Eli, & Yaaron (1999)	346 male Israeli 9th- and 10th-grade students	All goal conditions (easy, moderately difficult, and difficult) increased sit-ups over "do" and do-your-best goal conditions.	Moderate
Tenenbaum, Weinberg, Pinchas, Elbaz, & Bar-Eli (1991)	214 9th-grade Israeli students	Short-term, long-term, and short-term plus long-term goal conditions resulted in better performance on sit-up task compared with no-goal or do-your-best goal conditions.	Strong
Theodorakis (1995)	42 undergraduate physical education students	Setting goals significantly improved performance on swimming task trials compared with no-goal trials.	Strong
Theodorakis (1996)	48 undergraduate physical education students	Self-efficacy and goal setting were found to be predictors of performance on a tennis service task.	Moderate
Theodorakis, Laparidis, Kioumourtzoglou, & Goudas (1998)	18 male and 24 female undergraduate physical education students	Goal setting coupled with feedback resulted in increased performance and greater persistence on a bicycle-pedaling task.	Strong
Tzetzis, Kioumourtzoglou, & Mavromatis (1997)	78 boys associated with a basketball academy	Goal setting coupled with performance feedback on simple and complex basketball tasks improved performance more than did feedback alone.	Strong
Weinberg, Burton, Yukelson, & Weigand (1993)	678 intercollegiate male and female athletes	Nearly all subjects reported setting goals and perceived goals to be moderately to highly effective.	Strong
Weinberg, Burton, Yukelson, & Weigand (2000)	185 male and 143 female Olympic athletes representing 12 different sports	All subjects reported practicing some type of goal setting.	Strong
Weinberg, Garland, Bruya, & Jackson (1990)	87 undergraduate students in fitness courses	No difference was found between realistic, unrealistic, do-your-best, and no-goal conditions on a sit-up task.	Weak
Goal difficulty (support or partial support of goal difficulty predictions in 14 out of 24 studies)			
Anshel, Weinberg, & Jackson (1992)	54 undergraduate students	Difficult goals increased intrinsic motivation, whereas easy goals decreased intrinsic motivation on a juggling task.	Strong for goal difficulty
Bar-Eli, Levy-Kolker, Tenenbaum, & Weinberg (1993)	184 army trainees	No differences were found between easy, moderate, hard, very hard, do-your-best, and control goal-setting conditions on physical fitness tasks.	Weak for goal difficulty
Bar-Eli, Tenenbaum, Pie, Btesh, & Almog (1997)	364 male high school students	The difficult and realistic group exhibited the greatest increase in sit-up performance compared with the easy goal, do-your-best goal, and no-goal groups.	Strong for difficult, yet realistic goals

Study	Subjects	Results	Level of support
Boyce (1990a)	90 students in a rifle-shooting contest	Only the specific and difficult condition resulted in performance superior to the do-your-best condition on a shooting task.	Strong for goal difficulty
Boyce (1990b)	135 university riflery class participants	Specific and difficult goal conditions resulted in better performance than did the do-your-best condition on a rifle-shooting task.	Strong for goal difficulty
Boyce, Wayda, Johnston, Bunker, & Eliot (2001)	39 male and 117 female undergraduate beginning tennis students	Difficult and specific instructor-set goals enhanced performance more than did self-set goals.	Strong for goal difficulty
Frierman, Weinberg, & Jackson (1990)	45 novice and 27 intermediate bowlers	Long-term, specific, and difficult goal conditions resulted in better performance than did the do-your-best condition.	Strong for goal difficulty
Goudas, Ardamerinos, Vasilliou, & Zanou (1999)	17 male and 23 female undergraduate physical education students	Difficult assigned goals increased performance more than did personal goals.	Strong for goal difficulty
Gyurcsik, Estabrooks, & Frahm-Templar (2003)	28 male and 188 female arthritic aquatic exercise participants	Goal difficulty increased among low attendees, contrary to study and goal-setting theory hypotheses.	Moderate for goal difficulty
Hall, Weinberg, & Jackson (1987)	94 college males	No difference was found in hand dynamometer performance between goal condition to improve by 40 seconds and goal condition to improve by 70 seconds.	Weak for goal difficulty
Humphries, Thomas, & Nelson (1991)	60 college males	No difference was found in mirror-tracing performance between attainable and unattainable goal conditions.	Weak for goal difficulty
Jones & Cale (1997)	44 adult participants	Difficult goal condition resulted in better performance than did the very easy and do-your-best conditions on a series of perceptual speed trials.	Strong for goal difficulty
Lerner & Locke (1995)	60 participants	Both medium and hard goal groups significantly outperformed groups using the do-your-best condition on sit-up performance.	Moderate for goal difficulty
Nelson (1978)	100 college males	Students in the fictitious goal and norm group (highly difficult suggested goal and norm) performed best, compared with two realistic norm and goal groups and a control group.	Moderate for goal difficulty
Tenenbaum, Bar-Eli, & Yaaron (1999)	346 male Israeli 9th- and 10th-grade students	Easy, moderately difficult, and difficult (improbable or unattainable) goal conditions produced somewhat greater overall gains than did the do-your-best and "do" conditions.	Moderate for goal difficulty
Weinberg, Bruya, Jackson, & Garland (1986)	123 students enrolled in university fitness courses	No performance difference was found between participants using extremely hard goals, highly improbable goals, and do-your-best goals on a sit-up task.	Weak for goal difficulty
Weinberg, Bruya, Jackson, & Garland (1986)	30 students enrolled in university fitness courses	No performance difference was found between easy, moderate, and extremely hard goal conditions on a sit-up task.	Weak for goal difficulty

(continued)

Table 15.1 *(continued)*

Study	Subjects	Results	Level of support
Goal difficulty (support or partial support of goal difficulty predictions in 14 out of 24 studies) *(continued)*			
Weinberg, Burke, & Jackson (1997)	224 youth tennis players	Athletes preferred setting moderately difficult goals.	Moderate for goal difficulty
Weinberg, Burton, Yukelson, & Weigand (2000)	185 male and 143 female Olympic athletes representing 12 different sports	Difficult, realistic goals produced a higher level of performance for some athletes.	Moderate for goal difficulty
Weinberg, Butt, & Knight (2001)	8 male and 6 female adult high school sport coaches	Difficult, unrealistic goals produced frustration and motivational deficits.	Weak for goal difficulty
Weinberg, Fowler, Jackson, Bagnall, & Bruya (1991)	114 boys and 135 girls from third through fifth grades	No performance difference was found between easy, difficult, improbable, and do-your-best goal conditions on a sit-up task.	Weak for goal difficulty
Weinberg, Fowler, Jackson, Bagnall, & Bruya (1991)	50 college males and 50 college females	No performance difference was found between easy, moderately difficult, very difficult, highly improbable, and do-your-best goal conditions in basketball-shooting performance.	Weak for goal difficulty
Weinberg, Bruya, Garland, & Jackson (1990)	87 undergraduate students in fitness courses	No performance difference was found between realistic, unrealistic, do-your-best, and no-goal conditions on a sit-up task.	Weak for goal difficulty
Weinberg, Bruya, Garland, & Jackson (1990)	120 participants	No performance difference was found between moderately difficult, difficult, unrealistic, and do-your-best goal conditions on a hand dynamometer task.	Weak for goal difficulty
Goal focus (direct or indirect support for the use of multiple-goal focus strategies in 14 out of 15 studies)			
Burton (1989b)	29 collegiate swimmers	Setting performance goals enhanced both competitive cognitions and performance compared with a control condition.	Strong for performance goals
Burton, Weinberg, Yukelson, & Weigand (1998)	321 male and 249 female college athletes	Athletes who set process goals found goal setting more beneficial than did athletes who set outcome or product goals.	Moderate for process goals
Cobb, Stone, Anonsen, & Klein (2000)	104 community college fitness class students	Outcome goals (letter grades) significantly affected exercise adherence goals.	Strong for outcome goals
Filby, Maynard, & Graydon (1999)	40 adult participants	Multiple-goal strategies (outcome plus performance plus process goals) more effectively improved soccer performance compared with single-goal strategies.	Strong for multiple-goal focus strategies
Giannini, Weinberg, & Jackson (1988)	100 college male recreational basketball players	No performance difference was found between competitive, cooperative, and mastery goal conditions on a basketball task.	Weak for goal focus differential effects
Jones & Hanton (1996)	91 competitive swimmers	When athletes set multiple focus goals, high expectations of goal attainment increased facilitative anxiety perceptions compared with lower goal expectations.	Moderate for goal–anxiety relationship
Kingston & Hardy (1997)	37 club golfers	Both process goal and performance goal groups showed improvement in golf handicap; the process goal condition resulted in significant improvement more quickly.	Strong for process and performance goals

Study	Subjects	Results	Level of support
Munroe-Chandler & Hall (2004)	109 male and 140 female elite athletes representing 18 different sports	Outcome-related goals were set twice as often for competition, whereas subjective goals (train effectively, have fun, and make the most of practice) were used in practice.	Strong for outcome and performance goals
Pierce & Burton (1998)	25 female adolescent gymnasts	Performance-oriented athletes improved more than did success-oriented and failure-oriented athletes (respectively) during a goal-setting training program.	Strong for performance goals, weak for outcome goals
Weinberg, Burke, & Jackson (1997)	224 youth tennis players	Descriptive study findings identified three most important goals: to improve performance, to have fun, and to win.	Moderate for process, performance, and outcome goals
Weinberg, Burton, Yukelson, & Weigand (1993)	678 intercollegiate male and female athletes	Males set more outcome goals and fewer performance goals compared with females, and both groups reported goals to be effective.	Moderate for performance and outcome goals
Weinberg, Burton, Yukelson, & Weigand (2000)	185 male and 143 female Olympic athletes representing different sports	Process and performance goals were better for performance-oriented athletes, but outcome goals were better for win-oriented athletes.	Strong for process, performance, and outcome goals
Weinberg, Butt, & Knight (2001)	8 male and 6 female adult high school sport coaches	All coaches used outcome and performance goals.	Strong for outcome and performance goals
Zimmerman & Kitsantas (1996)	50 female high school physical education students	Process goals led to improved dart-throwing performance compared with product goals.	Strong for process goals
Goal proximity (support or partial support for setting both short- and long-term goals in 8 out of 13 studies)			
Annesi (2002)	100 Italian adult male exercise participants	Short-term goals to promote persistence were the most effective for exercise adherence.	Strong for setting short-term goals
Bar-Eli, Hartman, & Levy-Kolker (1994)	80 adolescents with behavior disorders	Although both conditions improved performance, the short-term plus long-term goal condition resulted in greater increases in sit-up performance than did the long-term-only goal condition.	Strong for setting both short- and long-term goals
Boyce (1992)	181 university students	No performance difference was found between short-term, long-term, and short-term plus long-term goal conditions on shooting task performance.	Weak for setting both short- and long-term goals
Boyce, Wayda, Johnston, Bunker, & Eliot (2001)	39 male and 117 female undergraduate beginning tennis students	More than half of the students achieved their long-term goals.	Moderate for setting long-term goals
Evans & Hardy (2002)	7 male and 2 female injured adult athletes	Athletes preferred long-term rehabilitation goals.	Strong for setting long-term goals
Frierman, Weinberg, & Jackson (1990)	45 novice and 27 intermediate bowlers	Of the four goal conditions (short-term, long-term, short- plus long-term, and do your best), only the long-term goal condition improved performance more than the do-your-best condition did.	Weak for setting both short- and long-term goals
Getz & Rainey (2001)	39 male college intramural basketball players	Flexible short-term goal condition promoted significant improvement in shooting.	Strong for setting short-term goals
Hall & Byrne (1988)	43 male and 11 female university weight training students	The two long-term plus intermediate goal conditions resulted in better performance than did the long-term only goal condition on an endurance task.	Moderate for setting both short- and long-term goals

(continued)

Table 15.1 *(continued)*

Study	Subjects	Results	Level of support
Goal proximity (support or partial support for setting both short- and long-term goals in 8 out of 13 studies) *(continued)*			
Howe & Poole (1992)	115 male undergraduate physical education students	No difference was found between short-term, long-term, and short-term plus long-term goal conditions on basketball-shooting performance.	Weak for setting both short- and long-term goals
Tenenbaum, Weinberg, Pinchas, Elbaz, & Bar-Eli (1991)	214 9th-grade white Israeli students	The short-term plus long-term goal condition resulted in better performance on a sit-up task compared with short-term-only or long-term-only goal conditions.	Strong for setting both short- and long-term goals
Weinberg, Bruya, & Jackson (1985)	96 students enrolled in university fitness courses	No performance difference was found between short-term, long-term, short-term plus long-term, and do-your-best goal conditions on a sit-up task.	Weak for setting both short- and long-term goals
Weinberg, Bruya, Longino, & Jackson (1988)	130 boys and 125 girls in grades 4 through 6	No performance difference was found between short-term, long-term, and short-term plus long-term goal conditions on a sit-up endurance task.	Weak for setting both short- and long-term goals
Weinberg, Butt, & Knight (2001)	8 male and 6 female adult high school sport coaches	Short-term goals were set for both practice and competition.	Strong for setting short-term goals
Goal specificity (strong or partial support for goal specificity predictions in 16 out of 26 studies)			
Bar-Eli, Levy-Kolker, Tenenbaum, & Weinberg (1993)	184 army trainees	No performance difference was found between four specific-goal conditions (easy, moderate, hard, very hard), do-your-best goal condition, and control condition on physical fitness tasks.	Weak for goal specificity
Bar-Eli, Tenenbaum, Pie, Btesh, & Almog (1997)	364 high school students	All specific goal groups (easy, difficult and realistic, and improbable and unrealistic) performed better than did nonspecific goal groups on sit-up task.	Strong for goal specificity
Boyce (1990a)	90 students in a rifle-shooting contest	Of three goal conditions (specific and difficult, specific and moderate, and do your best), specific and difficult condition was superior to do-your-best condition on a shooting task.	Moderate for specificity
Boyce (1990b)	135 university riflery class participants	Specific and difficult goal conditions resulted in better performance than did a do-your-best goal condition during a rifle-shooting task.	Strong for goal specificity
Boyce (1992a)	181 university students	Short-term, long-term, and short-term plus long-term goal conditions resulted in better performance on shooting task compared with do-your-best goal condition.	Strong for goal specificity
Boyce (1992b)	138 university riflery class participants	Both self-set and assigned goal conditions resulted in better performance than did the do-your-best condition during a rifle-shooting task.	Moderate for goal specificity
Boyce (1994)	30 experienced pistol shooters	No performance difference was found between instructor-set and do-your-best goal conditions on a pistol-shooting task.	Weak for goal specificity
Boyce & Bingham (1997)	288 college students performing a bowling task	No difference was found between self-set, assigned, and do-your-best goal conditions on bowling performance.	Weak for goal specificity
Burton (1989a)	16 male and 7 female undergraduate basketball students	Specific-goal condition resulted in better performance on most basketball skills compared with general-goal condition.	Moderate for goal specificity

Study	Subjects	Results	Level of support
Erbaugh & Barnett (1986)	52 elementary school children	Both goal conditions (goals, goals and modeling) enhanced rope-jumping performance compared with do-your-best goal condition.	Strong for goal specificity
Frierman, Weinberg, & Jackson (1990)	45 novice and 27 intermediate bowlers	Of the four goal conditions (short-term, long-term, short-term plus long-term, and do your best), only the long-term goal condition resulted in greater improvement than did the do-your-best condition.	Moderate for goal specificity
Giannini, Weinberg, & Jackson (1988)	100 college male recreational basketball players	Only the competitive goal condition (one of three specific-goal conditions) resulted in better performance than did the do-your-best-without-feedback goal condition on a basketball task.	Weak for goal specificity
Gyurcsik, Estabrooks, & Frahm-Templar (2003)	28 male and 188 female arthritic aquatic exercise participants	No difference was shown in goal specificity between high and low attendees.	Weak for goal specificity
Hall & Byrne (1988)	43 male and 11 female university weight training students	The two long-term plus intermediate goal conditions resulted in better performance than did a do-your-best goal condition on an endurance task.	Moderate for goal specificity
Hall, Weinberg, & Jackson (1987)	94 college males	The two specific-goal conditions resulted in better performance than did the do-your-best goal condition on a hand dynamometer endurance task.	Strong for goal specificity
Hollingsworth (1975)	90 junior high school students	No difference was found between a performance goal condition, a do-your-best goal condition, and a no-goal condition on a juggling task.	Weak for goal specificity
Jones & Cale (1997)	44 adult participants	Do-your-best goals improved performance more than very easy goals did, but they were less effective than very hard goals.	Moderate for goal specificity
Lee & Edwards (1984)	93 5th-grade physical education students	Specific goals (self-set and assigned) enhanced performance to a greater extent than do-your-best goals did on motor tasks.	Strong for goal specificity
Munroe-Chandler & Hall (2004)	109 male and 140 female elite athletes representing 18 different sports	Specific self-set goals enhanced practice sessions.	Strong for goal specificity
Tenenbaum, Bar-Eli, & Yaaron (1999)	346 male Israeli 9th- and 10th-grade students	Specific long-term goal condition improved task performance.	Strong for goal specificity
Tenenbaum, Weinberg, Pinchas, Elbaz, & Bar-Eli (1991)	214 9th-grade white Israeli students	Short-term plus long-term goal condition resulted in better performance on a sit-up task compared with do-your-best goal condition.	Strong for goal specificity
Weinberg, Bruya, & Jackson (1985)	96 students enrolled in university fitness courses	No performance difference was found between short-term, long-term, short-term plus long-term, and do-your-best conditions on a sit-up task.	Weak for goal specificity
Weinberg, Bruya, Jackson, & Garland (1986)	123 students enrolled in university fitness courses	No performance difference was found between participants using extremely hard goals, highly improbable goals, and do-your-best goals on a sit-up task.	Weak for goal specificity

(continued)

Table 15.1 *(continued)*

Study	Subjects	Results	Level of support
Goal specificity (strong or partial support for goal specificity predictions in 16 out of 26 studies) *(continued)*			
Weinberg, Bruya, Longino, & Jackson (1988)	130 boys and 125 girls in grades 4 through 6	Specific goals led to better performance on a sit-up endurance task compared with do-your-best goals.	Moderate for goal specificity
Weinberg, Garland, Bruya, & Jackson (1990)	87 undergraduate students in fitness courses	No performance difference was found between realistic, unrealistic, do-your-best, and no-goal conditions on a sit-up task.	Weak for goal specificity
Goal collectivity (support or partial support for the setting of group goals in 6 out of 8 studies)			
Brawley, Carron, & Widmeyer (1992)	167 college and recreational athletes	Group goals were general rather than specific, and although process goals predominated during practice, groups set both outcome and process goals during competition.	Group goals exploratory study
Brawley, Carron, & Widmeyer (1993)	145 adult and college athletes	Participation in team goal setting was strongly related to "groupness" variables, such as cohesion.	Strong for group goals
Bray (2004)	42 male and 69 female undergraduate students	Group goals contributed to increased performance on an interdependent muscular endurance task.	Strong for group goals
Dawson, Bray, & Widmeyer (2002)	155 male and 80 female collegiate athletes	Both individual goals for self and team and team goals for individual athletes and team were effective—more so for competition than for practice.	Strong for both group and individual goals
Johnson, Ostrow, Perna, & Etzel (1997)	36 male undergraduate bowling students	Of the three conditions (group goals, individual goals, and do-your-best goals), only the group goals condition improved bowling performance.	Strong for group goals
Lee (1988)	9 women's field hockey teams (96 women)	Team goals were positively related to winning percentage.	Strong for group goals
Weinberg, Butt, & Knight (2001)	8 male and 6 female adult high school sport coaches	Both group goals and individual goals were used.	Strong for both group and individual goals
Widmeyer & Ducharme (1997)	Not applicable	Position paper focused on enhancing team cohesion through team goal setting.	Not applicable
Goal participation (partial support for positive influence of self-set goals on task performance in 3 out of 10 studies)			
Baker, Marshak, Rice, & Zimmerman (2001)	2 male and 20 female physical therapists, 17 male and 56 female physical therapy patients age 65 and older	Assigned goal-setting conditions with patient input improved physical therapy outcomes.	Weak for goal-setting participation
Boyce (1992)	138 university riflery class participants	No difference was found between self-set and assigned goal conditions on rifle-shooting performance.	Weak for goal-setting participation
Boyce & Bingham (1997)	288 college students performing a bowling task	No difference was found between self-set, assigned, and do-your-best goal conditions on bowling performance.	Weak for goal-setting participation
Boyce & Wayda (1994)	252 female university weight-training students	Assigned goal condition resulted in better performance than did the self-set goal condition.	Weak for goal-setting participation

Study	Subjects	Results	Level of support
Boyce, Wayda, Johnston, Bunker, & Eliot (2001)	39 male and 117 female undergraduate beginning tennis students	Instructor-set goals resulted in better statistical performance, although both instructor-set and self-set goals were more effective than do-your-best goals.	Moderate for goal-setting participation
Cobb, Stone, Anonsen, & Klein (2000)	104 community college fitness class students	Self-set goals with investigator feedback resulted in greater self-motivation for exercise adherers.	Moderate for goal-setting participation
Fairall & Rodgers (1997)	67 track and field athletes	No difference was found between participation, assigned, and self-set goal conditions.	Weak for goal-setting participation
Hall & Byrne (1988)	43 male and 11 female university weight training students	No difference was found between long-term plus instructor-set intermediate goal condition and long-term plus self-set intermediate goal condition on an endurance task.	Weak for goal-setting participation
Lambert, Moore, & Dixon (1999)	4 female gymnasts	Gymnasts with a more internal locus of control benefited from self-set goals, whereas gymnasts with as external locus of control benefited from coach-set goals.	Moderate for goal-setting participation
Lee & Edwards (1984)	93 5th-grade physical education students	Assigned goals enhanced performance more than self-set goals did on two out of three motor tasks.	Weak for goal-setting participation
Task complexity (partial support for task complexity as a moderating variable of goal-setting effectiveness in 1 of 2 studies)			
Anshel, Weinberg, & Jackson (1992)	54 undergraduate students	All goal conditions (easy, difficult, and self-set) improved performance for both simple and difficult juggling tasks.	Strong for both simple and difficult tasks
Burton (1989a)	16 male and 7 female undergraduate basketball students	Specific-goal condition resulted in better performance than general-goal condition on low-complexity but not moderate- or high-complexity basketball tasks.	Moderate support for task complexity distinction
Goal interventions (support or partial support for goal setting as an effective intervention technique in 9 out of 11 studies)			
Anderson, Crowell, Doman, & Howard (1988)	17 male intercollegiate hockey players	Goal-setting intervention increased hitting performance during hockey games.	Strong for goal setting as an intervention strategy
Burton (1989b)	29 collegiate swimmers	Goal-setting intervention enhanced competitive cognitions and performance for collegiate swimmers.	Strong for goal setting as an intervention strategy
Galvan & Ward (1998)	5 collegiate tennis players	Goal setting, in part, reduced the number of inappropriate on-court behaviors immediately following the goal-setting intervention.	Strong for goal setting as an intervention strategy
Graham, Kowalski, & Crocker (2002)	67 male and 65 female teenage provincial all-star soccer players	Goal characteristics sometimes had direct effects on emotional responses.	Moderate for goal setting as an intervention strategy
Graham, Kowalski, & Crocker (2002)	84 male and 90 female teenage club team swimmers	Goal characteristics were significant across all emotions.	Strong for goal setting as an intervention strategy
Miller & McAuley (1987)	18 undergraduate students	No difference was found in free-throw performance between goal-training and no-goal-training conditions.	Weak for goal setting as an intervention strategy

(continued)

Table 15.1   (continued)

Study	Subjects	Results	Level of support
Goal interventions (support or partial support for goal setting as an effective intervention technique in 9 out of 11 studies) (continued)			
Poag-DuCharme & Brawley (1994)	99 adults enrolled in exercise classes	Participants set multiple goals and developed action plans and specific behavioral strategies for achieving the identified goals.	Moderate for goal setting as an intervention strategy
Swain & Jones (1995)	4 male collegiate basketball players	Goal-setting intervention enhanced basketball skills for three out of four subjects.	Moderate for goal setting as an intervention strategy
Theodorakis, Laparidis, Kioumourtzoglou, & Goudas (1998)	18 male and 24 female undergraduate physical education students	Experimental group significantly lowered their pretest heart rate and increased their performance standard when riding a cycle ergometer bicycle.	Strong for goal setting as an intervention strategy
Wanlin, Hrycaiko, Martin, & Mahon (1997)	4 female speed skaters	Goal-setting intervention enhanced skating performance.	Strong for goal setting as an intervention strategy
Weinberg, Stitcher, & Richardson (1994)	24 male Division III lacrosse players	Goal-setting intervention failed to improve performance significantly, although researchers identified a positive trend toward improvement.	Weak for goal setting as an intervention strategy
Goals and self-efficacy (support or partial support for goal setting as an effective mediator or enhancer of self-efficacy in 9 out of 9 studies)			
Evans & Hardy (2002a)	33 male and 6 female injured adult athletes	Goal-setting condition resulted in the highest level of self-efficacy during rehabilitation.	Strong for enhancing self-efficacy
Gyurcsik, Estabrooks, & Frahm-Templar (2003)	28 male and 188 female arthritic aquatic exercise participants	Task and scheduling self-efficacy and goal setting predicted enhanced aquatic exercise attendance.	Strong for efficacy enhancing attendance
Kane, Marks, Zaccaro, & Blair (1996)	216 high school wrestlers	Outcome goals mediated self-efficacy performance relationship for wrestlers at camp.	Strong for goals mediating efficacy and performance
Kingston & Hardy (1997)	37 club golfers	Both process goals and performance goals improved golfing self-efficacy; the process goal condition resulted in significant improvement more quickly.	Strong for enhancing self-efficacy
Lee (1988)	9 women's field hockey teams (96 women)	Setting specific and challenging team goals mediated the effect of self-efficacy on team performance (won–loss record).	Moderate for enhancing self-efficacy
Miller & McAuley (1987)	18 undergraduate students	Goal-training condition resulted in higher reported free-throw self-efficacy compared with no-goal-training condition.	Strong for enhancing self-efficacy
Poag & McAuley (1992)	76 adult female community conditioning participants	Goal efficacy predicted perceived goal achievement at the end of the program.	Strong for efficacy as a goal moderator
Theodorakis (1995)	42 undergraduate physical education students	Goals were found to be a mediator between self-efficacy and performance.	Strong for goals mediating efficacy and performance
Theodorakis (1996)	48 undergraduate physical education students	Self-efficacy and goal setting were found to be predictors of performance on a tennis service task.	Strong for efficacy as a predictor of performance

The review for the initial version of this chapter completed 14 years ago found only 14 sport and exercise goal studies, two-thirds of which revealed significant goal-setting effects, whereas the review in the second edition of the chapter demonstrated moderate to strong goal-setting effects in 44 of 56 goal-setting studies, a 79% effectiveness rate. Thus, as the number of goal-setting studies in sport increases, goal-setting results in sport have come to resemble general goal-setting findings.

Based on this overview of goal-setting basics, let us review the fundamental goal concept in sport and examine an updated version of our competitive goal-setting model that integrates the two notions of goals.

Updated Competitive Goal-Setting Model

The competitive goal-setting (CGS) model was originally proposed to advance the fundamental goal concept in sport, integrate discrete and global conceptions of goals, and account for personality influences on the goal-setting process. Although the model was proposed 14 years ago and has elicited a number of provocative comments from other goal-setting researchers, both pro and con, a paucity of research has directly tested model predictions. The major reason for the limited testing of the CGS model is probably the difficulty of empirically classifying people into appropriate goal-setting styles, an important prerequisite to testing model predictions. Nevertheless, several studies conducted by my colleagues, students, and me (e.g., Burton, 1989b; Burton et al., 2005; Burton & Sharples, 2001; Pierce & Burton, 1998) generally have supported model predictions, prompting us to believe that the model still has something to offer researchers who are attempting to understand the goal-setting process and ways to make it work more effectively in sport. As indicated in the introduction, we have found anecdotal evidence, gathered while working with coaches and athletes, more compelling than existing research in supporting the model.

Thus, we present here a modified third version of the model (i.e., CGS–3) and some specific suggestions for research to test key model predictions. We hope that this revision may promote independent research that will assess the viability of this conceptual framework. In this section, we first describe the fundamental goal concept. Next we present our most recent revision of the CGS model and briefly review important model predictions. Finally, we review the limited research that directly tests model predictions in sport and draw tentative conclusions about its viability. Those interested in the research that provided the empirical rationale for the model and its specific predictions are referred to the original edition of this text (see Burton, 1992).

Since proposing the competitive goal-setting (CGS) model a decade and a half ago, we have increasingly become convinced that focusing on process and performance rather than outcome goals is the fundamental goal concept in sport, and perhaps the most important concept in all of sport psychology (Burton, 1989b, 1992; Burton & Naylor, 2002; Burton et al., 2001; Kingston & Hardy, 1994, 1997).

Process goals refer to improving form, technique, and strategy. Performance goals focus on increasing overall personal performance (e.g., running a faster time, throwing farther, or shooting a lower score), and outcome goals emphasize outperforming competitors and achieving objective outcomes (i.e., placing high, winning). Thus, outcome goals such as winning or placing high in a 100-meter dash require the attainment of performance goals such as running the 100 meters in 10.22 seconds. To attain those performance goals, runners must achieve a series of process goals that focus on improving form, technique, knowledge, or strategy, such as getting a good start out of the blocks, working their arms as they tire, and running through the tape. In fact, these three types of goals might best be conceptualized on a continuum, with outcome goals on the product end of the continuum, process goals at the opposite end, and performance goals midway between the two.

Emphasizing Process and Performance Goals

In our society, those who achieve more are considered more competent. In sport, achievement is usually measured by one simple criterion—winning. Winning is seen as success, and losing as failure. Even the youngest athletes learn to adopt this achievement standard. When athletes make the mistake of basing their self-confidence on winning rather than on attaining process and performance goals, their self-confidence is likely to be highly unstable.

Many athletes quickly become overconfident after a win or two, only to lose and see their confidence plummet. When performers base their confidence on winning but do not win all the time, they usually feel helpless to do anything about their unstable self-confidence. They have become convinced that the only criterion for evaluating their competence is whether they win, and they are unable to separate their performance from its outcome. The only way for performers to stabilize their self-confidence and feel competent regardless of whether they win or lose is to replace the pervasive goal of winning with realistic process and performance goals. They must redefine success to mean attaining process standards and exceeding personal performance goals rather than surpassing the performance of others.

Effective goal-setting programs must help athletes understand the folly of basing their self-worth on factors beyond their control. It makes no sense for athletes to perform well and reach realistic process and performance goals, only to believe that they are failures because they lost the contest. Nor does it make sense for performers to perform poorly yet consider themselves successful because they beat a weak opponent or were lucky. Champions inevitably avoid getting caught up in constantly evaluating themselves based on every win or loss. Performers must set long-term objectives for themselves and then measure their progress toward those objectives by evaluating their performance in light of the quality of the competition, without regard to whether they win or lose.

The fundamental goal concept in sport has a powerful long-term effect on athletes' careers. Most athletes and teams set outcome goals, significantly fewer set performance goals, and fewer still establish process goals. Sadly, process and performance goals allow competitors to be more successful than do outcome goals. Specifically, outcome goals often create stress while decreasing motivation, confidence, and performance, whereas process and performance goals promote much more positive competitive cognitions and performance (Burton, 1989b). Intrinsic motivation occurs when performers feel competent and self-determining. To maximize intrinsic motivation, goals should possess two important characteristics:

■ Controllability—allows performers to maximize control over their own success, which ensures that they can take credit for their success as indicative of higher perceived competence

■ Flexibility—permits goals to be raised and lowered so that athletes can achieve consistent success on personally challenging tasks.

Maximizing Control Over Personal Success

One reason that process and performance goals are superior to outcome goals is that athletes have greater control over success, both their personal

athletic development (i.e., refining skill mechanics) and their performance, than they do over the outcome of the contest. It makes little sense for athletes to evaluate their success based on attaining goals that they only partially control. Process and performance goals identify specific behaviors to be achieved, and their attainment does not depend a great deal on the performance of others. Outcome goals, especially winning, are only partially controllable. Competitive outcome depends not only on the athlete's individual performance but also on the performance of teammates, the ability and performance of opponents, and the quality of coaching for each team. Numerous situational factors such as equipment, playing fields and courts, weather, officials, and luck also influence outcomes.

Ideally, all goals should be 100% controllable, but even skill development goals do not provide total controllability. Hence, all performers should strive to set goals that are as personally controllable as possible. A gymnast will find a goal to run through her floor exercise routine six times daily for the next week in preparation for an upcoming meet more controllable than scoring a 9.4 on her floor exercise routine, which, in turn, is more controllable than winning the meet in that event. Yet even this process-oriented training goal is not 100% controllable. Illness, injury, or midterm exam week at school may influence goal attainment. Although no goal is totally controllable, control increases as athletes move toward the process end of the continuum. As controllability increases, performers can more readily take credit for their success as indicative of high or increased perceived ability, prerequisites for raising self-confidence.

Creating Optimally Challenging Goals

Optimal goals are also flexible in that they can be raised or lowered to create optimal challenge. The more challenging the goal is, the greater are the motivation and self-confidence benefits that accrue from successful goal attainment. If goals become unrealistic, however, performers will no longer be confident of attaining them, and the resulting stress may lower motivation. Therefore, level of goal difficulty is always a compromise between creating the highest possible level of challenge to enhance motivation and maintaining a realistic opportunity to attain success necessary to maintain confidence and reduce stress. Ideal goals are flexible so that goal difficulty can be adjusted to ensure optimal challenge. Outcome goals offer little flexibility. Competition schedules normally determine opponents, sometimes years in advance, so adjusting outcome goal difficulty to create optimal challenge is virtually impossible. Conversely, process and performance goals are much easier to adjust. If a basketball player finds that hitting 80% of her free throws is too challenging, she can drop the goal to 75%. Conversely, if 80% is too easy, she can raise goal difficulty to 85%. Ideal goals have the flexibility to create optimal challenge, which, in turn, enhances motivation and self-confidence while boosting performance.

Integrating Process, Performance, and Outcome Goals

How coaches and athletes implement the fundamental goal concept is extremely important. Almost every athlete wants to perform well *and* win, even if doing both is not always feasible. Many performers get into sport, and even continue competing, for outcome reasons. Watching his or her heroes emerge victorious in the Olympics, World Series, Super Bowl, Masters, or Wimbledon may convince an athlete to pursue a particular sport. The big victories that athletes have in their careers are also critical for developing confidence and boosting long-term commitment. Outcome goals have an important motivational function in sport, primarily during practice because they remind performers why they are investing so much time and energy to improve their performance (Hardy, 1997). Outcome goals represent the ultimate destination, and process and performance goals establish the path to get there. That destination becomes attainable if competitors devise an action plan based on developing skills and strategies that promote good performance and if they manage their environment to ensure that they play their best. But too much focus on outcome without developing the action plan to achieve it, particularly the necessary process and performance goals, creates a number of problems.

When a great shooter like Reggie Miller hits a game-winning three-pointer with defenders in his face, he is not thinking about making the shot to win the game. Instead, he is thinking in a more process-oriented way such as "Stay relaxed, square up, good rhythm, and follow through." Those are examples of process goals that normally ensure success. In sport, in which lengthy practice intervals are required to master complex skills, process goals should function as the stepping-stones to achieving performance levels that will ultimately ensure desired outcomes. Moreover, the fundamental goal concept in sport provides a strong rationale for the need for our

updated competitive goal-setting model that will be described in the next section.

Competitive Goal-Setting Model Overview

The CGS model was initially advanced not to put forth a new theory of goal setting but simply to provide a heuristic tool to improve understanding of three important issues about goal setting. First, the model incorporates the fundamental goal concept. Second, the model attempts to integrate state and trait conceptions of goals into a single more comprehensive model that considers both the motivational and stress-related functions of goals. Third, the comprehensive model makes specific predictions that can aid our understanding and investigation of the goal-setting process in sport (figure 15.1). The CGS–3 model offers a slightly expanded version of previous models that is consistent with these purposes, maintains consistency with the huge influx of recent goal-setting research, and emphasizes key process variables that affect goal-setting effectiveness.

Consistent with the large body of cognitive motivation research (Duda & Hall, 2001; Dweck, 1999; Elliott & Dweck, 1988; Locke, 1968; Locke et al., 1981; Maehr, 1984; Nicholls, 1984a, 1984b), the CGS–3 model shown in figure 15.1 predicts that the motivational function of goals is most evident in the top portion of the model among links 1 through 6. First, beliefs about talent or intelligence determine goal orientations, which interact with perceived ability to prompt the development of three distinct goal-setting styles: performance oriented (link 1), success oriented (link 2), and failure oriented (link 3). These goal-setting styles, along with key situational variables such as situation type (i.e., practice versus competition), activity importance, task complexity, and performance expectancies, then dictate the specific goals set (i.e., process, performance, or outcome; link 4). Next, these discrete goals interact with key process variables such as perceived goal commitment and identification of obstacles and roadblocks to prompt specific goal responses—task choice, effort or intensity, strategy development, and persistence or continuing motivation (link 5). These goal responses significantly influence athletes' performance and competitive outcome (link 6).

Based on perceived ability theory and research (e.g., Duda & Hall, 2001; Dweck, 1999; Elliott & Dweck, 1988; Harter, 1981; Nicholls, 1984a, 1984b), the CGS–3 model further predicts that goals have an important self-evaluation function because they

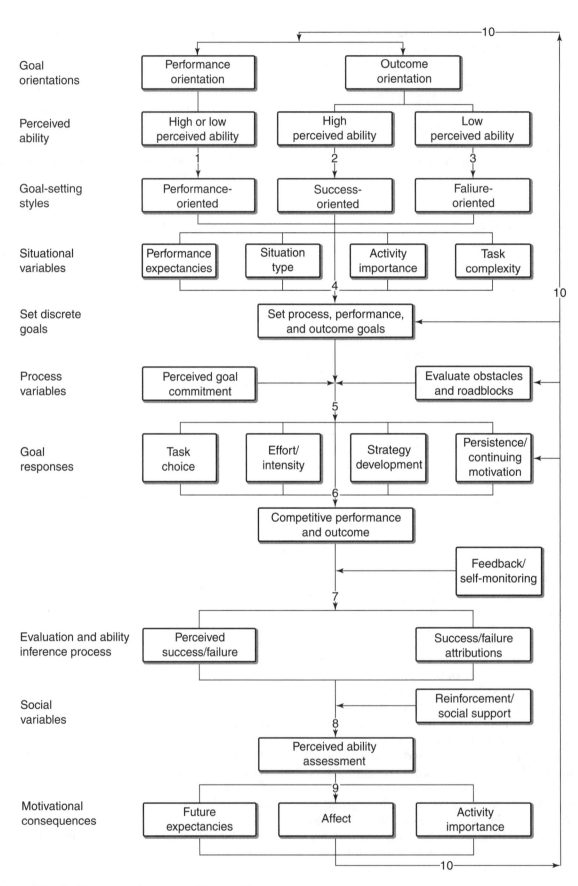

Figure 15.1 Updated competitive goal-setting model.

358

become the standards against which process, performance, and outcome are weighed to determine perceived success and failure and to assess specific success and failure attributions (link 7), the two primary antecedents of perceived competence or ability (link 8). Finally, the CGS–3 model predicts that perceived ability directly influences motivational consequent variables such as future expectancies, affect, and activity importance (link 9). Feedback loops then allow motivational consequent variables to influence beliefs, goal orientations, specific goals, goal process variables, and goal responses (link 10).

The CGS–3 model is depicted as a sequential process to facilitate understanding of the separate motivation and self-evaluation functions of goals. In reality, the process is probably more complex, and feedback loops are likely more extensive. Although the model does not attempt to resolve the dispute about the primacy of cognition versus affect, it emphasizes that these variables are related, probably in some reciprocal fashion. The CGS–3 model makes specific predictions about the types of practice and competitive goals set by athletes who adopt different goal-setting styles and the ways in which these goal patterns will affect competitors' cognitions and performance. In the next section, we briefly review each goal-setting style and make specific predictions about their preferred goal-setting patterns for each style.

Goal-Setting Styles The notion of goal-setting styles is based on motivation theory and research that combines the concept of global goal orientations with personal perceptions of ability. Contemporary conceptions of goal orientations are based on three theoretical premises (e.g., Duda & Hall, 2001; Dweck, 1999; Elliott & Dweck, 1988; Nicholls, 1984a, 1984b). First, perceived competence or ability is conceived as the critical underlying construct responsible for mediating motivational behaviors. Second, personal beliefs about talent and intelligence define two distinct ways of defining success (i.e., learning versus capacity). Third, individuals' goal orientations are hypothesized to mediate how perceived ability develops and how it affects achievement behavior.

According to Dweck (1999), beliefs about talent and intelligence underlie goal orientations. She postulated that beliefs fall into one of two major categories: learning or capacity. Learning beliefs view talent and intelligence as malleable and capable of change as long as performers put time and energy into upgrading their skills, prompting the development of a performance orientation. Effort is an essential component of learning beliefs because people believe that hard work will enhance

talent or intelligence and make success more probable. Conversely, capacity beliefs view talent and intelligence as fixed based on genetic factors. Thus, because talent and intelligence cannot be meaningfully altered, effort and hard work will have little effect on success. Capacity beliefs typically lead to the development of outcome orientations.

Athletes who adopt a performance orientation define success and failure in sport and related achievement domains predominantly according to whether they are able either to learn and master new tasks or to improve skills and performance. These performers believe that they can continue to refine ability and skill throughout their careers, and they define success in terms of self-referent standards such as learning, skill improvement, goal attainment, or task mastery. Perceived ability does not seem to mediate motivation for performance-oriented individuals, because athletes high or low in perceived ability demonstrate similar motivational patterns. Performance-oriented competitors assume that they can learn and improve if they put forth sufficient effort. Such a process focus frees them from worrying about demonstrating their competence and allows them to concentrate on ways of learning and enhancing their performance. Although these athletes certainly care about outcome, particularly winning, their top priority and the focus of their attention is process more than product.

Individuals who adopt an outcome goal orientation aim to "maintain positive judgments of their ability and avoid negative judgments by seeking to prove, validate, or document their ability and not discredit it" (Elliott & Dweck, 1988, p. 5). Outcome goal orientations define success or failure based predominantly on social comparison processes, thus making winning or positive social comparison essential to maintaining high perceived ability. For outcome-oriented performers, improvement and task mastery are important, but primarily as a means (i.e., process) to the desired end of achieving positive social comparison (i.e., product).

The CGS–3 model hypothesizes that goal orientation and level of perceived ability interact to create three distinct goal-setting styles: performance oriented, success oriented, and failure oriented. The general focus of each of these goal-setting styles is outlined in table 15.2, along with specific characteristics of each style.

Performance-Oriented Goal-Setting Style As indicated in columns 1 through 3 of table 15.2, performance-oriented (PO) athletes adopt learning beliefs about talent that define success predominantly in terms of learning and improvement

Table 15.2   Characteristics of Performance-, Success-, and Failure-Oriented Goal-Setting Styles

	1. How athletes define success and failure	2. Level of perceived ability	3. Normal goal priority	4. Competitive outlook	5. Attributions Success	5. Attributions Failure
Performance-oriented	Learning, improvement, and increasing self-referent ability	High or low as long as can learn and improve	1. Process 2. Performance 3. Outcome	Positive and optimistic	High effort (ability assumed)	• Often don't perceive failure • Effort
Success-oriented	Competitive outcome and positive social comparison as a means of demonstrating high ability	High ability—socially compares well (i.e., wins often)	1. Outcome 2. Performance 3. Process	Positive and optimistic	High ability	Internal, unstable, controllable factors (i.e., low effort or poor mental preparation)
Failure-oriented	Avoid competition and social comparison for fear of demonstrating low ability	Low ability—poor social comparison (i.e., loses often)	1. Outcome 2. Performance 3. Process	Negative and pessimistic	External or uncontrollable factors (i.e., luck or easy tasks)	Low ability

rather than demonstrating ability to others. Thus, high- and low-skilled PO performers should demonstrate similar motivational patterns in practice and competition. Ability comparison is a secondary issue for PO competitors because they are primarily interested in raising perceived ability through learning and skill development. PO athletes should view most situations as opportunities to learn and improve their skills, thus prompting high levels of intrinsic motivation.

Based on learned helplessness and perceived ability research (e.g., Diener & Dweck, 1978; Duda & Hall, 2001; Dweck, 1980, 1999; Elliott & Dweck, 1988; Nicholls, 1984a), the CGS–3 model predicts that PO athletes assume the ability to learn and improve, prompting them to attribute success primarily to effort (column 5). Moreover, PO competitors are predicted to view lack of success in a positive, constructive way, seldom making failure attributions (column 5). Because of their learning focus, PO competitors deal with lack of success by increasing effort or developing new problem-solving strategies (column 8).

Performers who adopt a PO goal-setting style are predicted to select challenging or difficult goals, even at the risk of making mistakes, because their primary objective is to increase competence (column 7). PO athletes also should exert high effort in most situations to maximize learning and performance improvement regardless of the level of task difficulty (column 6). Moreover, the model predicts that PO competitors should confront failure constructively, remain focused on the task, and develop more effective problem-solving strategies, thus demonstrating high persistence and continuing motivation for their sport (column 8).

The CGS–3 model predicts that PO athletes should perform consistently better than failure-oriented (FO) performers in all situations (column 9). Success-oriented (SO) and PO competitors should demonstrate similar levels of performance over the short run and in many success situations, but PO athletes should respond better to failure and come closer to reaching their performance potential over the course of their careers because they set more challenging goals, give consistently higher effort, use more effective problem-solving strategies, and persist longer in the face of failure (column 9). Moreover, because athletes maximize their chances of winning by performing their best, PO competitors also should win more over their careers than do SO or FO performers of similar ability.

6. Effort expenditure	7. Task choice preferences	8. Response to failure	9. Performance	10. Goal attribute preferences	11. Response to goal-setting program
Consistently high to maximize learning and improvement	• Prefer very hard tasks • Embrace all opportunities to learn and improve at risk of making numerous mistakes	Dramatically increased effort and improved problem solving	• Perform extremely well • Long-term athletes will closely approach performance potential	• Self-referenced • Specific • Difficult • Positive • Individual/team • Long-term/short-term	Improve performance significantly
Effort only as high as necessary to win and demonstrate positive social comparison	• Prefer moderately difficult tasks • Will sacrifice learning if risks extensive failure	Increased effort and improved problem solving	• Generally will perform well enough to win • Long-term potential depends on situational factors that prompt development of full capabilities	• Social comparative • Specific • Moderately difficult • Positive/negative • Individual/team • Long-term/short-term	Improve performance moderately
• Low effort on moderate tasks to confuse ability evaluation • High effort on easy tasks to avoid failure	• Prefer very hard or very easy tasks • Sacrifice learning to avoid failure and displaying low ability	Give up easily, reduce effort, and will drop out if can	Poor performance, which deteriorates with continued failure	• Social comparative • General • Moderately easy • Positive • Team • Long-term	Decrease performance slightly

Finally, the CGS–3 model predicts that PO athletes should experience positive motivational consequences from goal setting. The learning focus of PO competitors allows them to remain optimistic about their ability to learn and improve despite encountering plateaus or failure. In fact, low current ability in a valued area may motivate them to work hard to acquire skills needed to overcome their deficiency (Diener & Dweck, 1978; Dweck, 1999). The model also predicts that PO athletes should experience satisfaction and pride from success. Although they should perceive negative affect when unsuccessful, these mild negative emotions should prompt them to demonstrate even higher future motivation. Additionally, PO athletes are predicted to increase their commitment to challenging tasks that help them learn and improve.

Success-Oriented Goal-Setting Style Competitors with SO goal-setting styles adopt a capacity model of talent that views skill or competence as fixed and limited, with success defined based on social comparison and competitive outcome. But because they win consistently and socially compare well, SO competitors perceive that they have high ability (columns 1 through 3 of table 15.2). SO performers' primary objective is to win in order to demonstrate competence (columns 1 and 3). Although they view most situations as opportunities to demonstrate competence, SO competitors are optimally motivated, confident, and play their best only when matched against an opponent of similar ability (i.e., moderate task difficulty; column 7). SO athletes are predicted to attribute success to ability—an internal, stable, controllable factor that creates a positive and optimistic outlook toward competition. Conversely, failure normally is attributed to internal, unstable, controllable factors such as low effort, poor mental preparation, and the need to develop skills further (column 5). Although SO competitors still worry about failure, they normally respond to failure in a constructive way (column 8).

The CGS–3 model hypothesizes that competitors with SO goal-setting styles will avoid challenging goals if they perceive a risk of significant public failure or numerous mistakes (column 7). Instead, they are predicted to prefer to set moderately difficult goals on tasks at which they are already reasonably proficient to ensure that low ability is not revealed. SO competitors' effort expenditure is predicted to fluctuate, depending on task difficulty (column 6). For moderately difficult tasks, SO performers should put forth high effort to reach their goals. When the task is easy, however, SO competitors will expend as little effort as necessary to win, a strategy that allows them to demonstrate even higher ability. Finally, for extremely difficult tasks in which the probability of failure is high, SO athletes will exert high effort until they become convinced that successful social comparison is not possible; then they will concentrate their effort on other tasks at which they are more likely to be successful (column 6).

The CGS–3 model predicts that the relatively high perceived ability of SO athletes should help them approach failure in a positive way and allow them to manifest high confidence, remain task focused, and develop effective problem-solving strategies (column 8). But because of their need to continue to demonstrate high ability, the continuing motivation of SO performers eventually should deteriorate with extensive failure. The model also predicts that SO athletes generally will perform well (column 9). Compared with their PO counterparts, however, SO competitors are not expected to perform as close to their performance potential over the long run because their concern about demonstrating high ability to others reduces productivity in two ways. First, the importance of positive social comparison reduces the level of challenge of the goals set and limits how long SO athletes will persist in the face of failure. Second, the desire to maximize demonstration of ability prompts SO competitors to give low effort against weaker opponents and not look for ways to learn and improve unless pushed to do so in order to win. Such motivational patterns ultimately prevent SO performers from developing their full performance potential.

According to the CGS–3 model, SO athletes should experience positive motivational consequences from the goal-setting process. SO performers are predicted to maintain optimistic future expectancies because experience has told them that their normatively high ability will allow them to continue to socially compare well. The model also predicts that SO competitors should experience satisfaction and pride from success, whereas dissatisfaction over failure coupled with functional attributional patterns should prompt even higher motivation when they fail. Finally, SO athletes are predicted to increase activity importance for tasks at which they socially compare well to enhance their perceptions of ability.

Failure-Oriented Goal-Setting Style Performers with FO goal-setting styles are outcome oriented and adopt a capacity model of ability that views competence as fixed and limited, thus prompting them to define success in terms of social comparison. But FO competitors have low perceived ability because of their inability to socially compare well (columns 1 through 3 of table 15.2). A failure-oriented competitor's primary objective is to prevent others from finding out that he or she has low ability. Competitive situations become sources of fear because such situations may publicly reveal the FO performer's incompetence. Thus, FO athletes approach competition with diffidence and anxiety and often perform well below their capabilities. The CGS–3 model hypothesizes that FO competitors typically attribute failure to lack of ability, thus reinforcing their negative perceptions of competence (column 5). But they normally attribute success to external or uncontrollable factors such as luck or an easy task, thus doing little to increase feelings of competence (column 5). Regrettably, goals that foster increased success will not necessarily increase motivation for FO performers unless they take responsibility for their success and perceive that they can do something to turn failure into future success.

According to the CGS–3 model, FO performers have little interest in learning and normally demonstrate extreme task choice preferences (column 7). Because they are concerned with concealing their low ability from others, they normally set easy goals for tasks at which they are already experienced or proficient. Alternatively, they adopt extremely difficult goals so that they have an excuse for failure. The CGS–3 model predicts that the effort expenditure of FO competitors will fluctuate with the level of task difficulty (column 6). FO athletes who have not completely given up hope of demonstrating high ability should choose difficult tasks. Despite the high probability of failure, FO performers will exert high effort trying to "get lucky" and demonstrate high ability, because they are secure in the knowledge that they have a good excuse for almost certain failure. But after FO athletes become resigned to having low ability, they should prefer easy tasks and put forth high effort to ensure success (column 6). Moderately difficult tasks are predicted to be highly threatening to FO competitors, prompting them to respond by putting forth low effort as an ego defense mechanism. This token-effort strategy helps FO performers hide their low ability from others by creating confusion about whether failure was due to lack of ability or simply low effort (column 6).

The CGS–3 model hypothesizes that FO performers should demonstrate a significant deterioration in problem-solving skills when confronted with failure, probably because of the negative effects of diffidence and anxiety that prompt attentional distraction (column 8). Finally, FO athletes are predicted to demonstrate a sharp deterioration in persistence and continuing motivation, even with minimal failure. Fear of revealing low ability to others should prompt FO competitors to respond to failure by developing high levels of anxiety and self-doubt, by focusing internally on their own arousal and self-rumination, and by demonstrating severe deterioration in their problem-solving skills (column 8).

Conceptual arguments derived from the CGS–3 model predict that FO athletes normally should perform poorly (column 9). Fear of failure, because of inability to socially compare well, should elicit high levels of anxiety that significantly impair FO competitors' performance. Moreover, negative competitive cognitions coupled with the most dysfunctional types of goal responses—including easy goal difficulty, low effort expenditure, poor strategy development (particularly under failure), and low persistence—should ensure that performance deteriorates even further over time (column 9).

Finally, the model predicts that FO athletes should experience generally negative motivational consequences from the goal-setting process. FO performers are predicted to demonstrate negative future expectancies because of previous unsuccessful social comparison that they attributed to low ability. The model also predicts that FO competitors will experience minimal satisfaction from success, which they attribute to external, uncontrollable factors, whereas failure should promote extensive negative affect such as anxiety and shame that should impair performance and prompt a desire to drop out of sport. Additionally, FO athletes are predicted to devalue activities that force them to risk demonstrating low ability as a precursor to dropping out or changing activities.

Goal Attribute Preferences   Based on the goal-setting style profiles just outlined, the next section specifies CGS–3 model predictions for the goal attribute preferences of each goal-setting style, including goal specificity, difficulty, valence, proximity, and collectivity (column 10 of table 15.2).

Preferred Goal Attributes of PO Athletes   The CGS–3 model hypothesizes that PO athletes' learning orientation should prompt them to prefer self-referenced goals that are specific, difficult, and positive. Moreover, they should prefer to set both individual and team and long-term and short-term goals (column 10). Performers who adopt PO goal-setting styles are predicted to prefer goals with these attributes because such goals provide maximum information for developing new strategies to facilitate learning and performance improvement. PO competitors also are predicted to set long-term goals to provide direction for their skill development efforts, but they achieve those goals by developing action plans that focus on reaching specific short-term goals as realistic steps to obtaining their long-term objectives. But because PO performers are interested in learning as an extended ongoing process, they should focus more on long-term goals than either SO or FO competitors do, delaying gratification and accepting temporary setbacks as the price that they must pay to maximize learning and skill development (column 10).

Preferred Goal Attributes of SO Athletes   Because SO competitors adopt a capacity model of ability and define success in terms of positive social comparison, the CGS–3 model predicts that they should prefer specific and moderately difficult goals that include a combination of positive and negative, individual and team-oriented, and short- and long-term goals (column 10). SO performers should prefer specific and moderately difficult goals that maximize their chances of positive social comparison and ensure that they consistently demonstrate high ability. They also should benefit from positively focused goals for new or difficult skills but prefer more negatively focused goals that emphasize minimizing mistakes for well-learned skills. Model predictions suggest that both individual and team goals should facilitate social comparison, thus allowing SO competitors to demonstrate high ability. Athletes with SO goal-setting styles also should set a combination of short- and long-term goals (e.g., "I want to win the race this week as an important step toward my long-term goal of being an Olympic champion"). But because of their concern with demonstrating high ability to others, SO performers should emphasize short-term goals, sometimes retarding long-term skill development because focusing on development would cause a temporary decrease in performance that might hurt immediate social comparison (column 10).

Preferred Goal Attributes of FO Athletes   Finally, the CGS–3 model predicts that FO athletes should dislike competition because it threatens to reveal their low ability, thus prompting them to prefer goals that are general, team-oriented, extremely difficult or easy, long term, and positively focused (column 10). General and team-oriented goals make social comparison more difficult, thus lessening the threat. Extremely difficult goals allow the athlete to retain a small chance of demonstrating high ability while providing a built-in excuse for failure, whereas easy goals maximize the chances of winning. Finally, long-term goals delay the threatening evaluation process as long as possible, and because FO performers have a strong fear of failure, they are predicted to prefer positively focused goals that lessen concern about revealing low ability (column 10).

Moderating Variables   Two important moderating variables have an influence on goal-setting effects in the CGS–3 model: commitment and feedback. This section briefly describes the role that these variables play in influencing the goal–performance relationship.

Goal Commitment   For goals to have motivational value, performers must become committed to goal achievement. Goal commitment is an important component of Locke's (1968) goal-setting model. Without commitment, individuals probably will not do what it takes to achieve goals. Moreover, Locke postulated that factors such as participation in setting the goal, incentives for goal achievement, and trust and supportiveness of others in the organization, including coaches, teammates, and parents, are important to developing high commitment. In several meta-analyses, Locke and his colleagues (Locke, 1996; Locke, Latham, & Erez, 1988) emphasized that goal commitment is most important when goals are specific and difficult and that commitment is enhanced when goals are perceived to be important yet attainable.

The mechanism by which commitment influences goals is complicated. For example, Locke and Latham (1990) identified an interesting interaction between level of commitment and goal difficulty. Under low goal difficulty, low-commitment individuals perform better than their high-commitment counterparts, whereas under high goal difficulty, the opposite pattern occurs. These predictions suggest that highly committed performers will attempt to make their performance conform to their goals, whether they are easy or difficult, more than will less committed performers, thus highlighting the importance of maintaining challenging goals. General goal-setting research has confirmed that a number of factors can improve commitment, including the authority of the person assigning the goals (e.g., Latham, Erez, & Locke, 1988; Latham & Lee, 1986; Latham & Yukl, 1975; Oldham, 1975), peer influences (e.g., Matsui, Kakuyama, & Onglatco, 1987; Rakestraw & Weiss, 1981), competition (e.g.,

Locke & Shaw, 1984; Mitchell, Rothman, & Liden, 1985; Shalley, Oldham, & Porac, 1987), public disclosure of goals (e.g., Hayes et al., 1985; Hollenbeck, Williams, & Klein, 1989), incentives and rewards (e.g., Huber, 1985; Riedel, Nebeker, & Cooper, 1988; Terborg, 1976), and goal participation (e.g., Earley, 1985; Earley & Kanfer, 1985; Erez, 1986; Erez, Earley, & Hulin, 1985).

Somewhat surprisingly, Locke and Latham's (1990) review of the goal participation literature concluded that participation has a negligible effect on enhancing goal effectiveness through increased commitment. A number of studies (e.g., Boyce & Wayda, 1994; Earley & Kanfer, 1985; Erbaugh & Barnett, 1986; Hollenbeck et al., 1989; A.M. Lee & Edwards, 1984; Racicot, Day, & Lord, 1991) have demonstrated that assigned goals are more difficult and inspire higher levels of effort and commitment than do self-set goals. Interestingly, Hinsz (1995) found that despite the higher performance in the assigned goal condition, participants in the self-set goal condition had more positive affect toward setting goals.

Sport goal research (Fairall & Rodgers, 1997; Kyllo & Landers, 1995; Racicot et al., 1991; Theodorakis, 1996) strongly supports the view that participation in goal setting enhances commitment. A meta-analysis by Kyllo and Landers (1995) demonstrated an effect size of .62 for goal participation enhancing performance. Their findings suggest that athletes who are involved in the goal-setting process are more likely to be committed to their goals, more likely to have input in developing effective goal strategies, and subsequently more likely to attain their goals than are athletes with assigned goals. Recent research with Olympic athletes (Weinberg et al., 2000) demonstrated that a variety of factors can enhance commitment, particularly intrinsic (e.g., participation in setting goals and/or sharing goals with others), extrinsic (e.g., making national teams or winning rewards, sponsorships, endorsements, or international medals), and social support (e.g., support from others, help in shaping goals) factors. This research also confirmed that writing goals down and posting them enhanced commitment. Not surprisingly, more effective goal-setters could be distinguished from less effective goal-setters based on their commitment in two areas: social support from significant others and extrinsic rewards (Burton et al., 2001).

Feedback   Locke and Latham's (1990) goal theory contends that feedback is an essential part of the goal-setting process and is necessary to enhance performance. In the most comprehensive review to date on the role that feedback plays in goal setting, Locke and Latham reviewed 33 studies comparing the effectiveness of goals plus feedback with either goals or feedback individually. They found that 17 of 18 studies demonstrated that the combination of goals and feedback was significantly better than goals alone, and 21 of 22 studies revealed that the combination was superior to feedback alone. Moreover, Mento et al. (1987) demonstrated through their meta-analysis of goal-setting research that when feedback was added to goal setting, productivity increased an additional 17%. Thus, the consensus of the general goal-setting literature is that feedback is an important and necessary moderator of goal-setting effects. Subsequent self-monitoring research (Earley, Northcraft, Lee, & Lituchy, 1990; Hutchison & Garstka, 1996; Locke, 1996; Martens, Hiralall, & Bradley, 1997; Mesch, Farh, & Podsakoff, 1994; Roberts & Reed, 1996; Shoenfelt, 1996; Tzetzis, Kioumourtzoglou, & Mavromatis, 1997; Vance & Colella, 1990; Zagumny & Johnson, 1992; Zimmerman & Kitsantas, 1996) further confirmed the importance of feedback on goal attainment. Locke's (1996) meta-analysis revealed that goal setting is most effective when progress feedback is given. He cautioned, however, that feedback is only effective when taken constructively. If feedback is viewed negatively, self-efficacy and effort expenditure toward the goal may be compromised. Similarly, Vance and Colella (1990) compared two types of feedback and concluded that when goal discrepancy feedback became too negative (i.e., the individual was far from reaching his or her goal), goals were abandoned. Interestingly, when performers were given past performance and negative goal discrepancy feedback, they shifted their goal to exceeding past performance rather than achieving the more difficult current goal. Thus, it appears that people revert to a more self-referential form of comparison when objective goal difficulty is too high.

Research Testing the Competitive Goal-Setting Model–3

As mentioned earlier, the original CGS model elicited much discussion but little testing of model predictions. Based on initial justification for the development of the CGS model (Burton, 1992, 1993) and subsequent research that tested specific model predictions, we conclude from our most recent review that preliminary support is still solidly in place for the efficacy of the model as a conceptual framework for guiding goal-setting research and application.

Burton (1989b) did not test goal-setting styles or even compare performance versus outcome goals

directly. Pilot testing suggested that most collegiate athletes adopted outcome goals as their top priority, primarily because of the attractive extrinsic rewards attached to positive social comparison (e.g., medals, trophies, recognition, and fame). Thus, Burton (1989b) instituted a season-long goal-setting training (GST) program designed to teach members of a collegiate swim team to set performance goals as their highest priority. Burton then compared these swimmers' competitive cognitions and performance to another conference team that received no GST intervention and was assumed to set predominantly outcome goals. Across the five-month intervention, Burton found that with training, GST swimmers became more performance-oriented and more skilled at setting challenging but realistic goals. By the conference championships at the end of the season, GST swimmers demonstrated more positive competitive cognitions, particularly reduced cognitive anxiety and increased self-confidence, and greater performance improvement than did non-GST swimmers.

Kingston and Hardy (1997) also failed to test goal-setting styles directly. But if we can assume that the control group in this study focused on outcome to evaluate performance in the absence of any process or performance standards, then Kingston and Hardy demonstrated that performance-related goals are superior to their outcome-related counterparts in the development of positive competitive cognitions and performance improvement. Moreover, results revealed that golfing performance significantly improved for the process-goal group from the beginning to the middle of the intervention and for the performance-goal group from the beginning to the end of the intervention, whereas the control group did not significantly improve its golfing performance across the yearlong intervention. Competitive cognition data also confirmed that the two performance treatment groups reported lower cognitive anxiety than did the control group, whereas the process-goal group reported significantly higher self-efficacy, cognitive anxiety control, and concentration than did the performance-goal or control groups. Thus, these data provide partial support for the CGS–3 model.

Pierce and Burton (1998) designed a study to test model predictions directly in conjunction with an eight-week GST intervention program developed for female junior high school gymnasts. Gymnasts were categorized into goal-setting-style groups by both clinical and empirical procedures (i.e., 84% agreement on group assignment between methods), and SO, FO, and PO gymnasts were compared on competitive cognitions and performance across five meets. Consistent with model predictions, none of the FO gymnasts competed in even one event for all five meets, and most succeeded in avoiding social comparison by refusing to take part in weekly tryouts to win a spot in the competitive lineup. Results comparing gymnasts' performance for their most important event revealed a significant group-by-time interaction that was consistent with model predictions, whereas similar analyses for competitive cognitions demonstrated trends in the predicted directions, although greater variability in scores prevented these findings from reaching statistical significance for this relatively small sample. As predicted, PO gymnasts significantly improved their performance across meets, whereas somewhat surprisingly, SO performers experienced a slight decrease in their performance over the course of the season. Finally, results of postseason GST program evaluations revealed significant group differences; PO gymnasts rated the GST program more favorably than did SO or FO performers.

Similarly, Burton and Sharples (2007) conducted a GST intervention with three female collegiate cross-country runners: one PO, the second SO, and the third a SO athlete who became much more PO during the season. Case study results generally confirmed model predictions. First, the PO runner developed the most positive and productive competitive cognitions and improved her performance (i.e., both time and place) the most, both across the 13-week season and compared with the previous season. Second, the SO runner had the most anxiety and confidence problems throughout the season, particularly at big meets such as the conference championships, and her performance improved little during the season or compared with the previous season. Finally, the competitive cognitions and performance of the third runner, who started out SO but made a transition to PO by the end of the season, were intermediary to those of her PO and SO teammates. Her performance at the conference championships was significantly faster than what she had run the previous year, in part because she displayed her lowest anxiety and highest self-confidence levels of the season.

As part of a larger study on the goal patterns of Olympic athletes, Burton et al. (2007) generally supported theoretical predictions about the impact of goal-setting styles on athletes' goal patterns. The CGS–3 model predicts that SO and PO athletes will respond similarly over the short run and during success experiences whereas differences between these two goal-setting styles will only emerge slowly over time or under failure conditions. Burton and his colleagues tested these predictions by first assessing the goal-setting styles of 338 Olympic athletes in 12 sports using empirical procedures that grouped performers on their self-confidence and competitive orientation scores. Results investigating differences in the goal patterns of these goal-setting style groups revealed that most athletes were empirically categorized as PO (54%), followed by SO (24%) and FO (22%). Moreover, findings demonstrated little difference between the goal patterns of SO and PO athletes, although PO athletes were significantly higher on their frequency of setting long-term goals. FO athletes were significantly lower on almost all goal frequency, effectiveness, commitment, and barrier subscales than were the other two groups. Interestingly, PO athletes had more sport and goal-setting experience and made more international and Olympic teams than did SO athletes, who in turn were significantly higher on these four variables than were FO athletes. Overall, this survey investigation provides moderate support for the CGS–3 model, although it is the first to use cluster analysis to identify goal-setting styles.

Support for the CGS–3 model is not unanimous. Kyllo and Landers's (1995) meta-analysis of goal-setting research in sport and exercise offers the major contradictory finding. Their review concluded that outcome goals are superior to performance goals in stimulating performance improvement. Kyllo and Landers drew this conclusion based on several questionable assumptions. First, they concluded that "absolute goals," in which everyone is working toward the same standards, are superior to "relative goals," in which goals target individual performance objectives and performance levels. Kyllo and Landers argued that absolute goals are equivalent to outcome goals because of the common goal, and relative goals are similar to performance goals because they focus on individual performance. But their logic seems flawed. They defined absolute goals as "a standard shared or common to all athletes." Performers, however, may have both performance and outcome goals in common, making this argument shaky at best. Relative goals that focus on individual performance obviously may focus on both performance and outcome targets, again suggesting that the performance–outcome distinction is not consistent with Kyllo and Landers's absolute–relative dimension. Second, their performance–outcome conclusion is based on an interaction between goal difficulty and goal type, so that moderately difficult goals specified in absolute terms have significantly higher mean effect sizes

(.91) than do moderately difficult goals specified in relative terms (effect size = .36). Finally, Kyllo and Landers excluded the Burton (1989b) study from their analyses for methodological reasons (i.e., could not compute an effect size), even though it was the one study that most directly tested the performance-versus-outcome predictions of interest.

In a final major test of the CGS–3 model, Lerner and Locke (1995) attempted to test the mediating effects of self-efficacy and goal orientation on the goal–performance relationship. Consistent with Locke's (1991) predictions, personal goals and self-efficacy completely mediated the effects of motivational orientation on performance, suggesting that self-efficacy has a greater effect on performance than does motivational orientation. Several methodological problems, however, seem to confound their results. First, they used the total Sport Orientation Questionnaire score rather than individual subscale scores, so the effects of performance, outcome, and competitiveness were assessed in combination rather than individually. Second, goals were assigned to participants in this study, but accurate assessment of the role of motivational orientation requires that performers be free to set their own goals. Finally, the effects of goal orientation are most likely to affect performance for an ego-involving task in which success is highly important rather than the simple sit-up task that was used. Despite these methodology problems, Lerner and Locke (1995) confirmed that both goal orientation and self-efficacy were significantly related to performance, providing partial support for the CGS–3 model. Our review of goal focus research revealed that 14 of 15 studies (i.e., 93%) supported the efficacy of using a combination of process, performance, and outcome goals rather than using any of these goals individually (see table 15.1).

Two conclusions seem warranted from this review of research that tests the CGS–3 model. First, a great deal more testing of CGS–3 model predictions is needed. Second, the limited research to date provides moderate support for model predictions, although independent model tests using larger sample sizes in ecologically valid settings are needed to evaluate the true efficacy of the model.

Choosing the Right Type of Goal

Although the overall effectiveness of goals is clearly the most extensively researched goal-setting topic, goal attribute research has been a close second (Locke & Latham, 1990). Goal attribute research focuses on determining what types of goals are most effective in enhancing performance. This section highlights research that assesses the efficacy of five goal types frequently used in sport, including goal specificity, goal difficulty, goal valence, goal proximity, and goal collectivity.

Goal Specificity

Early reviews of the general goal-specificity literature (Chidester & Grigsby, 1984; Latham & Lee, 1986; Locke et al., 1981; Mento et al., 1987; Tubbs, 1986) concluded that goal specificity, or precision, enhances performance. Locke and his colleagues (1981) found that 51 of 53 goal-specificity studies partially or completely supported the premise that specific goals promote better performance than general, do-your-best goals or no goals, whereas several meta-analytic reviews (Chidester & Grigsby, 1984; Latham & Lee, 1986; Mento et al., 1987) confirmed that goal specificity consistently improved performance.

Locke and Latham's (1990) more recent revision of goal-setting theory, however, predicted that goal specificity is a less important goal attribute than goal difficulty and will contribute primarily to enhancing performance consistency rather than performance quality. Locke and Latham hypothesized that making difficult goals specific will further enhance performance because specific goals make it more difficult for a person to feel successful with performance that fails to meet the goal. They further argued that when goals are vague, people more readily give themselves the benefit of the doubt in evaluating performance and rate a relatively lower level of performance as acceptable. For example, Kernan and Lord (1989) found that when participants were provided with varying types of negative feedback, those with no specific goals generally evaluated their performance more positively than did those who had specific, difficult goals.

Locke and Latham (1990) concluded that goal specificity does not have a direct performance enhancement effect; rather, goal specificity interacts with goal difficulty to influence performance. Thus, specific, easy goals may actually be less effective than vague, hard goals (Locke, Chah, Harrison, & Lustgarten, 1989). Locke and Latham (1990) hypothesized that when goal difficulty is controlled, the major effect of goal specificity is to reduce performance variance by reducing interpretative leeway in evaluating success. In support of this prediction, Locke et al. (1989) separated the effects of goal difficulty and goal specificity and found that the more specific the goal was, the less the performance varied. Therefore, goal specificity seems to be an important attribute of effective goals, but its effect is most prominent when combined with goal difficulty to maintain stringent standards for success, thereby reducing performance variability. Interestingly, goal-specificity research in sport has not looked at the effects of specificity independent of goal difficulty, although approximately 16 of 26 studies in sport (i.e., 62%) have partially or strongly support the prediction that athletes who set specific goals perform significantly better than do performers who set general, do-your-best or no goals (see figure 15.1). It is unclear, however, whether these effects would remain if goal difficulty effects were partialled out.

Goal Difficulty

Locke and Latham's (1990) goal-setting theory postulates a positive linear relationship between goal difficulty and performance, primarily because difficult goals prompt greater effort and persistence than do easy goals. But goal-setting theory acknowledges that as people reach the upper limits of their ability at high goal difficulty levels, performance reaches a plateau. Nevertheless, the consensus of nearly 200 general goal-setting studies strongly supported this goal difficulty hypothesis. Locke and Latham found that 91% of the 192 goal difficulty studies that they reviewed demonstrated positive (140 studies) or contingently positive (35 studies) relationships between difficult goals and performance. Moreover, four meta-analyses of goal difficulty research (Chidester & Grigsby, 1984; Mento et al., 1987; Tubbs, 1986; Wood et al., 1987) demonstrated mean effect sizes ranging from .52 to .82, representing performance increments from 10.4% to 16.4%. Thus, general goal-setting reviews strongly support the goal difficulty hypothesis, and a number of more recent studies (Chesney & Locke, 1991; Ruth, 1996; White, Kjelgaard, & Harkins, 1995; Wood & Locke, 1990) have further supported this prediction. Nevertheless, research has shown that as goals exceed individuals' performance capability, people will abandon excessively difficult goals in favor of more realistic self-set goals.

Surprisingly, sport goal research generally contradicts the goal difficulty hypothesis (see table 15.1). Initial goal difficulty research by Weinberg and his colleagues (Hall, Weinberg, & Jackson, 1987; Weinberg, Bruya, Jackson, & Garland, 1986) was the first to question the goal difficulty hypothesis. Hall et al. (1987) compared hand dynamometer endur-

ance performance of performers randomly assigned to three goal conditions: Do your best, improve by 40 seconds, and improve by 70 seconds. Although the researchers confirmed that participants who were assigned to the two specific-improvement conditions performed better than their do-your-best counterparts, no goal difficulty effects were found between the specific goal conditions. Similarly, Weinberg et al. (1986) found no goal difficulty effects for participants assigned to easy, moderate, and extremely hard goal conditions who performed a sit-up task for five weeks.

Our review found that only 14 of 24 studies (i.e., 58%) supported goal difficulty predictions (see table 15.1). A number of studies not only failed to demonstrate hypothesized goal difficulty effects but also contradicted the prediction that unrealistically high goals will impair performance (see table 15.1). Interestingly, recent research surveying goal practices in sport (Weinberg et al., 1993, 2000) has demonstrated that most collegiate and Olympic athletes prefer moderately difficult, rather than difficult, goals and that more effective goal-setters (Burton et al., 1998, 2005) set moderately difficult goals more frequently than difficult ones. Moreover, reviews of sport goal research (Kyllo & Landers, 1995; Weinberg, 1994) have revealed that moderately difficult goals are more effective than difficult goals in sport, accounting for an effect size of .53.

Several explanations are offered for the contradictory findings for goal difficulty between the sport and general goal literatures. First, researchers' operationalization of goal difficulty may differ between general and sport domains. Locke (1991) suggested that a difficult goal is one that no more than 10% of participants can achieve, although there is little evidence that researchers in either general or sport goal research have consistently used this criterion. A goal that only 5% to 10% of performers can accomplish may be too difficult, prompting low goal acceptance and motivating performers to set more realistic goals on their own (i.e., spontaneous goal setting; Kyllo & Landers, 1995).

Second, Campbell and Furrer (1995) suggested that competition may mediate goal difficulty effects. Results investigating the effects of competition on goal-setting performance in a math class demonstrated that across three goal conditions (i.e., easy, moderate, and difficult), participants performing in the noncompetitive environment significantly outperformed their counterparts in the competitive environment. Although the mean number of problems attempted across conditions did not vary, competitive students made significantly more mistakes than did their noncompetitive classmates, suggesting that competition may reduce goal effects by either increasing anxiety or reducing concentration. Interestingly, Lerner and Locke (1995) found that competition did not mediate goal effects on sport performance. Because of the competitive nature of sport and the degree to which athletes compete in most situations, further investigation of the role of competition as a mediator of goal difficulty results seems warranted.

Goal Valence

Sport practitioners often encourage athletes to set goals in positive terms, focusing on what they want to accomplish (e.g., two hits in four at-bats) rather than what they hope to avoid (e.g., striking out or going 0 for 4; Gould, 2006). Kirschenbaum (1984), however, argued against the conventional wisdom of this goal-setting strategy. Based on an extensive review of research on self-regulation, Kirschenbaum (1984) concluded that positively focused goals are most effective for new or difficult skills (e.g., Johnston-O'Connor & Kirschenbaum, 1984; Kirschenbaum, Ordman, Tomarken, & Holtzbauer, 1982) but that negatively focused goals that emphasize minimizing mistakes are more effective for well-learned skills (e.g., Kirschenbaum, Wittrock, Smith, & Monson, 1984). We were unable to find any sport research on goal valence, suggesting that additional research is needed to clarify valence effects in sport domains.

Goal Proximity

Burton (1992) defined long-term goals as any objective whose attainment is expected six or more weeks into the future, whereas any goal of shorter duration is a short-term goal. Locke and Latham's (1990) goal-setting theory makes no specific predictions about the efficacy of short-term versus long-term goals. Existing reviews of goal proximity research (Kirschenbaum, 1985; Locke & Latham, 1990) have revealed equivocal results, prompting confusion about what specific goal proximity recommendations to make to practitioners. Consider these divergent conceptual perspectives on goal proximity.

Clinical researchers (e.g., Bandura, 1986) believe that short-term goals are more effective because they provide more frequent evaluation of success, thus stimulating development of self-confidence when goals are attained and motivation regardless of the outcome. Short-term goals should be critical in preventing procrastination and premature discour-

agement. Burton (1989b) emphasized other positive attributes of short-term goals, contending that short-term goals are more flexible and controllable. Because short-term goals are more flexible, they can be readily raised or lowered to maintain optimal challenge levels. Moreover, the controllability of short-term goals makes it easier for performers to take credit for success as indicative of high ability and a strong work ethic.

Proponents of long-term goals (e.g., Kirschenbaum, 1985) theorize that long-term goals facilitate greater performance improvement because they foster "protracted choice." They argue that too-frequent goal assessment may prompt excessive evaluation, making it difficult to remain focused on performance because social comparison concerns become more salient (Nicholls, 1984a, 1992). Performers may feel like pawns because they perceive goals as controlling rather than informational (e.g., deCharms, 1976; Deci & Ryan, 1985). Thus, long-term goals would allow short-term flexibility that prevents discouragement should people fail to attain daily goals.

Locke and Latham's (1990) review suggests that proximity has not been a popular topic for goal-setting research, perhaps because of the limited influence of this goal attribute on goal-setting efficacy or the lengthy duration of studies required to test this attribute. Although research conducted in both sport and nonsport settings (Bandura & Simon, 1977; Bar-Eli, Hartman, & Levy-Kolker, 1994; Borrelli & Mermelstein, 1994; Hall & Byrne, 1988; Kirschenbaum, 1985; Latham & Locke, 1991) suggests that long-term goals provide people with direction for their achievement strivings, these findings also confirm that the motivational effect of long-term goals depends on establishing short-term goals to serve as intermediate steps in the achievement process (Bandura & Simon, 1977; Hall & Byrne, 1988; Locke, Cartledge, & Knerr, 1970). In sport, goal proximity findings are similarly equivocal; the number of studies that investigate long-term versus short-term goals is limited. The consensus of sport goal proximity research (Kyllo & Landers, 1995; Tenenbaum, Weinberg, Pinchas, Elbaz, & Bar-Eli, 1991) is that long-term goals enhance performance most effectively when short-term goals are used to mark progress. Kyllo and Landers's (1995) meta-analysis of the sport goal research demonstrated an effect size of .48 for the combined effect of short- and long-term goals on performance. In our review, summarized in table 15.1, 8 of 13 sport studies (i.e., 62%) found that a combination of short- and long-term goals was superior to using either type of goal individually. This support for a combination of goal lengths was much stronger than the evidence found in our previous review. Future goal proximity research is needed not only to confirm the superiority of a combination of short-term and long-term goals but to also identify the most effective time frames for short- and long-term goals and to verify the relationship between these two types of goals.

Goal Collectivity

Group or team goals are objectives established for the collective performance of two or more people. According to Brawley, Carron, and Widmeyer (1992), team goals tend to be general rather than specific, and the focus of team goals often varies considerably between practice and competition. In practice, these authors found that team goals were process oriented (89.9%) rather than outcome oriented (10.1%), focusing on skill or strategy (66.1%), effort (29.3%), and fitness (4.6%). Conversely, competitive goals were almost evenly split between outcome (53.1%) and process (46.9%), focusing on skill or strategy (43.5%), outcomes (41.5%), and effort (15.0%). Team goals have been found to affect psychological variables such as team satisfaction, cohesion, and motivation as well as performance (Brawley, Carron, & Widmeyer, 1993).

Locke and Latham's (1990) goal-setting theory makes no predictions about the effectiveness of group or team goals versus individual goals, but available reviews of group goal-setting research (Carroll, 1986; Kondrasuk, 1981; Locke & Latham, 1990; Rodgers & Hunter, 1989) reveal that team goals enhance performance as effectively as do individual goals. Locke and Latham's review showed that 38 of 41 group goal-setting studies (93%) demonstrated positive or contingently positive performance enhancement effects, virtually the same success rate as that for individual goal-setting findings. Locke and Latham concluded that team goals, in addition to or instead of individual goals, are necessary or at least facilitative when the task is a group or team task rather than an individual one. Our review of goal collectivity research in sport demonstrated that six of eight studies (i.e., 75%) supported or partially supported the value of group or team goals.

Although the efficacy of group or team goals has been confirmed, direct comparisons of the effectiveness of group or team versus individual goals have been relatively limited, in both sport and nonsport settings (Hinsz, 1995; Larey & Paulus, 1995; Shalley, 1995). Larey and Paulus assigned participants to no-goal, individual-goal, and interactive-goal conditions for a brainstorming task. They found that individual-goal performers set more difficult goals (i.e., number of ideas generated) than did their counterparts in the team-goal condition. Low perceptions of other team members' ability were believed to lower the difficulty of team goals.

Goal collectivity is probably not an either–or proposition. Team goals offer direction for establishing appropriate types and levels of individual goals that result in the specific motivational benefits to individual performers. In fact, social-loafing research (e.g., C.J. Hardy & Latane, 1988; Jackson & Williams, 1985; Latane, 1986; Latane, Williams, & Harkins, 1979) predicts that group or team goals, without accompanying individual goals, may reduce performance by prompting social loafing. Social loafing is a group performance phenomenon in which individuals working together on a task tend to exert less individual effort than when they perform the same task alone (Jackson & Williams, 1985). Although not extensively studied in sport settings, social loafing has been shown to occur for a variety of physically demanding tasks (e.g., Ingham, Levinger, Graves, & Peckham, 1974; Kerr & Brunn, 1981; Latane et al., 1979).

Research has confirmed that social loafing diminishes or ceases to exist when individual performance is identifiable (Williams, Harkins & Latane, 1981) and when individuals perceive that they have made a unique contribution to the group effort or have performed difficult tasks (Harkins & Petty, 1982). Thus, the implication of social-loafing research for goal collectivity is that individuals who set group or team goals are prone to loaf and perform below their capabilities unless they also set individual goals that hold each team member responsible for a specific level of performance and are perceived as indispensable for team success. Teams need to use the role concept for setting individual goals to maximize identifiability and accountability. Thus, individual goals are set based on the role that each player needs to fulfill to maximize team effectiveness. Regrettably, goal collectivity predicts that a combination of group or team and individual goals should maximize performance have not been tested adequately to allow firm conclusions about team goals.

Based on the consensus of goal attribute research, the following recommendations can be made for the types of goals that practitioners should set in sport. First, performers should set a combination of process, performance, and outcome goals. Outcome goals should be focused primarily on increasing practice motivation, whereas during competition athletes should concentrate on process and performance goals. Second, to improve both the quality and the consistency of performance, goals should be specific, measurable, and moderately difficult. Third, goals should be positive and focused on attaining desirable performance outcomes rather than on either eliminating performance problems or avoiding potential pitfalls. Finally, although research on goal proximity and collectivity remains equivocal, practitioners should use a combination of short- and long-term goals and individual and team goals to promote maximal performance gains.

Measurement Issues in Goal Setting

As with most research in the behavioral sciences, measurement issues seem to dictate the quantity and quality of goal-setting research produced. The current status of goal-setting research suggests that two major measurement issues currently limit goal research and consequently limit our conceptual and practical understanding of how goals can be used most effectively. These issues include identifying the role of goal hierarchies in the goal-setting process and using measurement techniques to assess athletes' goal-setting styles more accurately.

Investigating Goal Hierarchies

A goal hierarchy is a systematic way of arranging and using goals based on a structured prioritization system. Most people set multiple goals for different aspects of their lives and various periods. Their goals typically focus on differential performance objectives. For example, athletes might concurrently have sport, academic, social, and career goals, all of which they value highly and pursue simultaneously. Similarly, athletes often set goals for a variety of periods, including dream, long-term, moderate-term, and short-term goals. Finally, athletes may set different types of goals that focus on different aspects of performance. These could include outcome goals (e.g., to win the next game), performance goals (e.g., to score 12 points, grab 10 rebounds, and make 4 assists), and process goals to accomplish those performance goals (e.g., to be prepared to shoot when receiving a pass, to block the opponent out as far from the basket as possible, and to turn and face the basket after receiving a pass).

The problem with multiple goals is developing a system to keep them straight and knowing when and how to focus on each type of goal at the appropriate time. For example, Hardy and his colleagues (L. Hardy, 1997; Kingston & Hardy, 1997) suggested that elite performers may focus outcome goals on long-term objectives, such as winning a world or Olympic championship, to sustain their motivation over long, difficult training periods or to increase motivation during a monotonous practice. In contrast, athletes use both performance and process goals to enhance short-term skill development and improvement, perform their best for a specific competition, or focus during critical moments of important competitions. These issues regarding goal focus and proximity are further complicated by athletes' needs to set goals in other domains to enhance their quality of life.

One of my former doctoral students, Greg South (2004), has tackled a goal hierarchy for short-, moderate-, and long-term goals using an approach he termed *the roadmap* (see figure 15.2). He has attempted to link goal temporality to self-confidence development, predicting that short-term goals promote increases in self-efficacy, moderate-term goals enhance state self-confidence, and long-term goals prompt changes in trait self-confidence. As indicated by the attached roadmap for tennis, short-term goals represent fundamental skills (i.e., component techniques and strategies) that the player develops systematically to form performance systems (e.g., forehand, backhand, serve, volley). As the intermediate goals represented by these feedback loops improve overall performance systems and become more accessible in actual play, they contribute to the player's overall game and help him or her progress up the ladder of success toward achieving a long-term goal such as playing the pro tour.

From a research standpoint, measurement strategies need to be developed to produce reliable and valid assessments of athletes' goal hierarchies, including goal focus and proximity factors across different achievement domains. Moreover, measurement techniques are needed to improve understanding of goal priorities, including how personal priorities are developed for different types of goals, how priorities might change across situations, and what situational factors prompt a change in priorities to athletes' goal hierarchies. From a practical standpoint, athletes need help understanding how to organize and prioritize their goals most effectively. Specific guidelines also are needed to help athletes prevent goal overload and to determine what types of goals they should focus on in specific situations to maximize motivation, self-confidence, and performance.

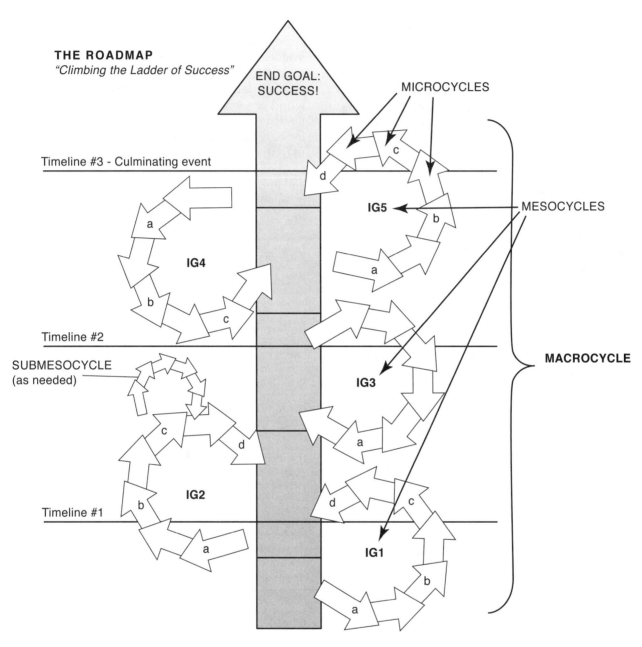

THE ROADMAP
"Climbing the Ladder of Success"

END GOAL: SUCCESS!

MICROCYCLES

Timeline #3 - Culminating event

IG4

IG5

MESOCYCLES

Timeline #2

SUBMESOCYCLE (as needed)

IG3

MACROCYCLE

IG2

Timeline #1

IG1

Intermediate goal 1: stroke mechanics

Short-term subgoals

a. Timing

b. Enhanced footwork skills

c. Positive and negative horizontal movement

d. Swinging vertically

Intermediate goal 2: physical conditioning

Short-term subgoals

a. Strength

b. Endurance

c. Stamina

d. Recovery

Intermediate goal 3: tactics

Short-term subgoals

a. Advanced tactical goals

b. Advanced tactical training

Intermediate goal 4: attacking skills

Short-term subgoals

a. Transitional strokes

b. Volleys

c. Overheads

Intermediate goal 5: psychological skills

Short-term subgoals

a. Goal-setting

b. Anger management

c. Arousal control

d. Self-talk

Note:

macrocycles = long-term goals

mesocycles = intermediate goals

microcycles = short-term subgoals

Figure 15.2 The goal roadmap.

Reprinted, by permission, from Col. Gregory South.

Measuring Goal-Setting Styles

The ultimate utility of goal-setting styles will hinge, in part, on researchers' ability to develop effective instruments to measure them. One approach to testing goal-setting styles is to conduct a laboratory study using a learned helplessness paradigm (Elliott & Dweck, 1988) in which goal orientation and perceived ability are experimentally manipulated to investigate their effect on motivation and performance variables. An additional need is to develop instruments that can measure existing goal-setting styles in real sport situations so that their consequences can be investigated in ecologically valid settings. Regrettably, the task of developing reliable and valid instruments to measure PO, SO, and FO goal-setting styles has proved challenging for three reasons. First, reliable and valid instruments must be identified or developed to measure both goal orientation and perceived ability. Second, joint scores for goal orientation and perceived ability that accurately bound each goal-setting style must be identified. Finally, because powerful situational factors seem to influence goal-setting styles, both state and trait versions of goal-setting style instrumentation must be developed.

Several reliable and valid instruments have been developed to measure goal orientation in sport, including Duda and Nicholls's (1992) Task and Ego Orientation in Sport Questionnaire, Gill and Deeter's (1988) Sport Orientation Questionnaire, Roberts and Balague's (1991) Perceptions of Success Questionnaire, and Vealey's (1986) Competitive Orientation Inventory. Duda and Whitehead (1998) provided a complete description of these goal perspective measures and their relative strengths and weaknesses. Both the Task and Ego Orientation in Sport Questionnaire and the Competitive Orientation Inventory have been used to assess goal-setting styles empirically, and both measures have problems with accurately categorizing athletes who are on the borderline between the two goal orientations. Further research is needed to determine which existing measure is most strongly related to goal setting as well as which best categorizes goal-setting styles.

At least two reliable and valid instruments have been developed to measure perceived ability-related constructs in sport, including Fox and Corbin's (1989) Physical Self-Perception Profile and Vealey's (1986, 1988) State–Trait Sport Confidence Inventory. Several reviews (Feltz & Chase, 1998; Fox, 1998) provide more complete descriptions of competence measures and their relative strengths and weaknesses. Both instruments have been used to assess goal-setting styles in sport, but results have been equivocal. The decision about which instruments provide the most valid measure of goal-setting styles awaits future research. In the meantime, researchers will have to select instruments to measure goal-setting styles in sport based on theoretical rationale and personal preferences.

Besides needing reliable and valid instruments that can assess goal orientation and perceived ability in sport, researchers need to identify the specific score profiles on each instrument that can define each goal-setting style. Moreover, the CGS–3 model views goal-setting styles as both (a) a general predisposition to set certain kinds of goals across most situations (i.e., psychological trait) and (b) a momentary goal-setting behavior that reflects the influence of particular situational factors (i.e., psychological state). For example, the volleyball team described in the introduction typically adopted a PO or SO goal-setting style but was influenced by powerful situational factors to adopt an FO style in that season. To assess the influence of goal-setting styles on motivation and performance accurately, researchers need to develop measurement instruments that assess both trait and state goal-setting styles so that research can assess the stability of these styles across situations.

Future Research Directions

Although goal setting is one of the most heavily researched areas in sport psychology, several important issues await future research. Three areas of research seem to be critical to obtaining a better understanding of goal setting and using goals to enhance performance in sport and exercise. First, we need to understand the optimal level of goal difficulty for specific individuals and situations as well as how to help practitioners adjust goal difficulty to optimal levels. Second, we need to know the effect of self-monitoring and evaluation on goal-setting effectiveness as well as the optimal amount and type of self-monitoring or evaluation. Finally, we need to know the role that action plans play in goal-setting effectiveness and ways to develop successful action plans.

Identify Optimal Goal Difficulty The CGS–3 model predicts that establishing goals that are too difficult for SO and FO athletes can prompt diffidence, anxiety, and attentional distraction that impair performance. This prediction suggests that goal-setting styles have an optimal goal difficulty range for best performance. Several researchers have attempted to provide strategies to determine appropriate levels of goal difficulty (e.g., O'Block & Evans, 1984), but few goal-setting studies have attempted to operationalize the goal difficulty level that will foster best performance. Although Burton and his colleagues (Burton, Daw, Williams-Rice, & Phillips, 1989) attempted to assess typical goal difficulty levels for different goal-setting styles in a basketball class, little is known about how well these goal difficulty ranges generalize to more competitive situations or other sports. Several additional questions concerning how to optimize goal difficulty need to be addressed: How should goal difficulty be adjusted as key situational factors, such as importance of the competition, change? How does personal goal difficulty influence performance? Is the relationship between goal difficulty and performance linear or curvilinear?

Quantify the Frequency of and Strategies for Goal Monitoring and Evaluation Kirschenbaum (1984) concluded that self-monitoring and self-evaluation are necessary but not sufficient to maintain effective self-regulation. Drawing on Carver and Scheier's (1981) self-focused attention model, Kirschenbaum and Tomarken (1982) argued that increasing self-awareness through self-monitoring typically increases attempts to match behavior to goals. But a trade-off seems to be inherent in self-monitoring and evaluation. If self-monitoring and evaluation are too infrequent, athletes will have difficulty perceiving improvement in competence, a necessary step to enhancing intrinsic motivation (e.g., Deci & Ryan, 1985; Vallerand, Gauvin, & Halliwell, 1986). But if monitoring and evaluation are too frequent, maintaining a performance orientation may be difficult because extensive evaluation heightens outcome concerns (e.g., Nicholls, 1984a). Frequent evaluation may also prompt people to feel like pawns because they perceive goals as controlling rather than informational (e.g., deCharms, 1976; Deci & Ryan, 1985; Vallerand et al., 1986). In fact, some self-regulation research (Kirschenbaum & Tomarken, 1982) suggests that moderately specific and longer-term plans may facilitate self-control to a greater degree than do specific, short-term plans. Indeed, anecdotal evidence from 25 years of practical goal-setting work with athletes confirms that maintaining the same goals for weekly intervals seems to facilitate improvement more than changing goals daily does. Goal monitoring and evaluation questions that require further research include the following: Does excessive self-evaluation lower perceived ability? If so, how? What is the most effective way to provide

feedback to encourage development of both self-confidence and motivation? Can social support (e.g., the buddy system) facilitate self-monitoring?

Environmental Engineering and Developing Action Plans Goal-setting research assessing the moderating effects of task complexity (Mento et al., 1987) suggests that the motivational benefits of goals work only when athletes are practicing skills correctly and have good action plans for long-term skill development (e.g., Hall & Byrne, 1988). Thus, optimal skill development requires developing sound technique and then practicing the skill until it becomes highly automated. For complex skills, athletes must find competent coaches who can help them develop correct technique. Moreover, coaches must understand the basic principles of periodization of training so that they can develop accurate action plans that help athletes adjust goals appropriately during different phases of training or skill development (Bompa, 1999). Heckhausen and Strang (1988) demonstrated that performers who were more effective at developing action plans to modify exertion performed better on a simulated basketball task, particularly under stressful conditions, than did less action-oriented performers. One of the most difficult aspects of skill development is understanding when a learning strategy is appropriate and needs only systematic practice to automate skills and when a strategy is limited or ineffectual. In the second case, a new strategy must be developed to allow the athlete to reach his or her performance potential. Abandoning an effective strategy too soon is undesirable and will only lengthen the time necessary to automate skills. On the other hand, practicing an ineffective technique will prevent optimal skill development. One of the talents that separates effective coaches from ineffective ones is the ability to know the correct approach to use in a particular situation. Research is needed on a number of environmental engineering and action plan questions: Would formal problem-solving training facilitate the development of new strategies necessary to enhance complex skills? How does the coach know when to encourage athletes to practice existing strategies more diligently and when to modify task strategies to maximize skill development?

Conclusion

This chapter introduced the mental training tool of goal setting and described the primary functions of goals. Next, the fundamental goal concept in sport was highlighted and an updated competitive goal-setting (CGS–3) model was presented as a heuristic tool to integrate the motivational and stress management functions of goals into an overall conceptual framework that hypothesizes three distinct goal-setting styles. This model makes specific predictions about the attributes of each goal-setting style and their effect on goal responses and motivational consequences. Research supporting the CGS–3 model was reviewed. These findings provided moderate support for the CGS–3 model and the notion of goal-setting styles. An examination of goal attribute research documented the types of goals to set for goal specificity, goal difficulty, goal valence, goal proximity, and goal collectivity. Two important measurement issues inherent in the model and goal-setting implementation were discussed. Finally, two future directions for goal-setting research were proposed. These research questions highlighted the role of individual differences and goal implementation strategies in goal-setting effectiveness.

CHAPTER 16

The Flow Perspective of Optimal Experience in Sport and Physical Activity

Susan A. Jackson, PhD ■ Jay C. Kimiecik, PhD

THE SECRET OF LIFE IS ENJOYING THE PASSAGE OF TIME.

James Taylor

To achieve our overall purpose of examining optimal experience in physical activity from a flow perspective, we have divided the chapter into four main sections. The first section provides a brief rationale, a history of the study of optimal experience, and an overview of peak performance and peak experience—two terms that parallel or overlap with flow. We have included in this section an overview of the positive psychology movement that is emerging as a major focus for mainstream psychology. Flow has been identified as a focus of positive psychology research, and thus an examination of positive psychology provides a useful context for grounding research on flow. The second section provides a basic description of the flow model and its relevance to life. The third section overviews the research that has examined flow in various physical activity contexts. Within this analysis and synthesis of the research on flow, we present some theoretical, paradigmatic, and measurement issues that researchers might consider when studying flow in physical activity. Lastly, we provide some ideas and possible directions for future research examining optimal experience in physical activity contexts.

Much of sport and exercise psychology research over the past 30 years has attempted to understand how cognitive processes are related to athletes' behavior and performance, which are then linked in a variety of ways to different kinds of outcomes (e.g., winning or losing, attaining medals). Certainly, this type of research is essential to understanding—and helping—athletes and coaches with performance enhancement issues and concerns. An overreliance on this research focus, however, tends to ignore the core element of what it means to be human—subjective experience. For instance, understanding the relationship between an athlete's perception of confidence and his or her performance in a specific sporting event is quite different from understanding the meaning, or lived experience, of that event for the athlete.

One way to view this distinction is to conceptualize our humanness as a behavior–cognition–affect triad that focuses on the periphery of experience (see figure 16.1). Subjective experience forms the core and connects these three areas to create meaning in our lives. Subjective experience is the "bottom line" of existence (Csikszentmihalyi, 1982). To understand

athletes in a sport context, we must seek to describe and understand the quality of their experience. DeCharms & Muir (1978, p. 107) made this observation thirty years ago:

> Theories and data abound. Are we making major advances in understanding motivation? Let us suggest that they are minor. We continually overlook our major source of knowledge—a personal, nonobjective source which is at the heart of each minitheory but not acknowledged. Our methodologies fall short because they lead us into more and more detailed specification of external conditions for producing behavioral effects and ignore the critical variable, namely the way the person *experiences* (not perceives) the conditions that we so elaborately contrive.

Subjective experience, or states of consciousness, can be conceptualized along a continuum, from psychic entropy (disorder in consciousness) to psychic negentropy (contents of consciousness are in harmony with each other) (Csikszentmihalyi, 1990). When subjective experience of sport and exercise participants has been studied, investigation has historically focused more on the negative pole, addressing such areas as stress and anxiety (see work by Scanlan, Stein, & Ravizza, 1989, and Wankel & Kreisel, 1985, as examples of exceptions). Hence, we know much less about athletes' positive, or optimal, experiences than we do about their negative, or stressful, ones. If subjective experience is the essence of what it means to be human, then it makes sense to study all kinds of experience, positive as

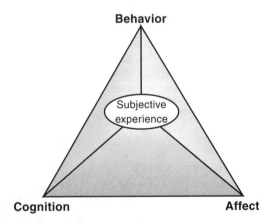

Figure 16.1 Subjective experience as the core of human experience.

well as negative. Sport and exercise contexts provide a rich laboratory for such exploration because participants' states of consciousness cover the entire gamut of the subjective experience continuum. The range of consciousness that physical activity elicits is remarkable, which makes it an ideal context in which to study subjective experience. We are using physical activity as the broad title and focus of our chapter to encompass the breadth of areas that could be addressed when examining the flow concept in settings involving human movement. As defined by Caspersen, Powell, and Christenson (1985), physical activity refers to any movement of the body associated with increases of energy expenditure above resting level. There are of course multiple motivations for engaging in physical activity, and it is our belief that flow has relevance to a myriad of forms and contexts. In this chapter, we review the expanding focus of flow research within sport and physical activity, and hope that others will recognize the significance of understanding optimal experience, and continue the development of research into this exciting phenomenon.

For a number of years both of us have been interested in learning more about the optimal experiences of sport and exercise participants, perhaps with the naive goal that we might optimize our own as well as others' physical activity experiences. A growing body of research in the area of positive activity experiences has the potential to broaden the knowledge base in sport and exercise psychology. We focus in this chapter on the research that has been conducted on optimal experience in physical activity from a flow perspective. Certainly, flow is not the only way to operationalize or examine optimal experience in physical activity. But flow is the optimal experience perspective with which we are most familiar, and it is the approach to studying optimal experience that has received the most attention in recent years.

Optimal Experience in Sport

More than thirty years ago, Csikszentmihalyi (1975) first published *Beyond Boredom and Anxiety*. This seminal work focusing on flow, which built on Maslow's (1968) pioneering efforts in the area of peak experience and self-actualization (Csikszentmihalyi, 1988), led to the development of optimal experience as an important area of study. At about this time Ravizza (1977) was also studying aspects of peak experience in sport. In the mid-1980s Garfield and Bennett (1984) and Loehr (1986) published

works that examined the characteristics of peak performance states in sport. Much overlap and considerable confusion pertain to the definition and operationalization of terms such as flow, peak performance, peak experience, joy, fun, and enjoyment. Authors such as Jackson (2000), Kimiecik and Harris (1996), and Wankel (1997) have attempted to address some of the ambiguity and overlap that exists with these kinds of constructs.

Optimal experience is a useful umbrella term for classifying positive states of consciousness in sport. Jackson and Wrigley (2004), drawing on recent well-being literature (e.g., Ryan & Deci, 2001), defined optimal experience as comprising multidimensional aspects of positive experiences in sport and exercise that provide both strong positive feelings associated with highest happiness (hedonistic psychology) and self-fulfilling experiences that result from exerting effort (eudaimonic psychology). Underneath this umbrella term *optimal experience* we can include concepts such as peak experience, peak performance, flow, enjoyment, and fun. Because of space constraints, we do not delve into a lengthy definitional discussion of these terms in this chapter. Those interested in definitional conundrums pertaining to optimal experience may wish to read articles, chapters, and books that review the topic (see Jackson, 2000; Jackson & Wrigley, 2004; Kimiecik & Harris, 1996; McInman & Grove, 1991; Podilchak, 1991; Privette & Bundrick, 1991; Wankel, 1997; Warner, 1987). Because peak performance and peak experience are closely aligned with flow states (Jackson, 1993), we will outline our views on these two forms of optimal experience as well as their potential link with flow.

Peak Performance

Peak performance is not inherently an optimal experience because the term has typically been defined as superior functioning that exceeds an individual's probable performance quality, or full use of potential, in any activity (Forbes, 1989; Privette, 1983). In the athletic realm, this term refers to the release of latent powers to perform optimally within a specific sport competition. Peak performance is idiosyncratic. An athlete who does not win the gold medal may still have a peak performance because she or he may have the performance of a lifetime. An athlete who goes well beyond any prior performance standard is likely to describe the event as a peak performance. An interesting question from a flow perspective concerns the kinds of psychological states that underlie a peak performance. Is a peak performance also an optimal experience? Studies typically show that athletes' thoughts and feelings are extremely positive when performing at their peak (see review by Williams & Krane, 1998). We have not found any evidence in the sport and exercise psychology research in which an athlete stated that he or she had a best performance and did not experience a variety of extremely positive psychological and emotional states. A number of studies support the notion that optimal, subjective experience underlies peak performances.

In a nonsport study, Privette and Bundrick (1991) found that full focus and a sense of self in clear process were the two primary elements of peak performance. In an interview study by Garfield and Bennett (1984), elite athletes reported such factors as being physically and mentally relaxed, confident, centered in the present, highly energized, extraordinarily aware, in control, and "in the cocoon" to describe their mental state during outstanding performances. In addition, these athletes had a sense that they were detached from the external environment and its distractions during their best performances. Loehr (1982) interviewed athletes about their experiences when performing at their best and cited a similar set of positive factors: high energy, fun and enjoyment, no pressure, optimism and positiveness, mental calmness, confidence, focused, and in control. In a qualitative study, Cohn (1991) found a set of peak performance factors reported by elite golfers that closely resemble those of Garfield and Bennett (1984) and Loehr (1982). Having a narrow focus of attention, being immersed in the present, feeling in control and confident, having no fear, and feeling physically and mentally relaxed were key characteristics of peak golfing performance. Eklund's (1994) interviews of collegiate wrestlers found that best performances were accompanied by an intense competitive focus and high confidence, findings that mirror those of Gould, Eklund, and Jackson (1992) based on their interviews with successful Olympic wrestlers.

We believe that flow serves as a useful concept for integrating the findings from previous studies that have examined the optimal psychological states or strategies typically associated with peak performances in sport contexts. As Jackson (2000) pointed out, flow states reflect optimal mental functioning, total focus, and complete absorption in a task. The notion that athletes perform their best when in flow is supported by findings from Jackson and Roberts (1992), who found correlational support for a link between flow and peak performance, operationally defined as one's best-ever performance. Qualitative analyses also supported a flow–peak performance

link; best performances were associated with flow state characteristics (Jackson & Roberts, 1992; Jackson, 1993). In a more recent study using the Flow State Scale (FSS; Jackson & Marsh, 1996), Jackson, Thomas, Marsh, & Smethurst (2001) found correlational support for relationships between flow and performance. Both an objective performance measure, finishing position, and (to a greater extent) a subjective measure of success correlated with flow scores on the FSS.

Although a close relationship between flow and peak performance is apparent, more research is needed to examine the specifics of the flow–peak performance link. For example, athletes in flow may not always perform at their peak. When does this occur? And conversely, when or how does an athlete perform at her or his peak without optimal mental states, such as flow? Future optimal experience research could address these kinds of questions. The empirical findings to date, however, along with an intuitive relatedness between flow and peak performance suggest that one important consequence of experiencing flow is optimal performance. Although we are intrigued by this relationship from a performance-enhancement perspective, we are hesitant in making too much of it. As Csikszentmihalyi (1988, p. 375) suggested, downplaying the connection between flow and peak performance may be best because "as soon as the emphasis shifts from the experience per se to what you can accomplish with it, we are back in the realm of everyday life ruled by extrinsic considerations."

Peak Experience

Maslow (1968) was one of the first researchers to examine peak experiences systematically across a variety of life dimensions. Maslow's work led him to define a peak experience as a moment of highest happiness in one's life. Although peak experiences are infrequent in the lives of most people, Maslow argued for their importance because they can lead to growth or actualization of the individual. Maslow developed an extensive list of peak experience factors, some of which were total attention, rich perceptions, time–space disorientation, perceptions of unity, and feelings of wonder and awe. Ravizza (1977, 1984) conducted one of the first attempts to examine the specific nature of athletes' peak experiences. He examined Maslow's concept of peak experience by asking athletes to describe their single most joyful moment while participating in their primary sport. Three common characteristics of sport peak experience emerged from Ravizza's analysis of the interview data: focused awareness leading to total absorption in the task, feelings of total control of self and the environment, and a sense of self-transcendence, in which the athlete described a complete merging of action and awareness. These three descriptors of peak experience in sport blend with those outlined earlier by Maslow.

Privette and Bundrick (1991) have been specifically interested in delineating the concepts of peak performance, peak experience, and flow. They define peak experience as intense joy, or a moment of highest happiness that is not necessarily performance related. The distinguishing characteristics of peak experience that Privette and Bundrick have uncovered are fulfillment, significance, and spirituality. In essence, peak experience seems to be more closely aligned with a positive emotions focus, whereas peak performance has more of a behavioral or outcome focus. Both may be considered extremely positive events that have some psychological and emotional commonalities. Note that studies that have examined peak experience in sport (e.g., Cohn, 1986; Ravizza, 1977) have focused on performance. We are not aware of any studies that found athletes' peak experiences to be unrelated to a peak performance. In addition, athletes' descriptions of their peak experiences (Ravizza, 1984) resemble closely the descriptions that athletes give of peak performances (Cohn, 1991).

In sum, peak performance is an episode of superior functioning, whereas peak experience is a moment of highest happiness and ecstasy. For example, for a basketball player a peak performance might be scoring 30 points in a game when he or she had been averaging 10 (superior functioning), and a peak experience may be a result of winning the conference championship (ecstasy, highest happiness). Note, however, that the player's peak experience may not be linked with his or her personal performance during the game. That is, the player may have performed poorly but because the outcome was extremely positive, a peak experience could still occur. Also, because peak experience is a subjective experience, winning the conference championship may or may not lead to a peak experience for every member of the team.

Relationships Among Flow, Peak Performance, and Peak Experience

The relationships among flow, peak performance, and peak experience can be complex. What do athletes think? We are only aware of one study (Jackson, 1993) where athletes have been asked their views

about the relationships among these three forms of optimal experience. Jackson defined these three constructs for elite athletes as (a) flow—a totally absorbing and rewarding experience, one that stood out from average; (b) peak performance—performing at an optimal level; and (c) peak experience—a time of highest happiness and fulfillment. She then asked the athletes how they viewed the relationship among these three experiences in their own sport participation. Predictably, the athletes offered a range of ideas about how these experiences were related. But there was little support from the athletes' perspectives for the independence of these constructs. Rather, support was found for the idea that boundaries between the three phenomena are flexible, and that often the same event may be a flow experience, a peak performance, and a peak experience. Seventy-five percent of the athletes said that flow was always part of their peak performances, and 71% said that flow was always involved in their peak experiences. The athletes viewed flow as an optimal mental state that led to their peak performances. Athletes who were able to achieve a peak performance without flow attributed the result to working very hard, being extremely fit, being able to control the performance, or being lucky.

Jackson (1993) also found that the athletes perceived both flow and peak experience to involve enjoyment, and this is where the athletes perceived the link between these two experiences to be strongest. The enjoyable aspect of flow stood out in the analyses of athletes' flow experiences as the most salient dimension, so the presence of a perceived interrelationship between flow and peak experience is not surprising. A peak experience that occurred without flow resulted from achievement of a valued goal, particularly through working hard, winning, exceeding expectations, or overcoming great odds. These views seem to lead to an identification of a peak experience after the fact, on reflection. For an experience to be enjoyed during its occurrence, a state involving flow seems more likely to be present than absent.

The findings with elite athletes, along with the other work examining peak experience and peak performance, indicate that understanding the role of optimal experience in sport is a complex task. Knowing to what extent these terms are describing the same or different experiences would help build a common understanding of optimal experiences. From a flow perspective, optimal psychological states probably underlie most peak performances, but we would be less certain in making such a connection between flow and peak experience. Peak experience may not necessarily involve flow (Jackson, 1993). As you will see shortly, flow states occur when perceived challenges and skills are in balance and above average. Based on this operationalization of flow, the intensity of a flow state can be much less than that of a peak experience. In addition, a peak performance may not lead to a peak experience, and an athlete can probably have a peak experience without having a peak performance. These relationships can become confusing, which means that this area is fertile ground for future research.

Although peak performance and peak experience are relevant to sport, these two concepts are not strongly grounded in psychosocial theory, which somewhat limits their usefulness for understanding athletes' experiences. Consequently, Csikszentmihalyi's work in the area of flow is appealing from a research perspective. Flow provides a theoretical framework with a substantive history of evidence from a diverse range of settings to support its contentions. In our view, flow is the essence of a positive performance state of mind, and it should become integral to the research examining the positive subjective experience of physical activity participants. In recent years, the body of research about flow has grown, both within and outside physical activity contexts, demonstrating the growing recognition of the criticality of the flow construct. Concurrently, a substantial shift has occurred in acceptance of what makes up the study of psychology. We will overview this latter development, which has included as part of its mission furthering the understanding of positive experiences such as flow.

Grounding Flow in Positive Psychology

The millennial issue of the *American Psychologist* was devoted to the exploration and advancement of positive psychology. Seligman & Csikszentmihalyi (2000) outlined three areas deemed to provide structure to the science of positive psychology: positive subjective experience, positive individual traits, and positive institutions. Each of these three areas can be further subdivided into specific psychological constructs. It is within the first area of subjective experience that flow (and happiness) stands out as the focus of present experience; the constructs of well-being, contentment, and satisfaction are the focus of past experience; and hope and optimism signal the future-oriented focus.

Seligman has described the aim of positive psychology as being "to catalyze a change in psychology from a preoccupation only with repairing the worst things in life to also building the best qualities in life"

(Seligman, 2002, p. 3). Historically, psychology has concerned itself with human ills and ways of correcting them. Seligman, whose work was recently highlighted in *Time Magazine* (January 9, 2005), believed that this effort involved trying to move people from a "minus five to a zero" (Wallis, 2005, p. 43). Seligman's goal in promoting positive psychology was to focus on how to get people "from zero to plus five" (Wallis, 2005, p. 43). As psychology works toward this goal, it has mirrored the direction that health has taken up, having prevention as its foreground. Prevention works best through building competency, not through trying to correct weakness (Seligman & Csikszentmihalyi, 2000). Among the myriad of human strengths that have been identified is the capacity for flow. Like the other strengths, this capacity for flow can be developed through building appropriate competencies. This area will be addressed in a later section. First, we will define and describe what flow is and what it can do for our lives.

Definition and Dimensions of Flow

Flow is a positive psychological state that typically occurs when a person perceives a balance between the challenges associated with a situation and his or her capabilities to accomplish or meet these demands (Csikszentmihalyi, 1990). A personally challenging situation in which perceived skills match the perceived demand opens up the opportunity for flow. The balance between the subjectively perceived challenges and skills directs the resultant quality of one's experience. Several flow characteristics, or dimensions, have been described by Csikszentmihalyi (1990, 1993) and supported in the sport and exercise environment through qualitative and quantitative research (e.g., Jackson, 1996; Jackson & Marsh, 1996). These dimensions will be briefly described here; more in-depth descriptions are available elsewhere (e.g., Csikszentmihalyi, 1990; Jackson & Csikszentmihalyi, 1999).

Challenge–Skill Balance According to Csikszentmihalyi's operationalization of flow, people will experience flow when they perceive that the challenges of the situation and their skills are in balance and above their average subjective experience (Csikszentmihalyi & Csikszentmihalyi, 1988). If skills and challenges are not in balance, people are not likely to experience flow. Instead, they will probably experience anxiety, relaxation, boredom, or apathy. Anxiety occurs when a person perceives the challenges of the situation to exceed perceived skills; relaxation or boredom results when the skills outweigh the challenges; and apathy occurs when both perceived challenges and skills are balanced and less than an individual's average experiences. Typically, the quality of an individual's experience is most optimal in flow, least optimal in apathy, and less than optimal in boredom or anxiety.

Merging of Action and Awareness Merging of action and awareness suggests that involvement is so deep that it becomes spontaneous or seemingly automatic (Csikszentmihalyi, 1990). Csikszentmihalyi reported that the sense of seemingly effortless movement associated with the word *flow* resulted in its being chosen to describe optimal experience. Individuals are no longer aware that they are separate from their actions. A person simply becomes one with the activity. Jackson (1992) found that elite athletes described this flow dimension with terms such as "being in the groove" or statements like "I am not thinking about anything . . . it just happens automatically."

Clear Goals and Feedback These two flow dimensions, clear goals and feedback, are frequently discussed concurrently (see Csikszentmihalyi, 1990). When in flow, goals are clearly defined by planning or are developed while engaging in the activity. When a person knows and understands the goals for an activity, he or she is more likely to become totally immersed or engaged. In addition, a clear goal allows easier processing of feedback, which provides messages that the actor is progressing with the goal. The powerful symbiosis between goals and feedback creates order in consciousness, which is at the core of the flow experience.

Total Concentration According to Csikszentmihalyi (1997, p. 31), "When goals are clear, feedback relevant, and challenges and skills are in balance, attention becomes ordered and fully invested. Because of the total demand on psychic energy, a person in flow is completely focused." The complete focus on the task at hand stands out as the clearest indication of flow. All distractions are kept at a minimum or nonexistent, and only a select range of information is allowed into awareness.

Sense of Control When in flow, a person feels in control of the situation without worrying about losing control. An athlete interviewed by Jackson (1992, p. 19) stated, "It feels like I can do anything in that (flow) state." The key to this dimension is the perception of control that one feels. Another athlete said, "As strange as it sounds, I don't feel

like I am in control of anything at all . . . my body just takes over. On the other hand, though, I feel like I am totally in control of everything." Because of the apparently contradictory statements such as this, Csikszentmihalyi first labeled this dimension the paradox of control. The possibility of control and the sense of being able to exercise control in difficult situations characterizes this flow dimension (Csikszentmihalyi, 1990).

Loss of Self-Consciousness When in flow, a person has no room for distractions or worry about how he or she is perceived by others. No self-consciousness is present; a sense of separateness from the world is overcome, which results in a feeling of oneness with the environment. The absence of self-consciousness does not mean that the person is unaware of his or her thoughts and bodily movements. Rather, it is a keen awareness that is not threatening. In essence, the self is fully functioning without the burden of the questioning voice that so often pervades our experience.

Time Transformation The perception of time may either speed up or slow down when in flow. In flow, the experience distorts time. For example, a distance runner in flow may not even recall what happened during a race and may perceive that it ended more quickly than it actually did. Time transformation is generally the least mentioned flow dimension in qualitative research (Jackson, 1996), and in psychometric scale work, time transformation has not been found to relate strongly to other flow dimensions (e.g., Jackson & Eklund, 2002; Jackson & Marsh, 1996). In addition, Csikszentmihalyi (1990) acknowledged that in some situations, being aware of the time is paramount, which could make experiencing transcendence of time difficult. Further research in various physical activity contexts is necessary to understand the role of the time transformation dimension of flow.

Autotelic Experience Csikszentmihalyi (1990) described an autotelic experience as the result of flow, one that is intrinsically rewarding. Statements such as "I was on a high" and "I really had a great experience" illustrate the product of a flow experience. A flow state is such a positive subjective state that the individual desires to perform the activity for its own sake. When a person has stretched her or his capacity to the fullest extent, has integrated mind and body, and is fully immersed in an activity, the outcome is likely to be autotelic, an activity done for its own sake, because it provides powerful intrinsic rewards.

Positive Outcomes of Flow Results of studies about flow states in a variety of contexts suggest that people consider flow to be an optimal and thoroughly enjoyable experience (e.g., Csikszentmihalyi & LeFevre, 1989; Jackson, 1992, 1996; Scanlan et al., 1989). For example, in a nonsport setting, Csikszentmihalyi and LeFevre (1989) found that people in flow at work had greater positive affect and potency than did workers not in flow. Findings from a study that examined children's physical activity experiences at a summer sports camp indicated that their flow experiences were positively related to "feeling good" and "perceived success" (Mandigo, Thompson, & Couture, 1998). Data from a variety of sources indicate a strong, positive relation between flow and positive affective experiences, which are important because "emotions focus attention by mobilizing the entire organism in an approach or avoidance mode" (Csikszentmihalyi, 1997, p. 25). By having many flow experiences in a specific activity that are intimately linked to positive affect, a person is likely to want to approach that activity again and again. Kimiecik and Harris (1996) have suggested a positive motivational cycle, whereby flow leads to positive affective experiences, which then enhances intrinsic motivation (i.e., the desire to do something for its own sake). That is, the activity becomes autotelic over time (Csikszentmihalyi, 1975, 1990). Note that the positive affect and potency tied to flow states typically occur following the activity, not during the activity (Csikszentmihalyi, 1997), and these affective experiences can vary in intensity.

Csikszentmihalyi (1997) suggested that the positive affective experiences related to flow states do more than enhance individuals' intrinsic motivation and transform a specific activity to one autotelic in nature. This process also leads to complexity and growth in consciousness. Csikszentmihalyi (1993) proposed that after a flow experience the organization of the self becomes more complex, through the opposing processes of differentiation and integration. Although space constraints do not allow us to delve into the intricacies of complexity, the basic notion is that flow contributes to the growth of the self through the process of complexification. Simply, flow increases potential for personal growth because this state involves the simultaneous interaction of differentiation and integration, which Csikszentmihalyi (1993) defined as follows:

> Differentiation refers to the degree to which a system . . . is composed of parts that differ in structure or function from one another. Integration refers to the extent to which the different parts communicate and enhance one another's goals. A system that is more differentiated and integrated than another is said to be more complex. (p. 156)

According to Csikszentmihalyi (1993), the process of differentiation occurs as one seeks out new and greater challenges, which provide greater opportunities for an individual to become unique and to explore limits and potential; integration occurs when an individual increases skills to master these new challenges. These skills then become part of the self, leaving one feeling more in tune with oneself and with the world in general. The optimal development of both integration and differentiation, through flow states, leads to a more harmonious self. By becoming more complex through flow, people experience personal growth. They have developed new skills and met new challenges, which enhances feelings about the self, produces positive emotions, and elevates a person above his or her daily, humdrum existence. To find flow in what one is doing in an ongoing way is to grow (Nakamura & Csikszentmihalyi, 2003).

In sum, flow is a positive experience that leads to an increased desire to perform an activity for the intrinsic rewards that it provides. Flow enhances quality of life and leads to personal growth through the process of increasing complexity. Some of the questions that we and other sport and exercise psychology researchers have been interested in are these: Do athletes experience flow in ways similar to those that Csikszentmihalyi has identified? Is flow relevant to the experiences of athletes, exercisers, and a range of physical activity participants? Can the factors influencing flow experiences in physical activity be identified? The next section presents research that has examined some of these questions.

Research Advances

Flow research in sport and exercise is in a developing stage, with still many more questions than answers. Much of the early research was conducted with elite athletes, and that is where we start. We then move on to review flow research with other types of physical activity participants. We also discuss the notion of the autotelic personality in the context of research that has examined psychological factors associated with flow in sport settings.

Flow in Elite Sport Contexts

When researching peak performance and optimal experience in sport, elite athletes have been the population of primary interest. Operationally, we define elite athletes as those who participate in U.S. Division I collegiate sport or higher, and the focal group will mostly have competed at an international level. From a flow perspective, the interest in elite athletes is based primarily on the assumption that athletes participating at a high skill level are more likely to be familiar with peak performance and flow experiences (Jackson, 1996). Csikszentmihalyi and Nakamura (1989) suggested that ability needs to be at a relatively high level before anything resembling a flow experience can occur.

Jackson (1992, 1996) was initially interested in establishing the relevance of Csikszentmihalyi's (1990) flow framework to elite athletes' flow experiences. The underlying question addressed in these two qualitative studies was this: How do athletes understand, interpret, and give meaning to the experience of flow? Specifically, how do athletes' descriptions of flow experiences compare with the dimensions of flow outlined in Csikszentmihalyi's (1990) flow model?

In her 1992 study, Jackson interviewed 16 former U.S. national champion figure skaters, and in her 1996 study, she interviewed 28 elite athletes from Australia and New Zealand. All athletes were asked to describe an optimal sport experience, one that stood out as being better than average. Many of the skaters' descriptions of optimal experience included feelings such as clarity, awareness, and perceived control of the situation. The skaters' clear and concise accounts of their flow experiences revealed that they were describing memorable and valued times. The "unique" state that the skaters recounted closely resembled Csikszentmihalyi's description of flow (1990). Therefore, the results indicated "a close agreement between the skater's perceptions of flow and the theoretical descriptions of the flow construct" (Jackson, 1992, p. 177).

The results of Jackson's 1996 study demonstrated a consistency of responses in elite athletes' experiencing of flow. For example, in describing flow experiences, this second group of elite athletes used terms such as awareness, automaticity, narrow focus, things happening in slow motion, and feeling in control, descriptions that the skaters also used. Of the 295 flow state descriptors, 97% could be classified into one of Csikszentmihalyi's nine flow dimensions. In addition, both groups of elite athletes provided rich descriptions of flow states, clearly showing that they were familiar with the flow experience and valued it highly.

In sum, the results of these two studies demonstrate strong support for the relevancy of flow

and its dimensions for elite athletes in a variety of sports. But both groups of athletes minimally endorsed the loss of self-consciousness and time transformation dimensions of flow. This issue will be addressed more fully in the measurement section. Briefly, studies using measures of flow designed for the physical activity setting also showed that time transformation and, to a lesser extent, loss of self-consciousness were weaker dimensions of a global flow construct from a psychometric perspective (Jackson & Eklund, 2002; Jackson, Kimiecik, Ford, & Marsh, 1998; Jackson & Marsh, 1996; Kowal & Fortier, 1999).

Facilitators of Flow for Elite Athletes

The results of the studies by Jackson (1992, 1996) support the notion that elite athletes experience flow at least some of the time in practice or competition, and in ways that correspond with Csikszentmihalyi's theoretical formulations of flow. These athletes also believe that the experience of flow is a motivating factor to participate in their sport on a regular basis. This work on the essence and relevance of the flow experience for athletes has been paralleled by a search for the factors that may facilitate such experiences. We have gone down this path cautiously, not wanting to destroy the magic and allure of flow states, which is partly related to the uncertainty about when such states occur. For an athlete, knowing that flow occurs but not knowing when it will occur is part of the joy of being a performer. Jackson (1992, 1995), however, has shown that many of the elite athletes in her research believe that flow is, to some degree, controllable. An elite figure skater commented on the perceived controllability of flow:

> Yeah, I think you can increase it. . . . It's not a conscious effort. If you try to do it, it's not going to work. I think maybe through trying you turn off the switch so it can't happen. . . . I think there are things, factors you can lessen, to make it happen more often. I don't think it is something you can turn on and off like a light switch. (Jackson, 1992, p. 174)

If elite athletes believe flow to be potentially controllable, it makes sense to examine the factors that may facilitate this optimal state. In her 1992 and 1995 studies, Jackson asked athletes about what they perceived to be the most important factors for getting into flow. She then developed categories of themes from inductive analysis of interview transcripts. Confidence, or positive mental attitude, was perceived by the athletes to be an important flow facilitator. This finding follows from flow theory, which states that flow will occur only when a person perceives that his or her skills match the challenge of the situation. To experience flow, an athlete must be confident in his or her abilities to meet the challenge of the situation. Another relevant flow facilitator from the 1995 study was the extent to which the athlete had prepared for the event and had a good plan for how she or he would perform. The importance of mental plans to optimal performance is well recognized in the applied sport performance literature (e.g., Orlick, 1998). By being well prepared and knowing clearly what he or she is going to do in an event, an athlete can focus on the task at hand. This ability to tune in to the event facilitates the occurrence of flow. Athletes perceived several others factors that could increase the probability that flow would occur, including being aroused to an optimal level, being highly motivated, feeling good during the performance, maintaining an appropriate focus, having optimal environmental and situational conditions, and being involved in positive team play and interaction (Jackson, 1992, 1995).

Besides asking athletes what factors they believed would help them get into flow, Jackson (1992, 1995) asked them about factors that prevent or disrupt flow. One of the most frequent responses to this question focused on nonoptimal environmental or situational conditions. This category included factors such as undesirable weather, uncontrollable event influences, and interactions with others before or during the event that proved distracting. Lack of physical preparation or readiness was also an obstacle to flow, as were physical problems such as injury or fatigue. As expected, lacking confidence or having a negative mental attitude was thought to make flow difficult to experience. Similarly, if motivation was lacking for the event, flow was less likely. Inappropriate focus, whether it was thinking too much, not being focused enough, or worrying about the competition, was an impediment to flow. Problems relating to performing as a team were also obstacles to flow.

This qualitative research by Jackson (1992, 1995) provided some interesting information about factors that elite athletes believed would affect their experience of flow during performance. In a quantitative approach to examining facilitators or correlates of flow, Jackson and Roberts (1992) conducted a study on positive performance states of 200 Division I college athletes. This study examined a possible link between athletes' goal orientations and their flow experiences. The researchers hypothesized that athletes high in a task orientation would report experi-

encing flow more often than athletes low in a task orientation and that an ego orientation would be unrelated to flow states. An additional hypothesis was that athletes high in perceived ability would report experiencing flow more often than would athletes low in perceived ability. As defined by Duda (1992) task orientation is a focus on the task at hand while relying on a self-referenced concept of ability. Conversely, ego involvement invokes normative comparison and concern with outcomes; success is based on doing better than others. Research in education (Deci & Ryan, 1987; Nicholls, 1984) and sport settings (Duda, 1988; Duda & Nicholls, 1992) indicated that task-involved individuals typically experience greater intrinsic interest in tasks, persist longer, and are more likely to be performing the task for its own sake.

In flow terms, being task involved should enable athletes to focus more on the task at hand, leading to task absorption, higher levels of concentration, and feelings of control, all characteristics of the flow state. Ego-involved athletes may experience flow less often because their ego involvement is more likely to produce counter states of flow, such as anxiety and boredom. For example, athletes who continually compare their ability to others are more likely to perceive competitive situations as overly challenging, which could lead to higher levels of anxiety. The flow literature and research on competitive anxiety (Martens, Vealey, & Burton, 1990) suggests that this state is not associated with positive performances. Boredom is also a greater possibility among ego-involved athletes because they may perceive opponents as less challenging than they really are to protect perceptions of competence. That is, they may underestimate the challenge, feign lack of interest, and act as if the whole thing is boring and unworthy of their talent. In contrast, whatever the level of ability (within reason) of a task-involved athlete's opponent, he or she will attempt to match challenges with skills, sometimes creatively, to learn the most from the situation and, perhaps, get into flow. Being task involved rather than ego involved may offer many advantages related to achieving flow. Orlick (1990, p. 16) has identified this relationship in a practical way:

> The ideal performance focus is total concentration to your performance. . . . Focusing on distracting thoughts (about final placing, others' expectations, the weather) interferes with an effective task focus. . . . Stay in the moment, which is the only one that you can influence anyway.

The findings of Jackson and Roberts (1992) support the hypothesized relationships among goal orientations, perceived ability, and flow. Athletes high in task involvement reported experiencing flow more frequently than did athletes low in task involvement, whereas ego orientation was unrelated to flow. These findings support the work and observations of applied sport psychology consultants (e.g., Loehr, 1986; Orlick, 1986) who suggest that focusing solely on outcome and comparisons of one's ability with other athletes—an ego orientation—does not lend itself to positive performance. As Orlick (1986, p. 10) pointed out, "The problem with thinking about winning or losing the event is that you lose focus of what you need to do in order to win." Jackson and Roberts (1992) also found perceived ability to be associated with experiencing flow. Focusing on perceived, rather than actual, ability is important because within the flow model "it is not the skills we actually have that determine how we feel, but the ones we think we have" (Csikszentmihalyi, 1990, p. 75).

A study by Norwegian researchers (Vea and Pensgaard, 2004) examined the relationship between perfectionism and flow in young elite athletes. Perfectionism has been shown to have negative implications, and the authors were interested in understanding the performance and well-being implications of perfectionism. Flow was selected as an indicator of potential to perform at optimal levels, as well as an indicator of subjective well-being. As expected, most of the perfectionism dimensions correlated negatively with flow dimensions, although there were a couple of unexpected positive associations.

Although a number of studies have focused on the use of psychological skills training (PST) to enhance elite athlete performance (see other chapters in part V of this volume), little research has attempted to link PST with flow states in elite athletes. One early attempt, by Straub (1996), involved a time series design in which five college wrestlers underwent a mental imagery program for a 5- to 10-week period after baselines were established for each participant. Four of the five wrestlers increased significantly in the self-reported frequency of flow states as measured by the challenge–skill balance. For example, one wrestler reported increasing his frequency of flow states from 33% of his matches during baseline to 77% of the matches during treatment. Although this study had limitations (e.g., small sample size), it demonstrated some of the exciting and creative possibilities of integrating PST with some of the findings on flow facilitators to build a foundation for optimal experience. Correlational support for the interplay between psychological skills and flow was demonstrated in a study by Jackson and colleagues (Jackson et al., 2001). Psychological skill use predicted flow states, with canonical correlational analyses showing the psychological skills of negative thinking, activation, emotional control, and relaxation to be most strongly related to both dispositional and state flow.

Pates and colleagues (e.g., Pates, Cummings, & Maynard, 2002; Pates, Karageorghis, Fryer, & Maynard, 2003) implemented single-subject multiple baseline designs to examine whether hypnosis and music could positively influence flow states. Three studies have examined the effects of hypnosis on flow states and performance in basketball and golf (Pates & Maynard, 2000; Pates, Oliver, & Maynard, 2001; Pates, Cummings, & Maynard, 2002), and one study examined the effects of music on flow and performance in netball (Pates et al., 2003). Although these single-subject designs involved a mix of player levels, all participants were competitive athletes, so the findings will be reported here. Each study found improvements in both performance and flow scores postintervention. The authors concluded that flow was accessible through hypnotic techniques, providing a key to increasing personal control over flow states. In the music study (Pates et al., 2003), which involved collegiate netball players, a music intervention was found to improve performance in all three participants and increase flow in two of the three participants. Speculating on the reason for the positive influence of music on flow, the authors suggested that music may trigger the emotions that are antecedent to the flow experience. The research approach of Pates and colleagues is a useful way forward for assessing the effect of intervention attempts on flow.

Wiggins and Freeman (2000) examined relationships between anxiety and flow in U.S. Division I college athletes. Higher flow scores, both at the global level, and for the dimensions of unambiguous feedback, concentration, and loss of self-consciousness, were obtained for athletes with facilitative anxiety perceptions compared with those who had debilitative anxiety perceptions.

In sum, the research with elite athletes demonstrates the relevance, centrality, and perceived controllability of flow experiences for this unique group of sport participants. In addition, both qualitative and quantitative studies have identified a set of factors that may facilitate flow experiences. In the qualitative work, elite athletes perceived such dimensions as confidence or positive mental attitude, competitive plans or preparation, maintenance of appropriate focus, and optimal physical preparation or readiness to be important for getting into flow. In the quantitative work, high task orientation and high perceived ability were associated with elite athletes' flow states. Connections between the findings of the qualitative and quantitative studies can be made. A task orientation would be intimately linked with the maintaining appropriate focus dimension, whereas perceived ability and the confidence or positive mental attitude dimension share some commonality. These kinds of connections pertaining to flow facilitators demonstrate the usefulness of using multiple research approaches to studying flow experiences in physical activity.

The Challenge of Experiencing Flow for Elite Athletes

Although we know that elite athletes experience flow, we also know that they experience it relatively infrequently. For example, 81% of the U.S. national champion skaters in the Jackson (1992) study said that they did not experience flow very often. Nonelite athletes may possibly have the opportunity to experience flow to a greater extent than elite athletes do, although their ability is at a lower level. Mitchell (1988) hypothesized that the highly competitive nature of elite sport and a competitive goal orientation can make it difficult to achieve a flow state. In other words, as sport participants move into more competitive environments that include greater emphasis on outcomes, a shift occurs in the many forms of play to the "earning of success, from means to an ends" (Mitchell, 1988, p. 55). Competition then becomes the dominant form of play, and winning the primary goal. Intrinsic satisfaction is replaced by extrinsic rewards such as profit and prestige. Because of this shift, the likelihood of experiencing flow may decrease because the sport environment is no longer conducive to positive psychological states of experience. The flow dynamics have changed. More value is placed on external rewards, such as scholarships and bonuses. For example, an athlete may focus more on winning the prize money in a race than on his or her experience in running the race. This focus on the future rather than the present may diminish the likelihood that flow experiences will occur.

Research that has examined the intrinsic and extrinsic motivation of scholarship athletes provides partial support for the view that an emphasis on the extrinsic aspects of competition can potentially minimize the quality of the sport experience. Ryan (1977) surveyed male scholarship and nonscholarship athletes at two institutions to examine the link between external rewards (i.e., scholarship) and

type of motivation emphasized by the athletes. He found that scholarship athletes cited more extrinsic reasons for participation and lower enjoyment levels than the nonscholarship athletes did. In a follow-up investigation with a larger sample, including male football players and wrestlers and female athletes in a variety of sports, Ryan (1980) found that football players on scholarship scored lower on intrinsic motivation than nonscholarship football players. But the wrestlers and female athletes on scholarship scored higher on intrinsic motivation than their nonscholarship teammates did. These findings suggest that because of the heavy emphasis on extrinsic orientation in collegiate football (i.e., win at all costs), scholarship football players are more likely to view their experience as controlling, whereas scholarship athletes in "minor" sports, such as wrestling, are more likely to view their sport experience from an intrinsic perspective.

Although the research by Ryan on scholarships and motivation could not establish causality, the results are particularly relevant to this discussion of the sport context and flow. According to Deci and Ryan (1985, p. 29), "When highly intrinsically motivated, organisms will be extremely interested in what they are doing and experience a sense of flow." Flow theory suggests that a focus on extrinsic aspects of the experience is a major barrier to facilitating optimal experience.

Furthermore, although participants may be good judges of their own enjoyment, they are stripped of this responsibility as judges and referees supervise the game. As Mitchell (1988, p. 55) stated, "Making decisions about the conduct of play becomes too critical to remain in the hands of the players themselves." As this shift from play to sport to highly competitive sport occurs, many of the precursors of the flow experience may be diminished or replaced. Therefore, the flow experience for elite athletes in highly competitive, extrinsic-focused environments may not occur as frequently as one might think, precisely because of the motivational processes identified by intrinsic motivation and flow theory.

The broader issue of competition and flow has been addressed in the sport of surfing, in which experiences in free surfing have been compared with those in competitive situations. Across three studies, flow was found to occur more frequently in free surfing than in competitions (Bennett & Kremer, 2000; Forch, 2004; Wagner, Beier, and Deleveaux, 2003). Forch commented that the rules and criteria of competitions may affect the achievement of flow. He found that most of the participants he interviewed believed that competition was detrimental to their finding flow because instead of being able to surf in whatever way they chose, they had to surf according to set criteria to earn good scores from the judges. In contrast, the free-surfing situation provided an autonomous, intrinsically motivating situation.

The forgoing is not to suggest that elite athletes do not experience flow or that competitive situations do not allow for flow experiences. Clearly, previous research on flow in sport, such as that reviewed in this chapter, shows that athletes (elite and otherwise) do experience flow during competition. What the discussion on the link between competition and subjective experience does suggest is that people who participate in less externally controlled physical activity environments could also experience flow, perhaps to a greater extent than elite, competitive athletes do. The nonelite participant may not be as immersed in the extrinsic-oriented aspects of the competitive environment as the elite athlete is. If nonscholarship athletes are likely to focus on the intrinsic aspects of competition, is it not possible that nonelite physical activity participants might also focus on intrinsic aspects of the experience? This intrinsic orientation could enhance the possibility of their experiencing flow.

Jackson (1996) pointed out that flow research in sport needed to go beyond the elite athlete to ascertain how generalizable the experiences described by elite athletes are to other types of participants. Do nonelite sport participants experience flow? Do they experience flow to a greater or lesser extent than elite athletes? Can facilitators or determinants of flow be identified in physical activity participants who are less skilled? Are flow states a motivating factor to participate in physical activity for the general population? In the next section, we discuss some interesting issues pertaining to the flow experience of nonelite sport participants, and present the empirical work that has been conducted on flow in more generalized physical activity contexts.

Flow in Nonelite Sport and Physical Activity Contexts

Nonelite sport participants are typically less skilled than elite athletes and do not compete for medals in national or international competitions. Most sport participants are of nonelite status, so studying the quality of their experience makes sense because findings could have long-term implications for understanding motivation, participation, and quality of life. As Wankel and Berger (1990) pointed out, little is known about the subjective quality of people's participation in leisure activities such as sport.

Interestingly, Csikszentmihalyi's (1975) original work on flow produced findings relevant to a discussion of the propensity of different types of physical activity participants for experiencing flow. In examining the flow states of rock climbers, composers, modern dancers, chess players, and basketball players, Csikszentmihalyi (1975, p. 18) found that the basketball players demonstrated a "deviant pattern." They were the only group that ranked "competition, measuring self against others" as most important. All of the other groups studied ranked "enjoyment of the experience and use of skills" as most important, whereas the basketball players ranked this item fifth out of seven choices. Csikszentmihalyi (1975, p. 18) explained this pattern in the following way:

> Possibly, however, the pattern reflects the activity [basketball], rather than the players' background. In other words, basketball, or other competitive sports, may provide a reward structure in which enjoyment comes from measuring oneself against others and from developing one's skills, rather than from experiencing the activity itself.

This quotation suggests that the very nature of competition could move its participants away from the intrinsic aspects (e.g., flow) of the sport experience. In addition, this notion leaves open the possibility that nonelite sport participants in less competitive environments could experience flow.

Using the flow framework, Chalip, Csikszentmihalyi, Kleiber, and Larson (1984) examined the subjective experiences of adolescents who participated in organized sport, informal sport, and physical education classes as well as in other life activities. The study examined subjective experience by means of the experience sampling method (ESM), in which each participant carried an electronic pager and a pad of self-report forms for one week. At random times the pager would go off, signaling the participant to fill out the report. This method has been found to produce valid and reliable data in previous studies of varied populations (Csikszentmihalyi & Graef, 1980; Csikszentmihalyi, Larson, & Prescott, 1977). Participants comprised 75 male and female students from a suburb of Chicago. The results indicated that organized sport provided substantially more positive experience than the rest of everyday life. The sense of control was highest in physical education class and lowest in informal sport. The perception of skill was highest in informal sport and lowest in physical education class, and more was perceived to be at stake in organized sport as compared with informal sport and physical education class. The relationship between motivation and the perception of skill varied significantly across all three groups. In physical education classes, the more highly the students perceived their skills, the more they wanted to do. The opposite was found for organized sport, and in informal sport no relationship was found between motivation and the perception of skill.

Furthermore, only in informal sports were challenges and skills positively related to enjoyment, and in organized sport and physical education class the relationship was negative. During organized sport, most participants regarded their challenges as outweighing their skills. A similar pattern was found in physical education class. Only in informal sport did a matching of perceived skill and perceived challenge exist. These results suggest that the informal sport context, in which no adults were present, provided the best environment for adolescents to experience flow. In the informal sport context, the participants had more control of the challenge–skill balance, which is typically how flow has been operationalized and measured (see Csikszentmihalyi, 1990). Perhaps nonelite sport participants have an advantage over elite athletes in being more able to control and structure their environment in a way that optimizes the skill–challenge balance and, in turn, the quality of their experience.

In sum, some data from Csikszentmihalyi and colleagues suggests that sport for the nonelite athlete, ranging from adolescent to adult, elicits a variety of flow experiences. Certainly more research is needed using an ESM-type approach on adult, nonelite participants to determine the quality of their experiences. Comparing varying samples of athletes according to skill level and across a variety of competitive contexts would also provide much needed information about the role of flow for elite versus nonelite participants. Similar to flow studies on the elite athlete, some recent research has examined the facilitators of flow for nonelite sport participants, and we review some of that work next.

Facilitators of Flow for Nonelite Sport Participants

Two general questions have been guiding the work that has examined facilitators of flow for nonelite sport participants: Are there psychological factors that might facilitate nonelite sport participants' flow states? How significant a role do these determinants play in participants' optimal experience?

Unlike Jackson's (1992, 1995) qualitative work examining facilitators of flow for elite athletes, the studies that have addressed this topic with nonelite

sport participants have mostly been grounded in the traditional, positivistic, quantitative approach. As you will see in a later section, the scientific paradigm that one adopts to study flow influences the type of studies conducted and subsequent findings and interpretations of the flow experience.

Stein, Kimiecik, Daniels, and Jackson (1995) conducted three studies investigating possible antecedents of flow in a variety of nonelite physical activity contexts—tennis, basketball, and golf. The initial tennis study focused on adults of varying ability participating in a parks and recreation weekend tournament. The next two studies used an ESM approach as recommended by Csikszentmihalyi (1988). The basketball study targeted college students enrolled in a physical activity course, and the golf study focused on older-adult golfers of average ability. Although the link between psychological antecedents of flow, such as goals, competence, and confidence, was weak, the results showed that optimal experience does occur for these kinds of participants. Most important, a difference seemed to exist between contexts that emphasized competition, in which above-average skill levels (regardless of challenge) produced a high-quality experience, and a context that emphasized learning, in which above-average skills and challenges (flow) were linked to a high-quality experience.

These findings support in part the argument in the previous section that as the emphasis on performance and outcome becomes more important in sport environments, the role of flow becomes less clear. For example, the golfers experienced nearly as much satisfaction, control, and concentration when in a bored state (skills above average and challenges below average) as when in a flow state (skills and challenges above average), and their performance was better in the bored state. These golfers were part of a league, and the good-natured competition involved small bets per hole or round, bragging rights for the day, and so forth. Other researchers who looked at flow relative to daily life experience found that high school students interpreted the context labeled *boredom* as more optimal than flow during productive and outcome-oriented situations (e.g., Carli, Fave, & Massimini, 1988). Recently, Csikszentmihalyi (e.g., Jackson & Csikszentmihalyi, 1999; Nakamura & Csikszentmihalyi, 2002) has moved toward using the label *relaxation*, rather than *boredom*, for the low-challenge, high-skill quadrant as it became clear that the state associated with this type of experience was "less aversive than originally thought" (Nakamura & Csikszentmihalyi, 2002, p. 97). From a quality of experience perspective, in competitive environments in which performance and winning or losing are highlighted, rating skill to be above average may optimize the experience for some participants to a greater extent than perceiving a balance between challenge and skill.

A study by Jackson et al. (1998) on the flow experiences of masters athletes supports the important role of perceived skill and the ambiguous role of challenge in influencing quality of experience in some samples. Using the Flow State Scale (FSS), Jackson and colleagues examined the relationships between flow and ratings of performance through measures of perceived success along with perceived skills and challenges following participation in one competitive event. Perceived success and perceived skills were significantly correlated with a number of the nine flow dimensions, whereas the perceived challenges variable was not correlated with any of the flow dimensions. Moneta and Csikszentmihalyi (1996) have also found differential patterns between perceived skills and challenges and quality of experience variables in a variety of life contexts outside sport. In their study, they found that concentration and involvement were positively related to ratings of challenge, whereas wishing to do the activity and happiness were negatively related.

When competition and emphasis on performance are introduced, some participants perceive high skill to be more desirable than high challenge because high skill, with minimal challenge, leads to desired outcomes (e.g., winning). At some point, however, one must wonder about the long-term effects of basing positive experience on the relationship between the desired outcome and the high skill–low challenge condition, which an overemphasis on the outcomes of sport can promote. Csikszentmihalyi (1988, p. 369) suggested that when "the flow experience is split, its motivational force is bound to be reduced." Csikszentmihalyi referred to the splitting of flow into two components: mental effort and strength when both challenges and skills are high, and happiness and motivation when skills outweigh challenges. For example, an athlete who perceives high skill–low challenge as optimal as compared with high skill–high challenge may experience happiness and a desire to be doing the activity but may not experience optimal concentration or involvement in the activity. In the short term, this kind of experience may produce a victory, but in the long term, splitting the flow experience may not be in the athlete's best interest. Can an athlete learn, grow, and develop without upping the challenge? As Moneta and Csikszentmihalyi (1996) pointed out, however, people face a perplexing problem

when they want to go for high challenge–high skill conditions, even though from an experience perspective those conditions produce the optimal psychological states. Increasing the challenge may mean a loss of happiness and a wishing not to be there, which could override the positive concentration and involvement that comes from high skill–high challenge experiences.

Perhaps individual differences, such as an autotelic personality, can account for some of the findings discussed here. The studies that have examined this possibility in sport are presented next.

The Autotelic Personality and Flow in Sport

Csikszentmihalyi (1975, 1990, 1997) has used the term *autotelic personality* to explain in part the large individual differences in people's flow experiences. For example, a study by Wells (1988) on mothers found that some mothers were in flow only 4% of the time, whereas others were in flow over 40% of the time. In our interpretation, Csikszentmihalyi views the autotelic personality as part of the individual that is influenced by both genetics and learning.

In essence, the autotelic personality notion refers to a person who generally does things for their own sake rather than to achieve some later external goal. That is, certain types of people may be more psychologically equipped, whatever the situation, to experience flow. Hypotheses have been forwarded to account for individual differences in the ability to experience flow. For example, differences in how people process information, with some people able to concentrate more efficiently, have been advanced as one possibility (Hamilton, 1981).

Other suggestions for why some people experience flow more easily than others include the idea that some people are better able to turn obstacles into challenges and thus realize their potential, without being self-conscious (Logan, 1988). Moneta and Csikszentmihalyi (1996) have suggested a possible link between hardiness and flow. This notion makes sense because Kobasa's (1979) conceptualization of hardiness includes a composite of perceptions of control, commitment, and challenge, which parallel the dimensions of flow outlined earlier in this chapter. In support of this possibility, a study by Perritt (1999) demonstrated a significant relationship between the control and commitment hardiness subscales and dispositional flow for collegiate track and field athletes.

Ellis, Voelkl, and Morris (1994) proposed self-affirmation as another personality variable that may differentiate people's flow experiences. Work in the area of intrinsic motivation (e.g., Deci & Ryan, 1985) suggested that those who feel more in control of their actions (i.e., self-determined) are more likely to be intrinsically motivated and that associations exist between flow and intrinsic motivation. Csikszentmihalyi (1988) suggested that we need to learn more about the configuration of traits associated with the large variability in people's flow states and then determine how much of this configuration people can learn or develop over time.

We have been intrigued by the possibility of the autotelic personality involved in people's flow experiences in sport. We take a general interactionist perspective following the framework presented by Kimiecik and Stein (1992). This framework suggests that certain dispositional (e.g., attentional style) and state (e.g., anxiety) psychological factors interact with various factors in the sport context (e.g., type of sport) to determine whether an athlete is likely to experience flow. In revisiting this framework, we would add intrinsic motivation to the list of dispositional factors because of the suggested link between intrinsic motivation and flow (Csikszentmihalyi, 1997; Deci & Ryan, 1985).

Little empirical work has been conducted on the situational factors and their role in flow states, although one can see how the previous discussion on the importance of competition and the competitive context could be relevant to optimal experience in sport. In addition, Jackson's (1995) work on elite athletes' beliefs about flow disrupters showed that nonoptimal environmental or situational conditions were the primary factors in getting athletes out of flow. These findings demonstrate the necessity for flow research in physical activity to begin to examine the dynamic interaction of person and situational factors and its influence on flow states.

Deciding which psychological factors might be associated with flow states in sport is a difficult task because little empirical data is available to direct such an endeavor. The few studies that have been conducted have focused primarily on dispositional factors (Jackson et al., 1998; Jackson & Roberts, 1992; Kowal & Fortier, 1999). In the next few sections, we present a number of dispositional factors that together could make up something resembling an autotelic personality in sport, and we discuss findings from studies that have examined the association of these person factors with flow states.

Goal Orientation   Goal orientation is a much studied concept in sport and exercise psychology (see chapter 8, this volume), one shown to be important in understanding the motivations of

people to engage in certain activities (e.g., Duda, 1992; Nicholls, 1992). Within the sport context, task and ego orientation seem to be particularly relevant because they relate to perceptions of ability, which are highly valued in athletic environments (Duda, 1992). Although it is possible to be high or low on either or both factors, individuals are thought to prefer a particular frame of reference within achievement situations. As reported earlier, Jackson and Roberts (1992) found correlational support for a positive association between task orientation and flow in college athletes. Athletes with a task orientation may be more likely to experience flow than do athletes with an ego orientation because those with the former orientation focus on the task rather than on anticipated outcomes. Task orientation would thus be expected to be positively associated with flow.

Perceived Sport Ability   Perceived ability is a factor that has been related positively to flow in both quantitative (Jackson and Roberts, 1992) and qualitative (Jackson, 1995) research. Csikszentmihalyi and Nakamura (1989) suggested that both challenges and skills must be relatively high before anything resembling a flow experience comes about. We focus on perceived sport ability because within the flow model "it is not the skills we actually have that determine how we feel, but the ones we think we have" (Csikszentmihalyi, 1990, p. 75). We would expect that perceived ability would have a positive relationship with flow.

Competitive Trait Anxiety   Competitive trait anxiety (CTA) is the "tendency to perceive competitive situations as threatening and to respond to these situations with feelings of apprehension or tension" (Martens, 1977, p. 23). From a flow perspective, high trait anxiety would be expected to prevent flow because the athlete's psychic energy is too fluid or erratic (see Gould, this volume, for an in-depth treatment of anxiety). A person cannot totally immerse him- or herself in an activity when worry or tension is the primary focus. Anxiety is the antithesis of flow in Csikszentmihalyi's (1975, 1990) flow model. An athlete cannot be in flow while experiencing high anxiety. Jackson (1995) found in her qualitative research that athletes recognized the importance of optimal arousal to achieving flow states. Hence, CTA would be expected to be negatively related to athletes' flow states.

Intrinsic Motivation   Intrinsic motivation is the "innate, organismic needs for competence and self-determination. The intrinsic needs for competence and self-determination motivate an ongoing process of seeking and attempting to conquer optimal challenges" (Deci & Ryan, 1985, p. 32). Self-determination is intimately linked to the concept of autonomy, a person's sense that intentional behavior is self-regulated, flexible, and occurs in the absence of pressure. In contrast, the concept of control refers to intentional behavior that the actor perceives to be coerced by intrapsychic and environmental forces. Theoretically, an individual who perceives autonomy should be more likely to experience flow than an individual who feels pressure toward particular outcomes because she or he will be extremely interested in the task at hand (Deci & Ryan, 1985). Jackson (1995) found high motivation to engage in the activity to be an important flow facilitator for elite athletes. Intrinsic motivation and autotelic experience (Csikszentmihalyi, 1990) are theoretically similar constructs; people engage in autotelic activities for their own sake, with no expectation of future reward. Thus, a positive relationship would be expected between intrinsic motivation and flow.

A study by Jackson and colleagues (Jackson et al, 1998) examined the role of these dispositional factors—task and ego orientation, perceived sport ability, competitive trait anxiety, and intrinsic motivation—in masters athletes' flow states at both the dispositional and state level. We used these potential autotelic personality factors as correlates of flow and expected that perceived ability, task goal orientation, and intrinsic motivation would be positively associated with flow and that competitive trait anxiety would be negatively related to flow. We expected that these dispositional factors would be more associated with a dispositional flow measure, the Dispositional Flow Scale (DFS; Jackson, et al., 1998; Marsh & Jackson, 1999), than a state flow measure, the Flow State Scale (FSS; Jackson & Marsh, 1996) but that there would still be significant associations at the state level. Results indicated that perceived sport ability, an intrinsic motivation factor, and competitive trait anxiety were related in the predicted way to dispositional and state flow, but task and ego goal orientation were unrelated to flow. We are uncertain about why task orientation did not relate to either dispositional or state flow in this study. Notwithstanding this unexpected finding, these findings lend credence to the notion that something akin to autotelic personality may exist. We have a long way to go, however, in figuring out the role of personality factors in understanding optimal experience in sport. Perceptions of sport ability seem to be crucial for flow states, and findings from Jackson et al. (2001) add further support.

These researchers assessed relationships between flow, as measured by both the DFS and the FSS, and psychological skills and strategies and athletic self-concept. Components of athletic self-concept positively related to flow, as assessed by the Elite Athlete Self-Description Questionnaire (Marsh, Hey, Johnson, & Perry, 1997), were mental and physical skills and perception of self as an overall skilled performer in one's event.

Catley & Duda (1997) set out to examine Jackson's (1992, 1995) qualitatively identified antecedents of flow using a quantitative approach. Using recreational golfers as the sample, they found that factors such as confident readiness, positive focus, pessimism, and golfers' skill level had significant relationships with flow.

Russell (2001), using qualitative and quantitative methods with a sample of college athletes, found a set of antecedent flow factors similar to those found by Jackson (1995) in her study of antecedent flow factors in elite athletes. Russell also examined scores on the FSS for any differences between gender or sport type and found none, leading him to conclude that his sample of college athletes experienced flow in the same way, regardless of type of sport or gender.

Flow in Exercise and Physical Activity

To date, much more attention has been paid to flow in sport contexts, with little research conducted on flow in exercise or recreational physical activity settings. Grove & Lewis (1996) provided an early exception with a study that examined hypnotic susceptibility and flowlike states during circuit training. The authors found that experience of flowlike states increased from early to late exercise and that this change was greater for the participants high in hypnotic susceptibility.

Wankel (1985) interviewed exercise program adherers and dropouts to examine the role of quality of experience factors, such as curiosity, social relationship, and developing skills in their exercise participation. Results show that both adherers and dropouts joined the program for health-related reasons such as losing weight and preventing disease. These factors did not differentiate between the adherers and the dropouts. Rather, it was the non-health-related, quality of experience variables that adherers cited as the primary reasons for their continued involvement in the program. Although this study did not examine flow states directly, the results indirectly suggest that optimal experience could be relevant to continued exercise participation.

In another interview study, Szabo and Kimiecik (1997) were interested in asking runners of varying ability and competitive orientation about their flow experiences. Findings suggest that runners who rarely enter races and consider themselves to have average running ability experience flow and view it as reason for running. A 32-year-old female runner in this category put it this way:

> I guess I'm thinking, well the potential for flow keeps you out there, whether or not, I mean I could have zero percent flow or very low percentage of flow experiences or opportunities for them, but the potential for them, because they are a good place to be, is enough to keep me going.

In a large study of aerobic dance exercise participants, Karageorghis, Vlachopoulos, and Terry (2000) found positive associations between flow and the postexercise feelings of revitalization, tranquility, and positive engagement. The authors of this study concluded that flow may encourage adherence to physical activity through the experience of positive postexercise feelings.

Jackson and colleagues have recently been examining the prevalence and relevance of flow to the physical activity experiences of adults engaged in recreational physical activity. Incorporating quantitative and qualitative approaches, these investigations have focused on understanding factors associated with physical activity involvement in nonelite, adult participants: women across different life stages (Jackson, 2007; Jackson & Lee, 2007), and older adults (50 years plus) facing the transition from work to retirement (Jackson et al., 2007). In both studies, there were positive associations between self-reported physical activity and flow experiences. Flow was also positively related to other psychological constructs such as physical dimensions of self-concept, and self-determined motivation. In-depth interviews with the women across lifestages (Jackson & Lee, 2007) demonstrated that flow is both understood and endorsed by female participants taking part in various forms of physical activity. This endorsement, while not true for every interviewee, held across the ages. From one 39-year-old participant came the following response to whether flow was important to her continued participation:

> Without a doubt. It's the only reason I go back. I would go back with sore muscles and difficulty getting child minding, whatever . . . that [flow] would always take me back there. I imagine you probably wouldn't continue [if you didn't get flow]. I imagine that's when people would give up.

One 53-year-old participant in cycling and jogging, when asked how relevant flow was to her participation, said,

> Well, I guess if it wasn't happening then it would be easy to talk yourself out of going, to not be motivated to get out there and I think it's all connected to that sort of thing [flow]. If it wasn't really happening or some factors of it started to sort of fall away, I think that the enjoyment as a whole of the activity would start to dwindle and then as you said you make excuses not to. You'd say, "Oh, I couldn't be bothered today" for more reasons than just that you were tired or it was hot. . . . I would think, "Why bother? There's no point."

Another participant, a 62-year-old swimmer, had this to say when asked how relevant flow was to her participation:

> I'd say it is fairly relevant because that's, you know, the feeling of being in, of enjoyment. So yes, if you didn't get flow, well you wouldn't do it unless you're a real martyr.

More research is needed on flow in various forms of physical activity, with a range of participants, to understand the role of optimal psychological states to participation in such activities. One context where there has been an increasing interest in flow is outdoor adventure, and examples of research conducted in this setting will be briefly summarized next.

Outdoor Adventure and Recreation

Not surprisingly, the setting of outdoor adventure and recreation has seen growth in flow research. Such settings involve participation in self-selected and physically challenging activities that could likely facilitate flow. Walker, Hull, and Roggenbuck (1998) examined the relationships between the quantity of optimal experience during an onsite phase of outdoor recreation and the quantity of benefits obtained offsite. Using a list of three item descriptions of flow developed for the study, participants were asked the extent to which they had experienced the characteristic represented by each item. Responses indicated a moderately high endorsement of the flow characteristics. Quantity of optimal experience during the onsite phase was found to be a predictor of three of four benefit categories measured during the recollection phase. Not all these relationships were linear, and the authors suggested there may be optimum amounts of optimal experience for attainment of postadventure experience benefits.

Jones, Hollenshurst, Perna, and Selin (2000) used a modified ESM to examine flow in white-water kayaking and found associations between the four-channel flow model and subjective experience, as well as support for the positive nature of flow experience. The authors did find that the flow and anxiety channels were experienced similarly during the extreme adventure of whitewater kayaking. Jones, Hollenhurst, and Perna (2003), in a more definitive examination of the four-channel flow model in whitewater kayaking, again found support for the model's predictions in an in-depth examination of experience in different degrees of kayaking difficulty.

An ambitious study examined the flow experiences of rock climbers on a Himalayan expedition (Delle Fave, Bassi, & Massimini, 2003). The climbers were identified as highly experienced, and with the degree of risk involved in the sport of high-altitude climbing, could be regarded as possessing strong psychological skills. By having climbers complete experience sampling forms, the researchers obtained repeated assessment of quality of experience in the various phases of alpine climbing. They found that flow occurred as predicted, when both challenges and skills were high. The authors concluded that motivation to take part in a risky expedition was associated with perceived opportunities to experience flow.

Measurement Challenges

One of the greatest challenges in flow research or any research involving subjective experiences, is finding ways to assess the experience itself accurately and reliably. As with most other sport psychology constructs, there is no one way to measure flow in sport. Flow is an optimal experience, a state of consciousness. Like all experiential phenomena, flow cannot easily be quantified by psychometrics or illuminated through investigative interviewing. No single measurement approach will be able to provide trouble-free assessments of the flow experience. The first author of this chapter has attempted to develop ways of researching flow, both quantitative and qualitative, that may uncover aspects of the experience that will make flow a more accessible concept to both researchers and practitioners.

Qualitative methods can provide rich accounts of flow, and Csikszentmihalyi (1975) used this approach in his first attempts to understand this phenomenon. Jackson, initially employing a primarily quantitative, questionnaire-based approach

(Jackson & Roberts, 1992) to study flow, also interviewed a small subsample of athletes about their flow experiences. The quality of information obtained through the interviews led Jackson to conduct two larger-scale interview-based studies of flow with elite athletes (Jackson, 1992, 1995, 1996). As reviewed earlier, these studies showed that elite athletes have a good experiential grasp of flow.

Certainly, qualitative approaches have limitations, including the retrospective element of interviews, the small samples conducive to this type of research, and the interpretive biases of the researchers, all of which influence understanding of the flow experience. But the fact that flow is amenable to understanding through open-ended interviews makes this approach an important means of continuing to study flow.

Wanting to be able to examine associations between flow and other psychological constructs, Jackson developed the Flow State Scale (FSS) and a corresponding dispositional version of the instrument, the Dispositional Flow Scale (DFS). The DFS is a dispositional assessment of the frequency with which people experience flow. The DFS was designed to assess the dispositional component of flow, whereas the FSS was designed to assess the state component. The FSS is designed to be answered after a specific event to assess the experience of flow in that event. The DFS is designed to assess the frequency with which respondents report experiencing flow in general during participation in their main activity. The assumptions underlying this dual measurement approach are that flow is a specific psychological state amenable to state-based assessments (using the FSS) and that people differ in their propensity to experience flow on a regular basis (using the DFS).

Both the FSS and DFS instruments underwent psychometric analyses and were found to have acceptable factor structure and reliability (Jackson & Marsh, 1996; Marsh & Jackson, 1999). Nine factors, corresponding to the nine flow dimensions, have been validated through confirmatory factor analyses (CFA) of the instruments. Both first-order (nine-factor) models and a higher-order model involving one global flow factor were supported through CFA. One of the factors, time transformation, has shown little relation to the global flow factor in the research with the scale to date. This absence of association may be partly due to the items used to assess this factor, but there is also a possibility that time transformation is not a central dimension to athletes' flow experiences. An additional factor, loss of self-consciousness, has not demonstrated relationships with the global flow measure as strong as those of the other flow factors.

Jackson and Eklund (2002) presented confirmatory factor analytic support for revised versions of the Flow Scales, the DFS–2 and the FSS–2. A small number of item modifications were made to improve the measurement of some of the flow dimensions. Both item identification and cross-validation samples demonstrated acceptable fit of the first-order (nine-factor) model and, to a lesser extent, the global higher-order model. Reliability estimates with both scales were also acceptable, ranging from .78 to .92 across item identification and cross-validation samples. Continuing research with the DFS–2 and FSS–2 should help to clarify the role and relationships among the multidimensional and higher-order flow models.

The Flow Scales provide a valid and reliable means of assessing flow in physical activity, and thus of furthering research on the experience of flow in such contexts. A test manual by Jackson and Eklund (2004) describes the Flow Scales and their use, presents information on their psychometric properties, and provides scoring profiles of different activity groups on the scales. Recent research by Jackson and colleagues (Jackson, Martin, & Eklund 2007; Martin & Jackson, 2007) has explored new, short versions of the Flow Scales, as well as continuing the validation of the DFS-2 and FSS-2. Complementing these 36-item flow scale versions, the short scales provide alternate means of assessing flow. Jackson and Martin, using a construct validity framework, present initial support for both a "composite" flow scale that provides a brief measure of flow according to the dimensional model, as well as a "core" flow scale that taps into the phenomenology of the experience itself.

The experience sampling method (ESM) (Csikszentmihalyi & Larson, 1987) is a popular approach to assessing flow and other subjective states of experience. Study participants wear a beeper or watch programmed to signal at eight random times during a day for a period of one week. ESM participants record measurements of mood, flow characteristics, and other factors such as their motivation to be doing the activity in self-report booklets. Using an operational definition of flow based on equivalence of challenges and skills, researchers assess quality of experience when in flow and when not in flow.

The ESM approach has had limited use in sport and exercise contexts, although there are notable exceptions (Delle Fave et al., 2003), and some researchers (e.g., Jones et al., 2000; Stein et al., 1995) have modified the approach to suit the setting. The idea of random beeping of athletes during performance is understandably greeted with skepticism. But the usefulness of the ESM approach, as evidenced in extensive research with this method (e.g., Csikszentmihalyi & Csikszentmihalyi, 1988; Csikszentmihalyi & Schneider, 2000), suggests that it should not be bypassed as an approach to assessing flow in physical activity. The ESM can be used to study a range of experiential states and cognitions and provides a tool for assessing experience as it occurs.

Jackson (2000) has suggested that a multimethod approach to measurement (i.e., both quantitative and qualitative) will yield the greatest amount and types of information about positive experiential states in sport. As the tools of measurement are refined, the possibilities for gathering important information about these experiences will increase significantly. As the research reviewed in this chapter indicates, both qualitative and quantitative approaches provide a unique understanding of factors that may be associated with flow experiences in sport. Every empirical approach used to study flow has limitations, but each has potential to provide some useful information about flow and the factors associated with this state. Continued expansion of the research base on flow is needed, using a variety of instrumentation and methodologies, to deepen understanding of what it is like to be in flow and to identify relevant antecedents and consequences to the flow experience. The next section provides a brief discussion on some of the issues from a scientific paradigmatic perspective relevant to the study of flow.

Scientific Paradigms

Flow as an area of scientific study serves as a rich metaphor for examining some of the paradigmatic issues that have been addressed by others in sport psychology (e.g., Dewar & Horn, 1992; Feltz, 1987; Martens, 1987) and by those who have examined the epistemology and paradigms of science (Fahlberg & Fahlberg, 1994; Lincoln & Guba, 1985; Valle, King, & Halling, 1989). We have many more questions than answers on these issues as they pertain to studying flow, but we believe that they are issues worth addressing.

Recent research on flow in physical activity has been attempting to examine correlates of flow, a subjective experience, with variables that could be categorized as cognitions or perceptions (e.g., perceived ability). The variables that have been used are important as demonstrated by the significant findings to date (e.g., Jackson et al., 1998, 2001; Kowal & Fortier, 1999), but they are removed from the phenomenology or lived experience of the individual. From a naturalistic paradigm (e.g., Lincoln & Guba, 1985) or existential phenomenological perspective (e.g., Valle et al., 1989), one would probably not search for antecedents of flow states.

According to Valle et al. (1989), mainstream psychology, based on the positivistic, hypothetico-deductive philosophy of science, is designed to deal only with the behavior half of the behavior–experience polarity. The major emphasis is on asking *why* questions through a cause–effect analysis. Hence, most of the psychological factors of interest to sport psychologists, such as self-efficacy and anxiety, have been developed and studied within this scientific paradigm. More important, they are used to explain, understand, and predict behavior.

The existential phenomenological approach, similar to interpretivistic philosophy of science espoused by Lincoln and Guba (1985), seeks to "explicate the essence, structure, or form of both human *experience* and human behavior as revealed through essentially descriptive techniques including disciplined reflection" (Valle et al., 1989, p. 6). In this approach, linear causality (cause–effect) thinking, hypothesis generation, and asking *why* questions are nonexistent. Rather, the emphasis is on elucidating lived experience by asking *what* questions

This issue is relevant for those interested in studying flow. The quantitative research assessing flow and variables related to its occurrence in sport come from interest among researchers in exploring the factors that affect the occurrence of flow in physical activity settings. This is an interesting topic from both a conceptual and an applied level. Because of the uniqueness of the flow experience, however, continuing to explore the phenomenology of this experience is also important. Different methodological approaches are suited to addressing different types of questions about flow. Although a quantitative approach can provide information about the relationship among different psychological variables with flow, qualitative methods fare much better when attempting to understand lived experience. Sparkes and Partington (2003) favor a specific line of qualitative inquiry known as narrative practice, and they have provided examples of how one could go about studying flow from this perspective.

Combining quantitative and qualitative perspectives is not without its problems from a philosophy of science perspective (Buchanan, 1992). A pragmatic approach, however, would suggest that it is useful to use whatever methods can answer the questions of interest (Patton, 1990). At this point, we certainly encourage multiple approaches, multiple methods, to the study of flow. Although we have provided the reader with some research possibilities throughout this chapter, we end this review with some additional future directions for those who want to continue to further the investigation of flow in physical activity.

Future Research Directions

A number of possibilities exist for creative researchers who are willing to deal with the ambiguity and challenge of studying flow in physical activity. Here we present some ideas for continuing to explore the role of flow in understanding physical activity experiences.

An interesting and fruitful research direction would be to examine the dynamic interaction between potential person and situational antecedents of flow experiences. What types of person factors (e.g., attentional style) interact with what kinds of contexts (e.g., type of sport situation) to produce the optimal physical activity experiences? Currently much of the research has examined either person factors or situational factors and their association with flow, but not both together. This interactive type of research may be complex and difficult but could open new doors of knowledge about flow states. Jackson and colleagues (e.g., 1998, 2001) have made some initial progress by using dispositional and state flow measures and examining associations with person-level and situational factors in sport.

Research on the different quadrants of experience in the flow model, such as flow, anxiety, relaxation, and apathy, will help deepen understanding of perceived quality of experience in physical activity. For instance, some research (Ellis et al., 1994; Mandigo et al., 1998; Moneta & Csikszentmihalyi, 1996; Stein et al., 1995) has found high skill–low challenge (i.e., the quadrant labeled "relaxation") to be a positive experiential state. Examining the four-channel flow model in different contexts would increase understanding of different types of subjective experiences that are defined by the relative balance of challenges and skills. Jones and colleagues (Jones et al., 2000, 2003) have provided examples of ways to examine the four-channel flow model in outdoor adventure settings. Sport, with its varying degrees of competition, is an ideal setting in which to study the effect of varying challenge and skill on quality of experience. A recent study by Stavrou, Jackson, Zervas,

& Karteroliotis (2007) examined the four channel flow model in a sample of competitive athletes. Athletes in the flow and relaxation quadrants reported the most optimal states, while athletes in the apathy quadrant reported the least optimal state. Perceived skills demonstrated stronger relationships with flow dimensions than perceived challenges.

An interdisciplinary approach would be useful in examining the link between flow states, hemispheric functioning, and sport performance. Integrating the psychosocial approach to studying flow with sport psychophysiology (Hatfield & Landers, 1983) would seem to be an ideal way in which to begin examining the role of optimal experience and its connection to psychophysiological phenomena. As Csikszentmihalyi (1988) pointed out, early neurophysiological studies by Hamilton (1976, 1981) showed that people who can turn boring situations into flowlike ones process information in a peculiar way. When they concentrate on a task, it seems that their cortical activation level, which measures their expenditure of mental effort, decreases from baseline, instead of increasing, as it normally should. This process could be a neurological indication of one of the central components of the phenomenology of flow, a measure of deep concentration on a limited stimulus field that excludes everything else from consciousness.

Sport researchers using psychophysiological approaches (e.g., Crews & Landers, 1990; Salazar, et al., 1990) have been interested in hemispheric asymmetries in EEG activity to examine attentional focus in a variety of sport tasks. The left hemisphere appears to process information analytically and is more involved in language, whereas the right hemisphere processes information holistically and is more adept at spatial cognitive processing and pattern recognition. In general, results from hemispheric studies in sport show that elite athletes (e.g., archers, marksmen) have a higher degree of alpha activity in the left hemisphere than in the right hemisphere in the seconds before performing their task. Alpha waves are indicators of relaxation, a state considered useful for sport performance. Their presence would mean that the left hemisphere is less active, thus reducing cognitions unnecessary to performance of the task (Boutcher, 1992).

Is there a connection between flow and brain wave patterns? Is the result of increased alpha activity in the left hemisphere an optimal state of mind? What comes first? Does flow lead to differential brain wave patterns? Psychophysiologists argue that retrospective self-report of optimal states views attentional functioning as an outcome rather

than a process and does not tell us much about the underlying process (see Boutcher, 1992; Hatfield & Landers, 1983). Certainly, using self-report to assess optimal attentional patterns has limitations, but we ask these questions: What is the cause of the differential brain wave patterns that the sport psychophysiological research has identified? How do elite archers, for example, suppress left-brain involvement in performance through an increase in alpha waves? How is the brain wave activity self-regulated? Boutcher (1992, p. 262) has suggested that this optimal brain wave pattern may be created by "the athlete who directs arousal away from task-irrelevant information and into the task itself." This notion would indicate that an optimal conscious thought process (i.e., flow) is needed to direct the athlete to the automatic processing aspect of attention, which some consider to be free of conscious monitoring (Schneider, Dumais, & Shiffrin, 1984). To address these issues, investigators could conduct creative and innovative research that integrates the psychosocial perspective with the psychophysiological perspective on optimal attentional processes and experiences in physical activity. Dietrich (2004) offered a related suggestion by calling for research to address neurocognitive mechanisms associated with flow. In this recent paper on how neurocognitive mechanisms might help explain the flow process, Dietrich theorized that flow occurs when a highly practiced skill is represented in the knowledge base of the implicit system without interference from the explicit system.

More research about optimal experience is needed on a wide range of physical activity participants. For example, elite athletes suggest that flow is important to their participation in their sport (Jackson, 1995). Do nonelite or recreational participants have similar views? This question becomes even more relevant as we cross over from a sport performance perspective to more of a physical activity and long-term health perspective. What motivates people who do not have high athletic ability to exercise regularly? As the surgeon general's report on physical activity and health suggests (U.S. Department of Health and Human Services, 1996), finding answers to this question is a high priority in the public health field. Does optimal experience play a role in people's continued participation in physical activity?

The findings from Jackson and colleagues' research in this setting (e.g., Jackson & Lee, 2007; Jackson et al., 2007) suggests that there is a relationship between flow and recreational physical activity involvement for adults. In particular, the in-depth investigation of the experiences of female physical activity participants (Jackson, 2007; Jackson & Lee, 2007) supports the idea that flow is a relevant, real, and important experience to the "everyday" athlete. The research that has been conducted outside of competitive sport settings suggest that regular physical activity participants both experience and value their optimal experiences in ways similar to elite athletes. Research on flow across all forms of meaningful physical activity will add to the existing knowledge base of flow in this broad context and has potential to enhance participation for all types of physical activity participants.

Along these same lines, work on flow could be integrated with some of the exciting work done on the role of emotions in exercise contexts (e.g., Gauvin, Rejeski, & Norris, 1996). Flow theory suggests that quality of experience is optimal when people experience flow. That is, individuals in flow typically experience greater postexperience positive affect and potency than do individuals in boredom, anxiety, or apathetic states (e.g., Csikszentmihalyi & LeFevre, 1989). In a study with women, Gauvin and colleagues (1996) found that acute bouts of vigorous physical activity were associated with significant improvements in affect and feeling states over a six-week period. Could positive experience during exercise be a mediating variable between exercise and feeling states? That is, do people who experience flow during exercise have greater positive affect than people who do not experience flow?

Research with the FSS–2, DFS–2 (Jackson & Eklund, 2002, 2004), the newly developed short versions of the Flow Scales (Jackson, Martin, & Eklund 2007; Martin & Jackson, 2007), and the ESM (e.g., Csikszentmihalyi & Larson, 1987) should provide useful quantitative information about the experience of flow in various physical activity contexts. One use of these instruments, perhaps conjointly, could include how quality of experience in physical activity relates to quality of experience in other areas of people's lives. In addition, the Flow Scales and the ESM provide opportunities to examine antecedents and consequences of flow as they occur in sport and exercise settings. Continued research using all viable methodologies will further understanding of the person and situational factors that underlie flow states in physical activity.

Conclusion

We began this chapter by suggesting that optimal experiences in physical activity provide a rich and valuable source for understanding participation. Flow, one form of optimal subjective experience, has been shown to play a central role in positive physical activity experiences. We need to know more about how person factors and the physical activity context shape and influence flow states. Measurement and scientific paradigmatic issues are both relevant and influence the approach to studying flow and the interpretation of findings.

In the end, the importance and relevance of flow in sport and other physical activity contexts is a matter of belief. Is there a state of mind in which a person is totally absorbed in the task with focused concentration, an optimal psychological state that stands out from everyday life? Do moments occur when everything is just right with the world, when an athlete, worker, or parent experiences magic? The empirical and anecdotal evidence suggests that such a state does exist, and that this state of mind has important implications for human development, quality of life, and performance. We believe that this optimal state of mind not only exists but is worthy of continued study in physical activity contexts, and that it is the "bottom line of existence." Flow is a way of getting at the meaning, or lived experience, of living. As Fahlberg and Fahlberg (1994, p. 108) stated,

> When we realize, finally, that human beings are more than mere objects to be manipulated and controlled, then we can truly understand the necessity of recognizing this human world through the described epistemologies. Meaning in life and the freedom to live that life then become concerns for reflection and inquiry. When human consciousness and meaning are recognized, a human science for movement is possible.

Flow should be at the core of any human science focused on understanding the links among consciousness, movement, and what it means to live a life.

Author's note: *Aspects of this chapter were supported by funding from the Australian Research Council to the first author.*

CHAPTER 17

Athletic Injury and Sport Behavior

■ Eileen Udry, PhD   ■ Mark B. Andersen, PhD ■

Many people today lead sedentary lives, and health professionals from a variety of realms spend considerable time and resources attempting, often with limited success, to increase activity levels among sedentary people. But for another group of people, namely athletes, being forced into physical inactivity, because of injuries, often constitutes a significant form of stress. Although the epidemiological evidence suggests that injury rates tend to vary by the type of sport and level of participation (Uitenbroek, 1996), injuries are endemic to sport. Recognizing that no athlete is immune to injuries, Richard Steadman, a prominent orthopedic surgeon, called sport injuries "the greatest equalizers" (Steadman, 1993).

Despite the best efforts to prevent injuries, they will never be eliminated. But it is of both theoretical and practical interest to ask whether there are ways to reduce the risk of injury by using what is known about the psychological factors associated with injuries. A related topic of interest is to examine ways to ameliorate the stress associated with athletic injuries after they occur and to facilitate recovery and rehabilitation. The purpose of this chapter is to explore these issues. The chapter is organized into four major sections. We begin with a discussion of operational definitions and measurement issues that are germane to understanding the psychological aspects of athletic injuries. These issues are important starting points, because the way that injury-related terms have been operationally defined in previous research has varied considerably, causing substantial confusion. Second, we review the literature pertaining to the psychological antecedents, or precursors, to athletic injuries along with interventions aimed at reducing injury risk. Third, we examine athletes' responses, both psychological and behavioral, to injuries. In the fourth section we provide directions for future research relative to both the antecedents and responses to injuries.

Definitions and Measurement Challenges

What is an athletic injury? How would one measure injury? We need to answer two extremely basic questions before research can progress. Unfortunately, these questions tend to be asked infrequently and are not satisfactorily answered in the psychologically based injury literature. Athletic injuries have been perfunctorily defined as any injury that results in missed practice or competition or alters participation (e.g., Blackwell & McCullagh, 1990). Athletes,

however, become injured from factors other than sport participation. If a football player slips in the shower and splits his chin open, is the injury an athletic injury? If a softball player on the way to practice has a bicycle accident and jams her knee, is the injury an athletic injury? One would hardly consider these athletic injuries, yet they would cause athletes to miss or modify their practice sessions. When we examined the literature, we found that some studies included any injury that occurred during a certain period of time (e.g., Hanson, McCullagh, & Tonymon, 1992) whereas others used athletic training reports and identified the situation of injury (e.g., game or practice; Petrie, 1993a). The former study presumably included nonathletic injuries, whereas the latter study did not mention what was done with data from nonathletic injuries.

Would an operational definition of athletic injury such as "those injuries occurring only in an athletic context that require missing or modifying practice or competition for one day or more" be valuable and more precise than the various definitions found in the literature? We do not believe that this definition is particularly helpful. The objective of all studies on athletic injury, and the ultimate goal of injury research, is improved health and welfare of athletes in and outside their sports. Thus, instead of looking at "athletic" injury, we would be better served by examining "athlete" injuries. A more thorough discussion of measurement and definitional issues is provided by Petrie and Falkstein (1998) and Andersen and Williams (1999).

After an injury has occurred, athletes typically are involved in some type of rehabilitation program. Knowing the degree to which athletes maintain their rehabilitation programs is frequently of interest. The terms *compliance* and *adherence* often are used interchangeably to describe rehabilitation-related behaviors. Using these terms in this manner, however, has also been a source of confusion. Agris (1989) contended that the term *compliance* should be used when referring to people who follow a regimen prescribed by a health care provider and that this term implies a relatively passive role on the part of the patient. In contrast, the term *adherence* suggests a more equitable role in which people participate in establishing the regimen and determining how they will reach various rehabilitation goals. In general, the more complex and long-term the health problem is, the more desirable it is to use an adherence approach rather than a compliance approach. Brewer (1998) noted that athletic rehabilitation programs are often relatively complex and may include instructions for restricting physical activity (e.g., workout limitations), completing home exercises, performing cryotherapy, attending physical therapy sessions, and taking prescribed medications in the proper dosages. Thus, sport injury rehabilitation may encompass a multitude of behaviors and take place in a number of settings (Brewer, 1998). Again, the term *adherence*, as opposed to *compliance*, may be more appropriate.

Injury Antecedents

Understanding the factors that might predispose athletes to increased risk of injury has been the focus of considerable research. These injury antecedents have been examined from a variety of perspectives, including physical and physiological (e.g., body composition), anatomical (e.g., biomechanical factors), and environmental (e.g., training surfaces). Although the influence of these factors is not disputed, the scope of this chapter is limited to examining the role that psychological factors may play in increasing the risk of injuries among athletes.

Research into the psychosocial antecedents of athletic injury has its roots in the landmark work of Holmes and Rahe (1967). Their work on the relationship between the stress of major life events and illness outcome sparked a revolution in behavioral medicine. They found that people who had experienced many major life events (e.g., death of a loved one, divorce, moving to a new place) over the previous year were much more likely to fall ill in the near future than those who had experienced lower levels of life events stress. They believed that the stress of adjusting to major life events left a person more susceptible to disease. In support of Holmes and Rahe, overwhelming evidence now shows that stress has negative effects on immune system function (O'Leary, 1990).

In 1970 Holmes used the Social and Readjustment Rating Scale (Holmes & Rahe, 1967) as a predictor of American football injuries, not illness. Holmes found that football players who had experienced many major life events were more likely to incur athletic injuries than those who had experienced few life events. Later, Bramwell, Masuda, Wagner, and Holmes (1975) modified the Social and Readjustment Rating Scale to fit American university athletes. Using that scale, they found similar results among football players, with the high life events group experiencing the most injuries. Cryan and Alles (1983), using the Social and Athletic Readjustment Rating Scale, replicated the findings of Bramwell et al. (1975) with another university football team.

Sarason, Johnson, and Siegel (1978) refined the measurement of life events by distinguishing between negative events and positive ones. Their Life Experiences Survey was modified for an athletic population by Passer and Seese (1983), who found that positive life events were not linked to football injury but negative life events were. Again, football players with more negative life events stress were more likely to be injured. Passer and Seese were also the first researchers to test for the influence of personality moderator variables (e.g., locus of control) on the effects of life events stress on injury outcome. They did not, however, find any significant connections between personality variables and likelihood of injury.

The available research suggests that the association between life events stress and sport injuries is robust. In a comprehensive review of the research literature, Williams and Roepke (1993) examined 20 studies (Blackwell & McCullagh, 1990; Bramwell et al., 1975; Coddington & Troxell, 1980; Cryan & Alles, 1983; Hanson et al., 1992; Hardy, O'Connor, & Geisler, 1990; Hardy, Prentice, Kirsanoff, Richman, & Rosenfeld, 1987; Hardy, Richman, & Rosenfeld, 1991; Hardy & Riehl, 1988; Holmes, 1970; Kerr & Minden, 1988; Lysens, Vanden Auweele, & Ostyn, 1986; J.R. May, Veach, Reed, & Griffey, 1985; J.R. May, Veach, Southard, & Herring, 1985; Passer & Seese, 1983; Petrie, 1992; R.E. Smith, Ptacek, & Smoll, 1992; R.E. Smith, Smoll, & Ptacek, 1990) and found significant positive associations between life events, stress, and athlete injuries in 18 of them. In a subsequent review, Williams and Andersen (1998) reported that of the 10 athletic injury and life events stress studies conducted since the Williams and Roepke review, 9 found similar associations (Andersen & Williams, 1999; Byrd, 1993; Fawkner, 1995; Kolt & Kirkby, 1996; Meyer, 1995; Perna & McDowell, 1993; Petrie, 1993a, 1993b; Thompson & Morris, 1994). Given that life events stress and injury relationships occurred across many different sports and came from studies that measured the variables in a variety of ways, these results are convincing. The relationship between life events stress and sport injuries, however, is complex, because at least one study (Petrie, 1993b) showed that even positive life events can be related to injury.

As noted previously, the early studies (e.g., Bramwell et al., 1975; Holmes, 1970) that tested the relationship between psychosocial variables and athletic injury produced findings that paralleled those from the field of psychoneuroimmunology, whereby an increased risk of life events stress was associated with an increased risk of illness. One difference, however, was that in the area of psycho-neuroimmunology, the immune system was clearly identified as the mediating link between life events stress and increased risk of illness. The connections between athletic injuries and life events stress did not have the same clear evidence of association between life events stress and immune system compromise. A sport-specific model for injury antecedents was needed. A comprehensive theoretical framework for the relationship between stress and athletic injury, along with proposed mechanisms behind that relationship, appeared in the literature in 1988 (Andersen & Williams, 1988). We now turn to a more complete description of this model and the related research.

A Stress-Based Model of Athletic Injury

By examining the stress–injury (see previously cited references), stress–accident, and stress–illness literatures (e.g., Stuart & Brown, 1981), Andersen and Williams (1988) developed a model that proposed possible factors and underlying mechanisms for the relationship between stress and athletic injury. The model is the most comprehensive and influential model concerning antecedents to athletic injury yet developed, and for that reason we limit our discussion to this framework. More specifically, this model includes three broad categories of psychosocial

factors (personality, history of stressors, and coping resources) along with two major categories of interventions aimed at reducing injury risk through addressing either the cognitive appraisal or the physiological and attentional aspects of the stress response. In 1998 Williams and Andersen reviewed the evidence for the viability of the model and revised its structure slightly. Figure 17.1 represents a schematic of the model in its updated form. In the following sections, we discuss the components of the model and their links with each other.

The Stress Response

The core of the model of stress and athletic injury is the stress response. The model suggests that when athletes confront potentially stressful athletic situations, they will make cognitive appraisals of the demands of the situation, their abilities to meet the demands, and the consequences of meeting (or not meeting) those demands. If athletes perceive that the demands of the situation are greater than their resources and that the consequences of failing to meet the demands are dire (e.g., being cut from the team), then their stress responses, and the accompanying physiological and attentional disruptions, may be substantial. Many physiological responses occur during stress (e.g., sympathetic nervous system activation), but one response that is most likely to influence injury outcome is peripheral narrowing, such as not detecting important peripheral

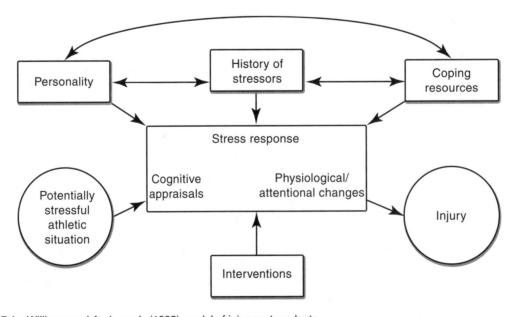

Figure 17.1 Williams and Andersen's (1998) model of injury antecedents.

visual (or auditory) cues that would alert the athlete to being in harm's way (e.g., a tackler coming in from the side in football).

Most of the research involving stress responsivity and perceptual or attentional changes has been laboratory based. Williams, Tonymon, and Andersen (1990, 1991) found that people who had recently experienced substantial life events stress and daily hassles exhibited greater peripheral narrowing during laboratory stress than did participants with opposite profiles, suggesting that those with more stressors in their lives have greater stress responses. Williams and Andersen (1997) also found that individuals with greater life events stress had more perceptual deficits in the central field of vision (greater distractibility). Additionally, they found that males with high life events stress, low coping resources, and low social support had the lowest perceptual sensitivity. Andersen and Williams (1999) also examined athletes' stress responses in the laboratory and then linked those responses to injuries recorded over the competitive season. The researchers found that peripheral narrowing during laboratory stress and major negative life events together accounted for 26% of subsequent injury incidence variance for athletes low in social support. Thus, the connection between life events, perceptual deficits, social support, and injury outcome was finally demonstrated.

Other laboratory research on life events stress and perceptual deficits during stress has produced some interesting results. Bum, Morris, and Andersen (1996) attempted to make laboratory conditions more ecologically valid by adding physiological and auditory stress to perceptual detection tasks. They found that as stress increased across experimental conditions (noise only, physical activity only, noise and physical activity together), perceptual deficits also increased, and the deficits increased more for those high in negative life events stress. Even more interesting, Bum, Morris, and Andersen (1998) found that a simple program of relaxation (autogenic training) for an experimental group resulted in better peripheral detection and response to central vision targets than what occurred in a nonintervention control group. These results suggest that simple interventions may help reduce stress responsivity and thus, possibly, injury risk.

Generalized muscle tension during stress is another obvious response that may predispose athletes to injury. Generalized muscle tension may lead to uncoordinated movements, awkward landings, and increased fatigue, especially in prolonged performance (e.g., a soccer match). Performing with antagonistic and agonistic muscles fighting each other can easily lead to a variety of musculoskeletal strains and sprains. Only one study (Andersen, 1989) examined muscle tension (through EMG) and stress under laboratory conditions, but it did not find a significant connection between life events stress and generalized muscle tension. EMG data, however, are notoriously labile, warranting further research in this area.

The laboratory research described in this section strongly suggests why people with high life events stress and low buffering factors have greater perceptual deficits during stress. Furthermore, Andersen and Williams (1999) established the connections between life events stress in laboratory situations, perceptual changes during stress, and subsequent injury in actual athletic contexts. Bum et al. (1996, 1998) attempted to make laboratory conditions closer to real competitive conditions, but the stress of competition is difficult to replicate. The work of Bum et al., however, needs to be expanded to include season-long injury data on athletes tested under laboratory conditions. In the future, with telemetry technology, researchers may be able to examine stress responsivity (but probably not perceptual deficits) and athletic injury as they occur in the field. Such research may provide more real-life information on the usefulness of the stress–injury model. For the most recent test of peripheral vision deficits and injury, see Rogers and Landers (2005).

History of Stressors

In the previous section we discussed the center of figure 17.1—the stress response. We now discuss the history of stressors, which is shown at the top middle portion of figure 17.1. The category of history of stressors includes three factors: life events stress, daily hassles, and previous injuries. The role of major life events stress and athletic injury was discussed extensively in the previous section. Kanner, Coyne, Schaefer, and Lazarus (1981) originally suggested that major life events may cause stress and disrupt lives because such events increase minor problems and hassles. For example, the death of a spouse may result in a wide range of demands being placed on the survivor (e.g., paying bills, transportation, settling an estate) that may be relatively minor but are chronic daily hassles. These chronic stressors may exert daily wear and tear on an individual.

Several research studies have examined the hypothesized connection between daily hassles and athletic injuries. Research into daily hassles and athletic injury, except for one study, has not produced a solid connection (e.g., Blackwell & McCullagh,

1990; Hanson et al., 1992; Meyer, 1995; R.E. Smith et al., 1990). The problem with the previous studies, however, is that daily hassles were measured at only one time or over monthly periods (e.g., Byrd, 1993; Meyer, 1995). Daily hassles are dynamic and need to be measured more frequently over the course of an athletic season. For university athletes, for example, one would expect an increase in hassles before each major competition and during both the end-of-season playoffs and the end-of-semester final exams. Measuring daily hassles only once, or monthly, over the course of an injury study seems to miss the point of examining this variable.

A study conducted by Fawkner, McMurray, and Summers (1999) demonstrated the value of measuring the construct of daily hassles more frequently. In this work, Fawkner et al. measured hassles every week during athletes' competitive seasons. They found a dramatic increase in hassles the week before, and the week of, athletic injuries. These results provide a strong rationale for the continued examination of this stress variable in athletic injury research. Bringer and Udry (1998), however, did not find a connection with biweekly measures of daily hassles and injury outcome. Thus, the role of daily hassles in injury research is still not firmly established and additional research in this area is needed.

The model of stress and athletic injury (Andersen & Williams, 1988) included previous injury as part of the history of stressors. This variable has not been examined extensively, but Lysens et al. (1984) found that if physical education students had a history of injury, then they also had a greater likelihood of a future injury. Increased likelihood of injury because of previous injury may stem from returning to full physical activity before being completely recovered physically or returning to physical activity before being psychologically ready. For example, athletes may be physically recovered but still have anxieties about returning to activities and possibly being injured again. Those anxieties may lead to substantial stress responses and thus may set up athletes for reinjury. Researchers may wish to examine previous injury and the related variable of psychological readiness to return to full activity as predictors of future injury, because these variables may have substantial relationships to who becomes injured again.

Personality

The personality section of figure 17.1 (upper left) has received considerably less attention from researchers than the history of stressors. Andersen and Williams (1988, 1993) hypothesized that the presence of certain personality traits, such as hardiness, would predispose athletes to view athletic situations as less threatening and more challenging, resulting in lower stress responses and thus lower injury risk. Other traits, such as competitive anxiety, would be hypothesized to predispose athletes to exhibit more pronounced stress responses in competitive situations and, consequently, injury risk would be greater. Research into personality and athletic injury has produced mixed results. Some studies have shown relationships between self-concept, locus of control, or trait anxiety and injury (e.g., Kolt & Kirkby, 1996; Pargman & Lunt, 1989). Others have shown no relationship between these variables (Hanson et al., 1992; Kerr & Minden, 1988; McLeod & Kirkby, 1995).

The personality trait and personality-related variables of sensation seeking and positive states of mind have emerged as predictors of injury outcome. R.E. Smith et al. (1992), in a study of 425 male and female high school athletes from a variety of sports, found a positive relationship between sport-related stressors and injury time loss only for athletes who tested low on the personality variable of sensation seeking. A secondary hypothesis, that high sensation seekers would incur more injuries because of greater risk-taking behavior, was not supported.

Positive states of mind, the ability to experience positive states such as maintaining focus, sharing with others, and staying relaxed, are also related to injury risk. Williams, Hogan, and Andersen (1993) showed that athletes who were able to experience more positive states of mind were less likely to become injured.

Although Andersen and Williams (1988) did not propose Type A personality as a predisposing factor for athletic injuries, research by K.B. Fields, Delaney, and Hinkle (1990) indicated that runners who scored higher on a type A personality scale were more likely to become injured. Meyer (1995) used a sample of runners to examine the personality traits of perfectionism and denial and found that people who scored high on both personality variables also had the strongest relationships to negative life events and injury. The athletes in both of the previously mentioned studies were long-distance runners, and many of their injuries were from overuse. As Williams and Andersen (1998) suggested, personality variables such as perfectionism may influence overuse or chronic injuries, which therefore may not be the product of an acute stress response. The studies mentioned here are provocative and suggest that personality and personality-related variables need more attention in psychosocial factors and athletic injury research.

As mentioned previously, the personality–injury research is a mixed bag. The equivocality of the personality results likely stems from measurement and methodological problems (e.g., sport versus general measures of personality, issues of statistical power, and definitions and measurements of injury). Because of space limitations, the complex problems of personality and injury research are not discussed in detail here. The interested reader should consult Williams and Andersen (1998) for an overview of the difficulties in personality, sport, and injury research.

Coping Resources

The third set of factors that Williams and Andersen (1998) proposed as having an effect on athletic injury is coping resources. This category, shown in the upper right portion of figure 17.1, includes such resources as general coping skills and strategies, stress management, and social support. Several studies have supported the link between general coping and athletic injuries. Specifically, in the Williams, Tonymon, and Wadsworth (1986) study with volleyball players, amount of coping resources was the only significant predictor of athletic injury; those low in coping resources had more injuries. Hanson et al. (1992) also found that amount of coping resources was the best discriminator for both severity and number of injuries. In a nonsport but related area, Noh, Morris, and Andersen (2005) found a moderate relationship between stress, coping skills, and frequency of injury among ballet dancers. Rogers and Landers (2005) demonstrated that life events stress and coping skills were significant predictors of athlete injuries and that peripheral narrowing mediated this relationship.

The research on the influence of social support on athletic injuries has not provided clear results. Some studies have shown a direct effect of social support on injury; athletes who were low in social support exhibited more injuries (e.g., Byrd, 1993; Hardy et al., 1987, 1990). Other studies have found that the relationship between social support and injury may occur only in extreme groups (Andersen & Williams, 1999; Petrie, 1992; R.E. Smith et al., 1990). Smith et al., for example, found a strong relationship between negative life events stress and injury outcome only for athletes who had both low social support and low coping resources, showing that the relationship between life events and injury is not simple. One of the goals of athletic injury research is to identify those at risk, and Smith et al. suggested that those with many major life events

are not the only ones who are vulnerable. Rather, their work suggests that athletes who are also low in psychosocial variables that operate in conjunction (i.e., low social support and low coping resources) are at risk. These findings should be carefully considered in any research on antecedent psychosocial factors and athletic injury.

In their stress-based models of athletic injury, Andersen and Williams (1988) and Williams and Andersen (1998) suggested that social support could have either a direct effect on stress responsivity and injury outcome or an indirect (buffering) effect by serving as a moderator of the history of stressors. These two paths of influence reflect current models of social support in the general health literature (Cohen & Wills, 1985). More support for the buffering model has appeared in the athletic injury research. Along with R.E. Smith et al. (1990), Petrie (1992) found a relationship between life stress and injury only for gymnasts who were low in social support. For gymnasts with high life events stress but also high social support, it appeared that social support buffered the negative effects of life stress. In a later study, Petrie (1993a) supported his 1992 findings but also found something not predicted. Starters on teams under conditions of low stress and high social support were more likely to be injured than were those with low levels of support. Petrie suggested that under low levels of stress and high social support, greater risk-taking behaviors may occur, placing athletes at higher risk of injury. Similarly, Hardy et al. (1991) also found some unexpected results. For example, high levels of social support among male athletes with object losses or high positive life events were associated with negative well-being.

To summarize, the influence of social support in particular, and coping more generally, is an important facet of understanding athletic injury outcomes. The relationship of social support to injury outcome, however, has produced some unexpected findings. One reason that the link between social support and injuries has been associated with unexpected findings may be related to the multidimensional nature of social support. That is, different types of social support (e.g., emotional challenge versus listening support) may have different relationships to injury risk.

Intervention, or Prevention, Research

The final component of the Williams and Andersen (1998) model, shown in the bottom portion of figure 17.1, focuses on intervention, or prevention, research as it relates to athletic injuries. According to

Williams and Andersen (1998), interventions that focus on injury prevention from a psychological perspective may occur because the intervention influences at least one of two possible pathways. One pathway predicted to reduce stress reactivity is through the cognitive appraisal of potentially stressful events (Williams & Andersen, 2007). This pathway would include interventions that focus on changing maladaptive thought patterns, developing and maintaining realistic expectations for performance, and optimizing coach–athlete interactions. The second predicted pathway for reducing stress reactivity is through dampening the physiological activation and attentional disruptions associated with the stress response. Interventions aimed at working though this pathway would include progressive muscle relaxation, meditation, and concentration training (Williams & Andersen, 2007).

Research conducted since the last edition of this chapter was published suggests that it may be possible to prevent injuries through thoughtfully planned psychologically based interventions. Davis (1991) conducted one of the first studies that approached injury prevention from a psychological perspective. Using a relaxation-based intervention, Davis reported reductions in injury rates that ranged from 33% for football players to 52% for swimmers. A limitation of this study, however, was the use of a retrospective design. Using a more rigorous design, Kerr and Goss (1996) provided gymnasts with a 16-session stress management program delivered over eight months. The program was essentially Meichenbaum's (1985) stress inoculation training (SIT). Although the injury incidence reduction indices for the control group and the experimental group receiving the training were not statistically significantly different from each other, there was an apparent reduction in injury (the effect size, Cohen's *d*, was .67, which is in the medium to large range). Andersen and Stoové (1998) suggested that Kerr and Goss' nonsignificant findings were more a problem of power and Type II error, and that given the effect size, there was substantial evidence that the stress management program was effective in reducing injury incidence.

Kolt, Hume, Smith, and Williams (2004) conducted an injury prevention intervention similar to that of Kerr and Goss (1996) in that it provided gymnasts with SIT training through 12 one-hour sessions over 24 weeks. No statistically significant differences in injuries were found between the control group and the gymnasts receiving the intervention. Williams and Andersen (2007) noted, however, that some evidence indicated that the intervention

was effective based on effect sizes. Specifically, as with the Kerr and Goss study, the sample size was small (*n* = 10 in each group), and sufficient statistical power may have been lacking.

Perna and colleagues (Perna, Antoni, Baum, Gordon, & Schneiderman, 2003) recently conducted a single-blind randomized clinical trial with competitive collegiate rowers. The experimental group received a structured seven-week intervention that was also based on SIT. To control for efficacy expectations and experimenter attention, the control group received a single educational session on stress management. Athletes in the experimental group had a significant reduction in the number of days lost to injury or illness and had half the number of health service visits as compared with the control group. Follow-up analyses indicated that the intervention effects were partially mediated by negative mood.

The work of Johnson, Ekengren, and Andersen (2005) highlighted the utility of targeting athletes who are at high risk for incurring injuries for intervention efforts. Participants in this research were soccer players identified as being at a high risk for injury based on profiles assessing sport anxiety levels, sport coping responses, and life events stress. Participants in the experimental group received brief therapy, which consisted of training in six mental skills (e.g., stress management, goal setting, relaxation) taught over a 19-week competitive season. Participants in the intervention group had significantly fewer injuries than did those in the control group. Specifically, in the experimental group 3 injuries occurred, whereas in the control group 21 injuries occurred and some athletes experienced multiple injuries. Other recent research supports Johnson et al.'s work. Specifically, Maddison and Prapavessis (2005) delivered a stress management intervention to a group of athletes who were identified as at risk based on their previous injuries, coping skills, and social support levels. Athletes in the treatment group lost less time to injuries as compared with those in the control group. Taken together these two studies suggest that targeting the individuals who are most at risk for injury allows researchers and practitioners to deliver psychologically based interventions more efficiently.

To conclude, recent research that has focused on injury prevention from a psychological perspective is compelling and suggests that injury rates can be attenuated through a variety of methods (e.g., progressive muscle relaxation, stress inoculation training, mental skills training). Interventions, however, should be carefully chosen based on the psychobiological demands of the sport or activity. For example, low muscle tension may be counterproductive in some sports (e.g., skiing; Raglin, 2001). Additionally, small sample sizes and low statistical power may have thwarted investigators' efforts to demonstrate the efficacy of intervention efforts in several studies. Related to the issue of sample size, Perna et al. (2003) noted that low baseline injury rates may reduce the feasibility of showing an effect on injury rates or even conducting an intervention in the first place. Researchers are advised to plan research interventions based on a priori power analyses and predictions of injury rates.

Conclusions Regarding Psychological Antecedents to Injury

Overall support for the current version of the Williams and Andersen (1998) model of stress and athletic injury is substantial. In regard to the personality category, the variables in the personality section of the model were originally posited as educated guesses. Clearly, however, the personality section of the model is its least explored facet and needs further examination.

In their revision of the model, Williams and Andersen (1998) suggested that bidirectional arrows be placed between personality and history of stressors, between personality and coping resources, and between coping resources and history of stressors. These arrows would indicate that these three categories of variables interact with one another to influence athletes' stress responses and ultimately their susceptibility to athletic injury. For example, the ability to experience positive states of mind may help an athlete cope better with major life events stress and daily hassles and be less vulnerable to athletic injury. Also, major life events stress may profoundly affect personality. Posttraumatic stress disorder (American Psychiatric Association, 2000) is an obvious example, and changes in personality after trauma often are observed (e.g., Kishi, Robinson, & Forrester, 1994). Traumatic events also can influence coping, such as having a loved one with cancer (e.g., Compas, Worsham, Ey, & Howell, 1996).

In the stress response section, Williams and Andersen suggested that perceptual changes in audition during stress also be investigated. Landers, Wang, and Courtet (1985) found peripheral auditory narrowing in high stress conditions. Athletes who do not hear well or who are slow to respond to auditory cues, especially of danger approaching, may be at greater risk of injury. Thus, the examina-

tion of perceptual changes during stress should be expanded to include audition. Finally, Williams and Andersen suggested that the model was probably most appropriate for acute injury etiology with its emphasis on acute stress responsivity. Chronic or overuse injuries probably occur through pathways other than an acute stress response (cf. Meyer, 1995).

The past decade has produced considerable support for the Andersen and Williams (1988) model. Although the Andersen and Williams model has been the dominant framework used by researchers to examine antecedents to injuries, viable alternative explanations may be available (see Junge, 2000, and Perna et al., 2003, for proposed modifications to the Andersen and Williams model).

Injury Responses

The previous section summarized the current literature relating to antecedents of athletic injuries and intervention strategies to reduce injury risk. As noted earlier, however, injuries will likely continue to occur despite our best efforts at prevention. The descriptive literature relative to injuries among athletes contains a number of relevant findings. First, perhaps not surprisingly, it has been documented repeatedly that injuries are a significant form of stress for athletes (Brewer & Petrie, 1995; Gould, Jackson, & Finch, 1993; Roh, Newcomer, Perna, & Etzel, 1998; Udry, 1997; Udry, Gould, Bridges, & Beck, 1997; Udry, Gould, Bridges, & Tuffey, 1997). For instance, injured athletes reported more depressed moods at one week postinjury than their injured nonathlete counterparts did, although there were no differences in mood between these two groups at one-month follow-up (Roh et al., 1998). Also, qualitative interviews with injured athletes have revealed that the psychological and interpersonal sources of stress tend to be more salient to an athlete than are the physical or medical concerns stemming from injuries (Gould, Udry, Bridges, & Beck, 1997).

Second, although psychological distress among athletes after injuries is relatively common, it appears that a subset of athletes, usually estimated at 5% to 24%, report psychological distress levels comparable to those seen among people seeking mental health treatment (Brewer, Linder, & Phelps, 1995; Brewer, Petitpas, Van Raalte, Sklar, & Ditmar, 1995; Leddy, Lambert, & Ogles, 1994). The rates at which injured athletes tend to experience high levels of psychological distress after injuries appear to be comparable to those found among patients who have been hospitalized for acute myocardial infarction (C.B. Taylor, Miller, Smith, & DeBusk, 1997).

Finally, research has demonstrated that those who play an important role in athletes' rehabilitation (e.g., sports medicine providers) often do not share athletes' perceptions regarding the severity of injuries or the amount of psychological distress that injured athletes typically experience (Brewer, Linder, & Phelps, 1995; Brewer, Petitpas, et al., 1995; Crossman & Jamieson, 1985). These findings are especially interesting in light of recent research suggesting that social support can moderate negative emotional responses to injury. Green and Weinberg (2001) found that athletes who were more satisfied with their social support networks displayed less mood disturbances after an injury than those who were less satisfied with their social support.

Clearly, researchers and practitioners need to understand athletic injuries not only from a physical (medical) viewpoint but also from a psychological perspective. To this end, the remainder of this chapter focuses on the psychological and behavioral responses to athlete injuries. We start by discussing the psychological responses (e.g., cognitive and emotional) to injuries. We then examine the behavioral responses related to injuries among athletes, namely the relationship between psychological processes and rehabilitation behaviors.

Understanding the complex quality of responses to a loss of health among physically active individuals has proven to be a challenge for researchers. In the main, two types of theoretical perspectives have been used to understand and conceptually organize injured athletes' psychological (cognitive and emotional) responses to injuries. These theoretical models include stage models and cognitive appraisal models, both of which are discussed in the following sections.

Stage Models

Although a variety of stage models (sometimes referred to as phase or grief models) have been forwarded (see Evans & Hardy, 1995, for a review), a conceptual similarity across various stage models is the assumption that when athletes become injured, they experience a somewhat predictable sequence of psychological responses. Most notably, Kübler-Ross (1969) developed a stage model based on her clinical experiences with terminally ill patients; this model subsequently has been adapted and applied to the area of sport injury response (e.g., Lynch, 1988). Specifically, Kübler-Ross suggested that when faced with a loss of health, people experience

the following reactions: denial, anger, bargaining, depression, and acceptance. Although some have interpreted these stages as sequential and invariant, Kübler-Ross herself indicated that people may skip stages or pass through stages more than once (Evans & Hardy, 1995).

Some researchers and theorists (e.g., Morrey, Stuart, Smith, & Wiese-Bjornstal, 1999; Rose & Jevne, 1993; A. Smith, 1996) have argued that because the experiences of terminally ill patients and injured athletes may be significantly different, the Kübler-Ross model may not be applicable to athletic injury. McDonald and Hardy (1990) and Heil (1993) posited stage models that were generated from work with injured athletes. McDonald and Hardy's model, the most parsimonious one, suggests a two-stage model of recovery that includes reactive and adaptive phases. Heil's (1993) affective cycle model suggests that athletes' injury recovery includes three processes: distress (shock, anger, bargaining, anxiety, depression, isolation, guilt, humiliation, helplessness); denial (viewed as both an ordinary process of selective attention and a clinical defense mechanism); and determined coping (varying degrees of acceptance of the injury and its influence on short- and long-term goals). Heil referred to his model as being one of cycles or phases rather than stages to account for the possibility that individuals may regress between phases based on their progress in rehabilitation and other factors. A shared feature of this model and other stage approaches, however, is its emphasis on the general tendency toward adaptation as rehabilitation proceeds (Evans & Hardy, 1995).

To summarize, numerous stage models have been proposed to explain injured athletes' responses to injury. These models differ relative to the number of stages that an injured athlete might be expected to experience and the specific stages that might occur. When stage models are tested, various components of the model can be scrutinized (Evans & Hardy, 1995). First, researchers can test the sequence of reactions; for example, does anger typically follow denial, as suggested by the Kübler-Ross (1969) model? Alternatively, researchers can test the range of emotional, cognitive, and behavioral responses; for example, does a model that has two dimensions adequately capture the range of injured athletes' experiences?

Udry and colleagues (Udry, Gould, Bridges, Beck; 1997; Udry, Gould, Bridges, & Tuffey, 1997) examined the range of emotions and cognitive responses reported by athletes who experienced season-ending injuries. The qualitative approach used in their study allowed participants to describe their psychological reactions to their injuries in their own words (i.e., free from the constraints imposed by existing models of injury response). The authors then compared the injured athletes' responses to three existing stage models of recovery, namely, the models of Kübler-Ross (1969), McDonald and Hardy (1990), and Heil (1993). Although retrospective interviews were used, injured athletes reported relatively few instances of denial—a psychological process encompassed by both Kübler-Ross' and Heil's models. This finding is consistent with research in health psychology by Carver et al. (1993), who found that denial was used relatively infrequently among a sample of cancer patients. The construct of denial, however, has proved to be both controversial and elusive for a variety of reasons. First, denial may not be a psychological process that is readily measurable through typical self-report instruments. Second, researchers and theorists have not always used uniform definitions of the construct and have disagreed over whether denial is an adaptive or maladaptive process. Finally, certain behaviors (e.g., continuing to compete when injured) may be labeled as denial by others but may result from athletes' lack of understanding about their injuries (Wiese-Bjornstal, Smith, & LaMott, 1995) or their ability to tolerate higher levels of pain than nonathletes (Jaremko, Silbert, & Mann, 1981). The construct of denial as it relates to stage models warrants continued refinement and exploration, but it is possible that denial plays a limited role in most athletes' responses to injury.

As part of a larger quantitative investigation examining the emotional effect of injuries, Pearson and Jones (1992) also conducted retrospective qualitative interviews with injured athletes. Although the interviews were conducted with a limited number of athletes (N = 6) and the severity of the injuries was not specified, the athletes tended to vacillate between emotional highs and lows. This oscillation of responses has been interpreted as characteristic of support for stage or phase approaches (Evans & Hardy, 1995), in that it speaks to the dynamic quality of emotional responses following injuries.

One criticism of stage models is that there is some assumption that the stages are discrete. For example, the Kübler-Ross model would predict that the third stage of the process would be distinguished by bargaining and would precede the fourth stage, which would be characterized by depression or depressed mood. Some evidence, however, suggests that athletes' mood responses to injuries may not be as specific or discrete as the stage models imply (e.g.,

injured athletes may have both anger and depressed mood at the same time). Specifically, A. Smith, Scott, O'Fallon, and Young (1990) and McDonald and Hardy (1990) found that the subscales of the mood disturbance inventories used tended to be highly intercorrelated (i.e., mood disturbances tend to be more global in nature). It is tempting to conclude from these findings that there is little evidence that the stages are discrete. Alternative explanations are that the assessment tools used to measure mood states are not sensitive enough to detect changes or that assessments need to be taken more frequently to pick up subtle changes in athletes' emotional states (Evans & Hardy, 1995).

Making firm conclusions regarding the utility of stage models is difficult because they have not been adequately tested and a variety of measurement issues may need to be addressed before these models can be subjected to scientific scrutiny. As Evans and Hardy (1995) noted, "In general, contemporary theorists have spent more time and effort criticizing and inconsistently conceptualizing classical approaches to grief (in particular stage approaches) than in proposing models of grief that can be empirically tested and verified" (p. 233). Thus, continued exploration of the viability of stage models is warranted.

Cognitive Appraisal Models

Some researchers and theorists who study sport injury response have examined psychological responses to injuries from what have been termed *cognitive appraisal* or *stress and coping* perspectives. Researchers have forwarded a variety of cognitive appraisal models (e.g., Brewer, 1994; Grove, 1993; Udry, 1997; Weiss & Troxel, 1986; Wiese-Bjornstal, 2004; Wiese-Bjornstal, Smith, Shaffer, & Morrey, 1998). Most are rooted in the stress and coping literature of general psychology (Cohen & Wills, 1985; Lazarus & Folkman, 1984). Space limitations preclude a detailed discussion of each model in this chapter. Wiese-Bjornstal and colleagues are responsible for the most enduring line of theory development and model construction related to the application of cognitive appraisal models among injured athletes (Wiese-Bjornstal, 2004; Wiese-Bjornstal & Smith, 2007; Wiese-Bjornstal et al., 1995, 1998). For that reason, the most recent cognitive appraisal model of Wiese-Bjornstal and colleagues (1998) will serve as the basis for this discussion (see figure 17.2).

Several aspects of figure 17.2 bear mentioning. First, one can observe similarities between figure 17.2, which focuses on postinjury factors, and figure

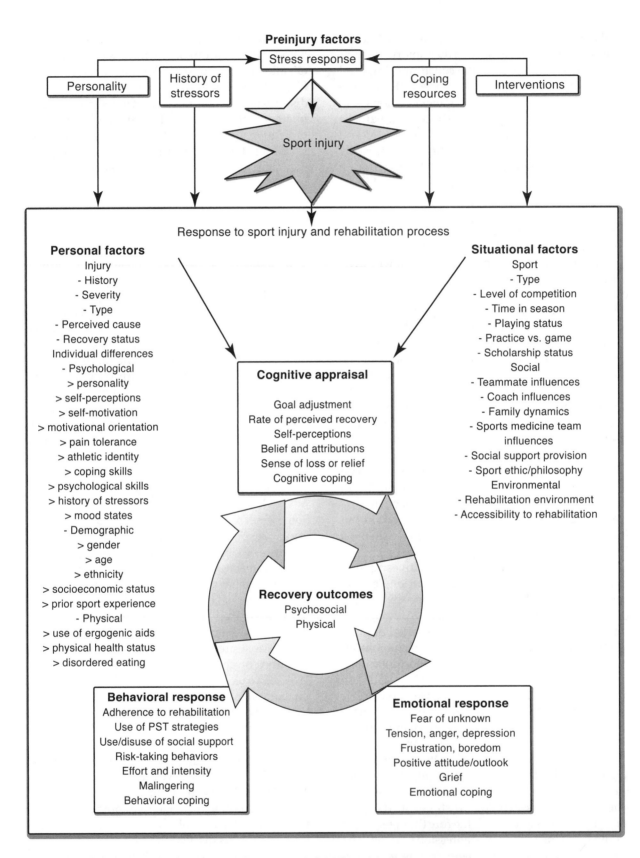

Figure 17.2 Wiese-Bjornstal, Smith, Shaffer, and Morrey's (1998) model of injury response.

17.1, which focuses on athletic injury antecedents. Wiese-Bjornstal and colleagues (1998) indicated that they developed their model as an extension of the Andersen and Williams (1988) antecedents-to-injury model. Specifically, Wiese-Bjornstal and colleagues thought that the factors that might predispose athletes to an increased risk of injury (e.g., low coping resources, personality dispositions) also might play a role in postinjury adjustment.

In addition, as shown in figure 17.2, Wiese-Bjornstal and colleagues (1998) suggested that a variety of personal (e.g., personality, developmental level, injury severity) and situational factors (e.g., time of season, accessibility to rehabilitation, sport ethos, available social support) influence the way that injured athletes cognitively appraise their injuries (e.g., threatening versus nonthreatening). In turn, how athletes cognitively appraise their injuries appears to influence their emotional (e.g., anger versus positive outlook) and behavioral responses (e.g., rehabilitation adherence, use or disuse of social support, malingering, use of psychological skills training). The potential behavioral responses to injuries as predicted by cognitive appraisal models are discussed later in this chapter. For now we wish only to point out that the model encompasses cognitive, emotional, and behavioral responses. Finally, injured athletes' cognitive, emotional, and behavioral responses may, in turn, have implications for both psychological and physical recovery outcomes.

Another notable aspect of the model shown in figure 17.2 is that it is recursive. That is, the model captures the dynamic nature of injury responses and rehabilitation. For instance, if an athlete experiences a setback in rehabilitation (e.g., reinjures a repaired knee), he or she may cognitively reappraise the injury in terms of its severity and consequences. Historically, cognitive appraisal models tended not to include this dynamic component (e.g., Brewer, 1994), and this was one of the ways in which cognitive appraisal models were thought to be distinct from stage approaches. The work of Wiese-Bjornstal and colleagues (Wiese-Bjornstal, 2004; Wiese-Bjornstal et al., 1998) provides a more comprehensive model that allows stage and cognitive appraisal models to be viewed as complementary rather than competing approaches.

The conceptual framework presented by Wiese-Bjornstal and colleagues (Wiese-Bjornstal, 2004; Wiese-Bjornstal et al., 1998) is significant for a variety of reasons. First, compared with the traditional stage approaches, it has been subjected to more extensive empirical testing. (For additional reviews,

see Wiese-Bjornstal, 2004; Wiese-Bjornstal et al., 1995, 1998.) Second, it is a sport-specific model that attempts to account for the distinct contextual factors that are associated with injuries in the athletic realm. For instance, Wiese-Bjornstal and colleagues (1998) reviewed research examining how the social networks and norms of certain sports may increase the likelihood that athletes will continue to practice and compete when injured (e.g., Nixon, 1992, 1993).

Until recently, the psychologically based injury response literature largely consisted of anecdotal and clinical accounts. This trend has changed dramatically in the last decade with the rapid increase in research and theory development relating to athletes' psychological responses to injuries. Two theoretical approaches—stage and cognitive appraisal approaches—have been forwarded as ways of understanding psychological responses to injuries. Although stage approaches and cognitive approaches historically have been presented as competing explanations, looking at these two approaches in an either–or light is not necessary. That is, both perspectives may help us understand athletes' responses to injury. For example, the information provided by stage models may shed light on *what* and *when* responses are experienced and, thus, compel researchers to pay attention to the dynamic quality of injuries. Alternatively, classic cognitive appraisal approaches may be better suited to answering *why* certain emotions are experienced. Thus, rather than choosing or deciding which type of theory is better, a more productive approach may be to recognize the contributions of the various theoretical postinjury response models.

Rehabilitation Adherence

The previous section covered the cognitive and affective responses to athletic injuries. Given the apparent complexity of athletes' psychological responses to injuries, it is not surprising that this topic has dominated the research. In returning to the model provided by Wiese-Bjornstal and colleagues (1998), we note the lower left part of the model includes the behavioral responses that athletes have to their injuries. Specifically, the behavioral responses of interest include, but are not limited to, adherence issues, use of psychological skills training, use or disuse of social support, coping responses, malingering, pain management, and the extent to which athletes engage in risk-taking behaviors. Because of space limitations, our discussion will focus only on adherence-related issues;

the interested reader should refer to other sources for more comprehensive discussions of these other topics (Kolt & Andersen, 2004; Pargman, 2007).

In a review article on sport injury adherence, Brewer (1998) cited evidence that adherence levels among injured athletes have ranged from 40% to 91% depending on how adherence is measured. Brewer (2004) noted that the reported levels of adherence among injured athletes are higher than those reported in the general medical literature, which have ranged from 4% to 92%. Working with a sample of severely injured athletes, Udry (1995) found that most athletes demonstrated relatively high levels of adherence. A subset of athletes, however, had very low adherence levels (i.e., attended less than 40% of their rehabilitation sessions) and, overall, rehabilitation adherence levels declined during the course of lengthy rehabilitation programs. A.H. Taylor and May (1996) noted that as rehabilitation programs (outside university settings) are increasingly becoming home based, the trend is for adherence levels to diminish. Finally, among injured athletes, some of whom may be highly motivated to return to physical activity, overadherence may be as problematic as underadherence. Based on the forgoing, we clearly need to further our understanding of the processes associated with rehabilitation adherence.

In this section, we review the literature on injury rehabilitation adherence and discuss several theoretical models that have been productive or appear to hold promise for future researchers. We discuss cognitive appraisal models, value-expectancy models, goal perspective theory, and the transtheoretical model. Due to space limitations we do not discuss measurement issues related to rehabilitation adherence. The interested reader should consult the work of Brewer and colleagues (Brewer, 2004; Brewer, Andersen, & Van Raalte, 2002).

Cognitive Appraisal Models   Earlier we introduced the rudiments of various cognitive appraisal models as they pertain to the psychological responses to injuries. We noted that cognitive appraisal models (see figure 17.2) also have been forwarded as a means of understanding rehabilitation adherence. We will now review some of the research on athletic injury rehabilitation adherence from a cognitive appraisal perspective.

A number of studies have examined the relationship between emotional responses to injuries and rehabilitation adherence. Daly, Brewer, Van Raalte, Petitpas, and Sklar (1995) found that individuals' cognitive appraisals of the difficulty of coping with injuries and their mood disturbances were nega-

tively correlated with rehabilitation adherence in a sports medicine clinic. These results were supported by findings from Brickner's (1997) investigation, which also reported an inverse relationship with mood disturbance levels and rehabilitation adherence. In contrast, however, Brewer et al. (2000) found no correlation between psychological distress and adherence.

Udry (1997) examined rehabilitation adherence levels among a sample of recreational athletes using a cognitive appraisal perspective. This study examined the effect on adherence levels of various types of coping: negative emotion (i.e., preoccupation with negative consequences of an injury), instrumental coping (i.e., problem-focused coping), distraction (i.e., thinking about other things or engaging in unrelated activities), and palliative coping (i.e., activities or responses that are soothing or alleviate the unpleasantness of an injury). Instrumental coping was positively linked to adherence levels, although this was true only in the later phases of rehabilitation. Alternatively, palliative coping was negatively linked to rehabilitation adherence, although this relationship was not detected until the later phases of rehabilitation.

In short, a number of investigators have used cognitive appraisal models to understand rehabilitation adherence behavior. See Brewer (2001, 2004) for a more comprehensive review.

Value-Expectancy Approaches   Another approach that has been used to examine adherence-related issues of injured athletes can be classified as a value-expectancy approach. Numerous value-expectancy models exist, including protection motivation theory (Maddux & Rogers, 1983; Rogers, 1975), the health belief model (Rosenstock, Strecher, & Becker, 1988), and the theory of planned behavior (Ajzen, 1988). A commonality among value-expectancy models is the premise that behavior can be predicted based on the value that people place on outcomes and their expectations that given behaviors will lead to those outcomes (Prentice-Dunn & Rogers, 1986). Value-expectancy theories have a well-established tradition in the social psychological and health-related realms, having been applied to a variety of health behaviors including cardiac rehabilitation (Oldridge & Streiner, 1990), exercise behavior (Slenker, Price, Roberts, & Jurs, 1984), emergency room care and follow-up appointments (Jones, Jones, & Katz, 1991), dental care, and seat-belt use (Rosenstock, 1990). Our discussion of value-expectancy models will be limited to a discussion of protection motivation theory (PMT; Prentice-Dunn & Rogers, 1986; Rogers, 1975). We limit our discussion to PMT because of space considerations and because it is one of the few value-expectancy models that have been applied to athletic injury rehabilitation adherence. Carter (1990) and Rosenstock (1990) provided a more comprehensive description of value-expectancy models.

PMT was originally formulated by Rogers (1975) and was subsequently modified by Maddux and Rogers (1983) and Prentice-Dunn and Rogers (1986). The revised version of PMT is the focus of this discussion. Figure 17.3 provides a schematic of PMT.

As shown in the left part of figure 17.3, environmental (e.g., verbal persuasion, modeling) and intrapersonal (e.g., personality variables, prior experience) information about a health threat is thought to initiate two cognitive processes: threat appraisal and coping appraisal. Threat appraisal accounts for factors that decrease or increase the probability that people will make maladaptive responses (e.g., responses that place them at risk, such as not attending rehabilitation). Factors that increase the chances of maladaptive responses are intrinsic rewards (e.g., bodily pleasure) and extrinsic rewards (e.g., social approval). Factors that decrease the probability of maladaptive responses are perceived severity, or the perceived degree of harm, discomfort, or damage that will result from health hazards, and vulnerability to threat, or the degree to which individuals perceive risks if they continue their unhealthy behavior (Prentice-Dunn & Rogers, 1986). Thus, intrinsic and extrinsic rewards minus perceived severity and vulnerability are thought to influence individuals' threat appraisal.

The second process that people engage in is coping appraisal (Maddux, 1993). Coping appraisal accounts for factors that decrease or increase the probability that people will make adaptive responses. Coping appraisal is primarily influenced by response efficacy, or individuals' perception of the effectiveness of a given coping strategy in preventing a negative health condition (e.g., attending rehabilitation will prevent scar tissue buildup) or encouraging positive health status (e.g., attending rehabilitation will speed recovery), and self-efficacy, or individuals' belief that they can successfully execute the behavior required to produce the desired outcome (Bandura, 1977; e.g., consistently attending rehabilitation sessions is possible). As response efficacy and self-efficacy increase, the probability of adherence should increase concomitantly. The probability of engaging in the behavior, however, should decrease in proportion to the perceived response costs (e.g., inconvenience, complexity, loss of social support; Maddux, 1993). Therefore, response efficacy and self-efficacy minus response cost will influence individuals' coping appraisal.

As indicated by the right side of figure 17.3, threat appraisal and coping appraisal combine to form individuals' protection motivation, and this motivation is an intervening variable that initiates, sustains, and directs behavior. In turn, the behavioral responses produced by protection motivation encompass both explicit behavior (e.g., completing rehabilitation exercises) and the inhibition of actions (e.g., refraining from activities that are likely

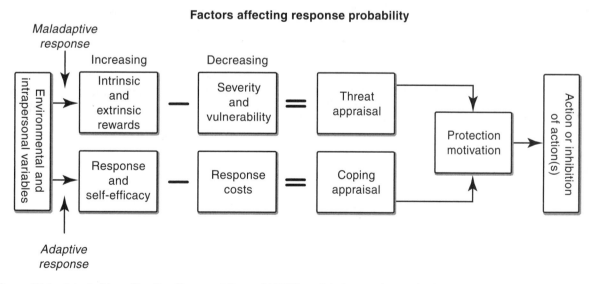

Factors affecting response probability

Figure 17.3 Adapted from Prentice-Dunn and Rogers' (1986) model of protection motivation theory.

S. Prentice-Dunn, and R.W. Rogers, "Protection motivation theory and preventive health: Beyond the health belief model," *Health Education Research* 1986, 1: 153–161 by permission of Oxford University Press.

to increase the risk of reinjury; Prentice-Dunn & Rogers, 1986).

A.H. Taylor and May (1996) conducted one of the first investigations that applied PMT to injury adherence behaviors. Using a questionnaire that had been developed to tap the constructs of PMT (i.e., the Sports Injury Rehabilitation Beliefs Survey, or SIRBS; S. May, 1995), 62 British university athletes completed self-assessments at various times during their rehabilitation. Athletes' responses on the SIRBS were compared with adherence levels that were assessed through both self-report measures and observations by sports medicine providers. The results partially supported the tenets of PMT, although the contribution of the constructs of PMT (e.g., severity, self-efficacy, and so on) varied with respect to whether the target behavior was adherence to an active rehabilitation program or adherence to a regimen of rest or modified activity. Unfortunately, the results of this investigation must be viewed cautiously because of measurement problems. Specifically, the subscale of the SIRBS that taps people's perception of severity had a reported internal consistency of only .52. Because other investigations related to injury adherence have been plagued by similar measurement issues (J. Fields, Murphey, Horodyski, & Stopka, 1995; Fisher, Domm, & Wuest, 1988), researchers in the future must use psychometrically sound assessment tools (Brewer, 1998).

Brewer and colleagues (2003) examined injury adherence levels using PMT and found that PMT constructs explained 43% of the variance in adherence levels. As in the A.H. Taylor and May study (1996), higher levels of adherence were positively related to treatment efficacy, self-efficacy, and susceptibility.

To summarize, PMT was developed to increase understanding of health-related behaviors. Research with injured athletes using this theoretical framework is currently limited. Despite such limitations, this theory and other value-expectancy theories may further our understanding of rehabilitation adherence among injured athletes.

Goal Perspective Theory Based within a social cognitive framework, goal perspective theory addresses the different types of behaviors that can be observed in various achievement settings (see Harwood et al. in this volume for a more comprehensive review). According to Nicholls (1984), people select and pursue goals in ways that will allow them to demonstrate competence, or at least their perceptions of competence. One way that individuals can view their abilities is through adopting a task orientation. A task orientation involves the use of self-referenced

strategies to define perceptions of ability and success. Another way that people can define ability is through the adoption of an ego orientation. An ego orientation makes greater use of normative-based assessments to interpret ability and success. In keeping with a social cognitive perspective, situational factors also are hypothesized to influence the goal perspectives that people adopt. For instance, if the environment emphasizes competition, individuals will tend to use normative strategies to interpret their abilities and successes (Nicholls). In turn, these differential motivational orientations and situational factors may influence individuals' expectations about tasks, the amount of effort they will invest in tasks, and their persistence.

Several studies have incorporated goal perspective theory to examine rehabilitation adherence levels among athletic populations. Duda, Smart, and Tappe (1989) found that injured athletes who believed in the efficacy of their treatments, perceived greater social support for their rehabilitation, were more self-motivated or goal directed, and emphasized a task orientation demonstrated higher rehabilitation adherence levels. Lampton, Lambert, and Yost (1993) found that injured athletes low in self-esteem and high in ego orientation tended to have lower rehabilitation adherence levels. In contrast to the work of Duda et al., their study indicated that task orientation was not related to treatment adherence. Given these preliminary findings, researchers may wish to consider the potential contribution that goal perspective might make to the study of injury rehabilitation adherence.

Transtheoretical Model The transtheoretical model (TM), sometimes referred to as the stages of change model or readiness for change model, is a process-organized model that addresses the psychological changes that people engage in when changing health-related behaviors (Prochaska & Marcus, 1994). The TM is not viewed as a competing model to the previous perspectives as much as one that integrates elements from various existing theoretical frameworks.

A central assertion of the TM is that people progress through distinct stages as they initiate and maintain health behaviors. Prochaska and Marcus (1994) suggested five stages of behavior change:

■ Precontemplation: The person is currently not involved in making behavioral change and does not intend to begin making a change.

■ Contemplation: The person is not currently engaged in making a behavioral change but is thinking about starting to in the future.

- Preparation: The person has started to engage in the behavioral change but does so on a limited or inconsistent level.

- Action: The person demonstrates less than six months of sustained behavioral change.

- Maintenance: The person demonstrates more than six months of regular participation in the behavior (or nonbehavior in the case of smoking cessation).

Research has shown that individuals who are in different stages of behavior change engage in different psychological processes regarding the behavior of interest (Marcus, Rossi, Selby, Niaura, & Abrams, 1992). For instance, people who are in the earliest stage of making a behavioral change have the lowest self-efficacy relative to their ability to engage in the behavior. Additionally, these individuals tend to perceive the greatest number of barriers and the fewest number of benefits resulting from behavioral changes.

The TM has been applied successfully to a diverse range of health-related behaviors including smoking, sunscreen use, high-fat diets, alcohol consumption, mammography screening, condom use (Prochaska et al., 1994), exercise behavior (Marcus et al., 1992), and cardiac rehabilitation adherence among older adults (Hellman, 1997). Research using the TM as it relates to sport injury rehabilitation is not well developed. In one of the initial studies in this area, Wong (1998) modified the questionnaires used to test the TM in the exercise domain for use in the sports injury domain and reported that the modified assessments appeared to be applicable. Udry, Shelbourne, and Gray (2003) used Wong's modified TM measures to examine athletes' psychological processes shortly before undergoing major knee surgery. Participants in the Udry et al. investigation reported relatively high levels of patient readiness for surgery (e.g., high levels of self-efficacy, more pros than cons associated with surgery) and an overall pattern of results that was somewhat different from that reported by Wong. With several initial studies completed, additional research is needed to determine whether injured athletes' self-reported readiness for change is linked to adherence and recovery outcomes.

A compelling implication of the TM is that it suggests that intervention efforts are most effective when they are stage matched (Marcus, Rakowski, & Rossi, 1992; Prochaska et al., 1994). Specifically, when applying the TM to exercise behavior, people who are in the precontemplation stage benefit from educational efforts that focus on the benefits of exercise.

In contrast, people who are in the action stage tend to benefit more from goal setting and incentive programs. Adopting this approach in the realm of injury rehabilitation could assist sports medicine providers in screening injured athletes before surgery. Specifically, injured athletes who perceive more barriers than benefits to injury rehabilitation and who are low in self-efficacy may benefit from postponing their surgeries or receiving more psychoeducational interventions about rehabilitation.

Brewer (1998) suggested that the value of the TM may be restricted because of the time-limited quality of injury rehabilitation. The TM, however, has been used to predict rehabilitation adherence among older adults after cardiac surgery—a condition that might also be presumed to be time limited (Hellman, 1997). Alternatively, the TM approach may prove to be more useful relative to working on adherence behaviors with athletes who have experienced chronic rather than acute injuries, in which the time-limited nature of injures is not as salient.

We have attempted to highlight the potential applications of the TM. Additionally, several studies have suggested that the TM may have some utility in understanding sport injuries. Further research in this area is needed, however, before the usefulness of the TM can be accurately assessed.

Conclusion Relatively little attention has been given to the issues surrounding injury rehabilitation adherence, and even fewer studies have been conducted within sound theoretical frameworks. Although we have provided an overview of several theoretical models and the corresponding research, several caveats are in order. First, the models that we have presented should not be viewed as constituting an exhaustive list. Certainly, other models (e.g., self-efficacy theory; Bandura, 1977) may ultimately prove more useful than the ones that we have outlined. Perhaps the most important message is the call for researchers to ground their research on rehabilitation adherence within a theoretical framework.

Second, although we have underscored the need for theory-based research, some classes of theories will likely be more productive than others in terms of their predictive capabilities. Behaviors in the health domain are often classified as (but are not limited to) preventive health behavior and sick-role behavior (Glanz, Lewis, & Rimer, 1990). Preventive health behaviors encompass activities undertaken by people who believe themselves to be healthy, or asymptomatic, for the purpose of preventing illness. In contrast, sick-role behavior entails activities undertaken by people who consider themselves ill or injured for the purpose of getting well. Sick-role behavior includes receiving treatment from medical providers and typically involves some level of exemption from ordinary responsibilities. Exercise adherence among apparently healthy individuals is more of a preventive health behavior, whereas athletic injury rehabilitation adherence behavior seems to fall closer to the category of sick-role behavior. A.H. Taylor and May's (1996) work with PMT in injury rehabilitation adherence found a different pattern of results compared with the pattern of results reported when PMT has been applied to exercise adherence. This differential pattern of results may have occurred because Taylor and May examined sick-role behavior rather than preventive health behavior. We agree with Duda et al. (1989), who suggested that it may not be wise to generalize the results from exercise adherence and the medical realm to athletic injury rehabilitation.

Third, although we have presented a number of theories pertaining to adherence that have been used in other domains, we do not mean to imply that sport-specific models of adherence should not be developed or that the existing theories should not be modified. The work of Scanlan and colleagues (Scanlan, Carpenter, Schmidt, Simons, & Keeler, 1993; Scanlan, Stein, & Ravizza, 1991), who have developed a model of sport commitment, is an excellent example of sport-specific model building. This type of theory building may be useful for researchers who study injury rehabilitation. Alternatively, in examining the exercise adherence theory and research, Maddux (1993) provided an integrated model of exercise behavior that captures many of the common elements of existing models of exercise behavior (e.g., theory of planned behavior, self-efficacy theory). Although forwarding a comprehensive model of injury rehabilitation adherence appears to be premature given the nascent character of the literature, the strengths of different models may be maximized when researchers can examine and test the conceptual similarities across various theoretical models.

Psychosocial and Physical Recovery Outcomes

In returning to the injury response model of Wiese-Bjornstal and colleagues (1998; see figure 17.2), we note that the center of the model suggests that injured athletes' cognitive, emotional, and behavioral responses may have implications for both psychological and physical recovery outcomes. In this section we briefly review some of the research that has examined the role that psychological and behavioral factors play in recovery outcomes. A number of studies in this area have examined both psychological and physical outcomes in the same investigation. For that reason we do not discuss psychological recovery separately from physical recovery.

Descriptive and correlational research provided the initial evidence suggesting that psychological factors were linked to postinjury psychological and physical outcomes in athletes (Gould, Udry, Bridges, & Beck, 1997b; Ievleva & Orlick, 1991). In one of the first studies conducted in the sport injury realm, Ievleva and Orlick used a retrospective design and found that athletes who healed faster reported using goal setting, positive self-talk, and healing imagery to a greater extent than did athletes who were slow healers.

More recently, a number of experimental interventions have been conducted that generally, although not uniformly, support the efficacy of using psychologically based interventions to facilitate psychological and physical outcomes. Some of this work has used a single intervention method to attempt to improve psychological or physical outcomes. For instance, Newsome, Knight, and Balnave (2003) used an imagery-based intervention to examine the effects of limb immobilization on flexion, extension, and grip strength. They found that participants in the experimental group did not experience deteriorations in physical functioning over a 10-day mobilization period whereas those in the control group did.

Evans and Hardy (2002a) examined the effects of a five-week intervention on injured athletes' rehabilitation adherence, self-efficacy, and affect. Participants were randomly assigned to one of three groups: goal setting, social support, or control. Athletes in the goal-setting group had significantly higher adherence levels and had the highest self-efficacy levels. Johnson (2000) examined the effectiveness of a variety of psychological interventions on mood among injured competitive athletes. Participants in the experimental group received a multimodal intervention that included sessions on stress management, goal setting, and relaxation and imagery. Participants in the experimental group reported more favorable mood states at the end of the five-week intervention as compared with those in the control group. Follow-up analyses indicated that the relaxation and imagery portion of the intervention contributed the most to mood improvements in the experimental group.

The studies described in this section focused mostly on facilitating athletes' psychological recovery from injuries. A number of studies have focused on psychological and physical outcome measures. Ross and Berger (1996) examined whether Meichenbaum's (1985) SIT program was successful in reducing postsurgery distress and improving physical recovery among injured athletes. The utility of the SIT with athletes has been demonstrated in studies on athletes coping with exertional pain (Whitmarsh & Alderman, 1993) as well as with reducing the risk of injuries (Johnson et al., 2005; Perna et al., 2003). Consistent with the previous research demonstrating the efficacy of SIT, Ross and Berger found that injured athletes who received SIT interventions experienced lower levels of postsurgical anxiety and pain and took fewer days to recover knee strength. Cupal and Brewer (2001) also examined the effectiveness of intervention efforts targeting injured athletes recovering from knee surgery. The intervention that they used was multifaceted and included imagery and relaxation training. The researchers found that injured athletes who received the intervention reported less reinjury anxiety, greater control over their recovery, and faster return to their desired levels of physical activities.

Several studies suggest that psychological interventions can have positive effects on psychological and physical outcomes in athletes following injuries. Note, however, that this research needs to be replicated and expanded before firm conclusions can be made. Some interventions in this realm have been multimodal (i.e., some combination of relaxation, imagery, stress management, goal setting, and social support) in their approach, and it has not been conclusively demonstrated which facets of the interventions are most critical to facilitating overall recovery in athletes.

Future Research Directions

We have discussed the psychology of athlete injuries from both an antecedents perspective and a responses perspective. These two areas of research have evolved in relatively distinct ways. As we conclude with recommendations for future research, we have organized our suggestions relative to these areas.

Injury Antecedents

First, although the early studies on the stress–injury relationship may have led researchers to conclude that the relationship was simple and direct, recent research has revealed that this is not the case. The

stress and athletic injury relationship is a complex one; numerous variables influence outcome (e.g., R.E. Smith et al., 1990). Research designs that can capture the complexities of the interrelationships between psychosocial factors are sorely needed. The issue of targeting athletes who are at high risk for injury based on profiles (e.g., athletes low in social support and high in stress) developed from conjunctive variables is important, but this type of research necessitates initially large samples (see Johnson et al., 2005).

Second, although a large body of research implicates psychosocial factors as antecedents to injuries, injuries clearly result from physiological (e.g., training loads), biomechanical, and field condition factors (Junge, 2000). The previous edition of this chapter included a call for more multidisciplinary research in this realm. In the last several years, a number of researchers have employed multidisciplinary perspectives to explore how stress interacts with other physiological and psychological factors in relation to injury vulnerability. In a nine-month prospective study of military officers in training, Gregg, Banderet, Reynolds, Creedon, and Rice (2002) found that acute injury rates were linked to increases in tension and anxiety and disturbances in sleep habits, although chronic injuries were not. Similarly, in a study of professional dancers, Adam and colleagues (Adam, Brassington, Steiner, & Matheson, 2004) found that dancers who missed more days of practice and performance reported higher levels of stress but also more negative mood states and sleep disturbances. Perna and colleagues (2003) have asserted (in an extension of the Williams and Andersen model) that increased autonomic activation and behavioral disruptions (e.g., sleep disturbances), stemming from negative mood, may act synergistically with the demands of heavy training loads to increase the likelihood of illness and injury. These investigators collected comprehensive baseline data from participants that included medical histories, mood states, stress levels, and cortisol levels.

Third, we are still in the initial stages of understanding the underlying mechanisms of athletic injuries. At this point, generalized muscle tension seems to be an intuitively appealing explanation. Unfortunately, only one study (Andersen, 1989) examined muscle tension during stress, and that study was inconclusive. Limitations of the Andersen study included the use of laboratory stressors (probably much lower than real-life stress) and the recruitment of participants from a general, not athletic, population. Measuring muscle tension in the field, however, would be difficult. Laboratory methods with greater ecological validity such as those of Bum et al. (1996, 1998), using physiological and auditory stressors, may help in examining the role that generalized muscle tension plays in stress responses and injury outcome.

Fourth, and related to the previous point, researchers may wish to attempt to make laboratory stress conditions more ecologically valid than the Bum et al. (1996, 1998) studies by adding other environmental variables such as high ambient heat and humidity. Bursill (1958) reported greater peripheral vision narrowing under such conditions. Many athletic competitions occur in stressful environmental conditions of high heat and humidity (e.g., the 1996 Olympics in Atlanta, the 1998 Commonwealth Games in Kuala Lumpur, Malaysia).

Fifth, studies with repeated measures of stressors and predictor variables are still needed. For example, as cited previously, Fawkner et al.'s (1999) study—in which daily hassles were measured on numerous occasions throughout the competitive season—is commendable. The study revealed that hassles tended to increase before injuries occurred. Along similar lines, Fawkner (1995) measured mood states of athletes weekly over the course of a competitive season with the Profile of Mood States (McNair, Lorr, & Droppelman, 1971) and found that as mood shifted negatively, the likelihood of injury increased. This work underscores the utility of using repeated assessments when the variable of interest (e.g., daily hassles, mood) may fluctuate considerably over time. A limitation of a number of prospective studies that have examined injury antecedents is that they assessed factors such as daily hassles, mood, and sleep disturbances only at the outset of the study, yet the research took place over several months (e.g., Byrd, 1993; Gregg et al., 2002).

A number of statistical and research design issues warrant consideration. Although a full discussion of these issues is beyond the scope of this chapter, the reader can refer to a number of excellent sources (Cupal, 1998; Petrie & Falkstein, 1998; Williams & Andersen, 2007). Williams and Andersen (2007) provided recommendations on the use of covariance structure modeling, logistic regression, repeated measure designs, and objective injury data. In the realm of injury intervention research, Cupal (1998) discussed the need for using larger samples, matching participants on critical variables, using random assignment of participants, and conducting the appropriate statistical analyses. Additionally, we suggest that it may be useful to obtain multiple outcomes measures (e.g., performance, pain toler-

ance) in addition to injury status when conducting injury prevention research. This recommendation is based on the findings that injury prevention interventions may influence (positively or negatively) athletic performance (Davis, 1991; Raglin, 2001) as well as psychological responses to pain (Williams & Andersen, 2007). Using multiple outcome measures will allow researchers and practitioners to develop a thorough and holistic understanding of the influence of injury intervention efforts.

Additionally, the antecedents to acute injuries are probably distinct from those related to chronic injuries. In a study of participants undergoing military training, the number of chronic injuries was approximately twice the number of acute injuries (Gregg et al., 2002). The point here is that depending on the setting, the time and resources lost because of chronic injuries can be significant, but research on the psychological factors that may predispose athletes to chronic injuries continues to lag behind research relating to acute injuries.

Finally, the ultimate goal of research into the antecedents of athletic injury has to be the development and implementation of interventions aimed at reducing injury risk. This reduction is the outcome of interest to most coaches, athletes, administrators, and investors (in professional sport). We hope that more intervention studies will be performed that follow the lead of the recent research in this area (e.g., Johnson et al., 2005; Maddison & Prapavessis, 2005; Perna et al., 2003) that has used rigorous research designs and screening procedures.

Injury Responses

The types of methodologies used to investigate the psychological and behavioral responses to injuries have become more sophisticated. Recently, researchers who have examined injury responses by using quantitative methods have used prospective and repeated-measures designs (e.g., Morrey et al., 1999; Udry, 1997) with control or comparison groups that in some cases have matched participants on one or more relevant variables (e.g., Cupal & Brewer, 2001; Evans & Hardy, 2002; Leddy et al., 1994; Ross & Berger, 1996). Investigators should continue to use these more rigorous designs.

We maintain that qualitative methodologies also stand to make significant contributions to our knowledge base regarding the responses to athletic injury. This approach, however, is not immune to the need to demonstrate rigor and should be used judiciously. For instance, qualitative approaches may be well suited for assessing psychological processes that might not be accessible given the current state of measurement (e.g., denial, bargaining). As Evans and Hardy (1995) noted, however, retrospective interviews may not be as useful in helping researchers understand the precise sequencing of emotions that injured athletes experience. Tracey (2003) provided an excellent example of how qualitative interviews can be used in a prospective manner. This work entailed multiple interviews with injured athletes over the course of their injury recovery, and the results were subjected to rigorous and detailed data analytic procedures. Work by Evans, Hardy, and Fleming (2000) met the criteria noted earlier and incorporated an action research approach in an attempt to facilitate injury rehabilitation processes among athletes.

We previously identified the need for researchers to explore the antecedents of injuries by making laboratory-based studies more ecologically valid. Along similar lines, investigations examining the responses to injuries often do not account for the way that injury rehabilitation actually occurs. For example, after an injury has occurred, researchers typically assess mood disturbances at some predetermined postinjury time (e.g., one week, two weeks). Often, however, no mention is made of whether any of the athletes experienced setbacks or additional injuries—factors that might significantly affect subsequent psychological distress levels. Although various conceptual models of injury response now encompass the dynamic quality of injuries, researchers have been slow to incorporate this facet into research designs and data analytic procedures.

The research that has been conducted on the psychological responses to injuries has tended to focus on the short-term negative emotional effect that injuries have on athletes. This research has provided us with useful information, but it may be limited in two ways. First, this approach tends to assume that the effect of injuries is uniformly negative and that injuries do not provide significant growth or learning opportunities for injured athletes. Qualitative interviews with athletes who experienced season-ending injuries have revealed, however, that approximately 95% of the athletes believed that they derived one or more long-term benefits from their injuries (Udry, Gould, Bridges, & Beck, 1997). These long-term benefits are consistent with a number of conceptual and theoretical models of stress, adversity, and personal development (see Udry, 2007, for a discussion) and should be further examined. A second assumption of much of the psychological response to injury research is that injured athletes are at similar cognitive-developmental levels (Harris, 2003; Wiese-Bjornstal, 2004) even though

studies commonly include participants who range in age from 16 to 40 years old. Several recent studies have shown that, compared with adults, adolescents are more likely to use "catastrophizing" as a form of coping with their injuries (Sullivan, Tripp, Rodgers, & Stanish, 2000) and are likely to experience higher levels of mood disturbances (Udry et al., 2003). Research studies that take into account possible cognitive-developmental differences in injured athletes are certainly needed.

As with the injury prevention literature, only a few studies have examined the efficacy of interventions aimed at the postinjury period. Evans and Hardy (1995) raised an intriguing point relative to the use of intervention work. Specifically, they suggested that researchers "explore theory driven interventions for use with injured athletes when they are in different grief/injury phases" (p. 243). This point is compelling in its own right but is also consistent with the transtheoretical approach. Simply put, if the psychological and behavioral responses to injuries are viewed as processes, then it makes sense to use intervention strategies that match the athlete's readiness to receive the intervention.

Finally, we note that investigators have not given much attention to the psychological responses of athletes who are recovering from concussions or chronic injuries. Several authors (Bloom, Horton, McCrory, & Johnston, 2004; Evans & Hardy 2003b; Tracey, 2003) have noted that athletes' psychological responses to acute injuries may be linked to the visual appearance of the injury. Specifically, as an acute injury heals, the injury typically becomes less visually apparent. As the injury becomes less visually obvious, athletes and significant others are reminded that the healing process is underway, and this, in turn, improves athletes' affect. With injuries that are less visually apparent (e.g., concussions or chronic injuries), different psychosocial responses may be at work. Of course, empirical work in this area is lacking. A number of authors have provided review articles on concussions (Bloom et al., 2004; Kontos, Collins & Russo, 2004; Putukian & Echemendia, 2003), but additional work in this area is warranted. Work in the area of concussions may be especially ripe for multidisciplinary efforts given the known effects of concussions on learning, memory, sleep, gait, and vision (Putukian & Echemendia).

Conclusion

Research and theory development related to the psychology of athlete injuries can be categorized as relating to either the antecedents or the responses to injuries. The research on antecedents to injury has been organized largely around the conceptual model presented by Andersen and Williams (1988) and subsequently modified by Williams and Andersen (1998). Overall, this model has received substantial support, and a number of areas within the model have been identified as particularly ripe for further research. Specifically, additional research is needed on the role of social support as it relates to the stress–injury relationship, the mechanisms underlying stress–injury relationships, and interventions aimed at reducing injury risk.

Regarding the responses to injuries, stage approaches and cognitive appraisal approaches have been used to understand how athletes psychologically respond to their injuries. Cognitive appraisal approaches have received consistent support in the literature, but there have been so few empirical tests of stage approaches that it is not possible to draw firm conclusions regarding their utility. Four theoretical approaches were forwarded relative to understanding injury rehabilitation adherence or the behavioral responses of athletes to injuries. The theoretical approaches discussed included cognitive appraisal, value expectancy, goal perspective, and the transtheoretical model. Research on the influence of interventions to reduce the psychological stress of injuries and to facilitate athletes' recovery is still in its early stages but has generally shown promise.

References

CHAPTER 1

Abernathy, B., Kippers, V., Mackinnon, N., Neal, L.T., & Hanrahan, S. (1997). *The biophysical foundations of human movement*. Champaign, IL: Human Kinetics.

Alderman, R.B. (1980). Sport psychology: Past, present, and future dilemmas. In P. Klavora & K.A.W. Wipper (Eds.), *Psychological and sociological factors in sport* (pp. 3–19). Toronto, ON: University of Toronto.

Andersen, M.B., & Williams, J.W. (1988). A model of stress and athletic injury: Prediction and prevention. *Journal of Sport and Exercise Psychology, 10*, 294–306.

Anshel, M.H. (1992). The case against the certification of sport psychologists: In search of the phantom expert. *The Sport Psychologist, 6*, 265–286.

Anshel, M.H. (1993). Against certification of sport psychology consultants: A response to Zaichowsky and Perna. *The Sport Psychologist, 7*, 344–353.

Bandura, A. (1977). Self-efficacy: Toward a unifying theory of behavioral change. *Psychological Review, 84*, 191–215.

Beuter, A., & Duda, J.L. (1985). Analysis of the arousal/motor performance relationship in children using movement kinematics. *Journal of Sport Psychology, 7*, 229–243.

Biddle, S.J. (1995). Introduction. In S.J. Biddle (Ed.), *European perspectives on sport and exercise psychology* (pp. xi–xviii). Champaign, IL: Human Kinetics.

Bond, C.F., & Titus, L.J. (1983). Social facilitation: A meta-analysis of 241 studies. *Psychological Bulletin, 94*, 265–292.

Brawley, L.R., & Martin, K.A. (1995). The interface between social and sport psychology. *The Sport Psychologist, 9*, 469–497.

Brawley, L.R., Martin, K.A., & Gyurcsik, (1998). In J.L. Duda (Ed.), *Advances in sport and exercise psychology measurement*. Morgantown, WV: Fitness Information Technology.

Bredemeier, B.J., & Shields, D.L. (1986). Game reasoning and interactional morality. *Journal of Genetic Psychology, 147*, 257–275.

Burton, D.A. (2000). Fellow agree: Time is right to explore major certification changes. *AAASP Newsletter, 15*, 11–12.

Carron, A.V. (1980). *Social psychology of sport*. Ithaca, NY: Mouvement.

Carron, A.V., Widmeyer, W.N., & Brawley, L.R. (1985). The development of an instrument to assess cohesion in sport teams: The Group Environment Questionnaire. *Journal of Sport Psychology, 7*, 244–266.

Chelladurai, P., Haggerty, T.R., & Baxter, P.R. (1989). Decision style choices of university basketball coaches and players. *Journal of Sport and Exercise Psychology, 11*, 201–215.

Cox, R.H. (1985). *Sport psychology: Concepts and applications*. Dubuque, IA: Brown.

Cratty, B.J. (1989). *Psychology in contemporary sport* (3rd ed.). Englewood Cliffs, NJ: Prentice Hall.

Dishman, R.K. (1983). Identity crises in North American sport psychology: Academics in professional issues. *Journal of Sport Psychology, 5*, 123–134.

Duda, J.L. (1987). Toward a developmental theory of children's motivation in sport. *Journal of Sport Psychology, 9*, 130–145.

Duda, J.L. (1998). *Advances in sport and exercise psychology measurement*. Morgantown, WV: Fitness Information technology.

Duda, J.L., & Nicholls, J.G. (1992). Dimensions of achievement motivation in schoolwork and sport. *Journal of Educational Psychology, 84*, 290–299.

Easterbrook, J.A. (1959). The effect of emotion on cue utilization and the organization of behavior. *Psychological Review, 66*, 183–201.

Fazey, J.A., & Hardy, L. (1988). *The inverted-U hypothesis: A catastrophe for sport psychology*. British Association of Sport Sciences Monograph No. 1. Leeds, United Kingdom: National Coaching Foundation.

Fédération Européene de Psychologie des Sports et des Activités Corporelles. (1993). *Directory of European sport psychologists*. Lund, Sweden: Author.

Feltz, D.L. (1982). Path analysis of the causal elements in Bandura's theory of self-efficacy and an anxiety-based model of avoidance behavior. *Journal of Personality and Social Psychology, 42*, 764–781.

Feltz, D.L. (1988). Self-confidence and sports performance. *Exercise and Sport Sciences Review, 16*, 151–166.

Feltz, D.L. (1989). Theoretical research in sport psychology: From applied psychology toward sport science. In J.S. Skinner, C.B. Corbin, D.M. Lenders, P.B. Martin, & C.L. Wells (Eds.), *Future directions in exercise and sport science research* (pp. 435–452). Champaign, IL: Human Kinetics.

Feltz, D.L., & Petlichkoff, L. (1983). Perceived competence among interscholastic sport participants and dropouts, *Canadian Journal of Applied Sport Sciences, 8*, 231–235.

Fujita, A.H., & Ichimura, S. (1993). Contemporary areas of research in sport psychology in Japan. In R.N. Singer, M. Murphey, & L.K. Tennant (Eds.), *Handbook of research on sport psychology*. New York: MacMillan.

Gauvin, L., & Spence, J.C. (1998). Measurement of exercise-induced changes in feeling states, affect, mood, and emotions. In J.L. Duda (Ed.), *Advances in sport and exercise psychology measurement* (pp. 325–336). Morgantown, WV: Fitness Information Technology.

Gilbourne, D., & Taylor, A.H. (1998). From theory to practice: The integration of goal perspective theory and life development approaches within an injury-specific goal-setting program. *Journal of Applied Sport Psychology, 10*, 124–139.

Gill, D.L. (1986). *Psychological dynamics of sport*. Champaign, IL: Human Kinetics.

Gill, D.L., & Deeter, T.E. (1988). Development of the Sport Orientation Questionnaire. *Research Quarterly for Exercise and Sport, 59*, 191–202.

Goldstein, J.H. (1979). *Sports, games, and play: Social and psychological viewpoints*. Hillsdale, NJ: Erlbaum.

Gould, D., Feltz, D., Horn, T., & Weiss, M. (1982). Reasons for attrition in competitive swimming. *Journal of Sport Behavior, 5*, 155–165.

Griffin, N.S., Keogh, J.F., & Maybee, R. (1984). Performer perceptions of movement confidence. *Journal of Sport Psychology, 6*, 395–407.

Hackfort, D. (1993). Contemporary areas of research in sport psychology in Germany. In R.M. Singer, M. Murphey, & L.K. Tennant (Eds.), *Handbook of research on sport psychology* (pp. 40–43). New York: MacMillan.

Hardy, L. (1996). Testing the predictions of the cusp catastrophe model of anxiety and performance. *The Sport Psychologist, 10,* 140–156.

Harter, S. (1978). Effectance motivation reconsidered: Toward a developmental model. *Human Development, 21,* 34–64.

Hatfield, B.D., & Landers, D.M. (1983). Psychophysiology—A new direction for sport psychology. *Journal of Sport Psychology, 5,* 243–259.

Hedley, A.A., Ogden, C.L., Johnson, C.L., Carroll, M.D., Curtin, L.R., & Flegal, K.M. (2004). Overweight and obesity among US children, adolescents, and adults, 1999–2002. *JAMA, 291,* 2847–2850.

Heide, F.J., & Borkovec, T.D. (1983). Relaxation-induced anxiety: Paradoxical anxiety enhancement due to relaxation training. *Journal of Consulting and Clinical Psychology, 51,* 171–182.

Heide, F.J., & Borkovec, T.D. (1984). Relaxation-induced anxiety: Mechanisms and theoretical implications. *Behavior Research and Therapy, 22,* 1–12.

Henry, F.M. (1981). Physical education: An academic discipline. In G.A. Brooks (Ed.), *Perspectives on the academic discipline of physical education* (pp. 10–15). Champaign, IL: Human Kinetics.

Hoffman, S.J. (1985). Specialization + fragmentation = extermination: A formula for the demise of graduate education. *Journal of Physical Education, Recreation and Dance, 56*(6), 19–22.

Janssen, J.P., Stoll, H., & Volkens, K. (1987). Short-term storage of power-time parameters: Studies with the rowing and bicycle ergometer for motor coding. *Psychologische Beitrage, 29,* 494–523.

Kantor, E., & Ryzonkin, J. (1993). Sport psychology in the former USSR. In R.N. Singer, M. Murphey, & L.K. Tennant (Eds.), *Handbook of research on sport psychology* (pp. 46–49). New York: MacMillan.

Klavora, P. (1978). An attempt to derive inverted-U curves based on the relationship between anxiety and athletic performance. In D.M. Landers & R.W. Christina (Eds.), *Psychology of motor behavior and sport 1977* (pp. 369–377). Champaign, IL: Human Kinetics.

Klint, K.A., & Weiss, M.R. (1986). Dropping in and dropping out: Participation motives of current and former gymnasts, *Canadian Journal of Applied Sport Sciences, 11,* 106–114.

Kontos, A.P., & Arguello, E. (2005, September). Sport psychology consulting with Latin American athletes. *Athletic Insight, 7*(3), Available from: www.athleticinsight.com/Vol7Iss3/LatinAmerican.htm.

Kontos, A.P., & Breland-Noble, A.M. (2002). Racial and ethnic diversity in applied sport psychology: A multicultural perspective for working with athletes of color. *The Sport Psychologist, 16,* 296–315.

Kroll, W. (1970). Current strategies and problems in personality assessment of athletes. In L.E. Smith (Ed.), *Psychology of motor learning* (pp. 349–367). Chicago: Athletic Institute.

Kuhl, J. (1985). Volitional mediators of cognitive-behaviour consistency: Self-regulatory process and action versus state orientation. In J. Kuhl & J. Beckmann (Eds.), *Action control: From cognition to behaviour* (pp. 101–128). New York: Springer-Verlag.

Landers, D.M. (1980). The arousal–performance relationship revisited. *Research Quarterly for Exercise and Sport, 51,* 77–90.

Landers, D.M. (1983). Whatever happened to theory testing in sport psychology? *Journal of Sport Psychology, 5,* 135–151.

Landers, D.M. (1989). Sport psychology: A commentary. In J.S. Skinner, C.B. Corbin, D.M. Landers, P.E. Martin, & C.L. Wells (Eds.), *Future directions in exercise and sport science research* (pp. 475–486). Champaign, IL: Human Kinetics.

Maehr, M.L., & Nicholls, J.G. (1980). Culture and achievement motivation: A second look. In N. Warr (Ed.), *Studies in cross-cultural psychology* (pp. 221–267). New York: Academic.

Mahoney, M. (1985). Open exchange and epistemic progress. *American Psychologist, 40,* 29–39.

Marsh, H.W. (1994). Sport motivation orientations: Beware of the jingle-jangle fallacies. *Journal of Sport and Exercise Psychology, 16,* 365–380.

Martens, M.P., Mobley, M., & Zizzi, S.J. (2000). Multicultural training in applied sport psychology. *The Sport Psychologist, 14,* 81–97.

Martens, R. (1970). A social psychology of physical activity. *Quest, 14,* 8–17.

Martens, R. (1974, March). *Psychological kinesiology: An undisciplined subdiscipline.* Paper presented at the meeting of the North American Society for the Psychology of Sport and Physical Activity, Anaheim, CA.

Martens, R. (1975). The paradigmatic crisis in American sport personology. *Sportwissenschaft, 5,* 9–24.

Martens, R. (1980). From smocks to jocks: A new adventure for sport psychologists. In P. Kalvora & K.A.W. Wipper (Eds.), *Psychological and sociological factors in sport* (pp. 20-26). Toronto: School of Physical and Health Education, University of Toronto.

Martens, R. (1989). Studying physical activity in context: Sport. In *Big Ten Leadership Conference Report,* Chicago (pp. 101–103). Champaign, IL: Human Kinetics.

Martens, R., & Landers, D.M. (1970). Motor performance under stress: A test of the inverted-U hypothesis. *Journal of Personality and Social Psychology, 16,* 29–37.

Martin, G.L., & Hrycaiko, D. (1983). *Behavior modification and coaching: Principles, procedures, and research.* Springfield, IL: Thomas.

Martin, S. (1999). To recruit division membership, get personal. *APA Monitor, 30,* 23–25.

Maxeiner, J. (1989). *Perception, attention, and memory in sports.* Schöndorf, Germany: Hofmann.

McCann, S.C., & Scanlan, T. (1995). A new USOC–AAASP partnership: Olympic world opens anew to interested certified consultants, AAASP. *AAASP Newsletter, 10*(3), 9.

McCormack, J.B., & Challip, L. (1988). Sport as socialization: A critique of methodological premises, *The Social Science Journal, 25,* 83–92.

McCullagh, P., & Noble, J.M. (1996). Education and training in sport and exercise psychology. In J.L. VanRaalte & B. Brewer (Eds.), *Exploring sport and exercise psychology* (pp. 377–394). Washington, DC: American Psychological Association.

Moore, R.L. (1998). Building strong academic programs for the future: Practical experience at the University of Colorado at Boulder. *Quest, 50,* 198–205.

Morgan, W.P. (1980). The trait psychology controversy. *Research Quarterly for Exercise and Sport, 51,* 50–76.

Morgan, W.P. (1989). Sport psychology in its own context: A recommendation for the future. In J.S. Skinner, C.B. Corbin, D.M. Landers, P.E. Martin, & C.L. Wells (Eds.), *Future directions in exercise and sport science research* (pp. 97–110). Champaign, IL: Human Kinetics.

Morris, T. (1995). Introduction. In T. Morris & J. Summers (Eds.) *Sport psychology: Theory, applications, and issues* (pp. xxii–xxxv). Milton, Queensland, Australia: Wiley.

Morris, T., & Summers, J. (1995). Future directions in sport and exercise psychology. In T. Morris & J. Summers (Eds.) *Sport psychology: Theory, applications, and issues* (pp. 592–604). Milton, QLD: Wiley.

Qiu, Y., & Qiu, Z. (1993). Contemporary areas of research in sport psychology in the People's Republic of China. In R.N. Singer, M. Murphey, & L.K. Tennant (Eds.), *Handbook of research in sport psychology* (pp. 50–51). New York: MacMillan.

Rejeski, W.J., & Brawley, L.R. (1983). Attribution theory in sports: Current status and new perspectives. *Journal of Sport Psychology, 5,* 77–99.

Rivenes, R.S. (1978). *Foundations of physical education.* Boston: Houghton Mifflin.

Roberts, G.C. (1989). When motivation matters: The need to expand the conceptual model. In J.S. Skinner, C.B. Corbin, D.M. Landers, P.E. Martin, & C.L. Wells (Eds.), *Future directions in exercise and sport science research* (pp. 71–84). Champaign, IL: Human Kinetics.

Roberts, G.C., Kleiber, D.A., & Duda, J.L. (1981). An analysis of motivation in children's sport: The role of a perceived competence in participation. *Journal of Sport Psychology, 3,* 206–216.

Ryan, E.D. (1968). Reaction to "sport and personality dynamics." In *Proceedings of the National College Physical Education Association for Men* (pp. 70–75).

Ryan, E.D. (1981). The emergence of psychological research as related to performance in physical activity. In G.A. Brooks (Ed.), *Perspectives on the academic discipline of physical education* (pp. 327–341). Champaign, IL: Human Kinetics.

Sachs, M.L., Burke, K.L., & Loughren, E.A. (2007). *Directory of graduate programs in applied sport psychology* (8th ed.). Morgantown, WV: Fitness Information Technology.

Scanlan, T., & Lewthwaite, R. (1986). Social psychological aspects of competition for male youth sport participants: Part 4. Predictors of enjoyment. *Journal of Sport Psychology, 8,* 25–35.

Schutz, R.W., & Gessarolii, M.E. (1993). Use, misuse, and disuse of psycho-metrics in sport psychology research. In R.N. Singer, M.M. Murphey, & L.K. Tennant (Eds.), *Handbook of research on sport psychology* (pp. 901–917). New York: MacMillan.

Selye, H. (1946). General adaptation syndrome and diseases adaptation. *Journal of Clinical Endocrinology, 6,* 117–230.

Singer, R. N. (1978). Sport psychology: An overview. In W. F. Straub, (Ed.), *Sport psychology: An analysis of athletic behavior* (pp.3-14). Ithaca, NY: Mouvement.

Smith, R.E. (1989). Scientific issues and research trends in sport psychol-ogy. In J.S. Skinner, C.B. Corbin, D.M. Landers, P.E. Martin, & C.L. Wells (Eds.), *Future directions in exercise and sport science research* (pp. 23–38). Champaign, IL: Human Kinetics.

Smoll, F.L., & Smith, R.E. (1989). Leadership behaviors in sport: A theo-retical model and research paradigm. *Journal of Applied Psychology, 19,* 1522–1551.

Straub, W.F., & Williams, J.M. (Eds.) (1983). *Cognitive sport psychology.* Lansing, NY: Sport Science Associates.

Treasure, D.C., & Roberts, G.C. (1994). Perceptions of success question-naire: Preliminary validation in an adolescent population. *Perceptual and Motor Skills, 79,* 607–610.

Vealey, R.S. (1986). Conceptualization of sport-confidence and competitive orientation: Preliminary investigation and instrument development. *Journal of Sport Psychology, 8,* 221–246.

Wankel, L.M. (1975). A new energy source for sport psychology research: Toward a conversion from D.C. (drive conceptualizations) to A.C. (attributional cognitions). In D.M. Landers (Ed.), *Psychology of sport and motor behavior* (Vol. 2, pp. 221–245). University Park, PA: Penn-sylvania State University.

Wankel, L.M. (1984). Audience effects in sport. In J.M. Silva & R.S. Wein-berg (Eds.), *Psychological foundations of sport* (pp. 293–314). Champaign, IL: Human Kinetics.

Weiss, M.R. (2004). *Developmental sport and exercise psychology: A lifespan perspective.* Morgantown, WV: Fitness Information Technology.

Weiss, M.R., & Bredemeier, B.J. (1983). Developmental sport psychology: A theoretical perspective for studying children in sport. *Journal of Sport Psychology, 5,* 216–230.

Weiss, M.R., Bredemeier, B.J., & Shewchuk, R.M. (1986). The dynamics of perceived competence, perceived control, and motivational orientation in youth sports. In M. Weiss & D. Gould (Eds.), *Sport for children and youth* (pp. 89–102). Champaign, IL: Human Kinetics.

Wicker, A.W. (1985). Getting out of our conceptual ruts: Strategies for expanding conceptual frameworks. *American Psychologist, 40,* 1094–1103.

Wiggins, D.K. (1984). The history of sport psychology in North America. In J.M. Silva & R.S. Weinberg (Eds.), *Psychological foundations of sport* (pp. 9–22). Champaign, IL: Human Kinetics.

Williams, J.W., & Andersen, M.B. (1998). Psychosocial antecedents of sport injury: Review and critique of the stress and injury model. *Journal of Applied Sport Psychology, 10*(1), 5–25.

Wilmore, J.H. (1998). Building strong academic programs for our future. *Quest, 50,* 103–107.

Zajonc, R.B. (1965). Social facilitation. *Science, 149,* 269–274.

CHAPTER 2

Aiken, L.S., & West, S.G. (1991). *Multiple regression: Testing and interpreting interactions.* Newbury Park, CA: Sage.

American Psychological Association (2001). *Publication manual of the Ameri-can Psychological Association* (5th ed.). Washington, DC: Author.

Baron, R.M., & Kenny, D.A. (1986). The moderator-mediator variable distinction in social psychological research: Conceptual, strategic, and statistical considerations. *Journal of Personality and Social Psychol-ogy, 51,* 1173–1182.

Bland, J.M., & Altman, D.G. (1995). Multiple significance tests: The Bonfer-roni method. *British Medical Journal, 310,* 170.

Brustad, R.J. (1998). Developmental considerations in sport and exercise psychology measurement. In J.L. Duda (Ed.), *Advances in sport and exercise psychology measurement* (pp. 461–470). Morgantown, WV: Fit-ness Information Technology.

Campbell, D.T. (1957). Factors relevant to the validity of experiments in social settings. *Psychological Bulletin, 54,* 297–312.

Cohen, J. (1962). The statistical power of abnormal-social psychologi-cal research: A review. *Journal of Abnormal and Social Psychology, 65,* 145–153.

Cohen, J. (1988). *Statistical power analysis for the behavioral sciences* (2nd ed.). Hillsdale, NJ: Erlbaum.

Cohen, J. (1992). A power primer. *Psychological Bulletin, 112,* 155–159.

Cook, T.D., & Campbell, D.T. (1979). *Quasi-experimentation: Design and analysis issues for field settings.* Chicago: Rand McNally.

Duda, J.L., & Allison, M.T. (1990). Cross-cultural analysis in exercise and sport psychology: A void in the field. *Journal of Sport and Exercise Psychology, 12,* 114–131.

Duda, J.L., & Hayashi, C.T. (1998). Measurement issues in cross-cultural research within sport and exercise psychology. In J.L. Duda (Ed.), *Advances in sport and exercise psychology measurement* (pp. 471–481). Morgantown, WV: Fitness Information Technology.

Fleiss, J.L. (1981). *Statistical methods for rates and proportions.* New York: Wiley.

Gill, D.L. (1992). Status of the *Journal of Sport & Exercise Psychology,* 1985–1990. *Journal of Sport & Exercise Psychology, 14,* 1–12.

Herek, G.M., Kimmel, D.C., Amaro, H., & Melton, G.B. (1991). Avoiding heterosexist bias in psychological research. *American Psychologist, 9,* 964–972.

Hume, D. (1739/2000). *A treatise of human nature.* New York: Oxford University Press.

Iijima-Hall, C.C. (1997). Cultural malpractice: The growing obsolescence of psychology with the changing U.S. population. *American Psycholo-gist, 53,* 642–651.

Journal citation reports: Science edition. (2004). Philadelphia: Thomson.

Krane, V. (1994). A feminist perspective on contemporary sport psychology research. *The Sport Psychologist, 8,* 393–410.

Landers, D.M., Boutcher, S.H., & Wang, M.Q. (1986). The history and status of the *Journal of Sport Psychology:* 1979–1985. *Journal of Sport Psychology, 8,* 149–163.

Landis, J.R., & Koch, G.G. (1977). The measurement of observer agreement for categorical data. *Biometrics, 33,* 159–174.

MacCorquodale, K., & Meehl, P E. (1948). On a distinction between hypothetical constructs and intervening variables. *Psychological Review, 55,* 95–107.

MacKinnon, D.P., Lockwood, C.M., Hoffman, J.M., West, S.G., & Sheets, V. (2002). A comparison of methods to test mediation and other interven-ing variable effects. *Psychological Methods, 7,* 83–104.

Mill, J.S. (1846). *A system of logic, ratiocinative and inductive: Being a connected view of the principles of evidence and the methods of scientific investigation.* New York: Harper.

Papaioannou, A., Marsh, H.W., & Theodorakis, Y. (2004). A multilevel approach to motivational climate in physical education and sport settings: An individual or a group level construct? *Journal of Sport and Exercise Psychology, 26,* 90–118.

Popper, K.R. (1959). *The logic of scientific discovery.* New York: Basic Books.

Ram, N., Starek, J., & Johnson, J. (2004). Race, ethnicity, and sexual orienta-tion: Still a void in sport and exercise psychology? *Journal of Sport and Exercise Psychology, 26,* 250–268.

Raudenbush, S.W., & Bryk, A.S. (2002). *Hierarchical linear models* (2nd ed.). Newbury Park, CA: Sage.

Roberts, R.M. (1989). *Serendipity: Accidental discoveries in science*. New York: Wiley.

Sedlmeier, P., & Gigerenzer, G. (1989). Do studies of statistical power have an effect on the power of studies? *Psychological Bulletin, 105,* 309–316.

Stouffer, S.A. (1950). Some observations on study design. *American Journal of Sociology, 55,* 355–361.

Sue, S. (1999). Science, ethnicity, and bias: Where have we gone wrong? *American Psychologist, 54,* 1070–1077.

Valenstein, E.S. (1998). *Blaming the brain*. New York: Free Press.

Weiss, M.R. (2004). *Developmental sport and exercise psychology: A lifespan perspective*. Morgantown, WV: Fitness Information Technology.

Weiss, M.R., & Bredemeier, B.J. (1983). Developmental sport psychology: A theoretical perspective for studying children in sport. *Journal of Sport Psychology, 5,* 216–230.

Weiss, M.R., & Raedeke, T.D. (2004). Developmental sport and exercise psychology: Research status on youth and directions toward a lifespan perspective. In M.R. Weiss (Ed.), *Developmental sport and exercise psychology: A lifespan perspective* (pp. 1–26). Morgantown, WV: Fitness Information Technology.

CHAPTER 3

Adler, P., & Adler, P.A. (1987). Role conflict and identity salience: College athletics and the academic role. *The Social Science Journal, 24,* 443–455.

Adler, P.A., & Adler, P. (1991). *Backboards and blackboards: College athletes and role engulfment*. New York: Columbia University Press.

Atkinson, P., & Hammersley, M. (1994). Ethnography and participant observation. In N.K. Denzin & Y.S. Lincoln (Eds.), *Handbook of qualitative research* (pp. 248–261). Thousand Oaks, CA: Sage.

Biddle, S.J.H., Markland, D., Gilbourne, D., Chatzisarantis, N.L.D., & Sparkes, A.C. (2001). Research methods in sport and exercise psychology: Quantitative and qualitative issues. *Journal of Sports Sciences, 19,* 777–809.

Brustad, R. (1997). A critical-postmodern perspective on knowledge development in human movement. In J.M. Fernandez-Balboa (Ed.), *Critical postmodernism in human movement, physical education, and sport* (pp. 87–98). Albany, NY: SUNY Press.

Brustad, R. (2002). A critical analysis of knowledge construction in sport psychology. In T.S. Horn (Ed.), *Advances in sport psychology* (2nd ed., pp. 21–37). Champaign, IL: Human Kinetics.

Brustad, R.J., & Ritter-Taylor, M. (1997). Applying social psychological perspectives to the sport psychology consulting process. *The Sport Psychologist, 11,* 107–119.

Capra, F. (1982). *The turning point: Science, society, and the rising culture*. New York: Simon & Schuster.

Capra, F. (1996). *The web of life: A new scientific understanding of living systems*. New York: Doubleday.

Collins, R. (1985). *Three sociological traditions*. New York: Oxford University Press.

Cote, J. (1999). The influence of the family in the development of talent in sport. *The Sport Psychologist, 13,* 395–417.

Cote, J., Salmela, J.H., Baria, A., & Russell, S.J. (1993). Organizing and interpreting unstructured qualitative data. *The Sport Psychologist, 7,* 127–137.

Culver, D.M., Gilbert, W.D., & Trudel, P. (2003). A decade of qualitative research in sport psychology journals: 1990–1999. *The Sport Psychologist, 17,* 1–15.

Dale, G.A. (1996). Existential phenomenology: Emphasizing the experience of the athlete in sport psychology research. *The Sport Psychologist, 10,* 307–321.

Dewar, A.M., & Horn, T. (1992). A critical analysis of knowledge construction in sport psychology. In T. Horn (Ed.), *Advances in sport psychology* (pp. 13–22). Champaign, IL: Human Kinetics.

Dzewaltowski, D.A. (1997). The ecology of physical activity and sport: Merging science and practice. *Journal of Applied Sport Psychology, 9,* 254–276.

Faulkner, G., & Biddle, S.J.H. (2004). Exercise and depression: Considering variability and contextuality. *Journal of Sport and Exercise Psychology, 21,* 52–69.

Faulkner, G., & Sparkes, A. (1999). Exercise as therapy for schizophrenia: An ethnographic study. *Journal of Sport and Exercise Psychology, 26,* 3–18.

Feyerabend, P.K. (1975). *Against method*. London: Verso.

Foon, A.E. (1987). Reconstructing the social psychology of sport: An examination of issues. *Journal of Sport Behavior, 11,* 223–230.

Gardner, H. (1985). *The mind's new science: A history of the cognitive revolution*. New York: Basic Books.

Gergen, K.J. (1985). The social constructionist movement in modern psychology, *American Psychologist, 40,* 266–275.

Gergen, K.J. (1991). *The saturated self: Dilemmas of identity in contemporary life*. New York: Basic Books.

Gould, D., Eklund, R.C., & Jackson, S.A. (1992a). 1988 U.S. Olympic wrestling excellence: I. Mental preparation, precompetitive cognition, and affect. *The Sport Psychologist, 6,* 358–382.

Gould, D., Eklund, R.C., & Jackson, S.A. (1992b). 1988 U.S. Olympic wrestling excellence: II. Thoughts and affect occurring during competition. *The Sport Psychologist, 6,* 383–402.

Gould, D., Jackson, S., & Finch, L. (1993). Sources of stress in champion figure skaters. *Journal of Sport & Exercise Psychology, 15,* 134–159.

Guba, E.G., & Lincoln, Y.S. (1994). Competing paradigms in qualitative research. In N.K. Denzin & Y.S. Lincoln (Eds.), *Handbook of qualitative research* (pp. 105–117). Thousand Oaks, CA: Sage.

Harris, J.C. (1981). Hermeneutics, interpretive cultural research, and the study of sports. *Quest, 33,* 72–86.

Harris, J. (1983). Broadening horizons: Interpretive cultural research, hermeneutics, and scholarly inquiry in physical education. *Quest, 35,* 82–96.

Hesse, M. (1980). *Revolutions and reconstructions in the philosophy of science*. Brighton, United Kingdom: Harvester Press.

Holstein, J.A., & Gubrium, J.F. (1995). Phenomenology, ethnomethodology, and interpretive practice. In N.K. Denzin & Y.S. Lincoln (Eds.), *Handbook of qualitative research* (pp. 262–272). Thousand Oaks, CA: Sage.

Holt, N.L., & Dunn, J.G.H. (2004). Toward a grounded theory of the psychosocial competencies associated with soccer success. *Journal of Applied Sport Psychology, 16,* 199–219.

Holt, N.L., & Sparkes, A.C. (2001). An ethnographic study of cohesiveness in a college soccer team over a season. *The Sport Psychologist, 15,* 237–259.

Krane, V., Andersen, M.B., & Strean, W.B. (1997). Issues in qualitative research methods and presentation. *Journal of Sport and Exercise Psychology, 19,* 213–218.

Kuhn, T.S. (1970). *The structure of scientific revolutions* (2nd ed.). Chicago: University of Chicago Press.

Martens, R. (1979). About smocks and jocks. *Journal of Sport Psychology, 1,* 94–99.

Martens, R. (1987). Science, knowledge, and sport psychology. *The Sport Psychologist, 1,* 29–55.

Mishler, E.G. (1986). *Research interviewing: Context and narrative*. Cambridge, MA: Harvard University Press.

Mutrie, N. (1997). The therapeutic effects of exercise on the self. In K.R. Fox (Ed.), *The physical self: From motivation to well-being* (pp. 287–314). Champaign, IL: Human Kinetics.

Pagels, H.R. (1982). *The cosmic code: Quantum physics as the language of nature*. New York: Simon & Schuster.

Rees, T., Smith, B., & Sparkes, A.C. (2003). The influence of social support on the lived experiences of spinal cord injured sportsmen. *The Sport Psychologist, 17,* 135–156.

Sands, R.R. (2002). *Sport ethnography*. Champaign, IL: Human Kinetics.

Scanlan, T.K., Ravizza, K., & Stein, G.L. (1989a). An in-depth study of former elite figure skaters: I: Introduction to the project. *Journal of Sport and Exercise Psychology, 11,* 54–64.

Scanlan, T.K., Ravizza, K., & Stein, G.L. (1989b). An in-depth study of former elite figure skaters: II: Sources of enjoyment. *Journal of Sport and Exercise Psychology, 11,* 65–82.

Scanlan, T.K., Stein, G.L., & Ravizza, K. (1991). Sources of stress in elite figure skaters. *Journal of Sport and Exercise Psychology, 13,* 103–120.

Schwandt, T.A. (1994). Constructivist, interpretivist approaches to human inquiry. In N.K. Denzin & Y.S. Lincoln (Eds.), *Handbook of qualitative research* (pp. 118–137). Thousand Oaks, CA: Sage.

Schwandt, T.A. (1997). *Qualitative inquiry: A dictionary of terms.* Thousand Oaks, CA: Sage.

Sparkes, A.C. (1992). *Research in physical education and sport: Exploring alternative visions.* Bristol, PA: Falmer Press.

Sparkes, A. (1998). Validity in qualitative inquiry and the problem of criteria: Implications for sport psychology. *The Sport Psychologist, 12,* 363–386.

Sparkes, A.C., & Partington, S. (2003). Narrative practice and its potential contribution to sport psychology: The example of flow. *The Sport Psychologist, 17,* 292–317.

Stake, R.E. (1994). Case studies. In N.K. Denzin & Y.S. Lincoln (Eds.), *Handbook of qualitative research* (pp. 236–247). Thousand Oaks, CA: Sage.

Strean, W.B., & Roberts, G.C. (1992). Future directions in applied sport psychology research. *The Sport Psychologist, 12,* 333–345.

Strauss, A., & Corbin, J. (1994). Grounded theory methodology: An overview. In N.K. Denzin & Y.S. Lincoln (Eds.), *Handbook of qualitative research* (pp. 273–285). Thousand Oaks, CA: Sage.

Strauss, A., & Corbin, J. (1998). *Basics of qualitative research: Techniques and procedures for developing grounded theory* (2nd ed.). Newbury Park, CA: Sage.

CHAPTER 4

Anderson, C.B. (2004). Athletic identity and its relation to exercise behavior: Scale development and initial validation. *Journal of Sport & Exercise Psychology, 26,* 39–56.

Asçi, F.H. (2003). The effects of physical fitness training on trait anxiety and physical self-concept of female university students. *Psychology of Sport & Exercise, 4,* 255–264.

Asçi, F.H., Asçi, A., & Zorba, E. (1999). Cross-cultural validity and reliability of the physical self-perception profile. *International Journal of Sport Psychology, 30,* 399–406.

Asçi, F.H., Eklund, R.C., Whitehead, J.R., Kirazci, S., & Koca, C. (2005). Use of the CY–PSPP in other cultures: A preliminary investigation of its factorial validity for Turkish children and youth. *Psychology of Sport & Exercise, 6,* 33–50.

Atienza, F.L., Balaguer, I., Moreno, Y., & Fox, K.R. (2004). El perfil de autopercepción física: Propiedades psicométricas de la versión española y análisis de la estructura jerárquica de las autopercepciones físicas (Physical Self Perception Profile: Psychometric properties in the Spanish version and validity of the physical self-perception hierarchical structure). *Psicothema, 16,* 461–467.

Baldwin, M.K., & Courneya, K.S. (1997). Exercise and self-esteem in breast cancer survivors: An application of the Exercise and Self-Esteem Model. *Journal of Sport & Exercise Psychology, 19,* 331–346.

Bandura, A. (1986). *Social foundations of thought and action: A social cognitive theory.* Englewood Cliffs, NJ: Prentice Hall.

Baumeister, R.F. (1987). How the self became a problem: A psychological review of historical research. *Journal of Personality & Social Psychology, 52,* 163–176.

Biddle, S.J.H. (1997). Cognitive theories of motivation and the physical self. In K.R. Fox (Ed.) *The physical self: From motivation to well-being* (pp. 59–82). Champaign, IL: Human Kinetics.

Blaine, B., & Crocker, J. (1993). Self-esteem and self-serving biases in reactions to positive and negative events: An integrative review. In R.F. Baumeister (Ed.), *Self-esteem: The puzzle of low self-regard* (pp. 55–86). New York: Plenum.

Bouffard, M. (1993). The perils of averaging data in adapted physical activity research. *Adapted Physical Activity Quarterly, 10,* 371–391.

Boyd, M., & Yin, Z. (1999). Cognitive, affective, and behavioral correlates of self-schemata in sport. *Journal of Sport Behavior, 22,* 288–302.

Brewer, B.W., Van Raalte, J.L., & Linder, D.E. (1993). Athletic identity: Hercules' muscles or Achilles heel? *International Journal of Sport Psychology, 24,* 237–254.

Byrne, B.M. (1996). *Measuring self-concept across the lifespan: Issues and instrumentation.* Washington, DC: American Psychological Association.

Campbell, R.N. (1984). *The new science: Self-esteem psychology.* Lanham, MD: University Press of America.

Chanal, J.P., Marsh, H.W., Sarrazin, P.G., & Bois, J.E. (2005). Big-fish-little-pond effects on gymnastics self-concept: Social comparison processes in a physical setting. *Journal of Sport & Exercise Psychology, 27,* 53–70.

Chase, L., & Corbin, C.B. (1995). Physical self-perceptions of older adults. *Medicine and Science in Sport and Exercise, 27,* S42.

Conroy, D.E., & Motl, R.W. (2002). Modification, cross-validation, invariance, and latent mean structure of the self-presentation in exercise questionnaire. *Measurement in Physical Education and Exercise Science, 7,* 1–18.

Conroy, D.E., Motl, R.W., & Hall, E.G. (2000). Progress toward construct validation of the Self-Presentation in Exercise Questionnaire (SPEQ). *Journal of Sport & Exercise Psychology, 22,* 21–38.

Cooley, C.H. (1902). *Human nature and the social order.* New York: Scribner.

Coopersmith, S. (1967). *The antecedents of self-esteem.* San Francisco: Freeman.

Crocker, P.R.E., Eklund, R.C., & Kowalski, K.C. (2000). *Children's physical activity and physical self-perceptions.* Journal of Sports Sciences, 18, 383–394.

Crocker, P.R.E., Sabiston, C., Forrestor, S., Kowalski, N., Kowalski, K., & McDonough, M. (2003). Predicting change in physical activity, dietary restraint, and physique anxiety in adolescent girls: Examining covariance in physical self-perceptions. *Canadian Journal of Public Health, 94,* 332–337.

Crocker, P.R.E., Snyder, J., Kowalski, K.C., & Hoar, S. (2000). Don't let me be *fat* or physically incompetent! The relationship between physical self-concept and social physique anxiety in Canadian high performance female adolescent athletes. *Avante, 6,* 16–23.

Cronbach, L.J., & Meehl, P.E. (1955). Construct validity in psychological tests. *Psychological Bulletin, 52,* 281–302.

Deci, E.L., & Ryan, R.M. (1995). Human autonomy: The basis for true self-esteem. In M. Kernis (Ed.), *Agency, efficacy, and self-esteem.* New York: Plenum.

Deci, E.L., & Ryan, R.M. (2002). *Handbook of self-determination research.* Rochester, NY: University of Rochester Press.

Diener, E. (2000). Subjective well-being: The science of happiness, and a proposal for a national index. *American Psychologist, 55,* 34–43.

Duda, J.L. (1998). *Advances in sport and exercise psychology measurement.* Morgantown, WV: Fitness Information Technology.

Eklund, R.C., Whitehead, J.R., & Welk, G.J. (1997). Validity of the children and youth physical self-perception profile: A confirmatory factor analysis. *Research Quarterly for Exercise and Sport, 68,* 240–256.

Epstein, S. (1973). The self-concept revisited or a theory of a theory. *American Psychologist, 28,* 405–416.

Epstein, S. (1991). Cognitive-experiential self-theory: Implications for developmental psychology. In M.R. Gunnar & L.A. Sroufe (Eds.), *Self-processes and development: The Minnesota Symposium on Child Development 23* . Hillsdale, NJ: Erlbaum.

Estabrooks, P., & Courneya, K.C. (1997). Relationships amongst self-schema, intention, and exercise behavior. *Journal of Sport & Exercise Psychology, 19,* 156–168.

Fitts, W.H. (1965). *Tennessee Self-Concept Scale: Manual.* Los Angeles: Western Psychological Services.

Fonseca, A.M., & Fox, K.R. (2002). Como avaliar o modo como as pessoas se percebem fisicamente? Um olhar sobre a versão Portuguesa do Physical Self-Perception profile (PSPP). *Revista Portuguesa de ciências do Esporto, 2,* 11–23.

Fortes, M., Delignières, D., & Ninot, G. (2004). The dynamics of self-esteem and physical self: Between preservation and adaptation. *Quality & Quantity: International Journal of Methodology, 38*, 735–751.

Fortes, M., Ninot, G., & Delignières, D. (2004). The hierarchical structure of the physical self: An idiographic and cross-sectional analyses. *International Journal of Sport Psychology, 2*, 119–132.

Fortes, M., Ninot, G., & Delignières, D. (2005). The autoregressive integrated moving average procedures: Implications for adapted physical activity research. *Adapted Physical Activity Quarterly, 22*, 221–236.

Fox, K.R. (1990). *The Physical Self-Perception Profile manual.* DeKalb, IL: Office for Health Promotion, Northern Illinois University.

Fox, K.R. (1997). The physical self and processes in self-esteem development. In K.R. Fox (Ed.). *The physical self: From motivation to well-being* (pp. 111–139). Champaign, IL: Human Kinetics.

Fox, K.R. (1998). Advances in the measurement of the physical self. In J.L. Duda (Ed.). *Advances in sport and exercise psychology measurement* (pp. 295–310). Morgantown, WV; Fitness Information Technology.

Fox, K.R. (2000). The effects of exercise on physical self-perceptions and self-esteem. In S.J.H. Biddle, K.R. Fox, & S.H. Boutcher (Eds.). *Physical activity and psychological well-being* (pp. 88–11) London: Routledge.

Fox, K.R. (2002). Self-perceptions and sport behavior. In T. Horn (Ed.), *Advances in sport psychology* (2nd ed., pp. 83–99). Champaign, IL: Human Kinetics.

Fox, K.R., & Corbin, C.B. (1989). The Physical Self-Perception Profile: Development and preliminary validation. *Journal of Sport and Exercise Psychology, 11*, 408–430.

Fox, K.R., Stathi, A., McKenna, J., & Davis, M.G. (2007). Physical activity and mental well-being in older people participating in the Better Ageing Project. *European Journal of Applied Physiology, 100*, 591-602.

Gagné, M., Ryan, R.M., & Bargmann, K. (2003). Autonomy support and need satisfaction in the motivation and well-being of gymnasts. *Journal of Applied Sport Psychology, 15*, 372–390.

Georgiadis, M.M., Biddle, S.J.H., & Chatzisarantis, N.L.D. (2001). The mediating role of self-determination in the relationship between goal orientations and physical self-worth in Greek exercisers. *European Journal of Sport Sciences, 1*(5).

Grove, J.R., Fish, M., & Eklund, R.C. (2004). Changes in athletic identity following team selection: Self-protection versus self-enhancement. *Journal of Applied Sport Psychology, 16*, 75–81.

Guérin, F., Marsh, H.W., & Famose, J.P (2004). Generalizability of the PSDQ and its relationship to physical fitness: The European French connection. *Journal of Sport & Exercise Psychology, 26*, 19–38.

Guidano, V.F. (1986). The self as mediator of cognitive change in psychotherapy. In L.M. Hartman & K.R. Blankstein (Eds.). *Perception of the self in emotional disorder and psychotherapy* (pp. 305–330). New York: Plenum.

Hagger, M.S., Biddle, S.J.H., Chow, E.W., Stambulova, N., & Kavvussanu, M. (2003). Physical self-perceptions in adolescence: Generalizability of a hierarchical multidimensional model across three cultures. *Journal of Cross-Cultural Psychology, 34*, 611–628.

Hall, S. (1992). The question of cultural identity. In S. Hall, D. Hell., & T. McGrew (Eds.), *Modernity and its futures* (pp. 374–325). Cambridge, UK: Polity.

Hart, E.A., Leary, M.R., & Rejeski, W.A. (1989). The measurement of social physique anxiety. *Journal of Sport and Exercise Psychology, 11*, 94–104.

Harter, S. (1978). Effectance motivation reconsidered: Toward a developmental model. *Human Development, 21*, 34–64.

Harter, S. (1985). *Manual for the Self-Perception Profile for Children.* Denver, CO: University of Denver.

Harter, S. (1988). *Manual for the Self-Perception Profile for Adolescents.* Denver, CO: University of Denver.

Harter, S. (1996). Historical roots of contemporary issues involving self-concept. In B.A. Bracken (Ed.), *Handbook of self-concept.* New York: Wiley.

Hayes, S.D., Crocker, P.R.E., & Kowalski, K.C. (1999). Gender differences in physical self-perceptions, global self-esteem and physical activity: Evaluation of the physical self-perception profile model. *Journal of Sport Behavior, 22*, 1–14.

Heian, E., Hagen, K.B., Abbott, J., & Nordheim, L. (2005). Exercise to improve self-esteem in children and young people. *The Cochrane Database of Systematic Reviews, 1*, 1–49.

James, W. (1892). *Psychology: The briefer course.* New York: Holt.

James, W. (1898). *Psychology: The briefer course.* New York: Holt.

Kerlinger, F.N. (1979). *Behavioural research: A conceptual approach.* New York: Holt, Rinehart, & Winston.

Kowal, J., & Fortier, M.S. (2000). Testing relationships from the hierarchical model of intrinsic and extrinsic motivation using flow as a motivational consequence. *Research Quarterly for Exercise & Sport, 71*, 171–181.

Kowalski, K.C., Crocker, P.R.E., Kowalski, N.P., Chad, K.E., & Humbert, M.L. (2003). Examining the physical self in adolescent girls over time: Further evidence against the hierarchical model. *Journal of Sport & Exercise Psychology, 25*, 5–18.

Kowalski, N.P., Crocker, P.R.E., & Kowalski, K.C. (2001). Physical self and physical activity relationships in college women: Does social physique anxiety moderate effects? *Research Quarterly for Exercise & Sport, 72*, 55–62.

Leary, M.R. (1992). Self-presentation processes in exercise and sport. *Journal of Sport & Exercise Psychology, 14*, 339–351.

Leary, M.R. (1995). *Self-presentation: Impression management and interpersonal behavior.* Dubuque, IA: Brown & Benchmark.

Leary, M.R. (2004). The sociometer, self-esteem, and the regulation of interpersonal behavior. In R.F. Baumeister & K. Vohs (Eds.), *Handbook of self-regulation.* New York: Guilford.

Leary, M.R., & Tangney, J.P. (2003). *Handbook of self and identity.* New York: Guilford.

Levy, S., & Ebbeck, V. (2005). The exercise and self-esteem model in adult women: The inclusion of physical acceptance. *Psychology of Sport & Exercise, 6*, 571–584.

Li, F., Harmer, P., Duncan, T.E., Duncan, S.C., & Chaumeton, N.R. (2002). Tai Chi as a means to enhance self-esteem: A randomized controlled trial. *Journal of Applied Gerontology, 21*, 70–89.

Lintunen, T. (1987). The perceived physical competence scale for children. *Scandinavian Journal of Sport Sciences, 9*, 57–64.

MacSween, A., Brydson, G., & Fox, K.R. (2004). Physical self-perceptions of women with rheumatoid arthritis. *Arthritis and Rheumatism, 51*, 958–963.

Markus, H. (1977). Self-schemata and processing information about the self. *Journal of Personality & Social Psychology, 35*, 118–133.

Markus, H. W, & Wurf, E. (1987). The dynamic self-concept: A social psychological perspective. *Annual Review of Psychology, 38*, 299–337.

Marsh, H.W. (1990). Causal ordering of academic self-concept and academic achievement: A multiwave, longitudinal panel analysis. *Journal of Educational Psychology, 82*, 646-656.

Marsh, H.W. (1992a). *Self-Description Questionnaire (SDQ) II: A theoretical and empirical basis for the measurement of multiple dimensions of pre-adolescent self-concept. A test manual and research monograph.* Macarthur, New South Wales, Australia: University of Western Sydney, Faculty of Education.

Marsh, H.W. (1992b). *Self-Description Questionnaire (SDQ) II: A theoretical and empirical basis for the measurement of multiple dimensions of adolescent self-concept. An interim test manual and research monograph.* Macarthur, New South Wales, Australia: University of Western Sydney, Faculty of Education.

Marsh, H.W. (1992c). *Self-Description Questionnaire (SDQ) II: A theoretical and empirical basis for the measurement of multiple dimensions of late adolescent self-concept. An interim test manual and research monograph.* Macarthur, New South Wales, Australia: University of Western Sydney, Faculty of Education.

Marsh, H.W. (1997). The measurement of physical self-concept: A construct validation approach. In K.R. Fox (Ed.) *The physical self: From motivation to well-being* (pp. 27–58). Champaign, IL: Human Kinetics.

Marsh, H.W., Asçi, F.H., & Marco, I.T. (2002). Multi-trait multi-method analyses of two physical self-concept instruments: A cross-cultural perspective. *Journal of Sport & Exercise Psychology, 24*, 99–119.

Marsh, H.W., & Hattie, J. (1996). Theoretical perspectives on the structure of self-concept. In B.A. Bracken (Ed.), *Handbook of self-concept* (pp. 38–90). New York: Wiley.

Marsh, H.W., & Perry, C. (2005). Self-concept contributes to winning gold medals: Casual ordering of self-concept and elite swimming performance. *Journal of Sport & Exercise Psychology, 27,* 71–91.

Marsh, H.W., Richards, G., Johnson, S., Roche, L., & Tremayne, P. (1994). Physical Self-Description Questionnaire: Psychometric properties and a multitrait-multimethod analysis of relations to existing instruments. *Journal of Sport & Exercise Psychology, 16,* 270–305.

Marsh, H.W., & Sonstroem, R.J. (1995). Importance ratings and specific components of physical self-concept: Relevance to predicting global components of self-concept and exercise. *Journal of Sport & Exercise Psychology, 17,* 84–104.

Martin Ginis, K.A., & Leary, M.R. (2004). Self-presentational processes in health damaging behavior. *Journal of Applied Sport Psychology, 16,* 59–74.

McDonough, M., & Crocker, P.R.E. (2005). Sport participation motivation in young adolescent girls: The role of friendship quality and self-concept. *Research Quarterly for Exercise & Sport, 76,* 456–467.

McGannon, K.R., & Mauws, M.K. (2000). Discursive psychology: An alternative approach for studying adherence to exercise and physical activity. *Quest, 52,* 148–165.

Messer, B., & Harter, S. (1986). *Manual for the Adult Self-Perception Profile.* Denver, CO: University of Denver.

Messick, S. (1995). Validity of psychological assessment: Validation of inferences from persons' responses and performances as scientific inquiry into score meaning. *American Psychologist, 50,* 741–749.

Murphy, G. (1947). *Personality: A biosocial approach to origins and structure.* New York: Harper & Row.

Neemann, J., & Harter, S. (1986). *Manual for the Self-Perception Profile for College Students.* Denver, CO: University of Denver.

Nicholls, J.G. (1989). *The competitive ethos and democratic education.* Cambridge, MA: Harvard University Press.

Ntoumanis, N. (2001). A self-determination approach to the understanding of motivation in physical education. *British Journal of Educational Psychology, 71,* 225–242.

Okasha, S. (2002). *Philosophy of science: A very short introduction.* Toronto, ON: Oxford University Press.

Ostrow, A.C. (1996). *Directory of psychological tests in the sport and exercise sciences* (2nd ed.). Morgantown, WV: Fitness Information Technology.

Phoenix, C., Faulkner, G., & Sparkes, A.C. (2005). Athletic identity and self-ageing: The dilemma of exclusivity. *Psychology of Sport & Exercise, 6,* 335–347.

Prentice, D., & Miller, D.T. (1992). When small effects are impressive. *Psychological Bulletin, 112,* 160–164.

Raudsepp, L., Kais, K., & Hannus, A. (2004). Stability of physical self-perceptions during early adolescence. *Pediatric Exercise Science, 16,* 138–146.

Raudsepp, L., Liblick, R., & Hannus, A. (2002). Children's and adolescent's physical self-perceptions as related to moderate to vigorous physical activity and physical fitness. *Pediatric Exercise Science, 14,* 97–106.

Roid, G.H., & Fitts, W.H. (1994). Tennessee Self-Concept Scale [Revised Manual]. Los Angeles: Western Psychological Services.

Rogasa, D. (1995). Myths and methods: "Myths about longitudinal research" and supplemental questions. In J.M. Gottman (Ed.), *The analysis of change* (pp. 3–66). Mahwah, NJ: Erlbaum.

Rosenberg, M. (1965). *Society and the adolescent self-image.* Princeton, NJ: University Press.

Ryan, R.M., & Deci, E.L. (2003). On assimilating identities to the self: A self-determination theory perspective on internalization and integrity within cultures. In M.R. Leary & J.P. Tangney (Eds.), *Handbook on self & identity* (pp. 253–274). New York: The Guilford Press.

Ryan, R.M., & Frederick, C.M. (1997). On energy, personality and health: Subjective vitality as a dynamic reflection of well-being. *Journal of Personality, 65,* 529–565.

Ryckman, R.M., Robbins, M.A., Thornton, B., & Cantrell, P. (1982). Development and validation of a physical self-efficacy scale. *Journal of Personality & Social Psychology, 42,* 891–900.

Sallis, J.F., & Owen, N. (1999). *Physical activity and behavioural medicine.* Thousand Oaks, CA: Sage.

Sarrazin, P., Vallerand, R., Guillet, E., Pelletier, L., & Cury, F. (2002). Motivation and dropout in female handballers: A 21-month prospective study. *European Journal of Social Psychology, 32,* 395–418.

Secord, P.F., & Jourard, S.M. (1953). The appraisal of body-cathexis: Body cathexis and the self. *Journal of Consulting Psychology, 17,* 343–347.

Seligman, M.E.P., & Czikszentmihalyi, M. (2000). Positive psychology: An introduction. *American Psychologist, 55,* 5–15.

Shavelson, R.J., Hubner, J.J., & Stanton, G.C. (1976). Self-concept: Validation of construct interpretations. *Review of Educational Research, 46,* 407–411.

Sheldon, K.M., Elliot, A.J., Kim, Y., & Kasser, T. (2001). What's satisfying about satisfying events? Comparing ten candidate psychological needs. *Journal of Personality and Social Psychology, 80,* 325–339.

Sherrill, C. (1997). Disability, identity, and involvement in sport and exercise. In K.R. Fox (Ed.), *The physical self: From motivation to well-being* (pp. 257–286). Champaign, IL: Human Kinetics.

Sonstroem, R.J. (1978). Physical estimation and attraction scales: Rationale and research. *Medicine and Science in Sports, 8,* 126–132.

Sonstroem, R.J., Harlow, L.L., Gemma, L.M., & Osborne, S. (1991). Test of structural relationships within a proposed exercise and self-esteem model. *Journal of Personality Assessment, 56,* 348–364.

Sonstroem, R.J., Harlow, L.L., & Josephs, L. (1994). Exercise and self-esteem: Validity of model expansion and exercise associations. *Journal of Sport and Exercise Psychology, 16,* 29–42.

Sonstroem, R.J., Harlow, L.L., & Salisbury, K.S. (1993). Path analysis of a self-esteem model across a competitive swim season. *Research Quarterly for Exercise & Sport, 64,* 335–342.

Sonstroem, R.J., & Kampper, K.P. (1980). Prediction of athletic participation in middle school males. *Research Quarterly for Exercise & Sport, 51,* 685–94.

Sonstroem, R.J., & Morgan, W.P. (1989). Exercise and self-esteem: Rationale and model. *Medicine & Science in Sports & Exercise, 21,* 329–337.

Sonstroem, R.J., & Potts, S.A. (1996). Life adjustment correlates of physical self-concepts. *Medicine & Science in Sports & Exercise, 28,* 619–625.

Sonstroem, R.J., Speliotis, E.D., & Fava, J.L. (1992). Perceived physical competence in adults: An examination of the Physical Self-Perception Profile. *Journal of Sport and Exercise Psychology, 14,* 207–221.

Spence, J.C., McGannon, K.R., & Poon, P. (2005). The effects of exercise on global self-esteem: A quantitative review. *Journal of Sport & Exercise Psychology, 27,* 311–334.

Standage, M., Duda, J.L., & Ntoumanis, N. (2006). Students' motivational processes and their relationship to teacher ratings in school physical education: A self-determination theory approach. *Research Quarterly for Exercise & Sport, 77,* 100–110.

Taylor, A., & Fox, K.R. (2005). Changes in physical self-perceptions: Findings from a randomised controlled study of a GP exercise referral scheme. *Health Psychology, 24,* 11–21.

Thogersen-Ntoumani, C., & Fox, K.R. (2005). Physical activity and mental well-being typologies in corporate employees: A mixed methods approach. *Work and Stress, 19,* 50–67.

Trochim, W. (2001). *The research methods knowledge base* (2nd ed.). Cincinnati: Atomic Dog.

Van de Vliet, P., Knapen, J., Fox, K.R., Onghena, P., David, A., Probst, M., Van Coppenolle, H., & Pieters, G. (2003a). Changes in psychological well-being in female patients with clinically diagnosed depression: An exploratory approach in a therapeutic setting. *Psychology, Health and Medicine. 8,* 399-409

Van de Vliet, P., Onghena, P., Knapen, J., Fox, K.R., Probst, M., Van Coppenolle, H., & Pieters, G. (2003b). Assessing the additional impact of fitness training in depressed psychiatric patients re. *Disability and Rehabilitation, 25,* 1344-1353.

Van de Vliet, P., Knapen, J., Onghena, P., Fox, K.R., David, A., Morres, I., Van Coppenolle, H., & Pieters, G. (2002a). Relationships between self-perceptions and negative affect in adult Flemish psychiatric in-patients suffering from mood disorders. *Psychology of Sport and Exercise, 3,* 309–322.

Van de Vliet, P., Knapen, J., Onghena, P., Fox, K.R., Van Coppenolle, H., David, A., Pieters, G., & Peuskens, J. (2002b). Assessment of physical self-perceptions in normal Flemish adults versus depressed psychiatric patients. *Personality and Individual Differences, 32,* 855–863.

Welk, G.J., & Eklund, R.C. (2005). Validation of the children and youth physical self-perception profile for young children. *Psychology of Sport & Exercise, 6,* 51–65.

White, R.W. (1959). Motivation reconsidered: The concept of competence. *Psychological Review, 66,* 297–333.

Whitehead, J.R. (1995). A study of children's physical self-perceptions using an adapted physical self-perception questionnaire. *Pediatric Exercise Science, 7,* 133–152.

Wilson, P., & Eklund, R.C. (1998). The relationship between competitive anxiety and self-presentational concerns. *Journal of Sport & Exercise Psychology, 20,* 81–97.

Wilson, P.M., & Rodgers, W.M. (2002). The relationship between exercise motives and physical self-esteem in female exercise participants: An application of Self-Determination Theory. *Journal of Applied Biobehavioral Research, 7,* 30–43.

Wilson, P.M., Rodgers, W.M., Fraser, S.N., Murray, T.C., & McIntyre, C. (2004). The relationship between psychological need satisfaction and self-perceptions in females. *Journal of Sport & Exercise Psychology, 26,* S200.

Wylie, R.C. (1979). *The self-concept: Vol. 2.* Lincoln: University of Nebraska Press.

Wylie, R.C. (1989). *Measures of self-concept.* Lincoln: University of Nebraska Press.

CHAPTER 5

Abma, C.L., Fry, M.D., Li, Y., & Relyea, G. (2002). Differences in imagery content and imagery ability between high and low confident track and field athletes. *Journal of Applied Sport Psychology, 14,* 67–75.

Allport, G.W. (1937). *Personality: A psychological interpretation.* New York: Holt.

Annesi, J.J. (1998). Applications of the individual zones of optimal functioning model for the multimodal treatment of precompetitive anxiety. *The Sport Psychologist, 12,* 300–316.

Atkinson, J.W. (1964). *An introduction to motivation.* Princeton, NJ: Van Nostrand.

Balaguer, I., Castillo, I., Tomas, I., & Vealey, R.S. (2004). *A cultural analysis of sources and levels of confidence in Spanish and American female athletes.* Paper presented at the Association for the Advancement of Applied Sport Psychology Conference, Minneapolis, MN.

Bandura, A. (1977). Self-efficacy: Toward a unifying theory of behavioral change. *Psychological Review, 84,* 191–215.

Bandura, A. (1986). *Social foundations of thought and action: A social cognitive theory.* Englewood Cliffs, NJ: Prentice-Hall.

Bandura, A. (1997). *Self-efficacy: The exercise of control.* New York: Freeman.

Bandura, A., & Jourden, F.J. (1991). Self-regulatory mechanisms governing the impact of social comparison on complex decision-making. *Journal of Personality and Social Psychology, 60,* 941–951.

Bandura, A., & Locke, E.A. (2003). Negative self-efficacy and goal effects revisited. *Journal of Applied Psychology, 88,* 89–99.

Bandura, A., & Wood, R.E. (1989). Effect of perceived controllability and performance standards on self-regulation of complex decision-making. *Journal of Personality and Social Psychology, 60,* 805–814.

Barker, J.B., & Jones, M.V. (2006). Using hypnosis, technique refinement, and self-modeling to enhance self-efficacy: A case study in cricket. *The Sport Psychologist, 20,* 94–110.

Beattie, S., Hardy, L., & Woodman, T. (2004). Precompetition self-confidence: The role of the self. *Journal of Sport & Exercise Psychology, 26,* 427–441.

Beauchamp, M.R., Bray, S.R., Eys, M.A., & Carron, A.V. (2002). Role ambiguity, role efficacy and role performance effectiveness: Multidimensional and mediational relationships within interdependent sport teams. *Group Dynamics: Theory, Research, and Practice, 6,* 229–242.

Beauchamp, M.R., & Whinton, L.C. (2005). Self-efficacy and other-efficacy in dyadic performance: Riding as one in equestrian eventing. *Journal of Sport & Exercise Psychology, 27,* 245–252.

Behets, D. (1997). Comparison of more and less effective teaching behaviors in secondary physical education. *Teaching and Teacher Education, 13,* 215–224.

Beilock, S.L., & McConnell, A.R. (2004). Stereotype threat and sport: Can athletic performance be threatened? *Journal of Sport & Exercise Psychology, 26,* 597–609.

Bond, K.A., Biddle, S.J.H., & Ntoumanis, N. (2001). Self-efficacy and causal attributions in female golfers. *International Journal of Sport Psychology, 31,* 243–256.

Bray, S.R., Balaguer, I., & Duda, J. (2004). The relationship of task self-efficacy and role efficacy beliefs to role performance in Spanish youth soccer. *Journal of Sport Sciences, 22,* 429–437.

Bray, S.R., Brawley, L.R., & Carron, A.V. (2002). Efficacy for interdependent role functions: Evidence from the sport domain. *Small Group Research, 33,* 644–666.

Brody, E.B., Hatfield, B.D., & Spalding, T.W. (1988). Generalization of self-efficacy to a continuum of stressors upon mastery of a high-risk sport skill. *Journal of Sport & Exercise Psychology, 10,* 32–44.

Brustad, R.J., & Ritter-Taylor, M. (1997). Applying social psychological perspectives to the sport psychology consulting process. *The Sport Psychologist, 11,* 107–119.

Bryk, A.S., & Raudenbush, S.W. (1992). *Hierarchical linear models: Applications and data analysis methods.* Newbury Park, CA: Sage.

Bull, S.J., Shambrook, C.J., James, W., & Brooks, J.E. (2005). Towards an understanding of mental toughness in elite English cricketers. *Journal of Applied Sport Psychology, 17,* 209–227.

Burton, D. (1989). Winning isn't everything: Examining the impact of performance goals on collegiate swimmers' cognitions and performance. *The Sport Psychologist, 3,* 105–132.

Burton, D., & Martens, R. (1986). Pinned by their own goals: An exploratory investigation into why kids drop out of wrestling. *Journal of Sport Psychology, 8,* 183–197.

Butt, J., Weinberg, R.S., & Horn, T. (2003). The intensity and directional interpretation of anxiety: Fluctuations throughout competition and relationship to performance. *The Sport Psychologist, 17,* 35–54.

Callow, N., & Hardy, L. (2001). Types of imagery associated with sport confidence in netball players of varying skill levels. *Journal of Applied Sport Psychology, 13,* 1–17.

Callow, N., Hardy, L., & Hall, C. (2001). The effects of a motivational general-mastery imagery intervention on the sport confidence of high-level badminton players. *Research Quarterly for Exercise and Sport, 72,* 389–400.

Carron, A.V., Colman, M.M., Wheeler, J., & Stevens, D. (2002). Cohesion and performance in sport: A meta analysis. *Journal of Sport and Exercise Psychology, 24,* 168–188.

Carver, C.S., & Scheier, M.F. (1981). *Attention and self-regulation: A control-theory approach to human behavior.* New York: Springer-Verlag.

Carver, C.S., & Scheier, M.F. (1988). A control-process perspective on anxiety. *Anxiety Research, 1,* 17–22.

Chartrand, J.M., Jowdy, D.P., & Danish, S.J. (1992). The Psychological Skills Inventory for Sports: Psychometric characteristics and applied implications. *Journal of Sport & Exercise Psychology, 14,* 405–413.

Chase, M.A. (1998). Sources of self-efficacy in physical education and sport. *Journal of Teaching in Physical Education, 18,* 76–89.

Chase, M.A. (2001). Children's self-efficacy, motivational intentions, and attributions in physical education and sport. *Research Quarterly for Exercise and Sport, 72,* 47–54.

Chase, M.A., Feltz, D.L., Hayashi, S.W., & Hepler, T.J. (2005). Sources of coaching efficacy: The coaches' perspective. *International Journal of Sport and Exercise Psychology, 1,* 7–25.

Chase, M.A., Feltz, D.L., & Lirgg, C.D. (2003). Sources of collective and individual efficacy of collegiate athletes. *International Journal of Sport and Exercise Psychology, 1*, 180–191.

Chase, M.A., Lirgg, C.D., & Feltz, D.L. (1997). Do coaches' efficacy expectations for their teams predict team performance? *The Sport Psychologist, 11*, 8–23.

Chen, G., Webber, S.S., Bliese, P.D., Mathieu, J.E., Payne, S.C., Born, D.H., et al. (2002). Simultaneous examination of the antecedents and consequences of efficacy beliefs at multiple levels of analysis. *Human Performance, 15*, 381–409.

Cleary, T.J., & Zimmerman, B.J. (2001). Self-regulation differences during athletic practice by experts, non-experts, and novices. *Journal of Applied Sport Psychology, 13*, 185–206.

Clifton, R.T., & Gill, D.L. (1994). Gender differences in self-confidence on a feminine-typed task. *Journal of Sport & Exercise Psychology, 16*, 150–162.

Corbin, C.B. (1981). Sex of subject, sex of opponent, and opponent ability as factors affecting self-confidence in a competitive situation. *Journal of Sport Psychology, 4*, 265–270.

Corbin, C.B., Landers, D.M., Feltz, D.L., & Senior, K. (1983). Sex differences in performance estimates: Female lack of confidence vs. male boastfulness. *Research Quarterly for Exercise and Sort, 54*, 407–410.

Corbin, C.B., & Nix, C. (1979). Sex-typing of physical activities and success predictions of children before and after cross-sex competition. *Journal of Sport Psychology, 1*, 43–52.

Corbin, C.B., Stewart, M.J., & Blair, W.O. (1981). Self-confidence and motor performance of preadolescent boys and girls studied in different feedback situations. *Journal of Sport Psychology, 3*, 17–29.

Courneya, K.S., & McAuley, E. (1993). Efficacy, attributional, and affective responses of older adults following an acute bout of exercise. *Journal of Social Behavior and Personality, 8*, 729–742.

Cousins, S.O. (1997). Elderly tomboys? Sources of self-efficacy for physical activity in late life. *Journal of Aging and Physical Activity, 5*, 229–243.

Cox, A.E., & Whaley, D.E. (2004). The influence of task value, expectancies for success, and identity on athletes' achievement behaviors. *Journal of Applied Sport Psychology, 16*, 103–117.

Cox, R.H., Martens, M.P., & Russell, W.D. (2003). Measuring anxiety in athletics: The revised Competitive State Anxiety Inventory–2. *Journal of Sport & Exercise Psychology, 25*, 519–533.

Craft, L.L., Magyar, T.M., Becker, B.J., & Feltz, D.L. (2003). The relationship between the Competitive State Anxiety Inventory–2 and sport performance: A meta-analysis. *Journal of Sport & Exercise Psychology, 25*, 44–65.

Crawford, M., & Griffin, N. (1986). Testing the validity of the Griffin/Keogh model for movement confidence by analyzing self-report playground involvement decisions of elementary school children. *Research Quarterly for Exercise and Sport, 57*, 67–78).

Crocker, P.R.E. (1989). A follow-up of cognitive-affective stress management training. *Journal of Sport & Exercise Psychology, 11*, 236–242.

Crocker, P.R.E., & Leclerc, D.R. (1992). Testing the validity of the movement confidence model in a high-risk dive by novices. *Journal of Sport & Exercise Psychology, 14*, 159–168.

Cunningham, G.B., Sagas, M., & Ashley, F.B. (2003). Coaching self-efficacy to become a head coach, and occupational turnover intent: Gender differences between NCAA assistant coaches of women's teams. *International Journal of Sport Psychology, 34*, 125–137.

Dirks, K.T. (2000). Trust in leadership and team performance: Evidence from NCAA basketball. *Journal of Applied Psychology, 85*, 1004–1012.

Durand-Bush, N., Salmela, J.H., & Green-Demers, I. (2001). The Ottawa Mental Skills Assessment Tool (OMSAT–3). *The Sport Psychologist, 15*, 1–19.

Eccles, J.S., & Wigfield, A. (2002). Motivational beliefs, values, and goals. *Annual Review of Psychology, 53*, 109–132.

Edwards, T., & Hardy, L. (1996). The interactive effects of intensity and direction of cognitive and somatic anxiety and self-confidence upon performance. *Journal of Sport & Exercise Psychology, 18*, 296–312.

Edwards, T., Kingston, K., Hardy, L., & Gould, D. (2002). A qualitative analysis of catastrophic performances and the associated thoughts, feelings, and emotions. *The Sport Psychologist, 16*, 1–19.

Eklund, R.C. (1994). A season-long investigation of competitive cognition in collegiate wrestlers. *Research Quarterly for Exercise and Sport, 65*, 169–183.

Eklund, R.C. (1996). Preparing to compete: A season-long investigation with collegiate wrestlers. *The Sport Psychologist, 10*, 111–131.

Escarti, A., & Guzman, J.F. (1999). Effects of feedback on self-efficacy, performance, and choice on an athletic task. *Journal of Applied Sport Psychology, 11*, 83-96.

Evans, L., Jones, L., & Mullen, R. (2004). An imagery intervention during the competitive season with an elite rugby union player. *The Sport Psychologist, 18*, 252–271.

Everhart, C.B., & Chelladurai, P. (1998). Gender differences in preferences for coaching as an occupation: The role of self-efficacy, valence, and perceived barriers. *Research Quarterly for Exercise and Sport, 69*, 188–200.

Eysenck, M.W., & Calvo, M.G. (1992). Anxiety and performance: The processing efficiency theory. *Cognition and Emotion, 6*, 409–434.

Fallby, J., Hassmen, P., Kentta, G., & Durand-Bush, N. (2006). Relationship between locus of control, sense of coherence, and mental skills in Swedish elite athletes. *International Journal of Sport and Exercise Psychology, 4*, 111–120.

Feather, N.T. (Ed.). (1982). *Expectation and actions: Expectancy-value models in psychology*. Hillsdale, NJ: Erlbaum.

Feltz, D.L. (1982). Path analysis of the causal elements in Bandura's theory of self-efficacy and an anxiety-based model of avoidance behavior. *Journal of Personality and Social Psychology, 42*, 764–781.

Feltz, D.L. (1988). Gender differences in the causal elements of self-efficacy on a high avoidance motor task. *Journal of Sport & Exercise Psychology, 10*, 151–166.

Feltz, D.L., & Chase, M.A. (1998). The measurement of self-efficacy and confidence in sport. In J.L. Duda (Ed.), *Advances in sport and exercise psychology measurement* (pp. 65–80). Morgantown, WV: Fitness Information Technology.

Feltz, D.L., Chase, M.A., Moritz, S.E., & Sullivan, P.J. (1999). A conceptual model of coaching efficacy: Preliminary investigation and instrument development. *Journal of Educational Psychology, 91*, 765–776.

Feltz, D.L., Landers, D.M., & Raeder, U. (1979). Enhancing self-efficacy in high-avoidance motor tasks: A comparison of modeling techniques. *Journal of Sport Psychology, 1*, 112–122.

Feltz, D.L., & Lirgg, C.D. (1998). Perceived team and player efficacy in hockey. *Journal of Applied Psychology, 83*, 557–564.

Feltz, D.L., & Mugno, D. (1983). A replication of the path analysis of the causal elements in Bandura's theory of self-efficacy and the influence of autonomic perceptions. *Journal of Sport Psychology, 5*, 263–277.

Feltz, D.L, & Riessinger, C.A. (1990). Effects on in vivo emotive imagery and performance feedback on self-efficacy and muscular endurance. *Journal of Sport & Exercise Psychology, 12*, 132-143.

Feltz, D.L., Short, S.E., & Sullivan, P.J. (2008). *Self-efficacy and sport*. Champaign, IL: Human Kinetics.

Fitzsimmons, P.A., Landers, D.M., Thomas, J.R., & van der Mars, H. (1991). Does self-efficacy predict performance in experienced weightlifters? *Research Quarterly for Exercise and Sport, 62*, 424-431.

Fletcher, D., & Hanton, S. (2001). The relationship between psychological skills usage and competitive anxiety responses. *Psychology of Sport and Exercise, 2*, 89–101.

Fung, L., Ng, J.K., & Cheung, S.Y. (2001). Confirmatory factor analysis of the trait sport-confidence inventory and state sport-confidence inventory on a Chinese sample. *International Journal of Sport Psychology, 32*, 304–313.

Garza, D.L., & Feltz, D.L. (1998). Effects of selected mental practice on performance, self-efficacy, and competition confidence of figure skaters. *The Sport Psychologist, 12*, 1–15.

Gayton, W.F., & Nickless, C.J. (1987). An investigation of the validity of the trait and state sport-confidence inventories in predicting marathon performance. *Perceptual and Motor Skills, 65*, 481–482.

George, T.R. (1994). Self-confidence and baseball performance: A causal examination of self-efficacy theory. *Journal of Sport & Exercise Psychology, 16*, 381–399.

George, T.R., Feltz, D.L., & Chase, M.A. (1992). Effects of model similarity on self-efficacy and muscular endurance: A second look. *Journal of Sport & Exercise Psychology, 14,* 237–248.

Gernigon, C., & Delloye, J. (2003). Self-efficacy, causal attribution, and track athletic performance following unexpected success or failure among elite sprinters. *The Sport Psychologist, 17,* 55–76.

Gould, D. (2006). Goal setting for peak performance. In J.M. Williams (Ed.), *Applied sport psychology: Personal growth to peak performance* (pp. 240–259). Boston: McGraw-Hill.

Gould, D., Dieffenbach, K., & Moffett, A. (2002). Psychological characteristics and their development in Olympic champions. *Journal of Applied Sport Psychology, 14,* 172–204.

Gould, D., Greenleaf, C., Chung, Y., & Guinan, D. (2002). A survey of U.S. Atlanta and Nagano Olympians: Variables perceived to influence performance. *Research Quarterly for Exercise and Sport, 73,* 175–186.

Gould, D., Guinan, D., Greenleaf, C.A., & Chung, Y. (2002). A survey of U.S. Olympic coaches: Variables perceived to have influenced athlete performances and coach effectiveness. *The Sport Psychologist, 16,* 229–250.

Gould, D., Guinan, D., Greenleaf, C., Medbery, R., & Peterson, K. (1999). Factors affecting Olympic performance: Perceptions of athletes and coaches from more or less successful teams. *The Sport Psychologist, 13,* 371–394.

Gould, D., Hodge, K., Peterson, K., & Giannini, J. (1989). An exploratory examination of strategies used by elite coaches to enhance self-efficacy in athletes. *Journal of Sport & Exercise Psychology, 11,* 119–127.

Gould, D., Jackson, S.A., & Finch, L.M. (1993a). Sources of stress in U.S. national champion figure skaters. *Journal of Sport & Exercise Psychology, 15,* 134–159.

Gould, D., Jackson, S.A., & Finch, L.M. (1993b). Life at the top: The experiences of U.S. national figure skaters. *The Sport Psychologist, 7,* 354–374.

Gould, D., Medbery, R., Damarjian, N., & Lauer, L. (1999). A survey of mental skills training knowledge, opinions, and practices of junior tennis coaches. *Journal of Applied Sport Psychology, 11,* 28–50.

Gould, D., Petlichkoff, L., & Weinberg, R.S. (1984). Antecedents of, temporal changes in, and relationships between CSAI–2 subcomponents. *Journal of Sport Psychology, 6,* 289–304.

Gould, D., & Weiss, M.R. (1981). The effects of model similarity and model talk on self-efficacy and muscular endurance. *Journal of Sport Psychology, 3,* 17–29.

Gould, D., Weiss, M.R., & Weinberg, R. (1981). Psychological characteristics of successful and nonsuccessful Big Ten wrestlers. *Journal of Sport Psychology, 3,* 69–81.

Grandjean, B.D., Taylor, P.A., & Weiner, J. (2002). Confidence, concentration, and competitive performance of elite athletes: A natural experiment in Olympic gymnastics. *Journal of Sport & Exercise Psychology, 24,* 320–327.

Greenleaf, C., Gould, D., & Dieffenbach, K. (2001). Factors influencing Olympic performance: Interviews with Atlanta and Nagano U.S. Olympians. *Journal of Applied Sport Psychology, 13,* 154–184.

Greenlees, I., Buscombe, R., Thelwell, R., Holder, T., & Rimmer, M. (2005). Impact of opponents' clothing and body language on impression formation and outcome expectations. *Journal of Sport & Exercise Psychology, 27,* 39–52.

Griffin, N.S., & Crawford, M. (1989). Measurement of movement confidence with a stunt movement confidence inventory. *Journal of Sport & Exercise Psychology, 11,* 26–40.

Griffin, N.S., & Keogh, J.F. (1982). A model for movement confidence. In J.A. Kelso & J. Clark (Eds.), *The development of movement control and coordination* (pp. 213–238). New York: Wiley.

Griffin, N.S., Keogh, J.F., & Maybee, R. (1984). Performer perceptions of movement confidence. *Journal of Sport Psychology, 6,* 395–407.

Grove, J.R., & Hanrahan, S.J. (1988). Perceptions of mental training needs by elite field hockey players and their coaches. *The Sport Psychologist, 2,* 222–230.

Grove, J.R., & Heard, N.P. (1997). Optimism and sport-confidence as correlates of slump-related coping among athletes. *The Sport Psychologist, 11,* 400–410.

Haberl, P., & Zaichowsky, L. (1999). The U.S. women's Olympic gold medal ice hockey team: Optimal use of sport psychology for developing confidence. In R. Lidor & K.P. Henschen (Eds.), *The psychology of team sports* (pp. 217–233). Morgantown, WV: Fitness Information Technology.

Hackman, J.R. (Ed.) (1990). *Groups that work (and those that don't).* San Francisco: Jossey-Bass.

Hale, B.D., & Whitehouse, A. (1998). The effects of imagery-manipulated appraisal on intensity and direction of competitive anxiety. *The Sport Psychologist, 12,* 40–51.

Hall, H.K., & Kerr, A.W. (1997). Motivational antecedents of precompetitive anxiety in youth sport. *The Sport Psychologist, 11,* 24–42.

Hambrick, D.C., & Aveni, R.A. (1988). Large corporate failures as downward spirals. *Administrative Science Quarterly, 33,* 1–23.

Haney, C.J., & Long, B.C. (1995). Coping effectiveness: A path analysis of self-efficacy, control, coping, and performance in sport competitions. *Journal of Applied Social Psychology, 25,* 1726-1746.

Hanin, Y.L. (1997). Emotions and athletic performance: Individual zones of optimal functioning. *European Yearbook of Sport Psychology, 1,* 29–72.

Hanin, Y.L. (2000). Successful and poor performance and emotions. In Y.L. Hanin (Ed.), *Emotions in sport* (pp. 157–187). Champaign, IL: Human Kinetics.

Hanton, S., & Connaughton, D. (2002). Perceived control of anxiety and its relationship to self-confidence and performance: A qualitative inquiry. *Research Quarterly for Exercise and Sport, 73,* 87–97.

Hanton, S., & Jones, G. (1999). The effects of a multimodal intervention program on performers: II. Training the butterflies to fly in formation. *The Sport Psychologist, 13,* 22–41.

Hanton, S., Mellalieu, S.D., & Hall, R. (2004). Self-confidence and anxiety interpretation: Qualitative investigation. *Psychology of Sport and Exercise, 5,* 477–495.

Hardy, J., Gammage, K., & Hall, C. (2001). A descriptive study of athlete self-talk. *The Sport Psychologist, 15,* 306-318.

Hardy, L. (1996). A test of catastrophe model of anxiety and sports performance against multidimensional anxiety theory models using the methods of dynamic differences. *Anxiety, Stress, and Coping: An International Journal, 9,* 69–86.

Hardy, L., Woodman, T., & Carrington, S. (2004). Is self-confidence a bias factor in higher-order catastrophe models? An exploratory analysis. *Journal of Sport & Exercise Psychology, 26,* 359–368.

Harwood, C., & Swain, A. (2002). The development and activation of achievement goals within tennis: II. A player, parent, and coach intervention. *The Sport Psychologist, 16,* 111–137.

Hays, K., Maynard, I., Thomas, O., & Bawden, M. (2007). Sources and types of confidence identified by world class sport performers. *Journal of Applied Sport Psychology, 19,* 434-456.

Hays, K., Thomas, W., Maynard, I., & Butt, J. (2006). *Profiling confidence for sport.* Paper presented at the Association for the Advancement of Applied Sport Psychology Conference, Miami, FL.

Heuzé, J., Raimbault, N., & Fontayne, P. (2006). Relationships between cohesion, collective efficacy and performance in professional basketball teams: An examination of mediating effects. *Journal of Sport Sciences, 24,* 59–68.

Heuzé, J., Sarrazin, P., Masiero, M., Raimbault, N., & Thomas, J. (2006). The relationships of perceived motivational climate to cohesion and collective efficacy in elite female teams. *Journal of Applied Sport Psychology, 18,* 201–218.

Highlen, P.S., & Bennett, B.B. (1979). Psychological characteristics of successful and nonsuccessful elite wrestlers: An exploratory study. *Journal of Sport Psychology, 1,* 123–137.

Hodges, L., & Carron, A.V. (1992). Collective efficacy and group performance. *International Journal of Sport Psychology, 23,* 48–59.

Jackson, S.A. (1995). Factors influencing the occurrence of flow states in elite athletes. *Journal of Applied Sport Psychology, 7,* 135-163.

Jackson, S.A. (2000). Joy, fun, and flow state in sport. In Y.L. Hanin (Ed.), *Emotions in sport* (pp. 135–155). Champaign, IL: Human Kinetics.

Jackson, S.A., Dover, J., & Mayocchi, L. (1998). Life after winning gold: I. Experiences of Australian gold medalists. *The Sport Psychologist, 12,* 119–136.

James, L.R., Demaree, R.G., & Wolf, G. (1984). Estimating within-group interrater reliability with and without response bias. *Journal of Applied Psychology, 69,* 85–98.

Janssen, J., & Dale, G. (2002). *The seven secrets of successful coaches.* Cary, NC: Winning the Mental Game.

Jones, G., & Cale, A. (1989). Precompetition temporal patterning of anxiety and self-confidence in males and females. *Journal of Sport Behavior, 12,* 183–195.

Jones, G., & Hanton, S. (1996). Interpretation of competitive anxiety symptoms and goal attainment expectations. *Journal of Sport & Exercise Psychology, 18,* 144–157.

Jones, G., & Hanton, S. (2001). Precompetitive feeling states and directional anxiety interpretations. *Journal of Sport Sciences, 19,* 385–395.

Jones, G., Hanton, S., & Connaughton, D. (2002). What is this thing called mental toughness? An investigation of elite sport performers. *Journal of Applied Sport Psychology, 14,* 205–218.

Jones, G., Swain, A., & Cale, A. (1991). Gender differences in precompetition temporal patterning and antecedents of anxiety and self-confidence. *Journal of Sport & Exercise Psychology, 13,* 1–15.

Kane, T.D., Marks, M.A., Zaccaro, S.J., & Blair, V. (1996). Self-efficacy, personal goals, and wrestlers' self-regulation. *Journal of Sport & Exercise Psychology, 18,* 36–48.

Kavanagh, D., & Hausfeld, S. (1986). Physical performance and self-efficacy under happy and sad moods. *Journal of Sport Psychology, 8,* 112–123.

Kenny, D.A., & La Voie, L. (1985). Separating individual and group effects. *Journal of Personality and Social Psychology, 48,* 339–348.

Kingston, K., & Hardy, L. (1997). Effects of different types of goals on processes that support performance. *The Sport Psychologist, 11,* 277–293.

Kitsantas, A., & Zimmerman, B.J. (2002). Comparing self-regulatory processes among novice, non-expert, and expert volleyball players: A microanalytic study. *Journal of Applied Sport Psychology, 14,* 91–105.

Kozlowski, S.W.J., & Hartrup, K. (1992). A disagreement about within-group agreement: Disentangling issues of consistency versus consensus. *Journal of Applied Psychology, 77,* 161–167.

Krane, V., & Williams, J.M. (1994). Cognitive anxiety, somatic anxiety, and confidence in track and field athletes: The impact of gender, competitive level and task characteristics. *International Journal of Sport Psychology, 25,* 203–217.

Landin, D., & Hebert, E.P. (1999). The influence of self-talk on the performance of skilled female tennis players. *Journal of Applied Sport Psychology, 11,* 263–282.

Lenney, E. (1977). Women's self-confidence in achievement situations. *Psychological Bulletin, 84,* 1–13.

Lent, R.W., & Lopez, F.G. (2002). Cognitive ties that bind: A tripartite view of efficacy beliefs in growth-promoting relationships. *Journal of Social and Clinical Psychology, 21,* 256–286.

Lerner, B.S., & Locke, E.A. (1995). The effects of goal setting, self-efficacy, competition, and personal traits on the performance of an endurance task. *Journal of Sport & Exercise Psychology, 17,* 138–152.

Lindsley, D.H., Brass, D.J., & Thomas, J.B. (1995). Efficacy-performance spirals: A multilevel perspective. *Academy of Management Review, 20,* 645–678.

Lirgg, C.D. (1991). Gender differences in self-confidence in physical activity: A meta-analysis of recent studies. *Journal of Sport & Exercise Psychology, 13,* 294–310.

Lirgg, C.D., & Feltz, D.L. (1991). Teacher versus peer models revisited: Effects on motor performance and self-efficacy. *Research Quarterly for Exercise and Sport, 62,* 217–224.

Lirgg, C.D., George, T.R., Chase, M.A., & Ferguson, R.H. (1996). Impact of conception of ability and sex-type of task on male and female self-efficacy. *Journal of Sport & Exercise Psychology, 18,* 426–434.

Locke, E.A., & Latham, G.P. (1990). *A theory of goal setting and task performance.* Englewood Cliffs, NJ: Prentice-Hall.

Maddux, J.E. (1995). Self-efficacy theory: An introduction. In J.E. Maddux (Ed.), *Self-efficacy, adaptation, and adjustment* (pp. 3–33). New York: Plenum.

Maddux, J.E. (1999). The collective construction of collective efficacy: Comment on Paskevich, Brawley, Dorsch, & Widmeyer (1999). *Group Dynamics: Theory, Research, and Practice, 3,* 223–226.

Maddux, J.E., & Lewis, J. (1995). Self-efficacy and adjustment. In J.E. Maddux (Ed.), *Self-efficacy, adaptation, and adjustment* (pp. 37–68). New York: Plenum.

Magyar, T.M., & Duda, J.L. (2000). Confidence restoration following athletic injury. *The Sport Psychologist, 14,* 372–390.

Magyar, T.M., Feltz, D.L., & Simpson, I.P. (2004). Individual and crew level determinants of collective efficacy in rowing. *Journal of Sport & Exercise Psychology, 26,* 136–153.

Mahoney, M.J., & Avenener, M. (1977). Psychology of the elite athlete: An exploratory study. *Cognitive Therapy and Research, 1,* 135–141.

Mahoney, M.J., Gabriel, T.J., & Perkins, T.S. (1987). Psychological skills and exceptional athletic performance. *The Sport Psychologist, 1,* 181–199.

Malete, L., & Feltz, D.L. (2000). The effect of a coaching education program on coaching efficacy. *The Sport Psychologist, 14,* 410–417.

Mamassis, G., & Doganis, G. (2004). The effects of a mental training program on juniors' precompetitive anxiety, self-confidence, and tennis performance. *Journal of Applied Sport Psychology, 16,* 118–137.

Man, F., Stuchlikova, I., & Kindlmann, P. (1995). Trait-state anxiety, worry, emotionality, and self-confidence in top-level soccer players. *The Sport Psychologist, 9,* 212–224.

Manzo, L.G., Silva, J.M., & Mink, R. (2001). The Carolina Sport Confidence Inventory. *Journal of Applied Sport Psychology, 13,* 260–274.

Marback, T.L., Short, S.E., Short, M.W., & Sullivan, P.J. (2005). Coaching confidence: An exploratory investigation of sources and gender differences. *Journal of Sport Behavior, 28,* 62–73.

Martens, R. (1975). *Social psychology of physical activity.* New York: Harper and Row.

Martens, R., Burton, D., Vealey, R.S., Bump, L.A., & Smith, D.E. (1990). Development and validation of the Competitive State Anxiety Inventory–2. In R. Martens, R.S. Vealey, & D. Burton, *Competitive anxiety in sport* (pp. 117–190). Champaign, IL: Human Kinetics.

Martin, J.J. (2002). Training and performance self-efficacy, affect, and performance in wheelchair road racers. *The Sport Psychologist, 16,* 384–395.

Martin, J.J., & Gill, D.L. (1991). The relationships among competitive orientation, sport-confidence, self-efficacy, anxiety, and performance. *Journal of Sport & Exercise Psychology, 13,* 149–159.

Martin, J.J., & Gill, D.L. (1995). The relationships of competitive orientations and self-efficacy to goal importance, thoughts, and performance in high school distance runners. *Journal of Applied Sport Psychology, 7,* 50–62.

Maynard, I.W., Hemmings, B., & Warwick-Evans, L. (1995). The effects of a somatic intervention strategy on competitive state anxiety and performance in semiprofessional soccer players. *The Sport Psychologist, 9,* 51–64.

Maynard, I.W., Smith, M.J., & Warwick-Evans, L. (1995). The effects of a cognitive intervention strategy on competitive state anxiety and performance in semiprofessional soccer players. *Journal of Sport & Exercise Psychology, 17,* 428–446.

McAuley, E. (1985). Modeling and self-efficacy: A test of Bandura's model. *Journal of Sport Psychology, 7,* 283–295.

McKenzie, A., & Howe, B.L. (1997). The effect of imagery on self-efficacy for a motor skill. *International Journal of Sport Psychology, 28,* 196–210.

McPherson, S.L. (2000). Expert-novice differences in planning strategies during collegiate singles tennis competition. *Journal of Sport & Exercise Psychology, 22,* 39–62.

Mellalieu, S.D., Hanton, S., & Jones, G. (2003). Emotional labeling and competitive anxiety in preparation and competition. *The Sport Psychologist, 17,* 157–174.

Miller, M. (1993). Efficacy strength and performance in competitive swimmers of different skill levels. *International Journal of Sport Psychology, 24,* 284–296.

Mills, B.D. (1996). Trait sport confidence, goal orientation and competitive experience of female collegiate volleyball players. *Perceptual and Motor Skills, 82,* 1085–1086.

Mills, K.D., Munroe, K.J., & Hall, C.R. (2000). The relationship between imagery and self-efficacy in competitive athletics. *Imagination, Cognition and Personality, 20,* 33–39.

Moore, W.E., & Stevenson, J.R. (1991). Understanding trust in the performance of complex automatic sport skills. *The Sport Psychologist, 5,* 281–289.

Moritz, S.E., Feltz, D.L., Fahrbach, K.R., & Mack, D.E. (2000). The relation of self-efficacy measures to sport performance: A meta-analytic review. *Research Quarterly for Exercise and Sport, 71,* 280–294.

Moritz, S.E., Martin, K.A., Hall, C.R., & Vadocz, E. (1996). What are confident athletes imaging?: An examination of image content. *The Sport Psychologist, 10,* 171–179.

Moritz, S.E., & Watson, C.B. (1998). Levels of analysis issues in group psychology: Using efficacy as an example of a multilayer model. *Group Dynamics: Theory, Research, and Practice, 2,* 285–298.

Murphy, S., & Tammen, V. (1998). In search of psychological skills. In J.L. Duda (Ed.), *Advances in sport and exercise psychology measurement* (pp. 195–209). Morgantown, WV: Fitness Information Technology.

Myers, N.D., & Feltz, D.L. (2007). From self-efficacy to collective efficacy in sport: Transitional issues. In G. Tenenbaum & R.C. Eklund (Eds.), *Handbook of sport psychology* (3rd ed., pp. 799-819). New York: Wiley.

Myers, N.D., Feltz, D.L., & Short, S.E. (2004). Collective efficacy and team performance: A longitudinal study of collegiate football teams. *Group Dynamics: Theory, Research, and Practice, 8,* 126–138.

Myers, N.D., Payment, C.A., & Feltz, D.L. (2004). Reciprocal relationships between collective efficacy and team performance in women's ice hockey. *Group Dynamics: Theory, Research, and Practice, 8,* 182–195.

Myers, N.D., Vargas-Tonsing, T.M., & Feltz, D.L. (2005). Coaching efficacy in intercollegiate coaches: Sources, coaching behavior, and team variables. *Psychology of Sport & Exercise, 6,* 129–143.

Nelson, L., & Furst, M. (1972). An objective study of the effects of expectation on competitive performance. *Journal of Psychology, 81,* 69–72.

Orlick, T. (2000). *In pursuit of excellence* (3rd ed.). Champaign, IL: Human Kinetics.

Paskevich, D.M., Brawley, L.R., Dorsch, K.D., & Widmeyer, W.N. (1999). Relationship between collective efficacy and team cohesion: Conceptual and measurement issues. *Group Dynamics: Theory, Research, and Practice, 3,* 210–222.

Passer, M.W. (1983). Fear of failure, fear of evaluation, perceived competence, and self-esteem in competitive trait-anxious children. *Journal of Sport Psychology, 5,* 172–188.

Patton, M.Q. (2002). *Qualitative research & evaluation methods* (3rd ed.). Thousand Oaks, CA: Sage.

Pensgaard, A.M., & Duda, J.L. (2002). "If we work hard, we can do it": A tale from an Olympic (gold) medalist. *Journal of Applied Sport Psychology, 14,* 219–236.

Perry, J.D., & Williams, J.M. (1998). Relationship of intensity and direction of competitive trait anxiety to skill level and gender in tennis. *The Sport Psychologist, 12,* 169–179.

Petruzzello, S.J., & Corbin, C.B. (1988). The effects of performance feedback on female self-confidence. *Journal of Sport & Exercise Psychology, 10,* 174–183.

Prapavessis, H., & Grove, J.R. (1994a). Personality variables as antecedents of precompetitive mood states. *International Journal of Sport Psychology, 25,* 81–99.

Prapavessis, H., & Grove, J.R. (1994b). Personality variables as antecedents of precompetitive mood state temporal patterning. *International Journal of Sport Psychology, 25,* 347–365.

Quinn, A.M., & Fallon, B.J. (1999). The changes in psychological characteristics and reactions of elite athletes from injury onset until full recovery. *Journal of Applied Sport Psychology, 11,* 210–229.

Rousseau, D.M., & House, R.J. (1994). Meso organizational behavior: Avoiding three fundamental biases. In C.L. Cooper & D.M. Rousseau (Eds.), *Trends in organizational behavior* (Vol. 1, pp. 13–30). London: Wiley.

Rudisill, M.E. (1989). Influence of perceived competence and causal dimension orientation on expectations, persistence, and performance during perceived failure. *Research Quarterly for Exercise and Sport, 60,* 166–175.

Sanguinetti, C., Lee, A.M., & Nelson, J. (1985). Reliability estimates and age and gender comparisons of expectations of success in sex-typed activities. *Journal of Sport Psychology, 7,* 379–388.

Savoy, C. (1993). A yearly mental training program for a college basketball player. *The Sport Psychologist, 7,* 173–190.

Scanlan, T.K., & Lewthwaite, R. (1984). Social psychological aspects of competition for male youth sport participants: I. Predictors of competitive stress. *Journal of Sport Psychology, 6,* 208–226.

Scanlan, T.K., & Lewthwaite, R. (1985). Social psychological aspects of competition for male youth sport participants: III. Determinants of personal performance expectancies. *Journal of Sport Psychology, 7,* 389–399.

Scanlan, T.K., & Passer, M.W. (1978). Factors related to competitive stress among male youth sport participants. *Medicine and Science in Sports, 10,* 103–108.

Scanlan, T.K., & Passer, M.W. (1979). Factors influencing the competitive performance expectancies of young athletes. *Journal of Sport Psychology, 1,* 212–220.

Scanlan, T.K., & Passer, M.W. (1981). Determinants of competitive performance expectancies of young male athletes. *Journal of Personality, 49,* 60–74.

Scheier, M.F., & Carver, C.S. (1993). On the power of positive thinking: The benefits of being optimistic. *Current Directions in Psychological Science, 2,* 26-30.

Schneider, W., Dumais, S.T., & Shiffrin, R.M. (1984). Automatic and control processing and attention. In R. Parasuraman & R. Davies (Eds.), *Varieties of attention* (pp. 1–27). Orlando, FL: Academic Press.

Shaw, J.M., Dzewaltowski, D.A., & McElroy, M. (1992). Self-efficacy and causal attributions as mediators of perceptions of psychological momentum. *Journal of Sport & Exercise Psychology, 14,* 134–147.

Sheldon, J.P., & Eccles, J.S. (2005). Physical and psychological predictors of perceived ability in adult male and female tennis players. *Journal of Applied Sport Psychology, 17,* 48–63.

Short, S.E., Apostal, K., Harris, C., Poltavski, D., Young, J., Zostautas, N., et al. (2002). Assessing collective efficacy: A comparison of two approaches. *Journal of Sport & Exercise Psychology, 24,* S115–S116.

Short, S.E., Bruggeman, J.M., Engel, S.G., Marback, T.L., Wang, L.J., Willadsen, A., et al. (2002). The effect of imagery function and imagery direction on self-efficacy and performance on a golf-putting task. *The Sport Psychologist, 16,* 48–67.

Short, S.E., Sullivan, P., & Feltz, D.L. (2005). Development and preliminary validation of the Collective Efficacy Questionnaire for Sports. *Measurement in Physical Education and Exercise Science, 9,* 181–202.

Sitkin, S.B. (1992). Learning through failure: The study of small losses. In B.M. Staw & L.L. Cummings (Eds.), *Research in organizational behavior* (Vol. 14, pp. 231–266). Greenwich, CT: JAI Press.

Smith, R.E., & Christensen, D.S. (1995). Psychological skills as predictors of performance and survival in professional baseball. *Journal of Sport & Exercise Psychology, 17,* 399–415.

Smith, R.E., Schutz, R.W., Smoll, F.L., & Ptacek, J.T. (1995). Development and validation of a multidimensional measure of sport-specific psychological skills: The Athletic Coping Skills Inventory–28. *Journal of Sport & Exercise Psychology, 17,* 379–398.

Solomon, G.B. (2001). Performance and personality impression cues as predictors of athletic performance: An extension of expectancy theory. *International Journal of Sport Psychology, 32,* 88–100.

Spink, K.S. (1990). Group cohesion and collective efficacy of volleyball teams. *Journal of Sport & Exercise Psychology, 12,* 301–311.

Stanimirovic, R., & Hanrahan, S.J. (2004). Efficacy, affect, and teams: Is momentum a misnomer? *International Journal of Sport and Exercise Psychology, 2,* 43–62.

Stewart, M.J., & Corbin, C.B. (1988). Feedback dependence among low confidence preadolescent boys and girls. *Research Quarterly for Exercise and Sport, 59*, 160-164.

Swain, A., & Jones, G. (1991). Gender role endorsement and competitive anxiety. *International Journal of Sport Psychology, 22*, 50–65.

Swain, A., & Jones, G. (1992). Relationships between sport achievement orientation and competitive state anxiety. *The Sport Psychologist, 6*, 42–54.

Tenenbaum, G., Kamata, A., & Hayashi, K. (2007). Measurement in sport and exercise psychology: A new outlook on selected issues of reliability and validity. In G. Tenenbaum & R.C. Eklund (Eds.), *Handbook of sport psychology* (3rd ed., pp. 757-773). New York: Wiley.

Tenenbaum, G., Levi-Kolker, N., Sade, S., Leiberman, D., & Lidor, R. (1996). Anticipation and confidence of decisions related to skilled performance, 293–307.

Theodorakis, Y. (1995). Effects of self-efficacy, satisfaction, and personal goals on swimming performance. *The Sport Psychologist, 9*, 245–253.

Theodorakis, Y. (1996). The influence of goals, commitment, self-efficacy and self-satisfaction on motor performance. *Journal of Applied Sport Psychology, 8*, 171–182.

Thomas, O., Maynard, I., & Hanton, S. (2004). Temporal aspects of competitive anxiety and self-confidence as a function of anxiety perceptions. *The Sport Psychologist, 18*, 172–187.

Treasure, D.C., Monson, J., & Lox, C.L. (1996). Relationship between self-efficacy, wrestling performance, and affect prior to competition. *The Sport Psychologist, 10*, 73–83.

Tsorbatzoudis, H., Daroglou, G., Zahariadis, P., & Grouios, G. (2003). Examination of coaches' self-efficacy: Preliminary analysis of the Coaching Efficacy Scale. *Perceptual and Motor Skills, 97*, 1297–1306.

Vadocz, E.A., Hall, C.R., & Moritz, S.E. (1997). The relationship between competitive anxiety and imagery use. *Journal of Applied Sport Psychology, 9*, 241–253.

Vallerand, R.J., Colavecchio, P.G., & Pelletier, L.G. (1988). Psychological momentum and performance inferences: A preliminary test of the antecedents-consequences psychological momentum model. *Journal of Sport & Exercise Psychology, 10*, 92–108.

Vancouver, J.B., & Kendall, L.N. (2006). When self-efficacy negatively relates to motivation and performance in a learning context. *Journal of Applied Psychology, 91*, 1146–1153.

Vargas-Tonsing, T.M., Myers, N.D., & Feltz, D.L. (2004). Coaches' and athletes' perceptions of efficacy-enhancing techniques. *The Sport Psychologist, 18*, 397–414.

Vargas-Tonsing, T.M., Warners, A.L., & Feltz, D.L. (2003). The predictability of coaching efficacy on team efficacy and player efficacy in volleyball. *Journal of Sport Behavior, 26*, 396–407.

Vealey, R.S. (1986). Conceptualization of sport-confidence and competitive orientation: Preliminary investigation and instrument development. *Journal of Sport Psychology, 8*, 221–246.

Vealey, R.S. (1988). Sport-confidence and competitive orientation: An addendum on scoring procedures and gender differences. *Journal of Sport and Exercise Psychology, 10*, 471-478.

Vealey, R.S. (2001). Understanding and enhancing self-confidence in athletes. In R.N. Singer, H.A. Haueseblas, & C.M. Janelle (Eds.), *Handbook of sport psychology* (2nd ed., pp. 550–565). New York: Wiley.

Vealey, R.S. (2007). Mental skills training in sport. In G. Tenenbaum & R.C. Eklund (Eds.), *Handbook of sport psychology* (3rd ed.,). New York: Wiley.

Vealey, R.S., & Campbell, J.A. (1988). Achievement goals of adolescent figure skaters: Impact on self-confidence, anxiety, and performance. *Journal of Adolescent Research, 3*, 227-243.

Vealey, R.S., Hayashi, S.W., Garner-Holman, M., & Giacobbi, P. (1998). Sources of sport-confidence: Conceptualization and instrument development. *Journal of Sport & Exercise Psychology, 20*, 54–80.

Vealey, R.S., & Knight, B.J. (2002, September). *Multidimensional sport-confidence: A conceptual and psychometric extension.* Paper presented at the Association for the Advancement of Applied Sport Psychology Conference, Tucson, AZ.

Vealey, R.S., & Sinclair, D.A. (1987, September). *The analysis and prediction of stability in sport-confidence.* Paper presented at the Association for the Advancement of Applied Sport Psychology Conference, Newport Beach, CA.

Watson, C.B., Chemers, M.M., & Preiser, N. (2001). Collective efficacy: A multilevel analysis. *Personality and Social Psychology Bulletin, 27*, 1057–1068.

Weinberg, R.S., Gould, D., & Jackson, A. (1979). Expectations and performance: An empirical test of Bandura's self-efficacy theory. *Journal of Sport Psychology, 1*, 320–331.

Weinberg, R.S., Gould, D., Yukelson, D., & Jackson, A. (1981). The effects of preexisting and manipulated self-efficacy on a competitive muscular endurance task. *Journal of Sport Psychology, 3*, 345–354.

Weinberg, R.S., Grove, R., & Jackson, A. (1992). Strategies for building self-efficacy in tennis players: A comparative analysis of Australian and American coaches. *The Sport Psychologist, 6*, 3–13.

Weinberg, R.S., & Jackson, A. (1990). Building self-efficacy in tennis players: A coach's perspective. *Journal of Applied Sport Psychology, 2*, 164–174.

Weinberg, R.S., Yukelson, D., & Jackson, A. (1980). Effect of public and private efficacy expectations on competitive performance. *Journal of Sport Psychology, 2*, 340–349.

Weiss, M.R., Barber, H., Sisley, B.L., & Ebbeck, V. (1991). Developing competence and confidence in novice female coaches: II. Perceptions of ability and affective experiences following a season-long coaching internship. *Journal of Sport & Exercise Psychology, 13*, 336–362.

Wiggins, M.S. (1998). Anxiety intensity and direction: Preperformance temporal patterns and expectations in athletes. *Journal of Applied Sport Psychology, 10*, 201–211.

Wilkes, R.L., & Summers, J.J. (1984). Cognitions, mediating variables, and strength performance. *Journal of Sport Psychology, 6*, 351–359.

Wilson, R.C., Sullivan, P.J., Myers, N.D., & Feltz, D.L. (2004). Sources of sport confidence of master athletes. *Journal of Sport & Exercise Psychology, 26*, 369-384.

Wise, J.B., & Trunnell, E.P. (2001). The influence of sources of self-efficacy upon efficacy strength. *Journal of Sport & Exercise Psychology, 23*, 268-280.

Woodman, T., & Hardy, L. (2003). The relative impact of cognitive anxiety and self-confidence upon sport performance: A meta-analysis. *Journal of Sports Sciences, 21*, 443–457.

Woolfolks, A.E., Rossoff, B., & Hoy, W.K. (1990). Teachers' sense of efficacy and their beliefs about managing students. *Teaching and Teacher Education, 6*, 137–148.

Yan Lan, L., & Gill, D.L. (1984). The relationships among self-efficacy, stress responses, and a cognitive feedback manipulation. *Journal of Sport Psychology, 6*, 227–238.

Zimmerman, B.J., & Kitsantas, A. (1996). Self-regulated learning of a motoric skill: The role of goal setting and self-monitoring. *Journal of Applied Sport Psychology, 8*, 60–75.

CHAPTER 6

Abramson, L.Y., & Martin, D.J. (1981). Depression and the causal inference process. In J.H. Harvey, W.J. Ickes, & R.F. Kidd (Eds.), *New directions in attribution research* (Vol. 3, pp. 117-168). Hillsdale, NJ: Erlbaum.

Abramson, L.Y., Seligman, M.E.P., & Teasdale, J.D. (1978). Learned helplessness in humans: Critique and reformulation. *Journal of Abnormal Psychology, 87*, 49–74.

Aiken, J.M., McClure, J., & Siegert, R.J. (1998). Outcome and game closeness effects upon individual and team sports attributions. *New Zealand Journal of Sports Medicine, 26*(1), 2–9.

Al-Mabuk, R.H., Dedrick, C.V.L., & Vanderah, K.M. (1998). Attribution retraining in forgiveness therapy. *Journal of Family Psychotherapy, 9*(1), 11–31.

Bandura, A. (1986). *Social foundations of thought and action: A social cognitive theory.* Englewood Cliffs, NJ: Prentice-Hall.

Bandura, A. (1989). Perceived self-efficacy in the exercise of personal agency. *The Psychologist: Bulletin of the British Psychological Society, 10*, 411–424.

Bandura, A. (1997). *Self-efficacy: The exercise of control.* New York: Freeman.

Belciug, M.P. (1991). Effects of prior expectancy and performance outcome on attributions to stable factors in high-performance competitive athletes. *Journal for Research in Sport, Physical Education and Recreation, 14*(2), 1–8.

Bem, D. (1972). Self-perception theory. In L. Berkowitz (Ed.), *Advances in experimental social psychology* (Vol. 6, pp. 1–62). New York: Academic Press.

Biddle, S.J.H., Hanrahan, S.J., & Sellars, C.N. (2001). Attributions: Past, present, and future. In R.N. Singer, H.A. Hausenblas, & C.M. Janelle (Eds.), *Handbook of sport psychology* (2nd ed., pp. 444–471). New York: Wiley.

Biddle, S.J.H., & Hill, A.B. (1992). Attributions for objective outcome and subjective appraisal of performance: Their relationship with emotional reactions in sport. *British Journal of Social Psychology, 31,* 215–226.

Bond, K.A., Biddle, S.J.H., & Ntoumanis, N. (2001). Self-efficacy and causal attribution in female golfers. *International Journal of Sport Psychology, 32,* 243–256.

Carlyon, W.D. (1997). Attribution retraining: Implications for its integration into prescriptive social skills training. *School Psychology Review, 26,* 61–73.

Chase, M. (2001). Children's self-efficacy, motivational intentions, and attributions in physical education and sport. *Research Quarterly for Exercise and Sport, 72,* 47–54.

Chatzisarantis, N.L.D., Hagger, M.S., Biddle, S.J.H., Smith, B., & Wang, C.K.J. (2003). A meta-analysis of perceived locus of causality in exercise, sport, and physical education contexts. *Journal of Sport & Exercise Psychology, 25,* 284–306.

Cleary, T.J., & Zimmerman, B.J. (2001). Self-regulation differences during athletic practice by experts, non-experts, and novices. *Journal of Applied Sport Psychology, 13,* 185–206.

Crocker, P.R.E., Eklund, R.C., & Graham, T.R. (2002). Evaluating the factorial structure of the revised causal dimensions scale in adolescents. *Research Quarterly for Exercise and Sport, 73*(2), 211–218.

Deci, E.L., & Ryan, R.M. (1985). *Intrinsic motivation and self-determination in human behavior.* New York: Plenum Press.

De Michele, P.E., Gansneder, B., & Solomon, G.B. (1998). Success and failure attributions of wrestlers: Further evidence of the self-serving bias. *Journal of Sport Behavior, 21,* 242–255.

Dieser, R.B., & Ruddell, E. (2002). Effects of attributions retraining during therapeutic recreation on attributions and explanatory style of adolescents with depression. *Therapeutic Recreation Journal, 36*(1), 35–47.

Dodds, J. (1994). Spelling skills and causal attributions in children. *Education Psychology in Practice, 10,* 111–119.

Faulkner, G., & Finlay, S.-J. (2002). It's not what you say, it's the way you say it! Conversation analysis: A discursive methodology for sport, exercise, and physical education. *Quest, 54,* 49–66.

Fincham, F.D., Paleari, F.G., & Regalia, C. (2002). Forgiveness in marriage: The role of relationship quality, attributions, and empathy. *Personal Relationships, 9,* 27–37.

Finlay, S.-J., & Faulkner, G. (2003). "Actually, I was the star": Managing attributions in conversation. *Forum: Qualitative Social Research, 4*(1), www.qualitative-research-net/fqs-texte/1-03/01-03finlayfaulkner-e.htm.

Forsterling, F. (1985). Attributional retraining: A review. *Psychological Bulletin, 98,* 495–512.

Forsterling, F. (1988). *Attribution theory in clinical psychology.* Chichester, West Sussex, United Kingdom: Wiley.

Forsterling, F. (2001). *Attribution: An introduction to theories, research and applications.* Munich: Psychology Press.

Fox, K.R. (Ed.). (1997). *The physical self: From motivation to well-being.* Champaign, IL: Human Kinetics.

Gernigon, C., & Delloye, J.B. (2003). Self-efficacy, causal attribution, and track athletic performance following unexpected success or failure among elite sprinters. *The Sport Psychologist, 17,* 55–76.

Gill, D.L., Ruder, M.K., & Gross, J.B. (1982). Open-ended attributions in team competition. *Journal of Sport Psychology, 4,* 159–169.

Graham, T.R., Kowalski, K.C., & Crocket, P.R.E. (2002). The contributions of goal characteristics and causal attributions to emotional experience in youth sport participants. *Psychology of Sport & Exercise, 3*(4), 273–291.

Grove, J.R., Hanrahan, S.J., & McInman, A. (1991). Success/failure bias in attributions across involvement categories in sport. *Personality and Social Psychology Bulletin, 17,* 93–97.

Grove, J.R., & Pargman, D. (1986). Relationships among success/failure, attributions, and performance expectancies in competitive situations. In L.V. Veldon & J.H. Humphrey (Eds.), *Psychology and sociology of sport: Current selected research* (pp. 85–95). New York: AMS Press.

Hamilton, P.R., & Jordan, J.S. (2000). Most successful and least successful performances: Perceptions of causal attributions in high school track athletes. *Journal of Sport Behavior, 23*(3), 245–254.

Hanrahan, S.J., Cerin, E., & Hartel, C. (2003, October). *Achievement goal orientations, attributional style, and motivational climate as predictors of performance and persistence.* Paper presented at the Association for the Advancement of Applied Sport Psychology annual conference, Philadelphia.

Hanrahan, S.J., & Gross, J. (2005). Attributions and goal orientations in masters athletes: Performance versus outcome. *Revista de Psicologia del Deporte, 14*(1), 43–56.

Hanrahan, S.J., & Grove, J.R. (1990a). Further examination of the psychometric properties of the Sport Attributional Style Scale. *Journal of Sport Behavior, 13,* 183–193.

Hanrahan, S.J., & Grove, J.R. (1990b). A short form of the Sport Attributional Style Scale. *Australian Journal of Science and Medicine in Sport, 22*(4), 97–101.

Hanrahan, S.J., Grove, J.R., & Hattie, J.A. (1989). Development of a questionnaire measure of sport-related attributional style. *International Journal of Sport Psychology, 20,* 114–134.

Hanrahan, S.J., & Seefeld, N. (2005). An intervention designed to enhance task orientation and improve attributions [Abstract]. *Association for the Advancement of Applied Sport Psychology 2005 Conference Proceedings, 53.*

Harter, S. (1978). Effectance motivation reconsidered: Toward a developmental model. *Human Development, 21,* 34–64.

Heider, F. (1944). Social perception and phenomenal causality. *Psychological Review, 51,* 358–374.

Heider, F. (1958). *The psychology of interpersonal relations.* New York: Wiley.

Jones, E. (1979). The rocky road from acts to dispositions. *American Psychologist, 34,* 107–117.

Jones, E.E., & Davis, K.E. (1965). From acts to dispositions: The attribution process in person perception. In L. Berkowitz (Ed.), *Advances in experimental social psychology* (Vol. 2, pp. 219–266). London: Academic Press.

Kelley, H.H. (1967). Attribution theory in social psychology. In D. Levine (Ed.), *Nebraska Symposium on Motivation* (Vol. 15, pp. 192–240). Lincoln: University of Nebraska Press.

Kelley, H.H. (1971). *Attribution in social interaction.* New York: General Learning Press.

Kelley, H.H. (1972). Causal schemata and the attribution process. In E.E. Jones, D.E. Kanouse, H.H. Kelley, R.E. Nisbett, S. Valins, & B. Weiner (Eds.), *Attribution: Perceiving the causes of behaviour* (pp. 1–26). Morristown, NJ: General Learning Press.

Kelley, H.H., & Michela, J. (1980). Attribution theory and research. *Annual Review of Psychology, 31,* 457–501.

Kozub, F.M. (2002). Expectations, task persistence, and attributions in children with mental retardation during integrated physical education. *Adapted Physical Activity Quarterly, 19,* 334–349.

Kruglanski, A.W. (1975). The endogenous-exogenous partition in attribution theory. *Psychological Review, 82,* 387–406.

Leith, L.M., & Prapavessis, H. (1989). Attributions of causality and dimensionality associated with sport outcomes in objectively evaluated and subjectively evaluated sports. *International Journal of Sport Psychology, 20*(3), 224–234.

Mark, M.M., Mutrie, N., Brooks, D.R., & Harris, D.V. (1984). Causal attributions of winners and losers in individual competitive sports: Toward a reformulation of the self-serving bias. *Journal of Sport Psychology, 6,* 184–196.

Markland, D. (1999). Self-determination moderates the effects of perceived competence on intrinsic motivation in an exercise setting. *Journal of Sport & Exercise Psychology, 21*, 351–361.

McAuley, E., Duncan, T.E., & Russell, D. (1992). Measuring causal attributions: The Revised Causal Dimension Scale (CDS–II). *Personality and Social Psychology Bulletin, 18*, 566–573.

McAuley, E., & Gross, J.B. (1983). Perceptions of causality in sport: An application of the Causal Dimension Scale. *Journal of Sport Psychology, 5*, 72–76.

McAuley, E., Poag, K., Gleason, A., & Wraith, S. (1990). Attribution from exercise programs: Attributional and affective perspectives. *Journal of Social Behavior and Personality, 5*, 591–602.

Miller, D.T., & Ross, M. (1975). Self-serving biases in the attribution of causality: Fact or fiction? *Psychological Bulletin, 82*(2), 213–225.

Minniti, A.M., & Hanrahan, S.J. (2005, August). *A qualitative investigation of elite triathletes' attributions: Comparisons across attribution retraining models.* Paper presented at the 11th World Congress of Sport Psychology, Sydney, Australia.

Miranda, A., Villaescusa, M.I., & Vidal-Abarca, E. (1997). Is attribution retraining necessary? Use of self-regulation procedures for enhancing the reading comprehension strategies of children with learning disabilities. *Journal of Learning Disabilities, 30*, 503–512.

Miserandino, M. (1998). Attributional retraining as a method of improving athletic performance. *Journal of Sport Behavior, 21*(3), 286–297.

Muller, J. (2005). *Attributional styles of exercisers versus non-exercisers.* Unpublished master's thesis, California State University at Fresno.

Munton, A.G., Silvester, J., Stratton, P., & Hanks, H. (1999). *Attributions in action: A practical approach to coding qualitative data.* Chichester, West Sussex, United Kingdom: Wiley.

Orbach, I., Singer, R.N., & Murphey, M. (1997). Changing attributions with an attribution retraining technique related to basketball dribbling. *The Sport Psychologist, 13*, 294–304.

Orbach, I., Singer, R.N., & Price, S. (1999). An attribution training program and achievement in sport. *The Sport Psychologist, 13*, 69–82.

Patchell, J.W. (2004). *Moderating effects of perceived team cohesion on attribution bias: Does it pay to be a member of a highly cohesive team?* Unpublished honours thesis, University of Queensland, Queensland, Australia.

Peterson, C. (1990). Explanatory style in the classroom and on the playing field. In S. Graham & V.S. Folkes (Eds.), *Attribution theory: Applications to achievement, mental health, and interpersonal conflict* (pp. 53–75). Hillsdale, NJ: Erlbaum.

Peterson, C., Maier, S.F., & Seligman, M.E.P. (1993). *Learned helplessness: A theory for the age of personal control.* New York: Oxford University Press.

Prapavessis, H., & Carron, V. (1988). Learned helplessness in sport. *The Sport Psychologist, 2*, 189–201.

Roberts, G.C., & Pascuzzi, D. (1979). Causal attributions in sport: Some theoretical implications. *Journal of Sport Psychology, 1*, 203–211.

Rotter, J.B. (1954). *Social learning and clinical psychology.* Englewood Cliffs, NJ: Prentice-Hall.

Rotter, J.B. (1966). Generalised expectancies for internal versus external control of reinforcement. *Psychological Monographs, 80* (Whole No. 609), 1–28.

Rotter, J.B. (1975). Some problems and misconceptions related to the construct of internal versus external control of reinforcement. *Journal of Consulting and Clinical Psychology, 43*, 56–67.

Rudisill, M. (1989). Influence of perceived competence and causal dimension orientations on expectations, persistence, and performance during perceived failure. *Research Quarterly for Exercise and Sport, 60*, 166–175.

Russell, D. (1982). The Causal Dimension Scale: A measure of how individuals perceive causes. *Journal of Personality and Social Psychology, 42*, 1137–1145.

Russell, D., McAuley, E., & Tarico, V. (1987). Measuring causal attributions for success and failure: A comparison of methodologies for assessing causal dimensions. *Journal of Personality and Social Psychology, 52*, 1248–1257.

Schacter, S., & Singer, J.E. (1962). Cognitive, social and physiological determinants of emotional state. *Psychological Review, 69*, 379–399.

Seligman, M.E.P., Abramson, L.Y., Semmel, A., & vonBaeyer, C. (1979). Depressive attributional style. *Journal of Abnormal Psychology, 88*, 242–247.

Singer, R.N., & McCaughan, L. (1978). Motivational effects of attributions, expectancy, and achievement motivation during the learning of a novel task. *Journal of Motor Behavior, 10*, 245–253.

Sinnott, K., & Biddle, S.J.H. (1998). Changes in attributions, perceptions of success and intrinsic motivation after attributions retraining in children's sport. *International Journal of Adolescence and Youth, 7*, 137–144.

Skinner, E. (1995). *Perceived control, motivation, and coping.* Thousand Oaks, CA: Sage.

Skinner, E. (1996). A guide to constructs of control. *Journal of Personality and Social Psychology, 71*, 549–570.

Stratton, P., Munton, A.G., Hanks, H., Hard, D.H., & Davidson, C. (1988). *Leeds Attributional Coding System (LACS) manual.* Leeds, United Kingdom: LFTRC.

Vallerand, R.J. (1987). Antecedents of self-related affects in sport: Preliminary evidence on the intuitive-reflective appraisal model. *Journal of Sport Psychology, 9*, 161–182.

Vallerand, R.J. (1997). Toward a hierarchical model of intrinsic and extrinsic motivation. In M.P. Zanna (Ed.), *Advances in experimental social psychology* (Vol. 29, pp. 271–360). New York: Academic Press.

Vallerand, R.J., & Richer, F. (1988). On the use of the Causal Dimension Scale in a field setting: A test with confirmatory factor analysis in success and failure conditions. *Journal of Personality and Social Psychology, 54*, 704–712.

Van Raalte, J.L. (1994). Sport performance attributions: A special case of self-serving bias? *Australian Journal of Science and Medicine in Sport, 26*(3/4), 45–48.

Vlachopoulos, S., Biddle, S., & Fox, K. (1997). Determinants of emotion in children's physical activity: A test of goal perspectives and attribution theories. *Pediatric Exercise Science, 9*, 65–79.

Wann, D.L., & Wilson, A.M. (2001). The relationship between the sport team identification of basketball spectators and the number of attributions they generate to explain their team's performance. *International Sports Journal, 5*(1), 43–50.

Weiner, B. (1972). *Theories of motivation: From mechanism to cognition.* Chicago: Rand McNally.

Weiner, B. (1979). A theory of motivation for some classroom experiences. *Journal of Educational Psychology, 71*, 3–25.

Weiner, B. (1980). *Human motivation.* New York: Holt, Rinehart & Winston.

Weiner, B. (1985a). An attributional theory of achievement motivation and emotion. *Psychological Review, 92*, 548–573.

Weiner, B. (1985b). Spontaneous causal thinking. *Psychological Bulletin, 97*, 74–84.

Weiner, B. (1986). *An attributional theory of motivation and emotion.* New York: Springer-Verlag.

Weiner, B. (1992). *Human motivation.* Newbury Park, CA: Sage.

Weiner, B. (1995). *Judgments of responsibility.* New York: Guilford Press.

Weiner, B., Frieze, I.H., Kukla, A., Reed, L., Rest, S., & Rosenbaum, R.M. (1972). Perceiving the causes of success and failure. In E.E. Jones, D.E. Kanouse, H.H. Kelley, R.E. Nisbett, S. Valins, & B. Weiner (Eds.), *Attribution: Perceiving the causes of behavior* (pp. 95–120). Morristown, NJ: General Learning Press.

Weiss, M.R., Ebbeck, V., McAuley, E., & Wiese, D.M. (1990). Self-esteem and causal attributions for children's physical and social competence in sport. *Journal of Sport & Exercise Psychology, 12*, 21–36.

Yamamoto, Y. (1983). A study on causal attribution for coaching. *Japanese Journal of Sport Psychology, 10*(1), 36–42.

Zientek, C.C., & Breakwell, G.M. (1988). Attributions made in ignorance of performance outcome. *International Journal of Sport Psychology, 19*, 38–46.

CHAPTER 7

Adler, P.A., Kless, S.J., & Adler, P. (1992). Socialization to gender roles: Popularity among elementary school boys and girls. *Sociology of Education, 65*, 169–187.

Alderman, R.A., & Wood, N.L. (1976). An analysis of incentive motivation in young Canadian athletes. *Canadian Journal of Applied Sport Sciences, 1,* 169–175.

Allen, J.B., & Howe, B. (1998). Player ability, coach feedback, and female adolescent athletes' perceived competence and satisfaction. *Journal of Sport & Exercise Psychology, 20,* 280–299.

Ames, C. (1992). Achievement goals, motivational climate, and motivational processes. In G.C. Roberts (Ed.), *Motivation in sport and exercise* (pp. 161–176). Champaign, IL: Human Kinetics.

Amiot, C.E., Gaudreau, P., Blanchard, C.M. (2004). Self-determination, coping, and goal attainment in sport. *Journal of Sport & Exercise Psychology, 26,* 396–411.

Amorose, A.J. (2001). Intraindividual variability of self-evaluations in the physical domain: Prevalence, consequences, and antecedents. *Journal of Sport & Exercise Psychology, 23,* 222–244.

Amorose, A.J. (2002). The influence of reflected appraisals on middle school and high school athletes' self-perceptions of sport competence. *Pediatric Exercise Science, 14,* 377–390.

Amorose, A.J. (2003). Reflected appraisals and perceived importance of significant others' appraisals as predictors of college athletes' self-perceptions of competence. *Research Quarterly for Exercise & Sport, 74,* 60–70.

Amorose, A.J. (2007). Coaching effectiveness: Exploring the relationship between coaching behavior and motivation from a self-determination theory perspective. In N. Chatzisarantis & M.S. Hagger (Eds.), *Self-determination in sport and exercise* (pp. 209-227). Champaign, IL: Human Kinetics.

Amorose, A.J., & Anderson-Butcher, D. (2007). Autonomy-supportive coaching and self-determined motivation in high school and college athletes: A test of self-determination theory. *Psychology of Sport and Exercise, 8,* 654-670.

Amorose, A.J., & Horn, T.S. (2000). Intrinsic motivation: Relationships with collegiate athletes' gender, scholarship status, and perceptions of their coaches' behavior. *Journal of Sport & Exercise Psychology, 22,* 63–84.

Amorose, A.J., & Horn, T.S. (2001). Pre- to post-season changes in the intrinsic motivation of first year college athletes: Relationships with coaching behavior and scholarship status. *Journal of Applied Sport Psychology, 13,* 355–373.

Amorose, A.J., & Smith, P.J.K. (2003). Feedback as a source of physical competence information: Effects of age, experience and type of feedback. *Journal of Sport & Exercise Psychology, 25,* 341–359.

Amorose, A.J., & Weiss, M.R. (1998). Coaching feedback as a source of information about perceptions of ability: A developmental examination. *Journal of Sport & Exercise Psychology, 20,* 395–420.

Baard, P.P. (2002). Intrinsic need satisfaction in organizations: A motivational basis of success in for-profit and not-for-profit settings. In E.L. Deci & R.M. Ryan (Eds.), *Handbook of self-determination research* (pp. 255–276). Rochester, NY: University of Rochester Press.

Babkes, M.L., & Weiss, M.R. (1999). Parental influence on cognitive and affective responses in children's competitive soccer participation. *Pediatric Exercise Science, 11,* 44–62.

Baumeister, R., & Leary, M.R. (1995). The need to belong: Desire for interpersonal attachments as a fundamental human motive. *Psychological Bulletin, 117,* 497–529.

Black, S.J., & Weiss, M.R. (1992). The relationship among perceived coaching behaviors, perceptions of ability, and motivation in competitive age-group swimmers. *Journal of Sport and Exercise Psychology, 14,* 309–325.

Bois, J.E., Sarrazin, P.G., Brustad, R.J., Chanal, J.P., & Trouilloud, D.O. (2005). Parents' appraisals, reflected appraisals, and children's self-appraisals of sport competence: A yearlong study. *Journal of Applied Sport Psychology, 17,* 273–289.

Bois, J.E., Sarrazin, P.G., Brustad, R.J., Trouilloud, D.O., & Cury, F. (2002). Mothers' expectancies and young adolescents' perceived physical competence: A yearlong study. *Journal of Early Adolescence, 22,* 384–406.

Bois, J.E., Sarrazin, P.G., Brustad, R.J., Trouilloud, D.O., & Cury, F. (2005). Elementary schoolchildren's perceived competence and physical activ-

ity involvement: The influence of parents' role modeling behaviours and perceptions of their child's competence. *Psychology of Sport and Exercise, 6,* 381–397.

Brown, B.A., Frankel, F., & Fennell, M. (1989). Hugs or shrugs: Parental and peer influence on continuity of involvement in sport by female adolescents. *Sex Roles, 20,* 397–412.

Brunel, P.C. (1999). Relationship between achievement goal orientations and perceived motivational climate on intrinsic motivation. *Scandinavian Journal of Medicine and Science in Sport, 9,* 365–374.

Brustad, R.J. (1988). Affective outcomes in competitive youth sport: The influence of intrapersonal and socialization factors. *Journal of Sport & Exercise Psychology, 10,* 307–321.

Brustad, R.J. (1993). Who will go out and play? Parental and psychological influences on children's attraction to physical activity. *Pediatric Exercise Science, 5,* 210–223.

Brustad, R.J. (1996). Attraction to physical activity in urban schoolchildren: Parental socialization and gender influences. *Research Quarterly for Exercise and Sport, 67,* 316–323.

Brustad, R.J., & Weiss, M.R. (1987). Competence perceptions and sources of worry in high, medium, and low competitive trait anxious young athletes. *Journal of Sport Psychology, 9,* 97–105.

Burton, D., & Martens, R. (1986). Pinned by their own goals: An exploratory investigation into why kids drop out of wrestling. *Journal of Sport Psychology, 8,* 183–197.

Carpenter, P.J. (1992). *Staying in sport: Young athletes' motivations for continued involvement.* Unpublished doctoral dissertation, University of California at Los Angeles.

Carpenter, P.J., & Coleman, R. (1998). A longitudinal study of elite youth cricketers' commitment. *International Journal of Sport Psychology, 29,* 195–210.

Carpenter, P.J., & Scanlan, T.K. (1998). Changes over time in the determinants of sport commitment. *Pediatric Exercise Science, 10,* 356–365.

Carpenter, P.J., Scanlan, T.K., Simons, J.P., & Lobel, M. (1993). A test of the sport commitment model using structural equation modeling. *Journal of Sport & Exercise Psychology, 15,* 119–133.

Centers for Disease Control and Prevention. (1997). Guidelines for school and community programs to promote lifelong physical activity among young people. *Morbidity and Mortality Weekly Report, 46*(No. RR-6), 1–36.

Chatzisarantis, N.L.D., & Biddle, S.J.H. (1998). Functional significance of psychological variables that are included in the Theory of Planned Behavior: A Self-Determination Theory approach to the study of attitudes, subjective norms, perceptions of control and intentions. *Journal of Social Psychology, 28,* 303–322.

Chatzisarantis, N.L.D., Biddle, S.J.H., & Meek, G.A. (1997). A self-determination theory approach to the study of intentions and the intention-behavior relationship in children's physical activity. *British Journal of Health Psychology, 2,* 343–360.

Chatzisarantis, N.L.D., Hagger, M.S., Biddle, S.J.H., Smith, B., & Wang, J.C.K. (2003). A meta-analysis of perceived locus of causality in exercise, sport, and physical education contexts. *Journal of Sport & Exercise Psychology, 25,* 284–306.

Clifton, R.T., & Gill, D.L. (1994). Gender differences in self-confidence on a feminine-typed task. *Journal of Sport & Exercise Psychology, 16,* 150–162.

Coakley, J.J., & White, A. (1992). Making decisions: Gender and sport participation among British adolescents. *Sociology of Sport Journal, 9,* 20–35.

Cox, A.E., & Whaley, D.E. (2004). The influence of task value, expectancies for success, and identity on athletes' achievement behaviors. *Journal of Applied Sport Psychology, 16,* 103–117.

Cresswell, S.L., & Eklund, R.C. (2005a). Motivation and burnout among top amateur rugby players. *Medicine & Science in Sports & Exercise, 37,* 469–477.

Cresswell, S.L., & Eklund, R.C. (2005b). Motivation and burnout in professional rugby players. *Research Quarterly for Exercise & Sport, 76,* 370–376.

deCharms, R. (1968). *Personal causation: The internal affective determinants of behavior.* New York: Academic Press.

Deci, E.L. (1975). *Intrinsic motivation*. New York: Plenum.

Deci, E.L., Koestner, R., & Ryan, R.M. (2001). Extrinsic rewards and intrinsic motivation in education: Reconsidered once again. *Review of Educational Research, 71,* 1–27.

Deci, E.L., & Ryan, R.M. (1985a). *Intrinsic motivation and self-determination in human behavior.* New York: Plenum.

Deci, E.L., & Ryan, R.M. (1985b). The general causality orientation sale: Self-determination in personality. *Journal of Research in Personality, 19,* 109–134.

Deci, E.L., & Ryan, R.M. (1987). The support of autonomy and the control of behavior. *Journal of Personality and Social Psychology, 53,* 1024–1037.

Deci, E.L., & Ryan, R.M. (1991). A motivational approach to self: Integration in personality. In R. Deinstbier (Ed.), *Nebraska Symposium on Motivation: Vol. 38. Perspectives on motivation* (pp. 237–288). Lincoln: University of Nebraska Press.

Deci, E.L., Ryan, R.M., Gagné, M., Leone, D.R., Usunov, J., & Kornazheva, B.P. (2001). Need satisfaction, motivation, and well-being in the work organizations of a former Eastern Bloc country. *Personality and Social Psychology Bulletin, 27,* 930–942.

Deeter, T.E. (1989). Development of a model of achievement behavior for physical activity. *Journal of Sport & Exercise Psychology, 11,* 1–12.

Deeter, T.E. (1990). Re-modeling expectancy and value in physical activity. *Journal of Sport & Exercise Psychology, 12,* 86–91.

Dempsey, J.M., Kimiecik, J.C., & Horn, T.S. (1993). Parental influence on children's moderate to vigorous physical activity participation: An expectancy-value approach. *Pediatric Exercise Science, 5,* 151–167.

Duda, J.L., Chi, L., Newton, M.L., Walling, M.D., & Catley, D. (1995). Task and ego orientation and intrinsic motivation in sport. *International Journal of Sport Psychology, 26,* 40–63.

Duncan, S.C. (1993). The role of cognitive appraisal and friendship provisions in adolescents' affect and motivation toward activity in physical education. *Research Quarterly for Exercise and Sport, 64,* 314–323.

Duncan, T.E., & Duncan, S.C. (1991). A latent growth curve approach to investigating developmental dynamics and correlates of change in children's perceptions of physical competence. *Research Quarterly for Exercise and Sport, 62,* 390–396.

Ebbeck, V. (1990). Sources of performance information in the exercise setting. *Journal of Sport & Exercise Psychology, 12,* 56–65.

Ebbeck, V. (1994). Self-perception and motivational characteristics of tennis participants: The influence of age and skill. *Journal of Applied Sport Psychology, 6,* 71–86.

Ebbeck, V., & Gibbons, S.L. (1998). The effect of a team-building program on the self-conceptions of grade 6 and 7 physical education students. *Journal of Sport & Exercise Psychology, 20,* 300–310.

Ebbeck, V., Gibbons, S.L., & Loken-Dahle, L.J. (1995). Reasons for adult participation in physical activity: An interactional approach. *International Journal of Sport Psychology, 26,* 262–275.

Ebbeck, V., & Weiss, M.R. (1998). Determinants of children's self-esteem: An examination of perceived competence and affect in sport. *Pediatric Exercise Science, 10,* 285–298.

Eccles, J.S., Adler, T.E., Futterman, R., Goff, S.B., Kaczala, C.M., Meece, J.L., et al. (1983). Expectancies, values, and academic behaviors. In J.T. Spence (Ed.), *Achievement and achievement motivation* (pp. 75–146). San Francisco: Freeman.

Eccles, J., Adler, T.F., & Kaczala, C.M. (1982). Socialization of achievement attitudes and beliefs: Parental influences. *Child Development, 53,* 310–321.

Eccles, J., Adler, T., & Meece, J.L. (1984). Sex differences in achievement: A test of alternate theories. *Journal of Personality and Social Psychology, 46,* 26–43.

Eccles, J.S., & Blumenfeld, P. (1985). Classroom experiences and student gender: Are there differences and do they matter? In L. Wilkison & C. Marrett (Eds.), *Gender influences in classroom interaction* (pp. 79–114). Orlando, FL: Academic Press.

Eccles, J.S., & Harold, R.D. (1991). Gender differences in sport involvement: Applying the Eccles' expectancy-value model. *Journal of Applied Sport Psychology, 3,* 7–35.

Eccles, J.S., & Midgley, C. (1990). Changes in academic motivation and self-perception during early adolescence. In R. Montemayor, G.R. Adams, & T.P. Gullotta (Eds.), *From childhood to adolescence: A transitional period?* (pp. 134–155). Newbury Park: CA: Sage.

Eccles, J.S., & Wigfield, A. (1995). In the mind of the actor: The structure of adolescents' achievement task value and expectancy-related beliefs. *Personality and Social Psychology Bulletin, 21,* 215–225.

Eccles, J.S., Wigfield, A.W., & Schiefele, U. (1998). Motivation to succeed. In W. Damon (Series Ed.) & N. Eisenberg (Vol. Ed.), *Handbook of child psychology: Vol. 3. Social, emotional, and personality development* (5th ed., pp. 1017–1095). New York: Wiley.

Evans, J., & Roberts, G.C. (1987). Physical competence and the development of children's peer relations. *Quest, 39,* 23–35.

Ewing, M.E., Feltz, D.L., Schultz, T.D., & Albrecht, R.R. (1988). Psychological characteristics of competitive young hockey players. In E.W. Brown & C.F. Branta (Eds.), *Competitive sports for children and youth* (pp. 49–61). Champaign, IL: Human Kinetics.

Feltz, D.L., & Brown, E.W. (1984). Perceived competence in soccer skills among youth soccer players. *Journal of Sport Psychology, 6,* 385–394.

Feltz, D.L., & Petlichkoff, L.M. (1983). Perceived competence among interscholastic sport participants and dropouts. *Canadian Journal of Applied Sport Sciences, 8,* 231–235.

Ferrer-Caja, E., & Weiss, M.R. (2000). Predictors of intrinsic motivation among adolescent students in physical education. *Research Quarterly for Exercise and Sport, 71,* 267–279.

Ferrer-Caja, E., & Weiss, M.R. (2002). Cross-validation of a model of intrinsic motivation in physical education with students enrolled in elective courses. *Journal of Experimental Education, 71,* 41–65.

Frederick, C.M., & Ryan, R.M. (1995). Self-determination in sport: A review using cognitive evaluation theory. *International Journal of Sport Psychology, 26,* 5–23.

Fredricks, J.A., Alfred-Liro, C.J., Hruda, L.Z., Eccles, J.S., Patrick, H., & Ryan, A.M. (2002). A qualitative exploration of adolescents' commitment to athletics and the arts. *Journal of Adolescent Research, 17,* 68–97.

Fredricks, J.A., & Eccles, J.S. (2002). Children's competence and value beliefs from childhood through adolescence: Growth trajectories in two male-sex-typed domains. *Developmental Psychology, 38,* 519–533.

Fredricks, J.A., & Eccles, J.S. (2004). Parental influences on youth involvement in sports. In M.R. Weiss (Ed.), *Developmental sport and exercise psychology: A lifespan perspective* (pp. 145–164). Morgantown, WV: Fitness Information Technology.

Fredricks, J.A., & Eccles, J.S. (2005). Family socialization, gender, and sport motivation and involvement. *Journal of Sport & Exercise Psychology, 27,* 3–31.

Freedson, P.S., & Evenson, S. (1991). Familial aggregation in physical activity. *Research Quarterly for Exercise and Sport, 62,* 384–389.

Gagné, M., Ryan, R.M., & Bargmann, K. (2003). Autonomy support and need satisfaction in the motivation and well-being of gymnasts. *Journal of Applied Sport Psychology, 15,* 372–389.

Garcia Bengoechea, E., & Strean, W.B. (in press). On the interpersonal context of adolescents' sport motivation. *Psychology of Sport and Exercise.*

Gibbons, S.L., & Bushakra, F.B. (1989). Effects of Special Olympics participation on the perceived competence and social acceptance of mentally retarded children. *Adapted Physical Activity Quarterly, 6,* 40–51.

Gill, D.L., Gross, J.B., & Huddleston, S. (1983). Participation motivation in youth sports. *International Journal of Sport Psychology, 14,* 1–14.

Glenn, S.D., & Horn, T.S. (1993). Psychological and personal predictors of leadership behavior in female soccer athletes. *Journal of Applied Sport Psychology, 5,* 17–35.

Goudas, M., Biddle, S., & Fox, K. (1994). Perceived locus of causality, goal orientations, and perceived competence in school physical education classes. *British Journal of Educational Psychology, 64,* 453–463.

Gould, D. (1987). Understanding attrition in youth sport. In D. Gould & M.R. Weiss (Eds.), *Advances in pediatric sport sciences: Vol. 2. Behavioral issues* (pp. 61–85). Champaign, IL: Human Kinetics.

Gould, D., Feltz, D., Horn, T., & Weiss, M. (1982). Reasons for attrition in competitive youth swimming. *Journal of Sport Behavior, 5,* 155–165.

Gould, D., Feltz, D., & Weiss, M. (1985). Motives for participating in competitive youth swimming. *International Journal of Sport Psychology, 6,* 126–140.

Gould, D., & Petlichkoff, L. (1988). Participation motivation and attrition in young athletes. In F.L. Smoll, R.A. Magill, & M.J. Ash (Eds.), *Children in sport* (3rd ed., pp. 161–178). Champaign, IL: Human Kinetics.

Guillet, E., Sarrazin, P., Carpenter, P.J., Trouilloud, D., & Cury, F. (2002). Predicting persistence or withdrawal in female handballers with social exchange theory. *International Journal of Psychology, 37,* 92–104.

Hagger, M.S., Chatzisarantis, N.L.D. (Eds.) (2007). *Self-determination theory in exercise and sport.* Champaign, IL: Human Kinetics.

Hagger, M.S., Chatzisarantis, N.L.D., Culverhouse, T., & Biddle, S.J.H. (2003). The processes by which perceived autonomy support in physical education promotes leisure-time physical activity intentions and behavior: A trans-contextual model. *Journal of Educational Psychology, 95,* 784–795.

Hagger, M.S., Chatzisarantis, N.L.D., & Harris, J. (2006). From psychological need satisfaction to intentional behavior: Testing a motivational sequence in two behavioral contexts. *Personality and Social Psychology Bulletin, 32,* 131–148.

Halliburton, A.L., & Weiss, M.R. (2002). Sources of competence information and perceived motivational climate among adolescent female gymnasts varying in skill level. *Journal of Sport & Exercise Psychology, 24,* 396–419.

Harter, S. (1978). Effectance motivation reconsidered. *Human Development, 21,* 34–64.

Harter, S. (1981a). A model of intrinsic mastery motivation in children: Individual differences and developmental change. In W.A. Collins (Ed.), *Minnesota Symposium on Child Psychology* (Vol. 14, pp. 215–255). Hillsdale, NJ: Erlbaum.

Harter, S. (1981b). The development of competence motivation in the mastery of cognitive and physical skills: Is there still a place for joy? In G.C. Roberts & D.M. Landers (Eds.), *Psychology of motor behavior and sport-1980* (pp. 3–29). Champaign, IL: Human Kinetics.

Harter, S. (1981c). A new self-report scale of intrinsic versus extrinsic orientation in the classroom: Motivational and informational components. *Developmental Psychology, 17,* 300–312.

Harter, S. (1982). The perceived competence scale for children. *Child Development, 53,* 87–97.

Harter, S. (1985). *Manual for the self-perception profile for children.* Denver, CO: University of Denver.

Harter, S. (1987). The determinants and mediational role of global self-worth in children. In N. Eisenberg (Ed.), *Contemporary topics in developmental psychology* (pp. 219–242). New York: Wiley.

Harter, S. (1988). *Manual for the self-perception profile for adolescents.* Denver, CO: University of Denver.

Harter, S. (1990). Causes, correlates, and the functional role of global self-worth: A life-span perspective. In R.J. Sternberg & J. Kolligan, Jr. (Eds.), *Competence considered* (pp. 67–97). New Haven, CT: Yale University Press.

Harter, S. (1992). The relationship between perceived competence, affect, and motivational orientation within the classroom: Processes and patterns of change. In A.K. Boggiano & T.S. Pittman (Eds.), *Achievement and motivation: A social developmental perspective.* New York: Cambridge University Press.

Harter, S. (1998). The development of self-representations. In W. Damon (Series Ed.) & N. Eisenberg (Vol. Ed.), *Handbook of child psychology: Vol. 3. Social, emotional, and personality development* (5th ed., pp. 553–618). New York: Wiley.

Harter, S. (1999). *The construction of the self: A developmental perspective.* New York: Guilford.

Harter, S., & Pike, R. (1984). The pictorial scale of perceived competence and social acceptance for young children. *Child Development, 55,* 1962–1982.

Hayashi, C.T., & Weiss, M.R. (1994). A cross-cultural analysis of achievement motivation in Anglo and Japanese marathon runners. *International Journal of Sport Psychology, 25,* 187–202.

Hellandsig, E.T. (1998). Motivational predictors of high performance and discontinuation in different types of sports among talented teenage athletes. *International Journal of Sport Psychology, 29,* 27–44.

Henderlong, J., & Lepper, M.R. (2002). The effects of praise on children's intrinsic motivation: A review and synthesis. *Psychological Bulletin, 128,* 774–795.

Hollembeak, J., & Amorose, A.J. (2005). Perceived coaching behaviors and college athletes' intrinsic motivation: A test of self-determination theory. *Journal of Applied Sport Psychology, 17,* 20–36.

Horn, T.S. (1984). Expectancy effects in the interscholastic athletic setting: Methodological considerations. *Journal of Sport Psychology, 6,* 60–76.

Horn, T.S. (1985). Coaches' feedback and changes in children's perceptions of their physical competence. *Journal of Educational Psychology, 77,* 174–186.

Horn, T.S. (2002). Coaching effectiveness in the sport domain. In T.S. Horn (Ed.), *Advances in sport psychology* (pp. 309–354). Champaign, IL: Human Kinetics.

Horn, T.S. (2004). Developmental perspectives on self-perceptions in children and adolescents. In M.R. Weiss (Ed.), *Developmental sport and exercise psychology: A lifespan perspective* (pp. 101–143). Morgantown, WV: Fitness Information Technology.

Horn, T.S., & Amorose, A.J. (1998). Sources of competence information. In J.L. Duda (Ed.), *Advances in sport and exercise psychology measurement* (pp. 49–64). Morgantown, WV: Fitness Information Technology.

Horn, T.S., Glenn, S.D., & Wentzell, A.B. (1993). Sources of information underlying personal ability judgments in high school athletes. *Pediatric Exercise Science, 5,* 263–274.

Horn, T.S., & Hasbrook, C.A. (1986). Informational components influencing children's perceptions of their physical competence. In M.R. Weiss & D. Gould (Eds.), *Sport for children and youths* (pp. 81–88). Champaign, IL: Human Kinetics.

Horn, T.S., & Hasbrook, C.A. (1987). Psychological characteristics and the criteria children use for self-evaluation. *Journal of Sport Psychology, 9,* 208–221.

Horn, T.S., & Weiss, M.R. (1991). A developmental analysis of children's self-ability judgments. *Pediatric Exercise Science, 3,* 312–328.

Jacobs, J.E., & Eccles, J.S. (1992). The impact of mothers' gender-role stereotypic beliefs on mothers' and children's ability perceptions. *Journal of Personality and Social Psychology, 63,* 932–944.

Jacobs, J.E., Lanza, S., Osgood, D.W., Eccles, J.S., & Wigfield, A. (2002). Changes in children's self-competence and values: Gender and domain differences across grades one through twelve. *Child Development, 73,* 509–527.

Johns, D.P., Lindner, K.J., & Wolko, K. (1990). Understanding attrition in female competitive gymnastics: Applying social exchange theory. *Sociology of Sport Journal, 7,* 154–171.

Kasser, T., & Ryan, R.M. (1996). Further examining the American dream: Differential correlates of intrinsic and extrinsic goals. *Personality and Social Psychology Bulletin, 22,* 80–87.

Kasser, T., & Ryan, R.M. (2001). Be careful what you wish for: Optimal functioning and the relative attainment of intrinsic and extrinsic goals. In P. Schmuck & K.M. Sheldon (Eds.), *Life goals and well-being* (pp. 116–131). Göttingen, Germany: Hogrefe and Huber.

Kasser, V., & Ryan, R.M., (1999). The relation of psychological needs for autonomy and relatedness to vitality, well-being, and mortality in a nursing home. *Journal of Applied Social Psychology, 29,* 935–954.

Kelley, H.H., & Thibaut, J.W. (1978). *Interpersonal relations: A theory of interdependence.* New York: Wiley.

Kimiecik, J.C., & Horn, T.S. (1998). Parental beliefs and children's moderate-to-vigorous physical activity. *Research Quarterly for Exercise and Sport, 69,* 163–175.

Kimiecik, J.C., Horn, T.S., & Shurin, C.S. (1996). Relationships among children's beliefs, perceptions of their parents' beliefs, and their moderate-to-vigorous physical activity. *Research Quarterly for Exercise and Sport, 67,* 324–336.

Klint, K.A. (1985). *Participation motives and self-perceptions of current and former athletes in youth gymnastics.* Unpublished master's thesis, University of Oregon, Eugene.

Klint, K.A., & Weiss, M.R. (1986). Dropping in and dropping out: Participation motives of current and former youth gymnasts. *Canadian Journal of Applied Sport Sciences, 11*, 106–114.

Klint, K.A., & Weiss, M.R. (1987). Perceived competence and motives for participating in youth sports: A test of Harter's competence motivation theory. *Journal of Sport Psychology, 9*, 55–65.

Koestner, R., Bernieri, F., & Zuckerman, M. (1992). Self-determination and consistency between attitudes, traits, and behaviors. *Personality and Social Psychology Bulletin, 18*, 52–59.

Kolt, G.S., Kirkby, R.J., Bar-Eli, M., Blumenstein, B., Chadha, N.K., Liu, J., et al. (1999). A cross-cultural investigation of reasons for participation in gymnastics. *International Journal of Sport Psychology, 30*, 381–398.

Kowal, J., & Fortier, M.S. (1999). Motivational determinants of flow: Contributions from self-determination theory. *The Journal of Social Psychology, 139*, 355–368.

Kunesh, M., Hasbrook, C.A., & Lewthwaite, R. (1992). Physical activity socialization: Peer interactions and affective responses among a sample of sixth grade girls. *Sociology of Sport Journal, 9*, 385–396.

Leff, S.S., & Hoyle, R.H. (1995). Young athletes' perceptions of parental support and pressure. *Journal of Youth and Adolescence, 24*, 187–203.

Lemyre, P., Treasure, D.C., & Roberts, G.C. (2006). Influence of variability in motivation and affect on elite athlete burnout susceptibility. *Journal of Sport & Exercise Psychology, 28*, 32–48.

Li, F. (1999). The Exercise Motivation Scale: Its multifaceted structure and construct validity. *Journal of Applied Sport Psychology, 11*, 97–115.

Li, F., & Harmer, P. (1996). Testing the simplex assumption underlying the sport motivation scale: A structural equation modeling analysis. *Research Quarterly for Exercise and Sport, 67*, 396–405.

Lirgg, C.D. (1991). Gender differences in self-confidence in physical activity: A meta-analysis of recent studies. *Journal of Sport & Exercise Psychology, 13*, 294–310.

Lirgg, C.D. (1993). Effects of same-sex versus coeducational physical education on the self-perceptions of middle and high school students. *Research Quarterly for Exercise and Sport, 64*, 324–334.

Lirgg, C.D. (1994). Environmental perceptions of students in same-sex and coeducational physical education classes. *Journal of Educational Psychology, 86*, 183–192.

Longhurst, K., & Spink, K.S. (1987). Participation motivation of Australian children involved in organized sport. *Canadian Journal of Sport Sciences, 12*, 24–30.

Mageau, G.A., & Vallerand, R.J. (2003). The coach–athlete relationship: A motivational model. *Journal of Sports Sciences, 21*, 883–904.

Markland, D. (1999). Self-determination moderates the effects of perceived competence on intrinsic motivation in an exercise setting. *Journal of Sport & Exercise Psychology, 21*, 351–361.

Markland, D., & Tobin, V. (2004). A modification to the Behavioral Regulation in Exercise Questionnaire to include an assessment of amotivation. *Journal of Sport & Exercise Psychology, 26*, 191–196.

Marsh, H.W., & Peart, N.D. (1988). Competitive and cooperative physical fitness training programs for girls: Effects on physical fitness and multidimensional self-concepts. *Journal of Sport & Exercise Psychology, 10*, 390–407.

Martin, J.J. (2006). Psychosocial aspects of youth disability sport. *Adapted Physical Activity Quarterly, 23*, 67–77.

McCann, P.S. (2006). Parent-coach and child-athlete retrospective perceptions of the dual role in youth sport. *Dissertation Abstracts International, 66* (9-A), 3250.

McClements, J., Fry, D., & Sefton, J. (1982). A study of hockey participants and drop-outs. In T.D. Orlick, J.T. Partington, & J.H. Salmela (Eds.), *Mental training for coaches and athletes* (pp. 73–74). Ottawa, ON: Coaching Association of Canada.

McCullagh, P., Matzkanin, K.T., Shaw, S.D., & Maldonado, M. (1993). Motivation for participation in physical activity: A comparison of parent child perceived competencies and participation motives. *Pediatric Exercise Science, 5*, 224–233.

McKiddie, B., & Maynard, I.W. (1997). Perceived competence of school children in physical education. *Journal of Teaching in Physical Education, 16*, 324–339.

McPherson, B., Marteniuk, R., Tihanyi, J., & Clark, W. (1980). The social system of age group swimmers: The perception of swimmers, parents, and coaches. *Canadian Journal of Applied Sport Sciences, 5*, 142–145.

Moore, L.L., Lombardi, D.A., White, M.J., Campbell, D.L., Olivera, S.A., & Ellison, R.C. (1991). Influence of parents' physical activity levels on activity levels of young children. *Journal of Pediatrics, 118*, 212–219.

Mullan, E., Markland, D., & Ingledew, D.K. (1997). A graded conceptualization of self-determination in the regulation of exercise behavior: Development of a measure using confirmatory factor analytic procedures. *Personality and Individual Differences, 23*, 745–752.

Newton, M., Duda, J.L., & Yin, Z. (2000). Examination of the psychometric properties of the Perceived Motivational Climate in Sport Questionnaire–2 in a sample of female athletes. *Journal of Sport Sciences, 18*, 275–290.

Ntoumanis, N. (2001). A self-determination approach to the understanding of motivation in physical education. *British Journal of Educational Psychology, 71*, 225–242.

Ntoumanis, N., Pensgaard, A., Martin, C., & Pipe, K. (2004). An idiographic analysis of amotivation in compulsory school physical education. *Journal of Sport & Exercise Psychology, 26*, 197–214.

Orlick, T.D. (1974, November/December). The athletic dropout: A high price for inefficiency. *Canadian Association for Health, Physical Education and Recreation Journal*, pp. 21–27.

Orlick, T.D., & Mosher, R. (1978). Extrinsic awards and participant motivation in a sport related task. *International Journal of Sport Psychology, 9*, 27–39.

Papaioannou, A., & Theodorakis, Y. (1996). A test of three models for the prediction of intention for participation in physical education lessons. *International Journal of Sport Psychology, 27*, 383–399.

Patrick, H., Ryan, A.M., Alfred-Liro, C., Fredricks, J.A., Hruda, L.Z., & Eccles, J.S. (1999). Adolescents' commitment to developing talent: The role of peers in continuing motivation for sports and the arts. *Journal of Youth and Adolescence, 28*, 741–763.

Paxton, R.J., Estabrooks, P.A., & Dzewaltowski, D. (2004). Attraction to physical activity mediates the relationship between perceived competence and physical activity in youth. *Research Quarterly for Exercise and Sport, 75*, 107–111.

Pelletier, L.G., Fortier, M.S., Vallerand, R.J., & Briére, N.M. (2001). Associations among perceived autonomy support, forms of self-regulation, and persistence: A prospective study. *Motivation and Emotion, 25*, 279–306.

Pelletier, L.G., Fortier, M.S., Vallerand, R.J., Tuson, K.M., Briére, N.M., & Blais, M.R. (1995). Toward a new measure of intrinsic motivation, extrinsic motivation, and amotivation in sports: The Sport Motivational Scale (SMS). *Journal of Sport & Exercise Psychology, 17*, 35–53.

Petlichkoff, L.M. (1993a). Group differences on achievement goal orientations, perceived ability, and level of satisfaction during an athletic season. *Pediatric Exercise Science, 5*, 12–24.

Petlichkoff, L.M. (1993b). Relationship of player status and time of season to achievement goals and perceived ability in interscholastic athletes. *Pediatric Exercise Science, 5*, 242–252.

Pintrich, P.R. (2003). A motivational science perspective on the role of student motivation in learning and teaching contexts. *Journal of Educational Psychology, 95*, 667–686.

Raedeke, T.D. (1997). Is athlete burnout more than just stress? A sport commitment perspective. *Journal of Sport & Exercise Psychology, 19*, 396–417.

Raedeke, T.D. (2004). Coaching commitment and burnout: A one-year follow-up. *Journal of Applied Sport Psychology, 16*, 333–349.

Raedeke, T.D., Granzyk, T.L., & Warren, A.H. (2000). Why coaches experience burnout: A commitment perspective. *Journal of Sport & Exercise Psychology, 1*, 85–105.

Raedeke, T.D., & Smith, A.L. (2001). Development and preliminary validation of an athlete burnout measure. *Journal of Sport & Exercise Psychology, 23*, 281–306.

Raedeke, T.D., Warren, A.H., & Granzyk, T.L. (2002). Coaching commitment and turnover: A comparison of current and former coaches. *Research Quarterly for Exercise & Sport, 73*, 73–86.

Rawsthorne, L.J., & Elliot, A.J. (1999). Achievement goals and intrinsic motivation: A meta-analytic review. *Personality and Social Psychology Review, 3,* 326–344.

Reeve, J. (2002). Self-determination theory applied to educational settings. In E.L. Deci & R.M. Ryan (Eds.), *Handbook of self-determination research* (pp. 161–182). Rochester, NY: University of Rochester Press.

Reeve, J., Jang, H., Hardre, P., & Omura, M. (2002). Providing a rationale in an autonomy-supportive way as a strategy to motivate others during an uninteresting activity. *Motivation and Emotion, 26,* 183–207.

Reinboth, M., & Duda, J.L. (2006). Perceived motivational climate, need satisfaction and indices of well-being in team sports: A longitudinal perspective. *Psychology of Sport and Exercise, 7,* 269–286.

Reinboth, M., Duda, J.L., & Ntoumanis, N. (2004). Dimensions of coaching behavior, need satisfaction, and the psychological and physical welfare of young athletes. *Motivation and Emotion, 28,* 297–313.

Reis, H.T., Sheldon, K.M., Gable, S.L., Roscoe, J., & Ryan, R.M. (2000). Daily well-being: The role of autonomy, competence, and relatedness. *Personality and Social Psychology Bulletin, 22,* 24–33.

Roberts, G.C., Kleiber, D., & Duda, J.L. (1981). An analysis of motivation in children's sport: The role of perceived competence in participation. *Journal of Sport Psychology, 3,* 206–216.

Rodriguez, D., Wigfield, A., & Eccles, J.S. (2003). Changing competence perceptions, changing values: Implications for youth sport. *Journal of Applied Sport Psychology, 15,* 67–81.

Roeser, R.W., & Eccles, J. (1998). Adolescents' perceptions of middle school: Relation to longitudinal changes in academic and psychological adjustment. *Journal of Research on Adolescence, 8,* 123–158.

Rose, B., Larkin, D., & Berger, B.G. (1994). Perceptions of social support in children of low, moderate and high levels of coordination. *ACHPER Healthy Lifestyles Journal, 41*(4), 18–21.

Rose, E.A., Markland, D., & Parfitt, G. (2001). The development and initial validation of the Exercise Causality Orientation Scale. *Journal of Sport Sciences, 19,* 445–462.

Rose, E.A., Parfitt, G., & Williams, S. (2005). Exercise causality orientations, behavioural regulation for exercise and stage of change for exercise: Exploring their relationships. *Psychology of Sport and Exercise, 6,* 399–414.

Rubin, K.H., Bukowski, W.M., & Parker, J.G. (1998). Peer interactions, relationships, and groups. In N. Eisenberg (Vol. Ed.), *Handbook of child psychology: Vol. 3. Social, emotional, and personality development* (5th ed., pp. 619–700). New York: Wiley.

Rusbult, C.E. (1980a). Commitment and satisfaction in romantic associations: A test of the investment model. *Journal of Experimental Social Psychology, 16,* 172–186.

Rusbult, C.E. (1980b). Satisfaction and commitment in friendships. *Representative Research in Social Psychology, 11,* 96–105.

Rusbult, C.E. (1983). A longitudinal test of the investment model: The development (and deterioration) of satisfaction and commitment in heterosexual involvements. *Journal of Personality and Social Psychology, 45,* 101–117.

Ryan, E.D. (1977). Attribution, intrinsic motivation, and athletics. In L.I. Gedvilas & M.E. Kneer (Eds.), *Proceedings of the National Association for Physical Education of College Men National Conference/National Association for Physical Education of College Women National Conference.* Chicago: University of Illinois at Chicago Circle.

Ryan, E.D. (1980). Attribution, intrinsic motivation, and athletics: A replication and extension. In C.H. Nadeau, W.R., Halliwell, K.M. Newell, & G.C. Roberts (Eds.), *Psychology of motor behavior and sport—1979* (pp. 19–26). Champaign, IL: Human Kinetics.

Ryan, R.M. (1982). Control and information in the intrapersonal sphere: An extension of cognitive evaluation theory. *Journal of Personality and Social Psychology, 45,* 736–750.

Ryan, R.M. (1995). Psychological need and the facilitation of integrative processes. *Journal of Personality, 63,* 397–427.

Ryan, R.M., & Connell, J.P. (1989). Perceived locus of causality and internalization: Examining reasons for acting in two domains. *Journal of Personality and Social Psychology, 57,* 749–761.

Ryan, R.M., & Deci, E.L. (2000). Self determination theory and the facilitation of intrinsic motivation, social development, and well being. *American Psychologist, 55,* 68–78.

Ryan, R.M., & Deci, E.L. (2002). An overview of self-determination theory: An organismic-dialectical perspective. In E.L. Deci & R.M. Ryan (Eds.), *Handbook of self-determination research* (pp. 3–33). Rochester, NY: University of Rochester Press.

Ryan, R.M., Koestner, R., & Deci, E.L. (1991). Ego-involved persistence: When free-choice behavior is not intrinsically motivated. *Motivation and Emotion, 15,* 185–205.

Ryckman, R.M., & Hamel, J. (1993). Perceived physical ability differences in the sport participation motives of young athletes. *International Journal of Sport Psychology, 24,* 270–283.

Ryckman, R.M., & Hamel, J. (1995). Male and female adolescents' motives related to involvement in organized team sports. *International Journal of Sport Psychology, 26,* 383–397.

Sapp, M., & Haubenstricker, J. (1978, April). *Motivation for joining and reasons for not continuing in youth sport programs in Michigan.* Paper presented at the American Alliance for Health, Physical Education, Recreation, and Dance annual conference, Kansas City, MO.

Sarrazin, P., Vallerand, R., Guillet, E., Pelletier, L., & Cury, F. (2002). Motivation and dropout in female handballers: A 21-month prospective study. *European Journal of Social Psychology, 32,* 395–418.

Scanlan, T.K., Carpenter, P.J., Lobel, M., & Simons, J.P. (1993). Sources of enjoyment for youth sport athletes. *Pediatric Exercise Science, 5,* 275–285.

Scanlan, T.K., Carpenter, P.J., Schmidt, G.W., Simons, J.P., & Keeler, B. (1993). An introduction to the sport commitment model. *Journal of Sport & Exercise Psychology, 15,* 1–15.

Scanlan, T.K., & Lewthwaite, R. (1986). Social psychological aspects of competition for male youth sport participants: IV. Predictors of enjoyment. *Journal of Sport Psychology, 8,* 25–35.

Scanlan, T.K., Russell, D.G., Beals, K.P., & Scanlan, L.A. (2003). Project on elite athlete commitment (PEAK): II. A direct test and expansion of the sport commitment model with elite amateur sportsmen. *Journal of Sport & Exercise Psychology, 25,* 377–401.

Scanlan, T.K., Russell, D.G., Wilson, N.C., & Scanlan, L.A. (2003). Project on elite athlete commitment (PEAK): I. Introduction and methodology. *Journal of Sport & Exercise Psychology, 25,* 360–376.

Scanlan, T.K., & Simons, J.P. (1992). The construct of sport enjoyment. In G.C. Roberts (Ed.), *Motivation in sport and exercise* (pp. 199–215). Champaign, IL: Human Kinetics.

Scanlan, T.K., Simons, J.P., Carpenter, P.J., Schmidt, G.W., & Keeler, B. (1993). The sport commitment model: Measurement development for the youth-sport domain. *Journal of Sport & Exercise Psychology, 15,* 16–38.

Scanlan, T.K., Stein, G.L., & Ravizza, K. (1989). An in-depth study of former elite figure skaters: II. Sources of enjoyment. *Journal of Sport & Exercise Psychology, 11,* 65–83.

Scanlan, T.K., Stein, G.L., & Ravizza, K. (1991). An in-depth study of former elite figure skaters: III. Sources of stress. *Journal of Sport & Exercise Psychology, 13,* 103–120.

Schmidt, G.W., & Stein, G.L. (1991). Sport commitment: A model integrating enjoyment, dropout, and burnout. *Journal of Sport & Exercise Psychology, 13,* 254–265.

Seifriz, J.J., Duda, J.L., & Chi, L. (1992). The relationship of perceived motivational climate to intrinsic motivation and beliefs about success in basketball. *Journal of Sport & Exercise Psychology, 14,* 375–391.

Shapiro, D.R., & Ulrich, D.A. (2002). Expectancies, values, and perceptions of physical competence of children with and without learning disabilities. *Adapted Physical Activity Quarterly, 19,* 318–333.

Sheldon, K., Ryan, R.M., & Reis, H.T. (1996). What makes for a good day? Competence and autonomy in the day and in the person. *Personality and Social Psychology Bulletin, 22,* 1270–1279.

Smith, A.L. (1999). Peer relationships and physical activity participation in early adolescence. *Journal of Sport & Exercise Psychology, 21,* 329–350.

Smith, A.L. (2003). Peer relationships in physical activity contexts: A road less traveled in youth sport and exercise psychology research. *Psychology of Sport and Exercise, 4*, 25–39.

Smoll, F.L., & Smith, R.E. (2002). Coaching behavior research and intervention in youth sport. In F.L. Smoll & R.E. Smith (Eds.), *Children and youth in sport* (pp. 211–231). Dubuque, IA: Kendall/Hunt.

Smoll, F.L., Smith, R.E., Barnett, N.P., & Everett, J.J. (1993). Enhancement of children's self-esteem through social support training for youth sport coaches. *Journal of Applied Psychology, 78*, 602–610.

Standage, M., Duda, J.L., & Ntoumanis, N. (2003a). A model of contextual motivation in physical education: Using constructs from self-determination and achievement goal theories to predict physical activity intentions. *Journal of Educational Psychology, 95*, 97–110.

Standage, M., Duda, J.L., & Ntoumanis, N. (2003b). Predicting motivational regulations in physical education: The interplay between dispositional goal orientations, motivational climate and perceived competence. *Journal of Sports Sciences, 21*, 631–647.

Standage, M., Duda, J.L., & Ntoumanis, N. (2005). A test of self-determination theory in school physical education. *British Journal of Educational Psychology, 75*, 411–433.

Standage, M., Duda, J.L., & Ntoumanis, N. (2006). Students' motivational processes and their relationship to teacher ratings in school physical education: A self-determination theory approach. *Research Quarterly for Exercise and Sport, 77*, 100–110.

Standage, M., & Treasure, D.C. (2002). Relationship among achievement goal orientations and multidimensional situational motivation in physical education. *British Journal of Educational Psychology, 72*, 87–103.

State of Michigan (1978). *Joint legislative study on youth sports programs, Phase II*. East Lansing: Michigan State University.

Stein, G.L., & Scanlan, T.K. (1992). Goal attainment and non-goal occurrences as underlying mechanisms to an athlete's sources of enjoyment. *Pediatric Exercise Science, 4*, 150–165.

Stephens, D.E. (1998). The relationship of goal orientation and perceived ability to enjoyment and value in youth sport. *Pediatric Exercise Science, 10*, 236–247.

Stipek, D., & Mac Iver, D. (1989). Developmental change in children's assessment of intellectual competence. *Child Development, 60*, 521–538.

Stuart, M.E. (2003). Sources of subjective task value in sport: An examination of adolescences with high or low value for sport. *Journal of Applied Sport Psychology, 15*, 239–255.

Theeboom, M., De Knop, P., & Weiss, M.R. (1995). Motivational climate, psychosocial responses, and motor skill development in children's sport: A field-based intervention study. *Journal of Sport and Exercise Psychology, 17*, 294–311.

Thibaut, J.W., & Kelley, H.H. (1959). *The social psychology of groups*. New York: Wiley.

Thomas, J.R., & Tennant, L.K. (1978). Effects of rewards on children's motivation for an athletic task. In F.L. Smoll & R.E. Smith (Eds.), *Psychological perspectives in youth sports* (pp. 123–144). Washington, DC: Hemisphere.

Ullrich-French, S., & Smith, A.L. (2006). Perceptions of relationships with parents and peers in youth sport: Independent and combined prediction of motivational outcomes. *Psychology of Sport and Exercise, 7*, 193–214.

Ulrich, B.D. (1987). Perceptions of physical competence, motor competence, and participation in organized sport: Their interrelationships in young children. *Research Quarterly for Exercise and Sport, 58*, 57–67.

Vallerand, R.J. (1983). The effect of differential amounts of positive verbal feedback on the intrinsic motivation of male hockey players. *Journal of Sport Psychology, 5*, 100–107.

Vallerand, R.J. (1997). Toward a hierarchical model of intrinsic and extrinsic motivation. In M.P. Zanna (Ed.), *Advances in experimental social psychology* (pp. 271–360). San Diego, CA: Academic Press.

Vallerand, R.J., Deci, E.L., & Ryan, R.M. (1987). Intrinsic motivation in sport. In K.B. Pandolf (Ed.), *Exercise and sport sciences reviews* (Vol. 15, pp. 389–425). New York: Macmillian.

Vallerand, R.J., & Fortier, M.S. (1998). Measures of intrinsic and extrinsic motivation in sport and physical activity: A review and critique. In J.L. Duda (Ed.), *Advances in sport and exercise psychology measurement* (pp. 81–101). Morgantown, WV: Fitness Information Technology.

Vallerand, R.J., & Ratelle, C.F. (2002). Intrinsic and extrinsic motivation: A hierarchical model. In E.L. Deci & R.M. Ryan (Eds.), *Handbook of self-determination research* (pp. 37–64). Rochester, NY: University of Rochester Press.

Vallerand, R.J., & Reid, G. (1984). On the causal effects of perceived competence on intrinsic motivation: A test of cognitive evaluation theory. *Journal of Sport Psychology, 6*, 94–102.

Vansteenkiste, M., Simons, J., Sheldon, K.M., Lens, W., & Deci, E.L. (2004). Motivating learning, performance, and persistence: The synergistic effects of intrinsic goal contents and autonomy-supportive contexts. *Journal of Personality and Social Psychology, 87*, 246–260.

Vansteenkiste, M., Simons, J., Soenens, B., & Lens, W. (2004). How to become a persevering exerciser? Providing a clear future intrinsic goal in an autonomy-supportive way. *Journal of Sport & Exercise Psychology, 26*, 232–249.

VanYperen, N.W. (1998). Predicting stay/leave behavior among volleyball referees. *The Sport Psychologist, 12*, 427–439.

Wang, J., & Wiese-Bjornstal, D.M. (1996). The relationship of school type and gender to motives for sport participation among youth in the People's Republic of China. *International Journal of Sport Psychology, 28*, 13–24.

Watkinson, E.J., Dwyer, S.A., & Nielsen, A.B. (2005). Children theorize about reasons for recess engagement: Does expectancy-value theory apply? *Adapted Physical Activity Quarterly, 22*, 179–197.

Weigand, D.A., & Broadhurst, C.J. (1998). The relationship among perceived competence, intrinsic motivation, and control perceptions in youth soccer. *International Journal of Sport Psychology, 29*, 324–338.

Weiss, M.R. (1993). Psychological effects of intensive sport participation on children and youth: Self-esteem and motivation. In B.R. Cahill & A.J. Pearl (Eds.), *Intensive participation in children's sports* (pp. 39–69). Champaign, IL: Human Kinetics.

Weiss, M.R. (2004). Motivating kids in physical activity. In C.B. Corbin, R.P. Pangrazi, & B.D. Franks (Eds.), *Physical fitness & activity: Selected topics* (Vol. 2, pp. 157–166). Scottsdale, AZ: Holcomb Hathaway.

Weiss, M.R., & Amorose, A.J. (2005). Children's self-perceptions in the physical domain: Between- and within-age variability in level, accuracy, and sources of perceived competence. *Journal of Sport & Exercise Psychology, 27*, 226–244.

Weiss, M.R., Bredemeier, B.J., & Shewchuk, R.M. (1985). An intrinsic/extrinsic motivation scale for the youth sport setting: A confirmatory factor analysis. *Journal of Sport Psychology, 7*, 75–91.

Weiss, M.R., Bredemeier, B.J., & Shewchuk, R.M. (1986). The dynamics of perceived competence, perceived control, and motivational orientation in youth sports. In M.R. Weiss & D. Gould (Eds.), *Sport for children and youths* (pp. 89–101). Champaign, IL: Human Kinetics.

Weiss, M.R., & Duncan, S.C. (1992). The relation between physical competence and peer acceptance in the context of children's sport participation. *Journal of Sport & Exercise Psychology, 14*, 177–191.

Weiss, M.R., & Ebbeck, V. (1996). Self-esteem and perceptions of competence in youth sport: Theory, research, and enhancement strategies. In O. Bar-Or (Ed.), *The encyclopaedia of sports medicine: Vol. VI. The child and adolescent athlete* (pp. 364–382). Oxford, United Kingdom: Blackwell Science.

Weiss, M.R., Ebbeck, V., & Horn, T.S. (1997). Children's self-perceptions and sources of competence information: A cluster analysis. *Journal of Sport & Exercise Psychology, 19*, 52–70.

Weiss, M.R., & Ferrer-Caja, E. (2002). Motivational orientations and sport behavior. In T.S. Horn (Ed.), *Advances in sport psychology* (2nd ed., pp. 101–184). Champaign, IL: Human Kinetics.

Weiss, M.R., & Frazer, K.M. (1995). Initial, continued, and sustained motivation in adolescent female athletes: A season-long analysis. *Pediatric Exercise Science, 7*, 314–329.

Weiss, M.R., & Fretwell, S.D. (2005). The parent-coach/child-athlete relationship in youth sport: Cordial, contentious, or conundrum? *Research Quarterly for Exercise and Sport, 76*, 286–305.

Weiss, M.R., & Hayashi, C.T. (1995). All in the family: Parent–child socialization influences in competitive youth gymnastics. *Pediatric Exercise Science, 7*, 36–48.

Weiss, M.R., & Horn, T.S. (1990). The relation between children's accuracy estimates of their physical competence and achievement-related characteristics. *Research Quarterly for Exercise and Sport, 61*, 250–258.

Weiss, M.R., Kimmel, L.A., & Smith, A.L. (2001). Determinants of sport commitment among junior tennis players: Enjoyment as a mediating variable. *Pediatric Exercise Science, 13*, 131–144.

Weiss, M.R., McAuley, E., Ebbeck, V., & Wiese, D.M. (1990). Self-esteem and causal attributions for children's physical and social competence in sport. *Journal of Sport & Exercise Psychology, 12*, 21–36.

Weiss, M.R., & Petlichkoff, L.M. (1989). Children's motivation for participation in and withdrawal from sport: Identifying the missing links. *Pediatric Exercise Science, 1*, 195–211.

Weiss, M.R., & Smith, A.L. (1999). Quality of youth sport friendships: Measurement and validation. *Journal of Sport & Exercise Psychology, 21*, 145–166.

Weiss, M.R., & Smith, A.L. (2002). Friendship quality in youth sport: Relationship to age, gender, and motivation variables. *Journal of Sport & Exercise Psychology, 24*, 420–437.

Weiss, M.R., Smith, A.L., & Theeboom, M. (1996). "That's what friends are for": Children's and teenagers' perceptions of peer relationships in the sport domain. *Journal of Sport & Exercise Psychology, 18*, 347–379.

Weiss, M.R., & Stuntz, C.P. (2004). A little friendly competition: Peer relationships and psychosocial development in youth sport and physical activity contexts. In M.R. Weiss (Ed.), *Developmental sport and exercise psychology: A lifespan perspective* (pp. 165–196). Morgantown, WV: Fitness Information Technology.

Weiss, W.M., & Weiss, M.R. (2003). Attraction- and entrapment-based commitment among competitive female gymnasts. *Journal of Sport & Exercise Psychology, 25*, 229–247.

Weiss, W.M., & Weiss, M.R. (2006a). *Determinants of sport commitment: Test of an expanded model.* Manuscript submitted for publication.

Weiss, W.M., & Weiss, M.R. (2006b). A longitudinal analysis of commitment among competitive female gymnasts. *Psychology of Sport and Exercise, 7*, 309–323.

Weiss, W.M., & Weiss, M.R. (2007). Sport commitment among competitive female gymnasts: A developmental perspective. *Research Quarterly for Exercise and Sport, 78*, 90-102.

Weiss, M.R., Wiese, D.M., & Klint, K.A. (1989). Head over heels with success: The relationship between self-efficacy and performance in competitive youth gymnastics. *Journal of Sport & Exercise Psychology, 11*, 444–451.

Weiss, M.R., & Williams, L. (2004). The *why* of youth sport involvement: A developmental perspective on motivational processes. In M.R. Weiss (Ed.), *Developmental sport and exercise psychology: A lifespan perspective* (pp. 223–268). Morgantown, WV: Fitness Information Technology.

White, R.W. (1959). Motivation reconsidered: The concept of competence. *Psychological Review, 66*, 297–330.

Whitehead, J., & Corbin, C. (1991). Youth fitness testing: The effect of percentile-based evaluative feedback on intrinsic motivation. *Research Quarterly for Exercise and Sport, 62*, 225–231.

Wigfield, A. (1994). Expectancy-value theory of achievement motivation: A developmental perspective. *Educational Psychology Review, 6*, 49–78.

Wigfield, A., & Eccles, J.S. (1992). The development of achievement task values: A theoretical analysis. *Developmental Review, 12*, 265–310.

Wigfield, A., & Eccles, J.S. (2000). Expectancy-value theory of achievement motivation. *Contemporary Educational Psychology, 25*, 68–81.

Wigfield, A., Eccles, J.S., MacIver, D., Reuman, D.A., Midgley, C. (1991). Transitions during early adolescence: Changes in children's domain-specific self-perceptions and general self-esteem across the transition to junior high school. *Developmental Psychology, 27*, 552–565.

Wigfield, A.W., Eccles, J.S., Yoon, K.S., Harold, R.D., Arbreton, A.J.A., Freedman-Doan, C., et al. (1997). Change in children's competence beliefs and subjective task values across the elementary school years: A 3-year study. *Journal of Educational Psychology, 89*, 451–469.

Wilko, A.M. (2004). *Influence of coaching behaviors and motivational climate on female adolescent athletes' psychosocial responses.* Unpublished master's thesis, University of Virginia, Charlottesville.

Williams, G.C., (2002). Improving patients' health through supporting the autonomy of patients and providers. In E.L. Deci & R.M. Ryan (Eds.), *Handbook of self-determination research* (pp. 233–254). Rochester, NY: University of Rochester Press.

Williams, G.C., Grow, V.M., Freedman, Z.R., Ryan, R.M., & Deci, E.L. (1996). Motivational predictors of weight loss and weight-loss maintenance. *Journal of Personality and Social Psychology, 70*, 115–126.

Williams, L. (1994). Goal orientations and athletes' preferences for competence information sources. *Journal of Sport & Exercise Psychology, 16*, 416–430.

Xiang, P., McBride, R., Guan, J., & Solmon, M. (2003). Children's motivation in elementary physical education: An expectancy-value model of achievement choice. *Research Quarterly for Exercise and Sport, 74*, 25–35.

CHAPTER 8

Aldenderfer, M.S., & Blashfield, R.K. (1984). *Cluster analysis.* Newbury Park, CA: Sage.

Allen, J.B. (2003). Social motivation in youth sport. *Journal of Sport and Exercise Psychology, 25*, 551–567.

Ames, C.A. (1984a). Achievement attributions and self instruction under competitive and individualistic goal structures. *Journal of Educational Psychology, 76*, 478–487.

Ames, C.A. (1984b). Competitive, cooperative, and individual goal structures: A cognitive-motivational analysis. In R. Ames & C. Ames (Eds.), *Research on motivation in education: Student motivation* (pp. 177–207). New York: Academic Press.

Ames, C. (1992a). Classrooms: Goals, structures, and student motivation. *Journal of Educational Psychology, 84*, 261–271.

Ames, C. (1992b). Achievement goals, motivational climate, and motivational processes. In G.C. Roberts (ed.), *Motivation in Sport and Exercise* (pp. 161–176). Champaign, IL: Human Kinetics.

Ames, C.A., Ames, R., & Felker, D. (1977). Effects of competitive reward structure and valence of outcome on children's achievement attributions. *Journal of Educational Psychology, 69*, 1–8.

Ames, C., & Archer, J. (1988). Achievement goals in the classroom: Students' learning strategies and motivation processes. *Journal of Educational Psychology, 80*, 260–267.

Atkinson, J. (1957). Motivational determinants of risk-taking behavior. *Psychological Review, 64*, 359–372.

Balaguer, I., Duda, J.L., & Crespo, M. (1999). Motivational climate and goal orientations as predictors of perceptions of improvement, satisfaction and coach ratings among tennis players. *Scandinavian Journal of Medicine and Science in Sport, 9*, 381–388.

Berlant, A.R., & Weiss, M.R. (1997). Goal orientation and the modeling process: An individual's focus on form and outcome. *Research Quarterly for Exercise and Sport, 86*, 317–330.

Biddle, S.J.H., Akande, A., Vlachopoulos, S., & Fox, K. (1996). Towards an understanding of children's motivation for physical activity: Achievement goal orientations, beliefs about sport success and sport emotion in Zimbabwean children. *Psychology and Health, 12*, 49–55.

Biddle, S., Cury, F., Goudas, M., Sarrazin, P., Famose, J.P., & Durand, M. (1995). Development of scales to measure perceived physical education class climate: A cross-national project. *British Journal of Educational Psychology, 65*, 341–358.

Biddle, S., Soos, I., & Chatzisarantis, N. (1999). Predicting physical activity intentions using goal perspectives and self-determination theory approaches. *European Psychologist, 4*, 83–89.

Biddle, S.J.H., & Wang, C.K.J. (2003). Motivation and self-perception profiles and links with physical activity in adolescent girls. *Journal of Adolescence, 26,* 687–701.

Biddle, S.J.H., Wang, C.K.J., Chatzisarantis, N.L.D., & Spray, C.M. (2003a). Motivation for physical activity in young people: Entity and incremental beliefs about athletic ability. *Journal of Sports Sciences, 21,* 973–989.

Biddle, S.J.H., Wang, C.K., Kavussanu, M., & Spray, C. (2003b). Correlates of achievement goal orientations in physical activity: A systematic review of research. *European Journal of Sport Sciences, 3,* 1–20.

Blumenfeld, P.C. (1992). Classroom learning and motivation—clarifying and expanding goal theory. *Journal of Educational Psychology, 84,* 272–281.

Boixadós, M., Cruz, J., Torregrosa, M., & Valiente, L. (2004). Relationships among motivational climate, satisfaction, perceived ability and fair play attitudes in youth soccer players. *Journal of Applied Sport Psychology, 16,* 301–317.

Carpenter, P.J., & Morgan, K. (1999). Motivational climate, personal goal perspectives, and cognitive and affective responses in physical education classes. *European Journal of Physical Education, 4,* 31–44.

Carpenter, P., & Yates, B. (1997). Relationship between achievement goals and the perceived purpose of soccer for semiprofessional and amateur players. *Journal of Sport and Exercise Psychology, 19,* 302–312.

Carr, S. (2006). An examination of multiple goals in children's physical education: Motivational effects of goal profiles and the role of perceived climate in multiple goal development. *Journal of Sports Sciences, 24,* 281-297.

Carr, S., & Weigand, D.A. (2001). Parental, peer, teacher and sporting hero influence on the goal orientations of children in physical education. *European Physical Education Review, 7,* 305–328.

Chan, D. (1998). Functional relations among constructs in the same content domain at different levels of analysis: A typology of composition models. *Journal of Applied Psychology, 83,* 234–246.

Chiu, C.-Y., Dweck, C.S., Tong, J.Y.-Y., & Fu, J.H.-Y. (1997). Implicit theories and conceptions of morality. *Journal of Personality and Social Psychology, 73,* 923–940.

Conroy, D.E., Elliot, A.J., & Hofer, S.M. (2003). A 2 X 2 achievement goals questionnaire for sport: Evidence for factorial invariance, temporal stability, and external validity. *Journal of Sport & Exercise Psychology, 25,* 456–476.

Conroy, D.E., Kaye, M.P., & Coatsworth, J.D. (2006). Coaching climates and the destructive effects of mastery-avoidance achievement goals on situational motivation. *Journal of Sport & Exercise Psychology, 28,* 69-92.

Cumming, J., Hall, C., Harwood, C., & Gammage, K. (2002). Motivational orientations and imagery use: A goal profiling analysis. *Journal of Sports Sciences, 20,* 127–136.

Cumming, S.P., Smoll, F.L., Smith, R.E., & Grossbard, J.R. (2007). Is winning everything? The relative contributions of motivational climate and won-lost percentage in youth sports. *Journal of Applied Sport Psychology, 19,* 322-336.

Cury, F., Da Fonseca, D., Rufo, M., & Sarrazin, P. (2002). Perceptions of competence, implicit theory of ability, perception of motivational climate, and achievement goals: A test of the trichotomous conceptualization of endorsement of achievement motivation in the physical education setting. *Perceptual and Motor Skills, 95,* 233–244.

Cury, F., Elliot, A., Sarrazin, P., Da Fonseca, D., & Rufo, M. (2002). The trichotomous achievement goal model and intrinsic motivation: A sequential mediational analysis. *Journal of Experimental Social Psychology, 38,* 473–481.

Cury, F., Famose, J.P., & Sarrazin, P. (1997). Achievement goal theory and active search for information in a sport task. In R. Lidor & M. Bar-Eli (Eds.), *Innovations in sport psychology: Linking theory and practice. Proceedings of the IX World Congress in Sport Psychology: Part I* (pp. 218–220). Netanya, Israel: Ministry of Education, Culture and Sport.

Csikszentmihalyi, M. (1990). *Flow: The psychology of optimal experience.* New York: Harper & Row.

Diener, C.I., & Dweck, C.S. (1980). An analysis of learned helplessness 2: The processing of success. *Journal of Personality and Social Psychology, 39,* 940–952.

Digelidis, N., Papaioannou, A., Laparidis, K., & Christodoulidis, T. (2003). A one-year intervention in 7th grade physical education classes aiming to change motivational climate and attitudes towards exercise. *Psychology of Sport and Exercise, 4,* 195–210.

Dorobantu, M., & Biddle, S.J.H. (1997). The influence of situational and individual goals on the intrinsic motivation of adolescents towards Physical Education. The European Yearbook of Sport Psychology, *1,* 145–168.

Duda, J.L. (1987). Toward a developmental theory of children's motivation in sport. *Journal of Sport Psychology, 9,* 130–145.

Duda, J.L. (1989). Relationship between task and ego orientation and the perceived purpose of sport among high school athletes. *Journal of Sport and Exercise Psychology, 11,* 318–335.

Duda, J.L. (1992). Motivation in sport settings: A goal perspective approach .In G.C. Roberts (Ed.), *Motivation in sport and exercise* (pp. 57–91). Champaign, IL: Human Kinetics.

Duda, J.L. (1993). Goals: A social-cognitive approach to the study of achievement motivation in sport. In R. Singer, M. Murphey, & L.K. Tennant (Eds.), *Handbook of research in sport psychology* (pp. 421–436). New York: Macmillan.

Duda, J.L. (2001). Achievement goal research in sport: Pushing the boundaries and clarifying some misunderstandings. In G.C. Roberts (Ed.), *Advances in motivation in sport and exercise* (pp. 129–182). Champaign, IL: Human Kinetics.

Duda, J.L., & Balaguer, I. (1999). Toward an integration of models of leadership with a contemporary theory of motivation. In R. Lidor & M. Bar-Eli (Eds.), *Sport psychology: Linking theory and practice* (pp. 213–229). Morgantown, WV: Fitness Information Technology.

Duda, J.L. and Chi, L. (1989). *The effect of task- and ego-involving conditions on perceived competence and causal attributions in basketball.* Communication to the Association for the Advancement of Applied Sport Psychology, University of Washington, Seattle, WA, September.

Duda, J.L., Chi, L., Newton, M.L., Walling, M.D., & Catley, D. (1995). Task and ego orientation and intrinsic motivation in sport. *International Journal of Sport Psychology, 26,* 40–63.

Duda, J.L., & Hall, H.K. (2001). Achievement goal theory in sport: Recent extensions and future directions. In R. Singer, H. Hausenblas, & C. Janelle (Eds.), *Handbook of sport psychology* (pp. 417–443). New York: Wiley.

Duda, J.L., & Hom, M. (1993). Interdependencies between the perceived and self-reported goal orientations of young athletes and their parents. *Pediatric Exercise Science, 5,* 234–241.

Duda, J.L., & Nicholls, J.G. (1992). Dimensions of achievement motivation in schoolwork and sport. *Journal of Educational Psychology, 84,* 290–299.

Duda, J.L., Olson, L., & Templin, T. (1991). The relationship of task and ego orientation to sportsmanship attitudes and the perceived legitimacy of injurious acts. *Research Quarterly for Exercise and Sport, 62,* 79–87.

Duda, J.L., & White, S.A. (1992). Goal orientations and beliefs about the causes of success among elite athletes. *The Sport Psychologist, 6,* 334–343.

Duda, J.L., & Whitehead, J. (1998). Measurement of goal perspectives in the physical domain. In J.L Duda (Ed.), *Advances in sport and exercise psychology measurement,* (pp. 21–48). Morgantown, WV: Fitness Information Technology.

Dunn, J.G.H., & Dunn, J.C. (1999). Goal orientations, perceptions of aggression, and sportspersonship in elite youth male ice hockey players. *The Sport Psychologist, 13,* 183–200.

Dweck, C.S. (1986). Motivational processes affecting learning. *American Psychologist, 41,* 1040–1048.

Dweck, C.S. (1999). *Self theories: Their role in motivation, personality, and development.* Philadelphia: Psychology Press.

Dweck, C.S., & Bempechat, J. (1983). Children's theories of intelligence: Consequences for learning. In S.G. Paris & G.M. Olson & H.W. Stevenson (Eds.), *Learning and motivation in the classroom* (pp. 239–256). Hillsdale, NJ: Erlbaum.

Dweck, C.S., Chiu, C.-Y., & Hong, Y.-Y. (1995a). Implicit theories and their role in judgments and reactions: A world from two perspectives. *Psychological Inquiry, 6,* 267–285.

Dweck, C.S., Chiu, C.-Y., & Hong, Y.-Y. (1995b). Implicit theories: Elaboration and extension of the model. *Psychological Inquiry, 6,* 322–333.

Dweck, C.S., & Elliott, E.S. (1983). Achievement motivation. In E.M. Hetherington (Ed.), *Handbook of child psychology: Socialization, personality and social development* (Vol. 4, pp. 643–691). New York: Wiley.

Dweck, C.S., & Leggett, E.L. (1988). A social-cognitive approach to motivation and personality. *Psychological Review, 95,* 256–273.

Ebbeck, V., & Becker, S.L. (1994). Psychosocial predictors of goal orientations in youth soccer. *Research Quarterly for Exercise and Sport, 65,* 355–362.

Elliot, A.J. (1997). Integrating the "classic" and "contemporary" approaches to achievement motivation: A hierarchical model of approach and avoidance achievement motivation. In M.L. Maehr & P.R. Pintrich (Eds.), *Advances in motivation and achievement* (Vol. 10, pp. 143–179). Greenwich, CT: JAI Press.

Elliot, A.J. (1999). Approach and avoidance motivation and achievement goals. *Educational Psychologist, 34,* 169–189.

Elliot, A. J. (2005). A conceptual history of the achievement goal construct. In A. J. Elliot & C. S. Dweck (Eds.), *Handbook of competence and motivation* (pp. 52-72). New York: The Guilford Press.

Elliot, A.J., & Church, M.A. (1997). A hierarchical model of approach and avoidance achievement motivation. *Journal of Personality and Social Psychology, 72,* 218–232.

Elliot, A.J., & Conroy, D.E. (2005). Beyond the dichotomous model of achievement goals in sport and exercise psychology. *Sport & Exercise Psychology Review, 1,* 17–25.

Elliot, A.J., & Covington, M.V. (2001). Approach and avoidance motivation. *Educational Psychology Review, 13,* 73–92.

Elliot, A.J., & McGregor, H.A. (2001). A 2 X 2 achievement goal framework. *Journal of Personality and Social Psychology, 80,* 501–519.

Elliot, A.J., & Thrash, T.M. (2001). Achievement goals and the hierarchical model of achievement motivation. *Educational Psychology Review, 13,* 139–156.

Epstein, J.L. (1989). Family structures and student motivation: A developmental perspective. In C. Ames & R. Ames (Eds.), *Research on motivation in education* (Vol. 3, pp. 259–295). San Diego, CA: Academic Press.

Escarti, A., & Gutierrez, M. (2001). Influence of the motivational climate in physical education on the intention to practice physical activity or sport. *European Journal of Sport Sciences, 1,* 1–12.

Escarti, A., Roberts, G.C., Cervello, E.M., & Guzman, J.F. (1999). Adolescent goal orientations and the perception of criteria of success used by significant others. *International Journal of Sport Psychology, 30,* 309–324.

Ewing, M.E. (1981). *Achievement orientations and sport behavior of males and females.* Unpublished doctoral dissertation, University of Illinois.

Fox, K.R., Goudas, M., Biddle, S., Duda, J., & Armstrong, N. (1994). Children's task and ego goal profiles in sport. *British Journal of Educational Psychology, 64,* 253–261.

Franiuk, R., Cohen, D., & Pomerantz, E.M. (2002). Implicit theories of relationships: Implications for relationship satisfaction and longevity. *Personal Relationships, 9,* 345–367.

Fry, M.D. (2001). The development of motivation in children. In G.C. Roberts (Ed.), *Advances in motivation in sport and exercise.* (pp. 51-78). Champaign, IL; Human Kinetics.

Fry, M.D., & Duda, J.L. (1997). A developmental examination of children's understanding of effort and ability in the physical and academic domains. *Research Quarterly for Exercise and Sport, 66,* 331–344.

Fry, M.D., & Newton, M. (2003). Application of achievement goal theory in an urban youth tennis setting. *Journal of Applied Sport Psychology, 15,* 50–66.

Gano-Overway, L.A., & Ewing, M.E. (2004). A longitudinal perspective of the relationship between perceived motivational climate, goal orientations, and strategy use. *Research Quarterly for Exercise and Sport, 75,* 315–325.

Gano-Overway, L.A., Guivernau, M., Magyar, T.M., Waldron, J.J., & Ewing, M.E. (2005). Achievement goal perspectives, perceptions of the motivational climate, and sportspersonship: Individual and team effects. *Psychology of Sport and Exercise, 6,* 215–232.

Gernigon, C., d'Arripe-Longueville, F., Delignieres, D., & Ninot, G. (2004). A dynamical systems perspective on goal involvement states in sport. *Journal of Sport and Exercise Psychology, 26,* 572–596.

Gervey, B.M., Chiu, C.-Y., Hong, Y.-Y., & Dweck, C.S. (1999). Differential use of person information in decisions about guilt versus innocence: The role of implicit theories. *Personality and Social Psychology Bulletin, 25,* 17–27.

Goudas, M., & Biddle, S. (1994). Perceived motivational climate and intrinsic motivation in school physical education classes. *European Journal of Psychology of Education, 9,* 241–250.

Goudas, M., Biddle, S., Fox, K., & Underwood, M. (1995). It ain't what you do, it's the way that you do it! Teaching style affects children's motivation in track and field lessons. *The Sport Psychologist, 9,* 254–264.

Guan, J., Xiang, P., McBride, R., & Bruene, A. (2006). Achievement goals, social goals, and students' reported persistence and effort in high school physical education. *Journal of Teaching in Physical Education, 25,* 58-74.

Hall, H. (1990). *A social cognitive approach to goal setting: The mediating effects of achievement goals and perceived ability.* Unpublished doctoral dissertation, University of Illinois at Urbana-Champaign.

Hall, H.K., & Kerr, A.W. (1997). Motivational antecedents of precompetitive anxiety in youth sport. *The Sport Psychologist, 11,* 24–42.

Hall, H.K., Kerr, A.W., & Matthews, J. (1998). Precompetitive anxiety in sport: The contribution of achievement goals and perfectionism. *Journal of Sport and Exercise Psychology, 20,* 194–217.

Harwood, C.G. (2002). Assessing achievement goals in sport: Caveats for consultants and a case for contextualization. *Journal of Applied Sport Psychology, 14,* 380–393.

Harwood, C.G. & Beauchamp, M.R. (in press). Group functioning through optimal achievement goals. In M.R. Beauchamp & M. Eys (Eds), *Group Dynamics in Exercise and Sport Psychology.* Routledge: London and New York.

Harwood, C.G., Cumming, J., & Fletcher, D. (2004). Motivational profiles and psychological skill use in elite youth sport. *Journal of Applied Sport Psychology, 16,* 318–332.

Harwood, C.G., Cumming, J., & Hall, C. (2003). Imagery use in elite youth sport participants: Reinforcing the applied significance of achievement goal theory. *Research Quarterly for Exercise and Sport, 3,* 292–300.

Harwood, C.G., & Hardy, L. (2001). Persistence and effort in moving achievement goal research forward: A response to Treasure and colleagues. *Journal of Sport and Exercise Psychology, 23,* 330–345.

Harwood, C.G., Hardy, L., & Swain, A. (2000). Achievement goals in competitive sport: A critique of conceptual and measurement issues. *Journal of Sport and Exercise Psychology, 22,* 235–255.

Harwood, C.G., & Lacey, K. (2001). *Partner perceptions and the intensity and direction of achievement goals in elite sport acrobats.* Paper presented at the annual meeting of the Association for the Advancement of Applied Sport Psychology. Orlando, FL, October.

Harwood, C.G., Smith, J., & Treasure, D.C. (2005). Motivational climate within individual sports: Initial developments of a multi-dimensional measurement tool. Paper presented at the World Congress of Sport Psychology. Sydney, Australia, August.

Harwood, C.G., & Swain, A.B. (1998). Antecedents of pre-competition achievement goals in elite junior tennis players. *Journal of Sport Sciences, 16,* 357–371.

Harwood, C.G., & Swain, A.B. (2001). The development and activation of achievement goals in tennis: I. Understanding the underlying factors. *The Sport Psychologist, 15,* 319–341.

Harwood, C.G., & Swain, A.B. (2002). The development and activation of achievement goals in tennis: II. A player, parent and coach intervention. *The Sport Psychologist, 16,* 111–137.

Harwood, C.G., Wilson, K., & Hardy, L. (2002). *Achievement goals in sport: Working towards an alternative model.* Paper presented at the 12th Commonwealth Games/British Association for Sport and Exercise Sciences Conference, Manchester, United Kingdom.

Hatzigeorgiadis, A., & Biddle, S. (1999). The effects of goal orientation and perceived competence on cognitive interference during tennis and snooker performance. *Journal of Sport Behavior, 22*, 479–501.

Hayashi, C. (1996). Achievement motivation among Anglo-American and Hawaiian physical activity participants: Individual differences and social contextual factors. *Journal of Sport and Exercise Psychology, 18*, 194–215.

Hodge, K., & Petlichkoff, L. (2000). Goal profiles in sport motivation: A cluster analysis. *Journal of Sport and Exercise Psychology, 22*, 256–272.

Jackson, S.A., & Roberts, G.C. (1992). Positive performance states of athletes: Toward a conceptual understanding of peak performance. *The Sport Psychologist, 6*, 156–171.

Kavussanu, M. (2006). Motivational predictors of prosocial and antisocial behaviour in football. *Journal of Sports Sciences, 24*, 575–588.

Kavussanu, M., & Roberts, G.C. (1996). Motivation in physical activity contexts: The relationship of perceived motivational climate to intrinsic motivation and self-efficacy. *Journal of Sport and Exercise Psychology, 18*, 264–280.

Kavussanu, M., & Roberts, G.C. (2001). Moral functioning in sport: An achievement goal perspective. *Journal of Sport and Exercise Psychology, 23*, 37–54.

Lemyre, P.N., Roberts, G.C., & Ommundsen, Y. (2002). Achievement goal orientations, perceived ability, and sportspersonship in youth soccer. *Journal of Applied Sport Psychology, 14*, 120–136.

Lintunen, T., Valkonen, A., Leskinen, E., & Biddle, S.J.H. (1999). Predicting physical activity intentions using a goal perspectives approach: A study of Finnish youth. *Scandinavian Journal of Medicine & Science in Sports, 9*, 344–352.

Liukkonen, J., Telama, R., & Biddle, S.J.H. (1998). Enjoyment in youth sport: A goal perspectives approach. *European Yearbook of Sport Psychology, 2*, 55–75.

Lloyd, J., & Fox, K. (1992). Achievement goals and motivation to exercise in adolescent girls: A preliminary intervention study. *British Journal of Physical Education: Research Supplement, 11*, 12–16.

Lochbaum, M.R., & Roberts, G.C. (1993). Goal orientations and perceptions of the sport experience. *Journal of Sport and Exercise Psychology, 15*, 160–171.

Maehr, M.L., & Nicholls, J.G. (1980). Culture and achievement motivation: A second look. In N. Warren (Ed.), *Studies in cross-cultural psychology* (Vol. 3, pp. 221–267). New York: Academic Press.

Magyar, T.M., & Feltz, D.L. (2003). The influence of dispositional and situational tendencies on adolescent girls' sport confidence sources. *Psychology of Sport and Exercise, 4*, 175–190.

Marsh, H.W., & Peart, N.D. (1988). Competitive and cooperative physical fitness training programs for girls: Effects on physical fitness and multidimensional self concepts. *Journal of Sport and Exercise Psychology, 10*, 390–407.

Miller, B.W., Roberts, G.C., & Ommundsen, Y. (2004). Effect of motivational climate on sportspersonship among competitive youth male and female football players. *Scandinavian Journal of Medicine and Science in Sport, 14*, 193–202.

Mueller, C.M., & Dweck, C.S. (1998). Praise for intelligence can undermine children's motivation and performance. *Journal of Personality and Social Psychology, 75*, 33–52.

Newton, M., & Duda, J.L. (1995). Relations of goal orientations and expectations on multidimensional state anxiety. *Perceptual and Motor Skills, 81*, 1107–1112.

Newton, M., & Duda, J.L. (1999). The interaction of motivational climate, dispositional goal orientations and perceived ability in predicting indices of motivation. *International Journal of Sport Psychology, 30*, 63–82.

Newton, M., Duda, J.L., & Yin, Z.N. (2000). Examination of the psychometric properties of the Perceived Motivational Climate in Sport Questionnaire–2 in a sample of female athletes. *Journal of Sport Sciences, 18*, 275–290.

Nicholls, J.G. (1984). Achievement motivation: Conceptions of ability, subjective experience, task choice, and performance. *Psychological Review, 91*, 328–346.

Nicholls, J.G. (1989). *The competitive ethos and democratic education.* Cambridge, MA: Harvard University Press.

Nicholls, J.G., Cheung, P.C., Lauer, J., & Patashnick, M. (1989). Individual differences in academic motivation: Perceived ability, goals, beliefs, and values. *Learning & Individual Differences, 1*, 63–84.

Nicholls, J.G., & Miller, A.T. (1984). Development and its discontents: The differentiation of the concept of ability. In J.G. Nicholls (Ed.), *Advances in motivation and achievement, Vol. 3: The development of achievement motivation* (pp. 185–218). Greenwich, CT: JAI Press.

Ntoumanis, N., and Biddle, S. (1998). The relationship between competitive anxiety, achievement goals, and motivational climates. *Research Quarterly for Exercise and Sport, 69*, 176–187.

Ntoumanis, N., & Biddle, S. (1999). A review of motivational climate in physical activity. *Journal of Sports Sciences, 17*, 643–665.

Ntoumanis, N., Biddle, S.J.H., & Haddock, G. (1999). The mediating role of coping strategies on the relationship between achievement motivation and affect in sport. *Anxiety, Stress, and Coping, 12*, 299–327.

Ntoumanis, N., & Vazou, S. (2005). Peer motivational climate in youth sport: Measurement development. *Journal of Sport & Exercise Psychology, 27*, 432-455.

Olympiou, A., Jowett, S., & Duda, J.L. (under review). The interface of the coach-created motivational climate and the coach-athlete relationship. *Group Dynamics: Theory, Research and Practice.*

Ommundsen, Y. (2001a). Self-handicapping strategies in physical education classes: The influence of implicit theories of the nature of ability and achievement goal orientations. *Psychology of Sport and Exercise, 2*, 139–156.

Ommundsen, Y. (2001b). Pupils' affective responses in physical education classes: The association of implicit theories of the nature of ability and achievement goals. *European Physical Education Review, 7*, 219–242.

Ommundsen, Y., & Roberts, G.C. (1999). Effect of motivational climate profiles on motivational indices in team sport. *Scandinavian Journal of Medicine and Science in Sport, 9*, 389–397.

Ommundsen, Y., Roberts, G.C., & Kavussanu, M. (1998). Perceived motivational climate and cognitive and affective correlates among Norwegian athletes. *Journal of Sport Sciences, 16*, 153–164.

Ommundsen, Y., Roberts, G.C., Lemyre, P.N., & Treasure, D. (2003). Perceived motivational climate in male youth soccer: Relations to social-moral functioning, sportspersonship and team norm perceptions. *Psychology of Sport and Exercise, 4*, 397–413.

Parish, L.E., & Treasure, D.C. (2003). Physical activity and situational motivation in physical education: Influence of the motivational climate and perceived ability. *Research Quarterly for Exercise and Sport, 74*, 173–182.

Papaioannou, A. (1994). Development of a questionnaire to measure achievement orientations in physical education. *Research Quarterly for Exercise and Sport, 65*, 11–20.

Papaioannou, A. (1998). Students' perceptions of the physical education class environment for boys and girls and the perceived motivational climate. *Research Quarterly for Exercise and Sport, 69*, 267–275.

Papaioannou, A., & Kouli, O. (1999). The effect of task structure, perceived motivational climate and goal orientations on students' task involvement and anxiety. *Journal of Applied Sport Psychology, 11*, 51–71.

Papaioannou, A.G., Marsh, H.W., & Theodorakis, Y. (2004). A multi-level approach to motivational climate in physical education and sport settings: An individual or group level construct? *Journal of Sport and Exercise Psychology, 26*, 90-118.

Papaioannou, A.G., Tsigilis, N., Kosmidou, E., & Milosis, D. (2007). Measuring perceived motivational climate in physical education. *Journal of Teaching in Physical Education. 26*, 236-259.

Pensgaard, A.M., & Roberts, G.C. (2000). The relationship between motivational climate, perceived ability and sources of distress among elite athletes. *Journal of Sport Sciences, 18*, 191–200.

Roberts, G.C. (1984). Achievement motivation in children's sport. In J.G. Nicholls (Ed.), *Advances in motivation and achievement, Vol. 3: The development of achievement motivation* (pp. 251–281). Greenwich, CT: JAI Press.

Roberts, G.C. (Ed.). (1992). *Motivation in sport and exercise*. Champaign, IL: Human Kinetics.

Roberts, G.C. (2001). Understanding the dynamics of motivation in physical activity: The influence of achievement goals on motivational processes. In G.C. Roberts (Ed.), *Advances in Motivation in Sport and Exercise*. Champaign, IL: Human Kinetics.

Roberts, G.C., & Ommundsen, Y. (1996). Effect of goal orientations on achievement beliefs, cognitions, and strategies in team sport. *Scandinavian Journal of Medicine and Science in Sport, 6*, 46–56.

Roberts, G.C., & Treasure, D.C. (1992). Children in sport. *Sport Science Review, 2*, 46–64.

Roberts, G.C., Treasure, D.C., & Balague, G. (1998). Achievement goals in sport: The development and validation of the Perception of Success Questionnaire. *Journal of Sport Sciences, 16*, 337–347.

Roberts, G.C., Treasure, D.C., & Kavussanu, M. (1996). Orthogonality of achievement goals and its relationship to beliefs about success and satisfaction in sport. *The Sport Psychologist, 10*, 398–408.

Sage, L. D., Kavussanu, M. & Duda, J. L. (2006). Goal orientations and moral identity as predictors of prosocial and antisocial functioning in male association football players. *Journal of Sports Sciences, 24*, 455-466.

Sarrazin, P., Biddle, S., Famose, J.P., Cury, F., Fox, K., & Durand, M. (1996). Goal orientations and conceptions of the nature of sport ability in children: A social cognitive approach. *British Journal of Social Psychology, 35*, 399–414.

Schneider, B., Salvaggio, A.N., & Subirats, M. (2002). Climate strength: A new direction for climate research. *Journal of Applied Psychology, 87*, 220–229.

Seifriz, J.J., Duda, J.L., & Chi, L. (1992). The relationship of perceived motivational climate to intrinsic motivation and beliefs about success in basketball. *Journal of Sport and Exercise Psychology, 14*, 375–391.

Smith, A.L. (1999). Perceptions of peer relationships and physical activity participation in early adolescence. *Journal of Sport and Exercise Psychology, 21*, 329–350.

Smith, A.L. (2003). Peer relationships in physical activity contexts: A road less travelled in youth sport and exercise psychology research. *Psychology of Sport and Exercise, 4*, 25–39.

Smith, J.M.J., & Harwood, C.G., (2001). *The transiency of goal involvement states in matchplay: An elite player case study*. Paper presented at the British Association of Sport and Exercise Sciences conference, Newport, September.

Spray, C.M., Wang, C.K.J., Biddle, S.J.H., Chatzisarantis, N.L.D., & Warburton, V.E. (2006). An experimental test of self-theories of ability in youth sport. *Psychology of Sport and Exercise, 7*, 255-267.

Standage, M., Duda, J.L., & Ntoumanis, N. (2003). Predicting motivational regulations in physical education: The interplay between dispositional goal orientations, motivational climate and perceived competence. *Journal of Sport Sciences, 21*, 631–647.

Stuntz, C.P., & Weiss, M.R. (2003). Influence of social goal orientations and peers on unsportsmanlike play. *Research Quarterly for Exercise and Sport, 74*, 421–435.

Swain, A.B., & Harwood, C.G. (1996). Antecedents of state goals in age-group swimmers: An interactionist perspective. *Journal of Sport Sciences, 14*, 111–124.

Theeboom, M., DeKnop, P., & Weiss, M.R. (1995). Motivational climate, psychological responses, and motor skill development in children's sport: A field-based intervention study. *Journal of Sport and Exercise Psychology, 17*, 294–311.

Thill, E.E., & Brunel, P.C. (1995). Ego-involvement and task-involvement: Related conceptions of ability, effort, and learning strategies among soccer players. *International Journal of Sport Psychology, 26*, 81–97.

Treasure, D.C., Duda, J.L., Hall, H.K, Roberts, G.C., Ames, C., & Maehr, M.L. (2001). Clarifying misconceptions and misrepresentations in achievement goal research in sport: A response to Harwood, Hardy and Swain. *Journal of Sport and Exercise Psychology, 23*, 317–329.

Treasure, D., & Roberts, G.C. (1995). Achievement goals, motivational climate and achievement strategies and behaviour in sport. *International Journal of Sport Psychology, 26*, 64–80.

Treasure, D., & Roberts, G.C. (1998). Relationship between female adolescents' achievement goal orientations, perceptions of the motivational climate, belief about success and sources of satisfaction in basketball. *International Journal of Sport Psychology, 29*, 211–230.

Treasure, D., & Roberts, G.C. (2001). Students' perceptions of the motivational climate, achievement beliefs, and satisfaction in physical education. *Research Quarterly for Exercise and Sport, 72*, 165–175.

Todorovich, J.R., & Curtner-Smith, M.D. (2002). Influence of the motivational climate in physical education on sixth grade pupils' goal orientations. *European Physical Education Review, 8*, 119–138.

Valentini, N.C., & Rudisill, M.E. (2004a). An inclusive mastery climate intervention and the motor skill development of children with and without disabilities. *Adapted Physical Activity Quarterly, 21*, 330–347.

Valentini, N.C., & Rudisill, M.E. (2004b). Motivational climate, motor-skill development, and perceived competence: Two studies of developmentally delayed kindergarten children. *Journal of Teaching in Physical Education, 23*, 216–234.

Vazou, S., Ntoumanis, N., & Duda, J.L. (2005). Peer motivational climate in youth sport: A qualitative inquiry. *Psychology of Sport and Exercise, 6*, 497-516.

Vealey, R.S., & Campbell, J.L. (1988). Achievement goals of adolescent figure skaters: Impact on self-confidence, anxiety, and performance. *Journal of Adolescence Research, 3*, 227–243.

Walling, M.D., Duda, J.L., & Chi, L. (1993). The Perceived Motivational Climate in Sport Questionnaire: Construct and predictive validity. *Journal of Sport and Exercise Psychology, 15*, 172–183.

Wang, C. K. J., Biddle, S. J. H., & Elliot, A. J. (2007). The 2 x 2 achievement goal framework in a physical education context. *Psychology of Sport and Exercise, 8*, 147-168.

Wang, C.K.J., Liu, W.C., Biddle, S.J.H., & Spray, C.M. (2005). Cross-cultural validation of the Conceptions of the Nature of Athletic Ability Questionnaire Version 2. *Personality and Individual Differences, 38*, 1245–1256.

Weiss, M.R., & Ferrer-Caja, E. (2002). Motivational orientations and sport behavior. In T.S. Horn (Ed.), *Advances in sport psychology* (2nd ed., pp. 101–183). Champaign, IL: Human Kinetics.

White, S.A. (1996). Goal orientation and perceptions of the motivational climate initiated by parents. *Pediatric Exercise Science, 8*, 122–129.

White, S.A. (1998). Adolescent goal profiles, perceptions of the parent initiated motivational climate and competitive trait anxiety. *The Sport Psychologist, 12*, 16–28.

White, S.A., Duda, J.L., & Hart, S. (1992). An exploratory examination of the parent-initiated motivational climate questionnaire. *Perceptual and Motor Skills, 75*, 875–880.

White, S.A., & Zellner, S. (1996). The relationship between goal orientation, beliefs about the causes of sport success, and trait anxiety among high school, intercollegiate, and recreational sport participants. *The Sport Psychologist, 10*, 58–72.

Whitehead, J. (1995). Multiple achievement orientations and participation in youth sport: A cultural and developmental perspective. *International Journal of Sport Psychology, 26*, 431–452.

Whitehead, J., Andrée, K.V., & Lee, M.J. (2004). Achievement perspectives and perceived ability: How far do interactions generalise in youth sport? *Psychology of Sport and Exercise, 5*, 291–317.

Williams, L. (1998). Contextual influences and goal perspectives among female youth sport participants. *Research Quarterly for Exercise & Sport, 69*, 47–57.

Wilson, K., Hardy, L., & Harwood, C.G. (2006). Investigating the relationship between achievement goals and process goals in rugby union players. *Journal of Applied Sport Psychology, 18*, 297-311.

Wylleman, P., & Lavallee, D. (2003). A developmental perspective on transitions faced by athletes. In M. Weiss (Ed.), *Developmental sport and exercise psychology: A lifespan perspective* (pp. 507–527). Morgantown, WV: Fitness Information Technology.

Xiang, P., & Lee, A. (2002). Achievement goals, perceived motivational climate, and students' self-reported mastery behaviours. *Research Quarterly for Exercise and Sport, 73*, 58–65.

Yoo, J. (1999). Motivational-behavioral correlates of goal orientation and perceived motivational climate in physical education contexts. *Perceptual and Motor Skills, 89,* 262–274.

CHAPTER 9

Ames, C.A. (1992). Achievement goals, motivational climate, and motivational processes. In G.C. Roberts (Ed.), *Motivation in sport and exercise* (pp. 161–176). Champaign, IL: Human Kinetics.

Aquino, K., & Reed, A. (2002). The self-importance of moral identity. *Journal of Personality and Social Psychology, 83,* 1423–1440.

Bandura, A. (1986). *Social foundations of thought and action: A social cognitive theory.* Englewood Cliffs, NJ: Prentice Hall.

Bandura, A. (1991). Social cognitive theory of moral thought and action. In W.M. Kurtines & J.L. Gewirtz (Eds.), *Handbook of moral behavior and development: Theory, research and applications* (Vol. 1, pp. 71–129). Hillsdale, NJ: Erlbaum.

Bandura, A. (1999). Moral disengagement in the perpetration of inhumanities. *Personality and Social Psychology Review, 3,* 193–209.

Bandura, A. (2002). Selective moral disengagement in the exercise of moral agency. *Journal of Moral Education, 31,* 101–119.

Bandura, A., Barbaranelli, C., Caprara, G.V., & Pastorelli, C. (1996). Mechanisms of moral disengagement in the exercise of moral agency. *Journal of Personality and Social Psychology, 71,* 364–374.

Bandura, A., Caprara, G.V., Barbaranelli, C., Gerbino, M., & Pastorelli, C. (2003). Role of affective self-regulatory efficacy in diverse spheres of psychosocial functioning. *Child Development, 74,* 769–782.

Bandura, A., Caprara, G.V., Barbaranelli, C., Pastorelli, C., & Regalia, C. (2001). Sociocognitive self-regulatory mechanisms governing transgressive behavior. *Journal of Personality and Social Psychology, 80,* 125–135.

Bandura, A., Ross, D., & Ross, S.A. (1961). Transmission of aggression through imitation of aggressive models. *Journal of Abnormal and Social Psychology, 63,* 575–582.

Beller, J.M., & Stoll, S.K. (1995). Moral reasoning of high school student athletes and general students: An empirical study versus personal testimony. *Pediatric Exercise Science, 7,* 352–363.

Bergman, R. (2002). Why be moral? A conceptual moral from developmental psychology. *Human Development, 45,* 104–124.

Berryman, J.W. (1996). The rise of boys' sports in the United States, 1900 to 1970. In F.L. Smoll & R.E. Smith (Eds.), *Children and youth in sport: A biopsychosocial perspective* (pp. 4–14). Madison, WI: Brown & Benchmark.

Boixados, M., Cruz, J., Torregrosa, M., & Valiente, L. (2004). Relationship among motivational climate, satisfaction, perceived ability, and fair play attitudes in young soccer players. *Journal of Applied Sport Psychology, 16,* 301–317.

Bovyer, G. (1963). Children's concepts of sportsmanship in the fourth, fifth, and sixth grades. *Research Quarterly, 34,* 282–287.

Bredemeier, B.J. (1985). Moral reasoning and the perceived legitimacy of intentionally injurious sport acts. *Journal of Sport Psychology, 7,* 110–124.

Bredemeier, B.J.L. (1994). Children's moral reasoning and their assertive, aggressive, and submissive tendencies in sport and daily life. *Journal of Sport & Exercise Psychology, 16,* 1–14.

Bredemeier, B.J.L. (1995). Divergence in children's moral reasoning about issues in daily life and sport specific contexts. *International Journal of Sport Psychology, 26,* 453–463.

Bredemeier, B.J., & Shields, D.L. (1984a). Divergence in children's moral reasoning about sport and everyday life. *Sociology of Sport Journal, 1,* 348–357.

Bredemeier, B.J., & Shields, D.L. (1984b). The utility of moral stage analysis in the investigation of athletic aggression. *Sociology of Sport Journal, 1,* 138–149.

Bredemeier, B.J., & Shields, D.L. (1985). Values and violence in sports today. *Psychology Today, 19* (10), 22–32.

Bredemeier, B.J., & Shields, D.L. (1986a). Moral growth among athletes and nonathletes: A comparative analysis. *Journal of Genetic Psychology, 147,* 7–18.

Bredemeier, B.J., & Shields, D.L. (1986b). Game reasoning and interactional morality. *Journal of Genetic Psychology, 147,* 257–275.

Bredemeier, B.J.L., & Shields, D.L.L. (1998). Moral assessment in sport psychology. In J.L. Duda (Ed.), *Advances in sport and exercise psychology measurement* (pp. 257–276). Morgantown, WV: Fitness Information Technology.

Bredemeier, B.J., Weiss, M.R., Shields, D.L., & Cooper, B.A.B. (1986). The relationship of sport involvement with children's moral reasoning and aggression tendencies. *Journal of Sport Psychology, 8,* 304–318.

Bredemeier, B.J., Weiss, M.R., Shields, D.L., & Cooper, B.A.B. (1987). The relationship between children's legitimacy judgments and their moral reasoning, aggression tendencies, and sport involvement. *Sociology of Sport Journal, 4,* 48–60.

Bredemeier, B.J., Weiss, M.R., Shields, D.L., & Shewchuk, R.M. (1986). Promoting moral growth in a summer sport camp: The implementation of theoretically grounded instructional strategies. *Journal of Moral Education, 15,* 212–220.

Bukowski, W.M., & Sippola, L.K. (1996). Friendship and morality: (How) are they related? In W.M. Bukowski, A.F. Newcomb, & W.W. Hartup (Eds.), *The company they keep: Friendship in childhood and adolescence* (pp. 238–261). New York: Cambridge University Press.

Catalano, R.F., Berglund, L., Ryan, J.A.M., Lonczak, H.S., & Hawkins, D. (2002). Positive youth development in the United States: Research findings on evaluations of positive youth development programs. Retrieved August 1, 2004, from http://aspe.os.dhhs.gov/hsp/PositiveYouthDev99/index.html.

Coakley, J.J. (1998). *Sport and society: Issues and controversies* (6th ed.). Boston: McGraw-Hill.

Commission for Fair Play. (1990). *Fair Play for Kids.* Ontario, Canada: Commission for Fair Play.

Conroy, D.E., Silva, J.M., Newcomer, R.R., Walker, B.W., & Johnson, M.S. (2001). Personal and participatory socializers of perceived legitimacy of aggressive behavior in sport. *Aggressive Behavior, 27,* 405–418.

Crick, N.R. (1995). Relational aggression: The role of intent attributions, feelings of distress, and provocation type. *Development and Psychopathology, 7,* 313–322.

Crick, N.R. (1996). The role of overt aggression, relational aggression, and prosocial behavior in the prediction of children's future social adjustment. *Child Development, 67,* 2317–2327.

Crick, N.R. (1997). Engagement in gender normative versus nonnormative forms of unsportsmanlike play: Links to social-psychological adjustment. *Developmental Psychology, 33,* 610–617.

Crown, J., & Heatherington, L. (1989). The costs of winning? The role of gender in moral reasoning and judgments about competitive athletic encounters. *Journal of Sport & Exercise Psychology, 11,* 281–289.

Cutforth, N.J. (1997). What's worth doing? Reflections on an after-school program in a Denver elementary school. *Quest, 49,* 130–139.

d'Arripe, F., Weiss, M.R., Pantaléon, N., & Raimbault, N. (2005, July). *Self-regulatory mechanisms governing beliefs about unsportsmanlike play in adolescent basketball players.* Presentation given at the international conference for the French Society for the Psychology of Sport, Reims, France.

d'Arripe-Longueville, F., Pantaléon, N., & Smith, A.L. (2006). Personal and situational predictors of sportspersonship in young athletes. *International Journal of Sport Psychology, 37,* 38–57.

Damon, W. (1984). Self-understanding and moral development from childhood to adolescence. In W.M. Kurtines & J.L. Gewirtz (Eds.), *Morality, moral behavior, and moral development.* New York: Wiley.

Damon, W. (1990). *The moral child.* New York: Free Press.

Damon, W. (2004). What is positive youth development? *Annals of the American Academy of Political and Social Science, 591,* 13–24.

DeBusk, M., & Hellison, D. (1989). Implementing a physical education self-responsibility model for delinquency-prone youth. *Journal of Teaching in Physical Education, 8,* 104–112.

Dubois, P.E. (1986). The effect of participation in sport on the value orientations of young athletes. *Sociology of Sport Journal, 3,* 29–42.

Duda, J.L., Olson, L.K., & Templin, T.J. (1991). The relationship of task and ego orientation to sportsmanship attitudes and the perceived legitimacy of injurious acts. *Research Quarterly for Exercise and Sport,* 62, 79–87.

Dunn, J.G.H., & Causgrove Dunn, J. (1999). Goal orientations, perceptions of aggression, and sportspersonship in elite male youth ice hockey players. *The Sport Psychologist,* 13, 183–200.

Duquin, M.E., & Schroeder-Braun, K. (1996). Power, empathy, and moral conflict in sport. *Peace and Conflict: Journal of Peace Psychology,* 2, 351–367.

Ebbeck, V., & Gibbons, S.L. (2003). Explaining the self-conception of perceived conduct using indicators of moral functioning in physical education. *Research Quarterly for Exercise and Sport,* 74, 284–291.

Eisenberg, N. (1995). Prosocial development: A multifaceted model. In W.M. Kurtines & J.L. Gewirtz (Eds.), *Moral development: An introduction* (pp. 401–429). Boston: Allyn & Bacon.

Eisenberg, N., & Fabes, R.A. (1998). Prosocial development. In N. Eisenberg (Ed.), *Handbook of child psychology, Vol. 3: Social, emotional, and personality development* (pp. 701–778). New York: Wiley.

Ennis, C.D. (1999). Creating a culturally relevant curriculum for disengaged girls. *Sport, Education, and Society,* 4, 31–49.

Ennis, C.D., & McCauley, M.T. (2002). Creating urban classroom communities worthy of trust. *Journal of Curriculum Studies,* 34, 149–172.

Ennis, C.D., Solmon, M.A., Satina, B., Loftus, S.J., Mensch, J., & McCauley, M.T. (1999). Creating a sense of family in urban schools using the "Sport for Peace" curriculum. *Research Quarterly for Exercise and Sport,* 70, 273–285.

Entzion, B.J. (1991). A child's view of fair play. *Strategies,* 4, 16–19.

Fisher, L.A., & Bredemeier, B.J.L. (2000). Caring about injustice: The moral self-perceptions of professional female bodybuilders. *Journal of Sport & Exercise Psychology,* 22, 327–344.

Fry, M.D., & Newton, M. (2003). Application of achievement goal theory in an urban youth tennis setting. *Journal of Applied Sport Psychology,* 15, 50–66.

Gano-Overway, L.A., Guivernau, M., Magyar, T.M., Waldron, J.J., & Ewing, M.E. (2005). Achievement goal perspectives, perceptions of the motivational climate, and sportspersonship: Individual and team effects. *Psychology of Sport and Exercise,* 6, 215–232.

Gardner, R.E., & Janelle, C.M. (2002). Legitimacy judgments of perceived aggression and assertion by contact and non-contact sport participants. *International Journal of Sport Psychology,* 33, 290–306.

Georgiadis, N. (1990). Does basketball have to be all W's and L's? An alternative program at a residential boys' home. *Journal of Physical Education, Recreation and Dance,* 61, 42–43.

Gibbons, S.L., & Ebbeck, V. (1997). The effect of different teaching strategies on the moral development of physical education students. *Journal of Teaching in Physical Education,* 17, 85–98.

Gibbons, S.L., Ebbeck, V., & Weiss, M.R. (1995). Fair Play for Kids: Effects on the moral development of children in physical education. *Research Quarterly for Exercise and Sport,* 66, 247–255.

Giebink, M.P., & McKenzie, T.C. (1985). Teaching sportsmanship in physical education and recreation: An analysis of intervention and generalization effects. *Journal of Teaching in Physical Education,* 4, 167–177.

Gilligan, C. (1982). *In a different voice: Psychological theory and women's development.* Cambridge, MA: Harvard University Press.

Gough, R. (1995). On reaching first base with a 'science' of moral development in sport: Problems with scientific objectivity and reductionism. *Journal of the Philosophy of Sport,* 22, 11–25.

Guivernau, M., & Duda, J.L. (2002). Moral atmosphere and athletic aggressive tendencies in young soccer players. *Journal of Moral Education,* 31, 67–85.

Haan, N. (1977). *Coping and defending: Processes of self-environment organization.* New York: Academic Press.

Haskins, M.J. (1960). Problem-solving test of sportsmanship. *Research Quarterly,* 31, 601–606.

Hellison, D. (1985). *Goals and strategies for physical education.* Champaign, IL: Human Kinetics.

Hellison, D. (1995). *Teaching responsibility through physical activity.* Champaign, IL: Human Kinetics.

Hellison, D., & Georgiadis, N. (1992). Teaching values through basketball. *Strategies,* 5, 5–8.

Hellison, D.R., Martinek, T.J., & Cutforth, N.J. (1996). Beyond violence prevention in inner city physical activity programs. *Peace and Conflict: Journal of Peace Psychology,* 2, 321–337.

Hellison, D., & Walsh, D. (2002). Responsibility-based youth programs evaluation: Investigating the investigations. *Quest,* 54, 292–307.

Hellison, D., & Wright, P. (2003). Retention in an urban extended day program: A process-based assessment. *Journal of Teaching in Physical Education,* 22, 369–381.

Horrocks, R.N. (1979). *The relationship of selected prosocial play behaviors in children to moral reasoning: Youth sports participation and perception of sportsmanship.* Unpublished doctoral dissertation, University of North Carolina at Greensboro.

Jantz, R.K. (1975). Moral thinking in male elementary pupils as reflected by perception of basketball rules. *Research Quarterly,* 46, 414–421.

Kavussanu, M. (2006). Motivational predictors of prosocial and antisocial behaviour in football. *Journal of Sports Sciences,* 24, 575–588.

Kavussanu, M., & Ntoumanis, N. (2003). Participation in sport and moral functioning: Does ego orientation mediate their relationship? *Journal of Sport & Exercise Psychology,* 25, 501–518.

Kavussanu, M., & Roberts, G.C. (2001). Moral functioning in sport: An achievement goal perspective. *Journal of Sport & Exercise Psychology,* 23, 37–54.

Kavussanu, M., Roberts, G.C., & Ntoumanis, N. (2002). Contextual influences on moral functioning of college basketball players. *The Sport Psychologist,* 16, 347–367.

Kleiber, D.A., & Roberts, G.C. (1981). The effects of sports experience in the development of social character: An exploratory investigation. *Journal of Sport Psychology,* 3, 114–122.

Knoppers, A., Zuidema, M., & Meyer, B.B. (1989). Playing to win or playing to play? *Sociology of Sport Journal,* 6, 70–76.

Kurtines, W.M., & Gewirtz, J.L. (1995). *Moral development: An introduction.* Hillsdale, NJ: Erlbaum.

Laparidis, K., Papaioannou, A., Vetakou, V., & Morou, A. (2003). Motivational climate, beliefs about the bases of success, and sportsmanship behaviors of professional basketball athletes. *Perceptual and Motor Skills,* 96(3, Part 2), 1141–1151.

Larson, R. (2000). Toward a psychology of positive youth development. *American Psychologist,* 55, 170–183.

Lemyre, P-N., Roberts, G.C., & Ommundsen, Y. (2002). Achievement goal orientations, perceived ability, and sportspersonship in youth soccer. *Journal of Applied Sport Psychology,* 14, 120–136.

Lerner, R.M., Almerigi, J.B., Theokas, C., & Lerner, J.V. (2005). Positive youth development: A view of the issues. *Journal of Early Adolescence,* 25, 10–16.

Lerner, R.M., Lerner, J.V., et al. (2005). Positive youth development, participation in community youth development programs, and community contributions of fifth-grade adolescents. *Journal of Early Adolescence,* 25, 17–71.

Levin, D.S., Smith, E.A., Caldwell, L.L., & Kimbrough, J. (1995). Violence and high school sports participation. *Pediatric Exercise Science,* 7, 379–388.

Loland, S. (2006). Morality, medicine, and meaning: Toward an integrated justification of physical education. *Quest,* 58, 60–70.

Long, T., Pantaléon, N., Bruant, G., & d'Arripe-Longueville, F. (2006). A qualitative study of moral reasoning of young elite athletes. *The Sport Psychologist,* 20, 330-347.

Loughead, T.M., & Leith, L.M. (2001). Hockey coaches' and players' perceptions of aggression and the aggressive behavior of players. *Journal of Sport Behavior,* 24, 394–407.

Martens, R. (1978). *Joy and sadness in children's sports.* Champaign, IL: Human Kinetics.

Martinek, T.J., & Hellison, D.R. (1997). Fostering resiliency in underserved youth through physical activity. *Quest,* 49, 34–49.

McAfee, R.A. (1955). Sportsmanship attitudes of sixth, seventh, and eighth grade boys. *Research Quarterly,* 26, 120.

McCloy, C.H. (1930). Character building through physical education. *Research Quarterly, 1*(3), 41–59.

Miller, B.W., Roberts, G.C., & Ommundsen, Y. (2004). Effect of motivational climate on sportspersonship among competitive youth male and female football players. *Scandinavian Journal of Medicine & Science in Sports, 16*, 193–202.

Miller, B.W., Roberts, G.C., & Ommundsen, Y. (2005). Effect of perceived motivational climate on moral functioning, team moral atmosphere perceptions, and the legitimacy of intentionally injurious acts among competitive youth football players. *Psychology of Sport and Exercise, 6*, 461–477.

Mugno, D.A., & Feltz, D.L. (1985). The social learning of aggression in youth football in the United States. *Canadian Journal of Applied Sport Sciences, 10*, 26–35.

Narváez, D., & Rest, J.R. (1995). The four components of acting morally. In W.M. Kurtines & J.L. Gewirtz (Eds.), *Moral development: An introduction* (pp. 385–399). Boston: Allyn & Bacon.

Nicholls, J.G. (1989). *The competitive ethos and democratic education.* Cambridge, MA: Harvard University Press.

Ommundsen, Y., Roberts, G.C., Lemyre, P.N., & Treasure, D. (2003). Perceived motivational climate in male youth soccer: Relations to social-moral functioning, sportspersonship and team norm perceptions. *Psychology of Sport and Exercise, 4*, 397–413.

Orlick, T.D. (1981). Positive socialization via cooperative games. *Developmental Psychology, 17*, 426–429.

Petitpas, A.J., Cornelius, A.E., Van Raalte, J.L., & Jones, T. (2005). A framework for planning youth sport programs that foster psychosocial development. *The Sport Psychologist, 19*, 63–80.

Petitpas, A.J., Van Raalte, J.L., Cornelius, A., & Presbrey, J. (2004). A life skills development program for high school student-athletes. *Journal of Primary Prevention, 24*, 325–334.

Priest, R.F., Krause, J.V., & Beach, J. (1999). Four-year changes in college athletes' ethical value choices in sports situations. *Research Quarterly for Exercise and Sport, 70*, 170–178.

Reed, A., & Aquino, K.F. (2003). Moral identity and the expanding circle of moral regard toward out-groups. *Journal of Personality and Social Psychology, 84*, 1270–1286.

Rest, J.R. (1984). The major components of morality. In W. Kurtines & J. Gewirtz (Eds.), *Morality, moral behavior, and moral development* (pp. 24–40). New York: Wiley.

Rest, J.R. (1986). *Moral development: Advances in research and theory.* New York: Praeger.

Romance, T.J. (1984). *A program to promote moral development through elementary school physical education.* Unpublished doctoral dissertation, University of Oregon, Eugene.

Romance, T.J., Weiss, M.R., & Bockoven, J. (1986). A program to promote moral development through elementary school physical education. *Journal of Teaching in Physical Education, 5*, 126–136.

Ryan, M.K., Williams, J.M., & Wimer, B. (1990). Athletic aggression: Perceived legitimacy and behavioral intentions in girls' high school basketball. *Journal of Sport & Exercise Psychology, 12*, 48–55.

Sage, L., Kavussanu, M., & Duda, J. (2006). Goal orientations and moral identity as predictors of prosocial and antisocial functioning in male association football players. *Journal of Sports Sciences, 24*, 455–466.

Sharpe, T., Brown, M., & Crider, K. (1995). The effects of sportsmanship curriculum intervention on generalized positive social behavior of urban elementary school students. *Journal of Applied Behavior Analysis, 28*, 401–416.

Sharpe, T., Crider, K., Vyhlidal, T., & Brown, M. (1996). Description and effects of prosocial instruction in an elementary physical education setting. *Education and Treatment of Children, 19*, 435–457.

Shields, D.L.L., & Bredemeier, B.J.L. (1995). *Character development and physical activity.* Champaign, IL: Human Kinetics.

Silva, J.M. (1983). The perceived legitimacy of rule violating behavior in sport. *Journal of Sport Psychology, 5*, 438–448.

Simmons, R. (2002). *Odd girl out: The hidden culture of aggression in girls.* New York: Harcourt.

Smith, M.D. (1974). Significant others' influence on the assaultive behavior of young hockey players. *International Review of Sport Sociology, 3-4*, 45–56.

Smith, M.D. (1975). The legitimation of violence: Hockey players' perceptions of their reference groups' sanctions for assault. *Canadian Review of Sociology and Anthropology, 12*, 72–80.

Smith, M.D. (1978). Social learning of violence in minor hockey. In F.L. Smoll & R.E. Smith (Eds.), *Psychological perspectives in youth sports* (pp. 91–106). Washington, DC: Hemisphere.

Smith, M.D. (1979). Towards an explanation of hockey violence: A reference other approach. *Canadian Journal of Sociology, 4*, 105–124.

Smith, M.D. (1988). Interpersonal sources of violence in hockey: The influence of parents, coaches, and teammates. In F.L. Smoll, R.A. Magill, & M.J. Ash (Eds.), *Children in sport* (pp. 301–313). Champaign, IL: Human Kinetics.

Solomon, G.B. (1997). Fair play in the gymnasium: Improving social skills among elementary school students. *Journal of Physical Education and Recreation, 68*, 22–25.

Solomon, G.B. (2004). A lifespan view of moral development in physical activity. In M.R. Weiss (Ed.), *Developmental sport and exercise psychology: A lifespan perspective* (pp. 453–474). Morgantown, WV: Fitness Information Technology.

Stephens, D.E. (2000). Predictors of likelihood to aggress in youth soccer: An examination of coed and all-girls teams. *Journal of Sport Behavior, 23*, 311–325.

Stephens, D.E. (2001). Predictors of aggressive tendencies in girls' basketball: An examination of beginning and advanced participants in a summer skills camp. *Research Quarterly for Exercise and Sport, 72*, 257–266.

Stephens, D.E., & Bredemeier, B.J.L. (1996). Moral atmosphere and judgments about aggression in girls' soccer: Relationships among moral and motivational variables. *Journal of Sport & Exercise Psychology, 18*, 158–173.

Stephens, D.E., Bredemeier, B.J.L., & Shields, D.L.L. (1997). Construction of a measure designed to assess players' descriptions and prescriptions for moral behavior in youth sport soccer. *International Journal of Sport Psychology, 28*, 370–390.

Stoll, S.K. (1999). Should character be measured? A reply to Professor Gough and the reductionist argument. *Journal of the Philosophy of Sport, 26*, 95–104.

Storch, E.A., Werner, N.E., & Storch, J.B. (2003). Relational aggression and psychosocial adjustment in intercollegiate athletes. *Journal of Sport Behavior, 26*, 155–167.

Stuart, M.E. (2003). Moral issues in sport: The child's perspective. *Research Quarterly for Exercise and Sport, 74*, 445–454.

Stuart, M.E., & Ebbeck, V. (1995). The influence of perceived social approval on moral development in youth sport. *Pediatric Exercise Science, 7*, 270–280.

Stuntz, C.P. (2005). *Social goal orientations in the physical domain: Links to moral functioning and psychosocial variables.* Unpublished doctoral dissertation, University of Virginia, Charlottesville.

Stuntz, C.P., & Weiss, M.R. (2003a). The influence of social goal orientations and peers on unsportsmanlike play. *Research Quarterly for Exercise and Sport, 74*, 421–435.

Stuntz, C.P., & Weiss, M.R. (2003b, October). *Beyond physical aggression: Alternative forms of aggression in sport.* Presentation given at the annual conference of Association for the Advancement of Applied Sport Psychology, Philadelphia.

Tod, D., & Hodge, K. (2001). Moral reasoning and achievement motivation in sport: A qualitative inquiry. *Journal of Sport Behavior, 24*, 307–327.

Tucker, L.W., & Parks, J.B. (2001). Effects of gender and sport type on intercollegiate athletes' perceptions of the legitimacy of aggressive behaviors in sport. *Sociology of Sport Journal, 18*, 403–413.

Turiel, E. (1998). The development of morality. In N. Eisenberg (Ed.), *Handbook of child psychology, Vol. 3: Social, emotional, and personality development* (pp. 863–932). New York: Wiley.

Underwood, M.K. (2003). *Social aggression among girls.* New York: Guilford.

Visek, A., & Watson, J. (2005). Ice hockey players' legitimacy of aggression and professionalization of attitudes. *The Sport Psychologist, 19,* 178–192.

Wandzilak, T., Carroll, T., & Ansorge, C.J. (1988). Values development through physical activity: Promoting sportsmanlike behaviors, perceptions, and moral reasoning. *Journal of Teaching in Physical Education, 8,* 13–23.

Webb, H. (1969). Professionalization of attitudes toward play among adolescents. In G. Kenyon (Ed.), *Aspects of contemporary sport sociology* (pp. 161–178). Chicago: Athletic Institute.

Weinstein, M.D., Smith, M.D., & Wiesenthal, D.L. (1995). Masculinity and hockey violence. *Sex Roles, 33,* 831–847.

Weiss, M.R. (2007, January). *'More than a game': Longitudinal effects of a life skills education program on positive youth development* (Year 2, 2006). Executive Report submitted to The First Tee National Home Office, St. Augustine, FL.

Weiss, M.R., with Bhalla, J.A., Price, M.S., Bolter, N.D., & Stuntz, C.P. (2006, October). *2005 research summary: Longitudinal effects of The First Tee life skills education programs on positive youth development.* St. Augustine, FL: The First Tee of the World Golf Foundation.

Weiss, M.R., & Bredemeier, B.J. (1986). Moral development. In V. Seefeldt (Ed.), *Physical activity and well-being* (pp. 373–390). Reston, VA: American Alliance for Health, Physical Education, Recreation and Dance.

Weiss, M.R., & Bredemeier, B.J. (1990). Moral development in sport. *Exercise and Sport Sciences Reviews, 18,* 331–378.

Weiss, M.R., & Gill, D.L. (2005). What goes around comes around: Re-emerging themes in sport and exercise psychology. *Research Quarterly for Exercise and Sport, 76*(2, Supplement), S71–S87.

Weiss, M.R., & Smith, A.L. (2002). Moral development in sport and physical activity: Theory, research, and intervention. In T.S. Horn (Ed.), *Advances in sport psychology* (2nd ed., pp. 243–280). Champaign, IL: Human Kinetics.

Weiss, M.R., & Stuntz, C.P. (2004). A little friendly competition: Peer relationships and psychosocial development in youth sport and physical activity contexts. In M.R. Weiss (Ed.), *Developmental sport and exercise psychology: A lifespan perspective* (pp. 165–196). Morgantown, WV: Fitness Information Technology.

White, S.H., & O'Brien, J.E. (1999). What is a hero? An exploratory study of students' conceptions of heroes. *Journal of Moral Education, 28,* 81–95.

Wiggins, D.K. (1996). A history of highly competitive sport for American children. In F.L. Smoll & R.E. Smith (Eds.), *Children and youth in sport: A biopsychosocial perspective* (pp. 15–30). Madison, WI: Brown & Benchmark.

CHAPTER 10

Bandura, A. (1977). Self-efficacy: Toward a unifying theory of behavioral change. *Psychological Review, 84,* 191–215.

Bandura, A. (1982). Self-efficacy mechanism in human agency. *American Psychologist, 37,* 122–147.

Bandura, A. (1986). *Social foundations of thought and action: A social cognitive theory.* Englewood Cliffs, NJ: Prentice-Hill.

Bandura, A. (1997). *Self-efficacy: The exercise of control.* New York: Freeman.

Bass, B.M. (1960). *Leadership, psychology, and organizational behavior.* New York: Harper.

Beauchamp, M.R., & Bray, S.R. (2001). Role ambiguity and role conflict within interdependent teams. *Small Group Research, 32,* 133–157.

Beauchamp, M.R., Bray, S.R., Eys, M.A., & Carron, A.V. (2002). Role ambiguity, role efficacy, and role performance: Multidimensional and mediational relationships within interdependent sport teams. *Group Dynamics: Theory, Research, and Practice, 6,* 229–242.

Beauchamp, M.R., Bray, S.R., Eys, M.A., & Carron, A.V. (2003). The effect of role ambiguity on competitive state anxiety. *Journal of Sport and Exercise Psychology, 25*(1), 77–92.

Bird, A.M., Foster, C.D., & Maruyama, G. (1980). Convergent and incremental effects of cohesion on attributions for self and team. *Journal of Sport Psychology, 2,* 181–194.

Bray, S.R., & Brawley, L.R. (2002). Role clarity, role efficacy, and role performance effectiveness. *Small Group Research, 33,* 245–265.

Bray, S.R., Brawley, L.R., & Carron, A.V. (2002). Efficacy for interdependent role functions: Evidence from the sport domain. *Small Group Research, 33,* 644–666.

Brawley, L.R., Carron, A.V., & Widmeyer, W.N. (1987). Assessing the cohesion of teams: Validity of the Group Environment Questionnaire. *Journal of Sport Psychology, 9,* 275–294.

Brawley, L.R., Carron, A.V., & Widmeyer, W.N. (1988). Exploring the relationship between cohesion and resistance to disruption. *Journal of Sport & Exercise Psychology, 10,* 199–213.

Brawley, L.R., Rejeski, W.J., & Lutes, L. (2000). A group-mediated cognitive-behavioral intervention for increasing adherence to physical activity in older adults. *Journal of Applied Biobehavioral Research, 5,* 47–65.

Brown, R. (1988). *Group processes: Dynamics within and between groups.* Oxford, United Kingdom: Blackwell.

Burke, S.M., Carron, A.V., Estabrooks, P.A., Hill, J.L., Loughead, T.M., Patterson, M.M., et al. (2005). Cohesion as shared beliefs in exercise classes. *Small Group Research, 36,* 267–288

Carron, A.V. (1982). Cohesiveness in sport groups: Interpretations and considerations. *Journal of Sport Psychology, 4,* 123–128.

Carron, A.V. (1988). *Group dynamics in sport.* London, ON: Spodym.

Carron, A.V., & Brawley, L.R. (2000). Cohesion: Conceptual and measurement issues. *Small Group Research, 31,* 89–106.

Carron, A.V., Brawley, L.R., Eys, M.A., Bray, S., Colman, M., Dorsch, K., et al. (2003). Do individual perceptions of group cohesion reflect shared beliefs? An empirical analysis. *Small Group Research, 34,* 468–496.

Carron, A.V., Brawley, L.R., & Widmeyer, W.N. (1990). The impact of group size in an exercise setting. *Journal of Sport & Exercise Psychology, 12,* 376–387.

Carron, A.V., Brawley, L.R., & Widmeyer, W.N. (1998). The measurement of cohesiveness in sport groups. In J.L. Duda (Ed.) *Advances in sport and exercise psychology measurement* (pp. 213–226). Morgantown, WV: Fitness Information Technology.

Carron, A.V., Brawley, L.R., & Widmeyer, W.N. (2002). Group dynamics. In T. Horn (Ed.), *Advances in sport psychology* (2nd ed., pp. 285–308). Champaign, IL: Human Kinetics.

Carron, A.V., Brawley, L.R., & Widmeyer, N.W. (2002). *The Group Environment Questionnaire: Test Manual (Electronic ONLINE & Text).* Morgantown, WV: Fitness Information Technology.

Carron, A.V., & Chelladurai, P. (1981). Cohesion as a factor in sport performance. *International Review of Sport Sociology, 16,* 21–41.

Carron, A.V., Colman, M.M., Wheeler, J., & Stevens, D. (2002). Cohesion and performance in sport: A meta-analysis. *Journal of Sport and Exercise Psychology, 24,* 168–188.

Carron, A.V., & Hausenblas, H.A. (1998). *Group dynamics in sport* (2nd.ed.). Morgantown, WV: Fitness Information Technology.

Carron, A.V., Hausenblas, H.A., & Eys, M.A. (in press). *Group dynamics in sport* (3rd ed.). Morgantown, WV: Fitness Information Technology.

Carron, A.V., Loughead, T.M., & Bray, S.R. (2005). The home advantage in sport competitions: The Courneya & Carron conceptual framework a decade later. *Journal of Sport Sciences, 23,* 395–407.

Carron, A.V., & Prapavessis, H. (1997). Self-presentation and group influence. *Small Group Research, 28,* 500–516.

Carron, A.V., & Spink, K.S. (1995). The group size-cohesion relationship in minimal groups. *Small Group Research, 26,* 86–105.

Carron, A.V., Spink, K.S., & Prapavessis, H. (1997). Team building and cohesiveness in the sport and exercise setting: Use of indirect interventions. *Journal of Applied Sport Psychology, 9,* 61–72.

Carron, A.V., Widmeyer, W.N., & Brawley, L.R. (1985). The development of an instrument to assess cohesion in sport teams: The Group Environment Questionnaire. *Journal of Sport Psychology, 7,* 244–266.

Carron, A.V., Widmeyer, W.N., & Brawley, L.R. (1988). Group cohesion and individual adherence to physical activity. *Journal of Sport & Exercise Psychology, 10,* 127–138.

Cartwright, D. (1972). Achieving change in people: Some applications of group dynamics theory. In E.P. Hollander & R.G. Hunt, *Classic contributions to social psychology* (pp. 352–361). New York: Oxford.

Cartwright, D., & Zander, A. (1968). *Group dynamics: Research and theory.* New York: Harper & Row.

Castellan, N.J. Jr. (1993). *Individual and group decision making: Current issues.* Hillsdale, NJ: Erlbaum.

Chelladurai, P. (1978). *A contingency model of leadership in athletics.* Unpublished doctoral dissertation, University of Waterloo, Waterloo, ON.

Cole, M. (1991). Conclusion. In L.B. Resnick, J.M. Levine, & S.D. Teasley (Eds.), *Perspectives on socially shared cognition* (pp. 399–417). Washington, DC: American Psychological Association.

Courneya, K.S., & Carron, A.V. (1992). The home advantage in sport competitions: A literature review. *Journal of Sport & Exercise Psychology, 14,* 28–39.

Dishman, R.K. (1994). *Advances in exercise adherence.* Champaign, IL: Human Kinetics.

Dion, K.R. (2000). Group cohesion: From "field of forces" to "multidimensional construct." *Group Dynamics: Theory, Research, and Practice, 4,* 7–26.

Doyle, Sir A.C. (1989). *The original illustrated 'Strand" Sherlock Holmes .* Ware, Hertfordshire, United Kingdom: Wordsworth.

Estabrooks, P.A., & Carron, A.V. (1999). Group cohesion in older adult exercisers: Prediction and intervention effects. *Journal of Behavioral Medicine, 22,* 575–588.

Estabrooks, P.A., & Carron, A.V. (2000). The Physical Activity Group Environment Questionnaire: An instrument for the assessment of cohesion in exercise classes. *Group Dynamics, 4,* 230–243.

Eys, M. A. (2000). Development of a measure of role ambiguity in sport. M.A. Thesis, University of Western Ontario, London, Ontario.

Eys, M.A., Carron, A.V., Beauchamp, M.R., & Bray, S.R. (2003a). Role ambiguity and athlete satisfaction. *Journal of Sport Sciences, 21,* 391–401.

Eys, M.A., Carron, A.V., Beauchamp, M.R., & Bray, S.R. (2003b). Role ambiguity in sport teams. *Journal of Sport and Exercise Psychology, 25*(4), 534–550.

Eys, M.A., Hardy, J., Carron, A.V., & Beauchamp, M.R. (2003). The relationship between task cohesion and competitive state anxiety. *Journal of Sport & Exercise Psychology, 25,* 66–76.

Feltz, D.L., Bandura, A., Albrecht, R.R., & Corcoran, J.P. (1988). *Perceived team efficacy in collegiate hockey.* Proceedings for the North American Society for the Psychology of Sport and Physical Activity.

Feltz, D.L., Corcoran, J.P., & Lirgg, C.D. (1989). *Relationships among team confidence, sport confidence and hockey performance.* Proceedings for the North American Society for the Psychology of Sport and Physical Activity.

Feltz, D.L., & Lirgg, C.D. (1998). Perceived team and player efficacy in hockey. *Journal of Applied Psychology, 83,* 557–564.

Fiedler, F.E. (1967). *A theory of leadership effectiveness.* New York: McGraw-Hill.

Florin, P., Giamartino, G.A., Kenny, D.A., & Wandersman, A. (1990). Levels of analysis and effects: Clarifying group influence and climate by separating individual and group effects. *Journal of Applied Social Psychology, 20,* 881–900.

Forsyth, D.R. (1983). *An introduction to group dynamics.* Belmont, CA: Wadsworth.

Frey, L.R. (1994). *Group communication in context: Studies of natural groups.* Hillsdale, NJ: Erlbaum.

Gardner, A., & Brawley, L.R. (2004, Nov.) *Moms in motion: Examining a short cognitive-behavioural physical activity intervention to influence exercise initiation.* Paper presented at the annual meeting of the Canadian Society for Psychomotor Learning and Sport Psychology, Saskatoon, SK.

Gill, D.L. (1979). The prediction of group motor performance from individual member ability. *Journal of Sport Psychology, 11,* 113–122.

Gossett, D., & Widmeyer, W.N. (1978, May). *Improving cohesion's prediction of performance outcome in sport.* Paper presented at the meeting of the North American Society for the Psychology of Sport and Physical Activity, Tallahassee, FL.

Granito, V.J., & Rainey, D.W. (1988). Differences in cohesion between high school and college football teams and starters and nonstarters. *Perceptual and Motor Skills, 66,* 471–477.

Gruber, J.J., & Gray, G.R. (1981). Factor patterns of variables influencing cohesiveness at various levels of basketball competition. *Research Quarterly for Exercise and Sport, 52,* 19–30.

Gruber, J.J., & Gray, G.R. (1982). Responses to forces influencing cohesion as a function of player status and level of male varsity basketball competition. *Research Quarterly for Exercise and Sport, 53,* 27–36.

Grusky, O. (1963). The effects of formal structure on managerial recruitment: A study of baseball organization. *Sociometry, 26,* 345–353.

Gully, S.M., Incalcaterra, K.A., Joshi, A., & Beaubien, J.M. (2002). A meta-analysis of team-efficacy, potency, and performance: Interdependence and level of analysis as moderators of observed relationships. *Journal of Applied Psychology, 87,* 819–832.

Hardy, C.J. (1989, June). Social loafing: Economizing individual effort during team performance. In L.R. Brawley (Chair), *Group size in physical activity: Psychological and behavioral impacts.* Symposium conducted at the meeting of the North American Society for the Psychology of Sport and Physical Activity, Kent, OH.

Hardy, J., Eys, M.A., & Carron, A.V. (2005). Exploring the potential disadvantages of high task cohesion in sport teams. *Small Group Research, 36,* 166–189.

Hare, P. (1992). *Groups, teams, and social interaction: Theories and applications.* New York: Praeger.

Harkins, S.G., Latané, B., & Williams, K. (1980). Social loafing: Allocating effort or taking it easy? *Journal of Experimental Social Psychology, 16,* 457–465.

Hinsz, V.B., Tindale, R.S., & Vollrath, D.A. (1997). The emerging conceptualisation of groups as information processors. *Psychological Bulletin, 121,* 43–64.

Ingham, A.G., Levinger, G., Graves, J., & Peckham, V. (1974). The Ringelmann Effect: Studies of group size and group performance. *Journal of Experimental Social Psychology, 10,* 371–384.

James, L.R., Demaree, R.G., & Wolf, G. (1984). Estimating within-group interrater reliability with and without response bias. *Journal of Applied Psychology, 69,* 85–98

Jowett, S., & Chaundy, V. (2004). An investigation into the impact of coach leadership and coach-athlete relationship on group cohesion. *Group Dynamics: Theory, Research, and Practice, 8,* 302–311.

Kahn, R.L., Wolfe, D.M., Quinn, R.P., Snoek, J.D., & Rosenthal, R.A. (1964). *Occupational stress: Studies in role conflict and role ambiguity.* New York: Wiley.

Karau, S J., & Williams, K.D. (1993). Social loafing: A meta-analytic review and theoretical integration. *Journal of Personality and Social Psychology, 65,* 681–706.

Kenny, D.A., & LaVoie, L. (1985). Separating individual and group effects. *Journal of Personality and Social Psychology, 48,* 339–348.

Kozlowski, S.W.J., & Hattrup, K., (1992). A disagreement about within-group agreement: Disentangling issues of consistency versus consensus. *Journal of Applied Psychology, 77,* 161–167.

Kozub, S.A. (1993). *Exploring the relationships among coaching behavior, team cohesion, and player leadership.* Unpublished doctoral dissertation, University of Houston, Houston, TX.

Kozub, S.A., & McDonnell, J.F. (2000). Exploring the relationship between cohesion and collective efficacy in rugby teams. *Journal of Sport Behavior, 23,* 120–129.

Kreft, I., & de Leeuw, J. (2002). *Introducing multilevel modeling.* Thousand Oaks, CA: Sage.

Landers, D.M., & Lüschen, G. (1974). Team performance outcome and cohesiveness of competitive co-acting groups. *International Review of Sport Sociology, 9,* 57–69.

Latané, B., Williams, K., & Harkins, S.J. (1979). Many hands make light the work: The cause and consequences of social loafing. *Journal of Experimental Social Psychology, 37*, 822–832.

Lee, H.K., Kim, B.H., & Lim, B.J. (1993). The influence of structural characteristics on team success in sport groups. *Korean Journal of Sport Science, 5*, 138–154.

Lewin, K. (1943). Forces behind food habits and methods of change. *Bulletin of the National Research Council, 108*, 35–65.

Loughead, T.M., & Carron, A.V. (2004). The mediating role of cohesion in the leader behavior-satisfaction relationship. *Psychology of Sport & Exercise, 5*, 355–371.

Loy, J.W., McPherson, B.D., & Kenyon, G. (1978). *Sport and social systems: A guide to the analysis, problems, and literature.* Reading, MA: Addison-Wesley.

Magyar, T.M., Feltz, D.L., & Simpson, I.P. (2004). Individual and crew level determinants of collective efficacy in rowing. *Journal of Sport and Exercise Psychology, 26*, 136–153.

Martens, R., Burton, D., Vealey, R.S., Bump, L.A., & Smith, D.E. (1990). The Competitive State Anxiety Inventory–2 (CSAI–2). In R. Martens, R.S. Vealey, & D. Burton, *Competitive anxiety in sport* (pp. 117–190). Champaign, IL: Human Kinetics.

McCullagh, P. (1987). Modeling similarity effects on motor performance. *Journal of Sport Psychology, 9*, 249–260.

McGrath, J.E. (1984). *Groups: Interaction and performance.* Englewood Cliffs, NJ: Prentice-Hall.

McKnight, P., Williams, J.M., & Widmeyer, W.N. (1991, October). *The effects of cohesion and identifiability on reducing the likelihood of social loafing.* Presented at the Association for the Advancement of Applied Sport Psychology Annual Conference, Savannah, GA.

Meichenbaum, D., & Turk, D. (1987). *Facilitating treatment adherence: A practitioner's guidebook.* New York: Plenum Press.

Mikalachki, A. (1969). *Group cohesion reconsidered.* London, ON: School of Business Administration, University of Western Ontario.

Moreland, R.L., & Levine, J.M. (1988). Group dynamics over time: Development and socialization in small groups. In J.E. McGrath (Ed.), *The social psychology of time: New perspectives* (pp. 151–181). Newbury Park, CA: Sage.

Moritz, S.E., & Watson, C.B. (1998). Levels of analysis issues in group psychology: Using efficacy as an example of a multilevel model. *Group Dynamics: Theory, Research, and Practice, 2*, 285–298.

Mudrack, P.E. (1989). Defining group cohesiveness: A legacy of confusion? *Small Group Behavior, 20*, 37–49.

Naylor, K., & Brawley, L.R. (1992, October). *Social loafing: Perceptions and implications.* Paper presented at the Joint Meeting of the Canadian Association of Sport Sciences and the Canadian Psychomotor learning and Sport Psychology Association Conference, Saskatoon, SK.

Paskevich, D.M. (1995). *Conceptual and measurement factors of collective efficacy in its relationship to cohesion and performance outcome.* Unpublished doctoral dissertation, University of Waterloo, Waterloo, ON.

Paskevich, D.M., Brawley, L.R., Dorsch, L.R., & Widmeyer, W.N. (1996). Implications of individual and group level analyses applied to the study of collective efficacy and cohesion. *Journal of Applied Sport Psychology, 7*(Suppl.), S95.

Paskevich, D.M., Brawley, L.R., Dorsch, K.D., & Widmeyer, W.N. (1999). Relationships between collective efficacy and team cohesion: Conceptual and measurement factors. *Group Dynamics: Theory, Research, and Practice, 3*, 210–222.

Paskevich, D.M., Estabrooks, P., Brawley, L.R., & Carron, A.V. (2000). Advances in cohesion research: Issues, correlates and new directions. In R.N. Singer & H. Hausenblas (Eds.), *The international handbook of research on sport psychology* (pp. 472–494), New York: Wiley.

Pollard, R. (1986). Home advantage in soccer: A retrospective analysis. *Journal of Sport Sciences, 4*, 237–248.

Prapavessis, H., & Carron, A.V. (1996). The effect of group cohesion on competitive state anxiety. *Journal of Sport & Exercise Psychology, 18*, 64–74.

Prapavessis, H., & Carron, A.V. (1997). Cohesion and work output. *Small Group Research, 28*, 294–301.

Prussia, G.E., & Kinicki, A.J. (1996). A motivational investigation of group effectiveness using social cognitive theory. *Journal of Applied Psychology, 81*, 187–198.

Raudenbush, S.W., & Bryk, A.S. (2002). *Hierarchical linear models: Applications and data analysis methods* (2nd ed.). Thousand Oaks, CA: Sage.

Rejeski, W.J., Brawley, L.R., Ambrosius, W.T., Brubaker, P.H., Focht, B.C., Foy, C.G., et al. (2003). Older adults with chronic disease: The benefits of group-mediated counseling in the promotion of physically active lifestyles. *Health Psychology, 22*, 414–423.

Resnick, L.B., Levine, J.M., & Teasley, S.D. (1991). *Perspectives on socially shared cognition.* Washington, DC: American Psychological Association.

Rosen, N. (1989). *Groups make a difference.* Hillsdale, NJ: Erlbaum.

Schafer, W. (1966, October). *The social structure of sport groups.* Paper presented at the First International Symposium on the Sociology of Sport, Koln, West Germany.

Schlenker, B.R., & Miller, R.S. (1977). Egocentricism in groups: Self-serving bias or logical information processing. *Journal of Personality and Social Psychology, 35*, 755–764.

Shaw, M.E. (1981). *Group dynamics: The psychology of small group behavior* (3rd ed.). New York: McGraw-Hill.

Shaw, M.E., & Costanzo, P.R. (1982). *Theories of social psychology* (2nd ed.). New York: McGraw-Hill.

Sherif, M., & Sherif, C.W. (1956). *On outline of social psychology* (Rev. ed.). New York: Harper & Row.

Sherif, M., & Sherif, C.W. (1969). *Social psychology* (Rev. ed.) New York: Harper & Row.

Spink, K.S. (1990). Group cohesion and collective efficacy of volleyball teams. *Journal of Sport & Exercise Psychology, 12*, 301–311.

Spink, K.S. (1995). Cohesion and intention to participate of female sport team athletes. *Journal of Sport & Exercise Psychology, 17*, 416–427.

Spink, K.S. (1998). Mediational effects of social cohesion on the leadership-intention to return relationship in sport. *Group Dynamics, 2*, 92–100.

Spink, K.S., & Carron, A.V. (1992). Group cohesion and adherence in exercise classes. *Journal of Sport & Exercise Psychology, 14*, 78–86.

Spink, K.S., & Carron, A.V. (1993). The effects of team building on the adherence patterns of female exercise participants. *Journal of Sport & Exercise Psychology, 15*, 39–49.

Spink, K.S., & Carron, A.V. (1994). Group cohesion effects in exercise groups. *Small Group Research, 25*, 26–42.

Spink, K.S., Nickel, D., Wilson, K., & Odnokon, P. (in press). Examining the relationship between task cohesion and team task satisfaction in elite ice hockey players: A multilevel approach. *Small Group Research.*

Spink, K.S., & Odnokon, P. (2001). Examining the effect of team cohesion on male ice hockey players' intention to return. *Journal of Sport & Exercise Psychology, 23*, S33.

Steiner, I.D. (1972). *Group process and productivity.* New York: Academic Press.

Turner, M.E. (2001). *Groups at work: Theory and research.* Mahwah, NJ: Erlbaum.

Van Bergen, A., & Koekebakker, J. (1959). "Group cohesiveness" in laboratory experiments. *Acta Psychologica, 16*, 81–98.

Watson, C.B., Chemers, M.M., & Preiser, N. (2001). Collective efficacy: A multilevel analysis. *Personality and Social Psychology, 27*, 1057–1068.

Watson, J.D., Martin Ginis, K.A., & Spink, K.S. (2004). Team building in an exercise class for the elderly. *Activities, Adapation, & Aging, 28*, 35–47.

Weiner, B. (1986). *An attributional theory of motivation and emotion.* New York: Springer Verlag..

Westre, K.R., & Weiss, M.R. (1991). The relationship between perceived coaching behaviors and group cohesion in high school football teams. *The Sport Psychologist, 5*, 41–54.

Widmeyer, W.N., Brawley, L.R., & Carron, A.V. (1985). *The measurement of cohesion in sport teams: The Group Environment Questionnaire.* London, ON: Sports Dynamics.

Widmeyer, W.N., Brawley, L.R., & Carron, A.V. (1990). The effects of group size in sport. *Journal of Sport & Exercise Psychology, 12*, 177–190.

Widmeyer, W.N., Brawley, L.R., & Carron, A.V. (1992). Group dynamics in sport. In T. Horn (Ed.), *Advances in sport psychology* (pp. 163–180), Champaign, IL: Human Kinetics.

Widmeyer, W.N., & Williams, J.M. (1991). Predicting cohesion in a coacting sport. *Small Group Research, 22,* 548–570.

Williams, J.M., & Hacker, C. (1982). Causal relationships among cohesion, satisfaction, and performance in women's intercollegiate field hockey teams. *Journal of Sport Psychology, 4,* 324–337.

Witte, E.H., & Davis, J.H. (1996). *Understanding group behavior: Consensual action by small groups* (Vol. I). Mahwah, NJ: Erlbaum.

Yukelson, D., Weinberg, R., & Jackson, A. (1984). A multidimensional group cohesion instrument for intercollegiate basketball. *Journal of Sport Psychology, 6,* 103–117.

Zaccaro, S.J., Blair, V., Peterson, C., & Zazanis, M. (1995). Collective efficacy. In J. Maddux (1995), *Self-efficacy, adaptation, and adjustment* (pp. 305–328). New York: Plenum.

Zander, A. (1979). The psychology of group processes. *Annual Review of Psychology, 30,* 417–451.

Zanna, M.P., & Fazio, R.H. (1982). The attitude-behavior relation: Moving toward a third generation of research. In M.P. Zanna, E.T. Higgins, & C.P. Herman (Eds.), *Consistency in social behavior: The Ontario symposium* (Vol. 2, pp. 283–301). Hillsdale, NJ: Erlbaum.

CHAPTER 11

Abraham, A., & Collins, D. (1998). Examining and extending research in coach development. *Quest, 50,* 59–79.

Allen, J.B., & Howe, B. (1998). Player ability, coach feedback, and female adolescent athletes' perceived competence and satisfaction. *Journal of Sport and Exercise Psychology, 20,* 280–299.

Ames, C. (1992a). Classrooms: Goals, structures, and student motivation. *Journal of Educational Psychology, 84,* 261–271.

Ames, C. (1992b). Achievement goals, motivational climate, and motivational processes. In G.C. Roberts (Ed.), *Motivation in sport and exercise* (pp. 161–176). Champaign, IL: Human Kinetics.

Amorose, A.J., & Horn, T.S. (1999). [An examination of athletes' perceptions of their coaches' behavior as a function of collegiate competitive level and number of available scholarships.] Unpublished raw data.

Amorose, A.J., & Horn, T.S. (2000). Intrinsic motivation: Relationships with collegiate athletes' gender, scholarship status, and perceptions of their coaches' behavior. *Journal of Sport and Exercise Psychology, 22,* 63–84.

Amorose, A.J., & Horn, T.S. (2001). Pre- to post-season changes in the intrinsic motivation of first year college athletes: Relationships with coaching behavior and scholarship status. *Journal of Applied Sport Psychology, 13,* 355–373.

Amorose, A.J., & Smith, P.J.K. (2003). Feedback as a source of physical competence information: Effects of age, experience, and type of feedback. *Journal of Sport and Exercise Psychology, 25,* 341–359.

Amorose, A.J., & Weiss, M.R. (1998). Coaching feedback as a source of information about perceptions of ability: A developmental examination. *Journal of Sport and Exercise Psychology, 20,* 395–420.

Avolio, B.J., & Bass, B.M. (2004). *Multifactor Leadership Questionnaire: Manual and Sampler Set* (3rd ed.). Redwood City, CA: Mind Garden.

Balaguer, I., Duda, J.L., Atienza, F.L., & Mayo, C. (2002). Situational and dispositional goals as predictors of perceptions of individual and team improvement, satisfaction and coach ratings among elite female handball teams. *Psychology of Sport and Exercise, 3,* 292–308.

Bandura, A. (1986). *Social foundation of thought and action: A social cognitive theory.* Englewood Cliffs, NJ: Prentice-Hall.

Bandura, A. (1997). *Self-efficacy: The exercise of control.* New York: Freeman.

Barnett, N.P., Smoll, F.L., & Smith, R.E. (1992). Effects of enhancing coach-athlete relationships on youth sport attrition. *The Sport Psychologist, 6,* 111–127.

Barrow, J. (1977). The variables of leadership. A review and conceptual framework. *Academy of Management Review, 2,* 231–251.

Bass, B.M. (1999). Two decades of research and development in transformational leadership. *European Journal of Work and Organizational Psychology, 8,* 9–32.

Beam, J.W., Serwatka, T.S., & Wilson, W.J. (2004). Preferred leadership of NCAA Division I and II intercollegiate student-athletes. *Journal of Sport Behavior, 27,* 3–17.

Beauchamp, M.R., Bray, S.R., Eys, M.A., & Carron, A.V. (2003). The effect of role ambiguity on competitive state anxiety. *Journal of Sport and Exercise Psychology, 25,* 77–92.

Becker, A.J., & Solomon, G.B. (2005). Expectancy information and coach effectiveness in intercollegiate basketball. *The Sport Psychologist, 19,* 251–266.

Black, S.J., & Weiss, M.R. (1992). The relationship among perceived coaching behaviors, perceptions of ability, and motivation in competitive age-group swimmers. *Journal of Sport and Exercise Psychology, 14,* 309–325.

Bloom, G.A., Crumpton, R., & Anderson, J.E. (1999). A systematic observation study of the teaching behaviors of an expert basketball coach. *The Sport Psychologist, 13,* 157–170.

Bloom, G.A., Durand-Bush, & Salmela, J. (1997). Pre- and post-competition routines of expert coaches of team sports. *The Sport Psychologist, 11,* 127–141.

Bloom, G.A., Durand-Bush, N., Schinke, R.S., & Salmela, J.H. (1998). The influence of mentoring in the development of coaches and athletes. *International Journal of Sport Psychology, 29,* 267–281.

Bloom, G.A., Stevens, D.E., & Wickwire, T.L. (2003). Expert coaches' perceptions of team building. *Journal of Applied Sport Psychology, 15,* 129–143.

Boixados, M., Cruz, J., Torregrosa, M., & Valiente, L. (2004). Relationships among motivational climate, satisfaction, perceived ability, and fair play attitudes in young soccer players. *Journal of Applied Sport Psychology, 16,* 301–317.

Brewer, C.J., & Jones, R.L. (2002). A five-stage process for establishing contextually valid systematic observation instruments: The case of rugby union. *The Sport Psychologist, 16,* 138–159.

Briere, N.M., Vallerand, R.J., Blais, M.R., & Pelletier, L.G. (1995). On the development and validation of the French form of the Sport Motivation Scale. *International Journal of Sport Psychology, 26,* 465–489.

Brooks, D., & Althouse, R. (2000). *Racism in college athletes: The African-American athlete's experience* (2nd ed.). Morgantown, WV: Fitness Information Technology.

Brophy, J.A. (1983). Research on the self-fulfilling prophecy and teacher expectations. *Journal of Educational Psychology, 75,* 631–661.

Butler, R. (2000). Making judgments about ability: The role of implicit theories of ability in moderating inferences from temporal and social comparison information. *Journal of Personality and Social Psychology, 78,* 965–978.

Cervello, E., Rosa, F.J.S., Calvo, T.G., Jimenez, R., & Iglesias, D. (2007). Young tennis players' competitive task involvement and performance: The role of goal orientations, contextual motivational climate, and coach-initiated motivational climate. *Journal of Applied Sport Psychology, 19,* 304-321.

Charbonneau, D., Barling, J., & Kelloway, E.K. (2001). Transformational leadership and sports performance: The mediating role of intrinsic motivation. *Journal of Applied Social Psychology, 31,* 1521–1534.

Chaumeton, N., & Duda, J. (1988). Is it how you play the game or whether you win or lose? The effect of competitive level and situation on coaching behaviors. *Journal of Sport Behavior, 11,* 157–174.

Chelladurai, P. (1978). *A contingency model of leadership in athletics.* Unpublished doctoral dissertation, University of Waterloo, Waterloo, ON.

Chelladurai, P. (1990). Leadership in sports: A review. *International Journal of Sport Psychology, 21,* 328–354.

Chelladurai, P. (2007). Leadership in sports. In G. Tenenbaum & R.C. Eklund (Eds.), *Handbook of sport psychology* (3rd ed.) (pp. 113-135). Morgantown, WV: Fitness Information Technology.

Chelladurai, P., & Arnott, M. (1985). Decision styles in coaching: Preferences of basketball players. *Research Quarterly for Exercise and Sport, 56,* 15–24.

Chelladurai, P., Imamura, H., Yamaguchi, Y., Oinuma, Y., & Miyauchi, T. (1988). Sport leadership in a cross-national setting: The case of Japanese and Canadian university athletes. *Journal of Sport and Exercise Psychology, 10*, 374–389.

Chelladurai, P., & Quek, C.B. (1991). Decision style choices of high school basketball coaches: The effects of situational and coach characteristics. *Journal of Sport Behavior, 18*, 91–108.

Chelladurai, P., & Riemer, H.A. (1998). In J.L. Duda (Ed.), *Advances in sport and exercise psychology* (pp. 227–253). Morgantown, WV: Fitness Information Technology.

Chelladurai, P., & Saleh, S. (1978). Preferred leadership in sports. *Canadian Journal of Applied Sport Sciences, 3*, 85–92.

Chelladurai, P., & Saleh, S. (1980). Dimensions of leader behavior in sports: Development of a leadership scale. *Journal of Sport Psychology, 2*, 34–45.

Coakley, J. (1994). Race and ethnicity. In J. Coakley, *Sport in society: Issues and controversies* (5th ed., pp. 239–273). St. Louis, MO: Mosby-Yearbook.

Coatsworth, J.D., & Conroy, D.E. (2006). Enhancing the self-esteem of youth swimmers through coach training: Gender and age effects. *Psychology of Sport and Exercise, 7*, 173–192.

Conroy, D.E., & Coatsworth, J.D. (2004). The effects of coach training on fear of failure in youth swimmers: A latent growth curve analysis from a randomized controlled trial. *Applied Developmental Psychology, 25*, 193–214.

Conroy, D.E., Kaye, M.P., & Coatsworth, J.D. (2006). Coaching climates and the destructive effects of mastery-avoidance achievement goals on situational motivation. *Journal of Sport and Exercise Psychology, 28*, 69–92.

Cote, J., & Salmela, J.H. (1996). The organizational tasks of high-performance gymnastic coaches. *The Sport Psychologist, 10*, 247–260.

Cote, J., Salmela, J.H., & Russell, S. (1995). The knowledge of high-performance gymnastic coaches: Competition and training considerations. *The Sport Psychologist, 9*, 76–95.

Cote, J., Salmela, J., Trudel, P., Baria, A., & Russell, S. (1995). The coaching model: A grounded assessment of expert gymnastic coaches' knowledge. *Journal of Sport and Exercise Psychology, 17*, 1–17.

Cote, J., Yardley, J., Hay, J., Sedgwick, W., & Baker, J. (1999). An exploratory examination of the Coaching Behaviour Scale for Sport. *Avante, 5*, 82–92.

Crocker, P.R.E. (1990). Facial and verbal congruency: Effects on perceived verbal and emotional feedback. *Canadian Journal of Sport Science, 15*, 17–22.

Cumming, S.P., Smith, R.E., & Smoll, F.L. (2006). Athlete-perceived coaching behaviors: Relating two measurement traditions. *Journal of Sport and Exercise Psychology, 28*, 205–213.

Cumming, S.P., Smoll, F.L., Smith, R.E., & Grossbard, J.R. (2007). Is winning everything? The relative contributions of motivational climate and won-lost percentage in youth sports. *Journal of Applied Sport Psychology, 19*, 322-336.

Cunningham, G.B. (2004). Strategies for transforming the possible negative effects of group diversity. *Quest, 56*, 421–438.

Cury, F., Famose, J.P., & Sarrazin, P. (1997). Achievement goal theory and active search for information in a sport task. In R. Lidor & M. Bar-Eli (Eds.), *Innovations in sport psychology: Linking theory and practice. Proceedings of the IX World Congress in Sport Psychology: Part I* (pp. 218–220). Netanya, Israel: Ministry of Education, Culture, and Sport.

Cushion, C.J., & Jones, R.L. (2001). A systematic observation of professional top-level youth soccer coaches. *Journal of Sport Behavior, 24*, 354–377.

d'Arripe-Longueville, F., Fournier, J.F., & Dubois, A. (1998). The perceived effectiveness of interactions between expert French judo coaches and elite female athletes. *The Sport Psychologist, 12*, 317–332.

d'Arripe-Longueville, F., Saury, J., Fournier, J., & Durand, M. (2001). Coach-athlete interaction during elite archery competitions: An application of methodological frameworks used in ergonomics research to sport psychology. *Journal of Applied Sport Psychology, 13*, 275–299.

Darst, P.W., Zakrajsek, D.B., & Mancini, V.H. (Eds.) (1989). *Analyzing*

Physical Education and Sport Instruction (2nd ed.). Champaign, IL: Human Kinetics.

Deci, E.L., Koestner, R., & Ryan, R.M. (1999). A meta-analytic review of experiments examining the effects of extrinsic rewards on intrinsic motivation. *Psychological Bulletin, 125*, 627–668.

Deci, E.L., & Ryan, R.M. (1985). *Intrinsic motivation and self-determination in human behavior.* New York: Plenum.

Duda, J.L. (2001). Achievement goal research in sport: Pushing the boundaries and clarifying some misunderstandings. In G.C. Roberts (Ed.) *Advances in motivation in sport and exercise* (pp. 129–182). Champaign, IL: Human Kinetics.

Duda, J.L., Balaguer, I., Moreno, Y., & Crespo, M. (October, 2001). The relationship of the motivational climate and goal orientations to burnout among junior elite tennis players. *AAASP 2001 Conference Proceedings* (p. 70). Denton, TX: RonJon.

Duda, J.L., & Kim, M.S. (1997). Perceptions of the motivational climate, psychological characteristics and attitudes toward eating among young female gymnasts. *Journal of Sport and Exercise Psychology, 19* (Suppl.), S48.

Duda, J.L., & Whitehead, J. (1998). Measurement of goal perspectives in the physical domain. In J.L. Duda (Ed.), *Advances in sport and exercise psychology measurement* (pp. 21–48). Morgantown, WV: Fitness Information Technology.

Dweck, C.S. (1986). Motivational processes affecting learning. *American Psychologist, 41*, 1040–1048.

Dweck, C.S. (1999). *Self-theories: Their role in motivation, personality, and development.* Philadelphia: Psychology Press.

Dweck, C.S., Chiu, C., & Hong, Y. (1995). Implicit theories and their role in judgments and reactions: A world from two perspectives. *Psychological Inquiry, 6*, 267–285.

Eccles, J.S. (2005). Subjective task value and the Eccles et al. model of achievement-related choices. In A.J. Elliott & C.S. Dweck (Eds.), *Handbook of competence and motivation* (pp. 105–121). New York: Guilford Press.

Eccles, J.S., Wigfield, A.W., & Schiefele, U. (1998). Motivation to succeed. In W. Damon (Series Ed.) & N. Eisenberg (Vol. Ed.), *Handbook of child psychology: Vol. 3. Social, emotional, and personality development* (5th ed., pp. 1017–1095). New York: Wiley.

Eccles, D.W., & Tenenbaum, G. (2004). Why an expert team is more than a team of experts: A social-cognitive conceptualization of team coordination and communication in sport. *Journal of Sport and Exercise Psychology, 26*, 542–560.

Elliot, A.J. (1999). Approach and avoidance motivation and achievement goals. *Educational Psychologist, 34*, 169–189.

Eys, M.A., Carron, A.V., Bray, S.R., & Beauchamp, M.R. (2005). The relationship between role ambiguity and intention to return the following season. *Journal of Applied Sport Psychology, 17*, 255–261.

Feltz, D.L., Chase, M.A., Moritz, S.E., & Sullivan, P.J. (1999). A conceptual model of coaching efficacy: Preliminary investigation and instrument development. *Journal of Educational Psychology, 91*, 765–776.

Franks, I.M., Johnson, R.B., Sinclair, G.D. (1988). The development of a computerized coaching analysis system for recording behavior in sporting environments. *Journal of Teaching in Physical Education, 8*, 23–32.

Frederick, C.M., & Morrison, C.S. (1999). Collegiate coaches: An examination of motivational style and its relationship to decision making and personality. *Journal of Sport Behavior, 22*, 221–233.

Fry, M.D., & Duda, J.L. (1997). A developmental examination of children's understanding of effort and ability in the physical and academic domains. *Research Quarterly for Exercise and Sport, 68*, 331–344.

Fry, M.D., & Newton, M. (2003). Application of achievement goal theory in an urban youth tennis setting. *Journal of Applied Sport Psychology, 15*, 50–66.

Gagne, M., Ryan, R.M., & Bargmann, K. (2003). Autonomy support and need satisfaction in the motivation and well-being of gymnasts. *Journal of Applied Sport Psychology, 15*, 372–390.

Gallimore, R., & Tharp, P. (2004). What a coach can teach a teacher, 1975–2004: Reflections and reanalysis of John Wooden's teaching practices. *The Sport Psychologist, 18*, 119–137.

Gano-Overway, L.A., Guivernau, M., Magyar, M., Waldron, J.J., & Ewing, M.E. (2005). Achievement goal perspectives, perceptions of the motivational climate, and sportspersonship: Individual and team effects. *Psychology of Sport and Exercise, 6*, 215–232.

Gernigon, C., d'Arripe-Longueville, F., Delignieres, D., & Ninot, G. (2004). A dynamical systems perspective on goal involvement states in sport. *Journal of Sport and Exercise Psychology, 26*, 572–596.

Gilbert, W.D., Cote, J., & Mallett, C. (2006). Developmental paths and activities of successful sport coaches. *International Journal of Sports Sciences and Coaching, 1* (1), 69-76.

Gilbert, W.D., & Trudel, P. (2001). Learning to coach through experience: Reflection in model youth sport coaches. *Journal of Teaching in Physical Education, 21*, 16–34.

Gilbert, W.D., & Trudel, P. (2004a). Role of the coach: How model youth team sport coaches frame their roles. *The Sport Psychologist, 18*, 21–43.

Gilbert, W.D., & Trudel, P. (2004b). Analysis of coaching science research published from 1970–2001. *Research Quarterly for Exercise and Sport, 75*, 388–399.

Gilbert, W.D., Trudel, P., & Haughian, L.P. (1999). Interactive decision making factors considered by coaches of youth ice hockey during games. *Journal of Teaching in Physical Education, 18*, 290–311.

Gould, D., Collins, K., Lauer, L., & Chung, Y. (2007). Coaching life skills through football: A study of award winning high school coaches. *Journal of Applied Sport Psychology, 19*, 16-37.

Gould, D., Guinan, D., Greenleaf, C., & Chung, Y. (2002). A survey of United States Olympic coaches: Variables perceived to have influenced athlete performances and coach effectiveness. *The Sport Psychologist, 16*, 229–250.

Griffin, P. (1998). *Strong women, deep closets: Lesbians and homophobia in sport.* Champaign, IL: Human Kinetics.

Halliburton, A.L., & Weiss, M.R. (2002). Sources of competence information and perceived motivational climate among adolescent female gymnasts varying in skill level. *Journal of Sport and Exercise Psychology, 24*, 396–419.

Hardin, B., & Bennett, G. (2002). The instructional attributes of a successful college baseball coach. *Applied Research in Coaching and Athletics Annual, 17*, 43–62.

Harris, M., & Rosenthal, R. (1985). Mediation of interpersonal expectancy effects: 31 meta-analyses. *Psychological Bulletin, 97*, 363–386.

Harry, J. (1995). Sports ideology, attitudes toward women, and anti-homosexual attitudes. *Sex Roles, 32*, 109–116.

Harter, S. (1981). A model of intrinsic mastery motivation in children: Individual differences and developmental change. In W.A. Collins (Ed.), *Minnesota Symposium on Child Psychology* (Vol. 14, pp. 215–255). Hillsdale, NJ: Erlbaum.

Harter, S. (1999). *The construction of the self: A developmental perspective.* New York: Guilford Press.

Harwood, C.G., Smith, J., & Treasure, D.C. (2005, August). *Motivational climate within individual sports: Initial developments of a multidimensional measurement tool.* Paper presented at the World Congress of Sport Psychology. Sydney, Australia.

Harwood, C., & Swain, A. (2002). The development and activation of achievement goals within tennis: II. A player, parent, and coach intervention. *The Sport Psychologist, 16*, 111–137.

Henderlong, J., & Lepper, M.R. (2002). The effects of praise on children's intrinsic motivation: A review and synthesis. *Psychological Bulletin, 128*, 774–795.

Heuze, J., Sarrazin, P., Masiero, M., Raimbault, N., & Thomas, J. (2006). The relationships of perceived motivational climate to cohesion and collective efficacy in elite female teams. *Journal of Applied Sport Psychology, 18*, 201–218.

Hollembeak, J., & Amorose, A.J. (2005). Perceived coaching behaviors and college athletes' intrinsic motivation: A test of self-determination theory. *Journal of Applied Sport Psychology, 17*, 20–36.

Horn, T.S. (1984). Expectancy effects in the interscholastic athletic setting: Methodological considerations. *Journal of Sport Psychology, 7*, 60–76.

Horn, T.S. (1985). Coaches' feedback and changes in children's perceptions of their physical competence. *Journal of Educational Psychology, 77*, 174–186.

Horn, T.S. (1987). The influence of teacher-coach behavior on the psychological development of children. In D. Gould & M.R. Weiss (Eds.), *Advances in pediatric sport sciences. Vol. 2: Behavioral issues* (pp. 121–142). Champaign, IL: Human Kinetics.

Horn, T.S., & Harris, A. (2002). Perceived competence in young athletes: Research findings and recommendations for coaches and parents. In F.L. Smoll & R.E. Smith (Eds.), *Children and youth in sport: A biopsychosocial perspective* (2nd ed., pp. 435–464). Dubuque, IA: Kendall/Hunt.

Horn, T.S., Lox, C.L., & Labrador, F. (2006). The self-fulfilling prophecy theory: When coaches' expectations become reality. In J.M. Williams (Ed.), *Applied sport psychology: Personal growth to peak performance* (5th ed., pp. 82–108). New York: McGraw-Hill.

Jambor, E.A., & Zhang, J.J. (1997). Investigating leadership, gender, and coaching level using the Revised Leadership for Sport Scale. *Journal of Sport Behavior, 20*, 313–322.

Jordan, J.V., Kaplan, A.G., Miller, J.B., Stiver, I.P., & Surrey, J.L. (1991). *Women's growth in connections: Writings from the Stone Center.* New York: Guilford Press.

Jowett, S. (2005). On repairing and enhancing the coach-athlete relationship. In S. Jowett & M.. Jones (Eds.), *The psychology of coaching: Sport and exercise psychology division* (pp. 14–26). Leicester, United Kingdom: British Psychological Society.

Jowett, S. (2006). Interpersonal and structural features of Greek coach-athlete dyads performing in individual sports. *Journal of Applied Sport Psychology, 18*, 69–81.

Jowett, S., & Chaundry, V. (2004). An investigation into the impact of coach leadership and coach-athlete relationship on group cohesion. *Group Dynamics: Theory, Research, and Practice, 8*, 302–311.

Jowett, S., & Cockerill, I.M. (2002). Incompatibility in the coach-athlete relationship. In I.M. Cockerill (Ed.), *Solutions in sport psychology* (pp. 16–31). London: Thompson Learning.

Jowett, S., & Cockerill, I.M. (2003). Olympic medallists' perspective of the athlete-coach relationship. *Psychology of Sport and Exercise, 4*, 313–331.

Jowett, S., & Meek, G.A. (2000). The coach-athlete relationship in married couples: An exploratory content analysis. *The Sport Psychologist, 14*, 157–175.

Jowett, S., & Ntoumanis, N. (2003). The Greek Coach-Athlete Relationship Questionnaire (GrCART-Q): Scale development and validation. *International Journal of Sport Psychology, 34*, 101–124.

Jussim, L., Eccles, J., & Madon, S. (1996). Social perception, social stereotypes, and teacher expectations: Accuracy and the quest for the powerful self-fulfilling prophecy. In M.P. Zanna (Ed.), *Advances in experimental social psychology* (Vol. 28, pp. 281–388). San Diego, CA: Academic Press.

Kavussanu, M., & Spray, C.M. (2006). Contextual influences on moral functioning of male youth footballers. *The Sport Psychologist, 20*, 1–23.

Kenow, L.J., & Williams, J.M. (1992). Relationship between anxiety, self-confidence, and evaluation of coaching behaviors. *The Sport Psychologist, 6*, 344–357.

Kenow, L.M., & Williams, J.M. (1999). Coach-athlete compatibility and athletes' perceptions of coaching behaviors. *Journal of Sport Behavior, 22*, 251–259.

Kerr, G., Berman, E., & DeSouza, M.J. (2006). Disordered eating in women's gymnastics: Perspectives of athletes, coaches, parents, and judges. *Journal of Applied Sport Psychology, 18*, 28–43.

Kilty, K. (2006). Women in coaching. *The Sport Psychologist, 20*, 222–234.

Kowall, J., & Fortier, M.S. (2000). Testing relationships from the hierarchical model of intrinsic and extrinsic motivation using flow as a motivational consequence. *Research Quarterly for Exercise and Sport, 2*, 171–181.

Krane, V. (1996). Lesbians in sport: Toward acknowledgement, understanding, and theory. *Journal of Sport and Exercise Psychology, 18*, 237–246.

Krane, V., Greenleaf, C.A., & Snow, J. (1997). Reaching for gold and the price of glory: A motivational case study of an elite gymnast. *The Sport Psychologist, 11*, 53–71.

Lacy, A.C., & Darst, P.W. (1984). Evolution of a systematic observation instrument: The ASU observation instrument. *Journal of Teaching in Physical Education, 3*, 59–66.

Landers, M.A., & Fine, G.A. (1996). Learning life's lessons in tee ball: The reinforcement of gender and status in kindergarten sport. *Sociology of Sport Journal, 13*, 87–93.

LaVoi, N.M. (2005). Interpersonal communication and conflict in the coach-athlete relationship. In S. Jowett & D. Levallee (Eds.), *The social psychology of sport*. Champaign, IL: Human Kinetics.

Levy, S.R., Stroessner, S.J., & Dweck, C.S. (1998). Stereotype formation and endorsement: The role of implicit theories. *Journal of Personality and Social Psychology, 74*, 1421–1436.

Li, W., & Lee, A. (2004). A review of conceptions of ability and related motivational constructs in achievement motivation. *Quest, 56*, 439–461.

Losier, G.F., Gaudette, G.M., & Vallerand, R.J. (1997). *A motivational analysis of the sportspersonship orientations of certified coaches from New Brunswick*. Paper presented at the annual conference of the Quebec Society for Research in Psychology, Sherbrooke, PQ.

Magyar, T.M., & Feltz, D.L. (2003). The influence of dispositional and situational tendencies on adolescent girls' sport confidence sources. *Psychology of Sport and Exercise, 4*, 175–190.

Magyar, T.M., Feltz, D.L., & Simpson, I.P. (2004). Individual and crew level determinants of collective efficacy in rowing. *Journal of Sport and Exercise Psychology, 26*, 136–153.

Mageau, G., & Vallerand, R.J. (2003). The coach-athlete relationship: A motivational model. *Journal of Sports Sciences, 21*, 883–904.

Malina, R.M. (1994). Physical growth and biological maturation of young athletes. In J.O. Holloszy (Ed.), *Exercise and sport science reviews* (Vol. 22, pp. 388–433). Baltimore: Williams & Wilkins.

Malina, R.M. (2002). The young athlete: Biological growth and maturation in a biocultural context. In F.L. Smoll & R.E. Smith (Eds.), *Children and youth in sport: A biopsychosocial perspective* (2nd ed., pp. 261–292). Dubuque, IA: Kendall/Hunt.

Mallett, C.J. (2005). Self-determination theory: A case study of evidence-based coaching. *The Sport Psychologist, 19*, 417–429.

Mallett, C., & Cote, J. (2006). Beyond winning and losing: Guidelines for evaluating high performance coaches. *The Sport Psychologist, 20*, 213–221.

McCormick, T.E., & Noriega, T. (1986). Low versus high expectations: A review of teacher expectation effects on minority students. *Journal of Educational Equity and Leadership, 6*, 224–234.

Messner, M.A. (2000). Barbie girls versus sea monsters: Children constructing gender. *Gender and Society, 14*, 765–784.

Messner, M.A., & Sabo, D.F. (Eds.) (1990). *Sport, men, and the gender order: Critical feminist perspectives*. Champaign, IL: Human Kinetics.

Miller, J.B., & Stiver, I.P. (1997). *The healing connection: How women form relationships in therapy and in life*. Boston: Beacon Press.

More, K.G., & Franks, I.M. (1996). Analysis and modification of verbal coaching behaviours. The usefulness of a data-driven intervention strategy. *Journal of Sports Sciences, 14*, 523–543.

Mueller, C.M., & Dweck, C.S. (1998). Praise for intelligence can undermine children's motivation and performance. *Journal of Personality and Social Psychology, 75*, 33–52.

Myers, N.D., Vargas-Tonsing, T.M., & Feltz, D.L. (2005). Coaching efficacy in intercollegiate coaches: Sources, coaching behavior, and team variables. *Psychology of Sport and Exercise, 6*, 129–143.

Nash, C., & Collins, D. (2006). Tacit knowledge in expert coaching: Science or art? *Quest, 58*, 465–477.

Newton, M.L., Duda, J.L., & Yin, Z. (2000). Examination of the psychometric properties of the Perceived Motivational Climate in Sport Questionnaire–2 in a sample of female athletes. *Journal of Sport Sciences, 18*, 275–290.

Nicholls, J.G. (1984). Achievement motivation: Conceptions of ability, subjective experience, task choice, and performance. *Psychological Review, 91*, 328–346.

Nicholls, J.G. (1989). *The competitive ethos and democratic education*. Cambridge, MA: Harvard University Press.

Ntoumanis, N., & Biddle, S.J.H. (1999). A review of motivational climate in physical activity. *Journal of Sports Sciences, 17*, 643–665.

Ntoumanis, N., & Vazou, S. (2005). Peer motivational climate in youth sport: Measurement development and validation. *Journal of Sport and Exercise Psychology, 27*, 432–455.

Ommundsen, Y., Roberts, G.C., Lemyre, P.N., & Treasure, D.C. (2003). Perceived motivational climate in male youth soccer: Relations to social-moral functioning, sportspersonship, and team norm perceptions. *Psychology of Sport and Exercise, 4*, 397–413.

Papaioannou, A. (1995). Differential perceptual and motivational patterns when different goals are adopted. *Journal of Sport and Exercise Psychology, 17*, 18–34.

Pease, D.G., & Kozub, S. (1994). Perceived coaching behaviors and team cohesion in high school girls' basketball teams. *Journal of Sport and Exercise Psychology, 16* (Suppl.), S93.

Pelletier, L.G., Fortier, M.S., Vallerand, R.J., & Briere, N.M. (2002). Associations among perceived autonomy support, forms of self-regulation, and persistence: A prospective study. *Motivation and Emotion, 25*, 279–306.

Pelletier, L.G., Seguin-Levesque, C., & Legault, L. (2002). Pressure from above and pressure from below as determinants of teachers' motivation and teaching behaviors. *Journal of Educational Psychology, 94*, 186–196.

Pelletier, L.G., Tuson, K.M., & Haddad, N.K. (1997). The Client Motivation for Therapy Scale (CMOTS): A measure of intrinsic motivation, forms of extrinsic motivation, and amotivation for therapy. *Journal of Personality Assessment, 68*, 414–435.

Pelletier, L.G., & Vallerand, R.J. (1996). Supervisors' beliefs and subordinates' intrinsic motivation: A behavioral confirmation analysis. *Journal of Personality and Social Psychology, 71*, 331–341.

Poczwardowski, A., Barott, J.E., & Jowett, S. (2006). Diversifying approaches to research on athlete-coach relationships. *Psychology of Sport and Exercise, 7*, 125–142.

Potrac, P., Brewer, C., Jones, R., Armour, K., & Hoff, J. (2000). Toward an holistic understanding of the coaching process. *Quest, 52*, 186–199.

Price, M.S., & Weiss, M.R. (2000). Relationships among coach burnout, coach behaviors, and athletes' psychological responses. *The Sport Psychologist, 14*, 391–409.

Ram, N., Starek, J., & Johnson, J. (2004). Race, ethnicity, and sexual orientation: Still a void in sport and exercise psychology? *Journal of Sport and Exercise Psychology, 26*, 250–268.

Reinboth, M., & Duda, J.L. (2004). The motivational climate, perceived ability, and athletes' psychological and physical well-being. *The Sport Psychologist, 18*, 237–251.

Reinboth, M., & Duda, J.L. (2006). Perceived motivational climate, need satisfaction, and indices of well-being in team sports: A longitudinal perspective. *Psychology of Sport and Exercise, 7*, 269–286.

Rejeski, W., Darracott, C., & Hutslar, S. (1979). Pygmalion in youth sports: A field study. *Journal of Sport Psychology, 1*, 311–319.

Riemer, H.A., & Chelladurai, P. (1995). Leadership and satisfaction in athletes. *Journal of Sport and Exercise Psychology, 17*, 276–293.

Riemer, H.A., & Toon, K. (2001). Leadership and satisfaction in tennis: Examination of congruence, gender, and ability. *Research Quarterly for Exercise and Sport, 72*, 243–256.

Rowold, J. (2006). Transformational and transactional leadership in martial arts. *Journal of Applied Sport Psychology, 18*, 312–325.

Ryan, R.M., Connell, J.P., & Deci, E.L. (1985). A motivational analysis of self-determination and self-regulation in education. In C. Ames & R.E. Ames (Eds.), *Research on motivation in education: The classroom milieu* (pp. 13–51). New York: Academic Press.

Ryan, R.M., & Deci, E.L. (2000). Self-determination theory and the facilitation of intrinsic motivation, social development, and well-being. *American Psychologist, 55*, 68–78.

Sarrazin, P., Vallerand, R., Guillet, E., Pelletier, L., & Cury, F. (2002). Motivation and dropout in female handballers: A 21-month prospective study. *European Journal of Social Psychology, 32*, 395–418.

Saury, J., & Durand, M. (1998). Practical knowledge in expert coaches: On-site study of coaching in sailing. *Research Quarterly for Exercise and Sport, 69,* 254–266.

Schunk, D.H. (1995). Self-efficacy, motivation, and performance. *Journal of Applied Sport Psychology, 7,* 112–137.

Seagrave, J.O., & Ciancio, C.A. (1990). An observational study of a successful Pop Warner football coach. *Journal of Teaching in Physical Education, 9,* 294–306.

Sherman, C.A., Fuller, R., & Speed, H.D. (2000). Gender comparisons of preferred coaching behaviors in Australian sports. *Journal of Sport Behavior, 23,* 389–402.

Shields, D.L.L., Gardner, D.E., Bredemeier, B.J.L., & Bostro, A. (1997). The relationship between leadership behaviors and group cohesion in team sports. *Journal of Psychology, 131,* 196–210.

Simons, J., Dewitte, S., & Lens, W. (2003). "Don't do it for me. Do it for yourself!": Stressing the personal relevance enhances motivation in physical education. *Journal of Sport and Exercise Psychology, 25,* 145–160.

Sinclair, D.A., & Vealey, R.S. (1989). Effects of coaches' expectations and feedback on the self-perceptions of athletes. *Journal of Sport Behavior, 12,* 77–91.

Skinner, E. (1995). *Perceived control, motivation, and coping.* Thousand Oaks, CA: Sage.

Skinner, E. (1996). A guide to constructs of control. *Journal of Personality and Social Psychology, 71,* 549–570.

Smith, R.E. (2006). Understanding sport behavior: A cognitive-affective processing systems approach. *Journal of Applied Sport Psychology, 18,* 1–27.

Smith, R.E., & Smoll, F.L. (1990). Self-esteem and children's reactions to youth sport coaching behaviors: A field study of self-enhancement processes. *Developmental Psychology, 26,* 987–993.

Smith, R.E., Smoll, F.L., & Barnett, N.P. (1995). Reduction of children's sport anxiety through social support and stress-reduction training for coaches. *Journal of Applied Developmental Psychology, 16,* 125–142.

Smith, R.E., Smoll, F.L., & Christensen, D.S. (1996). Behavioral assessment and interventions in youth sports. *Behavior Modification, 20,* 3–44.

Smith, R.E., Smoll, F.L., & Curtis, B. (1978). Coaching behaviors in Little League baseball. In F.L. Smoll & R.E. Smith (Eds.), *Psychological perspectives in youth sports* (pp. 173–201). Washington, DC: Hemisphere.

Smith, R., Smoll, F., & Hunt, E. (1977). A system for the behavioral assessment of athletic coaches. *Research Quarterly, 48,* 401–407.

Smith, R., Zane, N., Smoll, F., & Coppel, D. (1983). Behavioral assessment in youth sports: Coaching behaviors and children's attitudes. *Medicine and Science in Sports and Exercise, 15,* 208–214.

Smith, S.L., Fry, M.D., Ethington, C.A., & Li, Y. (2005). The effect of female athletes' perceptions of their coaches' behaviors on their perceptions of the motivational climate. *Journal of Applied Sport Psychology, 17,* 170–177.

Smoll, F.L., & Smith, R.E. (1989). Leadership behaviors in sport: A theoretical model and research paradigm. *Journal of Applied Social Psychology, 19,* 1522–1551.

Smoll, F.L., Smith, R.E., Barnett, N.P., & Everett, J.J. (1993). Enhancement of children's self-esteem through social support training for youth sport coaches. *Journal of Applied Psychology, 78,* 602–610.

Solomon, G.B. (2001). Performance and personality impression cues as predictors of athletic performance: An extension of expectancy theory. *International Journal of Sport Psychology, 32,* 88–100.

Solomon, G.B. (2002). Confidence as a source of expectancy information: A follow-up investigation. *International Sports Journal, 6,* 119–127.

Solomon, G.B., Golden, A.J., Ciapponi, T.M., & Martin, A.D. (1998). Coach expectations and differential feedback: Perceptual flexibility revisited. *Journal of Sport Behavior, 21,* 298–310.

Solomon, G.B., Wiegardt, P.A., Yusuf, F.R., Kosmitzki, C., Williams, J., Stevens, C.E., et al. (1996). Expectancies and ethnicity: The self-fulfilling prophecy in college basketball. *Journal of Sport and Exercise Psychology, 18,* 83–88.

Starkes, J., & Ericsson, K.A. (2003). (Eds.). *Expert performance in sports: Advances in research on sport expertise.* Champaign, IL: Human Kinetics.

Steele, C.M. (1997). A threat in the air: How stereotypes shape intellectual ability and performance. *American Psychologist, 52,* 613–629.

Steele, C.M., & Aronson, J. (1995). Stereotype threat and the intellectual test performance of African-Americans. *Journal of Personality and Social Psychology, 69,* 797–784.

Steinberg, G.M., Singer, R.N., & Murphy, M. (2000). The benefits to sport achievement when a multiple goal orientation is emphasized. *Journal of Sport Behavior, 23,* 407–422.

Strean, W.B., Senecal, K.L., Howlett, S.G., & Burgess, J.M. (1997). Xs and Os and what the coach knows: Improving team strategy through critical thinking. *The Sport Psychologist, 11,* 243–256.

Sullivan, P.J., & Kent, A. (2003). Coaching efficacy as a predictor of leadership style in intercollegiate athletics. *Journal of Applied Sport Psychology, 15,* 1–11.

Tharp, R.G., & Gallimore, R. (1976). What a coach can teach a teacher. *Psychology Today, January,* 75–78.

Trail, G.T. (2004). Leadership, cohesion, and outcomes in scholastic sports. *International Journal of Sport Management, 5,* 111–132.

Treasure, D.C. (2001). Enhancing young people's motivation in youth sport: An achievement goal approach. In G.C. Roberts (Ed.), *Advances in motivation in sport and exercise* (pp. 79–100). Champaign, IL: Human Kinetics.

Turman, P.D. (2003). Coaches and cohesion: The impact of coaching techniques on team cohesion in the small group sport setting. *Journal of Sport Behavior, 26,* 86–104.

Vallee, C.N., & Bloom, G.A. (2005). Building a successful university program: Key and common elements of expert coaches. *Journal of Applied Sport Psychology, 17,* 179–196.

Vallerand, R.J. (2001). A hierarchical model of intrinsic and extrinsic motivation in sport and exercise. In G.C. Roberts (Ed.), *Advances in motivation in sport and exercise* (pp. 263–320). Champaign, IL: Human Kinetics.

Vallerand, R.J., & Losier, G.F. (1999). An integrative analysis of intrinsic and extrinsic motivation in sport. *Journal of Applied Sport Psychology, 11,* 142–169.

Vargas-Tonsing, T.M., Myers, N.D., & Feltz, D.L. (2004). Coaches' and athletes' perceptions of efficacy-enhancing techniques. *The Sport Psychologist, 18,* 397–414.

Vazou, S., Ntoumanis, N., & Duda, J.L. (2006). Predicting young athletes' motivational indices as a function of their perceptions of the coach- and peer-created climate. *Psychology of Sport and Exercise, 7,* 215–233.

Vealey, R.S. (2005). *Coaching for the inner edge.* Morgantown, WV: Fitness Information Technology.

Vealey, R.S., Armstrong, L., Comar, W., & Greenleaf, C.A. (1998). Influence of perceived coaching behaviors on burnout and competitive anxiety in female college athletes. *Journal of Applied Sport Psychology, 10,* 297–318.

Weiner, B. (1986). *An attributional theory of motivation and emotion.* New York: Springer-Verlag.

Weiner, B. (1992). *Human motivation: Metaphors, theories, and research.* Newbury Park, CA: Sage.

Werthner, P., & Trudel, P. (2006). A new theoretical perspective for understanding how coaches learn to coach. *The Sport Psychologist, 20,* 198–212.

Williams, J.M., Jerome, G.J., Kenow, L.J., Rogers, T., Sartain, T.A., & Darland, G. (2003). Factor structure of the Coaching Behavior Questionnaire and its relationship to athlete variables. *The Sport Psychologist, 17,* 16–34.

Xiang, P., & Lee, A. (1998). The development of self-perceptions of ability and achievement goals and their relations in physical education. *Research Quarterly for Exercise and Sport, 69,* 231–241.

Zhang, J., Jensen, B.E., & Mann, B.L. (1997). Modification and revision of the Leadership Scale for Sport. *Journal of Sport Behavior, 20,* 105–121.

CHAPTER 12

Adler, P.A., Kless, S.J., & Adler, P. (1992). Socialization to gender roles: Popularity among elementary school boys and girls. *Sociology of Education, 65*, 169–187.

Akiyama, H., Elliott, K., & Antonucci, T.C. (1996). Same-sex and cross-sex relationships. *Journals of Gerontology Series B-Psychological Sciences and Social Sciences, 51*, 374–382.

Allen, J.B. (2003). Social motivation in youth sport. *Journal of Sport & Exercise Psychology, 25*, 551–567.

Andersen, M., & Williams, J. (1987). Gender role and sport competition anxiety: A reexamination. *Research Quarterly for Exercise and Sport, 58*(1), 52–56.

Babkes, M.L., & Weiss, M.R. (1999). Parental influence on children's cognitive and affective responses to competitive soccer participation. *Pediatric Exercise Science, 11*, 44–62.

Bales, R.F. (1950). *Interaction process analysis: A method for the study of small groups*. Reading, MA: Addison-Wesley.

Bandura, A. (1977). *Social learning theory*. Englewood Cliffs, NJ: Prentice-Hall.

Bandura, A. (1986). *Social foundations of thought and action: A social cognitive theory*. Englewood Cliffs, NJ: Prentice-Hall.

Bank, S.P. (1995). Before the last leaves fall: Sibling connects among the elderly. *Journal of Geriatric Psychiatry, 18*, 183–195.

Bank, S.P., & Kahn, M.D. (1982). *The sibling bond*. New York: Basic Books.

Baumeister, R.F., & Leary, M.R. (1995). The need to belong: Desire for interpersonal attachments as a fundamental human motivation. *Psychological Bulletin, 117*(3), 497–529.

Bigelow, B.J., Lewko, J.H., & Salhani, L. (1989). Sport-involved children's friendship expectations. *Journal of Sport & Exercise Psychology, 11*, 152–160.

Bigner, J.J. (1974). Second borns' discrimination of sibling role concepts. *Developmental Psychology, 10*(4), 564–573.

Bloom, B.S. (Ed.). (1985). *Developing talent in young people*. New York: Ballantine.

Bois, J.E., Sarrazin, P.G., Brustad, R.J., Trouilloud, D., & Cury, F. (2002). Mothers' expectancies and young adolescents' perceived physical competence: A year-long study. *Journal of Early Adolescence, 22*, 384–406.

Bowen, M. (1960). A family concept of schizophrenia. In D.D. Jackson (Ed.), *The etiology of schizophrenia*. New York: Basic Books.

Bowerman, B.K., & Dobash, R.M. (1974). Structural variations in inter-sibling affect. *Journal of Marriage and Family, 36*, 48–54.

Bronfenbrenner, U. (1979). *The ecology of human development: Experiments by nature and design*. Cambridge, MA: Harvard University Press.

Bronfenbrenner, U. (1993). The ecology of cognitive development: Research models and fugitive findings. In R.H. Wozniak & K.W. Fischer (Eds.), *Development in context: Acting and thinking in specific environments* (pp. 3–44). Hillsdale, NJ: Erlbaum.

Brustad, R.J. (1988). Affective outcomes in competitive youth sport: The influence of intrapersonal and socialization factors. *Journal of Sport & Exercise Psychology, 10*, 307–321.

Brustad, R.J. (1992). Integrating socialization influences into the study of children's motivation in sport. *Journal of Sport & Exercise Psychology, 14*, 59–77.

Brustad, R.J. (1993). Who will go out and play? Parental and psychological influences on children's attraction to physical activity. *Pediatric Exercise Science, 5*, 210–223.

Brustad, R.J. (1996). Attraction to physical activity in urban schoolchildren: Parental socialization and gender influences. *Research Quarterly for Exercise and Sport, 67*, 316–323.

Brustad, R.J., Babkes, M.L., & Smith, A.L. (2001). Youth in sport: Psychological considerations. In R.N. Singer, H.A. Hausenblas, & C.M. Janelle (Eds.), *Handbook of research in sport psychology* (2nd ed., pp. 604–635). New York: Wiley.

Buchanan, H.T., Blankenbaker, J., & Cotten, D. (1976). Academic and athletic ability as popularity factors in elementary school children. *Research Quarterly, 47*, 320–325.

Bukowski, W.M., & Hoza, B. (1989). Popularity and friendship: Issues in theory, measurement, and outcome. In T.J. Berndt & G.W. Ladd (Eds.), *Peer relationships in child development* (pp. 15–45). New York: Wiley.

Burhmester, C., & Furman, W. (1990). Perceptions of sibling relationships during middle childhood and adolescence. *Child Development, 61*, 1387–1398.

Butcher, K.F., & Case, A. (1994). The effect of sibling sex composition on women's education and earnings. *Quarterly Journal of Economics, 109*(3), 531–564.

Carter, B., & McGoldrick, M. (Eds.) (1989). *The changing family life cycle: A framework for family therapy*. Boston: Allyn & Bacon.

Casher, B.B. (1977). Relationship between birth order and participation in dangerous sports. *Research Quarterly, 48*(1), 33–40.

Chamrad, D.L., Robinson, N.M., & Janos, P.M. (1995). Consequences of having a gifted sibling: Myths and realities. *Gifted Child Quarterly, 39*, 135–145.

Chase, M.A., & Dummer, G.M. (1992). The role of sports as a social status determinant for children. *Research Quarterly for Exercise and Sport, 63*(4), 418–424.

Chelladurai, P. (1990). Leadership in sports: A review. *International Journal of Sport Psychology, 21*, 328–354.

Cicirelli, V.G. (1995). *Sibling relationships across the lifespan*. New York: Plenum Press.

Coakley, J. (1992). Burnout among adolescent athletes: A personal failure or social problem? *Sociology of Sport Journal, 9*, 271–285.

Colangelo, N., & Brower, P. (1987). Labeling gifted youngsters: Long-term impact on families. *Gifted Child Quarterly, 31*, 75–78.

Cote, J. (1999). The role of the family in the development of talent in sport. *The Sport Psychologist, 13*, 395–417.

Crick, N.R. (1996). The role of overt aggression, relational aggression, and prosocial behavior in the prediction of children's future social adjustment. *Child Development, 67*(5), 2317–2327.

Crick, N.R., & Gropeter, J.K. (1995). Relational aggression, gender, and social-psychological adjustment. *Child Development, 66*(3), 710–722.

Crispell, D. (1996). The sibling syndrome. *American Demographics, 18*, 24–30.

Csikszentmihalyi, M., & Rathunde, K. (1998). The development of the person: An experiential perspective on the ontogenesis of psychological complexity. In W. Damon (Ed.), *Handbook of child psychology* (5th ed., pp. 635–684). New York: Wiley.

Csikszentmihalyi, M., Rathunde, K., & Whalen, S. (1993). *Talented teenagers: The roots of success and failure*. New York: Cambridge.

Davison, K.K. (2004). Activity-related support from parents, peers and siblings and adolescents' physical activity: Are there gender differences? *Journal of Physical Activity & Health, 1*, 363–376.

Duncan, S.C., Duncan, T.E., Strycker, L.A., & Chaumeton, N.R. (2004). A multilevel analysis of sibling physical activity. *Journal of Sport & Exercise Psychology, 26*, 57–68.

Dunn, J. (1983). Sibling relationships in early childhood. *Child Development, 54*, 787–811.

Dunn, J. (1992). Sisters and brothers: Current issues in developmental research. In F. Boer & J. Dunn (Eds.), *Children's sibling relationships: Developmental and clinical issues*. Hillsdale, NJ: Erlbaum.

Dunn, J., & Kendrick, C. (1981). Social behavior of young siblings in the family context: Differences between same-sex and different-sex dyads. *Child Development, 52*, 1265–1273.

Ebihara, O., Ikeda, M., & Mylashita, M. (1983). Birth order and children's socialization into sport. *International Review of Sport Sociology, 18*, 69–90.

Eccles, J.S. (1993). School and family effects on the ontogeny of children's interests, self-perceptions, and activity choices. In J. Jacobs (Ed.), *Nebraska Symposium on Motivation, 1992: Developmental perspectives on motivation* (pp. 145–208). Lincoln: University of Nebraska Press.

Eccles (Parsons), J., Adler, T.F., Futterman, R., Goff, S.B., Kaczala, C.M., Meece, J.L., et al. (1983). Expectancies, values, and academic behaviors. In J. Spence & R. Helmreich (Eds.), *Achievement and achievement motives: Psychological and sociological approaches* (pp. 75–146). San Francisco: Freeman.

Eccles, J.S., Jacobs, J.E., & Harold, R.D. (1990). Gender role stereotypes, expectancy effects, and parents' socialization of gender differences. *Journal of Social Issues, 46,* 183–201.

Eccles, J.S., & Harold, R. (1991). Gender differences in sport involvement: Applying the Eccles' expectancy-value model. *Journal of Applied Sport Psychology, 3,* 7–35.

Eccles, J.S., Midgley, C., Wigfield, A., Buchanan, C.M., Reuman, D., Flanagan, C., et al. (1993). Development during adolescence: The impact of stage environment fit on adolescents' experiences in schools and families. *American Psychologist, 48,* 90–101.

Eccles, J.S., & Wigfield, A. (1995). In the mind of the actor: The structure of adolescents' achievement task values and expectancy-related beliefs. *Personality and Social Psychology Bulletin, 21,* 215–225.

Ericsson, K.A., Krampe, R.T., & Tesch-Romer, C. (1993). The role of deliberate practice in the acquisition of expert performance. *Psychological Review, 3,* 363–406.

Evans, J., & Roberts, G.C. (1987). Physical competence and the development of children's peer relations, *Quest, 39,* 23–35.

Felson, M.B., & Reed, M. (1986). The effect of parents on the self-appraisals of children. *Social Psychology Quarterly, 49,* 302–308.

Flowers, R.A., & Brown, C. (2002). Effects of birth order on state anxiety. *Journal of Sport Behavior, 25,* 41–56.

Fredricks, J.A., & Eccles, J.S. (2002). Children's competence and value beliefs from childhood through adolescence: Growth trajectories in two male sex-typed domains. *Developmental Psychology, 38,* 519–533.

Fredricks, J.A., & Eccles, J.S. (2004). Parental influences on youth involvement in sports. In M.R. Weiss (Ed.), *Developmental sport and exercise psychology: A lifespan perspective* (pp. 165–196). Morgantown, WV: Fitness Information Technology.

Fredricks, J.A., & Eccles, J.S. (2005). Family socialization, gender, and sport motivation and involvement. *Journal of Sport & Exercise Psychology, 27,* 3–31.

Frieze, I., & Bar-Tal, D. (1980). Developmental trends in cue utilization for attributional judgments. *Journal of Applied Developmental Psychology, 1,* 83–94.

Frome, P., & Eccles, J. (1998). Parents' influence on children's achievement-related perceptions. *Journal of Personality and Social Psychology, 2,* 435–452.

Furman, W., & Burhmester, D. (1985). Children's perceptions of the qualities of sibling relationships. *Child Development, 56,* 448–461.

Glenn, S.D., & Horn, T.S. (1993). Psychological and personal predictors of leadership behavior in female soccer athletes. *Journal of Applied Sport Psychology, 5,* 17–34.

Gould, D., Eklund, R., Petlichkoff, L., Peterson, K., & Bump, L. (1991). Psychological predictors of state anxiety and performance in age-group wrestlers. *Pediatric Exercise Science, 3,* 198–208.

Green, C.B., & Chalip, L. (1998). Antecedents and consequences of parental purchase decision involvement in youth sport. *Leisure Sciences, 20,* 95–109.

Greendorfer, S.L., & Lewko, J.H. (1978). Role of family members in sport socialization of children. *Research Quarterly, 49,* 146–152.

Greendorfer, S.L., Lewko, J.H., & Rosengren, K.S. (1996). Family and gender-based influences in sport socialization of children and adolescents. In F.L. Smoll & R.E. Smith (Eds.), *Children and youth in sport: A biopsychosocial perspective* (pp. 89–111). Madison, WI: Brown & Benchmark.

Grenier, M.E. (1985). Gifted children and their siblings. *Gifted Child Quarterly, 29,* 164–167.

Harter, S. (1978). Effectance motivation reconsidered: Toward a developmental model. *Human Development, 21,* 34–64.

Harter, S. (1981). A model of intrinsic mastery motivation in children: Individual differences and developmental change. In W.A. Collins (Ed.), *Minnesota Symposium on Child Psychology* (Vol. 14, pp. 215–255). Hillsdale, NJ: Erlbaum.

Harter, S. (1999). *The construction of the self: A developmental perspective.* New York: Guilford Press.

Hartup, W.W. (1995). The three faces of friendship. *Journal of Social and Personal Relationships, 12*(4), 569–574.

Hellstedt, J.C. (1988). Early adolescent perceptions of parental pressure in the sport environment. *Journal of Sport Behavior, 13,* 135–144.

Hellstedt, J.C. (1995). Invisible players: A family system model. In S.M. Murphy (Ed.), *Sport psychology interventions* (pp. 117–146). Champaign, IL: Human Kinetics.

Horn, T.S. (2004). Developmental perspectives on self-perceptions in children and adolescents. In M.R. Weiss (Ed.), *Developmental sport and exercise psychology: A lifespan perspective* (pp. 101-143). Morgantown, WV: Fitness Information Technology.

Horn, T.S., & Amorose, A.J. (1998). Sources of competence information. In J.L. Duda (Ed.), *Advances in sport and exercise psychological measurement* (pp. 49–63). Morgantown, WV: Fitness Information Technology.

Horn, T.S., & Hasbrook, C.A. (1986). Information components influencing children's perceptions of their physical competence. In M.R. Weiss & D. Gould (Eds.), *Sport for children and youths: Proceedings of the 1984 Olympic Scientific Congress* (pp. 81–88). Champaign, IL: Human Kinetics.

Horn, T.S., & Hasbrook, C.A. (1987). Psychological characteristics and the criteria children use for self-evaluation. *Journal of Sport and Exercise Psychology, 9,* 208–221.

Horn, T.S., & Weiss, M.R. (1991). A developmental analysis of children's self-ability judgments in the physical domain. *Pediatric Exercise Science, 3,* 310–326.

Jacobs, J.E., & Eccles, J.S. (1992). The influence of mothers' gender-role stereotypic beliefs on mothers' and children's ability perceptions. *Journal of Personality and Social Psychology, 63,* 932–944.

Kimiecik, J.C., & Horn, T.S. (1998). Parental beliefs and children's moderate-to-vigorous physical activity. *Research Quarterly for Exercise and Sport, 69,* 163–175.

Koch, H.L. (1960). The relation of certain formal attributes of siblings to attitudes held toward each other and toward their parents. *Monographs for the Society for Research in Child Development, 25*(4), 1–124.

Kochenderfer, B.J., & Ladd, G.W. (1996a). Peer victimization: Manifestations and relations to school adjustment in kindergarten. *Journal of School Psychology, 34*(5), 267–283.

Kochenderfer, B.J., & Ladd, G.W. (1996b). Peer victimization: Cause or consequence of school maladjustment? *Child Development, 67,* 1305–1317.

Kochenderfer, B.J., & Ladd, G.W. (1997). Victimized children's responses to peers' aggression: Behaviors associated with reduced versus continued victimization. *Development and Psychopathology, 9,* 59–73.

Kunesh, M.A., Hasbrook, C.A., & Lewthwaite, R. (1992). Physical activity socialization: Peer interactions and affective responses among a sample of sixth grade girls. *Sociology of Sport Journal, 9,* 385–396.

Ladd, G.W., Kochenderfer, B.J., & Coleman, C.C. (1996). Friendship quality as a predictor of young children's early school adjustment. *Child Development, 58,* 1168–1189.

Ladd, G.W., Kochenderfer, B.J., & Coleman, C.C. (1997). Classroom peer acceptance, friendship, and victimization: Distinct relational systems that contribute uniquely to children's school adjustment? *Child Development, 68*(6), 1181–1197.

Lasko, J. (1954). Parental behavior toward first and second children. *Genetic Psychology Monographs, 49,* 96–137.

Laursen, B., & Hartup, W.H. (2002). The origins of reciprocity and social exchange in friendships. *New directions for child and adolescent development, 95,* 27–42.

Lawson, A., & Ingleby, J.D. (1974). Daily routines of preschool children: Effects of age, birth order, sex, social class, and developmental correlates. *Psychological Medicine, 4,* 399–415.

Lee, M., Coburn, T., & Partridge, R. (1981). The influence of team structure in determining leadership function in association football. *Journal of Sport Behavior, 6,* 59–66.

Leff, S.S., & Hoyle, R.H. (1995). Young athletes' perceptions of parental support and pressure. *Journal of Youth and Adolescence, 24,* 187–203.

Lewin, K. (1934). *A dynamic theory of personality*. New York: McGraw-Hill.

Lewko, J.H., & Ewing, M.E. (1980). Sex differences and parental influence in sport involvement of children. *Journal of Sport Psychology, 2*, 62–68.

Longstreath, L.E. (1970). Birth order and avoidance of dangerous activities. *Developmental Psychology, 2*, 154

Martens, R. (1977). *Sport competition anxiety test*. Champaign, IL: Human Kinetics.

Martin, C.L. (1990). Attitudes and expectations about children with non-traditional and traditional gender roles. *Sex Roles, 22*, 151–165.

Martin, D.E., & Dodder, R.A. (1991). Socialization experiences and level of terminating participation in sports. *Journal of Sport Behavior, 14*(2), 113–127.

McCullagh, P., Matzkanin, K., Shaw, S.D., & Maldonado, M. (1993). Motivation for participation in physical activity: A comparison of parent-child perceived competence and participation motives. *Pediatric Exercise Science, 5*, 224–233.

Mendelson, M.J., DeVilla, E.P., Fitch, T.A., & Goodman, F.G. (1997). Adults' expectations for children's sibling roles. *International Journal of Behavioral Development, 20*, 549–572.

Minnett, A.M., Vandell, L.D., & Santrock, J.W. (1983). The effects of sibling status on sibling interaction: Influence of birth order, age spacing, sex of child, and sex of sibling. *Child Development, 54*, 1064–1072.

Newcombe, A.F., & Bagwell, C.L. (1995). Children's friendship relations: A meta-analytic review. *Psychological Bulletin, 117*(2), 306–347.

Nisbett, R.E. (1968). Birth order and participation in dangerous sports. *Journal of Personality and Social Psychology, 8*, 351–353.

Olweus, D. (1991). Bully/victim problems among school-children: Basic facts and effects of a school based intervention program. In D. Pepler & K. Rubin (Eds.), *The development and treatment of childhood aggression* (pp. 411–448). Hillsdale, NJ: Erlbaum.

Ommundsen, Y., & Vaglum, P. (1991). Soccer competition anxiety and enjoyment in young boy players: The influence of perceived competence and significant others' emotional involvement. *International Journal of Sport Psychology, 22*, 35–49.

Parker, J.G., & Asher, S.R. (1993). Friendship and friendship quality in middle childhood: Links with peer group acceptance and feelings of loneliness and dissatisfaction. *Developmental Psychology, 29*(4), 611–621.

Parsons, J., Adler, T.F., & Kaczala, C.M. (1982). Socialization of achievement attitudes and beliefs: Parental influences. *Child Development, 53*, 310–321.

Partridge, J.A. (2003). *Effects of peer influence on psychosocial outcomes in the sport domain*. Unpublished doctoral dissertation, University of Northern Colorado.

Passer, M.W. (1983). Fear of failure, fear of evaluation, perceived competence and self-esteem in competitive trait-anxious children. *Journal of Sport Psychology, 5*, 172–188.

Patrick, H., Ryan, A.M., Alfeld-Liro, C., Fredricks, J.A., Hruda, L.Z., & Eccles, J.S. (1999). Adolescents' commitment to developing talent: The role of peers in continuing motivation for sports and the arts. *Journal of Youth and Adolescence, 28*(6), 741–763.

Paulhus, D.L., Trapnell, P.D., & Chen, D. (1999). Birth order effects on personality and achievement within families. *Psychological Science, 10*(6), 482–488.

Perry, D.G., Kusel, S.J., & Perry, D.G. (1988). Victims of peer aggression. *Developmental Psychology, 24*, 807–814.

Phillips, D. (1984). The illusion of incompetence among academically competent children. *Child Development, 55*, 2000–2016.

Phillips, D. (1987). Socialization of perceived academic competence among highly competent children. *Child Development, 58*, 1308–1320.

Raedeke, T.D. (1997). Is athlete burnout more than just stress? A sport commitment perspective. *Journal of Sport & Exercise Psychology, 19*, 396–417.

Raudsepp, L., & Viira, R. (2000). Influence of parents' and siblings' physical activity on activity levels of adolescents. *European Journal of Physical Education, 5*, 169–178.

Scanlan, T.K. (1996). Social evaluation and the competition process: A developmental perspective. In F.L. Smoll & R.E. Smith (Eds.), *Children and youth in sport: A biopsychosocial perspective* (pp. 298–308). Madison, WI: Brown & Benchmark.

Scanlan, T.K., & Lewthwaite, R. (1984). Social psychological aspects of competition for male youth sport participants: I. Predictors of competitive stress. *Journal of Sport Psychology, 6*, 208–226.

Scanlan, T.K., & Lewthwaite, R. (1986). Social psychological aspects of competition for male youth sport participants: IV. Predictors of enjoyment. *Journal of Sport Psychology, 8*, 25–35.

Schachter, S. (1963). Birth order, eminence, and higher education. *American Sociological Review, 28*, 757–767.

Shantz, C.U., & Hobart, C.J. (1989). Social conflict and social development: Peers and siblings. In T.J. Berndt & G.W. Ladd (Eds.), *Peer relationships in child development* (pp. 71–94). New York: Wiley.

Smilkstein, G. (1980). Psychological trauma in children and youth in competitive sport. *Journal of Family Practice, 10*, 737–739.

Smith, A.L. (1999). Perceptions of peer relationships and physical activity participation in early adolescence. *Journal of Sport & Exercise Psychology, 21*, 329–350.

Stevenson, C.L. (1990). The early careers of international athletes. *Sociology of Sport Journal, 7*, 238–253.

Stocker, C.M., Furman, W., & Lanthier, R.P. (1997). Sibling relationships in early adulthood. *Journal of Family Psychology, 11*, 210–221.

Stoneman, Z., & Berman, P.W. (1993). *The effects of mental retardation, disability and illness on sibling relationships: Research issues and challenges*. Baltimore: Brookes.

Stoneman, Z., & Brody, G.H. (1982). Strengths inherent in sibling interaction involving a retarded child: A functional role theory approach. In N. Stinnett, B. Chesser, J. DeFrain, & P. Knaub, (Eds.). *Family strengths: Positive models for family life* (pp. 113–129). Lincoln: University of Nebraska Press.

Stoneman, Z., & Brody, G.H. (1993). Sibling relationship in the family context. In Z. Stoneman & P.W. Berman (Eds.), *The effects of mental retardation, disability, and illness on sibling relationships: Research issues and challenges* (pp. 3–30). Baltimore: Brookes.

Stoneman, Z., Brody, G.H., & MacKinnon, C. (1984). Naturalistic observations of children's activities and roles while playing with their younger siblings and friends. *Child Development, 55*, 617–627.

Sullivan, H.S. (1953). *The interpersonal theory of psychiatry*. New York: Norton.

Sutton-Smith, B., & Rosenberg, B.G. (1968). Sibling consensus on power tactics. *Journal of Genetic Psychology, 112*, 63–72.

Tesser, A. (1980). Self-esteem maintenance in family dynamics. *Journal of Personality and Social Psychology, 39* (1), 77–91.

Todd, S.Y., & Kent, A. (2004). Perceptions of role differentiation behaviors of ideal peer leaders: A study of adolescent athletes. *International Sports Journal, 8*(2), 105–118.

Tuttle, D.H., & Cornell, D.G. (1993). Maternal labeling of gifted children: Effects on the sibling relationship. *Exceptional Children, 59*, 402–410.

Walsh, W.M., & McGraw, J.A. (2002). *Essentials of family therapy: A structured summary of nine approaches* (2nd ed.). Denver, CO: Love

Waters, B. (1987). The importance of sibling relationships in separate families. *Australian and New Zealand Journal of Family Therapy, 8*, 13–17.

Weiss, M.R., & Barber, H. (1995). Socialization influences of collegiate female athletes: A tale of two decades. *Sex Roles, 33*, 129–140.

Weiss, M.R., & Chaumeton, N. (1992). Motivational orientations in sport. In T.S. Horn (Ed.), *Advances in sport psychology* (pp. 61–99). Champaign, IL: Human Kinetics.

Weiss, M.R., & Duncan, S.C. (1992). The relationship between physical competence and peer acceptance in the context of children's sports participation. *Journal of Sport & Exercise Psychology, 14*, 177–191.

Weiss, M.R., & Ferrar-Caja, E. (2002). Motivational orientations and sport behavior. In T.S. Horn (Ed.), *Advances in sport psychology* (2nd ed., pp. 101–183). Champaign, IL: Human Kinetics.

Weiss, M.R., & Hayashi, C.T. (1995). All in the family: Parent-child socialization influences in competitive youth gymnastics. *Pediatric Exercise Science, 7*, 36–48.

Weiss, M.R., & Petlichkoff, L.M. (1989). Children's motivation for participation in and withdrawal from sport: Identifying the missing links. *Pediatric Exercise Science, 1,* 195–211.

Weiss, M.R., & Smith, A.L. (1999). Quality of youth sport friendships: Measurement development and validation. *Journal of Sport & Exercise Psychology, 21,* 145–166.

Weiss, M.R., & Smith, A.L. (2002). Friendship quality in youth sport: Relationship to age, gender, and motivation variables. *Journal of Sport & Exercise Psychology, 24,* 420–437.

Weiss, M.R., Smith, A.L., & Theeboom, M. (1996). "That's what friends are for": Children's and teenagers' perceptions of peer relationship in the sport domain. *Journal of Sport & Exercise Psychology, 18,* 347–379.

Weiss, M.R., Wiese, D.M., & Klint, K.A. (1989). Head over heels with success: The relationship between self-efficacy and performance in competitive youth gymnastics. *Journal of Sport & Exercise Psychology, 11,* 444–451.

Wiersma, L.D. (2000). Risks and benefits of youth sport specialization: Perspectives and recommendations. *Pediatric Exercise Science, 12,* 13–22.

Wigfield, A., & Eccles, J.S. (1990). Test anxiety in elementary and secondary school students. *Educational Psychologist, 24,* 159–183.

Wigfield, A., Eccles, J.S., Yoon, K.S., Harold, R.D., Arbreton, A.J., Freedman-Daon, C.R., et al. (1998). Changes in children's competence beliefs and subjective task values across the elementary school years: A three year study. *Journal of Educational Psychology, 89,* 451–469.

Wittig, A., Duncan, S., & Schurr, K. (1987). The relationship of gender, gender-role endorsement and perceived physical self-efficacy to sport competition anxiety. *Journal of Sport Behavior, 11,* 192–199.

Wold, B., & Anderssen, N. (1992). Health promotion aspects of family and peer influences on sport participation. *International Journal of Sport Psychology, 31,* 555–572.

Yiannakis, A. (1976). Birth order and preference for dangerous sports among males. *Research Quarterly, 47,* 62–68.

Yukelson, D., Weinberg, R., Richardson, P., & Jackson, A. (1981). Interpersonal attraction and leadership within collegiate sport teams. *Journal of Sport Behavior, 6,* 29–36.

Zarbatany, L., Ghesquiere, K., & Mohr, K. (1992). A context perspective on early adolescents' friendship expectations. *Journal of Early Adolescence, 12,* 111–126.

Zarbatany, L., Hartmann, D.P., & Rankin, D.B. (1990). The psychological functions of preadolescent peer activities. *Child Development, 61,* 1067–1080.

CHAPTER 13

Abbott, A., & Collins, D. (2004). Eliminating the dichotomy between theory and practice in talent identification and development: Considering the role of psychology. *Journal of Sports Sciences, 22,* 395–408.

Abbruzzese, G., Trompetto, C., & Schieppati, M. (1996). The excitability of the human motor cortex increases during execution and mental imagination of sequential but not repetitive finger movements. *Experimental Brain Research, 111,* 465–472.

Abma, C.L., Fry, M.D., Li, Y., & Reylea, G. (2002). Differences in imagery content and imagery ability between high and low confident track and field athletes. *Journal of Applied Sport Psychology, 14,* 67–75.

Afremow, J., Overby, L.Y., & Vadocz, E. (1997). Using mental imagery to enhance sport and dance skills of children. *Journal of the International Council for Health, Physical Education, Recreation, Sport and Dance, 33,* 44–48.

Ahsen, A. (1984). ISM: The triple code model for imagery and psychophysiology. *Journal of Mental Imagery, 8,* 15–42.

Annett, J. (1988). Imagery and skill acquisition. In M. Denis, J. Engelkamp, & J.T.E. Richardson (Eds.), *Cognitive and neuropsychological approaches to mental imagery* (pp. 259–268). Martinus Nijhod: Dordrecht, Netherlands.

Baddeley, A.D. (1986). *Working memory.* Oxford, United Kingdom: Clarendon Press.

Baddeley, A.D. (2001). Is working memory still working? *American Psychologist, 56,* 851–864.

Bakker, F.C., Boschker, M.S.J., & Chung, T. (1996). Changes in muscular activity while imaging weight lifting using stimulus and response propositions. *Journal of Sport and Exercise Psychology, 18,* 313–324.

Bandura, A. (1977). Self-efficacy: Toward a unifying theory of behavioral change. *Psychological Review, 84,* 191–215.

Barr, K., & Hall, C. (1992). The use of imagery by rowers. *International Journal of Sport Psychology, 23,* 243–261.

Bird, E.I. (1984). EMG quantification of mental rehearsal. *Perceptual and Motor Skills, 59,* 899–906.

Bisig, T.B., & Spray, C.M. (2004). A psychological approach to golf: Relationships between motivation, performance and psychological strategies in competition. *Journal of Sports Sciences, 23,* BASES Annual Conference (2004), Liverpool, 161, ISSN 0264 0414.

Boschker, M.S.J., Bakker, F.C., & Rietberg, M.B. (2000). Retroactive interference effects of mentally imagined movement speed. *Journal of Sports Sciences, 18,* 593–603.

Budney, A.J., & Woolfolk, R.L. (1990). Using the wrong image: An exploration of the adverse effects of imagery on performance. *Journal of Mental Imagery, 14,* 75–86.

Bugelski, B.R., Kidd, E., & Segmen, J. (1968). Image as a mediator in one-trial paired-associate learning. *Journal of Experimental Psychology, 76,* 69–73.

Callow, N., & Hardy, L. (2001). Types of imagery associated with sport confidence in netball players of varying skill levels. *Journal of Applied Sport Psychology, 13,* 1–17.

Callow, N., & Hardy, L. (2004). The relationship between the use of kinaesthetic imagery and different visual imagery perspectives. *Journal of Sports Sciences, 22,* 167–177.

Callow, N., Hardy, L., & Hall, C. (2001). The effects of a motivational general-mastery imagery intervention on the sport confidence of high-level badminton players. *Research Quarterly for Exercise and Sport, 72,* 389–400.

Callow, N., & Waters, A. (2005). The effect of kinesthetic imagery on the sport confidence of flat-race horse jockeys. *Psychology of Sport and Exercise, 6,* 443–459.

Calmels, C., Berthoumieux, C., & d'Arripe-Longueville, F. (2004). Effects of an imagery training program on selective attention of national softball players. *The Sport Psychologist, 18,* 272–296.

Calmels, C., d'Arripe-Longueville, F., Fournier, J.F., & Soulard, A. (2003). Competitive strategies among elite female gymnasts: An exploration of the relative influence of psychological skills training and natural learning experiences. *International Journal of Sport and Exercise Psychology, 1,* 327–352.

Calmels, C., & Fournier, J.F. (2001). Duration of physical and mental execution of gymnastic routines. *The Sport Psychologist, 15,* 142–150.

Calmels, C., Holmes, P., Berthoumieux, C., & Singer, R.N. (2004). The development of movement imagery vividness through a structured intervention in softball. *Journal of Sport Behavior, 27,* 307–322.

Campos, A., Pérez-Fabello, M.J., & Gómez-Juncal, R. (2004). Gender and age differences in measured and self-perceived imaging capacity. *Personality and Individual Differences, 37*(7), 1383–1389.

Charlot, V., Tzourio, N., Zilbovicius, M., Mazoyer, B., & Denis, M. (1992). Different mental imagery abilities result in different regional cerebral blood flow activation patterns during cognitive tasks. *Neuropsychologia, 30,* 565–580.

Craik, F.I.M., & Lockhart, R.S. (1972). Levels of processing: A framework for memory research. *Journal of Verbal Learning and Verbal Behavior, 11,* 671–684.

Cumming, J., & Hall, C. (2002a). Athletes' use of imagery in the off-season. *The Sport Psychologist, 16,* 160–172.

Cumming, J., & Hall, C. (2002b). Deliberate imagery practice: The development of imagery skills in competitive athletes. *Journal of Sports Sciences, 20,* 137–145.

Cumming, J., Hall, C., Harwood, C., & Gammage, K. (2002). Motivational orientations and imagery use: A goal profiling analysis. *Journal of Sports Sciences, 20,* 127–136.

Cumming, J., Hall, C., & Shambrook, C. (2004). The influence of an imagery workshop on athletes' use of imagery. *Athletic Insight, 6.*

Cumming, J., Hall, C., & Starkes, J.L. (2005). Deliberate imagery practice: Examining the reliability of a retrospective recall methodology. *Research Quarterly for Exercise and Sport, 76,* 306–314.

Cumming, J.L., Nordin, S.M., Horton, R., & Reynolds, S. (2006). Examining the direction of imagery and self-talk on dart-throwing performance and self efficacy. *The Sport Psychologist, 20,* 257-274.

Cumming, J.L., & Ste-Marie, D.M. (2001). The cognitive and motivational effects of imagery training: A matter of perspective. *The Sport Psychologist, 15,* 276–287.

Decety, J. (1996a). Do imagined and executed actions share the same neural substrate? *Cognitive Brain Research, 3,* 87–93.

Decety, J. (1996b). The neurophysiological basis of motor imagery. *Behavioural Brain Research, 77,* 45–52.

Decety, J., & Grezes, J. (1999). Neural mechanisms subserving the perception of human actions. *Trends in Cognitive Science, 3,* 172–178.

Decety, J., & Ingvar, D.H. (1990). Brain structures participating in mental simulation of motor behavior: A neurological interpretation. *Acta Psychologica, 73,* 13–34.

Decety, J., Jeannerod, M., Germain, M., & Pastène, J. (1991). Vegetative response during imagined movement is proportional to mental effort. *Behavioural Brain Research, 42,* 1–5.

Djordjevic, J., Zatorre, R.J., Petrides, M., Boyle, J.A., & Jones-Gotman, M. (2005). Functional neuroimaging of odor imagery. *Neuroimage, 24,* 791–801.

Duda, J.L., Cumming, J., & Balaguer, I. (2005). Enhancing athletes' self regulation, task involvement and self determination via psychological skills training. In D. Hackfort, J. Duda, & R. Lidor (Eds.), *Handbook of research in applied sport and exercise psychology: International perspectives* (pp. 143–165). Morgantown, WV: Fitness Information Technology.

Efran, J.S., Lesser, G.S., & Spiller, M.J. (1994). Enhancing tennis coaching with youths using a metaphor method. *The Sport Psychologist, 8,* 349–359.

Eichenbaum, H. (2000). *Nature Reviews: Neuroscience, 1,* 41–50.

Epstein, M.L. (1980). The relationship of mental imagery and mental rehearsal to performance of a motor task. *Journal of Sport Psychology, 2,* 211–220.

Ericsson, K.A. (2003). The development of elite performance and deliberate practice: An update from the perspective of the expert-performance approach. In J. Starkes and K. A. Ericsson (Eds.), *Expert performance in sport: Recent advances in research on sport expertise* (pp. 49-81). Champaign, IL: Human Kinetics.

Ericsson, K.A., Krampe, R.T., & Tesch-Romer, C. (1993) The Role of Deliberate Practice in the Acquisition of Expert Performance. *Psychological Review, 100,* 363-406.

Ernest, C., & Paivio, A. (1971). Imagery and sex differences in incidental recall. *British Journal of Psychology, 62,* 67–72.

Etnier, J.L., & Landers, D.M. (1996). The influence of procedural variables on the efficacy of mental practice. *The Sport Psychologist, 10,* 48–57.

Evans, L., Jones, L., & Mullen, R. (2004). An imagery intervention during the competitive season with an elite rugby union player. *The Sport Psychologist, 18,* 252–271.

Farah, M.J. (1988). Is visual imagery really visual? Overlooked evidence from neuropsychology. *Psychological Review, 93,* 307–317.

Farah, M.J. (1989). Mechanisms of imagery-perception interaction. *Journal of Experimental Psychology: Human Perception and Performance, 15,* 203–211.

Feltz, D.L. (1984). Self-efficacy as a cognitive mediator of athletic performance. In W.F. Straub & J.M. Williams (Eds.), *Cognitive sport psychology* (1st ed., pp. 191–198). Lansing, NY: Sport Science Associates.

Feltz, D.L., & Landers, D.M. (1983). The effects of mental practice on motor skill learning and performance: A meta-analysis. *Journal of Sport Psychology, 5,* 25–57.

Feltz, D., & Reissinger, C.A. (1990). Effects of in vivo imagery and performance feedback on self-efficacy and muscular endurance. *Journal of Sport and Exercise Psychology, 12,* 132–143.

Fenker, R. M., & Lambiotte, J. G. (1987). A performance enhancement program for a college football team: One incredible season. *The Sport Psychologist, 1,* 224–236.

Finke, R.A. (1980). Levels of equivalence in imagery and perception. *Psychological Review, 87,* 113–132.

Fish, L., Hall, C.R., & Cumming, J. (2004). Investigating the use of imagery by elite ballet dancers. *AVANTE, 10,* 26–39.

Fletcher, D., & Hanton, S. (2001). The relationship between psychological skills usage and competitive anxiety responses. *Psychology of Sport and Exercise, 2,* 89–101.

Fournier, J.F., Calmels, C., Durand-Bush, N., & Salmela, J.H. (2005). Effects of a season-long PST program on gymnastic performance and on psychological skill development. *International Journal of Sport and Exercise Psychology, 3,* 59–78.

Franklin, E.N. (1996a). *Dance imagery for technique and performance.* Champaign, IL.: Human Kinetics.

Franklin, E.N. (1996b). *Dynamic alignment through imagery.* Champaign, IL.: Human Kinetics.

Gabriele, T., Hall, C., & Lee, T.D. (1989). Cognition and motor learning: Imagery effects on contextual interference. *Human Movement Science, 8,* 227–245.

Gallego, J., Denot-Ledunois, S., Vardon, G., & Perruchet, P. (1996). Ventilatory responses to imagined exercise. *Psychophysiology, 33,* 711–719.

Gammage, K., Hall, C., & Rodgers, W. (2000). More about exercise imagery. *The Sport Psychologist, 14,* 348–359.

Garza, D.L., & Feltz, D.L. (1998). Effects of selected mental practice on performance, self-efficacy, and competition confidence of figure skaters. *The Sport Psychologist, 12,* 1–15.

Gates, S.C., DePalma, M.T., & Shelley, G.A. (2003). An investigation of the relationship between visual imagery perspective, kinesthetic imagery and locus of control. *Applied Research in Coaching and Athletics Annual, 18,* 145–164.

Giacobbi, P.R., Hausenblas, H.A., Fallon, E.A., & Hall, C. (2003). Even more about exercise imagery: A grounded theory of exercise imagery. *Journal of Applied Sport Psychology, 15,* 160–175.

Giacobbi, P.R., Hausenblas, H.A., & Penfield, R.D. (2005). Further Refinements in the Measurement of Exercise Imagery: The Exercise Imagery Inventory. *Measurement in Physical Education and Exercise Science, 9,* 251-266.

Glisky, M.L., Williams, J.M., & Kihlstrom, J.F. (1996). Internal and external imagery perspectives and performance on two tasks. *Journal of Sport Behavior, 19,* 3–18.

Gordon, S., Weinberg, R., & Jackson, A. (1994). Effect of internal and external imagery on cricket performance. *Journal of Sport Behavior, 17,* 60–75.

Gorecki, J.J., Vadocz, E.A., Mensch, J.M., & French, K.E. (2002). Imagery content variation in expert-novice knowledge representations: A qualitative approach. *Journal of Sport and Exercise Psychology, 24,* S64.

Goss, S., Hall, C., Buckolz, E., & Fishburne, G. (1986). Imagery ability and the acquisition and retention of movements. *Memory and Cognition, 14,* 469–477.

Gregg, M., Hall, C., & Nederhof, E. (2005). The imagery ability, imagery use, and performance relationship. *The Sport Psychologist, 19,* 93–99.

Hale, B.D. (1982). The effects of internal and external imagery on muscular and ocular concomitants. *Journal of Sport Psychology, 4,* 379–387.

Hale, B.D., & Whitehouse, A. (1998). The effects of imagery-manipulated appraisal on intensity and direction of competition anxiety. *The Sport Psychologist, 12,* 40–51.

Hall, C. (1985). Individual differences in the mental practice and imagery of motor skill performance. *Canadian Journal of Applied Sport Science, 10,* 17S–21S.

Hall, C. (1997). Lew Hardy's third myth: A matter of perspective. *Journal of Applied Sport Psychology, 9,* 310–313.

Hall, C. (2001). Imagery in sport and exercise. In R.N. Singer, H. Hausenblas, & C.M. Janelle (Eds.), *Handbook of sport psychology* (2nd ed., pp. 529–549). New York: Wiley.

Hall, C., Bernoties, L., & Schmidt, D. (1995). Interference effects of mental imagery on a motor task. *British Journal of Psychology, 86,* 181–190.

Hall, C., & Buckolz, E. (1982). Imagery and the recall of movement patterns. *Imagination, Cognition and Personality, 2,* 251–260.

Hall, C., Buckolz, E., & Fishburne, G.J. (1992). Imagery and the acquisition of motor skills. *Canadian Journal of Applied Sport Sciences, 17,* 19 - 27.

Hall, C., Mack, D., Paivio, A., & Hausenblas, H. (1998). Imagery use by athletes: Development of the sport imagery questionnaire. *International Journal of Sport Psychology, 29,* 73–89.

Hall, C., & Martin, K.A. (1997). Measuring movement imagery abilities: A revision of the Movement Imagery Questionnaire. *Journal of Mental Imagery, 21,* 143–154.

Hall, C., Moore, J., Annett, J., & Rodgers, W. (1997). Recalling demonstrated and guided movements using imaginary and verbal rehearsal strategies. *Research Quarterly for Exercise and Sport, 68,* 136–144.

Hall, C., & Pongrac, J. (1983). *Movement Imagery Questionnaire.* London, ON: University of Western Ontario.

Hall, C., & Rodgers, W. (1989). Enhancing coaching effectiveness in figure skating through a mental skills training program. *The Sport Psychologist, 3,* 142–154.

Hall, C., Rodgers, W., & Barr, K. (1990). The use of imagery by athletes in selected sports. *The Sport Psychologist, 4,* 1–10.

Halpern, A.R., & Zatorre, R.J. (1999). When that tune runs through your head: A PET investigation of auditory imagery for familiar melodies. *Cerebral Cortex, 9,* 697–704.

Hanin, Y.L., & Stambulova, N.B. (2002). Metaphoric description of performance states: An application of the IZOF model. *The Sport Psychologist, 16,* 396–415.

Hanrahan, C. (1995). Creating dance images: Basic principles for teachers. *Journal of Physical Education, Recreation and Dance, 66,* 33–39.

Hanrahan, C., & Salmela, J.H. (1990). Dance images—Do they really work or are we just imagining things? *Journal of Physical Education, Recreation and Dance, 61,* 18–21.

Hanrahan, C., Tetréau, B., & Sarrazin, C. (1995). Use of imagery while performing dance movement. *International Journal of Sport Psychology, 26,* 413–430

Hanrahan, C., & Vergeer, I. (2000). Multiple uses of mental imagery by professional modern dancers. *Imagination, Cognition, and Personality, 20,* 231–255.

Hanrahan, S.J. (1996). Dancer's perceptions of psychological skills. *Revista de Psicologia del Deporte, 9-10,* 19–27.

Hanton, S., Mellalieu, S.D., & Hall, R. (2004). Self-confidence and anxiety interpretation: A qualitative investigation. *Psychology of Sport and Exercise, 5,* 477–495.

Hanton, S., & Jones, G. (1999). The acquisition and development of cognitive skills and strategies: I. Making the butterflies fly in formation. *The Sport Psychologist, 13,* 1–21.

Hardy, L. (1997). The Coleman Roberts Griffith address: Three myths about applied consultancy work. *Journal of Applied Sport Psychology, 9,* 277–294.

Hardy, L., & Callow, N. (1999). Efficacy of external and internal visual imagery perspectives for the enhancement of performance of tasks in which form is important. *Journal of Sport and Exercise Psychology, 21,* 95–112.

Harrigan, J.A., & O'Connell, D.M. (1996). How do you look when you feel anxious? Facial displays of anxiety. *Personality and Individual Differences, 21,* 205–212.

Harris, D.V., & Robinson, W.J. (1986). The effects of skill level on EMG activity during internal and external imagery. *Journal of Sport Psychology, 8,* 105–111.

Harwood, C., Cumming, J., & Fletcher, D. (2004). Motivational Profiles and Psychological Skills Use within Elite Youth Sport. *Journal of Applied Sport Psychology, 16,* 318-332.

Harwood, C., Cumming, J., & Hall, C. (2003). Imagery use in elite youth sport participants: Reinforcing the applied significance of achievement goal theory. *Research Quarterly for Exercise and Sport, 74,* 292-300.

Hausenblas, H., Hall, C., Rodgers, W., & Munroe, K. (1999). Exercise imagery: Its nature and measurement. *Journal of Applied Sport Psychology, 11,* 171–180.

Hecker, J.E., & Kaczor, L.M. (1988). Application of imagery theory to sport psychology: Some preliminary findings. *Journal of Sport and Exercise Psychology, 10,* 363–373.

Helsen, W.F., Starkes, J.L., & Hodges, N.J. (1998) Team sports and the theory of deliberate practice. *Journal of Sport and Exercise Psychology, 20,* 12-34.

Highlen, P.A., & Bennett, B.B. (1983). Elite divers and wrestlers: A comparison between open- and closed-skill athletes. *Journal of Sport Psychology, 5,* 390–409.

Hinshaw, K.E. (1991). The effects of mental practice on motor skill performance: Critical evaluation and meta-analysis. *Imagination, Cognition, and Personality, 11,* 3–35.

Hodges, N. J., & Starkes, J. L. (1996). Wrestling with the nature of expertise: A sport specific test of Ericsson, Krampe and Tesch-Romer's (1993) theory of deliberate practice. *International Journal of Sport Psychology, 27,* 400-424.

Holmes, P.S., & Collins, D.J. (2001). The PETTLEP approach to motor imagery: A functional equivalence model for sport psychologists. *Journal of Applied Sport Psychology, 13,* 60–83.

Holmes, P.S., & Collins, D.J. (2002). Functional equivalence solutions for problems with motor imagery. In I. Cockerill (Ed.), *Solutions in sport psychology* (1st ed., pp. 120–140). London: Thomson.

Ievleva, L., & Orlick, T. (1991). Mental links to enhanced healing: An exploratory study. *The Sport Psychologist, 5,* 25–40.

Ingvar, D.H., & Philipson, L. (1977). Distribution of cerebral blood flow in the dominant hemisphere during motor ideation and motor performance. *Annals of Neurology, 2,* 230–237.

Isaac, A., & Marks, D. (1994). Individual differences in mental imagery experience: Developmental changes and specialization. *British Journal of Psychology, 85,* 479–500.

Jacobson, E. (1930). Electrical measures of neuromuscular states during mental activities (part I). *American Journal of Physiology, 91,* 567–608.

Jeannerod, M. (1995). Mental imagery in the motor context. *Neuropsychologia, 33,* 1419–1432.

Jeannerod, M. (1997). *The cognitive neuroscience of action.* Oxford, United Kingdom: Blackwell.

Jeannerod, M., & Frak, V. (1999). Mental imaging of motor activity in humans. *Current Opinion in Neurobiology, 9,* 735–739.

Johnson, P. (1982). The functional equivalence of imagery and movement. *The Quarterly Journal of Experimental Psychology, A34,* 349–365.

Johnson-Laird, P.N. (1981). Cognition, computers, and mental models. *Cognition, 10,* 139–143.

Jones, M.V., Mace, R.D., Bray, S.R., MacRae, A.W., & Stockbridge, C. (2002). The impact of motivational imagery on the emotional state and self-efficacy levels of novice climbers. *Journal of Sport Behavior, 25,* 57–73.

Jordet, G. (2005). Perceptual training in soccer: An imagery intervention study with elite players. *Journal of Applied Sport Psychology, 17,* 140–156.

Jowdy, D.P., Murphy, S.M., & Durtschi, S. (1989). *An assessment of the use of imagery by elite athletes: Athlete, coach and psychologist perspectives.* Unpublished report to the United States Olympic Committee, Colorado Springs.

Kim, J., Singer, R.N., & Tennant, L.K. (1998). Visual, auditory and kinesthetic imagery on motor learning. *Journal of Human Movement Studies, 34,* 159–174.

Kohl, R.M., & Roenker, D.L. (1983). Mechanism involvement during skill imagery. *Journal of Motor Behavior, 15,* 179–190.

Kosslyn, S.M. (1994). *Image and brain: The resolution of the imagery debate.* Cambridge, MA: MIT Press.

Kosslyn, S.M., Ganis, G., & Thompson, W.L. (2001). Neural foundations of imagery. *Nature Reviews Neuroscience, 2,* 635–739.

Kosslyn, S.M., Seger, C., Pani, J.R., & Hillger, L. (1990). When is imagery used in everyday life? A diary study. *Journal of Mental Imagery, 14,* 131–152.

Kosslyn, S.M., Thompson, W.L., & Alpert, N.M. (1997). Neural systems shared by visual imagery and visual perception: A positron emission tomography study. *Neuroimage, 6,* 320-334.

Lang, P.J. (1977). Imagery in therapy: An information-processing analysis of fear. *Behavior Therapy, 8,* 862–886.

Lang, P.J. (1979). A bio-informational theory of emotional imagery. *Psychophysiology, 16*, 495–512.

Lang, P.J. (1985). Cognition in emotions: Concept and action. In C. Izard, J. Kagan, & R. Zajonc (Eds.), *Emotion, Cognitions, and Behavior* (pp. 192–225). New York: Cambridge University Press.

Lavallee, D., Kremer, J., Moran, A.P., & Williams, M. (2004). *Sport psychology: Contemporary themes*. Houndsmill, United Kingdom: Palgrave Macmillan.

LeDoux, J. (1996). *The emotional brain*. New York: Simon & Schuster.

LeDoux, J. (2002). *Synaptic self: How our brains become who we are*. New York: Penguin.

Li-Wei, A., Qi-Wei, M., Orlick, T., & Zitzelsberger, L. (1992). The effect of mental-imagery training on performance enhancement with 7–10 year old children. *The Sport Psychologist, 6*, 230–241.

Lotze, M., Montoya, P., Erb, M.., Hulsmann, E., Flor, H., Klose, U., et al. (1999). Activation of cortical and cerebellar motor areas during executed and imagined hand movements: An fMRI study. *Journal of Cognitive Neuroscience, 11*, 491–501.

Lutz, R.S. (2003). Covert muscle excitation is outflow from the central generation of motor imagery. *Behavioural Brain Research, 140*, 149–163.

MacIntyre, T., & Moran, A. (1996). Imagery use among canoeists: A worldwide survey of novice, intermediate, and elite slalomists. *Journal of Applied Sport Psychology, 8*, S132.

Mackay, D.G. (1981). The problems of rehearsal or mental practice. *Journal of Motor Behavior, 13*, 274–285.

Mahoney, M.J., & Avener, M. (1977). Psychology of the elite athlete: An exploratory study. *Cognitive Therapy and Research, 1*, 135–141.

Marks, D.F. (1999). Consciousness, mental imagery and action. *British Journal of Psychology, 90*, 567–585.

Martin, K.A., Moritz, S.E., & Hall, C. (1999). Imagery use in sport: A literature review and applied model. *The Sport Psychologist, 13*, 245–268.

McClelland, J.L. (1992). Parallel-distributed processing models of memory. In L.R. Squire (Ed.), *Encyclopedia of learning and memory* (pp. 583–596). New York: Macmillan.

Meyers, A.W., Schleser, R., Cooke, C.J., & Cuvillier, C. (1979). Cognitive contributions to the development of gymnastics skills. *Cognitive Therapy and Research, 3*, 75–85.

Mills, K.D., Munroe, K., & Hall, C. (2000). The relationship between imagery and self-efficacy in competitive athletes. *Imagination, Cognition, and Personality, 20*, 33–39.

Monsma, E.V., & Overby, L.Y. (2004). The relationship between imagery and competitive anxiety in ballet auditions. *Journal of Dance Medicine and Science, 8*, 11–18.

Moran, A. (1996). *The psychology of concentration in sport performers: A cognitive analysis*. Hove, East Sussex, United Kingdom: Psychology Press.

Moran, A. (2004). *Sport and exercise psychology: A critical introduction*. Hove, East Sussex, United Kingdom: Routledge.

Moran, A., & MacIntyre, T. (1998). "There is more to an image than meets the eye": A qualitative study of kinaesthetic imagery among elite canoe-slalomists. *Irish Journal of Psychology, 19*, 406–423.

Moritz, S.E., Hall, C., Martin, K.A., & Vadocz, E. (1996). What are confident athletes imaging? An examination of image content. *The Sport Psychologist, 10*, 171–179.

Morris, T., Spittle, M., & Perry, C. (2004). Mental imagery in sport. In T. Morris & J. Summers (Eds.), *Sport Psychology: Theory, Applications and Issues* (2nd ed., pp. 344–387). Milton, Australia: Wiley.

Mulder, T., Zijlstra, S., Zijlstra, W., & Hochstenbach, J. (2004). The role of motor imagery in learning a totally novel movement. *Experimental Brain Research, 154*, 211–217.

Mumford, B., & Hall, C. (1985). The effects of internal and external imagery on performing figures in figure skating. *Canadian Journal of Applied Sport Psychology, 10*, 171–177.

Munroe, K., Giacobbi, P.R., Hall, C., & Weinberg, R. (2000). The four Ws of imagery use: Where, when, why, and what. *The Sport Psychologist, 14*, 119–137.

Munroe, K., Hall, C., Simms, S., & Weinberg, R. (1998). The influence of type of sport and time of season on athletes' use of imagery. *The Sport Psychologist, 12*, 440–449.

Munroe-Chandler, K.J., & Hall, C.R. (2004). Enhancing the collective efficacy of a soccer team through motivational general-mastery imagery. *Imagination, Cognition, and Personality, 21*, 51–67.

Munroe-Chandler, K.J., Hall, C.R., Fishburne, G.J., & Shannon, V. (2005). Using cognitive general imagery to improve soccer strategies. *European Journal of Sports Sciences, 5*, 41–49.

Murphy, S.M. (1986). Emotional imagery and its effects on strength and fine motor skill performance. *Dissertation Abstracts International, 47*, 383B. (University Microfilms No. DA 8604844)

Murphy, S. (1994). Imagery interventions in sport. *Medicine and Science in Sports and Exercise, 26*, 486–494.

Murphy, S.M., & Jowdy, D.P. (1992). Imagery and mental practice. In T. Horn (Ed.), *Advances in Sport Psychology* (pp. 221–250). Champaign, IL: Human Kinetics.

Murphy, S., & Martin, K.A. (2002). The use of imagery in sport. In T. Horn (Ed.), *Advances in Sport Psychology* (2nd ed., pp. 405–439). Champaign, IL: Human Kinetics.

Neisser, U. (1978). Anticipations, images and introspection. *Cognition, 6*, 169–174.

Nisbett, R., & Wilson, T. (1977). Telling more than we can know: Verbal reports on mental processes. *Psychological Review, 84*, 231-259.

Nordin, S.M., & Cumming, J. (2005a). More than meets the eye: Investigating imagery type, direction, and outcome. *The Sport Psychologist, 19*, 1–17.

Nordin, S.M., & Cumming, J. (2005b). Professional dancers describe their imagery: Where, when, what, why, and how. *The Sport Psychologist, 19*, 395–416.

Nordin, S.M., Cumming, J., Vincent, J., & McGrory, S. (2006). Mental training or spontaneous play? Examining which types of imagery constitute deliberate practice in sport. *Journal of Applied Sport Psychology, 18*, 345-362.

Nougier, V., Stein, J.F., & Bonnel, A.M. (1991). Information processing in sport and orienting of attention. *International Journal of Sport Psychology, 22*, 307–327.

Orlick, T., & McCaffrey, N. (1991). Mental training with children for sport and life. *The Sport Psychologist, 5*, 322–334.

Overby, L.Y. (1990). The use of imagery by dance teachers—development and implementation of two research instruments. *Journal of Physical Education, Recreation and Dance, 61*, 24–27.

Overby, L.Y., Hall, C., & Haslam, I.R. (1997). A comparison of imagery used by dance teachers, figure skating coaches, and soccer coaches. *Imagination, Cognition, and Personality, 17*, 323–337.

Page, S.R., Sime, W., & Nordell, K. (1999). The effects of imagery on female college swimmers' perceptions of anxiety. *The Sport Psychologist, 13*, 458–469.

Paivio, A. (1971). *Imagery and verbal processes*. New York: Holt, Rinehart and Winston.

Paivio, A. (1985). Cognitive and motivational functions of imagery in human performance. *Canadian Journal of Applied Sport Sciences, 10*, 22S–28S.

Paivio, A. (1986). *Mental representations*. Oxford, United Kingdom: Oxford University Press.

Pascual-Leone, A., Nguyet, D., Cohen, L.G., Brasil-Neto, J.P., Cammarota, A., & Hallet, M. (1995). Modulation of muscle responses evoked by transcranial magnetic stimulation during the acquisition of new fine motor skills. *Journal of Neurophysiology, 74*, 1037–1045.

Perry, C., & Morris, T. (1995). Mental imagery in sport. In T. Morris & J. Summers (Eds.), *Sport Psychology: Theory, applications and issues* (pp. 339–385). Brisbane, Australia: Wiley.

Pietrini, P., Guazelli, M., Basso, G., Jaffe, K., & Grafman, J. (2000). Neural correlates of imaginal aggressive behavior assessed by positron emission tomography in healthy subjects. *American Journal of Psychiatry, 157*, 1772–1781.

Pinker, S., & Kosslyn, S.M. (1983). Theories of mental imagery. In A. Sheikh (Ed.), *Imagery: Current theory, research and application* (pp. 43–71). New York: Wiley.

Podgorny, P., & Shepard, R.N. (1978). Functional representations common to visual perception and imagination. *Journal of Experimental Psychology: Human Perception and Performance, 4*, 21–35.

Poon, P.P.L., & Rodgers, W.M. (2000). Learning and remembering strategies of novice and advanced jazz dancers for skill level appropriate dance routines. *Research Quarterly for Exercise and Sport, 71*, 135–143.

Pylyshyn, Z.W. (1973). What the mind's eye tells the mind's brain. *Psychological Bulletin, 80*, 1–24.

Ranganathan, V.K., Siemionow, V., Liu, J.Z., Sahgal, V., & Yue, G.H. (2004). From mental power to muscle power: Gaining strength by using the mind. *Neuropsychologia, 42*, 944–956.

Richardson, A. (1967). Mental practice: A review and discussion (part I). *Research Quarterly, 38*, 95–107.

Rodgers, W., Hall, C., & Buckolz, E. (1991). The effect of an imagery training program on imagery ability, imagery use, and figure skating performance. *Journal of Applied Sport Psychology, 3*, 109–125.

Rotella, R.J., Gansneder, B., Ojala, D., & Billing, J. (1980). Cognitions and coping strategies of elite skiers: An exploratory study of young developing athletes. *Journal of Sport Psychology, 2*, 350–354.

Ruiz, M.C., & Hanin, Y.L. (2004). Metaphoric description and individualized emotion profiling of performance states in top karate athletes. *Journal of Applied Sport Psychology, 16*, 258–273.

Rushall, B.S. (1988). Covert modeling as a procedure for altering an athlete's psychological state. *The Sport Psychologist, 2*, 131–140.

Rushall, B., & Lippmann, L. (1998). The role of imagery in physical performance. *International Journal of Sport Psychology, 29*, 57-72.

Sackett, R.S. (1934). The influences of symbolic rehearsal upon the retention of a maze habit. *Journal of General Psychology, 10*, 376–395.

Salmon, J., Hall, C., & Haslam, I.R. (1994). The use of imagery by soccer players. *Journal of Applied Sport Psychology, 6*, 116–133.

Sawada, M., Mori, S., & Ishii, M. (2002). Effect of metaphorical verbal instruction on modeling of sequential dance skills by young children. *Perceptual and Motor Skills, 95*, 1097–1105.

Schmidt, R.A. (1987). *Motor control and learning* (2nd ed.). Champaign, IL: Human Kinetics.

Shambrook, C.J., & Bull, S.J. (1996). The use of a single-case research design to investigate the efficacy of imagery training. *Journal of Applied Sport Psychology, 8*, 27–43.

Shaw, D.F., & Goodfellow, R. (1997). Performance enhancement and deterioration following outcome imagery: Testing a demand-characteristics explanation. In I. Cockerill & H. Steinberg (Eds.), *Cognitive enhancement in sport and exercise psychology* (pp. 37–43). Leicester, United Kingdom: British Psychological Society.

Short, S.E., Bruggeman, J.M., Engel, S.G., Marback, T.L., Wang, L.J., Willadsen, A., et al. (2002). The effect of imagery function and imagery direction on self-efficacy and performance on a golf-putting task. *The Sport Psychologist, 16*, 48–67.

Short, S.E., Hall, C.R., Engel, S.R., & Nigg, C.R.. (2004). Exercise imagery and the stages of change. *Journal of Mental Imagery, 28*, 61–78.

Short, S.E., Monsma, E.V., & Short, M. (2004). Is what you see really what you get? Athletes' perceptions of imagery functions. *The Sport Psychologist, 18*, 341–349.

Singer, J., & Antrobus, J.S. (1972). Daydreaming, imaginal processes, and personality: A normative study. In P. Sheehan (Ed.), *The function and nature of imagery* (pp. 175–202). New York: Academic Press.

Slade, J.M., Landers, D.M., & Martin, P.E. (2002). Muscular activity during real and imagined movements: A test of inflow explanations. *Journal of Sport and Exercise Psychology, 24*, 151–167.

Smith, D., & Collins, D. (2004). Mental practice, motor performance, and the late CNV. *Journal of Sport and Exercise Psychology, 26*, 412–426.

Smith, D., Collins, D., & Holmes, P. (2003). Impact and mechanism of mental practice effects on strength. *International Journal of Sport and Exercise Psychology, 1*, 293–306.

Smith, D., & Holmes, P. (2004). The effect of imagery modality on golf putting performance. *Journal of Sport and Exercise Psychology, 26*, 385–395.

Sordoni, C., Hall, C., & Forwell, L. (2000). The use of imagery by athletes during injury rehabilitation. *Journal of Sport Rehabilitation, 9*, 329–338.

Sordoni, C., Hall, C., & Forwell, L. (2002). The use of imagery in athletic injury rehabilitation and its relationship to self-efficacy. *Physiotherapy Canada, Summer*, 177–185.

Suinn, R. (1993). Imagery. In R.N. Singer, M. Murphey, & L.K. Tennant (Eds.), *Handbook of research on sport psychology* (pp. 492–510). New York: Macmillan.

Taylor, S.E., Pham, L.B., Rivkin, I.D., & Armor, D.A. (1998). Harnessing the imagination: Mental simulation, self-regulation, and coping. *American Psychologist, 53*, 429–439.

Taylor, J., & Shaw, D.F. (2002). The effects of outcome imagery on golf-putting performance. *Journal of Sports Sciences, 20*, 607–613.

Vadocz, E., Hall, C., & Moritz, S.E. (1997). The relationship between competitive anxiety and imagery use. *Journal of Applied Sport Psychology, 9*, 241–253.

Vealey, R.S., & Greenleaf, C.A. (2001). Seeing is believing: Understanding and using imagery in sport. In J.M. Williams (Ed.), *Applied sport psychology: Personal growth to peak performance* (4th ed., pp. 247–272). Mountain View, CA: Mayfield.

Vecchio, L., & Bonifacio, M. (1997). Different images in different situations: A diary study of the spontaneous use of imagery. *Journal of Mental Imagery, 21*, 147-170.

Vergeer, I. (2003). An exploration of factors affecting vividness of physically-orientated mental imagery. In R. Stelter (Ed.), *New approaches to exercise and sport psychology—theories, methods and applications. Proceedings of the XIth European Congress of Sport Psychology* (pp. 180). Copenhagen, Denmark: FEPSAC.

Vergeer, I., & Hanrahan, C. (1998). What modern dancers do to prepare: Content and objectives of preperformance routines. *AVANTE, 4*, 49–71.

Weinberg, R., Butt, J., Knight, B., Burke, K.L., & Jackson, A. (2003). The relationship between the use and effectiveness of imagery: An exploratory investigation. *Journal of Applied Sport Psychology, 15*, 26–40.

White, A., & Hardy, L. (1995). Use of different imagery perspectives on the learning and performance of different motor skills. *British Journal of Psychology, 86*, 169–180.

White, A., & Hardy, L. (1998). An in-depth analysis of the uses of imagery by high-level slalom canoeists and artistic gymnasts. *The Sport Psychologist, 12*, 387–403.

Woods, E. (2005, July 14). *Tiger prints.* [Television broadcast on the Golf Channel].

Woolfolk, R.L., Murphy, S.M., Gottesfeld, D., & Aitken, D. (1985). Effects of mental rehearsal of task motor activity and mental depiction of task outcome on motor skill performance. *Journal of Sport Psychology, 7*, 191–197.

Woolfolk, R.L., Parrish, W., & Murphy, S.M. (1985). The effects of positive and negative imagery on motor skill performance. *Cognitive Therapy and Research, 9*, 335–341.

Yue, G., & Cole, K.J. (1992). Strength increases from the motor program: Comparisons of training with voluntary and imagined muscle contractions. *Journal of Neurophysiology, 67*, 1115–1123.

CHAPTER 14

Abernethy, B. (2001). Attention. In R.N. Singer, M. Hausenblas, H.A., & Janelle, C.M (Eds.), *Handbook of sport psychology* (pp. 53–85). New York: Wiley.

Albrecht, R.A., & Feltz, D.L. (1987). Generality and specificity of attention related to competitive anxiety and sport performance. *Journal of Sport & Exercise Psychology, 9*, 231–248.

Bacon, S. (1974). Arousal and the range of cue utilization. *Journal of Experimental Psychology, 102*, 81–87.

Badgaiyan, R.D. (2000). Executive control, willed action, and nonconscious processing. *Human Brain Mapping, 9*, 38–41.

Bauer, R.H. (1976). Short-term memory: EEG alpha correlates and the effect of increased alpha. *Behavioral Biology, 17*, 425–433.

Baumeister, R.F. (1984). Choking under pressure: Self-consciousness and paradoxical effects of incentives on skillful performance. *Journal of Personality and Social Psychology, 46*, 610–620.

Boutcher, S.H. (1990). The role of performance routines in sport. In G. Jones & L. Hardy (Eds.), *Stress and performance in sport* (pp. 231–245). London: Wiley.

Boutcher, S.H., & Crews, D.J. (1987). The effect of a preshot routine on a well-learned skill. *International Journal of Sport Psychology, 18*, 30–39.

Boutcher, S.H., & Rotella, R.J. (1987). A psychological skills educational program for closed-skill performance enhancement. *The Sport Psychologist, 1*, 127–137.

Boutcher, S.H., & Zinsser, N. (1990). Cardiac deceleration of elite and beginning golfers during putting. *Journal of Sport Psychology, 12*, 37–47.

Brisswalter, J., Collardeau, M., & Arcelin, R. (2002). Effects of acute physical exercise characteristics on cognitive performance. *Sports Medicine, 32*(9), 555–566.

Broadbent, D.E. (1958). *Perception and communication*. London: Pergamon Press.

Camras, L.A., Holland, E.A., & Patterson, M.J. (1993). Facial expression. In M. Lewis & J.M. Haviland (Eds.), *Handbook of emotions* (pp. 199–208). New York: Guildford Press.

Carver, C.S., & Scheier, M.F. (1978). Self-focusing effects of dispositional self-consciousness, mirror presence, and audience presence. *Journal of Personality and Social Psychology, 36*, 324–332.

Carver, C.S., & Scheier, M.F. (1981). *Attention and self-regulation*. New York: Springer-Verlag.

Colcombe, S., & Kramer, A.F. (2003). Fitness effects on the cognitive function of older adults: A meta-analysis study. *Psychological Science, 14*(2), 125–130.

Cote, J., Baker, J., & Abernethy, B. A developmental framework for the acquisition of expertise in team sports. In Starkes, J.L., & Ericsson, K.A. (Eds.), *Expert performance in sports* (pp. 90–113). Champaign, IL: Human Kinetics.

Crews, D.J., & Boutcher, S.H. (1986). The effects of structured preshot behaviors on beginning golf performance. *Perceptual and Motor Skills, 62*, 291–294.

Crews, D.J., & Boutcher, S.H. (1987). An observational analysis of professional female golfers during tournament play. *Journal of Sport Behavior, 9*, 51–58.

Crews, D.J., & Landers, D.L. (1992). Electroencephalographic measures of attentional patterns prior to the golf putt. *Medicine and Science in Sports and Exercise, 25*, 116–126.

Csikszentmihalyi, M. (1975). Play and intrinsic rewards. *Journal of Humanistic Psychology, 15*, 41–63.

Deeny, S.P., Hillman, C.H., Janelle, C.M., & Hatfield, B.H. (2003). Cortico-cortical communication and superior performance in skilled marksman: An EEG coherence analysis. *Journal of Sport and Exercise Psychology, 25*, 188–204.

Duval, S., & Wicklund, R.A. (1972). *A theory of objective self-awareness*. New York: Academic Press.

Easterbrook, J.A. (1959). The effect of emotion on cue utilization and the organization of behavior. *Psychological Review, 66*, 183–201.

Ekman, P., & Friesan, M.V. (1975). *Unmasking the face*. Englewood Cliffs, NJ: Prentice Hall.

Elder, S.T., Grenier, C., Lashley, J., Martyn, S., Regenbogen, D., & Roundtree, G. (1985). Can subjects be trained to communicate through the use of EEG biofeedback? *Biofeedback and Self-Regulation, 10*, 88–89.

Hatfield, B.D., & Landers, D.M. (1983). Psychophysiology—a new direction for sport psychology. *Journal of Sport Psychology, 5*, 243–259.

Hatfield, B.D., Landers, D.M., & Ray, W.J. (1984). Cognitive processes during self-paced motor performance: An electroencephalographic profile of skilled marksmen. *Journal of Sport Psychology, 6*, 42–59.

Haufler, A.J., Spalding, T.W., Santa Maria, D.L., Hatfield, B.D. (2000). Neuro-cognitive activity during a self-paced visuospatial task: Comparative EEG profiles in marksmen and novice shooters. *Biological Psychology, 53*, 131–160.

Helin, P., Sihvonen, R., & Hanninen, O. (1987). Timing of the triggering action of shooting in relation to the cardiac cycle. *British Journal of Sports Medicine, 21*, 33–36.

Hirst, W. (1986). The psychology of attention. In J. LeDoux & W. Hirst (Eds.), *Mind and brain* (pp. 105–141). Cambridge, United Kingdom: Cambridge University Press.

Hockey, G. (1970). Effects of loud noise on attentional selectivity. *Quarterly Journal of Experimental Psychology, 22*, 28–36.

Gould, D., Greenleaf, C., & Krane, V. (2006). Arousal-anxiety and sport behavior. In T. Horn (Ed.), *Advances in sport psychology*. Champaign, IL: Human Kinetics.

Izard, C.E. (1977). *Human emotions*. New York: Plenum Press.

Jackson, G.M., & Eberly, D.A. (1982). Facilitation of performance on an arithmetic task as a result of the application of a biofeedback procedure to suppress alpha wave activity. *Biofeedback and Self-Regulation, 7*, 211–221.

Jackson, S.A. (1996). Toward a conceptual understanding of flow experience in elite athletes. *Research Quarterly Exercise and Sport, 67*, 76–90.

James, W. (1890). *Principles of psychology* (Vol. 1). New York: Holt.

Janelle, C.M., Hillman, C.H., Apparies, R.J., Murray, N.P., Meili, L., Fallon, E.A., et al. (2000). Expertise differences in cortical activation and gaze behaviour during rifle shooting. *Journal of Sport and Exercise Psychology, 22*, 167–182.

Janelle, C.M., Singer, R.N., & Williams, A.M. (1999). External distraction and attentional narrowing: Visual search evidence. *Journal of Sport and Exercise Psychology, 21*, 70–91.

Kahneman, D. (1973). *Attention and effort*. Englewood Cliffs, NJ: Prentice Hall.

Keele, S.W. (1973). *Attention and human performance*. Pacific Palisades, CA: Goodyear.

Kerick, S.E., Douglas, L.W., Hatfield, B.D. (2004). Cerebral cortical adaptations associated with visuomotor practice. *Medicine and Science in Sports and Exercise, 36*, 118–129.

Kerick, S.E., McDowell, K., Hung, T.-M., Santa Maria, D.L., Spalding, T.W., & Hatfield, B.D. (2001). The role of the left temporal region under the cognitive motor demands of shooting in skilled marksman. *Biological Psychology, 58*, 263–277.

Kerr, B. (1973). Processing demands during mental operations. *Memory and Cognition, 1*, 401–412.

Kimble, G., & Perlmuter, L. (1970). The problem of volition. *Psychological Review, 77*, 361–384.

Kissin, B. (1986). *Conscious and unconscious programs in the brain*. New York: Plenum Press.

Klinger, E. (1984). A consciousness-sampling analysis of test anxiety and performance. *Journal of Personality and Social Psychology, 47*, 1376–1390.

Kocel, K., Galin, D., Ornstein, R., & Merrin, E.L. (1972). Lateral eye movements and cognitive mode. *Psychonomic Science, 27*, 223–224.

Konttinen, N., & Lyytinen, H. (1999). Brain slow potentials and postural sway behaviour during sharpshooting performance. *Journal of Motor Behavior, 31*, 11–20.

Konttinen, N., & Lyytinen, K. (1992). Physiology of preparation: Brain slow waves, heart rate, and respiration preceding triggering in rifle shooting. *International Journal of Sports Psychology, 23*, 110–127.

Konttinen, N., Lyytinen, K., & Konttinen, R. (1995). Brain slow potentials reflecting successful shooting performance. *Research Quarterly for Exercise and Sport, 66*, 64–72.

Krings, T., Topper, R., Foltys, H., Erberich, S., Sparing, R., Willmes, K., et al. (2000). Cortical activation patterns during complex motor tasks in piano players and control subjects. A functional magnetic resonance imaging study. *Neuroscience Letters, 278*, 189–193.

Landers, D.M. (1980a). Arousal, attention, and skilled performance: Further considerations. *Quest, 33*, 271–283.

Landers, D.M. (1980b). Motivation and performance: The role of arousal and attentional factors. In W.F. Straub (Ed.), *Sport psychology: An analysis of athlete behavior* (pp. 91–125). New York: Mouvement.

Landers, D.M. (1981). Arousal, attention, and skilled performance: Further considerations. *Quest, 33,* 271–283.

Landers, D.M. (1985a, May). *Beyond the TAIS: Alternative behavioral and psychophysiological measures for determining an internal vs. external focus of attention.* Paper presented at the North American Society for the Psychology of Sport and Physical Activity Conference, Gulfport, MS.

Landers, D.M. (1985b). Psychophysiological assessment and biofeedback: Application for athletes in closed-skill sports. In J. Sandweiss & S. Wolf (Eds.), *Biofeedback and sports science* (pp. 65–105). New York: Plenum Press.

Landers, D.M., Boutcher, S.H., & Wang, M.Q. (1986). A psychobiological study of archery performance. *Research Quarterly for Exercise and Sport, 57,* 236–244.

Landers, D.M., Christina, R., Hatfield, B.D., Doyle, L.A., & Daniels, F.S. (1980). Moving competitive shooting into the scientists' lab. *American Rifleman, 128,* 36–37, 76–77.

Landers, D.M., Han, M., Salazar, W., Petruzzello, S.J., Kubitz, K.A., & Gannon, T.L. (1994). Effects of learning on electroencephalographic and electrocardiographic patterns in novice archers. *International Journal of Sport Psychology, 25,* 313–330.

Landers, D.M., Petruzzello, S.J., Salazar, W., Kubitz, C.A., Crews, D.J., Kubitz, K.A., et al. (1991). The influence of electrocortical biofeedback on performance in pre-elite archers. *Medicine and Science in Sports and Exercise, 23,* 123–129.

Landers, D.M., Qi, W.M., & Courtet, P. (1985). Peripheral narrowing among experienced and inexperienced rifle-shooters under low- and high-stress conditions. *Research Quarterly for Exercise and Sport, 56,* 122–130.

Langer, E.J., & Imber, L.G. (1979). When practice makes imperfect: Debilitating effects of overlearning. *Journal of Personality and Social Psychology, 37,* 2014–2024.

LeDoux, J.E., Wilson, D.H., & Gazzaniga, M.S. (1977). Manipulo-spatial aspects of cerebral lateralization: Clues to the origin of lateralization. *Neuropsychologica, 15,* 743–750.

Logan, G.D. (1988). Automaticity, resources, and memory. Theoretical controversies and practical implications. *Human Factors, 30,* 583–598.

McKee, G., Humphrey, B., & McAdam, N.W. (1973). Scaled lateralization of alpha activity during linguistic and musical tasks. *Psychophysiology, 10,* 441–443.

Molander, B., & Backman, L. (1989). Age differences in heart rate patterns during concentration in a precision sport: Implications for attentional functioning. *Journal of Gerontology: Psychological Sciences, 44,* 80–87.

Moran, A. (1996). *The psychology of concentration in sport performers.* Hove, United Kingdom: Psychology Press.

Morgan, W.P., & Pollack, M.L. (1977). Psychologic characterization of the elite distance runner. *Annals of the New York Academy of Sciences, 301,* 382–403.

Navon, D., & Gopher, D. (1979). On the economy of the human processing system. *Psychological Review, 86,* 214–255.

Nideffer, R. (1976a). *The inner athlete: Mind plus muscle for winning.* San Diego, CA: Enhanced Performance Associates.

Nideffer, R. (1976b). Test of attentional and interpersonal style. *Journal of Personality and Social Psychology, 34,* 394–404.

Nideffer, R. (1976c). *An interpreters' manual for the test of attentional and interpersonal style.* Rochester, NY: Behavioral Research Applications Group.

Norman, D. (1969). Toward a theory of memory and attention. *Psychological Review, 75,* 522–536.

O'Donnel, B.F., & Cohen, R.A. (1993). Attention: A component of information processing. In R.A. Cohen (Ed.), *The neuropsychology of attention* (pp. 11–28). New York: Plenum Press.

Parasuraman, R. (1998). *The attentive brain.* Cambridge, MA: MIT Press.

Pashler, H.E. (1998). *The psychology of attention.* Cambridge, MA: MIT Press.

Posner, M.I., & Bois, S.J. (1971). Components of attention. *Psychological Review, 78,* 391–408.

Privette, G. (1982). Peak performance in sports: A factorial topology. *International Journal of Sport Psychology, 13,* 242–249.

Privette, G. (1983). Peak experience, peak performance, and flow: A comparative analysis of positive human experiences. *Journal of Personality and Social Psychology, 43,* 1361–1367.

Rogers, T.J., Alderman, B.L., & Landers, D.M. (2003). Effects of life event stress and hardiness on peripheral vision in a real life stress situation. *Behavioral Medicine, 29,* 21–26.

Rogers, T.J., & Landers, D.M. (2005). Mediating effects of peripheral vision in the life event stress/athletic injury relationship. *Journal of Sport and Exercise Psychology, 27,* 271–288.

Salazar, W., Landers, D.M., Petruzzello, S.J., Han, M., Crews, D.J., & Kubitz, K.A. (1990). Hemispheric asymmetry, cardiac response, and performance in elite archers. *Research Quarterly for Exercise and Sports, 61,* 351–359.

Sarason, I.G. (1972). Experimental approaches to tests anxiety: Attention and the uses of information. In C.D. Spielberger (Ed.), *Anxiety: Current trends in theory and research* (Vol. 2, pp. 380–403). New York: Academic Press.

Scheier, M.S., Fenigstein, A., & Buss, A.H. (1974). Self-awareness and physical aggression. *Journal of Experimental Social Psychology, 10,* 264–273.

Schmidt, A., & Peper, E. (1998). Strategies for training concentration. In J. Williams (Ed.), *Applied Sport Psychology* (pp. 316-328). California: Mayfield.

Schmidt, R.A. (1999). *Motor control and learning.* Champaign, IL: Human Kinetics.

Schneider, W., Dumais, S.T., & Shiffrin, R.M. (1984). Automatic and control processing and attention. In R. Parasuraman & R. Davies (Eds.), *Varieties of attention* (pp. 1–27). Orlando, FL: Academic Press.

Schomer, H.H. (1986). Mental strategies and the perception of effort of marathon runners. *International Journal of Sport Psychology, 17,* 41–59.

Schomer, H.H. (1987). Mental strategy training programme for marathon runners. *International Journal of Sport Psychology, 18,* 133–151.

Schwartz, G.E., Davidson, R.J., & Maer, F. (1975). Right hemispheric specialization for emotion: Interactions with cognitions. *Science, 190,* 286–290.

Schwartz, G.E., Davidson, R.J., & Pugwash, E. (1976). Voluntary control of patterns of EEG parietal asymmetry: Cognitive concomitants. *Psychophysiology, 13,* 498–504.

Shiffrin, R.M. (1976). Capacity limitations in information processing, attention, and memory. In W.K. Estes (Ed.), *Handbook of learning and cognitive processes* (Vol. 4, pp. 117–136). Hillsdale, NJ: Erlbaum.

Sperry, R.W. (1968). Hemisphere deconnection and unity in conscious awareness. *American Psychologist, 23,* 723–733.

Springer, S.P., & Deutsch, G. (1998). *Left brain-right brain: Perspectives from cognitive neuroscience.* New York: Freeman.

Stroop, J.P. (1935). Studies of interference in serial verbal reactions. *Journal of Experimental Psychology, 18,* 643–662.

Styles, E. (1997). *The psychology of attention.* Hove, East Sussex, United Kingdom: Psychology Press.

Suter, S., Griffin, G., Smallhouse, P., & Whitlach, S. (1981). Biofeedback regulation of temporal EEG alpha asymmetries. *Biofeedback and Self-Regulation, 6,* 45–56.

Tomkins, S. (1983). Affect theory. In P. Eckman (Ed.), *Emotion in the human face* (2nd ed., pp. 353–395). New York: Cambridge University Press.

Tomporowski, P.D. (2003). Effects of acute bouts of exercise on cognition. *Acta Psychologica, 112,* 297–324.

Tucker, D.M., Shearer, S.L., & Murray, J.D. (1977). Hemispheric specialization and cognitive behavior therapy. *Cognitive Therapy and Research, 1,* 263–273.

Van Schoyck, S.R., & Grasha, A.F. (1981). Attentional style variations and athletic ability: The advantage of a sports-specific test. *Journal of Sport Psychology, 3,* 149–165.

Vickers, J.N. (1996a). Visual control while aiming at a far target. *Journal of Experimental Psychology: Human Perception and Performance, 22,* 342–354.

Vickers, J.N. (1996b). Control of visual attention during the basketball free throw. *American Journal of Sports Medicine, 24,* S93–S97.

Vickers, J.N., & Adolphe, R.M. (1997). Gaze behavior during a ball tracking and aiming skill. *International Journal of Sports Vision, 4,* 18–27.

Wachtel, P.L. (1967). Conceptions of broad or narrow attention. *Psychological Bulletin, 68,* 417–429.

Wickens, C.D. (1984). Processing resources in attention. In R. Parasuraman & R. Davies (Eds.), *Varieties of attention* (pp. 63–102). Orlando, FL: Academic Press.

Wine, J. (1971). Test anxiety and direction of attention. *Psychological Bulletin, 76,* 92–104.

Zaichkowsky, L.D. (1984). Attentional styles. In W. Straub & J. Williams (Eds.), *Cognitive sport psychology* (pp. 140–150). New York: Sports Science Associates.

Wulf, G. (2007). *Attention and Motor Skill Learning.* Champaign, IL: Human Kinetics.

CHAPTER 15

Anderson, D.C., Crowell, C.R., Doman, M., & Howard, G.S. (1988). Performance posting, goal setting, and activity-contingent praise as applied to a university hockey team. *Journal of Applied Psychology, 73,* 87–95.

Annesi, J.H. (2002). Goal-setting protocol in adherence to exercise by Italian adults. *Perceptual and Motor Skills, 94,* 453–458.

Anshel, M.H., Weinberg, R.S., & Jackson, A. (1992). The effect of goal difficulty and task complexity on intrinsic motivation and motor performance. *Journal of Sport Behavior, 15,* 159–176.

Baker, S.M., Marshak, H.H., Rice, G.T., & Zimmerman, G.J. (2001). Patient participation in physical therapy goal setting. *Physical Therapy, 81,* 1118–1126.

Bandura, A. (1986). *Social foundations of thought and action: A social cognitive theory.* Englewood Cliffs, NJ: Prentice Hall.

Bandura, A., & Simon, K.M. (1977). The role of proximal intentions in self-regulation of refractory behavior. *Cognitive Therapy and Research, 1,* 177–193.

Bar-Eli, M., Hartman, I., & Levy-Kolker, N. (1994). Using goal setting to improve physical performance of adolescents with behavior disorders: The effect of goal proximity. *Adapted Physical Activity Quarterly, 11,* 86–97.

Bar-Eli, M., Levy-Kolker, N., Tenenbaum, G., & Weinberg, R.S. (1993). Effect of goal difficulty on performance of aerobic, anaerobic and power tasks in laboratory and field settings. *Journal of Sport Behavior, 16,* 17–32.

Bar-Eli, M., Tenenbaum, G., Pie, J., Btesh, Y., & Almog, A. (1997). Effect of goal difficulty, goal specificity and duration of practice time intervals on muscular endurance performance. *Journal of Sport Sciences, 15,* 125–135.

Barnett, M.L. (1977). Effects of two methods of goal setting on learning a gross motor task. *Research Quarterly, 48,* 19–23.

Barnett, M.L., & Stanicek, J.A. (1979). Effects of goal-setting on achievement in archery. *Research Quarterly, 50,* 328–332.

Beggs, A. (1990). Goal setting in sport. In G. Jones & L. Hardy (Eds.), *Stress and performance in sport* (pp. 135–170). Chichester, United Kingdom: Wiley.

Bompa, T.O. (1999). *Periodization training for sports.* Champaign, IL: Human Kinetics.

Borrelli, B., & Mermelstein, R. (1994). Goal setting and behavior change in a smoking cessation program. *Cognitive Therapy and Research, 18,* 69–83.

Boyce, B.A. (1990a). Effects of goal specificity and goal difficulty upon skill acquisition of a selected shooting task. *Perceptual and Motor Skills, 70,* 1031–1039.

Boyce, B.A. (1990b). The effect of instructor-set goals upon skill acquisition and retention of a selected shooting task. *Journal of Teaching in Physical Education, 9,* 115–122.

Boyce, B.A. (1992a). Effects of assigned versus participant-set goals on skill acquisition and retention of a selected shooting task. *Journal of Teaching in Physical Education, 11,* 220–234.

Boyce, B.A. (1992b). The effects of goal proximity on skill acquisition and retention of a shooting task in a field-based setting. *Journal of Sport and Exercise Psychology, 14,* 298–308.

Boyce, B.A. (1994). The effects of goal setting on performance and spontaneous goal-setting behavior of experienced pistol shooters. *The Sport Psychologist, 8,* 87–93.

Boyce, B.A., & Bingham, S.M. (1997). The effects of self-efficacy and goal setting on bowling performance. *Journal of Teaching in Physical Education, 16,* 312–323.

Boyce, B.A., & Wayda, V.K. (1994). The effects of assigned and self-set goals on task performance. *Journal of Sport and Exercise Psychology, 16,* 258–269.

Boyce, B.A., Wayda, K.W., Johnston, T., Bunker, L.K., & Eliot, J. (2001). The effects of three types of goal setting conditions on tennis performance: A field-based study. *Journal of Teaching in Physical Education, 20,* 188–200.

Brawley, L.R., Carron, A.V., & Widmeyer, W.N. (1992). The nature of group goals in sport teams: A phenomenological analysis. *The Sport Psychologist, 6,* 323–333.

Brawley, L.R., Carron, A.V., & Widmeyer, W.N. (1993). The influence of the group and its cohesiveness on perceptions of group goal-related variables. *Journal of Sport and Exercise Psychology, 15,* 245–260.

Bray, S.R. (2004). Collective efficacy, group goals, and group performance of a muscular endurance task. *Small Group Research, 35,* 230–238.

Burton, D. (1989a). The impact of goal specificity and task complexity on basketball skill development. *The Sport Psychologist, 3,* 34–47.

Burton, D. (1989b). Winning isn't everything: Examining the impact of performance goals on collegiate swimmers' cognitions and performance. *The Sport Psychologist, 3,* 105–132.

Burton, D. (1992). The Jekyll/Hyde nature of goals: Reconceptualizing goal setting in sport. In T. Horn (Ed.), *Advances in sport psychology* (pp. 267–297). Champaign, IL: Human Kinetics.

Burton, D. (1993). Goal setting in sport. In R.N. Singer, M. Murphey, & L.K. Tennant (Eds.), *Handbook of research on sport psychology* (pp. 467–491). New York: Macmillan.

Burton, D., Daw, J., Williams-Rice, B.T., & Phillips, D. (1989, October). *Goal setting styles: The influence of self-esteem on goal difficulty preferences.* Paper presented at the meeting of the Canadian Society for Psychomotor Learning and Sport Psychology, Victoria, BC.

Burton, D., & Naylor, S. (2002). The Jekyll/Hyde nature of goals: Revisiting and updating goal-setting in sport. In T. Horn (Ed.), *Advances in sport psychology* (2nd ed., pp. 459–499). Champaign, IL: Human Kinetics.

Burton, D., Naylor, S., & Holliday, B. (2001). Goal setting in sport: Investigating the goal effectiveness paradox. In R.N. Singer, H.A. Hausenblas, & C.M. Janelle (Eds.), *Handbook of sport psychology* (2nd ed., pp. 497–528). New York: Wiley.

Burton, D., & Sharples, P. (2007). *The impact of goal setting styles on the effectiveness of a goal setting training program for women's collegiate cross country runners.* Manuscript in preparation.

Burton, D., Weinberg, R.S., Yukelson, D., & Weigand, D. (1998). The goal effectiveness paradox in sport: Examining the goal practices of collegiate athletes. *The Sport Psychologist, 12,* 404–418.

Burton, D., Pickering, M.A., Weinberg, R.S., Yukelson, D., & Weigand, D. (2007). The competitive goal effectiveness paradox revisited: Examining the goal practices of Olympic athletes. Manuscript submitted to *The Sport Psychologist.*

Campbell, D.J., & Furrer, D.M. (1995). Goal setting and competition as determinants of task performance. *Journal of Organizational Behavior, 16,* 377–389.

Carroll, S.J. (1986). Management by objectives: Three decades of research and experience. In S.L. Rynes & G.T. Milkovich (Eds.), *Current issues in human resource management.* Plano, TX: Business Publications.

Carver, C.S., & Scheier, M.F. (1981). *Attention and self-regulation: A control-theory approach to human behavior.* New York: Springer-Verlag.

Chesney, A., & Locke, E. (1991). Relationships among goal difficulty, business strategies, and performance on a complex management simulation task. *Academy of Management Journal, 34,* 400–424.

Chidester, T.R., & Grigsby, W.C. (1984). A meta-analysis of the goal setting-performance literature. In J.A. Pearce & R.B. Robinson (Eds.), *Academy of management proceedings* (pp. 202–206). Ada, OH: Academy of Management.

Cobb, L.E., Stone, W.J., Anonsen, L.J., & Klein, D.A. (2000). The influence of goal setting on exercise adherence. *Journal of Health Education, 31,* 277–281.

Croteau, K.A. (2004). A preliminary study on the impact of a pedometer-based intervention on daily steps. *American Journal of Health Promotion, 18,* 217–220.

Dawson, K.A., Bray, S.R., & Widmeyer, W.N. (2002). Goal setting by intercollegiate sport teams and athletes. *Avante, 8,* 14–23.

deCharms, R. (1976). *Enhancing motivation: Change in the classroom.* New York: Irvington.

Deci, E.L., & Ryan, R.M. (1985). *Intrinsic motivation and self determination in human behavior.* New York: Plenum Press.

Diener, C.I., & Dweck, C.S. (1978). An analysis of learned helplessness: Continuous changes in performance, strategy, and achievement cognitions following failure. *Journal of Personality and Social Psychology, 36,* 451–462.

Duda, J.L., & Hall, H. (2001). Achievement goal theory in sport: Recent extensions and future directions. In R.N. Singer, H.A. Hausenblas, & C.M. Janelle (Eds.), *Handbook of sport psychology* (2nd ed., pp. 417–443). New York: Wiley.

Duda, J.L., & Nicholls, J.G. (1992). Dimensions of achievement motivation in schoolwork and sport. *Journal of Educational Psychology, 84,* 1–10.

Duda, J.L., & Whitehead, J. (1998). Measurement of goal perspectives in the physical domain. In J.L. Duda (Ed.), *Advances in sport and exercise psychology measurement* (pp. 21–48). Morgantown, WV: Fitness Information Technology.

Dweck, C.S. (1980). Learned helplessness in sport. In C.H. Nadeau, W.R. Halliwell, K.M. Newell, & G.C. Roberts (Eds.), *Psychology of motor behavior and sport-1979* (pp. 1–12). Champaign, IL: Human Kinetics.

Dweck, C. (1999). *Self theories: Their role in motivation, personality, and development.* Philadelphia: Psychology Press/Taylor and Francis.

Earley, P.C. (1985). Influence of information, choice, and task complexity upon goal acceptance, performance, and personal goals. *Journal of Applied Psychology, 70,* 481–491.

Earley, P., & Kanfer, R. (1985). The influence of component participation and role models on goal acceptance, goal satisfaction, and performance. *Organizational Behavior and Human Decision Processes, 36,* 378–390.

Earley, P., Northcraft, G., Lee, C., & Lituchy, T (1990). Impact of process and outcome feedback on the relation of goal setting to task performance. *Academy of Management Journal, 33,* 87–105.

Elliott, E.S., & Dweck, C.S. (1988). Goals: An approach to motivation and achievement. *Journal of Personality and Social Psychology, 54,* 5–12.

Erbaugh, S.J., & Barnett, M.L. (1986). Effects of modeling and goal-setting on the jumping performance of primary-grade children. *Perceptual and Motor Skills, 63,* 1287–1293.

Erez, M. (1986). The congruence of goal setting strategies with sociocultural values, and its effect on performance. *Journal of Management, 12,* 585–592.

Erez, M., Earley, P.C., & Hulin, C.L. (1985). The impact of participation on goal acceptance and performance: A two-step model. *Academy of Management Journal, 28,* 50–66.

Evans, L., & Hardy, L. (2002a). Injury rehabilitation: A goal-setting intervention study. *Research Quarterly for Exercise and Sport, 73,* 310–319.

Evans, L., & Hardy, L. (2002b). Injury rehabilitation: A qualitative follow-up study. *Research Quartery for Exercise and Sport, 73,* 320–329.

Fairall, D.G., & Rodgers, W.M. (1997). The effects of goal setting method on goal attributes in athletes: A field experiment. *Journal of Sport and Exercise Psychology, 19,* 1–16.

Feltz, D.L., & Chase, M.A. (1998). The measurement of self-efficacy and confidence in sport. In J.L. Duda (Ed.), *Advances in sport and exercise psychology measurement* (pp. 65–80). Morgantown, WV: Fitness Information Technology.

Filby, W C.D., Maynard, I.W, & Graydon, J.K. (1999). The effect of multiple-goal strategies on performance outcomes in training and competition. *Journal of Applied Sport Psychology, 11,* 230–246.

Fox, K.R. (1998). Advances in the measurement of the physical self. In J.L. Duda (Ed.), *Advances in sport and exercise psychology measurement* (pp. 295–310). Morgantown, WV: Fitness Information Technology.

Fox, K.R., & Corbin, C.B. (1989). The physical self-perception profile: Development and preliminary validation. *Journal of Sport and Exercise Psychology, 11,* 408–430.

Frierman, S.H., Weinberg, R.S., & Jackson, A. (1990). The relationship between goal proximity and specificity in bowling: A field experiment. *The Sport Psychologist, 4,* 145–154.

Galvan, Z.J., & Ward, P. (1998). Effects of public posting on inappropriate on-court behaviors by collegiate tennis players. *The Sport Psychologist, 12,* 419–426.

Getz, G.E., & Rainey, D.W. (2001). Flexible short-term goals and basketball shooting performance. *Journal of Sport Behavior, 24,* 31–41.

Giannini, J.M., Weinberg, R.S., & Jackson, A.J. (1988). The effects of mastery, competitive, and cooperative goals on the performance of simple and complex basketball skills. *Journal of Sport and Exercise Psychology, 10,* 408–417.

Gill, D.L., & Deeter, T.E. (1988). Development of the sport orientation questionnaire. *Research Quarterly for Exercise and Sport, 59,* 191–202.

Goudas, M., Ardamerinos, N., Vasilliou, S., & Zanou, S. (1999). Effect of goal-setting on reaction time. *Perceptual and Motor Skills, 89,* 849–852.

Gould, D. (2006). Goal setting for peak performance. In J.M. Williams (Ed.), *Applied sport psychology: Personal growth to peak performance* (5th ed., pp. 240–259). Mountain View, CA: Mayfield.

Graham, T.R., Kowalski, K.C., & Crocker, P.R.E. (2002). The contribution of goal characteristics and causal attributions to emotional experience in youth sport participants. *Psychology of Sport and Exercise, 3,* 273–291.

Gyurcsik, N.C., Estabrooks, P.A., & Frahm-Templar, M.J. (2003). Exercise-related goals and self-efficacy as correlates of aquatic exercise in individuals with arthritis. *Arthritis Care and Research, 49,* 306–313.

Hall, H.K., & Byrne, A.T.J. (1988). Goal setting in sport: Clarifying recent anomalies. *Journal of Sport and Exercise Psychology, 10,* 184–198.

Hall, H.K., Weinberg, R.S., & Jackson, A. (1987). Effects of goal specificity, goal difficulty, and information feedback on endurance performance. *Journal of Sport Psychology, 9,* 43–54.

Hardy, C.J., & Latane, B. (1988). Social loafing in cheerleaders: Effects of team membership and competition. *Journal of Sport and Exercise Psychology, 10,* 109–114.

Hardy, L. (1997). The Coleman Roberts Griffith address: Three myths about applied consultancy work. *Journal of Applied Sport Psychology, 9,* 277–294.

Harkins, S.G., & Petty, R.E. (1982). Effects of task difficulty and task uniqueness on social loafing. *Journal of Personality and Social Psychology, 43,* 1214–1229.

Harter, S. (1981). The development of competence motivation in the mastery of cognitive and physical skills: Is there still a place for joy? In G.C. Roberts & D.M. Landers (Eds.), *Psychology of Motor Behavior and Sport-1980* (pp. 3–29). Champaign, IL: Human Kinetics.

Hayes, S.C., Rosenfarb, I., Wulfert, E., Munt, E.D., Korn, Z., & Kettle, R.D. (1985). Self-reinforcement effects: An artifact of social standard setting? *Journal of Applied Behavior Analysis, 18,* 201–214.

Heckhausen, H., & Strang, H. (1988). Efficiency under record performance demands: Exertion control—an individual difference variable? *Journal of Personality and Social Psychology, 55,* 489–498.

Hinsz, V. (1995). Goal setting by groups performing an additive task: A comparison with individual goal setting. *Journal of Applied Social Psychology, 25,* 965–990.

Hollenbeck, J.R., Williams, C.R., & Klein, H.J. (1989). An empirical examination of the antecedents of commitment to difficult goals. *Journal of Applied Psychology, 74*, 18–23.

Hollingsworth, B. (1975). Effects of performance goals and anxiety on learning a gross motor task. *Research Quarterly, 46*, 162–168.

Howe, B., & Poole, R. (1992). Goal proximity and achievement motivation of high school boys in a basketball shooting task. *Journal of Teaching in Physical Education, 11*, 248–255.

Huber, V.L. (1985). Comparison of monetary reinforcers and goal setting as learning incentives. *Psychological Reports, 56*, 223–235.

Humphries, C.A., Thomas, J.R., & Nelson, J.K. (1991). Effects of attainable and unattainable goals on mirror-tracing performance and retention of a motor task. *Perceptual and Motor Skills, 72*, 1231–1237.

Hunter, J.E., & Schmidt, F.L. (1983). Quantifying the effects of psychological interventions on employee job performance and work force productivity. *American Psychologist, 38*, 473–478.

Hutchison, S., & Garstka, M.L. (1996). Sources of perceived organizational support: Goal setting and feedback. *Journal of Applied Social Psychology, 26*, 1351–1366.

Ingham, A., Levinger, G., Graves, J., & Peckham, V. (1974). The Ringlemann effect: Studies of group size and group performance. *Journal of Experimental Social Psychology, 10*, 371–384.

Ivancevich, J.M. (1974). Changes in performance in a management by objectives program. *Administrative Science Quarterly, 19*, 563–574.

Jackson, J.M., & Williams, K.D. (1985). Social loafing on difficult tasks: Working collectively can improve performance. *Journal of Personality and Social Psychology, 49*, 937–942.

Johnson, S.R., Ostrow, A.C., Perna, F.M., & Etzel, E.F. (1997). The effects of group versus individual goal setting on bowling performance. *The Sport Psychologist, 11*, 190–200.

Johnston-O'Connor, E.J., & Kirschenbaum, D.S. (1984). Something succeeds like success: Positive self-monitoring for unskilled golfers. *Cognitive Therapy and Research, 10*, 123–136.

Jones, G., & Cale, A. (1997). Goal difficulty, anxiety and performance. *Ergonomics, 40*, 319–333.

Jones, G., & Hanton, S. (1996). Interpretation of competitive anxiety symptoms and goal attainment expectancies. *Journal of Sport and Exercise Psychology, 18*, 144–157.

Kane, T.D., Marks, M.A., Zaccaro, S.J., & Blair, V. (1996). Self-efficacy, personal goals, and wrestlers' self-regulation. *Journal of Sport and Exercise Psychology, 18*, 36–48.

Kernan, M.G., & Lord, R.G. (1989). The effects of explicit goals and specific feedback on escalation processes. *Journal of Applied Social Psychology, 19*, 1125–1143.

Kerr, N.L., & Brunn, S.E. (1981). Ringlemann revisited: Alternative explanations for the social loafing effect. *Personality and Social Psychology Bulletin, 7*, 224–231.

Kingston, K.M., & Hardy, L. (1994). Factors affecting the salience of outcome, performance, and process goals in golf. In A. Cochran & M. Farrally (Eds.), *Science and golf 2* (pp. 144–149). London: Chapman-Hill.

Kingston, K.M., & Hardy, L. (1997). Effects of different types of goals on processes that support performance. *The Sport Psychologist, 11*, 277–293.

Kirschenbaum, D.S. (1984). Self-regulation and sport psychology: Nurturing an emerging symbiosis. *Journal of Sport Psychology, 6*, 159–183.

Kirschenbaum, D.S. (1985). Proximity and specificity of planning: A position paper. *Cognitive Therapy and Research, 9*, 489–506.

Kirschenbaum, D.S., Ordman, A.M., Tomarken, A.J., & Holtzbauer, R. (1982). Effects of differential self-monitoring and level of mastery on sport performance: Brain power bowling. *Cognitive Therapy and Research, 6*, 335–342.

Kirschenbaum, D.S., & Tomarken, A.J. (1982). On facing the generalization problem: The study of self-regulatory failure. In P.C. Kendall (Ed.), *Advances in cognitive behavioral research and therapy* (Vol. 1, pp. 121–200). New York: Academic Press.

Kirschenbaum, D.S., Wittrock, D.A., Smith, R.J., & Monson, W. (1984). Criticism inoculation training: Concept in search of a strategy. *Journal of Sport Psychology, 6*, 77–93.

Kondrasuk, J.N. (1981). Studies in MBO effectiveness. *Academy of Management Review, 6*, 419–430.

Kyllo, L.B., & Landers, D.M. (1995). Goal-setting in sport and exercise: A research synthesis to resolve the controversy. *Journal of Sport and Exercise Psychology, 17*, 117–137.

Lambert, S.N., Moore, D.W., & Dixon, R.S. (1999). Gymnasts in training: The differential effects of self- and coach-set goals as a function of locus of control. *Journal of Applied Sport Psychology, 11*, 72–82.

Larey, T.S., & Paulus, P.B. (1995). Social comparison and goal setting in brainstorming groups. *Journal of Applied Social Psychology, 25*, 1579–1596.

Latane, B. (1986). Responsibility and effort in organizations. In P. Goodman (Ed.), *Groups and organizations* (pp. 277–303). San Francisco: Josey-Bass.

Latane, B., Williams, K.D., & Harkins, S.G. (1979). Many hands make light the work: The causes and consequences of social loafing. *Journal of Personality and Social Psychology, 37*, 823–832.

Latham, G.P., Erez, M., & Locke, E.A. (1988). Resolving scientific disputes by the joint design of crucial experiments by the antagonists: Application to the Erez-Latham dispute regarding participation in goal setting. *Journal of Applied Psychology, 73*, 753–772.

Latham, G.P., & Lee, T.W. (1986). Goal setting. In E.A. Locke (Ed.), *Generalizing from laboratory to field settings: Research findings from industrial-organizational psychology, organizational behavior, and human resource management* (pp. 101–117). Lexington, MA: Heath.

Latham, G.P., & Locke, E.A. (1991). Self-regulation through goal setting. *Organizational Behavior and Human Decision Processes, 50*, 212–247.

Latham, G.P., & Yukl, G.A. (1975). Assigned versus participative goal setting with educated and uneducated woods workers. *Journal of Applied Psychology, 60*, 299–302.

Lazarus, R.S. (1991). *Emotion and adaptation*. New York: Oxford University Press.

Lazarus, R.S. (1999). *Stress and emotion: A new synthesis*. New York: Springer.

Lazarus, R.S., & Folkman, S. (1984). *Stress, appraisal and coping*. New York: Springer.

Lee, A.M., & Edwards, R.V. (1984). Assigned and self-selected goals as determinants of motor skill performance. *Education, 105*, 87–91.

Lee, C. (1988). The relationship between goal setting, self-efficacy and female field hockey team performance. *International Journal of Sport Psychology, 20*, 147–161.

Lerner, B.S., & Locke, E.A. (1995). The effects of goal setting, self-efficacy, competition and personal traits on the performance of an endurance task. *Journal of Sport and Exercise Psychology, 17*, 138–152.

Lerner, B.S., Ostrow, A.C., Yura, M.T., & Etzel, E.F. (1996). The effects of goal-setting and imagery training programs on the free-throw performance of female collegiate basketball players. *The Sport Psychologist, 10*, 382–397.

Locke, E.A. (1968). Toward a theory of task motivation and incentives. *Organizational Behavior and Human Performance, 3*, 157–189.

Locke, E.A. (1991). Problems with goal-setting research in sports—and their solution. *Journal of Sport and Exercise Psychology, 8*, 311–316.

Locke, E.A. (1996). Motivation through conscious goal setting. *Applied and Preventative Psychology, 5*, 117–124.

Locke, E.A., Cartledge, N., & Knerr, C.S. (1970). Studies of the relationship between satisfaction, goal setting, and performance. *Organizational Behavior and Human Performance, 5*, 135–158.

Locke, E.A., Chah, D.O., Harrison, S., & Lustgarten, N. (1989). Separating the effects of goal specificity from goal level. *Organizational Behavior and Human Decision Processes, 43*, 270–287.

Locke, E.A., & Latham, G.P. (1990). *A theory of goal setting and task performance*. Englewood Cliffs, NJ: Prentice Hall.

Locke, E.A., Latham, G.P., & Erez, M. (1988). The determinants of goal commitment. *Academy of Management Review, 13*, 23–39.

Locke, E.A., & Shaw, K.N. (1984). Atkinson's inverse-U curve and missing cognitive variables. *Psychological Reports, 55*, 403–412.

Locke, E.A., Shaw, K.N., Saari, L.M., & Latham, G.P. (1981). Goal setting and task performance: 1969–1980. *Psychological Bulletin, 90,* 125–152.

Maehr, M.L. (1984). Meaning and motivation. In R. Ames & C. Ames (Eds.), *Research on motivation in education: Student motivation* (Vol. 1, pp. 115–144). New York: Academic Press.

Maehr, M.L., & Braskamp, L. (1986). *The motivation factor: A theory of personal investment.* Lexington, MA: Heath.

Maehr, M.L., & Nicholls, J.G. (1980). Culture and achievement motivation: A second look. In N. Warren (Ed.), *Studies in cross-cultural psychology* (pp. 341–363). New York: Academic Press.

Martens, B.K., Hiralall, A.S., & Bradley, T.A. (1997). A note to teacher: Improving student behavior through goal setting and feedback. *School Psychology Quarterly, 12,* 33–41.

Matsui, T., Kakuyama, T., & Onglatco, M.L. (1987). Effects of goals and feedback on performance in groups. *Journal of Applied Psychology, 72,* 407–415.

Mento, A.J., Steel, R.P., & Karren, R.J. (1987). A meta-analytic study of the effects of goal setting on task performance: 1966–1984. *Organization Behavior and Human Decision Processes, 39,* 52–83.

Mesch, D., Farh, J., & Podsakoff, P. (1994). Effects of feedback sign on group goal setting, strategies, and performance. *Group and Organizational Management, 19,* 309–333.

Miller, J.T., & McAuley, E. (1987). Effects of a goal-setting training program on basketball free-throw self-efficacy and performance. *The Sport Psychologist, 1,* 103–113.

Mitchell, T.R., Rothman, M., & Liden, R.C. (1985). Effects of normative information on task performance. *Journal of Applied Psychology, 70,* 48–55.

Munroe-Chandler, K.J., & Hall, C.R. (2004). A qualitative analysis of the types of goals athletes set in training and competition. *Journal of Sport Behavior, 18,* 58–74.

Nelson, J.K. (1978). Motivating effects of the use of norms and goals with endurance testing. *Research Quarterly, 49,* 317–321.

Nicholls, J.G. (1984a). Conceptions of ability and achievement motivation. In R. Ames & C. Ames (Eds.), *Research on motivation in education: Student motivation* (Vol. 1, pp. 39–73). New York: Academic Press.

Nicholls, J.G. (1984b). Achievement motivation: Conceptions of ability, subjective experience, task choice, and performance. *Psychological Review, 91,* 328–346.

Nicholls, J.G. (1992). The general and the specific in the development and expression of achievement motivation. In G.C. Roberts (Ed.), *Motivation in sport and exercise* (pp. 31–56). Champaign, IL: Human Kinetics.

O'Block, F.R., & Evans, F.H. (1984). Goal setting as a motivational technique. In J.M. Silva & R.S. Weinberg (Eds.), *Psychological foundations of sport* (pp. 188–196). Champaign, IL: Human Kinetics.

Oldham, G.R. (1975). The impact of supervisory characteristics on goal acceptance. *Academy of Management Journal, 18,* 461–475.

Pierce, B.E., & Burton, D. (1998). Scoring the perfect 10: Investigating the impact of goal-setting styles on a goal-setting program for female gymnasts. *The Sport Psychologist, 12,* 156–168.

Poag, K., & McAuley, E. (1992). Goal setting, self-efficacy and exercise behavior. *Journal of Sport and Exercise Psychology, 14,* 352–360.

Poag-DuCharme, K.A., & Brawley, L.R. (1994). Perceptions of the behavioral influence of goals: A mediational relationship to exercise. *Journal of Applied Sport Psychology, 6,* 32–50.

Racicot, B., Day, D., & Lord, R. (1991). Type A behavior pattern and goal setting under different conditions of choice. *Motivation and Emotion, 15,* 67–79.

Rakestraw, T.L., & Weiss, H.M. (1981). The interaction of social influences and task experience on goals, performance, and performance satisfaction. *Organizational Behavior and Human Performance, 27,* 326–344.

Rawsthorne, L.J., & Elliot, A.J. (1999). Achievement goals and intrinsic motivation: A meta-analysis. *Personality and Social Psychology Review, 3,* 326–344.

Riedel, J.A., Nebeker, D.M., & Cooper, B.L. (1988). The influence of monetary incentives on goal choice, goal commitment, and task performance. *Organizational Behavior and Human Decision Processes, 42,* 155–180.

Roberts, G., & Reed, T. (1996, Fall). Performance appraisal participation, goal setting and feedback. *Review of Public Personnel Administration,* pp. 29–61.

Roberts, G.C., & Balague, G. (1991). *The development and validation of the Perception of Success Questionnaire.* Paper presented at the FEPSAC Congress, Cologne, Germany.

Rodgers, R.C., & Hunter, J.E. (1989). *The impact of management by objectives on organizational productivity.* Unpublished manuscript, School of Public Administration, University of Kentucky, Lexington, KY.

Russell, W., & Branch, T. (1979). *Second wind: The memoirs of an opinionated man.* New York: Random House.

Ruth, W. (1996). Goal setting and behavior contracting for students with emotional and behavioral difficulties: Analysis of daily, weekly, and total goal attainment. *Psychology in the Schools, 33,* 153–158.

Shalley, C. (1995). Effects of coaction, expected evaluation, and goal setting on creativity and productivity. *Academy of Management Journal, 38,* 483–503.

Shalley, C.E., Oldham, G.R., & Porac, J.F. (1987). Effects of goal difficulty, goal-setting method, and expected external evaluation on intrinsic motivation. *Academy of Management Journal, 30,* 553–563.

Shoenfelt, E.L. (1996). Goal setting and feedback as a post-training strategy to increase the transfer of training. *Perceptual and Motor Skills, 83,* 176–178.

Smith, M., & Lee, C. (1992). Goal setting and performance in a novel coordination task: Mediating mechanisms. *Journal of Sport and Exercise Psychology, 14,* 169–176.

South, G. (2004). *The roadmap: Examining the impact of periodization, particularly goal term length, on the self-confidence of collegiate tennis players.* Unpublished doctoral dissertation, University of Idaho, Moscow.

Swain, A., & Jones, G. (1995). Effects of goal-setting interventions on selected basketball skills: A single-subject design. *Research Quarterly for Exercise and Sport, 66,* 51–63.

Tenenbaum, G., Bar-Eli, M., & Yaaron, M. (1999). The dynamics of goal-setting: Interactive effects of goal difficulty, goal specificity and duration of practice time intervals. *International Journal of Sport Psychology, 30,* 325–338.

Tenenbaum, G., Weinberg, R.S., Pinchas, S., Elbaz, G., & Bar-Eli, M. (1991). Effect of goal proximity and goal specificity on muscular endurance performance: A replication and extension. *Journal of Sport and Exercise Psychology, 13,* 174–187.

Terborg, J.R. (1976). The motivational components of goal setting. *Journal of Applied Psychology, 61,* 613–621.

Theodorakis, Y. (1995). Effects of self-efficacy, satisfaction, and personal goals on swimming performance. *The Sport Psychologist, 9,* 245–253.

Theodorakis, Y. (1996). The influence of goals, commitment, self-efficacy and self-satisfaction on motor performance. *Journal of Applied Sport Psychology, 8,* 171–182.

Theodorakis, Y., Laparidis, K., Kioumourtzoglou, E., & Goudas, M. (1998). Combined effects of goal setting and performance feedback on performance and physiological response on a maximum effort task. *Perceptual and Motor Skills, 86,* 1035–1041.

Tubbs, M.E. (1986). Goal setting: A meta-analytic examination of the empirical evidence. *Journal of Applied Psychology, 71,* 474–483.

Tzetzis, G., Kioumourtzoglou, E., & Mavromatis, G. (1997). Goal setting and feedback for the development of instructional strategies. *Perceptual and Motor Skills, 84,* 1411–1427.

Vallerand, R.J., Gauvin, L.I., & Halliwell, W R. (1986). Effects of zero-sum competition on children's intrinsic motivation and perceived competence. *Journal of Social Psychology, 126,* 465–472.

Vance, R., & Colella, A. (1990). Effects of two types of feedback on goal acceptance and personal goals. *Journal of Applied Psychology, 75,* 68–76.

Vealey, R.S. (1986). Conceptualization of sport-confidence and competitive orientation: Preliminary investigation and instrument development. *Journal of Sport Psychology, 8,* 221–246.

Vealey, R.S. (1988). Sport-confidence and competitive orientation: An addendum on scoring procedures and gender differences. *Journal of Sport and Exercise Psychology, 10,* 471–478.

Wanlin, C.M., Hrycaiko, D.W., Martin, G.L., & Mahon, M. (1997). The effects of a goal-setting package on the performance of speed skaters. *Journal of Applied Sport Psychology, 9,* 212–228.

Weinberg, R.S. (1994). Goal setting and performance in sport and exercise settings: A synthesis and critique. *Medicine and Science in Sports and Exercise, 26,* 469–477.

Weinberg, R.S., Bruya, L.D., & Jackson, A. (1985). The effects of goal proximity and goal specificity on endurance performance. *Journal of Sport Psychology, 7,* 296–305.

Weinberg, R.S., Bruya, L.D., Jackson, A., & Garland, H. (1987). Goal difficulty and endurance performance: A challenge to the goal attainability assumption. *Journal of Sport Behavior, 10,* 82–92.

Weinberg, R.S., Bruya, L.D., Longino, J., & Jackson, A. (1988). Effect of goal proximity and specificity on endurance performance of primary-grade children. *Journal of Sport and Exercise Psychology, 10,* 81–91.

Weinberg, R.S., Burke, K.L., & Jackson, A. (1997). Coaches' and players' perceptions of goal setting in junior tennis: An exploratory investigation. *The Sport Psychologist, 11,* 426–439.

Weinberg, R.S., Burton, D., Yukelson, D., & Weigand, D. (1993). Goal setting in competitive sport: An exploratory investigation of practices of collegiate athletes. *The Sport Psychologist, 7,* 275–289.

Weinberg, R.S., Burton, D., Yukelson, D., & Weigand, D. (2000). Perceived goal setting practices of Olympic athletes: An exploratory investigation. *The Sport Psychologist, 14,* 279–295.

Weinberg, R.S., Butt, J., & Knight, B. (2001). High school coaches' perceptions of the process of goal setting. *The Sport Psychologist, 15,* 20–47.

Weinberg, R.S., Fowler, C., Jackson, A., Bagnall, J., & Bruya, L. (1991). Effect of goal difficulty on motor performance: A replication across tasks and subjects. *Journal of Sport and Exercise Psychology, 13,* 160–173.

Weinberg, R.S., Garland, H., Bruya, L., & Jackson, A. (1990). Effect of goal difficulty and positive reinforcement on endurance performance. *Journal of Sport and Exercise Psychology, 12,* 144–156.

Weinberg, R.S., Stitcher, T., & Richardson, P. (1994). Effects of seasonal goal setting on lacrosse performance. *The Sport Psychologist, 8,* 166–175.

White, P.H., Kjelgaard, M.M., & Harkins, S.G. (1995). Testing the contribution of self-evaluation to goal-setting effects. *Journal of Personality and Social Psychology, 69,* 69–79.

Widmeyer, W.N., & Ducharme, K. (1997). Team building through team goal setting. *Journal of Applied Sport Psychology, 9,* 97–113.

Williams, K.D., Harkins, S.G., & Latane, B. (1981). Identifiability as a deterrent to social loafing: Two cheering experiments. *Journal of Personality and Social Psychology, 40,* 303–311.

Wood, R.E., & Locke, E.A. (1990). Goal setting and strategy effects on complex tasks. *Research in Organizational Behavior, 12,* 73–109.

Wood, R.E., Mento, A.J., & Locke, E.A. (1987). Task complexity as a moderator of goal effects: A meta-analysis. *Journal of Applied Psychology, 72,* 416–425.

Zagumny, M., & Johnson, C. (1992). Using reinforcement and goal setting to increase proof reading accuracy. *Perceptual and Motor Skills, 75,* 1330.

Zimmerman, B.J., & Kitsantas, A. (1996). Self-regulated learning of a motoric skill: The role of goal setting and self-monitoring. *Journal of Applied Sport Psychology, 8,* 60–75.

CHAPTER 16

Asakawa, K. (2004). Flow experience and autotelic personality in Japanese college students: How do they experience challenges in daily life? *Journal of Happiness Studies, 5,* 123–154.

Bakker, A. (2004, July). *Flow at work: The WOLF.* Paper presented at the 2nd European Conference on Positive Psychology, Italy.

Bassi, M., & Delle Fave, A. (2004). Adolescence and the changing context of optimal experience in time. *Journal of Happiness Studies, 5,* 155–179.

Bennett, R., & Kremer, P. (2000, July). *The psychology of peak performance among elite surfers.* Paper presented at the 2nd annual Monash University Sport Psychology Conference, Melbourne, Australia.

Boutcher, S. (1992). Attention and athletic performance: An integrated approach. In T. Horn (Ed.), *Advances in sport psychology* (1st ed., pp. 251–265). Champaign, IL: Human Kinetics.

Buchanan, D. (1992). An uneasy alliance: Combining qualitative and quantitative research methods. *Health Education Quarterly, 19,* 117–135.

Byrne, C., MacDonald, R., & Carlton, L. (2003). Assessing creativity in musical compositions: Flow as an assessment tool. *British Journal of Music Education, 20,* 277–290.

Carli, M., Fave, A.C., & Massimini, F. (1988). In M. Csikszentmihalyi & I. Csikszentmihalyi (Eds.), *Optimal experience: Psychological studies of flow in consciousness* (pp. 288–306). New York: Cambridge University Press.

Caspersen, C.J., Powell, K.E., & Christenson, G.M. (1985). Physical activity, exercise, and physical fitness: Definitions and distinctions for health-related research. *Public Health Reports, 100,* 126–131.

Catley, D., & Duda, J.L. (1997). Psychological antecedents of flow in golfers. *International Journal of Sport Psychology, 28,* 309–322.

Chalip, L., Csikszentmihalyi, M., Kleiber, D., & Larson, R. (1984). Variations of experience in formal and informal sport. *Research Quarterly for Exercise and Sport, 55,* 109–116.

Chan, T.S., & Repman, J. (1999). Flow in web based instructional activity: An exploratory research project. *International Journal of Educational Telecommunications, 5,* 225–237.

Chen, H., Wigand, R.T., & Nilan, M.S. (1999). Optimal experience in web activities. *Computers in Human Behavior, 15*(5), 585–608.

Chen, H., Wigand, R.T., & Nilan, M.S. (2000). Exploring web users' optimal flow experiences. *Information Technology and People, 13*(4), 263.

Click Online. (2002). www.bbcworld.com/content/clickonline_archive_30_2002.asp.pageid=666&co_pageid=3 Retrieved July 25, 2002.

Cohn, P. (1986). *An exploration of the golfer's peak-experience.* Unpublished manuscript, California State University at Fullerton.

Cohn, P. (1991). An exploratory study of peak performance in golf. *The Sport Psychologist, 5,* 1–14.

Crews, D., & Landers, D. (1990). Electroencephalographic measures of attentional patterns prior to the golf putt. *Medicine and Science in Sports and Exercise, 25,* 116–126.

Csikszentmihalyi, M. (1975). *Beyond boredom and anxiety.* San Francisco: Jossey-Bass.

Csikszentmihalyi, M. (1982). Toward a psychology of optimal experience. In L. Wheeler (Ed.), *Review of personality and social psychology* (pp. 13–36). Beverly Hills, CA: Sage.

Csikszentmihalyi, M. (1988). The future of flow. In M. Csikszentmihalyi & I. Csikszentmihalyi (Eds.), *Optimal experience: Psychological studies of flow in consciousness* (pp. 364–383). New York: Cambridge University Press.

Csikszentmihalyi, M. (1990). *Flow: The psychology of optimal experience.* New York: Harper & Row.

Csikszentmihalyi, M. (1993). *The evolving self.* New York: Harper & Row.

Csikszentmihalyi, M. (1997). *Finding flow.* New York: Harper Collins.

Csikszentmihalyi, M., & Csikszentmihalyi, I. (1988). Measurement of flow in everyday life: Introduction to Part IV. In Csikszentmihalyi, M. & Csikszentmihalyi, I. (Eds.). *Optimal experience: Psychological studies of flow in consciousness* (pp. 251–265). New York: Cambridge University Press.

Csikszentmihalyi, M., & Graef, R. (1980). The experience of freedom in daily life. *American Journal of Community Psychology, 8,* 401–414.

Csikszentmihalyi, M., & Larson, R. (1987). Validity and reliability of the experience-sampling method. *Journal of Nervous and Mental Disease, 175,* 526–536.

Csikszentmihalyi, M., Larson, R., & Prescott, S. (1977). The ecology of adolescent activity and experience. *Journal of Youth and Adolescence, 6,* 281–294.

Csikszentmihalyi, M., & LeFevre, J. (1989). Optimal experience in work and leisure. *Journal of Personality and Social Psychology, 56,* 815–822.

Csikszentmihalyi, M., & Nakamura, J. (1989). The dynamics of intrinsic motivation: A study of adolescents. In C. Ames & R. Ames (Eds.), *Research on motivation in education, Vol. 3: Goals and cognitions* (pp. 45–71). New York: Academic Press.

Csikszentmihalyi, M., & Schneider, B. (2000). *Becoming adult: How teenagers prepare for the world of work*. New York: Basic Books.

Custodero, L. (2002). Seeking challenge, finding skill: Flow experience and music education. *Arts Education Policy Review, 103*, 3–10.

DeCharms, R., & Muir, M. (1978). Motivation: Social approaches. *Annual Reviews in Psychology, 29*, 91–113.

Deci, E.L., & Ryan, R.M. (1985). *Intrinsic motivation and self-determination in human behavior*. New York: Plenum Press.

Deci, E., & Ryan, R. (1987). The support of autonomy and the control of behavior. *Journal of Personality and Social Psychology, 53*, 1024–1037.

Delle Fave, A., Bassi, M., & Massimini, F. (2003). Quality of experience and risk perception in high-altitude rock climbing. *Journal of Applied Sport Psychology, 15*, 82–98.

Dewar, A., & Horn, T. (1992). A critical analysis of knowledge construction in sport psychology. In T. Horn (Ed.), *Advances in sport psychology* (1st ed., pp. 13–22). Champaign, IL: Human Kinetics.

Dietrich, A. (2004). Neurocognitive mechanisms underlying the experience of flow. *Consciousness and Cognition, 13*, 746–761.

Duda, J.L. (1988). The relationship between goal perspectives and persistence and intensity among recreational sport participants. *Leisure Sciences, 10*, 95–106.

Duda, J.L. (1992). Motivation in sport settings: A goal perspective approach. In G. Roberts (Ed.), *Motivation in sport and exercise* (pp. 57–92). Champaign, IL: Human Kinetics.

Duda, J.L., & Nicholls, J.G. (1992). Dimensions of achievement motivation in schoolwork and sport. *Journal of Educational Psychology, 84*, 290–299.

Egbert, J. (2003). A study of flow in the foreign language classroom. *Modern Language Journal, 87*, 499–518.

Eklund, R. (1994). A season long investigation of competitive cognition in collegiate wrestlers. *Research Quarterly for Exercise and Sport, 65*, 169–183.

Ellis, G., Voelkl, J., & Morris, C. (1994). Measurement and analysis issues with explanation of variance in daily experience using the flow model. *Journal of Leisure Research, 26*, 337–356.

Fahlberg, L.L., & Fahlberg, L.A. (1994). A human science for the study of movement: An integration of multiple ways of knowing. *Research Quarterly for Exercise and Sport, 65*, 100–109.

Feltz, D. (1987). Advancing knowledge in sport psychology: Strategies for expanding our conceptual framework. *Quest, 39*, 243–254.

Forbes, J. (1989). The cognitive psychobiology of performance regulation. *Journal of Sports Medicine and Physical Fitness, 29*, 202–207.

Forch, T. (2004). *Flow in surfing: A comparison between competitive and recreational contexts*. Unpublished BEd (Hons.) thesis, University of Otago, New Zealand.

Garfield, C., & Bennett, Z. (1984). *Peak performance*. New York: Warner Books.

Ghani, J.W. (1991). Flow in human-computer interactions: Test of a model. In J. Carey (Ed.), *Factors in management information systems: An organizational perspective*. Norwood, NJ: Ablex.

Ghani, J.W., & Deshpande, S.P. (1994). Task characteristics and the experience of optimal flow in human-computer interaction. *Journal of Psychology, 128*(4), 381–391.

Gauvin, L., & Rejeski, W., & Norris (1996). A naturalistic study of the impact of acute physical activity on feeling states and affect in women. *Health Psychology, 15*, 391–397.

Gould, D., Eklund, R., & Jackson, S. (1992). 1988 USA Olympic Wrestling Excellence II: Competitive cognition and affect. *The Sport Psychologist, 6*(4), 383–402.

Grove, J.R., & Lewis, M.A.E. (1996). Hypnotic susceptibility and the attainment of flowlike states during exercise. *Journal of Sport and Exercise Psychology, 18*, 380–391.

Gunderson, J.A. (2003). *Csikszentmihalyi's state of flow and effective teaching.* Unpublished doctoral dissertation, Claremont Graduate University, Claremont, CA.

Hamilton, J.A. (1976). Attention and intrinsic rewards in the control of psychophysiological states. *Psychotherapy and Psychosomatics, 27*, 54–61.

Hamilton, J.A. (1981). Attention, personality, and self-regulation of mood: Absorbing interest and boredom. In B.A. Maher (Ed.), *Progress in experimental personality research, 10* (pp. 282–315). New York: Academic Press.

Hatfield, B., & Landers, D. (1983). Psychophysiology: A new direction for sport psychology. *Journal of Sport Psychology, 5*, 243–259.

Jackson, S.A. (1992). Athletes in flow: A qualitative investigation of flow states in elite figure skaters. *Journal of Applied Sport Psychology, 4*, 161–180.

Jackson, S.A. (1993). Elite athletes in flow: The psychology of optimal experience in sport. (Doctoral dissertation, University of North Carolina at Greensboro, 1992). *Dissertation Abstracts International, 54*, 124A.

Jackson, S.A. (1995). Factors influencing the occurrence of flow states in elite athletes. *Journal of Applied Sport Psychology, 7*, 135–163.

Jackson, S.A. (1996). Toward a conceptual understanding of the flow experience in elite athletes. *Research Quarterly for Exercise and Sport, 67*, 76–90.

Jackson, S.A. (2000). Joy, fun, and flow state in sport. In Hanin, Y. (Ed.), *Emotions in sport* (pp. 135–156). Champaign, IL: Human Kinetics.

Jackson, S.A. (2007) *Subjective experience in physical activity I: A quantitative perspective on perceptions of physical activity for women across life stages.* Manuscript in preparation.

Jackson, S.A., & Csikszentmihalyi, M. (1999). *Flow in sports: The keys to optimal experiences and performances*. Champaign, IL: Human Kinetics.

Jackson, S.A., & Eklund, R.C. (2002). Assessing flow in physical activity: The Flow State Scale–2 (FSS–2) and Dispositional Flow Scale–2 (DFS–2). *Journal of Sport and Exercise Psychology, 24*, 133–150.

Jackson, S.A., & Eklund, R.C. (2004). *The flow scales manual*. Morgantown, WV: Fitness Information Technology.

Jackson, S.A., Kimiecik, J., Ford, S., & Marsh, H.W. (1998). Psychological corrrelates of flow in sport. *Journal of Sport and Exercise Psychology, 20*, 358–378.

Jackson, S.A, & Lee, J. (2007) *Subjective experience in physical activity II: A qualitative perspective on perceptions of physical activity for women across life stages.* Manuscript in preparation.

Jackson, S.A., & Marsh, H.W. (1996). Development and validation of a scale to measure optimal experience: The flow state scale. *Journal of Sport and Exercise Psychology, 18*, 17–35.

Jackson, S.A., Martin, A.J., & Eklund, R.C. (2007). *Standard and brief measures of flow: Examining construct validity of the FSS-2, DFS-2, and brief counterparts*. Manuscript submitted for publication.

Jackson, S.A., Miller, Y., Brown, W., Martin, A.J., Marsh, H.W., Cotterill, T., & O'Dwyer, S. *Physical activity in the lives of Australian older adults: The relative contribution of demographic, psychological, social, and environmental correlates*. Manuscript submitted for publication.

Jackson, S.A., & Roberts, G.C. (1992). Positive performance states of athletes: Toward a conceptual understanding of peak performance. *The Sport Psychologist, 6*, 156–171.

Jackson, S.A., Thomas, P.R., Marsh, H.W., & Smethurst, C.J. (2001). Relationships between flow, self-concept, psychological skills, and performance. *Journal of Applied Sport Psychology, 13*, 154–178.

Jackson, S.A., & Wrigley, W.J. (2004). Optimal experience in sport: Current issues and future directions. In T. Morris & J. Summers (Eds.), *Sport psychology: Theory, applications, and issues* (2nd ed., pp. 423–451). Milton, Queensland, Australia: Wiley.

Jones, C.D., Hollenhorst, S.J., & Perna, F. (2003). An empirical comparison of the four channel flow model and adventure experience paradigm. *Leisure Sciences, 25*, 17–31.

Jones, C.D., Hollenhurst, S.J., & Perna, F., & Selin, S. (2000). Validation of the flow theory in an on-site whitewater kayaking setting. *Journal of Leisure Research, 32*(2), 247–61.

Karageorghis, C.I., Vlachopoulos, S.P., & Terry, P.C. (2000). Latent variable modeling of the relationship between flow and exercise-induced feelings: An intuitive appraisal perspective. *European Physical Education, 6*, 230–48.

Kimiecik, J., & Harris, A. (1996). What is enjoyment?: A conceptual/definitional analysis with implications for sport and exercise psychology. *Journal of Sport and Exercise Psychology, 18*, 247–263.

Kimiecik, J., & Stein, G. (1992). Examining flow experiences in sport contexts: Conceptual issues and methodological concerns. *Journal of Applied Sport Psychology, 4*, 144–160.

Kobasa, S. (1979). Stressful life events, personality, and health: An inquiry into hardiness. *Journal of Personality and Social Psychology, 37*, 1–11.

Kowal, J., & Fortier, M. (1999). Motivational determinants of flow: Contributions from self-determination theory. *Journal of Social Psychology, 139*, 355–368.

Kraus, B.N. (2003). Musicians in flow: Optimal experience in the wind ensemble rehearsal. *Dissertation Abstracts International, 64*, 839.

Lincoln, Y.S., & Guba, E.G. (1985). *Naturalistic inquiry.* Newbury Park, CA: Sage.

Loehr, J. (1982). *Mental toughness for sports: Achieving athletic excellence.* New York: Forum.

Loehr, J. (1986). *Mental toughness training for sports.* Lexington, MA: Stephen Green.

Logan, R.D. (1988). Flow in solitary ordeals. In M. Csikszentmihalyi & I. Csikszentmihalyi (Eds.), *Optimal experience: Psychological studies of flow in consciousness* (pp. 172–180). New York: Cambridge University Press.

Mandigo, J., Thompson, L., & Couture, R. (1998, June). *Equating flow theory with the quality of children's physical activity experiences.* Paper presented at the annual North American Psychology of Sport and Physical Activity Conference, St. Charles, IL.

Marsh, H.W., Hey, J., Johnson, S., & Perry, C. (1997). Elite Athlete Self-Description Questionnaire: Hierarchical confirmatory factor analysis of responses by two distinct groups of elite athletes. *International Journal of Sport Psychology, 28*, 237–258.

Marsh, H.W., & Jackson, S.A. (1999). Flow experiences in sport: Construct validation of multidimensional hierarchical state and trait responses. *Structural Equation Modelling, 6*, 343–71.

Martens, R. (1977). *Sport Competition Anxiety Test.* Champaign, IL: Human Kinetics.

Martens, R. (1987). Science, knowledge, and sport psychology. *The Sport Psychologist, 1*, 29–55.

Martens, R., Vealey, R.S., & Burton, D. (1990). *Competitive anxiety in sport.* Champaign, IL: Human Kinetics.

Martin, A.J., & Jackson, S.A. (2007). *Brief approaches to assessing task absorption and enhanced subjective experience: Examining "composite" and "core" flow in diverse performance settings.* Manuscript submitted for publication.

Martin, J.J., & Cutler, K. (2002). An exploratory study of flow and motivation in theater actors. *Journal of Applied Sport Psychology, 14*, 344–352.

Maslow, A. (1968). *Toward a psychology of being.* New York: Van Nostrand.

McInman, A., & Grove, J. (1991). Peak moments in sport: A literature review. *Quest, 43*, 333–351.

Mitchell, R.G. (1988). Sociological implications of the flow experience. In M. Csikszentmihalyi & I. Csikszentmihalyi (Eds.) *Optimal experience: Psychological studies of flow in consciousness* (pp. 36–59). New York: Cambridge University Press.

Moneta, G.B. (2004a). The flow experience across cultures. *Journal of Happiness Studies, 5*, 115–121.

Moneta, G.B. (2004b). The flow model of intrinsic motivation in Chinese: Cultural and personal moderators. *Journal of Happiness Studies, 5*, 181–217.

Moneta, G., & Csikszentmihalyi, M. (1996). The effect of perceived challenges and skills on the quality of subjective experience. *Journal of Personality, 64*, 275–310.

Nakamura, J., & Csikszentmihalyi, M. (2002). The concept of flow. In C.R. Snyder & S.J. Lopez (Eds.), *Handbook of positive psychology* (pp. 89–105). Oxford, United Kingdom: Oxford University Press.

Nakamura, J., & Csikszentmihalyi, M. (2003). The construction of meaning through vital engagement. In C.L. Keyes & J. Haidt (Eds.), *Flourishing: Positive psychology and the life well-lived* (pp. 83–104). Washington, DC: APA.

Nicholls, J. (1984). Achievement motivation: Conceptions of ability, subjective experience, task choice, and performance. *Psychological Review, 91*, 328–346.

Nicholls, J.G. (1992). The general and the specific in the development and expression of achievement motivation. In G. Roberts (Ed.), *Motivation in sport and exercise* (pp. 31–56). Champaign, IL: Human Kinetics.

Novak, T.P., Hoffman, D., & Duhachek, A. (2003). The influence of goal-directed and experiential activities on online flow experiences. *Journal of Consumer Psychology, 13*, 3–16.

Novak, T.P., Hoffman, D.L., & Yung, Y.F. (2000). Measuring the customer experience in online environments: A structural modeling approach. *Marketing Science, 19*, 22–42.

O'Neill, S. (1999). Flow theory and the development of musical performance skills. *Bulletin of the Council for Research in Music Education, Summer*, 129–134.

Orlick, T. (1986). *Psyching for sport.* Champaign, IL: Human Kinetics

Orlick, T. (1990). *In pursuit of excellence.* Champaign, IL: Human Kinetics.

Orlick, T. (1998). *Embracing your potential.* Champaign, IL: Human Kinetics.

Pates, J., Cummings, A., & Maynard, I. (2002). Effects of hypnosis on flow states and three-point shooting performance in basketball players. *The Sport Psychologist, 16*, 34–47.

Pates, J., Karageorghis, C.I., Fryer, R., & Maynard, I. (2003). Effects of asynchronous music on flow states and shooting performance among netball players. *Psychology of Sport and Exercise, 4*, 415–427.

Pates, J., & Maynard, I. (2000). Effects of hypnosis on flow states and golf performance. *Perceptual and Motor Skills, 91*, 1057–1075.

Pates, J., Oliver, R., & Maynard, I. (2001). The effects of hypnosis on flow states and golf-putting performance. *Journal of Applied Sport Psychology, 13*, 341–354.

Patton, M.Q. (1990). *Qualitative evaluation and research methods* (2nd ed.). Newbury Park, CA: Sage.

Perritt, N. (1999). *Hardiness and optimism as predictors of the frequency of flow athletes experience in sport.* Unpublished master's thesis, Miami University, Oxford, OH.

Perry, S.K. (1999). *Writing in flow.* Cincinnati, OH: Writer's Digest.

Podilchak, W. (1991). Establishing the fun in leisure. *Leisure Sciences, 13*, 123–136.

Privette, G. (1983). Peak experience, peak performance, and flow: A comparative analysis of positive human experiences. *Journal of Personality and Social Psychology, 45*, 1361–1368.

Privette, G., & Bundrick, C.M. (1991). Peak experience, peak performance, and flow. *Journal of Social Behavior and Personality, 6*, 169–188.

Ravizza, K. (1977). Peak experiences in sport. *Journal of Humanistic Psychology, 17*, 35–40.

Ravizza, K. (1984). Qualities of the peak-experience in sport. In J. Silva & R. Weinberg (Eds.), *Psychological foundations of sport* (pp. 452–461). Champaign, IL: Human Kinetics.

Russell, W.D. (2001). An examination of flow state occurrence in college athletes. *Journal of Sport Behavior, 24*(1), 83–99.

Ryan, E. (1977). Attribution, intrinsic motivation, and athletics. In L. Gedvilas & M. Kneer (Eds.), *Proceedings of the National Association for Physical Education of College Men National Conference/National Association for Physical Education of College Women National Conference.* Chicago: University of Illinois at Chicago Circle.

Ryan, E. (1980). Attribution, intrinsic motivation, and athletics: A replication and extension. In C. Nadeau, W. Halliwell, K. Newell, & G. Roberts (Eds.), *Psychology of Motor Behavior and Sport—1979* (pp. 19–26). Champaign, IL: Human Kinetics.

Ryan, R.M., & Deci, E.L. (2001). On happiness and human potentials: A review of research on hedonic and eudaimonic well-being. *Annual Review of Psychology, 52*, 141–166.

Salazar, W., Landers, D., Petruzello, S., Myungwoo, H., Crews, D., & Kubitz, K. (1990). Hemispheric asymmetry, cardiac response, and performance in elite archers. *Research Quarterly for Exercise and Sport, 61,* 351–359.

Scanlan, T.K., Stein, G.L., & Ravizza, K. (1989). An in-depth study of former elite figure skaters: II. Sources of enjoyment. *Journal of Sport and Exercise Psychology, 11,* 65–83.

Schneider, W., Dumais, S., & Shiffrin, R. (1984). Automatic and control processing and attention. In R. Parasuraman & R. Davies (Eds.), *Varieties of attention* (pp. 1–27). Orlando, FL: Academic Press.

Seligman, M.E.P. (2002). Positive psychology, positive prevention, and positive therapy. In C.R. Snyder & S.J. Lopez (Eds.), *Handbook on positive psychology* (pp. 3–9). Oxford, United Kingdom: Oxford University Press.

Seligman, M.E.P., & Csikszentmihalyi, M. (2000). Positive psychology: An introduction. *American Psychologist, 55,* 5–14.

Sparkes, A.C., & Partington, S. (2003). Narrative practice and its potential contribution to sport psychology: The example of flow. *The Sport Psychologist, 17*(3), 292–317.

Stavrou, N.A., Jackson, S.A., Zervas, Y., & Karteroliotis, K. (2007). Flow experience and athletes' performance with reference to the orthogonal model of flow. *The Sport Psychologist, 21,* 438–457.

Stein, G., Kimiecik, J., Daniels, J., & Jackson, S.A. (1995). Psychological antecedents of flow in recreational sport. *Personality and Social Psychology Bulletin, 21,* 125–135.

Straub, C. (1996). *Effects of a mental imagery program on psychological skills and perceived flow states of collegiate wrestlers.* Unpublished master's thesis, Miami University, Oxford, OH.

Szabo, C., & Kimiecik, J. (February, 1997). *Flow and running.* Paper presented at the Midwest Sport and Exercise Psychology Conference, Ball State University, Muncie, IN.

U.S. Department of Health and Human Services. (1996). *Physical activity and health: A report of the Surgeon General.* Atlanta, GA: U.S. Department of Health and Human Services, Centers for Disease Control and Prevention, National Center for Chronic Disease Prevention and Health Promotion.

Valle, R.S., King, M., & Halling, S. (1989). An introduction to existential-phenomenological thought in psychology. In R.S. Valle & S. Halling (Eds.), *Existential-phenomenological perspectives in psychology* (pp. 3–16). New York: Plenum Press.

Vea, S., & Pensgaard, A.M. (2004, September). *The relationship between perfectionism and flow among young elite athletes.* Paper presented at the Advancement of Applied Sport Psychology Annual Conference, Minneapolis, MN.

Wagner, P., Beier, K., & Delaveaux, T. (2003). *Assessing flow in surfing a comparison of competitive and recreational surfing.* Paper presented at the XI European Congress of Sport Psychology, University of Bayreuth, Germany.

Walker, G.J., Hull, IV, R.B., & Roggenbuck, J.W. (1998). On-site optimal experiences and their relationship to off-site benefits. *Journal of Leisure Research, 30*(4), 453–472.

Wallis, C. (2005, January 9). The new science of happiness. *Time.* www.time.com/time/magazine/article/0,9171,1015902-1,00.html Retrieved January 9, 2005.

Wankel, L. (1985). Personal and situational factors affecting exercise involvement: The importance of enjoyment. *Research Quarterly for Exercise and Sport, 56,* 275–282.

Wankel, L. (1997). "Strawpersons," selective reporting, and inconsistent logic: A response to Kimiecik and Harris's analysis of enjoyment. *Journal of Sport and Exercise Psychology, 19,* 98–109.

Wankel, L.M., & Berger, B.G. (1990). The psychological and social benefits of sport and physical activity. *Journal of Leisure Research, 22*(2), 167–182.

Wankel, L.M., & Kreisel, P.J. (1985). Factors underlying enjoyment of youth sports: Sport and age group comparisons. *Journal of Sport Psychology, 7,* 51–64.

Warner, R. (1987). *Freedom, enjoyment, and happiness.* Ithaca, NY: Cornell University Press.

Wells, A. (1988). Self-esteem and optimal experience. In Csikszentmihalyi, M. & Csikszentmihalyi, I. (Eds.). *Optimal experience: Psychological*

studies of flow in consciousness (pp. 327-341). New York: Cambridge University Press.

Wiggins, M.S., & Freeman, P. (2000). Anxiety and flow: An examination of anxiety direction and the flow experience. *International Sports Journal, 4,* 78–87.

Williams, J., & Krane, V. (1998). Psychological characteristics of peak performance. In J. Williams (Ed.), *Applied sport psychology* (3rd ed., pp. 158–170). Mountain View, CA: Mayfield.

Wrigley, W.J., (2005). *An examination of ecological factors in music performance assessment.* Unpublished doctoral thesis, Griffith University, Brisbane, Australia.

CHAPTER 17

Adam, M.U., Brassington, G.S., Steiner, H., & Matheson, G.O. (2004). Psychological factors associated with performance limiting injuries in professional ballet dancers. *Journal of Dance Medicine and Science, 8,* 43–46.

Agris, W.S. (1989). Understanding compliance with the medical regimen: The scope of the problem and a theoretical perspective. *Arthritis Care Research, 2*(Suppl.), S2–S7.

Ajzen, I. (1988). *Attitudes, personality, and behavior.* Chicago: Dorsey Press.

American Psychiatric Association. (2000). *Diagnostic and statistical manual of mental disorders* (4th ed., text rev.). Washington, DC: Author.

Andersen, M.B. (1989). Psychosocial factors and changes in peripheral vision, muscle tension, and fine motor skills during stress. *Dissertation Abstracts International, 49*(10-B), 4580.

Andersen, M.B., & Stoové, M.A. (1998). The sanctity of $p < .05$ obfuscates good stuff: A comment on Kerr and Goss. *Journal of Applied Sport Psychology, 10,* 168–173.

Andersen, M.B., & Williams, J.M. (1988). A model of stress and athletic injury: Prediction and prevention. *Journal of Sport & Exercise Psychology, 10,* 294–306.

Andersen, M.B., & Williams, J.M. (1993). Psychological risk factors and injury prevention. In J. Heil (Ed.), *Psychology of sport injury* (pp. 49–57). Champaign, IL: Human Kinetics.

Andersen, M.B., & Williams, J.M. (1999). Athletic injury, psychosocial factors, and perceptual changes during stress. *Journal of Sports Sciences, 17,* 735–741.

Bandura, A. (1977). Self-efficacy: Toward a unifying theory of personality change. *Psychological Review, 84,* 191–215.

Blackwell, B., & McCullagh, P. (1990). The relationship of athletic injury to life stress, competitive anxiety, and coping resources. *Athletic Training, 25,* 23–27.

Bloom, G.A., Horton, A.S., McCrory, P., & Johnston, K.M. (2004). Sport psychology and concussion: New impacts to explore. *British Journal of Sports Medicine, 38,* 519–521.

Bramwell, S.T., Masuda, M., Wagner, N.H., & Holmes, T.H. (1975). Psychological factors in athletic injuries: Development and application of the Social and Athletic Readjustment Rating Scale (SARRS). *Journal of Human Stress, 1,* 6–20.

Brewer, B.W. (1994). Review and critique of models of psychological adjustment to athletic injury. *Journal of Applied Sport Psychology, 6,* 87–100.

Brewer, B.W. (1998). Adherence to sport injury rehabilitation programs. *Journal of Applied Sport Psychology, 10,* 70–82.

Brewer, B.W. (2001). Psychology of sport injury rehabilitation. In R.N. Singer, H.A. Hausenblas, & C.M. Janelle (Eds.), *Handbook of sport psychology* (2nd ed., pp. 787–809). New York: Wiley.

Brewer, B.W. (2004). Psychological aspects of rehabilitation. In G.S. Kolt & M.B. Andersen (Eds.), *Psychology in the physical and manual therapies* (pp. 39–53). Edinburgh, Scotland: Churchill Livingstone.

Brewer, B.W., Andersen, M.B., & Van Raalte, J.L. (2002). Psychological aspects of sport injury rehabilitation: Toward a biopsychosocial approach. In D.L. Mostofsky & L.D. Zaichkowsky (Eds.), *Medical and psychological aspects of sport and exercise* (pp. 41–54). Morgantown, WV: Fitness Information Technology.

Brewer, B.W., Cornelius, A.E., Van Raalte, J.L., Petitpas, A.J., Sklar, J.H., Pohlman, M.H., et al. (2003). Protection motivation theory and adherence to sport injury rehabilitation revisited. *The Sport Psychologist, 17,* 95–103.

Brewer, B.W., Linder, D.E., & Phelps, C.M. (1995). Situational correlates of emotional adjustment to athletic injury. *Clinical Journal of Sports Medicine, 5,* 241–245.

Brewer, B.W., Petitpas, A.J., Van Raalte, J.L., Sklar, J.H., & Ditmar, T.D. (1995). Prevalence of psychological distress among patients at a physical therapy clinic specializing in sports medicine. *Sports Medicine Training and Rehabilitation, 6,* 139–145.

Brewer, B.W., & Petrie, T.A. (1995). A comparison between injured and uninjured football players on selected psychosocial variables. *Academic Athletic Journal, 9,* 11–18.

Brewer, B.W., Van Raalte, J.L., Cornelius, A.E., Petitpas, A.J., Sklar, J.H., Pohlman, M.H., et al. (2000). Psychological factors, rehabilitation, adherence, and rehabilitation outcome after anterior cruciate ligament reconstruction. *Rehabilitation Psychology, 45,* 20–37.

Brickner, J.C. (1997). *Mood states and compliance of patients with orthopedic rehabilitation.* Unpublished master's thesis, Springfield College, Springfield, MA.

Bringer, J.D., & Udry, E. (1998). Psychosocial precursors to athletic injury in adolescent competitive athletes [Abstract]. *Journal of Applied Sport Psychology, 10*(Suppl.), 126.

Bum, D., Morris, T., & Andersen, M.B. (1996). Stress, life stress, and visual attention. In D. Kenny (Ed.), *Proceedings (edited abstracts): International Congress on Stress and Health* (p. 37). Sydney, NSW, Australia: University of Sydney.

Bum, D., Morris, T., & Andersen, M.B. (1998, August). *Stress, stress management, and visual attention.* Paper presented at the International Congress of Applied Psychology, San Francisco.

Bursill, A.E. (1958). The restriction of peripheral vision during exposure to hot and humid conditions. *Quarterly Journal of Experimental Psychology, 10,* 113–129.

Byrd, B.J. (1993). *The relationship of history of stressors, personality, and coping resources with the incidence of athletic injuries.* Unpublished master's thesis, University of Colorado, Boulder.

Carter, W.B. (1990). Health behavior as a rational process: Theory of reasoned action and multiattribute utility theory. In K. Glanz, F.M. Lewis, & B.K. Rimer (Eds.), *Health behavior and health education* (pp. 63–91). San Francisco: Jossey-Bass.

Carver, C.S., Pozo, C., Harris, S.D., Noriega, V., Scheier, M.F., Robinson, D.S., et al. (1993). How coping mediates the effect of optimism on distress: A study of women with early stage breast cancer. *Journal of Personality and Social Psychology, 65,* 375–390.

Coddington, R.D., & Troxell, J.R. (1980). The effect of emotional factors on football injury rates: A pilot study. *Journal of Human Stress, 6,* 3–5.

Cohen, S., & Wills, T.A. (1985). Stress, social support, and the buffering hypothesis. *Psychological Bulletin, 98,* 310–357.

Compas, B.E., Worsham, N.L., Ey, S., & Howell, D.C. (1996). When Mom or Dad has cancer: II. Coping, cognitive appraisals, and psychological distress in children of cancer patients. *Health Psychology, 15,* 167–175.

Crossman, J., & Jamieson, J. (1985). Differences in perceptions of seriousness of disrupting effects of athletic injury as viewed by athletes and their trainer. *Perceptual and Motor Skills, 61,* 1131–1134.

Cryan, P.O., & Alles, E.F. (1983). The relationship between stress and football injuries. *Journal of Sports Medicine and Physical Fitness, 23,* 52–58.

Cupal, D.D. (1998). Psychological interventions in sport injury prevention and rehabilitation. *Journal of Applied Sport Psychology, 10,* 103–123.

Cupal, D.D., & Brewer, B.W. (2001). Effects of relaxation and guided imagery on knee strength, reinjury anxiety, and pain following anterior cruciate ligament reconstruction. *Rehabilitation Psychology, 46,* 28–43.

Daly, J.M., Brewer, B.W., Van Raalte, J.L., Petitpas, A.J., & Sklar, J.H. (1995). Cognitive appraisal, emotional adjustment, and adherence to rehabilitation following knee surgery. *Journal of Sport Rehabilitation, 4,* 23–30.

Davis, J.O. (1991). Sports injuries and stress management: An opportunity for research. *The Sport Psychologist, 5,* 175–182.

Duda, J.L., Smart, A.E., & Tappe, M.K. (1989). Predictors of adherence in the rehabilitation of athletic injuries: An application of personal investment theory. *Journal of Sport & Exercise Psychology, 11,* 367–381.

Evans, L., & Hardy, L. (1995). Sport injury and grief responses: A review. *Journal of Sport & Exercise Psychology, 17,* 227–245.

Evans, L., & Hardy, L. (2002a). Injury rehabilitation: A goal-setting intervention study. *Research Quarterly for Exercise and Sport, 73,* 310–319.

Evans, L., & Hardy, L. (2002b). Injury rehabilitation: A qualitative follow-up study. *Research Quarterly for Exercise and Sport, 73,* 320–329.

Evans, L., Hardy, L., & Fleming, S. (2000). Intervention strategies with injured athletes: An action research study. *The Sport Psychologist, 14,* 188–206.

Fawkner, H.J. (1995). *Predisposition to injury in athletes: The role of psychosocial factors.* Unpublished master's thesis, University of Melbourne, Australia.

Fawkner, H.J., McMurray, N.E., & Summers, J.J. (1999). Athletic injury and minor life events: A prospective study. *Journal of Science and Medicine in Sports, 2,* 117–124.

Fields, J., Murphey, M., Horodyski, M., & Stopka, C. (1995). Factors associated with adherence to sport injury rehabilitation in college–age recreational athletes. *Journal of Sport Rehabilitation, 4,* 172–180.

Fields, K.B., Delaney, M., & Hinkle, S. (1990). A prospective study of type A behavior and running injuries. *Journal of Family Practice, 30,* 425–429.

Fisher, A.C., Domm, M.A., & Wuest, D.A. (1988). Adherence to sports-related rehabilitation programs. *The Physician and Sportsmedicine, 16*(7), 47–52.

Glanz, K., Lewis, F., & Rimer, B. (1990). Health education and health behavior: The foundations. In K. Glanz, F. Lewis, & B. Rimer (Eds.), *Health behavior and health education* (pp. 3–32). San Francisco: Jossey-Bass.

Gould, D., Jackson, S., & Finch, L. (1993). Sources of stress in national champion figure skaters. *Journal of Sport & Exercise Psychology, 15,* 134–159.

Gould, D., Udry, E., Bridges, D., & Beck, L. (1997a). Stress sources encountered when rehabilitating from season-ending ski injuries. *The Sport Psychologist, 11,* 361–378.

Gould, D., Udry, E., Bridges, D., & Beck, L. (1997b). Coping with season-ending injuries. *The Sport Psychologist, 11,* 379–399.

Green, S.L., & Weinberg, R.S. (2001). Relationships among athletic identity, coping skills, social support, and the psychological impact of injury in recreational athletes. *Journal of Applied Sport Psychology, 13,* 40–59.

Gregg, R.L., Banderet, L.E., Reynolds, K.L., Creedon, J.F., & Rice, V.J. (2002). Psychological factors that influence traumatic injury occurrence and physical performance. *Work, 18,* 133–139.

Grove, J.R. (1993). Personality and injury rehabilitation among sport performers. In D. Pargman (Ed.), *Psychological basis of sport injuries* (pp. 99–120). Morgantown, WV: Fitness Information Technology.

Hanson, S.J., McCullagh, P., & Tonymon, P. (1992). The relationship of personality characteristics, life stress, and coping resources to athletic injury. *Journal of Sport & Exercise Psychology, 14,* 262–272.

Hardy, C.J., O'Connor, K.A., & Geisler, P.R. (1990, October). *The role of gender and social support in the life stress injury relationship.* Paper presented at the annual conference of the Association for the Advancement of Applied Sport Psychology, San Antonio, TX.

Hardy, C.J., Prentice, W.E., Kirsanoff, M.T., Richman, J.M., & Rosenfeld, L.B. (1987, June). Life stress, social support, and athletic injury: In search of relationships. In J.M. Williams (Chair), *Psychological factors in injury occurrence.* Symposium conducted at the annual meeting of the North American Society for the Psychology of Sport and Physical Activity, Vancouver, BC, Canada.

Hardy, C.J., Richman, J.M., & Rosenfeld, L.B. (1991). The role of social support in the life stress/injury relationship. *The Sport Psychologist, 5,* 128–139.

Hardy, C.J., & Riehl, M.A. (1988). An examination of the life stress-injury relationship among noncontact sport participants. *Behavioral Medicine, 14,* 113–118.

Harris, L.L. (2003). Integrating and analyzing psychosocial and stage theories to challenge the development of the injured collegiate athlete. *Journal of Athletic Training, 38,* 75–82.

Heil, J. (1993). *Psychology of sport injury.* Champaign, IL: Human Kinetics.

Hellman, E.A. (1997). Use of the stages of change model in exercise adherence among older adults with a cardiac diagnosis. *Journal of Cardiopulmonary Rehabilitation, 17,* 145–155.

Holmes, T. (1970). Psychological screening. In *Football injuries: Paper presented at a workshop* (pp. 211–214). Sponsored by Subcommittee on Athletic Injuries, Committee on the Skeletal System, Division of Medical Sciences, National Research Council, February 1969. Washington, DC: National Academy of Sciences.

Holmes, T., & Rahe, R.J. (1967). The Social and Readjustment Rating Scale. *Journal of Psychosomatic Research, 11,* 213–218.

Ievleva, L., & Orlick, T. (1991). Mental links to enhanced healing: An exploratory study. *The Sport Psychologist, 5,* 25–40.

Jaremko, M.E., Silbert, L., & Mann, T. (1981). The differential ability of athletes and nonathletes to cope with two types of pain: A radical behavioral model. *Psychological Record, 31,* 265–275.

Johnson, U. (2000). Short-term psychological intervention: A study of long-term-injured competitive athletes. *Journal of Sport Rehabilitation, 9,* 207–218.

Johnson, U., Ekengren, J., & Andersen, M.B. (2005). Injury prevention in Sweden: Helping soccer players at risk. *Journal of Sport & Exercise Psychology, 27,* 32–38.

Jones, S.L., Jones, P.K., & Katz, J. (1991). Compliance in acute and chronic patients receiving a health belief model intervention in the emergency department. *Social Science in Medicine, 32,* 1183–1189.

Junge, A. (2000). The influence of psychological factors on sports injuries. *The American Journal of Sports Medicine, 28*(5), S-10–S-15.

Kanner, A.D., Coyne, J.C., Schaefer, C., & Lazarus, R.S. (1981). Comparison of two modes of stress management: Daily hassles and uplifts versus major life events. *Journal of Behavioral Medicine, 4,* 1–39.

Kerr, G., & Goss, J. (1996). The effects of a stress management program on injuries and stress levels. *Journal of Applied Sport Psychology, 8,* 109–117.

Kerr, G., & Minden, H. (1988). Psychological factors related to the occurrence of athletic injuries. *Journal of Sport & Exercise Psychology, 10,* 167–173.

Kishi, Y., Robinson, R.G., & Forrester, A.W. (1994). Prospective longitudinal study of depression following spinal cord injury. *Journal of Neuropsychiatry and Clinical Neurosciences, 6,* 237–244.

Kolt, G.S., & Andersen, M.B. (Eds.). (2004). *Psychology in the physical and manual therapies.* Edinburgh, Scotland: Churchill Livingstone.

Kolt, G.S., Hume, P.A., Smith, P., & Williams, M.M. (2004). Effects of a stress-management program on injury and stress of competitive gymnasts. *Perceptual and Motor Skills, 99,* 195–207.

Kolt, G., & Kirkby, R. (1996). Injury in Australian female competitive gymnasts: A psychological perspective. *Australian Physiotherapy, 42,* 121–126.

Kontos, A.P., Collins, M., & Russo, S.A. (2004). An introduction to sports concussion for the sport psychology consultant. *Journal of Applied Sport Psychology, 16,* 220–235.

Kübler-Ross, E. (1969). *On death and dying.* New York: Macmillan.

Lampton, C.C., Lambert, M.E., & Yost, R. (1993). The effects of psychological factors in sports medicine rehabilitation adherence. *Journal of Sports Medicine and Physical Fitness, 33,* 292–299.

Landers, D.M., Wang, M.Q., & Courtet, P. (1985). Peripheral narrowing among experienced and inexperienced rifle shooters under low- and high-stress conditions. *Research Quarterly for Exercise and Sport, 56,* 122–130.

Lazarus, R.S., & Folkman, S. (1984). *Stress, appraisal, and coping.* New York: Springer-Verlag.

Leddy, M.H., Lambert, M.J., & Ogles, B.M. (1994). Psychological consequences of athletic injury among high level competitors. *Research Quarterly for Exercise and Sport, 65,* 347–354.

Lynch, G.P. (1988). Athletic injuries and the practicing sport psychologist: Practical guidelines for assisting athletes. *The Sport Psychologist, 2,* 161–167.

Lysens, R., Steverlynck, A., Vanden Auweele, Y., Lefevre, J., Renson, L., Claessens, A., et al. (1984). The predictability of sports injuries. *Sports Medicine, 1,* 6–10.

Lysens, R., Vanden Auweele, Y., & Ostyn, M. (1986). The relationship between psychosocial factors and sports injuries. *Journal of Sports Medicine and Physical Fitness, 26,* 77–84.

Maddison, R., & Prapavessis, H. (2005). A psychological approach to the prediction and prevention of athletic injury. *Journal of Sport & Exercise Psychology, 27,* 289–310.

Maddux, J.E. (1993). Social cognitive models of health and exercise behavior: An introduction and review of conceptual issues. *Journal of Applied Sport Psychology, 5,* 116–140.

Maddux, J.E., & Rogers, R.W. (1983). Protection motivation and self-efficacy: A revised theory of fear of appeals and attitude change. *Journal of Experimental Social Psychology, 19,* 469–479.

Marcus, B.H., Rossi, J.S., Selby, V.C., Niaura, R.S., & Abrams, D.B. (1992). The stages and processes of exercise adoption and maintenance in a worksite sample. *Health Psychology, 11,* 386–395.

May, J.R., Veach, T.L., Reed, M.W., & Griffey, M.S. (1985). A psychological study of health, injury, and performance in athletes on the U.S. alpine ski team. *The Physician and Sportsmedicine, 13,* 111–115.

May, J.R., Veach, T.L., Southard, S.W., & Herring, K. (1985). The effects of life change on injuries, illness, and performance. In N.K. Butts, T.G. Gushkin, & B. Zarins (Eds.), *The elite athlete* (pp. 171–179). Jamaica, NY: Spectrum Books.

May, S. (1995). *An investigation into compliance with sports injury rehabilitation regimens.* Unpublished doctoral dissertation, University of Brighton, Eastbourne, England.

McDonald, S.A., & Hardy, C.J. (1990). Affective response patterns of the injured athlete: An exploratory analysis. *The Sport Psychologist, 4,* 261–274.

McLeod, S., & Kirkby, R.J. (1995). Locus of control as a predictor of injury in elite basketball players. *Sports Medicine, Training, and Rehabilitation, 6,* 201–206.

McNair, D., Lorr, M., & Droppelman, L. (1971). *Manual for the Profile of Mood States.* San Diego, CA: Educational and Industrial Testing Service.

Meichenbaum, D. (1985). *Stress inoculation training.* New York: Pergamon Press.

Meyer, K.N. (1995). *The influence of personality factors, life stress, and coping strategies on the incidence of injury in long-distance runners.* Unpublished master's thesis, University of Colorado, Boulder.

Morrey, M.A., Stuart, M.J., Smith, A.M., & Wiese-Bjornstal, D.M. (1999). A longitudinal examination of athletes' emotional and cognitive responses to anterior cruciate ligament injury. *Clinical Journal of Sports Medicine, 9,* 63–60.

Newsome, J., Knight, P., & Balnave, R. (2003). Use of mental imagery to limit strength loss after immobilization. *Journal of Sport Rehabilitation, 12,* 249–258.

Nicholls, J.G. (1984). Achievement motivation: Conceptions of ability, subjective experience, task choice, and performance. *Psychological Review, 91,* 328–346.

Nixon, H.L. (1992). A social network analysis of influences on athletes to play with pain and injuries. *Journal of Sport and Social Issues, 16,* 127–135.

Nixon, H.L. (1993). Accepting the risks of pain and injury in sport: Mediated cultural influences on playing hurt. *Sociology of Sport Journal, 10,* 183–196.

Noh, Y.E., Morris, T., & Andersen, M.B. (2005). Psychosocial factors and ballet injuries. *International Journal of Sport & Exercise Psychology, 1,* 79–90

Oldridge, N.B., & Streiner, D.L. (1990). The health belief model: Predicting compliance and dropout in cardiac rehabilitation. *Medicine and Science in Sports and Exercise, 22,* 678–683.

O'Leary, A. (1990). Stress, emotion, and human immune function. *Psychological Bulletin, 108,* 363–382.

Pargman, D. (Ed.). (2007). *Psychological bases of sport injuries* (3rd ed.). Morgantown, WV: Fitness Information Technology.

Pargman, D., & Lunt, S.D. (1989). The relationship of self-concept and locus of control to the severity of injury in freshman collegiate football players. *Sports Medicine, Training, and Rehabilitation, 1,* 201–208.

Passer, M.W., & Seese, M.D. (1983). Life stress and athletic injury: Examination of positive versus negative events and three moderator variables. *Journal of Human Stress, 9,* 11–16.

Pearson, L., & Jones, G. (1992). Emotional effects of sports injuries: Implications for physiotherapists. *Physiotherapy, 78,* 762–770.

Perna, F.M., Antoni, M.H., Baum, A., Gordon, P., & Schneiderman, N. (2003). Cognitive behavioral stress management effects on injury and illness among competitive athletes: A randomized clinical trial. *Annals of Behavioral Medicine, 25,* 66–73.

Perna, F., & McDowell, S. (1993, October). *The association of stress and coping with illness and injury among elite athletes.* Paper presented at the annual meeting of the Association for the Advancement of Applied Sport Psychology, Montreal, PQ, Canada.

Petrie, T.A. (1992). Psychosocial antecedents of athletic injury: The effects of life stress and social support on female collegiate gymnasts. *Behavioral Medicine, 18,* 127–138.

Petrie, T.A. (1993a). The moderating effects of social support and playing status on the life stress-injury relationship. *Journal of Applied Sport Psychology, 5,* 1–16.

Petrie, T.A. (1993b). Coping skills, competitive trait anxiety, and playing status: Moderating effects of the life stress-injury relationship. *Journal of Sport & Exercise Psychology, 15,* 261–274.

Petrie, T.A., & Falkstein, D.L. (1998). Methodological, measurement, and statistical issues in research on sport injury prediction. *Journal of Applied Sport Psychology, 10,* 26–45.

Prentice-Dunn, S., & Rogers, R.W. (1986). Protection motivation theory and preventive health: Beyond the health belief model. *Health Education Research, 1,* 153–161.

Prochaska, J.O., & Marcus, B.H. (1994). The transtheoretical model. In R.K. Dishman (Ed.), *Advances in exercise adherence* (2nd ed., pp. 161–180). Champaign, IL: Human Kinetics.

Prochaska, J.O., Velicer, W.F., Rossi, J.S., Goldstein, M.G., Marcus, B.H., Rakowski, W., et al. (1994). Stages of change and decisional balance for 12 problem behaviors. *Health Psychology, 13,* 39–46.

Putukian, M., & Echemendia, R.J. (2003). Psychological aspects of serious head injury in the competitive athlete. *Clinics in Sports Medicine, 22*(3), 617–630.

Raglin, J.S. (2001). Psychological factors in sport performance. *Sports Medicine, 31,* 875–890.

Roh, J.L., Newcomer, R.R., Perna, F.M., & Etzel, E.F. (1998). Depressive mood states among college athletes: Pre- and post-injury [Abstract]. *Journal of Applied Sport Psychology, 10*(Suppl.), 54.

Rogers, R.W. (1975). A protection motivation theory of fear appeals and attitude change. *Journal of Psychology, 91,* 93–114.

Rogers, T.J., & Landers, D.M. (2005). Mediating effects of peripheral vision in the life event stress/athletic injury relationship. *Journal of Sport & Exercise Psychology, 27,* 271–288.

Rose, J., & Jevne, R.F. (1993). Psychological processes associated with athletic injuries. *The Sport Psychologist, 7,* 309–328.

Rosenstock, I.M. (1990). The health belief model: Explaining health behavior through expectancies. In K. Glanz, F.M. Lewis, & B.K. Rimer (Eds.), *Health behavior and health education* (pp. 39–62). San Francisco: Jossey-Bass.

Rosenstock, I.M., Strecher, V.J., & Becker, M.H. (1988). Social learning theory and the health belief model. *Health Education Quarterly, 15,* 175–183.

Ross, M.J., & Berger, R.S. (1996). Effects of stress inoculation training on athletes' postsurgical pain and rehabilitation after orthopedic injury. *Journal of Consulting and Clinical Psychology, 64,* 406–410.

Sarason, I.G., Johnson, J.H., & Siegel, J.M. (1978). Assessing the impact of life changes: Development of the Life Experiences Survey. *Journal of Consulting and Clinical Psychology, 46,* 932–946.

Scanlan, T.K., Carpenter, P.J., Schmidt, G.W., Simons, J.P., & Keeler, B. (1993). An introduction to the sport commitment model. *Journal of Sport & Exercise Psychology, 15,* 1–15.

Scanlan, T.K., Stein, G.L., & Ravizza, K. (1991). An in-depth study of former elite figure skaters: III. Sources of stress. *Journal of Sport & Exercise Psychology, 13,* 103–120.

Slenker, S.E., Price, J.H., Roberts, S.M., & Jurs, S.G. (1984). Joggers versus nonexercisers: An analysis of knowledge, attitudes, and beliefs about jogging. *Research Quarterly for Exercise and Sport, 55,* 371–378.

Smith, A. (1996). Psychological impact of injuries in athletes. *Sports Medicine, 22,* 391–405.

Smith, A., Scott, S., O'Fallon, W., & Young, M. (1990). Emotional responses of athletes to injury. *Mayo Clinic Proceedings, 65,* 38–50.

Smith, R.E., Ptacek, J.T., & Smoll, F.L. (1992). Sensation seeking, stress, and adolescent injuries: A test of stress-buffering, risk-taking, and coping skills hypotheses. *Journal of Personality and Social Psychology, 62,* 1016–1024.

Smith, R.E., Smoll, F.L., & Ptacek, J.T. (1990). Conjunctive moderator variables in vulnerability and resiliency research: Life stress, social support, and coping skills, and adolescent sport injuries. *Journal of Personality and Social Psychology, 58,* 360–369.

Steadman, R. (1993). A physician's approach to the psychology of injury. In J. Heil (Ed.), *Psychology of sport injury* (pp. 25–31). Champaign, IL: Human Kinetics.

Stuart, J.C., & Brown, B.M. (1981). The relationship of stress and coping ability to incidence of diseases and accidents. *Journal of Psychosomatic Research, 25,* 255–260.

Sullivan, M.J.L., Tripp, D.A., Rodgers, W.M., & Stanish, W. (2000). Catastrophizing and pain perception in sport participants. *Journal of Applied Sport Psychology, 12,* 151–167.

Taylor, A.H., & May, S. (1996). Threat and coping appraisal as determinants of compliance with sports injury rehabilitation: An application of protection motivation theory. *Journal of Sports Sciences, 14,* 471–482.

Taylor, C.B., Miller, N.H., Smith, P.M., & DeBusk, R. (1997). The effect of a home-based, case-managed, multifactorial risk-reduction program on reducing psychological distress in patients with cardiovascular disease. *Journal of Cardiopulmonary Rehabilitation, 17,* 157–162.

Thompson, N.J., & Morris, R.D. (1994). Predicting injury risk in adolescent football players: The importance of psychological variables. *Journal of Pediatric Psychology, 19,* 415–429.

Udry, E. (1995). *Examining mood, coping, and social support in the context of athletic injuries.* Unpublished doctoral dissertation, University of North Carolina, Greensboro..

Udry, E. (1997). Coping and social support among injured athletes following surgery. *Journal of Sport & Exercise Psychology, 19,* 71–90.

Udry, E. (2007). The paradox of injuries: Unexpected positive consequences. In D. Pargman (Ed.), *Psychological bases of sport injuries* (3rd ed.). Morgantown, WV: Fitness Information Technology.

Udry, E., Gould, D., Bridges, D., & Beck, L. (1997). Down but not out: Athlete responses to season-ending injuries. *Journal of Sport & Exercise Psychology, 19,* 229–248.

Udry, E., Gould, D., Bridges, D., & Tuffey, S. (1997). People helping people? Examining the social ties of athletes coping with burnout and injury stress. *Journal of Sport & Exercise Psychology, 19,* 369–395.

Udry, E., Shelbourne, K.D., & Gray, T. (2003). Psychological readiness for anterior cruciate ligament surgery: Describing and comparing the adolescent and adult experiences. *Journal of Athletic Training, 38,* 167–171.

Uitenbroek, D.G. (1996). Sports, exercise, and other causes of injuries: Results of a population survey. *Research Quarterly for Exercise and Sport, 67,* 380–385.

Weiss, M.R., & Troxel, R.K. (1986). Psychology of the injured athlete. *Athletic Training, 21,* 104–109.

Whitmarsh, B.G., & Alderman, R.B. (1993). Role of psychological skills training in increasing athletic pain tolerance. *The Sport Psychologist, 7,* 388–399.

Wiese-Bjornstal, D.M. (2004). Psychological responses to injury and illness. In G.S. Kolt & M.B. Andersen (Eds.), *Psychology in the physical and manual therapies* (pp. 21–38). Edinburgh, Scotland: Churchill Livingstone.

Wiese-Bjornstal, D.M., & Smith, A.M. (1999). Counseling strategies for enhanced recovery of injured athletes within a team approach. In D. Pargman (Ed.), *Psychological bases of sport injuries* (2nd ed., pp. 125-155). Morgantown, WV: Fitness Information Technology.

Wiese-Bjornstal, D.M., Smith, A.M., & LaMott, E.E. (1995). A model of psychologic response to athletic injury and rehabilitation. *Athletic Training, 1,* 17–30.

Wiese-Bjornstal, D.M., Smith, A.M., Shaffer, S.M., & Morrey, M.A. (1998). An integrated model of response to sport injury: Psychological and sociological dynamics. *Journal of Applied Sport Psychology, 10,* 46–69.

Williams, J.M., & Andersen, M.B. (1997). Psychosocial influences on central and peripheral vision and reaction time during demanding tasks. *Behavioral Medicine, 26,* 160–167.

Williams, J.M., & Andersen, M.B. (1998). Psychosocial antecedents of sport injury: Review and critique of the stress and injury model. *Journal of Applied Sport Psychology, 10,* 5–25.

Williams, J.M., & Andersen, M.B. (2007). Psychosocial antecedents of sport injury and interventions for risk reduction. In G. Tenenbaum & R.C. Eklund (Eds.), *Handbook of sport psychology* (3rd ed., pp. 379-403). New York: Wiley.

Williams, J.M., Hogan, T.D., & Andersen, M.B. (1993). Positive states of mind and athletic injury risk. *Psychosomatic Medicine, 55,* 468–472.

Williams, J.M., & Roepke, N. (1993). Psychology of injury and injury rehabilitation. In R.N. Singer, M. Murphey, & L.K. Tennant (Eds.), *Handbook of research on sport psychology* (pp. 815–839). New York: Macmillan.

Williams, J.M., Tonymon, P., & Andersen, M.B. (1990). Effects of life-event stress on anxiety and peripheral narrowing. *Behavioral Medicine, 16,* 174–181.

Williams, J.M., Tonymon, P., & Andersen, M.B. (1991). Effects of stressors and coping resources on anxiety and peripheral narrowing in recreational athletes. *Journal of Applied Sport Psychology, 3,* 126–141.

Williams, J.M., Tonymon, P., & Wadsworth, W.A. (1986). Relationship of stress to injury in intercollegiate volleyball. *Journal of Human Stress, 12,* 38–43.

Wong, I. (1998). *Injury rehabilitation behavior: An investigation of stages and processes of change in the athlete-therapist relationship.* Unpublished master's thesis, University of Oregon, Eugene.

Index

Note: The italicized *f* and *t* following page numbers refer to figures and tables, respectively.

About the Editor

Thelma S. Horn, PhD, is an associate professor and member of the graduate faculty at Miami University of Ohio. Horn is the former editor and a current editorial board member of the *Journal of Sport and Exercise Psychology*; associate editor of the *Journal of Applied Sport Psychology*; and an editorial board member for *Measurement in Physical Education and Exercise Science*.

Horn received her PhD in psychology of sport and physical activity from Michigan State University. She earned a master of arts degree in coaching behavior from Western Michigan University at Kalamazoo and a bachelor of science degree in psychology from Calvin College in Grand Rapids, Michigan.

Besides editing the first and second editions of *Advances in Sport Psychology*, Horn has also contributed chapters to several other books and has published many articles and proceedings on sport psychology. In 1999, she was co-winner of the research writing award from *Research Quarterly for Exercise and Sport*; and in 1993, Miami University honored her with the Richard T. Delp Outstanding Faculty Award. In her free time, Horn enjoys reading, running, and watching amateur athletic contests.

About the Contributors

Anthony J. Amorose, PhD, is an associate professor in the school of kinesiology and recreation at Illinois State University. His research focuses on understanding the psychological and social development of sport and physical activity participants, including an emphasis on how significant others such as parents, peers, and coaches influence athletes' motivational orientations and self-perceptions.

Mark B. Andersen, PhD, is a registered and licensed psychologist in Australia and the United States. He is a professor in the school of human movement, recreation, and performance at Victoria University in Melbourne. Dr. Andersen lives in St. Kilda, Victoria, and actively supports many restaurants in his neighborhood.

Stuart J.H. Biddle, PhD, is professor of exercise and sport psychology in the school of sport and exercise sciences at Loughborough University. He was Head of School from 2001-2007. Dr. Biddle is an honorary fellow of BASES, the British Association of Sport & Exercise Sciences, and Distinguished International Scholar of AASP. In 2006 he was the Dorothy V. Harris memorial scholar at Penn State and in 2004 was the Pease Family Visiting Scholar at Iowa State. Stuart is co-author of the text *Psychology of Physical Activity* (Routledge) and will have new co-edited book published by Human Kinetics in 2008 on youth physical activity. He is married to Fiona and has two sons, Jack and Greg.

Stephen H. Boutcher, PhD, is an associate professor in the department of physiology and pharmacology at the University of New South Wales' School of Medical Science. He is a keen golfer and jogger, and he lives in Sydney with his wife, Yait.

Lawrence R. Brawley, PhD, is a professor and Canada Research Chair in Physical Activity in Health Promotion and Disease Prevention, College of Kinesiology, University of Saskatchewan. His longstanding collaboration with Dr. Carron reflects mutual interests in group dynamics. Recently, he has focused on using the group as an agent of behavior and self-regulatory change for interventions to promote adherence to physical activity in different populations. He is currently Chair, Board of Directors, for the Canadian Fitness and Lifestyle Research Institute (CFLRI), and an Affiliate Scientist, Centre for Behavioral Research and Program Evaluation (CBPRE), a National Cancer Institute of Canada center. For more information visit his web site at www.usask.ca/crc/profiles/brawley.php.

Robert J. Brustad, PhD, is professor of sport and exercise science at the University of Northern Colorado in Greely. His major research focus has been in the social psychology of sport and physical activity with primary attention dedicated to parental socialization influences upon children's physical activity and sport involvement. Current research interests include cross-cultural research in youth development and the study of the effects of after school sport and physical activity programs on the psychological and social development of youth. He is a former editor and associate editor for the *Journal of Sport and Exercise Psychology* and also served as the Social Psychology chair of the Association of the Advancement of Applied Sport Psychology (AAASP). He enjoys traveling and also teaches at the University of Porto in Porto, Portugal and the University of Diego Portales in Santiago, Chile.

Damon Burton, PhD, is the coauthor of *Competitive Anxiety in Sport*. Dr. Burton uses goal-setting extensively in mental skills consulting with high school, college, and Olympic athletes. He enjoys the outdoors of Idaho and watching and coaching his three sons.

Albert V. Carron, EdD, is a professor in the school of kinesiology at the University of Western Ontario in London, Ontario. The principal focus of his research is the nature of group dynamics in sport and exercise groups. Dr. Carron is a fellow in the American Academy of Kinesiology and Physical Education, the Association for the Advancement of Applied Sport Psychology, and the Canadian Psychomotor Learning and Sport Psychology Association. Currently, Carron is a member of the editorial board of the *International Journal of Sport Psychology* and *Small Group Research*.

Melissa A. Chase, PhD is an associate professor in the department of kinesiology and health and associate dean for the school of education and allied professions at Miami University in Oxford, Ohio. Her scholarly interests are in the area of self-efficacy beliefs and motivation. Her research has focused on the sources of self-efficacy beliefs and consequences of these beliefs on motivational intentions in a physical education or sport setting.

David E. Conroy, PhD, is an associate professor of kinesiology in the department of human development and family studies at The Pennsylvania State University. Dr. Conroy received the IOC Prince de Merode Award (2002) as well as the Dorothy V. Harris Memorial Award (2001) from the Association for Applied Sport Psychology. He serves as a member of the editorial board for a number of journals, including *Assessment, Journal of Sport & Exercise Psychology, Journal of Applied Sport Psychology, Measurement in Physical Education & Exercise Science*, and *International Review of Sport & Exercise Psychology*.

Jennifer Cumming, PhD, is a lecturer in the school of sport and exercise sciences at the University of Birmingham. Dr. Cumming is the former section editor of the *European Journal of Sport Science* and currently sits on the editorial board of *The Sport Psychologist* and the *Journal of Imagery Research in Sport and Physical Activity*. She holds the gold medal for highest general proficiency in the physical education program from McGill University and now turns her energy towards research in imagery in sport, exercise, and dance. In her spare time she enjoys dancing, reading good books, and wine tasting.

Deborah L. Feltz, PhD, is coauthor of *Self-Efficacy in Sport* with Sandra Short and Philip Sullivan. Dr. Feltz is an American Psychological Association fellow, former president of the American Academy of Kinesiology and Physical Education, served on the sport psychology advisory committee to the U.S. Olympic Committee, and is president of the North American Society for the Study of Sport and Physical Activity. Dr. Feltz's research has included studies of modeling influences of self-efficacy on anxiety and sport performance, gender influences on self-efficacy in sport, and the influence of collective efficacy in sport terms. Her most recent scholarship has focused on the development of a model of coaching efficacy and testing its antecedents and consequences.

Kenneth R. Fox, PhD, is professor and research fellow in the department of exercise, nutrition and health sciences at the University of Bristol. He is an International Fellow of the American Academy of Kinesiology and Physical Education, and also a Fellow of the British Association of Sport and Exercise Sciences, and UK Association for Physical Education. He was Scientific Editor for the *UK Chief Medical Officer's Report (2004) on Physical Activity and Health*. He is also editor of *The Physical Self: From Motivation to Well Being* and coeditor of *Physical Activity and Psychological Well Being*.

Stephanie J. Hanrahan, PhD, is an associate professor in the schools of human movement studies and psychology at The University of Queensland. Dr. Hanrahan is the 1997 recipient of the University of Queensland's Excellence in Teaching Award, is a fellow of Sports Medicine Australia, and current editor of the *Journal of Applied Sport Psychology*. She is the coauthor of *The Coaching Process: A Practical Guide to Improving Your Effectiveness, Game Skills: A Fun Approach to Learning Sport Skills, The Biophysical Foundations of Human Movement, The Sociocultural Foundations of Human Movement*, and an upcoming title on cultural sport psychology to be published by Human Kinetics in 2008. In her free time, she enjoys travel and Latin dance.

Chris Harwood, PhD, is a senior lecturer in sport psychology at Loughborough University. His research, teaching, and training interests lie in the areas of achievement motivation, motivational climate, and psychological skill-related education for youth sport coaches, athletes, and parents. He is a BASES high performance sport accredited psychologist and registered chartered psychologist with the British Psychological Society. As an applied researcher and practitioner, Chris serves on the editorial board for the *Journal of Applied Sport Psychology* and *The Sport Psychologist*, as well as the managing council for *FEPSAC*. He has consulted widely with national governing bodies, professional clubs, and athletes over the past 15 years and currently works within junior and senior professional tennis, youth soccer, and cricket.

Susan A. Jackson, PhD, is a sport and performace psychology researcher, writer, and consultant. She is coauthor of *Flow in Sports: The Keys to Optimal Experiences and Performances* with Mihaly Csikszentmihalyi. Dr. Jackson has developed an internationally recognized program of research focusing on investigating the flow phenomenon in physical activity and other performance domains. Sue lives in Queensland, Australia with her husband and two sons. She is currently engaged in private practice while continuing to hold an adjunct appointment in the School of Human Movement Studies at the University of Queensland.

Miranda P. Kaye is a PhD candidate specializing in the psychology of movement and sport at The Pennsylvania State University.

Richard Keegan, MSc, is a doctoral student at Loughborough University, UK where his research focuses on motivational influences across stages of development in youth sport. He is also a lecturer in sport psychology at the University of Lincoln. He gained his MSc in sport psychology at Loughborough and a BSc (Honors) in psychology at the University of Bristol. He is a BASES accredited sport psychologist working in across a variety of sports and levels.

Jay C. Kimiecik, PhD, is an associate professor in exercise science at Miami University in Oxford, Ohio where he is engaged in work focused on well-being, optimal experience, and healthy living. Dr. Kimieck is the director of Miami University's Employee Health & Well-Being. He is author of *The Intrinsic Exerciser: Discovering the Joy of Exercise,* and his writing has also appeared in numerous publications such as *Runner's World* and *Psychology Today.* Jay also developed and authored the *Y Personal Fitness Program,* an exercise behavior change program for inexperienced individuals that has been used in over 500 YMCAs in North America. His most recent book, *Runner as Hero,* is an autoethnographic tale of his experiences in becoming a competitive masters runner. Jay runs and plays sports of all sorts with his wife and two children in Oxford, Ohio.

Anthony P. Kontos, PhD, received the 2000-2001 Dissertation of the Year Award from the Sport and Exercise Psychology Academy of the National Association for Sport and Physical Education. Dr. Kontos currently directs research and applied activities at the Behavioral Performance Lab and provides sport psychology consulting to collegiate athletes as part of the Sports Medicine staff at the University of New Orleans. His research interests include perceived risk and risk taking, psychology of injury, sport concussion, youth sports, and applied sport psychology issues.

Shane Murphy, PhD, is an associate professor at Western Connecticut State University. He was the U.S. team sport psychologist at the Olympic Games in Seoul and Albertville, and a consultant to the U.S. Olympic Committee on mental preparation for the 2000 Summer Games in Sydney as well as the 2002 Winter Games in Salt Lake City. Dr. Murphy was given the Distinguished Professional Practice Award by the Association for the Advancement of Applied Sport Psychology (AAASP) in 2000. He is the author of *Sport Psychology Interventions, The Achievement Zone, The Cheers and the Tears,* and *The Sport Psych Handbook.* He also serves as editor for both the *Journal of Clinical Sport Psychology* and the *International Review of Sport and Exercise Psychology.* Shane lives in Trumbull, Connecticut, with his wife, Annemarie, and children, Bryan and Theresa.

Sanna Nordin, PhD, is a research fellow in the psychology of dance and sport at the London Sport Institute, Middlesex University. She completed her doctoral thesis under the supervision of Dr. Jennifer Cumming on the topic of imagery in dance at the University of Birmingham, UK. Current research continues to focus on dance, with topics such as perfectionism, self-confidence, anxiety, and motivation added to the main topic of imagery. She is further interested in how these and similar topics apply to dance in education and the community, including in programs with disadvantaged youth. She has begun to explore the applied side of performance psychology through consulting work with dancers, teaches the psychology module of the MSc in Dance Science at Wolverhampton University, and guest lectures at a number of other institutions in England and Sweden.

Julie A. Partridge, PhD, is an assistant professor in the department of kinesiology at Southern Illinois University Carbondale. Her research focuses on social influence in youth sport and physical activity, shame, and coping in sport. Dr. Partridge is a current member of AASP and NASPSPA and also served as editorial assistant for the *Journal of Sport & Exercise Psychology* in 1999. She lives in Carbondale, Illinois with her husband Phil Anton and their beagle, Buddy, where they spend time hiking, playing volleyball, and golfing.

Lindsey H. Schantz, earned a MS degree in the psychology of movement and sport, with a minor in industrial/organizational psychology, from The

Pennsylvania State University. Lindsey currently serves as a consultant for Novations Group, Inc., a global professional-services firm committed to helping organizations meet their strategic goals by improving the performance of their people.

Alan L. Smith, PhD, is an associate professor of health and kinesiology and director of graduate studies in the department of health and kinesiology at Purdue University. His research focuses on youth social and psychological development in physical activity contexts. He is particularly interested in peer relationships and motivational processes in the physical domain. Dr. Smith is an associate editor for the *Journal of Sport & Exercise Psychology* and a consulting editor for *Child Development*, as well as a fellow of the research consortium of AAHPERD. He lives in Lafayette, Indiana with his wife, Sarah, and children Austin and Emma, where he enjoys running.

Christopher M. Spray, PhD, is a senior lecturer in sport and exercise psychology at Loughborough University, and a registered chartered psychologist of The British Psychological Society. His research focuses on achievement motivation in young people, with particular regard to approach-avoidance achievement goals in school physical education and sport.

Megan Babkes Stellino, EdD, is an associate professor in the school of sport and exercise science, University of Northern Colorado, where she received the College of Health and Human Sciences 2004-2005 College Scholar Excellence Award. Her research focus is on family influence on youth motivation and emotion in sport and physical activity, and motivation for free time physical activity in connection with childhood obesity. Dr. Stellino is an active member of AASP, NASPSPA, and the AAHPERD research consortium, and has served as a guest reviewer for numerous journals including *JSEP, JASP, PES, RQES* and *APAQ*. She lives in Denver, Colorado with her husband Vince and son, Evan, where she enjoys a wide variety of outdoor sports, sewing, scrapbooking, and spending time with her family and friends.

Cheryl P. Stuntz, PhD, is an assistant professor in the department of psychology at St. Lawrence University. Her research focuses on social influence in sport with a focus on motivational and moral issues. Dr. Stuntz lives in Canton, New York, with her husband and two children.

Eileen Udry, PhD, is an assistant professor in the department of physical education at Indiana Uni-versity-Purdue University Indianapolis. Dr. Udry's research focuses on examining psychosocial aspects of sport injuries. She lives in Indiana where she enjoys working out and trying to remain injury free.

Robin S. Vealey, PhD, is a professor in the department of kinesiology and health at Miami University in Ohio. Dr. Vealey has authored two books, *Coaching for the Inner Edge* and *Competitive Anxiety in Sport*. She has served as a sport psychology consultant for the U.S. Nordic Ski Team, U.S. Field Hockey, elite golfers, and athletes and teams at Miami University and in the Cincinnati area. Dr. Vealey is a fellow, certified consultant, and past president of the AASP and former editor of *The Sport Psychologist*. She is a fellow of the American Academy of Kinesiology, a member of the United States Olympic Committee Sport Psychology Registry, and received the Distinguished Scholar Award from the College of Sport Psychologists in the Australian Psychological Society. A former collegiate basketball player and coach, she now enjoys the mental challenge of golf.

Cheryl Weiss, MFA, EdM, has been a professional singer, actor, and pianist for over 30 years, having won the Music Teacher's National Association national voice competition and a Baldwin Piano Award. At the University of Idaho, Cheryl is an adjunct instructor in voice at the Hampton School of Music and is a PhD student of Damon Burton. Her principle area of research interest is the parent-child dynamic in youth sport. She also teaches mental skills for athletes, works as a research assistant in the Center for ETHICS in the department of health, physical education, recreation and dance, and is currently the northwest region student representative to AAASP. Cheryl lives in Pullman, Washington with her husband John, and in her free time she enjoys attending college athletic events, cooking, power walking, knitting, and spoiling her daughter Amy and granddaughter Samantha.

Maureen R. Weiss, PhD, is professor and co-director of the Tucker Center for Research on Girls & Women in Sport in the school of kinesiology, and adjunct professor in the Institute of Child Development at the University of Minnesota-Twin Cities. Her research focuses on the psychological and social development of children and adolescents through participation in sport and physical activity, with interests in self-perceptions, motivation, character development, and social relationships. Previously, she was a faculty member at University of Virginia (1997-2007) and University of Oregon (1981-1997).

Weiss has published over 110 refereed articles and book chapters in her areas of expertise, and edited or co-edited 4 books on youth sport and physical activity: *Competitive Sport for Children and Youths, Advances in Pediatric Sport Sciences: Behavioral Issues, Worldwide Trends in Youth Sport,* and *Developmental Sport and Exercise Psychology: A Lifespan Perspective.*

Philip M. Wilson, PhD, is an assistant professor in the Department of Physical Education and Kinesiology at Brock University. His research interests focus on the interplay between measurement and theory for understanding motivational processes involved in promoting health behaviors.

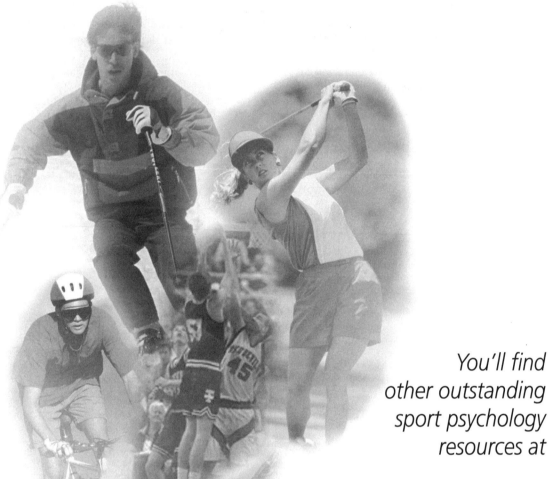